Bull Of Heaven

The Mythic Life of Eddie Buczynski
And the Rise of the New York Pagan

Bull of Heaven

The Mythic Life of Eddie Buczynski And the Rise of the New York Pagan

Michael G. Lloyd

Hubbardston, Massachusetts

Asphodel Press
12 Simond Hill Road
Hubbardston, MA 01452

Bull of Heaven:
The Mythic Life of Eddie Buczynski
and the Rise of the New York Pagan

© 2012 by Michael G. Lloyd
ISBN 978-1-938197-04-8

All rights reserved. No part of this publication may be reproduced, distributed, or transmitted in any form or by any means, including photocopying, recording, or other electronic or mechanical methods, without the prior written permission of the publisher, except in the case of brief quotations embodied in critical reviews and certain other noncommercial uses permitted by copyright law. For permission requests, write to the publisher.

Foreword © 2012 by Margot Adler.

Eddie Buczynski's writings © Edmund Buczynski, Jr. estate. Used with permission.

Author image courtesy of Debby Drake.

Cover image of Eddie Buczynski © Terry Gianniotis. Used with permission.

Cover design & artwork by Carvin Rinehart (www.carvinrinehart.com).

Title page photo: Eddie Buczynski at the Welsh Outer Court of Branwen and Bryce, ca. early 1972.

First Paperback Edition
Printed in the United States of America

Printed in cooperation with
Lulu Enterprises, Inc.
860 Aviation Parkway, Suite 300
Morrisville, NC 27560

*For Mom and Dad
Who from a very early age
Encouraged me to read voraciously*

and

*My Brothers of the Between the Worlds community
Who continuously humble me with their
Zest for Life and Quest for Knowledge*

Contents

Acknowledgements i
Proemium iv
Foreword ix

Puer Aeturnus

Chapter 1: A Bull At The Beginning 1
Chapter 2: One If by Broom, Two If by Sea 12
Chapter 3: It Takes a Village 27
Chapter 4: Cry Havoc 64
Chapter 5: The Lamed Smith and the Bright Child 87
Chapter 6: The Cauldron of Wisdom 94
Chapter 7: A Little Occult Emporium 108
Chapter 8: Birth-wail of the Child of Light 122
Chapter 9: Ye Shall Know Them by Their Ways 135
Chapter 10: The Kids Are Alright 145
Chapter 11: The Changing of the "Gard" 150
Chapter 12: Breaking Up is Hard to Do 158
Chapter 13: What's My Line? 168
Chapter 14: Perverts in the Craft 181
Chapter 15: The Edge of the Cold Moon's Blade 212
Chapter 16: The "Wars of the Witches" 221
Chapter 17: Breaking with Tradition 277
Chapter 18: Black and White and Rede All Over 288
Chapter 19: The Cubits of Plenty 295
Chapter 20: "I Think I've Met Him." 308
Chapter 21: The Cubits of Death 314
Chapter 22: Last Dance, Last Chance 321
Chapter 23: The Dockside of the Force 341
Chapter 24: The End of the Line 365
Chapter 25: A Place of Our Own 383
Chapter 26: Gay Spirit 403
Chapter 27: The Necronomicon Affair 423
Chapter 28: Babalon Comes to Babylon 442
Chapter 29: Letting Go of the Life That Was Planned 456

Regius Senex

Chapter 30: The Hunter College Years 479
Chapter 31: The Bryn Mawr College Years 506
Chapter 32: A Bull at the End 527

Senex Et Puer
    Chapter 33: Epilogue 545

Chapter Notes 574
Bibliography 669
Photo Credits 682
Publications of Earth Religions Supplies and
    Magickal Childe Publishing 682

Index 687

Acknowledgements

I would like it clearly understood that I never started out with any conscious intent to write Eddie Buczynski's biography. This project began its life with lesser expectations, such as the hope for a few simple answers to a few simple questions about an interesting fellow. But, as we all know, interesting people tend to be very complex individuals, and simple questions about such people usually end up having anything but simple answers. Thus, each of my questions inevitably led to more questions, or partial answers or, worse (for an engineer, which I am), maddening inconsistencies, which then led to yet more questions. Like a stone rolling down a hill, before long there was an avalanche, and by the time I realized what was happening, it was too late to stop. For better or worse, the dust is now settling, and you're the one who's left holding the incident report.

Eddie Buczynski demonstrated an understanding of Taoist philosophy when he wrote that "however important the final destination may be, it is the road leading to it that makes the lasting impression."[1] From that perspective, I have been blessed with and impressed by so many gifted and interesting wayfarers in the walking of this tale. Without the many kindnesses and forbearance of these individuals the story of Eddie's life might have continued its fade into rumor and speculation, eventually transforming itself into the mythology that comprises the dreamtime of all cultures. First and foremost, I would like to thank Eddie's spiritual children for their stories, documents, and photographs, as well as their patience, as I covered the same ground over and over again with them in the necessary act of fact-checking.[2] Their dedication to the preservation of Eddie's memory and the history of his times was a driving force for this project.

I am also deeply indebted to Eddie's professors, friends, and classmates at Hunter College CUNY, Bryn Mawr College, and the 1982 summer session of the American School of Classical Studies at Athens. Their continuing respect and fond memories of Eddie were truly a delight to both record and recount. To the many elders of the community who took the time to answer my numerous questions, the gratitude that I express for your help, as well as for your ongoing service — whether in the arts, history, spirituality, or other pursuits — seems dim compensation indeed. Special thanks go to Llewellyn Worldwide for providing unfettered access to the Weschcke Library and to Circle Sanctuary for opening their extensive Earth Religion archives to me. And to those who loved Eddie in his mortal guise — his parents and siblings, and his lovers Bennie Geraci, Gene Muto, and the late Herman Slater — I hope that I have done right by you in attempting to reflect at least a glimmer of what he meant to you all.

I would be remiss if I did not name the many individuals and organizations who assisted in the research and preparation of this book, and I do so now, for this is also their story: Acorn Books (Columbus, OH), Alobar, George Arthur, Laura Austan, Nikolaos Axas, Bruce Baldwin, Curt Bargren, Karen Bartlett, Julia Belham-Payne (Centre for Pagan Studies, United Kingdom), Richard Berman, Isaac Bonewits, William Breeze (Hymenaeus Beta, Frater Superior, Caliph, O.T.O.), Lori Bruno (Leo Martello Estate), Dr. Raymond Buckland, Frank Buczynski, Zsuzsanna Budapest, Carol Bulzone, Robert "Monte" Burns, Alan Cabal, Khem and Emily Caigan, Joseph Caldiero, Robert Carey, Cheiron, Chas S. Clifton, Columbus Metropolitan Library Tech Center, Peter Conte, Steven Critchley, Kerr Cuhulain, Sara Cunningham-Carter, Joseph Cupolo, Phyllis Curott, Ken Dalton, Charlie Dandelakis, Michael Davis, Marianne Davy, Dr. Alice Donohue (Bryn Mawr College), Justin Crockett Elzie, Alisha Engeleit, Nancy Enright (SW CARE Center, Santa Fe, NM), Janet Farrar, Dr. John Fischer (Wabash College, ret.), Ed Fitch, Kay Flagg (Smith), Riley Foster, Star Foster, Selena Fox and Dennis Carpenter (Circle Sanctuary), Kathryn Frank, Pat Garrard (Capitalist Reporter), Bruce-Michael Gelbert, Bennie Geraci, Cathy Gere (University of California, San Diego), Terry Gianniotis, Catherine Gorlin, Dr. Tamara Green (Hunter College CUNY), Josiah Gromley, Derek and Lisa Harrison, Dr. Lena Hatzichronoglou, William Heidrick, Frank Heimans (Cinetel Productions), Helios, Philip Heselton, J. Julian Hill, Dr. Mark Hillery (Hunter College CUNY), Dr. Hans Holzer, Andrew Honigman (*FATE* magazine), Michael Hornum, Dr. Ronald Hutton (University of Bristol, United Kingdom), The Internet Archive (Wayback Machine), Artie Jamison, Shahla Jannetta and Colleen Quinn (Sala One Nine), Randy Jones, Raven Kaldera, Will Kale (The Centre for Pagan Studies, United Kingdom), Dr. Janice Kamrin (Supreme Council of Antiquities, Cairo, Egypt), Tzipora Katz, Wayne Kernochan, Kenny Klein, Dr. Nancy Klein, Sardi Klein, Tom and Judy Kneitel, Larry Kirwan, Dr. Robert Koehl (Hunter College CUNY), William Krause (Llewellyn Worldwide, Ltd.), Charlie Kyle, Jean-Pierre Laffont, Frederic Lamond, Paul Larson, John Lauritsen, Peter Levenda, Kenny Lowenstein, Eugenia Macer-Story, Eileen Markson (Bryn Mawr College, ret.), Rebekah McKendry (*Fangoria* magazine), Judith McNally, Nathan Meyer, Jason Miller, Malcolm Mills, Herb Mitchell, James Mitchell (American Folk Art Museum), Julia Moore, Kevin Moscrip, Leon Moses and Jeremy Bredeson, Harold Moss (Church of the Eternal Source), Gene Muto, Billy Name, Ed and Marie Nascosto, Tommy Nascosto, Edgar Neidel, Jeremiah Newton, New York Men's Open Pagan Circle, Jonathon Nightshade, Father John O'Brien, Dr. Asli Özyar (Boğaziçi University, Istanbul, Turkey), Lynn Pacifico, Jason Pitzl-Waters (The Wild Hunt Blog), Adam Donaldson Powell, Roger Pratt, Dr. Brunilde Sismondo Ridgway (Bryn Mawr College, ret.), Carvin Rinehart, Ria and Sandra Rivera, Tom Robinson, Lexa Roséan, Len Rosenberg, Dr. Susan Rotroff (Washington University), Owen Rowley, Michael Saperton, Sheila Saperton, Dr. Phyllis Saretta (New York

University), Denny Sargent, William Schell, Steve Scott-Schudin, Kim and Lisa Schuller, Melissa Seims, Dennis Stevens, Zanoni Silverknife, Giani Siri, Steven Skinner, Dr. Alden Smith (Baylor University of Monmouth College), Alexander Smith, Marcella Smith, Allan Tannenbaum, Joshua Tenpenny, Gary Suto, Jonathon Tapsell, Alaric Terrason, Renate Springer, Andrew Theitic, Michael Thorn, Jonathon Tominar, Tuan Cú Mhara, Pamela Webb (Bryn Mawr College), Professor Aledyis van de Moortel (University of Tennessee — Knoxville), Rich Wandel (National History Archive, New York LGBT Community Center), Jim Ward, James Wasserman, Carl and Sandra Weschcke (Llewellyn Worldwide, Ltd.), William Wheeler, Don Wildgrube, Jean Williams, Doric Wilson, Dr. James Wright (Bryn Mawr College), Aubrey Wyatt, Oberon and Morning Glory Zell.

To each and every one of you, I give my profound thanks for your help, for the friendships which I have made, and for the friendships among you that have been renewed during this project. A hat tip to my homes away from home — Claddagh, Brewery District (Columbus, OH) and Rusty Bucket (Bexley, OH) — for their accommodation, support, fellowship, and bottomless wells of iced tea. I am extremely grateful for Margot Adler's help and for her sensitive and erudite Foreword from the standpoint of one who was there. A very special thank you goes to my faithful NYC guide, go-between, manuscript reader, and brother — Matthew Sawicki — for all of his help in navigating the canyons and denizens of Mannahatta and surrounds. Hekate works through you, my friend. I would also like to thank my other readers — Christopher Penczak, Steve Kenson, Sally Eaton, and Julie Scott-Schudin — for their comments and improvements to the text. Much gratitude to my editor, Kathy Moore, for her assistance in rendering this into a readable tale, and to Paul Patton and Michael Pistrui for their help in indexing this behemoth. As always, all errors may be laid at the author's feet.

Proemium

> *Yes: I am a dreamer. For a dreamer is one who can only find his way by moonlight, and his punishment is that he sees the dawn before the rest of the world.*
>
> –Oscar Wilde, *Intentions*

It was a time of ferment, rage, and hope. The 1960s and 1970s marked a period of significant social upheaval in the United States where Americans witnessed a tug-of-war between conservatives and progressives that, to at least some observers, had the potential to pull the country apart at the seams. Everywhere one turned, sociopolitical movements were springing up or becoming re-energized, in some cases militantly so, demanding that their issues be acknowledged and addressed. These included the anti-war movement, the women's movement, the environmental movement, and the more aggressive factions within the black and gay civil rights movements following the 1967 and 1968 riots in black communities throughout the United States and the 1969 Stonewall riots in New York City

During these years, two spiritual movements arose in reaction to the perceived ills of the time. In the case of evangelical Christianity, the perception that society had strayed dangerously from inerrant Biblical teachings was apparent from the signs all around, from the deterioration of sexual mores, the legalization of birth control (and later abortion), the advent of the modern gay rights movement, and the social chaos resulting from increasing challenges to the economic and political might of the United States from without and to the power of authorities both secular and spiritual from within.

Forming a counterpoint to this were the practices and beliefs that condensed to form the nucleus of an occult revival, or what is now loosely called the modern New Age and the contemporary Pagan movement in the United States. Popularly represented at that time by Gardnerian Wica and similar spiritual paths of Witchcraft,[†] this movement stressed the

---

[†] **A short note on terminology.** The treatment of various terms within this book is explained herein to avoid confusion. "Occult" is generally used in this book to refer to all practices that fall under the umbrellas of Neo-Paganism and the New Age. This usage is far from perfect, but it was the common parlance of the era, particularly within the news media, and it is still widely considered to be the catch-all term even today. The term "Neo-Pagan" is meant to include all aspects of modern Pagan religion, including Witchcraft. Again there is disagreement in this usage; some Witches claim not to be Neo-Pagan, and some putatively Neo-Pagan faiths (e.g., Asatru) refuse to be associated with Neo-Pagans, and especially Wiccans. Again, while not perfect, that is the treatment herein. The term "Neo-Paganism" has been largely supplanted by "contemporary Paganism" in modern

individual as the arbiter of his or her own spiritual well being. Its practitioners, known collectively as Witches, generally believe in a multiplicity of Gods, the interchangeability of magick* and prayer as tools to transform both self and the world, and the decentralization of authority in matters spiritual. Wica arose from a variety of inspirational sources — folklore, anthropology, mythology, Oriental religions, Theosophy, Freemasonry, the Golden Dawn and the Ordo Templi Orientis (O.T.O.), spiritualism, archaeology and romantic fiction. It is this second movement, that of Wica, its spiritual fellow travelers, and others comprising the Neo-Pagan movement, that forms the backdrop of this book.

New York City, as a world center for finance and media, and as an important crossroads for immigration into the country, bore first-hand witness to the upheaval of these times and, indeed, contributed largely to it. Gardnerian Wica established its first significant toehold in North America via Raymond and Rosemary Buckland in 1964 on Long Island in the shadow of the Big Apple, assisted to a large extent by popular media and a dynamic and ever-changing countercultural movement that called the city home. From that foray, and others, modern Witchcraft spread far and wide in the United States, forming the core of arguably one of the fastest-growing spiritual movements in the country today.

Many characters have wandered into and out of the story of Neo-Paganism over the last forty years. One of the more interesting was a tall, thin fellow with the mien of a rock star, who didn't originally start out seeking fame as a leader in Witchcraft community. As a boy from a

---

writings, but was in common usage at the time covered by this work and so is retained herein. When the term "Wica" is used, it generally refers to a specific type of Witchcraft, e.g., Gardnerian Wica. "Wicca," in this book, is usually applied to the forms of Witchcraft that either derive from Gardnerian Wica or that developed semi-independently from Wica after its establishment in the United States but, as the reader will see, this application is not consistent, even amongst Gardnerians, who variously use Wica, Wicca, Witchcraft, and the Craft to describe their path.

In all cases, religions and religious/spiritual movements and their adherents are capitalized, e.g., Christianity=Christian, Satanism=Satanist, Witchcraft/Wica/Wicca=Witch/Wican/Wiccan. Some would object that Witchcraft/Wica/Wicca is more akin to a philosophy or practice than a religion and should not be capitalized or treated in the same manner as Christianity, Catholicism, etc. However, these practices usually invoke God-forms by name, and make sacrifice and direct prayers to those God-forms. These are, by most definitions, religious practices, and thus worthy of the same treatment and respect granted to other religions, and even philosophical schools of thought are usually capitalized.

* The process of exerting one's Will upon the Universe via prayer or ritual in order to effect change is referred to herein as "magick." This follows the nomenclature adopted by a significant portion of the occult and Neo-Pagan communities in order to differentiate this process from that of stage magic.

Catholic family, Edmund Buczynski (pronounced "boo-CHIN-ski") had initially dreamed of becoming a Jesuit priest after having lost his biological father at a young age. However, those plans and his life were abruptly turned upside down after he was confronted by the hatred engendered by his homosexuality. This eventually resulted in his devotion to a more sympathetic spiritual path, one that would most kindly be described as apostate by his former church. To paraphrase Joseph Campbell's ideal of the archetypal hero of mythology, he let go of the life he had planned, so as to accept the one that was waiting for him.

Eddie Buczynski's life was a quest, with the thread of mythology running deeply through its pattern. Shortly after abandoning his quest for the priesthood, he dropped out of high school and ran away to Greenwich Village, where he witnessed and partook of the delights that the Hippie subculture had to offer. Despite his initial aspirations to the Catholic priesthood, he went on to found a world-famous Witchcraft supply store with the first great love of his life, and a Witchcraft tradition devoted to gay and bisexual men with the second. Under the influence of his third and last love, Buczynski garnered his high school equivalency diploma and then set his sights on college. Earning degrees in classics and archaeology, with a special devotion to Minoan Crete, Eddie succumbed on the threshold of his doctoral studies to complications associated with acquired immune deficiency syndrome. On his deathbed, Buczynski returned full circle to the Catholicism of his youth, thus completing the quest cycle that is the mark of Campbell's mythic hero.

It was an era of sexual and racial discrimination, infighting and upheaval as the occult movement, and the community that coalesced around it, grew and changed. And while Buczynski's contributions to the Neo-Pagan movement in the United States do not rise to the level of a Gerald Gardner, the effects of his actions certainly continue to echo throughout that community, whether in the presence of occult-oriented bookstores and mail order (and now internet-based) services scattered across the country, in the living traditions of Witchcraft that he founded, and in the opportunities he offered to men and women of different racial backgrounds and sexual orientations to practice their faith openly. A life such as Buczynski's can thus be used as a lens through which to examine the history of the occult community during this period, for Eddie Buczynski's presence in New York City in the 1970s under the particular circumstances of that time influenced the history of the occult revival in the United States to a notable extent. This reason alone would make his life a worthy subject for study. But more fundamentally, his is a story of the alchemy of a man's life. It is a story of hope, if tinged with the pathos of a Greek tragedy. Buczynski's life demonstrates the ability of a person to look beyond his past, to take the essence of who and what he is and focus it to effect change in himself and his fellows. This, simply put, is the definition of magick. Myth and magick were the clear mountain streams in which Eddie bathed throughout his short life.

Ironically, Buczynski's life was becoming mythical (in the worst sense of the term) as those closest to him passed on or their memories began to fade. The loss of history is always of particular concern in minority subcultures, where change is often rapid and the accurate preservation of historical details is of secondary interest to merely living life and getting by. Moreover, every work of history is itself an act of audacity, for it is difficult enough for those present at events to agree upon what happened in general terms, let alone to come to consensus in the multi(ne)farious details. How much more challenging, then, is it for one separated from those events by time and geography to spin a golden tale from the straw of past harvests? This story is no different, for the subject was a complex man, and purposefully ambiguous even to his family, his lovers and his closest friends. It is fitting, therefore, that Eddie chose Hermes as the initiatory name by which he would first be known in the Craft community. As the classical scholar R. F. Willetts, whom Eddie would later use as a source for his own writings, wrote, "In many ways, Hermes is the most sympathetic, the most baffling, the most confusing, the most complex, and therefore the most Greek of all the Olympian gods."[1] These epithets accurately establish the boundaries of our subject.

Trying to document the life of a leader in the Neo-Pagan community is perhaps one of the thorniest, most frustrating tasks on which one could choose to spend one's free time. Eventually, if one is fortunate, a critical mass of writings, recordings, stories and photographs can be accumulated to the point that an outside observer might naively muse, like Adele in Gertrude Stein's Q.E.D., "Why, it's like a bit of mathematics. Suddenly it does itself and you begin to see." However, the path to that point is in reality often a rocky, sometimes hidden one fraught with dead ends, precipices and bewildering switchbacks. One must deal with family members, fearful of the odium that they perceive may taint the name of their loved one. Friends and associates may be reticent to speak either ill or fairly of the subject, concerned over the reactions that either response may engender. One must navigate through a maze of occult oaths and secrets, mindful that while one should not bite the hand that offers succor in the quest for knowledge, neither should one accept unsupported assertions that everything is secret and thus off-limits to discussion. One must also assuage egos, gently coax fragile memories, rub liniment on old war wounds, and fill in as best as one can the painful gaps left by the dead — who always know, but seldom can be bothered to speak.

In short, one is more often than not faced with a tangle of facts, apocrypha and contradictions that more closely resembles the Gordian knot than a simple bedtime story. Like Alexander, there is always the temptation to simplify matters and cut to the chase, but such tactics do little to reveal the true complexities of a person, and risk dishonoring that person's memory by turning a life into a salacious cartoon. Far better, then, for the writer to gently tease loose the threads of a man's story, and then weave it into a tapestry that does justice to the life that he led. This has the added advantage of saving the boline's edge for fending off the author's critics afterwards.

There will likely be few tales produced as this one has been, with the collaboration and encouragement of the communities that bookend the major aspects of Eddie's life — namely, the occult, as typified by the many different strains within modern Neo-Paganism, and the academia of Classical and Near Eastern archaeology. Under normal circumstances, these two worlds overlap only tentatively, the Bacchante lightly dancing out of the academician's clinical reach, the Apollonian skittishly avoiding the ecstatic's otherworldly touch. Yet Eddie walked between these worlds, reveling in both the Dionysian and the Apollonian aspects of humanity, much like the Dictaean Zeus he so honored and loved. The people of ancient Crete found no contradiction in the worship of a youthful, boundary-breaking, dying and rising God of wine and dance who was also the elder law-giver. The bull, so full of piss and seed, of stamping power and the steaming blood of sacrifice, is sacred to both. Leaping ebulliently to heaven, his back speckled with starry sweat, the curve of his horns marks the course of the glowing moon — the same moon that shines
upon the dreams of academic and Pagan priest alike. The Bull of Heaven thunders between these two worlds, breathing hot life into both. Ia Zoë!

MICHAEL LLOYD
COLUMBUS, OHIO
1 JANUARY 2011 C.E.

Μαΐου, η Θεών Διατηρήστε την Αδελφότητα

(από τόν αφτον τόυς)

Foreword

I first met Eddie Buczynski in 1972. He was charismatic, gorgeous and somewhat intimidating to me, a newbie Pagan. He seemed to carry deep secrets.

I found myself in the Brooklyn Pagan Way, and then joined a Welsh training coven. While the Pagan Way materials were mostly created by writer Ed Fitch, the Welsh material — much of it beautiful and poetic — turned out to be written by Eddie.

At that time, many Pagans were creating fictitious tales of their tradition's origins, perhaps out of the insecurity of a newly created religion, even if based on old roots, mythology and history. The tradition created by Eddie Buczynski, Herman Slater and Leo Martello was no exception. I and my fellow newbies were told our Welsh tradition was twelve thousand years old and unbroken. When I and others realized this could only be a fiction, we left, feeling it was a lie. I saw very little of Eddie ever again. But I kept his Welsh Book of Shadows, since some of the poems, invocations and rituals were among the most beautiful I encountered in Wicca.

For years I wondered about this brilliant man and his secrets. I didn't know a tenth of it.

Michael Lloyd has written the untold story, not only Eddie Buczynski's history, but how that history intersects with a broad swath of Pagan and magical history in New York and the United States. Eddie's journey encompasses Celtic Paganism, the Egyptian based Church of the Eternal Source, the Crowley based Ordo Templi Orientis, the Minoan Brotherhood, the gay movement in New York, the AIDS crisis, and so much more.

For those who are encountering modern Paganism for the first time in these pages, remember that if you go far enough back, all of our ancestors were Pagans — that is, they followed spiritual and religious traditions that were tied to the earth and its seasonal cycles. Almost all of us in the United States had those traditions torn from us, for good or ill. If we are African American, the traditions were torn from us by slavery; if we are Native American, the traditions were destroyed, or almost destroyed, by colonialism — and if we are white Europeans, our grandparents or great grandparents or great, great grandparents tried to assimilate or adapt as fast as possible and threw away most of those earth-based traditions. Now, some of those traditions were authoritarian, so good riddance. But throwing them out also meant throwing out the lullabies, the dances, the coming of age ceremonies, the connection with nature, the juice of the ecstatic practice of indigenous peoples, who we all once were. Contemporary Paganism is the attempt to connect with that juice. Eddie Buczynski was one of those people who knew how to make a pathway to that creative, vital center.

Now, in 2012, contemporary Paganism is becoming mainstream. There are Pagan headstones in Arlington Cemetery, peer reviewed Pagan scholarly journals, Pagan charities and blood drives, Pagan pastoral counselors and much more. But when this movement began, it was rebellious and anarchistic in both good and bad ways. One of its problems was that there was little support for those with deep needs that religions often help.

The early growth of the Pagan Movement is filled with stories of people who left because the movement could not help them with their troubles. I think of Aidan Kelly, the Pagan Thealogian who went back to Catholicism to find an AA group to deal with his alcoholism and came back later. I think of Joe Caldiero, a gay man who was on the skids economically and became a Mormon; he got a job, a wife, a family, thereby missing the AIDS epidemic where many of his friends died. He later left the church, and embraced his gay identity. And I think of brilliant Eddie Buczynski, who finally left Pagan activism to become a serious scholar of the classics and was brought down by AIDS much too early, before his new life could fully flower.

Michael Lloyd's biography is a window into so many worlds. It brings alive a creative man who many of us erroneously thought we knew, but clearly did not. By bringing Buczynski into the light, Lloyd also brings to light the often hidden history of many of the political and spiritual groups and movements of the 1970's and 1980's.

>   MARGOT ADLER
>   NEW YORK CITY
>   14 FEBRUARY, 2012 C.E.

Puer Aeturnus

Chapter 1: A Bull At The Beginning

Beautiful Little Boy

In the beginning there was the word, and that word was a formless roar of shock and indignation as the newborn babe was extracted from the comforting warmth of his mother's womb and thrust into a bright, cold world. Edmund Buczynski, Jr. arrived on the 6th day of a waxing moon at the Coney Island Hospital in Brooklyn, New York. He was born at 8 AM on the morning of Tuesday January 28, 1947 to Edmund Joseph and Marie C. Buczynski. For his mother, the squalling child couldn't have come a moment too soon. "I was in labor for seventeen hours," Marie stated. "I cried the entire time, and I thought that the doctor was going to slap me."[1] A chubby little guy with jet black hair and piercing sky blue eyes, Eddie was a beautiful little boy, and one nurse took the unusual step of carrying the newborn around the ward to show him off to the other nurses, doctors and patients.[2] This kind of adoration would take place throughout Eddie's life, whether he was at the local Charming Child contest in 1949, or out at the gay bars in 1979. Many years later, his last lover would remark that "Eddie got all of the looks in the family."[3]

If one believed in astrology, as many of Eddie's fellow countrymen were increasingly prone to do in these post-War years, then a glance at his natal horoscope would give cause for a cocked eyebrow, or two. With a double grand trine in both air and fire, Buczynski was destined to be a visionary — an intensely curious and spiritual man, a fast thinker, and a communicator who could forge his ideas into actions. Indeed, if he followed the course suggested by his chart, he couldn't *not* make things happen, particularly in matters both esoteric and intimate. However, with no earth signs to anchor him and all of his water planets in Scorpio, his inquisitive and adventuresome nature had the potential to manifest in impulsive, fickle and rootless behavior.[4, 5] But we're getting ahead of ourselves in this tale. Such matters were far from anyone's ken at the head of this path, with the squalling newborn still "stained with blood and with the waters of his mother's womb," as Plutarch wrote, "more like someone just killed than someone just born."[6] As with all people, he began in blood and ended in blood, but endings were still many years away for young Eddie on this crisp morn as the thin Aquarian sun shone through the dawn-tinted windows of his mother's hospital room.

Eddie's father, Edmund, was the youngest son of eastern European immigrants — a Polish mother and a Russian father of Polish extraction. He was raised in a Brooklyn tenement at 143 Williams Avenue with his four brothers and two sisters. Edmund's father was a tailor, an occupation that he brought from Minsk in the chaos after the Czar's fall.[7] But tailoring wasn't in Edmund's destiny. When he turned sixteen, war was raging across the world. Edmund lied to the Navy about his age and enlisted in 1943 as part of the Naval Armed Guard. His entry port was the US Naval Armed Guard Center at 52nd Street and 1st Avenue in Brooklyn.[8, 9, 10]

During World War II, the Brooklyn Armed Guard Center was used to train men to be members of Navy gun crews, radiomen, or signalmen on troop ships and Liberty ships — merchant vessels transporting war materiel and goods in the Atlantic and Pacific sea lanes. Buczynski was later shipped to the armed guard training center at Camp Shelton near Norfolk, Virginia, which prepared gun crews — known as "bluejackets" — for their role in protecting merchant ships. From Norfolk, Buczynski sailed as a Naval Armed Guard aboard two Liberty ships, the SS John Howland and the SS José Marti. *(Ibid n#8)*

It was a perilous occupation, with lightly armed vessels running singly or in convoys being attacked by enemy surface ships, submarines and planes. In 1942 alone, the first full year that the United States was involved in the war, 1006 ships were sunk.[11] Between 1940 and 1947, almost 2,200 Naval Armed Guard personnel were killed guarding merchant vessels. One of those fallen was a buddy, shot down dead next to Edmund during one particularly vicious attack in the mid-Atlantic. Though poorly equipped in comparison to the foe they were up against, the Naval Armed Guard was the lucky rabbit's foot of merchant vessels running the supply routes between America and Europe. It was stressful work, filled with gun drills, nervous watches and boredom interspersed with periods of sheer terror as enemy vessels were sighted or, worse, reported to be operating unseen in the area.[12] Letters from a sweetheart back home sometimes made all the difference between a sailor keeping his head on straight and losing it to an enemy gunner.

Enter Marie Mauro, the granddaughter of immigrants from southern Italy. Marie grew up in a 6th Avenue apartment house in Brooklyn just a short walk from the Naval Armed Guard Center. Brooklyn during the war was an exciting and busy place, with ships being built or refitted for service and launched from the Navy Yard on the East River. Over seventy thousand men and women worked to strengthen the US fleet, and many thousands more servicemen and women passed through the borough on their way to war.

Edmund first met Marie as a pen pal in 1944, as she and several of her girlfriends had decided to do their part for the war effort by writing to local servicemen overseas. They met face-to-face for the first time when Edmund was home on leave, and he was smitten with the dark-haired teenager. Buczynski's interest in Marie was understandable, for she was a knockout. From that point onward he became a more diligent correspondent, gently pushing for a deeper commitment, while she remained somewhat aloof. "I was writing to several guys at the time," Marie remembered. "I wanted to keep my options open. I was only sixteen, after all!"[13]

After several successful cross-Atlantic runs, Edmund was returned stateside for training in cargo handling in Brooklyn and later in conducting Landing Ship Tank operations at Camp Bradford in Norfolk, Virginia. *(Ibid n#8)* At the end of the war, Edmund returned to Brooklyn and civilian life. He entered the United States Naval Reserve and took a job as a track maintenance worker with the B-1 Division of the New York Metropolitan Transportation Authority (MTA). It was 1945 and the nineteen-year-old, returning home far worldlier and more mature than when he left, was ready to settle down and start a family. When he finally asked for Marie's hand in marriage, she was also ready to make the commitment. However, both her parents and Edmund's reacted with horrified prejudice at the prospect. Edmund's father did not want him to marry into an Italian family. For his part, Marie's father didn't want her wedding "a Pollack," and went so far as to enter the seventeen-year-old into a bathing suit contest in an effort to attract more acceptable suitors. Marie won the contest, but told her father that she *was* marrying Edmund anyway. *(Ibid n#13)* And that was that.

Despite the lingering reservations of their families (Edmund's father was still trying to talk his son out of the marriage on the train en route to the ceremony), the young couple was wed on April 27, 1946 and settled down in Brooklyn. It wasn't long afterward that they found out that Marie was pregnant, and they eagerly looked forward to their first child. Eddie was born exactly nine months later into a world that stood on the cusp of things wondrous, worrisome and weird.

It was the year that the radiocarbon method was first proposed as a dating technique for archaeology, and the year that the first Dead Sea Scrolls were discovered that would later be subjected to this new technique. In a converted ice-skating rink at the New York City Building in Queens, Palestine was divided by a cabal of world leaders, thereby setting the stage for many decades of bloody conflict in the Middle East. The Indian subcontinent was also partitioned, resulting in a massive upheaval in the population and violence that killed an estimated one million people. The last major outbreak of smallpox occurred in New York City in late March, prompting what was then the largest mass vaccination in the nation's history in response to a potential pandemic outbreak.[14] The crash of a strange aircraft outside of Roswell, New Mexico, in combination with an ill-considered Air Force press release, ignited the public's imagination and spawned an industry of government conspiracy theorists and UFO-logists that remains with us to this day. LaGuardia Airport was dedicated, and commercial television broadcasting began in earnest in the United States — and in December, Aleister Crowley, a ceremonial magickian and outer head of the Ordo Templi Orientis (O.T.O.), known as the "wickedest man in England" and the most visible occultist of his time, passed away.

Though the pall of world war had thinned, it never quite cleared as the great alliance against fascism slowly crumbled to starkly reveal the competing interests that had lain dormant behind the façade of necessary cooperation. The Truman Doctrine was announced in May, marking the official start of the Cold War between the democracies of the West and the spread of Soviet-enabled Communism in the East, and forty years of low-level conflict by proxy. The sunny days of optimism at the victory over fascism quickly became clouded with the fears of communist conspiracies. The country steadily grew more suspicious and conservative, even as it shifted to a more urban and middle class society. By June, the State Department began instituting steps to remove homosexuals from sensitive positions on the grounds of national security. The so-called "Hollywood 10" were indicted for contempt of Congress in November for refusing to testify before the House Un-American Activities Committee.

But all was not gloom and doom. The world into which Eddie was born was also one of boundless opportunity, particularly so if one were white, heterosexual and middle class. But even for those who weren't, greater New York City in the immediate aftermath of World War II was a bustle of growth and opportunity as the country shook off the trappings of the war economy to settle back into patterns of normalcy. Jackie Robinson broke the color barrier in major league baseball, playing his first game for the Brooklyn Dodgers. The Presidential committee on civil rights submitted its report in October, recommending the establishment of a permanent Fair Employment Practices Committee (FEPC) with enforcement powers. Racial segregation in the armed forces was ended, federal legislation was promulgated to punish lynching and abolish the poll tax, and the first known lesbian publication in the United States — *Vice Versa* (subtitled "America's Gayest Magazine") — began publication on the West Coast in June.

With the outbreak of hostilities in Korea, the elder Edmund was briefly called back to active duty from the Navy Reserves. Shortly before Christmas in 1950, he was shipped to the Fleet Training Center in San Diego, California. There as a boatswain's mate shipboard he helped train sea crews aboard the USS Glynn (APA-239) — a Haskell Class Attack Transport. *(Ibid n#8, 10)* He later assisted in the transfer of the Glynn to Norfolk, Virginia, where it engaged in peacetime training exercises in the Atlantic. Edmund was finally discharged once and for all from active duty in October 1951 at Portsmouth, Virginia and returned to his family in Brooklyn and his job with the MTA.

Ed Buczynski bought a house in the New York suburb of Ozone Park in the borough of Queens, moving his family there in September 1952. *(Ibid n#1)* In the 1940s and 1950s, as now, first-time homeowners were moving from Brooklyn and the Bronx to the farther suburbs because of their relatively low housing costs. Many white families had also begun to flee Brooklyn as middle-class blacks began pushing out from Harlem. Ozone Park was originally created in 1882 from farmland in the borough of Queens as a bedroom community for New York City. In those days, "ozone" suggested clean, fresh air from the ocean and bay to city dwellers who were looking to escape the crowding and tuberculosis of the tenements.

By the time the Buczynskis moved in, Ozone Park had settled down into a solidly middle-class Italian-Catholic neighborhood.[15, 16, 17] Writer Jack Kerouac, known by his friends as the "Wizard of Ozone Park" had written his Beat masterpiece *On the Road* while living with his parents just blocks from where the Buczynskis set up house. Actress Bernadette Peters and musician Cyndi Lauper grew up in Ozone Park, and the neighborhood would later play host to the Gotti crime family and all of the unwelcome attention that would entail. What fresh air there was in Ozone Park by then was generally left up to one's imagination in the face of overdevelopment and industry, and ozone. Still, the small but tidy houses of the neighborhood beat apartment living in Brooklyn any day, and the Buczynskis were grateful for the opportunity. Eddie quickly grew tall and thin in this environment and explored his kingdom as all young boys do.

In 1952, Eddie was tested for school admission and was rated a 1A student of exceptional intelligence. That fall, at age five-and-a-half, he was admitted to Kindergarten at Public School 63 in Queens, also known as Old South Elementary in Ozone Park. Eddie was a precocious and good child in school, and Marie remembered that they were always very proud of his grades. A sensitive boy who loved music, Eddie was always reading, drawing and painting and had a very active imagination. Childhood friend Terry Gianniotis said that "he was just very creative, no matter what he did. There was creativity involved in anything he did. He saw things differently. There was definitely a very art[istic] element to Eddie."[18] Eddie's grade school years were extremely happy ones, according to his mother.

The sedate rhythm of the family was pleasantly interrupted in August 1954 with the arrival of a younger brother, Frank, who was named after Ed Buczynski, Senior's eldest brother. Eddie was an involved and loving brother, despite the seven year difference in the boys' ages. Frank remembered him as "the best big brother anyone could ever have."[19] The Buczynskis and the family next door threw summer parties together, building a shared barbecue pit in the fence line between the houses and serving cold beer in wooden kegs to family and friends. The family was, by all counts, a normal and happy one. Ed Buczynski, Senior was a big, burly man who would help other homeowners with such projects as hanging suspended ceilings. He was a nice guy and the neighbors had a lot of respect for him, recalled Gianniotis. *(Ibid n#18)*

Eddie developed into a contemplative child and became interested in nature and history and the interconnectedness of things at an early age. Writing as an adult, Eddie noted that "my dearest memories, especially religious memories, are connected with my father."[20] Through walks in the neighborhood and visits to parks, the library, and museums, the elder Buczynski was credited with teaching Eddie of his "kinship with the other living things of earth ... and a reverence for the past." *(Ibid n#20)* Gianniotis offered an anecdote that illustrated her friend's early love of history. "My first memory of Eddie was of him [walking down the street pulling] me in a wagon. He was Antony and I was Cleopatra," she recalled, laughing. "That wasn't my idea. It was his." *(Ibid n#18)*

It was during this period that Eddie began to take an earnest interest in spirituality. Buczynski recalled that "My mother honored the Virgin Mary, the 'Mother of God' ... but my father did not practice his Catholicism. Instead he revered Nature in his own way." *(Ibid n#20)* And yet, Edmund honored his wife's path and solemnly told the youngster that if he was ever troubled, he shouldn't hesitate to seek out the Mother and pray to Her. Eddie wondered if this wasn't an oblique reference to Goddess worship; an unlikely possibility, but one that he sometimes pondered in years to come.[21] In reality, Mary was a hot topic in the Catholic Church of the 1950s, as it had only recently endorsed the dogma of the Assumption of Mary via the Apostolic Constitution *Munificentissimus Deus* of Pope Pius XII on November 1, 1950.

Buczynski recalled playfully experimenting with Pagan worship in these formative years. "My father was the first to teach me about [ancient] Egypt. He told me the names of the Gods as we walked together through museums. ... My first contact with the Deities and ways of ancient Egypt was when I went to see the movie *The Ten Commandments* [in 1956]. It was as though I was looking at splendors that I had once known. From that moment on, I devoured as much as I could about the ancient Egyptians and their religious beliefs. I worshipped the sun daily, sacrificing fruits and flowers and milk. My father never disapproved ... my mother never knew." *(Ibid n#20)*

Eddie's experimentation paralleled that of several friends and acquaintances, including Giani Siri, whom he would meet many years later in Brooklyn Heights. "[My father] was a fundamentalist atheist. 'There's no god and you better fucking get used to it.' He tried to raise me that way and failed miserably," Siri wrote of her own upbringing. "I believe that all kids are born little pagans. If you don't send us to Sunday school it doesn't get beat out of us. I have never stopped having the magical thinking of a child. I've had a sense of the luminous numinous since I was 3. I built my first altar in a sheltered area in some bushes near my home when I was 8."[22] Similarly, Eddie was said to have made offerings to a Wisteria vine at home. "He liked the 'dark side' of things," said Gianniotis. "He was always interested in mystical things." *(Ibid n#18)*

Despite some prevailing opinions on the subject, Paganism is actually no more prone to "the dark side of things" than any other religion. Regardless of one's spiritual path, the dark side of human nature manifests itself when we abandon our humanity in the face of fear or tragedy. A foretaste of tragedy occurred in 1958 when Eddie's father badly injured his leg on the job and was forced to recuperate at home while it healed. But even worse would befall the family later that year when, on August 28, the elder Buczynski passed away suddenly in the upstairs bedroom from a massive heart attack. Eddie was eleven years old.[23, 24] Frank, who was just days shy of his fourth birthday at the time of the disaster, remembers the house being filled with police officers on the day his father passed away. The family physician, Dr. Robertson, was called to the house and shook his head grimly as he came downstairs after examining the body. Ed's death at age thirty-one devastated the family both emotionally and financially.

The sudden death stunned the neighborhood, according to Terry Gianniotis, who believes that Marie was not equipped to deal with the sudden loss of her husband, with two young sons to care for and a house to keep. Gianniotis thinks that the incident left the newly widowed mother questioning her faith, and recalled that Marie subsequently refused to attend funerals. *(Ibid n#18)* After recovering from the shock of losing her husband, Marie was forced to look for work in order to make ends meet. Her mother moved in with the family to help raise the boys and got her daughter a job at the St. Mary Gate of Heaven Parish in Ozone Park where she worked. Marie was placed in charge of maintaining the wardrobes of the twenty-five priests who served the parish. *(Ibid n#13, 19)*

Terry noticed that her childhood friend was very melancholy during this period. *(Ibid n#18)* According to his mother, Eddie tightly held in his feelings after his father's death, never crying once.[25] But the strain was there nonetheless, and much of the innocence had evaporated from his life. His father's death didn't immediately affect Eddie's performance at school, but his behavior began to gradually erode with no adult male in the house. This became more pronounced when Marie began dating again. A year after Edmund's death, a nun at the parish told Marie that she needed to start looking toward the future for her own sake and that of her sons. Marie initially rejected this advice, but the thought stayed in the back of her mind. Her family privately agreed with the nun's advice, and it wasn't long before Marie's sister, Ann, introduced the widow to a potential suitor.

Edward Nascosto was a gentle, soft-spoken man who had a good job at Madison Square Garden. From the outset, he treated Eddie and Frank with respect and kindness, realizing that seeing their mother with another man would be difficult for them. The younger Frank barely remembered what his father looked like, but Eddie's memories of the elder Buczynski were still vivid, and he initially rejected Edward's overtures. Nascosto was a patient man, however, and bided his time until he eventually won the young man over. Three years after Edmund's death, Marie asked Eddie if he wouldn't mind her remarrying, and Eddie assented. Edward and Marie were wed on November 3, 1961. From that point forward, Edward treated the two boys as if they were his own.

Suffer the Children

The Buczynskis had never really been staunch church-goers, even though both parents came from Catholic families. This didn't change when Edward and Marie married; both remained nominally Catholic but were not particularly religious. Frank Buczynski notes that Edward Nascosto tended more toward atheism than Catholicism. *(Ibid n#19)* However, in the years following his father's passing, Eddie had become even more spiritual. Eddie wrote that when his biological father died, he retreated into the golden ages of past civilizations, turning for protection and guidance to the Pagan Gods whose representations he had first encountered on museum forays with his father. "My pantheon consisted of the Gods of Egypt, the Gods of Greece, and ... the Gods of the Sabaeans of Southern Arabia. My closest affinity was with female deities and deities of love and parenthood – perhaps because my parenthood was incomplete." *(Ibid n#20)* It was at this time that Eddie made his first attempts at working magick.[26]

By the time Buczynski turned thirteen, he had decided that religion was to play a major role in his life. Along with his Pagan interests, he began to study his native Roman Catholicism. "I had realized that I was born to the priesthood," he writes. "[But] since I felt that I was the only Pagan left in the world, I turned to the Catholic priesthood." *(Ibid n#20)* While Eddie may also have been influenced in this by his interactions with the priests with whom his mother worked at St. Mary Gate of Heaven, it was most likely his relationship with his favorite uncle, a Catholic Priest named Father Michael, that guided him in this direction. In early 1961, he was confirmed in the Catholic Church, taking the confirmation name of Michael in honor of his uncle. From this point onward he used Michael as his middle name, even though it wasn't part of his legal name. *(Ibid n#10)* Eddie informed Marie that same year that he wished to transfer from the public schools to a Catholic high school. This was, he said, the first step to prepare the way for eventually taking orders with the *Societas Iesu*, also known as the Jesuits. Marie assented, and in September 1961, at age fourteen, Eddie began his freshman year at Monsignor McClancy Memorial High School in the East Elmhurst neighborhood of Queens.

Operated by the French Catholic Order "Brothers of the Sacred Heart," Monsignor McClancy had a superior academic curriculum that suited Buczynski's intellect. However, in marked contrast to his grade school days, Marie noted that Eddie's time in high school was sad. *(Ibid n#2)* Eddie began to have problems almost immediately. Not having attended a Catholic grade school placed him somewhat at a disadvantage with regard to the culture of the private school, which was different from his public school experience. His tendency toward bookishness and effeminacy, and his general disinterest in sports, also marked him as an outsider, and he was beginning to mature sexually in a way that diverged from his fellow students. His fellows, with the primal sense of such things that youngsters often possess, recognized that Eddie wasn't like them — and they made him pay for it.

Eddie's freshman year at Monsignor McClancy was very difficult. Although he was stimulated in his academic studies, he was not socializing well. He was called names and beaten up for being "queer" on a number of occasions, and he received little support from the school administration. His attitudes toward the teachings of the Church also began to change during this period. "I respected the teachings of Christ to the greatest degree, but I was confused about the teachings of His Church, especially because of the period I was going through. Sex, life, pleasures, wildness, *et cetera* were all part of my teenage experience, and yet in school I was taught that these things were wrong. I could not understand why the Natural was so utterly repressed by the Christian ways and replaced by guilt and mortification. I caused havoc in my Religion classes and subsequently was expelled." *(Ibid n#20)*

This experience soured Eddie on the Catholic Church, and by the end of his freshman year in High School he had abandoned any prospect of taking priestly vows. After being expelled from McClancy, he transferred back to the New York public school system in his sophomore year and began attending John Adams High School in Ozone Park in September 1962. The return to public school, however, proved to be no panacea. Eddie was bored in the classroom, which wasn't able to challenge him intellectually. His social problems followed him from one school to another — only this time he couldn't even escape them in his own neighborhood.

Unbeknownst to Marie and Edward, Eddie had become painfully aware of differences between himself and other boys his age. He was pretty for a boy and effeminate, both traits that tend to mark one as a target in the brutal jungle of male adolescence. Life in Ozone Park was particularly hard for Eddie, who had been effeminate from a very early age. "I think [our] street was kind of hard on Eddie," said Terry Gianniotis. "His mother, of course, was loving to him. But [our] street was pretty bigoted, and outside of the home it was pretty hard for him to be on [our] street. ... People on [the] street were very critical of him. Eddie was different. From his youth, he was different. Different — he was feminine. He wasn't '[our] street.'" *(Ibid n#18)* Eddie and Terry used to joke in later years that it was if an alien spaceship had landed and colonized their tiny part of the neighborhood.

What remained of his childhood came to an abrupt end once he started attending John Adams. Rumors that he was gay began circulating almost immediately. Kids started tormenting Eddie at school, then in his home neighborhood, calling him a faggot. Regular beatings were administered by the neighborhood kids, who Marie disgustedly characterized as a bunch of "macho bastards." Eddie's discipline both at home and at school suffered as he began to act out his frustrations. He began to smoke Marlboros and experiment with drugs. His younger brother, Frank, remembers seeing Eddie smoking a joint on the front stoop of their house one day and asked him if he was out of his mind for being so blasé about it. Pot use in 1962 was still relatively uncommon in the suburbs, and Eddie shrugged off Frank's concerns by saying that no one would know what it was. *(Ibid n#19)*

In September 1962, Marie gave birth to Tommy Nascosto. Edward and Marie were proud parents, and Eddie and Frank welcomed their newborn brother with open arms. Still, Tommy's birth took attention from Eddie when he was going through a difficult period in his life, and the addition of a new person to their tiny Ozone Park home added its own degree of stress. Even within the extended family, there were signs that all was not well. While his immediate family and Marie's relatives remained loving and supportive, there was a growing distance between Eddie and the Buczynski side of the family. His father's relatives looked askance at the teen and talked about him behind his back. Eddie tried not to let his hurt show, retreating further into his beloved books, but the mounting pressure simply became too much for him to bear. Before his junior year was out, Buczynski had attempted suicide twice by overdosing on downers.

"I knew that he suffered from bouts of depression," Gianniotis said. "And I think it was [due to his] coming to terms with who he was. I mean [our] street was really not an easy place to grow up on, and being in Eddie's shoes, I just can't imagine everything he went through. But I'm not surprised." *(Ibid n#18)* The Nascostos, on the other hand, were stunned. *(Ibid n#24)* Following this cry for help, they took Eddie to the family physician. Marie said many years later that "it was the best thing we ever did for him." *(Ibid n#25)* The doctor said that there was nothing physically wrong with Eddie, and recommended that the family take him to a counselor. Frank Buczynski said that his mother believed that someone had made Eddie gay, but the counselors dissuaded Marie from that notion. The conclusion was that Eddie's problems resulted from other people's reactions to him, not from any intrinsic maladjustment on his part. *(Ibid n#19)* For 1963, when homosexuality was still considered to be a mental illness and homosexual acts were a crime in the New York penal code, this was an unusually sympathetic diagnosis for a young male exhibiting these traits.

To their credit, Edward and Marie never turned their backs on Eddie or judged him, unlike so many other parents in the early 1960s when confronted with gay offspring. "I've never been prejudiced," Marie stated in a 2010 interview. "It didn't matter whether you were black, brown, green, or whatever. I've always just treated people as people." *(Ibid n#1)* Unfortunately, it simply wasn't enough. "I think that Marie didn't know what to do with Eddie many times," recalled Terry Gianniotis. "She loved him but she, you know, just didn't know what to do with him. She couldn't talk to anybody about him, I think. Maybe she talked to her sister. I think she talked a bit later on to my mother. ... It was tough for her. She really adored him, but she really didn't know how to manage him at all. Or manage Eddie in the context of the social pressures of her [life]." *(Ibid n#18)*

Although he never attempted to take his life again, Eddie struggled with depression for the rest of his life. No longer able to stomach the daily torment of attending high school or even living in the only place he knew as home, he dropped out of John Adams High School in March 1964 just two months shy of an early graduation. Contributing to his feelings of rootlessness was the fact that Eddie had completely given up on religion after his dismissal from Catholic school. "I lived for a long time without any religion whatsoever. By the time I was finished with High School, I was totally irreligious. The Hippy movement was beginning to come in strongly and I moved into it readily. It seemed to fill a void that had taken root in my life." *(Ibid n#20)* As Frank and Tommy grew older, there was also less room in the house for a moody seventeen-year-old. While he loved his family dearly, he needed to get out. Eddie packed his bags and left the oppression of Ozone Park behind, hopping a train into Manhattan to begin sorting out who he was. Buczynski landed in Greenwich Village and discovered a different sort of life — one that didn't involve being beaten on a regular basis by neighborhood thugs.

Chapter 2: One If by Broom, Two If by Sea

The British Witches Are Coming

A new spiritual influence came ashore in the United States in late 1963, one that would eventually influence the course of Eddie's life. It was at this time, according to some, that British Traditional Witchcraft "officially" crossed the Atlantic in the persons of Raymond and Rosemary Buckland. They and their spiritual practice arrived in the Unites States two years before the Beatles did, and with considerably less fanfare from the American press. Since 1954, Gerald Brousseau Gardner, the spokesman (some say the creator) of what came to be called Gardnerian Wica, had embarked on a mission of rescuing Witchcraft from the dustbin of history by spreading his vision and version of it as widely as possible.

Through the 1950s and early 1960s, the public was becoming aware of the existence of Witchcraft covens and of opportunities for training and worship that were not as widely known (or as available) in the past. Most of the press coverage of the day poked fun at its practitioners. A frequent charge was that Gardnerian Witches were engaged in Satanic worship and blasphemous rites, which some detractors described as "a strange hodge-podge of filth, beauty and idiocy."[1, 2] Enough factual details leaked out through the pejorative wall erected by the media that a small but steady stream of people of sound character were drawn to seek out Craft teachers. Inquiries also came from unsavory or otherwise unqualified seekers who wanted to participate in Witchcraft for a variety of reasons, none of them having to do with its purpose as defined by Gardner.

At the same time, people who followed other extant paths of Witchcraft — some related to Gardner's, some not — resented the publicity and the arrogance of the "Gardnerians" in what they considered to be public grandstanding. "Gardnerian" Wica was initially a pejorative label used by other Witchcraft practitioners to describe Gerald Gardner's followers. It was an attempt to dismiss Gardner's dream as a cult of personality, despite the evidence that many of these other forms of Witchcraft were themselves being influenced either by Gardner's ideas or by the earlier sources that had informed his outlook. As a result, for many years, Gardner's followers resisted using the term "Gardnerian" to describe their form of Witchcraft. Some still do today, instead preferring terms such as the Old Religion, the Craft, or just plain Witchcraft. They believed that focusing on the recent efforts of a single individual distracted from their claim to an unbroken spiritual tradition dating back to the dim mists of time. But, rightly or wrongly (with most observers tending towards the former), the Gardnerian label stuck.

The growth of Witchcraft that initially resulted from Gardner's efforts was accompanied by conflict, which is the coin (and often the doom) of all great human endeavors. Simply put, many of the people Gardner raised to leadership positions could not seem to tolerate one another. Gardner fretted over the inability of his priestesses to get along, and was dismayed when the inevitable fights occurred — the most famous of which was his own break with his former high priestess Doreen Valiente, to whom Gardner owed so much. For her part, Valiente was so hurt by being overthrown for a younger high priestess that she omitted any mention of Gardner in her first book on the subject of Witchcraft in 1962. She did, however, take an oblique swipe at the public promotion of Wica by Gardner and others — a bone of contention between the two — by noting that "The very last thing a possessor of real secrets does is to seek cheap publicity."[3] Surviving correspondence, news articles and letters in British occult publications dispels any notion of a Golden Age of Wica by demonstrating that the Craft community that Gardner had created was involved in continuous low-level squabbles by the early 1960s. That conflicts occurred is not surprising, given the type of personality needed to rise to the demands of coven leadership, combined with the decentralized nature of the tradition.

Toward the end of his life, Gerald Gardner brought in his last High Priestess, Monique Wilson (Craft name *Olwen*). By 1961, Wilson had established two covens in Scotland and was fielding inquiries from seekers sent to her by Gardner. One of these inquiries was from Raymond Buckland, a man who would have a profound impact on the history of the Craft movement. Buckland had contacted Gerald Gardner after reading a copy of Gardner's 1954 book *Witchcraft Today.* He was fascinated by the concepts that Gardner and other writers of the period were beginning to promote concerning the survival of Pagan religious practices into modern times, and he undertook a long period of correspondence with Gardner, and later with Monique Wilson, to explore this spiritual avenue. This correspondence continued even after Raymond and his wife, Rosemary, had emigrated from England to the United States in February 1962.

Buckland eventually prevailed on Gardner to bring him into the Craft, which Gardner did by asking that Monique take him on as a student. On November 18, 1963, Raymond Buckland traveled to Perth, Scotland, where Wilson trained him over a period of ten days and initiated and elevated him.[4] Buckland took the Craft name *Robat*. Such a rapid advancement through the Degree system is not normally recommended, but this depends also upon the age, maturity and experience of the recipient, and Buckland passed muster in these regards. However, such "quickie degrees" are far more common than some in the Craft community would like to admit. (It is not unusual, for instance, for a person to initiate and elevate his/her own spouse up through the ranks in rapid order, often in a single night.) Upon returning to the United States, Raymond initiated and elevated Rosemary, who took the Craft name *Rowen*, and made her his High Priestess. Together, they formed a teaching coven that began operating out of their home on Long Island in the community of Brentwood, New York.[5, 6]

Rosemary was appointed by Monique on November 30, 1963 to act as the maiden of the New York Covens and deputy high priestess in her absence.[7, 8] *(Ibid n#5)* Wilson was, by all appearances, pleased with the enthusiasm and competence the Bucklands brought to the Craft, and with the fact that they were starting off with a group of eight students. She wrote to Gardner expressing her confidence in their abilities on December 3, 1963.[9] The Bucklands' coven began operating shortly after New Year's in 1964. Rosemary's appointment, in combination with Raymond's working relationship with Gerald Gardner, gave the appearance that the Bucklands had been "chartered" as the spokespersons for the Gardnerian brand of Witchcraft in the United States. Perceptions notwithstanding, from this point through the remainder of Wilson's active participation in the Craft, all inquiries directed to Gerald Gardner and Monique Wilson from seekers in the United States were forwarded on to the Bucklands to handle. It was from these letters and Raymond's deft handling of the press that the Bucklands found the people who became the first members of their Long Island coven. *(Ibid n#6)* In mid-1964, Rosemary traveled to the Isle of Man, where Monique Wilson facilitated the re-doing of all three of her degrees and declared her Witch Queen on July 13, 1964.[10] By August 1965, the Bucklands were pleased to have the first new coven break away from theirs (a process known as "hiving off"). This was the coven of Fran and Gerry Fisher (Craft names *Theo* and *Thain*) of Louisville, Kentucky. *(Ibid n#6, 10)*

On November 14, 1963, Dr. Margaret Murray passed away at age 100. Her 1921 treatise on the survival of Witchcraft — *The Witch Cult in Western Europe* — helped jumpstart modern Witchcraft and spur its subsequent growth, and it greatly influenced both Gerald Gardner and Raymond Buckland. Gardner himself passed away a few months later on February 12, 1964 while on a voyage in the Mediterranean. Monique Wilson was named as Gardner's beneficiary, along with Eleanor Bone, Patricia Crowther, Doreen Valiente and several others. However, it was to Monique that the ownership of Gerald Gardner's Witchcraft Museum and all of its contents passed, and this bequest from Gardner to his last high priestess was the source of bitter feelings amongst his other priestesses.[11] Nevertheless, Monique and her husband and high priest Campbell (Craft name, *Loic*) weathered the resentment and continued with their teaching, initially receiving relatively positive publicity from the British press.

However, one news article eventually prompted a charge of child abuse against the couple by some unfriendly neighbors. After struggling for several years with the legal problems and opprobrium arising from this issue, Monique's husband negotiated the sale of the entire contents of the Witchcraft Museum to the Ripley's Believe It or Not Museum in the United States and moved the family to Spain in 1971. This action, seen by many of Gardner's initiatory descendents as having robbed England of its Craft patrimony, sparked outright hatred against the couple. The bulk of Gerald Gardner's library and papers — including Gardner's Book of Shadows, *Ye Bok of ye Art Magical* — were eventually acquired from Ripley's by Richard and Tamarra James of the Wiccan Church of Canada (Toronto, Ontario), and so were repatriated within the bounds of the Commonwealth if not to Great Britain herself. Nevertheless, for their actions, Monique and Campbell Wilson continue to be reviled by many British Witches long after their deaths, even as they are honored by many in the United States for their patronage of the Bucklands and their support of Witchcraft in the United States.

Land of Opportunity

Although Ray Buckland had originally moved to the United States for employment, the opportunity for expanding the reach of Gardnerian Wica on these shores did not go unrecognized. When the Bucklands began their New York Coven in 1964, there were few publicly known covens in the United States. It has been said that a number of hereditary Witchcraft traditions pre-dated the Bucklands' arrival, and that even some practitioners from lineages of Gardnerian Wica other than Monique Wilson's had already arrived on the shores of North America (e.g., in Nova Scotia). The influx of occult ideas and philosophies into the United States certainly did not originate with the arrival of the Bucklands in the 1960s. Indeed, successive waves of mystical and occult ideas had been lapping America's shores since before the Republic's founding.

Some argue the first wave was at the Ma-re settlement in the Puritan Massachusetts Bay Colony, where renegade English trader Thomas Morton erected a huge Maypole around which he and other English danced and drank with Native Americans in the 1620s. The actions of Morton, who was at least putatively an Anglican Christian, caused great consternation to his Puritan neighbors.[12] As early as the 1690s, Hermetic and Rosicrucian concepts were being incorporated into the spiritual practices of some religious sects in eastern Pennsylvania under the leadership of such folks as German immigrant Johannes Kelpius.[13,14] The Amish, Dunkers, and Mennonites, grouped under the common term "Pennsylvania Dutch," have preserved a rich tapestry of powwow and *hexerei* folklore and beliefs for at least two hundred years.[15] Loners or families of healing Witches have been known to exist in the remote hills of Kentucky since the 1800s.[16] The practice of Vodoun, imported with newly-arrived slaves from Haiti and Equatorial Guinea, had a sufficient presence in New Orleans by the late 1700s to be considered a civil threat. Root workers practicing the art of Hoodoo weren't far behind.[17]

The Virginia Statute for Religious Freedom, when passed into law by the Virginia legislature in 1786, was a public acknowledgement of the religious diversity that already existed in the country at that time. Of its passage, Thomas Jefferson rejoiced that there was finally freedom "for the Jew and the Gentile, the Christian and the Mahometan, the Hindoo, and Infidel of every denomination."[18] And of course the shamanism and magic practiced by the native peoples of North America had never completely disappeared, despite the depredations of European colonialism, and some of the ideas from these native traditions eventually came to influence the spiritual practices of other groups in the United States.

Another wave of the mystical and occult to affect the United States was Spiritualism. With its emphasis on mediumship with the dead, Spiritualism swept the country beginning in the 1840s in Upstate New York.[19] It grew in leaps and bounds following the Civil War, and again in the early twentieth century after the influenza pandemic and World War I. This was in some ways echoed by the mystical Ghost Dance that swept the Plains tribes in the late 1860s, brought on by the stress of war and the extermination of the vast buffalo herds upon which the tribes depended for bodily and spiritual sustenance. Madame Blavatsky and Civil War veteran Colonel Henry Olcott founded the Theosophical Society in New York City in 1875. Theosophy, with its blending of Hinduism, Buddhism and western occultism, influenced a number of influential American thinkers of the late nineteenth and early twentieth centuries.[20] Following in the spiritual footsteps of Walt Whitman and Henry David Thoreau, Oscar Wilde toured the nation in 1892 preaching the unspoken gospel of romantic Paganism that underlay his beloved Aesthetic Movement. Buddhists and practitioners of the Hindu faiths began immigrating to the United States in the 1890s.

Also beginning in the 1890s, Great Britain began experiencing the widespread emergence of a new esoteric spirituality and a proliferation of the so-called "New Age" groups that went hand in hand with a renewed interest in medieval and Renaissance myths.[21] This, in turn, spurred the development of groups such as the Hermetic Order of the Golden Dawn and, later, the O.T.O. The O.T.O. was the spiritual descendant of the many underground occult societies that flourished in Europe in the 1890s, including French Satanism, Rosicrucianism and Witch cults, American Theosophy, and the Occult-Scientific societies and fragmenting Masonic orders of Austro-Hungary. Later, under the leadership of the O.T.O.'s most famous spokesman, Aleister Crowley, the Order was influenced by the ceremonial sex cults of Weimar Germany.[22]

This spiritual movement quickly spread to the United States via the establishment of mystical lodges. The Golden Dawn broke up in 1900, and a successor organization — Alpha et Omega (A.O.) — was founded by its former leader, Samuel Liddell MacGregor Mathers, sometime after 1903. Two of the former Golden Dawn temples in the United States, located in Chicago and New York City, became part of the A.O., and it was to the New York Temple that future genius of the tarot, Paul Foster

Case, was drawn. Three more temples were founded in Philadelphia, Los Angeles, and San Francisco after World War I; however, all appear to have vanished by the end of World War II after the Golden Dawn's secret teachings were published by Israel Regardie.[23, 24, 25] The collapse was due in no small part to Mathers' death in 1918, followed by the high-handed incompetence of his wife in the aftermath. Case eventually published his lifetime's knowledge of the Tarot, which also incorporated secret teachings of the Golden Dawn, in his book *The Tarot* (1947).[26] The modern tarot has another link to New York City, it being the birthplace of its most famous promoter, Arthur Edward Waite, the co-designer of the Rider-Waite-Smith deck.[27]

Aleister Crowley traveled to America in 1914 to spread the message of Thelema — emphasizing Will and personal power — and his particular practice of ceremonial magick. He came to help found a new and greater Pagan cult in the New World.[28] The first O.T.O. group in North America, Agapé Lodge, was founded in Vancouver, British Columbia in 1912. It migrated to the United States with the chartering of the Agapé Lodge No. 2 in Los Angeles, California in 1935.[29, 30, 31] Crowley spent a good deal of his time in the United States ensconced in Greenwich Village on Washington Square where, it was wryly said, he "made many converts." Reporter Nigel Trask, when recalling that period, wrote "I was in that city at the time and attended several of [Crowley's] séances where the 'black mass' was read. There were blue lights, spirals of blue smoke, and Crowley, in dark monkish garb, sitting just outside the magic circle, intoning the words of his demoniac services."[32]

Crowley alternated his time between travel, publishing, meditative retreats, seduction, spying for the Allies, and paid public performances in order to help make ends meet.[33] During one of his retreats he painted "Do What Thou Wilt Shall Be the Whole of the Law" and "Every Man and Woman is a Star" on the cliffs on both sides of Oesopus Island in the middle of the Hudson River, no doubt to the puzzlement of the local farmers who rowed over to investigate the doings of the charming and eccentric Englishman. It was at his Washington Square studio in New York that Crowley met Leah Hirsig, who would become his magickal partner, his "Scarlet Woman" — the earthly representative of Babalon, the Goddess of his Thelemic magickal system.[34] He tried his hand at painting during this period, advertising for deformed and freakish models and staging a "Dead Souls" art exhibition in Greenwich Village in 1919.[35] But New York City was merely a way station for Crowley, who left with Hersig for Cefalu, Italy in 1920. There, he founded and ran his orgiastic Abbey of Thelema until 1923, when Mussolini's government had him expelled for his excesses. Fascists, it seems, are only tolerant of the perversities hidden behind their own closed doors.

In 1915, American businessman and philosopher H. Spencer Lewis incorporated the Rosicrucian Order, AMORC, in New York City. By the

1920s, occult temples and organizations of various types were ensconced in most major metropolitan areas.[36, 37] There are some indications that Witchcraft groups may also have been operating in the United States at the turn of the twentieth century in such scattered locations as the West Coast, Boston, and New York, the latter reportedly having two covens run by a European antiques dealer.[38] Occult bookstores and groups were certainly thriving in New York City by this time, as evidenced by the contemporary correspondence of horror writer H.P. Lovecraft.[39] The used and rare book shops on "Book Row," which ran along 4th Avenue, between Union Square and Astor Place, catered to the tastes of New York's many discerning and unusual bibliophiles.

Yet another wave of the United States mystical experience began with the Italian immigrants who began arriving in New York City beginning in the 1880s and 1890s. These immigrants brought with them rural beliefs in herbs, Witches (*Strega*), occult powers, the "evil eye," and charms. A demographic study of Greenwich Village in the 1920s documented Italian residents — both immigrants and their first-generation offspring — patronizing *Strega* for love potions and spell powders. Demand for herbs and herbal remedies was great enough in this community to support the presence of several herb stores, and even "an enterprising dealer of doubtful reputation [who made] a business of Indian herb remedies."[40] Italian customers often crossed ethnic lines to shop at botanicas for necessary ingredients and ready-made spells.[41]

In addition, fortune tellers of various stripes appear to have long made New York City their home. *The New York Times* reported an estimated 1000 fortune tellers operating in every neighborhood throughout the city in 1909.[42, 43, 44] All told, these oracles were taking in a staggering ten thousand dollars a day (almost a quarter million dollars in 2010 valuation). One astrologer, Evangeline Smith Adams, flourished in turn-of-the-twentieth century New York despite being arrested twice, in 1911 and 1914, for the crime of fortune-telling.[45] And Hollywood used the presence of fortune tellers in 1920s-era Greenwich Village to convey to audiences the exotic nature of that neighborhood, as illustrated by Carmen Miranda's "Princess Querida" character in the film *Greenwich Village* (1944).[46]

Reports of Witchcraft and the occult regularly appeared in the pages of *The New York Times* from the mid-1800s until the 1930s, then fell off before picking up again in the 1960s. The authorities and reporters were, not surprisingly, generally skeptical of the claims of occult practitioners. The hysterical bewitchment claims made by a Miss Susan Hook of Paterson, New Jersey against her neighbor Mrs. Josephine Kievit is one such example from 1895.[47] News reports in 1900 and 1903 detail the arrests of "occult seeresses" in Brooklyn, one of whom also appeared to be working love, luck and revenge spells for her clients. In a case from 1914, postal inspectors jailed the Supreme Ruler of the Iridescent Order of the Iris for selling to hundreds of clients "luck-stones," which the inspectors alleged to be nothing more than common lodestones.[48] It has been claimed that Greenwich Village during the 1920s was awash with Witchcraft, some genuine, some masquerading as Satanism, but mostly fake.[49]

Santeria made its first public appearance in New York City with the growing population of Hispanic immigrants after World War I. Alberto Rendon opened his "West Indies Botanical Garden" botanica at 60 East 116th Street in Harlem in 1921 to serve this community.[50] The *New York Times* of August 14, 1925 reported that police in Atlantic City, New Jersey seized twelve thousand price lists sent from a "Voodoo Doctor" operating in Brooklyn.[51] By the late 1950s, a new wave of practitioners of African diasporic spiritualities — Santeria, Vodou, Candomblé — made New York their home, beginning with the refugees of the Cuban revolution in 1959 and increasing with an influx of Haitians and others following the easing of United States immigration restrictions from the Third World in 1965.[52] Vodou, in particular, had sparked the public's imagination and appetite for Third World popular culture in the 1950s through the 1970s, much as the cultures and spirituality of Asia, such as the practice of Zen Buddhism, were brought to our shores by veterans returning from the Pacific Theatre in the 1940s.

A spate of sensationalistic, disrespectful and even racist books on African-oriented spirituality was published to satisfy this curiosity.[53] Persecution of practitioners of African diasporic faiths continued well into the twentieth century. In 1962, New York Commissioner of Markets Albert Pacetta ordered a crackdown on the retail markets owned by the city. After sending samples of various "voodoo objects" to laboratories for testing and determining them all to be fraudulent, he banned their sale.[54, 55] Some of those affected by his acts threatened to curse Pancetta, though others worked magic in his favor because he was rooting out the frauds (who were also their competitors). As one writer of the era noted, "Witchcraft, like politics, has many factions in New York City."[56]

By the end of the decade, politicians had bigger fish to fry, and the botanicas were left alone as long as the items they sold were truthfully labeled. By this time, the production and marketing of prepackaged Witchcraft spells was reported to have had blossomed into a nationwide business pulling in millions of dollars annually.[57] Markets and shops catering to believers continued to thrive, particularly in Harlem and the Bronx. One of the largest, known simply as "La Marqueta," spread its awning under the elevated tracks along Park Avenue between 111th and 112th Avenues.[58] Tolerance of these activities was, as is so often the case, not the same as acceptance. As Rena LeBlanc asked in a 1974 article in *Probe the Unknown* magazine, "Voodoo priests are nice people ... but would you want one living next door?"[59]

While imported practices were fruitful and multiplied on American soil, native groups also sprang into being across the United States From the 1800s, scattered assemblies of people practiced varieties of folk magick that employed a mishmash of Ceremonial, Spiritualist, Masonic, and astrological practices.[60] A few of these survived to gain the notice of the modern era, such as Olney Richmond's Order of the Magi in Chicago. The Long Island Church of Aphrodite was established in 1938 by Gleb Botkin in West Hempstead, New York. Worshipping the Greek Goddess of Love, the Church of Aphrodite was most likely the first Reconstructionist Pagan group in the country, although it was essentially a monotheistic cult rather than a polytheistic one.[61] *Life* magazine covered New York's issuance of a state certificate of incorporation to the church in 1939. "The new and frankly pagan church is complete with a congregation of 35, a high priest — its founder Gleb Botkin — [and] a concrete manifestation of its divinity in a plaster model of the Medici Venus.'"[62] The Church of Aphrodite was never very large, nor was it particularly influential in its day. However, some of the church's philosophy carried over into the 1960s and 1970s through the actions of one of its former members, W. Holman Keith.

Frederick Adams founded the California-based Fellowship of Hesperides in 1957, a classically-inspired spiritual, artistic and cultural group. The Fellowship experimented with forming an intentional community long before communes became popular in the 1960s.[63] The seeds of what would become the Feri tradition sprouted shortly after Gerald Gardner published *Witchcraft Today* (1954), although Feri itself did not become a formalized system until 1970. Victor Anderson, the founder of the Feri tradition, stated that he had been inculcated into a folk practice in the 1930s. While Victor took inspiration from Gardner's book, forming a coven and teaching his own unique spiritual philosophy in the 1950s, it is clear that Feri bears no resemblance to Gardner's Wica.[64] An organization called Atl, the Aztec word for "water," was formed in 1962 by several university students, including Lance Christie and Tim Zell. Atl would evolve by 1967 into The Church of All Worlds, which would become arguably the most influential Neo-Pagan group in the United States during the 1970s.[65] In 1963, Harold Moss began to hold an annual Egyptian-themed summer party that in 1970 became the Church of the Eternal Source, a reconstructionist group of the religion of ancient Egypt.[66]

Moonrise over New York

Apart from Gerald Gardner's Wica, there is some indication that other Witchcraft traditions or practices were present in the United States prior to late 1963, or else arrived soon thereafter. Some were Satanic groups. Many were traditional groups, hedge Witches, and Cunning men who had adopted Gardner's methodology beginning in the 1950s and had thus begun to migrate into the Gardnerian sphere.[67] Others cleaved more closely to their original forms. One of these was an alleged unnamed family tradition in Wichita, Kansas into which airman Joseph Wilson was initiated in 1963. After joining, Wilson began to correspond with British Witches via an ad placed in the last issue of the occult magazine *Pentagram*.[68]

Wilson was encouraged by this wider view of the Craft to start his own United States-based publication, *The Waxing Moon*, in early 1964. This newsletter republished a great deal of information from newsletters and writers from England and was an important early source of cross-pollination between the two continents. One of Wilson's British correspondents was Roy Bowers (a.k.a. Robert Cochrane), who was said to have provided the young American with information on his own family tradition, which he called the "Clan of Tubal Cain."[69] Wilson went on to found the 1734 tradition of Witchcraft in the late 1960s based upon the information provided by his initial family tradition, Roy Bowers, and Ruth Wynn-Owen, a practitioner of the Welsh Hereditary Family of "Y Plant Bran."[70]

British Witch Sybil Leek visited the States on a book tour in early 1964 and fell in love with the country. Leek was already a minor celebrity in her native land. Well-known in England as a "white Witch," broadcaster and antiques shop owner, Leek practiced, in the New Forest area a tradition called Horsa, which she claimed was related to Gardner's Wica and Celtic Witchcraft. Because of the publicity she attracted, Leek had outstayed her welcome as far as the landlord of her shop in the village of Burley, Hampshire was concerned, and she was looking for greener pastures. Ironically, it was the United States edition of her 1962 book *A Shop in the High Street*, which told the story of her time as a shop-owner, that launched her career as an author and public speaker in America. Sensing an opportunity to start afresh across the Atlantic, Sybil emigrated from England to the United States in 1964, just as the Bucklands had done two years previously.[71, 72]

While Sybil's first visit to the United States was filled with interviews and appearances, Raymond Buckland was still very much an unknown in his adopted land. Buckland, however, was on good terms with Leek at this time, going out to dinner with the New Forest refugee shortly after she arrived in New York. The matronly Leek, with her British accent and dry wit, became a much-sought-after interviewee.[73] Taking his cue from Leek's reception in 1964, Raymond also began to engage the press. Buckland granted his first interview on Witchcraft to the *New York Daily News* in October 1964 in what was to become a predictable, and tiresome, media tradition of parading stories of real live Witches before the public at Hallowe'en. *(Ibid n#5)* Witches really were working against the tide of history on this point; as people had been dressing up as their fairy-tale counterpart at Hallowe'en for the better part of the twentieth century. Buckland and Leek, sans warts and pointy hats, made for a cultured, non-threatening, yet still exotic team when they began participating in joint speaking engagements, and the networks ate it up. One of their early appearances together was in 1966 on *The Alan Burke Show*, a controversial conservative talk show on WNEW Channel 5 in New York. *(Ibid n#5)*

Inspired by Gerald Gardner's Witchcraft Museum on the Isle of Man, Raymond Buckland founded The Buckland Museum of Witchcraft & Magick in 1966. Raymond operated his museum during limited hours out of the basement of his family's home in Bay Shore, New York. That same year, he published his first pamphlet on Gardnerian Wica — *Witchcraft: The Religion* — which was Number 1 in the "Museum Handbook Series." By this time, covens descended from the Bucklands' Long Island group were located in New York, New Jersey, Kentucky, California, Washington, D.C., Ohio, and Ontario, Canada. Raymond had also become a professional on the lecture circuit and became one of the first Witches to be represented by an agent — Richard Fulton in Manhattan.[74]

Being the public face of Wica provided Buckland with hitherto unaccustomed access to free publicity. Raymond began not only fielding inquiries from interested seekers, but also consulting on the subject in cooperation with college and university professors who taught classes that touched on the occult. While these activities caused some consternation in Craft circles, arguably his most controversial move was to respond to interview requests from the American media, who were thrilled to have a Witch in their own backyard to feed the growing occult interests of the public. The publicity further whetted the appetite of the American public, and seekers besieged the Bucklands and others for the opportunity to train and practice to become Witches.

Witchcraft — the spiritual practice, as opposed to the fantasy — was still very much a novelty to the vast majority of the United States public at this time. Certainly information on the practice of modern Witchcraft in Great Britain — the news coverage, books and magazines — was not released in a vacuum. Americans with an interest in the occult had access to virtually everything being published on the other side of the Atlantic — particularly in the New York metropolitan area, given the city's place as a media hub. Anyone keen to do so would have had ample opportunity to read about, and even independently contact, Witches in Britain, and a number of Americans did.

One example of early coverage of British Witchcraft by the American media can be found in the April 1962 issue of the popular pulp paranormal publication *Fate*, which contained a short article about Gardnerian Witches Monique and Campbell Wilson.[75] Another example is the November 13, 1964 issue of *Life* magazine, in which two articles discussed the coven of Gardner initiate Eleanor Ray Bone. This issue of *Life* was groundbreaking for two reasons. First, it contained a number of photographs, including one picture depicting a skyclad (nude) rite that is likely the first such photograph to have appeared in print in the United

States.[76] Secondly, one of the articles was written by Bone herself, and was one of the earliest first-person accounts written by an active practitioner of Gardnerian Wica to appear in a nationally-circulated periodical in the United States. The articles were surprisingly balanced for the day, with Bone's account expressing in thoughtful words some of the romanticism that makes modern Wica so appealing.[77]

> *In this age of science ... one might think that there was no place left for the witch. But the sun still rises in the morning and sets in the evening; at night the moon watches over us. ... We know that come what may, "another sun will rise tomorrow."*

Both the sun and the moon were very definitely rising on Witchcraft in the United States In 1952, Pennethorne Hughes had published his book, *Witchcraft*. Released two years before Gardner's *Witchcraft Today*, Hughes' book provided an overview of the history of the practice, and a pronouncement that "witchcraft, as a cult belief in Europe, is dead. As a degenerate form of a primitive fertility belief, incorporating the earliest instructive wisdom, the practice is over. Conjurors, wisewomen, palmists, and perverts may be called witches, but it is using an old stick to beat a dead dog."[78] Hughes declared that Christianity and rationalism had won the day, and that it was only a matter of time before a rising standard of living accomplished the same for the developing world. Within the span of two decades, history would prove the certainty of Hughes' convictions to be utterly misplaced. Indeed, the seeds for his failure as an oracle, in the form of the Brentwood coven, were already being sown in the United States when Penguin reissued the book in 1965.

Americans had long been fascinated with the idea of Witches and magick. This may be intimately tied to the Puritanistic suppression of sex that was the dark underbelly of the country's unique Protestant inheritance. Witches, positioned by the arts and media to represent those who stand outside the boundaries of polite society, in some cases romantically so, may have represented a fantasy world where the forbidden fruit was, if not sanctioned, then at least more accessible. This temptation, and the resulting sexual tension between Witches and "normals", resurfaced in books and the performing arts throughout the latter half of the twentieth century. Indeed, it could be argued that the depiction of Witchcraft in the popular culture laid the groundwork for the rise of the Witchcraft religion in the United States.

The 1939 movie *The Wizard of Oz* is one indication of this phenomenon. Loosely based on the beloved series of children's books by L. Frank Baum, Witches in the Land of Oz were portrayed as representing opposing forces for good and evil: the Good Witch of the North and the Wicked Witch of the West. The story presented to the audience is a classic morality play, where the loyalty of the protagonists to one another and their bravery in standing up to the threats of the Wicked Witch — all done under the light guiding hand of the Good Witch — are rewarded. Witches are shown as nearly elemental beings of power and wisdom, able to either help or harm as their own particular nature dictates.

Likewise, Witches are a breed apart in the much gloomier *Dark of the Moon*. This 1942 Broadway play by William Berney and Howard Richardson explores the efforts of the "witch boy," John, to become human after bedding a mortal woman on his mountaintop abode. With its portrayal of Witchcraft, religious fundamentalism, infanticide and rape, it is not surprising that the story ends badly for its characters. Despite being quite controversial at the time it debuted, the play has been popular with high school, college and community theatrical groups for over sixty years.

The unhappy ending of *Dark of the Moon* is reversed with an upbeat one in the romantic comedy film *I Married a Witch*, which was released that same year. The film is a comedy of errors resulting from the attempts of a Witch and her father to seek revenge on the descendant of the man who was responsible for having them both burned at the stake for their crimes in 1672. The Witches in *I Married a Witch* break with previous portrayals in that they are human, but with extraordinary powers. The mundane protagonist, instead of being destroyed by his erstwhile enemy, the Witch, ends up happily married to her. He is rewarded by becoming a wildly successful politician as a result of his wife's magickal interference in his election bid. The vapid, unquestioning support of the voters upon whom the spell was cast is a tongue-in-cheek commentary on the electoral process if ever there was one. The story ends with the proud parents settling down to raise their broomstick-riding child. Unlike *Dark of the Moon*, the antagonist-turned-heroine can find redemption in the end despite being a Witch.

The themes of these latter two stories would be twisted together in John Van Druten's 1950 Broadway production of *Bell, Book and Candle*. In this comic play, Witches represent an "other" that lives amongst the humans and toys with them for sport. A Witch initially pursues a mortal man for fun, only to become romantically entangled herself, thereby losing her powers and her place in her own society as a result of her love for the man. *Bell, Book, and Candle* had a good run on Broadway and was made into a moderately successful movie of the same name in 1958. Starring Kim Novak and James Stewart, the film was eagerly anticipated, as demonstrated by its placement as the cover story in *Life* magazine in November 1957.[79]

The Witches and Warlocks in *Bell, Book, and Candle* are residents of Greenwich Village. Writer Leslie Ellen Jones points out that they were portrayed in the movie as Beatniks, so as to emphasize their status as social outsiders.[80] The Beat subculture was also known as a haven for the sexually disreputable, counting among its members such "notorious" homosexuals and bisexuals such as Alan Ginsberg, Jack Kerouac, and

William S. Burroughs. Thus, to be labeled as a Beat was often akin to being called a queer. Certainly the two were treated similarly on the streets of Greenwich Village, both by New York's finest and by many of the neighborhood's immigrant residents. Van Druten, who was himself gay and a resident of the Village, may also have used the Witches and Warlocks who affected Beat dress and mannerisms as euphemisms for the lesbians and gay men who lived there.[81] These interlocking identities produced a series of Wildean puzzle boxes that only the hip audience members were able to solve.

This story is further complicated by Van Druten's apparent belief that practicing Witches actually did live in Greenwich Village in the 1950s.[82] Given New York's occult history and the steady rise in interest on this subject during that decade, Van Druten's notion is not outside the realm of possibility. *Look* magazine looked into the question and ended up interviewing three female Witches.[83] Sybil Leek was both amazed and appalled by the sheer number of psychics she found in New York City during her first visit, writing "I began to study the newspapers and various psychic magazines. I was disturbed to find that there are thousands of psychics who charge regular fees for consultation." Upon her return to New York in 1964, she saw that many of the psychics from her previous trip were still practicing their trade. Yet, despite the proliferation of services and readers on practically every street corner, Leek observed that there remained a great deal of discontent and unhappiness. "In America," she concluded sadly (and somewhat ironically), "occultism is big business."[84]

This big business was advanced and sustained, in part, by the sheer number of media outlets, some of which catered specifically to those interested in the occult. One example is Samuel Weiser Publishing, which was founded in 1956. Weiser originally began in 1926 as a used bookstore on the 4th Avenue "Book Row." Soon after its opening, it began to specialize in metaphysical books and Eastern religions. Branching out into publishing allowed Weiser to serve a growing market in esoteric books. The company soon developed into one of the world's foremost specialists in that genre, so it stands to reason that *someone* must have been purchasing those occult titles. Another merchant of esoteric books was the Orientalia Bookstore, which also got its start in the 1920s. Occult-related magazines, such as *Fate*, were yet another means of providing information to a fascinated, and somewhat credulous, public.

Sybil Leek entirely owed her own popularity to the publishing industry by releasing her more than 60 books on various occult topics throughout her life, beginning in 1965 with *Mr. Hotfoot Jackson* (published in the United States in 1966 as *The Jackdaw and the Witch*). Hans Holzer, a New York paranormal investigator who began publishing books on the subject shortly before Leek immigrated (beginning with *Ghost Hunter* in 1963), asked her to team up with him to investigate hauntings throughout the country. These ghost-hunting trips were publicized in news stories and in the pages of Holzer's numerous books on the subject.[85] Such activities, in addition to Leek's own interviews, columns and books, helped to popularize the dowdy eccentric.

Popular culture also continued to play a role in preparing the public for the arrival of the Craft on these shores. Unfortunately, much of this was utter schlock; witness *The Naked Witch* (1961), a film about a university student who uncovers the remarkably preserved corpse of a Witch. Removing the stake from her heart permits the naked Witch (hence the title) to wander the campus killing people. On the other hand, some popular products were quite good, such as a 1963 short story, written by Norman Mailer, which appeared in *Harper's Weekly Magazine*. Titled "The Witch of Westport," it told the tale of a modern-day Witch who had married a mortal man and proceeded to settle down into a closeted suburban lifestyle. Mailer's story was inspired by and invokes elements of *I Married a Witch* and *Bell, Book, and Candle*. It eventually became the basis for the hit television sitcom *Bewitched*, which debuted in September 1964.

Bewitched hit the airwaves the same year that the Bucklands began teaching in the United States and Leek moved to New York. Other television shows portraying magic (*I Dream of Jeannie*, 1965) and Witches (*The Addams Family* and *The Munsters*, both 1964, and *Dark Shadows*, 1966) also became quite popular during this era. One could argue that *Bewitched* and the other television programs piqued the public's curiosity about Witchcraft by portraying it in a hip, non-threatening and even positive light, using the very American media of commercial television. That public interest attracted the attention of network executives, who began casting about for real live Witches to interview. This then is one means by which Sybil Leek, Ray Buckland, and others began to capture the public's interest.

There is little doubt that the commercial success of the movie *Bell, Book and Candle* in 1958 made it possible for *Bewitched* to reach television screens across the country in 1964. Stepping from the big screen to the small ratcheted up the number of people touched by this white magick social meme. "Here again was something spreading the witchcraft word, albeit in a fantasy, situation-comedy manner," writes C.H. Wallace. "The significant point about this program, however, is that not so many years ago no television network would have dared consider it. Witchcraft, as a theme for mass media, would have been unthinkable."[86]

From the campy antics of Paul Lynde as the fey warlock Uncle Arthur, one can see echoes of those gay men and lesbians in Greenwich Village who were the models for Van Druten's Beatnik Witches.[87] But Witchcraft in the United States — the spiritual practice, not the fantasy — was still a rarity, and New York would continue to play a part in its development and growth for some time to come.

Chapter 3: It Takes a Village

And the Beats Go On

Author Jon Margolis has written that 1964 was the year when what we think of as "the Sixties" truly began. "[If] some people had smoked marijuana, dressed exotically, embraced Eastern mysticism, written or painted erotica, and spoken openly about sex in earlier years," Margolis writes, "it was in 1964 that this kind of behavior burst out of its Bohemian ghetto."[1] Certainly, from Eddie Buczynski's perspective, 1964 was the year when the course of his life was fixed. When Eddie took the train into Manhattan that summer, he landed at one of the key subcultural crossroads of the United States. Buczynski began his journey as an explorer, a voluntary exile from a loving home who sought to find his own way in the world while trying to understand his place in it. In this he differed from many of the young gay men who would journey to New York over the next twenty years, escaping or thrown unloved from their homes in the hinterlands and drawn to the bright lights, opportunities and freedom (limited as it was at the time) that the Big Apple had to offer. Even Aleister Crowley, who set out for Greenwich Village from England some fifty years previous, had arrived in Manhattan as an exile, beyond the reach of both creditors and cuckolds in his native land. Eddie, by contrast, was one of the lucky ones. He could always move back home if things got too bad, and he did so several times over the course of the next decade.

Buczynski picked a time of intense upheaval for his first foray into Greenwich Village — though, as outside observers and denizens alike might wryly note, every era is a time of upheaval in the Village, which is constantly reinventing itself. Greenwich Village, with its angled streets and odd lots, is one of the last remaining shadows of the old, organic villages that had sprouted from amongst the original Dutch farms on the island of Manhattan. Others were slowly wiped away, beginning in the 1800s, as the city modernized. Bounded by Broadway on the east and the Hudson River to the west, Houston Street on the south, and 14th Street on the north, Greenwich Village has maintained an aura of coherent quirkiness, with its brownstones and converted stables, narrow one-way streets, mature trees and small shops.

The Village seems to have encouraged a contrarian mindset in its residents for much of the last century. Some have attempted to explain this effect by citing the Village street plan, where alleys and byways in some cases still follow old stream beds and game paths, in contradiction to the sterile, rectilinear layout of the new city. Writer Ross Wetzsteon wrote that Greenwich Village had become a "self-conscious bohemian and radical community" by 1912 and the eventual "home of half the talent and half the eccentricity in the country."[2] By the beginning of World War I, the

Village was known for its homosexual residents and visitors. This reputation solidified through the 1920s until by the 1930s Greenwich Village was referred to as "the Mecca for exhibitionists and perverts of all kinds."[3]

Throughout the twentieth century, the neighborhoods of Greenwich Village and the Lower East Side had provided a hothouse environment for the arts, culture and politics — as well as the "sex, life, pleasures and wildness" that Eddie had embraced as an integral part of his teenaged life. Whether as an incubator for the Beats in the 1950s or a home to the folk music scene of the 1960s, a studio and stage for artists or a laboratory for social and political activists, the Village had literally something for everyone. So long as they were prepared to rub elbows with all of the other somethings that had attracted everyone else to the neighborhood, intrepid explorers might even have a decent enough time while seeking out their own poisons and epiphanies.

Property values and rents had begun rising in New York City during the 1950s, mainly because new laws, building codes and tax abatement programs restricted the construction or conversion of buildings to single room occupancy (SRO) uses and rooming houses, and which encouraged the conversion of SRO units into other uses.[4] Greenwich Village had by the late 1950s already begun to receive a slow influx of middle class investors who began buying up and clearing out the low income properties. This led to increased pressure on the established residents who were occupying existing housing stock in the neighborhood. Protest meetings and marches were organized by many long-time residents, who demanded that the city crack down on illegal coffee houses and the activities of the Beatniks, homosexuals, prostitutes, drug dealers, street performers, teenagers, vendors and tourists (in tour buses, no less) that these establishments attracted.[5]

Responding to resident complaints, the city passed the New York Coffeehouse Law in 1962. This regulation specifically targeted the Beatnik fringe by restricting spoken word performances in licensed establishments. Equipped with this tool, the Department of Licenses began cracking down on such venues in 1963 and 1964. The police also joined in this repression by targeting art houses that showed *avant-garde* films which were labeled obscene by the authorities. Prints of such works as Jack Smith's *Flaming Creatures* and Jean Genet's *Un Chant d'Amor* were seized along with the projection equipment, and theatre staff and sometimes even the audience members were arrested.[6] Despite these actions by the authorities, the frustration of long-time residents eventually erupted into an open revolt in the part of the neighborhood along MacDougal Street in 1965.

Many of the Beats who had once called Greenwich Village home began to migrate to the Lower East Side in the early 1960s, driven out by the higher rents, the tourists and the depredation of police who answered the complaints of the working-class Italian residents of the neighborhood.[7] Lamenting the loss of artists from the Village, Eli Waldron noted in 1964 that "Today only the well-heeled, the very well-heeled, can afford the rents prevailing in Greenwich Village. The ill-heeled and the struggling are fleeing to a new Bohemia. This is the former ghetto of the Lower East Side."[8,9]

With the influx of artists and Beats from Greenwich Village, the Lower East Side — an area roughly defined by the Bowery and 3rd Avenue on the west and Avenue D on the east — soon came to be called the "East Village." In the 1950s and early 1960s, the East Village was filled with flophouses and brothels serving the winos, junkies, and down-and-outs that had once engendered its dubious fame as New York's skid row district. As a result of this diaspora, Greenwich Village became less gritty in the 1960s, eventually serving as the nursery for the folk music scene of that period with the likes of Bob Dylan, Peter, Paul & Mary, and others. The East Village, conversely, emerged in the 1970s as an orphanage for punk rock in the miasma of lowered expectations that marked New York City as it limped through that decade. Like lions trailing a herd of antelope, city repression followed the wake of this migration into the East Village. Ed Sanders notes that the police were particularly persistent in raiding and shutting down squatter communes in the Lower East Side such as those organized by James Leroy "Groovy" Hutchinson which primarily served the needs of homeless street youth.10

The Beat subculture that developed in the mid-1950s was a rebellion against the dominant culture in the United States. As religion scholar Robert Ellwood notes, some Beats also considered their struggle to be an underground spiritual movement in opposition to conservative attempts to recast the country as a Christian bulwark against Godless Communism. For example, the Beat generation adopted Zen Buddhism because it represented freedom from the "follies of the West and its self-righteousness and angry God."[11] The Beats' flexible interpretation of Zen tenets, according to Ellwood, offered the promise of "utter freedom and spontaneity to meet personal rather than socially defined objectives." In 1959, the Maharishi Mahesh Yogi began teaching Transcendental Meditation (TM) in the United States Known disparagingly as "Hippie mysticism" in the 1960s, TM had spread throughout the country, first from Hawaii and later from California to New York City. The Beats, by adopting these spiritual traditions and living in counterpoint to the majority and, most importantly, by communicating their philosophy to a wider public through books and poetry, helped to preserve and foster spiritual diversity in America at a time when fear and uncertainty was being used as a tool to enforce conformity. *(Ibid n#11)* Yoga was another practice that began to sweep through the Village. Introduced into the United States at the turn of the nineteenth century, and quite popular among the elite at the turn of the twentieth century while spread by the Transcendentalists and Theosophists, it saw a revival in the late 1960s.[12]

With the advent of the Sixties, the Beats gradually yielded the stage to the Hippies. The Hippie subculture was a countercultural youth movement that was spawned by, and eventually absorbed much of, the aging Beat generation. Like the Beats, its adherents were antiestablishment in their outlook, believing in self-determination and freedom from the rules of society, including those that limited sexual freedom and the right to expand one's consciousness as a means to understand, and even touch, the face of Creation. Other spiritual practices and ideas crept into the mix – the environmental poetry of Henry David Thoreau and Walt Whitman; the psycho-mythological studies of Mircea Eliade, Joseph Campbell, C. G. Jung and Erich Neumann; and the Sufi mysticism of Kahlil Gibran's *The Prophet*.

The Hippie subculture was likewise compared to a religious movement. "If life to the hippies has any 'purpose' in the ordinary context of the word," *Look* magazine writer William Hedgepeth reported, then "that purpose is religious discovery."[13] Cultural anthropologist William Partridge observed by 1973 that the "hippies have reformulated the Judeo-Christian tradition of individual salvation, individual guilt and sin, the journey of spiritual growth, and created an ideology we have seen to be the 'quest for self-knowledge.'"[14] Pot, sex and loafing were certainly in there somewhere as well, but there isn't any rule that says those pursuits couldn't also be imbued with a spiritual significance (and they were).

Although the Hippies generally held their Beat predecessors in high regard, the feelings of admiration were not always mutual. Beat writer Jack Kerouac, in his last published piece before his death in 1969, railed against the Hippies and the radicals of the anti-war movement, whom he compared to parasites.[15] And yet, in debating the similarities and differences between the Beats and the Hippies on William F. Buckley Jr.'s television show *Firing Line* in 1968, Kerouac acknowledged that the Hippies were a continuation of the Beats, but also "apparently some kind of Dionysian movement in late civilization, which I did not intend, any more than, I suppose, Dionysos did."[16]

Hot Child in the City

It was this exciting subculture that had attracted the young Eddie Buczynski to Greenwich Village. In a way, Eddie was trying to escape the pain of what he perceived as his stillborn dreams. His father's death still hurt him badly, even after six years, and his rejection by the Catholic Church closed down his hope of joining the priesthood almost from the outset. So, for a time, Eddie rebelliously threw himself into the very things that rankled Church authorities. But life in the Village was not easy, even for the adults who called the neighborhood home. How much worse, then, were the hardships faced by a seventeen-year-old living on the streets for the first time?

Disaffected youths were flocking to the Village in order to escape from unhappy family situations or just to take their chances in the thriving scene. Many of these young men and women faced some rather unpleasant choices when it came to their basic survival.[17] If one were really lucky, he or she might quickly make friends with others who were already established and get an invitation to "crash" with them. It wasn't uncommon for substandard New York lofts to be crowded with Beat, and later Hippie, youths sleeping wall-to-wall in a proto-communal arrangement of rented crash pads and squats. These living conditions may well have provided the necessary social training and negotiating skills for the advent of a hallmark of the Hippie subculture — the establishment of communes and intentional communities — beginning in the mid-to-late 1960s. But even if one had no associates in the Village, there was always the 63rd Street YMCA. Edmund White, who stayed there himself upon reaching New York in 1962, noted that the Greenwich Village YMCA had so many gay residents that it was referred to as a "fairy palace."[18]

As with the homeless of today, the least fortunate were forced to sleep on the street, in parks, on rooftops or in stairwell landings. Others resorted to prostitution or depended on hookups with a series of lovers in order to keep a roof over their heads. The area around West 42nd Street and 8th Avenue, for example, was well known as a notorious hustler corner as far back as the 1920s. Another very active cruising area was the West 70s, between Central Park and the Hudson River.[19] Male prostitution in New York was surprisingly organized by early in the decade. A number of gay bars in uptown Manhattan catered to trade; that is to say, men who had sex with other men for money. A few of these specialized in "chicken hawks" — older men who are sexually attracted to younger men of quasi, or questionable, legal age. There were even male prostitution rings, with stables of young hustlers run by Misters instead of Madams.[20] Eddie admitted to several of his friends that he had occasionally resorted to hustling in the Village in order to survive during the 1960s.[21,22] As the old-timers are wont to say, needs must when the Devil drives.

Crime was more of a problem in the Village than it was in Ozone Park. But things were tough everywhere in New York City in 1964, as the murder and rape of Kitty Genovese in Kew Gardens, Queens demonstrates. Crime in the Village was aggravated by Italian street toughs, who regularly set upon those they viewed as undesirable interlopers on their turf. The problems began in the early 1950s, when the customers of the mob-run transvestite bars along 7th Avenue started getting jumped by street gangs. After a syndicate representative came up from Jersey City to give a health lecture to the perpetrators, the incidents died down for a while before flaring up once again in 1961 and 1962. By then it was the blacks, even more than the Beats and homosexuals, who were a particular target of the residents' ire.[23]

Blacks had begun to move into the area in larger numbers to escape the troubles of Harlem and Bedford-Stuyvesant, which had experienced race riots in 1964. They were drawn to the Village by the egalitarian atmosphere fostered by the Beat subculture. Writer Ned Polsky notes that "the social bonds uniting members of any deviant culture tend to override race prejudice in large degree, and thus nearly every such subculture is more racially integrated than is 'respectable' society."[24] This was certainly true of the Beats and the Hippies, and it was much the same for the gay community in the early 1960s, where the underground nature of the culture encouraged people to band together. Gay activist Jim Fouratt recalled, "We had blacks and whites living together, a lot of gay men, a few gay women, jazz. Rent was cheap. You did what you had to do to survive."[25]

In the minds of those in power, the coloreds, commies, and queers represented an implicit threat to the status quo. There is a case to be made that the established residents of the Village were lashing out at the vulnerable and easily identifiable scapegoats who were within easy reach, thereby transferring their rage from the well-heeled — and untouchable — uptown investors who were really responsible for ringing down the curtain on their way of life.[26] Still, it is fairer to say that everyone had their turn at stirring the pot. Conditions were even worse in other areas of the city, including parts of the East Village, where grinding poverty, alcoholism, drug dealing and prostitution, and the violent crime that exists side-by-side with them, were rampant.

Drugs were an integral part of the Beat scene and, later, the Hippie subculture. The Hippies, like their Beat progenitors, enjoyed their marijuana. Beat psychonauts like Alan Ginsberg and the Hippies were much more open to experimenting with psychoactives such as peyote, mescaline, mushrooms, and chemist Albert Hofmann's problem child — LSD. Just as Aleister Crowley once extolled the use of drugs to break patterns of behavior in order to open oneself to new ideas and experiences, so too did drugs play, for many, a vital role in the consciousness-raising that was an integral part of the spiritual experimentation in the 1960s. This concept was well-established within the countercultural movement by the middle of the decade, as reflected in Frank Herbert's epic 1965 novel *Dune*, where the spice *melange* is used to awaken the consciousness of trained minds. Brian Herbert, in his father's biography, notes the influence of psychedelic drugs on Frank Herbert's development of the literary concept of *melange*.[27]

By 1962, Timothy Leary was actively promoting the use of psychoactive substances for their purported spiritual and therapeutic benefits. After being fired from Harvard University in 1963, Leary participated in a communal experiment in a mansion near Millbrook, New

York, with his activities underwritten by heirs to the Mellon fortune. Writing later about his time at the Millbrook commune, Leary stated that "we were attempting to create a new paganism and a new dedication to life as art."[28] A number of spiritual groups whose philosophies revolved around or otherwise involved the use of psychedelic substances were formed throughout the 1960s. These included the Psychedelic Peace Fellowship, founded in New York City by Michael Itkin, a gay rights advocate and early proponent of Liberation Theology.[29]

Like many youngsters in the scene, Eddie Buczynski experimented with drugs, including pot and acid. He was also rarely without a stash of Quaaludes. Also called "ludes" and "disco biscuits," the drug sensitized and relaxed its users while lowering their inhibitions — important properties when one is in the midst of a sexual revolution. However, he did not allow drugs to rule or ruin his life as some his age had.[30] It is unknown whether his experiments with psychoactive substances influenced his thinking, although Eddie would later associate cannabis with the ambrosia of Greek mythology and extol its use as a mind-opening and mood-setting adjunct.

Eddie also dove head first into the sexual theme park that the Village had to offer. Gay activist and philosopher Arthur Evans recalls that his own move to Greenwich Village was prompted by an article in *Life* magazine in 1963 that reported many homosexuals living there.[31] By the early 1960s, there were bars catering to gays in all the boroughs of New York City, even in the Jamaica neighborhood of Queens close to where Eddie grew up. In Manhattan itself, gathering places were numerous, crowded as they were along 7th and 8th Avenues through Greenwich Village, as well as up and down 2nd and 3rd Avenues in the East Village, and elsewhere.[32] *(Ibid n#23)* There was a certain danger in frequenting such establishments, both for the customers and for the business, as it was against the law for homosexuals to gather in public or to be served alcohol at licensed bars.

Bath houses, bars, gymnasiums, parks and men's rooms were often notorious pickup spots, and the "respectable" establishments spent a great deal of time policing the behavior of their clientele in order not to develop a "fast" reputation that could get them raided by the authorities or drive away their other clientele. It could be very dangerous to importune strangers for sex, since criminals and undercover police were constantly on the lookout for gay prey. The gangs that ran Hell's Kitchen north of Greenwich Village regularly beat and robbed gay men who were lured away from places like Times Square — another favorite cruising spot — on the promise of sex. Despite the opportunities that were available to him, Eddie didn't spend his entire Manhattan stay bed-hopping. At one point he settled down and dated an older fellow named Jerry, who, according to Eddie's brother Frank, seemed like a nice enough guy but bore an unfortunate resemblance to Jethro Bodine from the TV show *The Beverly*

Hillbillies.[33] Still, as one lover would later admit, "Eddie wasn't a one-man kind of guy." In this he was certainly not unique. One person who knew him a few years later wrote, "If Ed was ever without a partner, it was strictly by his own choice. The guy could be a magnet (to both sexes), and he was well aware of it."[34]

Not every moment of every day in the Village was spent in grubbing for survival or in indulging the more pleasurable needs of the body. Eddie picked up the guitar at some point from one of his Hippie friends, though he would later admit that he would never be very good at it no matter how much he practiced.[35] Somehow he managed to eke out an existence in the Village. But Eddie also maintained close contact with his family, particularly his mother, with whom he spoke on the phone at least weekly. He tried very hard to make it back home on the train every weekend for Sunday dinner with his family. When the grind eventually got to be too much for Eddie, he made the decision to move back home. Over the next several years, he moved back and forth between Manhattan and Ozone Park several times. After each time away, he returned home a little wiser and a little more street smart than during his previous stint.

Despite his embrace of the hedonism that the Village scene had to offer, Eddie still tried to satisfy his spiritual needs. Yet, as the decade wore on, he felt that the Hippie scene, so full of promise in its early days, was becoming sterile and empty. In the beginning, he wrote that "it seemed to fill a void that had taken root in my life, a void because of the abandonment of my [chosen] vocation – the priesthood." But as time went on, he began to vegetate, despairing that the "movement was going nowhere and was turning sour." Disappointed in the continuing emptiness in his life, he tried to return to the Church, probably in mid to late 1966 during one of his Manhattan sojourns. *(Ibid n#30)*

Eddie's attempt at reconciliation may have been motivated by his belief that the Church was loosening its reliance on dogma in the wake of the Second Ecumenical Council of the Vatican, otherwise known as "Vatican II." One of the Council's goals when it met from the fall of 1962 until the fall of 1965 was to try, in the face of massive change in the world, to integrate the modern human experience with Christian dogma. It was hoped that social change, in particular the increasing visibility of homosexuals in Western societies, would result in a modification and softening of the Church's views on homosexuality. At least, that was the belief of gay and lesbian Catholics, who were excited by the prospects of finally being accepted by Holy Mother Church. This turned out to be a hope in vain, for the most likely place for the Council to address the issue of homosexuality – *Schema XIII*, known as the "Church in the Modern World" – was utterly silent on the subject.

In this, the homosexuals shared their disappointment with the large number of American Catholics who had hoped that the Church would change its stance on the use of artificial birth control.[36,37] With the issuance of the *Humanae Vitae* encyclical on July 25, 1968, the Church reaffirmed its stance against artificial methods of contraception. By rejecting the realities of rubbers for population control and disease prevention "in the modern world" in blind favor of dogma, the Church signaled that the promise of change implied by Vatican II was only skin deep. The rejection of birth control virtually guaranteed that the case of gay and lesbian Catholics would also not be given a fair hearing, a point that was underlined in the 1980s when Pope John Paul II went so far as to forbid chapters of the organization of gay Catholics — Dignity USA — from meeting on Church property, and a few Bishops began to withhold communion from "unrepentant" homosexuals. These strictures led to the bizarre situation of male priests, who were referred to as the "brides of Christ," actively discriminating against gay men.

Ironically, some have blamed Vatican II for loosening the strictures on sexual conduct and facilitating the later child sexual abuse scandals in the Church. But, as research sponsored by the United States Conference of Catholic Bishops shows, gay men did not begin enrolling in seminaries in greater numbers until the rate of abuse was already in decline.[38] The fact remains that any liberality in the Council's conclusions had no widespread effect in the church. Jack Fritscher, commenting in 1979 on the number of lapsed Catholics he knew in the gay community, said "Scratch a queer ... and get a Catholic."[39] Yet for all of the talk of a "lavender mafia" in the Church hierarchy, the Vatican continued to teach the masses that "penises belonged in vaginas and in wedlock, and nowhere else."[40]

Whatever changes were wrought within the Church also produced no leniency in Eddie's particular case. On the one hand, if the post-Vatican II Church was truly being run by a homosexual cabal, as implied by its ultraconservative critics, then accepting the services of a bright, energetic and handsome young man like Eddie should have been a mere formality, especially since the Church was at that time suffering a severe loss of priests. On the other hand, given his obvious effeminacy and unorthodox spiritual views, including what some must have seen as a disturbing tenderness toward the Pagan faiths of old (a tenderness shared, one must admit, by many a Classical scholar and Catholic priest), it is perhaps less surprising that Eddie could find no suitable place for himself within the Church.[41]

The character of the Church was particularly apparent in the Archdiocese of Manhattan, which was still in the iron grip of the ultra-conservative Francis Cardinal Spellman — a "made man" in the lavender mafia if ever there was one. Whatever the reason for his failure at reconciliation, Eddie wrote that "after a year of fighting with the Priests and becoming totally fed up with the hypocrisy that has sprung up like an evil weed in the pleasant fields of Christianity, I sunk into a heavy depression and lost my hopes in life." *(Ibid n#30)* It was at this point that he gave up on the Catholic Church completely, turning away from it until the end of his days.

Eddie's belief that the Manhattan scene was spiritually empty simply isn't fair on the face of it. Plenty was going on, even if none of it may have appealed to him at that time. But his perspective was perhaps understandable. Buczynski was drawn to the ritual, history and majesty of the Catholic Church, its pomp and circumstance, the incense and candles — all of those things that he imagined to be distant reflections of the glory once found in the Pagan temples of old. As far as he could tell, none of this was available within any of the new spiritual innovations that were being played out in the countercultural laboratory of the Village. But change was continuing on multiple levels, spurred on by a relaxation of Christianity's grip on the levers of political power.

The 1950s and 1960s saw an unprecedented decoupling of religion from many of the public policy decisions of American society. Examples of this process include United States Supreme Court decisions such as *Abington Township School District v. Schempp*, 374 United States 203 (1963), which was one of a string of rulings that eliminated forced prayer in public schools; *Griswold v. Connecticut*, 381 United States 479 (1965), which established a right to privacy for married couples, including their right to use contraceptives; and *Epperson v. Arkansas*, 393 United States 97 (1968), which invalidated an Arkansas statute that prohibited the teaching of evolution in the public schools on the grounds that the law violated the Establishment Clause of the First Amendment.[42] In the Abington Township School District case, United States Supreme Court Justice Tom Clark wrote, "The very purpose of a Bill of Rights was to withdraw certain subjects from the vicissitudes of political controversy, to place them beyond the reach of majorities and officials and to establish them as legal principles to be applied by the courts. One's right to ... freedom of worship ... and other fundamental rights may not be submitted to vote; they depend on the outcome of no elections."

With the Second Vatican Council, God was no longer unchanging. With the Supreme Court rulings that took the Bible out of the classroom, God was no longer unassailable. With the arrival of modern Feminism, God was no longer male; and with the advent of Eastern mysticism, God was no longer Judeo-Christian. While the older generation equated God with country, the younger generation, choosing such prophets as Timothy Leary and Robert Heinlein over God, dropped out of country and became gods themselves. As the 1960s progressed into the 1970s, this period proved to be a seminal time for the occult in the United States, where a number of related social trends came together with a simultaneously rich and abundant array of information on non-traditional spirituality. New York City was a nexus for many of these developments.

The United States saw a tug-of-war continuing to develop between conservatives and progressives that, to at least some observers, had the potential to pull the country apart at the seams. Everywhere one turned, sociopolitical movements were springing up or becoming re-energized, in some cases militantly so, demanding that their issues be acknowledged and addressed by society. These included the anti-war movement, the women's movement, the Native American movement, and the rise of more aggressive factions within the black and gay civil rights movements after the summer of '67 and '68 riots in black communities throughout the United States and the 1969 Stonewall riots in New York City. It was the era of the Black Panthers, the Gay Liberation Front, and the National Organization for Women.

Environmental issues, which had steadily gained support in the years following the publication of Rachel Carson's book *Silent Spring* (1962), also came to the forefront by the late 1960s. The "earthrise" photo taken during the Apollo 8 mission in December 1968 helped put mankind's place in the Universe in perspective and provided a touchstone for people concerned about what we were doing to the planet. Public awareness and concern about air and water pollution were growing, sparked in part by fires on the Cuyahoga River near Cleveland, Ohio. Undersea explorer Jacques Cousteau produced wildly popular television documentaries depicting the beauty and plight of the oceans, and nature films premiered at local theatres in those pre-Imax days. On April 22, 1970 the first Earth Day was held, with an estimated 20 million Americans participating. This event is widely believed to mark the official coming-out party of the modern environmental movement in the United States. For many, interest and involvement in nature-affirming spiritual movements seemed a natural progression from their initial environmental awareness and concerns.

A new generation of young men and women had also become dissatisfied with the exercise of power and authority in society, its destruction of the planet's natural resources, and enforcement of an unpopular military draft due to the increasingly unpopular "police action" in Vietnam. While future leaders — the likes of George W. Bush, Dick Cheney and Paul Wolfowitz — supported the war from the safety of their privileged connections or draft deferments, other young men were being torn from their lives and dreams and thrust into the seemingly insatiable maw of Indochina. Peaceful protests were increasingly eclipsed in news reports by strident confrontations in the wake of the Tet offensive and the resulting United States counteroffensive in 1968.

The depth of the counterculture's animosity over the war, and the contempt of the establishment for its critics, was laid bare in Chicago that year when anti-war protesters, innocent bystanders, reporters, and even politicians were violently crushed in what was afterward called a "police riot." The carnage, orchestrated by Chicago Mayor Richard Daley, was played out on national television during the coverage of the Democratic National Convention. Following as it did on the heels of Senator Robert Kennedy's murder in California, the scandal shattered the already fragile

Democratic coalition and threw the party into disarray. This infighting and the public's horror over the images shown on television from Chicago arguably helped pave the way for Richard Nixon's election as President. Eric Alterman, writing about the origins of neo-conservatism and the Vietnam War, observed that the methods employed by anti-war movement were often counterproductive. "Many Americans didn't like the war but they really hated the counterculture," writes Alterman. "If supporting Nixon was a way to get back at the hippies and protesters and rioters, they were willing to do it."[43] Peaceful anti-war protests continued to be carried out throughout the remaining years of the Vietnam War, but the movement was forever tarred with the brush of Chicago.

In the New York City of the 1960s, home to Francis Cardinal Spellman, to be anti-war was to be seen as not just anti-American but also as anti-Church and even anti-Christian, given that United States involvement was positioned as a fight against Godless Communism.[44] New York, for the better part of a century, had seen successive waves of Catholic immigration as the Irish, Italians, Polish and Hispanics came to start new lives. The post-World War II years in New York City saw the rise of a robust and conservative Catholicism. Spellman offers a special insight into the grip on power, and its eventual loss, by conservative Christians in New York City.

Allegedly a closeted homosexual, Francis Cardinal Spellman was a close friend and ally of the equally-closeted Roy Cohn. Together with the alcoholic and possibly-closeted Republican Senator Joseph McCarthy and others, these men worked against liberal causes and helped destroy the lives of other gay men and leftists during the communist and homosexual witch hunts of the 1950s.[45, 46] Spellman became a kingmaker in New York politics and a confidant of Presidents. His support of the formation of South Vietnam's puppet government in the 1950s arguably helped to set the stage for the Vietnam War.[47] His ardent promotion of the conflict throughout the 1960s caused antiwar activists in New York to label it "Spellman's War" and to protest in front of his residence and at St. Patrick's Cathedral in Manhattan. Spellman's death in 1967 began a waking-up process for New York that allowed people to begin questioning the hypocrisy and power of a church that had come to be intimately identified with such a brutal and costly conflict.[48]

The right to freedom of worship, spelled out in the United States Constitution and yet given lip service throughout so much of the country's history, became such a cause célèbre during the 1960s and 1970s that even the Catholic Church was forced to recognize the principle that "no man can be coerced in his beliefs."[49] The call for ecumenical dialogue that resulted from Vatican II had, ironically, a countereffect within conservative Protestantism, which looked with suspicion on any attempt by the Catholics to undo the divisions in the Christian faith community wrought by Martin Luther's heresy and the Church's counter-Reformation.[50] These misgivings and doubt helped cultivate and maintain a spiritual plurality within the United States that might have been threatened if those calling for one Christian faith succeeded. The diversity of religious belief in the United States continued to widen throughout the 1960s and 1970s, with some of the greatest changes and growth occurring in the New Age and occult movements.

Pop Goes the Witchcraft

As noted by religious scholar J. Gordon Melton, "all of the primary elements constituting the 'New Age' had been around for a century or more prior to the emergence of the movement. That is, there was very little about the New Age that was new."[51] Repackaged and presented to a new generation of seekers, these old concepts were still finding traction. By 1975, Melton had acknowledged "the occult world in general as an important molder of popular culture."[52] The drive to explore alternative spiritual paths was fueled in part by resentment and rebellion and also by a burgeoning media interest on the subject of the occult and eastern religions, which was played out in popular culture via magazines, newspapers, movies and television. It was spurred on by the experimentation and personal beliefs of the social heroes of youth culture — rock musicians, movie stars, writers, artists and other celebrities.

Traditional religious authorities concluded early on that the increasing presence of the occult in pop culture was a threat to their hegemony. The television show *Dark Shadows* (1966-1971), which presented a story line populated by Witches, vampires, ghosts and werewolves, was singled out in the inevitable backlash by fundamentalist Christians, who labeled it "Satan's favorite TV show."[53] The dark tone of the occult in shows like *Dark Shadows* was more than offset by the light humor of those such as *Bewitched* (1964-1972), *The Munsters* (1964-1966), *The Addams Family* (1964-1966), and *I Dream of Jeannie* (1965-1970). Yet traditional religious authorities were not enamored with the trend of turning what they viewed as Satanism into an acceptable, even friendly, entertainment medium.

The popularity of Witches as fantasy characters has been explained by positing it as a public reaction to the unfulfilling strictures imposed by rationalism. Paranormal investigator and author Hans Holzer noted that society's "renewed interest in the occult in all its manifestations is not so much the result of a quest for greater knowledge as the reaction against the failure of the materialistic establishment to deliver the goods."[54] According to Holzer, the occult appealed to those whose lives had already lost meaning. "To regain the enthusiasm of life, they seek solutions in other areas, and the occult promises to deliver both irrationally and personally, that is, on a direct level without a necessary intermediary." *(Ibid n#54)* It follows that if Christians could claim to achieve results through prayer to a Higher Power, why then was a Witchcraft ritual or a spell-casting, which called upon the powers of ancient Gods to assist the practitioner, any different? This drive towards sustaining the individual, exemplified by the quest for a *personal* relationship with Deity, also played a role in the rising popularity of Evangelical Christianity in the late 1960s.

In light of this development, it's not surprising that the hold of traditional religions on the reins of society was beginning to slip, especially in large urban centers in the north and particularly among the youth culture. Writing of this young generation, Alan Ehrenhalt said, "If you were born in 1947, as I was, then the odds are you spent your childhood learning one set of social customs and moral rules and the prime years of your youth throwing them overboard."[55] By the late 1960s and early 1970s, many younger men and women in urban areas had begun to drift away from established mainline churches, leaving their childhood faiths completely and switching to more liberal or conservative churches, or else abandoning Christianity altogether and gravitating toward non-traditional spiritual pursuits in order to find meaningful answers to the questions and concerns of the time.[56] Evangelical author Joseph Bayly, in his book *What About Horoscopes?* (1970), wrote that "to many people, today's church seems impotent because it is identified with the problems it should be solving. They see the church as a mere authenticator of the Establishment."[57, 58]

People began to explore the boundaries of religion as never before, assisted by a flood of imported ideas and philosophies. Some traditional religious groups began sounding the alarm at this turn of events. Ambassador College, affiliated with the World Church of God, warned the Christian public in *Hippies, Hypocrisy and Happiness* (1968) that the "Hippie religion" was nothing more than a cult of drugs, sexual immorality, and rebellion. Implying that mainstream religious leaders seemed blind to the danger, the pamphlet stated that "most theologians are not alarmed about the hippie religion. They just see it as a mixture of drugs, poetry, paganism and pseudo-intellectual Orientalism."[59]

History professor Theodore Roszak, writing in 1968, declared that the United States was now in a post-Christian period characterized not by the grey, atheistic landscape of George Orwell, but rather by a youth counterculture that had embraced a new, eclectic religious revival. "What began as Zen," Roszak wrote, "has now rapidly, perhaps too rapidly, proliferated into a fantasmagoria of exotic religiosity." Roszak believed that it was precisely because the movement had once held such promise that made its ultimate degeneration into one that was "vaguely wicked and ultimately trivial" so disappointing.[60] His opinion on this "miscellaneous heaping together" of material resonated with the opinion of anthropologist William Partridge, who described the Hippie subculture as "a conglomeration of Christian mysticism, Vedic teachings, revolutionary tracts, Madison Avenue pop-psychology, hedonism, pseudo-American religiosity, and the particularly American virtues of Horatio Alger such as individualism, independence, and frontier courage." Partridge believed that what society was witnessing wasn't so much a great awakening as it was "an agonizing disorientation."[61]

This disorientation was augmented to some extent by changes in federal immigration policy. The Immigration and Nationality Act of 1965 eliminated national quotas for immigrants, thus allowing a new wave of Third World immigrants into the country. Neighborhoods in New York began to change rapidly as these newest immigrants moved into the city, bringing with them the cultural and spiritual traditions of their homelands. This influx displaced those who had previously occupied these areas, leading to the latest in a long series of ethnic neighborhood-shufflings.[62] It was immigration — from Great Britain rather than the Third World — that provided the source of the spiritual path that finally caught Eddie's eye. Yet without the influx and impact of fresh blood and different perspectives from the Third World, it is unclear whether any lasting change in the religious profile of the country would have occurred.

One beneficiary of the loosened immigration policy was Srila Prabhupada, who in 1966 founded the Hare Krishna movement — the International Society for Krishna Consciousness (ISKCON) — in a converted storefront on 2nd Avenue in the Bowery on the Lower East Side of New York City. ISKON provided fodder for the burgeoning public interest in orientalist spirituality, as well as ammunition for its cultural critics. Such practices as vegetarianism and yoga, and such beliefs as reincarnation and karma — all first introduced by Theosophists and ceremonial magicians at the turn of the twentieth century — were reintroduced to popular culture through the street proselytization of the Hare Krishnas and, later, through its influence on pop culture figures, such as Beatle George Harrison (whose 1974 solo album "Dark Horse" and associated concert tour was used as a platform for promoting his vision of Krishna Consciousness). Starting with the countercultural elements in Greenwich Village — the Beats, Hippies, and anti-war activists — the Krishna movement soon spread like the Galli of the ancient Near East to the Hippie neighborhood of Haight-Ashbury in San Francisco.[63] Thus were the West Coast's gifts of Zen and TM to Greenwich Village in the 1950s returned a decade later with the smell of incense, the flash of bright saffron, and the jangling of tambourines.

The Beats weren't just into Zen Buddhism and meditation. Some were fully capable of working the shadows, too. Beat musician and poet Bill Heine was introduced to the joys of ceremonial magick by the likes of Harry Smith and Lionel Ziprin in the 1960s. Heine developed a reputation as a black magician that people feared to cross, but he suggests that this was wildly exaggerated. Yet Heine, who studied texts by Aleister Crowley, Madame Blavatsky, Erasmus of Rotterdam, Dr. John Dee, Eliphas Levi and others, also described a ritual wherein he allegedly summoned a leopard sex demon using Crowley's translation of The Lesser Key of Solomon.[64]

The Beats trended towards nihilism and misogyny, whereas the Hippies tended to be more cooperative and with a softer outlook, though they were, surprisingly, no more egalitarian toward women.[65] Greenwich Village resident Jim Fouratt remembers, "Women were still treated as sex objects and Hippie mommas still did all the cooking."[66] Any progress made by women was influenced by the women themselves, who were becoming more assertive about their place in society. Betty Friedan published *The Feminine Mystique* in 1963, helping to touch off the 1960s-era wave of the feminist movement that had its roots in the suffragettes of the late-nineteenth and early-twentieth centuries.

The availability of legal contraceptives in the wake of the 1965 Supreme Court ruling ensured that women were freed from pregnancy to pursue their own interests and careers. This freedom eventually led to an exploration of the roles of sex and gender in spirituality. Casting about for a framework that would function both spiritually and politically as a tool to promote an empowered feminine ideal, some women began to experiment with Witchcraft and its archetypal Goddess figure. This certainly wasn't the first time that a feminist perspective had found its way into occult-magickal teachings. At the turn of the twentieth century, Philadelphia feminist and Theosophist Ida Craddock wrote several works on sexuality and the occult that were admired by the likes of Aleister Crowley. Hounded by the authorities of her day for obscenity and immorality, she committed suicide at the age of 42 rather than submit to a lengthy prison sentence.[67,68]

Artists also played a role in preparing the public for this spiritual revolution. Sally Banes, in her book Greenwich Village 1963, noted the forces at work in the Village's artistic community and illustrated how the new generation of artists themselves were agents for change in this evolving spiritual landscape. Noting the inadequacy of modern religious, philosophical, and artistic thought to provide "routes of access to the absolute," Banes writes that "'New' religions — that is, old religions from other cultures, like Buddhism, Taoism, and Hinduism, as well as such latter-day cults as Aleister Crowley's — offered an attractive alternative to some, providing as well themes, techniques, and images for art."[69]

Others such as Andy Warhol, who was himself a practicing Byzantine Rite Catholic and as much a pop phenomenon as the art he produced, promoted the occult without participating in it directly. Because so much of his mystique and attraction as an avant-garde artist was intrinsically bound up with his indifference to the mores of polite society, it was perhaps inevitable, even desirable, that Warhol would foster an environment around him in which occult ideas and practices could be played with and studied. People in the Warhol crowd who dabbled in or seriously delved into the occult included photographer Billy Name, musician Lou Reed, the sometime-actor-personality Ondine, actresses Candy Darling and Edie Sedgwick, director Chuck Wein, and others.[70,71,72]

Many of Warhol's Factory clique appear to have become involved in the occult as a social dalliance or affectation, the type of people that writer John Fritscher would later describe as "acid-freak poseurs in the occult."[73] These may represent some of the earliest examples of the "cool kids" using Witchcraft and the occult as fashion accessories. One of these was Factory habitué Orion de Winter, also known as "Orion, the Witch of Bleecker Street." Together with actress Dorothy Podber and Beat poet Diane de Prima, the trio has been described as a coven of self-styled Witches who were part of the Factory's "amphetamine rapture group" (referred to by Warhol as the "A-heads").[74,75] Not everyone was impressed with the public face that the pop elite presented for the occult. Long-time ceremonial practitioner Sally Eaton writes, "Don't get me started about most of the Warhol crew."[76] As it turned out, while many in that crowd dabbled in the occult, very few took it further than that. Clinton Stevens (aka "Chanel 13") and Billy Name did, but few of the others made it a serious part of their philosophy.

Lou Reed's interest in the occult was more serious than that displayed by many of the others in the Factory.[77] Reed, according to one popular story, was said to have loaned three books by Theosophist and mystic Alice Bailey to "Factory Fotographer" Billy Name in November 1968, after which Billy retreated into his darkroom and allegedly had a breakdown.[78] Name did have difficulties during that period, but it was not due to his studies of Alice Bailey, whose system of esoteric science and occult philosophy is rather benign in comparison with, say, Crowley's abyss workings where one is expected to face and overcome one's own fears and limitations in the form of the demon Choronzon. Billy was also made of sterner stuff than that, having studied occult topics for most of that decade, beginning when he started working at the Orientalia Bookstore after moving to Manhattan in 1958. Name recalls when he delved into his first occult book in Orientalia's stacks, a treatise on astrology by Alan Leo, an early Theosophist who taught astrology from a metaphysical viewpoint: "This was my first glimpse into the hidden worlds. I went on to the series of books by W.Y. Evans-Wentz, also an early Theosophist, and John Woodroofe (aka, Arthur Avalon) on kundalini/serpent power, yoga, Tibetan Buddhist liberation, and the *Tibetan Book of the Dead.* [Orientalia] was a hub of Oriental/mystical interest at the time with customers like avant-garde composer John Cage ... who introduced Zen concepts into the experimental art scene at the time."[79]

Therefore, it is doubtful that Billy Name's mind would have been unhinged by the words of the British esotericist. Name himself blames his withdrawal in late 1968 as a reaction to the trauma the entire Factory staff suffered after the shooting of Andy Warhol in June of that year by Valerie

Solanas, a radical lesbian feminist and author of the anarchistic, antiestablishment S.C.U.M. Manifesto.[80] His recollections of additional aspects of the occult and spiritual-oriented mystical situations in New York during the 1960s, insofar as he was aware of them, are enlightening.

Billy Name: *(Ibid n#79)*

Many eastern sages and gurus had established ashrams, centers for study and meditation and various disciplines in the New York City area. For instance, Meher Baba, George Gurdjieff, Swami Satchidananda, George Ohsawa (Macrobiotics founder), Prabupada (Hare Krishna founder), Rudolf Steiner (Anthroposophy), Rammurti Mishra (Raja and Hatha yoga), and, no doubt, numerous others with whom I did not come into contact. All of the above had international influence in orienting the Western awareness to the existance of 'hidden worlds' of power and potential development available to the seeker.

Freudian psychology and existentialism were at the waning years of their powers in the early Sixties, and Buddhism and Taoism were becoming the primary philosophical interests of the arts/mystical-oriented New York culture. Everyone knew the Tao Te Ching, the I Ching, and numerous Buddhist sutras (Diamond, Lotus, Platform, etc.). These Oriental philosophies introduced new parameters for living everyday life completely unattached to traditional European western philosophical and religious cultures. Zen was as powerful as LSD and the chemical revolution which took off simultaneous with this wind from the east. It was a whole new world which seemed to be known only to the artists and mystics.

Other than Steiner's Anthroposophy and the Theosophical movement, which was mostly a translation of Eastern views into the fabric of Western Euro-culture, the repudiation of Christianity and dead religions, and the introduction of hidden Eastern school concepts, such as the Great White Lodge of white magicians at Shamballa and the finer points of Buddhism, vedanta, and yoga, not much 'Western' [Magick] was going on. I was not aware of much activity of the Golden Dawn magicians, Crowley, the O.T.O. or the Rosicrucians; nothing Satanic (other than S & M sexuality), but I'm sure it was going on in some esoteric places as New York has always housed all movements cutting away established, dead culture. No strong winds from the runes and Odin, tarot was not 'popular' yet, and astrology was still 'strange'. The most magic in the sense of 'magick' I knew of was coming from Tibetan tantric Buddhism and Chinese Taoist alchemy.

Always having been a hermitic hermetic guy, I did not join any groups or gatherings of like souls (other than in the arts) so I can't really give you a sense of how the roots of Western magick sprung up except to say that people I know who moved in that direction frequently got their early inspirations in the chemical and drug, anarchistic, and revolutionary fields, and I think I could say that Ed Sanders was a prime mover in the field. Mostly hetero/peacenik and successors to the Beat generation, these early heroes of American culture were the grass roots of the movement which was insisting on 'authenticity' of relationships and natural spirit and natural inherent magical powers which at that time were the hope to change the dead world to a living one. Be-ins in Central Park with thousands of hip enlightened people high on acid were an awe-inspiring view into what was 'our world' and what we wanted it to become. The magick that was experienced was less ritual than inherent blooming of natural magical talent within each of us. Tompkins Square Park and the Psychedelicatessen on the Lower East Side were typical haunts of the magic living flora/fauna coming to the fore.

Name was not the only "hermitic hermetic" person out there at that time. Occult practices in the United States, after the collapse of the magickal orders after World War II and before the spread of Neo-Pagan/Witchcraft groups in the late 1960s, tended to be an avocation of individualists. "The European occult enters here with influence from the Surrealists, Kabbalists and a variety of sophisticated practitioners," explains playwright and UFOlogist Eugenia Macer-Story. "There is a difference in approach between the European and United States *gris gris* practitioners. Of course, it's a similar practice, but the European mystique has less of a speakeasy or illicit quality to it applied from the surrounding culture."[81] It was this "illicit quality" that explains some of the attraction that the occult held for individualists.

Presentations on the occult had a long history of titillating the purportedly serious audiences of New York City. One of the earliest recorded examples is a lecture on ancient and modern Witchcraft that was presented to the Protestant Episcopal Brotherhood by Dr. Edward H. Parker at the Clinton Hall opera house on December 4, 1855.[82] But whereas these earlier lectures were conducted under the rubric of scientific curiosity within a Christian framework, one hundred years later occult presentations were aimed at spiritual explorers, without any assumption of religious dogma. Examples may be found in 1964, with the renowned New School for Social Research offering a course on "Witchcraft, Magic and Sorcery."[83] The Institute for Research at the old 4th Street Theatre offered seminars on astrology, Witchcraft, and the paranormal, including a lecture on "flying saucers and other off-beat topics" by The Amazing Randi, in 1965 and 1966.[84,85] By 1967, even public universities were getting in on the act. New York University offered a non-credit course titled "Witchcraft,

Magic and Sorcery" taught by Joseph Kaster.[86] Described by one student as "a regular W.C. Fields," Kaster joked and disparaged his way through a semester-long historical overview of his subject matter which concentrated on the Medieval/Satanic aspects of Witchcraft.[87]

Certain bookstores also catered to these students of the esoteric. In addition to disseminating literature, they began to act as informal gathering spots where people could exchange ideas. One such shop was the Gotham Book Mart on West 47th Street. Its owner, Frances Steloff, was an aficionado of books on Oriental religions and the Spiritualist movement. However, for Orientalist books, the Gotham was outstripped by the Orientalia Bookstore. Located on East 12th Street between 5th and University during the 1950s and 1960s, Orientalia, as its name implied, specialized in books on Eastern philosophy, history, design and life. Many artists, writers, musicians and spiritual explorers worked or hung out there, including the previously mentioned Billy Name, as well as pop artist Ray Johnson and musician John Cale (later of the Velvet Underground).

Yet another community center catering to metaphysicians was the Peace Eye Bookstore that was run by Beat poet and musician Ed Sanders. Sanders opened his "book scene, freak center, and scrounge lounge" in late 1964 in a former kosher meat market at 383 East 10th Street in the East Village.[88] The Peace Eye quickly became an underground gathering place for the countercultural movement, what *Life* magazine would later call "a foxhole for psychic revolutionaries on the Lower East Side."[89] Sanders was a student of Latin and Greek. He was also fascinated with Egyptology, so much so that his teaching of a course on Revolutionary Egyptology at the Free University in the summer of 1965 earned a mention in the files the FBI maintained on the anti-war activist.[90,91] A 1969 ad for the store offered "Books on magic, poetry, smut, revolution, underground newspapers, perv, astrology, dope, religion, Indianlore, sodomy."[92]

Name writes that "the only real influence that I can recall relating to Western magic or mysticism [in New York City at the time] was Ed Sanders and his Peace Eye Bookstore. Ed was a radical anarchist/revolutionary and founding member of the Sixties revolutionary movement. One of his areas of study was the activity of anarchist/radicals during the Egyptian dynasties, and their similarity of inspiration to the New York underground at the time. The Eye of Horus was the logo for his bookstore." *(Ibid n#79)* Sally Eaton concurs, writing that the Peace Eye "was a truly seminal New York occult bookstore. I first saw it in 1965. Ed Sanders dabbled in magick, astrology, and the Tarot." *(Ibid n#76)* In 1965, Sanders formed a rock band called the Fugs, which was used as a platform to protest the Vietnam War nationwide.

The basement of Samuel Weiser Books also became a nucleus of the nascent community of ceremonial practitioners in New York. Punk rocker Patti Smith recalled the time when occultist filmmaker and musician Harry

Smith introduced her and photographer Robert Mapplethorpe to Weiser's circa 1970. She described the bookstore at that time as having the greatest selection of esoteric books in the city.[93] Samuel Weiser Publishing pumped out a steady stream of esoteric titles throughout the 1960s on parapsychology, astrology, auras, ceremonial magick, and the like. So successful was this market that by the early 1970s, Weiser's stocked five thousand different occult titles.

From the 1950s onward, publishers seemed more willing to produce books that touched on occult and paranormal themes. In 1961, Carl Weschcke purchased Llewellyn Publishing for $40,000 and steered the company from one that had been primarily concerned with astrological publications into one that fed the New Age movement with titles by Dion Fortune, Aleister Crowley, Israel Regardie, and other authors. More publishers entered the fray, including Citadel and University, which produced a number of Witchcraft titles by the late 1960s. Pulp publishers, such as Key, Dover, and Ace Books, developed their own paranormal lines to meet consumer demand. Occult writer Leo Martello started his own occult publishing house, Hero. The Universe Book Club, catering solely to the occult market, was started in 1968, and by 1970 it had a hundred and fifty thousand subscribers.[94]

It wasn't a given within the small world of esoteric publishers that public interest in the occult would continue to grow. Carl Weschcke recalls that, "Back in the Fifties I used to visit New York often and would always stop in Weiser's bookstore. When I told [Weiser owner Don Weiser] that I had purchased Llewellyn, he intimated that I was crazy and that the occult interest of the 1930s would never have a comeback."[95] And yet the genre did grow in leaps and bounds, with occult book suppliers and book clubs doubling by the mid-1960s.[96] Occult titles were grossing more than $1 billion in overall sales by 1996.[97]

Many influential titles stand out during this period, including the *I Ching*, *The Tibetan Book of the Dead*, James Frazier's *The Golden Bough*, Carl Jung's *The Archetypes and the Collective Unconscious*, and Aleister Crowley's *Magick in Theory and Practice*. All of these were reprints and translations of earlier (in some cases, *much* earlier) works; however, one new title that was noteworthy in its effect was Louis Pauwels' and Jacques Bergier's best-selling book *The Morning of the Magicians* (1960).[98] *The Morning of the Magicians* stands out for two important reasons. First, it provided an overview of a wide range of occult and paranormal topics that was accessible to a popular audience. Second, and more importantly, it spurred a renewed interest in the works of writer Arthur Machen and, though him, H.P. Lovecraft. The book explored Machen's membership in the Order of the Golden Dawn, leading new readers to investigate the philosophy and practices of that occult organization.[99, 100] And those seeking the Golden Dawn would eventually stumble upon the ceremonial magick of the O.T.O., which by 1963 was teetering on the edge of Choronzon's abyss following the death of Aleister Crowley's chosen successor, Karl Germer.

The theatre also continued to play a role in disseminating occult ideas to the general public. One such place was the Caffe Cino at 31 Cornelia Street, the original off-off-Broadway venue. At Cino, the astrological vibe of the playwright seeking to get a play to stage was said to have had more influence than the quality of the work. Doric Wilson, one of the first playwrights to present at Caffe Cino, said that whenever he was asked what his sign was, "My stock answer was I didn't have one, my family was too poor."[101] Caffe Cino owner, Joe Cino, believed that Arthur Rimbaud and Aleister Crowley would have felt right at home at the coffeehouse.[102] "That was strictly wishful thinking on his part," says Wilson. "Near the end the Cino was overrun by Andy [Warhol's] 'artists' and drugs came pouring in. ... Crowley and Rimbaud would have sneered." *(Ibid n#101)* It was the stage at the Caffe Cino that H.M. Koutoukas reflected in his 1977 play *When Turtles Dream*, with its amphetamine-fueled cobra cult.

By the end of the 1960s, interest in magic and the occult was widespread in countercultural circles and was influencing the theatre. Examples of this influence include Broadway productions such as *Hair* (1968), with Sally Eaton's performance as the Hippie Witch. *Hair* announced the dawning of a new age with a defiant production that pulled together all of these concurrent social threads — rebellion against the war, drugs, racial injustice, the rights of women and gays, sexual freedom, environmental awareness, and Witchcraft — and shoved the whole writhing, orgiastic mass under the collective nose of the public. The play was a smash hit.[103] Meanwhile, off-Broadway offered up such presentations as Richard Schechner's homoerotic antiestablishment reworking of Euripides' *Bacchae* in *Dionysus in 69* (1968), which was later documented on film by Brian De Palma.[104,105] And off-off-Broadway venues offered plays such as *Keystone Communal* (1969). Communal, with its interest in magick and the occult, has been described as "partly inspired by possession rituals described in the writings of Aleister Crowley."[106]

Avant-garde film and rock music were also active participants in disseminating occult thought and symbolism in America. In 1967, The Rolling Stones had revealed their own involvement with the occult upon the release of their album *Their Satanic Majesties Request*. Aleister Crowley devotee Kenneth Anger, who had previously released *The Inauguration of the Pleasure Dome* in 1954, provided the public with the latest in his Magic Lantern Cycle on ceremonial magick with his *Invocation of My Demon Brother*. This movie, starring Church of Satan founder Anton LaVey in the role of Satan, opened in 1969.[107] The Stones were connected to Anger via a shared interest in ceremonial magic.[108] Front man Mick Jagger worked on the soundtrack of *Invocation of My Demon Brother* and was originally slated for the title character in Anger's 1972 film *Lucifer Rising*.

Another musician-occultist, Led Zeppelin guitarist Jimmy Page, was supposed to produce the soundtrack for *Lucifer Rising* but was dismissed from the project by Anger. Led Zeppelin's most successful album, *Led Zeppelin IV*, with its hit track "Stairway to Heaven," was released in 1971. Page was a devotee of Aleister Crowley, and if that wasn't obvious before the release of *Led Zeppelin IV*, then the engraving "Do what thou wilt — So mete it be" in the center of the first pressings of the album would dispel any thoughts to the contrary.[109] "Stairway to Heaven" was said to be Zeppelin singer Robert Plant's homage to Robert Graves' book *The White Goddess*.[110] The Who's 1971 song "Baba O'Riley" seemed to sum up the attitude of this new generation of spiritual seekers.

British psychedelic rock was born in 1967 with the release of Pink Floyd's *Piper at the Gates of Dawn*, an album whose inspiration was the wild, ancient magick of the great God Pan — a magick accessed by using modern adjuncts such as LSD. But one can go back even further, say to Harry Smith's spacey, hermetic film *Heaven and Earth Magic* (1959-1961), for signs of things to come.[111, 112] In 1969, a band called Coven released a psychedelic occult/Satanic-inspired album titled *Witchcraft Destroys Minds & Reaps Souls* that contained an alleged black mass. But for pure authenticity and showmanship, Coven couldn't compete with Anton LaVey's 1968 release of the live recording *The Satanic Mass*. Gentler fare could be found in the late 1960s and early 1970s with traditional/folk groups such as Pentangle, and in the 1970s with the rock group Steeleye Span. This theme would be taken up later by Jethro Tull, whose *Songs from the Wood* (1977) would provide the background music for many Witchcraft rituals.

Drugs, the bogeyman of the 1950s (and the escape valve and inspiration for many of its artists and writers), became commonplace by the 1960s as a modern shortcut to the Philosopher's Stone. But in the latter years of the decade, hard drugs like cocaine and methamphetamine began to invade the Hippie scene and, some say, hastened its demise.[113] Beat author Jack Kerouac, while admitting that the Hippies were engaging in the pursuit of spiritual knowledge through their use of psychoactive substances such as LSD, still distrusted the instant enlightenment seemingly granted by those adjuncts, noting that "Walking on water wasn't made in a day."[114]

Regardless of the spiritual uses to which they put them, neither the Hippies nor their Beat antecedents were immune from the repercussions of their drug taking and merchanting. Snorting and shooting up crystallized speed, and the social and medical troubles this engendered, had gotten its start not in the gay clubs and trailer parks of post-twentieth century America, but in the subcultures of beautiful people in the early 1960s, such as Warhol's "A-heads," and later in places such as the "Hashbury District" of San Francisco and in what *Time* magazine called "the turned-on squalor of hippie life in the East Village."[115, 116] In 1967, *The New York*

Times reported on the brutal East Village murder of a pretty prep school graduate named Linda Fitzpatrick. The 18-year-old Hippie and self-proclaimed Witch and her male companion, Groovy Hutchinson, were on a speed binge when their heads were caved in with a furnace brick in the basement boiler room of their Avenue A flophouse.[117] While Fitzpatrick's death was what garnered the headlines of a rabid New York press, it was the loss of Groovy and his commune organizing skills which was most keenly felt by the members of the Hippie underground in the East Village.[118]

Drugs had even invaded paradise, as TM's founder Maharishi Mahesh Yogi found to his dismay when he discovered his most famous students engaging in drug use during their 1968 visit to his ashram in the Himalayas. The TM movement's popularity did not suffer unduly for this violation of trust, although its innocence was somewhat soiled by the revelation. In 1971, Raymond Buckland wrote, "Never do Witches use drugs of any kind; the reason being that they are not found necessary."[119] Yet this attitude was not universally held in Witchy circles. Sybil Leek noted that "There's a place in religion for drugs, not only in pagan religions, but in many orthodox religions. But the thing is, when the Indian decides to take peyote, he's prepared for it. He doesn't take it as a kick to escape life, because he knows he will never get any benefit from it. He prepared himself with seven days of religious fasting and duties. Preparation is the secret."[120]

For critics to argue that drug use went hand in hand with the occult would be as wrong as those who denied that any in the metaphysical community who partook of drugs did so as an integral part of their spiritual practice, or as a simple mood-setting adjunct. The coverage in magazines such as *Fate*, which ran a number of articles related to the mystical aspect of drug use — "Quest for the Sacred Mushroom" (1957), "Magic Mushrooms Heal the Sick" (1958), "The Finding of the Sacred Mushroom" (1961), "Can Drugs Lead You to God?" (1963) — certainly demonstrates that the interest was there. Occult magazines in the 1970s, such as *Gnostica News* ("Drugs: Detrimental or Perfecting," April/May 1974; "Tantra, Modern Witchcraft and Psychedelic Drugs," December 1974) and *Earth Religion News* ("Drugs and the Craft," December 1973), would continue the sometimes heated debate on the use of drugs as part of one's spiritual practice. Beloved "faerie shaman" Gwydion Pendderwen was depicted in an advertisement for his album *Songs for the Old Religion* (1976) offering the reader a large chalice and a joint in *Gnostica News* while urging them to "GET HIGH ... on Witches music."[121] And one of the semi-regular columns in the Neo-Pagan magazine *Green Egg* during the 1970s was entitled "Dry Mouth Musings," an unsubtle reference to the condition suffered by many ganja smokers.[122]

Rimbaud may have loved his absinthe and Crowley his opiates and hash, but pot and wine were the undisputed kings of the Witchcraft scene in the 1970s. Many post-millennial Neo-Pagans make a point of clucking their tongues disapprovingly and continue to proclaim that drugs and Neo-Pagan spirituality *never* mix, but that is more an artifact of Reagan-era drug education than historical fact. This attitude certainly doesn't reflect the realities on the ground in the 1960s and 1970s, despite the fact that there were anti-drug occult practitioners even back then. But many (though not all) of them were also hypocrites or else willingly donned blinders in order to present a whitewashed image to the public and, more importantly, to law enforcement. This was, after all, the age of Carlos Castaneda, whose long career of writing about turned-on Shamanism began in 1968 with his publication of *The Teachings of Don Juan.*

Notwithstanding the debates about the factual basis for the specifics of Castaneda's alleged work with the Yaquis, the fact is that psychotropic adjuncts formed a historical basis for Shamanic practice over thousands of years. This correlation has been exhaustively documented by various writers and researchers, including Wasson, Schultes, McKenna, Ott, Pendell and many others.[123] Modern armchair shamans who criticize the ritualistic (as opposed to recreational) use of drugs and alcohol by others are mostly non-native poseurs who couldn't hold a candle to the approach of many native practitioners who draw on the experience of hundreds of generations of ancestors to journey to the otherworld on the currents of *amanita muscaria*, iboga, cannabis, peyote, Ayahuasca, and a hundred other plant spirits. Even the *Ur*-tobacco used by South American Shamans — *nicotiana rustica* — would blow the top off of the skull of an urban practitioner not accustomed to its effects. Can one journey between worlds without the use of chemical adjuncts — say, through long periods of drumming, sleep deprivation and starvation? Absolutely. But a people raised in a modern hothouse culture of television, video games, porn, iPods, cell phones, mega-doses of caffeine, instant-messaging and instant gratification are generally ill-equipped to rally the concentration and Will necessary to honestly achieve these mind states. Dishonestly, they do it all the time — and then give $9000-a-head weekend workshops about it where they kill their participants in poorly constructed and managed sweat lodges.[124]

The Shamans seemed poised to pick up the slack from the Spiritualists in this era. Although not as numerous as in the post-war periods in the late 1800s and early 1900s, Spiritualists were still quite active throughout the 1960s, providing an integral beachhead into the changing spiritual layout of the country. One of the most famous of these during this time was Clifford Bias, a clairvoyant who lived on the West Side in the Ansonia Hotel and who at one time was a spiritual advisor to Franklin D. Roosevelt and was friends with his wife, Eleanor. From his apartment, Bias ran a spiritualist group in the mid-1960s that included Laura Austan's mother, a Spiritualist minister named Kenn Coulter, Ceil Clay, and Bertha Brown.[125]

Laura Austan: *(Ibid n#125)*

> *Thing is, there was a big mélange of all the non-regular spiritual types — everyone from any idea, all flew around together in those days. [There were] three general centers — the Village, Bay Ridge Brooklyn, and Cliff's apartment. But there were psychic fairs constantly in those days, and between those attending, teaching or reading, it was a circus life. So Spiritualists and Co-Masons and Buddhists and Krishnas would all be at any one gathering of anything, at any time. It was the 60s. ...*
>
> *[The] men all looked like Felix Unger in those circles. The Spiritualists went thru a disgruntlement and split into factions around 1971 — the Associateds vs. the Universal Independents. Come to think, I never recall knowing a male Spiritualist minister who wasn't gay! After the old broads who were still Fox Sister devotees, like Bertha and my Grandmothers, died, the gay men took over the organizations.*

Astrology appeared to capture the attention of the public throughout the 1960s. Warhol, ever the observer of American pop culture, noticed a marked increase in public interest at the beginning of 1968, commenting that "there were suddenly Zodiac signs everywhere."[126] The Broadway musical *Hair* may have had an influence, with its song about the dawning of the Age of Aquarius, but the fact is that astrology was already deeply entrenched in the American imagination. Present since the founding of the Republic, astrology underwent a renaissance in the 1940s and 1950s.

But interest in the ancient divination technique exploded during the 1960s. Suddenly, every major newspaper in the country had a daily or weekly horoscope section, many of them attributed to psychic and syndicated astrologer Jeane Dixon, whose best-selling biography, *A Gift of Prophecy: the Phenomenal Jeane Dixon*, was published in 1965.[127] Sybil Leek had her own monthly astrology column in the *Ladies Home Journal* by late 1966. Leek even acted as the California governor's personal astrologer, through the auspices of his wife, Nancy Reagan. Dixon would provide that same service to the future First Lady in the 1980s, much as she did as Richard Nixon's "soothsayer" during his time as President. It was estimated in 1969, when New Yorker Linda Goodman published her first book on the technique, that there were at least ten thousand full-time and a hundred and seventy-five thousand part-time astrologers in the United States.[128, 129] By 1976, astrology had become a $200 million-a-year business in America.[130] Other divination methods were also experiencing a renaissance, with tarot cards being sold in mainstream bookstores like New York's 8th Street Bookshop by 1969.[131]

Eugenia Macer-Story concurs that the arts also had an effect on strengthening and promoting occult ideas beginning in the 1960s "in the sense of the flashy *gris gris* and the black magick ethos of certain rock bands and film makers like Polanski and Bergmann. But the 'occult' has always been around, and Fellini is my personal metaphysics favorite of that era in mass market films. His stuff has the flavor of the authentic *commedia* which has very ancient origins."[132] Media attention on the black magick aspect of the occult intensified with the ritualistic undertones of the August 1969 Tate-LaBianca murders by the Manson cult and the psychotic antics of the Zodiac killer in California. Manson, according to *Life* writer Paul O'Neil, controlled his followers by tailoring his message so that it was in tune with their confused sense of self and community. The movement towards communal living could increase the potential for the exploitation of people through the isolation of its members from outsiders who might provide a reality check on the groupthink being promoted from within. One way of achieving this is by appealing to the innate spirituality of those attracted to this type of living arrangement. "The communal thing is very spiritual," wrote O'Neil. "Belief in magic, astrology, cosmic consciousness — that explains everything. One of the characteristics [of a commune] is to have a spiritual leader and, violence aside, Charlie Manson as a spiritual leader is probably more common than we care to believe."[133]

Bewitched, Bothered and Bewildered

The increased media attention was not always a healthy trend, as demonstrated by reporters tying the villainies of Manson to his belief, however tenuous, in the occult. *Esquire* magazine ran a large section in its March 1970 issue, focusing on the rise of "evil" in California. Inspired by the Manson cult murders, the feature appeared to contextualize many of the social trends taking place on the West Coast at the time — drugs, the Hippie subculture, Witchcraft and the occult — in terms of the growth of Satanism and evil.[134] The chivalric Order of the Garter, started by King Edward III, was long rumored to be associated with a secret order of Witches for whom the garter was a mark of membership (hence the use of the garter by modern Gardnerians to denote a Witch Queen). The rumor states that the Countess of Salisbury's garter slipped while at a ball, thereby revealing her to be a Witch. The King allegedly picked up the garter and pinned it to himself, saying "Shame be to him who thinks evil of it," thereby throwing a cloak of protection over the erstwhile Witch. Henceforth, the motto of the Order became *Honi soit qui mal y pense*.[135] By using this motto as the title of the cover story, one wonders whether the *Esquire* editors weren't just having a good laugh at their readers' expense.

Lawyers also hopped onto the occult bandwagon in an attempt to score points by using the Witch as boogeyman. Richard Nixon, an accomplished "Witch hunter" from the 1950s, was at one time a senior partner in the law firm of Nixon, Mudge, Rose, Guthrie and Alexander. Before he resigned to run for President in 1968, a client of his old firm,

General Cigar de Utaudo of Puerto Rico, disputed a union vote organized by the International Association of Machinists. The law firm, in making its case before the National Labor Relations Board, argued that the election results should be overturned because union organizers had successfully used Witchcraft to influence the vote. The firm duly presented a white paper purporting to prove that "Belief in witchcraft and sorcery has been an important part of the development of the history and culture of the Western world..." The Union openly mocked the company, declaring that its officials did not ride broomsticks to the election. The NLRB denied the appeal, and the press clucked its tongue at the seeming foolishness of such an august law firm.[136, 137, 138]

However, it was important to remember that The Press, as the modern news media are called, was also the name for a medieval device used to torture Witches. Engaging The Press was a two-edged sword for those who openly practiced their faith, especially for those whose attention the media actively courted. For example, in an article in the October 27, 1968 edition of the *New York Sunday News*, staff writer Lisa Hoffman published the Bucklands' names and address despite her own assurances to the couple that she would not.[139] A large photo accompanying the article shows four Witches who were nude from the waist up with a sensationalistic and unsympathetic caption that read, "Long Island witches gyrate in bare and bizarre ceremony based on rituals of ancient nature cultists."[140]

Raymond Buckland describes what followed in decidedly mixed terms. "During the ensuing weeks after Hoffman's article appeared," he writes, "we were plagued with unwelcome visitors. We had rocks thrown through our windows. We had the front door and screen kicked in. We had a car set on fire. We — my wife and children especially — suffered verbal abuse whenever they went out, all thanks to Ms. Hoffman. ... However, Hoffman's cavalier attitude did actually have one positive aspect to it. Now that the cat was out of the bag — or the Witch was out of the broom closet — it meant that I would be able to do far more, for I still believed that it was a duty to persevere with trying to straighten the misconceptions. So now I could do television and radio, and magazine and newspaper articles, without having to worry about my name being given since it was already out there." *(Ibid n#139)*

Buckland couches the event in terms of a betrayal of trust; however, the hardest blow was more likely the loss of the naïve assumption that they could forever control how the press depicted them. After all, even though they had insisted on being identified as *Robat* and *Rowen* in interviews for some years, the Bucklands' pictures had been published locally and they had appeared on television. They also had begun running a Witchcraft Museum out of the basement of their home in 1966, and admitted that their neighbors had known that the couple was operating a coven from their home within 18 months of their moving into the Brentwood, New

York suburb in 1963. People do talk. Therefore, to blame Hoffman alone for lifting the veil, so to speak, seems rather harsh. As any member of an initiatory mystery tradition must surely realize, an open secret is hardly a secret at all. Still, when a reporter — or a reporter's editor — fails to honor a commitment, it erodes the public's trust in the press and ultimately drags the conversation down into the gutter in disservice to the truth.

Playing on the public's newly-awakened interest and fears, writers and filmmakers also realized the potential commercial possibilities of creating stories of sexed-up and violent mystic cults lurking just beneath the surface of polite society. Many books and films, such as Roman Polanski's *Rosemary's Baby* (1968), Malcolm Leigh's *Legend of the Witches* (1970), and Luigi Scattini's *Witchcraft '70* (1970), continued to link Witchcraft with Satanism in the public mind.[141] Witches of that time often cite *Rosemary's Baby* as a particularly vexing problem because this widely released, highly publicized and commercially successful film portrayed Witches as Devil-worshippers. The linkage of Witchcraft with Satanism, a relationship that was categorically denied by the Bucklands and others involved with Gardnerian Wica, was a media headache for those who chose to be points of public contact.

This publicity also helped position Wica as a rebellious alternative to the status quo. But for Gardnerians, this was no better a reason for becoming a Witch than mistaking Wica for Devil worship (rebellion, after all, being an identified Luciferian trait). However, the attention also attracted many well-intentioned people who were disaffected with mainstream religion. In contrast, Witches in Great Britain had already dealt with this problem for several years. In 1964, British Witch Robert Cochrane wrote that this publicity has been something of a two-edged sword attracting, on the one hand, people looking for a simpler life. On the other hand, it seemed that "In many cases the Craft has become a funkhole, in which those who have not been successful in solving various personal problems hide."[142]

The occult phenomenon in New York was sufficiently well established by the early Seventies to become the butt of popular satire and commentary. James Herlihy, the writer of *Midnight Cowboy*, also penned *Season of the Witch* (1971), a half-hearted condemnation of the Aquarian Age.[143] In the novel, 17-year-old Gloria Random of Belle Woods, Michigan runs away to New York with her homosexual sidekick, John, to live in a Greenwich Village commune and experiment with free sex, drugs, organic food and encounter groups. A reviewer in *The Rolling Stone* pronounced the book "dull" and criticized the writer for his "random judgments."[144]

As the number of different occult pathways multiplied and spread within the United States at this time, publishing houses became *de facto* participants in the process by both spurring and feeding on the public's interest in the phenomenon. The number of books published in English that mentioned Witchcraft spiked dramatically in the late 1960s.[145] Before then, most books about Witchcraft were written by outsiders who had very little actual knowledge of the Craft. However, from 1969 through 1971, this situation had reversed, and a number of the new Witchcraft books were written by, or in collaboration with, self-described Craft practitioners.

Louise Huebner, the "Official Witch of Los Angeles," published her self-promotional book *Power Through Witchcraft* in 1969.[146] This was followed by the semi-biographical work on Alex Sanders, *King of the Witches* (1969), Leo Martello's *Weird Ways of Witchcraft* (1969) and Ray Buckland's first book on Gardnerian Wica, *Ancient & Modern Witchcraft* (1970).[147] In 1971, Witchcraft books were published by Sybil Leek, Ray Buckland, Isaac Bonewits, and Stewart Farrar, among others.[148] Ritual magick, a mainstay for specialty publishers such as Samuel Weiser in Manhattan, began to experience a renaissance with the United States release of a Crowley biography by Kenneth Grant and John Symonds, along with reprints of some of Crowley's books in 1971. A reprint of Israel Regardie's massive work on the Golden Dawn also appeared in 1971, as did Colin Wilson's influential retrospective *The Occult*.[149]

The modern New Age movement was also represented during this period with such books as the ubiquitous *Be Here Now* (1971), affectionately known as the "Hippie Bible," by former Harvard drug researcher turned Eastern guru Ram Dass [Richard Alpert].[150] Even the wholesomely American Sears, Roebuck & Company Christmas Catalogue began to list occult-related toys over which nominally good children could salivate. These included Kenner's "Mystic Skull" voodoo game (1964); the "Green Ghost Game" (1966) and "Ka-Bala – The Mysterious Game that Foretells the Future" (1967), both by the Transogram Company; Parker Brothers' "Ouija – Mystifying Oracle" (1967); and Milton Bradley's "Which Witch" (1970).[151] By 1970, the occult had become one of the hottest trends in the toy industry.[152] In between building pyramids for Pharaoh out of glass marbles in Sunday school and summoning Captain Howdy on their Ouija boards, kids could sit down to watch Jimmy and his magic flute defeat the evil antics of Witchiepoo on the trippy *H.R.Pufnstuf* (1969-1970).

One also should not underestimate the effects of popular interest in UFOs and psychic phenomena on the growth of the occult in the 1960s. As June Johns noted in 1969, "the upsurge in interest in psychic phenomena – be they flying saucers or ESP [extrasensory perception] – is conducive to the revival of witchcraft."[153] Interest was so high for a time that New York had a shop, the Flying Saucer News Bookstore, devoted to publications on such topics.[154] Often, lectures on Witchcraft were held right alongside those for UFOs.[155] Timothy Beckley, who had been presenting seminars on psychic powers since the late 1960s, was an avid UFOlogist in New York City.[156]

While not strictly a UFO magazine, *Fate* had, since its inception in 1949, reported a wide variety of stories, including UFO lore, metaphysics, ghost stories, magick, Pagan history, and other tales of occult interest. Other evidence of the crossover between the UFO community and the occult movement can be seen in the advertising accepted by UFO publications throughout the 1960s. The Rosicrucians were heavily advertising for members in these magazines by the beginning of the decade, while full-page ads by advertisers such as The Universe Book Club, which offered books like Sybil Leek's *Diary of a Witch* and Richard Cavendish's *The Black Arts*, were not uncommon by its end.[157, 158]

Reports of UFOs have been made throughout recorded history, but the number and variety of these instances exploded after World War II. By the early 1950s, inspired in part by Cold War fears of invasion and conquest by the implacable and poorly understood alien cultures of the Soviets and Red Chinese, the public had become enamored with the possibility that Earth was being visited by extraterrestrials. The United States Air Force stated that there was no evidence for alien visitation, thereby convincing a segment of the public in the 1960s that a government cover-up was well underway.[159] This belief eventually evolved into an elaborate conspiracy – promoted by such authors as Erich von Däniken (*Chariots of the Gods*, 1968) – positing that alien visitors were responsible for not only molding mankind into its current form, but also for most of the greatest accomplishments of ancient civilizations.[160]

But von Däniken's theme wasn't new. For example, Desmond Leslie and George Adamski speculated about the influence of UFO-traveling aliens on ancient societies in India, Britain and Egypt in *Flying Saucers Have Landed* (1953).[161] Carl Jung, analyzing the UFO craze in 1959, speculated that the mythology underlying Western civilization could, in an increasingly materialistic and science-driven world, be replaced by one involving the heavenly, superhuman beings posited to be behind the phenomenon.[162] Jung's sober analysis was in marked contrast to that of many UFOlogists, who often walked hand in hand with New Age theorists, such as those promoting pyramid power. Pyramidology, which had been around since the Victorian era, was linked with esoteric schools and Christian mystics alike.[163] Egyptians such as Zahi Hawass, former secretary-general of Egypt's Supreme Council of Antiquities, have long taken offense at these speculations and referred to those promoting them as "pyramidiots" for dismissing the capabilities and pride of an ancient culture.[164]

Paralleling the UFO craze was a revived and equally popular interest in millennialism and catastophism, exemplified by such works as Hal Lindsey's *The Late, Great Planet Earth* (1970) and Immanuel Velikovsky's *Worlds in Collision* (1950), which was almost continuously in print throughout the late 1960s and 1970s. Immanuel Velikovsky, moving to New York City before World War II, began to develop and write about his catastrophist theory, which would later prove so popular among people in the UFOlogy and occult communities. Such groups had a variety of magazines and newsletters to communicate their ideas. These included, among many others, *Fate Magazine*, which began publishing accounts of the strange and unknown in 1948, and *Mystic Magazine*, an occult non-fiction magazine started in 1953. *Fate*, in particular, published a number of in-depth articles on Witchcraft and ancient Pagan cults from the 1940s through the 1960s.[165]

David Techter of *Fate* magazine noted in the 1970s that the current health of psychic-occult publishing owed a debt to the steady stream of paranormal paperbacks from authors like Brad Steiger (*Strangers From the Skies*, 1966; *Beyond Unseen Boundaries*, 1967; *The Tarot*, 1969).[166] Occult fiction, which saw a resurgence in popularity in the late 1960s and early 1970s, also prepared the ground for things to come. Many of horror writer H.P. Lovecraft's stories were being reprinted in 1971, as well as a number of Lovecraft-inspired works by August Derleth and other authors. These would later play an unlikely inspirational role in the development of chaos magick through the auspices of another book. The year 1971 also saw William Blatty publish *The Exorcist*, from which much of the genre of modern horror fiction has evolved, and to which the use of the Ouija board will ever be tied.

One character among the many that called New York home was the street musician and poet Louis Thomas Hardin, who called himself "Moondog." Frequenting the northeast corner of 54th Street and 6th Avenue in Manhattan, Hardin became known in the 1960s as the Viking of 6th Avenue because of his habit of dressing as a Viking in handmade clothing, from rough leather footwear to horned helmet to spear.[167] Moondog was something of an otherworldly outsider, but his music and poetry were admired by many, including Artur Rodziński, the conductor of the New York Philharmonic and folksinger Bob Dylan, and was influential to composer and one-time roommate Philip Glass. Spiritually, Moondog referred to himself as a "Gothic" and an opponent of what he called "panchristianity." A follower of the Norse God Thor, Moondog had developed his personal philosophy from the 1940s through the 1970s, long before the current incarnation of Norse/Germanic spirituality fired the imaginations of most American descendants of those ethnic backgrounds. In today's Neo-Pagan parlance, Moondog would be described as a Heathen.[168, 169]

In trying to contextualize Hardin with the events of the day, his biographer, Robert Scotto, echoes the thoughts of anthropologist William Partridge, writing, "The 1960s sometimes elevated the mere eccentric to the status of hero. Beneath the kinky glamour, the political vitality, and the shimmering variety lay a confusion that a hundred antiheroes could not dispel, and shaky underpinnings of a rebelliousness that was a symptom, not a cure."[170] Admittedly Moondog and many of the others mentioned in this chapter individually had very little influence on the spiritual trajectory of the United States. For all of their admirers and detractors, they were still little more than a symptom of the changes that were taking place in society. By themselves, they could be ignored by society at large like individual drops of water that might presage nothing worse than a brief summer shower. But by ignoring these drops, one risks missing the warning signs of an advancing flash flood that threatens to sweep away many of the things that one has taken for granted.

Ceremonial magickian Simon believes that it is just as well that the spiritual adventurers of this era were not more politically active. He writes, "The occultist of the 1960s was a revolutionary of the soul and as such could not be bothered by the more materialistic revolution promised by Marx and Engels, Lenin and Mao. While the occultist may have short-circuited himself or herself politically, the service done to society as a whole has yet to be evaluated. If nothing else, the self-centered and self-involved American occultist of the 1960s was removed from the great social upheavals of the anti-war movement, in the sense that he or she did not bring any sophisticated cultic influence to bear on the political aspect of that movement unlike the influence of the Teutonic mystics on the German political movements of the post-World War I era. For that, we have to be thankful; the occultist of the period did not have the political intelligence or social skills to create a new movement that blended — in a positive, life-affirming, liberty-affirming way — both spirituality and political organization."[171]

Simon may be correct in his assessment that the postmodern occult movement was in its infancy in the 1960s, but the stage was being set for its practitioners to graduate from the nursery and move out onto the playground in the coming decade. The churn produced by the likes of Warhol and Moondog, Sanders and Cino, Anger and Page kept the cultural pot stirred and allowed things to pop to the surface that might otherwise have gone unremarked. It was through this process that politically conscious individuals began to awaken to the existence of spiritual philosophies that challenged the individual to become active in determining his or her own future — and it was through this process that the Pagan religions began to creep back into the periphery of society.

Frederick Adams' Fellowship of Hesperides was succeeded in 1967 by his Goddess-worshipping Feraferia ("wilderness festival"). Adams was inspired by the Greek concept of the Kore, or sacred Maiden Goddess, and he constructed elaborate and beautiful rituals to honor the feminine principle in nature. In this, he approximated some of the earlier work of Gleb Botkin — so much so that, after leaving Botkin's Long Island Church of Aphrodite, W. Holman Keith joined Feraferia and helped blend some of that Church's philosophy and teachings with those of his new spiritual home.[172] Keith had written an early blueprint on incorporating sexuality into worship within a Westernized structure (*Divinity as the Eternal*

Feminine, 1960), and this was used as a guiding principle of the worship of the divine feminine, known as the *Kore*.[173]

The Church of All Worlds (CAW) was born over Labor Day weekend in 1967 from the remnants of the youthful college group called Atl. CAW was an egalitarian group from its start. Founded on the principles of water-kinship set out in Robert A. Heinlein's science fiction novel *Stranger in a Strange Land*, CAW's worship of a generic Mother Goddess and a Father God paralleled to some extent the extant practice of Witchcraft covens.[174] In March 1968, CAW began publishing what would become the most influential Neo-Pagan magazine of its day, *Green Egg*.[175,][176] Spanish émigré Frederic de Arechaga founded his mystic Middle Eastern temple, the Sabaean, in Chicago in 1968, using his mother's El Sabarum occult supply store as its base of operations.[177] Victor Anderson's Feri tradition, which emphasizes a close connection with the spirits of nature, became a formalized spiritual system in 1970.[178]

Gardnerian Wica, under the guidance of the Bucklands and their initiates, slowly began to increase in numbers and visibility in the United States throughout the 1960s. By June 1971, the Buckland Museum of Witchcraft and Magick had outgrown the Buckland home (and Rosemary's patience), and was moved a two-and-a-half storey Victorian frame house at 6 First Avenue in Bay Shore, New York, where it received 5000 visitors in its first four months of operation.[179] Alexandrian Witchcraft, an offshoot of Gardnerian Wica, was developed by Alex Sanders in England in the mid-1960s and was established in the United States by the late 1960s. While not a Neo-Pagan religion, the Church of Satan, founded in 1966 by Anton LaVey in San Francisco, would promote the concept of Satanic Witchcraft as a counterbalance to both the dominant Judeo-Christian faith communities and the growing influence of what the Satanists derided as the "white" magic of the Gardnerian Witches and their kind. Dubbed the "Barnum of Beelzebub," the goateed former carnival roustabout and calliope player was a publicity hound and character who astutely and joyfully filled the role of a twisted alternative to such others as Raymond Buckland on the media circuit.[180]

These avant-garde religious practices — Witchcraft, Neo-Paganism, Satanism, the occult, the New Age — swept the entire country in the 1960s, settling in both major metropolitan areas and in smaller communities throughout the United States. Sometimes, it was received as just another fad; a brief relief from boredom. Writer C. H. Wallace observed that the adoption of occult themes by irreverent fashion cognoscenti ultimately introduced these ideas into popular culture. "The rise of camp in the early 1960s undoubtedly helped to spread the use of witchcraft artifacts in these circles," wrote Wallace. "New York, as the capital of camp, seems to have been at least partially responsible for the meeting of witchcraft with the sometimes talented, frequently peculiar, fashion bullies who clothe, shape, paint and decorate the restless rich." But the association with camp does not preclude serious practice by those who had originally picked up the trappings as fashion accessories. "Campy beginnings," Wallace reluctantly concludes, "may well lead to practiced witchcraft within a relatively short space of time."[181]

Like the mustard seed of Christ, all of this convergent information fell upon disturbed soil and began to produce a very large crop. Where they took root inevitably determined their future focus and flavor. There appeared to be a difference in philosophy between how occult knowledge was pursued in New York versus how it was practiced in the West Coast centers. But appearances can be deceiving. As a Los Angeles resident explained to *Esquire* writer Tom Burke, "New York is a together place. You've got to take care of business, or get out. People come here [to LA] purposefully to freak. They do things here they'd never have dreamed of back in St. Paul or somewhere." Drawn by the illusion that Cali is a never-ending beach party, they instead find themselves trapped in the middle of a nightmare from which there is no escape.[182] The fact is that the West Coast held many serious occultists (Israel Regardie, for example), while New York occultists were just as likely to be skating on the thin edge of dissolution as their West Coast brethren. Still, unfairly or not, New York was generally seen in a more impersonal, hard-edged commercial light, while California was characterized by a certain (for lack of a better term) "woo-woo" factor. This image remains ingrained, unfairly or not, as a "fruits, nuts and flakes" stereotype to this day in popular culture.

Coverage of occult themes in the mainstream American media morphed throughout the 1960s, from articles on the quaint beliefs of British Witches after Gardner went public to cover stories and salacious exposés of occult practices in America's own back yard.[183, 184] Witches, psychics, Satanists, UFOlogists and others appeared regularly on the TV circuit and in the newspapers. The most notable of these included people like Hans Holzer, Rolla Nordic, Raymond Buckland, and Sybil Leek in the New York City media market. *Look* magazine ran a highly visible cover story titled "Witchcraft is Rising," in which an appropriately Satanic-looking Anton LeVey stared out at the reader from the cover with skull in hand. Other occult figures of the day were also covered in this article, including Long Island resident Raymond Buckland. Writer Frank Smyth, in commenting on the late 1960s scene in New York City, observed that "New York's Greenwich Village area — always a hidden source of occult doings — broke out in a rash of fortune tellers, black magicians, astrologers, spirit mediums, ghost hunters, and witches of the 'Gardnerian' type as soon as the more permissive attitude to such things became apparent, while at the same time in other areas of the city, New York's hotch-potch of nations delved into their memories and produced the beliefs of their own, old countries."[185]

Despite all these signs and portents, Eddie Buczynski had found nothing to satisfy his spiritual appetite in lieu of his hoped-for career with the Jesuits. Worse, the Hippie subculture, the social-spiritual movement that had once so attracted him, seemed to be disintegrating before his eyes — and in full view of the rest of the country. The 1967 "Summer of Love" had to share center stage with a "long hot summer" of race riots, including a horrific six-day siege in Newark, New Jersey that left twenty-six people dead and $10 million in property damage. In April 1968, Dr. Martin Luther King, Jr.'s assassination sparked riots in 125 cities nationwide. New York City remained relatively calm during this time, mainly due to the actions of Mayor Lindsey and other community leaders; however, violence broke out in Brooklyn near Coney Island, which was uncomfortably close to Buczynski's family. Eddie decided to move back once again to Ozone Park. He wrote of this time, "I finally returned home to my family with my tail between my legs, to try to pick up the pieces and start anew." *(Ibid n#30)*

At home, Eddie doted on his younger brothers — particularly Frank, who was now old enough to accompany Eddie on the occasional excursion into the City. Frank remembered Eddie as being the best big brother that a guy could have. *(Ibid n#33)* Little Tommy was awestruck by his older brother. Eddie took the time to read to him and teach him about the mythology and history of ancient Greece, Rome and Egypt. His guitar-playing, while not the best, inspired the musically talented Tommy to pick up the instrument himself, and in later years he became a successful rock musician.[186] Eddie took over part of the basement as his own, as Frank was now sharing the small bedroom with Tommy that he had once occupied with Eddie.

Eddie Buczynski lived unobtrusively with his family until the summer of 1971, when he stumbled across a recent reprint of Gerald Gardner's 1954 book *Witchcraft Today*. It was a book that would change his life.

> *I remember reading it from cover to cover on a family expedition to the Bronx Zoo. I was overjoyed! There were still Pagans in the world and, although it wasn't the kind of Paganism that was natural to me, I knew that I must join it. It was so much better than [having] nothing at all akin to my beliefs. I would adjust. (Ibid n#30)*

Discovering that Witchcraft actually existed allowed Eddie a chance to rekindle his youthful interest in Paganism. Intrigued by the promise that it held, he began his quest to seek out someone who could introduce him to the practice of Wica.

This leads one to question why Eddie would ever have been tempted to pick up a copy of *Witchcraft Today* in the first place. It isn't as if Wica fit neatly into the worldview of a gay man struggling to find acceptance within Catholicism — at least not in an obvious way to someone unfamiliar with the practice (this despite the Wiccan adage "Scratch a Catholic, find a Witch"). Eddie himself notes that "I had been raised a Roman Catholic. While Christianity provided me with a cohesive view of the spiritual world, it lacked (or so I thought) anything comparable [to Wica] where man's place in nature is concerned. Pagan mysticism provided both a way to salvation and a way to 'plug-in' to the cosmos."[187] As his childhood friend Terry Gianniotis noted, Eddie had always been interested in the mystical, and by the time he moved back home, this had translated into an interest in Witchcraft and the occult. *(Ibid.n#21)*

It is possible that one or more articles in the popular press at that time that may have piqued Eddie's interest in Witchcraft and prompted his search for a copy. Certainly related stories were published regularly in the New York metro newspapers, particularly on or about Hallowe'en. One such example is a Witchcraft lecture presented by Raymond Buckland that was advertised in the *Village Voice* in September 1969.[188] Another example is an October 1969 article in the *New York Times* featuring Sybil Leek and the Bucklands.[189] However, it is more likely that what caught Eddie's eye was a regular column on gay Witchcraft that was published in one of the local gay community newspapers beginning in December 1970. Eddie's search took him once more to Manhattan and to the columnist in question, who had organized a large and highly publicized gathering of Witches in Central Park just a year earlier. The writer in question was a darkly handsome Italian named Leo Martello.

Chapter 4: Cry Havoc

A Rebel with Many Causes

Leo Louis Martello was a lanky, hungry scrapper with piercing eyes, the face of a dark angel, and a mouth like a bear trap. The nimbus of hair that fell like a curtain of shadow down to his shoulders made him look like a black-maned lion, and, when roused, he was quite capable of acting like one as well. Martello was both blessed and cursed with a strong personality and a desire to assert his own place in the world. Dismissive of both fools and whiners, Martello believed that you had to make your own way through life. It is not without reason then that the saying for which he is best remembered cuts to the heart of who he was — "The weak find an excuse, the strong find a way."[1]

Martello was born on September 26, 1930 in the small town of Dudley, Massachusetts. His first years were spent on a small farm that was worked by his father, Rocco Luigi Martello, who was a Sicilian immigrant. Beginning in 1931, a series of economic missteps in the United States resulted in the collapse of farm exports. This in turn caused many American farmers to default on loans that were necessary for procuring land, seed, and equipment. Caught up in the destruction of small family farms in the early years of the Great Depression, the Martellos were forced off the land, moving first to Worcester, Massachusetts and then 19 miles away to Southbridge.

It was in Southbridge, Massachusetts that young Leo was finally baptized into his native Catholic faith. His parents divorced not long after moving to the small town, and Leo's father placed the young man in a Catholic boarding school in Worcester to begin his education. The preparatory school was operated by Assumption College, which was a small Catholic school founded by the Augustinians of the Assumption. Leo told friends that the six years he spent at the boarding school were the unhappiest of his life, perhaps understandable given the Catholic Church's stance on divorce. Often in trouble during his stay at the boarding school, Leo did not endear himself to the Church, or vice versa. However, the time away from home and the deprivation of his younger years strengthened his character. The stated mission of Assumption College is to form graduates known for critical intelligence, thoughtful citizenship and compassionate service. In Leo Martello's case, at least, the Augustinians were successful, though he ultimately chose the freedoms offered by apostasy and the occult over the bindings of mother Church.

As a child, Leo had had many psychic experiences that led him to explore the occult. By his early teens, he was studying palmistry and tarot with a Gypsy woman named Marta. His earliest claim to fame was as a graphologist, or handwriting analyst, at which he became particularly skilled. By the time he was sixteen, he had begun making radio appearances, and giving handwriting analyses and selling stories to magazines. Occult gifts, it seems, ran in his family. According to Leo's father, the younger Martello physically resembled his paternal grandmother, Maria Concetta. He had also inherited her temperament and psychic abilities. Maria was a well-known *Strega Maga* — "Great Witch" — in her hometown of Enna, Sicily, and was both hated and envied by the priests, according to Leo.[2] She was a card-reader, and was also said to have used her skills to help the local townsfolk. In one instance, she reputedly caused the heart attack that killed a local Mafioso who threatened her husband for failing to pay protection money. Whatever the truth, it was a given that you did not rattle the cage of a Sicilian *Strega* or *Stregone* (male Witch) without expecting consequences. They protected their own.

As Leo approached adulthood, his father informed him that he had cousins in New York City who wished to meet him. Martello alleges that he was told that these cousins followed the ancient ways of the old country. Martello journeyed to New York and met with his cousins, who told him they had been watching him for years for signs that he had inherited the psychic gifts that would confirm his potential as a practitioner of the Old Religion, or *La Vecchia*. He moved to New York City and continued his studies at Hunter College and the Institute for Psychotherapy. On Leo Martello's 21st birthday, in 1951, he was purportedly initiated into his cousins' Sicilian coven, at which point he became a *mago* — a mage (another term for *Stregone*). The initiation involved a blood oath never to reveal the secrets of the coven or its members or any of the secret teachings. To do so would be to be labeled *Infamia*, and an oath-breaker.

There is really very little information that can be used to independently corroborate Martello's story concerning how he came into Witchcraft. A number of contemporary critics scoffed at his claims of being an initiate of a Continental form of Witchcraft that differed markedly from Gardnerian Wica. Citing the secrecy of the tradition, Martello provided no hard proof to back up his claims. One person who knew him in New York City stated that Leo had told her and her husband in the early 1980s that he had never been initiated into any Witchcraft tradition, but had only jumped on the occult bandwagon in the 1960s in order to make a living. Regardless of the true story, it is clear that he had demonstrated a skill with paranormal subject matter at an early age. Well ahead of the main body of the Witchcraft wave in the United States, he presented a well-developed, though often highly confrontational, view of Witchcraft to the public. Arising seemingly from nowhere, Leo Martello stands as a unique personage of this time and place.

During his early years in New York, Leo was involved in a number of enterprises stemming from his interest in the occult. In 1950, he founded the American Hypnotism Academy in New York, and he directed the organization until 1954. From 1955 to 1957, he served as the treasurer of the American Graphological Society, which was founded by Louise Rice in New York City in 1926. During this time, Martello was also actively engaged in writing articles for various fringe magazines associated with graphology and occult topics. He also used his talents as graphologist to examine the handwriting of job candidates for various corporate clients, including the Unifonic Corporation of America and the Associated Special Investigators International, and for eight years he wrote a column "Your Handwriting Tells" for the *Chelsea Clinton News* in New York. Another thing that Leo discovered in the Big Apple was the burgeoning gay night life in the post-War years. Free of the strictures and guilt of the Catholic Church, Martello made himself right at home.

Martello was awarded a Doctorate of Divinity degree in 1955 by the National Congress of Spiritual Consultants, a non-accredited organization that performed roughly the same function as the Universal Life Church, that is, as a clearing house for registering unaffiliated ministers. That same year, as a Spiritual-Nonsectarian minister, he became the founder and Pastor of the Temple of Spiritual Guidance. He also founded the Spiritual Independents Movement in an effort to represent "non-aligned" spiritual practitioners. Martello withdrew from his position as Pastor of the Temple in 1960 in order to devote himself to his writing and his research into his philosophy of "psychoselfism." As he delicately put it in his 1966 author's bio, he gave up his ministry because he could no longer practice and preach moral doctrines in which he disbelieved. Martello refused to give his moral sanction "to the 'creed of need versus deed' when the evidence revealed that the popular idea of altruism, of 'living for others,' provoked, produced and pandered to parasites."[3] This "up by your own bootstraps" philosophy was to set the tone for the remainder of Leo's life. He chose instead to pursue occult interests in Witchcraft, parapsychology, psychology, and philosophy. In 1961, Martello published his first book, *Your Pen Personality*, which was a discussion of what handwriting reveals about the personality of the writer.[4]

Leo moved to Tangier, Morocco during the summer of 1964 to study oriental religion, magick, and Witchcraft, researching the history of the tarot at the University of Fez.[5] The culmination of this effort was his 1964 book on cartomancy titled *It's in the Cards*.[6] Returning to the United States in 1965, he moved into an apartment in Greenwich Village to be near the subcultural center of the city and began writing and publishing once again. This time he produced a book on astrology titled *It's Written in the Stars* and another on psychic protection titled *How to Prevent Psychic Blackmail*.[7] *(Ibid n#3)* Laura Austan notes that it was around this time that Leo began showing up at gatherings of the Spiritualist group operated out of the Ansonia Hotel by Clifford Bias.[8]

As the 1960s wore on, Witchcraft was becoming a more public spiritual vocation in the United States. This was particularly true in New York City. Apart from media mainstays such as Ray Buckland and Sybil

Leek, others were being noticed by the press. By 1970, a booking agency — Psychic Dimensions, Inc. — had even been founded specifically to represent astrologers, Witches, graphologists and the like.[9] For an oddball Hallowe'en piece in October 1967, an Associated Press journalist interviewed a 29-year-old Greenwich Village artist named Martin Carey. Carey spoke earnestly about a new kind of magick "that seems very pervasive among young people," noting that "By combining art, science and magic with the catalyst of meditation, I have been able to rise beyond the time-space relationships and live in the past, future and present all at once, and see the universe as a whole."[10] Carey's understanding of magick appeared to derive as much from the fictional talents of the Kwisatz Haderach of Frank Herbert's 1965 science fiction novel *Dune* as it did from the tenets of Ceremonial Magick; however, this philosophy and his willingness to express it were indications of how occult ideas and eastern mysticism were spreading amongst the younger generation in the bohemian precincts of late 1960s Manhattan.

The intersection of Marxism, the anti-war movement, eastern philosophy and magick was manifest on October 21, 1967, when approximately fifty thousand anti-war protestors provided a visible display of "People Power" by attempting to levitate the Pentagon through force of Will.[11] The ritual was written by Ed Sanders with the help of ceremonial magickian Harry Smith. Sanders led his band The Fugs in an "exorcism" of the building to drive out the generals with chants of "Out Demons, Out!" Alan Ginsberg attempted the same feat using Tibetan chants. Kenneth Anger was reportedly present for the rite but was working his own magick. Michael Bowen, Beat artist, metaphysical Shaman, and former resident of the Lower East Side, was responsible for the distribution of the daisies that were placed in the rifle barrels of the Military Police guarding the Pentagon, thus giving rise to the anti-war movement's iconic phrase "Flower Power."[1]

Some believe that the attempt by Sanders and the others was a joke. However, a handout prepared by the Peace Eye's owner and distributed at the time shows that it was, in fact, a fully integrated "magick rite to exorcize the Spirits of murder, violence & creephood from the Pentagon."[13] Attending the event was writer Norman Mailer. Mailer observed a tectonic shift in the outlook of those who participated, from New Age goody two-shoes to spiritual warriors:[14]

> Now suddenly an entire generation of acid-heads seemed to have said goodbye to easy visions of heaven, no, now the witches were here, and rites of exorcism, and black terrors of the night — hippies being murdered. Yes, the hippies have gone right from Tibet to Christ to the Middle Ages, now they were revolutionary Alchemists.

While the efficacy of the Pentagon action was debatable — given that the Vietnam War lasted another six and a half years — the attempt was significant in that it represented the first large-scale public magickal working in the United States.[15] Sanders and company followed up with an exorcism of Senator Joseph McCarthy's gravesite in Appleton, Wisconsin in February 1968, and performed a magickal rite against a Los Angeles obscenity prosecutor in April of that year.[16] Many of those responsible for organizing the protest march and the initial magickal working — including Hoffman, Ginsberg, Sanders, and Bowen — were representative of the vibrant Village counterculture that was rocking the establishment in the late 1960s.

Public ritual workings popped up every so often after the Pentagon affair. On July 21, 1968, Louise Huebner and a coven of Witches cast a large public spell at the Hollywood Bowl designed to raise levels of romantic and emotional vitality throughout Los Angeles County, California. The Los Angeles County "Spellcast," involving eleven thousand immediate participants, is often incorrectly credited as the first large-scale public ritual in the country.[17] The Pentagon working was copied three years later at an anti-war protest in front of the Internal Revenue Service building on Church Street in New York City, where, on April 15, 1970, a group of protestors attempted to levitate the building nine inches through the use of Witchcraft.[18] Many years later, Sally Eaton still expressed admiration for the chutzpah exhibited by the organizers of the protest. "[It was] ten years before Starhawk started doing that at nuke plants in California, but still the same idea — and a good one, if you ask me!"[19]

Not everyone was as thrilled by these public displays. Leo Martello watched this street theatre and read what passed for objective information on Witchcraft with mixed feelings. Although the Witchcraft tradition to which he belonged was underground and secret, he felt that someone should be speaking out to counter the public perceptions formed by the publicity hounds and clowns of the occult fringe. In early 1969, Leo sought the acquiescence of his coven to go public as a Witch. They concurred on the condition that he remain true to his oath of secrecy that he took to guard their rites and teachings. One of Martello's first acts after coming out of the broom closet as a Sicilian Witch was to start the Witches International Craft Associates as a way to network and promote the Craft in the United States. He also wrote two books in 1969, one on hypnotism and another on the current state of Witchcraft in the United States. It was the latter book that was to garner him the most attention and set him at the forefront of the fight for the rights of Witches.[20] Its title was *Weird Ways of Witchcraft*.[21]

On April 18, 1969, Leo Martello interviewed a 27-year-old male Witch, Elijah Hadynn (aka Elijah "Lige" Hayden Clarke), for *Weird Ways of Witchcraft*. A transplant to New York City, Lige grew up in the "hills and hollers" of eastern Kentucky before joining the Army. After his military service, he became the lover of gay activist John Ross "Jack" Nichols. Together, the two men had been involved in the struggle for gay rights since 1965, having founded the Florida chapter of the Mattachine Society with their friend Richard Inman, and later participating in Mattachine activities in Washington, D.C. and New York City (Nichols, in fact, had helped Franklin Kameny start the Washington, D.C. chapter of the Mattachine Society in 1961).[22, 23] Nichols and Clarke organized the Mattachine Society's first protest at the White House on April 17, 1965. In 1967, the couple made television history in the United States by appearing as openly gay men in an interview with Mike Wallace during the first CBS documentary on homosexuality. Therefore, it's fair to say that Lige wasn't quite the retiring lad portrayed by Martello in his book. On the contrary, he was not only openly gay, but already possessed a significant depth of experience in and connections with the nascent gay rights movement in the United States.

In the Martello interview, Clarke stated he was a hatha yoga instructor in Manhattan and a solitary practitioner of Witchcraft. Martello described Clarke as living a hip, vegetarian lifestyle in the East Village with Jack Nichols in an apartment strewn with throw pillows in lieu of sofas and chairs. Lige occasionally modeled and wrote articles on the occult for Strange Unknown as well as for other magazines, such as Personal Horoscope.[24, 25] Nichols biographer J. Louis Campbell writes that Lige's Witch persona was a fictional construct that he used when writing articles for Nichols' magazines.[26] If that were the case, one would think that he would have dropped the act after Nichols had stopped editing the publications; but instead, he continued using it into the early 1970s.

Campbell describes Lige as having a "mystic personality," and this is likely true.[27] Clarke, with his Appalachian upbringing, was more likely a practitioner of rural folk magick and Hoodoo, rather than one of the Witchcraft traditions coming to prominence at the time. He always took the resulting publicity with a grain of salt, laughing once with Jack over a photo shoot where he is depicted as a Warlock with a photo caption that read, "At Last! A Male Witch Speaks!"[28] Martello wasn't the only writer with whom Lige spoke, having also been interviewed by Florence Hershman for her book Witchcraft USA. (1971). Clarke's exposure in magazines and books, in combination with his youthful appeal, caused him to receive many inquiries from teenagers and men looking to become Witches themselves.[29, 30]

Jack, who had arranged for the interview with Martello, had just completed a stint as editor of the magazines *Strange Unknown* and *Companion* for Countrywide Publications. In 1969, Nichols became the first managing editor of Al Goldstein's new adult magazine, *Screw*. Dedicated to an era of free love, *Screw* broke many boundaries when it hit the newsstands on November 3, 1968. One of those broken boundaries was a column for gays in the decidedly straight, but hardly narrow, publication. Called "The Homosexual Citizen," the popular column was penned by Lige and Jack beginning with the inaugural issue of the magazine, and reflected their experiences in the gay community. The following year, *Screw* broke ground again when the couple appeared in a nude photo shoot of male-male lovemaking in the May 16, 1969 issue.[31] Nichols and Clarke were soon co-authoring the "New York Notes" column of the new Los Angeles-based biweekly paper, *The Advocate*. Not content with writing columns, Nichols and Clarke dreamed of one day launching their own newspaper.[32] Only after the gay community began to seriously organize in order to assert their rights would the couple realize their dream — and that change was just around the corner.

Hail Aquarius

In 1967, *Look* magazine devoted had an entire issue to the American man. Senior editor Jack Starr wrote an article on the status of gay men in American society that, while generally bleak, offered some hope that attitudes were beginning to change — at least in the larger cities.[33] The off-Broadway production of Mart Crowley's play *The Boys in the Band* opened on April 14, 1968. While sticking to the safe themes of sardonic, miserable and self-loathing homosexuals, Crowley's play also offered a somewhat sympathetic view of the societal pressure and resulting dysfunction with which gay men were forced to live. In 1968 and 1969, police across the United States raided liquor establishments that allowed gay and lesbian people to gather together in public. The repression was neither coordinated nor given much thought by those in power as anything more or less than an appropriate response to what they perceived as a rising tide of perversion that was enabled, in large part, by bars catering to "disorderly" elements or operating without the required permits or payoffs.[34,35]

Gay men, lesbians, transvestites, hustlers and others on the sexual fringe had come to expect a certain level of risk — to be harassed, arrested, assaulted and blackmailed — in exchange for the chance to congregate with one another during a night out on the town. Vice squads regularly preyed on the gay bars in each city, with corrupt officers shaking down bar owners who were often themselves affiliated with the mob, and ruining the lives of patrons caught up in the sweeps. Many states and municipalities had draconian laws designed to prevent the congregation of homosexuals in public (and in some cases, in private), ranging from prohibiting the serving of alcohol to homosexuals, to minimum requirements for gender-appropriate dress, to prohibitions against public displays of affection, dancing, or importuning. But even though a 1968 court ruling in New York essentially struck down many of these prohibitions in 1968, the police in New York City were still given wide latitude in dealing with the "homosexual problem" in neighborhoods where gay men and lesbians liked to congregate, such as Greenwich Village.[36] Given the general rise in expectations among gays and lesbians, particularly those younger men and women who had been weaned on the fight for civil rights throughout the 1950s and 1960s and the anti-war movement, this situation could not last indefinitely.

In 1966, the Stonewall Inn at 53 Christopher Street in Greenwich Village was a burned out storefront that investors were trying to turn into a discotheque.[37] Shortly afterward, "Fat" Tony Lauria opened a gay bar in the space for the Genovese crime family.[38] The Stonewall was a typical mob-run hangout for gay and bi men, lesbians, and drag queens. "The Stonewall, from the outside of the bar, was pretty typical for Gay bars at the time," recalls Joe Caldiero, who had begun sneaking into the bar at age 16. "It was rundown and painted with dull, unattractive colors so it would not attract the wrong kind of attention. Once inside, there was a man at the door (a bouncer) who would check our ID. They had a few different guys there, but my favorite bouncer's name was Chuck. He was straight, but still very nice to us. If straight guys would follow us into the bar, he would bounce them out. There were plenty of times I had to run into the bar for safety from straight hitters and Chuck was always good to take care of his little fairies (that's what he called us). The bar was divided into two sections. As you went in, there was a real long bar with a big dance floor at the end of it. In the upper left corner near the ceiling was a go-go cage with a guy dancing in it. I think there may have been a girl in it once in a while, especially when we knew the police were walking through. It may have been a drag queen come to think of it. There were plenty of drag queens there to choose from. The ones that stand out in my mind the most were: "Putasa," a Puerto Rican who was a model for Vogue magazine, a Black Queen called "Twiggy" who took care of us younger gay boys by kicking ass if she had to in order to keep us safe, and "Bubbles" who was so pretty, all of us loved her/him."[39]

On the night of June 27-28, 1969, a vice squad entered and began rounding up, harassing and arresting the staff and members of the crowd at the Stonewall Inn. In the prior three weeks, at least five bars in the Village that catered to homosexuals had been raided by the police, including the Stonewall.[40] A fight started when some of society's outcasts — the hustlers, homeless gay runaways, drag queens, lesbians, gay men and others — decided that they had had enough on that particular night. The predominant theme that night was "this shit has got to stop."[41] A large crowd had gathered in the streets and park outside the Stonewall, including patrons the police had thrown out of the bar in their quest to separate the employees from the customers. While the scene started out docile, with drag queens on their way to the paddy wagons taking their bows before the gathered onlookers, at some point the crowd turned ugly.

Joe Caldiero, who went by the name "Maxine" (later "Max"), recalls the scene that night.

Joe Caldiero: *(Ibid n#39)*

The bar was loud, smoky and I was speeding on some pills I took. As the evening went on everything was what I figured to be normal, when all of a sudden the lights went on and the music stopped. The cops came racing in blowing whistles and yelling at everybody to go here or there. They were so rude and nasty to us. The bar owners had a licensing problem, but they needed no excuse to harass us in those days.

They took all of those people with ID to one side of the room and made the rest of us pile into the front room and line up along the long bar. The jukebox was playing "In the Year 2525" in the front room and they turned it off. We put it back on again and they unplugged it. As the cops passed by us, they would punch us in the side or the stomach when they thought no one was looking. My friend was so frightened he wet himself a little. We helped him dry off and tried to wait out the raid hoping no one would get badly hurt. The police were such bullies and whispered threats to us and tried to scare us. They did a good job of that, we were scared to death. Some of the older queens tried to comfort us by telling us things would be OK and to just be quiet. But that is not the way it would happen that night for us, for any of us.

One by one we were questioned and then made to leave the bar. When it was my turn, I was asked my name and age. I gave the name that was on the ID (my draft card) I had purchased and said I was 18 years old. The cop said I looked awful young for 18 so I smiled and thanked him for the compliment. He called me a few names, names I was used to and shoved me into a corner. He said he would deal with me later. He shoved me so hard my ribs hurt for days after that. Imagine a big cop pushing around a 16-year-old child. I was so frightened; I was not sure what to do. I had this numb feeling all over me.

Soon enough, the cop took me into the other part of the bar and started to yell at me and slap me around until I just couldn't hold back the tears anymore. I yelled back at him, telling him that I was just dancing and trying to have fun. I told him that I wasn't hurting anyone and to leave me alone. At that point, someone from outside started yelling "Maxine! Where is Maxine?" I yelled back, "I'm here! Help me!" Then, the cop kicked me in the butt and pushed me outside. I was grabbed by someone (I think it was Twiggy) and brought to Sheridan Square Park across the street. My friends checked me out to see if I had been seriously hurt. I hid behind the statue of General Sheridan until I could walk without falling over.

The police told all of us to "go the fuck home" and we started to yell back. I'm sure this took them by surprise. They were used to us all running and hiding from them. But not that night. I was beaten, a bit bloody, but I was not afraid anymore. The older guys had us younger guys stay in the background while they fought off the police attacks. We all stood arm in arm doing high kicks and singing "The Stonewall Girls Song:"

*"We are the Stonewall girls,
we wear our hair in curls,
we wear no underwear,
we show our pubic hair,
we wear our dungarees,
above our nelly knees!"*

After a little while what seemed an endless riot broke out. The streets were full of cops in riot gear. I was still numb all over. But that didn't stop me from yelling at them and throwing stuff at them to keep them away from us. When I couldn't find anything more to [throw], I started throwing my shoes as well as some articles of clothing including my belt. I loved that belt; wish I still had it now! A large group of us eventually made it through the crowd to the nearby subway station and headed for Queens, where my friend lived. We stayed there for a few days hoping things would calm down. Things never calmed down and wouldn't for a long time.

Who threw the first punch remains in dispute. The police were eventually forced to retreat into the bar under a barrage of bottles, pennies, bricks and garbage. Some rioters tried to set fire to the storefront, behind which the police with drawn guns had barricaded themselves while awaiting reinforcements. Rioters and police both ran amok through the night, though remarkably no one was killed or even seriously injured. Artie Jamison, who would later become a high priest in the same coven of Welsh Witchcraft that Joe Caldiero would join, stood across the street from the Stonewall hooting and hollering and watching the action.[42] Order was eventually restored early in the morning, but confrontations erupted several more times over the coming days.[43]

Word of the events at Sheridan Park and its surrounds quickly spread within New York City, and the story made its way to gay communities elsewhere in the United States in publications such as *The Advocate*. Gays and lesbians who were tired of attempting to accommodate society's contempt began instead to form activist groups in large cities across the country. In doing so, they borrowed heavily from the lessons learned and alliances formed during the civil rights and anti-war demonstrations of the 1960s. Some activists wrung their hands and agonized over the inevitable reprisals. Others, however, recognized that something fundamental had changed in the social equation. As Allan Ginsberg remarked following an impromptu post-riot visit to the Stonewall Inn, "You know, the guys there were so beautiful — they've lost that wounded look that fags all had 10 years ago."[44] However it was Kevan Liscoe, a resident of Greenwich Village, who perhaps best summed up the post-riot vibe when he wrote, "The age of the scared little queens is gone. Hail Aquarius." *(Ibid n#40)*

So-called homophile groups had been organizing in the United States to promote civil rights for homosexuals since the 1950s, with the creation of such groups as the Mattachine Foundation (Los Angeles, 1950) and the Daughters of Bilitis (San Francisco, 1955).[45] These organizational, educational and lobbying activities were the beginning of what John Lauritsen and David Thorstad refer to as the "second wave" of gay liberation.[46] The New York chapter of the Mattachine Society was founded in 1955 to educate and lobby for change within New York City and its surrounds. The officers of Mattachine-New York reacted with horror not only to the violence of the Stonewall rioters, but also to the reports of drag queens openly taunting the police. For them it was a public relations disaster that threatened their ability to work behind the scenes to effect change. The leaders of Mattachine-New York wanted to calm the anger in the gay community and channel it into their stock response to the outrages inflicted upon homosexuals, namely public education and the respectful engagement of politicians in backroom discussions aimed at a gradual change in attitudes and laws. A public meeting to be hosted by the Mattachine Action Committee was called for July 16, 1969 in order to do just that. Unfortunately for Mattachine's leaders, the events on the ground had already outstripped their ability to put the djinn back into the bottle.[47]

At the outset of the July 16 meeting, Leo Martello unleashed his legendary temper on the audience. He castigated the attendees for buying into society's treatment of homosexuality as a mental illness and for their own resulting feelings of self-loathing.[48] Martello refined his remarks and later published them as a call to action to the gay community. In his essay, Leo asked the reader to carefully and objectively examine his own thoughts, to ponder his own origins, to modify his own actions and reactions to his repression — including his self-repression and his repression of others like him — and to lay claim to his inalienable rights. He exhorted gay men to reject society's expectations of what it means to be a homosexual. "Homosexuality is not a problem in itself," he wrote. "The problem is society's attitude towards it."[49] These ideas would later find their way into the 1971 London Gay Liberation Front Manifesto and the self-published pamphlet, *With Downcast Gays* (1974).[50]

After Leo spoke, Dick Leitsch, the leader of Mattachine-New York, took over the meeting. But the gathering soon devolved into chaos after Jim Fouratt and others declared the Mattachine accomodationist strategy to be weak and ineffective. In reaction to what they saw as a conciliatory approach to police harassment, the more radicalized members of the community had decided that the time had come for a more confrontational engagement with the powers that be. Throwing off what they felt to be the straitjacket of the Mattachine rulebook, these activists chose instead to form a new group, calling it the Gay Liberation Front (GLF). Their number included Arthur Evans, Arthur Bell, John Lauritsen, Lige Clarke, and Jack Nichols.[51] Sixteen-year-old Joe Caldiero would also join to walk the picket lines. *(Ibid n#39)* Leo Martello was elected as the fledgling organization's first Moderator.[52] Being in a leadership position was an unusual step for the Sicilian. Asked once if he saw himself as a leader, Leo replied, "No. I don't relish the idea of being followed!"[53] Nevertheless, he took his role seriously.

The GLF's statement of purpose condemned "this rotten, dirty, vile, fucked-up capitalist conspiracy" that had its foot on the throat of the social underclass.[54] Martello volunteered to help further the GLF's agenda by preparing articles for the press and for the newsletter of the organization – *Come Out!* One of the first actions GLF took was against the *Village Voice* on September 12, 1969 to protest its refusal to accept any advertisement or story with the word "gay" in it. The position of the *Voice* editorial board was that "gay" was considered an obscenity when used in reference to homosexuals. The *Voice* had proposed that the term "homophile" be used in place of "gay." Although groups like Mattachine had used "homophile" for almost twenty years to describe their movement, the newest generation of activists, as represented by the GLF, was inclined to make a clean break with the past. Martello sneeringly rejected the term, saying that it sounded like a nail file for homosexuals.[55] The GLF eventually won the fight, publicizing the victory in the first issue of *Come Out!* Years later, gay activist John Lauritsen reminisced on the behind-the-scenes struggle to produce the GLF article that described the heady events of 1969 – "The Summer of Gay Power and the *Village Voice* Exposed!"[56]

> *The two main authors, Mike Brown and Leo Louis Martello, and I were in Martello's apartment. (Leo was a practicing witch, and kept a boa constrictor under the bed.) They were having a fiery argument about something or another, and I was sitting at a typewriter in-between them. Mike would yell in my left ear, Leo would yell in my right ear, and I would bang something on the typewriter, which might be a compromise or even something that I myself wanted to say.*[57]

That sort of chaotic creativity was generally how most things operated in GLF. To be fair, the GLF was able to accomplish a number of actions that furthered the quest for gay rights in those early months following the Stonewall riots. However, the organization was from its inception a loose amalgam of competing interests that were concerned with righting a multitude of social wrongs, gay rights being only one of many. Attempts to narrow its agenda to a list of attainable goals proved difficult. Parliamentary procedure was rejected in favor of an anarchic consensus approach, a process guaranteed to ensure that any attempt to come to final closure on an item of business was tedious at best. There was no assurance that an issue settled in one meeting would not be reopened for debate at a later meeting by a completely different set of attendees, and an atmosphere of political correctness and Marxist/anarchist ideology stifled open debate and encouraged *ad hominem* attacks on friend and foe alike.

Arthur Evans became disenchanted by the open-ended approach to debate that allowed anyone and everyone to bog down the decision-making process. Meanwhile, in one meeting Clarke and Nichols watched as their friend Leo Martello — usually quite the firebrand himself — tried to unsuccessfully moderate a debate, only to be shouted down by the radical elements present. A number of people began to feel disenfranchised by the GLF's anarchic process or unhappy with some of the organization's actions. The final straw was the membership voting to provide political and monetary support to the homophobic Black Panthers in mid-November. This provoked a mass walkout of many members, including Evans, Bell, Clarke, Nichols, and Martello.[58, 59, 60, 61, 62]

At roughly the same time, publicity was already churning for the film version of *The Boys in the Band*, which was scheduled for release the following March. Ironically, only a year after its off-Broadway run the story, with its "safe" stereotype of the self-loathing homosexual, already seemed like a hopelessly dated period piece in this new post-Stonewall paradigm of gay empowerment and pride. An article in *Look* magazine on the film's production gave Jack Star, who had written about "the sad 'gay' life" less than two years previous, an opportunity to revisit the topic. While studiously avoiding any mention of the Stonewall riots or the increasing politicization of the gay community, Star openly broached the topic of whether society's view of homosexuals was perhaps outdated.[63, 64] It's hard to say how the magazine's national audience of middle-class housewives might have reacted had Star come clean and said not only that society's was view hopelessly out of step with the times, but also that homosexuals were organizing to shove this new paradigm into the national spotlight, and down their pearl-draped throats if necessary.

A select group of people who had left the GLF were invited by Jim Owles to a private meeting on November 24, 1969 with the intention of forming a new activist group to do just that. Amongst the thirteen in attendance were Owles, Marty Robinson, Arthur Evans, Arthur Bell and

Leo Martello. Evans was chosen to draft the preamble to the Constitution of a new group, which was to focus exclusively on attaining equality for gays and lesbians. The size and composition of the organizational group was controlled in order to both keep the agenda on track and to lessen the risk that members of the GLF might try to disrupt the process. The name of the new organization would be the Gay Activist Alliance (GAA). The preamble was written and amended over the next several weeks and was ratified at a meeting at Arthur Bell's apartment on December 21, 1969. The date of the Winter Solstice was a propitious time for birthing new ventures, as the *Stregone* Martello surely knew. Lige Clarke and Jack Nichols soon joined the fledgling organization.

Owles became the first President of the GAA, serving in that capacity until 1971.[65] Evans became known as GAA's theoretician and, with others, he honed the tactic known as the "zap" that was used with great effect to publicly confront politicians and gain much-needed publicity for its cause in the mainstream media.66 Evans also pushed for the adoption of *Robert's Rules of Order* as the standard process for holding GAA meetings. There would be no repeat of GLF's unending debate or hijacked meetings. In an interview, Evans expressed what had changed since Frank Kameny, the theoretician of Mattachine-Washington, coined the phrase Gay is Good: "Today we not only know that gay is good, gay is angry."[67] Arthur Bell volunteered to act as public relations coordinator and write a regular GAA column for the newspaper *Gay Power*.[68] Having Lige Clarke and Jack Nichols as members also ensured that GAA's activities would be covered in other media outlets.

It was in Clarke and Nichols *Screw* column "The Homosexual Citizen" that the first nationally-distributed report on the Stonewall riots appeared, describing the incident to the straight community from the perspective of the gay community. After Stonewall, the columnists convinced *Screw*'s owner, Al Goldstein, to invest $25,000 to start a newspaper written by and for the gay community. "The Homosexual Citizen" column had proven to be so popular, and the post-Stonewall activity in the gay community so charged with energy, that the liberal publisher felt he was making a fairly safe bet. Called *GAY*, the New York based newspaper was launched on December 1, 1969. Nichols and Clarke edited *GAY* from 1969 to 1973, sharing the same floor as the offices for *Screw*. During their tenure, *GAY* became the second-most widely read gay newspaper in the country, and certainly the largest one edited by a gay Witch. *(Ibid n#32)* The paper attracted some of the best and brightest writers and thinkers in the gay community at that time, such as Arthur Bell, Leah Fritz, Kay Tobin, Vito Russo, Dick Leitsch, and Lilli Vincenz. For the next four years, Lige and Jack would use *GAY* as a rapier to prick those individuals and institutions they saw as standing in the way of gay equality, maintaining the focus on lifestyle at the expense of outright ideology.

Leo Martello had an agreement with the duo to write a regular column for *GAY* titled "The Gay Witch." Beginning with the first edition of *GAY*, he educated the public on aspects of modern Witchcraft and Paganism, and answered questions sent in to him by readers.[69, 70] Writer James Sears notes that Martello's occult column, despite its then-controversial subject matter, "raised scarcely an eyebrow."[71] This may have been due to Leo's matter-of-fact handling of the topic as much as it was the hip staff and readership of the newspaper. It could also be that, in the heady times following Stonewall when generations worth of protective self-restraint were beginning to fade away, the community had simply developed a higher standard for what constituted outré material. Writing for *GAY* provided Martello with arguably the largest audience he had ever had for his work. One month after the paper's debut, it had a circulation of approximately twenty-five thousand.[72, 73] Martello's contribution to the newspaper was remembered long after it had folded. In responding to his own critics, Jack Nichols remembered that "In *GAY*, back in 1969, The Gay Witch, Dr. Leo Louis Martello, revealed to our readers what he called 'the curse that never fails.' What's the curse? It goes like this: 'I wish you upon yourself!'"[74]

Leo continued to participate in the GAA, writing news stories and assisting when he could. Certainly there was plenty to write about, despite the organizational efforts of the gay community in the aftermath of the riots, police raids on bars and bath houses had not subsided. In one instance, 23-year-old Diego Vinales jumped from an upper story window of a precinct house after being taken in on a raid of the Snake Pit. Martello wrote about the raid and its grisly aftermath, when the Argentinean national became impaled on the iron fence outside the police station after his jump.[75] Leo also helped on the GAA Police Power Committee and in the planning and execution of zaps of Mayor John Lindsay in late 1970 for failing to rein in police abuse of homosexuals.

In the debate over the approval of the second GAA zap, to take place at an anti-war rally at the Loeb Student Center of New York University, Martello is quoted as saying "We are not there so much to zap Lindsay as we are to dramatize our plight. This is the only recourse open to us."[76] Regardless of their own membership in the organization, Clarke and Nichols were their own men, and GAA activities were not always reported in a positive light. For example, the October 12, 1970 edition of *GAY* criticized the GAA's zap of Mayor Lindsay and his wife at the Imperial Theatre on the opening night of the New York Metropolitan Opera, and called into question the effectiveness of that protest technique.[77]

Rights and Rites

Throughout 1970, Leo began to focus some of his energies on agitating for the rights of Witches to worship when, where and how they pleased. Martello had not neglected his commitments to the Old Religion during his time with the GLF and GAA. With everything else that was going on in 1969, he had also managed to release two books — *The Weird Ways of Witchcraft*, featuring his interview with Lige Clarke, and *Hidden World of Hypnotism*.[78] In early 1970 he founded the Witches International Craft Associates (WICA) and began to edit *The WICA Newsletter*. The purpose of WICA was to provide information to the general public on the Witchcraft movement in the United States, as well as providing an "encounter bureau" where occult practitioners could contact one another. The newsletter also reported on the large volume of correspondence with Leo's supporters and detractors, the troubled, and the merely curious that this venture inspired.

Buoyed by his post-Stonewall experiences in GLF and GAA, Leo felt a sense of optimism that by challenging the system head-on, progress could be made for the cause of Witchcraft and Paganism to secure equal standing in society with the likes of Christianity. Gay Witches had helped feed into the process for lobbying for gay rights. Now those experiences and energy could be spun off to help lobby for the rights of Witches. Several events that year would inspire him to do just that.

April 1970 found Leo attending the Festival of Occult Arts in New York.[79] This event provided one of the first real opportunities for the Big Apple's Craft practitioners, card readers, psychics, authors, shop owners, and those on the far fringe of the spiritual bell curve to gather together in one place. It was an eye-opening experience for many, as the occult had been largely a pursuit of solitary practitioners or small groups. In early April, Martello appeared on the Emmy award-winning documentary series *Helluva Town*, hosted by Gene Rayburn on WNEW-TV Channel 5 (now NNYW). Together with his assistants, Martello was filmed in Central Park as he performed a Witchcraft ritual to honor the four elements. *(Ibid n#69)*

Later in that same month, New York also saw huge crowds turn out for the first Earth Day celebration on April 22. Upwards of a hundred thousand people spent the day in Central Park at an ecology fair aimed at raising environmental awareness, and on Sunday June 28, the first Christopher Street Gay Liberation Day parade marched from Sheridan Square to Central Park in commemoration of the Stonewall riots. There, in the Sheep Meadow, as many as ten thousand men and women gathered for a "Gay-In."[80] The phenomenal crowds associated with the Earth Day and Gay Liberation Day activities in New York City, and the sense of the potential for a larger and more public Craft movement as evidenced by the Festival of Occult Arts, may be what inspired Leo's next move.

In 1970, Witchcraft wasn't yet strongly identified with the environmental movement, although that would change throughout the 1970s as it was transformed into a "nature religion."[81] However, home-grown Pagan traditions, such as Feraferia and the Church of All Worlds, and some older ones, such as the Continental Witches, *Hexerei*, and Cunning folk, had closer ties to the land. Martello, a *Stregone* who had spent some of his youth in the country, was one of these latter. Having already demonstrated the value of getting out in nature to work magick and ritual, as evidenced by his *Helluva Town* appearance, he realized that there was an obvious opportunity to hold a large gathering of Witches out in nature.

The Pagan festival scene, which would eventually be spawned by a matrix of Science Fiction conventions and Society for Creative Anachronism events, had not yet manifested into the days-long camping extravaganzas that would become more common by the late 1970s. New Yorkers, in particular, were often starved for contact with nature in the concrete and brick canyons that they called home. Most coven meetings were being held in cramped and stuffy apartments. Lige Clarke and Jack Nichols noted, "We'll do almost anything for a glimpse of leaves, no matter how ignoble the withered branches to which they're attached."[82] Where better, then, to hold a Sabbat celebrating the turning of the seasons than out in nature? New York's tradition of using Central Park as a public square also made it an ideal platform for consciousness-raising. Martello was also likely to have been inspired in his choice of venues, and by the name of his proposed event, by the spontaneous "Be-In" in Central Park on Easter Sunday 1967, where ten thousand hippies and fellow travelers gathered to celebrate spring.[83]

Late in the summer of 1970, Leo Martello approached the New York City Parks Department for permission to stage what he referred to as a "Witch-In" in the Sheep Meadow. The Sheep Meadow is a 15-acre green space in the south end of Central Park. Originally intended as an open space to serve as a military parade ground, it was used instead to graze a flock of city-owned sheep from 1864 to 1934. By the 1960s, the Sheep Meadow was being used for large-scale concerts and gatherings, and the Apollo 11 lunar landing was televised live there on July 20, 1969. The spacious lawn, surrounded by mature hardwood trees, was an ideal location for a gathering of city Witches to celebrate a Sabbat. Martello intended the Witch-In to be held on All Hallows, which is also known variously as Samhain to the Witches and Hallowe'en to mundane folk. Samhain, along with Beltane — also known as May Day or Lady Day — represent the two most important Sabbats of the yearly cycle for Witches and are often referred to as the axis of the year. Thus Martello's choice of a Samhain event at Central Park was understandable.

Groups wishing to use Central Park for public or private events had to obtain a permit from the New York City Parks Department to do so. Under the auspices of WICA, Martello applied for a permit to hold his Witch-In. He heard no word for several weeks, and then out of the blue he received a phone call stating that permission to use the Sheep Meadow had been denied. Puzzled, he inquired of the man at the other end of the phone the reason for the denial. The representative of the Parks Department responded with a hostile tone that "It does not serve the purpose of the park." Martello responded "I thought the park existed to serve the purpose of the people. Anyway, we will congregate for our Witch-In as *individuals.* Even witches have civil rights." The Parks representative then said that he would notify the police of the impending illegal gathering.[84]

Leo was hardly surprised at the brush-off he received from the city bureaucrat. After all, the possibility of Witches gathering on Hallowe'en probably conjured up images of diabolical and perverse Satanic rites in the fevered imaginations of the Parks management. Doubtless they were also nervously thinking back to the 1967 "Be-In" that took officials by surprise and trod the grassy Sheep Meadow into a muddy mess. Regardless of their underlying motives, Martello was infuriated by the threat of police harassment of a peaceful religious event and the possible arrest of its organizers and attendees. He promptly contacted the New York Civil Liberties Union (NYCLU) and was put in touch with Barbara Shack, who agreed to take on the case. The NYCLU sent a letter to the New York City Parks Department explaining that denying access to city services and infrastructure on the basis of religion was a violation of the First Amendment and could result in a civil rights suit against the city.

The legal back and forth between the two organizations eventually culminated in a meeting on Thursday October 29, 1970. Leo Martello and NYCLU attorney Shack met with the attorney and the Deputy Commissioner for the New York City Parks Department just two days before the scheduled event. The Parks representatives were very cordial and informed Martello and Shacks that the decision to deny the permit had been reversed; however, they requested that the name of the event be changed in order to avoid controversy. Martello refused the request, saying "Since the Sheep Meadow in Central Park once had sheep, and since the symbolic God of the Witches is a goat, what could be more appropriate? It's a good thing I didn't apply for a Goat-In!"[85] Leo left the meeting with the Witch-In permit in hand.

The Parks representatives probably felt that they could afford to be magnanimous with the trouble-maker because it was now far too late for WICA to organize more than a token turnout that would – hopefully – be ignored by the media. If the city was banking on that, they were mistaken on both counts. On the evening of Friday, October 30, Martello and friends held a pre-Witch-In public meeting at the Willkie Memorial Building at 20 West 40th Street. The meeting space was standing room only, and it was reported that as many as 200 people had to be turned away. Martello gave a lecture on the history and meaning of Witchcraft, and then conducted a ritual with his high priestess, Witch Hazel. During the ritual, audience members were invited to banish negative aspects in their lives – a common Wiccan ritual at All Hallows. A lively question and answer session was held at the end of the event.[86] Martello encouraged those who planned on coming the next day to dress for the event in ritual garb and to be prepared to have a good time. He also asked people to bring candles, incense and food but, in deference to the sensibilities of the news media and the Park Police, both of whom would likely be present in force, he advised coven members to leave their swords, ritual knives and cauldrons at home.[87]

Saturday October 31, 1970 was a gorgeous sunny day. Surrounded on all sides by trees whose leaves were a luminescent palette of yellows, oranges and greens, several hundred people gathered on the Sheep Meadow for WICA's Witch-In. Dozens of reporters, photographers and television cameras covered the event. A documentary film of the event, made by the Global Village collective, was shown many times on WNET-TV Channel 13 in New York. The celebrants, Witches and non-Witches alike, eventually gathered together in a wide circle. Holding hands and dancing the Witches reel, the crowd sang "London Bridge is Falling Down" with new words composed by a Connecticut Witch: *(Ibid n#1)*

Witches meet in Central Park, Central Park, Central Park,
Witches meet in Central Park. For our Lady!

One person who was fascinated and somewhat perturbed by Martello's very public presence as a Witch was Roger Pratt. Roger first encountered Leo Martello and his assistant Witch Hazel in 1969 on 81st Street across from the Planetarium during an outing with a group of friends. "The two of them were swanning along the street in flowing black capes with red satin linings. People with me asked, 'Who is that?' and I replied, 'Witches, by the look of them.' ... I really was on the outskirts of that world then. I was at his 'Witch-In' ... the same year in Central Park. It was a wild circle run round and that's all I can remember. It was picnicky in feel, and lasted perhaps 2 hours or so. ... I was rather overwhelmed at the Witch-In and I remember being with a few friends and finding a secluded hill (right off 5th Ave) and doing some small thing there instead. My biggest problem is that I was raised that witchcraft is to be practiced in secret. The rites aren't supposed to be exploited."[88]

Whether an exploitation or a straightforward assertion of First Amendment rights, Martello's Witch-In constituted the first victory in the push and pull between Witches in New York and a city bureaucracy that was heavily influenced by the Catholic Church and Orthodox Judaism. Truth be told, it also represented the only time that Witches had made any demand of the bureaucracy. Yet Martello's fight with the city, while successful, angered him simply because of the need to have to do it. He was also dismayed by the lack of Neo-Pagan resources to assist others in such conflicts.[89] To ensure that other Witches had someone whom they could turn to if faced with similar attempts at religious discrimination, he founded the Witches Anti-Defamation League (WADL).

It was with an eye toward the heady rhetoric of the gay rights movement that Martello then threw down the gauntlet by publishing a brash essay that he dubbed "The Witch Manifesto."[90] It demanded that the Catholic Church be subject to an international tribunal for crimes committed against those accused of Witchcraft during the Inquisition, and also demanded millions of dollars in reparations, both for victims of the Catholic Church and for descendants of those persecuted during the Salem Witch trials. The Witch Manifesto brims with a condemnation of and contempt for the Christian church for the wrongs it had inflicted upon mankind that could only be summoned up by a recovering Catholic. Martello also leveled his finger at the civil authorities, claiming that actions taken by the state to discriminate against Witchcraft practitioners were a violation of the First Amendment. Battles of the type he had just waged, whether against the profound injustices or the petty prejudices directed against those who stray from the accepted norm, were the result of allowing society's laws to be held hostage to the overwhelming influence of Judeo-Christian theology in United States government.

It is not unfair to note that Leo's Catholic boarding school experience could be at the heart of his seething rage against the Church. However, it is entirely too easy to blame the unresolved anger of this young man for his strong reaction to what he essentially saw as a bully running roughshod over the smaller kids on the playground. As Lori Bruno puts it: *(Ibid n#1)*

> *The Witch must not condone injustices. Leo's own philosophy, as outlined in his 1966 book "How to Prevent Psychic Blackmail," is one of psychoselfism, and sensible selfishness versus senseless self-sacrifice.*

Two contemporary events may also have informed Martello's decision to write his manifesto and the form that it took. The first involved Carl Wittman, an anti-war activist and former member of the national council of Students for a Democratic Society (SDS). Wittman left the SDS, disillusioned by the widespread homophobia of the New Left, and in 1969 he migrated to San Francisco, where he eventually became involved in the struggle for gay rights. Beginning in May of that year, Wittman began writing the essay titled "Refugees from Amerika: A Gay Manifesto." Published in January 1970, the Gay Manifesto begins with a declaration of the place of homosexuals in society:[91, 92, 93]

> *San Francisco is a refugee camp for homosexuals. We have fled here from every part of the nation, and like refugees elsewhere, we came not because it is so great here, but because it was so bad there. By the tens of thousands, we fled small towns*

> *where to be ourselves would endanger our jobs and any hope of a decent life; we have fled from blackmailing cops, from families who disowned or 'tolerated' us; we have been drummed out of the armed services, thrown out of schools, fired from jobs, beaten by punks and policemen.*

John Lauritsen notes that Leo's political views differed from his own, and therefore Wittman's, socialist world-view at the time.[94] Yet Martello's description of the atrocities that the Church visited on its declared enemies resonated with Wittman's theme of a people oppressed and reviled by an unsympathetic majority in society. "The Gay Manifesto" called on homosexuals to come out, to liberate themselves, to fight oppression, and to band together into coalitions with other like-minded supporters.

Wittman's manifesto, widely reprinted and distributed in the United States, was a powerful and influential essay of the times. It was not the only one of its day, as the late 1960s and early 1970s was a time of Marxist-anarchist influenced ideologies communicated via broadside and newsletter; nor was it the only gay- or Witch-oriented manifesto of the era.[95] In 1967, Valerie Solanas wrote her anarchist, anti-establishment, anti-male screed, the S.C.U.M. Manifesto.[96] The next year, the Women's International Terrorist Conspiracy from Hell (W.I.T.C.H.), an activist feminist street theatre group in New York City, issued their "W.I.T.C.H. Manifesto" that called upon modern feminists to emulate the Witches of old:[97,98]

> *WITCH is an all-woman Everything. It's theatre, revolution, magic, terror, joy, garlic flowers, spells. It's an awareness that Witches and Gypsies were the original guerillas and resistance fighters against oppression — particularly the oppression of women — down through the ages. ... Whatever is repressive, solely male-oriented, greedy, puritanical, authoritarian — those are your targets. Your weapons are theatre, satire, explosions, magic, herbs, music, costumes, cameras, masks, chants, stickers, stencils and paint, films, tambourines, bricks, brooms, guns, voodoo dolls, cats, candles, bells, chalk, nail clippings, hand grenades, poison rings, fuses, tape recorders, incense — your own boundless beautiful imagination. Your power comes from your own self as a woman, and it is activated by working in concert with your sisters. The power of the Coven is more than the sum of its individual members, because it is together.*

W.I.T.C.H. got its start in a day-long protest action called "Up Against Wall Street" that took place in the New York financial district on Hallowe'en 1968. In Chicago, W.I.T.C.H. members protested at the trial of the Chicago Seven on Hallowe'en 1969. "Our sister justice lies chained and tied," they chanted. "We curse the ground on which she died."[99, 100] While its members called it a "coven," W.I.T.C.H. was more about political action and less about worship, a point made by the group's quotation of the Biblical book of Judges – "For rebellion is as the sin of witchcraft."[101] Martello acknowledged the debt modern Witches owed to the feminists and the homosexuals in his crusade, and the debt that all three groups owed to their Pagan forebears. He writes, "The female witch was the first suffragette, the forerunner of today's Women's Liberation Front, and the Women's International Terrorist Corps [sic] from Hell (W.I.T.C.H.). The latter are political witches using street and guerilla theatre, as have the Hippies, the Yippies, the Crazies, and many other radical groups. Combining the profound, the profane and the put-on, modern political witches are using the same techniques [as] the Medieval Mattachines." *(Ibid n#69)*

The second incident that may have informed Martello's decision to write the Witch Manifesto occurred in front of the First Congregational Church of Los Angeles on February 23, 1970. There, GLF-Los Angeles co-founder Morris Knight, dressed in Papist drag as His Holiness Pope Morris I, tacked a bill for 90 billion dollars to the door of the church. The amount represented "$10,000 for each of 9 million homosexuals which historical records indicate were executed at the instigation of the clergy." The San Francisco Free Press quoted the so-called Gay Pope as saying "The Congregational or Puritan Church is particularly guilty; they murdered thousands of people for sodomy in New England during the 17th and eighteenth centuries."[102] The antics of "Pope Morris," which were reported in the gay press in New York City shortly after the Witch-In, may have inspired Martello's demand for reparations for the atrocities of Salem and the Inquisition.[103]

The Christian church, both Catholic and Protestant, was also a target of *GAY* and *Screw* editorialists Jack Nichols and Lige Clarke during this time. A more balanced view of Christianity's role in the early gay movement in the United States would acknowledge the fact that liberal churches of various Protestant denominations had given many fledgling gay rights groups a space in which to meet, often when no other safe accommodations could be had. One example is the Church of the Holy Apostles at 9th Avenue and 28th Street, which gave the West Side Discussion Group, at that time one of New York City's oldest homophile organizations, a meeting place shortly after the Stonewall riots.[104] But generally speaking, Christian churches, like the armed forces, law enforcement, and marriage, were considered to be bulwarks of the opprobrium society levied against homosexuals. In their 1972 autobiography, the duo wrote, "People chained in the pews of orthodox temples will never be truly self-reliant. ... If we must have temples and churches, let us center them in our own free minds. In their spacious aisles, we can find good friends from throughout the globe; and in their hymnals, songs of love from every clime."[105]

Nichols and Clarke saved some of their strongest criticisms for those, such as the Reverend Troy Perry and his Metropolitan Community Church (MCC), who they felt were selling the movement down the river by promoting Christianity within the gay community. *(Ibid n#71)* Doing so, they believed, was at best "substituting a wheelchair for a crutch."[106] At worst, it would send homosexuals back into the arms of their oppressors at the very brink of victory and freedom:

> *The prime enemy of the homosexual has always been the Church. We hoped at one time that gays would learn to abandon absurd vestiges of superstition and dogma. Troy Perry, the good gay reverend, has proved our hopes in vain.*[107]

This pronouncement was somewhat cheeky, given Jack's stint as the editor for *Strange Unknown,* Lige's own involvement in astrology and (at least peripherally) Witchcraft, and the dubious standing of both of those pursuits in the court of public opinion. This was somewhat unfair, given that the MCC was hardly an "orthodox temple" by any stretch of the imagination. Yet because modern Witchcraft was in harmony with the ideals of this Aquarian Age — that an individual is responsible for his own spiritual well-being — their sentiment was understandable. When asked to state his own beliefs in relation to Christianity and Witchcraft, Clarke told Leo Martello that he wanted nothing to do with any religion organized around a vindictive God:

> *The most unhappy people I know are very religious. What has witchcraft ever ever done in this world to compare with the bloodshed and tyranny caused by organized religion? When I think of this, if I wasn't a witch, I'd have to become one.*[108]

At the time Lige spoke these words to Leo, Eddie Buczynski had come to much the same conclusion.

Chapter 5: The Lamed Smith and the Bright Child

"Horrible" Herman Slater

It was in the autumn of 1971 that Eddie tracked down Leo Martello. During his frequent stints in Manhattan, he had seen Leo around the Village. Martello was well-known in the gay community for his activities in the GLF and GAA and for his regular column "The Gay Witch" in the local newspaper *GAY*. He had also achieved a certain notoriety via his published books and for the "Witch-In" that he had organized in Central Park and that had attracted so much media interest in 1970. Leo liked the younger man and took Eddie under his wing. However, he would not agree to take Eddie on as a student of his Continental Witchcraft. This is not, as some have speculated, due to Eddie's Polish surname. After all, Eddie's mother was from southern Italian rootstock, and Leo firmly believed that the propensity for Witchcraft was passed down through the family by the women. Rather, Martello was cautious because he was somewhat conservative, as fit his practice, and because Eddie was a newcomer to Witchcraft.

But Leo also had extensive contacts in the occult community through his numerous books and *WICA Newsletter*, and he corresponded with the leaders of many occult groups in the New York metropolitan area and beyond. These contacts he gladly shared with Buczynski. The time Eddie spent with Leo spurred his thirst for occult knowledge and, most importantly, experiential opportunities. Using the contact information and references gleaned from Martello's personal files and from the *Stregone's* "Witches Encounter Bureau," Eddie began writing to covens around the country. Leo also began introducing Eddie to people in the immediate community and taking him to the shops that were in existence at the time. On one such adventure, he dragged Buczynski along on a house call to see Herman Slater.

Slater was a short, somewhat dumpy man with mousy brown hair that, by the late 1960s, was rapidly thinning on top. He had a wild cast to his left eye that was fairly pronounced, to the point that folks with whom he was speaking sometimes weren't sure where he was looking. His face had a striking profile, with his Kissinger-like beak of a nose. Politically speaking, Herman was a hard-core New York Jewish liberal. That is to say, he came from a working-class background with Socialist roots — the type of folks who brought the Labor Movement to the sweatshops of the Lower East Side. While his family came from Poughkeepsie and New Paltz, Herman was born in Queens, New York on February 6, 1938. He grew up in a lower-middle class Jewish neighborhood in the Brooklyn borough.[1]

Slater joined the Navy after high school, going through basic at the United States Navy Naval Training Center (USNTC) in Bainbridge, Maryland. After leaving the service in 1958, Herman moved to southern California where he took up hair dressing. He often told the story of the Marine boyfriend he had in the 1960s who had gone AWOL, and whose hair Slater had dyed blonde in an effort to conceal his identity from the Military Police. Upon his return to New York City, Slater meandered through various educational pursuits, studying business administration at New York University, liberal arts at Hunter College City University of New York (CUNY), and traffic management at the Traffic Management Institute. From 1958 to 1969, he had a series of jobs in business management, traffic expediting and insurance claims investigation for the Post Office. *(Ibid n#1)*

From 1965 to 1969, Herman was said to have operated a small store on West 4th Street in Greenwich Village dealing in antiques and bric-a-brac.[2,3,4,5] Another story locates the shop in the basement of the Ansonia Hotel at Broadway and West 73rd Street in the space later occupied by the straight bathhouse Plato's Retreat.[6] While there is no conclusive proof that Herman Slater operated a shop at either location, the Ansonia Hotel story is intriguing because he is known to have attended Spiritualist meetings upstairs at the time according to his friend, Laura Austan.

Laura Austan:[7]

Herman was part of the NYC gay Spiritualists bunch that my mother, Kenn Coulter, Ceil Clay, Cliff Bias and Bertha Brown ran with in the mid-60s. ... Herman was friends with Cliff Bias, who lived in the Ansonia [Hotel], and under whose coat rack I slept a lot as a kid. Kenn Coulter was the minister of a Spiritualist Church, they all were – Clay, Brown, my mom, and all traveled in the same circles. I was very young, [and] this all started in my family in 1964. There was a kinda inner circle of gay mediums. Herman never was a medium, but he hung with them, for sure. That's how Leo [Martello] entered the scene, thru Cliff Bias. ... It's all a blur of séances and billet readings to me. ...

They had some study group in Cliff's place, once, sometimes twice a week, and held a séance after each. I'd be snoring by then, under the coats. [They] sat in armchairs in a circle in his big living room with all the marble, notebooks on their laps. It was after the hotel psychic fairs that they'd congregate in parties. I never saw any of them drunk, ever. Herman was always a disgusting eater and Leo hated me and, I think, all children. Cliff was like a grumpy great-uncle to me. His high school graduation present to me was a long [psychic] reading, but I don't remember much of it. Except that he was right about the guys I was with ...

Herman had known Leo Martello since the mid-1960s when Herman had opened his shop in the Village, and the two may even have had a fling for a short period of time.[8] Slater was aware of Martello's own occult interests from the time he spent with the *Stregone,* however he had always approached it with a degree of skepticism. It also isn't clear whether Herman was retailing occult-related items during this period, but as the occult revival began to gather steam, Herman might have decided to get with the times by expanding into this line of goods. If he did, Leo Martello may have influenced Slater's decision by appealing to his business sense. He would have had to have used an argument along those lines, as Slater was hardly an adherent of any occult tradition at that point in his life. If anything, he was highly skeptical of Witchcraft and magick, and if he was willing to cater to that market, it was only because he was able to make money by doing so. A contemporary book on the occult referred to "a storekeeper in Manhattan who, though skeptical of witch magic, nevertheless stocks a huge supply of monkey skulls, black candles, Dragon's Breath Powder, ointments, oils, charms and *fith faiths* (ritual dolls) with accompanying pins." It is not unreasonable to conclude that the author may have been writing of Herman's Greenwich Village shop circa 1969.[9]

Herman took on another job working as a dispatcher at Manpower, a job placement center in Times Square. But by late 1969, Herman had to stop working due to failing health.[10] His mobility was impaired by a tubercular infection that had buried itself in his hip bone. The hip joint deteriorated, and Slater was forced to undergo hip replacement surgery at New York University Medical Center in Manhattan. He spent the latter part of 1969 through the first half of 1971 in the hospital, immobilized in a massive cast.[11] Replacement surgery in those days was not a perfect solution, and the affected leg with its new stainless steel hip was several inches shorter than his good leg. The damage was severe enough for his doctors to express doubt that Slater would ever be able to walk again. *(Ibid n#1, 4)* They obviously did not know their patient.

Herman left the hospital in early 1971 and moved into a small apartment at 428 Atlantic Avenue in Brooklyn Heights. The area was home to a number of antiques stores in the 1960s, much as it is today. Shops of all kinds were doing a brisk business as Brooklyn Heights and Cobble Hill were in the very early stages of gentrification. *(Ibid n#8)* Brooklyn Heights and other neighborhoods in the boroughs east of Manhattan had begun seeing a large influx of gay and lesbian residents in the 1960s as rents and crime rose in the city core. There was an active gay subculture in Brooklyn since at least the 1940s, and by the 1960s there were bars and political organizations springing up to serve the displaced populace, particularly in the heady times immediately following the Stonewall riots. Unfortunately, between return visits to the hospital for rehabilitation, Slater was forced to spend until early 1972 lying abed in his apartment recuperating and regaining his strength. *(Ibid n#11)* The slow pace of his healing and the crushing medical bills were ruining any attempt to get his finances in order.

To alleviate the boredom while he was laid up, Herman voraciously read all of the science fiction, fantasy, and horror that he could lay his hands on. It was not unusual for his bedside table to boast books by both Aleister Crowley and H.P. Lovecraft. One day he claimed to have had an experience of levitation — not an uncommon effect with bed-bound persons, often caused by a combination of long-term body restriction and painkillers that affects a person's sense of kinesthesia. The experience, in combination with some of the ideas that crossed his path during his readings, intrigued him. Herman was not a particularly observant Jew himself, perhaps attending Passover with family every other year. *(Ibid n#2)* Nevertheless, he was willing to entertain the possibility that there was more out there than normally meets the eye.

During one of Herman's rehabilitation stints at New York University Medical Center, Leo offered to come in and perform a healing ritual to help speed his recovery. The bedridden man, desperate to recover enough mobility to start making a living once more, took him up on the offer. Assisting Leo in this rite was the 24-year-old Eddie Buczynski. Slater, while still skeptical of many of the claims made by occult practitioners, was impressed enough with the results of this ritual to credit it with helping his recuperation. He later told writer Dan Greenberg that he believed strongly in the power of the human mind to mend the body, and attributed this belief to his own recovery.[12] *(Ibid n#4)* He was equally insistent on the power of magick to heal. To a writer at *New York* magazine, Slater remarked that he had studied Witchcraft and credited it with helping him to walk again. "I tried to stay neutral," Herman said, "but after that I couldn't. Witchcraft's too beautiful. It's not worshipping death. It's worshipping life and nature." *(Ibid n#10)*

Although he eventually returned to full health, Herman would thereafter walk with a pronounced limp, and was later dependent upon a cane. Yet Sally Eaton notes that in later years he would turn this disability to an advantage. "His cane was far more of a magickal tool than one would suppose. He could slow people down to his pace with it, get them on his wavelength." *(Ibid n#8)* Whether it was his own willpower, Martello's spiritual powers, or the powerful fluttering of Herman's heart at the sight of Buczynski's handsome, lithe body that ultimately healed Slater, we may never know. However, it was clear that Herman was powerfully attracted to the younger man. At age thirty-three, it was not uncommon for Herman to enjoy the company of men in their early twenties (and sometimes younger) who flocked to New York's gay bars, some of whom hoped to cultivate the attentions of older men for both emotional and economic support.[13] Herman was, as his friends admit, a chicken hawk who was in the habit of cruising for young rough trade in the bars of Manhattan on the

West Side, like Uncle Paul's at 8 Christopher Street, and the area of 53rd and 3rd — a hustling spot made famous in a 1976 song by the Ramones.

Eddie wasn't particularly "rough" as these things go. Indeed, as Randy Jones recalls, Buczynski was something of an anomaly, given Herman's usual taste in men. "To know Herman, you have to realize that the type of guys he liked were generally drug addicted hustlers," writes Jones. "He was also into really raunchy sex. ... The guys Herman had around him were not bright at all." *(Ibid n#2)* But Eddie *was* a bright young man, and he was attracted to huskier men like Herman — men who are now referred to in the gay community as bears. It wasn't long before Buczynski and Slater became an item. While he was laid up, Slater taught Buczynski how to color hair, and Eddie used this skill for several years to supplement his meager income. He experimented on himself so often that friends noted that his hair never stayed the same color for very long, and he even referred to himself as a "hair burner" or hair stylist when asked what he did for a living.[14] Buczynski continued living with his parents in Ozone Park until June 1972, when he and Herman moved into a space in Brooklyn Heights.

After they actually moved in together, Roger Pratt, who met the men nearer the beginning of their relationship, wondered what the attraction was between the two. "I remember thinking, ONE bedroom (and a double bed at that), and I somehow couldn't imagine him sleeping with Herman," Pratt wrote.[15] Malcolm Mills expressed similar bewilderment about how the two had ever ended up together. "I met Herman and Ed near the end of their relationship," Mills notes. "I confess I wondered from time to time why Ed would associate with someone like Herman, but never had the opportunity to question either Herman or Ed about what the attraction was."[16] The answer to that question is relatively simple. They were in love.

Like Martello, Slater wasn't always the easiest man to get along with. Herman could be quite charming and erudite when he wished to be, but he wasn't afraid to speak his mind, or to call people out with a wickedly sharp tongue. "Herman was a walking conflict," recalled Ken Dalton, a former employee. "He could switch almost instantly from a sincere persona promoting the earth based mystery religions, to a greedy merchant mentality. He did have a wicked sense of humor and a finely honed gift for sarcasm. He could be funny, he could be cold. I liked him, but never really trusted him. It was not easy to get close to him."[17] Carl Weschcke remembers Herman as "a New York far-left liberal with a lot of animosity toward anything that had the smallest appearance of being 'Establishment.'"[18] Harold Moss referred to the abrasive aspect of Slater's personality as "the Tao of New York — 'keep shoving until someone shoves back.'"[19] As Tommy Kneitel recalls, "Herman impressed me as being artificial and overly ingratiating, which made me question his sincerity."[20]

In other words, Herman was a businessman through and through. People were either put off by Herman's look and attitude, or else taken by it. Good friendships were sometimes founded by those who took the chance to get to know him (and who were able to break through that hard exterior). Slater friend Larry Kirwan notes, "Herman struck me straight off as a satyr-type individual with a quirky smirk which I later came to know as a grin. I did not have a favorable impression of him at first, but really grew to like him. He seemed devious and on the make on first impression, but I grew to like his humor and sense of the absurd. He was very welcoming to me down through the years."[21]

Herman was basically a good soul, according to Judith McNally. "He could be exasperating. He was idiosyncratic. I'd never ask him to set up a budget for me — he'd be completely honest, but ye gods, he was disorganized! It was impossible to stay angry at the man, at least for me."[22] Carol Bulzone agrees, saying, "Everyone said 'You loved Herman in spite of himself.'"[23] Kay Smith recalls that "Herman was Herman. Even Eddie looked at him once or twice and said 'Herman, you can be such a troll.' But they really loved each other. Eddie saw that Herman was a good guy." When asked why then so many people took such a dislike to Slater, she replied "I think it's because Herman had such a formidable, imposing visage, that I think people disliked Herman because of the way he looked. They shouldn't have, but they did. And he was really a sweet guy. He could get cranky, but can't we all? He was by no means mean. And he was very good to Eddie."[24] Eddie, in turn, helped soften Herman's sharper edges — some of them, at any rate.

Now that he was truly beginning to mend, Herman began looking for a way to make a living. In addition to reading science fiction and horror, Herman had begun to focus on the occult, with an emphasis on Witchcraft. He could sense an opportunity, and began to investigate further.[25] Several factors played into his investigations. First was his experience with the healing ritual, which had given him pause and forced him to re-evaluate his skepticism of magick. His bedside reading also pointed to the continuing growth of public and media interest in the occult. Finally, there was the gentle influence of Eddie, whose enthusiasm in his search for a coven was rubbing off on Herman. Though still cautious, Slater began to develop his own close association with the basic Moon Goddess/Horned God paradigm intrinsic to the various paths of Wica.[26]

This wasn't a gimmick that Slater simply exploited to make a living, as some have suggested. "His interest in, and devotion to the Craft was sincere," asserted Judith McNally. "He was never any kind of scholar, but he was an idealist — who probably trusted people too easily sometimes."[27] Peter Levenda concurs, writing, "He was very serious about paganism and Wicca. ... In those days political consciousness and religious consciousness were mixed up with each other. He saw paganism as a counter-culture movement in every way: as an anti-War, anti-sexist platform that included not only spiritual aspects but political and social ones as well."[28]

In his search for a Witchcraft coven, Eddie began writing to a number of known elders in various Witchcraft traditions throughout the United States, beginning in the autumn of 1971. These included Fran and Gerry Fisher (*Theo* and *Thain*), leaders of a Gardnerian coven from Louisville, Kentucky.[29] While friendly with Buczynski, the couple was not interested in taking on long-distance students. Also, like most Gardnerian covens at the time, they were reluctant to bring in single students of either sex, preferring instead to initiate male-female couples who would act as working partners within the coven.[30] Eddie also contacted Mary Nesnick, who was originally initiated into Gardnerian Wica by the Bucklands in 1967.[31] She later became a high priestess in Alexandrian Witchcraft and an important figure in that tradition in the United States. By 1972, Nesnick was in the process of forming the Algard tradition in New York, which blended the practices of Gardnerian and Alexandrian Wica. Although she corresponded with Buczynski on several occasions, Nesnick wouldn't agree to take him on as a student, in part because she was reticent about bringing in an openly gay student.[32] Of this encounter, Buczynski wrote, "I was distinctly told of the homosexual taboo and was refused initiation."[33]

Buczynski also wrote to Kitty Lessing, a Traditionalist Witch living in Hollywood, Florida with whom he hoped to become a long-distance student. Kitty, too, was reluctant to train him, though in this case as much because of the formidable distance involved as Eddie's sexual orientation. *(Ibid n#32)* Most Witchcraft teachers and traditions are not amenable to distance learning unless it is augmented with regular visits to the coven, feeling that the student is hampered by the loss of the face-to-face experience within the coven environment.

"I vaguely remember a bit of friction with Eddie and Kitty," recalls Joe Caldiero. "He was so up front about his gayness and so many at that time were so afraid of what others may think. I'm sure Kitty was one of those who in spite of her religious position was still afraid the Alexandrians would be seen as just another gay thing and that was why I think she may have had problems with him."[34] Nevertheless, it may have been Lessing who first suggested that Eddie seek out another Traditionalist Witch who was located closer to him and who she considered to be a Traditionalist peer and good friend.[35] This person was Phyllis Ruth Thompson (née Healy), who was known to people in the Craft as Gwen Thompson.[36]

Chapter 6: The Cauldron of Wisdom

Celtic Traditionalist Witchcraft

Phyllis Ruth Thompson lived in North Haven, Connecticut, where she had been initiating students since the late 1960s into what she claimed was a hereditary Celtic tradition of Witchcraft, or "fam-trad." The origins of this tradition rested with a packet of letters tied with a red ribbon, which Thompson said had been passed down to her in an old trunk from her paternal grandmother, Adriana Porter, who had died in 1946. According to the story she related to her own initiates, Thompson had been initiated as a child by her mother and grandmother, receiving the Craft name of Gwen. Her mother eventually married a conservative Protestant and gave up the practice of Witchcraft, simultaneously isolating young Phyllis from her grandmother Porter and any further contact with the tradition.

The story goes that after Porter died and the letters came into her possession, Gwen realized that they contained the essence of a Witchcraft tradition that had been passed down within her family since at least the late 1600s. The materials are said to have originated in Somerset, England, having been brought to the United States by way of Nova Scotia. Gwen claimed that she burnt the letters after she had copied out and arranged the information that they contained within a three-ring binder.[1] The resulting book is a cogent manual that follows the general outline of what would today be called a Book of Shadows.[2,3]

In 1985, Thompson wrote a letter to her downline explaining that she was the family member who had spent many years bringing this material together into one book, which she named *The Cauldron*.[4] Those familiar with the material and who also knew Gwen Thompson believe that she could not have been the author of *The Cauldron* because Thompson, as writers go, simply wasn't very good.[5] This begs the question: did Thompson copy the work of others to produce her Book of Shadows, or was she actually the recipient of authentic materials that had been handed down within her family?

With regard to the latter, Leo Martello, who some say claimed to have written a portion of Thompson's material, asserted that she had never been initiated by anyone.[6] Gwen Thompson's burning of the only evidence to support her tale throws considerable doubt on the origins of these materials, especially given the unlikelihood that any loving granddaughter would willingly destroy such cherished heirlooms. The lack of documentary evidence, in conjunction with Gwen's claim to have also been initiated as a child by her grandmother into a family Witchcraft tradition that had been kept secret for centuries, leads critics to question the veracity of her story.[7] There is an alternate explanation, which Gwen Thompson is alleged to have told some members of the Baltimore

Alexandrian coven in 1972. In this story, Thompson claimed that she had been initiated in England while serving there as a nurse during World War II. This also seems unlikely, as Thompson, who was born in 1927, would only have been 17 years old when the war ended in 1945.

Some such histories prove to have been constructed by people who, for whatever reason, wish to obscure the modern origins of the founding documents of their spiritual tradition. Neo-Pagan scholars call these histories, whether fraudulent or true, "grandmother tales." Writing about this phenomenon, Ed Fitch noted that "someone will tell of a Grandmother possessed of shadowy and arcane knowledge, portending much, who initiates just the one fortunate youngster of the one family...but who is inevitably dead by the time it is all printed in Neo-Pagan/Craft newsletters or in the public news media."[8] Leo Martello crystallized this skepticism, noting, "Nowadays everyone's grandmother seems to have been a Witch."[9] This is a rather ironic remark on Martello's part, given that he claimed his own grandmother tale. Years later, Herman Slater, who would have his own credibility issues regarding the origins of a Witchcraft tradition, criticized the phenomenon. "For years now," he noted, "while former 'Pagans' were turning into hereditary Witches, we have been fighting to educate outsiders as much as possible."[10]

Seeing limited interest within her family to continue the tradition, Thompson is said to have started bringing in a few trusted outsiders in the late 1960s in order to keep the tradition alive. In 1972, Gwen and a few of her early initiates were in the process of forming the New England Covens of Traditionalist Witches (N.E.C.T.W.), and were thus actively seeking new students. It was in this state that Eddie found her tradition early in that year. Leo Martello was an acquaintance of Gwen's through correspondence via his *WICA Newsletter*.[11] He had guested with Gwen's coven on several occasions, and so it was logical that he be the one who finally introduced Eddie to Gwen in a visit by the two men to her home in North Haven.[12] Gwen was immediately taken by Eddie's beauty and charm. Based on this first impression and on Martello's recommendation, Thompson agreed to take on Buczynski as a student of her Traditionalist coven.

Eddie was initiated into the Neophyte grade in the spring of 1972, taking the name of the Greek God, Hermes, as his public initiatory name in the Craft.[13] *(Ibid n#12)* Buczynski chose the name primarily because his natal chart places the planet Mercury, the Roman name for Hermes, within close proximity (four degrees) of his sun sign. Eddie's choice of name was appropriate for two other reasons; first, because Hermes, whom Gore Vidal's Julian called "the swift intelligence of the universe," was a God of communication — the mainstay of writers and teachers, both of which professions Eddie aspired to. Second, Hermes was a God of sexual fluidity, and His ancient worshippers included those men who especially favored the homoerotic aspect of human sexuality. Gwen, whose own name within the North Haven coven was Minerva (for the Roman Goddess of commerce, poetry, and war) approved. Judith McNally notes that, "[Ed] was proud of her background and lineage. ... He obviously felt she was a knowledgeable Witch and a good teacher."[14]

Every few weeks, Eddie trekked the 80-odd miles between New York City and North Haven, Connecticut to study and participate in ritual, riding the train that runs from Grand Central Station in New York to Union Station in New Haven. From there, he was usually shuttled to the covenstead in North Haven by Gwen or one of the local initiates. Although Eddie usually returned home the same night, a number of these trips involved overnight stays, given the train schedules and the timing of the sabbat and esbat rites. Eddie stayed at Gwen's house when this was necessary, and this arrangement soon became a source of friction between Eddie and Herman.

One of the new initiate's first assignments was to begin the arduous task of hand-copying the Neophyte portions of the Traditionalist Book of Shadows under the watchful eyes of Gwen or an elder initiate.[15] Eddie's copy of *The Cauldron* was carefully transcribed and lovingly illustrated in colored inks, providing evidence of his care and respect for the materials with which he was entrusted. Its 210 pages of material provide a wealth of mythology, prayers, rituals, spellworkings, essays and instructional material, containing Welsh, Scottish, Irish and Brythonic materials. *(Ibid n#5, 13)* Eddie composed a few original pieces of poetry for his book. In "To the Cowan," Buczynski explains to the non-Witch (presumably Christian) what attracts a man or woman to Witchcraft:[16, 17]

> *Night has brought the Full Moon, Round*
> *And warm her silver rays heat,*
> *While sacred earth's great breasts abound*
> *With flowing fruit and flowers, sweet*
> *With Spring's bright promise of Re-birth.*
> *Upon the hills and deep in woods*
> *The children of the Lady sway,*
> *For heaven's gifts and earthly goods*
> *We summon in the Wiccan way.*
>
> *Our hearts beat wild with cosmic Joy*
> *And Wiccan blood pumps hot and red*
> *With flowing hair and heads raised high,*
> *Around the sacred place we tread.*
> *Between the Worlds, in ecstasy*
> *We slip, to meet the Mighty Ones*
> *We camp behind eternity*
> *And realize we are not alone.*

Through the glowing candle light
Away from worry, fear and harm
The Horned One prances with Delight
The Goddess comes with open arms.
Thus, we, the Wicca, dance and sing
In worship <u>you</u> don't understand
Yet, in this way, to man we bring
The gifts of Earth (Love) and Peace of Mind.

Remember, though we burn and hang
(And these things, to us, you again may do)
While <u>only</u> Sunday's hymns you sang,
<u>Our Lives</u> we loved and lost for <u>You</u>!
So, to you all I proudly say
Though you be stubborn, cruel, or blind
"The Witches follow the Ancient Way,
To aid the Good of All Mankind!"

Buczynski's words provide the reader with a vision of the passion and mystery that forms the basis of most Witchcraft traditions. The prose also reflected an antagonism to Christianity that would resurface several times in Eddie's writings over the years. The vision in "To the Cowan" is tainted with the practicing Witch's apocalyptic fear of being discovered by the "stubborn, cruel, or blind" non-Witch and being subjected once again to the punishments of the Burning Times.[18] It is ironic that the Christian vision of the end times, with its paranoia of heathen forces overrunning the world, should prompt such fear and secrecy in practicing Witches, given that the latter's ability to overrun the world is often limited by the inability of thirteen Witches to peacefully co-exist in Circle together. Terry Pratchett struck uncomfortably close to the truth many years later when he described a similar inability get along regarding Granny Weatherwax and the other Witches of Discworld.[19]

A constant state of tension is an apt descriptor of the relationship between Gwen and Eddie, for the relationship between teacher and pupil was at times tumultuous because of their dominant personalities and inborn stubbornness. Gwen was a middle-aged woman who had ridden three husbands down in the traces, as it were. She was a very fiery personality: independent-minded, used to having her way and protective of her tradition. Eddie was forever the 17-year-old runaway: street-smart, intelligent, opinionated, flamboyant, charismatic, driven and, true to his Craft name, often governed by mercurial emotions. He could be fiery, and he had a vicious temper when someone angered him, which admittedly was not easy to accomplish. *(Ibid n#5)* Quarrels between Slater and Buczynski would often end with Herman accusing Eddie of being bull-headed, followed by Eddie "putting on the horns" and charging him with a

Mooo! How the two Aquarians lived and loved under the same roof without blowing the place apart is anyone's guess. The Goddess of War also clashed frequently with this mercurial temper, usually over power issues; yet for all of this, Gwen adored Eddie. Eddie, in turn, was grateful for Gwen's teachings. He fashioned a needlepoint of Gwen and the Horned God in which he was rumored to have incorporated some of his own pubic hair — likely into the image of the Horned God itself.[19] That bit of sympathetic magic, intentional or not, would prove to have some rather unwelcome consequences for the young Witch.

The importance of Eddie's relationship with Gwen Thompson during this time cannot be overstated. Eddie was a prolific reader, and he readily retained and understood whatever he read. However, these "book smarts" will only take one so far in any occult area of study. Many an armchair occultist can explain how something should be done but may have absolutely no experience in actually doing it himself. Gwen gave Buczynski the first formal training that he had ever had in Witchcraft, and also the first opportunity to put what he had learned into practice within the bounds of a working coven. She also introduced Eddie to other practitioners, thereby expanding his circle of acquaintances and friends within the Craft and according him further opportunities for learning and growth. Zanoni Silverknife of the Georgian tradition of Witchcraft is one elder who recalls meeting Eddie through the auspices of Gwen Thompson. "Pat Patterson [the founder of the Georgian tradition] had gotten in contact with [Gwen] early on in the forming of the Georgian tradition and as the co-founder and First Georgian Priestess, I also wrote to her," Zanoni recalls. "She was very generous in sharing knowledge and introducing me to her Priest, Eddie, who then started writing to me, as well."[21, 22]

As spring turned slowly to summer, Eddie's training toward Second Degree proceeded apace. Lady Gwen began to use him as her high priest at some point in the summer of 1972. This was not unusual, as Thompson used males of any degree to act in the role of high priest for a night as the need arose or as training dictated. *(Ibid n#12)* However, it is also likely that Eddie was elevated to the Second Degree sometime between the Summer Solstice and the cross-quarter Sabbat of Lammas. One piece of evidence for this is the use of the second Craft name, Dionysus, in the book. In a number of Witchcraft traditions, the student adopts a different name as he progresses through degrees. Thus Buczynski records his name in the book as Hermes Dionysus. Buczynski chose Dionysus after the Greek God of ecstasy and madness. *(Ibid n#13)* It is believed that Eddie was at least a Second Degree primarily because of the materials that he had in his possession.

While Gwen only recorded Buczynski as being initiated to First Degree, there are those who believe that Gwen had shared a lot more with him, as he had in his possession certain portions of the N.E.C.T.W.

Second Degree materials. *(Ibid n#5)* While his elevation to the Second Degree is not recorded in the coven register, Buczynski's copy of The Cauldron contains a copy of the Second Degree Initiation ritual inscribed in the same loving hand as the materials recorded on either side of it in the book.[23] A Neophyte in N.E.C.T.W. would not be expected to have a copy of this, because it is a ritual that he or she would not yet have gone through and was thus beyond his or her grade. That it is present in Eddie's book, neatly and in sequence, strongly indicates that Buczynski was, in fact, elevated to Second Degree. Herman Slater, in a letter printed in the October 1972 issue of *Green Egg*, refers to Eddie as "the High Priest of the New England Traditionalists."[24] Generally speaking, the period between the First and Second Degrees is traditionally considered to be a year and a day, though there is no requirement that a high priestess hew to this. That Gwen may have advanced Eddie at an accelerated pace spoke not only of her satisfaction with his mettle and progress, but also, perhaps, her growing infatuation with the younger man.

This attitude on Gwen's part, if it existed, may be linked to Eddie's failure to reciprocate the desires she felt toward the younger man. It was during this time that Gwen began to pressure Eddie to have sex with her. The role of high priestess and high priest is inherently a sexual one, for Witchcraft covens generally celebrate nature-based fertility rituals, even in traditions that treat it as a more cerebral exercise. The Traditionalist Witchcraft path that Gwen practiced does not have a Great Rite, *per se*, where the high priestess and high priest join with one another "in true," which is to have sex — high priest to high priestess — in the ritual. Nevertheless, the rituals fostered an inherent sexual tension, which was especially problematic given that the 44-year-old Thompson was already drawn to the attractive 25-year-old Buczynski. This is not to say that she was besotted with the younger man, but she had the normal drives of a mature and strong-willed widow. The overnight stays allowed her ample opportunity to flirt with Eddie.

For his part, Eddie was made increasingly uncomfortable by the amorous attentions of his High Priestess. "He was very upset about it," remembers Karen Bartlett, because Eddie said that "if he sleeps with a woman he goes crazy for weeks." Bartlett attributed this to "some kind of sexual identity crisis," but it is more likely because Buczynski was what would have been described as a typical Kinsey 6 homosexual male.[25,26] The situation in which he found himself was largely of Eddie's own doing. Having been rejected by Mary Nesnick because of his homosexuality, Buczynski said he was admitted into Gwen's coven after "conveniently forgetting to inform them of my homosexuality."[27] Herman, hearing of her advances to his lover, became very unhappy with the situation and fumed at every meeting that required Eddie to stay overnight at Gwen's home.[28] Gwen, in turn, grew to despise Herman, though it remains unclear whether it was because she began to suspect the truth about Eddie's rejections of her favors or because she sensed Herman's own animosity toward her. *(Ibid n#5)* Eddie apparently believed it was the former, telling Judith McNally that he felt that Gwen was possibly jealous of his life with Herman. *(Ibid n#14)*

Under pressure from both Herman and Gwen, Eddie began to tire of the situation and dreamed of starting his own coven away from Gwen's unwelcome attentions. Yet when he broached the topic to her, Thompson rebuffed his proposal. Eddie complained to others on several occasions that Gwen was "holding him back" and "didn't think he was ready." *(Ibid n#14)* In Thompson's defense, it seems reasonable to believe that someone who had been practicing in the Craft for only five or so months probably wasn't ready to hive off and start a coven of his own, no matter how much of a prodigy he might be. But how much of her decision was based on his readiness, and how much on a desire to keep him close for her own personal reasons, remains unknown. Regardless, Buczynski secretly began making plans to form his own group in New York City. He did so quietly, for is word of his plans filtered back to Thompson, she was likely to expel him from her coven. His state of mind at the time might be reflected in some prose he composed in his copy of *The Cauldron*. In "To Approach the Priesthood" Buczynski wrote:[29]

> *Now to His service I do render*
> *Body, soul and mind.....*
> *To Her Love I now surrender*
> *The virginity of human pride.*
> *Wildly, in my numbing fright,*
> *I struggle from within Her womb*
> *To ponder in orgasmic splendour,*
> *That I am but the Birth-wail of the Child of Light.*

Emblematic of Buczynski's "struggle from within Her womb" was his continued search for other Witchcraft traditions during his time with Thompson. In May 1972, Eddie and Herman attended a Pagan Way group in Riverdale, the Bronx, which was led by Terry Madden. Also at this meeting was Roger Pratt, who had been elevated to Second Degree in March by Donna Cole Schultz of Chicago and his high priestess, Kathy. An impromptu Pagan Way rite was held in the kitchen, after which those gathered sat and talked for much of the night. "Before we left," Roger remembered, "Herman and Eddie approached Kathy and I, and asked if we'd initiate them into the Craft. Kathy asked them 'Why?' and Herman responded, 'We're about to open a witch shop and we want to be initiates before then.' I don't remember having any response, but I DO remember telling my mother who said, 'One doesn't have to be a witch to run a shop!' She was also appalled at the thought of purchasing 'tools' [instead of making them]. 'That's what puts the CRAFT in WitchCRAFT!' she said."[30]

Kathy and Roger were noncommittal about the request, but at the next meeting of their coven they polled the members for their opinions. All of them believed that their coven was like a family and felt that suddenly adding strangers to the mix wasn't such a good idea. At the Bronx Pagan Way meeting in June, Kay and Roger turned down Herman and Eddie's request. "From then on," Pratt writes, "Herman told EVERYONE ... that we'd turned them down because they were gay! Well, being gay myself, that seemed a bit implausible, and I don't know if Herman meant it or if it was a joke. But he did say it every time we saw him! So it became a running 'joke.'" *(Ibid n#30)*

Pratt visited the shop over the years before opening his own occult shop, Altar Egos, in 1989. A good friend of Roger's named Michael Ravenspirit (*née* Massone) worked for Herman at the time, and innocently thought it would be okay to place a flier advertising the new competitor on the shop's community bulletin board. Herman promptly tore it down in a rage. "[Michael] returned to my shop and I asked him how he could be so stupid? He stopped me by telling me that Herman saw my name as he tore the poster up and said, *Do you KNOW him?* Michael timidly replied, 'Yes.' Herman then said, 'Listen and learn from him. He's one of the ORIGINALS!' I was so touched, and so moved, that I still regret our NOT initiating them way back in 1972! It was a side of Herman that I didn't know existed." *(Ibid n#30)* In hindsight, it's a pity that Roger hadn't done so. It might have saved everyone a great deal of grief in the long run.

1. Eddie Buczynski (age 11), Ozone Park, Queens. 1958.

2. Eddie Buczynski, back room of the Warlock Shop, ca. 1972.

3. The Warlock Shop, 300 Henry Street, Brooklyn Heights. ca. 1974.

4. Herman Slater in the tarot and book section, Warlock Shop. April 1974.

5. David Farnham (left) and an unidentified shop employee at the front counter, Warlock Shop. April 1974.

6. The main aisle of the Warlock Shop looking from the front door to the kitchen door. April 1974.

7. David Farnham (left) weighing herbs for a customer, in the Warlock Shop in April 1974.

8. Judith McNally, Eddie Buczynski, and Kay Flagg (from left to right), Traditionalist Gwyddoniaid, Brooklyn Heights. Yule rite, December 1972.

9. The Children of Branwen, Traditionalist Gwyddoniaid, Brooklyn Heights ca. 1974.

10. Leo Martello, Traditionalist Gwyddoniaid, Brooklyn Heights. ca. 1973.

11. Occult author Hans Holzer.

12. Radio journalist and author Margot Adler.

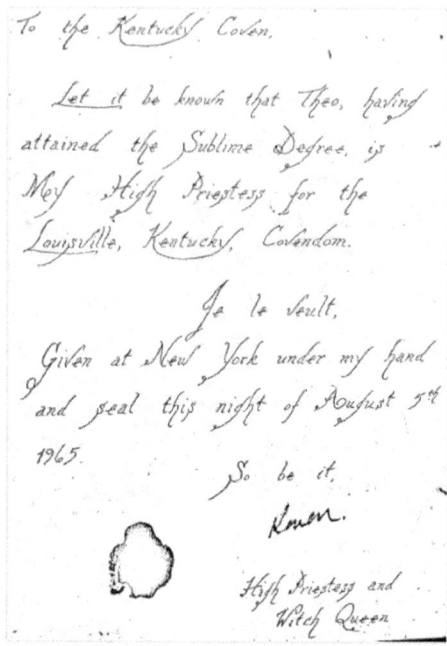

13. The disputed Gardnerian Wica vouch of Fran Fisher (*Theo*), Brentwood, New York. 1965

14. Harold Moss (left) and Eddie Buczynski, Witchmeet room party, Minneapolis, Minnesota. April 1974.

15. The green issue of *Earth Religion News* featuring the New York Coven of Witches (The Wica). June 1974.

16. Eddie Buczynski (lower left) at a New York Coven of Witches sabbat, Brooklyn. April 1974.

Chapter 7: A Little Occult Emporium

The Warlock Shop

The economic situation in New York City in the late 1960s and into the following decade was, in a word, dismal — and it was going to get much worse. Whereas the press had lauded New York in 1964 as "the brilliant metropolis that plays host to the world," by 1969 it was asking if the dream city had turned into a nightmare.[1,2] In the early 1970s, the *Village Voice* began referring to New York as the "Rotten Apple." Crime was increasing and corporations were forced to bribe executives with hazard pay to come into the city to work. Still unable to work full time and saddled with medical bills, Herman Slater was forced to file for bankruptcy protection in January 1972. He was listed as unemployed, with $7798 in liabilities and $400 in assets.[3,4] While this provided relief from his crushing debt, Herman still needed to find a way to make money.

From his reading and by speaking to Martello and friends, Slater knew that the market for Witchcraft and the occult was experiencing continued growth. In late 1971 Raymond Buckland was complaining that one of the problems in setting up a coven is that there were "no witch supply stores listed in the telephone directory."[5,6] Yet by 1973, author Jack Fritscher wrote that "Witchcraft ... has been willfully merchandised into a business even more brisk than the average Christian Book and Art Supply Store."[7] It is unclear whether Buckland's lament proved to be the "Aha!" moment for Herman, or whether he simply noted that other mainstream businesses were cashing in on the occult market. What is known is that Herman conceived a business plan that could satisfy both the public's growing needs and his own. Judith McNally notes that "retailing was the trade he knew, so opening some kind of occult shop seemed logical."[8] And given that Herman already had some experience catering to that niche, he decided to take a chance once more, only this time he would plunge in completely. In this he was whole-heartedly supported by Eddie.

The company Slater envisioned — Earth Religions Supplies, Inc. — would stock every conceivable need for an occult practitioner, regardless of "flavor." They would eventually distribute goods nationally via mail order and locally through a brick-and-mortar store. The concept of a one-stop-shop for occult supplies was relatively new. Shopping in large metropolitan areas has always been an à la carte process, with the consumer hopping from one small neighborhood store to the next. Therefore, if you wanted esoteric books, you went to a bookshop such as Samuel Weiser at 734 Broadway for New Age and ceremonial books, or Mason's Bookstore (789 Lexington Avenue) which, though specializing in books on astrology, stocked thousands of occult titles.[9] By 1970, however, one could also purchase such books in mainstream booksellers such as

Manhattan's Scribner's on 5th Avenue where, *Time* magazine sourly observed, "books on the occult have completely taken over a counter that was once reserved for more traditional religious books (theological, inspirational and other churchly volumes are now relegated to a side bookcase)."[10] Scribner's was in competition with Brentano's Books at 586 5th Avenue, which held a "Séance for the Press" in 1970 to celebrate the opening of its occult, paranormal and New Age book section, the so-called "Mystique Boutique."[11] The presence of this special occult section marked a trend in mainstream booksellers to capitalize on the public's increasing interest in esoterica.[12]

Carl Weschcke, President of Llewellyn Worldwide, the largest publisher of occult titles in the world, places this growth in perspective. "You have to realize that the occult scene wasn't much in those days," Weschcke writes. "There were a few specialized stores like our Gnostica in Minneapolis — in New York, Chicago, San Francisco, and Los Angeles — but most of the occult book business originated in antiquarian book stores and a few herb shops. Rather large book stores like the Controversial Book Store in San Diego had occult sections, as did the Pickwick in Los Angeles. The first tide of growth came from large independent book stores. Beyond these there were several mail order operations — including our own — that dominated the retail field."[13] On the West Coast, one of the earliest occult bookstores was the Church of Light on Sixth Street in Los Angeles. Dating from the 1930s, Elbert Benjamine's Church of Light group operated the store until the 1970s, when it was eclipsed by the Bohdi Tree in West Hollywood.[14]

In New York City, if one wanted occult jewelry, one generally went to a place like Amulets & Talismans at 33 Christopher Street, or else had it hand-made to order by any number of talented artisans in the city. For essential oils, one went to a place like Berje Chemical on 23rd Street. Herbs, resins, incense, and oils could also be found at a botanica, such as Original Products in the Bronx, or Arara on Amsterdam Avenue at West 74th Street in Manhattan. Or one could venture into The Original Head Shop at McDougal Street right off 8th Street, or to any number of organic health food emporiums that sprang up in that era of environmental awareness. Swords could be found in the Masonic supply shop in the old Flatiron Building at 23rd Street and 5th Avenue. For candles, charcoal and "ritual equipment," such as censers, patens and chalices, one went to a Catholic supply store, such as the one in the area soon to be occupied by the future World Trade Center — assuming that the buyer had the proper church *bona fides* to shop there.[15] The irony of shopping for Witchcraft accoutrements at church supply stores has been an in-joke of long standing among Craft practitioners.

Occult classes were offered by many societies, such as The Center for the Exploration of Consciousness at 120 West 28th Street; the InnerVision School of the Occult & Psychic Sciences, which gave a series of 10-week lectures at the New York Advertising Club at 23 Park Avenue; the New York Occult Center at 217 West 14th Street; and those old stalwarts the New York Theosophical Society at 242 East 53rd Street, the American Society for Psychical Research (5 West 73rd Street) and the New York Astrology Center (127 Madison Avenue). Mainstream colleges and universities also got into the act. New York University's Joseph Kaster had offered a popular course titled "Witchcraft, Magic and Sorcery" since 1967.[16, 17] Long Island University taught a seminar on occult sciences in 1971.[18] And a course on "Magic, Mysticism and Metaphysics" was taught at St. Peter's College in Jersey City in 1972 by a Jesuit Priest *cum* astrologer.[19] But this wasn't just a phenomenon of the liberal north, for schools in the Bible Belt, such as the University of Alabama and the University of South Carolina, also offered courses on the occult.

Additionally, there were already several small occult stores in New York City at the time. These included Blessed Are the Blessed Be (239 East 53rd Street), Yemaya House (3147 Broadway), and The Magician (177 West 4th Street). The Blessed Be was rumored to be a front for a religious cult, while Yemaya House and The Magician had Satanic connections, the former advertising Satanic rites and classes. The proprietor of The Magician (or Magickal Occult Service Corporation) — Ronald Barrett — was a Second Degree member of the Church of Satan's Lilith Grotto, and somewhat more discreet than the owners of Yemaya House in his connections.[20]

There were other shops in the general vicinity of New York City, including The Occult Shop, which had opened in 1970 in Smithtown, New York, and The Cauldron, which operated a mail order business out of Rego Park in Queens in 1972. *(Ibid n#18)* There was plenty of competition, and most shops serving the metro New York occult community were located in Manhattan, which had the advantage of a denser, more eclectic population and greater ease of access than Brooklyn Heights. So Slater and Buczynski were going to have to work hard if they wanted to make a go of the business.

In the spring of 1972, the couple located a quasi-commercial space at 300 Henry Street just north of Atlantic Avenue in Brooklyn Heights.[21] With the recent bankruptcy on his record, Herman would have had difficulty leasing a space in his name. Therefore, it is possible that Eddie's relatively clean credit history allowed them to lease the building. Originally built in 1845, it had only two external clapboard and stucco walls of its own, front and back, wedged as it was between the bare brick walls of the buildings on either side. The small two-story frame building was converted into a one-family brick-faced condominium in 1976, but it stands today much as it did then, tucked in between two larger brick buildings and seemingly constructed as an afterthought. Long-time shop employee Robert Carey mused, "God knows what the current yuppies had to do to exorcise it and bring it up to code."[22]

The duo needed several thousand dollars to get the shop off the ground. They had to cover the first and last month of the lease, make at least a few cosmetic improvements to the space, and stock the initial inventory. A bank wasn't very likely to float a loan to open an occult shop in 1972, even if the lender was willing to overlook the fact that one proprietor was a recent bankrupt coming off of a debilitating illness, while the other was a former Hippie without two spare pennies to rub together. But somehow the two managed to scrape together enough money, most likely from Slater's family, to lease the space and buy some store furnishings and stock so that the shop could get off to a wobbly start.

Soon after they took possession of the property, a sign was placed alongside a human skull in the front windows announcing the impending opening of "The Warlock Shop." For several months the tree-lined residential street of brownstones awaited the birth with curiosity and, perhaps, a touch of unease. Herman walked the short distance from his Atlantic Avenue apartment to the Henry Street location several times a week to work on readying the space for business. Until June, Eddie commuted in from his parents' home in Ozone Park to help.

To be sure, an occult shop wasn't the first oddity to grace this area. Brooklyn Heights was Manhattan's first suburb, developed from the rich country estates that dotted the area before the population of the city swelled and people began to seek an escape to the fresh air of the countryside. Once the suburban home of the upper middle class, by the early twentieth century it had become largely urbanized, and parts of it were somewhat seedy and populated with a mix of working class immigrants. In 1925 and 1926, horror writer H.P. Lovecraft lived at 169 Clinton Street, just two blocks away from the 300 Henry Street location. There he crafted tales that reflected his disdain for "the gangs of young loafers & herds of evil-looking foreigners that one sees everywhere in New York."[23]

By the early 1970s, as a result of men fleeing the increasing rents in Manhattan, Brooklyn Heights and nearby Cobble Hill were home to a large gay population and its accompanying infrastructure, including several bars and a Man's Country bathhouse. A thriving Arab community, with many Middle Eastern restaurants and an office of the Red Crescent Society (the Islamic equivalent of the Red Cross), peacefully coexisted alongside the gays. The area was also a hotbed of antiestablishment, anti-war left-wing activity.[24] The architecture and ambience of Brooklyn Heights was such that a movie director chose an apartment building several blocks away from the shop to serve as a gate to hell in the 1977 occult film *The Sentinel*. None of the above would likely have prompted a charitable revision of Lovecraft's jaundiced views of humanity. But to Eddie and Herman, it was a vibrant, hip and — most importantly — inexpensive location for their new venture.

The Warlock Shop opened for business on the Neo-Pagan holy day of the Summer Solstice — June 21, 1972 — just three days after Nixon White House operatives were arrested for burglarizing the offices of the Democratic National Committee in the Watergate Hotel office towers. There was something ironic about this next step in the growth of the Craft in the United States, occurring as it did during the first steps towards the disintegration of Nixon's paranoid administration. In many respects the wine-bibbing Craft represented the worst nightmares of the bourbon and branch water supporters of Republican hegemony. Rosemary's baby had now truly come into its own.

In the new shop, the walls were whitewashed and the floor was laid in black and white linoleum, usually grimy despite Herman's obsessive sweeping. A small counter comprising two glass cases and bookshelves was located on the left. A floor-to-ceiling wall of herb jars on rickety shelves was on the right, along with more shelves of candles and cauldrons and oils, a modest selection of books, and a number of pamphlets on séances, numerology, herbs, tea leaf reading and the like, and not much else.[25, 26] Other flotsam and jetsam would accumulate over the years. It wasn't unusual for a customer poking among the herb containers to find, shoved to the back of a shelf, a sealed glass jar full of dark liquid with herbs and a rubber baby doll floating in it like some macabre anatomy specimen. When questioned about it, Eddie would shrug and say, "Oh, that's my Witches' bottle. Just leave it there."[27]

On its opening day, one of the very first customers to ring the cowbell on the shop door was 21-year-old Peter Levenda. A slender, dark-haired, bookish and self-taught student of the occult, Levenda lived in the neighborhood and had been eagerly awaiting the shop's opening since first setting eyes on the "coming soon" sign in the window.[28] As with many occult shops that are even today open and operate on a shoestring, the stock was very limited in the beginning. Levenda helpfully jotted down a list of books that he recommended that they stock, and he soon became a regular, even manning the store when Herman had other things to do. Levenda himself provided a few of the pamphlets that were sold at the shop.[29] "It was the start of a beautiful friendship," he remarked some years later. *(Ibid n#28)*

At its opening, the Warlock Shop had something less than $2000 invested in stock.[30] The store eventually sported a tarot case that was described as one of the most complete and diverse of the time. In 1973, Slater told *New York* magazine, "We get our stuff from all over the world. Half of it comes in from smugglers."[31] One could believe this when perusing what was on offer. The front windows often had unusual and provocative displays, at various times including, apart from the human skull, a lion's heart in a jar of formaldehyde and a hanging mummified monkey. "Any item of shock value always had commercial value where Herman was concerned. He knew his rubes, after all," laughed long-time

Slater friend and employee Sally Eaton.[32] Roger Pratt offered a slightly different take. "The shop was beautiful," he writes, "and they had a great selection of hand crafted items. ... Henry Street was a very quiet street though they were almost at the busy corner of Atlantic Avenue. Upstairs looked out over a quiet bird filled garden. It was an ideal spot."[33]

Joe Caldiero, who came to work for Herman and Eddie at the shop that first year, and who briefly lived with them there, remembers the impression that the place made on the younger spiritual explorers who walked through its door. "The Warlock Shop was a fascinating place, especially for those of us who were very young in years and in the craft," Caldiero recalled in 2010. "Some weird people came there but most of the customers were wonderful people. The shop had shelves loaded with charms, herbs, tonics, and books of spells, magazines, and some free printed pages with information on the craft. People would come from everywhere to shop and some of them would come in the back and sit to tea and talk. It was fun and exciting to listen and learn from so many who knew so much about the Gods."[34]

Ken Dalton, who worked for Herman from 1974 until 1976, concurred. "The never-ending parade of characters that came through the door would provide material for a book itself," Dalton recalled. "[There was] the guy dressed head to toe in black wearing dark glasses who had a praying mantis on his shoulder held by a purple ribbon "leash", the man ... who bought hundreds of dollars worth of books, but who was remarkable for the multicolored tattoo on his forehead, complete with a pentagram running down the length of his nose, and so on. ... The clientele was generally odd but sincere."[35] Like Caldiero, Dalton also felt personally enriched by his time at the store. "It was probably my favorite job ever!" he recalled. "It was a great time to be there, no pressure and lots of freedom. ... I spent a good deal of time reading (the place was never busy) and answering questions about the Craft, paganism and history both in person and on the phone. I must also say that as the only straight guy there at the time it was, to put it politely, helpful. After all, it was the '70's and I was 22 or 23. Enough said. It was a part time job, the money wasn't great but it didn't matter. I made a lot of friends, learned a lot and had great experiences." *(Ibid n#35)*

Launching a store of this nature in 1972 was not an easy thing to do, and this opening wasn't entirely without its problems. The foremost of these was their rather unfortunate choice of a name. Incorporating the term "warlock" into the name of the shop was a controversial act on Herman and Eddie's part, and one that would dog their steps for several years. The word itself is said to derive from the Middle English, *warloghe*, which means "one that breaks faith" or, more bluntly, "oath-breaker." Those are fighting words among people who follow spiritual traditions based upon oath-bound Mysteries.

Kathryn Frank states that the name of the store was the result of a misunderstanding on Herman's part, writing, "Herman did tell me a story once about how he was so unaware of things at the time that he didn't even know that warlock was not a nice term in the Wiccan world."[36] The Warlock is also an actual title in Gardnerian Wica, referring to the person in charge of "warricking" (binding and unbinding) people in Circle. But it isn't clear that the men understood that meaning when they chose it in 1972. In the first mail-order catalogue for the store, issued in January 1973, the two admitted that the name was chosen for its shock value.[37, 38] One can sense some frustration on the part of the proprietors, perhaps from being subjected to lectures on their decision to use the name, when they noted in a flier prepared in late 1972,[39]

> *We are quite aware that "Warlock" within the Craft, doesn't have such a nice meaning ... we use it for publicity purposes only.*

This was not the first time that someone associated with the occult made use of the word as a means to provoke a negative reaction. In 1918 the composer and occultist Philip Heseltine adopted the pen name "Peter Warlock" after several review articles he had penned under his own name had been rejected for publication.[40] Heseltine was himself incorrectly rumored in his day to be a Satanist, and his involvement with the occult was widely regarded as a contributing factor in his suicide at age thirty-six. So even then the choice of the term was not a positive one.[41, 42]

The Warlock Shop was quite small, occupying the front room of the first floor of a narrow building that only had a footprint totaling about 450 square feet, and a total area of something less than 1000 square feet.[43, 44] The larger front room was approximately 300 square feet in area. The smaller back room occupied the remainder of the first floor and was separated from the main shop by a doorway screened with a beaded curtain. The back room functioned as a combination parlor, dining room and kitchen for the small upstairs apartment. It held a cheap set of iron ice cream parlor furniture comprising a round, marble-topped table and six straight-backed chairs, a sofa, and a loveseat in addition to a small refrigerator, stove and sink. Stairs leading up to the second floor, and a small bathroom with a shower stall, were located in a rear corner of the kitchen. A back door led out onto a small paved courtyard that was lined with potted herbs and flowers. Robert Carey notes that the back yard belonged to a funeral parlor around the corner, and that on hot summer nights you could hear the morticians "goofing around with the corpses." *(Ibid n#22)* This is the likely source of a coffin that found its way into the basement of the Warlock Shop. When the kitchen was occupied, it was a challenge to edge your way around both the people and furniture. But the coffee pot was rarely empty, making it a focal point for friends and honored guests.

Herman, Eddie, and Herman's black Saluki, Ptolemy, set up house together in a small two-room apartment above the shop. Rickety stairs led up to the second floor. The bedroom/living room was located in the front of the building, with an east-facing window overlooking Henry Street. A large brass bed was placed here, and over time Eddie would display his green thumb by nurturing a small garden of potted plants on the back stoop and a white-blossomed Hawaiian wood rose that he would drape and twine around the headboard of the bed.[45] A large tropical fish tank that was Eddie's pride and joy burbled away in the bedroom. The apartment, with its white walls, dark trim and bilious green carpet, was decorated in what was variously described as a "nouveau Pagan style" or "early cheap."[46] *(Ibid n#27)* Like the first floor, it was very cramped for space. A small Pagan altar graced a dresser on one wall. Few visitors were allowed upstairs, and socializing was done mainly in the back room on the first floor. Warlock Shop business, as well as Eddie's studies and writing, was conducted at a desk in a small back room that occupied the remainder of the second floor. With a typewriter and a filing cabinet, this comprised the shop's office.

Getting Down to Business

Eddie and Herman were listed in ads and in press interviews as the co-proprietors of the store.[47] It was general knowledge that they were equal partners in the venture, but to this day its unknown whether that business relationship was founded on anything other than a handshake or kiss.[48,49] Regardless, everyone knew that Herman was the hard-nosed businessman in charge of the day-to-day operations of the store.[50] During business hours, he could usually be found sitting behind the glass display case and checkout counter, chain-smoking while reading the newspaper. A wire displaying a long line of pewter and brass talismans and pendants ran the length of the counter a bit above head height, forcing Herman to bend down in order to peer up owlishly at the customers through a forest of pentacles, ankhs, and the like. From behind this screen he could keep an eye on things, responding to customers' questions and occasionally ordering someone to "Get outta my shop!" when they annoyed his sensibilities, seemed on the verge of shoplifting or were just loafing about and unlikely to spend any money. "Herman was a very good businessman," Kathryn Frank asserted, "in that he understood the idea of branding before it became a common term. And whatever else happened, gods help you if you screwed with his business." *(Ibid n#36)*

Sally Eaton remarked, "I think [Herman] lived his politics every day of his life — a rebel and a pioneer in a time when truth and justice were far more important than financial success. 'Tolerance' was clearly Herman's watchword — yet true to his Hermetic nature, he took it to extremes and became more than a bit intolerant himself." *(Ibid n#46)* For example, early on it became clear to some that, despite the help he had received from Leo Martello's healing ritual, Herman wasn't giving the benefit of the doubt to many of the Craft practitioners with whom he did business. While his attitude may be understandable, given the number of outlandish stories and claims the average occult shop owner hears every week, his close-mindedness appears to have irritated at least a few of those who were close to him. As Kenny Lowenstein tells it, "A group of [Witches that Herman knew] got together and they decided to prove to him that Witchcraft was real. So they decided to conduct a Circle and dance around, run around the Circle and raise the cone of power, and they said 'We're going to raise so much energy that we're going to kick him on his butt.' And they did that, and he went flying on his butt. And then he decided 'Well there must be something to this.'"[51] He at least became more open-minded on the subject.

The Warlock Shop soon developed a persona all its own. Artie Jamison described it in much the same way as many other habitués did, "The shop was a wonderful little hole in the wall. It was so magickal and so mysterious. It just reeked of Witch-dom. It just was not only the books and the smell of the herbs, and the jewelry, but it was just the store itself. It was just a nice, wonderful, crazy energy."[52] The business certainly began to attract an eclectic, rag-tag assortment of hangers-on early in its run, from Witches to Ceremonial Magickians to Satanists, and from authors to mere curiosity-seekers. Community leaders such as Ray Buckland (Gardnerian Wica), Terry Madden (Bronx Pagan Way), Leo Martello (Wica Newsletter), and Lilith (Church of Satan) were regulars at the shop by September.[53] One rumor has John (Sonny) Wojtowicz and his cohorts planning their August 22, 1972 robbery of the Gravesend, Brooklyn branch of the Chase Manhattan bank at the shop. The bumbling caper became the basis for the movie *Dog Day Afternoon* (1974), starring South Bronx native Al Pacino.[54] While this story is unlikely, Wojtowicz was known to be friends with Herman Slater. Sonny was also a member of the GAA and a regular at that group's weekly firehouse dances. He would therefore have also known Leo Martello, at least in passing.[55]

As time went on, the back room came to be used as a place to fill mail orders for the shop and as a social center for its denizens, in addition to dispensing coffee. Friends and "in" acquaintances could often count on being allowed into the back room to gossip or kibbutz. During one particularly raucous discussion in the back room, Leo Martello, tacitly acknowledging his role as Buczynski's and Slater's early mentor in the Craft, was said to have jokingly stated, "As the mother of you all, I should have had an abortion!"[56] Tommy Kneitel described the Warlock Shop's back room as *the* place to be:[57]

> *The small back room was the site of what seemed to be a day/nite (by invitation only) gathering place for assorted pagans,*

witches, magicians, tarot readers and others. It was where to go to be "seen," to make contacts, pick up gossip, exchange or create rumors. It was both the best, and the most insidious, occult place in New York. It was where to go when you had nothing else to do. Eddie was the host, the focal point, and ringmaster there, circulating, talking to attendees, gossiping, telling funny stories, and being "on stage." Eddie was in his natural element, and in his full glory, there. Mostly, Herman remained in the front of the shop dealing with customers.

Ken Dalton concurs. "The Warlock Shop was 'Pagan Central,' a meeting place and clearing house for the community. It was where people (myself included) learned of the Craft's existence and became involved. ... It was where you got the gossip, the incense and supplies, your books, jewelry, robes. It was a warm, welcoming place, especially when Eddie was there. The NYC Craft community could not have existed without the Warlock Shop."[58]

As much as the local community counted on it, the shop was simply too small to function as a Neo-Pagan community center. Indeed, it was so crowded with floor-to-ceiling witchy-odd merchandise that it was little better than an Addams Family fire trap. Most of the regular customers were not allowed in the back room, nor were they encouraged to loiter on the premises. With the store resembling an occult bodega, aisle space was at a premium and bills were always due. Herman's business philosophy was simple, as expressed by a sign in the shop: "Attention, tourists, sightseers and natives: This is a religious supply store. Buy or bye!"[59, 60]

Yet though Herman was sometimes a grump, he also had a wicked sense of humor that could manifest itself at the oddest moments. He would sometimes hide under the stairs leading to the second story with a bulb horn, squeezing it like Harpo Marx when Ria Farnham, then a part-time helper, was coming down the stairs burdened with an armload of files. She would inevitably shriek, and then grumble about an old troll living under the bridge as she picked up the scattered papers.[61] She could hold her own with him, though. In Circle one night, Herman splashed cold water from a cauldron on Ria's naked body just to make her jump, and she ended up dumping the entire thing over his head.[62]

Eddie's contribution to the enterprise was just as important as Herman's, though less structured. While he helped with the day-to-day operations, he was at heart a people person. "Eddie and Herman had a good working and personal relationship, each with a well defined role," recalls Tommy Kneitel. "Herman ran the business. He was strictly out for a buck. Herman was introverted. Eddie was the star ... [and] was totally disarming. Eddie was handsome as well as charming, with a great sense of humor. He took fullest advantage of his outgoing personality and youthful good looks. Many people thought he resembled Mick Jagger." *(Ibid n#57)*

With his raunchy good looks and a mane of hair (the color of which he changed almost as often as his mood), the twenty-five-year-old attracted the gaze of men and women alike. Buczynski wanted very much to be a respected leader in the Craft movement, and he had both the charisma and intelligence to pull it off. With the Warlock Shop as his base of operations, he set out to do just that and, in the process, to build a loyal customer base for the business — in effect by pulling in or making new customers.

It may sound surprisingly mercenary, but business really was the ultimate goal of the Warlock Shop — as anyone who knew Herman would tell you. Good business sense also meant that the shop needed to develop a demand for its services, and the best way to do that was by helping to grow a community in need of those services. That is what many regard as the lasting legacy of the Warlock Shop. As Kay Smith remembers, "There were always people in the Warlock Shop. There were always people coming in and out. And, well, they made money off of this. They had to eat. And where else are you going to get this stuff? They were performing a service for us. You know, where else were you going to get all these books in one place? Herman gave away more books than he sold. I mean he did sell books, but Eddie was always giving books to people. And loaning books to people. If you couldn't afford to buy the book he'd loan you his copy. But, you know, they did all right."[63] Yet from the very beginning Herman jockeyed to keep prices low in order to ensure "that all Crafters, no matter how short on bread, will be able to be accommodated."[64]

Herman also understood the value of advertising, the necessity to pay attention to trends and the need to be quick off the mark. The first print ad for the Warlock Shop appeared in *The Village Voice* in August, just two months after the business opened.[65] Before that, the other occult shops in town had done very little print advertising. With the notable exception of the ever-present fortune-tellers, the occult population in New York City was small and relatively quiet in those days. News tended to travel fast, usually through word of mouth, so print advertising wasn't seen as a necessity. From the first Warlock Shop ad, however, weekly print ads became *de rigueur*. Within three weeks of the Warlock Shop's first paid ad, The Blessed Are the Blessed Be shop began to advertise regularly in *The Village Voice*. Within five weeks, The Magician began to advertise there as well. Notices and ads began appearing in Neo-Pagan publications, such as *Green Egg*, by October. *(Ibid n#64)* Herman also wasn't opposed to less-mundane means of attracting attention. On some days he would dress in black robes and walk down the block to heavily trafficked Atlantic Avenue, where he would walk up and down "cleansing the street" with a sword and censer trailing frankincense smoke.[66]

Installing a business phone was an expensive proposition in 1972, comparatively much more so than it is today; however, it was a necessity for a merchant who wanted to expand, especially for one with an eye toward catalogue sales. As Herman had big plans for both, a phone was essential. He got around the expense by having the telephone company install a pay phone on the wall of the shop. By late fall he was using it to conduct business, placing the number in the shop's paid advertisements in November and getting yet another jump on the competition.[67]

Herman didn't steal a march on the others every time, but he paid attention to what was going on and was, for the most part, both flexible and quick to respond. For example, the Taurus-Risen Company manufactured and displayed capes and robes at its 151 Montague Street location in Brooklyn Heights. It also supplied other stores with its goods, including occult shops in Manhattan, and advertised those locations in its print ads. When the Blessed Are the Blessed Be shop was highlighted in a Taurus ad promoting capes and robes for All Hallows Eve, Herman made sure that the Warlock Shop was also mentioned in the following week's advertisement.[68, 69] In another instance, Blessed Are the Blessed Be offered Wicca and magick lectures by "Walli" on October 6 and 7, 1972.[70, 71] Not to be outdone, in the following week's print ad, Herman unveiled a series of lectures scheduled for November.[72]

Weekly classes on a variety of occult topics became a standard means of outreach and marketing for the shop almost from its beginning. Very small workshops were occasionally held in the kitchen, and one would sometimes see people smoking and kibitzing out front before or after a talk. One early attendee remembered, "We used to have those study groups and there'd be people sitting in the bathroom on the toilet, there'd be people sitting up the stairs. And there were people out into the shop. And Eddie would hold court." *(Ibid n#63)* But because the Warlock Shop had no room for larger meetings, these took place at various venues in Brooklyn Heights. Simon notes that when he began lecturing for the Warlock Shop in 1972, some of the first classes were taught at the St. George Hotel at 100 Henry Street.[73] At one time a grand old hotel, the St. George was worn down by the 1970s but still catered to a homosexual clientele as it had since the 1940s.[74] Classes were also taught at the Pierrepont Street chapel of the First Unitarian Church in Brooklyn Heights, and also at the apartments of several of the store's regulars.

One such place was a shabby and rundown brownstone apartment building located on Columbia Place at the foot of Joralemon Street, known pejoratively as "Vaseline Flats" for the large number of gay men who lived there. Folks from the Warlock Shop would gather for workshops or to conduct rituals at the apartments of regulars of the shop who resided in the building at 30 Joralemon Street.[75, 76] Kay Flagg fondly remembers the building. "During the War it was an SRO [rooming house] and hookers used to ply their trade down there close to the docks. Before the [Brooklyn-Queens Expressway] was built it was a huge complex with a central courtyard. They tore down half of it to build the raised road. The courtyard reverted to almost a wood. Unfortunately it wasn't private or large enough for Circles. It is still quite a structure. All the floors and walls are stone and brick with outside exposed walkways and circular staircases of stone worn down in the center. It was like living in a castle."[77]

Below the first floor of the Warlock Shop, a rough basement with a hard-packed earthen floor and a barely functional furnace was used for storage and eventually as a tiny makeshift temple space. The "dungeon," as the workers called it, was filled mostly with bags, barrels and boxes of excess inventory, and was accessible via a trap door in the front room on the first floor. To reach it, one had to negotiate a very steep, almost ladder-like, set of stairs. *(Ibid n#22)* The location of the trap door made it a safety hazard for customers who, looking for a copy of Aleister Crowley's "Book of the Law," might suddenly find themselves falling into a real abyss. Herman would sometimes suddenly pop his head up out of the trap door, not unlike Grandpa Munster coming up from the lab, and scatter the startled customers.[78] Eventually Herman and Eddie constructed a small temple in the basement for their own use. They also rented it out to others, including a ceremonial magick group, Witchcraft covens, and even Satanists, in order to make a little cash on the side.

One of the more humorous incidents in the shop happened when some people were downstairs doing ritual in the temple. They had left the trap door open to help clear out the smoke from all the incense they were burning. As Kenny Lowenstein remembers, "They were trying to do an invocation of some kind of a Goetic being, almost like a devil or something. And just at the moment they finished the invocation, somebody fell through the trap door from the floor above them and landed right in the middle of their Circle." *(Ibid n#51)* After the customer accidentally fell down the rabbit hole, Herman decided to solve the safety problem by eliminating the need for the ladder and trap door by cutting through and extending the back staircase into the basement. This remodeling, which was done without notifying the landlord, involved slicing a main support beam for the structure. The modifications were almost too much for the building, says Robert Carey. "We all sat in the kitchen watching it done and I'd swear the whole place dropped at least six inches." *(Ibid n#22)*

To celebrate the ecumenical spirit resulting from a very successful lecture series in November, an informal get-together of practitioners was held in the back room of the Warlock Shop after the final presentation on Wednesday, November 29. The group, consisting of high priests, high priestesses, and elders of five occult groups representing the Pagan Way, Welsh, Gardnerian and Continental Witches, met to drink wine and talk shop. Present were Herman and Eddie, Leo Martello, and Raymond and Rosemary Buckland, among others. The gathering ended with the following invocation:[79, 80, 81]

Answer us, O Ancient Horned One,
Provender and Power are Thine.
Hear and answer, Gracious Goddess,
Grant us laughter, wit, and wine.
Descend on us, O Thou of blessings,
Come among us, make us glad.
Since Thou art Chief of Our Creation,
Why, O why, should we be sad?
Beam on us, O joyous Bacchus,
Banish heavy-hearted hate.
Accept our Craft, O Greatest Mother,
Let cheerful brightness be our fate.
SO MOTE IT BE!

It was, alas, a sentiment that did not last for long in the rough-and-tumble occult subculture of New York.

Chapter 8: Birth-wail of the Child of Light

A Woman Scorned

Eddie voraciously devoured everything he could on mythology. Apart from the Egyptian, Greek and Roman pantheons, the mythology of the British Isles was a subject with which he had long been fascinated. Since childhood he had been attracted to the tales of King Arthur and the Knights of the Round Table. Arthur is said to have been a Welsh war leader who held his people together sometime after the Romans withdrew from Britannia and in the face of invasions from other kingdoms. This connection to Wales naturally led Eddie to explore other examples of Welsh mythology. The historical sources he examined included *The Mabinogion*, a collection of Welsh epics written between the twelfth and fourteenth centuries and translated and published by Lady Charlotte Guest in several volumes beginning in 1838, and *The Barddas* of Iolo Morganwg, a book of controversial origin and content first published in 1862. Other historical sources may have included *The Black Book of Caermarthen, The Book of Taliesin, The Book of Aneurin,* and *The Red Book of Hergest*.[1] The Mabinogi novels of Evangeline Walton — *The Virgin and the Swine* (1936, republished as *The Island of the Mighty* in 1970), *The Children of Llyr* (1971), and *The Song of Rhiannon* (1972) — also provided him with inspiration, along with Arthur Machen's *The Great God Pan* (1894) and other works.[2,3] When he began studying with Gwen Thompson, the Celtic material he encountered in her Book of Shadows convinced him that something of those ancient ways may have survived into the present.[4]

It is not known exactly when Buczynski made a conscious decision to create his own Witchcraft tradition. Some might argue that he went into his relationship with Gwen Thompson with the intent of harvesting her materials for his own use; however, there is no proof of this, nor that he had any real notion of what Gwen's tradition had to offer before first cracking the cover of *The Cauldron*. What is known is that by the early summer of 1972, Eddie began a serious effort to collect and modify materials from all of these sources.[5] He also began writing additional original material to help weld the pieces together. With sensitivity to the original material, he isolated the Welsh aspects of Thompson's Book of Shadows and incorporated them into the materials that he was compiling.[6] Attracted to both the poetic beauty and the seeming authenticity of Welsh literature describing a native Pagan mythology, and inspired by what he thought to be an authentic survival of Pagan practices native to Great Britain, Eddie molded elements of these materials into a cogent Witchcraft tradition. Herman Slater took considerable interest in Eddie's project and ordered books to help him in his research. There was a certain amount of self-interest in Herman's assistance; given the friction between him and Gwen, he would have done anything to help Eddie break that connection. However, Slater's desire to help Eddie was sincere, and his own fascination with Arthurian and Celtic mythology hardly made the task an onerous one.

Soon after the Warlock Shop opened in June 1972, a husky and brusque hair salon owner named Kay Smith walked in off the street. As she tells it, "I went into the Warlock Shop to look at books. The Goddess had fascinated me since high school, when I read about the Greek and Roman Gods and Goddesses. Ever since my childhood as a Lutheran, Mary had always held more interest for me than that poor dead thing on the cross. Of course now I know he was an Old One. I felt at the time as a female child, talking to his mother made more sense. After all, she had a direct line to God. So when I found the Goddess in so many cultures the transition was easy. I struck up a friendship with Eddie immediately. You know the proverbial 'known you forever' feeling? We both had it."[7]

Smith became interested in Eddie's research into Welsh mythology, and the two began a lively friendship. Kay had a very earthy personality with an infectious belly laugh, and she could just as easily sing like an angel and swear like a sailor on shore leave while smoking like the chimneys of a Con Ed power plant. Like the proprietors and many of the early folks who shopped at the Warlock, she ended up socializing in the lively Brooklyn Heights gay bar scene.[8] She was enthusiastic about Eddie's ideas about forming a Welsh tradition and began studying with him almost immediately, both at the Warlock Shop and at her apartment in Vaseline Flats. Eddie was already living dangerously, having previously taken on another student named Judith McNally, the assistant of writer Norman Mailer. *(Ibid n#7)* But the group continued to grow throughout the summer. McNally recounted how "[Ed] began telling us about his plans to start a coven in Brooklyn, and had taken a small group — 5 or 6 perhaps, of which I was one — as his students. ... I had the impression that he thought of continuing to work with Gwen while starting a second coven in NYC."[9] Taking on students of his own was risky, given that Eddie was still studying with Gwen Thompson and did not have her permission to teach others.[10] Such an act would be seen as a challenge to the authority of his high priestess and grounds for his immediate expulsion from the coven.

Relations between Gwen and Eddie grew more strained as the summer wore on. There is some indication that Gwen continued to pressure Eddie to have sex with her. *(Ibid n#7)* Some of Eddie's friends from the time, such as Kay Smith, have said that Buczynski told them that Thompson was in love with him, insisting that he sleep with her, and also that she wanted Eddie to conduct the Great Rite "in true" with her during ritual as part of the fertility magick inherent in Witchcraft. *(Ibid n#7)* However, as the archivist of the N.E.C.T.W., Andrew Theitic, points out, "Gwen might have pressured Eddie to have sex with her, but not the Great

Rite. Our Tradition doesn't have a Great Rite so to speak." This assertion is supported by Eddie's copy of *The Cauldron*, which includes no such rite in its pages, and by the fact that the Welsh Witchcraft that Buczynski was working on, which derives in part from the N.E.C.T.W. materials, also did not incorporate a Great Rite "in true," though it does include a variation of the symbolic Great Rite, conducted using ritual tools.[11]

It was during one of Eddie's overnight stays at the Autumnal Equinox of September 1972 that things finally came to a head between him and Gwen. An argument took place at Thompson's home in North Haven, Connecticut, with each accusing the other of power trips and ego issues. The fight escalated well beyond any of their previous ones. Sexual tension/frustration may have added fuel to the fire. Whatever the underlying reason, they parted with considerable acrimony and Eddie was "released" from the coven.[12] *(Ibid n#10)* "My suspicion is [that] the break came when he told her he was definitely starting a coven in New York," writes Judith McNally. "Knowing Ed, I assume that he worded himself quite diplomatically, but he was essentially *telling* her his plans, not asking her permission to proceed, and Gwen probably took exception to the 'take it or leave it' between the lines. .... Whatever the details of his plans, I don't think he anticipated how strong her objections would be." *(Ibid n#9)*

Two stories purport to tell what happened. In the first, told right after the conflict, Eddie mentioned to several friends and students that he received a letter from Gwen informing him that he was no longer welcome in the North Haven coven. He never showed the letter to anyone else, but said that he released it onto the wind which carried it away. The listeners believed the tale far too theatrical to be completely true, and suspected that there was more than what was being said. However, given the circumstances, no one was keen to dig further. "Ed's demeanor was very sorrowful, very melodramatic," recalls McNally. "It didn't occur to me at the time to wonder why he was answering a question none of us had asked. I, for one, would have considered it appalling rudeness to ask to *see* that letter. It was only months later that I felt certain that business of letting the letter vanish on the street was well-planned to forestall any requests to see Gwen's actual communication." *(Ibid n#9)*

In the second story, Eddie claimed that his fight with Gwen resulted from his refusal to have sex with her after she had elevated him to Second Degree. He said he went to bed after the fight and when he awoke the next morning, Gwen was nowhere to be seen. However, he found a note, informing him that he was removed from the coven, pinned to (or weighted down on) the pillow next to his head with his own athame. Eddie did not relate this story to Kay, Herman and a few others until mid-1973, some months after the alleged event.[13, 14] While these stories are not mutually exclusive, neither are they necessarily a complete or accurate portrayal of the fight and its immediate aftermath.

There is some question as to whether or not Buczynski was officially banished from the N.E.C.T.W. Both Gwen and Eddie used the term "banished" in later conversations with others, but Andrew Theitic states that there is no record or recollection of Gwen actually having performed the N.E.C.T.W. Banishment Rite on his name. *(Ibid n#10)* Her use of the term may significantly post-date the event, and might be more indicative of Gwen's renewed anger in subsequent months and years after finding out that Eddie used materials from *The Cauldron* in constructing his Welsh tradition. However, an initiate of Thompson's line who was also friendly with Eddie states that Buczynski informed him that he had indeed been banished by Gwen after attaining the Second Degree in her coven.[15] Other Craft associates of Buczynski, including Judith McNally and Kay Flagg, likewise state that he specifically used the term "banishment" at the time to refer to what had taken place. Gwen was certainly capable of banishing members of her group, having done so to her own son, James, in 1985.[16]

Regardless of the circumstances, the break between the two was permanent, particularly after Eddie's use of N.E.C.T.W. materials in writing his Welsh book became known. When Gwen kicked Eddie out, she did so completely and refused to speak of him for a long while after. But even though they never healed the rift between them, Gwen did eventually come to regard Eddie as one of the brightest personalities who had ever come to her. *(Ibid n#6)* Regardless of whether either one had any nostalgic second thoughts about their relationship, there was certainly no love lost between Gwen and Herman in the aftermath of the split. Theitic notes, "Many years after Gwen died, Herman told me that he had no ill feelings toward her, but he said it with a frown on his face." *(Ibid n#10)*

Eddie's own treatment at Gwen's hands instilled in him a very conscious understanding of the potential for abuse of power by persons in coven leadership positions. Judith McNally notes that the impact of the banishment on Eddie was profound. "Either that day [when he told of the banishment] or very soon after, Ed said he would never banish anyone from any coven of his — it was simply too hurtful. If he ever found himself at odds with a covener, he would make them Third Degree with all reasonable speed and give them every assistance in founding their own coven. I can attest that he stuck to that policy when I knew him." *(Ibid n#9)* Formed as it was at an early point in his association with the Craft, this viewpoint was to be reinforced in the coming years as the Craft continued to grow in New York and conflict became more commonplace.

Welsh Traditionalist Witchcraft

Buczynski had continued to develop the Welsh materials through the summer into autumn, but his Book of Shadows was not complete by the time Gwen released him from her coven; for example, only four Sabbat rituals, which would eventually number eight rites, were present at the time of the split. There is clear evidence that Eddie borrowed N.E.C.T.W. materials from The Cauldron to construct his Welsh Book of Shadows. A side-by-side comparison of an early copy of the Second Degree Initiation ritual in Eddie's Welsh Book of Shadows with the Rite of Initiation contained in his copy of The Cauldron demonstrates that the former was derived from the latter. The same can be said of the Welsh First Degree Initiation ritual and the N.E.C.T.W. Neophyte Initiation ritual.[17] By one estimate, as much as 70 percent of the initial Welsh First Degree material was taken from Thompson's book. Others familiar with both books say that the percentage of copied material was actually much lower; however, all agree that copying certainly occurred. Major aspects were changed from the original, including the God and Goddess names, totems, coven colors, and Sabbat oil recipe. *(Ibid n#10)*

Practically speaking, there were real limits on what Eddie could borrow from Gwen because as a First Degree — or even as a newly made Second Degree — he simply hadn't had the time or opportunity to access much of The Cauldron's higher-level material. One person who is knowledgeable in both traditions notes, for example, that the Welsh tradition created by Buczynski does not have the full degree system that N.E.C.T.W. had because he left before gaining access to much of the higher-degree information. This assertion is confirmed upon an examination of Eddie's personal copy of Gwen's book, which ends within a few pages of the Second Degree ritual being inscribed. While Gwen's Book of Shadows is said to be one of the thickest ever seen (the First Degree section alone is said to cover 400 pages), Eddie's hand-copied version of that book comes to only 210 pages. *(Ibid n#6)* Gwen Thompson was constantly tinkering with her materials and likely continued adding material to her book after Eddie ended his studies with her.[18] With one notable exception, the material in Eddie's personal copy of The Cauldron appears to be consistent with what one would expect to find in the book of a recently elevated Second Degree initiate of a Witchcraft tradition.

The noted exception in question refers to an "Elder Initiation" ritual, which is present in Buczynski's version of *The Cauldron.* This N.E.C.T.W. ritual is roughly equivalent to a Third Degree elevation ritual in, say, Gardnerian Wica. It represents a graduation ceremony of sorts for a student, a final investiture of the priest or priestess, and it usually contains the innermost Mysteries of a Witchcraft tradition. Once he or she has gone through that ritual, the student becomes a master, able to hive from the mother coven and begin training his or her own students. Neither a Neophyte nor a Second Degree student would ever, under any legitimate circumstances, have a copy of this ritual in his or her Book of Shadows. In addition to the anomalous presence of this ritual in Eddie's copy of the book, there is circumstantial evidence that he may have copied this material under some duress. The ritual is the last piece of instructional material written in his copy of *The Cauldron*. And, whereas great care had been taken in the transcribing of all other material into the book, the text in question is scrawled, as if the writer were copying it in great haste.[19]

Some believe that Gwen may have shared upper-level material with Eddie, and this may be true, given the apparent speed with which she was advancing him. *(Ibid n#6)* But it is highly unlikely that she would have allowed him to copy the Elder Initiation ritual unless he had already gone through the ceremony, and that also seems unlikely. It is quite possible that Gwen Thompson may have failed to register Eddie's Second Degree elevation in a fit of pique if their final fight followed close upon the heels of his elevation. Certainly Thompson never publicly referred to Eddie as anything other than "a former First Degree student."[20] However, even if Buczynski had been elevated to the Second Degree, for her to then have elevated him to Elder so quickly after achieving Second Degree, while possible and certainly not unheard of, seems doubtful. Therefore, the presence of the Elder Initiation ritual in his copy of The Cauldron and its peculiar state raises unanswered questions as to how it came to be there.

The N.E.C.T.W. Elder Initiation ritual appears to have contributed to the Third Degree ritual that appears in Eddie's early Welsh book. However, it is unclear how great the influence was because only the first page of the N.E.C.T.W. text remains intact in Eddie's copy of The Cauldron, the remainder having been roughly ripped from the book at some time after it was penned in the journal book.[21] A story has been widely circulated that either the N.E.C.T.W. Elder Initiation ritual or the Welsh Third Degree ritual (or both) was originally written by Leo Martello.22 Martello had been friends with Thompson for a few years, but after the split between Buczynski and Thompson, he decided to side with Eddie. One friend remembers Leo as a contentious character who was close to Eddie when Eddie first left Gwen's coven. But Leo also had a strong connection to Gwen, and they remained good friends for a long while until they had a major falling out.

According to William Wheeler, Leo said that they fell out because he loaned Gwen money that she never paid back, but some doubt that was the real reason.[23] *(Ibid n#6)* Martello himself did refer in 1973 to having loaned $240 to a high priestess in order to keep her from being evicted, and said that he had never been repaid. But he said the falling out had more to do with her constant negativity rather than the money itself.[24, 25, 26, 27]
It is possible that the fight between Gwen and Leo may have had more to do with the support he lent to Eddie's creative efforts, which she would most certainly have interpreted as a betrayal of their friendship. However, Martello may not have gone on to author the Welsh Third Degree Initiation ritual, since the early version of that rite points to its derivation from the text of the Elder Initiation rite in Eddie's copy of The Cauldron. If Martello was involved at all, it is more likely that he adapted the

N.E.C.T.W. Elder Initiation rite for use by the Welsh tradition at a later date.[28]

By early August, the Welsh instructional materials, mythology and rituals were sufficiently developed for Buczynski to begin putting them to use. On the night of October 8, 1972, under the cusp of a dark moon, Eddie initiated Kay Smith into his Welsh tradition, and then handed his creation into her hands by elevating her to be his high priestess. Kay chose as her public Craft name Vivienne, while within the coven she was known as Melusine.[29] *(Ibid n#7)* That same night, Eddie took the Inner Court Craft name Gwydion to signify not only his break with the past, but also to more closely associate himself with the Welsh mythology upon which his new tradition was based. *(Ibid n#29)* Gwydion is a character in the Fourth Branch of The Mabinogion. A powerful magician, Gwydion misuses his powers by helping his brother Gilfaethwy to rape the maiden Goewyn, for which he was punished and eventually redeemed by his uncle, Math, the maiden's master. That he chose a name which figures so prominently in a Welsh story of condemnation and redemption is perhaps one of the most telling insights into Eddie's thoughts during this period.[30]

Buczynski officially founded his Welsh Witchcraft tradition — the "Traditionalist Gwyddoniaid" — in a ceremony held in Kay's apartment on Joralemon in Brooklyn Heights. The night of October 21, 1972 was chosen for the ceremony because it was a full moon and thus considered propitious for new beginnings.[31] The first Traditionalist Gwyddoniaid coven was named the New York Coven of Welsh Traditionalist Witchcraft, with Kay Smith (Vivienne/Melusine) as its high priestess and Eddie Buczynski (Hermes/Gwydion) as her high priest. Herman Slater and Leo Martello were initiated and brought up to Third Degree that same night. *(Ibid n#7)* Slater, because of his own limp and the cast of his left eye, chose the Craft name Hephaestus in honor of the lame Greek God. His inner coven name was Govannon in honor of yet another lame smith, this one a God of the Welsh, which aligned more closely with the current of the tradition. Martello, to no one's great surprise, took the name Nemesis — the Greek spirit of balance and divine retribution against society's bullies and self-dealers.

The night was a joyous one and not without some humor as the assembled worshippers, still working through and memorizing the ritual text, stumbled on occasion. However, not all was honey and rosewater from the start. Judith, who had been passed over for the position of high priestess, was initiated to the First Degree that night and was chosen instead to become the maiden of the coven. The role of maiden is an important one. She is the deputy to the high priestess and has a role to play in every rite, and she is in charge of the coven in the absence of the high priestess. The maiden is also deputed to do certain chores, such as setting up the altar for ritual. Although she performed her duties admirably, this drudge work didn't sit well with her, as Kay recalls. "When

I started studying with Eddie, Judith had been coming to the shop for longer than me. When I was chosen over her as high priestess, she was not amused, but held her continence." *(Ibid n#7)*

Many of the original members of the coven were drawn from local sources. "As far as I know Kay and many/most of the early folks were linked thru the Brooklyn Heights gay bar scene of the time," recalled Robert Carey.[32] Initially, the coven met every Saturday. Rumors that Eddie was now heading a previously unknown Witchcraft tradition began to circulate shortly after its birth. The rumors were confirmed in New York City when a Warlock Shop advertisement appeared in the Village Voice to promote a Welsh lecture to be given by Buczynski on November 8, 1972.[33] The news made the rounds nationally in November when Leo Martello wrote in *Gnostica News* of attending the Samhain Sabbat of the coven on October 28, 1972.[34] At that rite, Leo was elevated to the Third Degree in the Welsh tradition.[35] In the May 1973 edition of *Gnostica News'* regular "Wiccan Sects" column, Buczynski described the tradition as more properly "Brythonic Traditions of Gwyddoniaid (Wicca). ... Our Laws and some of our Rituals are closely related to Gardnerian and American-Celtic and Dianic form, though most of them are distinctly unique."[36] Eddie's mention of an "American-Celtic" influence is the closest that he ever came to publicly admitting a connection to Thompson's N.E.C.T.W.

Eddie's actions, coming so soon after his dismissal from Thompson's North Haven coven, would eventually provoke near unanimous hostility from members of the N.E.C.T.W. As it became known that he had altered their teachings and incorporated them into his own Book of Shadows, they were loath to recognize Buczynski's Welsh tradition or any of its initiates as being related in any way to their tradition. *(Ibid n#10)* There was also some question of Eddie's authority to lead a coven, given that he had been unceremoniously removed from the North Haven coven and was by their records only a First Degree. Eddie appears to have addressed this issue by placing a statement in the Welsh Book of Shadows, asserting that he was a Third Degree initiate of a branch of British Traditional Witchcraft:

> *I, Gwydion, having received proper initiation at the hands of the Lady Rhiannon, do hereby set down this Book of Shadows for the benefit of all who come after me along this path.*
>
> *I received First Degree at Oimelc, 1965 C.E. Second Degree at Oimelc, 1967 C.E., and Third Degree...the Sublime Degree...at Midsummer's Eve, 1968 C.E. I was duly prepare[d] and made High Priest at Lughnasad, 1970 C.E.*[37]

Eddie publicly repeated this claim in Hans Holzer's 1973 book *The Witchcraft Report*, stating that "my original high priestess brought me in when I was eighteen years old and in 1970 I was finally made high priest."[38] It must be said that the likelihood of Buczynski having been elevated to the Third Degree by anyone in 1968 is quite low. Covens hewing to British Traditional Witchcraft were still quite rare in the United States at that time. The Bucklands had only begun to teach in Brentwood, New York in early 1964, and Buczynski was not one of their students, according to Raymond Buckland.[39] Eddie would have just been a few days into his eighteenth year in early February 1965 and, struggling as he was to survive in Greenwich Village, had few resources at his command to conduct what was then a long and often frustrating search for a coven. According to Welsh high priestess Judith McNally, "He never said Word One to me about a 1965 initiation or 'Lady Rhiannon' .... That would mean, of course, she was training Ed when he was a 17-year-old. At that time and place, it's hard to imagine a sensible High Priestess training someone underage unless he was a blood relative."[40]

At least one print reference — albeit a pejorative one — questions Buczynski's bona fides to lead a coven, pointing out that Eddie had written multiple Craft elders as a seeker only months before founding the Traditionalist Gwyddoniaid in 1972.[41] Furthermore, the N.E.C.T.W. archivist recalls Gwen Thompson stating that Buczynski told her that she was his first initiator.[42] At least one person who knew both Eddie and Kay appears to support this assertion, writing that, as far as he was aware, Eddie didn't come into the Craft until years after the claimed 1965 First Degree initiation. *(Ibid n#6)* There is also the issue of Eddie's attempted rapprochement with the Catholic Church, which likely occurred sometime in 1966 after the closing session of Vatican II. It is implausible that Buczynski would have been pursuing relations with the Catholic Church while actively engaged in the practice of Witchcraft.

Eddie was remarkably consistent over a period of eleven years in claiming to having been initiated in 1965. These citations include the frontispiece of the Welsh Book and the response to Hans Holzer in 1972, two other Books of Shadows written in early 1974 and late 1976, and a report written in 1983.[43] However, an autobiographical paper written by Buczynski in September 1974 makes no mention of this initiation into British Traditional Witchcraft in the 1960s and appears to contradict the dates he cited, casting further doubt on his claimed 1965 initiation.[44] Thus, while Buczynski's 1960s-era lineage via "Rhiannon" cannot be conclusively ruled out, there is no known independent documentary or testamentary evidence to support it, and considerable circumstantial evidence to cast doubt upon it.

One possible motive for citing "Rhiannon" as the originator of this material is that, by referring to a period that predates his involvement with Gwen Thompson, Eddie was constructing a plausible defense against future charges that he had used Thompson's Book of Shadows to construct his Welsh tradition. Another possible motive for Buczynski's forging a Craft lineage, if that is indeed what happened, may well lay in his concern about how potential students would perceive his authenticity. Being unable to cite a lineage granting authority to lead a coven was a sticking point in 1972 for any putative high priestess or high priest. Independent covens were still fairly rare and looked upon with some skepticism by seekers, many of whom were searching for the "real deal." In this respect, Eddie's assertion bears a striking similarity to that of Alex Sanders, who also claimed an unbroken and ancient lineage of Welsh Witchcraft for his Alexandrian tradition. Writer Elizabeth Guerra notes that Sanders "needed this story to gain respect and admiration from his followers."[45] And this habit of citing *tradition ancienne* did not start with Buczynski, Sanders, or even Gardner. That honor, at least in modern occult history, can be laid at the feet of the occult Brotherhoods of the 1800s, such as the Hermetic Order of the Golden Dawn.[46]

But persons who seek out groups that offer access to this purported authenticity eventually end up with one of two choices: either so-called hereditary traditions whose grandmother tales ultimately cannot withstand independent verification, or lineaged traditions whose documentary evidence peters out after at most a few generations. Neo-Pagan author Kerr Cuhulain sums it up this way: "The 'older is better' argument is a logical fallacy: Truth is truth, whether it was discovered five minutes ago or a thousand years ago. Age has nothing to do with it."[47] In reality, lineage counts for little if the person wielding the title is not a competent ritualist, teacher, or magickian. As one high priestess bluntly put it when speaking of those who, through vanity or insecurity, falsify their credentials, "You either have the energy or you don't."[48] Few who stood in Circle with him would argue that Eddie was not a competent Witch, and his energy was due in large part to the training received at Thompson's hands, and also to his own native charisma and force of Will.

Buczynski's use of N.E.C.T.W. materials would fuel recriminations over his actions in the years to come by N.E.C.T.W. initiates and others in the Craft. Initiation into a Witchcraft tradition was, and still remains, freighted with explicit expectations for secrecy, personal responsibility and accountability. Oaths are required of the initiate, who pledges, among other things, to protect the teachings from revelation to or profanation by outsiders. Thompson's fam-trad was no different in this, as the initiates swore on their blood to keep the secrets of the coven and, to seal this oath, daubed a drop of their blood into the coven register next to their name.[49] To be forsworn was to risk being labeled an oath-breaker. That many of those doing the labeling might also indulge in similar activities, or benefit from their occurrence, is quite beside the point.

Covens both then and now often allow initiates of other traditions to guest with them at Sabbat, although the practice was more prevalent in the past. *(Ibid n#15)* Certainly Gwen's North Haven coven did so, for they frequently hosted Leo Martello, who was not an initiate of Celtic

Traditionalist Witchcraft; and it is a parochial Witch indeed who does not possess a Book of Shadows from at least one or two traditions besides his or her own, even if purchased from a local bookstore. Some Witches boast of owning a dozen or more books from traditions into which they have not been initiated, and these are often received in exchange for copies of their own books as an act of courtly good will amongst the high priestesses and high priests of disparate traditions.[50]

Many of these collectors, if pressed, would acknowledge that they, their predecessors, or their downlines have incorporated materials gleaned from such exchanges into their own practices.[51] Indeed, it has been shown that Gardnerian Wica made use of materials from diverse sources, such as Aleister Crowley, the Golden Dawn, Margaret Murray, and a smattering of nineteenth and early twentieth century classicists, writers and poets.[52, 53] It seems clear that Gwen also borrowed from others, for example the Gardnerians, in the construction of her Rede of the Wiccae. Yet by no means are any of the Witches who participate in these exchanges considered by their peers to be thieves. In general, despite the fact that guests of coven sabbats and recipients of coven materials are not bound by oath to do so, they endeavor to keep the secrets of other covens safe and secure from the prying eyes of non-Witches. They do this not only because it is right and honorable to do so, as one Witch to another, but also because both sides in the exchange would be under a mutually implicit threat, both of having their own Mysteries revealed to outsiders and of being held in contempt by other Craft practitioners.[54]

There was a rumor in circulation at this time that Eddie had shared oathbound material from Gwen Thompson's *Cauldron* with members of the Georgian tradition. George "Pat" Patterson had co-founded the Georgian tradition early in 1971 in Bakersfield, California with his first high priestess, Zanoni Silverknife. Patterson and Silverknife both corresponded with many Craft elders throughout the country during this formative process and afterwards. "We had help from Ed Fitch, who wrote the Pagan Way material, Lady Gwen [Thompson] who assisted us in numerous ways, and Doris and Sylvester Stuart of Sussex, England who also corresponded with us to guide us," wrote Silverknife in 2004. "Later, Eddie [Buczynski] and *Siobhan* also wrote to me, as well as Leo Martello, Bonnie Sherlock and T. Camisa and Gwydion Pendderwen; a plethora of people."[55] Silverknife was at one point corresponding with over sixty different individuals across the country. Noting that the lingering spirit of the 1960s encouraged people to be more open and friendly to newcomers in those days, she recalled that "we all had influence upon one another; we brainstormed through multitudes of letters and newsletters and infrequent phone calls. Can you imagine how we could have expanded had we the use of the internet 33 years ago?"[56]

After Eddie left Gwen's coven in late 1972, he continued to write to Zanoni. Buczynski's direct contributions to the Georgian tradition appear to have taken the form of moral support and advice, with in-depth technical support from members of his Welsh downline. Silverknife explains, "There is not a lot I can tell you about the impact that Eddie had on the Georgian tradition actually; while he was a very strong influence in my life (we corresponded almost weekly for about two and one-half years) his presence in the Georgian tradition was as [being named] an honorary elder by Pat. ..... I also corresponded with Kay, his High Priestess, a lovely, warm person. More to the point, the way that Eddie influenced the Georgian tradition was through two of his Third Degrees, *Lord Pygmalion* and *Lady Siobhan*. They were instrumental in teaching me many things and sharing much material that wended its way into my own Book of Shadows and my practices. One of my Second [Degree students] later went back over to Pat's Coven after having copied much of my book [along with] with the relevant material from *Lady Siobhan's* 'Order of the Silver Wheel Coven' which she led with *Lord Pygmalion* (Tommy Zielinsky, now deceased [also a Third Degree from Eddie]). This person took that material to Pat and it became integrated into the rest of the Tradition's Book of Shadows." *(Ibid n#56)* Herman Slater was also named as an honorary elder of the Georgian tradition by Patterson.[57]

Siobhan and Tommy Zielinsky began helping Silverknife as early as late 1972 while they were still with Eddie, and continued after they had hived off their own Welsh coven in Brooklyn in 1973. Zanoni remembers that they "were never anything but [Welsh]; neither were interested in being Georgian. But, I did share bits of knowledge and spells with them as they did with me."[58] It appears, therefore that accusations that Eddie violated his Celtic Traditionalist oath by providing material assistance to the Georgian tradition were misplaced. Such charges also seem somewhat hypocritical, given that Gwen Thompson was also assisting to Patterson and Silverknife during that time. One must also take into consideration the fact that it was Gwen who introduced Eddie to the Georgians while she was helping them, which seemingly amounted to a tacit approval of such assistance.

Of course, none of this explains the larger question of why Buczynski initially sought out Celtic Europe as a spiritual homeland during this period of his life (or, as Pagan historian Chas Clifton asks, "Why does a boy from Queens with a Polish name want to be 'Welsh', for Rhiannon's sake?")[59] There was certainly no Celtic background on either side of his family which might have inspired him to take a keen interest in that area. And Herman, though a solid and loyal supporter of Eddie's Welsh tradition, was of New York Jewish rootstock, so there is nothing in that corner on which to hang a hypothesis. Eddie's childhood attraction to the Arthurian myths no doubt played a role in his choice, as did the Celtic "lure" that was manifesting during those years (and indeed continues today). Historian Marion Bowman refers to this latter phenomenon — the attraction of peoples from all cultures and races to a New Age vision of a noble and idealized Celtic mythology — as "a thing of spirit, not of heritage". Some refer to it as being one of the "cardiac Celts" — i.e., in your heart, you know you're Celtic.[60] *(Ibid #59)* Eddie's exposure to the inner workings of Witchcraft with his involvement in Gwen Thompson's Celtic Traditionalist path would also have exerted an immediate influence on his thoughts and ambitions. Expediency may also have played an important factor in his direction; as he had ready access to Gwen's material, which he genuinely believed to be ancient and authentic (and Celtic), repurposing parts of it would have been the fastest path to constructing a tradition of his own. They say that imitation is the sincerest form of flattery, and this certainly appears to be backed by the history of Neo-Paganism, which is rife with similar examples of borrowing during this period.

Still, Buczynski was on shaky ethical ground from the moment he began combing through Gwen Thompson's Book of Shadows for materials to use in the creation of his Welsh tradition, and this often led others to a presumption of guilt whenever his subsequent activities came under scrutiny. This presumption was not, as some have alleged over the years, because Buczynski stole the materials from the N.E.C.T.W; as a N.E.C.T.W. initiate, he was clearly entitled to possess the bulk of the material he used from his copy of *The Cauldron*. It was also not because he revealed the Mysteries to outsiders, because by revealing the materials only to oathbound initiates, he effectively provided at least the same level of protection to the materials as was expected by oath of N.E.C.T.W. initiates, and by Craft courtesy of guests to the North Haven coven. Indeed, the language of the Welsh book is considerably harsher in its pronouncements against those who would reveal the Mysteries therein to outsiders than that contained in *The Cauldron* itself, a point that Eddie emphasized. *(Ibid n#36)* Beyond this, Eddie did attempt to obscure the true origins of the N.E.C.T.W. materials used in his Welsh book by telling students over the next several years that he possessed pieces of an unnamed traditional Book of Shadows, and that he created the Welsh book from this material by fleshing it out with additional writings of his own. *(Ibid n#8)*

All of this was certainly true as far as it went. But whether this obfuscation was intended to protect the original source of the so-called traditional materials he used, or to conceal his own role in their unauthorized adaptation, or both, remains unknown. In the end, Buczynski's greatest offense was arguably one of infidelity or disobedience to his high priestess. It is fair to say that Eddie did misuse what he was given, for he was not chartered by Gwen Thompson to adapt the materials in the ways that he did. And angering one's high priestess can often result in unwelcome and unforeseen consequences down the road.

Chapter 9: Ye Shall Know Them by Their Ways

The Brooklyn Heights Pagan Way

Unlike occult bookstores such as the Warlock Shop, most covens in the 1960s and early 1970s shied away from publicity. Those that chose to reveal themselves to the public usually did so in venues whose focus and circulation was narrowly tailored so as to limit their exposure to unfriendly elements within their home communities. These venues included occult newsletters and magazines and postings on bulletin boards in shops likely to be frequented by spiritual fellow travelers. A coven usually publicized its existence because it was willing to entertain inquiries from persons interested in studying Witchcraft. In the early years, covens such as the one operated by Rosemary and Raymond Buckland had practiced a strict philosophy in the selection and training of initiates. Seekers were subjected to a rigorous screening process. Seekers who expressed an interest in black magic, Satanism, personal power, sexual gratification and other illegitimate motivations were refused. Other considerations also played a role, such as the resistance on the part of many covens to admit homosexuals or people of different racial backgrounds.

Those who made the initial cut were interviewed either in person or via correspondence to further ascertain their motivations, level of maturity, and commitment. One technique that was employed was to stall and draw out the seeker for a period of time in order to discern unhealthy signs of poor socialization or deceptive practices. This process could take upwards of a year, at the end of which, if the prospective student had demonstrated behaviors conducive to training, he or she might be selected for initiation. Judy Kneitel stated that it took over a year from her initial correspondence with the Bucklands before the couple consented to initiate her and her husband Tommy.[1] This technique is not a bad thing in and of itself, and can save a coven a great many headaches and heartaches in the long run. Once a candidate entered a coven, training was often rigorous. Pains were taken to observe a year-and-a-day between degrees to further ensure that the initiate was growing into a mature, dependable and properly socialized Witch who was able to function within the coven environment. One would be hard-pressed to fault this methodology even today.

Yet, in the 1960s teachers like the Bucklands were often criticized for their caution, generally by those who had been turned away for one reason or another before eventually being accepted by another coven. Raymond Buckland recalled how he had been accused of being "snooty" and the Brentwood Coven of being "overly selective" in its vetting process.[2] But even with a precautionary air, any coven could occasionally make embarrassing mistakes in their judgment of people. In one extraordinary case in 1967, a new First Degree initiate named Mary Nesnick had allegedly copied out materials from Brentwood Coven's Book of Shadows without permission. After adding some material from the Kabbalah, she then abandoned the Bucklands and subsequently proclaimed to the national media that she was the Lady Dionysia, Grand High Priestess of the United States and Canada of a previously unheard of Witchcraft tradition. The betrayal hurt and angered the Bucklands, but such events were a concern to all coven leaders.[3,4]

Despite the rise of interest in the occult and the resulting flood of unsuitable applicants, those covens that advertised never wanted for a constant supply of qualified candidates. Indeed, the supply was always greater than the existing covens could handle, and it was all one could do to keep from being overcome when trying to drink from the fire hose of applicants. The scarcity of covens and the slow process of inculcation severely limited the number of people who could be brought in. The overall growth of Witchcraft during this period was slow, because it took several years of training to create the elders who could hive off to create new covens to help ease the pressure.

In the mid-1960s, Ed Fitch was a member of the United States Air Force. Moving around according to his military postings, he eventually ended up at Hanscom Air Force Base in Bedford, Massachusetts. As a result of his interest in Witchcraft, Fitch struck up a correspondence with Raymond Buckland. He began making weekend trips to Brentwood, New York, where he was initiated into Gardnerian Wica by the Bucklands in the spring of 1967, and elevated to high priest in 1968. He compiled a Book of Shadows based upon Dion Fortune's concept of an "outer court," which was designed to provide a Gardnerian training system that did not violate the oaths of those doing the training. "It could be used," according to Fitch, "for training and evaluating new people without putting the Book of Shadows at risk."[5,6]

Fitch met with Susan Roberts on one trip to New York to provide input to a manuscript on Witchcraft that she was writing. Its publication in 1971 as *Witches USA.* helped accelerate the growth of Witchcraft in the United States. Ed was also a correspondent of Joseph Wilson, who, like Fitch, was also in the Air Force and was posted around the country. In 1965 he had begun a newsletter, *The Waxing Moon*, which provided the first public encounter list for Craft contacts and correspondence in the United States. The lack of training venues, or even points of contact, for those interested in Witchcraft was becoming a problem by 1970.

Also of concern was the appearance of groups inappropriately claiming descent from Gardnerian, Alexandrian and other established traditions. Books of Shadows were becoming publicly available, either obtained from legitimate initiates, cobbled together piecemeal from published works, written from scratch and then claimed as ancient works handed down within families, or some combination thereof. This is not to say that there are no surviving volumes of pre-Gardnerian lore, herbology, folk cures, or practices that might, loosely, fall under the rubric of "Books of Shadows." However, none that have surfaced have withstood authentication by independent scholars, and until that is done, all such claims must be taken with a grain of salt. The pre-electronic age practices of hand-copying one's personal book from the example provided by the coven leaders, and the alleged practice of burning the book upon the death of the owner, tend to work against the likelihood of finding an "ancient" Book of Shadows. If you don't want your claims of antique knowledge to be publicly challenged, then you probably shouldn't be making them in public. As Marcello Truzzi so eloquently put it, "[W]hen such claims are extraordinary ... we must demand extraordinary proof."[7]

In 1971, *The Book of Shadows* of Lady Sheba was published.[8] Suddenly, a version of a Gardnerian-derived Book of Shadows was being mass-produced and made available to anyone who wanted it, regardless of whether they had the training or mental stability to lead a coven, and regardless of their motives for doing so. As Raymond Buckland stated:[9]

> *Groups of self-styled Witches started springing up all over the place. True and sincere seekers after the Wica that Gardner and Murray had extolled were sidetracked, many being taken into pseudo-covens and given an irreversible dose of negative Witchcraft that would drive them from the true Craft forever.*

This marked the beginning of a sustained period of divergence within the Craft that continues to this day. Individuals and groups were helped in this by do-it-yourself books on Witchcraft that began to appear in bookstores — The *Do-It-Yourself Witchcraft Guide* (1971) and *The Book of Shadows* (1971), to name but two examples — as well as newspapers and magazines.[10] In the late 1960s, ads for occult training were placed in such alternative newspapers as *The Village Voice* and the *East Village Other*, the latter of which ran a classified ad reading, "Bored? Why not try WITCHCRAFT?" and gave details on joining a "real" coven.[11] One might be justified in titling an honest account of Wica in the latter half of the twentieth century, *Ex Uno Plura*.

This was not an entirely harmful process in the long run; a great number of very good and dedicated people who otherwise had no opportunity to study or work within a Gardnerian coven were now able to practice a spirituality to which they felt deeply and sincerely attuned. Any number of these people eventually went on to join covens of Gardnerian Wica and related paths when the opportunities arose, but in the early 1970s, with unconnected covens popping up and attempting to pass themselves off as Craft insiders, the trend had the makings of a disaster for traditions that were based both on mystery and on the passing of legitimacy and a spiritual current of power from generation to generation.

Ed Fitch originally wrote the *Outer Court Book of Shadows* and an accompanying *Grimoire of Shadows* to help Gardnerian covens train and evaluate people without placing the secrets of the Book of Shadows at risk. Yet there were individuals and small groups of people who were not affiliated with nearby Gardnerian covens who also clamored for the tools to train themselves in Witchcraft. In response to this increasing demand for instructional materials, Fitch wrote additional materials to provide a system for unaffiliated seekers. *(Ibid n#6)*

Called the "Pagan Way", this system was designed to provide training materials for individuals who might not otherwise have access to a coven. In the idealistic spirit of the era, the material had no bylines indicating its authorship. It was meant to be in the public domain so that it could be freely distributed to those who needed it.[12] Thomas Giles, who published the *Crystal Well* newsletter with Ed Fitch, established a mailing center in Philadelphia to distribute the materials. Fitch operated another mailing center in Minot, South Dakota where he was stationed by the Air Force on his return to the country from Vietnam. Within these mailings could be found information on Neo-Pagan beliefs and rituals that individuals or groups could practice without any previous specialized knowledge or background in Craft magickal techniques and training. The Pagan Way system provided a foundation that could allow a qualified candidate a better chance of eventually being accepted as a student in an established coven. However, for those who had no desire for in-depth coven-based studies, or who were not for whatever reason able to find a place in an established coven, the system provided a way to practice Neo-Pagan spirituality.[13, 14]

The Pagan Way proved so successful that the demand began to outstrip the ability of Giles and Fitch to meet it. Some of the first recipients of the Pagan Way and outer court materials included the Louisville, Kentucky coven of Fran and Gerry Fisher (*Theo* and *Thain*), Gardnerian siblings of Fitch from the Buckland coven, who began to share the materials with interested people in the south. Soon other mailing centers were established to handle the load. As Joseph Wilson recalled, "Our purpose was to create something for every seeker no matter who they were or what their background was, to be available either without cost, or for the cost of printing and postage alone." *(Ibid n#12)*

While the Pagan Way system did not require a coven-like environment to be effective, such groups began to self-organize almost from the beginning. As the Pagan Way organizers felt it was inappropriate to refer to them as covens, the name "grove" was used to name these groups. Judy Harrow states that "Pagan Way was primarily a gateway to pre-Initiatory training, for those who felt called to make that commitment."[15] The first Pagan Way grove was arguably formed in

Chicago by Donna Cole Schultz and Herman Enderle, who had begun writing additional training materials for distribution by at least 1971.[16] Established covens began to use Pagan Way groves to screen seekers, with the groves sometimes functioning as an "outer court" training group for the coven (the "inner court" comprising those who were already initiated). The Bucklands founded the first Pagan Way grove in New York to perform this function for their Brentwood coven. By the end of 1973, Pagan Way groves existed throughout the United States in such places as Philadelphia, Pennsylvania; Commack, New York; Brooklyn, New York; Bronx, New York; Manhattan, New York; Passaic, New Jersey; Chicago, Illinois; Louisville, Kentucky; Woonsocket, South Dakota; and Pasadena, California. *(Ibid n#13)* Contacts included Ed Fitch, Joe Wilson, Thomas Giles, Fred & Martha Adler, Gwydion Pendderwen and Susan Roberts in the United States; and Tony Kelly and John Score in Great Britain. *(Ibid n#16)*

The Brooklyn Pagan Way grove was formed in late 1972 and operated out of the Warlock Shop. It was originally under the umbrella of the Chicago Pagan Way through Herman's contacts with Donna Cole Schultz and Ed Fitch.[17] Its first leader was a man named Justin, who taught it as a Neo-Pagan-oriented system without ties to any particular tradition. Other Pagan Way groups eventually met under the Brooklyn Heights umbrella, as well as several Welsh outer courts that were taught by Eddie Buczynski and Kay Smith and others. Although Herman Slater publicly expressed a reluctance to use Pagan Ways as farm teams tied to specific covens, in practice this often occurred throughout the country. The Brooklyn outer court covens pulled most of their members from the Pagan Way.

Ken Dalton, who first came into the scene in the summer of 1974, recalls "There were a number of covens in Brooklyn, primarily Welsh and Gardnerian. There were groups for somewhat older witches (in their late 20's and early 30's?) There was a group of really young pagans (late teens) and most in their mid-20's. As you've probably heard, it was, for many, a big group dating/sex scene. There were however some groups which were genuinely into the spirituality of the Craft."[18]

The Pagan Ways and outer court covens met in people's apartments, with Smith's Joralemon Street walk-up being the busiest of the lot in the early days.[19] Welsh outer court training began in late 1972, soon after the founding of the New York Coven of Welsh Traditionalist Witchcraft. In January of the following year, Buczynski and Smith added an advanced outer court coven to accommodate the First Degree initiates.[20] As they attained the Second Degree, these members left the advanced outer court and joined the inner court for higher-level training and practice. *(Ibid n#19)*

Training in the New York Pagan Way was based on materials received from the Chicago mailing center operated by Donna Cole and Herman Enderle and, as such, was essentially Gardnerian in its orientation. Slater was also assisted through his contact with Ed Fitch. *(Ibid n#17)* When questioned on the intersection of Gardnerian and Welsh teachings, Kay Flagg confirmed this outer court relationship:[21]

> *That was Welsh Pagan Way, yeah. But we had by that time imported some of the Gardnerian stuff, and the Gardnerian Pagan Way ... We used it because we didn't really have a set ritual for Pagan Way. So there is the truth to the story that we took Gardnerian rituals. We took the Gardnerian Pagan Way because we didn't have set rituals for Pagan Way, so we used the Gardnerian Pagan Way because we liked it.*

Eddie later admitted publicly that, while the laws and rituals in the Traditionalist Gwyddoniaid were unique, they were closely related to Gardnerian Wica, amongst other traditions.[22] There were, in truth, a number of similarities between the practices of the Welsh and Gardnerian traditions. For example, like Gardnerian Wica, polarity was observed in Welsh rites, whether in inner or outer courts. Welsh covens performed a symbolic Great Rite similar to that of Gardnerian Wica. The covens of the Traditionalist Gwyddoniaid also had three degrees. As Buczynski explained in 1973:[23]

> *The degrees are symbolic of the Three Degrees of Learning and Change that the God Gwidion and his Brother Gilfaethwy underwent in the Mabinogi of Math ap Mathonwy. The First is the Deer Degree (Male – Stag, Female – Hind) ... The Second is the Pig Degree (Male – Boar, Female – Sow) ... The Third is the Wolf Degree (Male – Wolf, Female – She Wolf) ... As Gwidion and Gilfaethwy were transformed into three different animals in order to learn about life, so too do we undergo three degrees in order to learn life's secrets.*

Some of the similarities between the traditions can be explained by the slow diffusion of Gardnerian practices into the occult subculture and their adoption by others. One manifest example of this can be found in the Laws as laid down in the Welsh Book of Shadows circa 1972. With only minor changes, the Welsh Laws are virtually identical to those published in Lady Sheba's *The Book of Shadows*, from which they were adapted.[24,25,26] There were some marked differences between the two traditions as well. The format and content of Traditionalist Gwyddoniaid rituals were more derivative of Gwen Thompson's Celtic Traditionalist practices than of Gardnerian Wica. Welsh covens, in marked contrast to the Gardnerians, did not purify their members with binding and scourging, nor did they conduct skyclad rituals, instead wearing red floor-length hooded cloaks. It was the differences between Welsh and Gardnerian practices that helped fuel the debate concerning the Craft legitimacy of the Welsh tradition, not just the similarities between the two traditions.

Some of the differences were fairly revolutionary. For example, the Traditionalist Gwyddoniaid offered membership to those who were not Caucasian. Some of the earliest photographs of Welsh gatherings show Hispanic, black and Caucasian participants unselfconsciously mixed together, in marked contrast to most covens of the day. While polarity was strictly observed in Welsh covens, they were also among the first to openly welcome gay, lesbian, bisexual, and transgender (GLBT) practitioners.[27] In an interview with Hans Holzer, Eddie stated "We do not discriminate against those who, within their private lives, have found love with those of their own sex. However, we work female to male within the circle. Such sexual discrimination has never been a part of paganism, as we see it."[28] Margot Adler, who joined the Welsh outer court coven in 1973, later recalled the "irony of all these gay men in the Craft stressing that magick had to be hetero in nature with male-female polarities observed in Circle."[29] Judith McNally concurs: "Obviously, the GLBT [practitioners] were completely welcome. BUT [Ed] stuck to the old ways of a co-ed coven and teaching and initiation passing male-to-female and vice versa. He pointed out that gays and lesbians who broke out in hives around the opposite sex would have trouble fitting in."[30]

That isn't to say that questions didn't arise. McNally recalls that Eddie was "unsure how to handle the training of one student who declared he was 'a woman in a man's body.' Now how, [Ed] wondered, would a deity be 'drawn down' when the time came along? Well, said the young man (who had a superb sense of humor — and I guess that's the only way the cross-gendered keep their mental health intact), he *knew* he was a woman but he actually did ACT like a man in critical ways, so ... my recollection is the conversation turned non-serious (and a bit raunchy) at that point. I remember saying, 'Well, we could invoke both and see who shows up.' Not the world's worst approach, perhaps. In any case, [Ed's] first NYC coven was a thorough mix of gay, straight, bi and the young man above who defied categorization. A similar mix worked fine in my own coven. I think gays and lesbians who wanted no part of mixed groups simply never approached Ed." *(Ibid n#30)*

The Books of Pagan Rituals

The Brooklyn Heights Pagan Way was typical of others at the time. Students would pay the Warlock Shop for the cost of copying the Pagan Way handouts. Some of those went on to share materials with their fellows, passing these papers from hand to hand to be tediously hand-copied or taken to copy centers for reproduction. However, if the former method was wearisome, the latter was an expensive proposition for most students, with copies running ten cents a page or more (50 cents a page in 2007 dollars), and the common thermographic copiers of the day, with their heat sensitive, bad-smelling and curling paper, left something to be desired. While the Pagan Way mailing centers only charged enough to recoup the cost of copying and postage, the expenses added up.

Part of Herman Slater's business plan for Earth Religions Supplies, Inc. involved establishing a publishing arm for occult works that could then be marketed through the Warlock Shop and through mail order. With the tremendous growth of the Pagan Way in the United States, and particularly with the intense local demand for these materials, Slater saw an opportunity. He decided that instead of running off copies of the materials to be handed out, it was simply more efficient and economical to publish them as a unit. That way, he could print inexpensive copies of the Pagan Way materials and sell them to students while simultaneously using this property as a trial run for breaking into the publishing business. Thus it was that by March 1974, Earth Religions Supplies, Inc. began offering a hardbound edition of the Pagan Way materials via catalogue sales and through the Warlock Shop.[31] The materials were also offered in two softbound volumes, *Pagan Rituals – Volume I* and *Pagan Rituals – Volume II*, the former covering basic Pagan rituals and the latter presenting more advanced materials. The printing quality was very low, with the softbound copies resembling cheaply made bibles, but the prices were well within the means of any student and were certainly cheaper than those of a copying center.[32,33]

Slater had received the materials from the Philadelphia Pagan Way in 1973 that eventually became *Pagan Rituals – Volume I*. The material in Volume I was mostly written by Ed Fitch and Tony Kelly (one notable exception being the Cauldron ritual, which was written by English ceremonial magician William Gordon Gray).[34] Herman procured other material, written mainly by Donna Cole Schultz and Herman Enderle, from the Chicago Pagan Way. That material became the basis for *Pagan Rituals (Advanced) – Volume II*. *(Ibid n#34)* Jonathon Nightshade, an initiate of Donna Cole Schultz, notes that "there was a version of an Anti-War spell which was originally from *Potions and Spells of Witchcraft by Osirus*, 1970. Also, the *Abracadabra Spell* and *Radiant Health Spell* may have come from *Book of Legendary Spells* by Elbee Wright, 1968 ([according to] my research)." *(Ibid n#16)* Although he took the next logical step in their distribution, Slater clearly did not have the copyright clearance to legally publish the Pagan Way rituals and accompanying instructional materials. He just happened to be the first off the mark with a mass market publication incorporating the material. The copyright actually rested with the original authors of those materials, who included Ed Fitch (aka 'Ed Sitch'), Herman Enderle, Donna Cole Schultz, William Gordon Gray, Tony Kelly and others.

Slater and Buczynski guested with the Chicago Temple of the Pagan Way on the first leg of their trip to a Witchmeet gathering in Minneapolis right after the books were released, and left a copy of Volume I for Donna Cole Schultz.[35] *(Ibid n#34)* The Chicago Pagan Way had articles published in the Earth Religion News at the same time that these books were being advertised for sale, so it is highly unlikely that Schultz and Enderle were unaware of them. While there appears to have been no immediate outward reaction to their publication, Nightshade notes that Donna's husband said that she may have been unhappy at the time that their efforts were not credited. *(Ibid n#34)* Even as late as April 1975, Slater was publicly writing of his role in printing the Pagan Way rituals as if it were a matter of public service.[36]

The authors' failure to exercise any controls or even provide a notice of authorship over the Pagan Way materials certainly left the door wide open for their rights to be abused. But the backlash, when it finally surfaced, was the result of Slater's decision to sell the publication rights of the materials to Samuel Weiser, Inc. for $1500 in late 1975. Herman was in a financial bind at the time and needed to raise some cash in order to satisfy outstanding subscription obligations for the *Earth Religion News*, a Pagan-oriented newspaper he started in late 1973.[37] The final combined edition of the newspaper was printed around February 1976. Slater arranged the Pagan Way material for publication by Weiser, wrote the introduction, and also wrote some material to fill what he perceived as gaps in the text to make it flow. Samuel Weiser published the collected material as *The Book of Pagan Rituals* in June 1978. This first Weiser edition noted that the material had been first published in two volumes in 1974 and 1975 by Earth Religious [sic] Supplies, New York. No editor or author information was given in this book, though subsequent editions listed Herman Slater as its editor. *(Ibid n#33)*

Perhaps most egregious in the eyes of many was the fact that the volume published by Weiser did not credit any of the original authors for their work, and certainly no remuneration was directed their way. The books published by Earth Religions Supplies had little chance of making any serious money, but a Weiser imprint was on a higher plane of publishing altogether. Donald Weiser, who headed the firm at the time, reportedly knew nothing of the true origins of the work and thus may be excused for his part in this episode, although the book continues to be published by Weiser/Red Wheel, still with no acknowledgement of its original contributors.[38] Slater was certainly aware of who was involved in authoring the materials, because he was in contact with most of them. In revisiting the issue many years later, Herman insisted that those from whom he obtained the materials were aware of his intention to publish them in order to make the whole more widely available.[39] Ed Fitch, for his part, acknowledged that he expected his work to be freely passed from coven to coven in the spirit of the 1960s. Back then, he never intended for it to be copyrighted or even formally published. In hindsight, Fitch noted sardonically, "I don't think I would be so idealistic if I were to do it again." *(Ibid n#6)*

Joseph Wilson was blunter in his assessment. Writing that the authors of the Pagan Way materials had opted for anonymity in order to encourage its transmission, Wilson complained that Herman Slater had taken advantage of their good will and optimism. Regarding the publication of the Pagan Way materials, Wilson noted, "We'd have been better off doing that ourselves, and maintaining the credit. But then this was the free Hippie era, and freedom was our ideal. Or at least mine."[40] Wilson's romantic memory of the era is somewhat at odds with his reputation for spying on anti-war protestors on behalf of the federal government in 1971, an activity that he confirmed in his own writings and for which he was criticized by some within the Pagan community at the time.[41, 42, 43, 44] Nevertheless, Wilson was correct in that the unauthorized publication and sale of the rights to the Pagan Way materials rightly remains a focus of criticism for Slater's detractors in the Craft.

Chapter 10: The Kids Are Alright

The Children of Branwen

Robert Carey was a fifteen-year-old budding occultist when he began hanging out at the Warlock Shop in late 1972. Herman, recognizing that the teen was both eager to learn and always underfoot, finally offered him a position doing odd jobs that would last until he entered college. Working part-time on weekends while school was in session, and full-time during the summer, Carey cycled through practically every job in the store, from working the counter to stocking and packing herbs, to preparing catalogues and mailings, to ordering books. "I also hung out a lot," he admitted. "In the days before videos I used to loan Herman shopping bags of science fiction. He devoured them and always returned more books than I loaned him."[1]

Carey had become interested in the occult a few years before Buczynski and Slater opened the Warlock Shop, and had written away for Pagan Way materials. "[Joe Wilson] was one of my first Wiccan contacts. I took his correspondence course well before the little shop of warlocks landed from outer space. I also had some nice talks with Ray Buckland when his museum was in Long Island early on."[2] Thus already being somewhat familiar with the Pagan Way teachings and many of the major players in the Craft, Carey and several other teens who hung out at the shop (one as young as fourteen) lobbied to be allowed to study in the Pagan Way and Welsh outer court in spite of their youth.

Inquiries from underage seekers was an issue that was beginning to arise with increasing frequency as information on the Craft was disseminated in the media. Hans Holzer wrote about the phenomenon of youngsters approaching him for help in contacting covens once he began writing about the increasing popularity of Witchcraft as an alternative to mainstream religions. "Some of these are twelve and thirteen year olds whose chances of being introduced to a coven or even a solitary practitioner of 'The Old Religion' are practically nil until they reach the age of reason, or what passes as the legal age. In matters of changing one's religion, people may of course choose their own way but not until they are beyond the reach of parental authority."[3]

This was a problematic situation, especially where the Warlock Shop was concerned. The societal issues and legal liabilities associated with teaching teenagers Witchcraft were serious enough in 1972 on their own account without factoring in homosexual adult males and skyclad rituals. Eddie, Herman and Kay debated how to settle the matter. The risk-averse "just say no" mentality of the litigious and uptight Eighties was still a decade in the future, and to flatly turn people away ran counter to the spirit of the Seventies era and the personalities of those involved. Any underage seeker who wished to study with the Pagan Way was evaluated for emotional maturity and seriousness, and if the seeker passed muster, he or she would be allowed to study — with a letter of permission signed by at least one parent or guardian. As Robert Carey explains, teenaged seekers were required to provide a "letter of permission (of dubious legality) before we could prance about naked waving knives for religious purposes." *(Ibid n#1)*

Still, there was a legal obligation for the adults running the Pagan Way meetings to safeguard their charges while acting in loco parentis. Herman, in particular, took his responsibility seriously. "Mother Herman was always very protective of us," said Carey, "and he may have nurtured the illusion that sex and drugs and Rock & Roll were less prevalent among our group. Possibly a bit less sex, but I'd suspect more of the other two. Nevertheless, there was a tendency to sort of shield us." *(Ibid n#1)* Karen Bartlett, another young member of the group, confirms this: "We were kept out of a lot of the politics that went on at the time."[4]

Like everyone else, the teens and young adults went through Pagan Way meetings and outer court training first, then graduated to the full coven experience. Karen Bartlett (née Chiecorecalls, "The [teenage] Coven formed basically because me, Eddie Chieco), Robert Carey, and Frances [Ronno], were all kids at the time, had gotten into the Pagan Way, and hung around the Warlock Shop almost every day, bought every book we could on Magick and Wicca, and hung on every word of Herman and Eddie. All I can tell you about Eddie really is that I was totally infatuated with him. He was like the Sun God to me. Herman and Eddie thought we were very good [students] and very devoted, and so it was decided by them and other Elders that we should be in our own 'teenage' group, I assume out of the goings on of some of the 'adult' covens that were around. No posting or advertising was done."[5] *(Ibid n#4)*

This coven of younger people took the name Children of Branwen, chosen by Kay to honor the Welsh Goddess of love and beauty. The notion of a teenaged coven appealed to Herman, who may have believed that he could exercise more control and mold their young minds to his way of doing things. "Not that he would cause us any harm," writes Bartlett. "In fact he was extremely protective of us. We went to a Pagan gathering once in the neighborhood. I recall where [an] unstable person who was present decided to sniff roach spray and nearly killed himself. I recall Herman showing up out of nowhere and getting us (the Children of Branwen) all out of there immediately before the cops came." *(Ibid n#5)*

The coven originally comprised Robert Carey, Denny Sargent, Karen and Eddie Chieco, Joe Engeleit, Frances Ronno, Hal Geller, Ria and David Farnham, Artie Jamison and several others. Some people, such as Herman, shuttled back and forth between the adult coven and the teenaged one, while others, such as Artie, Ria and David, quickly graduated into the adult coven. Carey notes, "At times our group was well over the traditional thirteen [members] and very active, with lots of guests. This was our social life. We were not all teenagers, but sure looked like a bunch of hippies, and in some ways we teens found ourselves in charge of [the] adults." *(Ibid n#1)*

By early 1973, the New York Coven of Welsh Traditionalist Witchcraft had very active inner and outer courts. Smith was holding weekly outer court sessions on Sunday afternoons at her apartment. To accommodate the growth in the outer court, the inner court was maturing quickly. While Eddie and Kay continued training the outer court Pagan Way grove, the teaching duties of the "intermediate" outer court coven were eventually given over to the maiden and summoner of the inner court coven.[6] The first few meetings of the Children of Branwen were officiated by Smith and Buczynski as high priestess and high priest beginning in December of 1972.

As Buczynski became more involved with the adult coven and the "intermediate" outer court, he left the youngsters in Kay's hands. The Children of Branwen continued to meet under Kay Smith's watchful eye at her Vaseline Flats apartment. Melda Tamarack (Craft name Katrin) gradually took over from Kay as high priestess of the Children of Branwen at the same time that she began her stint as the maiden of Kay's adult coven.[7] Various males, including Robert Carey and Artie Jamison, acted as high priest for the youth group. As a training coven, everyone was expected to participate and to officiate at some point. Karen became the maiden of the coven, and was soon placed in charge of the Children of Branwen's own outer court.

While they did not openly advertise the existence of the group and generally kept quiet about their activities, word gradually leaked out about the existence of a teenaged coven. The fault partially lay with Eddie Buczynski, who wanted to make a splash in the local community. Zanoni Silverknife remembers that Eddie "had a high sense of theater, which evidenced itself in his artwork and several public rituals he either organized or participated in ... most notably, the Midsummer in Central Park where all [the participants] wore gossamer wings and crowns from a costume and theater supply house. I understood it to be over 50 people at least [in size,] and the public — what the hey — it's NYC!"[8,9]

The fault also lay with Slater, whose protectiveness of the teens had its limits, competing as it did with his desire to publicize the Warlock Shop and promote the growth of the Craft. In October 1973, Herman invited a French film crew, led by director Michel Parbot, to film a ritual of the Children of Branwen at his place on Atlantic Avenue. The members of the coven were supposed to be allowed to view the film before it was released, but the French company reneged on this part of the agreement. It also failed to secure waivers from the participants or their legal guardians, even though many of them were still underage. "I heard it got released in Europe where they didn't need our permission," Karen recalled, "and that they made it really Satanic looking when it was supposed to be a legit documentary. Eddie Chieco said he found it in a Village video place one day." *(Ibid n#4)* The film, *Oh! America*, was released by Antégor in France on October 22, 1975.

Growing Up and Moving On

The Children of Branwen weathered the political storms within the Craft that manifested in 1973 and 1974. Its teenaged members matured and became competent practitioners in their own right. Citing personal reasons, Melda left the coven in 1975. At that point Smith was considering disbanding the group; however, Karen asked to take over as high priestess. Kay was reluctant to endorse that move, which was controversial given that Karen was only sixteen at the time, but she finally agreed, and Karen (Craft name *Althea*) was elevated to the position of high priestess by Herman Slater. Under Karen's leadership, a portion of the group hived off and moved to Borough Park in Brooklyn soon after her installation. There she ran a more eclectic version of the coven with Eddie Chieco (Craft name *Fenris*), whom she had recently married, as her High Priest. *(Ibid n#1, 4)*

Dan Greenberg from Playboy magazine finagled an invitation from Slater to attend the coven for a few weeks in October 1975. Greenberg's experience was written up in his book Something's There (1976).[10] Karen recalls: *(Ibid n#4)*

> *He came to several of our meetings and was quite polite and quiet. I did not know that he wrote for Playboy and Herman thought it was funny when I was a bit shocked by his writing after it was published. I was 16 maybe going on 17 at the time. Dan called me Sheilah in the chapter and described his sexual fantasies about me. He changed our names because we were underage.*

By the late 1970s, the group began to gradually dwindle as the members grew up and went their separate ways. The coven split again. Robert Carey, who was in college at this point, formed a smaller group called the Grove of the Star & the Snake with Denny Sargent and a few others. They were influenced by Aleister Crowley, Austin Osman Spare, Robert Anton Wilson and Chaos magick, and they soon became affiliated with Kenneth Grant's Typhonian O.T.O. Their Grove formed a relationship with Soror Nema, the author of *Maat Magick*. *(Ibid n#1)*

Karen left Eddie Chieco when he began to heavily abuse downers and experiment with heroin. The parting was hard for Karen, who had known Chieco since she was thirteen and they had formed a blood pact as magickal partners. The self-proclaimed street warrior, whose personality, Sicilian good looks, and love of magick and Wicca had first attracted

Karen's attention, journeyed down a dark road after the breakup. He shot heroin and speedballs, and was eventually jailed on suspicion of manslaughter. When Karen finally crossed paths with him again in the mid-1980s, Chieco had contracted AIDS from a Haitian woman he had married and with whom he had shared needles.

A year later on a return visit to New York, Karen saw a glimmer of the old Fenris once more. Chieco had cleaned himself up and, with a local vigilante group, had begun battling neighborhood crack dealers affiliated with a Columbian cartel. He was rumored to be working with an HIV-positive Drug Enforcement Agency agent (whom he was also dating). However, one Sunday the street warrior's luck ran out. Karen and a former covener named Maria Parra, concerned that they had not heard from him for several days, found Chieco's bludgeoned and bloody corpse in the bathroom of his ransacked apartment. At the morgue he could be identified only by virtue of a tattoo of his ex-wife's name, Jeneese – ink that he had been in the process of having removed when death struck him down. *(Ibid n#5)*

The day of Eddie Chieco's cremation saw the worst snow storm to hit New York City in one hundred years. Karen was stuck in the area, and was also stuck with arranging Chieco's funeral as his family wanted nothing to do with the task. She had a series of haunting experiences during this time – unplugged televisions and stereos suddenly coming to life, shower knobs turning on by themselves, the smell of roses where none existed, and visions of blood pouring from the box that held Eddie's cremains. "When Eddie and I were teens we promised that whoever died first would attempt to let the other know they were still around," Karen wrote. "I thought of that with all these phenomena." *(Ibid n#5)* To put his spirit to rest, Karen contacted Ria Farnham, who pulled together a number of members from the old coven for a rite of remembrance where Chieco was proclaimed a God. At this point, the restless spirit seemed to calm down and things returned to normal. Karen eventually remarried, this time to alchemist and occult author Robert Bartlett. All of Branwen's children had grown up and left the nest.

Chapter 11: The Changing of the "Gard"

Rowen and Robat Retire

By 1972, after a nearly a decade of leading the Brentwood Coven, Rosemary Buckland was approaching the end of her time as its high priestess. One major contributing factor to her withdrawal was the increasingly strident environment of the Craft, which was a far cry from the way it had been in the relatively quiet days of the early 1960s when she and Raymond had first started the journey. The internal squabbling within Gardnerian Wica, which had arisen in the aftermath of Gerald Gardner's passing in 1964, had not abated. Sybil Leek, who was not a Gardnerian but who did consider her Horsa tradition to be a kindred path of Witchcraft, wrote in 1971 that "The most unexplained fact about witchcraft today is that it is a religion with a serious schismatic problem; there are almost as many causes for dissension here as in the Protestant faith. Added to this, there are a large number of personality clashes upcoming."[1]

Leek noted that those who followed in Gerald Gardner's footsteps as leaders in the Gardnerian tradition didn't seem to hold a candle to the old man in terms of their attitude or style. Of course, some argued that Gardner was just as self-serving in his approach to the Craft as those who came after him, whether he was courting the press or younger priestess candidates. Yet Gardner, with his grandfatherly mien and wild hair, also had a certain panache and *auctoritas* that seemed lacking in many of the elders in the following generations of Witches. The petty spitefulness demonstrated by the personal fights between individuals, covens and traditions, particularly in the United States, was certainly attractive to the press, but was hardly helping the public image of the Craft. Arguing that many of those who professed to practice Witchcraft seemed to have more in common with Satanism, Leek warned, "What is happening here is sometimes pathetic but mostly horrible, and it will be the greatest detriment to witchcraft's making the fine comeback which seemed to be its potential when the Anti-Witchcraft Laws were repealed. At least Gardner had his merits and was not vicious even to those who were a little different in their ideas." *(Ibid n#1)*

The viciousness to which Leek referred was not only the battles within the Gardnerian tradition, but also the conflict between the Gardnerians and practitioners of other Witchcraft paths. The latter argued that Witches other than those of the Gardnerian persuasion had existed before Gerald Gardner seized the "Witch" label and made it his own. There is some limited evidence to support this claim, both in the United States and elsewhere. Yet many Gardnerian practitioners insisted that modern Witchcraft be viewed solely through the lens of their own tradition, and dismissed anyone who claimed to be a Witch but who was not of a proven Gardnerian lineage. For better or worse, just as with the Saulists in early Christianity, the Gardnerians had both the better press agent in Gerald Gardner, and later in Raymond Buckland, as well as the added desire to take center stage. However, as Susan Roberts wrote in *Witches, USA* (1971), not all Witches were pleased with this publicity-seeking, noting that the Gardnerians did not accomplish this without incurring the resentment of these other groups. As one of her interviewees bitterly complained, "The Gardnerians — particularly because they are Johnny-come-latelies — should be looking for similarities with other American witches, not looking down their noses at us because of our differences."[2] This attitude, though relatively widespread among non-Gardnerian Witches, was also somewhat disingenuous, given the evidence that a number of such groups incorporated Gardnerian materials in their own practices, or formed only after Gardner first began publishing, or even were wholly derivative of Gardnerian Wica.

As bad as the community-wide antagonism could at times be, it was an external problem that could generally be ignored. Of greater concern were internal issues, which led Rosemary to question whether she could trust those within the coven's own ranks. One such incident involved Mary Nesnick, a First Degree member of the coven. Before Nesnick's initiation, the Bucklands' strategy for bringing postulants into the Brentwood Coven had typically been to require upwards of a year of training prior to initiating the student.[3] Hans Holzer, who had spent some time interviewing Nesnick for his book *The Truth About Witchcraft* (1969), reported that this extended training strategy appears to have broken down in Nesnick's case after some resistance by the impatient student.[4] The Bucklands relented and, after a shortened training regimen, initiated Nesnick into Gardnerian Wica on October 30, 1967. *(Ibid n#4)* Mary, who chose the Craft name *Dionysia*, practiced with the group only for a short while before allegedly leaving the group under less than salutary conditions while still a First Degree student. She thereafter applied for recognition as a high priestess in the Alexandrian tradition, within which she became an important figure in the United States. In 1972, Nesnick used the Gardnerian and Alexandrian materials she had received to formulate a new tradition that she called "Algard." There is some indication that her failure with Nesnick damaged Rosemary's confidence in her own ability to adequately evaluate prospective students, and that afterward she hesitated to initiate people for a couple of years.[5]

Perhaps the final issue that precipitated Rosemary's retirement, however, was the unraveling of her marriage with Raymond. Common gossip has it that Raymond was caught having an affair with another woman, though Raymond states that he left Rosemary after discovering that she was having an affair with another man. Regardless of who was at fault (and in many such cases there's usually more than enough blame to go around), the resulting fissure between the reigning high priestess and her high priest threatened the existence of the coven. As their marriage deteriorated, Rosemary decided to go into full retirement and let another couple lead the Brentwood Coven. By doing so, she also effectively removed Raymond Buckland as the high priest of the coven. Two other Third Degree couples were first approached to fill the leadership positions before Rosemary finally settled on replacements for the coven's high priestess and high priest.[6]

Under the waxing gibbous moon of Friday, November 17, 1972, leadership of the Brentwood Coven was passed into the hands of two members, Judith and Thomas Kneitel (Craft names *Theos* and *Phoenix*, respectively).[7] After they gave up their positions, Rosemary and Raymond became elders and advisors of the coven. In the case of Rosemary, this status lasted until 1985, when she withdrew completely from the Craft.[8] For Raymond, this period was considerably shorter. The Kneitels immediately moved the coven four miles from the old covenstead in Brentwood to their home in Commack, New York. The members who were willing and able to make the drive did so with enthusiasm.

Good Omens Gone Bad

Although Eddie had been banished from Gwen Thompson's coven, his desire to find a legitimate lineage within traditional Witchcraft did not abate. Before the troubles in the Brentwood Coven, Buczynski and Slater tentatively considered asking Raymond whether the Bucklands would take them on as Gardnerian students. For some reason, though, they never came right out and asked for initiation. Both men liked Raymond personally, did business with him through the shop, and worked with him out in the community. Their reticence may have had to do with Buckland's apparent dismissal of homosexuals in the Craft in his book *Ancient & Modern Witchcraft* (Castle Books, 1970). Each man would also have had to come to the Bucklands with a female working partner.[9] But after Raymond's retirement as the high priest for the coven, the point was moot as Eddie and Herman no longer had an insider who they believed might have the pull to sponsor them.

Upon assuming control of the coven, Judy and Tommy Kneitel took care to immediately step into their leadership roles so as to provide the group with stability and a sense of continuity. As part of assuming the mantle, the couple made the rounds of local occult shops to introduce themselves to the various proprietors. This outreach was important, given that nearly all coven recruitment was conducted within the shops either by word of mouth or via postings on bulletin boards. One of the establishments that the Kneitels visited was the Warlock Shop. As Tommy Kneitel recalled,[10]

> *Theos and I [first] met Eddie at the shop in Brooklyn not long after we took the coven reins from the Bucklands in late 1972. We showed up one evening and introduced ourselves. Eddie made a big fuss about meeting us, taking us into the shop's back room where he introduced us to those assembled there. ... We dropped in there quite a number of times. It was where to go when you had nothing else to do.*

The two owners, but particularly Eddie, seemed to hit it off with the Kneitels, and over time Judy and Tommy also grew friendlier with them. Judy was a professional astrologer, and Buczynski asked her to draw up his horoscope. Judy did this for him partly as a favor, and partly because Eddie and Tommy shared the same birth date (though Tommy was fourteen years Eddie's senior) and she was curious to see the result. *(Ibid n#10)*

Eddie and Tommy had some interesting conversations during this period. One in particular stuck out in Kneitel's memory many years later. "I had a lengthy discussion with Eddie about the various names of the gods used in Wicca," Tommy wrote. "We both agreed that several of the more commonly encountered names had been publicized, misused and abused to the point where they had become virtually meaningless and useless within the context of a mystery religion. I mentioned that I had stumbled upon a totally obscure and virtually unknown Roman goddess whose name had never been thrown to the wolves. Even scholars argued about who this mystery deity was. Therefore, I liked to regard her as my own personal deity. Eddie's eyes welled up. I could see that he had been caught off guard. He said, 'Don't tell me, she is Angerona.' I was amazed he knew the name. He said that he had once learned that she was the goddess of secret sorrow, and was always depicted with her mouth bound shut. Eddie had never told anyone else, but Angerona was also his own secret personal deity. I was the only other person he ever met who mentioned her."[11] This shared understanding helped forge a closer bond between the two men, and that nascent friendship would prove vital to the survival of the Warlock Shop in very short order.

Early in 1973, the Warlock Shop hit the first of several bad financial patches and was in desperate need of financial help. This problem likely coincided with the need to pay business taxes on their first months of operation, which was a perpetual struggle for Herman. Going to the bank for a small business bridge loan was a non-starter, and most of their friends and fellow occultists were likewise in no position to help the shopkeepers. But, as it so happens, their new Gardnerian friends appeared to be financially stable. The Kneitels ran a mail order business from their home. Judy also held down a job as president of an electronics firm, and Tommy was a writer and editor.[12] The duo decided to go for broke and explained their situation to the Kneitels. "Eddie asked if we could give him a personal loan," writes Tommy Kneitel. "We liked Eddie, and felt this shop was a valuable Craft resource. On a handshake, we loaned him the money. I think we had loaned Eddie maybe two or three thousand dollars. There was no interest charged. Eddie duly repaid most of it in cash within a short time, but asked if he might use merchandise to repay the balance. We accepted this offer as reasonable. Theos and I considered this loan as having been fully and honorably satisfied." *(Ibid n#10)*

The influx of money helped float the Warlock Shop long enough to recover, and Slater and Buczynski were quickly able to increase the store's inventory. With the breathing room afforded by the Kneitel's generosity, they expanded the herb selection and began what officially came to be called the "oils office," a place for mixing essential oils to order for personal scents and for use in spells and incense preparation. For this job they hired a young New Orleans transplant named Clinton Stevens. Clinton, according to his good friend Sally Eaton, "was a nice, well-bred white boy born and raised in New Orleans. He was the epitome of Southern charm, which enabled him to work at a variety of upscale venues and occupations. A florist by trade, Clinton was also a very gifted artist, painter, and clothing designer, as well as a social engineer who arranged introductions, events, parties, et cetera. Clinton was close with the Warhol Factory crowd, especially Candy Darling. He and his friends formed part of her entourage."[13,14]

"I remember Candy with Clinton at one of my own singing gigs in the early 1970s. She was gorgeous even when she was dying," Eaton continues. "Candy Darling had a female roommate [who] ... did spells and so forth, which I think Clinton helped her with." *(Ibid n#14)* Clinton's *nom de guerre* around Warhol's Factory was "Chanel 13." As many people called him Chanel around the Warlock Shop as they did Clinton. The nickname was an arch juxtaposition of Chanel perfume – a nod both at Clinton's skill at blending essential oils and Andy Warhol's own involvement in the marketing of that perfume brand – and WNET New York Channel 13, the same station that had broadcast coverage of the Central Park Witch-In in 1970. "[H]is skill with potions [was] based on the essential oil formulas he had first started collecting as a kid in New Orleans," remembers Eaton. *(Ibid n#14)*

While Clinton was not an initiated *brujo* or *santero*, he had studied with those practitioners in his native New Orleans and brought that knowledge with him to New York. *(Ibid n#6)* Stevens' pleasant nature and mastery of his craft ensured that he was a very popular figure at the shop. While Clinton was friends with Eddie, one of his adoring fans was Ria Farnham, who wrote, "With a choir boy face of innocence, pouty lips, and the most delicate expressions I have ever seen, he could spin magic and voodoo out of nothing. Spells, blending oils, and making mojo were his domain."[15]

In an effort to foster an ecumenical spirit between the Brooklyn Heights Coven and the Commack Coven, the two groups began exchanging guests with one another. "In more pleasant days, Eddie and Herman had visited our coven as guests," Tommy recalled. "Our coven, in turn, visited Eddie's Welsh group in 1973 to celebrate a sabbat. Theos and I also were guests at a couple of his esbats. We liked Eddie's people very much." *(Ibid n#10)* They liked Eddie's people a bit too much, as it later developed.

This open-armed reception stands in marked contrast to the welcome accorded occult author Hans Holzer. Eddie had refused a request by Holzer in December 1972 to attend a ritual of the Welsh coven to improve Holzer's understanding of the group for *The Witchcraft Report*, a book he was working on at the time. In reply to Holzer's request, Eddie replied that the elders of the coven had refused the request. "Very rarely do we invite a witch from another tradition to our rites."[16] And yet, in that same time frame, Eddie was entertaining an entire coven of Witches from another tradition. The reason behind this may have had to do with the cost of such exposure versus the benefit that it provided. From Eddie's perspective, the potential risk of intimate scrutiny before a local audience so soon after the Welsh tradition's founding was outweighed by the benefit of cultivating a close relationship with the Kneitels. The same could not be said for a visit from Holzer, whose writing style and accuracy on the topic of Neo-Paganism Buczynski did not trust.[17] It is not known whether Herman, who was all for free publicity when the opportunity presented itself, concurred with this assessment. But Eddie's decision stood, nonetheless.

Some observers were dismissive of this emphasis on community-building, regardless of the social station of the individuals involved. "The inter-coven socializing, Craft 'ecumenism' and other hallmarks of the Craft community were (for me, at any rate) a waste of time," writes Welsh initiate Judith McNally. Ceremonialist Peter Levenda admits, "I was consumed by curiosity about the Craft for awhile until I began to see that it represented a kind of lumpenproletariat form of occultism rather than a more intellectual, deadly serious approach."[18] From Levenda's perspective, the effort needed to construct and maintain that sense of community was a distraction from the Work that was the basis for being involved with the occult to begin with. But others, while accepting the need for community, described an almost a yobs-versus-jocks kind of dichotomy within the Craft subculture. In this respect, it was odd that the Brooklyn Heights and Commack covens would get along at all, given their differences in composition.

Sally Eaton notes that "Most people associated with the Warlock Shop affected a mysterious, diffident air which included dressing in Ren Faire garb, long black capes or proto-Goth garb." *(Ibid n#6)* Margot Adler adds, "A lot of them were like street kids. And there was a certain thing about the Brooklyn Pagan Way and the Brooklyn [Heights] coven that was very much kind of working class, a little druggie, you know? Most people were really sort of on the outs and they ... were slightly rebellious but they were also not. They weren't going to be the kind of rebellious people who were going to write treatises that were going to get published in alternative journals. They were just very on the outs. People [who] were not what I would call ... making it in the real world in any kind of deep way, except maybe Herman." *(Ibid n#7)*

Conversely, Adler wrote that "the Gardnerians, Long Island people ... they were what I would call middle class. I mean, there were a lot of cops, and firefighters and the people in that coven were like right out of Archie Bunker Middle America. And it was so odd. It was mostly straight, but not entirely." *(Ibid n#7)* Judy Kneitel, in describing her coven to Leo Martello, stated "We are mostly married suburban couples. The gals tend to talk about kids, the PTA, the orthodontist, the new secretary at their husbands' offices, etc."[19] In other words, the two groups were very nearly polar opposites of one another in the social spectrum. Under those circumstances, a close connection couldn't possibly last and, indeed, it didn't, which is a shame.

The fraternization between the two covens began to break down at the Welsh sabbat held on the first weekend of February in 1973. Kneitel remembers the evening as generally being a very happy one. "On that occasion, [Eddie] proclaimed Theos as the Welsh tradition Witch Queen, presenting her with a document signed by all his group's members. She accepted the honor, but only for that one evening. The sabbat our coven attended as guests of Eddie's coven was a lavish and festive event. A lot of people attended. There was abundant food and wine, music, laughter and warm feelings all around. We brought along Rosemary Buckland (Lady Rowen). Eddie conducted the rites, with his usual perfection." *(Ibid n#11)*

Nevertheless, the rite ended on a jarring note. Tommy continues, "There stood upon the altar a large (about two foot tall) and impressive goddess figurine. Just as Eddie was about to end the evening's rituals, he accidentally bumped the altar, ever so slightly. The figurine promptly toppled over and crashed to the floor, shattering loudly into dozens of shards. Everyone was stunned into shock, taking it as a bad omen. This cast a pall on the entire evening. Interestingly, that sabbat marked the beginning of events that triggered the slow and unfortunate disintegration of our relationship with Eddie." *(Ibid n#11)*

It was after the February sabbat that Eddie eagerly put forth his petition to the Kneitels for initiation into Gardnerian Wica. *(Ibid n#10)* The effort invested in the sabbat celebration may have been orchestrated to position Buczynski's request in the best possible light. If that was the case, then it was all for naught. One of the Kneitel's biggest concerns had to do with the end uses that Buczynski would make of their materials.

Eddie had given the Kneitels a First Degree copy of his Traditionalist Gwyddoniaid Book of Shadows. *(Ibid n#10)* "I still have the Book of Shadows Eddie gave me," Tommy Kneitel writes. "His Welsh Tradition Book of Shadows was a work in progress. [T]hese rites were all beautifully written. Eddie was as spiritual as he was gifted as a writer, with natural feel for creating these rituals. He always insisted that [it] was handed down to him. I was told that his higher degree material consisted of Gardnerian stuff, [while he was] telling his coveners it had been handed down to him as Traditional. This eventually created a problem for him." *(Ibid n#10, 11)*

There was certainly some reason for the Kneitels to be cautious in this respect. Mary Nesnick had formed the Algard tradition in 1972 by blending the materials of the Gardnerian and Alexandrian traditions. The allegation that Nesnick made use of the Bucklands' Book of Shadows in this effort sensitized the members of that line to any possibility that their materials could again be placed in danger. Since material from other traditions had already found its way into Buczynski's Welsh book, Judy and Tommy were uneasy about giving him access to their own Book of Shadows. "Basically, various items appeared to be oathbound rites and teachings from several [traditions]. We expressed to him our concern about this reckless approach, fearing that he might publish all or parts of our Book of Shadows. He was unwilling or unable to provide adequate assurance [to us that this wouldn't happen]. ... At that time, Gardnerian materials had experienced minimal publication. We were paranoid. ... Ultimately, we decided against offering him initiation. He became rather cold towards us at that point." *(Ibid n#10)* If the Kneitels felt that the camaraderie between the two camps had cooled at this juncture, it was to become positively frigid with what followed.

Chapter 12: Breaking Up is Hard to Do

Open Questions

The Traditionalist Gwyddoniaid attracted interested seekers from its inception, hungry as they were for a chance to study Witchcraft and heretofore denied the opportunity for one reason or another, primarily due to the scarcity of covens with which to train. Two such seekers, Claudia and Gerard Nero, had become members of Smith's and Buczynski's New York Coven of Welsh Traditionalist Witches within a month of its founding, taking the Craft names of Branwen and Bryce, respectively. By the end of 1972 — a fast advancement, even for experienced practitioners — the couple was placed in charge of an Outer Court Welsh coven for the purposes of training seekers who were ready to advance beyond the Pagan Way system. First Degree initiates were trained within the Outer Court coven as they were ready for advancement to Second Degree, at which time they were moved to the inner Court. Claudia was the maiden of the Inner Court coven, and Gerard was its summoner.[1] The couple began gathering a nucleus of students around them by the end of the year. One of these was twenty-six-year-old Margot Adler, a student who had been initiated by Eddie and Kay in the Welsh tradition after studying for a short time in the Brooklyn Heights Pagan Way.[2]

Adler, who describes herself as a "Cold War red diaper baby," busied herself throughout the 1960s as a member of the Free Speech Movement, protesting the Vietnam War, organizing voters in Mississippi, and showing solidarity with workers in Cuba. She earned a master's degree from the Columbia University Graduate School of Journalism in New York only two years before becoming involved in the Pagan Way, and in early 1973 was hosting a talk show on Pacifica Radio's WBAI (99.5 FM) in New York City. It is fair to say, therefore, that she was both an intelligent and extremely inquisitive woman who was professionally trained to gather, analyze and present information in a cogent manner. These are traits that tend to react poorly to the prevarication that is often associated with Craft history, and the Welsh tradition in early 1973 proved to be no exception to this.

The Welsh Outer Court students had been studying with the Neros for only a month before they began asking their teachers some rather pointed questions about the origins of the tradition. Their questioning started out innocently enough; like many students, they were curious about the history of the material that they were studying. Claudia and Gerard weren't entirely sure of the answers themselves, and in the beginning they could not provide a satisfactory explanation. One of the students' major problems with the history of the Traditionalist Gwyddoniaid, as related by

Eddie and the other initiates, was its alleged age. Margot Adler recalls that "Herman and Eddie were extremely bad about being communicative to new people. ... I was getting more involved in stuff and started reading stuff and I remember Roger and some other people who were in our group just started feeling that there was something wrong. ... [W]e were constantly trying to call up Eddie and Herman and say 'Could we talk to you? Could you really tell us the real history of the tradition?' And they were just completely closed-mouthed, you know, they didn't want to talk about it."[3]

Part of the problem was that there was simply no consistency in the telling of the tale. To Eddie's students, the tradition was positioned as having its origins in the Paleolithic some twelve thousand years in the past. The story that Witchcraft dated back to the Stone Age — what might be referred to as the ultimate "grandmother tale" — was widely circulated in the 1960s and 1970s. Inspired by Margaret Murray's *God of the Witches*, which had been continuously reprinted from the 1930s onward, this highly implausible mythology influenced the writing of respected Witchcraft authors, such as Gerald Gardner and Raymond Buckland.[4] Thus, Eddie was in good company when he repeated this story, even if he had no more basis for it than any of the others.

However, in an interview with Leo Martello in 1973, Eddie told a different story about the age of the Welsh materials, stating that "as far as my own tradition (or any other of the various forms of the Welsh tradition) there are no [published] books of rituals; they have been kept a closely guarded secret for centuries."[5] Buczynski repeated a similar claim in his description of the tradition to *Gnostica News* in May 1973, adding that their rituals and mythologies are "definitely pre-Druidic."[6] Yet the history as related to Hans Holzer in January 1973 had his Welsh tradition dating back only to the twelfth century and involving a family heritage.[7] What Eddie failed to add was that the family to which he was referring was Gwen Thompson's, from whose purported hereditary tradition he had extracted and adapted much of the material that went into the Welsh Book of Shadows. But the original source material that he brought over from *The Cauldron* is believed, by the N.E.C.T.W., to date back only to around the 1600s. Furthermore, even among those who understood and acknowledged *The Cauldron* as the wellspring of the Welsh Book of Shadows, there was a healthy skepticism concerning the provenance of that document and its own grandmother tale.

Eddie's assertion that his Welsh tradition dated at least from the twelfth century was based primarily on the fact that he had incorporated material from the *Mabinogion* into his Book of Shadows. The purported age of the source material from the Mabinogi was thereby conflated with the claimed age of the Welsh book itself in order to lend an air of authenticity to the Traditionalist Gwyddoniaid. Those who knew Eddie confirmed that he regularly informed prospective students and others that the tradition could be traced back to Llewellyn the Great when, in fact, it couldn't be traced back beyond Gwen Thompson's family.[8] Herman Slater was to concede this point some years later, noting "I have been initiated into several traditions. All of their origins are questionable."[9]

This was commonplace in the 1950s through the 1970s, as evidenced by purported hereditary traditions that claimed ancient roots but used variations of the twentieth century Gardnerian Book of Shadows as the basis for their practices.[10] Gardnerian initiate Frederic Lamond wrote that while Gerald Gardner implied that their practice dated in an unbroken line from a time prior to the Witch hunts, "...We all knew that this was improbable."[11] Ronald Hutton, in his ground-breaking book *Triumph of the Moon* (1999), noted "that the terms with which Gardner announced the existence of Wicca ... made it impossible for about thirty years for anybody to gain credibility for a coven unless it likewise claimed to be part of an ancient and enduring line."[12] However, it is one thing to claim that one's teachings are inspired by or derived from an ancient work, but something altogether different to insinuate that they comprise an ancient work in themselves.

Historian Elliot Rose puts a fine point on this, writing that "Few indeed have been those with the audacity to stand forth as the inventor of a spell, a charm, an invocation; few have felt so self-reliant as to admit that they taught themselves what they know of hidden truths. Formal, Faustian sorcery by the individual magus in his study has always been led astray by forged grimoires, concocted ancient traditions and spurious claims to private sources of spiritual information."[13] Tom DeLong (Craft name *Gwydion Pendderwen*), in writing to the *Green Egg* in response to questions about the age of the Gardnerian Book of Shadows, noted that "If a tradition is valid because it is harmonious with the fundamentals of Witchcraft, or if it is derived from an extant tradition, hereditary or otherwise, there is no reason why the Witch should try to antique it further by dummying up an ancient tome, replete with 'ancient' spells and lore."[14]

This caution is as applicable to any current occult tradition that claims antique origins as much as it is to the Traditionalist Gwyddoniaid. For Buczynski to dig in his heels and stake the legitimacy of his tradition on such a shaky foundational myth was a mistake, for by doing so he directed attention away from the beauty and efficacy of his creation and focused it on issues irrelevant to its inherent worth to the spiritual seeker. This focus led to questions about the provenance of the Welsh Book of Shadows, which threatened in turn to undercut its appeal by rendering it wholly specious. Judith McNally ponders this intersection of motivation and outcome with regard to the patrimony of the Welsh tradition.

Judith McNally:[15]

> *I think my comments and recollections [have] made clear that, eventually, I had less than complete faith in Ed's veracity. What I never figured out even to my own satisfaction*

was how much of his uneasy relationship with the truth was conscious manipulation and to what degree he might have convinced himself of his own PR — or, at any rate, that what he saw as a worthy end justified not-too-awful means. I suspect there was quite a tangle of mixed motives at work in him back in the 72-74 period when I knew him. At the least, a sincere spiritual quest was well-mixed with the desire for "an easy gig" that would let him earn a livelihood doing what he most enjoyed — or so it seemed to me. In any event, the "explosion" of interest in the Craft/pagan community back then led many besides Ed down the very tricky path of power-tripping and politicking — many of whom, it would be fair to say, had far more life experience than Ed and presumably should have known better. That doesn't absolve Ed from responsibility for his own actions, of course, but it's only fair to point out that he was hardly the only person on the scene who fell into the trap of sacrificing good judgment and proven methods for quick results that, often as not, backfired.

Similar arguments were made concerning Gerald Gardner's Wica after his passing. As Gardner initiate Lois Bourne notes in her autobiography *Dancing with Witches*, "Whether his portrayal of the craft is an accurately ancient one or a modern invention is only important to pendants [sic] and historians. In the final analysis, the magic works."[16] Of that there is no doubt, at least not among those whose lives have been improved through its practice. Still, were it not for the influence of credulous seekers, whose equation of antiquity with authenticity helped drive the marketing of such claims, occult teachers like Gardner or Buczynski might have sooner evinced the audacity and self-reliance that Elliot Rose found lacking in modern Witchcraft. Closing this loop of purveyor and client, Rose observed that those driven to unlock the secrets of the Universe for personal gain were simply not to be stopped by the lack of the tools to do so. Echoing the words of Lige Clarke, Rose noted, "[If] indeed it was not to be found, it must be invented."[17] Of course, both charlatans and prophets have an odd habit of leap-frogging their way across the pages of the history books. After all, Saul was a despised tax-farmer for Rome who had never actually met Yeshua in the flesh, and yet look at the ultimate influence he wielded in the Christian Church.

Cerridwen's Cauldron Cracks

In appreciation for his work in the Craft and as recognition of his place as a Third Degree elder in the Traditionalist Gwyddoniaid, the New York Coven presented Leo Martello with a silver wolf's head chalice on February 2, 1973.[18] Late the previous year, as a payment in kind for bringing him into the Traditionalist Gwyddoniaid, Leo had inducted

Eddie into his own coven of La Vecchia and raised him to the Third Degree.[19] Martello himself led the blindfolded Buczynski into the initiation site. When the blindfold was removed, Eddie found himself surrounded by a black-robed and masked coven of Continental Sicilian Witches.[20]

Buczynski's initiation into the Sicilian coven and its tradition marked one of the few times an outsider had been allowed into their secretive ranks, according to Martello. While Eddie kept to his oaths after the rite, never revealing to outsiders what took place, he was never truly at home in the tradition. "I have participated in Sicilian rituals which are both grizzly and frightening," Buczynski wrote in 1983. "As far as I can tell, they are extremely old. A mother and daughter Goddess are worshipped who are identical in all respects to Demeter and Persephone."[21] Perhaps, as Colleen McCullough's Lucius Cinna said of the northern Italians, they were "too basic, too close to the old gods," and thus too unnerving for Eddie's comfort.[22]

While his affection for Leo was genuine, Eddie's recognition and embrace of such a prominent member of New York's occult subculture may also have subtly helped establish the bona fides of his coven. Not everyone was impressed with the closeness exhibited between Buczynski and Martello, and at least one writer to *Green Egg* accused Martello of being suckered into the coven by Eddie and Herman.[23] But whatever Buczynski's motivation for awarding the honorarium, the skepticism within the Craft over the legitimacy of his Welsh tradition did not fade, but continued to grow. The questioning did not prevent Eddie from attracting new students, but cracks soon appeared in the united front presented by the Welsh elders he had gathered around himself.

As it turned out, Claudia and Gerard, like Eddie, were also interested in Gardnerian Wica — and, like Eddie, they had struck up a dialogue with Judy and Tommy Kneitel, whom they had met at joint gatherings of the two covens. What passed between the elders of the two traditions was a rather frank discussion, wherein the Kneitels conveyed to the Neros their concerns about Eddie's bona fides to lead a coven and expressed their own doubts about the validity of Eddie's Book of Shadows, which they had had a chance to study for themselves.[24] *(Ibid n#8)* The Kneitels, who had received a copy of the Traditionalist Gwyddoniaid Book of Shadows as a gift from Eddie in 1972, knew the core basics of the Welsh tradition and were able to show the Neros where Eddie had obtained some of his material. As Tommy Kneitel remembered, "Eddie ... began incorporating Gardnerian material into his Welsh Book of Shadows. His Welsh High Priestess, Branwen, rebelled. She recognized this material as having been taken from Gardnerian sources. In the spring of 1973, she quit Eddie's group and asked that Theos and I train her as a Gardnerian."[25]

At a coven meeting in late February of 1973, the Neros made the startling announcement to their students that they were switching traditions. Margot Adler recalled, "I don't know what was happening ... with

Branwen and Bryce, whether they had their own issues and they were suddenly not happy with Eddie, so I don't know exactly what was going on, but ... they finally came to us and said 'We have decided to go Gardnerian. We have decided to change. And you have to make a decision ... whether you're going to come with us or stay with Eddie and Herman and the Welsh tradition.'" *(Ibid n#3)*

This situation might not have arisen if Eddie had been more forthright in his answers to the questions raised by his spiritual family. Margot and several of the other students in the coven, including Lynn and Dwight Hall (Craft names Branwen and Taliesin, respectively), were concerned enough to make a trip to the Warlock Shop to confront Eddie and Herman with the situation. Margot Adler says: *(Ibid n#3)*

> *[T]hat's when we actually went down to Eddie and Herman and said "Look, we have been told that our coven is becoming Gardnerian and that we're leaving and we would like you to explain to us ... the questions we have about the tradition, including this 12,000-year-old stuff." And they wouldn't answer it. Eddie and Herman were both at the store and Eddie was basically kind of like "If you want to question us, then leave. You either trust us, you either believe us, or you don't." That was it. It was sort of like "take it or leave it." And I remember thinking at the time ... "well, the Gardnerian tradition doesn't make any claims except that it went back to 1939. And it's a lot easier to believe a tradition went back to 1939 than it went back 12,000 years. So, I'm not sure I want to continue in a tradition that's based on a lie." That's really the way I was looking at it. It may not have been the way Branwen and Bryce were looking at it, but Branwen and Bryce became Gardnerians.*

Kenny Lowenstein concurred with this version of the event and cut to the heart of the issue, stating, "Eddie lied to his initiates [about the Traditionalist Gwyddoniaid] being Welsh, because he didn't tell them the tradition came from Gwen Thompson and that he changed it a little bit and it was a reconstruction. And there's nothing wrong with [that] if he'd come out and said that up front. Instead he told all of the initiates this went back thousands of years and it's exactly the way it was down thousands of years only with minor changes in a continuous line."[26]

Following the impasse at the Warlock Shop, the students regrouped and made the unanimous decision to stick with Claudia and Gerard. In early March, they gathered together one final time as a Welsh Outer Court coven. Clad in their red robes, all six students were initiated into the First Degree in the Traditionalist Gwyddoniaid. The ritual took several hours to complete. As Margot Adler recalls, afterwards Claudia "suddenly said 'Okay, take off your robes.' And we all threw our robes off, [and] she said 'You're Gardnerians now. Now ... we're going to train you to be Gardnerians. We're going to take you out to Theos and ... you're gonna basically go through the stuff.'" *(Ibid n#3)*

For the next three months, the group traveled out to Commack, New York every week or two for fast-tracked Outer Court training in Gardnerian Wica. On June 2, 1973, Claudia and Gerard were initiated into the Gardnerian tradition and elevated through the Second and Third Degrees.[27] Their students began to be initiated into Gardnerian Wica shortly thereafter. Adler was initiated in early June 1973 and completed her training with her elevation to the Third Degree on December 22, 1974. After their jump to the Long Island coven, the Neros handed over a copy of the Welsh traditionalist Gwyddoniaid Book of Shadows to the Kneitels. Judy Kneitel was then said to have taken the entire Welsh Book and appended it to the Third Degree section of her Gardnerian Book of Shadows and labeled each page with "From an old book of shadows."[28, 29]

There is evidence to support the claim made by some that the Kneitels took an active role in encouraging Eddie's people to abandon him. On July 2, 1973, Roger Pratt visited the Kneitels' home. "Judy took me to the sunroom to show me a 'sham' [Book of Shadows], which was Eddie's Welsh Book," recalls Roger Pratt. "I looked it over, thoroughly impressed by the scholarship and I told her I didn't think it to be [a] sham. She was absolutely CERTAIN it was faked, and had written to them all [Branwen and Bryce's coven] insisting they come and get Re-initiated as Gardnerians and therefore [become] validated. And run they did. There's a note [in my journal] that says they were all going out to be 'initiated' as Gardnerians on June 2nd 1973. Something I looked down upon them for at the time. I was young, but principled, and I didn't understand how much people needed reassurance."[30, 31]

The irony in Judy Kneitel's denunciation of Eddie's Book of Shadows is that, even if one were to believe that Gerald Gardner was given fragmentary Witchcraft rituals by the membership of the Rosicrucian Theatre, we are still left with the fact that Gardner, Doreen Valiente, and others added the bulk of the core material that comprises what we know today as the Gardnerian Book of Shadows. By doing so, they substantially changed it and made it their own — in other words, they turned out a book that was as much a "sham" as Judy insisted of Eddie's Book of Shadows. Kneitel might just as well have declared Gwen Thompson's Book of Shadows to be a fake, and one could argue that she in fact did so by dismissing Eddie's book, which was based in large part on Thompson's. But saying it directly would have made far more enemies than were gained by simply poking a stick at Buczynski's fledgling group.

Despite the turmoil and controversy that followed in the wake of the defection, the Welsh tradition continued to grow as seekers were attracted to the inherent beauty and strength of the rituals and teachings, as well as its relative accessibility. Several people are keen to note that most of

Eddie's people walked out on him, but this isn't true. The Outer Court coven left, but the Inner Court coven remained. The Children of Branwen were unaffected by the crisis and continued to meet mainly under Smith's and Slater's tutelage. Leo Martello noted in May 1973 that "The Pagan Grove of Brooklyn, N.Y. under direction of High Priest Ed Buczynski (Hermes) and Kay Smith (Lady Vivienne) had over 50 people in attendance recently. This rapidly growing Wicca-oriented group enables people to practice Paganism and acts [as] a sort of Outer Court coven and clearing house for prospective covens."[32]

Covens continued to hive off of Kay's and Eddie's Inner Court coven after the breakup.[33] The growth was sufficient to warrant the splitting of Kay's and Eddie's coven into two groups at midsummer of 1973. Smith's coven became known as the Brooklyn Heights Coven of Welsh Traditionalist Gwyddoniaid, and she conducted initiations and elevations throughout that year.[34,35] Eddie remained the high priest of the New York Coven of Welsh Traditionalist Witchcraft, finally taking Judith as his high priestess in June. By August 1973, there were two Outer Court covens in New York City, and one each in Philadelphia, Pennsylvania and Hopewell, Virginia.[36]

Kay Smith elevated Terry Parker (Craft names *Dylan* and *Arawn*) at Midsummer's Eve and took him as her high priest. *(Ibid n#34)* Terry was no newcomer to the Craft. A lapsed Roman Catholic, he had been initiated and elevated in Alexandrian Witchcraft in 1970 by Mary Nesnick in her Brooklyn coven. While acting as Nesnick's high priest, Parker fell out with her over "doctrinal differences" and went his own way later that same year. Hans Holzer devoted the first pages of his book *The New Pagans* (Doubleday, 1972) to Terry's attempts after that break to start a new coven in Manhattan in December 1970.[37] Smith was initiated into Alexandrian Witchcraft by Parker in 1973, in what is now a time-honored tradition of degree-swapping between friends.[38]

Whatever disappointments the Welsh initiates of Claudia and Gerard's Outer Court coven felt toward Eddie's prevarication about the origins of his Welsh tradition, several of them still saw much to value in the rituals and mythology he compiled. According to Kenny Lowenstein, several unauthorized covens based on the Welsh Book came into being within months of the "big breakup," as it came to be called, including one that he joined later that year. "I was initiated into Welsh [in] October of 1973, and I actually joined a group in August of 1973 and that was right after two of the people decided they would start their own ... Welsh group without permission, but they decided to change it and to create their own tradition. They started a group called the Coven of Kyarliad." *(Ibid n#26)*

Another of the early results of this blending of Eddie's Welsh material with that of other traditions was Blue Star Wica, started in 1975 by peace activist Frank Duffner, who had earned a Third Degree in the Traditionalist Gwyddoniaid from Kay Smith.[39] Even Simon, a ceremonial magickian and friend to both Herman and Eddie, was accused of using materials from the Welsh Book of Shadows in lectures he held in Manhattan in 1973 — a claim that he steadfastly denied and that, on the face of it, made little sense, given that his own area of interest was Ceremonial Magick.[40]

Apart from those who were content to continue practicing in the Welsh tradition — and there were many still — and those who were inspired to adapt the Welsh materials for their own, albeit unauthorized, uses, there remained a reservoir of skepticism, if not animosity, toward Eddie and his Traditionalist Gwyddoniaid in the occult community. "For many years Eddie was not looked upon favorably by the N.E.C.T.W. Family, [and] neither was his downline of Covens in the New York Welsh Trad," wrote N.E.C.T.W. archivist Andrew Theitic. "Actually, the N.E.C.T.W. Family didn't recognize the [Traditionalist Gwyddoniaid] people as being of the same family." *(Ibid n#24)*

This hostility was not limited to the N.E.C.T.W. There is some evidence that the outward friendliness initially displayed by the Commack Coven may have been superficial, and that Eddie's Welsh tradition was considered something of a joke by the Gardnerians, particularly after Judy and Tommy had a chance to glance at the contents of the Welsh book. Gwilym Dafydd recalls, "The perceived conflict escalated in 1975 to a stage where [Long Island] Gardnerian covens maintained that a Third Degree Welsh was really only equivalent to a First Degree Gardnerian, or to Gardnerian postulants, because Gwyddoniaid High Priestesses and High Priests weren't snogging and penetrating on the floor in the Circle."[41]

Some have tried to explain this conflict as resulting from an intellectual gap between factions within the community. "I remember that the Gardnerians on Long Island (not Ray or Rosemary Buckland but some of their inductees) were pretty aggressively blue collar," writes Simon. "They were anti-intellectual for the most part (as were many Wiccans then), and looked down at the Welsh Trads for being 'stuck up' emotionally or sexually or something; sort of 'holier than thou.'"[42] While Khem Caigan concurs that many people in the community thought that the intellectual side of the Craft was just "weird," he believes that this mindset was not limited to any one tradition or lineage. As proof, he notes that far fewer books flew off the shelves of the Warlock Shop than did the oils, candles and other material, as demonstrated by the amount of dust that would built up on the merchandise. But he also acknowledges that those who had the greatest animosity for Eddie and his teachings may have been touchy about their own ignorance.[43]

After many years, much of this hostility has gone by the wayside. One demonstration of this sea change in attitude was the effort made by several people in the 1990s to fold certain aspects of the Traditionalist Gwyddoniaid back into the N.E.C.T.W., forming the Welsh Rite branch of that tradition. *(Ibid n#8)* To this day, Kay doesn't know what to make of the big breakup, but she is amused by "all these people calling me Mother. I hear there are still groups who call me Witch Queen." On a more somber note, she adds that she doesn't understand those who badmouthed Buczynski but not her. "Some people gave Eddie a hard time, but accepted me. [But] I came out of him!" *(Ibid n#38)*

Adler was not one to look back, setting aside the Welsh tradition and separating herself as much as practicable from the Brooklyn Heights crowd following her conversion to Gardnerian Wica. With a gay working partner, she left the Brooklyn Pagan Way and started the Manhattan Pagan Way, which began meeting at her Central Park West apartment in the spring of 1973.[44] Margot and Eddie never again spoke with one another after the split. "He didn't really want to have much to do with us. That was all. That was the feeling – you made your decision and that's it. Herman was much more effusive, being Herman, you know. He was a business man. He wanted to maintain your relationship." *(Ibid n#3)* In the first years after severing her ties with Buczynski, Adler was blunt in her assessment of his veracity when asked, although her opinion did eventually mellow with time. *(Ibid n#8)* In her 2006 revision to *Drawing Down the Moon*, she fondly remembered Eddie for the extremely beautiful rituals and poetry of his Welsh tradition.[45]

In the immediate aftermath of the big breakup, Eddie and Herman placed the blame for what happened squarely on the Kneitels, whom they accused of poaching students from the Welsh tradition. *(Ibid n#29)* Regardless of where the ultimate fault for the conflict lay, that was an unseemly act, given the façade of courtliness that was otherwise expected of Craft practitioners. Tommy Kneitel stated that this marked the end of cordial relations between the two groups, writing, "When we agreed to [initiate Branwen], most of Eddie's Welsh people also walked out and sought Gardnerian initiation. That ended Eddie's tolerance for Theos and I on any level whatsoever."[46] It seems difficult to fault Eddie for feeling thus. Looking at it from his perspective, with the big breakup following as close as it did on the heels of the Kneitels' rejection of him for initiation into Gardnerian Wica, the whole bore closer resemblance to an unwarranted vendetta against him rather than an unpleasant series of unrelated events. Once amicable, relations between the leaders of the Commack Coven and the proprietors of the Warlock Shop were to take on the characteristics of a Cold War.

Chapter 13: What's My Line?

The Kentucky Lineage of Gardnerian Wica

In April 1973, shortly after receiving his Third Degree in the Traditionalist Gwyddoniaid, Leo Martello went on sabbatical from the New York Welsh coven. He left the country for six months to do research with Patricia and Arnold Crowther in England. Pat Crowther, who had been one of the last high priestesses to be initiated by Gerald Gardner in 1960, had taken a fancy to the brash Sicilian-American writer who wasn't afraid to speak his mind. Later that April, Martello stated that he had been brought into Gardnerian Wica "up to third" by the Crowthers, for whom he wrote the introduction to their 1974 book *The Secrets of Ancient Witchcraft with the Witches Tarot.*[1,2] Leo's claim of Third Degree status has been disputed by some, although Crowther initiate Steven Critchley confirms that Patricia told him that Leo had been brought in.[3] That Leo respected the independence and scholarship of the Crowthers, and their loyalty to the memory of Gerald Gardner, was clear in the text he wrote for them. It was these traits that persuaded the *Stregone* to seek initiation into a tradition for which he had publicly stated that he had no use, based in large part on the actions of its adherents in the States. Martello's initiation heightened Eddie Buczynski's desire for Gardnerian credentials.

When Eddie sought initiation into Gardnerian Wica via Judy and Tommy Kneitel in early 1973, his inquiry was rebuffed. Relations between the Warlock Shop and the Commack, New York coven deteriorated further after it was revealed that the Kneitels had interfered with the Outer Court Welsh coven of Claudia and Gerard Nero in late February of that year. Buczynski's hopes of persuading any of the New York Covendom to initiate him were further stymied by the loyalties those covens owed to the Kneitels via the Long Island Line.[4] Eddie began looking outside of New York for a high priestess who would be willing to initiate him into Gardnerian Wica, and he found just such a woman in Patricia Siero of Paterson, New Jersey. Buczynski and Slater had met Siero at the shop and knew that she shared an interest in the Gardnerian tradition. Tommy Kneitel believes that Herman Slater arranged to fly Patricia Siero to Louisville in order to be given all three Gardnerian degrees in one day. The story goes that this he did this with the understanding that Siero would return and initiate Slater and Buczynski.[5] Whether or not that was true, what is known is that Patricia traveled to Louisville, Kentucky to receive all three degrees in Gardnerian Wica from Fran Fisher under a dark moon on the evening of Saturday June 30, 1973.[6]

Fran claimed to have been elevated to the Third Degree in Gardnerian Wica at the hand of Rosemary Buckland and, under the Craft name of *Theo*, was placed over the Louisville, Kentucky Covendom on

August 5, 1965.⁷ With her chosen high priest and husband, Gerald (Craft name *Thain*), Fran began what later came to be called the Kentucky Line of Gardnerian Wica in Louisville, Kentucky. Raymond Buckland remembered in a 2007 interview that "The very first coven to branch off from ours was in 1965 ... with Fran and Gerry Fisher (*Theo* and *Thain*) from Kentucky."[8, 9] Patricia Siero (Craft name *Sira*) was placed over the New Jersey Covendom by Fran. *(Ibid n#6)* Siero took as her high priest her husband, Glenn Siero (Craft name *Ragnar*). Eddie had struck up a correspondence with the Fishers in 1971 when he was searching for a coven in which to be initiated.[10] Another common link between the two was Ray Buckland, who was on good terms both with the Fishers and with the owners of the Warlock Shop.

Patricia made the perfect bridge between Louisville and the greater New York area, being not only friendly with the folks on both ends but also, to paraphrase Herman Slater's words, "independent of the Long Island conspiracy" that had thus far prevented Eddie and himself from being brought into Gardnerian Wica.[11] The weekend after she returned from Kentucky, Siero initiated Buczynski and Slater into Gardnerian Wica.[12] Both men were elevated through the Second and Third Degrees, thus achieving the standing in the Craft for which Eddie had so earnestly been searching.[13, 14, 15] Even better, he was now a Gardnerian initiate who was not in the Kneitels' downline, and therefore not answerable to them. Having finally achieved his goal, Buczynski now needed a high priestess of his own in order to run a Gardnerian coven, and he found one in a German transplant to the States, Renate Springer.

Renate had first wandered into the Warlock Shop in late 1972 to pick up some books on Witchcraft that Ray Buckland had recommended during her visit to his museum. "I was interested in Wicca from reading *Witchcraft from the Inside* and I went to see Buckland ... and he told me what books I should read to help me, and I guess he must have told me about Herman's store."[16] Renate was a tall, beautiful blonde with a pronounced German accent and a worldly mien. Peter Levenda recalls her as "a striking European woman with a great deal more sophistication than the Warlock Shop could easily contain. She was interested in occult manuscripts and grimoires, especially those in German, Italian, etc. and seemed more of an all-around occultist than the kind of woman Wicca was attracting in those days."[17] She was very comfortable around gays and lesbians, having hung out in the arts community in Berlin in the 1950s, and so wasn't put off by Slater's or Buczynski's open, and sometimes rather flamboyant, homosexuality. *(Ibid n#6)*

Eddie was bedazzled by the older woman's European refinement, and Renate was impressed with the younger man's intelligence, Craft knowledge and good looks. Renate was thirty-eight years old at the time, while Eddie was just shy of his twenty-sixth birthday. This was yet another instance of Buczynski being attracted to serve as high priest with a strong older woman. Their talks over the next few months strayed, unsurprisingly, to their mutual interest in Gardnerian Wica, and Buczynski thought that Renate would make an excellent high priestess and working partner if he could ever secure his own initiation into the tradition.

Once he was initiated and elevated to Third Degree, Eddie lobbied Patricia Siero to make Renate a Gardnerian high priestess so that they could form a coven of their own. Patricia readily consented, the prospect of already having a hived coven to her credit being a powerful draw in an era when the title of "Witch Queen" was becoming a *de rigueur* expression of one's standing within Craft social circles. Renate was initiated and elevated to Third Degree in Gardnerian Wica in Paterson, New Jersey, on the evening of July 11, 1973 and, as the Lady Hela, was placed over the Brooklyn Heights Coven of the New York Covendom.[18] Buczynski acted as the presiding high priest at this ceremony.[19] Renate formally took Eddie as her High Priest that same evening, and together they formed and ran the Brooklyn Heights Coven. Slater was then elected to this coven.[20] *(Ibid n#14)*

Though ostensibly based out of the Warlock Shop, along with an accompanying Gardnerian Outer Court coven, in reality the groups met at the Brooklyn apartment where Renate lived with her husband and two small children. Renate's familiar, an ornery black cat named Pent, would lay in wait during these visits, jumping out of cupboards at coveners and trying to pull Eddie's athame from his satchel when he set it within reach. *(Ibid n#16)* Kathryn Frank remembers Eddie telling her of a time in the middle of ritual where the cat decided to fix his claws onto Eddie's bare calf. "Oh man, I levitated, I was so scared," he laughingly told Frank. "I didn't know what the hell we'd managed to invoke."[21]

Roger Pratt recalls being in the Warlock Shop on a Saturday in early March 1973 with his high priestess when Slater popped out of the back room and asked if they wouldn't mind running down the block to check on the Gardnerian Outer Court group. "He gave us the address and we popped on round to what appeared to be someone's garage (there was a motorcycle in the center of the circle)," Pratt recalls. "A woman named Renate was the high priestess and someone named Wayne was the High Priest. As everyone circled round and round the energy felt like a dryer when your sneakers make it all weighted incorrectly and it keeps banging. The energy was very wrong." It turned out that Renate and Roger's High Priestess, Kathy, were the only women in the circle. All of the other "women" present turned out to be men in drag. "Afterwards, we rushed back to the shop to tell Herman that he should have warned us, [only] to be answered with, 'Oh yeah, you hate gays!' Oh man. He was consistent."[22,23]

After taking Terry Parker as her high priest, Kay Smith continued to shepherd her flock of Welsh students and hived covens. She too expressed interest in being brought into Gardnerian Wica. Since she had been using the Gardnerian Pagan Way materials for the better part of a year to train Welsh students, Kay already had a basic understanding of the Gardnerian approach to ritual and magick. Renate traveled out to a cabin in Cherry Grove on Fire Island where Kay liked to spend some of her free time. There, on the Full Moon of September 12, 1973, Springer and Buczynski initiated Smith and elevated her to the Third Degree in Gardnerian Wica. Kay took the Gardnerian name of *Goewyn* and was placed over the Riverside Coven of the New York Covendom.[24] She acknowledged Renate's leadership with a signed letter stating, "Let it be known that we, the Riverside Coven of the New York Covendom, recognize the Lady Hela as our Witch Queen." *(Ibid n#16)* Terry was then brought into Gardnerian Wica by Kay and became her Gardnerian high priest, in addition to his role as her high priest in the Welsh and Alexandrian traditions. That same evening, Kay cross-initiated Renate into the Traditionalist Gwyddoniaid. *(Ibid n#19)*

The Arte of Legitimancy

Under the circumstances, having been rejected by the Long Island Line for initiation and then suffering the loss of an entire Outer Court Welsh coven to the Kneitels, it was probably too much to expect Slater and Buczynski to go about their business quietly after joining the Gardnerian tradition. Herman in particular felt a perverse need to wave their newly minted credentials in Judy's and Tommy's faces, and did so late in the summer of 1973. It was with some surprise, then, that Judy Kneitel's response was to inform Slater that Fran Fisher was not a legitimate Third Degree Gardnerian high priestess. As a result, Judy continued, Slater's and Buczynski's initiations were invalid and unrecognizable, as far as she was concerned. Now the Fishers' Louisville Coven had been operating since 1965 and significantly pre-dated the advent of the Kneitels to the Craft, it being the first coven to hive from the Buckland's Brentwood Coven.[25] The Fishers were not in Judy Kneitel's downline, but rather traced their lineage to the recently retired Rosemary and Raymond Buckland. Therefore, Judy's pronouncement should have carried absolutely no weight of authority. However, her claim was bolstered by Rosemary, who (the Kneitels said) asserted that she had never raised Fran Fisher to the Third Degree.

The basis for Judy and Tommy Kneitel's opinion that Fran Fisher was not a legitimate Third Degree lay in what Rosemary Buckland had allegedly told them, which is to say that "Theo was a [Second Degree] who had split with Rowen's coven years earlier, and was not heard from by Rowen again. She was not of sufficient degree to initiate [others]." *(Ibid n#5)* As Kneitel explained it, "The story goes that Herman paid the airfare to fly Ray to Louisville in order to cast the circle and elevate Theo to [Third Degree]. The Gardnerian tradition does not recognize male cast circles as valid." *(Ibid n#5)* Therefore, Fran Fisher's elevation to Third Degree was not accepted by the Commack Coven.

Raymond Buckland, on the other hand, denies this, stating that he did not elevate Fran in 1972 and that any talk of Herman paying for him to travel to Louisville was preposterous. Buckland's point does seem to be supported by Slater's well-known parsimoniousness, not to mention his perpetual shortage of funds in those first years of the Warlock Shop. Raymond has consistently stated that the Fishers stayed with the Bucklands in Brentwood, New York in 1965 and received all three degrees there at that time. "Rosemary and I brought in Theo and Thain in August of 1965," Buckland writes. "Theo was initiated on August 1, took 2nd on August 3, and 3rd on August 5. Thain the same dates. Theos, of course, was not brought in until April 10, 1973."[26] *(Ibid n#9)*

Buckland also noted that in every case but one, he has always abided by the American rule on female-cast initiatory circles. As he said in a 2007 interview, "The one single exception had been when I originally brought-in and raised Rowen so that we could start the American line of Wica, back in 1964. But that had been done under the express 'orders,' one might say, of Gerald Gardner himself after conferring with Olwen and others, and it was seen as the only possible way of getting things started in the United States." *(Ibid n#8, 9)* Gardnerian Wica has no equivalent to the Papal *epistola decretalis*, that is say a vehicle to set aside its own Laws. Thus, Rosemary Buckland's own tenure as high priestess had to have at least started out as invalid under this rule, since she had practiced and taught for almost 6 months based solely on Raymond's cognizance before her degrees were all re-done by under the supervision of Monique Wilson in mid-1964.[27]

By this same reasoning, one could argue that many of the British lines might also be considered invalid (from the Long Island standpoint, at any rate), as Gardner sometimes made high priestesses without female-cast initiatory circles, and this error would have propagated through entire downlines. Dr. Ronald Hutton, author of *Triumph of the Moon*, believes that this would have been in character with how other of Gardner's high priestesses were made over the years. "[This] certainly was the case when he brought in Doreen Valiente, Olive Greene, Patricia Crowther, and others," writes Hutton.[28] Two other such examples, according to Gardnerian researcher Philip Heselton, are Barbara Vickers and Olwen Greene.[29] Dr. Hutton continues, "In 1950s Britain, with so few Wiccans around, it was considered sufficient for any second-degree person to initiate another of the opposite sex, single-handed. Among old-fashioned British Gardnerians, this is still the case, and the sensible rule for a religion which grew from very small numbers and it is still thin on the ground in some places." *(Ibid n#28)*

Gardnerian elder Frederic Lamond hedges on this interpretation, however, writing, "Gerald tried generally to have one of his High

Priestesses from an earlier line of his present, at least for the 1st degree, so that she could draw the circle. Lois Bourne ... drew the circle for the initiation of Eleanor Bone, and probably did for Monique Wilson as well. Once a priestess had got her 1st degree, Gerald assisted her in drawing the circle for her 2nd and 3rd degrees, which followed very quickly."[30] But, as Philip Heselton, writes, "I think the necessity for a High Priestess to cast the circle originated in America. It may be that Monique Wilson always cast the circle herself, for reasons unconnected with precedent or rule, and that this was misinterpreted by those who took the Craft to America. This idea never caught on in England. ... I've certainly never come across anything which suggested that it was Gerald's practice to require a High Priestess to cast a circle."[31]

Heselton's understanding is supported by descendants of Eleanor Bone in the United States. "Donna [Cole Schultz], and I, come from the Rae Bone branch, now referred to as the Whitecroft Line," writes Roger Pratt. "In this English Gardnerian line, Second Degree witches can initiate others up to 2nd Degree, and the Priestess runs the Circle from Beltane through Samhain, and the Priest from Samhain to Beltane. Also, the circle can be drawn by either the Priestess or the Priest, or anyone who is designated to do so. We don't have that 'Lady's only' thing that Monique [Wilson] must have added." *(Ibid n#22)*

It appears, then, that this practice has not been followed everywhere, and that the patriarch of Gardnerian Wica, Gerald Gardner, did not even consistently follow it himself. This would seem hardly to constitute the hard and fast rule that certain American practitioners have made of it. This precedent appears to have been set when Gardnerian Wica crossed the Atlantic, and was instituted by Monique Wilson shortly after the death of Gerald Gardner in February 1964. The change in requirements was likely accepted by Rosemary Buckland when she agreed to travel to Perth in mid-1964 to have her degrees redone, and was then subsequently institutionalized by the Brentwood Coven.

Consequently, there may be some justification for Herman Slater's 1989 opinion that the American practitioners of Gardnerian Wica, following the precedent set by Monique Wilson, had emasculated the high priest by taking away his equality to the high priestess.[32] It is unclear why Slater would have remained so bitter over this issue, and for so long. On the one hand, it might support the Kneitels' charge — that Raymond Buckland did cast the circle to elevate Fran Fisher to the Third Degree in violation of the rule instituted in Monique Wilson's line of Gardnerian Wica — despite the fact that the evidence points against this. Conversely, however, one could argue that Slater's residual disgust with the rule had more to do with how it was abused in supporting a decision that was totally without merit and based upon an untruth — which is to say, that same accusation against Raymond Buckland.

But, all this aside, why had issues of a person's legitimacy within the Craft even risen to this level of conflict? Buckland himself, unfortunately, seems to have played a role in raising this issue in 1970 when he began to rail against "pseudo-witches and spurious covens" who were riding the coattails of the Witchcraft movement because it was the "in" thing.[33] During the 1960s and 1970s, there was a perceived need to erect a defense against poseurs who were, with increasing regularity, attempting to infiltrate the ranks of or pass themselves off as Gardnerians. As with the Masons, initiates of Gardnerian Wica used pass-phrases to determine whether an unknown claimant was truly an initiate of the tradition — the most important of which being the secret names of the Goddess and the God that are used at each degree level. Another means of assessing their legitimacy was through the presentation of lineage documents. A Gardnerian high priestess or high priest, upon reaching the Third Degree, was typically given a copy of the lineage document for each high priestess in their lineage dating back to Monique Wilson (*Olwen*).

The lineage document, also called a "vouch," initially came into use as an additional way for initiates to prove from which high priestess and coven they originated, a means to establish their spiritual consanguinity, as it were. Various combinations of features were used, depending upon the high priestess, to authenticate the vouch. These could include a signature, a photograph of the initiating high priestess taken nude while in Circle (and in a specific pose), a sigil or wax seal ring impression, and the use of particular phrases (e.g., *Je le Veult* — I Will [It]). The pursuit of such documentation, and the endless quibbling over lineage "purity" that it came to engender, later caused cynics both within the Craft and without to derogate the collection of vouches given to a Third Degree initiate as "puppy papers," so-called for the documents issued for registered dogs. However, unlike an American Kennel Club registration, the possession of an otherwise authentic vouch (or even knowledge of the secret names) was not an immutable statement of legitimacy.

When the Kneitels first called Buczynski's and Slater's initiations into question, Herman sent Judy Kneitel a copy of Fisher's 1965 lineage document to prove their case. As Tommy Kneitel later recalled, "It was in Ray's distinctive handwriting, including the signature. It did not appear that there was even any attempt to make a reasonable facsimile of Rowen's signature. Rowen came over to our house and looked at it, laughed, then wrote 'This is not my signature! Rowen' across the letter. Then the letter was mailed back to Herman."[34, 35] Raymond Buckland disputes the notion that the vouch was counterfeit, writing, "Rosemary never did say it was a forgery (since she and I were the ones who initiated her)." *(Ibid n#35)* While acknowledging that the calligraphy of Fran Fisher's vouch was in his hand, as were several from his tenure as High Priest of the Brentwood coven, he steadfastly maintained that the signature on the document was that of *Rowen*. Upon being presented with a copy of the vouch in question, Raymond responded, "Yes, that's the 'official' note from Rowen to Theo. It was actually penned in my own fair hand and then signed and sealed by Rowen. It was given to Theo on being taken to Third IN NEW YORK (again, no trip [by me] to Louisville), perfectly validly."[36, 37] *(Ibid n#9)* Unfortunately, it appears that Rosemary never publicly refuted the Kneitel's assertion that it was a forgery, either.

The very idea that the vouch was forged was belied by the fact that as early as 1966, a booklet published by the Buckland Museum of Witchcraft & Magick acknowledged the existence of a Gardnerian coven in Kentucky that was descended from the Brentwood Coven.[38] After Rosemary Buckland's retirement, Gerald Fisher confirmed his own belief in Fran's status by referring to their Louisville coven as being "led by the Lady Queen Theo...the oldest active Gardnerian high priestess and Witch Queen in the United States today."[39] Under the rules of Gardnerian Wica in place at that time in the United States, a coven could not hive until the high priestess placed in charge of it had reached the Third Degree. Ed Fitch, in his book *A Grimoire of Shadows*, writes of exchanging Pagan Way and Outer Court training information in the late 1960s with the "original Gardnerian coven in Louisville, Kentucky," whom he writes of as working to expand Gardnerian Wica in the south during that period.[40] The "very strong and influential Louisville coven" to which Fitch refers was that of Fran and Gerald Fisher.[41] *(Ibid n#10)* Presumably, Rosemary Buckland had had at least six years in which to dispute the validity of the Louisville coven, but did not do so until late in the summer of 1973. So how could Rosemary claim that she never raised Fran when the evidence overwhelmingly supported the conclusion that she, in fact, had?

The answer to this question may lay in the manner in which control is exercised within the American branch of Gardnerian Wica. Order is maintained within a coven by the High Priestess, and within groups of downline covens by their titular "Witch Queen," the upline high priestess to whom they owe their position (or their fealty, following this *fausse noblesse* posturing to its conclusion). In theory, covens operated independently of one another. In reality, however, an upline high priestess could apply considerable pressure to a downline high priestess — essentially for life — to ensure that they toed the line drawn by the upline high priestess. This pressure could be applied through several means. Banishment, for example, is a tool a High Priestess may use to rid her own coven of persons who, for whatever reason, are out of step with the leadership or the group. Banishment, however, does not necessarily disenfranchise an initiate, who could theoretically apply to join another coven or, if of sufficient level, start their own coven.

A more forceful method of control was for an initiator to "recule" their initiate. From the French word *reculer*, meaning "to go backwards," to recule a Gardnerian initiate was essentially for an initiator to unmake his or her initiate as if they had never been initiated. By doing so, every initiation conducted by the reculed high priestess or high priest would also be rendered void. It was a rather dramatic way to deal with a troublesome initiate — but not nearly as final as when an initiate's "measure" was used against him or her. The measure, taken during the initiation ritual, is a string knotted in a certain manner to show various body measurements of the initiate, and containing samples of the initiate's blood and hair. Usually kept by the initiating high priestess for the life of the initiate, the measure is a symbolic representation of the initiate's body and soul that can be used to curse and destroy the offender in a ritual.[42] Reculing an initiate or using their measure against them are acts generally reserved for the worst bad seeds in the tradition, such as oath-breakers who endanger their tradition or their fellows.

A high priestess could also opt to exercise control in a more moderate manner simply by revoking the vouch given to an initiate. By revoking a vouch, the high priestess refuses to acknowledge to others that the reputed initiate had ever been hers. While this action does not concurrently revoke the degrees earned by the initiate as a reculing would, it does call his or her legitimacy into question, since there is no independent way of verifying that he or she is genuine. In cases where the upline high priestess is deceased, a fellow coven mate or other vouched-for initiate who has circled with the person in question might be called upon to vouch for the initiate. However, this rarely occurs when the upline high priestess is still alive and has refused to vouch for the initiate herself. The covenmate might also find his or her own vouch in jeopardy for having the temerity to speak up for the one who is currently out of favor.

What this usually means for the initiate is that Gardnerian practitioners in that lineage and others will shun and refuse to recognize them or their downlines. This, in turn, could also cause potential students to avoid the high priestess or high priest selected for this punishment. In some cases, this shunning may be augmented by the ungallant *schadenfreude* that others experience while planting their tongues, like sharpened bolines, into the reputation of the hapless recipient. Therefore, presenting lineage papers to another as proof of one's lineage is of little help to an initiate when the purported initiating high priestess refuses to validate them to others. In that case, the vouch is quite literally not worth the paper upon which it is written.[43] Like a reversal of Peter to Christ, all an initiator had to do was to deny the initiate.

Patricia Crowther notes, "Perhaps choosing members for a coven is the most difficult thing to do, as people who want to find out what something is will put on a wonderful act of sincerity and promise anything. Once they are accepted, their real self comes out and the veneer of sincerity is quickly broken. A coven can easily initiate the wrong kind of person if they take them at face value."[44] When used responsibly, the three control methods discussed above can act as a safety mechanism to bring to heel truly noisome individuals who have either successfully slipped through the vetting and training process undetected, or who have otherwise completely run off the tracks later in life.

The flaw in this system of control is that the word of a Gardnerian high priestess is law, and that all three methods can be exercised unilaterally. It is also assumed that the high priestess exercising this authority is mentally stable, mature in outlook, even in temperament and consistent in her application of the rules. Unfortunately, this is not always the case (if it were so, then such methods of control might never have been considered necessary). With no one to gainsay her, such a coven leader could arbitrarily mete out punishment for even the most petty of reasons. For example, if the high priestess in question were a homophobe or a racist, she might revoke the vouch of an initiate who, against her wishes, brought a homosexual or a person of color into her downline.

To be fair, Gardnerian Wica was not the only occult group known to toss people out. Neo-Pagan groups were known to have done so, as well as ceremonial groups such as the O.T.O. Mainstream churches have all expelled both priests and laity from time to time. The difference between the Christian churches and Wiccan covens is that the churches usually have a procedure for assessing the "guilt" and the appropriate actions to be taken in any given case, and the process is almost never under the control of a single individual — especially one who has, like the Queen of Hearts, the unchecked power to "behead" anyone who disagrees with her. In the case of Rosemary Buckland, a combination of issues may have led to the allegation that she had not signed Fran Fisher's vouch. The most likely explanation is that Fisher's vouch had not been forged; it had been revoked.

Several factors could have influenced a decision by Rosemary to revoke Fisher's vouch. Certainly one of the Kneitels' main concerns in admitting Buczynski into Gardnerian Wica was that they knew that Eddie already had a track record of taking material from one tradition and converting it to an unauthorized use, as demonstrated by the Traditionalist Gwyddoniaid Book of Shadows. Judy and Tommy feared that the same thing might happen with the Gardnerian Book of Shadows (just as it had with the Gardnerian Pagan Way materials), or worse — that they would be exposed through publication.[45] *(Ibid n#5)* Of course, one could argue that once Buczynski had been given the materials by Patricia Siero in July 1973, the horse had effectively left the barn, rendering further protests moot. At that point, the conflict seemed to shift from doctrinal concerns to personal animosities.

During this period, considerable anger was directed toward Raymond Buckland and anyone perceived to be allied with him by members of the Commack Coven and its downline. Originally, the reason for this anger was most likely rooted in the circumstances surrounding Raymond's divorce from Rosemary. As has sometimes occurred in other covens down through the years, the finger-pointing and choosing of sides within the coven following the breakup of their relationship disrupted the relatively fragile social and spiritual fabric of the local Craft community. Such was the case with the Buckland divorce, which, one observer noted, nearly split the Kneitels' coven at its outset.[46]

The extended membership of the Commack Coven generally, though not unanimously, came down on Rosemary's side and closed ranks against Raymond. Undercut by the very group he had founded, Buckland left the coven in early 1973. *(Ibid n#5)* Shortly thereafter, he moved to Weirs Beach, New Hampshire, where in 1974 he married Joan Helen Taylor (Craft name, *Taza*).[47] Raymond re-opened his Buckland Museum of Witchcraft and Magick and began teaching mail-order courses. He sold cassette tapes and Craft merchandise to make some additional income, gave lectures and made public appearances to promote his books, and taught classes at New Hampshire Technical College.[48] *(Ibid n#5)*

Buckland also continued to write. In his fury against what he called the power-over politics and ego-tripping that had forced him from the coven that he had founded nearly a decade earlier, Buckland began to isolate himself from Gardnerian circles. He took off in a new direction, focusing his efforts on developing the material that was eventually published in 1974 as *The Tree: the Complete Book of Saxon Witchcraft*.[49, 50] The first rite of the tradition that he named "Seax-Wica" occurred at Samhain 1973.[51]

Seax-Wica officially debuted in the pages of the Yule 1973 issue of the *Earth Religion News*. In his announcement, Buckland made no bones about the fact that he had created Seax-Wica, something which he had formerly criticized in other paths that arose in modern times while the myth of Wica as an ancient survival still held the popular imagination. The Seax-Wica tradition was designed to minimize the chances for an entrenched, abusive hierarchy by providing for the election and removal of persons in leadership positions. Raymond also made it clear from the outset that gays and lesbians were welcome in this path, even covens made up solely of homosexuals — a concept that he had also criticized just four years earlier.[52] *(Ibid n#33)* But perhaps the greatest irritant to Buckland's critics within Gardnerian Wica was that Seax-Wica allowed for self-initiation by people who went through no screening process whatsoever, using a book accessible to anyone who could come up with the cover price, thereby removing all the Mystery from the process. After *The Tree* was published, Tommy Kneitel felt compelled to challenge Buckland's actions, charging that his former high priest had abandoned in the name of profit the very principles on which he had for so long lectured his students and the public.[53]

The Kneitels considered Raymond's actions — leaving the Commack Coven and, soon thereafter, developing Seax-Wica — tantamount to a complete abandonment of the practice of Gardnerian Wica. In rejecting Fran Fisher's vouch and Eddie's lineage, Tommy noted, "Ed's claims to being a valid Gardnerian initiate were based solely upon a document we deemed as counterfeit, plus the vouch of someone [Raymond Buckland] who had left the Gardnerian Trad for another system before the fact. We did not accept that as proof of valid Gardnerian lineage. Incidentally, neither did other Gardnerians known to us."[54] However, in none of Raymond Buckland's public criticisms of Gardnerian Wica did he disavow his place in that tradition, nor did he destroy or leave behind any of the books and papers associated with his practice as someone who intended to leave the practice might reasonably be expected to do. Furthermore, this "other system" to which Kneitel refers was Seax-Wica, the creation of which Buckland did not announce to the world until December 1973, long after the storm over Eddie's and Herman's legitimacy within the Gardnerian tradition had broken. *(Ibid n#49)* Regardless of his involvement with this new system, Raymond had continued to practice Gardnerian Wica as a solitary and with other working partners, and he wrote and lectured on the subject for decades afterward.

Certainly other practitioners of Gardnerian Wica had claimed membership in other occult traditions without being required to surrender their Gardnerian credentials; the most prominent example of this being Gerald Gardner himself, who had owned an O.T.O. Charter bestowed upon him by Aleister Crowley in 1947. Given that Raymond was made by Monique Wilson (who had retired to Torremolinos, Spain by that time) with the approval of Gardner (who was deceased), there was no one with sufficient authority to make the determination of Buckland's validity within the tradition, except Buckland himself. Even then, the accepted adage in the Craft was, and still remains, "Once a Witch, always a Witch."

Regardless of the reasons, the friendship that once existed between the Kneitels and Ray Buckland was irretrievably shattered.[55] Not everyone treated Raymond as a scoundrel or a sellout. He remained on very good terms with the Fishers in Louisville, noting that they were "two of the most responsible leaders of the Gardnerian tradition in the country."[56] Buckland had also, over the preceding year, become good friends with Eddie and Herman, who had promoted his books and lectures and carried his merchandise in the Warlock Shop. *(Ibid n#5)* He even stayed with the duo in their tiny apartment above the store when he returned to New York from New Hampshire for a lecture in 1973.[57] Buczynski referred in print to Raymond and Joan as "very dear friends of ours" after a trip he and Herman made to visit with them. *(Ibid n#47)*

One may point to the close relations between Brooklyn Heights and Raymond Buckland as the reason for Buczynski and Slater being swept up by the internal squabble affecting the downline of Rosemary Buckland. There is some circumstantial evidence to support the conclusion that pressure was applied to those who opted to remain close to Ray Buckland. Ariane and Abraxas, the high priestess and high priest of a Gardnerian coven downline of the Commack Coven, announced that they were severing their ties and those of their own downline with Judy and Tommy over the Kneitels' continued attacks on Ray Buckland. "Covens are supposed to be autonomous, but we find now that this is untrue," wrote Ariane in a letter to *Green Egg* dated November 25, 1975. "Why should anyone be told they must make a choice between the Circle they work in and personal friendships they have? Are we back in the times of persecutions, only this time it is brother pitted against brother?"[58]

Others, however, point to a less salubrious reason to explain the actions taken by Rosemary and the Kneitels; namely, a rampant atmosphere of anti-gay bias that was present in the Craft at the time.

Chapter 14: Perverts in the Craft

Some Acts of Love and Pleasure Need Not Apply

An issue relevant to any discussion of Buczynski's acceptance within Gardnerian Wica is the status of homosexuals within that tradition and related spiritual paths in the occult scene at that time. Despite the slow movement in the Christian faith community in the 1960s and 1970s toward acknowledging the needs of their homosexual congregants, the overwhelming majority of Christian churches were ecumenically steadfast in their rejection both of homosexuality — the state of the being — and homosexuals — the beings themselves. But if the Christians were in denial regarding their gay and lesbian members, the various traditions of Witchcraft in existence at that time were arguably no more enlightened. Up until the 1980s, the status of homosexuals in the various paths of Witchcraft was ambivalent at best. Many covens refused to knowingly initiate or work with homosexuals, and for those that did, the homosexuals were forced to subsume their identities and play roles that did not honor their own unique threads in the warp and weft of Creation's tapestry. This produced the ironic situation wherein gay men and lesbians throughout the 1970s were, in some cases, more likely to be welcomed to take vows within the Roman Catholic Church than to be elevated to the rank of high priestess or high priest within a coven. The situation wasn't much better in many other esoteric groups.

Nevertheless, many homosexuals flocked to the occult because such groups offered the opportunity to escape the judgmental atmosphere of mainstream religions, locked as they were in a dogma-fostered status quo. This was true whether the persons in question were merely curious dabblers, such as Candy Darling, Lige Clarke, and Samson De Brier, or more serious practitioners like Leo Martello, Zsuzsanna "Z." Budapest, Billy Name, or Eddie Buczynski. But, like the mainstream religions, the paths of Witchcraft have been conflicted when trying to fit their homosexual siblings into the mythos and the magick that comprise their worldviews.

Some Craft elders had gone so far as to say that because gay men and lesbians do not participate in the creation of life, they have no place in the ritual or mythology of Witchcraft. These attitudes appear to derive mainly from the residual conservative sexual mores of Great Britain and those of Protestant America. Modern Witchcraft developed under the influence of a post-Edwardian conservative atmosphere in Great Britain. At that point, the sensationalistic trials of Oscar Wilde — which had crushed the life out of the Aesthetic Movement and its romantic Paganism and had driven the nascent struggle for gay rights in England deep underground — were still in living memory. Anti-gay attitudes were still harsh enough in England after

World War II to compel some men to suicide after having their homosexuality revealed publicly — Alan Turing, the brilliant mathematician who helped break the Nazi codes, being but one sad example.[1]

Conservative leaders of the various occult traditions of the early to mid twentieth century were predisposed to bias against minority sexual practices, largely because the mores common to the people most active in the movement were those of middle and upper middle class British society.[2] This bias was rooted as much in a constrictive brand of Judeo-Christian morality particular to that breed as it was in the unwritten rules of duty and privilege that underlay the rigid class structure of the society. One example of this attitude may be found in the writings of Violet Firth, known to the world as Dion Fortune. Ms. Fortune was an occult practitioner during the first half of twentieth century, a former member of Alpha et Omega whose teachings on the subject of ritual magick are lauded to this day in the occult community. Yet her own background was heavily influenced by Christian mysticism, and Fortune condemned homosexuality as a perversion and an infectious mental disease.[3]

If we examine the basis of her philosophy, as expressed in her book *The Cosmic Doctrine*, we find that Fortune had divided the Universe into polar opposites: good and evil, evolution and devolution, Right Hand Path and Left Hand Path, love (life) and death.[4] Following her logic, because the homosexual act does not involve a union of opposites, it goes against the laws of the Universe. A path in such disharmony with the Universe cannot possibly involve love and is therefore of the Left Hand Path. Because it cannot result in the creation of life, homosexuality must then, by definition, be a squandering of the potential of the individuals involved, resulting in devolution and death. This is a complete misunderstanding of what the Left hand Path represents. Nevertheless, persons clinging to this type of belief system, whether a hermeticist or a Christian fundamentalist, will often raise the issue of the advent of the AIDS crisis to prove their point. (This ignores the fact that heterosexuals, who should be immune to such a "polarity disease," are infected just as easily as everyone else, given the right conditions; one need look no further than sub-Saharan Africa for proof.)

Similarly, then, Fortune's philosophy would have us declare that the fusion at the heart of every star, and to which all life owes its very existence, is a manifestation of pure evil, yet we have no writings from Fortune or her supporters criticizing the Sun for its homo-hydrogenic orgy. Individuals following this judgmental philosophy can become quite agitated when faced with the reality of men or women in loving, happy homosexual relationships. To remove this contradiction to their simplistic worldview, they may even go out of their way to erase this happiness, and sometimes the individuals themselves, thereby making miserable all those who dare flout these so-called "laws of nature." Misery may be meted out whether the individual is famous, as in the case of Oscar Wilde, or a relative nobody, such as Matthew Shepard or Gwen Araujo.

Fortune's opinions on homosexuality were common at the time and were based, in part, on a flawed understanding of the nature of human sexuality. But they also, to some extent, reflect a reaction amongst occult practitioners against the excesses of Aleister Crowley and the bad reputation by association that he and other rebellious spirits gave to occult studies. Crowley's bisexual tendencies did not go down well with the heterosexual practitioners who largely comprised the occult societies of his day. It is reported that Adepts of the London chapter of MacGregor Mathers' Golden Dawn originally blocked Crowley's initiation to the grade of Adeptus Minor in 1899 on the basis that a mystical society was not an appropriate moral reformatory for Crowley's homosexual tendencies.[5]

After taking over as head of the O.T.O. in 1925, Crowley was able to promote his own magickal philosophy. His experimentation in sex magick for partners of the same sex led to the development of the XI°, the highest ranking one could achieve within the O.T.O. By following the homosexual magickal workings devised by Aleister Crowley with his working partner, Victor Neuberg, ceremonial practitioners could occupy a place of "otherness" that was outside the strictures of Western society's norms.[6,7] As Crowley wrote of those who dared to follow in his footsteps, "When they can contemplate any given sexual idea without emotion of any kind, they are well on their way to freedom."[8] Not surprisingly, given the prevailing opinion on the subject, his ideas were not universally accepted, and few took up the challenge.

Crowley, though certainly the most controversial of the lot, was not the only homophile of his generation to walk occult paths. In 1893, writer George Cecil Ives founded the Order of Chaeronea as a secret society for homosexuals. Its purpose was part legal reform, part mystical order, and it claimed among its members such men as occult author Montague Summers, Uranians John Symington and Edward Carpenter and, allegedly, poet and playwright Oscar Wilde.[9] Unfortunately, the ambitions of this forerunner to today's gay rights organizations were subsumed by the wave of moral outrage that erupted in the wake of the Wilde trials of 1895. Wilde himself moved in the circles of the Theosophical Society, and his wife, Constance, was briefly a member of it, as well as of the Hermetic Order of the Golden Dawn. Nevertheless, the prevailing opinion within the occult circles of Victorian England was clear. Avocation of mystical androgyny was acceptable, but physical manifestations — masturbation, sodomy, or anything smacking of Henry Du Pré Labouchère's concept of "gross indecency" between men — were not.[10]

Things did not improve during the Edwardian period in England, nor for some time thereafter. While Crowley and his antics continued to dominate the field of Ceremonial Magick through the first half of the century, another artist and poet, Ralph Chubb, was developing his own occult pathway. Chubb's philosophy was "an amalgam of Blake, occultism, and pederasty" that incorporated elements of Theosophy, alchemy, astrology, numerology, Christianity, and Celtic mysticism.[11] But unlike Ives' Order of Chaeronea, which was largely a mystic order devoted to the protection of homosexuals and the celebration of homosexuality, Chubb attempted to synthesize a creed that preached the Advent of the Boy-God. In doing so, he carried boy-love to an extreme by elevating it to the status of a religion.[12] It is probably for the best — both for the occult and specifically for homosexual occultists — that Chubb was virtually unknown and that his ideas had no great influence on the public's perception of it or them.

Homophobia remained evident within the extended community of ceremonial practitioners in the latter half of the twentieth century. After Aleister Crowley's death in 1947, many ceremonialists tried to sweep the more socially radical aspects of his philosophy under the rug. However, in the years following the Stonewall riots, the debate seemed to explode back out of the closet. Kenneth Grant, who had been expelled from the O.T.O. in 1954 by Karl Germer, had consistently found fault with Crowley's homosexual sex magick in his own writings, for example in *Aleister Crowley: The Hidden God* (1974) and *The Nightside of Eden* (1995). In referring to it as the "blasphemy of the homosexual formula," Grant appears to reflect the primeval horror that many a tightly-wrapped Christian has of sodomitical acts, the threat and temptation of which require the intervention of Angelic intercessors and Holy Ghosts to be overcome.[13] This judgment, and the underlying weakness it reveals, would probably have caused Crowley — the self-named "Beast 666" — to smirk. To this day, the merest suggestion that Aleister Crowley was a bisexual prompts heated exchanges in Thelemic discussion groups. Yet, as Robert Brett Sherry writes in *Behutet* magazine, there "is irrefutable evidence that The Great Beast had many homosexual experiences throughout his life and felt very comfortable with his sexuality."[14]

Grant is not alone in his opinion amongst ceremonialists. The Ordo Templi Ashtart (OTA), a ritual magick lodge founded in 1970, noted that it was an heir to the Gnostic tradition of the O.T.O., yet was careful to distance itself from Crowley's influence by stating, for example, that it did not adhere Crowley's Law of Thelema.[15,16] In describing the qualifications for membership in the OTA, the lodge insisted that "There is no place in the O∴T∴A∴ for the social dropout, the illegal drug user, the sexual deviate or the political extremist."[17] Applicants were also screened for evidence of mental illness, physical handicaps and felony records, and emphasis was placed on the moral character of those seeking membership. Together, these screening criteria seemed aimed at discouraging Hippies, lefties and homosexuals from applying.

The head of the OTA, Carroll "Poke" Runyon (*Frater Aleyin*, later *Frater Thabion*), was a former Captain in the Green Berets whose conservative bent appeared to hold the counterculture and anything that smacked of "perversion" in contempt.[18, 19] Yet looks can sometimes be deceiving, for the OTA was present at a California Pagan Ecumenical Council weekend meeting in June 1974 where, at the behest of the all-gay Order of the Golden Calf (an offshoot of the Psychedelic Venus Church), the member groups voted unanimously in favor of abolishing discrimination based upon sexual preference.[20]

Another example from the realm of Ceremonial Magick was John Phillips Palmer, who bluntly dismissed Crowley's methodology, writing that "Thelemite sex magick ... can only be described as a bestial and degenerate excuse for promiscuity."[21] Palmer, a self-proclaimed devotee of the long-defunct Order of the Golden Dawn, was yet another in a long line of Christian mystics pandering an anti-homosexual line. He briefly made a name for himself in the mid-1970s through a short-lived attempt to resuscitate the Golden Dawn through his Tennessee-based Bennu Phoenix Temple. Bennu Phoenix rejected Aleister Crowley's teachings and discriminated in its membership against those it termed "sexual sociopaths."[22, 23] In a 1974 article published in *Gnostica News*, Palmer attacked Crowley and his followers for their alleged depredations against the Order of the Golden Dawn. Yet he reserved his most malicious words for homosexual practitioners of the art.

Relying on the teachings of Fortune and an outmoded medical theory of homosexuality that had been abandoned by the American Psychiatric Association a year earlier, Palmer declared homosexuals to be mentally unstable and condemned homosexual ceremonialists as practitioners of the Left Hand Path. Signing his article as "King of all the elves and feys," Palmer argued that homosexuals were unqualified for practicing the magickal arts, declaring: "homosexuality is a pathology characteristic of disequilibrium, instability and the penetrable aura and we even posit the existence of an obsessing or possessing homosexual elemental. At any rate, homosexual behavior may be regarded as an impurity of character which renders one unfit for magical practice [or] mystical study."[24] In this, he echoed a theory of demonic possession postulated by Gavin and Yvonne Frost — the leaders of the Church and School of Wicca to explain homosexuality — although to their credit the Frosts never used a royal charter from the realm of Faerie to bolster their claims. But Palmer's *bona fides* aside, one wonders at a world view that allows for the existence of "homosexual entities" but not homosexual people.

Not every ceremonial practitioner supported Palmer's position. Golden Dawn expert and author Israel Regardie blasted Palmer as an ignoramus, writing that "freedom of speech is one thing and publishing idiocy predicated on a total lack of comprehension, is another!"[25] Phillip Hansford, an occult practitioner and teacher, took Palmer and all occultists to task for judging people based on personal irrelevancies. "It has never been proven that sexual orientation has anything to do with success or failure at anything, magic included," Hansford noted, continuing, "One's sexual orientation is a private matter and need be of no concern to any true occult group or order."[26] It was during this same period that Llee Heflin published *The Island Dialogues* (1973), which advocated the ritual and loving ingestion of semen in order to usher gay men toward enlightenment.[27] Heflin was initiated into the O.T.O. by Grady McMurtry, who was eventually recognized as the outer head of the Order (OHO), albeit with the help of the federal courts. Yet McMurtry was reported to dislike "weak sisters" (i.e., homosexuals), and refused to accept the literal meaning of Crowley's XI° rite.[28]

An alchemist named Metacalus answered Palmer's incendiary attack with his own article, charging that Western dualism was to blame for the rage felt by certain ceremonialists over Crowley's recognition that the homosexual current in magick was as valid as that of the heterosexual. Sexism, racism and prudery were a modern phenomenon and formed the true degeneracy in what passed for Ceremonial Magick after Crowley's time, he argued. Bigots of all stripes who play at being visionaries and ground-breakers risk damaging themselves and those they seek to instruct. "Since many feel, with good reason, that sex is the power of True Magick," Metacalus cautioned, "the uninitiated should be warned against the preachers of sexual chauvinism, sex hatred, misogyny, and homophobia."[29]

As Metacalus and others pointed out, homosexuals were abhorred not because they allegedly ran afoul of nature — for individuals of a homosexual orientation kept arising spontaneously for generation after generation, despite overwhelming cultural pressures to the contrary — but because their very existence was contrary to the artificial standards of society. In a July 1966 article in *American Astrologer* magazine, Robert R. Shanks addressed the issue of homosexuality from an astrological perspective. Succinctly defining the inherent contradictions that arose when those in the occult/New Age movement were called upon to factor homosexuality into their worldview, Shanks noted that,[30]

> *Homosexuality must be considered as both a natural and abnormal phenomenon. Natural because in its broadest sense everything which exists in nature is that. Abnormal because it contravenes the prevailing moral standards of most societies and their commonly held conception of a particular physiological function in nature vital to the continuation of life itself.*

It was these "prevailing moral standards" and "commonly held conceptions" that allowed persons in positions of authority to enshrine their personal beliefs, dislikes and phobias into the structural framework of both law and medicine, thus providing further cover for the repression of homosexuals, and these legal and medical judgments were used as a basis for excluding homosexuals from membership in esoteric groups.

The Times They Are A-Changing

In August 1974, an anonymous writer published an article titled "Gay Magick?" in *Earth Religion News*. "Gay Magick?" asked readers to open their minds to the possibility that gay sex magick, as practiced within the XI° rite of the O.T.O., might have its place in the broader scope of ceremonial magick. In response to the anticipated arguments against such practices, the author chided the opponents for their own seeming hypocrisy. "Where there are Taboos, there may well be lack of understanding," the anonymous writer stated. "To the 'straight', the 'gay' often appears unable to settle down, seems to be constantly changing partners and unable to establish meaningful relationships, appears promiscuous and seems to select his partners on the superficial basis of 'looks' rather than on the deeper level of spiritual attainment. Needless to say, all of the same charges can be leveled at heterosexual males ... the heterosexual who is guilty of all charges he directs at the homosexual is blind to his own folly."[31]

Church of the Eternal Source (CES) co-founder Harold Moss asserts that homophobia was not as common in the Neo-Pagan organizations of the time as it was in the ceremonial and Witchcraft groups. Church of All Worlds co-founder Oberon Zell concurs that Neo-Pagan groups were generally more open to all in the 1970s. "We always had gay members of CAW – along with straight, poly, mono, whatever. And various races as well. Eventually we got [transsexuals], too, and folks into BDSM and all kinds of things. So? Why would any of that be an issue?"[32] Why, indeed?

The problem of homophobia was also, to some extent (though not entirely), geographical in nature, according to Moss. "[West Coast] Paganism prospered because gays and non-whites were welcome in Pagan groups," he writes, "but not in the existing occult scene which consisted mostly of 'magickal lodges' or 'witchcraft covens' – barely camouflaged wife swapping clubs consisting mostly of homophobic retired military officers and their wives. The traditional occult personalities – Dane Rudhyar, Elbert Benjamine, Max Heindel – were all virulently homophobic, perhaps in reaction against [Aleister] Crowley. So far as I know, so was [Gerald] Gardner."[33]

There are certainly examples of West Coast Neo-Pagan groups whose memberships were open to homosexuals. These include Moss' own CES, which counted homosexuals among its members and in leadership roles. In another case, a group of people meeting to organize what would eventually become the New Reformed Orthodox Order of the Golden Dawn (NROOGD) decided in 1975 that people of any sexual orientation would be both welcome and treated equally.[34] But Neo-Pagan groups across the country, running the gamut from the CES (California) through the CAW (Missouri) to the highly hedonistic Psychedelic Venus Church (with its roots in New York), openly welcomed gay and lesbian members.

Some were even led by homosexuals and bisexuals, the CES having been co-founded by a gay man, while the Pontifex of the Sabaean Religious Order (Illinois) was a bisexual.[35] Yet even the Church of the Eternal Source was concerned about perceptions, not wanting to appear to be *too* gay.

It should be noted that a homophobic attitude was also mirrored to some extent in the 1960s and 1970s by practitioners in the revitalized New Age movement, influenced as it was by Spiritualism and Christian mysticism. One example of this intolerance is author and journalist Jess Stearn. A former editor of *Newsweek*, Stearn published a number of books that explored the paranormal, covering such subjects as the life of psychic Edward Cayce, reincarnation, yoga, miracles, immortality and astrology. These books were generally quite supportive of the New Age movement, in stark contrast to Stearn's explorations of New York's homosexual underground. His published works on that topic, *The Sixth Man: A Startling Investigation of the Spread of Homosexuality in America* (1961) and *The Grapevine: A Report on the Secret World of the Lesbian* (1964), were positioned as shocking exposés of a subculture that was alternately depicted as both degenerate and pathetic. Designed to titillate the public at the expense of his subjects rather than to objectively inform, both books were regarded by the gay community as hatchet jobs. Thus it can be seen that being an adherent of New Age practices and philosophies — or at least an enthusiastic booster thereof — did not necessarily indicate open-mindedness on other subjects, such as homosexuality.

As demonstrated by these examples, the occult community remained unsympathetic to homosexuals well into the twentieth century, eventually bleeding over into the early Witchcraft traditions that were influenced by the Masonic and ceremonial systems. While fed by the prevailing opinion of British society, this attitude also reflected the views of some of those whose works influenced the early years of the Witchcraft revival. One such author was British poet and novelist Robert Graves, whose works include *The White Goddess* (1948), *Seven Days in New Crete* (1949), and *The Greek Myths* (1955). In his prologue to *The White Goddess*, a book that discusses the mythological sources of poetry, Graves advanced the theory that homosexuals like Socrates, by rejecting their duty to women, were really rejecting the Goddess who was the source of their intellect and of all creative ventures and supplanting Her with a world-view which he labeled platonic or "ideal" homosexuality. "[T]hough the Goddess as Cybele and Ishtar tolerated sodomy even in Her own temple-courts," wrote Graves, "ideal homosexuality was a far more serious moral aberrancy — it was the male intellect trying to make itself spiritually self-sufficient."[36]

Socrates, as we are all taught, was sentenced to death for corrupting the youth of Athens. This is often simplistically interpreted to mean that he was punished for practicing what the British referred to, in E.M. Forster's bitter words, as "the unspeakable vice of the Greeks."[37] In fact, the offence for which Socrates was sentenced to death was not the corruption of youth in the ways of the body; rather, it was for teaching his students to question the existence of the Gods, all Gods, male and female alike. Taken at face value, Graves' argument seems more a general indictment of impiety, where the Gods do not receive their due measure of sacrifice, respect, or even belief. Such impiety endangered the State, which was dependent upon the favor, or *kharis*, bestowed by the Gods for its continued strength and prosperity.

That Socrates was impious by the standards of his time is not in question. However, by interjecting the issue of homosexuality into the argument, Graves would have us believe that Greek boy-love, couched as the chimera of the woman-hating homosexual when viewed through the lens of Christian morality, was at the root of this impiety. In denying women his affections, Graves reasons, the homosexual overturned the natural order and cast down the Goddess from Her rightful place. But the fault for displacing the Goddesses from power within the Greek sphere could hardly be laid at Socrates' doorstep. That process had been ongoing for more than a thousand years by his time, perhaps since the fall of Minoan Crete or since the advent of the Mycenaean civilization and the rise of Doric culture.

The "ideal homosexuality" with which Graves concerned himself appears to be more a symptom of the later Christian Church, with its emphasis on a singular male Creator, than of poor old Socrates, who didn't appear to have much use for Gods of either sex. However, homosexuality could hardly be blamed for this phenomenon. After all, why would the Goddesses tolerate homosexuality even unto their sacred temple precincts, as Graves so readily concedes, if the very existence of this practice was anathema to Their worship? Indeed, his objection withers in the face of evidence that homosexuals throughout Classical history acted as priests of various Goddesses — Inanna, Ishtar, Artemis, Athirat, Isis and Cybele being but a few examples — a role that many also strove to fulfill in modern Witchcraft.

Finally, following Graves' argument to its logical conclusion, one would have to acknowledge the woman-loving lesbian as representing the highest possible virtue in Greek society, an argument that found new traction during the AIDS crisis in Western society, when it was shown that lesbians were among those least likely to become infected with the human immunodeficiency virus (HIV). While Sappho might not quibble with that finding, it is doubtful that was Graves' intent in proffering his thesis. In his disparagement of Greek love, Graves may have been, as some have suggested, overcompensating for his own admitted "honourably chaste and sentimental" homosexual experimentation in school.[38]

Gerald Gardner used portions of *The White Goddess* in his evolution of the Gardnerian Book of Shadows — *Ye Bok of ye Art Magical*,[39] but what is not known is to what extent, if any, Graves' opinions on homosexuality influenced Gardner and, by extension, the development of what came to be known as Gardnerian Wica. It may be that Graves' opinion was merely one of many that were in concord with Gardner's own feelings on the subject. But, whatever the source of this strongly-held opinion, Lois Bourne, a close friend of Gerald Gardner and former high priestess of the Bricket Wood Coven, confirmed that the grandfather of modern Witchcraft loathed homosexuals and considered them to be the antithesis of the fertility-based Craft. In her memoir, *Dancing with Witches*, Bourne describes Gardner's reaction when the subject arose in a conversation with Jack Bracelin:[40]

> *"There are no homosexual witches, and it is not possible to be a homosexual and a witch"* Gerald almost shouted. *No one argued with him.*

From a historical perspective, Gardner's disgust at homosexuals was particularly egregious given the veneration of the Goddess Diana by his Witchcraft tradition. Diana was served in ancient times by priestesses (the *Melissae*) and priests (the *Megabyzoi*) who practiced gender variance and same-sex eroticism in their rites. But given the prevailing opinion of sexual diversity in Great Britain at the time, it is no surprise that ignorant personal biases of this nature should find their way into the pages of the Gardnerian Book of Shadows and Gerald Gardner's other writings. In the foreword to his 1952 book *Witchcraft Today*, Gardner wrote "I have been told by witches in England: 'Write and tell people we are not perverts. We are decent people, we only want to be left alone.'"[41] It is ironic that Gardner felt obligated to preface his work with this statement, in light of his correspondence with and alleged use of materials from Aleister Crowley in the writings that eventually became part of Gardnerian Wica.[42]

The Gardner-Valiente Book of Shadows cemented this attitude in the tradition.[43] Regarding the invocation of Deity by same-sex couples, the Book states that "woman and woman should never attempt these practices together, and may all the curses of the Mighty Ones be on any who make such attempt."[44] It is an unusual warning, given that feminist-lesbian Witchcraft generally did not manifest itself until almost twenty years later, after Gardnerian Wica crossed the Atlantic.[45, 46] Up through the 1970s, many Witchcraft covens would not allow gay men, lesbians, or bisexuals of either sex to practice with them. The few covens that did openly welcome homosexuals in the 1970s were often criticized both publicly and privately by those that did not. It was not uncommon for covens to ruthlessly purge members who were discovered to be gay after having admitted them under the assumption that they were straight. Indeed, for many years, the only covens that publicly welcomed homosexuals were lesbian-Dianic covens, such as Z. Budapest's Susan B. Anthony Coven (beginning in 1970) and Eddie Buczynski's Traditionalist Gwyddoniaid (beginning in 1973).[47]

If one were tasked to name a point when the debate concerning homosexuality in the occult community came to a head, that year might have been 1973. Magazines and newsletters in both the United States and abroad devoted many column-inches of space to debating the advisability of admitting homosexuals into the Craft. A newsletter that functioned as a mouthpiece of Gardnerian Wica in England, *The Wiccan*, reflected its anti-homosexual prejudice primarily through the opinions of its editor, John Score (Craft name *M*).[48] Refusing to pass on to readers the names of Witchcraft covens or interested seekers suspected of being gay, *The Wiccan* gave notice:[49]

> *Black, and/or homosexual groups please don't bother. Enquirers please note we are NOT a queers' contact service. We are, so to say, heterosexual!*

By "black," *The Wiccan* was referring not to a person's race but to those who follow the Left Hand Path (i.e., engage in black magick). But, as Leo Martello noted, Score's choice of terminology intentionally brought with it its own heavily-loaded baggage. The juxtaposition of homosexuals and black magickians, according to Martello, was no different from Christians calling all Witches Devil-worshippers. "Once again," he wrote, "a minority becomes the dumping depot for all of the garbage that exists in other people's souls."[50] In his *Witch Manifesto*, Martello tied racial politics to the Christian church's habit of color-coding sin, and accused the church of fomenting the same racial stereotyping in its denouncement of Witches.[51] This habit of linking homosexuals with the Left Hand Path demonstrates that fundamentalist Witches shared some attitudes in common with fundamentalist Christians, an unpleasant fact that would no doubt have disturbed members of both groups.[52] As Katon Shual would write some years later about those who were quick to label others as black magicians, "As in the accusation of Witchcraft, it is the accuser one should see in a bad light. One often discovers these same people making lots of money out of magick, and they obviously see no contradiction between materialist values and so-called 'white Magick.'"[53]

This argument continues to the present day, with many Wiccan practitioners shunning those they perceive as practicing the black arts, while most Ceremonialists deny that that there even is such a thing as "black" or "white" magick. Non-Wiccan Witches often tend to straddle the fence on this subject, depending upon the "whether" — that is to say, whether or not someone has really pissed them off. For example Victor Anderson, the founder of the Feri Tradition, was fond of saying that "White magic is poetry and black magic is anything that works."[54] Ceremonial Magickians are generally disgusted with the entire public airing of the topic, believing that the conversation inevitably goes pear-shaped whenever non-ceremonials discuss the matter.

This difference in opinion has carried over into popular culture. Author Kim Harrison uses the term "black magic" as a significant plot device in her "Hollows" series of books, e.g., *Black Magic Sanction* (Harper Collins, 2010). The life of Harrison's character, Rachel Morgan, demonstrates that the boundary between the two practices is much more fluid than most people choose to admit. Ben Aaronovitch's protagonist, on the other hand, has a different problem with the terminology in *Moon Over Soho* (DelRey, 2011). A police detective, apprentice sorcerer and black man, Aaronovitch's Peter Grant objects to the use of "black magician" to describe a criminal who murders people through magic. Though his teacher chides him for being obtuse by conflating the racial term with the ethical label, Grant categorically states that he prefers the term "ethically challenged magical practitioner" to describe their opponent.[55]

Martello criticized the continued reliance on "black" and "white" as descriptive terms in the occult because of this rather unavoidable racial baggage, which exists regardless of which side of the Atlantic one casts a Circle. "I must also point out that those [Witches] who are the most guilty of this are basically white racists," he notes. "Not one of them has any black coven members." *(Ibid n#50)* Isaac Bonewits, writing in 1975, observed that "Those of African descent are not the only ones denigrated by the followers of the Western Mainstream Occult Tradition — Oriental Pagans, Chicanos, Native Americans, Polynesians — all receive racist slurs ... Racism in the American occult community is widespread, and though it is usually genteel, it is frequently quite harsh."[56]

The community appeared not to have a great deal of interest in broaching this issue. George "Pat" Patterson, the founder of the Georgian tradition of Wica, wrote to contacts around the country in the early 1970s seeking information on blacks in the Craft and found nothing. In 1973, the Georgian covens in Bakersfield and Sacramento, California began admitting black members.[57] Buczynski's Traditionalist Gwyddoniaid also offered membership to non-Caucasians, and some of the earliest photographs of Welsh Witchcraft gatherings show Hispanic and black participants, in marked contrast to most covens of the day. Herman Slater, writing as late as 1989, noted that there was an untold story of racism and sexual discrimination in the Craft from the 1970s.[58]

In mid-1973, Jonathon Zotique wrote an article for *Green Egg* entitled "A Manifesto of Ideals for the New Age." Zotique's "manifesto" was rather more of a rambling missive at whose heart was a denunciation of the Neo-Pagan community, and more specifically the various paths of Witchcraft, for their denial of a place for gays in the Craft. "We sadly realize that many leaders of Wicca are openly 'anti-gay' and that some have attempted to 'banish' us from the craft to leave us in that perpetual Limbo created by the Bishops of Rome. Have any of you analyzed your prejudices and hang-ups? — most of them very real Old Testament hang-ups to be sure."[59]

Zotique lamented the continued influence of Jewish and Christian thinking on the movement, noting the disconnect in thinking that allowed modern practitioners to believe the then-popular myth that six million Witches perished in the Burning Times, and yet to refuse to give credence to the well-documented history of homosexuals in the various Pagan cults of the ancient world. "No one race, or even religion — or colour — or sexual group — has a monopoly on God's great truth of Love. To claim such is a vain ignorance and folly. ... If the Gods and High Priests of the Ancients embraced one another in passion, then how can the 'teachers' of today say that 'a homosexual cannot raise a cone of power?'" Zotique ended with a plea for his fellow Witches to remember the words of the Goddess, who declared that "all acts of love are my ritual." *(Ibid n#59)* Writing as the leader of the Little Grove of Ganymede in the Aquarian Family of covens, Jonathan Vartan Zotique was himself an absolute contradiction. Born Thomas William Brennand, he changed his name to Zotique upon taking orders as a Priest in the Old Catholic Church (OCC). In 1973, Zotique was simultaneously high priest of his coven and a practicing OCC priest.[60] Zotique variously described himself as straight, bisexual, and finally gay before leaving the Aquarian Family and Wicca soon after his manifesto was published. His abandonment of Wicca appears to have been precipitated by a fight between himself and his former high priestess, Nan Wyllie, whom he had derogated as a Satanist in his manifesto — a charge she later denied in *Green Egg*.[61]

Roy Dymond, an Alexandrian high priest who practiced with Wyllie and who was also slighted in the manifesto, responded with a broadside of his own that was insulting to all homosexuals, Craft practitioners or not. Objecting to Zotique's quotation of the Charge of the Goddess as justifying the right of gays to participate in traditional Witchcraft, Dymond threw the words back into his face, writing, "Now you are just being obscene and profane in suggesting that the homosexual act fits this description [i.e., Love]."[62] While he certainly was not the only Witch to hold to that opinion, the hostility of Dymond's words indicates an animosity which went far beyond that which can be readily explained by simple annoyance over the antics of one unstable individual. This stance is also ironic, given that the Alexandrian tradition of which he was an initiate was founded by a bisexual man whose own antics were excoriated in Craft publications during this same period.

Expanding on Zotique's subject, Leo Martello wrote an article that was published in August 1973. Titled "The Gay Pagan," Martello's article aimed to further refute the argument that homosexuals were ill-suited to and unqualified for participation in the Craft. However, rather than presenting a dispassionate case that would achieve his goal by persuading opponents to his position, Martello instead personalized the debate and angrily lashed out at those who held the opposing viewpoint. In doing so, he lost the opportunity to bring the discussion out of the emotional realm and onto a more rational playing field. To make matters worse, Martello tied his presentation to the earlier Zotique manifesto — unfortunate timing, since the mental stability and motives of its author were being openly questioned by some in the community, including Martello himself.

Looking beyond Martello's by-now trademark pejorative tone, his conclusions were sound. Calling out those who hid behind the fertility religion argument for excluding gays even when their own tradition or coven did not practice the Great Rite in true, Martello wrote, "Homosexuals in the Craft and in Paganism, those who are self-accepting and secure, can easily relate to and identify with the Mother Goddess. I wonder how many heterosexual High Priests would be willing to make the supreme sacrifice for the Goddess if She requested it, like the devotees of Cybele?"[63] Of course, it isn't clear how many gay or bisexual Neo-Pagans of the day would have been willing to make the same sacrifice of self-castration as the Galli to whom Martello referred, particularly coming, as they were, out of an eons-long prohibition of their sexual expression that had been imposed upon them by the dominant culture.

Of those named in Martello's article, Gavin Frost, along with his wife, Yvonne, responded in the next issue of *Green Egg* with an article of their own titled "The Craft and Homosexuality: A New Look at an Old Topic."[64] Placing themselves on the opposite side of the line drawn by Zotique's "Ganymede Manifesto," the Frosts provided an analysis of the origins of homosexuality, and the implications for the potential of such individuals to practice within a Craft environment, that was eyebrow-raising from almost anyone's perspective. The Frosts identified three underlying causes for the homosexual condition.

In the first case, they conflated homosexuality with the misassignment of gender at birth, a mistake often made with newborns who exhibit the condition of intersexuality. This ignorance displayed the tendency of medical/psychiatric dabblers, which the Frosts certainly were, to confuse gender with sexual attraction. One common example of this dabbling is the discredited explanation that the gay male is simply a woman trapped in a man's body.[65] This intersexual condition and the alleged shift in the "polarity" of the subjects were said to be detectable with dowsing wands or electrical field measurement — claims that have never been backed by any repeatable, peer-reviewed scientific study.

In the second case, homosexuality was said to be caused by dominant possession of the subject by a spirit of opposite polarity "which normally seems to inhabit the lower part of the body." In other words, men and women in this category were homosexual because they were possessed by demons that made them think with their gonads in ways opposite to their "true" nature. According to the authors, this condition could also be revealed by dowsing.

In the final case, men and women were said to turn to homosexuality in order to hide from persons of the opposite sex because they've been hurt by something in their past that prevents them from adhering to society's expectations for normalcy. For these homosexuals, the Frosts recommended guidance and healing by exposure to a person of the opposite sex. In their opinion, only the victims of the first condition could form a functioning same-sex coven, and even then only if their polarities were balanced. The Frosts' theories and treatment regimen in some ways resembled those of certain fundamentalist Christians who would, in years to come, foist the quackery of the "ex-gays movement" on a credulous and ignorant segment of the public. As nineteenth century educator Horace Mann observed, "Ignorance breeds monsters to fill up the vacancies of the soul that are unoccupied by the verities of knowledge."[66]

Responding to the Frosts' claims, Morris Kight, President of the Gay Community Services Center of Los Angeles, denounced the article as enormously oppressive to an entire class of people. "We do engage in 'guidance' and 'healing,'" Morris wrote, "and in those areas we guide one another away from people who believe their own sexual orientation makes them 'more fortunate,' and into 'healing,' principally from being healed of any notion that heterosexuality is a superior lifestyle to ours, which is nonsense. It's just great for the heterosexuals, but just all wrong for us."[67] Leo Martello mocked the Frosts' pseudo-scientific research into the causes of homosexuality and repeated a point that he had first made in 1969 when writing for the GLF in the months following Stonewall — that the "homosexual problem" was really all about heterosexual attitudes toward and maltreatment of gay men and lesbians.[68] Writing in *Gnostica News*, Martello observed that if the homophobic Crafters weren't careful, they could find themselves on the receiving end of a GLF picket line.[69]

The topic flared up again in the pages of *Green Egg* in March 1974, where a letter to the Forum savaged Herman Slater and Eddie Buczynski. Couched in an *ad hominem* attack on the homosexuality of the Warlock Shop's owners, the pseudonymous writer called into question the validity of the Welsh tradition that Eddie founded in 1972.[70] After the letter was published, Herman Slater telephoned Morning Glory Zell to vent his outrage that *Green Egg* would run such a transparently homophobic screed. Herman's outrage was not just as a gay man, but as someone who up to then had been on good terms with the editors and who was also an advertiser in the magazine. Morning Glory cited *Green Egg*'s position that the magazine did not censor its content and pointed out that Tim Zell had followed "Spock's" letter with an editorial note calling him to task for his views, but Herman was not to be placated. The ensuing argument left Morning Glory in tears, but she did not back down.[71]

In the end, Slater and his backers had to settle for the opportunity to respond with a letter of their own. This they did in the May issue, not only attacking the original correspondent, but also belittling the magazine's position of non-censorship and arguing that freedom of the press did not excuse the printing of slander and libel.[72] Morning Glory wrote an open letter to the readership in that same issue, stating that the editorial staff of the magazine would not succumb to outside pressure to censor what was printed in its pages, and warning everyone that they shouldn't dish it out if they can't take it. Zell also reminded the public that *Green Egg* had gone out of its way to give space not only to those who hold anti-gay opinions, but also to "Gay Liberationists in the Craft to state their position and to defend themselves in print against the attacks of those who claim that gays have no place in the Craft." *(Ibid n#72)* This episode caused a permanent rift in what had otherwise been an amicable relationship between Slater and the *Green Egg* management team. In recalling the controversy many years later, the former *Green Egg* editor noted, "I guess we in CAW never really understood what the fuss was among Witches about gays. ... Not being Witches, we figured that was their problem, not ours. So we happily printed stuff in *Green Egg* by [supporters of] homosexuality in the Craft. And also stuff by those on the other side. And we just let them duke it out. We had no dog in that fight."[73]

Gnostica News also ventured into these troubled waters in June 1973. In their regular column, "The Brotherhood Messenger," Lady Sheba's American Order of the Brotherhood of the Wicca (AOBW) took a stand against admitting homosexuals into the Craft. The columnist quoted the Laws that proclaim "a man may be taught by a woman and a woman by a man and that woman and woman and man and man should never attempt these practices together. And, may all the Curses of the Mighty Ones be on any who make such an attempt."[74] On this basis, the AOBW writer went on to assert that "Witchcraft is for man and woman. And the Laws of Witchcraft plainly indicate that the Wiccan way has no place for homosexual acts."[75] Of course, the Laws were originally written not by the Gods, nor even by ancient ancestors, but by Gerald Gardner in 1957.[76] And there is certainly room to question how much Gardner allowed his own personal beliefs to color the tradition that bears his name, as well as those who had branched off of it.

The dispute over the place of homosexuals in the Craft continued throughout the 1970s on both sides of the Atlantic. An example from 1978 shows how controversy could erupt over one high priestess even broaching the possibility of working with homosexuals. In the pages of the occult journal *Aquarian Arrow*, a Western Mysteries group protested the idea of working with homosexuals, stating that "any genuinely contacted fraternity could not countenance working with sexual deviants of any sort."[77] Intolerance manifested at large gatherings of Witches and Neo-Pagans until late in the decade. A survey conducted at the 1979 Pan-Pagan Festival, for example, found that ninety percent of respondents viewed homosexuality as "immoral" — a stunning admission in a community that often prided itself on rejecting the judgmental dogma of Christianity and related religions.[78] Negative reaction to an all-women's circle led by Z. Budapest at the 1980 Pan-Pagan Festival further contributed to the belief that homosexuals were second-class citizens there. This perception eventually led to a split in that festival community, with many gay and lesbian participants leaving to establish a "faerie camp" in a new festival founded by Circle Sanctuary, which had, up to that point, been a major backer of Pan-Pagan.

While many Gardnerians continued to advocate the total exclusion of homosexuals from the Craft well into the 1980s — with some practitioners fussing over the place of gays and lesbians even into the 1990s — this was by no means the only Witchcraft path that practiced such discrimination.[79] Fred and Martha Adler, followers of a Celtic Traditionalist path, were quoted in 1972 on the subject as saying, "I don't believe that drug users or homosexuals have the positive vibrations for White Magic; these things are part of the Left-Hand Path ... Black Magic that destroys the people who try to use it."[80] Another example was the Aquarian Family of covens based in Watertown, New York, whose high priestess was quoted in 1974 as saying, "As with many other groups, we do not allow ... indulgence in homosexuality since we feel it is detrimental to the training" — an odd stance for a tradition purportedly descended from the Fairy people.[81] Alex Sanders, founder of the Alexandrian tradition in the 1960s, was said to have spent a period of his youth disporting in bisexual and homosexual practices.[82] Yet he later disavowed those actions as being "Left Hand Path." Whether his disavowal resulted from a change of heart or whether it was induced by the cagey pragmatism and business acumen of an up-and-coming occult leader is unknown. Still, in his final years, Sanders again formed working relationships with gay and bisexual men in the Craft.[83, 84]

Apart from the deeply-ingrained prejudice against homosexuality that was prevalent in Western society, the three reasons most often cited for denying homosexuals a place in the Craft were issues associated with fertility-polarity magick, mental illness, and criminality. With regard to fertility-polarity magick, the rationale most often used to justify this discrimination was the equation of magickal power to that of an electrical current, with dipolar — positive/negative — opposition being essential for magick to manifest. By this reasoning, male-female sexual polarity was seen as the only basis for valid magickal-spiritual workings. Groups that practiced with male-female polarity — that is to say, paired male and female working partners — were said to be genuinely "contacted." Ronald Hutton characterizes this as "the hostility to homosexuals which Gardner embedded in the Book of Shadows and which was deeply implicit in the Wiccan emphasis on gender polarity." *(Ibid n#84)*

In short, heterosexuality was seen as part of the natural world, while homosexuality was judged to be unnatural — a disease of civilization and the product of a deeply flawed character or mental illness. But this was certainly not the only opinion on the subject within the greater Neo-Pagan community. Writing in 1960, Temple of Aphrodite member W. Holman

Keith (later associated with Feraferia) asserted in a highly sympathetic assessment of the treatment of homosexuals that:[85]

> *The personality disorders that are characteristic of homosexuals are quite largely the consequence of society's refusal to accept them and the arbitrary moral stigma attaching to homosexuality. ... Human sexuality is, potentially, highly polymorphous. It can find expressions far removed from what would seem its direct, natural expression. Hence, given an entirely different set of mores and conditionings in tender years, there might well be a society in which the noblest passion and intimacy was Lesbian.*

To be fair to the heterosexual practitioners of that time, there were few studies on the prevalence of homosexuality in nature, and those few were unavailable to the public or to academics.[86] Homosexuals, in one prevalent psychological theory of the day, were assumed to be people of one sex trapped in the bodies of those of the opposite sex. Therefore, by definition, the homosexual did not have the correct polarity to function effectively in Circle, i.e., they could never be "contacted." In this, the Wiccans were the recipients of outdated theories on sexuality that were based on Theosophical investigations into reincarnation and its effect on gender.[87] Even after this theory lost ground in the medical community, some in the Craft who believed that it was not just the gender of the individuals involved that mattered, but also the *potential* for sexual attractedness — the sexual tension inherent between heterosexual men and heterosexual women — that powered the magick of the coven.

For many, these arguments trumped even those gay and lesbian practitioners who were willing to toe the tradition's heterocentric line in Circle, and this mindset predominated in spite of the numerous cases of bisexual and predominantly homosexual men and women who had children, a sure sign that many were most certainly "contacted" at some point by the opposite sex, and so could indeed function effectively where male-female sexual polarity was concerned. John Score — as "M," the editor of the influential British Craft newsletter, *The Wiccan* — went so far as to advocate that candidates be required to supply proof of their heterosexual orientation. A letter to Leo Martello from Score dated June 26, 1970 — the eve of the first anniversary of the Stonewall riots — read:[88]

> *White Witchcraft is specifically heterosexual. One of our difficulties over here is to weed out the applicants who are immature sexually in this way. Thus the suggested ruling that no single male should be initiated without good evidence of heterosexual attainment, or should be initiated with his sexual partner ..., married or not. (One well known and highly publicized*

male high priest ... so called ... is 'ambisextrous' ... and we are horrified and dismayed at the amount of publicity he has been able to obtain over here.)

The high priest in question was Alex Sanders, proving that even men who could provide 'good evidence of heterosexual attainment' — Alex was married to his wife, Maxine, at the time and the two had had a child together — needn't apply if that attainment happened to swing both ways. Martello, an openly gay practitioner of Sicilian *Strege* and recent veteran of the struggle for gay rights in the United States, was not about to put up with homophobes dictating who was or was not permitted to call themselves Witches. He laughingly derided the proposed "stud requirement" as worthy of the Catholic Pope.[89]

In 1970, a gay man in the United States had expressed his intention to form a gay coven. As gay men were often rejected for membership in (nominally) straight covens, the frustration motivating this action was understandable. Alarmed by the post-Stonewall assertiveness of gays in the United States, Score quashed the notion that such individuals could form covens. "We wish to categorically repudiate the suggestion which has been raised in the USA. that homosexual covens exist," he wrote in Issue 12 of *The Wiccan*. "A coven is a group of witches. Witches are heterosexual, and unlike some other religions have both a God and a Goddess as deities. We have no doubt that that homo groups exist, and we feel sorry for those who have failed to mature to normality, but they are not witch covens; though they may practice B.M. [black magick] and thus fall into the category of Black Magicians."[90]

A year after the riots, John Score was not the only practitioner of British Traditional Witchcraft to comment on this issue. Raymond Buckland summarized the majority opinion of the American branch of Gardnerian Wica when, in response to the same report of the gay Witch forming a gay coven, he wrote, "A 'gay witch' would be an absolute contradiction in terms. Being a religion of nature the witch is very much heterosexual; there must be male and female, equal numbers of each, in a coven."[91] Buckland and Score were addressing the same issue. But whereas Buckland had merely rejected such groups because they did not practice opposite-sex pairings of working partners, Score went much further by declaring that the magick practiced by such homosexual groups was "black" — evil — in nature. Freud's increasingly questionable theory on the origins of homosexuality may have informed *The Wiccan* editor's understanding of the psychology behind the trait, but Score was clearly coloring outside the lines by parlaying this into a moral basis for his judgment.

Such discrimination, while directed mainly at gay men, was also applied to lesbians. Irish Witch Sharon Devlin explained Z. Budapest's legal problems as the predictable outcome of sexual politics. "I think Z has been persecuted because she is a threat to everything straight people represent," Devlin told Margot Adler in a 1976 interview, concluding, "and if you ain't a threat, then you ain't worth much."[92] In his *Green Egg* review of Z. Budapest's book, *The Feminist Book of Lights and Shadows*, Gwydion Pendderwen supported this conclusion, noting that the Dianic Tradition was perceived as a threat because they were self-sufficient, sex-segregated and unabashedly lesbian-supportive. "[W]hat really irks most objectors," wrote Pendderwen, "is its denial of the mysteries to men, its total independence from 'masculine virtues' (competition, aggressiveness, domination) and the fact that it is probably the most successful tradition going. It is riding on the crest of the feminist wave, and it is very appealing to women of all ages."[93]

While Pendderwen's statement that Dianics were a women-only tradition was disputed in the next issue of *Green Egg* by Dianic Witch Morgan McFarland, she conceded that there were separate women's Mysteries within the tradition.[94] If lesbian practitioners of Witchcraft were somewhat less likely to be an affront to members of Gardnerian Wica and other related paths, it may have been because women were at the top of the coven power structure within those traditions. As feminist author Ellen Willis noted, lesbians in the 1970s were more interested in female solidarity than they were in sexual liberation.[95]

The stated reason for the anti-homosexual bias of the Craft was the association of Witchcraft with fertility magick that required male-female polarity, the practice of which homosexuals were thought to have no inherent aptitude. But while the argument against this policy cited the remaining Judeo-Christian prejudices of its adherents as its true origins, there were some who dryly noted that the bias appeared to be much stronger within covens that practiced skyclad rites.[96] This led more than one observer to privately quip that the basis for the ban had more to do with the paranoia of straight suburbanite males, who were uncharacteristically protective of their virginity, than for any other reason. Louise Huebner, the so-called "Official Witch of Los Angeles," certainly provided no cover for the fragile ego of male practitioners of the Craft when she declared to the readership of the second-largest tabloid in the United States that all male Witches have "homosexual tendencies."[97] As all aspects of society had up to that point drilled into straight men both the need to aggressively defend their cultural primacy and the incentive to deride gay men as weak and disgusting beings, none of this speculation did anything to endear the cause of homosexual men to their heterosexual counterparts.

Modern social mores notwithstanding, the anti-gay prejudice of many Craft practitioners had no basis in the history of Pagan religious practices of ancient Europe or the Near East. There is ample evidence for homoeroticism and gender variance in Pagan religions and for the existence of bisexual Gods. Putting aside the more recent disrepute allegedly fostered by Crowley's activities, there was also a clear and unmistakable record that homosexuals and bisexuals had long engaged in occult pursuits.[98] This evidence would not have been a problem for the Gardnerians and others if they had simply created a completely new religion out of whole cloth. However, whether because of a genuine desire to return to the old ways or in an attempt to provide a façade of antiquity to their practices, they incorporated ancient mythologies, Gods, Goddesses, history and religious practices into their modern spiritual paths. Having done so, they were now stuck with the inconvenient baggage associated with that history. Whether the straight Witches chose to accept it or not, there *was* a history of homosexuals and bisexuals in the occult.

Occult practitioners had also maintained an unofficial prohibition against indoctrinating mentally unstable persons. While in theory some of the techniques taught to Craft practitioners, such as meditation, visualization, and mental discipline, could be helpful to certain categories of the mentally ill, in practice they could be extremely disorienting even to the mentally fit. The potential for ill effects by the fact that very few covens had anyone with formal training in counseling or mental health to call on for assistance. Because homosexuality was officially classified as a mental illness until the 1970s, most coven leaders could justify excluding homosexuals on the basis that they were unstable and therefore unqualified for initiation. In the United States, the "sickness theory" of homosexuality, as formalized in the Diagnostic and Statistical Manual (DSM II) of the American Psychiatric Association (APA), was overturned in late 1973. The stage for this reversal was set in 1964, when Jack Nichols lobbied Mattachine-Washington, DC to begin to address the issue through the APA. He was supported in this by Frank Kameny, also of Mattachine-Washington; Barbara Gittings, editor of the Daughters of Bilitis magazine *The Ladder*; and others.

A decade of lobbying, including the later use of the confrontational tactics that had come to characterize the post-Stonewall gay rights movement, eventually led the APA Board of Trustees to remove homosexuality from the list of mental and emotional disorders on December 15, 1973. The vote was by no means unanimous, yet two years later the American Psychological Association passed a resolution in support of this removal.[99,100] This validation did not silence the opinions of dissenting mental health practitioners who, supported by a few tormented souls, continued to argue that homosexuality could be "cured."[101] The debate erupted again in the early 1980s with the rise of evangelical conservatism.[102] But since that time, it has mainly been those whose scientific background is limited by their fundamentalist religious beliefs, downright quackery, or both who have continued to hew to the old line. This pushback would eventually mutate into the so-called ex-gays movement. Thus, while in 1970 homosexually was still officially classed as a mental illness and coven leaders could claim some justification for their decision to deny membership on this basis, after 1973 (and certainly by the close of 1975) this excuse was no longer valid.[103]

Finally, there was the issue of criminality. In 1970, sodomy was illegal in New York and 48 other states in the United States, as well as the District of Columbia and the protectorates and territories of American Samoa, Guam, Puerto Rico, Northern Mariana Islands and the Virgin Islands. Punishment for violating these laws ranged anywhere from a misdemeanor fine to a felony life sentence. In explaining the social environment, Mart Crowley, the screenwriter for *The Boys in the Band*, said "There were still, not just attitudes, there were laws against one's being; against the core of one's being."[104] Thus, homosexuals could be, and indeed often were, portrayed as not only psychologically deviant, but also of a criminal bent. In reality, however, as the decade wore on these laws were enforced less and less, except occasionally for retaliation; and as was the case in the medical community, the country was already moving steadily toward decriminalizing private sexual behavior between consenting adults in all but the most entrenched states. By the end of the decade, nearly half of these statutes were to fall by the wayside, and the rest would eventually be declared unconstitutional, either by state courts or by the United States Supreme Court in a 2003 ruling.[105, 106]

In Great Britain, the criminal status of homosexual acts had been debated since the release of the "Wolfenden Report" in 1957. The recommendations of Lord Wolfenden's committee led to the passage of the Sexual Offences Act of 1967, which resulted in a limited decriminalization of homosexual sodomy in England and Wales. Thus, it would seem on the surface that the British Witches had an even weaker excuse for their continued harassment of their homosexual brethren on these grounds than the American Witches. Yet, oddly enough, the backlash against gays in the Craft originated primarily from Great Britain.

The Stonewall riots in 1969 had galvanized the modern gay rights movement in New York City and elsewhere, but this effect did not provoke an immediate positive change in attitudes within either the then-conservative Craft movement or the United States as a whole. In fact, as gays and lesbians became more active and visible in their quest for equal treatment under the law, pressure began building to oppose them politically. Much the same thing happened in Great Britain after passage of the Sexual Offences Act. The GLF, which formed to lobby for gay rights in New York City in the aftermath of the Stonewall riots, quickly spread to other cities in the United States and to Great Britain. The London chapter of the GLF held its first meeting on October 13, 1970 and grew rapidly afterwards. By late the next month, it was conducting actions against those opposed to equal rights for homosexuals.[107, 108] Raymond Buckland, writing in 1971, stated, "A spokesman for the Craft in England recently said that a move was being made to 'root out of the movement the large number of thrill seekers and deviates.'" This spokesman was John Score, who began to turn up the editorial heat in order to keep gay and bi men out of the Craft.[109]

With homosexuality largely decriminalized in Great Britain, the lot of British homosexuals should have improved. But, in truth, things didn't change all that much after the passage of the Sexual Offences Act. British society still widely disapproved of "poofters," who were generally viewed as sick individuals who simply couldn't help being what they were. Historian and activist Lisa Power notes that "many of the politicians supporting [the Act] saw it primarily as a humanitarian attempt to minimize blackmail against homosexuals and were horrified at the growth in gay visibility which followed."[110] The remaining aura of hatred and warnings of a backlash were expressed in some of the lyrics voiced by punk rocker and gay rights activist Tom Robinson, who summed up society's attitude by asking what more were the buggers after?[111] In truth, the buggers wanted a lot more.

Despite legal advances, there were disturbing indications that it was business as usual for police and prosecutors in Great Britain. Police authorities simply found new ways to take enforcement actions against homosexuals by using draconian "under suspicion" *(sus)* laws, often rounding up, beating and arresting gays on the flimsiest of charges. Gay clubs and pubs were routinely raided and shuttered, community newspapers were declared obscene and silenced, and the age of consent remained several years older for gay men than for straight couples. *(Ibid n#108)* Perhaps the most telling single event was the prosecution of the underground newspaper *International Times* in 1970 on charges of pandering obscenity due to the presence of gay singles ads in its pages. As Lisa Power describes it, "the prosecution was based on the assumption that while certain homosexual acts between adult gay men had been decriminalized, the basic criminality of homosexuality had not been removed. This meant that encouragement of homosexual acts, whether they were legal or not, was still immoral and those publishing such advertisements were liable to prosecution."[112] The publishers were found guilty, and the verdict stood on final appeal in 1972.

While the Stonewall uprising itself may have had some very limited effect on inflaming opinions in the British Craft community, other factors likely sparked in the mind of John Score and his like an image of radical gay activists spreading, unchallenged, like a metastasizing cancer from the decadent colonies to the motherland. These included the increased visibility of British homosexuals and the public antics of the GLF in London and other cities in Great Britain, as well as the audacity of openly gay Witches like Leo Martello in haranguing "normal people" through occult books and magazines in the United States and abroad. In combination with Score's own personal prejudices and the general residuum of dislike of homosexuality, these additional irritants motivated Score's campaign to rid the Craft of homosexuals.

Score was entirely unsympathetic to the plight of the homosexual segment of the population, and, in the newly coined parlance of the gay rights movement, he was declared a homophobe and an enemy of gay Witches. Church of Eternal Source co-founder Harold Moss noted that the editor of *The Wiccan* "has equated homosexuality with the sweaty hypererotic explorations of adolescents, with the phony celibacy of Catholic priests — 50% of whom are practicing homosexuals — and with the reproachful, loud, badmouthing by Leo Martello."[113] But Martello's continuing attacks on Score's stance on this issue since 1970 resulted simply from Score's own unrelenting efforts and vituperative language. Others, such as Herman Slater, eventually joined the fray, with Slater lumping Score in with con artists and the passers of bad checks within the community.[114]

Moss states that Score attempted to explain his rationale for attacking gays. "Since I never flaunted my homosexuality, M probably assumed I was straight," Moss writes. "He wrote me a personal letter explaining that he was compelled to be anti-gay by a karmic debt from a past life and he hoped I would not hold it against him personally."[115] As far as excuses for hating others go, that was an interesting approach, given that it places the impulse within a framework that cannot be challenged by any outsider. But while John Score was one of the most vocal advocates of excluding gays from the Craft, his was far from the lone viewpoint on either side of the Atlantic, and this attitude continues at some level to dog the steps of gay and bisexual practitioners in Great Britain to this day.

Steven Critchley, who was brought into Gardnerian Wicca in 1997 by Patricia Crowther in her Sheffield coven, states that he has been the target of many homophobic comments in the British Neo-Pagan/Craft community. "I have often been examined with a curious eye when known to be a gay high priest and have been asked many times if I performed the Great Rite either in token or 'truly' with Patricia when I became 3rd degree Wiccan," Critchley writes. "It's like they are asking 'oh my god — how can he really work polarity!' I am sure that you know that prejudice against homosexuals has been rife in the occult world in many movements besides Wicca — such as in Dion Fortune's Society of the Inner Light — mainly on the grounds of understandings of 'polarity', but [also] in some cases where traditional Hebraic moralistic and religious views have been subscribed to."[116]

Satanists in the Woodpile

Public relations also played a key role in the marginalizing of homosexuals in Wica. Harold Moss believed this to be a leading reason for the anti-gay Witch-hunt in the Craft, writing, "[Score] feels — perhaps rightfully, for I do not know the English legal scene — that homosexuals in the alternative religious movement could undermine the work accomplished to make ordinary citizens see Pagans and Witches in a sympathetic light."[117] Christian moralists who despised Witchcraft, perversion and Satanism certainly went out of their way to purposefully conflate them, a stance that the press did not always question when reporting on such matters.[118] Masturbatory fantasies, such as *Sex and Modern Witchcraft* (1969), passed for truth in portraying the sodomitical degradation of adolescent boys in Satanic rites as a cautionary tale against the readers themselves getting involved in the occult.[119]

To confuse matters further, there *were* homosexuals involved in Satanic groups, and in sadomasochistic groups that engaged in ritualistic practices modeled on a fantasy vision of modern Satanism or on those of the historical Hellfire Clubs, just as surely as there were heterosexual participants in both of these camps.[120] Photographer Robert Mapplethorpe, who was later celebrated by mainstream critics for his erotic photographs of flowers and reviled for those featuring sado-masochism, dabbled in Satanism throughout the 1970s (partly as an artistic conceit) and was heavily into BDSM. Candy Darling was another who was intrigued by Satanism, and she traveled with a copy of Anton LaVey's *Satanic Bible*, which she studied and underlined.[121]

Some of the antipathy to homosexuals within the occult community can, perhaps, be blamed on the historical (if not entirely accurate) association of sodomy with the practices of the Knights Templar, who were said to worship an androgynous God named Baphomet that the Catholic Church equated with Satan. Leo Martello wrote of a gay S/M group in New York who adopted pseudo-Templar rites in order to worship Satan in the form of Baphomet.[122] *Esquire* magazine's March 1970 cover spread, "Evil Lurks in California," described a gay S/M ritual in 1969, with Hellfire Club overtones, to support the thesis that the West Coast was quite literally going to the Devil.[123]

Gay men, like straight ones, could be found on the membership roll of the Church of Satan (CoS). One noted example was Gavin Arthur, who was a noted astrologer in the San Francisco Bay area and a grandson of Republican President Chester A. Arthur.[124] On the heterosexual end of the Kinsey scale one could find former CoS member Isaac Bonewits, who, in the documentary *Satanis: The Devil's Mass* (1969), can be observed asking Lucifer to bestow a blessing upon his manhood.[125, 126]

The Bonewits case illustrates the double standard that functioned within the occult community in the 1970s. At a time when homosexuals were being smeared with the Satanist/Left-Hand-Path epithet within the occult community, Bonewits' actual Satanic interlude was eventually laughed off as a youthful indiscretion and did no lasting harm to his own standing in that same community. He became the editor of *Gnostica News* in 1973 after his stint in the CoS, and went on to found the Druid fellowship Ár nDraíocht Féin in 1983. Yet despite the fervent wishes of the more homophobic Witches, homosexuals were involved in Wica, and many of them were there for the same reason that their straight siblings were — to rise above the hidebound and judgmental attitudes of the mainstream Abrahamic faiths.

The true irony of this insistence that all homosexual occultists were, by definition, "black" practitioners is that the Satanists themselves were sometimes just as disparaging of homosexuals as the so-called "white" Witches or the Christians. CoS founder Anton LaVey stated in *The Satanic Bible* that "Satanism condones any type of sexual activity which properly satisfies your individual desires — be it heterosexual, homosexual, bisexual, or even asexual, if you choose."[127] As if to prove this point, LaVey is shown in a 1987 documentary conducting a "prayer-response" during one of his rituals in which a male member of his coven asks for Satan's help in seducing someone named Roger.[128]

This egalitarian ideal of the CoS did not always prevail in practice. An example is the treatment that Ronald Barrett, a Second Degree member of the CoS' Lilith Grotto in New York City, received at the hands of Anton and Diane LaVey, who had turned against him. Writing to Michael Aquino in 1973, Diane LaVey said, "If you sense a subtle hostility on our part towards him, please understand that it is not him personally to whom we object, but rather to the homophile's personality in general, which we find extremely mercurial."[129] One homosexual Satanist, in a 1970 letter to *The Proceedings of the Church of Satan*, complained that "all of the articles written for the *Cloven Hoof* that I have seen covering the aspect of sex have covered only the heterosexual aspect. As I am sure that I am not the only homosexual Satanist, I believe there is a need for an article covering the homosexual aspect of sex from a Satanic viewpoint."[130] Thus, while LaVey publicly promoted the CoS as being tolerant of gays, in private the church's record was not spotless. Still, on the whole the Luciferian record on this score was far better than that of the so-called White Witches, whom they despised.[131] Even a rank sexploitation film like *Sex Ritual of the Occult* (1970) cut closer to the truth than the Gardnerian party line when it placed homosexual acts within the context of ritual and noted that "These practices can be traced back to ancient times."[132]

Frederic Lamond, in a romantic look back at the history of the Wica, proclaimed that "more than 10 years before the flower child period of the late 1960s [Gardnerians] already lived their values."[133] This positioning of Gardnerian covens as egalitarian groups studiously avoids the conservative origins of Wica which was certainly not in the progressive spirit of that period. However, it can be argued that the ill-treatment of sexual minorities by the leadership of many lineaged covens on both sides of the Atlantic did arguably fit into that pattern, even if their treatment of racial minorities did not. It was not enough to claim that homosexuals and, in many cases, bisexuals were intrinsically incapable of fulfilling the roles that would be required of them by the prevailing theory of magickal operations within a "genuinely contacted" coven, nor was it apparently sufficient to say that homosexuals were rejected from Wica on the basis of mental illness or criminal intent, however spurious those arguments might be. To avoid being tarred by society with the same brush as that used against the homosexuals, many Witches felt obligated to repeat Gardner's plea in *Witchcraft Today*, pointing out to anyone who would listen the differences between themselves and the real perverts.

Leo Martello noted the hypocrisy of the Witches who adopted this position, writing that by lumping together homosexuals and black magick these "'protest too much' witches of the 'white, right hand path' have adopted the same prejudicial weapons of their Christian persecutors."[134] In other words, by unjustifiably labeling homosexuals as evil and Satanic in order to look good by comparison, many Witches committed harm against other human beings, thereby violating the Wiccan Rede. The fact that it was done unthinkingly within the social matrix of the times is no defense, for the Witch is supposed to possess what Lamond calls "a personal moral autonomy" independent of the fossilized dogma of prior movements.[135] In light of societal developments, this continued insistence on the deviancy of homosexuals and their unsuitability for participating in Wica began to look like nothing more than a rearguard action to sustain public support for their own deeply-held prejudices.

Raymond Buckland's negative reaction in *Ancient & Modern Witchcraft* (1970) was directed more against the concept of a same-sex coven than it was toward disbarring men who happened to be homosexual and who wished to practice Gardnerian Witchcraft. The Bucklands had, in fact, initiated at least one gay man by the time Raymond's words on the subject were been published. However, to be a successful candidate of in Brentwood Coven, a gay man had to practice the rites with a straight face, as it were.[136] Donna Cole Schultz was another Gardnerian elder who was open to working with homosexuals. A descendent of Madge Worthington and Arthur Eaglen's Whitecroft Gardnerian line, as well as having worked with Lois Bourne and with Ruth Wynn Owen of the Plant Bran traditional family group among other Craft people, Donna's *bona fides* were as impressive as Raymond's. One of her initiates writes, "Donna was very progressive for a Wiccan Leader at that period in history. Hers was one of the first Gardnerian lines to be very accepting of gays in the Craft. ... There were always gay members of [her coven,] the Temple of the Sacred Stones."[137]

As the inner workings of most Gardnerian covens tend to be masked from the public, it is unsurprising, particularly given the era in which it occurred, that the presence of homosexuals in the Bucklands' and Schultz-Enderle covens would pass unremarked for so long. The outspoken homophobia of many Craft practitioners on both sides of the Atlantic virtually guaranteed that those who were willing to work with homosexuals would not publicize the fact lest they themselves risk being ostracized for their liberality. The apparent absence of gays in the Craft very likely aggravated their situation, because while familiarity may sometimes breed contempt, complete ignorance will almost assuredly do so. As one gay Gardnerian high priest noted in a 1982 interview with the Craft newsletter *The Hidden Path*, "I do hope that people will make some effort to understand how difficult it is to be a gay male witch. It's a position in which you're not understood by your gay peers or your Craft ones. It's really a minority within a minority."[138]

While bisexuals and homosexuals had been practicing — albeit quietly and invisibly — within the Craft since its advent on American shores, the heightened visibility of gays in the aftermath of Stonewall seemed to provoke a visceral response within certain members of the Craft against their admittance, particularly in Great Britain. In an attempt to spur public discussion on this subject, Sybil Leek devoted an entire chapter to the place of homosexuals in the Craft in her book *The Complete Art of Witchcraft* (1971). There, she made a remarkably poignant case for allowing gay men and lesbians to practice Witchcraft openly, particularly given the era and her own upbringing in England. However, it was a cautious rather than a whole-hearted endorsement, for Leek stated on one hand that "I think that within witchcraft we could find a place for the homosexuals of society," yet on the other hand she noted that "I do not think that they could rise to be part of the inner hierarchy of Wicca."[139] Martello and others criticized Leek's timid endorsement, yet even backhanded acceptance was better than nothing at all. *(Ibid n#63)*

Gay men and lesbians were beginning to demand access and equal footing within the Craft movement just as they were within the framework of society's political structures. However, many in positions of authority within the Craft saw no reason to change. As in society at large, charges of perversion remained one of the preferred means of smearing one's opponents in the ongoing conflicts within the Craft. No matter how often the words of the Goddess passed over their tongues in ritual, some could still not abide in their hearts that all acts of love and pleasure really *are* sacred to Her.[140] Of all the possible areas to share common ground with the Catholic Church, this was probably the most reprehensible. Echoing the conclusions of Metacalus, author Jack Fritscher scolded prudish Witches who sought to limit the practice of the Craft to heterosexuals, saying — quite correctly — that any sex act will provide the underlying power source for magick. "People who claim to be witches can be tested with this rede," Fritscher asserted, "if they are sexual Puritans, they are not really witches."[141]

Thus the question returns to the role that homosexuality may have played in the decision to cut Eddie Buczynski and Herman Slater off from the Gardnerian current, given that both men were openly gay (and sometimes flamboyantly so). Known homosexuals were blacklisted in some Gardnerian lineages, particularly in England where a move was underway to root out "deviates," and enormous peer pressure was brought to bear to ensure that the party line was toed in this respect. *(Ibid n#109)* Alex Sanders' antics in the late 1960s reinforced the opinion in England that homosexuals and bisexuals were inherently unstable and poor candidates for initiation. Regarding allegations of instability, it was not until December 1973 that the APA Board of Trustees ruled that homosexuality would no longer be classified as a "mental disorder" in the United States.[142] Homosexual acts were still considered a criminal offense in most states, even at that time.

Was Buczynski's and Slater's homosexuality the underlying reason for Fran Fisher's vouch being denied? Clearly, Eddie believed that it was a factor, bitterly laying the blame at the feet of Monique Wilson and her American downline. "The taboo against homosexuality was exalted by this woman, who was an avowed 'fag hater,'" he wrote in 1977. "And so the 'Gardnerian' witches (as they are now called) took the public lead in representing paganism and witchcraft in the modern age. And with it the homosexual taboo grew. Where once it was only forbidden to practice homosexuality during the rites, now homosexuals were even forbidden entry into the cult, on the premise that, because of the nature of their sexual preferences, homosexuals would never be able to function in the presence of the opposite sex."[143]

Others, such as Sally Eaton, agreed, saying that if homophobia was present in the American branch of the Craft, one need look no further than its progenitor, Monique Wilson. "I am told *Olwen* was a flaming homophobe who didn't tolerate Gays, but openly rejected them," Eaton writes. "Although Ray isn't homosexual, he was far more tolerant than *Olwen* had been."[144, 145] Tommy Kneitel implied that homophobia may have played a role in restricting the entrance of gays into the Craft in the United States, writing, "The Bucklands had never (and would never have) initiated a homosexual. They felt there was an unwritten law not to bring gays into Wicca. This was something they had picked up in England, where they came from and where they had been initiated."[146]

"There was a lot of conflict among the covens as to whether or not a gay man or woman could function successfully within the [Witchcraft] cult," observed Peter Levenda. "The Craft emphasizes the male-female polarity in everything they do: high priest and priestess, the priest drawing down the moon into the priestess, etc. Thus, how does a gay man, for instance, fit into this structure? Is he 'male enough' to be a high priest, etc.? I heard Eddie proclaim that he was male, i.e. 'straight', within the circle in the sense that he was purely a high priest channeling 'male energy', but I don't know if that was politics, hyperbole, or the unvarnished truth."[147]

Raymond Buckland's own words from *Ancient and Modern Witchcraft* (1970) do raise the question of homophobia. *(Ibid n#91)* And yet it was Raymond, and not the Kneitels, who ended up supporting Herman Slater and Eddie Buczynski in their claim of Gardnerian lineage in 1973. Raymond Buckland stated that neither he nor Rosemary was opposed to working with homosexuals: *(Ibid n#136)*

> *Rosemary is not a homophobe. As I never was. [This] was a case of people misinterpreting what had originally been said. We stated — as we had been taught — that the coven (Gardnerian) had to have equal number of male and female. Because of that it seemed to us that gays or lesbians would not be attracted to that tradition, but that didn't mean that they were excluded if they were willing to work with someone of the opposite sex. In fact, from the very start — the first coven we had — we had a homosexual in it. He worked with a female. No problem. No homophobes!*

Buckland's recollection is bolstered by his December 1973 letter to the first edition of the Warlock Shop's newspaper, *Earth Religion News*, where he publicly clarified his position on the subject. "In recent years we have seen a general 'mellowing' of this approach [to homosexuals in the Craft] (I personally think it is a good thing). With the greater acceptance of homosexuality, Gardnerian covens, along with other traditions, are quite willing to accept individuals of whatever mind. The criterion is — as it should be — how one relates *within* the Circle. What one does outside the Circle is, as it has always been, one's own concern. Homosexuality is today, therefore, no more reason for exclusion from Gardnerian covens than race or color."[148]

But the timing of Raymond's letter seems to imply that Buczynski's and Slater's homosexuality may have been a factor in the behind-the-scenes bickering during that year, to the point where he felt the need to present a countering opinion. However, just as the evidence does not support the accusation that either of the Bucklands was overtly homophobic in their treatment of gays, it also appears to demonstrate that the Kneitels' opposition to Buczynski's and Slater's initiations didn't arise from overt dislike of homosexuals. When asked by Leo Martello in a 1973 interview whether gays were welcome to study with their coven, Judy Kneitel stated that a homosexual preference was not an impediment, provided that the person in question could work within the Gardnerian system. "I suppose that if there was a person who was a homosexual who could establish a social rapport with our members, had a [working] partner of the opposite sex, and was otherwise suitable for membership — there is a possibility that they would be considered for Initiation. ... I don't feel that a homosexual offers any affront to the Craft as it is practiced in our coven, insofar as the philosophical aspect of it being a fertility-based religion."[149]

Tommy Kneitel repeated this affirmation in 2005. Commenting on their refusal to initiate Buczynski in 1972, Tommy wrote, "Eddie's lifestyle played no part in our decision not to initiate him. ... We trained, initiated and worked with openly gay people right from the start. Sexual preference was never a factor in our decision as to whether to initiate." *(Ibid n#146)* The presence of homosexuals in the Kneitels' coven was confirmed by Gardnerian initiate Michael Thorn, who said that he personally knew of at least three gay men who were members of that coven in the 1970s.[150] Margot Adler concurs: "I think that's probably true. I don't know how many, but I think that's probably true. Certainly there were gays ... in our coven with Branwen and Bryce from the beginning."[151] Roger Pratt, a gay Gardnerian high priest descended from Donna Cole Schultz through the lines of both Eleanor "Ray" Bone and Judy Kneitel, also supported this assertion. "The Kneitels hadn't any problem with gay craft members," Pratt writes. "There were quite a few while I was around. Of course one's working partner had to be female — it's just SO Gardnerian."[152]

This is not to say that the Kneitels didn't try to stay on good terms with the likes of John Score and others who weren't open to allowing gays into the Craft. In a 1974 article in the *Earth Religion News*, Leo Martello lambasted such efforts, implying that the Kneitels were hoodwinking Score by hiding the fact that they not only had gays in their own coven, but also had loaned two gay men money to keep their occult shop afloat.[153] The Kneitels could not be seriously faulted for maintaining cordial relations with Score, as it was an accepted part of Craft etiquette. As to the latter point, it was typical of Martello's acerbic wit to highlight the fact that in happier days, the Kneitels had actually helped to keep the Warlock Shop financially solvent, thereby losing the opportunity to rid themselves of these troublesome priests.

Finally, Eddie's high priestess, Renate Springer, states that she isn't aware of anyone making an issue out of Eddie's homosexuality. "I never heard anything that people had said 'Oh Eddie is gay' or something like this. Never. I never heard that. And I never had the feeling that anybody had anything against his [being] gay."[154] Thus, while gays were far from universally accepted in the Craft in 1974, it cannot be proved that Eddie's and Herman's sexual orientation was an overriding factor in their treatment at the hands of Rosemary Buckland and Judy Kneitel. But regardless of its root cause, the end result was the same — conflict.

Chapter 15: The Edge of the Cold Moon's Blade

As Brothers, Fight Ye

In the face-off between Long Island and Kentucky, the covens in Louisville, Kentucky, Paterson, New Jersey, Brooklyn Heights, New York and Riverside, New York chose to support Raymond Buckland. This overt expression of amity by the Warlock Shop and the so-called "Kentucky Line" won them no friends among the initiates of the Long Island Line; however, given what had already passed between these Lines so far, Buczynski and Slater considered it to be a small matter. Of greater concern was the impact of this friendship on the Fishers' own standing in Gardnerian Wica, for the Long Island Line was spreading the story that the Kentucky Line was fraudulent, placing them on par with the faux "Witches' Farthings" that Buckland was selling to credulous tourists through the Warlock Shop.

When the controversy broke out over her legitimacy in the Gardnerian tradition, Patricia Siero realized that she had gotten far more than she had bargained for. The constant bickering was a huge drain on her energy and a distraction from her duties as high priestess. Whether or not Fran Fisher was a legitimate Gardnerian high priestess was no longer the issue. Having only been a member of the tradition for a few months, Siero was already facing the prospect of her entire future downline being unrecognized by a significant portion of the Gardnerian lineage in the United States. Thus, when Judy Kneitel offered Patricia an olive branch in the form of a Gardnerian initiation in the fall of 1973, she took it. Siero renounced her own initiation from Fran Fisher and went on to revoke the vouches of all the initiations she had conducted as a Gardnerian high priestess, including those of Eddie and Herman.[1] Both men were outraged. Siero's decision had, in essence, publicly acknowledged that Fran Fisher's vouch was forged. In one fell swoop, the local rivals to the Kneitels' authority in the Gardnerian tradition had been effectively neutralized.[2]

Despite Siero's actions, Fran and Gerald Fisher were not shy about continuing to publicly assert their own place in the Gardnerian hierarchy. They came out fighting in December with an announcement in the inaugural edition of the *Earth Religion News*. Appearing a year after Rosemary Buckland's retirement, Gerald Fisher's article claimed the precedence of the Louisville Coven in the Craft, stating "It is hoped that all Gardnerian Covens and all persons desiring to become Gardnerian will contact The Lady Theo."[3] This last was a direct challenge to Rosemary Buckland's chosen successor, Judy Kneitel. If that was insufficient for a knockout, the Fishers also announced that on December 16, 1973 they had incorporated Gardnerian Wica in the state of Kentucky:[4,5]

> *In accordance with the laws of the land, Gardnerian Wicca has been incorporated as a legal, non-profit religious corporation, and now has the same status as any legal religion in the United States and will enjoy legal protection under the law.*

A further jab was administered with a statement that appeared on the banner of the inaugural edition of the *Earth Religion News* — "This is the Official Organ for 'Gardnerian Wicca, Inc.' in the United States of America." This assertion led to a growing perception that perhaps Slater's ultimate goal was to control, or to at least dominate, a post-Buckland Gardnerian Wica in the United States.[6] "Herman told me that he was setting up a Gard hierarchy to rival that of Theos', and asked me to join," recalls Ed Fitch.[7] But this made no sense to those who knew Herman. One acquaintance stated that Herman had never really cared about being a Gardnerian, even though he had gone along with Eddie's quest to become Gardnerian; Slater's first love was the Traditionalist Gwyddoniaid, and he remained a devoted Welsh initiate to the end of his life.[8] A former employee of Slater, Peter Conte, confirms this. "You've probably been told of his love of money, cheap gin and blondes, but I saw a different Herman," Conte writes. "He had an undying love of the 'Welsh Tradition' and just the mention of it would bring Herman into a very serious focus."[9]

But while Slater may not have cared all that much about his own Gardnerian credentials, he knew that Buczynski felt differently about the matter and so fought to protect his lover's reputation. Herman also didn't like to back down in a fight, especially when he believed that the Fishers had both the requisite lineal, and now legal, standing to fend off any counterclaims of legitimacy. The first issue of the *Earth Religion News* was the end result of this maneuvering. Though Eddie was listed as the paper's editor, the assault on the Kneitels within its pages had the fingerprints of its publisher, Herman Slater, all over it.

The rumor that Slater was attempting to take over the Gardnerian Tradition was somewhat ironic, given that the Kneitels themselves were, from Herman's perspective, exercising undue influence over the rest of that tradition in the United States.[10] This opinion was reflected in the pages of Earth Religion News with a picture of an antique woodcut subtitled "Four Gardnerian Witch Queens Dividing up the World!"[11] In that same issue, an article by Raymond Buckland off-handedly dismissed the Commack Coven as "Kneitel-Gardnerian," or a Gardnerian-adapted tradition on the same order as Mary Nesnick's Alexandrian-Gardnerian "Algard" tradition — a terrible insult from a Gardnerian point of view, in light of the events between the Bucklands and Nesnick in 1967. Buckland lamented the abuse of power, the bastardizing of the Gardnerian Tradition and the ego-trip that some covens engage in, each trying to outdo the other, not only between traditions but within them. He also first gave voice to an oft-repeated complaint against Judy Kneitel: "It is said of one (Long Island, New York) Priestess that she initiates anyone who happens to drive slowly past her house."[12, 13]

Slater friend and author Simon recalls that Herman was "a notorious gossip and delighted in causing trouble, but anyone who knew him understood that it was not malicious but ... well, 'mischievous' might be the better word."[14] Tommy Kneitel disagreed with that assessment, remembering "a spate of false statements and rumors about our coven that tracked directly to the back room at the [Warlock Shop]." *(Ibid n#1)* Herman admittedly reveled in being a mischief maker at times, as evidenced by a sign in the shop reading, "If you heard a rumor, it probably started here." Ria Farnam said, "If you look at the universe as a great cauldron, Herman Slater was the wooden spoon in the Goddess' hand. He was a shit stirrer."[15] Tommy claimed that the Kneitels did not respond to any of these provocations, but while they may not have responded publicly, there was an inevitable tit-for-tat exchange of put-downs that played out through the proxies of both groups. This point was tacitly acknowledged by Judy Kneitel when she noted the involvement of Gardnerians in creating "the present state of misery."[16]

"They each had their stories about each other," said Kenny Lowenstein, recalling that one of the slanders directed against Buczynski by the Long Island camp had him going down to "The Tombs" (otherwise known as the Manhattan House of Detention at 125 White Street) and offering to bail out people in exchange for their accepting initiation at his hand.[17] Aside from the implication that Eddie accepted criminals into his covens, there is the smell of anti-gay bias in this particular accusation, as Miguel Piñero's production "Short Eyes", which depicted homosexual rape and child molesters in the Tombs, was playing in New York at the time.[18] Eddie, for his part, tended to avoid the conflict and focus instead on the work, according to Ed Fitch. "To Ed Buczynski's credit and in line with his more quiet personality, he did not take part in any mud-slinging, and instead preferred to take a low-key approach, writing and researching for what would become part of an upcoming Book of Shadows," writes Fitch. "I believe that he did not care for all the high emotions and hard feelings that were going on around him. At least that was the impression that I received in my last letters exchanged with Eddie." *(Ibid n#7)*

On more than one occasion, the detritus of baneful spell-workings, and other debris that is best left undescribed, was deposited at the front door of the Warlock Shop by persons unknown. Rumors have long circulated of other, even less respectable, exchanges — rocks thrown through windows, murdered pets, Witches outed at their places of employment and fired from their jobs.[19] While none of these claims have ever been independently substantiated, their persistence over the years points to the substantial feelings of ill-will within the community at the time.

One theme that appears throughout this period is the urgency with which the two sides appeared to be trying to grow their numbers. "[It] all centered on questions of empire-building and legitimacy," Judith McNally writes. "A few really wanted a power base of covens and daughter covens, and quickly. The question of who was or was not a 'real witch' seemed a major preoccupation for many as well."[20] At least one person noted that the joke about people driving slowly past Judy Kneitel's house on Long Island isn't that far-fetched if you examine the size of the Gardnerian lineage descending from her.[21]

Leo Martello, in a transparent poke at the Kneitels, observed that this fast pace could backfire, with initiates turning on their initiators when the quantity of candidates was favored over their inherent quality.[22] It is somewhat unusual for a lineaged Gardnerian coven to advertise for members in a national publication, as the Commack Coven eventually did in the pages of *Gnostica News* and *Fate* magazine in 1975 and 1976.[23] But Eddie was hardly an innocent himself when it came to the numbers game. McNally asserts that in 1972, "Ed was in a tearing hurry to have a good-sized [Welsh] coven, and then in a rush to have a daughter coven." She recalled having to turn away students he sent to her because she and her high priest were unable to keep up. *(Ibid n#20)*

The main result of the sustained low-level conflict between these two sides was a corrosive miasma that was not beneficial to any of the parties in their efforts to present a reasoned face to interested seekers, scholars or the public. Martello friend and long-time Gardnerian practitioner Patricia Crowther noted the overall divisive climate within the Craft with disapproval, writing, "I'm afraid that there is a lot too much muck throwing, and too many people trying to get on the bandwagon. I believe that the Craft should be a Brotherhood, like freemasonry, and not everyone tearing each other to pieces."[24]

Unhappy Hela Days

Renate Springer (*Hela*) was of a like mind with Crowther. Like Siero, Springer was not a political creature. She just wanted to be able to practice her Craft with good German efficiency and a minimum of hassle, and at this juncture that was just not in the cards. With Siero's abdication and submission to the Kneitels, Renate was in an awkward position. With her own place as a Gardnerian high priestess now undeniably forfeit, she could continue on as she had, at the center of a maelstrom and recognizing that her downline initiates would be considered illegitimate, or she could make a change and hope that things would blow over.

In the few short months since she had been made a high priestess, Springer had become increasingly unhappy with the hostile climate in which she had to operate. She blamed much of this on Slater's schemes to get back at the Kneitels.[25] Granted, she had also benefited from her association with Slater, for example by appearing on television with him and Eddie to speak about Wica.[26] However, these small opportunities did not make up for having her name dragged into a Witch War.

Springer also recognized that Buczynski was not entirely faultless in creating her situation; for Eddie's overriding desire to be a successful and respected Gardnerian high priest, laudable as that might be, was the driving force behind Slater's actions. Like it or not, the Warlock Shop, as the most active and visible occult store in the New York Metropolitan area, and its owners were, as Simon would later write, "a magnet for Wiccan politicking and gossip."[27] Eddie seemed either unable or unwilling to bring Herman to heel. Tommy Kneitel believed it was the former. "I don't know for sure the role Eddie played in [*Earth Religion News*], as opposed to what Herman did — but I suspect that Herman was calling all the shots, with Eddie having virtually no say in what got published." *(Ibid n#1)*

Apart from the stress of riding the Brooklyn Heights whirlwind, tension had begun to build between Renate and Eddie on how the coven was to be run almost from its beginning. Like a barely restrained young bull, Eddie was eager to charge off, wanting a greater say in how the coven was run than was usual in Gardnerian Wica. Renate, meanwhile, was resisting his energetic attempts to take the lead. *(Ibid n#25)* As Renate and Kay would say to one another when Eddie got on a roll, "*Er ist etwas* (He is something)."[28] Buczynski had wooed Ria Farnham away from her Welsh duties by Samhain of 1973 in favor of studying Gardnerian Wica, and both Ria and David Farnham were initiated into the Gardnerian Outer Court coven at that time.[29] Eddie spent almost the next two months trying to convince Springer to initiate the couple and some other candidates from the Pagan Way into the inner court, but Springer kept putting off the decision to do so. He tried to keep these problems from the Pagan Way students, but it was obvious to them that something was amiss.

Magickally speaking, the two worked well together. "When I look at the Book [of Shadows]," Renate remembers, "the way [Eddie] put it together, he was very helpful and loving to the high priestess. He was a good high priest. That I know for sure."[30] However, there were some differences in how the tradition was practiced in the Brooklyn Heights Coven versus other covens of Gardnerian Wica. One example is the Great Rite, the sexual union between the high priestess and high priest that is representative of the relationship between the Goddess and the Horned God. "We never did [the Great Rite]," Renate laughs. "No, no ... not with Eddie. I was married and I had two children and ... so that didn't happen to do with Eddie being gay. But I never even thought about it. I mean, it never occurred to me to perform the Great Rite with Eddie." *(Ibid n#30)* Yet the two did perform the Great Rite, perhaps semi-symbolically, a point confirmed by Buczynski friend Kathryn Frank, who said that Eddie had told her so.[31]

For those Gardnerian purists who insist that the Great Rite must be practiced both as a sexual, and a symbolically representative, act, this was an obvious problem in how the rites and magick of the tradition were implemented within the Brooklyn Heights Coven. It also raises one of the main objections of many straight Gardnerians of the day regarding the initiation of gay men in Gardnerian Wica or, for that matter, to straight men or women where only one partner in a monogamous marriage is a Craft practitioner.

For this reason, many Gardnerian high priestesses in the 1960s to mid-1970s preferred that women and men be brought in and elevated together as both working partners and as lovers. However, this preference represented a conservative interpretation of what Judy Kneitel had explained to Leo Martello as the "philosophical aspect of [Gardnerian Wica] being a fertility-based religion." Gardnerians might point to the failure of Renate and Eddie to engage in the Great Rite "in true" as a source of the disconnect that eventually developed between the two, although they were certainly not unique in eschewing the practice even within the Long Island Line of the Gardnerian Tradition.[32,33] Regardless of the reasons, whether mundane or magickal, or both, Buczynski was failing in his relationship with Renate as high priest to high priestess.[34]

Nevertheless, Renate finally agreed to initiate Ria and David Farnham into the coven at the Yule Sabbat, to be held on Friday, December 21. Preparations were underway when the confrontational Yule edition of the *Earth Religion News* came out. For Springer, this was the final straw. She decided that a change in coven leadership was needed in order to insulate the Brooklyn Heights Coven from the increasingly personalized attacks between the Warlock Shop and the Long Island Line. With that in mind, Springer requested a meeting with Eddie at her apartment on Friday and told him that she intended to elevate coven member Gilbert Littlebear (Craft name *Set*) to the Third Degree and take him on as her high priest. Buczynski was welcome to remain as an elder in the coven if he chose to do so, but he could no longer function as her high priest. Eddie was stunned. Ria and David were working in the Warlock Shop with Herman and Glenn when Eddie returned from the meeting. In tears, Buczynski informed the Farnhams that he was no longer the high priest of the coven and that he didn't know whether or not they would be initiated that night. *(Ibid n#34)*

Herman tried to calm Eddie down, but Buczynski was having none of it. He rounded on Slater, blaming him for the circumstances because of the fighting between him and the Long Island Gardnerians. Eddie also blamed the new high priest, accusing Littlebear of maneuvering behind the scenes to usurp his position in the coven. *(Ibid n#34)* But it was Herman who bore the brunt of his anger as they carried the fight to their upstairs apartment. Ria and David Farnham stood in shock as the battle took place. In the meantime, Gil Littlebear began calling the Warlock Shop, pressuring Ria to decide whether or not she and David were going to be present at Sabbat that night in order to be initiated.[35] During one of these phone calls between Hela's apartment and the Warlock Shop, Littlebear told Ria that she and David did not belong with Eddie because he was gay, and that Eddie wasn't going anywhere in the Craft because of his homosexuality. Littlebear informed Ria that she and David had a simple choice to make — they could either stay with Eddie and Herman, or they could go with Hela and Gil where they would be recognized as legitimate Gardnerians.[36]

Ria and David had been practicing Witches for a little over a year at this point. They had fallen in love with the Craft on their very first visit to the Warlock Shop in 1972. Ria had been given a copy of *The Gypsy Fortune Teller* for her birthday and from that had become enamored with the idea of learning to scry using a crystal ball. The couple paid the Warlock Shop a visit around September 20, 1972 near their wedding anniversary. "I first met Eddie in the store, when I was buying a crystal ball, and [David] was buying a skull. It was our anniversary and I had wanted a crystal ball so I went searching in the Village Voice for the ad for the Warlock Shop. I walked into the Craft that day and never left." *(Ibid n#29)* The Farnhams were immediately taken by the ambience of the place and impressed with the knowledge of its owners. Ria, in particular, fell hard for Buczynski. "When I first laid eyes on Eddie," Ria remembers, "I said to myself 'Ah, here is the epitome of the androgynous God.'"[37]

Herman Slater recruited Ria and David on the spot for the Sunday afternoon Pagan Way classes at Kay Smith's apartment in Vaseline Flats. "Eddie would come to Pagan Way for a sabbat or if he felt like getting away from Herman. I kept going to the store every Sunday and then started frequenting the shop one or two days a week. It was Herman who [looked forward to seeing] us in the beginning, not Eddie. We were good spenders. I was infatuated with Eddie from the beginning. I would make sure I spoke to him each time we came to the shop, which by October was about three times a week."[38] *(Ibid n#29, 34)*

The couple began helping out at the store in return for being allowed to hang out there. Ria helped ship out orders and receive merchandise, while David handled the mail. When choosing a Craft name, Ria complained that she couldn't find a Goddess name to which she was drawn. Nothing spoke to her. Eddie happened to be walking around the shop in a bathrobe and said to her, "Why don't you just use your own name? It's one of my favorite Goddesses," and started to waltz up the stairs. Ria ran after him and asked, "There's a Goddess named Ria?" After telling her the correct spelling of the name, Eddie said she should go look it up. Thus did Ria Farnham choose *Rhea* as her Craft name. *(Ibid n#35)*

It is fair to say that Ria worshipped the ground Eddie walked on, and her loyalties were not in question. "My initiation was still on if I wanted to go with Hela and Gil Littlebear, but I wouldn't leave Eddie," Ria said in a 2005 interview. *(Ibid n#35)* She informed Littlebear that they would not be present for the Yule Sabbat. Several more phone exchanges that day resulted in the same answer. Meanwhile, the fight overhead continued unabated. *(Ibid n#35)* Hearing the turmoil over the telephone, Renate came into the shop that afternoon and went upstairs to speak with Eddie, who had calmed down by this point. She came back downstairs a short time later and, in the same back room where much of the politicking and gossip allegedly took place, Springer snapped to Slater, "He says this is *you* causing this." Herman coldly responded that it was Renate's and Gil's fault: "*You* ripped Eddie's heart apart over this." *(Ibid n#35)* Springer left the shop, never to return. She and Eddie did not speak again to one another after that, although they did exchange several cassette tapes by post, which rehashed their grievances with one another but did nothing to resolve them. In early 1974, Renate moved from Brooklyn to Long Island and ceased running her own coven. She began to visit with the Kneitels once or twice a month, and was eventually initiated and elevated by them in the Long Island Line of Gardnerian Wica.[39]

For all intents and purposes, the Long Island Line had won the day in New York. A cartoon on the front cover of the March issue of *Earth Religion News* seemed to bitterly acknowledge this reality. It depicted a skyclad Witch standing before an altar. On the wall next to her hung a framed vouch signed by "The Queen of All Wicca."[40] One can almost imagine the Ed Sanders tune "Priestess" playing softly in the background as it was being sketched.[41] Slater eventually took his revenge by printing in the final issue of *Earth Religion News* the contents of *Witch*, a pamphlet originally issued by *Rex Nemorensis* (Charles Cardell) in 1964.[42] Cardell had used *Witch* to attack Gerald Gardner, with whom he had once been on friendly terms, and Doreen Valiente. More significantly, the pamphlet (and article) revealed a significant amount of the Gardnerian Book of Shadows.[43] The Warlock Shop received many complaints about its publication, but Slater turned a deaf ear. Besides, the secret was already out.

In the end, a vouch, no matter who signs it, isn't worth the paper it's written on if the beauty and power of the tradition it represents are not also written upon the heart of its owner or, indeed, the one that confers it. When that that power is truly present (which happens less often than one would hope in any spiritual path, including the Gardnerian tradition), the vouch itself is like wrapping paper, concealing the real gifts of peace and harmony the tradition presents to the seeker. Joe Wilson touched on this point in reference to Leo Martello's Continental tradition, writing in 1971 that "I think it makes no difference whether anyone invented the names and rites they use or not. Sincerity is the key here."[44]

Ed Fitch echoed this sentiment in response to the in-fighting of 1973. "Pedigrees are not of importance, and antiquity is not really needed," wrote Fitch. "We would all be better off with less time and emotion placed on them."[45] This is not to say that Eddie was wrong to pursue a Gardnerian lineage, for he truly believed that the tradition offered a legitimate spiritual path for him, and there is clearly much to recommend it to those looking to explore the soul of the Universe. But, ultimately, each person sees Creation from his or her own perspective in this quest. One cannot force one's own vision upon others, any more than one can paper over one's differences with any number of vouches.

Reflecting on Buczynski's quest, Tommy Kneitel wrote, "The determination of one's legitimacy (or lack thereof), it seems to me, comes down to two basic points ... who will acknowledge someone as having been validly initiated into a given Tradition, and who will work with them as such. It's not necessarily a question of what claims a person makes on their own behalf. Those who can vouch for someone are willing to work with them in a particular tradition. Those who don't accept them are unwilling to work with them in a given tradition. Ed claimed to be a Gardnerian, but we didn't accept him as such. There are many people who have made various claims of legitimate Gardnerian lineage. It only became a question or issue if/when they sought or demanded acceptance or validation from us. Those who didn't care what we thought, and/or didn't seek to work with us, couldn't be prevented from making whatever claims they liked."[46] And yet during that time a fierce debate *was* raging in the Craft to determine who could — or could not — claim to be a Witch, Gardnerian or otherwise.

Chapter 16: The "Wars of the Witches"

The Media and the Message

Mass media coverage of occult themes continued to increase throughout the 1970s. This was not necessarily a healthy trend, as many books such as *The Complete Book of Magic and Witchcraft* (1970) and films such as the oft-cited *Rosemary's Baby* (1968) continued to link Witchcraft with Satanism in the public's mind, with an attendant spike in inquiries from "inappropriate" personalities.[1,2] Books also began to appear on the market, some from authors who were at least nominally marketed as Witches, advocating the use of Witchcraft to achieve personal power over others, including through the use of harmful magick.[3]

Witches of that time point to *Rosemary's Baby* as a particularly vexing problem. Its portrayal of Witches as stereotypical Devil-worshippers would not have been a serious problem, given that this story line had been played out in "B" movies many times over the years. However, the book became a best seller soon after it was published in 1967, and the movie was one of the most-anticipated summer releases of 1968.[4] Adding to the pop interest was the rumored participation in the film of a rising star in the occult community. Anton LaVey (1930-1997), founder of The Church of Satan and an advocate of Satanic Witchcraft, was alleged to have played the part of the Devil in the movie. Though this rumor was untrue, it added to his cachet and created a delicious shiver amongst the credulous film-goers who heard it. LaVey was a showman and advocate of an Objectivistic up-by-your-own bootstraps form of Satanism. When he spoke of Witchcraft, LaVey was expressing an affinity between modern Satanism and the medieval understanding of the term, defined as the practice of magick and ritual by anti-Christian socio-religious rebels.

Although LaVey demurred any association with *Rosemary's Baby*, he was involved in a number of other film projects. He appeared in Kenneth Anger's film *Invocation of my Demon Brother* (1969), and was a subject of two documentaries, *Satanis* (1970) and *Witchcraft '70* (1970), which was released in Europe as *Angeli Blanca, Angeli Negra* (1970). Between these films, his numerous media interviews, and his books — *The Satanic Bible* (1969), *The Complete Witch* (1971), and *The Satanic Rituals* (1972) — LaVey's image was firmly cemented in the public's mind as a representative of modern Witchcraft. It probably did not help the cause of Gardnerian Wica that its main spokesperson, Raymond Buckland, cultivated a goatee and mustache similar to those sported by LaVey at the time.

Satanism is generally defined as a spiritual belief system that falls within the penumbra of Christianity — which is to say that it has absolutely nothing to do with any form of Neo-Paganism. While this point was acknowledged by certain academics of the time, such as American religious scholar J. Gordon Melton of the Institute for the Study of American Religion, it was a minority opinion.[5] Neo-Pagan practitioners, including Witches of the Gardnerian-derived traditions, do not ascribe to or even believe in the mythology of the Zoroastrian opponent that forms the basis of the God-Satan duality of Christianity. For their part, the Satanists didn't particularly care what the Gardnerians — whom many of them derisively dismissed as "White Witches" — thought on the subject, and were somewhat amused by the discomfort the unwelcome association provoked in Wiccans. Citing history as the basis, they also believed that they had as much right to the use of the term "Witch" as anyone else.

The Satanists were both correct and incorrect. Certainly while the medieval concept of a Witch as the worshipper of the Christian Opponent fell into their bailiwick, the Witch of the Classical period did not. This distinction was complicated by the fact that modern Witches, helped along by Margaret Murray and others, tended to blur these two distinct types of Witches, and for good measure threw in traits from the Classical period associated solely with the priestly castes of the ancient temples. But the Witch of Classical history was not a member of the organized temple priesthoods, which were highly structured organizations concerned with maintaining social harmony by tending to relations between the worlds of Gods and men. Temples therefore were often necessarily the repositories of history, law, oracles, ritual and healing that were integrally woven into the fabric of, and often financially supported by, a city-state or nation. Priests and priestesses were specialists, honoring all of the Gods of their culture's pantheon, yet usually devoted to and serving one Deity in particular.

Witches, on the other hand, were usually solitary practitioners of magick, wortcunning, and divination who used their knowledge to heal, poison, curse, bless and guide individuals. They were generalists, skilled at striking pacts with many different Gods and spirits, bullying, cajoling and bribing Them in order to get their way. Because Witches usually operated outside the strictures of society they were often viewed with suspicion and fear even by those who made use of their services. However, in Classical times, individuals were also fully capable of communing with the Gods and spirits on their own behalf, making sacrifices and prayers without the intercession of others, and certainly without being viewed by their fellows as either priests or Witches. In the old days, a priestess would have taken great offense at being addressed as a Witch, and a Witch would have laughed at being referred to as a priestess. Then along came Margaret Murray and her theory of the survival of a degenerated form of Pagan worship, and suddenly the two were joined together like a spiritual jackalope.

Many Satanists also used the medieval concept of the devil-worshipping Witch to project a bogeyman purposefully designed to discomfit and unbalance their Christian detractors. A sizable percentage of Christian believers firmly held that any spiritual pursuit deviating from the Christian orthodox faith is in some way tainted by the Devil. So for the occult community, anything that drew a comparison between modern Witchcraft or Neo-Paganism and Satanic practices was problematic from a public relations standpoint. This was another way in which Hans Holzer stepped afoul of his critics in the occult community. Beginning with *The Truth About Witchcraft* in 1969, he included chapters on Satanic Witches in his books on the occult. This inclusion, more an egalitarian nod by Holzer to others who claimed the title of "Witch" than an actual linkage between Devil-worshippers and the modern Craft, still made many occult practitioners uneasy.

To some Christians, everyone who was not of their faith, sect or church was of Satan. The conflation of Witchcraft with Satanism, a relationship categorically denied by the Gardnerians and most other members of the modern occult movement at every opportunity, was a public relations headache for those who chose to serve as media points of contact (a recurring headache to this day). When given the choice between a discussion of boring, ethical white Witchcraft and one covering the (imagined) salacious dark arts, the media were always ready to jump on the message that was guaranteed to spur ratings or sell publications.

Given the potential for profit, it was inevitable that the sex industry would begin releasing tawdry, occult-themed soft and hard core pornography. One such short film was *Sex Ritual of the Occult* (1970), which featured staged scenes of black magic and Vodoun designed to titillate jaded voyeurs through its incorporation of sado-masochism, orgies and homosexuality.[6] Yet even the respectable mainstream media tend to err on the side of profit in these matters. Sybil Leek recounts her disastrous appearance on the *Today Show* with Hugh Downs and Barbara Walters where the matronly Witch "was expected to stir a cauldron while mouthing the usual 'Double, double, toil and trouble' bit out of Shakespeare, and to look as cackling and evil as possible."[7] The *Today Show* moderators were recalibrated during a commercial break and the interview was salvaged, but not every such instance turned out for the better. Regardless of the message that Witchcraft practitioners tried to convey, there were those who simply refused to believe that they were anything other than pawns of Satan and yet another sign that Western civilization was on the verge of total collapse.

Evangelical Christianity had undergone a renewal in the United States in the wake of wars and economic collapse in the early to mid-twentieth century. By the early 1970s, evangelicals had begun to engage the disruptive social changes that were sweeping the country. The rise of interest in the occult and its influence on popular youth culture was perceived to threaten the future place of Christianity in the United States. Preachers were fulminating against the dangers of the occult long before fantasy games incorporating magic, demons and ancient Gods, such as *Dungeons and Dragons* (1974), became the whipping boy for the religious right in 1979. With the increasing public exposure of Witchcraft and the revival of Pagan worship and interest in occult-linked activities, such as card-reading and astrology, right-wing Christians began to quite literally fan the flames of religious fury.

Occult-related books and other materials were burned regularly in public around the country in the early to mid-1970s. This trend did not go unnoticed in the occult press, where publications like *Green Egg* reported on such incidents as the book burning in 1974 in Rock Island, Iowa during a large public ceremony.[8] In response to a book-burning in Minneapolis, Llewellyn owner Carl Weschcke wrote a scathing editorial in *Gnostica News* that compared the book burners to the Inquisition and the followers of Hitler and Stalin. "Books are the building blocks of culture, the tools by which humanity raises itself from mob-thinking to personal responsibility — without which mankind has no soul," the publisher fulminated. "Books are keys to personal freedom, for with books, access to knowledge is not limited to 'official dogma.'"[9] A number of municipalities went so far as to ban the publication and sale of occult material, in violation of the First Amendment to the United States Constitution. Because the ban included material on astrology, *Fate* magazine wondered how long it would be before the newspapers and women's magazines, most of which published syndicated horoscope columns from such nationally known astrologers as Sidney Omarr and Sybil Leek, would begin howling about limits on the freedom of the press.[10] Yet others in the press, such as the *Christian Science Monitor*, openly questioned the rise of the occult and wondered whether the increased interest in "the cultic underground" represented the spiritual degeneration of the nation.[11]

The editors of the *Christian Science Monitor* might well have directed the same question at the other end of the spiritual spectrum, where such evangelists as Billy Graham constantly equated Witchcraft and magic with Satanism, drug use and evil. Graham, whom Isaac Bonewits labeled the "Führer of the New Witchburners," was a formidable opponent to occult practitioners because he had not only a national audience, but also the ear of powerful politicians.[12] Evangelical superstars like Graham could influence listeners across the nation to act locally on their narrow interpretation of scripture, whether by banning or burning "un-Godly" books, shutting down the stores that sold them, or praying for God to strike down those who had gone against His word. (One wonders why those who so often promote their God as being both omnipotent and omnipresent would see any need to direct His attention to what He must surely already know.)[13]

But if Graham's record-breaking crusade gatherings were comparable to a Broadway smash hit, the travelling freak show known as the

"Witchmobile" was its off-off-Broadway equivalent. Unveiled by charismatic evangelist Morris Cerullo, alleged ex-Satanist Mike Warnke, and public relations man Dave Balsiger in January 1972, this specially outfitted trailer — packed with Tarot decks, album covers with occult overtones, amulets, occult books, a human skull, and a plethora of occult-pop bric-a-brac — was designed to "educate" people on the evils of the occult and to "reconvert witches by education, not by hangings."[14,15] (That hangings were even mentioned was perhaps an indication of the evangelists' innermost thoughts on the preferred backup plan in case their educational efforts proved insufficient.) Warnke claimed to have been a high priest in a Satanic coven early in his adult life. Freeing himself from its influence was the basis for his popular book *The Satan Seller* (1973).

Unfortunately for him, critics pointed out that the available evidence did not appear to support the allegations Warnke made in his semi-autobiographical account; but that was no impediment to him as he grabbed the national spotlight for his Warholian fifteen minutes of fame.[16] Indeed, the more outlandish and horrific the reputed acts of occult criminal behavior were said to be, the more likely it seemed that a credulous and fearful audience of the churched would lap up fiction of this Christian pulp genre as if it were Gospel served with a side of tipsy cake. Reporter Andrew Rice, in examining the more recent connection between American evangelicals and those advocating the death of homosexuals in Uganda, observed that "The world is full of evangelists who confess all sorts of heinous past sins; a non-believer might say that exaggeration makes their testimony about subsequent redemption all that much more powerful."[17]

The story of another alleged ex-Satanist, Hershel Smith's *The Devil and Mr. Smith* (1974), was also built on this fantasy world of occult conspiracy, though it appeared to have no more basis in fact than Warnke's tale. Having wrung out what publicity they could from the Witchmobile, Cerullo sold the gimmick to Smith, who began his own evangelical tour. Hooting his battle cry "Thou shalt not suffer a witch to live!", Smith's peripatetic sideshow crisscrossed the countryside campaigning for the enactment and rigid enforcement of anti-occult laws.[18] *(Ibid n#14)* At Smith's St. Louis stop in November 1972, Tim Zell and others attempted to respond to his challenge to publicly debate anyone on the occult. Finally faced with a group of willing opponents, Smith failed to show at the appointed time. Instead, Zell and several like-minded fellows were reportedly roughed up by what was described in the press as an "Evangelical goon squad." Satisfied at having shown a spotlight on the true nature of their opponents, Zell presented Smith's wife with an award in recognition of Smith's advancing the cause of Neo-Paganism.[19] The beginnings of the Satanic panic and fears of ritual child abuse that swept the nation in the 1980s (e.g., the McMartin Preschool scandal and books such as *Michelle Remembers*) can be traced to the occult hype foisted on a gullible public by evangelical charlatans of this ilk in the 1970s.[20]

Witches, Neo-Pagans and others were now being covered in various media all over the country at that time. In the past, the problem in the United States had generally been one of trying to get the press to pay any attention at all, apart from the occasional Hallowe'en article or background story on a crime with "occult" overtones, where alternative spiritualities were trivialized or mocked.[21] Now people within the community fixated on a different problem: who among them was being approached to play the role of spokesperson, what were their qualifications to speak on the subject, and how they were being covered? Illustrative of the problems that an unscrupulous press could cause in this sensationalistic environment was the interview granted in late 1973 by Buczynski and Slater, which later appeared in the tabloid *National Star* under the title "Ed Buczynski — His Warlock Shop is a Satanist Supermarket." Published in early 1974 to coincide with the local appearance of Hershel Smith and his second-hand Witchmobile, the article featured Herman Slater discussing the business side of the Craft, while Eddie Buczynski spoke to its romantic side, of "feel[ing] the wind in my face and the scent of the forest." These humdrum, somewhat goofy details of the Warlock Shop and its residents were jarringly juxtaposed against Smith's outlandish claims of a brutal national crime wave spawned by "the occult scene," replete with murders, dismemberment and cannibalism.[22]

Slater was criticized by a local business competitor for being suckered into granting the *National Star* an interview, when other area stores had allegedly been approached by the paper and had turned down the request.[23] Yet the rather boring details of the Warlock Shop had the palliative effect of making the evangelical claims about the occult look even more disconnected from reality than they might have appeared if they stood alone and unchallenged. Regardless of whether Slater and Buczynski made the right decision in agreeing to the interview, the article was read by a wide audience, and free press was free press. This wasn't to say that Herman was cavalier about such mixed blessings. But he had no editorial control over how the Warlock Shop was to be presented in the paper, and he certainly hadn't been informed up front of the slant the article would take. Slater noted that the *National Star* had retracted its "Satanic Supermarket" characterization of the Warlock Shop the following week, likely as the result of his protest.[24]

This interview wasn't the first time the Warlock Shop was associated with Satanism in the press. A "Playboy Potpourri" blurb in the October 1973 issue of the magazine wrote up a promotional blub for the store under the title "That Old Black Magic." Playboy told its readers, "Despair no more, you witches, warlocks and weirdos [sic] of the cosmos — this is your chance to come out of the closet in style."[25,26] It wasn't as if Herman and Eddie were the first "out" Witches to be lumped in with the Satanists; Raymond Buckland had appeared alongside Anton LaVey in the high-profile national cover story "Witchcraft is Rising" in *Look* magazine in 1971.[27] In the end, it wasn't fair to blame the owners of the Warlock Shop for the failings of the editorial staff of the *National Star* any more than it was to hold them responsible for the objectification of women promoted by *Playboy* magazine. Nevertheless, media misrepresentations like the *National Star's* might have gone unremarked in the past but now began to draw a strong response from occult practitioners.

Witches began to actively work to change public opinion on the occult. Various groups and individuals within the occult movement in the United States had been educating the public for close to a decade by this point. Raymond Buckland, Sybil Leek, Leo Martello and others had appeared on television and radio and granted print interviews for years in the metropolitan New York media market. Others made similar efforts across the country and throughout Europe. The early 1970s saw the continuation of the 1960s trend of interviewing Witches, Warlocks, occultists, paranormals, Satanists and UFOlogists on radio and TV. Producers of talk shows actively scouted out people from the spiritual edge for the "freak factor" they presented to the audience, and as the number of occult practitioners, pseudo-practitioners and just plain fringe-walkers multiplied, there were ample choices for stirring up public controversy and boosting ratings. Welsh Witch Robert Carey writes, "[There was always a] big call for speakers at Samhain. I once got paid to speak at the Young Men's & Women's Hebrew Association. I was probably 17 then."[28] On Hallowe'en in 1972, Buckland and Martello appeared together in an hour-long double-header on the *Straight Talk* television show on New York's Channel 9 (WOR-TV).[29]

But whereas the media, under the constant prodding of anti-occult crusaders, such as Graham, Warnke and Smith, often lumped all aspects of occult practice in with Satanism, occult practitioners throughout the country began to challenge reporters and editors to take note of the differences between Satanism and other aspects of the movement, such as astrology, Neo-Paganism, and Witchcraft. One group of activists even labored to rewrite the pejorative definition of "Witchcraft" in the dictionary.[30] These attempts to engage critics of the occult were an important step in seizing the initiative and redirecting the conversation along more constructive paths.

But the occult spokespersons also had to satisfy certain societal expectations in dress and comportment if they were to be effective representatives of their organizations to the public. While practitioners such as Raymond Buckland and Sybil Leek came from a generation and a culture that encouraged conservative dress and behavior in public, this was generally a difficult message to get across in a newly coalescing community that drew many of its members from a counterculture that despised establishment mores. Hans Holzer commented on this point when writing about an appearance by CAW leaders and *Green Egg* co-editors Tim and Julie "Morning Glory" Zell in fancy dress at a science fiction convention. "[W]hen a leader of a group ... appears in public, he represents that organization."[31]

The Zells certainly weren't alone in their counterculture appearance. Leo Martello recalled an incident during the taping of a television show where the assistant of Louise Huebner (the "Official Witch of LA") had said that he looked like an abortionist.[32] Kay Flagg recalls challenging Martello on his personal appearance. "Leo used to dress like a rag-picker, and someone said one night 'Leo what do you do, get your clothes from a dumpster?' and Leo said 'Yes. I never buy clothing. I go through when people throw clothing out and I take it. Why should I spend money on clothes? What do I need it for? Do I go and lecture at colleges?' And I said 'Yes, you do.' And he replied 'Well, then I wear something a little better. Then I wear something that somebody gave me.'"[33]

Comportment, particularly maintaining one's cool in the midst of a heated debate, could be challenging, yet it was also an essential part of the job if one was to be effective in educating the public on behalf of Witchcraft and Neo-Paganism. It was important to come across as knowledgeable and intelligent, rather than as an airhead or an arrogant ass — especially when debating a critic in a live broadcast. One oft-cited example is an exchange on an American television program between Eleanor Bone and Sybil Leek, two English Witches who weren't on the best of terms with one another. Bone, a Gardnerian high priestess, was asked by the program's host to turn Sybil Leek, the practitioner of Celtic Witchcraft, into a toad. "Why should I improve on nature?" she drily responded.[34]

A self-styled critic of the occult in New York City named Owen Rachleff also used the asinine and disrespectful "turn me into a toad" challenge, which periodically resurfaces even to this day. Rachleff's run-ins with occult practitioners began with the publication of his book *The Occult Conceit* (1971). Members of the Craft were angered by his stated goal of debunking the occult, which he characterized as being "founded in the most primitive reaches of human fear and nurtured in the darkest ages of human history" and as "a snake oil for the twentieth century."[35] Rachleff also taught "Witchcraft, Magic and Sorcery," an admittedly biased, yet very popular, course on the subject at New York University.[36] Though a professed atheist, Rachleff tended to dismiss modern Witchcraft by defining it with the same pejorative terminology used by the Christian church since the Middle Ages. As reported by Time magazine in 1972, Rachleff took a dim view of the whole occult movement. "Most occultniks," he said, "are either frauds of the intellectual and/or financial variety, or disturbed individuals who frequently mistake psychosis for psychic phenomena."[37] For his objectionable opinions, Rachleff was awarded the

1972 Bigot of the Year Award by the Friends of the Craft and Leo Martello's WICA Newsletter.

The Friends of the Craft was an association formed by Herman Slater, Eddie Buczynski, Peter Levenda and a few others in late 1972, primarily to disseminate information on the occult, but also with an eye towards increasing the Warlock Shop's visibility. With Slater as its President, the group kicked off its activities with a series of public lectures on Neo-Paganism, Wica and related topics at the First Unitarian Church in Brooklyn Heights throughout November 1972. The speakers were Justin (Pagan Way), Eddie Buczynski (Welsh Traditionalist Witchcraft), Raymond Buckland (Gardnerian Wica), Leo Martello (Sicilian Stregeria), and Rolla Nordic (Tarot interpretation).[38] By making a point of including several well-known personalities in its lineup, the Warlock Shop guaranteed that Brooklyn Heights would be the place people in the New York metro area thought of — when they thought of the occult at all. Several of the lectures, including Buczynski's and Buckland's, were tape-recorded. It became a common practice to sell cassette tapes of these lectures in the Warlock Shop, usually with the permission of the guest speaker, but sometimes without.[39]

Local newspapers picked up on the novelty of an occult lecture series being held in a church. Tipped off by the canny shopkeeper, the papers quoted Slater as saying, "Such cooperation between an established church and the still largely underground religion of Witchcraft is, to the best of our knowledge, a first, really an ecumenical landmark."[40] He may have been correct in the ground-breaking aspect of the lecture series; it wasn't until 1987 that the Unitarian Universalist Association of Congregations embraced the Neo-Pagan movement as yet another legitimate expression of spirituality, resulting in the formation of an independent affiliate organization within the church known as the Covenant of Unitarian Universalist Pagans (CUUPs). Herman gleefully noted that "Through these seminars, we are responding to the tremendous popular interest in the occult with something more meaningful than the all-too-prevalent sensationalism." *(Ibid n#40)* Buczynski was later invited back to the First Unitarian Church to teach a children's Sunday school class some Witchcraft reels, which are songs used to raise energy during ritual. Afterwards, parents of the children visited the Warlock Shop to ask questions of the proprietors. *(Ibid n#40)*

The publicity the Warlock Shop received during this period infuriated the monsignor of the Roman Catholic Church in Brooklyn Heights, who declared that everything in the shop was blessed by the Devil. Slater challenged the priest's assertions. "I called him up and said 'Is the Devil in Hong Kong?' and he said 'No. Why?'" Slater recalled. "And I said 'Well you just said that the Devil blessed everything in my shop, and specifically the chalices come from Hong Kong.' And he hung up on me."[41] The monsignor threatened to quit the Brooklyn Heights ecumenical council because of their support for the Warlock Shop's outreach efforts.

Church of Satan member Michael Aquino recalled an exchange between himself and Leo Martello at the Friends of the Craft lecture on Stregheria taught by the latter on November 22, 1972. Aquino had received a decidedly frosty reception by the audience and organizers when he walked into the church and couldn't quite fathom why, as he was sure that none of those present knew him. To Aquino's amusement, Martello informed him afterwards that the audience reaction resulted from his being mistaken for Owen Rachleff, whom he slightly resembled. Rachleff, who had been declared *persona non grata* in occult circles after his book was published, had been thrown out of the Warlock Shop earlier in the week, where he had been caught lurking and taking notes. It was presumed that Rachleff would also try to attend the night's lecture in order to gather more fodder for his writing and teaching.[42] *(Ibid n#36)*

Rachleff was a particular thorn in Martello's side. Leo had been unsuccessfully trying to corner the author into a public debate for some time. *(Ibid n#36)* An opportunity to resolve the standoff presented itself in October 1973, when Slater and Martello made a Hallowe'en appearance on the talk show of conservative radio personality Barry Farber on WOR-AM (New York). During the show, Owen Rachleff's name came up, and Farber expressed admiration for him. Frustrated by Rachleff's stonewalling of Martello, Herman Slater offered to give $100 to Farber's favorite charity if he could produce the occult critic for a one-on-one debate with the Sicilian Witch. Farber accepted the challenge.

Finally, on December 18, 1973, Owen Rachleff sat down with Leo Martello on Farber's show. The two spoke at cross-purposes for the entire program, with Martello insisting on discussing Witchcraft as a legal religious movement, while Rachleff persisted in defining Witches as either Devil worshippers or as pop freaks. Rachleff referred to the Craft as having an anal, rather than oral, history. Martello accused Rachleff of being a Judeo-Christian pimp and kept calling him Draculeff.[43, 44] While one might conclude that the geniality of talk radio hasn't much improved over the intervening decades, this event was significant in that it marked the first occasion when a Witch was able to publicly debate a well-known critic of the Craft on a syndicated radio broadcast in the United States.

Popular entertainment also proved to be a legitimate target of the Neo-Pagan community's ire. On October 14, 1973, an episode of the mystery show *McMillan and Wife* aired on the NBC television network. The episode, titled "The Devil You Say," sparked a controversy in Craft circles because certain aspects of Wiccan ritual, and phraseology such as "Blessed Be," were presented in a plot involving Satanic ritual murder. Herman Slater took umbrage at the show's portrayal of Witchcraft. It isn't clear what in particular about the *McMillan and Wife* episode set him off. After all, it was merely one in a long line of films and shows that exploited

Witchcraft in order to make a buck — and, as was pointed out by others in the community, Wicca was not the only religion to be so treated. Perhaps it was the wide exposure that "The Devil You Say" gained by being on a popular network program that galvanized Slater to act in this particular instance.

Whatever the reason, Herman managed to secure an invitation to appear on NBC's Today Show on October 31 for the annual media tradition of showcasing the occult for the public's amusement at Hallowe'en. However, rather than meekly submitting to the standard low-intensity ridicule, Slater turned the tables on the hosts and blasted the television network for its insensitivity. Before a national audience, he presented NBC with the second annual Inquisitional Bigot of the Year Award on behalf of the Friends of the Craft, the Witches Anti-Defamation League and the Witches Liberation Movement "in recognition of their gross misrepresentation of the valid religion of WICCA, a peace-loving nature-oriented celebration of life." Herman ended up in an argument with the show's producer, Mr. Gottlieb, because he felt he had not been given enough time to counter the Witchcraft stereotype promoted by the network on *McMillan and Wife*. The appearance ended with Gottlieb physically removing Slater from the studio. From there, Herman flew to Washington, DC for an interview on Metromedia's Panorama television show (WTTG Channel 5) with Gore Vidal, who indicated that he was supportive of Paganism.[45]

It would become increasingly popular to protest unflattering media depictions of minority communities in the coming years, including those involving Witchcraft.[46] Some, such as Leo Martello, who drew upon his experience in the post-Stonewall gay rights movement, had always advocated direct confrontation in these situations. "Witches have to define themselves — challenge the stereotyped roles forced on them," he told writer Peter Haining. "We'll get nowhere being timid. We've been pushed around too long."[47] But others didn't believe that protests like Slater's would have much impact on a system that was driven by advertising dollars and targeted the majority culture. Instead, leaders such as Tommy Kneitel urged people to go after the advertisers in an attempt to starve offensive shows of their income.[48]

NBC-TV continued to play to stereotypes with yet another show. The Snoop Sisters, which ran on NBC during the 1973-74 season, was a formulaic mystery series similar to McMillan and Wife. Only five episodes were produced, of which Episode 4 was titled "The Devil Made Me Do It." That episode, another association of Witchcraft with Satanism that used actual Gardnerian chants, originally aired on March 5, 1974 and was repeated on September 20, 1974.[49] The Aquarian Anti-Defamation League (AADL) urged readers to write to the show's sponsors. Others would use this tactic in the future to some effect, including conservative Christians, environmentalists, gay rights groups and anti-Apartheid protestors. Meanwhile, activists such as Isaac Bonewits and his AADL worked behind the scenes to educate the network, as well as the occult community.

AADL published a *Guidelines for Media* handbook, and community members were instructed to write to networks not just to protest negative portrayals of the occult but also to praise TV shows that depicted it in a fair light.[50, 51, 52] This was an important point to make, as not every media depiction of Witchcraft in this era earned a black mark. Bruce Kessler's *Simon, King of the Witches* (1971) is one example of a film that didn't start out to exploit the occult – and even though the studio tried to recut the film into one that would do so, enough of the humor and authenticity remained to defeat the attempt (although it also made the film a box office failure).[53] Simon also playfully incorporated a subtext of homosexuality, which made it even more hip to open-minded audience members.[54] Another relevant film from this period was *The Wicker Man* (1973), starring Christopher Lee as Lord Summerisle, leader of an isolated island community whose inhabitants still worshipped the old pre-Christian Celtic Gods.[55] While intended as a horror film with its sacrifice of a Christian police officer, *The Wicker Man* actually became something of a cult classic among the Neo-Pagan set for its portrayal of a living Pagan community that managed to hold its own against intrusive and authoritarian outside forces. Lee's enthusiastic performance as the spritely high priest of mythical Summerisle has endeared him to two generations of Neo-Pagan audiences.

Rather than rely upon the mainstream media, which was often perceived as indifferent if not outright hostile, other community members worked to provide an independent means of communicating more sympathetic alternative viewpoints to the public. One example was Raymond Buckland's Museum of Witchcraft & Magick. After visiting the museum in 1973, Michael Aquino described it in rather unflattering terms in the pages of the Church of Satan's newsletter *Cloven Hoof,* referring to it as an "utter shock" due to the unpolished nature of its displays and for its negative portrayal of Satanism.[56] Buckland never claimed to be a professional curator or a booster for Satanism, but he was at least putting himself out there in an attempt to educate the public. Despite its flaws, the museum served as an initial starting point in the late 1960s through the early 1970s for many people in the New York metropolitan area who were interested in exploring the Craft.

Individuals also played an important role in educating the public. Kathryn Frank writes, "I was once criticized for having May Day parties (which I did for over 20 years) and inviting non-Pagans to them. Isaac [Bonewits] defended what I was doing, basically saying, 'who knows, people might come to the Craft because of such an experience, and besides, why should we practice in secret?' We used to dance the May Pole at midnight on my roof, which my neighbors found pretty funny."[57]

Those associated with the Warlock Shop were also involved in proactive education, not just in public confrontation for perceived wrongs, and as far as museum exhibits, few could top the opportunity that dropped in Eddie and Herman's lap at the end of 1972. Shortly after the Warlock Shop appeared in the newspapers because of the November lecture series at First Unitarian Church, the couple was approached by Herbert Hemphill, Jr. to help with an exhibit scheduled for early 1973 at the Museum of American Folk Art (now The American Folk Art Museum). Titled OCCULT, it was to be the third Discovery Exhibit in the series "Grassroots Folk Art." The installation would feature artwork, ritual objects and tools associated with various occult traditions in the United States.[58] Hemphill, who was a founder of the museum in 1961 and its first curator, was to curate the exhibit with William Harris.

To be asked to participate in this project was a real feather in their cap. Buczynski and Slater accepted the offer on the spot and even arranged for a few more contributors to help round out the materials that Hemphill had already gathered. Simon was asked to provide pieces that were representative of ceremonial magick.[59] Ray Buckland was also asked to provide input on Witchcraft, drawing on the resources of his museum exhibits. *(Ibid n#28)* Eddie and Herman decided that their contribution would be a full Welsh tradition altar, and they selected items from the Warlock Shop inventory to place in the display. *(Ibid n#19)* An opening party was given for the museum membership and the press on Monday, January 15, 1973. A dozen red-robed members of the New York Coven of Welsh Traditionalist Witches greeted the guests. A bubbling cauldron of punch was served, and tarot readings were given by members of the InnerVision School. The Warlock Shop and the Friends of the Craft stepped into the media glare of the world press as a host of national and international print, radio, and television media covered the event. The opening was written up in *The New York Times*, *The New Yorker*, and the *London Times*.[60]

The exhibit opened to the public on January 16 with a lecture series by various speakers and proceeded with daily tarot readings by the InnerVision school, the proceeds of which were donated to the museum. Eddie's coven participated in the lecture series, speaking on the subject of Witchcraft.[61] The exhibit was so successful that it was extended an additional five weeks past its scheduled closing, and the museum reported a sixty percent increase in attendance over the corresponding period of the previous year.[62] The OCCULT exhibit, among others organized in the early 1970s, is widely regarded to have been the epitome of Bert Hemphill's (d. 1998) curatorial career.[63] Reflecting on the media attention that the exhibit brought to the occult movement, Robert Carey notes, "I think the Craft was always happy to see anything that looked vaguely genuinely traditional; it helped everyone's self-image. I helped set up some of that exhibit and it got some good mass-media coverage at the time. It was really kind of unifying and inspirational and vindicating for a very odd subculture. Even my poor parents got to see it." *(Ibid n#28)*

Given the level of exposure the OCCULT exhibit offered, it is not surprising that Herman took full advantage to promote the Warlock Shop. The store's first catalogue and pricing guide was available as a handout at the exhibit, as were a flier for the store and a press release where Herman offered himself to the media for interviews.[64, 65] Herman and Eddie began the task of putting together the first Earth Religions Supplies, Inc. catalogue late in 1972. The booklet provided 34 pages of merchandise, including books, pamphlets, magazines and greeting cards; ritual tools and altar accessories; divination tools; jewelry; ritually formulated incenses, oils and essences; herbs; records and tapes; talismans; statues; robes; and curios. Jewelry could also be made to order. While this certainly wasn't the first mail order operation of its kind in the United States (others, such as The Hermetic Workshop in Los Angeles, had offered incenses, oils and books for sale via magazine ads), it had probably one of the most sophisticated and wide-ranging inventories of its time, with literally hundreds of different items available for purchase.[66] Hans Holzer said of the catalogue, "Anyone who cannot find everything he needs for his particular coven or witchcraft activities simply doesn't know what it is all about."[67] It was the catalogue perhaps more than anything else, that placed the Warlock Shop on the map as an occult supplier.

Released in January 1973, the Earth Religions Supplies catalogue was a work of love — and a good thing, too, given the difficulty of assembling the text, drawings and photos with the tools of the day. Putting the catalogue together was a group effort, with Slater writing descriptions, Buczynski providing illustrations, and other store employees contributing their efforts to the final product. As Robert Carey remembers, "I did some paste-up work on catalogues, worked on labeling and sorting by zip code on mailings (a time of primitive technology, typewriters, mimeographs and temperamental Xeroxes)." *(Ibid n#28)* In later years, the catalogues would be professionally designed by Jim Wasserman of Studio 31.[68] Up to that point, Slater had confined his ads to local newspapers and a few occult newsletters of limited circulation. With the advent of the catalogue, he began expanding the advertising outreach of the Warlock Shop nationally into such movement magazines as Llewellyn Publishing's *Gnostica* and the CAW's *Green Egg*. However, the Warlock Shop ad in the March 1973 issue of *FATE*, a magazine of paranormal phenomena that was sold door-to-door and on newsstands across the country, marked the widest circulation to date.[69]

As another means of countering negative public perceptions of the occult, the movement began to develop its own media outlets. Authors with street credibility, such as Doreen Valiente, Raymond Buckland and Leo Martello, had been dealing mainly with the few publishing houses that catered substantially to members of the occult movement. These included

Llewellyn Publications, Samuel Weiser, Castle and University Books. As the public's demand for occult books increased in the 1970s, others also began to get into the publishing business to fill this niche, including such firms as 93 Publishing in Canada, which specialized in texts on ceremonial magick, and Slater and Buczynski's Earth Religions Supplies, Inc.

Lesser-known authors also wrote books on occult subjects, some with little or no connection to any recognizable part of the movement itself; and many of those authors dealt with non-occult publishers who weren't particularly scrupulous about checking their authors' claimed *bona fides* or knowledgeable enough to vet the stories they pandered. Nor were many of these publishers morally opposed to twisting the manuscripts and the advertising copy in order to stir a bit of controversy and boost their book sales. However, occult authors also began to find mainstream publishers who were open to providing fair and balanced outlets for their work. In one notable instance, Margot Adler announced in 1976 that she had been given a book contract by Viking Press to author the first wide-ranging study of the Neo-Pagan movement in the United States written from the perspective of a movement insider.[70] This was a marked departure from the plethora of "how-to" books and misleading historical retrospectives that continued to link modern Witchcraft with the Burning Times and to the Satanic groups of the eighteenth and nineteenth centuries. Adler noted in a 2004 interview how important it was to her that a more intellectual approach to Neo-Paganism be presented, one that was only beginning to manifest on a national level during this period.

Margot Adler: [71, 72]

> *That whole scene down at the Warlock Shop and [elsewhere], it was like the Craft that was there and so it was the Craft that I joined. But what was fascinating to me, and probably the reason that I wrote "Drawing Down the Moon," was that I began through the Green Egg mainly and through Nemeton at the time to suddenly realize that there was this other Wicca and other Paganism that was going on that was much more intellectual, much more interesting. And all you had to do was read the letters to the Green Egg and it was clear that what they were talking about was so much more interesting than what was going on in this little coven in Brooklyn that I was in or in the one that I was going to when I went into Gardnerian. And so it became clear that I had to go elsewhere. It's funny, Starhawk and I have often joked that the books we wrote (she wrote "Spiral Dance"), which came out on the same day in the same year on opposite coasts, that they were really, on some deep level that's hard to talk about, the Craft that we wanted to be and not the Craft that existed. And that on some level it was almost like a spell to bring that Craft into creation.*

Newspapers and newsletters, as previously discussed, had long been a disseminator of information on the occult movement in the United States, though they had a mixed record as an educational tool to reinforce a positive image for the public. Periodicals were often tied to individual spiritual groups or communities. These included Feraferia's *Korythalia*, the Church of All Worlds' *Green Egg*, Nemeton's *Nemeton Newsletter*, the OTA's *Seventh Ray*, Thelema's *Oriflamme*, Windwalker Coven's *The Hidden Path*, and, later, Circle Sanctuary's *Circle Network News*. Less frequently, publications might be associated with occult-oriented businesses (e.g., Llewellyn's *Gnostica News* and Earth Religions Supplies' *Earth Religion News*). Few, such as *The Crystal Well*, were truly independent publications, though such independent sources would become more common in the 1980s.

Reflecting the unstable economics of the publishing business as much as the subculture itself, most occult periodicals folded within a few months or years of their debut. Although the *Earth Religion News* is often cited as a newspaper of influence during the mid-1970s, its lifespan was no better than most other occult periodicals from that period, despite a circulation of twenty thousand as reported in its final issue.[73] Contrast this with *Gnostica News*, whose circulation was sixty thousand (of which three thousand were paid subscriptions) and *Green Egg*, whose own paid subscriptions never exceeded two thousand in the 1970s.[74] While its editor and publisher never made *Green Egg*'s mistake of allowing the letters section to run (and financially ruin) the paper, the *Earth Religion News* was no less controversial, nor financially more solvent, than its rivals. While it had a respectable United States and international subscriber base, the *Earth Religion News* stumbled through 1975 without printing a single issue, then folded early in 1976 after publishing a massive combined issue to satisfy its outstanding subscription obligations.[75, 76] *Green Egg* soon followed it over the precipice at the end of 1976, but like the proverbial Green Man (and unlike the *Earth Religion News*), *Green Egg* would cycle through deaths and rebirths for the next three decades.

Herman and Eddie had launched the *Earth Religion News* in 1973 in order to promote both the Warlock Shop and the Craft, following Herman's philosophy that anything that built up an occult community would eventually improve business. Although Slater advertised the Warlock Shop in the *Earth Religion News*, he never treated the newspaper as the shop's catalogue, which was always published separately. Herman also accepted advertising from the Warlock Shop's local suppliers, such as Samuel Weiser Books, and even from its competitors. One criticism leveled against the paper was the overwhelming influence of its publisher's acerbic personality on its editorial character. There is no doubt that Slater's penchant for calling things as he saw them found its way into every aspect of the newspaper's production — and sometimes he was known to print information that wasn't accurate but that made for good copy.

Tommy Kneitel notes that he once complained to Eddie when a fictitious "Legend of the Witches' Farthing" appeared in the *Earth Religion News* under his byline.[77] Kneitel had written the piece as a favor to Raymond Buckland, who sold the fake coins as souvenirs to visitors of his Witchcraft museum. Each coin was accompanied by a handout containing the fraudulent description penned by Kneitel; however, when the description appeared in print with Kneitel's name associated with it, Tommy was livid. Although Buczynski was the putative editor of the paper, when Kneitel complained to him about the article, Eddie replied that the matter was solely in Slater's hands. Herman, who also sold the farthings at the Warlock Shop, shrugged off Tommy's protest and instead badgered him to write more articles for the newspaper. As Kneitel later recalled,[78, 79]

> *Ultimately, I sent him a feature that told of my initiation into a brotherhood of Tibetan shamans. I provided intricate details of this ritual and how it was performed at a secret location by Tibetan lamas in New York. There wasn't a shred of truth to this yarn, but I figured it was due retribution for [the Earth Religion News] and Herman. Herman received the manuscript and called to say it was exactly what he wanted. When it ran in [the paper], everyone I knew was in on the joke, and we all had a horselaugh on poor, gullible Herman. Herman sent me a check to pay for the story. I returned the check with a note saying he'd been had by my hoax story. Herman couldn't have cared less, saying he loved it, anyway. He even forwarded me a batch of serious letters from readers asking how much I charge to initiate seekers as Tibetan shamans. These letters trickled in for months. I could have been the Gerald Gardner of Tibetan shamanism!*

Regardless of these editorial lapses, the overall message conveyed by *Earth Religion News* was one of striving to improve the standards of the movement by providing a venue for occult writers to educate the public. Herman also used the paper as a bully pulpit to selectively root out those he considered to be charlatans and con artists. He was particularly hard on those whom he suspected of using the Craft predominantly as a means to gain sexual favors or money (or both) from naïve and inexperienced seekers. Slater took such stands while at the same time, and with a straight face, selling the aforementioned Witches' Farthings to gullible tourists, or even the chicken bones from his lunch as a magickal spell ingredient.[80] Imperfect business ethics marked a complexity (some might say hypocrisy) in his worldview, where the wheels of commerce were usually greased with a dollop of snake oil regardless of what business you were in.

Nevertheless, Herman was by and large a strong advocate for the serious practitioners of the Craft, even as he profited from those who he considered to be poseurs and tourists. The motto of his newspaper — "Guard the Mysteries, Reveal Them Constantly" — was not an exhortation to break one's oath but, rather, to make the Craft a living, thriving practice that could not be stamped out by the forces of intolerance in the United States. In this, the *Earth Religion News* and its fellow publications across the country succeeded beyond their wildest expectations. Judith McNally notes that the paper "was never as influential as *Green Egg*, mainly because it was published irregularly. To be kind, the production values left something to be desired. Old [*Earth Religion News*], though, was around when a growing pagan audience was hungry for anything in print."[81]

While newsletter publishing was available to any group or individual with access to a mimeograph machine, the broadcast media were a different matter altogether, requiring special equipment, training and airtime. The occult movement had relied upon the coverage of mainstream media, which obviously had its limitations. Public access cable television and public and community radio stations also provided outlets for occult broadcasting. Pagan Way rituals had been broadcast on local cable, for example, as well as special events such as the Witch-In organized by Leo Martello in 1970, which was filmed by the Global Village collective and shown on WNET TV Channel 13 in New York. However, these efforts reached relatively limited audiences.

On Sunday January 27, 1974, when Margot Adler began hosting a monthly radio program called "Pagan Press Review" on the Pacifica radio network's WBAI-FM in New York. Using music, poetry and articles of interest to the occult subculture, the show provided a creative, sensitive and non-sectarian venue that was acclaimed by the community.[82] Despite Adler's well earned accolades, hers was not the first regularly-broadcast occult-oriented radio program. That honor goes to Marion Weinstein's weekly program "Marion's Cauldron," which premiered on WBAI in 1968.[83] The first regularly-broadcast television show dedicated to the Old Religion was aired on April 27, 1975. Hosted by John and Jacquie Nielson, *Witchcraft Today* appeared weekly on Channel 9 in Winnipeg, Ontario.[84] By comparison, Herman Slater, who had become a minor celebrity in New York City through his appearances in the mainstream media, didn't begin hosting his own show until over a decade later.[85]

Slowly but surely, the occult movement began to make inroads into the realms formerly held by mainstream media types alone. This increased awareness of the need to "manage" the public image of the occult, combined with the egos of those attempting to guide this process, caused some of the greatest battles in the occult movement in the early to mid-1970s. But it also led to the greatest progress in creating a community from a wide range of practitioners and spiritual paths that held little in common with one another.

The Neo-Pagan/New Age movement harbored many disparate groups beneath its overarching umbrella. These ran the gamut from the rational to the intuitive, with ceremonial magick, Neo-Platonism, science fiction and paranormal research rubbing elbows with Witchcraft, Neo-Pagan cults and the various strains of the New Age movement. Adding to this spiritual smorgasbord was a bleedover of Gnostic philosophies, as well as Spiritualists, Cabalists, astrologers, UFOlogists, ghost hunters and the like. Some seekers who swam these waters were choosy, with a measure of consistency and staying power in their approach. Others were far more credulous, taking it all in and accepting it at face value, or else flitting from interest to interest like spiritual butterflies. A spirit of eclecticism and exploration ran through the movement just as it did with society in general. Many people embraced and rejected ideas and philosophies in an ongoing search for truth, picking up and discarding various teachings seemingly with changes in the seasons, or even in the weather. Herman Slater, who in comparison to many was downright orthodox in his beliefs, often self-deprecatingly answered any criticism of his own approach to spirituality by saying, "I also change my underwear when it gets dirty."[86]

Beginning about 1970 and continuing through that decade, there was a debate within the occult community over who could call themselves a Witch. The topic was initially broached by the Gardnerians, who generally disparaged non-Gardnerians who called themselves Witches. To confuse matters more, the term "Pagan" — as in "Pagan Way" — appears to have been applied by Witches mainly to the portion of Wica having to do with the worship of Deities, as opposed to the practice of magick. "Once I received my First Degree in Welsh, I became a teacher in the Pagan Way," explained Welsh practitioner Artie Jamison. "It's amazing that most Witches, and I don't belittle them at all, none of them really know what Paganism is really about. And this is my whole concept, that you have to learn to love the Goddess and the religion first. ... Because everybody comes in and goes 'I want to learn magic, I want to do this, I want to do that.' [But] you've got to learn to love the Goddess first, and to understand that first."[87] However, there were Neo-Pagan groups such as the CES, non-Witches who were curious and unhappy at being lumped in with the Wiccans by the media, and even some of the Wiccans. The situation was not helped when the Christian critics of the New Age movement slapped a generic Neo-Pagan/Heathen/Satanic label on everything that was not of their own blinkered sect.

The Pen is Mightier than the Athame

By the early 1970s, a small but very vocal minority of the occult community had taken to publicly airing these complaints, and others, in the editorial pages of the various occult publications of the day. The duels, fought via pen and typewriter, ran the gamut, from personal attacks over petty insults to disputes over dogma to accusations of outright sexual misconduct or fraud. The readership of some of the smaller newsletters, such as *The New Broom* and *The Hidden Path*, tended to be somewhat more genteel in their exchanges. Other publications, such as the *WICA Newsletter*, *Earth Religion News*, *Nemeton*, and *Green Egg* could be more confrontational, with letters sections packed issue after issue, from header to footer, with the obligatory obloquies. This call-and-response often ranged across publications due to shared readerships and to the actions of editorial staff, who were often responsible for cross-publishing controversial exchanges within rival journals. The Forum section of *Green Egg* magazine in particular was a prime battleground. *Green Egg's* wide circulation certainly played a large part in this; however, its role as a town square of choice resulted mainly from its hands-off editorial policy. Fully half of every issue might be taken up with letters to the editor, and the refusal to consistently edit or limit reader responses eventually contributed to the sinking of *Green Egg* under the weight of printing and postage costs.[88, 89, 90]

From this reading, it might seem that much of the bickering centered on New York City, but that was clearly not the case. Those on the West Coast fought among themselves, and with the East Coasters, about as much as those in the East battled each other and those in the West. Nor was this problem limited to the coasts. "There were Witch Wars in the mid-west too," notes Carl Weschcke. "The trouble was that anyone who stuck their head above the rest was attacked as either a traitor, a fraud, or a farce. Immediately people were accused of vague crimes, most often involving drug dealing, and warnings were given that 'the occult police' would take care of the offenders. It was a time of adolescent nonsense."[91]

The stated reasons for these disputes are as numerous as the writers themselves; however, in the simplest terms, the motivation generally boiled down to human ego. Many of those with the greatest propensity for public displays of drama were people of essentially no consequence outside their own lives and limited circle of friends. Ceremonial magickian and author Simon explains this by noting that the small size of covens allowed for relative underachievers to attain positions of prominence.[92] Having achieved a title or a place in the vaporous hierarchy of the movement, some were keen to throw a bit of weight around by issuing pronouncements on various subjects, leveling curses at their detractors and generally making nuisances of themselves. Others, meanwhile, enjoyed twitching the tails of the pompous and then sitting back to watch the resultant yowling without regard to the lingering damage these fights did to the stability of the underlying community. Reflecting on the causes of such in-fighting, Ed Fitch wrote that "It is entirely too easy to claim a fantastically long pedigree (and maybe some equally inflated titles) merely to cover-over one's emotional problems and to inflate one's sagging ego."[93]

In many ways, little seems to have changed some forty years on, with the advent of the internet.

This phenomenon is certainly not limited to the occult. Like modern Neo-Paganism, which was still very much in its infancy in the early 1970s, doctrinal disputes wracked the early Christian church. American author Gore Vidal described these conflicts in delightfully cynical detail in his 1964 novel *Julian*, and one is hard-pressed to tell those early Christians apart from early modern Neo-Pagans based solely on the nature of their disagreements and means of settling disputes. Yet even in the now mature Christian faith community, storefront churches will form one day and then split up the next due to dogmatic quibbling, with the disgruntled parishioners leaving with half of the chairs to occupy a new storefront tabernacle. Much the same occurs when covens come into conflict, although ostensibly fewer chairs are involved.

While Neo-Pagan and occult practitioners treated the squabbling of the early 1970s as if it was a new phenomenon, such was clearly not the case. Such dust-ups were regular occurrences among practitioners of ceremonial magick from the late 1800s onward; in the 1950s, Gerald Gardner fretted over his priestesses' inability to get along and was dismayed by the inevitable fights and severed relationships. The most famous of these was his own break with his former high priestess, Doreen Valiente. Surviving correspondence, as well as articles and letters in British occult publications, demonstrates that by the early 1960s the tradition that Gardner had created was involved in continuous low-level drama. Echoes of these tiffs continued to resound in the Craft, even as new ones arose between more recent initiates over issues both wan and weighty. This is not to say that there were never any legitimate reasons for taking people to task in the forums of occult publications. However, this manner of discipline was often just as destructive as the underlying concern that was being addressed.

It is difficult to gauge what effect, if any, this war of correspondents had on the public's perception of the occult at the time. Certainly within the subculture itself there was a diversity of opinion as to whether these exchanges were a helpful airing of differences, a self-destructive cancer, or merely a boring display of childishness. Tommy Kneitel complained about "the morbid obsession that some people seem to display on 'digging out the dirt' on the internal workings on someone else's coven or tradition" and the people within the Craft who fed them this information.[94] In an oblique reference to Herman Slater, Leo Martello and others, Kneitel castigated those "who never seem to have anything constructive or nice to say or report about their Craft affiliation, whose sole function within the Pagan movement seems to be to masturbate their insecure egos by using the Pagan press by babbling away with feuds, vendettas, personal attacks, scandals, lies, bickering, suspicion, innuendo, childishness, jealousy, and fear."[95]

Kneitel believed that this airing of dirty laundry diminished the chances that the various occult traditions would attract the participation of responsible people who had valuable things to add, and suggested that practitioners would be better off ignoring those "who attempt to split apart our movement with dissension and suspicion."[96] *(Ibid n#94)* Yet even he admitted that "perhaps we ourselves are guilty too, to some extent, of feeding this mill with grist for its operation."[97] Craft elder Sybil Leek clearly thought that the Gardnerians shared the blame for any bad press, writing that "What emerges now, from what is termed Gardnerian witchcraft, is often some pretty petty spitefulness which is not worthy of those who are involved in witchcraft. This personal spitefulness, of course, is meat and drink to an avid press, anxious to give the worst possible representation of witchcraft in the newspapers of the world."[98] To be fair, it must be said that Sybil herself, like most other players of the day, was not above a good dust-up from time to time. On this score, separating the guilty from the innocent was at times the work of angels.

The effect of this ongoing bickering could have on newcomers to the Craft is illustrated by an exchange that Margot Adler recalls having with Herman Slater at the Warlock Shop in late 1972 concerning the contents of *Green Egg*: "[One] of these memories that I have never forgotten is walking into the store and Herman ... looking at a copy of the *Green Egg* and telling me that it was an 'Inner Court document' or something like that — that it wasn't appropriate for people who were not initiates to read. I mean, it's like one of these completely bizarre things." *(Ibid n#71)* While Slater was only joking, from his perspective an injunction warning off a fresh-faced student made perfect sense. Given the amount of backbiting evident in the pages of *Green Egg's* Forum, some of which originated with denizens of the Warlock Shop, including Slater, any newcomer seeking to understand the Craft might, after reading page after page of invective, write off the entire Neo-Pagan movement as a bunch of maladjusted kooks and return to a mainstream temple or church. Better the devil you know, after all.

These fights propagated from magazines to books, or books to magazines, or television or radio to newspapers, to books, and back again. It was the rare author, shop owner, group leader or student who could say or write anything on any topic within the occult sphere and come out of the experience unsavaged. During 1973 and 1974, author Hans Holzer was the recipient of a considerable share of this ire, and not, it must be admitted, without some reason. Since the late 1950s, Holzer had made a career of writing about the paranormal. He already had an impressively long list of books to his credit when he began looking into the rise of modern Witchcraft in *The Truth About Witchcraft* (1969). Three later books on the Neo-Pagan movement that Holzer had released in this period — *The New Pagans* (1972), *The Witchcraft Report* (1973), and *The Directory of the OCCULT* (1974) — employed a chatty, tabloid-esque first-person style of reporting that worked the nerves of various occult leaders.

Some felt that Hans was an imposter, an outsider who claimed Craft credentials simply to gain the trust of occult practitioners and groups so that he could write about their activities. There was also a feeling in certain quarters that Holzer had committed lèse majesté for failing to pay certain leaders or groups in the movement the level of respect or attention that they felt was due them. Of course nobility, even the faux nobility embodied by the titled Lords, Ladies, Primates and Poobahs so common in Neo-Paganism, also implies a certain standard of *noblesse oblige* on the part of the putative title-holders, something that was often lacking within segments of the community. Their disobliging nature was evident in the public and private treatment they meted out to Holzer.

Holzer's book *The New Pagans* had stirred some discontent, primarily in Tim Zell, who savaged it in a June 1972 *Green Egg* book review for, among other things, failing to capitalize "Pagan" and providing CAW with insufficient coverage.[99] However, it was Holzer's follow-on book, The Witchcraft Report, that provoked the most negative reaction. While some of the criticism of Holzer centered on accusations that his research was slipshod, most of the animus was directed at his reporting on the interpersonal and inter-group conflicts within the occult movement.[100] Along with the mundane aspects of group operations, he placed the over-the-back-fence gossip and schoolyard brawls before a much wider audience of non-Pagans. Of the *Green Egg*, for example, he wrote that "substantial sections of the magazine are nothing more than faithful reproductions of the correspondence between people expressing opposing views. Much of it is very boring — except to those who wrote the letters. Some of it is downright embarrassing. The magazine contains useful information too, of course, and could do without the public bickering in its back pages."[101]

It is true that many Neo-Pagans believed *Green Egg* to be divisive. But many others, such as Margot Adler, felt that the magazine "was a key to the movement's vitality" and posited that dissension may actually have had some benefit in keeping Neo-Pagans separated and safe from persecution until their numbers were sufficient to provide strength.[102] *(Ibid n#82)* This assumes, of course, that they don't first run out of chairs. CES co-founder Harold Moss, a Forum regular, comes at it from a different perspective, writing that the controversy generated within the Forum pages was actually beneficial to keeping the community together. "The real glue holding Neo-Paganism together was *Green Egg* magazine," writes Moss. "Everybody had to get every issue to find out what people were saying about them."[103] Leo Martello, whose own public pronouncements often contributed to the antagonistic climate within the Craft, believed that it was better to get the disputes out into the open rather than to go along like "good Germans" while the true state of things festered in a background rife with backstabbing and hypocrisy. *(Ibid n#44)* And, as Martello noted, the Gardnerians hardly had clean hands in this, a point that Judy and Tom Kneitel had previously conceded.[104] Responding to a reader's criticism of the "back pages," *Green Egg* co-editor Julie "Morning Glory" Zell wrote that "As for battles within the Forum of [*Green Egg*], we are an 'inside' publication of the Neo-Pagan Movement, and the Forum is partly meant to be an escape valve for hot air; there is a difference between our readership and Holzer's."[105]

This sounded like much the same argument that Herman Slater made when discussing *Green Egg* with Margot Adler. However, since the *Green Egg* had an open subscription policy and could even be purchased from some of the same booksellers across the country that sold Hans Holzer's books, the difference in readership to which Morning Glory referred was somewhat debatable. Moss also rejected the characterizations that the *Green Egg Forum* was either an embarrassment to or an "escape valve" for the community, preferring instead a much simpler explanation: "It was simply a forum. People who had no other platform could be heard [there]."[106] It would be imprudent not to acknowledge the rich resource that these Forum sections have left behind. As American religious scholar J. Gordon Melton noted, "Through its 'forum,' the *Green Egg* has become the major chronicle of the [Neo-Pagan] movement as a whole."[107]

For Holzer's critics, the core issue was that revealing any controversy to the general public risked placing the entire occult movement in a bad light. But the message that Holzer was trying, albeit imperfectly, to get across was that it was impossible for the emerging Neo-Pagan movement to be taken seriously as a faith community (which many of its adherents desperately wanted) when many of its leaders and practitioners behaved so execrably both in public and in private.[108, 109] As Robert Carey pointed out, "It is purely the Pagans' fault that there was anything to report. The squawks about [*The Witchcraft Report*] sound suspiciously like people being forced to face the consequences of their own actions. You don't want the public to know that you act that way? Don't act that way."[110] Carey's covenmate and co-editor of *Mandragore* magazine, Denny Sargent, was more succinct: "How are we going to be the priests of a New Age when we can't even be priests to ourselves?"[111] Many readers during that period agreed, writing letters to *Green Egg* and other publications to urge for restraint and comity on their fellows.

In Holzer's defense, although his research could sometimes be outdated or skewed towards the unseemly side of things, he was generally well-disposed to the subject matter, if not to all the particular players.[112] And a sympathetic ear was hardly the typical reception that the occult community could expect in the arena of mass-market publishing. However, if the attacks on Holzer sometimes resembled a shoot-the-messenger approach to dealing with the criticisms he raised in his books, the communal response was largely due to his unfortunate tendency to take sides in the stories that he covered. It should be noted, for example, that Zell's criticism of *The New Pagans* followed closely on the heels of the Council of Themis meltdown of May 1972. Holzer then went out of his way the following year to shine a positive light on Carroll Runyon's part in that event in the pages of *The Witchcraft Report*, while simultaneously calling into question Tim Zell's reputation and CAW's right to even call itself a Neo-Pagan organization. This partisanship was a sordid deed, and it irreparably damaged Holzer's ability to claim that he reported objectively and dispassionately on the community and its members. However, *Green Egg* acted rashly as well, referring to Holzer as "an enemy of the Craft and of the Pagan movement, a Christian who collects Craft Initiations like a dog collects fleas, and with no apparent regard for the sanctity of the bonds thus created."[113] This clearly was not the case, and the charges were somewhat ironic, given that a number of leaders in the occult movement had already been aiming similar accusations at one another for several years.

By allowing himself to be drawn into the conflicts, Hans Holzer overshadowed the positive message that he was trying to get across. He also permitted his involvement to color his opinion of the groups and individuals with whom he was in conflict, thereby opening himself to charges of stirring controversy in order to sell books. Holzer's lack of objectivity was particularly noticeable in *The Directory of the OCCULT*, where he rated groups (a bad idea) and assigned generally lower ratings to groups and individuals who were critical of him (a worse idea). Leo Martello, in commenting on the reasons behind Hans Holzer's increasingly negative reporting, asked, "Was Holzer an enemy or was Holzer made into one? You can't keep attacking people and then expect them to praise you."[114] But that blade cuts both ways, as Leo himself well knew.[115] Nevertheless, a retaliatory reaction could be expected from an author such as Martello, who made no bones about being first and foremost an activist, many occult leaders had expected more balance from Holzer, the ghost-hunter whom they accused of turning Witch-finder.

Of course, part of the problem was that in the early to mid-1970s, occult practitioners had little sense of what one might call an actual "community," in that various traditions and interests had no fraternal sense of group belonging and generally-shared values. As Sally Eaton recalls of New York in those days, "I'd say the term 'community' is *way* too touchy-feely to apply to Witches of that period. Blatant revisionism, in fact! People back then were *Witches*, thank-you-very-much, not 'Neo-Pagans' or 'Wiccans.' There was no attempt to be semi-mainstream 'clergy' — or even 'respectable.'"[116] However, the groundwork for a community of occult groups and practitioners was already being laid in some of the first national meetings of heretofore insular groups. Despite the in-fighting within the pages of national publications, there were definite signs that a kind of concordance was developing across the country, and not just within spheres of related practices such as the various permutations of Witchcraft or ceremonial magick.

Growing Pains

The prospect of a return to the Witch hunts of yore weighed heavily on the minds of some Witches and Neo-Pagans during early to mid-1970s. After all, the various traditions of Witchcraft had, since the appearance of Gerald Gardner's Witchcraft Today (1954) incorporated a recital of the excesses of the Catholic Inquisition and the Protestant Reformation against Witches into their foundational mythologies.[117] Published during the Cold War, Gardner's linkage of historical Witch hunts and the Burning Times with the history of modern Witchcraft might well have resonated with readers who were at that time witnessing the events of America's McCarthy era, which many saw as arising from the same stagnant pool as the brutish forces that caused so much pain from the fourteenth to the seventeenth centuries. The push by Witches and other allied Neo-Pagan and occult traditions for greater freedom to practice their religious beliefs was representative of the greater struggle for self-determination that marked the era. It was not surprising, then, that concerns arose over the prospect that stories of modern occult activities might instill fear in the minds of the public and, more worrisome, the authorities.[118]

Several groups were formed in the early 1970s specifically to address the civil rights concerns of occultists. The first was Leo Martello's Witches Anti-Defamation League (WADL). Using his experience in helping organize the gay community after the Stonewall riots, Martello built on his success in the wake of his battle with the New York City Parks Department to found WADL in 1970. By the late 1980s, Martello claimed that WADL had established chapters in every state in the country.[119] Another group, the Aquarian Anti-Defamation League (AADL), was organized by Isaac Bonewits and others in 1973 while Bonewits was the editor of *Gnostica News*. Both groups could count some minor victories in their efforts to protect civil rights in the community, but neither was particularly effective, especially when compared to such well-established organizations as the American Civil Liberties Union or the Anti-Defamation League. Their limitations resulted mainly from the fact that the WADL and AADL suffered from a lack of monetary support and an abundance of disorganization within the movement, both of which impeded their ability to provide legal help to those requesting assistance.[120] The AADL attempted to capitalize on the fear of a modern Witch hunt in its fundraising materials, using the spectre of the Burning Times in an effort to solicit donations. "Remember, the New Witchburners have a stake in your future. *Do you*?"[121]

These fears weren't totally misplaced. There was circumstantial evidence that discrimination against people who held minority religious beliefs was a continuing, if not systematic or widespread, problem in American society. If Joseph McCarthy's own communist "witch hunts" were still a painful memory to progressives of the mid-1970s, then the excesses of the FBI and police departments across the country in their crackdowns on countercultural activities and anti-War protests were a raw wound. Nixonian paranoia had infected the country's youth, where winning the popular guessing game of "Who's the Narc?" took on a greater sense of urgency. Within the occult community, this mindset was reinforced by the knowledge that at least one prominent member had been fingered as a government anti-war informant.[122] But despite these portents, the civil rights efforts within the Neo-Pagan community never received much support from its constituents during the 1970s.

Gwydion Pendderwen attempted to explain why Witches weren't more politically active. "Over the centuries, Witches have lost their taste for mixing it up with the political establishment," he wrote. "The memories of the burnings and the Inquisition, as well as a desire to practice their religion unmolested, have helped to foster the notion that they should be apolitical. To this day, most Witches shy away from allying their religion with any sort of political or social movement."[123] Pendderwen's citation of historical causes for the lack of Neo-Pagan participation in the political process was revisionist nonsense, as any "memories of the burnings and the Inquisition" had been artificially implanted by the likes of Margaret Murray, Gerald Gardner, and others only in the last twenty or so years before he wrote this statement. Even if they were converts from the Hippie movement or the Renaissance Faire circuit, American Witches in the 1970s didn't live in a medieval headspace any more than they did in one mapped on a post-Empire Great Britain of the 1950s and 1960s.

However, Pendderwen was correct in that most who followed a Neo-Pagan/occult path just wanted to practice their faith in peace. Many of them participated in the political process at the local, state and federal level, even if it was to do nothing more than cast a vote on election day. However, those who did so rarely politicized their religious beliefs; and even though they may have voted for candidates who most closely reflected their own personal outlook, they did so not as outwardly-identifiable members of the occult subculture. Few were "out of the broom closet," and fewer still had any social standing.

The reasons for this inaction are varied, but the deciding factor may be that most people just didn't see the need. Evidence of the widespread and systematic persecution of Neo-Pagans, Witches and other metaphysical practitioners simply didn't exist as it did for homosexuals, blacks or women, and the individual cases cited by the AADL and others to make this case weren't sufficient motivation for most people to be bothered to get involved. The "middle, middle class" initiates noted by Margot Adler, many of whom otherwise led relatively quiet and conservative lives, certainly weren't going to jeopardize their standing in the greater community by sticking their heads up too far.

The Hippies and their like, on the other hand, were being hassled anyway for reasons that had nothing to do with their choice of religion. Many of them were already heavily involved in various political causes — women's rights, black civil rights, the anti-war movement, drug legalization, gay rights, the environment — and Neo-Pagan rights were, pragmatically speaking, relatively low on the priority list during this period. Yet others, generally distrustful of any establishment authority, took Timothy Leary's advice and simply dropped out of the political process altogether. Some observers, such as Malon Wilkus, argue that by 1968 sufficient numbers of these inwardly-directed "me first" individuals had withdrawn from the political process to have enabled a rightward drift in United States politics.[124]

One can sense the frustration of some movement leaders at this lack of engagement, while others fulminated against those who put everyone at risk, as they saw it, by tarring the entire subculture with their bad behavior. "These people are not Craft at all, regardless of their claims," wrote Tommy Kneitel. "They are our enemies, the enemies of every Pagan, and consequently they are an affront to The Lady." *(Ibid n#95)* Cold War rhetoric aside, the issue of presenting a respectable public face for Witchcraft and Neo-Paganism became a matter of concern for community leaders at this time, even though no one could agree on exactly what that face might be, or even who or what constituted a community leader. As in most groups, people who rose to leadership positions in the occult were often rather parochial in their outlook, mainly concerned about holding onto enough power to guide their own little tribes — or Donner parties, as the case may be — through the wilderness.

Many within the greater movement didn't recognize either the need for or the authority of leaders, self-appointed or otherwise. "I have always criticized organized religious movements and spiritual movements since they suffer from the same stupid internal politics as, say, the SDS did during the 60's or the Catholic Church still does," Simon wrote in a 2002 interview. "The organization soon becomes more important than its members and the leaders more important than anyone else. ... Religions are the effluvia of someone else's enlightenment and there is always value to be found in examining religion carefully and cautiously. But leadership? To paraphrase Goering, 'Once I hear the word 'guru' I reach for my revolver.'"[125] Simon's attitude could be attributed to his devotion to ceremonial magick, which buds off loners like a bubbling yeast culture. But he was not alone in his pointed observation that swelling egos were often a concurrent side-effect of the swelling of an organization's ranks.

Nevertheless, a number of far-sighted individuals and organizations recognized a growing need to formally communicate with one another in order to coordinate responses to internal and external threats. Doing so seemed the safest approach for avoiding the potential for damage from the twin pressures of media interest in and evangelical opposition to anything that smacked of the occult. These pressures, if left unchecked, could eventually result in regulatory actions by government authorities, with the resultant intervention by law enforcement (as demonstrated by the Z. Budapest case). Ceremonial magickian and author Simon notes that "The idea that government might actually crack down on witches — as absurd as it seems today — was considered a very real possibility then." *(Ibid n#118)* Developing concurrently with the civil rights organizations, networking organizations began to coalesce around the notion of dealing with the emerging political and media relations issues. This level of cooperation was made possible in part by the nascent Neo-Pagan festival circuit, where people who had been corresponding with one another for years finally began meeting face to face for the first time.

Neo-Pagan, Occult and New Age conferences and festivals evolved out of the sense of community arising from and the efficacy demonstrated by several sources in the 1960s and 1970s. These included fantasy and science fiction conventions, historical re-enactment groups, "psychic awareness" fairs and conferences, and events sponsored by motivated individuals and diverse groups such as bars, occult bookstores, and booksellers associations. Fantasy and science fiction conventions have been held in the United States since the late 1930s. Certainly since the 1960s, there has been considerable crossover between devotees of this genre of literature and the men and women who were interested or actively participating in the various forms of occult spirituality spreading across the country. One example demonstrating its profound influence is Robert A. Heinlein's novel *Stranger in a Strange Land* (1961), which provided the inspiration for the co-founding of CAW in 1967 by Tim Zell. Tim and Morning Glory Zell were regular attendees at such conventions. A similar venue that also had some effect was the phenomenon of UFO conventions that dotted the landscape throughout the 1960s. The first national convention of the Amalgamated Flying Saucers Clubs of America, for example, attracted 2000 people in 1966.[126] Smaller regional events had been held much earlier, such as the 1960 Space Age Convention in Chicago, and local gatherings and clubs began springing up as early as the 1950s.[127]

If fantasy and science fiction was a robust incubator for the birth of modern Neo-Paganism, medieval reconstructionist groups, such as the Society for Creative Anachronism (SCA), proved no less influential. Founded in the late 1960s, the SCA began with a 1966 graduation party/"Last Tournament" held in the back yard of then medieval studies student Diana Paxson (who in later years became a Neo-Pagan writer).[128]

Modern Neo-Pagans owe a grateful nod to these romantic re-enactors, for their contribution extends well beyond the peasant shirts, capes and robes that have infiltrated the movement to include an emphasis on the scholarly, even obsessive, pursuit of ancient knowledge and practices that form the basis of many reconstructionist and adaptive spiritual practices and traditions.

Businesses, especially entertainment venues, also looked to cash in on the occult fad, with little or no regard to the effect of this frippery on the movement they were strip-mining for party ideas and profit. The Manhattan nightclub Cheetah at Broadway and 53rd Street, the so-called granddaddy of large commercial discotheques, had tried to enlist Hans Holzer to help persuade Sybil Leek to preside over their 1969 Hallowe'en party because they wanted "a genuine witch in charge." Holzer declined to even make the attempt, so sure was he of Leek's negative response to "this type of commercial enterprise which has nothing to do with genuine practice of the Old Religion, or any religion for that matter, except for the worship of Mammon."[129] Eventually the Cheetah settled for a twenty-two-year-old "East Village-type Witch" as its mistress of ceremonies.

Other members within the movement, such as Leo Martello and his assistant, Witch Hazel, occasionally blurred the lines between Witchcraft and Satanism. Roger Pratt remembers attending the opening of *Blood on Satan's Claw*, a film about witchcraft and Satanism, in the summer of 1971 at the Criterion in Times Square. "Leo and Witch Hazel were at the door as a promo," recalls Pratt, "and [theater-goers] wrote a wish on a slip of paper and they threw it into a suspended cauldron (no fire) as you went into the theatre. They were the only reason I went to the opening."[130, 131] Conversely, Martello turned down a request from promoters to tie his planned May Day festival to the release of the film *Simon, King of the Witches* (1971), even though *Simon* was written by an occultist and wasn't half bad as such things usually go (and certainly a damn sight better than *Claw*).[132]

The participation of Martello and his assistant in these types of publicity stunts seems fundamentally at odds with the threat he would make just a year later to file suit against radio and television stations for permitting "fundamentalist bigots to continue to call us 'in league with the devil' and 'evil.'" *(Ibid n#36)* This contradictory side of Leo's public stance did not go unnoticed at the time. In his May 1972 reply to Eddie Buczynski's complaint of *Green Egg* editor Tim Zell's review of Martello's recent book *Black Magic, Satanism and Voodoo*, Zell noted that Martello's "earlier efforts at promoting the Craft may have been more in the line of sensationalism than some of us would have wished."[133]

UFOlogist Timothy Green Beckley also played the Satanism card by promoting an annual rock and occult festival in the early 1970s, emceed by Witch Hazel and featuring Satan "The Eternal Fire Man" as the special guest.[134, 135] Yet this tradition of throwing occult-themed parties became an honored tradition within the metaphysical community in New York and beyond, whether it was harvest festivals held in Chelsea's Inferno Disco in the late 1970s, occult-arts happenings at the Bells of Hell in the 1970s and 1980s, or competing New York Witches Balls of the 1990s and beyond.

Other influences include small regional fairs, such as the April 1970 Festival of Occult Arts in New York City (noted in Susan Roberts' book *Witches USA.*); the Psychic Awareness Weekend (where ritualist and UFOlogist Eugenia Macer-Story produced her play *The Autobiography of Morgan LeFay* in 1977); the annual Edgar Allan Poe Bizarre Bazaar (which featured mystics, soothsayers and magicians); local activist-organized events, such as Leo Martello's 1970 Witch-In; and bookseller trade shows through which the various occult publishers and vendors nationwide made contact with one another on a professional level.[136,137,138,139] *(Ibid n#129)*

Carl Weschcke recalls first meeting Herman Slater at the American Bookseller's Association Trade Show (now called BookExpo America) in New York City sometime in the early 1970s. The Warlock Shop was a small customer of Llewellyn's at the time. *(Ibid n#91)* While one would think that book trade shows would be rather dry and a bit dull, Carl tells the story of how Slater spiced up the floor at one event when he wasn't getting enough foot traffic at his own booth. "We were all at the ABA Trade Show in New Orleans," Weschcke writes. "[Llewellyn] had Ray Marborough doing a thing in our booth using eggs to cleanse volunteers [auras] — including a lady from 'Good Morning America.' Herman hated it, and kept badgering the news people for all their crimes. In the meantime, he hired a lady to come to his booth wearing a boa constrictor and not much else to compete with Ray."[140]

One of the earliest national metaphysical conferences was sponsored by the Llewellyn Publications' Gnostica Bookstore. The first Gnostic Aquarian Festival was held at the Leamington Hotel in St. Paul, Minnesota on September 3-6, 1971.[141] When Gnostica Bookstore opened in 1971, it benefitted from substantial TV and newspaper coverage and attracted several hundred attendees. The crowds at Gnostica's weekly open houses continued to grow, and this popularity did not go unnoticed. Llewellyn President Carl Weschcke describes how these open houses eventually transformed into Neo-Pagan conventions in 1970s.

Carl Weschcke:[142]

> *One day, the convention manager of one of the largest hotels — the one that actually did more convention business than all the others put together — called and proposed the idea of what became the Gnosticon and offered to help in numerous ways including basic expenses in exchange for a share of the profits. Well, it worked but it wasn't profitable so that hotel was not interested for the next one. We, however, were excited by it and*

> *continued them for several years. We eventually had an additional weeklong event for astrology and for Tantra, and then the separate Witch Meet. ... As a 'commercial' venture it was not profitable, but it did start the trend for psychic fairs and such all over the world. Had it been non-commercial, i.e., with volunteer labor rather than Llewellyn and Gnostica employees, it would have been. ... When I say it wasn't profitable I do have to qualify that point. Had we been a large enough business at that time so that we could measure the indirect benefits from 'spreading the word,' attracting and developing new authors, utilizing market research for new book ideas, etc., I am sure it would have been considered a remarkable success by MBA types.*

By the end of the decade, such large regional and national gatherings were becoming commonplace throughout the country. The Pan-Pagan festival began in the summer of 1977 at the Tuco campground in Indiana, hosted by the Midwest Pagan Council.[143] By 1978, the Gathering of the Tribes event hosted by the Association of Cymmry Wicca was meeting annually in Georgia.[144] Rites of Spring was begun by the Athanor Fellowship in the Boston area in May 1979.[145] Pagan Spirit Gathering, held in the Madison, Wisconsin area beginning in June 1980, started as a Midsummer Festival hosted by Circle Sanctuary and the Minneapolis Coven of Lothlorian that had hived off of the Pan-Pagan Festival.[146, 147] The Starwood festival, hosted by the Chameleon Club (later ACE) began in the summer of 1981.[148] Apart from the obvious advantages of exposing a wide variety of teachers, authors, goods, and services to people who might not otherwise have access to them, one of the greatest follow-on benefits of these festivals, gatherings and conferences was the networking meetings and discussions that took place between the leaders of far-flung organizations. It was these interactions, and those fostered through the medium of newsletters and magazines, that led to the development of national umbrella organizations for the modern Neo-Pagan movement. The first of these was the Council of Themis.

Founded in 1969 as a Neo-Pagan ecumenical alliance, the Council of Themis was chartered to authorize spokespersons and issue policy statements representing the stance of its member organizations. The Council of Themis began meeting in southern California in 1970. Some twenty-four groups eventually joined, including the Church of All Worlds (CAW), Feraferia, the Order of the Temple of Astarte (OTA), and the Church of the Eternal Source (CES). The Council was inevitably riven by what was characterized as disagreements in organization, philosophy, and leadership; in other words, virtually everything that defines a group.[149] Things came to a head in 1972 with the concerns that some of the member organizations raised in connection with the antics of one fellow member, the Psychedelic Venus Church (PsyVen).

PsyVen was founded in 1969 by the Rev. Jefferson Poland as "a pantheistic nature religion, humanist hedonism, a religious pursuit of bodily pleasure through sex and marijuana."[150] Functioning like the Merry Pranksters of the Neo-Pagan set, PsyVen openly flaunted sex and drugs in its rituals, thereby tweaking the Establishment's nose. Upon paying a five dollar registration fee, new recruits to the church were mailed two joints and instructed to use them in their own personal meditations. Friday Church ceremonies usually began with a sacramental smoking up and liturgical readings of erotica and leftist material, and ended with an orgy.[151] Public rituals revolved around the solar year and typically involved the invocation of Kali and Shiva, followed by the erotic "genital sacrifice" of a male and female member of the cult. Naked and with their genitals smeared with honey, the couple would submit to the oral attentions of the other worshippers in the crowd. Poland stated that the church's deity was "the sex goddess Venus-Aphrodite...in her psychedelic aspect. We see her presiding over nude orgies of fucking and sucking and cannabis: [a] truly venereal religion."[152]

To PsyVen's credit, there was no discrimination regarding the sexual orientation of the worshippers, so that men or women could lavish their attention whither they would. An auxiliary group associated with PsyVen in Berkeley, California — the Order of the Golden Calf — specifically "ministered to" the gay community. Even the name of one of the organization's newsletters, *Nelly Heathen*, reflected this openness to sexual diversity. But bisexuality and homosexuality weren't merely an afterthought to PsyVen; rather, Poland had built them into his vision of sexual liberation from the very beginning. While this was very forward-thinking on Poland's part, PsyVen sabbats weren't a complete free-for-all. Attendees at PsyVen's Friday services were limited to heterosexual couples and gay males in an effort to keep the events from being overwhelmed by mobs of horny straight men.[153]

PsyVen's devotional exercises were on the far fringe of spiritual exploration, but there is no reason to think they weren't authentic and heart-felt. Also, PsyVen certainly was not the only contemporaneous group to advocate the use of drugs as part and parcel of spiritual practice. The Neo-American Church, with its motto "Victory Over Horseshit!", was even more aggressive than PsyVen in this. "We have the *right* to practice our religion, even if we are a bunch of filthy, drunken bums," declared Neo-American Church founder, Art Kleps.[154] PsyVen's organizers also seemed to believe in what they were trying to accomplish, and it certainly embodied the energy and ideals of the psychedelic age of free love in a way that few spiritual groups dared. However, this in-your-face advocacy of group sex and drug use made a few members of the Council of Themis very nervous.

One of those who took issue with PsyVen's membership in the Council of Themis was Carroll "Poke" Runyon of the OTA. According to

Harold Moss of the CES, Runyon's belief in the threat that Jefferson Poland posed was based less on the issues of perversion and pot than on Poland's role as a political agitator, which Moss said Runyon viewed as part of an "alleged secret Communist plot to infiltrate Neo-Paganism." *(Ibid n#103)* Communist infiltration of the Council of Themis would certainly present a problem for the group, attracting as it would the unwanted attention of the FBI's Counter Intelligence Program (COINTELPRO) against political dissidents, as well as the interest of other law enforcement entities. However, in light of the PsyVen's public use of marijuana and its use of the US Postal Service to ship the drug to members (which already offered ample provocation for law enforcement to open an investigation into their activities and relationships), Runyon's concern over Poland's political orientation seems somewhat picayune, if not selective in nature. The latter point is especially relevant given the libertarian political leanings of one of the Council's major members, CAW.[155]

Runyon's beef against PsyVen was complex, stemming in part from what he termed the "drugs and sex-perversion" of the group.[156] The OTA, which Runyon founded and led as its Grand Master, excluded drug users and so-called sexual perverts from its own ranks, so his objection to the PsyVen could certainly be tied to the hedonistic group's emphasis on marijuana, public nudity and the free exercise of sexuality, particularly bisexuality and homosexuality. All these traits would have been at odds with his own conservative nature. But it was PsyVen's courting of the media to make its case for changing society's views on sex and drugs, and the collateral damage that this type of media attention might generate for the other Council members, that likely caused Runyon the greatest heartburn. Runyon admitted having crossed paths with the venereal activist in Florida as early as 1962, and described him as a professional agitator for a number of causes.[157]

Runyon was correct in stating that Jefferson Poland had a long history of activism. But Poland was not the bomb-throwing sort of anarchist, nor was he a rustic Bolshevik with blood dripping from hand tools pressed into the service of the Revolution. During this period, Poland was first a civil rights activist and then a sexual revolutionary who not only challenged the moral underpinnings governing society's regulation of sex, but society's very right to intrude into the personal lives of its citizens. By 1972, he had dedicated a decade of his life to various causes, whether protesting the arrest of comedian Lenny Bruce on obscenity charges in San Francisco in 1961, campaigning for the availability of contraceptives in the campus store at San Francisco State University, or registering black voters in Alabama in 1963.

In 1964, together with early New York gay activist Randy Wicker and future Fugs vocalist Tuli Kupferberg, Poland founded the Sexual Freedom League in New York City.[158] A number of Beat luminaries formed common cause with SFL, including Alan Ginsberg, Ed Sanders and Diane di Prima. The League formed chapters across the country, lobbying for changes in laws on prostitution, public nudity, contraception, gay rights and other issues touching on human sexuality.[159, 160] Campaigning for the right of blacks to register to vote, for free access to contraceptives, and for equal rights for gays and lesbians was certainly disturbing in those times to those of a counter-counterculture mindset.

The Council of Themis "crisis" developed when CAW and PsyVen began to discuss the possibility of merging their two groups as a way to head off Runyon's lobbying to oust PsyVen from the Council. Tim Zell tried to reassure Runyon that CAW would remain unaffected by the merger, and he was probably correct in this because CAW was already a staunch advocate of free love, ritual nudity and the right to sacramentally partake of drugs. *(Ibid n#156)* But CAW's approach tended to be somewhat subtler (all things being relative), whereas PsyVen was anything but discreet and there was no reason to expect that it would change. Merging with CAW would also have provided a national vehicle for Poland's political activities through *Green Egg* magazine. After failing to convince Tim Zell to rescind CAW's support of PsyVen, Runyon and Feraferia's Fred Adams decided to unilaterally revoke PsyVen's membership in the Council of Themis.

On the OTA's home turf of Pasadena, California, Fred Adams and Carroll Runyon held a rump meeting of the Council on May 10, 1972. With Adams as Chair and Runyon as acting secretary, the decision was made to expel PsyVen from the Council of Themis along with a British member organization called the Hellenic Order, which advocated a return to animal sacrifice as practiced in the Classical world. The expulsion notice stipulated that the determination was final and irrevocable, and further decreed that the remaining members were forbidden from incorporating the expelled entities within their own organizations. *(Ibid n#157)*

Questions immediately arose over the legitimacy of what Runyon had later labeled an "emergency action." *(Ibid n#157)* Other member organizations protested the high-handed action on the part of Runyon and Adams that allowed for neither the input nor the concurrence of the other Council members.[161, 162] Furthermore, the stipulation against incorporating the expelled groups within the remaining member organizations was a clear and unacceptable interference in the internal workings of those organizations, and seemed aimed primarily at undermining CAW's effort to protect PsyVen's status within the Council. The controversy continued throughout 1972, and ultimately resulted in the disintegration of the Council of Themis.

In an interview with Hans Holzer, Carroll Runyon said he believed that PsyVen and CAW had ultimately hoped to turn the Council of Themis into a militant organization for promoting all manner of antiestablishment left-wing causes, including drugs and sexuality. *(Ibid n#108)* But Runyon's explanation did nothing to justify the actions of the Executive Committee, which many considered to be the undemocratic takeover of that same organization in order to protect their own vision. Nor does Runyon's explanation align with the fact that CAW's own place on the Council remained unchallenged. Harold Moss, whose relatively conservative CES pulled out of the Council of Themis to protest the action, dismisses Runyon's rationale: "[It] had to do with [Runyon] attempting to set himself up as dictator of Council of Themis. Every member of the Council except Feraferia consequently resigned from the Council and most of them joined into a new 'Council of Earth Religions.' … Fred Adams [of Feraferia] apologized to me almost at once for being gulled by Runyon, but he and Runyon (and Holzer) remained friends."[163]

Meanwhile, the remnants of the Council of Themis, backed by Holzer's written account of the event and its aftermath in *The Witchcraft Report* (1973), tried to project the image that the organization was stronger than ever. Yet only members of the OTA and Feraferia, the two groups responsible for precipitating the crisis, were represented in the interview. Hans Holzer had previously criticized PsyVen's membership on the Council of Themis in his book *The New Pagans* (1972), writing, "When such extremist groups join with other pagan groups in overall organizations, they tend to embarrass the more seriously orientated movements."[164] Given this assertion and Holzer's own public sparring with Tim Zell and CAW, who were in the opposing camp, it was perhaps no surprise to find him backing Runyon's version of events. However, Leo Martello contradicted Holzer's tale that same year, reporting that most of the Council members had broken away to form the Council of Earth Religions (COER).[165] Margot Adler later blamed Holzer's inaccurate coverage of the story for making a bad situation worse.[166]

Adler referred to these events as the "Council of Themis War," while Leo Martello assigned the vaguely dismissive title "the War of the Witches" to the acrimonious state of affairs in 1973.[167] The sad truth is that most metaphysical groups in the modern era — Witchcraft, ceremonial, and Neo-Pagan alike — have been plagued with infighting at one time or another. In the end, this most recent struggle essentially boiled down to who would be accepted as part of the movement "mainstream" (if even such a term could be applied), and who would not.

Reflecting on the state of things, Leo Martello observed that, "The new trend in Witchcraft is for organization and cooperation between the various groups, though each one retains its own autonomy. Unfortunately, there are some prima donnas who have a vested interest in keeping the Craft divided. They really don't care about the Old Religion — just what they can get out of it."[168] Citing her music industry experience with insular groups such as the Yippies, Kathryn Frank notes that "There is nothing like small fringe organizations for infighting. Many times they spend more time fighting each other than the cause to which they are dedicated."[169] With a community or movement made up of diverse groups, such as Neo-Paganism, this dysfunction is magnified. Writer and Feraferia member W. Holman Keith noted that "Sectarianism is the bane of the neopagan movement. There is freedom, which is all to the good, but unity is lacking."[170]

Following the rupture of the Council of Themis, the CAW, CES, and a number of other former Council members began discussing their options. The decision was made later that year to form an alternative umbrella organization, which Harold Moss proposed to call the Council of Earth Religions (COER).[171, 172] *(Ibid n#162)* According to an announcement sent out by Moss, COER was founded on August 31, 1972 "as a democratic association of Nature religions groups allied to promote the common cause of love and service to our Holy Mother Earth and all forms of life; to promote [active] communication among our various groups thus increasing mutual understanding of our various viewpoints; and to provide for the common defense."[173] The charter members of the Council were the CAW, the CES, the Dancers of the Sacred Circle, and Rainbow Coven. By January 1973, COER had added six additional members, including the Philadelphia Pagan Way and a group from Italy. Eddie Buczynski's newly minted New York Coven of Welsh Traditionalist Witches had joined the Council in a bid to establish a national presence for the Traditionalist Gwyddoniaid. The Pagan Way associated with the Fishers' Louisville Coven was voted in as a member in the fall of 1973. *(Ibid n#172)* The CAW offered the pages of *Green Egg* for use as the official journal of the Council, and the CES Board provided the fledgling organization with stationery and postage.

The COER's initial activities promised great things, including, ironically enough, a carefully crafted membership admission process. Members debated the need to draw up formal standards for member groups — for example, for determining whether activist groups (referring to the PsyVen issue) would be admitted. One issue that the members appeared to agree upon was a "Bill of Rights" to ensure that the majority could not interfere with the inner workings of the individual members "in matters of taste or opinion." Yet despite these and other grand plans, the COER foundered.

"The Council was intended by the founding group as an alternative to the former Council [of Themis]. We wanted a democratic organization instead of a dictatorial one," Harold Moss wrote in a 1975 letter to *Green Egg*.[174] Explaining what went wrong, Moss noted that many of the member groups had either folded or merged, thus reducing the pool of support. Many of the remaining members seemed unable or unwilling to shoulder any of the burden to help run the Council. Like most volunteer organizations, COER relied upon a small coterie to get things done. After standing in as the acting Coordinator of the group to kick it off, Moss expected elections to fill the posts so he could return his attention to his duties in the CES. When the COER members did not step up to do so by the end of 1973, the Council collapsed. *(Ibid n#103)* Various efforts were undertaken to revive it through 1975, though none were successful.

In an ironic footnote to the story, the newly-formed COER turned down the membership request of PsyVen, albeit this time via legitimate means. Moss writes, "we democratically voted to deny Poland membership in the Council, which Poland respected. So Runyon's panic was ... completely unnecessary." *(Ibid n#103)* The Psychedelic Venus Church, which reportedly had 700 members by 1971, grew to 1000 members at its height. But because of various internal problems, membership dropped to 250 by 1974, and the organization was defunct by the close of the decade. Yet it had still managed to survive both the Council of Themis and the Council of Earth Religions. *(Ibid n#152, 153)*

When it became obvious in 1973 that COER was not working out, Carl Weschcke, owner of Llewellyn Publications, stepped in to try to find a workable solution. Weschcke had previously overseen a plenary session titled "Where Do We Go From Here?" at the second Gnostic-Aquarian Festival in Minneapolis on September 25, 1972. A number of positive ideas came out of this meeting, including the possibility of establishing an "occult hot line" to answer questions and providing a news media monitoring and response service to counter inaccurate reporting on occult issues. Weschcke's suggestion that the group consider forming an organization — the Gnostic Aquarian Society — to meet those needs and others was greeted with enthusiasm by those assembled.[175] Because the Council of Themis was crumbling and COER was struggling to establish itself at this time, many of the session's participants recognized that something needed to be done; and yet nothing came of it.

However, at the third annual Gnostic-Aquarian Festival in Minneapolis on September 20-23, 1973, the organizer took a different approach. Instead of a plenary session open to all comers, arrangements were made to have nightly meetings with attendance limited only to initiated Witches. Called "Witchmeets," these meetings attracted a total seventy-three individuals from the festival who worked together over the course of the festival to establish mutual rapport. Despite their different philosophies and a history of mistrust amongst some of the attendees, defenses were gradually lowered and important connections began to develop between individuals and groups.

By the end of the third night, those assembled agreed to form an informal and unofficial Council of American Witches (COAW) that would work to establish clear lines of communication and resolve issues in areas of mutual benefit. These issues included the definition of what comprises the "Craft," a Code of Ethics defining the responsibilities of Witches toward one another, the publication of common statement, and a commitment to reach out to other Witches who had not been present at these meetings. Carl Weschcke (Craft name *Gnosticus*) agreed to act as the "unofficial and informal" chairman. The COAW decided to convene a Witchmeet in the spring of 1974 to follow up on these goals.[176] As the COER was for all intents and purposes a dead entity at this point, these actions seemed proper if there was to be any forward movement in establishing an umbrella organization, however limited its scope.

Fighting Frosts with Fire

No event better illustrated the need for such coordination, and deliberation by cooler heads, than the publication of *The Witch's Bible*.[177] Gavin and Yvonne Frost, the authors of the book, had founded the Church of Wicca in 1968. After moving to the town of St. Charles, Missouri near St. Louis, they developed a correspondence course in 1972 that became the basis for their School of Wicca. *The Witch's Bible*, released in 1972 by Nash Publishing, contained information about the practices of the Church of Wicca and was intended to attract potential students to the correspondence school.

The Frosts' brand of Wicca was unlike any other Witchcraft tradition in the United States or Great Britain. One of the greatest differences between it and Gardnerian-derived Witchcraft was its pronouncement that Wicca was a monotheistic religion with an asexual God, a claim that no other Wiccan group publicly supported. Other distinctions included practices that seemed to be alternately Pentecostal and ascetic in nature, such as the casting out of demons, abstemious behavior prior to ritual, and multiple mentions of the Christian God and belief system. However, it also had some similarities in practice with other Witchcraft traditions, such as the casting of a circle, dancing to raise energy, and the emphasis on the heterosexual fertility aspect of nature. However, even here, the Church and School of Wicca differed from other Witchcraft paths in that theirs was a robust heterosexuality. A symbolic Great Rite would not do. Sex between working partners wasn't just encouraged; it was required, with every woman mounting her working partner introitus within the Circle in an act designed to raise and direct magickal energy.[178]

These practices were detailed in *The Witch's Bible*, the title of which was irritating to other practitioners for two reasons. First was the use of the word "Bible" as a descriptor for a book of Witchcraft, which grated on the nerves of many Witches, given its association with the book that forms the basis for Christianity. The book's many mentions of Christianity did not help its image on this count. Second was the choice of the definite article "the," which implied that the book described the only way Witchcraft was practiced.[179] Perceptions were not helped on this count, either, by indications that the Frosts believed that theirs was the only true way of

Witchcraft even though its public appearance in the late 1960s long postdated that of Gardnerian Wica.[180]

But these were all minor issues in comparison to the Frosts' most controversial revelations, including advocating the use of dildoes on virginal novice girls in order to prepare them for their role in the sex magick rites of the Church. The Church required the father of the girl or an unrelated male coven sponsor to assist the girl in using the dildoes if necessary. Detailed instructions were even provided in *The Witch's Bible* on the construction and use of the artificial phalloi to be used.[181] The book promoted the practice of having a child lose his or her virginity as early as possible through the assistance of either the mother or a physician. For example, the mother was instructed to pull back the foreskin of her son and cut the membrane to allow it to fully retract.[182] These practices, and speculation about the age of the girls and boys who could be subjected to them, raised serious questions about incest and childhood sexual abuse in the minds of outside observers. This concern was heightened by the legal advice offered by *The Witch's Bible* with respect to bending or breaking local laws, along with an example, under the title "Carnal Knowledge," of initiating a sixteen-year-old girl.[183] Many Witches at that time recoiled in horror from the practices described in The Witch's Bible, and many still do to this day because these practices have remained a part of Church doctrine for almost 40 years. Other statements, such as openly discouraging the formation of mixed-race covens, led to additional charges of racism on the part of the authors.[184]

Roger Pratt tells of receiving a copy of the Frost manuscript from one of his coven contacts in Great Britain in 1972 before the book was published. "I was appalled!" he writes. "I couldn't believe anyone would make stuff like that up!" *(Ibid n#130, 131)* Pratt went so far as to give the manuscript to someone he thought might be able to stop its publication, to no avail. On December 17, 1972, Pratt accompanied another man to the Warlock Shop in order to consecrate a dagger the younger guy had received as a gift from Joe Lukach. Leo Martello was there with Herman Slater. After introductions were made, Slater noted that Roger had a copy of *The Witch's Bible* manuscript. According to Pratt, *(Ibid n#130, 131)*

> *Leo cornered me with his most terrifying look. "I must read it! You must get it for me!" I replied that I'd lent it to John Hansen (who had studied with Joe Lukach) and when it was returned I'd drop it off. Leo started ranting about "We Sicilian Witches take images of the gods and when they don't answer us we put their heads in the toilet and flush till we get our way." And he wouldn't listen to my protests that I'd have it back until finally I said, "You kneel and worship what's in the TOILET! And you've the nerve to advise ME!" And Leo collapsed in laughter and hugged me and we got on from that day forward.*

It was only logical that after publication *The Witch's Bible* would first show up in occult and metaphysical book stores, including the Warlock Shop. When the book arrived, Herman Slater began skimming through it out of curiosity. What he found between the book's covers infuriated him. Herman was already predisposed to dislike the Frosts because of their bizarre theories on the origins and detection of homosexuality in individuals and on the suitability of gays to practice in a coven. An article by the couple earlier that year in *Green Egg* had theorized, among other things, that homosexuality was caused by demonic possession.[185]

The Frosts' practiced a form of Witchcraft that specifically excluded homosexuals, and the couple stated that they had never admitted a known homosexual to their rites.[186] In The Witch's Bible, the Frosts promoted their path as one that celebrated the fertility of its members. Expressing their concern about human overpopulation, Gavin and Yvonne Frost called for the use of responsible contraception (which did not include abortion) to ensure that only children who are wanted and loved are brought into the world — a worthy goal, regardless of the advocate.[187] Yet while they wrote approvingly of non-procreative heterosexuality, they dismissed "sterile unisex relationships" and discussed them in the same context as drug abuse and sexual perversion. Homosexuality, they declared, was not condoned by Wicca.[188] Margot Adler has suggested that if the Frosts had merely stuck to stating their beliefs on homosexuality in terms of the qualifications and limits they placed on their own students and practices, their stance might not have aroused the ire it did when they occasionally strayed into making blanket statements about the ill-qualification of homosexuals to practice Witchcraft.[189]

The basis for Slater's outrage upon reading *The Witch's Bible* stemmed primarily from the Frosts' labeling of their religion as Wicca, when it included many practices and concepts that bore little or no resemblance to that family of paths as it had been generally understood since Gardner's day. Peter Levenda writes, "From what I understand, it was the perception that somehow the Frosts were promoting incest and child abuse. And there was that stuff with the dildoes. That made a lot of problems for Herman. In the first place, he objected strongly to the incest/child abuse scenario, of course, and also found the 'sacred dildo' approach ridiculous. In the second place, he felt strongly that this gave Wicca extremely negative publicity, after all Herman and others had gone through to promote a healthy view of Wicca. The attacks on the Frosts were visceral, heartfelt, and sustained over a long period of time."[190]

Slater also had a very personal reason for his visceral objection to what the Frosts were passing off as Wicca. During this same period, Craft practitioners commonly referred to homosexuals as perverts and barred them from participating in their rites for fear of the disrepute that they might bring on Wica. Indeed, society generally looked with suspicion on any situation that placed homosexuals, particularly gay men, in close contact with children, and yet here were the Frosts publicly describing nude sexual contact in the Circle with underage children, the deflowering of underage girls with wooden dildoes by their fathers as part of their initiation into Witchcraft, and the cutting of a boy's foreskin by his mother. Given the Frosts' own stance on homosexuality and perversion, there was something incredibly hypocritical and unfair about this in Herman's mind, and he simply wasn't willing to let it pass.

In late December 1972, Slater sent out a letter to a long list of community leaders, organizations, publications, and stores. Writing as the President of the Friends of the Craft, he set himself up as the *bête noire* of the Frosts by delivering a scathing attack on *The Witch's Bible*:[191]

> *NOTE TO ALL OF THE OLD RELIGION,*
>
> *A new "WITCH-CRAP" book is on the market. The debunkers like Rachleff and the sensationalists like Haining are Christian angels compared to this book..."THE WITCHES BIBLE" by Gavin and Yvonne Frost.*
>
> *The people that wrote it are very nice people and perhaps friends of many of you ... however, the book is a mockery and an obscenity to all those who worship the Goddess. It is nothing but an excuse for apparently CHRISTIAN wife-swapping and sex. WICCA is not trademarked...witches do not use the "Lord's Prayer"...Witches worship the Goddess and the Horned God...Witches do not use three [sic] different sized artificial phalli wrapped in plastic wrap for new female initiates to ready them for initiation...female witches do not mount male witches in the circle to the point of orgasm and then stop...the great rite is not a mass orgy sung to the tune of "She'll be coming round the mountain" or "San Francisco" (shades of Lawrence Welk).*

While Slater's letter acknowledged that the Church of Wicca was a legitimate earth religion, he denied that they were Wiccan. Although he stated that people have a right to worship as they see fit, he rejected the Frosts' attempt to redefine the term "Wicca" to fit their unique and, in his view, perverse practices, which placed all other Wiccans at risk by comparison. "After reading the book," Slater wrote, "think to yourself...'What if I weren't a Witch and read this book ... What would I think of WICCA?' The answer will horrify you." Herman suggested that Craft practitioners borrow and read *The Witch's Bible* for themselves, write letters of protest, and then burn the book, a rather repugnant notion in itself given that evangelicals were organizing public burnings of occult materials at the time. As Hans Holzer dryly observed, "Imagine a witch suggesting a burning!" *(Ibid n#108)*

Harold Moss sent out a letter to the COER membership in early January, acknowledging receipt of Slater's broadside. "I received from

Herman Slater a warning about the book <u>Witches Bible</u>; CES sent out on its letterhead to local libraries and bookstores a greeting letter with a copy of Mr. Slater's warning. This is an example of our Council [of Earth Religions] in action!"[192] But not everyone was supportive of this position. By February 1973, the debate about the Frosts began hitting the editorial and letters pages of the metaphysical magazines. Carl Weschcke, publisher of *Gnostica News*, delivered a withering criticism of Slater's call for action.

Weschcke noted the "hue and cry" that Slater had raised since the publication of the Frosts' book, but made it clear that no one had any right to tell others that what they practiced was not Wicca. "The Wicca by its nature is a jigsaw puzzle of beliefs, motives and practices," wrote Weschcke. "Every sect differs from the other, and even between affiliated covens practices differ. The Wiccan way is based upon the worship of nature and the control of the natural powers. Aside from this, there is as yet, no further definition."[193]

But it was precisely this inability to define who belonged within the big tent of Witchcraft and Neo-Paganism that was causing issues within the community, thereby setting up a replay of the same struggle which brought down the Council of Themis in 1972. Literally anyone could claim to be a Witch or Neo-Pagan, seize the media spotlight, and drag the entire movement down through any manner of outlandish and unsupported statements, or promote practices that could arguably be labeled as criminal. Even Carl Weschcke eventually came to acknowledge the desirability of the community having a "self-policing mechanism."[194] In lieu of such a mechanism, however, the community was left to fall back on the actions of individuals and small groups of like-minded people, which often as not failed to reflect the consensus of the community at large. There was also a tendency in the Neo-Pagan community, then as now, to err on the side of acceptance even when the evidence tended to point toward reprehensible behavior. This tendency stemmed from the movement's historic position in the United States as a countercultural, even fringe, element of society, and it may explain why otherwise thoughtful people in leadership roles were willing to give the Frosts the benefit of the doubt, even when faced with evidence of highly questionable beliefs and behavior.

Herman Slater did make a concerted effort to rally support for a boycott of *The Witch's Bible*, beginning with his initial fusillade in December 1972. Late in January 1973, he wrote privately to Hans Holzer, providing the paranormal author with copies of his correspondence concerning the controversy and urging him not to give the Frosts a platform from disseminate their views. "Deep in your heart you know the truth," Herman wrote in an attempt to sway Hans' opinion, fearful that the writer would be interested in examining the couple in his next book on the occult.[195] Holzer, however, was intrigued by the Frosts' unique perspective and wanted to explore why they raised the hackles of so many people. It must also be said that Holzer's opinion of Herman was not entirely positive, and this may well have played in his decision to decline climbing aboard an anti-Frost bandwagon being driven by his fellow New Yorker. Far from remaining neutral in the matter, there is some indication that Holzer may have shared with the Frosts the correspondence he received about them from Slater in an effort to elicit a reaction from them.

Slater may have shot himself in the foot with his overt publicity and pressure tactics by piquing the interest of people like Holzer, thus affirming Oscar Wilde's aphorism that the only thing worse than being talked about was *not* being talked about. Cognizant of the burgeoning controversy surrounding the Frosts and their book, Holzer arranged to meet the couple backstage of *Regis Philbin's Saturday Night in St. Louis* at the studios of KMOX-TV, where he had just filmed an appearance on his old friend's show. The resulting interview provided favorable coverage of the Frosts when *The Witchcraft Report* was published in September 1973, helped in no small part by Holzer's interview technique which failed to challenge the historical claims behind or modern legality of the most objectionable of the practices that they promoted.

The Frosts themselves didn't sit on their hands while Slater was scourging them in public and in private. The couple agreed to speak free of charge to any group who would bother to hear them. This was a savvy public relations move, indicating that they weren't afraid to face questions about their beliefs and practices up front. On a personal level, Gavin tried to persuade Herman to drop the matter, but his manner seemed purposefully designed to infuriate the Welsh initiate and prolong the conflict. Gavin jammed a metaphorical thumb in Herman's eye by implying that the New York Welsh Witches didn't know anything about Welsh Witchcraft, and questioned the success of their rites.[196] On the one hand, Gavin Frost claimed that they didn't wish to add further divisions in the community. Yet on the other, he declared that their attorneys had deemed Slater's letter to be libelous, and demanded either that he issue a retraction or that he provide a list of those to whom the original broadside was sent so that the Frosts could send out a rejoinder.

Herman instead responded by dismissing the Frosts' alleged concerns over splitting the Craft as impossible "since you're not a part of the Craft." Slater wrote, "You may be Pagan. You may read, write or speak Welsh. BUT ... YOU ARE NOT WITCHES." He suggested instead that the Frosts have their publisher withdraw all remaining copies of *The Witch's Bible*. Echoing a charge that he would bring against another in years to come, Slater widened his attack to note that the School of Wicca was charging a fee to teach students through its mail order courses. "Witches have never, nor will ever charge students for their teachings."[197]

The gist of Slater's argument was correct, insofar as all Witches who adhere to the Wiccan Laws are supposedly forbidden to take money in exchange for teaching. Yet, as Hans Holzer pointed out, a number of well-known Witches of the time — Sybil Leek, Sara Cunningham and Alex

Sanders, among others — charged a teaching fee.[198] But the Wiccan Laws were not a part of the teachings of the Church of Wicca; nor, indeed, was much of anything else that had been previously recognizable as "doctrinaire" Wica. Therefore, it is unclear why the Laws would be thought to apply to the Church and School of Wicca. Herman seemed hardly in a position to suggest enforcing Laws that were also not, in fact, part of the Traditionalist Gwyddoniaid to which he himself belonged.

Despite failing to secure Slater's list of correspondents, Gavin Frost sent out his own broadside to as many people as possible in an attempt to reach everyone who received Slater's original letter of denunciation. Slater was indirectly addressed in the missive with a bare-toothed threat of using candle and cord magick against him. *(Ibid n#198)* Gavin's attitude appeared in marked contrast to his own admonishment in *The Witch's Bible* against doing harmful magick to others.[199] However, adherents of the Church and School of Wicca were not always required to turn the other cheek, and the Frosts didn't, launching an *ad hominem* attack that questioned Slater's motivation for attacking their work and his basic competence for judging others. The Frosts compared the Jewish shopkeeper to "a fundamentalist Christian haranguing from his pulpit" and an "under-achieving sex-fantasizer" who was "cross-eyed with desire on reading the book." *(Ibid n#196)* The Frosts dismissed Herman as an incompetent for his inability to count phalli, and as an oaf for objecting to their advocating the use of relatively comfortable dildoes instead of the types of dildoes that had allegedly been used for rituals in ancient times. This sidestepped the actual objection that Slater and others had raised to the Frosts' teachings — which was that they advocated practices likely to raise suspicions of ritual sexual abuse, statutory rape, and incest.

Further exchanges between the two sides ensued, culminating in a final volley from the Frosts that referred to Slater as "Herman Bradwr" — "bradwr" being Welsh for "traitor," a play on words referring to the Warlock Shop — and accusing him of slandering the Church and School of Wicca. Judging by the continued hostility emanating from Brooklyn Heights, Gavin and Yvonne had decided that it was pointless to try reasoning any further with Herman. They chose, instead, to unnerve him while at the same time proving that he didn't know as much as he thought he did about either them or the Craft. The Frosts announced that their coven had decided to respond to Slater's attacks by sending a hex his way. "As a dog returns to its vomit," they wrote, "go back to your cellar under the traitor's shop and call upon Beelzebub or any other two-bit god or goddess you wish."[200] While on its face this appears to be another example of the Frosts violating their own admonition against cursing, the letter to Herman was both menacing and humorous — a send-up designed to return insult for insult, and also to rattle the New Yorker's cage.

One telling clue for this is one of the side effects of the hex noted by the Frosts (premature ejaculation during heterosexual intercourse) which was a pointed dig at Herman's homosexuality. Their mention of the ritual room beneath the Warlock Shop put Herman on notice that they knew the layout of the store and of the ritual space below, although they had never visited there. The Frosts ended the letter by offering up the hope that an effective protection against the hex could be obtained by Dennis Wheatley on the edge of the New Forest. The only problem with this was that Wheatley was not a practitioner with any known occult skills; rather, he was a well-known British writer of black magic thrillers that were said to have influenced Church of Satan founder Anton LaVey. [201, 202, 203] Hans Holzer, who continued to receive copies of all the correspondence from both sides in the fight, got the jokes and admitted to having a good laugh after reading the Frosts' reply. But he also cautioned, "I don't think that tempting the Goddess, so to speak, is a good idea. It's just possible that the hex might work."[204]

Herman took the threat with a grim seriousness, however, and it was at this point that people in the community began to worry that things were getting out of hand. Holzer wrote that in February he had started interceding to try to stop the public attacks before they escalated further. It is clear, however, that if he truly made such an attempt, it had virtually no effect. Leo Martello joined the fight later in the year with his publication of *Witchcraft: The Old Religion.* In a section of his book where he heaped scorn on false Witches and those who made money at the expense of the religion, Martello attacked the Frosts and their book, but without mentioning them by name. He charged that they, with their dildoes and circumcision and "excerpts from Christian grimoires and their own masturbatory fantasies" were nothing more than perverse Christians who advertise their Witchcraft courses in the sex columns of the *Los Angeles Free Press.*[205] Worrying that books of this nature would be used against the movement, Martello wrote, "Their book makes no distinction between the various traditions of Wicca, but presents its garbage as something true of all Witches. ... Their book of course will be avidly quoted by the fundamentalist fascists — a false book giving false ammunition to the Biblical bigots." *(Ibid n#205)*

The sniping continued throughout the summer, and Herman used the first print ad for the Warlock Shop in *Gnostica News* as a platform for hammering at the Frosts. The ad copy, which read "Member Friends of the Craft – BOYCOTT WITCH CRAP BOOKS!", was probably chosen to counter the support initially offered to the Frosts by Llewellyn's *Gnostica News* in opposition to Slater's call for a boycott.[206] Given the hubbub over the claims by The Church and School of Wicca, and the unblinking coverage of the Frosts in Hans Holzer's book *The Witchcraft Report,* it was no surprise that one of the primary topics for discussion at the September 1973 Witchmeet sponsored by Llewellyn Worldwide would be to cobble together a consensus definition of what actually constitutes the Craft.

Carl Weschcke, in reporting on the results of the evening Witchmeet sessions, was perhaps overly optimistic about the hurdles involved in this undertaking when he wrote, "The attempts at definition of the Craft and resolution of other problem areas ... demonstrated that major barriers to the program outlined the first night really did not exist." Despite this hope, the Witchmeet broke up on September 23 without resolving the fundamental question of the gathering, namely "a definition of the Craft that is widely inclusive — and yet that will be a standard which will afford the public a protection against the wild claims of both our detractors and glamour-seekers alike."[207]

Others came away from the event with a less rosy opinion, with one critic bluntly stating that "the goings-on resembled a Chinese fire-drill at a Southern Baptist Convention."[208] Tim Zell set a more cautious tone when describing the progress made during the Witchmeet. Noting that each participant at the festival had been asked to provide a 25-words-or-less definition of Witchcraft, Zell concluded, "We spent some time discussing these matters ... and didn't get very far." *(Ibid n#180)* While the majority of attendees were able to agree on several characteristics that could be used to define the Craft — recognition and worship of the Goddess and Her Divine Consort, the Horned God, being the primary one — even this trait was not universally held, and was contrary to the theology of The Church and School of Wicca, whose founders claimed Witchcraft to be a monotheistic religion devoted to an unnamed and asexual being. "At the Gnostica Festival, Gavin and Yvonne were quite clear in stating that their religion bears no relation to the religion of all others who call themselves 'Witches,'" Zell continued. "However, they feel that they are the only TRUE Witches, and all the OTHERS are faking it." *(Ibid n#180)* This assertion would likely have hardened Slater's position, vindicating in his mind the belief that the Frosts would end up giving Witchcraft a black eye and thereby justifying his continued attacks on them.

Gavin and Yvonne were present for the entire event. It is possible that, had they not been, the Witchmeet might have achieved a consensus on the Frosts' place within the greater Wiccan community. As it turned out, however, there was sufficient disagreement to prevent anything from happening. Gavin Frost offered up a means to settle the matter of disciplining alleged misbehavior within the Wiccan community. "In order to establish a means by which those who transgress the basic law shall be judged," Frost proposed, "the five leaders of five traditions shall demand explanation of warlock acts. If no satisfactory explanation is forthcoming, the person(s) involved shall be declared a warlock and his name shall be communicated to all."[209]

This mechanism not only neatly sidestepped the qualification issue that was causing such consternation at the gathering, but also made it virtually impossible to bring charges against anyone — because where would five Witchcraft traditions ever find sufficient common cause to demand such a hearing? The other issue that no one was eager to face had to do with determining the qualifications of individuals seeking to be empanelled for any such hearing. The arguments about who could be considered the "leaders" of traditions made up of loose confederations of related covens could delay any hearing for months or years (or even forever). Although his proposal went nowhere, Gavin Frost would nevertheless regret ever having uttered it.

In December, Herman and Eddie published the first edition of their own newspaper, the *Earth Religion News*. Herman's various feuds, first with the Frosts and later with the Long Island Gardnerians, may have been the single major contributing factor in his decision to publish, as it would give him a soapbox to project his views, unfettered by the editorial decisions of others. As Slater wrote in the paper's first editorial — *Directions That This is Going* — "This paper will follow the purpose set forth by (Friends of the Craft) and expose filth and garbage, as was done with the Witches Bible and the School of WICCA (Complete Christian Sex Filth) and continue on that road as much as we can! ... we will attack what is ripe for attacking and expose what is ripe for exposing and not put up with the wishy washy, backbiting phonyness that is all too prevalent in the organized Craft today, especially by the bought (fence sitters) who are on their own self decepting power and ego trips. Blessed Be ... Herman Slater ... Publisher ... If you feel personally slighted ... Blessed was!!"[210] Despite the many positive things that the *Earth Religion News* would do, Slater's antagonistic opening volley set the mood for the paper over its short run.

But being on the polar end of a disagreement wasn't necessarily a bad thing. Whereas *Earth Religion News* was clearly against the Frosts and *Gnostica News* tended to support them, it was *Green Egg* that took the most flak, perhaps because its editorial staff had tried to air both sides of the issue. This neutrality did nothing, however, to insulate them from charges that they were taking sides. For example, in an attempt to characterize The Church of Wicca in its "Yellow Pages" section, *Green Egg* had listed it under Pagan groups instead of "Witches and Covens," eliciting a protest from some who felt that the magazine was trying to insert itself into the debate over who could claim the title of Witch.

In defense of the magazine's action, Tim Zell noted that it wasn't at all clear where the Frosts' organization belonged within the occult movement. "As far as I'm concerned, their trip is thoroughly Pagan, and hence should be listed in the 'Yellow Pages' — which is a listing of Pagan groups in North America," Zell wrote in response to one reader's complaint. "But now Yvonne [Frost] tells me that they are not Pagan at all, so what should I do? Should I list them anyway even though they have excluded themselves from the very classification on which the Directory is based?" Addressing the issue of whether or not the Frosts' group was Wiccan, he continued, "I am only a 1st initiate of Wicca and therefore I must bow before the authority of the High Priest & High Priestesses of the many various traditions of the Craft, ALL of whom seem to agree that neither the 'Church of Wicca' nor the 'Baal Sathanas' [a Satanic group] are forms of Witchcraft. I have yet to hear from any in the Craft who disagree with this majority opinion."[211, 212]

In an article in the March edition of *Earth Religion News*, Zell went even further, declaring, "I have not received, ever, a single letter of support for the Frosts from ANY members of the Craft, anywhere in the world. On the contrary, all the letters we received, from leaders of all kinds of traditions, unanimously denied that the Frosts teach Witchcraft. ... [If] Witches themselves have no right to define what is or is not Witchcraft, then who has?" *(Ibid 180)* Nemeton co-founder Gwydion Pendderwen summed up the matter this way: "Ultimately, of course, the standards of Witchcraft belong to the individual traditions and covens. In concert, we may disqualify some individuals or groups (e.g., the Frosts) by a consensus of opinion. Individually, we can only live up to our own standards behind the title Witch."[213]

Yet, despite this apparent support for his anti-Frost position, Herman Slater grew frustrated by what he saw as *Green Egg*'s tendency to cut the Church of Wicca an inordinate amount of slack while the magazine simultaneously, and vociferously, took sides against Hans Holzer. Accusing the *Green Egg* editor of having changed since the September Witchmeet, Slater wrote that Zell had regressed to "Fence sitting and kissing ass for Llewellyn" (publisher of *Gnostica News*) and had turned his magazine into a rag sheet.[214] Zell repudiated those characterizations, claiming that the policy of *Green Egg* had always been to "treat others as we would wish to be treated. ... We believe that full expression of ALL diverging viewpoints is essential if the truth is ever to be gotten at."[215] He claimed that *Green Egg* did not publish anonymous letters and complained about the tendency for Neo-Pagans to go at each others' throats, noting that "Vituperative attacks on fellow Pagans pains us greatly, and you, Herman, are far from exempt from these!" But his argument was not helped when, in this same issue, *Green Egg* published a pseudonymous letter with no return address, defaming Herman Slater, Eddie Buczynski, Leo Martello, and anyone else who frequented the Warlock Shop.[216] The resulting row between Slater and *Green Egg* co-editor Morning Glory left the latter in tears and soured the relationship between the two groups even further.[217]

Thus it is perhaps an understatement to say that tempers were frayed in the run-up to the April 1974 Witchmeet. Things became hotter yet when Slater published a bombshell in the pages of *Earth Religion News*. In the March edition of the newspaper, Slater wrote that he would take Gavin Frost up on his idea for holding hearings against alleged "warlocks" by proposing that a mock trial be conducted during a workshop period as a proof of the concept. "The several Tradition Leaders will be chosen hopefully by Gnosticus, Tim Zell and myself ... none of whom shall sit on the Council," Herman wrote. "It is ironic that I, who have been battling with the Frosts since the publication of the (GARBAGE bible) should use their own words to call this Council which will sit in Judgment on them upon charges drawn up by myself, the end result hopefully being that they be read out of the Pagan Movement, Officially." *(Ibid n#209)* With this, the gauntlet was thrown down. Almost as an afterthought, Herman scheduled a final Warlock Shop advertisement including the phrase "Boycott Witch Crap Books" to run in the edition of *Gnostica News* that would be available to the Witchmeet attendees in April.[218]

Leaving the shop in the hands of Burt Cicciotto, the husband of their bookkeeper, Slater and Buczynski boarded a United Airlines flight to Chicago in the second week of April to begin their trip to the spring Witchmeet. They were met at the Chicago airport by Ginny Brubaker, High Priestess of the Chicago Temple of the Pagan Way. Ginny and Herman recognized each other by the slogan buttons they wore — hers saying "In Goddess We Trust," his "Blessed Be." Brubaker drove the duo to a restaurant for a hearty meal. There they met Herman Enderle, High Priest of the local Pagan Way and author of some of the Pagan Way materials used by covens nationwide to train new members.

After dinner, the group was driven to the building housing the Pagan Way temple. It was a three-story house at 1125 West Wellington Street, with the temple in the finished basement and Pagans, Witches and Magickians residing communally in the upper floors. The temple itself was spacious, comfortable and well-appointed. Eddie was instantly smitten with it, writing that it "was the most fantastic place I've ever seen. ... Walking into the temple was like walking out of the world of frenetic men and into a world of peace and sanctuary."[219] Waxing poetic about the entire scene, Buczynski admitted "that I fell in love with Ginny [Brubaker] and Herman [Enderle] simultaneously and immediately. I have been many places in this country, with many Pagans, and never have I experienced the warmth that I experienced in Chicago with these people."

Eddie and Herman stayed for several days with Ginny, who was a delightful host in every way. Together, they explored the museums, restaurants, and occult shops the Windy City had to offer. One such side trip included a visit with Frederick de Arechaga at his El-Sabarum shop, which also housed the temple of the Sabaean Religious Order that de Arechaga led. Herman and Eddie were truly impressed with the amount of work and attention to detail that Frederick put into the Order. The New Yorkers — residents of, as Eddie put it, the "Antarctic of the Eastern USA" — were simply not used to the openness and friendly faces they encountered during their stay. The hospitality led Eddie to wistfully ask Herman if they couldn't just pull up stakes and move their operation to Chicago. At the close of their Chicago trip, the two boarded an Amtrak train bound for Minneapolis, joined by a Gardnerian High Priestess from the Temple of the Pagan Way who was also going to the Witchmeet.

The spring Witchmeet was held in Minneapolis on Thursday through Sunday, April 11-14, 1974. Slater and Buczynski arrived on Thursday and made it to the venue, Holiday Inn Central, in time to unpack and set up the Warlock Shop vendor table. Tim Zell and Morning Glory were both at the Witchmeet, along with Morning Glory's four-year-old daughter, Rainbow. Now Rainbow had been present during the telephone argument between Morning Glory and Herman in March, and was still upset that her mommy had been brought to tears by this "Herman Slater" person. As Zell later remembered, Herman was setting up his display when "This adorable little 4-year-old girl in a pink fairy tutu accosted him in front of everyone, accusing him fiercely, 'Are you Herman Slater? You're a bad man! You made my mommy cry!'" Zell continues, "Someone got hold of Morning Glory and brought her over, where Herman was cowering behind his table, [saying] 'I'm sorry, Lady! Call off your kid!'" *(Ibid n#217)*

That evening, Eddie and Herman circulated through the various parties that were taking place amongst the attendee rooms. Herman introduced Eddie to Carl Weschcke, the owner of Llewellyn Publishing and host of the event, whom Slater had previously met at book conventions. "I remember [that Herman had] a broad smile when he was happy," Weschcke recalls, "and I know there was a kind of proud look when he introduced me to Eddie." *(Ibid n#91)* Pleasantries out of the way, Herman drew Carl aside to discuss the plans for the "mock trial" scheduled for Saturday. The Witchmeet attendees were certainly abuzz about Herman's "Special Council," which many referred to as "the Inquisition." The schedule notice read:[220]

> *Saturday, April 13, 2-4 PM. Herman Slater will convene a council to accuse and demand judgment on certain persons he believes to be Warlocks, not Witches, and therefore traitors to the Craft.*

Herman may have hoped that by naming people from the pro, anti, and neutral camps to appoint the panel, the hearing would be more palatable to everyone. He had already conceded that he would not be sitting on the panel himself, nor would it have been reasonable for Slater to do so since he had no claim to being the leader of a tradition. This concession was also likely a sop to those who would have pointed to his lack of objectivity in the matter, given that he had been waging a crusade for over a year to discredit the Frosts. However, the antagonistic wording of the schedule, combined with the mood of the attendees, indicated that the support that Herman had been counting on at the event had evaporated. Eddie's presence at the Witchmeet was also likely orchestrated by Herman, who may have counted on him to be one of the panel selectees since he was the leader of the Traditionalist Gwyddoniaid.

But Eddie showed no apparent interest in the trial. Peter Levenda notes that "Eddie was as much part of [the fight] as anyone else in the Craft at the time, although I had the feeling that he wanted to remain aloof from the squabbles as much as possible." *(Ibid n#190)* While Herman was lobbying others for support, Buczynski was meeting with Harold Moss and his lover, Jim Kemble, both of the CES. Buczynski had begun corresponding with Moss when the latter had attempted to kick-start the COER into existence in 1972. Eddie's own interest in ancient Egypt guaranteed that he would not pass up the opportunity to speak in person with a co-founder of the CES. Thus, while Herman was endeavoring to make sure that the show trial would go on, Eddie was off talking about Egyptian hieroglyphic grammar with Kemble and attending a room party with the couple.[221]

On Friday morning, Tim Zell and Morning Glory presented a workshop titled "Paganism, Witchcraft and Neo-Paganism: The Old Religion and the New Religion." The purpose of the workshop, which was to provide an overview of the article of the same name that Zell had published in *Earth Religion News* in March, was a technical analysis of what constituted a practitioner of Witchcraft.[222] The presentation covered the topic in a far more organized manner than had been applied at the previous Witchmeet in September 1973 and provoked a number of side-discussions that went on into the evening.[223] The points raised in this ongoing dialogue provided considerable food for thought among those who attended it, and this in turn had a profound effect on the remainder of the Witchmeet.

Weschcke, Zell and others continued to work on Herman to get him to back down from his prosecution/persecution of the Frosts on Saturday. Movement leaders sensed that there was little support for conducting a hearing, and they were not eager to put their names on the line by assisting in its execution. Herman eventually bowed to the inevitable, likely realizing that to force the issue was to lose all credibility. Pressured to abandon his antagonistic approach to the Frosts and to look at the bigger picture, he capitulated — but he exacted a price for his cooperation. When the time came for the trial to begin, the assembled crowd waited with bated breath.

According to CAW member Lewis Scheiber, "Herman called for a circle to be cast and asked that people who wished to participate enter the circle to raise power and use it to establish an atmosphere of 'Perfect Love and Perfect Trust.'" *(Ibid n#223)* In Herman's own words, "There was no trial. There was a Craft Circle formed and people [were] told only to enter if they bore no animosity and respected Perfect Love and Perfect Trust. I know it sounds corny but for some reason the feeling was there."[224] The very fruitful discussion that followed, attended by upwards of sixty Witches from around the country, lasted well into the afternoon with, as Schreiber notes, "only a few breaks in the atmosphere of 'Perfect Love and Perfect Trust.'"[225] *(Ibid n#223)*

As Carl Weschcke noted many years later, "The Frost trial didn't happen because no one wanted it to happen, and the concept itself is absurd. There was no 'authorized body' before which such a trial would be meaningful, and any 'judgment' would be meaningless. Even though one of the anticipated outcomes of that Witchmeet was the creation of a Council of American Witches ... the only result of a trial could have been to deny the Frosts membership. The news of such could possibly have hurt their mail order business (correspondence course), but what else?"[226]

Bowing to the desires of the other movement leaders gave Slater leverage to push for a *quid pro quo*. Seizing this opportunity to address the bigger picture, Slater forced the assembled representatives to face up to the ugly presence of racial and sexual discrimination in the Craft. "There was a confrontation on basic issues of bigotry and all sides were heard," Herman wrote. "The basic contention on my part was that a Homosexual, either Male or Female, or a Black was no different than anyone else in the workings of Covens and Magick. There was much dispute, which brought about the general adoption [of] among other things [an antidiscrimination motion on] Sexual Preference." He continued, "It was interesting to note that the basically straight or bisexual females were the only ones to defend my stand, except for some beautiful people from Colorado and Tim Zell. The known homosexuals sat and shivered in their chairs. But as I said to the audience, 'If you people don't get off your asses and start pulling it together there's going to be another burning time and this FAGGOT IS NOT GOING TO BE THROWN ONTO THE FIRE.'" *(Ibid n#224)*

After considerable debate, some of it heated, the group came to consensus on three main points. First, any person, regardless of race or sexual preference, can be balanced within a coven, given enough time and energy. Second, covens have the absolute right to admit or reject people at will, with the understanding that they should try to refer the rejected applicants to other covens where they may fit better. Third, just because a set of standards works for one coven, they should not expect every other coven to follow it. *(Ibid n#223)*

By the close of the meeting the attendees had managed to hammer out a statement titled "Principles of Wiccan Belief," which stated in part,[227]

> It is in the spirit of welcome and cooperation that we adopt these few principles of Wiccan Belief. In seeking to be inclusive, we do not wish to open ourselves to the destruction of our group by those on self-serving power trips, or to philosophies and practices contradictory to those principles. In seeking to exclude those whose ways are contradictory to ours, we do not want to

> *deny participation with us to any who are sincerely interested in our knowledge and beliefs, regardless of race, color, sex, age, national or cultural origins or sexual preference.*

"I had drafted 'The Principles of Wiccan Belief' as a means for the organized discussion, and with few changes everyone endorsed it and adopted it," wrote Witchmeet host Carl Weschcke. "We did agree that Maleness and Femaleness was not limited to or fully defined by physical gender, and that so long as there was balance of these spiritual or psychological sexual energies, the God and Goddess were served. The Council of American Witches was great, and I always considered my role in drafting the Principles of Wiccan Belief the most important thing I ever did." *(Ibid n#225)* The Principles were ground-breaking in that, for the first time, diversity of race and sexual orientation were explicitly embraced within the larger context of the Craft by a wide cross-section of traditions.

By agreeing to swallow his pride and take the high road, Herman Slater helped counter the efforts of people like the UK's John Score, who was actively working to turn back the clock on gay rights by pushing homosexual practitioners from the Craft. This acceptance of diversity marked a turning point in the maturation of the movement. During the first week of June that same year, the member groups of the California Pagan Ecumenical Council also voted unanimously in favor of abolishing discrimination within Neo-Paganism based upon sexual preference.[228] Change is often slow in human systems, and the Craft is certainly no different in this. However, from this point onwards, it became less and less acceptable to discriminate against race or sexual orientation within Witchcraft or the greater Neo-Pagan movement. It is interesting to note that although the issue of ritual child abuse and incest faded from the discussion at this point, it never completely disappeared. On May 22, 1988, at the height of the child ritual abuse scare which was then sweeping the country, the CAW sponsored an "Earth Religion Anti-Abuse Resolution" at the Ancient Ways festival in northern California. It was not unanimously endorsed.[229]

"We called ourselves 'The Council of American Witches,'" Weschcke recalled with fondness, "and it was a triumph with Gavin and Herman shaking hands and agreeing to stop calling each other names, and then Isaac [Bonewits] did a wedding service for Morning Glory and Tim [Zell]. Among other things, we did a distant healing for Lady Sheba with a resultant cure of her tumor." *(Ibid n#225) Gnostica News* wrote afterward that the event had been "Acclaimed by the attendees as one of the most fruitful and productive convocations of Witches and Neopagans ever held."[230] This was high praise indeed for an event that had started under a cloud. As it turns out, the Council of American Witches, founded in this climate of optimism, was not fated to survive and soon faded into history. However, it and its predecessors set the stage for the formation of the

Covenant of the Goddess at the Summer Solstice of 1975, and that successor organization remains viable to this day.[231] But as the attendees dispersed home in the afterglow of the 1974 Witchmeet, there was, at least for a brief period, a general sense of goodwill, hope and accomplishment within the greater community.

To paraphrase Dickens, Slater was better than his word. When he arrived back home in Brooklyn Heights, he began making amends for some of the angry rabble-rousing he had done in the name of the Craft. He solicited an article from Gavin Frost for publication in the next issue of *Earth Religion News*, and went so far as to run a free ad for The Church and School of Wicca in that section of the paper.[232] Impressed after meeting Isaac Bonewits in person, Herman declared him to be a younger version of Leo Martello (an act not guaranteed to win Martello's approval) and apologized for some of the things that *Earth Religion News* had printed about him. Bonewits was likewise offered space in the paper to answer his critics, which he accepted.[233]

In announcing to the community that "THE WAR OF THE WITCHES ... is over," Slater agreed that the Frost tradition was as valid as anyone else's "and though it is not where my head is at, there are many sincere followers of that Tradition, as well as The Leaders Gavin and Yvonne Frost. I like them!" *(Ibid n#224)* The *Earth Religion News* solicited input from a wide variety of traditions, promising them cost-free, ad-free, and autonomous space within the newspaper. Apart from The Church and School of Wicca, the Chicago Temple of the Pagan Way (now renamed "Uranus"), the CES, and Seax-Wica each had a place in the paper.

Earth Religion News wasn't the first publication to offer space to outside organizations; *Green Egg* had been printing a short newsletter by Tommy Kneitel, "Gardnerian Aspects," for over a year. Still, it was a generous attempt at ecumenical outreach within the community. Outreach efforts within the New York community were already being made by such people as Kay Smith, who published a long article in the February issue of *Earth Religion News* calling for the formation of a study and discussion group for all those of the Third Degree, regardless of tradition.[234] On returning from the April 1974 Witchmeet, Herman pushed this effort onto the front burner. He brought together representatives of the various warring factions within the Craft, meeting in the cramped confines of the back room of the Warlock Shop in Brooklyn Heights in an effort to achieve some kind of truce. *(Ibid n#118, 190)*

"Herman had a knack for insulting everyone and thereby stripping them of their defenses and their egos enough so that they could start laughing and begin the process of healing," wrote Simon of the truce meeting.[235] Nevertheless, the meeting was neither tidy nor organized, according to Khem Caigan. "People who were willing to talk showed up and others did not," he noted. "Nobody buried the hatchet who didn't have an interest in doing so, [and] nobody put an end to the Witch wars [which are] still going on today."²³⁶

"We held our WitchMeet to try to settle things between Herman and Gavin," Weschcke writes. "And, as far as I know, neither continued the vendetta after shaking hands and agreeing that the 'Principles of Wiccan Belief' summed up the 'theology' of Wicca." *(Ibid n#91)* This is true up to a point, but past hurts were not entirely forgotten or forgiven. Gwilym Dafydd recalls that "Herman kept the Frosts' original flame-letter and his reply pinned to the wall until it rotted, and refused to take it down. He was always his own worst enemy."²³⁷

Lest one think poorly of Herman for nursing old grudges, one should consider that Gavin Frost also continued to express resentment about the events of April 1974. In an interview with PaganNews.com, Frost characterized Slater's actions as "the ravings of a single egotistical wannabe leader" and accused Carl Weschcke of putting them on trial.²³⁸ The Frosts continue to bring up the circumstances surrounding the 1974 Witchmeet in their interviews and workshops and on the Church and School of Wicca website. The latter lists a "Myth-History of Modern Wicca" which accuses Carl and Sandra Weschcke, Herman Slater, and Lady Sheba of trying them in a court.²³⁹

This refusal to let go presents what might be considered a textbook case of the Wiccan "Law of Return" in action. By obstinately keeping the details of the Witchmeet before the public, it could be argued that the Frosts inadvertently encouraged the same accusations of child abuse and perversion to resurface in 2007. As in 1974, the 2007 accusations also resulted in threats to take action against the Frosts and their Church at a Pagan gathering.²⁴⁰ Although this, too, ended in nothing more than mere sound and fury, Gavin and Yvonne's names were once more dragged through the mud. But, to paraphrase Quentin Crisp, after the first thirty years the dirt doesn't get any worse.²⁴¹

Chapter 17: Breaking with Tradition

The New York Coven and "The Wica"

After leaving Renate Springer's coven at Yule of 1973, Eddie's first task was to gather together whatever loyal students he could muster in order to form a new coven. He asked Jane Cicciotto (Craft name *Coreatha*), who was a First Degree initiate in the old Gardnerian Outer Court coven, if she would be his high priestess. Jane, Eddie and Herman both believed, was a trusted and known quantity. She worked as the Warlock Shop's bookkeeper, while her husband, Burt, made custom jewelry for the shop. Cicciotto gladly accepted the position and was elevated to Second and Third Degree by Eddie Buczynski and Kay Smith. She became high priestess to a reconstituted Brooklyn Heights Coven, which began meeting in the Cicciottos' Brooklyn apartment. Eddie became her high priest and assumed a dominant role in the coven from the very beginning.[1]

Buczynski and Smith both continued to claim their Gardnerian lineage, even though it had essentially been erased by Patricia Siero's declaration that her own initiation was invalid and her subsequent re-initiation by the Kneitels.[2] Eddie and Kay both continued to initiate and advance candidates in their covens, albeit without the bona fides of a traceable Gardnerian lineage. Ria and David Farnham, whose initiation had been delayed by the disastrous Yule confrontation, were brought in at a delayed Yule Sabbat of the newly-formed Brooklyn Heights Coven held later in December 1973. They were elevated to the Second and Third Degree at an Imbolc Sabbat on February 2, 1974. Ria took the Craft name *Rhea*, and David chose *Ammon*.[3,4] Kay Smith elevated two high priestesses to the Third Degree in her Riverside coven by the Spring Equinox of 1974.[5,6] The Brooklyn Heights and Riverside covens continued to operate normally, despite the de facto expulsion of Buczynski and Slater from the Gardnerian tradition and in spite of the opinions of any elders of the Long Island Line.

Given his experiences within the Celtic Traditionalist and Gardnerian paths, Eddie had concluded that a coven — or, worse, an entire tradition — having a single leader in the form of an infallible dictator, even a benevolent one, was a prescription for abuse. In his mind, this arrangement was just as dysfunctional as that of the Catholic Church, which he had left a decade earlier. Buczynski wanted to operate as a high priest within a Witchcraft coven where his opinion was not only valued but was also not subject to being overruled at the whim of his high priestess. In short, what he was looking for was neither a matriarchy nor a patriarchy, but rather a partnership. However, he would not find this equality within Gardnerian Wica, whose Laws say that the high priest must resign all his power to the high priestess, the representative of the Goddess. In his opinion, if the foundation of the tradition was contributing to its weakness, then the solution was to shore up what worked and rip out and replace what didn't.

Shortly after his split with Renate, Eddie began thinking about the problems he saw in Gardnerian Wica. Taking as his start the Gardnerian Book of Shadows that he had received from Patricia Siero, Eddie began to weed out anything that he felt was no longer valid in the modern day, underlining Laws to be retained while leaving in place those that were deemed outmoded as a historical reminder.[7] As Eddie noted in the new Book of Shadows, "Since the Wicca now have religious freedom once again, many of the old laws are archaic and unimportant. Those that are underlined, either in part or in whole, are those that are still used today, either in part or in whole. The others are left as a remembrance of those times when we were not free to worship our Gods in peace."[8] One might reason that as a gay man, Buczynski would take this opportunity to do away with the Law constraining same-sex practice within the Craft. However, he did not do so when crafting the Welsh tradition, and he did not do so in the new tradition. The rewritten Book of Shadows retained the requirement that "A man may only be taught be a woman, and a woman by a man, and that man and man or woman and woman should never attempt the practices together." However, the obligatory "curses of the Mighty Ones" upon those who disobeyed this injunction was relegated to the dust-bin of history.[9,10]

An entire page of "New Laws" was added to the book in order "to meet with the current way of life and the laws of the land." *(Ibid n#9)* These Laws were extremely forward-thinking (Craft traditionalists might say radical, even heretical) in their scope. Several dealt specifically with the abuse of power that was alleged to have occurred in some Gardnerian covens. To begin with, the power structure within the coven was shifted so that the high priest was co-equal with the high priestess in running the ritual and administering the coven. This co-equality extended to the Sabbats, which were nevertheless divided unevenly between the two. The high priestess was to lead all rituals from Imbolc (February 1) through Samhain (October 31). The high priest was given the rituals from Samhain through Imbolc — in other words, the darkest months of the year. Bolder yet was the provision enabling each coven to elect the high priestess and/or high priest from the pool of eligible Third Degree members at a meeting immediately prior to the Autumnal Equinox Sabbat. The incumbent, upon being voted out, was required either to resign the office and return to the pool of coven elders, or to hive off and form a new coven after installing the newly-elected high priest or high priestess within the old coven. Finally, the new Laws set a limit of seven years on the time any High Priestess or High Priest could remain in their office as head of a coven.

In instituting these changes, Eddie's Book of Shadows reflects many of the same concepts put forth by Raymond Buckland, who was then in the process of creating his Seax-Wica tradition.[11, 12] This similarity is not surprising, as Buczynski, Slater and Buckland spoke to and corresponded with one another, and editorialized in the pages of Earth Religion News about the power trips within Gardnerian Wica. Eddie's Book of Shadows, which contained these concepts, was essentially complete by March 1974, leading some to believe that Buczynski may have had a hand in writing Buckland's book, *The Tree*, which wasn't published until June of that year. Raymond denies that the two men collaborated on the manuscript of *The Tree*, and he is supported in this circumstantially by the fact that he had already published several of these concepts in the Earth Religion News in December 1973, when he introduced Seax-Wica to the world.[13] However, it is clear that the two men were in close contact, with Eddie and Herman traveling to New Hampshire during this period to spend time with Raymond and his new wife.[14] There is little doubt that the men had shared their thoughts on rectifying the problem of power-hungry leaders in the Craft, or rather, in those segments of it in which they might wield some influence. Buckland's ongoing friendship with Buczynski and Slater also appears to have had some effect on his public statements concerning homosexuals in the Craft.

Buckland went out of his way to support the right of gays and lesbians to practice Gardnerian Witchcraft, a concept still considered radical at the time, especially in light of the pushback coming from Great Britain in the form of John Score and his supporters. With regard to his own Seax-Wica, Buckland went on to write, "Although it seems unlikely that a homosexual would be attracted to a religion which is definitely male-female based, it does sometimes happen. If this should be the case then Saxon Witchcraft seem[s] more able to 'absorb' [them] than many of the other traditions. (In fact it is not unknown for homosexuals, or lesbians, to work together exclusively as a Seax-Wica coven; or to blend quite happily with others.)"[15] Thus did Raymond Buckland with his Seax-Wica, and Eddie Buczynski with what he came to call The Wica, take the first step toward eliminating doctrinaire excuses for discrimination of homosexuals within modern Witchcraft.

Buczynski knew that by changing the Gardnerian Book of Shadows he could no longer claim to be running an authentic coven of Gardnerian Wica. Therefore, he abandoned any pretense and called his new tradition a neo-Gardnerian path known simply as "The Wica." He publicized this new tradition in the pages of the Earth Religion News, explaining his rationale for the changes he made to the Book of Shadows:[16, 17]

The New York Coven of Witches
What we're all about..........

Ever since the Witchcraft Laws were repealed in Britain in 1951, Witch Covens have been literally "popping up" all over the world. All of these covens have one thing in common: they have proceeded to categorize themselves by naming themselves of this tradition or that (i.e. Gardnerian Wicca, Alexandrian Wicca, Traditionalist Wicca, Hereditary Wicca, etc.) and it is because of these 'Traditions' that the covens have been bickering amongst themselves ever since their emergence. "My tradition is older than yours...", "Our rituals are more authentic than yours...", "My tradition gives us 'Lineage papers'", "Our Magick works more often than yours...", etc., etc., <u>AD NAUSEUM</u>!

Nine years ago, in 1965, Gwydion, the current High Priest of the New York Coven of Witches, was initiated by a Welsh woman into the Craft. Since then, he has been initiated to the highest degrees of four different 'Traditions', finding the bickering everywhere that he went. After studying several other traditions of the Wicca as well as working as High Priest in his four initiated 'Traditions', he discovered the apparent cause of the dissension within the structure of the Craft today. As a Revival of a Survival, the Craft ... or more correctly, the people within it ... has been too concerned with constructing <u>what might have been</u>, never thinking of re-evaluating What is Now and so, by working under Laws both written and oral which have no possible use or meaning to life in our times, the Craft very rarely "works" and most covens wind up disbanded because of general Disharmony and the pressures of discontent and power trips in the hierarchy.

And so, knowing the causes, we have <u>eliminated</u> them, without disturbing the hereditary structure of the Old Pagan ways ... and revised those things that should have been revised years ago.

We call ourselves "The Wica" because that's exactly what we are ... No Tradition labels. We are merely plain Witches. Our Book of Shadows is the result of nine years of hard work and extensive study. It contains, we believe, the best of everything put to the best possible uses. The Power of our covens is controlled by the Coven itself ... not one or two people within it, but All people involved ... therefore, it is impossible for any one person to go off on a Power-Trip. We are a Democracy, working within a democratic society.

And THAT'S what We're all about!

This message carried echoes of the much earlier accusatory letter that Lillian Giese wrote to MacGregor Mathers' widow, Moina Mathers, when the latter expelled her and her lover, Paul Foster Case, from the Golden Dawn. In it Giese declared, "I am convinced that no Order can claim the private ownership of ways to perform magic. Apparent disappointments have turned out to be blessings in disguise and now our freedom from an old alliance is another step towards realizing what we consider our life's work."[18]

The pugnacious and accusatory tone of Buczynski's coming-out statement, regardless of the validity of any of its underlying bases, virtually ensured that the efforts of The New York Coven of Witches would not be well-received within the part of the community that hewed to the Gardnerian Book of Shadows. Ironically, it was the Long Island coven's dismissal of Eddie's and Herman's validity within Gardnerian Wica, and the derision with which any non-Gardnerian practitioner of Witchcraft was met by many of this downline, which ultimately prompted Buczynski's reworking of the Gardnerian materials.[19] Raymond Buckland publicly admitted this problem of tradition snobbery within Gardnerian Wica as something in which he himself had indulged in the past. *(Ibid n#13)*

Others took exception to the argument that somehow Gardnerian Wica, as practiced in the United States, had reduced the role of the high priest to that of a "glorified altar boy" or "merely being present for purposes of gratifying the psychological and sexual needs of the [high priestess]."[20] Ferran Cassals, in the August 1974 issue of Earth Religion News, maintained that those who minimized the role of the High Priest simply didn't understand the importance of duality in Wica. He was correct in arguing that a successful Gardnerian ritual requires both high priestess and high priest working in harmony; however, he also acknowledged that it is the high priestess who calls the shots and bears the responsibility for the outcome. By assuring his readers that he was not calling for a redefinition of the role of the high priest, Cassals essentially agreed with keeping the high priest in a subordinate role and glossed over the issues he had raised about how "pettiness and ego trips and awful lack of communication" infected covens where only one person was in charge. Cassals was writing as the Magus of Patricia Siero's Passaic Coven of Gardnerian Wica, so it is likely his letter was meant to obliquely counter Eddie's public dissatisfaction with the Gardnerian book and rituals. It is unclear how Cassals' statements reflected the inner workings of Patricia Siero's Passaic coven, but it should be noted that in the same issue of Earth Religion News, several of her people announced that they had resigned from her coven.

Given his past experiences, Eddie considered the potential for others to harass the practitioners of his version of Wica to be a serious matter and a looming threat. To counter this concern, the new Laws prohibited initiates of the path from revealing the fact that they were members of The New York Coven of Witches to those outside their own coven, except with the permission of their high priestess or high priest. The Laws went one step further, stating that members weren't even permitted to associate with Witches outside their own coven without being granted leave to do so. These prohibitions, particularly the last one, strayed dangerously close to cult-like behavior, where members of the group might be denied contact with others who might cause them to question the group's philosophy and actions It is likely that Eddie's experiences to date simply led him to try to protect initiates of The Wica from attacks. But he also appears to have recognized the potential for abuse within this path as well, for he followed up by admonishing initiates to avoid those who set themselves up as cult leaders, who claimed to represent the only "true" Wica, or who insisted upon adherence to Laws that were not set down in the Book of Shadows. (Ibid n#8)

Buczynski went one step further, establishing a "black list" in the front of his Book of Shadows that prohibited specific individuals from being initiated into The Wica or being permitted to see or possess a copy of the Book of Shadows.[21] This prohibition was not unusual; many covens at the time had such a list of individuals who were determined, for whatever reason, to be inappropriate candidates for initiation. Monique Wilson, for example, was alleged to have issued such a list after Gerald Gardner's death.[22] Some covens generated these lists from their own screening efforts. Some black lists were also well networked and enforced via peer pressure amongst covens in a lineage.[23] The black list at the front of The Wica Book of Shadows reads like a Who's Who of persons whom Buczynski believed had betrayed him at one point or another since his early involvement in the Craft. Not surprisingly, the Kneitels found their way onto the list, along with others in the Long Island Line.

In a few cases, persons were included on the list because of some action that was deemed harmful to the Craft in general. For example, John Score, editor of the British Witchcraft newsletter The Wiccan, is listed in Eddie's Wica black list because of his ongoing attacks against gay Witches.[24] However, the list also includes gay Witch and long-time friend, Leo Martello, likely for doing something to anger Eddie at the time. The last names on the list appear to have been added by mid to late 1974, after which the list became static. Although many of the persons on the black list have since passed away, it is still faithfully included, unaltered, in all copies of the Book of Shadows that are passed down to new initiates. It is curious and somewhat ironic that Buczynski would make use of such a tool in his Book of Shadows. Rightly or wrongly, black lists had been used to keep known or suspected homosexuals and bisexuals out of the Craft. While "enemies lists" could certainly be seen as fashionable during those last, paranoid days of Richard Nixon's Presidency, some who knew Eddie referred to the very existence of a black list as an embarrassment.[25] When asked to comment on the list, Ria Rivera notes that one shouldn't place too much emphasis on its contents, as Eddie eventually made his peace with some of those who were named therein.[26]

Although some of the new Laws of The New York Coven operated seem intended to shield the group members from the occult community, it also appeared that the coven went out of its way to court public attention. One case involved the coven's response to the March 1974 letter in *Green Egg* from "Spock," which had stirred the ire of the denizens of the Warlock Shop.[27] Spock's letter, a homophobic attack against Buczynski and Slater, was primarily used to question the legitimacy of Buczynski's Welsh tradition and to mock Leo Martello. Slater answered it in the next issue of the magazine, with Buczynski and Cicciotto as signatories to the response. Cicciotto signed as "Lady Koretha [sic], HPs, New York Coven."[28] Other than to bolster support for Eddie, there seems little reason for Jane to have signed Slater's reply, nor to have brought The New York Coven into the debate; which was, after all, about the Traditionalist Gwyddoniaid and not The Wica. Yet this may also have been an attempt to keep The New York Coven's name in the public eye. Jane Cicciotto also tried her hand at writing for the Earth Religion News at this time, penning two articles.[29, 30] Eddie and Jane settled down and ran the coven much as before, albeit now without the fig leaf of Gardnerian lineage.

Perhaps because they were now for all intents and purposes in the same Gardnerian lifeboat together, the friendship shown between the proprietors of the Warlock Shop and Raymond Buckland continued to grow throughout 1974. Slater gave Buckland space in Earth Religion News to print what would eventually become his Seax-Wica newsletter, Seax-Wica Voys, because Raymond was short on cash and could not fund its launch by himself.[31, 32] That isn't to say that everything was perfect between Buckland and Slater, judging by an incident involving a sword designed by Gerald Gardner. As Raymond tells it, "Herman ... (in his inimitable style) ... talked me into letting him have an original Gardnerian sword hilt and cross-guard, made by Gerald. I gave it to him on the understanding that it was for the use of his own coven, and not to be duplicated. Needless to say in less than a month Herman was selling them at the store and from his catalog! Ah, well — that was Herman."[33, 34] Still, such minor disputes raised barely a whisper on the windy stage of Pagan politics and squabbling. But when the matter touched on financial peculation, things were very different.

Sale of the Titties

While Herman and Eddie were away at the Witchmeet in Minneapolis in April 1974, they left Jane's husband, Burt, in charge of the shop. Upon their return, Slater was taken ill for a week. After recovering from his illness, Herman was horrified to discover that Burt was missing, along with over $3000 of the Warlock Shop's funds and some merchandise. According to Slater and other contemporaries, Burt was a heroin addict who had suffered a relapse and absconded with the money and goods. Skipping the country for merry old England, he was said to be staying with Maxine Sanders, who was allegedly going to sponsor his detoxification treatment through the British Heroin Program.[35] That Cicciotto would seek out Maxine for help is not implausible, given that she and her former husband, Alex Sanders, had claimed to be able to cure drug addiction using Witchcraft.[36] By 1970, their basement flat in London had become an unofficial outpatient clinic for drug addicts, and Maxine kept the apartment even after she and Alex split up in 1973.[37] Adding insult to injury, Slater alleged that Burt was showing up stoned at occult stores in Great Britain and claiming to represent the Warlock Shop. *(Ibid n#35)*

The loss of so much money was catastrophic. Not only did it represent the bulk of the Warlock Shop's operating capital, but a number of checks had already been written to suppliers based on these funds, and Herman and Eddie were forced to scramble to make good on them. Phone service to the store was cut off, and the May issue of *Earth Religion News* was skipped, with publication not resuming until June. Frustrated and demoralized by the violation of their trust, Herman stated their intent to put the brick-and-mortar store up for sale.[38] As Burt's wife and, more importantly, as the Warlock Shop's bookkeeper, Jane Cicciotto was tainted by association. In the wake of the scandal, she left her position at the shop in May and stepped down as high priestess of The New York Coven.

After Jane's departure, it was decided that Ria Farnham would take over as the new high priestess of The New York Coven, with David Farnham as her high priest. With that, the remaining members picked up and moved from Brooklyn Heights to the Bronx and met in Ria's and David's apartment, since they had no other place of sufficient size in which to meet. Ria and David liked this arrangement, as they had been commuting to and from the Bronx to work at the Warlock Shop and attend coven meetings and sabbats. Unfortunately, this situation didn't last for long because the rest of the coven membership tired of the long commute. Eddie and Herman were the first to step down, and they became inactive elders in the coven by the end of May. *(Ibid n#7)* While Eddie occasionally popped back in, Herman had essentially washed his hands of Gardnerian Wica and its offshoots, returning to his beloved Welsh tradition. Ria and David continued to practice as a couple well into 1975, when fate would intervene again in the form of a Witch lately from Salem, Massachusetts.

The New York Coven had already dissolved by the time the June 1974 edition of the *Earth Religion News* hit the stands bearing a photo of the coven in all its full-frontal skyclad glory on its cover.[39] Although some community wags have suggested that blue might have been a more appropriate cover color, the so-called "green" issue of *Earth Religion News* was a hotly sought collectible that fairly flew off the shelves as soon as the ink set. The photograph, showing coven members Eddie, Jane, Artie, Tony, Dagda, Katrynn, Ria, and David, was taken at a specially arranged gathering of The New York Coven at Jane Cicciotto's Brooklyn apartment earlier that spring. *(Ibid n#7)* It was part of a photo series taken by Jean-Pierre Laffont for an article on Witchcraft titled "Le Grande Retour a la Nature," which was to appear in the French magazine *Elle*. The main topic of the article was the Warlock Shop and the modern movement toward nature-based religions.

Laffont had formed the Sygma Photo News Agency in New York with his wife Elaine in late 1973. The combined photo spread and article was one of the agency's first commercial efforts. Appearing in the original French along with several photos of the coven raising power in Circle, the full text of the article appeared in the August issue of *Earth Religion News*. The shop was portrayed much more sympathetically and enthusiastically by Elle than another article that same year in the National Star:[40]

> *I met Herman Slater and Ed Buczynski in their strange shop in Brooklyn, 300 Henry Street. Its name "The Warlock [Shop]." Books on the different religions and on sorcery, voodoo, ghosts, objects for every sort of adoration; magic herbs of every hue; and so on. "The Warlock" shop is above all an atmosphere, an odor, and a multitiude of experiences one finds nowhere else. ... The religion of Wicca is the religion of sorcerers. A Witch or Warlock. The very word if mysterious and terrifying, be it the wicked Witch in Snow White or the Witch Doctor in Africa. "I think that this misconception should change," says Ed. "Because I am a Warlock!" Ed doesn't look like a sorcerer. I shouldn't say it, but he reminds me of a Greek God.*

While critics dismissed this article as yet another bit of puffery arranged by Herman Slater to promote the Warlock Shop, it was the accompanying photographs that stirred some controversy, and not a little admiration, from others in the community. In the pages of *Green Egg*, Gwen Thompson primly observed that "Old Religionists who allow themselves to be photographed by the news media in the 'altogether' (skyclad), and often in positions that suggest obscene practices, are not doing the Old Religion any service whatsoever, but rather giving it a very black eye." Thompson, whose own tradition practiced robed, went on to complain, "We live in a clothed society which is not all that ready to accept what some Witches or Pagans do."[41]

Of course, skyclad pictures of Witches had been published in the mainstream media for some time, both in the United States and in Great Britain. Examples of Gardnerian Witches appearing skyclad in the press can be seen as early as 1965 in the British press and 1964 in the American press.[42,43] And Alex Sanders seemed to have made a career of touting nude pictures of staged Alexandrian rituals.[44] Thompson's protest seemed both quaint and out of step with the times, coming as it did at the height of the sexual revolution, and printed as it was within the pages of a sex-positive Pagan periodical that occasionally featured buxom female fantasy nudes.[45]

"Obscenity," or just plain old lust, has always been good for sales. Before the financial catastrophe of April, Slater had tried his hand at publishing books under the Earth Religions Supplies, Inc. imprint when he had some excess funds that were not otherwise committed to other projects, such as paying taxes. One result of Herman's interest in breaking into the publishing business was the first United States edition of Aleister Crowley's *White Stains*.[46] It was a rare book in the United States. Most copies of the original private printing of White Stains were reportedly seized and burned by British Customs officers in 1924 over charges of obscenity, and a modern reprint by Gerald Duckworth & Company had only been published in Great Britain the previous year. It is difficult to argue with the conclusions of the British Customs service, given the mores of those days and the fact that the book's poems deal with a range of outré sexual topics, including masturbation, oral sex, paedophilia, and diseased rent boys. It is just as well that Crowley published this book pseudonymously; if the authorities had caught up with him, the 22-year-old writer of the love poem "Necrophilia" might have joined his books on the pyre or spent the rest of his days confined to an asylum, and the world would now be bereft of all that was to come.

This combination of rarity and perversity made *White Stains* an interesting choice for the Warlock Shop's first hardcover imprint, and was perhaps intended to set the store apart as a fearless promoter of the free exchange of information. Of course, it is very likely that this free exchange hinged on Slater's ability to copy the text of the Gerald Duckworth & Company edition, for it is doubtful that he had access to an extremely rare copy of the first edition from which to work.

Slater wasn't the only publisher taking advantage of the public's new-found interest in the Great Beast. Curiosity in the occult and in all things Crowley had continued its steady rise since the late 1960s and showed no sign of abating. Samuel Weiser was marketing reprints of Crowley works, and 93 Publishing ran an advertisement in the Earth Religion News for several Crowley titles. *White Stains* helped to plug the Warlock Shop into that marketplace and made it a player, albeit a minor one, in the boutique world of occult publishing. This marked the apex of the open, Wild West period of publishing Crowleyana. Crowley had passed away in 1947, and by the mid-1970s the copyrights to much of his work were drifting in a grey fog of uncertainty. Within a decade of *White Stains*' publication, the burgeoning market potential of the Crowley brand would see an end to that free-for-all.

Other titles that came out of Earth Religions Supplies at this time included the hardbound edition of the Pagan Way materials and the first edition of Eddie Buczynski's *Witchcraft Fact Book*.[47,48] Eddie's book, first issued as a pamphlet priced at two dollars, was listed as Number 2 in the "Museum Handbook Series" by Earth Religions Supplies, Inc. in conjunction with the Buckland Museum of Witchcraft and Magick. It provided a basic description of modern Witchcraft and outer court information that was accessible to non-Witches who were trying to understand this growing phenomenon. The book remained in print more or less continuously for the next fifteen years, even though its author's aspirations for legitimacy in the Gardnerian tradition had suffered a setback and his neo-Gardnerian coven had stagnated. Eddie had not given up his search for legitimacy within British Traditional Witchcraft; however, this desire was moved to the back burner by the middle of 1974 in light of another, more immediate opportunity.

Chapter 18: Black and White and Rede All Over

Revealing the Rede of the Wiccae

In March 1974, an anonymous poem appeared in the Earth Religion News. As printed in the newspaper, the poem reads:[1]

The Wiccan Rede

Bide the Wiccan Rede laws ye most [sic],
In perfect love and perfect trust
Live and let live, fairly take and fairly give
Cast the circle thrice about to keep all evil spirits out
To bind the spell every time, let the spell be spoken in rhyme
Soft of eye and light of touch, speak little and listen much
Deosil go by waxing moon, chanting out the Wiccan rune
When the Lady's moon is new, kiss the hand to her times two
When the moon rides at her peak, then your heart's desire seek
Heed the north wind's mighty gale. Lock the door and drop the sail
When the wind comes from the South,
Love will kiss thee on the mouth
When the moor wind blows from the West,
Departed spirits have no rest
When the wind blows from the East, expect the new and set the feast
Nine woods in the cauldron go, burn them quick and burn them slow
Elder be Ye Lady's tree, burn it not or cursed you'll be
When the wheel begins to turn, let the Beltane fires burn
When the wheel has turned to Yule,
Light the log and the Horned One rules
Heed ye flower, bush and tree, by the Lady Blessed Be
Where the rippling waters go, cast a stone and truth you'll know
When ye have need, hearken not to others' greed
With no fool a season spend, or be counted as his friend
Merry meet and merry part, bright the cheeks and warm the heart
Mind the threefold Law ye should,
Three times bad and three times good
When misfortune is enow, wear the blue star on thy brow
True in love ever be, unless thy lover's false to thee
Eight words the Wiccan Rede fulfill — an ye harm none, do what ye will.

The Wiccan Rede is a poetic hodgepodge of advice, observations and folklore, the purpose of which appears to be to communicate a few of the basic guiding principles of the Craft to its practitioners. While many covens have since adopted the gist of the Wiccan Rede in a number of different forms, this article in the Earth Religion News marked the first time that any long version of the rede had been published. As the poem appeared without attribution, there was no way for an uninformed reader to discern its origin. Readers who were members of the N.E.C.T.W., however, knew at first glance that it derived from the *Celtic Traditionalist Book of Shadows* — the same book that Eddie had hand-copied two years earlier when he was Gwen Thompson's student. The rede's publication was guaranteed to cause a flare-up in the dormant conflict between Gwen Thompson and Eddie Buczynski.

The Wiccan Rede appeared in *Earth Religion News* shortly after the first anniversary of the "Big Breakup" of the Traditionalist Gwyddoniaid, the event in late February 1973 where Branwen and Bryce's Welsh Outer Court coven went over to the Long Island Line of Gardnerian Wica. This raises the question of whether the timing of the article was mere coincidence or if Eddie and/or Herman published the Wiccan Rede as a way of embarrassing Gwen Thompson and the N.E.C.T.W. for what they believed to be their interference in the operation of the Traditionalist Gwyddoniaid. It is certainly possible that the duo thought Thompson was at least partly to blame for the split that occurred in Eddie's Welsh Tradition. However, Slater may simply have viewed the poem as pertinent material to fill space in the newspaper.

While it isn't at all clear that either Buczynski or Slater purposefully set out to avenge themselves on Thompson by their action, they must surely have known or suspected that the publication of the rede would anger N.E.C.T.W. initiates. However, an entire year passed between the appearance of the rede in *Earth Religion News* and Gwen Thompson's public response. As a March 1975 article in *Green Egg* made clear, Lady Gwen was rather put out by the poem's publication the previous year.[2] "Many different traditions have different redes," she wrote. "Our own particular Rede, however, has appeared in the past year in a perverted form. That is to say, the wording has been changed. This is sad for those who are seeking the Light of the Old Religion, because it confuses them." Gwen Thompson appeared to go against the secrecy of her tradition not only by confirming the source of the rede that appeared in *Earth Religion News*, but also by taking it upon herself to publish the rede of her Celtic Traditionalist path in its entirety.[3] The act was curious one for someone concerned about protecting the oathbound material of her tradition, of which her "Rede of the Wiccae" was a part.

The *Green Egg* version of the rede is virtually identical with "Ye Rede of Ye Wiccae" as it appears in Buczynski's *Welsh Book of Shadows* and in his copy of the *Celtic Traditionalist Book of Shadows*, from which the Welsh version was derived.[5,6] The so-called "perversion" of Thompson's "Rede of the Wiccae," as represented by its published form in the Earth

Religion News, is mostly the result of minor editorial changes and transcription errors, typically involving the replacement of some of the rede's debatably antique language with modern wording. One marked exception to this is the omission in the *Earth Religion News* of the couplet that states when it is appropriate to circle "widdershins," or counter-clockwise. Given the poor quality of copy editing present in the newspaper, a point agreed upon by virtually everyone from that era, this omission was most likely a typesetting mistake. This conclusion is bolstered by the fact that the wording in question does appear both in Eddie's copy of *The Cauldron* and in his *Welsh Book of Shadows*.

There has been considerable debate over the origins of the rede. Perhaps it is helpful to first clarify that two works are referred to interchangeably as "the rede." The first is what may be termed the "short" rede, comprising the couplet:

> *Eight words the Wiccan Rede fulfill – an it harm none, do what ye will.*

This admonishment is what people normally think of when they speak of the Wiccan Rede. The "eight words" couplet is subsumed in a larger poem that is also referred to as the Wiccan Rede, and which is sometimes called the "long" rede so as to distinguish it from the couplet. Gwen Thompson admitted that other redes existed at the time of her *Green Egg* article, although she provided no evidence of this. Thompson also claimed that her tradition's version of the rede originated with her maternal grandmother, Adriana Porter (d. 1946). Historian Robert Mathiesen, who reviewed the language used in Thompson's "long" rede for the book *The Rede of the Wiccae: Adriana Porter, Gwen Thompson and the Birth of a Tradition of Witchcraft*, concluded that he could not rule out the possibility that it originated in the late nineteenth or early twentieth century during Porter's lifetime.[7] However, this conclusion is not the same as confirming that the N.E.C.T.W. rede was actually written during that period, and several points argue against the Rede of the Wiccae as having originated, at least in its entirety, with Adriana Porter.

To begin with, the opening couplet of the Rede of the Wiccae refers to "Wiccan laws." The Laws were originally written to define a common framework of rights and responsibilities, and to set some limits on practitioners of Gardnerian Wica. They came about during a period of conflict when others in the Craft challenged Gardner's publicity-seeking. Some, such as Doreen Valiente, argued that their true goal was to dilute the authority of the high priestess.[8,9] The Laws were not introduced into Gardnerian Wica until 1957, eleven years after Porter's death, and did not become widespread outside of Gardnerian or Alexandrian Wica until the publication of June Johns' *King of the Witches* (1969) and Lady Sheba's *The Book of Shadows* (1971).[10] In fact, the so-called hereditary traditions, presumably including Thompson's Celtic Traditionalist Witchcraft, tend to disparage the use of contemporary Gardnerian-derived materials like the Wiccan Laws except when the materials underlying those traditions have become so adulterated by materials from other groups or traditions that they have become indistinguishable.

That the Celtic Traditionalist Witchcraft did not incorporate such Laws is confirmed by an examination of Buczynski's copy of *The Cauldron*, which contains most or all of Thompson's First Degree material circa 1972. The Laws are among the first things taught to Wiccan initiates in those traditions that utilize them, and their absence from Buczynski's copy of *The Cauldron* suggests that Thompson's tradition did not at that time possess the Wiccan Laws to which this couplet refers. This implies that the wording in question is an artifact carried over from the author's borrowing of unrelated material. Additionally, the phrase "in Perfect Love and Perfect Trust" is taken directly from the Gardnerian First Degree Initiation ritual. The phrase first appeared in print three years after Porter's death in Gerald Gardner's novel *High Magic's Aid* (1949).[11,12] All of this together argues against the first couplet of the Rede of the Wiccae as originating with Adriana Porter.

The "Threefold Law" referenced in couplet 23 also appears to have originated outside of the Celtic Traditionalist path. A hint of this ethical admonishment appeared in Gardner's *High Magic's Aid* (1949), and Raymond Buckland, who recalls being taught the concept of the Threefold Law by Monique Wilson in the early 1960s, gave what may be the first published reference to the use of this principle in Wica via an October 1968 interview "I Live with a Witch" in *Beyond* magazine.[13,14]

Finally, the "short" rede comprising the final couplet of Thompson's Rede of the Wiccae is widely acknowledged to have originated with an address made by Doreen Valiente at a dinner organized by the British Witchcraft newsletter Pentagram on October 3, 1964. The couplet "Eight words the Wiccan Rede fulfil, An' it harm none, do what ye will," was reported in the November 1964 edition of the *Pentagram* and was subsequently reprinted in Joseph Wilson's newsletter *The Waxing Moon*.[15] Wilson noted that Gwen Thompson to have been one of his early correspondents and a subscriber to his publication, and she may have first encountered the wording there.[16] Justine Glass also quoted a variant of the "eight words" couplet without attribution in her widely circulated book *Witchcraft: The Sixth Sense* (1965).[17] Thompson's "Rede of the Wiccae (Being knowne as the counsel of the Wise Ones)" tracks very closely to Glass' "The Wiccan Rede (i.e. Counsel or advice of the Wise Ones)."[18] It seems very unlikely, therefore, that the final couplet of the Rede of the Wiccae, or even the title of the "long" rede itself, was part of the materials allegedly left behind by Adriana Porter.

A detailed analysis of Gwen Thompson's materials is certainly not the focus of this biography, and it may well be that the remainder of the rede she published did originate within her Witchcraft tradition. The presence of such borrowings in the Rede of the Wiccae does not detract from the beauty of the poem, though in hindsight it should blunt the criticisms of Buczynski by N.E.C.T.W. initiates for his own uncredited borrowings and reworkings of Thompson's materials in crafting the Traditionalist Gwyddoniaid. The process illustrates a point made by occult artist and esotericist Khem Caigan when questioned about the implications of Buczynski's unauthorized adaptation of material from *The Cauldron*: "Everyone borrows from everyone else."[19]

Regardless of the rede's source, it can be argued that its publication by either Gwen Thompson or the owners of the Warlock Shop was a violation of one or more oaths that were designed, in part, to protect the material from public disclosure. It is not certain whether Buczynski had a hand in the publication of the Wiccan Rede in the *Earth Religion News*. By 1974, it was quite clear to some people that Slater called all the shots in producing the paper, even though Buczynski was its titular editor. But even if Herman could be proved to have placed the rede in the newspaper without Eddie's knowledge, Eddie was still ultimately responsible for its revelation because he had given Slater access to Gwen's material via the *Welsh Book of Shadows*. However, Herman has his own responsibility for its publication, for he too made his own oath to the Gods to protect the materials when he joined the Traditionalist Gwyddoniaid, and he failed to do so. Likewise, Gwen Thompson was no innocent in this matter. Rather than leading by example and remaining silent in order to safeguard her tradition's secrets as she expected of her students, she revealed the Rede of the Wiccae to the public in a seeming bid to claim her share of the credit for the heretofore unattributed poem.

Thompson's mood did not improve when the editors of *Green Egg* inadvertently referred to her spiritual tradition in the March article's byline as "Welsh Tradition Wicca." This error led to an exchange of letters from the high priestess that were reprinted in the June and August issues of the magazine, where Gwen strongly asserted that her spiritual path was Traditionalist or Celtic Traditionalist, and not Welsh.[20] Writing in June 1975, Thompson explains, "A former first degree member of my Coven broke off and formed a Welsh coven of his own, which may be what you are thinking of. Due to the fact that this person was quite publicity-prone, I can understand where impressions could have been misconstrued."[21] Thompson's pointed criticism of Buczynski as a publicity-seeker might have raised questions for an investigative reporter, coming as it did on the heels of her public revelation of secret materials from her own tradition. However, the incongruity slipped by *Green Egg* co-editor Tim Zell who, expressing remorse at his error, agreed with Thompson's statement. "It was the thing of one of your initiates claiming to be Welsh Trad that got me confused," wrote Zell, "as I would have assumed that one's Trad is the one he was initiated into."[22] Buczynski would likely have agreed with this last, insofar as his Gardnerian bona fides were concerned. Nevertheless, it was a rather cheeky statement for the founder of one previously nonexistent spiritual tradition (the CAW) to make in reference to the founder of another (Traditionalist Gwyddoniaid).[23]

The Usual Suspects

A final controversy regarding Buczynski's and Slater's handling of the Celtic Traditionalist materials surfaced more than a decade later, when it was rumored that Herman Slater had given William Wheeler a copy of the *Traditionalist Gwyddoniaid Book of Shadows*. Wheeler (Craft name *Rhuddlwm Gawr*) is a founder of the Witchcraft tradition known as the Church of Y Tylwyth Teg ("the fair family," in Welsh) and has published a number of books since the 1980s on his variety of Welsh Witchcraft. Of the event in question, N.E.C.T.W. archivist Andrew Theitic writes, "It was said that Herman gave much of the [New York Welsh Tradition] materials to William Wheeler and it was published. Even though it was now second or third hand and had lost some pages and changed even more, the N.E.C.T.W. Council was enraged."[24] This accusation was similar to the baseless rumor that arose in the early 1970s, alleging that Eddie shared Gwen's materials with members of the Georgian Tradition.

William Wheeler and Herman Slater had known one another beginning in the mid-1970s from their activities in the occult community, and Herman had even lectured at one of the Gathering of the Tribes festivals hosted by the Church of Y Tylwyth Teg, although he showed up in a "Witch Queen" t-shirt in a calculated attempt to stir unrest among the gathering's more heterophilic attendees.[25] The two men also had some business dealings, with Slater arranging for the publication of Wheeler's *Pagan, Occult, New Age Directory* (1978).[26] However, Wheeler denies that he received any Welsh materials from Herman Slater. "Herman would have laughed his butt off if someone told him he had given me Eddie's Book of Shadows," Wheeler wrote. "I never saw a copy of any of Eddie's stuff at any time."[27]

Instead, he asserts that Gwen Thompson had authorized her last initiate, a man named Henry Carter (Craft name *Taliesin*), to give a copy of The Cauldron to Wheeler to compare to the Welsh materials he clamed to have received from his elders in Betys-y-Coed, Wales. "This was in 1987, four years after I wrote *The Way*," Wheeler stated. "When I went to Wales in 1991, I met a High Priestess who was of a related tradition to ours. She had a Book of Shadows which contained a great deal of the same material as Gwen's Book of Shadows. So all I can deduce from all of this was that Gwen's tradition (to the second degree) is related to ours. ... I haven't seen a New York Welsh Tradition book so I can't say for sure Eddie's material is the same."[28, 29]

However, Carter had never actually been initiated by Gwen Thompson, although he studied with her for three or four months before her death from cancer in New Hampshire on May 22, 1986.[30] According to N.E.C.T.W. archivist Andrew Theitic, Carter entered Gwen's apartment after she had passed away and took her copy of The Cauldron.[31] "Gwen's [Book of Shadows] passed through Henry's hands after she died," writes Theitic. "He told me that he didn't copy any of it, but felt it to be too much of a burden (with the curse Gwen put on in it and all). Rather, he looked for someone to give it to and he decided to give it to Bill Wheeler of Georgia."[32]

However, it isn't clear that Gwen Thompson ever fully trusted Wheeler, and Theitic believes that she would never have agreed to hand over a copy of *The Cauldron* to a non-initiate.[33] Given that Gwen forcefully denied being a priestess of a Welsh path, it also seems doubtful and somewhat ironic that she would have cooperated with Wheeler's effort to link her Book of Shadows to one said to have originated in Wales. Thompson's repudiation of ties to any Welsh tradition may have been motivated more by a desire to further distinguish her path from Eddie Buczynski's Traditionalist Gwyddoniaid than from any in-depth understanding of her material's origins. As one initiate of Thompson's path notes, although there is an identifiable stream of Welsh mythology in *The Cauldron*, it was by no means the overwhelming influence in the materials, which contain Scottish and Irish influences as well.[34] Thus, Celtic Traditionalist seems as good a title as any for the path.

Wherever the final truth of the matter lies is anyone's guess. However, it should be noted that within two years of Wheeler's obtaining a copy of Thompson's Book of Shadows, he published a similarly-named book, *The Cauldron: Celtic Mythology and Witchcraft* (Camelot Press, 1989).[35] Buczynski's *Welsh Book of Shadows*, by contrast, does not bear the "Cauldron" name. In a final parting shot, Slater wrote, in his introduction to *Pagan Rituals III* (1989), that "A very careful reading will reveal the Welsh Book mixed in with the material in *The Quest* and *The Way* (Camelot Press) written by William Wheeler." *(Ibid n#25)* Both of the books that Slater mentions were published in 1985.

Taking Wheeler at his word that Slater did not give him Eddie's *Welsh Book of Shadows*, and given that Wheeler could not have possessed Gwen's book before her passing in 1986, it remains unclear exactly what Slater was trying to say in that introduction — or to whom. He may have been trying to further muddy the origins of the Traditionalist Gwyddoniaid. However, it is more likely that he was merely tweaking the collective nose of the N.E.C.T.W. by implying an association between their material and that of the Church of Y Tylwyth Teg, and since *Pagan Rituals III* was written in defense of Eddie's legacy, this latter explanation better fits the circumstances, particularly in light of Herman's sense of humor and his long-standing grudge against Gwen Thompson.

Chapter 19: The Cubits of Plenty

The Church of the Eternal Source

With its palm-lined thoroughfares bustling with the potentates of entertainment empires, "Beautiful downtown Burbank", the same town that played host to the imagination factories that shaped so much of pop culture, is the obvious home for a church devoted to a romantic reconstruction of the religion of ancient Egypt. Founded in 1970, the CES was an attempt to resurrect the religion of ancient Kemet as it existed prior to the invasions of the kingdom and contamination of its mythology and religious practices by other Near Eastern cultures. Indeed, the goal of the CES was not only to reconstruct that religion, but also to bring it into the modern day. The CES is a polytheistic federation of independent cults, each dedicated to an individual Egyptian God or Goddess.[1]

The idea for the CES originated in an annual Egyptian-themed summer party that Harold Moss had been hosting since 1963. He originally practiced a form of what he terms the "Amarna Heresy," referring to the monotheistic worship of the sun disk, or "Aten", that was practiced during the reign of the Pharaoh Akhenaten. Abandoning Aten worship in 1967, Moss reverted to a practice of Kemetic orthodoxy that focused on the cult of the Egyptian God Horus. He joined the Feraferia path of Frederick Adams that same year, where he met Donald Harrison. Together with Sara Cunningham, the two men formed the CES in 1970. Moss was ordained as a Priest of Horus in 1971 and began a tradition of public outreach for the group, attending many regional and national conferences and festivals within the Neo-Pagan community.[2] One of these outreach visits was to the Witchmeet that was held in Minneapolis, Minnesota during the weekend of April 12-14, 1974.

Eddie Buczynski met Harold Moss and his lover, Jimmy Kemble, in person for the first time on the opening night of the Witchmeet. While Herman Slater consulted with the festival organizers and other leaders in the occult community about the feasibility of holding an inquiry into the matter of Gavin and Yvonne Frost, Eddie had an animated conversation with Jimmy about ancient Egyptian hieroglyphic grammar.[3] Up to that point, the two men had known each another chiefly through correspondence. Harold had been active in the Forum section of *Green Egg* on a variety of topics; however, it was his letters on the subject of homosexuals and their place in the Neo-Pagan movement that had initially attracted Eddie's interest.

Buczynski remained fascinated with ancient religions and, since his founding of the Traditionalist Gwyddoniaid in 1972, had continued his search for a Neo-Pagan spiritual path that was authentically inspired by ancient religious practices. The CES was one of the few extant spiritual paths that came close to fitting that description, and Eddie was fortunate in that a CES temple was located near Brooklyn, in Flushing, New York. At that time, the temple was run by Jane and Burt Cicciotto, who had been given that opportunity in 1973 upon the recommendation of Herman Slater.[4,5] Eddie knew and got along well with the Cicciottos, and they encouraged him to check out the CES. Buczynski had begun corresponding with Moss in 1973, ostensibly to discuss Moss' involvement in establishing the COER in 1972. But Eddie also began to explore what the CES had to offer, and he eventually broached the topic of joining its priesthood after his tumultuous association with Gardnerian Wica ended.

A small part of Harold's mission at the 1974 Witchmeet was to get a closer look at Eddie, and to report back to the church membership and Board on Buczynski's suitability for the priesthood. Moss had a decidedly mixed view before the meeting, particularly because of Eddie's personal relationship with Herman Slater. Slater's very public squabbles with various personalities in the community were distasteful to Moss. "I didn't like Herman at all, and avoided him as much as possible, although I defended him publicly from attacks by the straight chauvinist community," Moss admits. "He was effeminate, unattractive, undignified, prone to embarrassing angers, to very loudly saying things he, and others, regretted later. However, we were allies, so I tolerated him as necessary."[6,7]

After his meeting with Eddie, Moss agreed to put Buczynski's case to the CES Board to be brought in as a Priest. Yet, after the Witchmeet, Moss was still of two minds about the New Yorker. On the one hand, Buczynski was obviously a very intelligent, charismatic and well-read individual. But he was also an effeminate homosexual, and given the number of gay men who were already present in the CES, Moss was concerned that the CES might be perceived as a gay church, even though he was himself a gay man. *(Ibid n#7)* Buczynski had also developed a reputation, within the community, of jumping from coven to coven. Moss noted that most members of the CES had only changed religions once or twice at most, and for Eddie to have hopped groups three times in such a short period just seemed excessive. Also, because he had approached the CES within only a few months after his rejection by his Gardnerian coven, there was some concern that Eddie's interest was more attributable to looking for a port in the storm than to a serious consideration of the CES as a spiritual home. *(Ibid n#7)* In addition, there was also a question about his qualifications to be a member of the CES Priesthood.

To be ordained in the CES, a candidate was required to be at the eighth level on the pyramid of initiation, corresponding to the level of Priest of a given Deity. The candidate also needed to receive unanimous approval from all active priests and priestesses within the church, followed by the concurrence of and installation by the Board. Ordination was granted after twelve years of study or its equivalent. As Harold Moss points out, "[Ordination] is not an introductory handshake, it is a culmination."

(Ibid n#7) In Buczynski's case, both Moss and the Board had reservations about Eddie's ordination as a Priest. He was a newcomer to the church, after all, and had not progressed through the preceding seven levels, nor had he studied for the requisite period of time. On the other hand, the CES itself had only been around for four years, not twelve, so no one else in the Church at that time could have met the strict interpretation of the rules. Still, one has to start somewhere.

Eddie assumed that the Board would reciprocally credit his past works and initiations as equivalent to serving time in grade to the level of Priest in the CES. This argument by itself would never have carried the day; however, Buczynski had clearly demonstrated an overwhelming exuberance about becoming a CES Priest. Embarking on a writing frenzy, by July he had already drafted an initial set of Egyptian rituals for the proposed New York Temple. He had also worked on a design for a silver amulet of the Goddess Asat, developed a cast bronze temple ankh based on the carved design of one of his students, and made plans to produce bronze statuettes of Asat and Nebt-het, all of which would be offered to CES members at a discount through the Earth Religions Supplies catalogue.

But the upheaval in the Warlock Shop in the wake of Burt Cicciotto's alleged peculations in late April clinched the matter, for the New York Temple run by Jane and her husband immediately ceased to exist.[8] If the CES wanted to salvage its New York presence, it would need to appoint someone in short order to take charge of the situation, and Eddie was the only local candidate who came close to meeting the qualifications and who was also willing to take on the task. Otherwise, it might be several years before a temple could be organized under another Priest. Still, the CES Board was skeptical, and it was only after some debate that Buczynski was ordained as a Priest at the annual meeting on July 19, 1974.[9]

Although the letter to Buczynski mentioned nothing of it, Harold Moss later stated that at his suggestion the ordination was a provisional one. *(Ibid n#5)* The CES had never before decided to provisionally ordain a Priest, and it was indicative of the Board's view of Buczynski's candidacy that the members unanimously agreed to this path rather than risk a split decision over granting full ordination. A review was to be scheduled later to determine whether the Board was satisfied with Eddie's performance; if it was, the ordination would be made permanent. Because of Eddie's provisional status, his certificate of ordination was prepared but neither signed nor mailed to him, pending the outcome of the future review. *(Ibid n#5)*

It isn't clear, however, that Eddie was aware of his provisional status. He likely considered himself a shoo-in for the position, as he was already identifying himself as a member of the CES by June 1974.[10] The ordination letter said nothing of a provisional ordination, stating that his certificate was being prepared and would be mailed as soon as possible.

Subsequent correspondence seemed to indicate that the certificate was delayed due to a series of unfortunate happenstances. In reality, although Buczynski referred to himself from this point onwards as an ordained Priest of Isis, he never actually received an ordination certificate from the CES Board. The original certificate remains on file with the church to this day. The ordination letter does provide some insight into the Board's concerns, stating, *(Ibid n#9)*

> *Divinations show that a problem may develop in relations between your local office and the main office with respect to influence from non-Egyptians. We remind you that you and you alone are a priest and an Egyptian, and should accept advice and guidance first from Church fellows and other Egyptians, and second from friends and associates and members of other Churches. ... Rev. Jim W. Kemble has asked that discussion that he has held with you regarding his personal concerns with your situation be included in the conditions.*

These cautions were a veiled warning that Eddie should resist any attempts to be drawn into the various fights of others within the community that could sully the reputation of the CES. The discussion with Kemble was almost certainly a reference to the CES's concern over Eddie's own status within the New York community regarding his conflict with the Kneitel's Long Island Line of Gardnerian Wica. Moss later suggested that Eddie should write to Judy Kneitel and try to patch up their differences. Eddie responded was that there was no need to do so, as had made his peace with Judy some time ago.[11] Eddie was likely referring to the peace accord that Slater negotiated in the wake of the Witchmeet held that Spring. However, given that the Kneitels remained blacklisted by Buczynski in the Wica tradition Book of Shadows, it is unlikely that he genuinely believed that there was no longer any enmity between the two groups at that time.

The Board chose to overlook their concerns, primarily because of their assumption that Eddie's application to join the CES was motivated by a sincere desire to experience the mysticism of Egyptian ritual and explore the Egyptian philosophical system. *(Ibid n#5)* Yet doubts remained. Reflecting on this wariness, Moss writes, "I was always convinced that Ed was 'collecting initiations,' and that he never took his CES priesthood seriously. His ordination occurred when he was 'on the rebound' after his brutal rejection by his [Gardnerian] coven and their approach to the Long Island coven." *(Ibid n#5)* But Moss' judgment of the seriousness of Buczynski's commitment is harsher than the facts at hand warrant, at least as far as Eddie's initial involvement with the CES was concerned.

There is little doubt that Eddie was still stinging from his treatment by Renate Springer's Gardnerian coven in December 1973. Yet he had never stopped working with his Welsh covens, and he had also been working with Jane Cicciotto as the high priest of a new Gardnerian-derived coven by the time he began corresponding with Harold Moss about the CES. Therefore, his impetus to find safe harbor in another spiritual group was not pronounced. It was clear, however, that Eddie was still searching for *something*, and this drive certainly inspired some admiration in Harold. "He was obviously a pan-spiritualist into every kind of spiritual practice, later especially as they related to gay sex magic," Moss notes. "The one thing we shared was a determination to understand everything."[12] It was this drive to understand and to experience that led Buczynski to the CES, and that first brought him to Harold's attention. But whether Eddie's search would be satisfied by his involvement with the Neo-Pagan church would only become clear with time.

One thing was certain about Eddie's motivations for joining the CES: he was truthfully fed up with Craft politics, at least for the time being. Of his recent experiences, Buczynski wrote, "I was determined to make the best of Wica for myself. But the bickering, the nonsense, and the utter bullshit of it all — where I was concerned — put me into chronic depression and utter unhappiness. It is a beautiful and joyous religion ... but NOT for ME."[13] A few years later, he would repeat his complaint, writing, "I stuck it out [in Wica] until my late twenties. Finally, sick of all the shit flying back and forth from coven to coven (mainly concerning me), along with threats, death curses, slander, etc., I decided that, in order to find fulfillment in my religious beliefs, I must find a pagan cult which would welcome me as I am ... a proud gay man." *(Ibid n#11)* Moss acknowledged his own belief that, based on Buczynski's correspondence, Eddie felt more like a Priest in the CES than he ever did in Wica.[14]

The CES was ambivalent about the role of Wica in the Neo-Pagan community and its relationship, if any, to the teachings of the CES. On the one hand, it saw a kinship between the Witches and Egyptian Neo-Paganism. "CES looks upon Wicca as one of the surviving Egyptian religious forms," Moss wrote in a letter to *Earth Religion News*. "We see in Wicca some important elements of our religion, and we see it as one way to serve some of the Great and Eternal Gods. Wicca represents a natural evolution of Egyptian religion under the conditions of European Climate and Christian persecution. In America, neither of these conditions is exactly found, so an alternative evolution is appropriate, hence the CES."[15] Yet it was the continued involvement in Wica by CES co-founder Sara Cunningham that led to the first split in the church in 1972. In explaining Cunningham's departure to Hans Holzer in 1973, Moss said that when the CES found out about her activities, "the inevitable showdown occurred." *(Ibid n#5)* This heightened sensitivity to keeping the boundaries between the two paths unblurred would cause Eddie's writings on behalf of the CES to be scrutinized for any evidence of his continued devotion to Wica.

Before his ordination, Eddie had chosen as his patron the Goddess Isis, and he took as his name "Un-Nefer." Buczynski described his visions of meeting with Isis to anyone who would listen. Moss notes that "[Eddie] went to a great deal of effort to convince us of his sincere interest in Egyptian religion, describing dreams and visions." *(Ibid n#5)* Karen Bartlett recalls Eddie regaling his Welsh students that summer with stories of astral initiations and meeting the Goddess Isis and becoming one with Her.[16] In a letter printed in the June 1974 issue of *Green Egg*, he described a waking dream where he met Isis and was both commanded to be Her Priest and given his Egyptian name.[17]

Eddie's choice of Isis was an interesting one, in that it marked the first time he had dedicated himself to serving as the Priest of one specific Deity. He had off-handedly mentioned to Ria Farnham in 1973 that the Greek Goddess Rhea was his favorite from the ancient world, and Isis was in many respects the Deity from ancient Kemet most closely corresponding to the Aegean Great Mother. The priest-name that he adopted, Un-Nefer, is derived from the Kemetic words *Un* (to make manifest) and *neferu* (good things/beauty). It is one of the names of Osiris, the God of the Egyptian underworld and the brother and husband of the Goddess Isis. Herman Slater commissioned a silver seal ring with "Un-Nefer" in hieroglyphs to commemorate Eddie's ordination. Shortly afterward, Eddie began using the *Tyet* — an ankh-like pictogram with downward-curving arms — as a signature in his CES correspondence. Also called "the Knot of Isis," among other names, the *Tyet* was an ancient symbol of the Goddess Isis and was a potent representation of Her magick. The archaeologist E. A. Wallis Budge believed the *Tyet* to represent the place whence the blood of Isis came (i.e., the vulva or uterus), and thereby may have represented the awesome and mysterious powers of creation or rebirth.[18] It may also be related to the Minoan and Greek sacral knot, themselves perhaps a representation of the tied-off umbilical cord.

With a typical burst of enthusiasm at the outset of a grand project, Eddie began organizing a New York Temple of the CES, which would be based out of the Warlock Shop in Brooklyn Heights. He set for himself the ambitious goal of having a permanent physical temple of Isis in New York City within three years.[19] By the June 1974 edition of the *Earth Religion News*, Eddie had begun publishing a newsletter for the New York Temple called *Esbat*, a name that Harold Moss told Herman Slater was equivalent to the Egyptian word for "Star."[20] This issue of *Esbat* listed "Ed Buczynski, Initiate of Isis" as the contact for the New York Center of the CES. The Pyramid of Initiation printed in that issue defined an "Initiate" as a VII level member of CES.[21]

By the next issue of *Esbat* in August, Buczynski had announced an ambitious class schedule for an associated temple school he was starting.[22] The first semester of the school was to run from September 8 to December 22. Classes could be taken independently, and attendance at

CES rites was not a prerequisite. Only two of the eight classes were specifically tailored to the Egyptian religion; the rest were introductory studies that could apply to any Pagan Way group. This distribution of subject matter is unsurprising in and of itself, as the classroom materials were already available and fit into the CES vision of producing a priesthood with a broad knowledge of the occult community.

By early September, Buczynski had informed Moss that he had three active students who were, in his opinion, nearly ready to be ordained via the New York Temple. One of these was Melda Tamarack, one of Eddie's Welsh downline from the coven of Kay Smith and Terry Parker. Two others, Denny Sargent and Robert Carey, had also studied occasionally with Eddie in the New York Temple, although they mainly relied on mail order lessons from the main temple in Burbank, California. But despite Eddie's best efforts, there weren't many people in the core group.[23]

Eddie went out of his way to describe how much effort he had been putting into the New York Temple, writing, "I have been working day and night with these persons ... I am currently VERY DEEP into Theological Hypotheses and working twenty-four hours a day on study and organization. The above three persons have been of tremendous help in this. The rituals have been revised and a third volume will be ready in a manner of months."[24] Obviously Buczynski was not working twenty-four hours a day. No person could sustain that kind of effort regardless of their enthusiasm, and Eddie's optimism of his students' readiness for the priesthood was premature because, as things turned out, none of them was ever ordained within the CES.

Eddie achieved more success with the revision of the two volumes of rituals that he had earlier drafted. Volume One, *The Temple Ritual*, provided purification rites, a litany of Names of the Goddess, mythology, and festivals and rituals.[25] Volume Two, *The Rituals of Khem*, contained magickal spells and a section on theology that contained guidance for the priesthood on qualifications, teaching, counseling, and the like.[26] The arrangement and content of these volumes were to form the basis of Buczynski's writing style in the coming years. These volumes met with considerable approval from members of the CES, including Harold Moss and Martha Adler.[27] The public rituals hosted by the New York Temple were said to be quite beautiful were reminiscent of those conducted by Fred Adams' Feraferia.[28]

Dissension in the Ranks

Yet relations weren't perfect between the California headquarters and New York, as tensions arose between Eddie and others within the CES. Some of this had to do with Eddie's rather flamboyant personality. "I am homosexual myself but I find effeminate men disgusting, and was really only able to communicate with Ed in writing," Moss admitted. "Our relationship was what my generation called a 'clothespin alliance,' referring to the putting of a clothespin on the nose to hold the nostrils shut and keep out a disagreeable smell while one went ahead and did one's duty. I avoided telephoning him although that was my preferred means of communicating with others." Yet Moss admitted that Eddie also had a sexual charisma that could be unsettling to some. "[A] confirmed, nay, militantly, heterosexual man confided to me once that although he hated homosexuality and couldn't understand it, the erotic power of Ed's personality showed him a little about how it could be possible to be homosexual, although he still had no interest in trying it." *(Ibid n#5)* Despite his discomfort in dealing with Eddie in person, Moss found him to have a sharp and engaging intellect. "Ed was obviously extremely intelligent and deeply committed to whatever he was doing at the moment. When writing [to him] I could forget everything else and share ideas with enthusiasm." *(Ibid n#7)*

In contrast, the working relationship between Eddie and the CES secretary, Ron Myron, alternated between geniality and outright hostility. This was a serious issue, as Ron's position in the CES required continuous close contact with the church personnel in the field, including Eddie. Moss believed that Myron privately despised Eddie from the beginning, but was too professional to allow that to color his treatment of the New Yorker. *(Ibid n#7)* Eddie, however, was sensitive to Myron's brusqueness, despite Moss' assurances that Ron treated everyone that way. A great deal of Harold's time appears to have been spent smoothing ruffled feathers and keeping the lines of communication open between the two men.

Buczynski and Myron's relationship was further complicated by the fact that Myron was also a worshipper of Isis and so had a vested interest in what the church published on this subject. Ron may also have resented Eddie's elevation above him in the church hierarchy of the Cult of Isis. Privately, Moss urged Eddie to practice humility in his Priesthood and admit that, despite the fact that even though he outranked everyone in the Cult of Isis, including Martha Adler, the opinions of others regarding Her practices were also valid. He was also cautioned that, as a Priest of Isis, he was not at liberty to pick and choose who came to worship in Her name as he might do in the Craft.[29] Eddie replied that he was mature enough to function as a Priest with those who did not like him personally or vice versa. He also ruefully admitted his failings, noting, "I strive towards humility – but it is a difficult task (you know me, Harold). Yet, I will succeed."[30] Buczynski appeared to be sensitive to this issue at times, going out of his way to acknowledge Myron's time in the service to Isis and eliciting his feedback on Eddie's work. The August 1974 edition of *Esbat* featured an article written by Myron on incense, herbs and stones used in Egyptian magick and religion.[31]

It is no surprise that Myron had definite opinions on Buczynski's approach to CES ritual. Ron believed that Eddie's first draft of the CES rituals incorporated too much of the mechanics and philosophy of Wica. He was particularly concerned that Buczynski was adapting the basic ritual structure of the Catholic Church for use in the New York Temple rites. Eddie sought to assuage Ron's alarm, but did not offer to alter his basic approach. "It is important to supply the lay-worshipper with symbols, words and gestures which convey decipherable meanings to his intellect," Eddie wrote. "What may have meant something 5000 years ago, in most cases, would mean little, if nothing, to the average worshipper of today. ... Religion must adapt to the society in which it is practiced – I am trying to compromise this with the comparable experiences of the ancients as understood by the scholars of this age. ... This in no way detracts from the spiritual concept of Isis worship since Judeo-Christianity has purloined an unbelievable mass amount from the worship of the Isis-Osiris-Horus Triad. This I have learned from the years from my Catholic training and from my learned friends who are Catholic and Orthodox priests and Bishops (of which I at one time aspired to become). I am sure that, with these points in mind, you can come to understand the nature and purposes of my rituals."[32]

On the subjects of obsession and possession, Eddie went on to note that "I have been assured by both my research and the Bishop of Brooklyn [Simon] ... that the **RITUALE ROMANUM** was borrowed from Egyptian, Graeco-Roman, Sumerian sources and is almost as old as civilization. I do not like to discuss this matter as it concerns experience which is very close to me. The ritual works, and that is what matters." *(Ibid n#32)* With regard to the inherent incongruity of introducing the Wiccan Circle into his ritual work, Buczynski appeared to be unconcerned, writing "I don't think that the Ancients used the Circle; however, I am used to this as a protective device from the Wica ... and isn't Wica very closely associated related to Isis worship? Many who are notable in Wica-craft recognize this as fact." *(Ibid n#32)* Although Eddie was reflecting some of the same thoughts that Harold Moss had expressed to the readership of the *Earth Religion News* in June, this statement probably cemented Myron's belief that Buczynski would not be able to discard the trappings of Wica and transition to the purely Pagan practices of the CES.[33] In this case, the adage "Once a Witch, always a Witch" appeared to work against the New Yorker.

Myron was also concerned that Buczynski was trying to interject an element of sexual magick into the rites of Isis. Ron made his opinion on the subject abundantly clear in a letter later published in *Green Egg*. "Sex Magic(k)," Myron wrote, "is a symptom of psychic adolescence, that period of time or practice in which one has not yet learned to effectively 'use' or integrate sexually-derived energies into the totality of one's nature/being so as to act with wholeness and integration. The practice of

Sex Magic(k) is a large step backwards for many people or perhaps a regression to the starting point for serious work which has already been entered into."[34] With that mindset, it seems reasonable that he would question Buczynski's placement of a phallus in the altar arrangement proposed in the first volume of rituals. Eddie countered that "The phallus does not denote Sex Rituals — whatever gave you that idea? It is merely a re-enactment of the actions of Isis in the legend. [D]id she not raise up the inert phallus of her dead husband and conceive thereby? Does this not represent the hopes of all men to find resurrection from the dead through the intercession of the great Mother Isis? The aspergillum represents the phallus in the act of ejaculation — is not the Holy water the semen of the Gods which purify and fertilize the Temple and the souls of the people?" *(Ibid n#32)*

But while Eddie was debating the fertility of the people, his own relationship with Herman was withering on the vine. Devoted as they had been to one another, neither man was particularly cut out for a committed, monandrous relationship. Karen Bartlett characterized their relationship as polyamorous.[35] But, while Slater was often derided for his wandering eye, which fell more often than not on younger rough trade, Eddie was hardly a June Cleaver sitting at home waiting on his man. He too was known to play the field himself from time to time. Joe Caldiero confirms this, writing, "I recall Eddie and I went to the Pierrepont Baths a few times and Herman was all upset about that. Eddie didn't seem to mind him being upset so I didn't give it another thought."[36]

Certainly the near-failure of the Warlock Shop that spring placed a considerable and ongoing stress on both men. Correspondents across the country contacted them to ask whether the Warlock Shop had closed. Eddie, who had never run to fat, had begun to lose weight under the pressure. Judith McNally notes that because the two men lived within their business premises, they really had little opportunity to foster a healthy home life, even under the best of conditions. "The Warlock Shop opened late-ish (11 AM?), seven days a week, and [Eddie] and Herman locked up and shooed out the inevitable guests in the back room late in the evening and finally, I assume, had some time to themselves. The two rooms upstairs were off-limits to casual visitors, but given the proximity of the shop and their home, and the demands of running the business, it probably took real work to carve out a private life."[37]

But another insight into the deteriorating relationship between Slater and Buczynski is shown by the banner notice of the first issue of *Esbat* which was printed in the June 1974 edition of *Earth Religion News*. In it, Buczynski stated that "[*Esbat*] is printed within the pages of the 'Earth Religion News' eight times a year ... We do not, however, necessarily agree with the Editorial policy of Earth Religion News, maintaining that we are a completely separate publication with our own Editorial policy."[38] In this remarkable statement, Eddie appeared to be distancing himself from the editorial policy a publication of which he was the named editor. Some in the community had long suspected that Buczynski wasn't in a true position of authority, either on the newspaper or at the Warlock Shop itself.

Tensions had been simmering between Eddie and Herman since the Gardnerian imbroglio of the previous year. For his part, Eddie had grown weary of Herman's meddling and picking of fights throughout the occult community. The Frost controversy, peaking as it did on the heels of the Gardnerian blowup, had further strained their relationship. "To Ed Buczynski's credit and in line with his more quiet personality, he did not take part in any of the mud-slinging, and instead preferred to take a low-key approach," remembers Ed Fitch. "I believe that he did not care for all the high emotions and hard feelings that were going on around him."[39] The *Esbat* declaration seems to indicate that Buczynski was tiring of his role as a figurehead authority at the newspaper, and perhaps also in the operation of the business. That assessment may be bolstered by the August issue of the *Earth Religion News*, in which Eddie was no longer listed as the editor. Herman Slater was now the paper's lone Publisher-Editor.[40]

Having gradually fallen out of lust with one another over the last two years, and with the strain of running several different spiritual groups and a business weighing on them both, the two men had begun to squabble almost constantly. Karen Bartlett recalls that during this period Herman and Eddie were always fighting like cats and dogs.[41] The breakup, when it happened, was final. The two men moved out of the Warlock Shop to Slater's apartment on Atlantic Avenue. By the summer of 1974, Eddie and Herman were only roommates. Ken Dalton remembers that "Eddie was still living at the apartment on Atlantic Avenue, but not for long."[42]

When Buczynski finally left, he took what he could — his precious books and writings, clothing, guitar, record albums and ritual equipment — and moved back to his parents' home in Ozone Park. But if he was searching for peace, he was not to find it — at least not in the short term — because his life went to pieces from the moment he left Herman in late August.

When his relationship with Slater ended, Buczynski lost not only his main source of income but also the daily face-to-face contact with his many friends and covenmates he had come to count on. Now jobless and broke, Eddie often couldn't afford to travel to the Warlock Shop, nor was he made to feel particularly welcome there when he did manage to return. This was a marked change from when he had been living and working there as Herman's lover and business partner. In addition, Eddie had to pull out of active coven work by late September 1974. *(Ibid n#16)* Some of the Welsh initiates did not take this well, particularly the teens in the Children of Branwen who idolized him. "I remember being so sad that Eddie B was leaving that I almost cried, and he said something really harsh to me, like 'Oh stop it! One day you'll see that everyone's in the Craft for themselves!'" wrote Karen Bartlett. "I just really lost it then and started crying. He softened then and wiped my tears and apologized to me, and reassured me that he would still be around." *(Ibid n#41)* Keeping that promise would be beyond Eddie's ability for a while, given his situation. Ironically, this also meant that he was unable to follow through with the coursework he had planned for the fall semester of the New York Temple School, and the idea died unrealized.

Occupying the basement of his parents' house once more, Buczynski managed to make the best of his situation. He managed to stay sporadically connected with others, via letters or telephone. Occasionally some of his covenmates and friends came to visit. His eleven-year-old brother, Tommy, was fascinated by the mysterious adult goings-on in the bare-bulb-and-candlelight world beneath his feet. "[Eddie] had an altar and a large red pentagram on the floor in our basement. He and his friends used to hang out down there," Tommy remembers. Those who gathered below were all young and good looking. With their longish hair, and mysterious ways, they seemed like very magical beings. These exotic, beautiful people only came around at night, leading the boy to fancifully conclude that they were all vampires.[43]

Much to his surprise, despite being flat broke and somewhat isolated, Eddie was happier than he'd been in a long time. He wrote of coming to terms with his life outside of the Warlock Shop: "I have found this situation of mine to be a blessing in disguise, for now I can begin a new life all over again. ... I have a lot of time to continue my studies. ... I am out of touch with what is happening on the Pagan/Craft scene now. I am happy to be so. I have become weary of the fucking bullshit back and forth and around and around. Since I have been away from it all, my composure is 100 times better, I have put on some weight and I'm looking and feeling great."[44] Moss empathized with this feeling, confiding some months later in a letter to Eddie that he too was fed up with "the nuts" in the community and in serious need of a vacation. *(Ibid n#27)*

By October, Eddie was no longer in touch with Herman. "They seemed fairly distant when I first met them," Ken Dalton writes. "After Eddie moved out he rarely spoke about Herman. My impression was that the relationship was frosty. I continued to work at the shop and Eddie was rarely mentioned." *(Ibid n#42)* Eddie complained of this state of affairs to Harold Moss' lover, Jim Kemble, writing, "The fact that he hasn't telephoned me once since I have been here shows me exactly what I mean to him — especially since I called him every other day for the first month [after I left]." Almost as an afterthought, Buczynski added, "I'm really not as bothered about it as I may seem to be." *(Ibid n#44)* Yet it was clear that the situation troubled him, aggravated as it was by the fact that Slater also failed to forward Eddie's mail from Brooklyn Heights to Ozone Park. For Eddie, who relied heavily on correspondence with friends and students, this came as a severe blow, and he couldn't just transfer his mailing address to his parents' home. Aside from the fact that he knew they wouldn't appreciate the substantially increased volume of post coming through their mail slot, he also didn't want his parents' address in wide circulation (a prudent course then as now, given some of the characters the community attracts).

Despite his troubles with Herman, Eddie busied himself with putting his life back in order. He took a part-time job at the BookMasters Bookstore at 1482 Broadway in Times Square, or as he called it, "the sin center" of New York. The pay was poor, and the hours were absolutely lousy. Eddie had to commute by train from Times Square back to Ozone Park after 11 PM from Tuesday through Thursday. On Friday and Saturday nights, he had to push his way through crowds of hustlers and whores, porn theatre barkers, derelicts, drunks, drug addicts, pickpockets and sex tourists when he left work at 1 AM. Nevertheless, he was grateful for the job in the deteriorating economy of New York. *(Ibid n#44)* Eddie's schedule left him with little free time to pursue his spiritual practices, but he read voraciously. Working at a bookstore certainly had its advantages for an inveterate bookworm, and even the rotten hours would eventually prove a boon.

Chapter 20: "I Think I've Met Him."

The Big Easy Meets the Big Apple

Bennie Geraci was born in 1950. The youngest of three children, including an older half-brother and half-sister from his mother's previous marriage, Bennie had spent the first years of his life in the bustling river city of New Orleans. That changed on September 10, 1965 when hurricane Betsy slammed into the city with winds of 125 mph. Fifteen-year-old Bennie and his mother weathered the storm alone in their home. Bennie's father, like the other employees of the city's Water and Drains commission, was on duty out in the storm in an attempt to save the city. New Orleans, which did not have the rings of dikes it now possesses, suffered the worst flooding that it had seen in decades due to the 10-foot storm surge caused by the hurricane. Mother and son retreated to the second floor of their flooded home, where they spent a terrible night waiting out the storm. Emergency workers in boats rescued them the next day. As they were rowed to safety, the family had to come to grips with the fact that they had lost everything.

Bennie's older sister lived a short distance away in Gretna, Louisiana. She and her new husband took in her parents and young brother until the family could get on its feet again. They lived together, cramped and yet somehow comfortable in the young couple's two-bedroom home, for the year that it took Bennie's father to have a new home built in Gretna a short distance from Bennie's sister. Life in Gretna, a working class suburb of New Orleans, was a bit slower than in New Orleans proper, but the young man managed the transition well.

Bennie grew up nominally Catholic, like most of his classmates, but his outlook on life never quite fit in with that of the majority of his community. This may have resulted in part from an incident that occurred when he was attending Catholic elementary school. While going through catechism, one day Bennie's teacher informed him that he was a bastard because he had been sired by a man other than his divorced mother's first husband. The upset youngster told this story to his mother that evening. The next day she yanked him from the school, thus ending the family's formal relationship with the Catholic Church. Another thing that greatly influenced Bennie's outlook was his realization by the time he reached high school that he was gay. This factor, his abrupt removal from a judgmental and overbearing sect of Christianity, and the influence of an independent-minded mother would color much of his subsequent life.

After graduating from high school, Bennie moved back into the Big Easy, where he spent a short stint at the University of New Orleans. However, he eventually dropped out of college in order to earn a living. In 1972, the twenty-two-year-old was employed by day at a brokerage firm in

New Orleans, and working part-time in the evenings at the front desk of the New Orleans Bathhouse. Bennie lived comfortably in a small apartment in the French Quarter — "where all the action was" — with his roommate, Charlie Dandelakis. Charlie and Bennie had been friends and roommates since 1970, when they met during a party at Bennie's place. Charlie was three months younger than Bennie and worked in purchasing at a local supply house. He was smooth, blonde and curly-haired in contrast to the dark-haired, mustachioed and hirsute Bennie. In modern parlance, Charlie was a twink and Bennie was a cub, but these were the days before the counterproductive subdivision of the gay community into separate "scenes." To the men of the 1970s, it was all *the* scene. The two became good friends and set up house together soon after meeting.

By late 1972, life in New Orleans was beginning to pall with the slow pace and slumping economy. The country was changing. Since the end of World War II, gay men and lesbians had been migrating to the large, mainly coastal, cities of the United States and establishing enclaves and social networks to cater to their needs. Certainly New Orleans had long been an environment where the fey and perverse (in Society's eyes) were if not openly welcomed, then at least able to get by with a wink and a nod. However, by the early 1970s, the two biggest draws were the emerging gay ghettos of New York City and San Francisco. In some ways the nation resembled a gigantic bar magnet, with gay men being pulled like little iron filings toward the poles represented by the communities on either coast. While some urban gay activists were just beginning to argue against the ghettoization of the movement, many rosy-cheeked youths from the hinterlands were eagerly lining up to answer the Siren's call. Like so many gay men in the nation's midsection, Bennie and Charlie felt the pull and headed to the East Coast.

With their friend, David Roberts, they took an exploratory trip to New York City over Thanksgiving weekend in 1972. David was the first gay friend that Bennie had made at the gay bars after coming out in 1969. All three men thought it would be a fun adventure to visit Gail Howard and Dawn Fazend, lesbian friends of theirs who had recently moved there from New Orleans and had invited them to visit. The young men explored the city, carousing through its night life and cruising the bridle paths off Central Park West, and they all decided that the Big Apple was the place to be. David was so enamored with New York that he decided then and there to remain with the women when Bennie and Charlie went home at the end of the weekend. On returning to Louisiana, Charlie and Bennie saved their money and laid the plans for their own move in April of 1973. To save on expenses, they arranged to transport a car to New York City for its owners. Packing the car with their bags, they set off again for the East Coast and completed the 1,300-mile trip in one long push, with short stops for gas along the way. They hit the ground in New York with less than a thousand dollars between them.

Bennie and Charlie each landed a job at Chase Manhattan Bank exactly one day after their arrival. Bennie worked as a Certification Clerk in the Brokers Loan Department at Chase Manhattan Plaza, while Charlie was hired into the Purchasing Department down the street at 1 New York Plaza. They had arranged to stay on 63rd Road in Rego Park, Queens in the one-bedroom apartment of their friend Charlie Kyle (nicknamed "Poule d'Eaux") until they could find a place of their own. Poule d'Eaux was a *real* Cajun from Franklin, Louisiana; a cute little guy with a tremendous personality that had earned him many trinkets at Mardi Gras. He was to be a great help to the men as they learned their way around the city and its denizens.

After a month of searching, Bennie and Charlie managed to rent a one-bedroom apartment right around the corner from Poule d'Eaux on 63rd Drive in Rego Park, Queens. Rego Park was a neighborhood of Queens that the Real Good Construction Company developed in the 1920s as a bedroom community for New York City. In the 1970s, it was a quiet neighborhood and home to many Western Russian Jews, as well as gay men in search of cheap rentals that were still close to Manhattan. The two men moved into their new flat in May 1973. For the next several months, the aptly numbered Apartment 3X would be their home base as they explored and sampled the wicked, glorious and decidedly gay metropolis for the next several months. As they weren't lovers, sharing a one-bedroom apartment sometimes proved inconvenient for them both. When one brought a trick home, the other was forced to yield the bed and spend the night on the sofa. When they both brought men back, they sometimes decided the matter with a coin toss. Because sex was so readily available, this situation was not a rare occurrence.

The night life of New York City in mid-1970s provided sex clubs, bathhouses (called "the tubs"), bars, dance clubs and dirty bookstores which vied with the opera, symphony, theatre, art galleries, museums and restaurants to create a 24-hour cultural smorgasbord. It was the scene of Andy Warhol, of the wandering homeless, of S&M clubs and poetry readings, of gay-bashings and gay rights activists, of a rough, young Robert Mapplethorpe and a finely-seasoned Leonard Bernstein, of Central Park, heroin addicts, Times Square peep shows, the waterfront with its docks where men had sex in empty buildings, and the Statue of Liberty – the great old Queen who lifted her skirts for *anyone*. It justly earned its millennialist nickname "Babylon" as a crossroads of all that was lush, vicious, seedy and sublime.1 Weekends could be spent carousing in the dance clubs where the disco phenomenon was just beginning its reign. Or, with just a little more trouble, the train and ferry trip over to Cherry Grove on Fire Island opened up a private world of tea dances, nude sunbathing and non-stop cottage parties – and in either locale there was sex. *Lots* of sex. As Bennie puts it, "We fit into the scene like a glove."

They made friends quickly through introductions by Poule d'Eaux and others, and from meeting and socializing with the other gay men in their building and at the bars. The bars and establishments in Greenwich Village provided a carousel of entertainment for their off-hours — Julius, a long-time gay bar on West 10th Street, the Ninth Circle down the block from the Stonewall Inn, the Limelight, Badlands, and the International Stud. Even the more sedate local bars in Queens were good for an occasional relaxing foray, and the Continental Baths, where Bette Midler and Barry Manilow got their start performing in 1970 for handsome young men clad only in towels and flip-flops, was a pleasure dome in its own right. But while Bennie and Charlie certainly made judicious use of the opportunities presented them, neither man ever became so immersed in the subculture as to lose his way. After all, even in Babylon a guy's got to pay the rent.

By September 1973, David Roberts was looking for a new place to live, having roosted with Gail and Dawn since arriving in town. Charlie and Bennie decided to move into Apartment 3M, a two-bedroom flat in the same building on 63rd Drive. David moved in with them, allowing them to save on rent. David was dating a Puerto Rican named Louie Morales, who lived in New Jersey, so David spent most of his free time there and used the apartment mainly as a place to stash his work clothes. By the spring of 1974 they had added a fourth roommate, Kevin McClung, so they could divvy up the rent into even smaller chunks. Bennie and Charlie continued to expand their circle of friends as they settled into the routines of the city. There was so much to see and do that it seemed at times that they would never run out of new places to explore.

Cherry Grove on Fire Island held a particular appeal to them. The Grove had long been a resort where gay men and lesbians could get away from the oppression of mainland society. The quaint cottages, the beaches, the boardwalks, the tea dances and cottage parties, and the wild and wooded dunes between Cherry Grove and the neighboring Pines created a fantasy world where gay men could indulge themselves in relative safety.[2] Indeed, it was so well known as a gay haven that as early as 1962 it was dubbed "Paradise Island" by Jess Stearn in his New York Times best-selling book *The Sixth Man*.[3] By the mid-1970s, the local economy had become heavily reliant on income from mainland tourists to support a plethora of gay-owned and operated shops, bars and restaurants. Bennie and Charlie made the two-hour trip over to the island as often as they could afford it (which was generally one weekend a month during the summer). They usually stayed at an affordable guesthouse such as The Carousel, and they danced their nights away with a large crowd of gay men and lesbians at The Ice Palace. The Ice Palace had the distinction being one of the first commercial discos in the world, opening in 1970 to serve the gay weekenders who frequented the island.[4] It was in this vivid, loose and raucous atmosphere that Bennie and Charlie met Joseph Cupolo one Saturday night in August 1974.

Joey Cupolo was living with his parents at the time in Sayville, New York on Long Island and working at a local electronics company. Sayville was the home port of the Fire Island ferry, and Cupolo often hopped over to Fire Island. After a night of dancing at The Ice Palace, Joey and Charlie became infatuated with one another. Joey couldn't tear his eyes off the lithe, blonde Charlie as he gyrated across the Palace's polished wooden dance floor, while Charlie was smitten with Joe's darkly handsome looks. Bennie was introduced to Joey that same night and also took a liking to the cocky, young Italian. "You look tired, open up," said Bennie, who popped a benzedrine into Joey's mouth. The men had a great time that weekend, forging a friendship that lasted for decades. Once back on the mainland, Joe and Charlie soon became an item, and it wasn't long before Joe moved out of his parents' home and in with the Louisiana transplants. Bennie, for his part, bowed gracefully to the situation and left the bedroom for Charlie and Joey, moving into the other bedroom with Kevin.

The "circus apartment" (as Bennie called it) began to attain something of a madhouse atmosphere, with the men and their friends coming and going at all hours, parties on some weekends, regular forays to the three B's (bookstores, baths, and backrooms), trips to Cherry Grove, and some occasional downtime. Every Wednesday and Friday night, the men would play poker with some seriously cute and allegedly straight boys from the building. They often made so much racket, with the poker games on some days and David Roberts hanging out the third floor window serenading the neighborhood with Diana Ross tunes on others, that the landlord might have asked them to leave were it not for the fact that every time a vacancy opened up they immediately encouraged their friends to move into the building. The twice-weekly poker party became a ritual of cigarettes, whiskey and sexual innuendo that lasted for the entire time the men roomed together. Bennie paid for many trips back to New Orleans from the proceeds of these weekly sheep-shearings.

In general, the guys didn't drive around town, since cars were expensive to maintain in the city, and parking was scarce. For a short time Joey managed to keep a lime green Yugo, but the car (to no one's great surprise) constantly broke down and was eventually seized by the city for a raft of unpaid parking tickets. So for the most part, they walked or used the subways, trains and the occasional cab to get around. It was one such train ride late in 1974 that was to have a profound impact on Bennie's life.

On the evening of November 2, Bennie was bored and restless. He decided to take the train to Chelsea to visit one of the tubs — Man's Country at 28 West 15th Street, known for its several floors of orgies. Like most other bathhouses, it contained both private rooms and public areas devoted to the single-minded goal of facilitating sexual conquest. Bennie spent that evening cruising the sauna and watching TV, but in the end he just wasn't into the scene. Still feeling bored, he left after 1 AM and hopped on the local Westside subway line. At the Times Square/42nd Street station, he switched to the E train back to Queens. A tall, attractive man boarded and sat down across from Bennie, his nose buried in a book. Bennie's skin prickled as he realized he was being cruised. Looking across the aisle he saw a pair of blue-grey eyes staring back at him from under a mop of auburn hair. The eyes snapped back down to the text before slowly edging up over the top of the book again.

The Louisiana native was spellbound, and returned the cruise for all he was worth. The game continued for the entire trip until, all too soon, their stop approached. As they both reluctantly stood up to exit the Express at the Roosevelt Avenue/Jackson Heights Station, the man suddenly came up behind him and urgently whispered "call me" in his ear while thrusting a piece of paper with his phone number written on it into Bennie's hand. Bennie boarded the local for 63rd Drive as the stranger walked towards the bus transfer station. A short time later as he walked up 63rd in the dark, Bennie's heart was still thumping from the encounter. Joe and Charlie were still awake as he entered the apartment in the wee hours of November 3rd. Bennie flopped down on their bed and declared, "I think I've met him."

What Eddie thought or felt about the chance encounter on the way home from his job at BookMaster's that night is lost to time, but Bennie did call him the next day, and the two men spent several hours talking over coffee on Monday the 4th. They hit it off right away, and by December Eddie was making plans to move into the 63rd Drive apartment. While he was close to his mother and stepfather, the twenty-seven-year-old chafed under their roof and longed to continue his work in the Craft community outside the scrutiny of his parents.

Despite his mother's concern, Eddie ran off once more to join the "circus" in January 1975. Kevin moved out of the bedroom he had occupied with Bennie and onto the sleeper sofa in the living room so that Eddie could take up with his new lover. Apartment 3M now held five permanent residents, with David as an occasional sixth. There were some definite differences between Eddie and Bennie that took some getting used to, not the least of which was their different patterns of speech. Ken Dalton notes, "I still chuckle [when] thinking about the incredible War of the Accents between Eddie and Benny."[5] And while the agnostic Bennie had learned of Eddie's spiritual path during that first date over coffee, the subject of religion had never really come up before with the other men. Still, it didn't take long for them to realize that there was something different about their new roommate: a Witch had moved lock, stock and cauldron into their nest. This didn't bother Bennie as much as it might have with some other southern boy. He was from New Orleans, after all. And, as Eudora Welty's character Leota, says in *The Petrified Man*, "Ever'body in New Orleans believes ever'thing spooky."[6]

Chapter 21: The Cubits of Death

Up the Nile Without an Oar

Eddie settled in very quickly with the boys. Cramped as the apartment was, it was a definite improvement over his parents' basement. Though he was still working long hours and late shifts, he occasionally managed to find time to go out to the clubs and tubs with the others. Bennie was fascinated with his new lover. Bookish, intelligent and sometimes moody, Eddie was unlike anyone he'd ever met before. From Buczynski's perspective, Geraci was radically different in personality from Slater. Whereas Herman could be abrasive and sarcastic, Bennie was generally a happy-go-lucky type, as well as a rare species of benign smart-ass. The lovers were often shut up in one of the two bedrooms of the apartment, where they would go at it like rabbits for hours at a time, according to Bennie. Although they would eventually open up their relationship, for the first two years they were generally monandrous.

Buczynski practiced the Craft as much as he was able in the cramped apartment, much to the bemusement of his roommates, who weren't sure what to make of his beliefs. One activity that Bennie recalls vividly was what he jokingly refers to as "restraining orders" or "restraints." These were binding spells that involved writing the name of a person who was giving Eddie problems onto a piece of paper and then "freezing them out" in ice cubes. Bennie said that Eddie always had a few trays in the freezer section of the refrigerator that they were covered with a paper warning "DO NOT TOUCH!"[1]

Despite his perceived need to conduct these binding spells, Eddie felt that his happiness was virtually complete. Unfortunately, this optimism did not last. By mid-January he had been laid off from his job at BookMasters, yet another victim of the recession that plagued New York City. He had not worked long enough to qualify for unemployment compensation, and so he was once again penniless and forced to scramble for work. During this period Eddie suffered from bouts of severe, brooding depression, leading Bennie to think that Eddie might have been a borderline manic-depressive (now termed "bi-polar"). His mood wasn't helped by the antagonistic tone of a letter received from CES secretary Ron Myron who was troubled by the fact that important church correspondence was going unanswered; Eddie, as the only CES Priest on the East Coast, was responsible for inquiries originating from the entire northeastern United States. Myron pointedly informed the head of the New York Temple that he was developing a reputation for unresponsiveness within the church. Eddie's reply was equally blunt, telling Ron that much of his time was taken up trying to find work, adding that "I have fallen in love, and whatever spare moments I do have are spent, needless to say, NOT writing."[2]

In trying to explain why he was falling behind on correspondence, Buczynski also informed Myron that Herman was still not forwarding Eddie's mail from Brooklyn Heights and also voiced the suspicion that Herman was secretly destroying it, rather than holding it for pickup. To be fair, Eddie was not the only Church member having trouble keeping up with correspondence. Harold Moss admitted to readers of *Green Egg* that "CES tries to answer every letter within 24 hours, but doesn't succeed all of the time. Some letters have sat in my basket for a year or so."[3] Nevertheless, communications issues were to dog Eddie throughout the coming year as he failed to keep up with the correspondence expected of him as the New York representative of the CES. The people in and around New York City who made initial inquiries to the church had been directed to Eddie for follow-up, and his failure to contact some of these interested parties in a timely manner (or at all) led them to complain about Buczynski to CES headquarters in Burbank. For within the CES, Eddie's perceived unresponsiveness and laxity reinforced their earlier misgivings about his suitability for the Priesthood.

By mid-February, fortune began smiling once more in Eddie's direction when he landed a job as an office boy with J. Aron and Company, a commodities trading company on Wall Street that specialized in gold and silver futures and coffee.[4,5] The business of precious metals futures was booming in those times of economic uncertainty, and Eddie's position paid quite well despite his menial status as a mail room worker, fetcher of coffee, and occasional messenger for the traders in the Cocoa exchange. Between this job and Bennie's at Chase Bank, the two had enough income to live comfortably. Eddie's job could be demanding at times, but it allowed him to get outside a lot and also gave him access to copying machines, which he used for his personal research and writings. Herman had also begun to forward all of the correspondence that had been piling up for Eddie at the Warlock Shop, allowing him to begin catching up with the backlog, although he never seemed to completely satisfy Ron Myron. *(Ibid n#5)* Freed once more from the scramble for basic survival, Eddie began writing again, and by early March he had finished typing up the final addition to the Egyptian rituals that he had prepared for the New York Temple. He sent off this addendum of ritual, prayers, blessings and guidance to Harold Moss, who wrote back that Martha Adler was very impressed with the results. Moss assured Eddie that his long-overdue ordination certificate would be signed and in the mail by Monday, March 24, "barring Isis' intervention."[6]

Despite Eddie's welcome additions to the church's storehouse of writings, it had become clear in the past months that the New York Temple and School weren't developing as Buczynski and the CES Board had hoped. Although New York City had a rich history of flirting with the outer veils of the Egyptian religion (witness the past presence of Aleister Crowley and Madame Blavatsky, both of whom had a strong attraction to Isis), and despite the world-class Egyptian exhibit at the New York Metropolitan Museum of Art and the excellent Egyptology program at nearby Pennsylvania State University, the Egyptian religion, as offered by the CES, simply did not attract a great deal of serious, which is to say committed, interest. There were perhaps several reasons for New York's tepid response.

Egypt has generally been considered a very mysterious, a very exotic and a very dead place given the press's morbid emphasis on mummies, tombs and treasure. By contrast, the civilizations of Classical Greece and Rome continue to live on, in however diffuse a manner, within our own society, and their stories are a living cornerstone of our education, art and government. Egypt's location in Africa and the ancient Near East has made its religion and mythology feel uncomfortably foreign to most Americans who, when they think about it at all, do so through the prism of the Biblical Exodus, complete with Charleton Heston wagging his wand at Pharaoh every Easter. In fact Greece and Rome were far more dependent upon slave labor than Egypt ever was, but history is often unfair (just as opinions are often uninformed). As a result, few people gave serious consideration to the religion of ancient Egypt as a choice for a living body of mythology and ritual. This is not to say that those few who did follow the path laid down by the CES were not sincere; the CES presented some of the most elaborate, beautiful and heartfelt rituals to grace modern Neo-Pagan practice. But it takes a person with a certain flexibility of imagination and outlook to be able to lift him or herself completely into a culture that has not been seen on this earth for the better part of seventeen hundred years. Early on, the CES recognized this impediment to the church's ability to attract a wider audience. However, it was never really able to overcome this hurdle, and indeed the church remains quite small to this day.[7]

Also by this time, the field of alternatives was already rather crowded, even with the large number of potential students in New York City. At least five Pagan Way groups existed in the greater metropolitan area by 1974 — Brooklyn Heights, Bronx, and Manhattan in New York City; Commack on Long Island; and Paterson, New Jersey — as well as a large number of covens and other groups, such as yoga centers, Krishna Consciousness devotees, and gurus with their circles of disciples. These groups competed avidly for the admittedly small segment of the population that was receptive to their messages. One might also postulate that a religion birthed by a riparian culture on the edge of a desert might play better in the dry heat of southern California, where the CES was headquartered, than in the chill winters of New York City.

Nevertheless, some in the CES placed the blame squarely on Eddie for failing to follow through on his commitments to the church: "Ed claimed to be working very hard and accomplishing a lot, but we never saw much to substantiate this. Our quondam secretary, Ronald Myron, jumped on Ed over this lack of substantiation."[8] Whether Eddie's heart was completely in the job or not, the CES was not entirely fair in making him bear the cumulative burden for the New York area's failure area to live up to the CES' expectations, a failure that more likely began with the sudden collapse of Burt and Jane Cicciotto's efforts. Regardless, these objections to Eddie's performance probably kept him from receiving his ordination certificate in March. Instead, in mid-April 1975, Myron sent a letter to Buczynski that was extremely critical of his performance as a Priest in the CES. He further questioned the direction in which Eddie was taking the cult of Isis. Eddie fired off a bitter complaint to Harold Moss later that month:[9]

> *I refuse to be insulted any further by this man. Under the circumstances, I have been doing as much as humanly possible in the Church here in New York. If C.E.S. does not require my services anymore — let me know. I also refuse to be drawn into an internal "bickering" in any religion, anymore (having had enough of it in Wicca)...*

Eddie ended the letter by threatening to resign if he was forced to deal any further with Ron Myron. Moss attempted to soothe Buczynski's feelings, pointing out that Myron's manner was often brusque with others in the church. But Harold firmly reminded Eddie that Ron, as the church secretary, was required to communicate with Eddie and other Church officials, and that Eddie was obligated to respond to Ron's requests for information that was required by the state of California. On the subject of Myron's concerns about Buczynski's teachings and practices, Moss wrote, "Ron says to me that he is concerned that you are too 'witchy' and that you tend to substitute generalizations for what he would like to see in the way of specific teachings about Isis — his Goddess as well as yours. He is urging you to be more frank with him. ... It's a shame that he rubs you the wrong way. But he is a member of the Isis group in CES and the two of you will have to find some way to get along, because you both have information that the other needs. You will meet people in your future Church work who are much harder to get along with than Ron. ... But, as a Priest of Isis, you do not have the option of turning away any seeker or worshipper from your door, and certainly do not have the option of refusing to discuss your religion with another member of your cult within the church. Something must be worked out."[10]

Moss suggested that the two men avoid writing to one another except for official church business. It is not known whether either of them took this advice, but for a short while things did calm down somewhat. Buczynski was also told that the church officials recognized his efforts in

New York "and are very pleased by them." However, on the subject of the much-delayed ordination certificate, there was grim news. Moss noted that they had made an appointment with Martha Adler to finish inscribing the certificate, "but the Gods intervened — pointedly. There can be no doubt that the series of weird 'coincidences' that have prevented us from completing your certificate can no longer be dismissed as accidents. Perhaps the Gods are saving you for yet one more crucial test, and intend the arrival of your certificate as a new reaffirmation of your mission." *(Ibid n#10)* Whether the Nile Goddess personally intervened or a more worldly power chose to do so is unclear; however, the ordination certificate never did make it into Eddie's hands.[11]

June brought one more minor tiff between Eddie and Ron. An alleged seeker had written to CES headquarters complaining that Eddie had been taking up to six months to answer mail from him, and that when he did respond it was usually perfunctorily. Myron aksed Buczynski whether his performance would improve or whether Eddie would rather limit his church duties to New York City alone, instead of the entire northeastern district.[12] Eddie chose not to respond to that letter, instead writing a reply to an inquiry that was sent to all district representatives on June 15 asking for a status report on active church contacts. To that letter, Eddie replied that he had handled all of the approximately sixty referrals in his district by sending out two introductory letters to each contactee, and noted that he was in active correspondence with seekers in Port Jefferson Station and Jamaica in New York, Philadelphia and Barnesboro in Pennsylvania, and Laconia in New Hampshire. He also informed Myron that the seeker who had prompted the rebuke on June 5 was in fact a sixteen-year-old dabbler with whom he had been corresponding since before Eddie joined the CES. Buczynski concluded, "He needs a pen pal, not a priest ... I write when I have spare time."[13]

Unbeknownst to Moss or the other officials of the CES, and despite his consistent disparagement of the politics associated with its practice, Eddie had begun drifting back into Wica during the summer of 1975. Buczynski's taking up the pentacle once more was a foreshadowing of what was to happen later that summer. On August 1, 1975, he submitted his resignation from the active priesthood of the CES. In his resignation letter, Eddie noted that his work and living arrangements had become overwhelming and that he could no longer find time to attend to his duties as a priest of Isis. Rather than slow down the progress of the church in the east, Buczynski believed that it was better to resign: "I cannot help but feel that I cannot, during this lifetime, fulfill, satisfactorily, the task set before me by Mighty Isis — I am just not knowledgeable enough. Many are called, few are chosen!"[14]

It was not entirely clear to Moss or the others what motivated Eddie's decision to abandon the CES. In truth, he was being asked to handle only a moderate amount of correspondence as the representative of the northeast district of the CES. Still, Eddie had no office space for processing it within the crowded confines of the apartment he and Bennie shared with four other men. Bennie recalls that Eddie was constantly typing letters during this period, and this mundane paper-pushing may not have been what he had in mind when he signed up for the position. Perhaps Eddie had also become fed up with his treatment by the CES bureaucracy. This was most notably symbolized by the CES' inability to deliver his promised ordination certificate after a year of waiting. Or it may be that he perceived his own lack of progress in building a sustainable New York Temple as a personal failure. In the end, Eddie's admission that he was just not up to the task might have been a ruse to cover both his frustration over the personal and interpersonal hurdles that seemingly barred his way in the CES and his renewed interest in Wica.

In his resignation letter to Harold Moss, Buczynski also wrote that he was planning to move from New York City to New Orleans. However, while this move would have taken him from the northeast district of the CES, he could still have remained a Priest of Isis. Church representatives were thinly scattered, and such a move would normally have opened up an opportunity to serve another district, if he had wanted to. On the other hands, Eddie may not have seriously intended to move to New Orleans. Bennie Geraci stated that he personally had no intention of moving back home to Louisiana at that time, and Eddie had not yet visited the city. So it may be that Buczynski merely daydreamed about escaping the political swamp in which he found himself but had not actually planned to do so, at least not as far as Bennie knew.[15]

Harold expressed sorrow for Eddie's decision, but also remarked that the church was in the process of retrenching and directing its energy toward goals closer to its corporate base. Buczynski recommended one of his current students for consideration as a replacement to run the New York Temple, but Moss was noncommittal, writing that the church did not know the person in question and that person should begin the process of establishing his own relationship with the CES. The student apparently did not follow up, and the New York Temple failed to survive the loss of its founder. Although Eddie had stated that he wanted to remain a member of the CES, once he resigned his post he dropped off the church's radar, and the prospect for establishing a permanent presence in New York seemed to vanish with him. "It vanished in a tick," according to Moss. "We had no contact with New York after Ed left CES." *(Ibid n#8)*

One final issue of *Esbat* was printed in the last combined issue of *Earth Religion News*, which was published in May 1976, some nine months after Buczynski's withdrawal from the CES. This article was probably slated for publication in the summer of 1975; however, a lack of finances resulted in another lapse in the *Earth Religion News* printing schedule, and the article remained in the slushpile with the other submittals until Slater could afford the final run of the newspaper.[16] This final edition of *Esbat* deals mostly with what Eddie refers to as the adaptation or restoration of the practice of sexual rites in the special context of the Egyptian religion. To make his case for an Egyptian practice of sex magick, Eddie relied heavily on the practices of peoples outside ancient Kemet, such as the Hebrew Qaballah, the Tantras, the Tao, and Gnostic and Sufi teachings.

If Buczynski had been the head of the Cult of Isis, his article would likely have caused a great deal of consternation within the CES, since it appears to confirm Ron Myron's belief that Eddie was trying to incorporate sexual practices into the core of the Kemetic faith. Myron himself resigned from his position and membership in the CES in July 1976 for personal reasons, but not before stirring controversy by publicly laying out his criticism of the practice of sex magick within the Neo-Pagan community.[17, 18] Despite the CES' lack of interest in this topic, Eddie's research in this field and his time in the Church were to pay dividends in the future, for he had now touched upon all of the concepts that he would later use to develop his final contribution to modern Witchcraft.

Chapter 22: Last Dance, Last Chance

Of Quarrels, Cats and Poppets

Eddie and Herman spent some time during the spring and summer of 1975 patching up things between them. Although their relationship would never be the same as when they were lovers, the two were civil with one another, and they gradually adjusted themselves to being friends. Despite now holding down a full-time job at J. Aron, Buczynski managed to occasionally teach classes and fill in behind the counter at the Warlock Shop after the dust had settled. Several years later, when asked about his past dealings with Slater, Eddie was heard to quip, "Oh, I was in business with Herman once, but I forgave him."[1]

After their breakup, the men had moved out of the upstairs apartment at the shop and back into Slater's old apartment on Atlantic Avenue before Eddie moved back home to Ozone Park. "I was only at [Herman's] apartment once or twice to drop off the day's receipts," Ken Dalton recalled. "It was, on those occasions, dark, poorly lit, cluttered, messy, and again, not too clean. By then Eddie had been gone for months. The building itself was (is) old. A narrow walk-up plagued by mice and roaches. (Quite a contrast to the apartment in Queens shared by Eddie and Bennie!)"[2] After Slater and Buczynski had moved out, the front bedroom of the Warlock Shop apartment was converted into an office and mailroom. "The apartment above the shop was a post-cyclonic disaster. Messy, cluttered, not particularly clean," Dalton continues. "Upstairs was just as ramshackle as the first floor. I remember that there was a cot of sorts, tons of papers strewn about, a rusty file cabinet or two and a desk. The place always looked like the aftermath of a natural disaster." *(Ibid n#2)*

The back room became a bedroom for one of the shop's employees, a slightly pickled but gentle redneck named Glenn, who was known for stashing pint bottles in various nooks and crannies throughout the shop. Glenn was a thin, blonde southern man in his twenties who had a serious crush on Ria Farnham. This disturbed Ria, partly because Glenn was in the habit of writing unsolicited (and bad) poetry and love letters to her even though he knew she was a married woman, but also because he had slept in a coffin in the basement storeroom when he first came to work for Herman. Glenn was also known to occasionally sell the fish bones from his dinner to customers as talismans, an idea that Herman was not averse to copying on occasion.[3,4]

Herman was lonely after Eddie left, even though he wasn't always alone. He never got over his feelings for Buczynski, but was also never able to find a substitute that would allow him to move on. As a result, many of Herman's subsequent lovers were just pale imitations of Eddie. Given his age, his wandering eye, and his limp, of which he was extremely self-conscious, Herman had some serious issues with his own self-image, often leading him to seek companionship at bars catering to rough trade and hustlers.[5] Some of the men he met ended up moving in with him; however, these relationships always seemed to end badly.

Ria tells the story of how she once responded to a call from Herman, who desperately begged her to help get rid of a fellow upon whom he had previously asked Ria to cast a love spell. This German man, to whom Ria refers as "the Frankenstein monster," stood six feet five inches, from his knee-length black riding boots to his shaved, skull-like head. Herman really wanted this guy, and Ria had constructed two anatomically-correct poppets, one of Herman and the other of his beau, and bound them together. Unfortunately for Herman, not only was Ria's spell marvelously efficacious, but the fellow towards whom it was directed was exquisitely nuts.

"Frankenstein" had convinced Herman to purchase a bunch of equipment so that they could extract their own oils for the shop. "So Herman has all of this Frankenstein equipment in the back of the shop and he was trying to figure out how to extract oils," Ria recalls. "Then the guy turned out to be a nightmare and Herman wanted rid of him." Ria brought the poppets to the shop and conducted a ritual to break the connection and make the former object of Herman's affections go away. "So I do the whole ritual and take the poppets apart, and Herman grabs the guy's poppet and feeds it to his dog, Ptolemy," Ria continues. The love spell was overpowered and the now-former beau was sent packing.[6] Herman would later recall the event, saying, "I did love magick once, and I was sorry. I always tell people [to] never do love magick, 'cause once you get the person you can't get rid of them (laughing)."[7]

His own experiences with relationships could sometimes make Herman cynical and unlikely to empathize with the personal problems of others. He could be the dearest man in the world one moment, and its nastiest bitch in the next. *(Ibid n#5)* "If you didn't have a good reason to cry, [you didn't] cry in front of him." Ria remembers. "He'd say, 'Get over it, dear. Get your tits together!'"[8] Yet he also cared for and supported his fellow coveners when they truly needed help.

Well into 1975, the Warlock Shop was still suffering from the repercussions of Burt Cicciotto's alleged pecuniary misdeeds of 1974. While things weren't fantastic, at least the shop wasn't sinking beneath a tide of red ink. One indication of the state of the business was how deeply Slater had gotten into arrears in his buying account with Samuel Weiser, Inc. over the course of that year. "When I started working at Samuel Weiser's, I was under the impression that Herman had carte blanche," remembers Jim Wasserman. "Originally Don Weiser handled Herman's credit personally, then I took on his account. It seemed to me that Donald was very warm to him and [Herman] could basically do whatever he wanted. I ran his account for one year until one day Don was horrified to find that it was up to $3500." Slater graciously settled the account when asked to do so.[9]

But there was no money left over to continue publishing the Earth Religions Supplies catalogue, let alone the *Earth Religion News*. As a result, catalogue sales, which had been a significant percentage of the shop's overall income, were declining. With the newspaper down, if not out, Herman had also lost his bully pulpit. This didn't stop him from responding to the jabs of others or from picking fights, sometimes unwisely; he just had to do it on someone else's turf. One example was the unfortunate confrontation between Slater and feminist Witch Z. Budapest.

Beginning in May 1975, several occult newspapers began picking up on the story of Z. Budapest's arrest in February of that year for violating the Los Angeles ordinance against fortune-telling.[10,11] She was a refugee of the 1956 Hungarian Revolution who eventually found her way to Los Angeles. In 1970, she became a part of the women's liberation movement and founded the Susan B. Anthony coven of what came to be known as feminist Dianic Witchcraft. By the time of her arrest, Budapest was on the verge of publishing *The Feminist Book of Lights and Shadows* (1975), the book that would make her name in feminist Neo-Pagan circles. At this point in her life, however, the Hungarian feminist was still a relative unknown. Her arrest by the Los Angeles police, who had vowed to shut down her Craft store, catapulted Budapest into the national spotlight in the struggle for Neo-Pagan civil rights.

Many Neo-Pagans viewed the Budapest fortune-telling case as an example of things to come. The general feeling was that if authorities could get away with enforcing this type of medieval ordinance in a major metropolitan area like Los Angeles, similar laws throughout the country would prove difficult, if not impossible, to fight.[12] Furthermore, Budapest and her attorney asserted, the real reason that Budapest was arrested was her high-profile role in the women's liberation movement in Los Angeles. As Budapest told *Fate* magazine, "If prediction is against the law in this country, then why haven't people like Criswell, Jeane Dixon, and Sybil Leek been arrested? What about all these psychic seminars all over the place? No, they were out to get me."[13] While it isn't at all clear that the authorities had singled out Budapest for enforcement, *Green Egg*'s follow-up article detailing the trial and subsequent conviction was sympathetic to her cause, and the Neo-Pagan community was urged to contribute money for a court challenge to overturn the verdict.[14]

But not everyone took Budapest's side in the battle, and one of those dissenters was Herman Slater. In dismissing her appeal to the community for help, Slater made two main points. First, he insisted that Budapest, in engaging in a quasi-commercial activity — reading tarot cards, whether for donations or for fee — was in effect "selling the Craft" in violation of the Wiccan Laws. "'Friends of the Craft' which I represent does not go for the charging of monies for divination as a copout that it is part of the religion,"

Slater asserted. "Money & Craft do not mix and it is against all precepts of the Craft."[15, 16] This was the same objection that Slater had raised during his fight with the Frosts in 1973-74 concerning teaching the Craft for payment.

Yet these were odd claims for Slater to make given that he and Buczynski were engaging in the act of "selling the Craft" daily through their various business activities. Indeed, before the embezzlement and theft which had brought them to the brink of financial ruin, Herman had proudly boasted of the success of his business to reporters when interviewed by a reporter for the *National Star* in late 1973. "A year and a half ago we had $2000 invested in the store," said Slater. "Now we have $80,000 of stock."[17] Hans Holzer, when writing about the *Earth Religion News*, the Warlock Shop, and its "fascinating" catalogue, said, "Make no mistake about it, Herman and Ed have made Witchcraft pay, and what they have started as a sideline has become a major occupation for them."[18] Within a year, Herman would even install tarot readers for hire in the store, taking a cut from the fees they charged to read for paying clients.

In his second, and perhaps more telling, objection, Slater declared that Budapest was a violent and anti-male radical who was unworthy of the community's support. Writing as the President of the Friends of the Craft, Slater stated that Budapest's claim of "'RELIGIOUS DISCRIMINATION' is just an effective cover for her Violent and Man Hating Tendencies." According to Herman, it all came down to "MONEY & QUESTIONABLE POLITICS under the guise of 'Religious Discrimination' in the name of the Goddess and 'Her Hereditary Representative' Z. Budapest! Pagan leaders should speak out against this Woman & her Bigoted, Violent, Man hating ideals, or we will be grouped in with the Violent Radicals and lose any political gain we have made in the last few years as Legitimate Earth Religions."[19] Herman also expressed contempt for rebels who retreated to the community for support when their needs outstripped their resources. In this, he was merely communicating his disdain for people who couldn't dig themselves out of their own messes, as he had had to do so often as a business owner.

On the surface, it is hard to understand why Z. Budapest inspired this level of visceral reaction in Herman Slater. Herman was certainly not a "woman hater", a charge often leveled at gay men by straight society (and some feminists); he worked with women in his store, submitted to women in his covens and was friends with women in his personal life. Nor was Slater opposed to lesbians, for he encouraged an open lesbian to join the Farnhams' coven at roughly the same time he was fulminating over the negative image that Budapest's lesbian feminist Goddess worshippers might give the Craft.[20] Herman was also a firm believer in equality between the sexes. However, he was adamantly opposed to the concept of segregation, either in society or in the gay rights movement.

With regard to the practice of Witchcraft, Slater believed that the sexes should both be present in Circle and equal before the Gods. Many of the early proponents of the feminist Goddess movement, particularly on the West Coast, were both anti-establishment and anti-male in their worldview, thus placing them at odds with the philosophy of Gardnerian Wica and many of its spiritual fellow-travelers. As John Lauritsen pointed out in 1976, straight feminists of the day were just as likely to oppress gay men as the rest of straight society.[21] Thus it seems likely that, in Herman's view, lesbian separatism of the type represented by Z. Budapest — radical, revolutionary, and vocal — was not just dangerous to the public image of what he called the "Legitimate Earth Religions," it was also an affront to the Gods. Yet, as a young historian named Laurel Thatcher Ulrich would observe in 1976, "Well-behaved women seldom make history."[22]

Despite his attempt to label her as a "radical" (the term itself was more an acknowledgement than a denunciation on both coasts in the mid-1970s), Budapest's mild reply to Slater made the Warlock Shop proprietor look rabid by comparison, and his insinuations that she was a radical bomb-thrower seemed rather silly. "I certainly hate to lose you as an ally," she wrote in *Green Egg*, "especially when the foundation of your rejection is rooted in shortsightedness and may be a bit of the emotional backlash that the Women's Movement has sparked amongst even the best of males. I feel you [focused on] our 'slogan' [Hands Off Women's Religion] and threw out the baby with the wash. ... I pray to Athena to awaken your consciousness and challenge you to influence your times along with us as an ally and not as a misguided pagan who internalizes his oppression and can't see political advancement for being blinded by his hubris."[23]

Tim Zell responded to this exchange with an editorial that, while supporting Budapest's court fight, also raised questions about the seeming lack of respect accorded to the God by her group in marked contrast to the honor they gave to the Goddess. He also dismissed her assertion that a matriarchal society was superior to a patriarchal one, writing, "A revolution which merely changes the genders of the rulers is no revolution at all! Matriarchy is just as patristic as patriarchy, and we oppose both."[24]

Slater wasn't alone in his view of this issue. His contempt for Budapest's cause was echoed by, of all people, Gavin Frost. It is hard to imagine Frost and Slater making common cause on any issue, but in the case of Z. Budapest they did, though coming at it from different angles. Frost advocated for Witches to work within the system instead of pretending that the system didn't apply to them and then alleging discrimination when their tactics failed to impress the authorities. He also said that people in the community should "stop using the Craft and its associated churches as a pressure group for other causes like Gay Lib and Lesbianism ... Let them fight their own battles; we have more than enough to do."[25]

Gavin's reasoning was essentially the same as that used to justify the split between the Gay Liberation Front and the Gay Activists Alliance in

1969, and even Herman did not publicly fault him for it. Isaac Bonewits, writing as the President of the Aquarian Anti-Defamation League, also criticized Budapest's grandstanding and the alleged misinformation she was spreading about the Craft, as well as the appearance that she was using her case to advance the feminist cause at the expense of the Neo-Pagan community at large.[26] Slater's opposition to Budapest, while heartfelt, was in retrospect an unfortunate diversion. But Slater's introduction to *Pagan Rituals III* (1989), where he wrote, "*East Coast Feminists* thank you for opening a door, *West Coast Feminists* thank you by kicking you in the ... (well, you all know what!)," demonstrated that the animus resulting from the spat was long-lasting.[27]

Long-lasting might also describe the fallow period in which Ria and David Farnham found themselves. They had kept the former Brooklyn Heights Coven together for occasional sabbats after moving it to the Bronx, but they were generally not active. Patty and Mike Salucca were initiated into the coven in the Bronx in the latter half of 1974, and by 1975 they were running an Outer Court coven in Queens that answered to Ria even though she was not currently running an inner court coven.[28] The Farnhams still worked part-time at the Warlock Shop, and it was Herman who eventually lit a torch under them to become active once more. Around the middle of June 1975, Slater telephoned Ria out of the blue, and noted that it had been a while since she had run a coven. To entice Ria to consider picking it up again, he suggested that she and David might want to meet with a woman he had met that day at the shop.

Carol Bulzone had dropped by the Warlock Shop in order to sell a large brass ankh altar piece she had previously purchased there, which was likely one of those that Eddie had had specially manufactured during his involvement with the CES. She had just returned to New York City after spending time with Laurie Cabot in Salem, Massachusetts. Newly arrived and unemployed, she had hoped to raise some ready cash to help with rent.

Bulzone had her initial brush with the Craft on the first night of Woodstock on August 15, 1969. She was attracted to the sounds of tambourines and chanting and stumbled across a ritual at a huge bonfire where a large group of people were dancing. In 1970, she started going to Salem on weekends, where she met Laurie Cabot. She was befriended by Laurie and became "one of the kids," helping the Craft leader with decorations for her Witches Ball and hanging out in Salem searching for a Wiccan coven. "I did this for a couple of years, back and forth, back and forth," she recalls. "Eventually, I moved there for a period of about three months with a lover, but it didn't pan out and so I came back home and went to the Warlock Shop." *(Ibid n#20)* Laurie and Carol had planned to open a shop in Salem, but the landlord with whom they were negotiating stole their deposit money, so their plans for the business were stillborn. Although Cabot invited her to remain, Carol had not found a coven after several years of searching. Carol's relationship with her girlfriend had also failed at this time and, frustrated with both the Craft and with love, she gave up and returned to New York.

Carol had first visited the Warlock Shop in 1972 after seeing an ad in the *Village Voice*. She didn't feel a pull to the place or its owners at that time, but did periodically stop by to see what was new. On her return visit in 1975, she told Herman her story about returning to New York with nothing to show for it and he asked her, "But what about the Craft?" Carol's reply was blunt. "What do you mean 'What about the Craft?' Fuck the Craft! I've busted my ass for four years now and I just can't [find a coven]. I'm on my own." *(Ibid n#20)* Although Herman had a firm dislike of Laurie Cabot, he took a shine to Carol and suggested that she speak with Ria and David. He even went so far as to give her the Farnhams' telephone number. After Carol left, Herman called Ria and gave her Carol's phone number and told her she should call.

The next day Ria telephoned Carol and set up a meeting for that evening. Carol nervously drove up to the Bronx and knocked on the door, not sure what to expect. Instead of this matronly older woman she had been envisioning, the gorgeous, dark-haired Ria answered the door in a red, one-piece swimsuit. Carol was quite taken by Ria's looks and noted that, "The attraction was quite mutual." *(Ibid n#20)* The trio hit it off immediately and spent most evenings together for the next two weeks. One night they went out to a bar, and while building a pyramid out of their empty beer cans, Carol began talking about the Craft to whoever would listen.

As the evening wore on, David and Ria gradually grew more concerned because Carol was regaling complete strangers with the details of Witchcraft mysteries that she shouldn't even have known about. Finally at their wit's end, the couple each grabbed an arm and escorted Carol back to their apartment. There, at 5:30 AM on July 9, 1975, Carol was brought into the Wica tradition and elevated through the Second and Third Degrees.[29] *(Ibid n#20, 28)* For her Craft name, she chose *Miw*, Egyptian for "Cat," which had been her nickname since childhood. Afterward, the three went to the Bronx Botanical Garden, where they believed that they heard Pan's pipes playing softly in the morning air. From that point forward, they were leading a functioning inner court coven once again.

Eddie was also gradually working his way back into the Craft during this period. Despite his misgivings concerning the petty aspects of Witchcraft (or, to be fair, the pettiness of some of its practitioners), Eddie's sabbatical from that spiritual path had been brief, lasting for less than a year. Even before he announced his resignation from the CES in August, Buczynski was making new connections with other Witches in New York. One of these was a forty-three-year-old housewife and commercial voiceover artist from Huntington Station on Long Island.

Sheila Saperton (Craft name *Khrysis*) had come to the Craft late in life, spurred on by a failure of her twelve-year marriage and an unrequited love affair that followed.[30] Initiated at the same time as Judy and Tommy Kneitel, she studied in the Bucklands' Pagan Way group in Brentwood, New York from 1970 until the Kneitels took over the coven in late 1972.

Saperton had a fundamental disagreement with how the Kneitels were running the coven, and she left for greener pastures without taking any further degrees.[31] Early in 1973, Saperton formed a circle with several other like-minded local practitioners. She stayed in touch for a while with Raymond Buckland, who occasionally sent her rituals he had written; however, the two eventually drifted apart. The coven to which Sheila belonged broke up by early 1974 as several of its other members sought initiation into the "real thing." She continued to practice by herself, filling in her time by lecturing at universities and appearing on television as a spokesperson for the Craft.

Sheila had not heard from Raymond Buckland for almost a year when, out of the blue, he sent her a copy of the Seax-Wica information sheet he had published in the May 1974 edition of *Green Egg*.[32] Excited by what she read, Sheila telephoned him to ask about the new tradition. In response, Buckland invited her to visit him in Weirs Beach, New Hampshire. Accompanied by her older son, Sheila traveled to New Hampshire in mid-May. Raymond answered her questions and allowed her to read the manuscript of his book, *The Tree*, which was to be published later that year. Sheila was pleased by the fact that the priest and priestess in Seax-Wica were co-equal and interchangeable.

"I had always felt that the role of the priest was little more than 'Altar Boy' until now," she wrote in the *Earth Religion News*. "It felt good; it felt right for me; it was where I belonged."[33] With Ray and Joan as witnesses, she self-initiated into Seax-Wica and became its first initiate, taking the Craft name *Khrysis*. During the initiation ritual, Sheila read "The Myth of the Goddess" from Buckland's book manuscript. This was, the tradition's founder remarked, the first time that it had been read in circle. Saperton wrote of her moving experience in the pages of *Earth Religion News* in June. By August 1974, Saperton announced the formation of a Seax-Wica coven in Huntington Station, New York.[34]

It was at about this same time that twenty-two-year-old Ken Dalton walked into the Warlock Shop for the first time. "As best as I can remember, there was an article in one of the New York newspapers about paganism in the City, with a bit about the shop and a picture of Eddie," Dalton recalls. "I do remember taking the subway to Brooklyn Heights, going to the shop for the first time and meeting Eddie. ... [I]t was he who put me in touch with Ray Buckland, with whom I had extensive correspondence. Ray had just written the 'The Tree' and Eddie thought I might be interested in exploring [Seax-Wica]. ... Eddie viewed it as a relatively decent introduction to paganism, a sort of witchcraft with training wheels. ... I don't remember now if it was Eddie or (probably) Ray himself who forwarded my info to Sheila." *(Ibid n#2)*

Dalton received an invitation to attend the August 8, 1974 meeting Saperton had called at her home in Huntington Station to discuss the formation of a Seax-Wica coven on Long Island.[35] "There were probably about a dozen people there, and that was the basis of the initial coven. I was a member from that evening on," writes Dalton. "What a wonderful group of people! Mostly in their early 20's, some a few years younger, one or two older people, including one married couple. Sheila was in her mid 40's at that time and lived there with her 2 sons. We met in the living room which could be sectioned off from the rest of the house with drapes/curtains. We'd follow Buckland's instructions and spend most of the night afterwards drinking mead. I often had a guitar and we'd all get a little drunk and sing together. Remember, we were still the Woodstock Nation at that time." *(Ibid n#2)*

The first person Sheila Saperton initiated was a man in his forties who took the position of high priest of the coven. Taking the post of *Thegn* (scribe) was Ken Dalton, the second person Sheila initiated. The coven was run using as a guide a copy of the unpublished manuscript for *The Tree* which Buckland had given to Saperton.[36] This was the second Seax-Wica coven to be formed (the first being the one run by Ray and Joan Buckland). Because of this, there was a certain amount of experimentation and shaking out that took place. Participants in the rites of Seax-Wica covens are usually robed for ritual but Sheila, perhaps already wishing a return to the Gardnerian practices with which she was familiar, eventually began to lobby the members of the group to practice skyclad. As Ken Dalton remembers, "Some [were] in favor, some opposed. Eventually we came up with the 'compromise' of going skyclad but with a belt which suspended the seax (athame). Eddie thought this was just plain silliness when he first heard of it. When he visited and saw it, he changed his mind, pronouncing it to be quite sexy!" *(Ibid n#2)*

The first crisis weathered by the new coven was the loss of its High Priest. A married man in his forties, he was forced to withdraw not long after the coven began practicing skyclad by his wife, who had become suspicious of what was going on at the Sabbats. Sheila Saperton asked Ken Dalton to move up and take over the position, which he did. At Dalton's invitation, Eddie Buczynski occasionally visited the coven as a guest in the first half of 1975, although he was never initiated into Seax-Wica. There was no need for secrecy since Buckland had published the rites in late 1974.

The Huntington Coven

It isn't clear when Saperton and Buczynski first met. Dalton believes that it may have been at his instigation. "I could be very seriously mistaken about this, but I think he decided to be involved in the Huntington group following my suggestion that he come and visit," he recalled. "I know that afterwards I'd almost always pick him up and we'd drive to Long Island together, usually with Godwyn [my girlfriend] in the beginning, and then by myself. This is when he lived in Brooklyn and then later when he was at his mom's place in Queens." *(Ibid n#2)* Sheila may have first come to Eddie Buczynski's attention because she had allegedly been the target of a smear campaign, and he would have felt empathy for the fellow former Gardnerian. The two would have known of one another informally, both through the auspices of the *Earth Religion News* and via the inveterate gossip of the local grapevine.

A friend and initiate of Saperton asserts that the Long Island Gardnerians were spreading terrible stories about the Huntington Station resident.[37] Ken Dalton confirms that relations between Saperton and supporters of the Kneitels were strained. "Sheila was originally involved with [the Kneitels], but she came to be very negative about them and was very mistrustful," said Dalton. "Theos somehow became a Voldemort — like 'She Who Must Not Be Named.'" *(Ibid n#2)* Saperton may have become a particular focus of the Kneitels' ire because of her continuing friendship with Ray Buckland, whom the Long Island Line had come to despise. Whatever black mark this may have placed against her name, however, likely paled in comparison to her decision to join with Buckland's new spiritual tradition. The Kneitels at this time were making no secret of their displeasure over Ray Buckland's actions, attacking his founding of the Seax-Wica tradition in the pages of *Green Egg* and elsewhere.[38] To have Saperton, a former member of the Brentwood Coven (rejected or not), turn her back on Gardnerian Wica and publicly embrace Seax-Wica as its first "convert" was perhaps too much to bear.

Likewise, relations between Eddie and the Long Island crowd were still unsettled. Despite Eddie's assurances to Harold Moss in September 1974 that things had been patched up between him and the Kneitels, there are indications that such was not the case. Ken Dalton asserts that a lot of back and forth sniping was still taking place between the two groups at that time. "Like so many sectarian issues, the competing claims of orthodoxy were paramount," writes Dalton. "Eddie and Herman frequently accused the Long Island group's leadership of being un-authentic and motivated by greed and a desire to control the Craft in the Northeast, if not in the United States as a whole." *(Ibid n#2)* Saperton and Buczynski most likely found common cause in their status as outsiders.

Saperton's stint in Seax-Wica ended up lasting less than a year before she returned to Gardnerian Wica.[39] By the summer of 1975, Eddie and Sheila were already discussing the possibility of transitioning the coven from Seax-Wica to Gardnerian practice. "With Eddie present we were moving increasingly in that direction anyway," Dalton recalls, "and I know that I was happy with that progression. Sheila was of course ecstatic." *(Ibid n#2)* It took some time to convince the rest of the group, but once the decision was made to make the switch change came swiftly. "By the late Autumn of 1975, we were functioning as a Gardnerian group with Eddie as [high priest]. ... [O]nce we transitioned to a non-Saxon tradition Eddie just assumed the role, pretty much by unspoken assent; it was a natural, organic transition without any fanfare," Dalton remembered. *(Ibid n#2)* "From my perspective it was just amazing to have him as part of the circle and was happy to cede the position to him."[40] It may be that Eddie's increasing involvement with the Huntington Coven energized him at the end of July 1975, spurring Buczynski to clear his slate by dumping the CES and its never-ending paperwork.

There is some indication that the pressure on Eddie may even have intensified during this period. He is alleged to have used two high priestesses, *Artemis* and *Thelema*, as intermediaries to contact a Witch in Great Britain both to introduce himself and to complain of his treatment at the hands of the Long Island line. This British Witch, known only as *Jana*, was supposedly a high priestess in British Traditional Witchcraft. According to Saperton initiate Curt Bargren, Buczynski corresponded with the elderly surviving members of the Dorothy Clutterbuck coven, the same coven that had brought Gerald Gardner into the Craft in 1939.[41] *(Ibid n#39)* Bargren writes that Gardner initiate Eleanor "Ray" Bone supposedly knew of this group, but that few others were aware of its existence. *Jana* identified herself as the eldest of the high priestesses and high priests of Hampshire.

Jana reportedly agreed to correspond with Eddie only after she was satisfied that he had been legitimately brought into the Craft. He was able to prove this by giving her the correct answer to the question, "How were you brought in to the Circle?"[42, 43] *Jana* wrote that she was also assured by *Thelema* that Eddie also knew the correct God and Goddess names, and that the photograph Eddie sent to *Jana* depicting him in Circle demonstrated that he was giving the correct hand sign. *Artemis* also provided *Jana* with a copy of Eddie's book which he had mailed to her. This book, according to *Jana*, was mostly in line with what she herself used, its failings being blamed on Gardner and its subsequent transmissions down the line.[44] Eddie may have believed that this contact with British Witches afforded him the opportunity to finally achieve legitimacy in British Traditional Witchcraft, and to do so via an authority that was completely independent of Monique Wilson and her Long Island downline.

Eddie's status in Gardnerian Wica had been considered illegitimate since 1973 when his initiating high priestess, Patricia Siero, had renounced her own initiation, along with Eddie's and Herman's. That was all supposed to change on August 22, 1975 when Eddie is allegedly said to have received a letter from *Jana* in response to another missive from him earlier that month complaining of further outrages taken against him. This letter and the previous hint that some of his distress was caused by a reaction to Eddie's homosexuality and its stated incompatibility with the practice of the Craft. On August 4, *Jana* wrote "Concerning your particular situation, it is not uncommon. As long as your behavior in Circle is according to the Law, it is (and always was) permissable [sic]." *(Ibid n#44)* On August 22, she wrote again to comfort Eddie regarding his situation, saying "there is little, if nothing, that you can really do about it (save trust the Gods to see you through). Remember, it cannot go on forever."[45] Seeking to help him reclaim his legitimacy, *Jana* is said to have enclosed a vouch that recognized Eddie and his downline: *(Ibid n#43)*

> *Gwydion has been properly prepared and Initiated. He has passed through the Pentacle grade and has truly passed the Test of Third. Therefore, as representative of the High Priestesses of Hampshire, I hereby vouch for and recognize him as a true High Priest and Magus. And we accept all Initiations and Elevations by his hand as being both Valid and Proper.* <u>So</u> <u>be</u> <u>it</u> <u>ardane</u>.

With the *Jana* vouch, Eddie believed that he could once more claim that he was a legitimate initiate of a line of British Traditional Witchcraft. Buczynski had the added bonus of no longer needing to concern himself with what the Long Island Line thought of him, because *Jana*'s coven supposedly predated the Bucklands' (and, hence, the Kneitels') and was based in the mother country whence Wica originated. What possible motive could Witches in Hampshire, England have for issuing a vouch to someone in the United States who they had never met? A clue may rest in an article written by Saperton, which states:[46]

> *The Witches of Southern Britain can be traced back as far as the Twelfth Century A.D. ... They are not initiating presently, nor do they want to be known by the outside world. The Elders of this tradition are aware that their numbers are dwindling in Europe and look to America for hope in carrying on their Heritage.*

Shortly after *Jana* allegedly issued the August 22 vouch, Eddie is said to have received copies of her coven's Book of Shadows. If so, he must have received it via the mail, as he did not possess a passport and lacked the means to travel outside the country. Sheila Saperton admitted that she wasn't sure that Eddie and *Jana* ever met face to face, and certainly the surviving correspondence indicates that they did not. *(Ibid n#42)* An upline high priestess simply giving away a Book, without insisting that the recipient copy it out longhand under a watchful eye, was an exceedingly rare occurrence in those days. Furthermore, not only was the high priestess in question not the recipient's initiator, but she had never even met him in person. These improbable happenings (despite *Jana's* expressed desire that Eddie come to England for proper training) indicate that the story of how the Book of Shadows came to be in Eddie's hands may not be entirely trustworthy. *(Ibid n#44)*

With *Jana's* vouch and Book of Shadows in hand, Eddie proceeded with his plans to re-enter British Traditional Witchcraft. Eddie elevated Sheila to the Third Degree in Gardnerian Wica, most likely on the full moon of December 19, 1975. Buczynski later recalled this period in a letter to Sheila's coven. "As some of you may know," Eddie wrote, "not long ago I took a 'Leave of Absence' from the Craft. When I finally returned, it was because I was guided by the Gods to establish a marvelous and old tradition here in America, and also to Validate the Lady Khrysis after her seemingly endless trials. These things have now been accomplished."[47] Sheila's gratitude with Eddie's help in securing her place in British Traditional Witchcraft was expressed in a heartfelt poem ("To My High Priest — Gwydion") that is included as part of the Huntington Coven's Book of Shadows.[48]

Ken and his girlfriend (and working partner) spent the weekend after Christmas 1975 with Eddie and Bennie in Rego Park, New York in order to be brought into the tradition. On Friday December 26, Eddie initiated and elevated Ken's girlfriend up through the Third Degree in his Brooklyn Coven, whereupon she took the Craft name *Godwyn*.[49] The next evening, *Godwyn* initiated and elevated Ken up to the Third Degree and he took the Craft name *Cerdic*.[50] The coven began to acquire new members who were a little older and more mature, attracted through the adult education classes on Neo-Paganism that Saperton occasionally gave at Smithtown High School. *(Ibid n#2)* It was as a Gardnerian that Eddie had installed Sheila, and he "began referring to the group as the Huntington Coven of the [Hampshire] Tradition," writes Ken Dalton. *(Ibid n#40)*

Now that a functioning coven had been started in the United States, *Jana* is said to have issued a follow-up pronouncement that Eddie was to be the official point of contact between America and the coven in Great Britain. This was delineated in a letter dated December 1975:[51]

> *As duly vouched-for representative of the High Priestesses and High Priests of Hampshire, and as Elder-most of the same, I say:*
>
> *We, the Elders of the Craft in Southern Britain, do hereby name Gwydion---a properly prepared High Priest and Magus---as first bearer of the Red Garter, and thereby, Messenger of the Gods in America. So be it ardane.*

Sheila was then to be recognized by the New Forest Coven as the legitimate high priestess for their line in the United States. "Eddie acted as the go-between for the New Forest coven and those of us who are the direct descendents," she wrote. "I was told in writing that I was to be the High Priestess and Witch Queen of all the Americas." *(Ibid n#42)* Curt

Bargren confirms this, writing, "Saperton was appointed by the (very old) survivors of the Clutterbuck coven [as] their high priestess to the Americas, and [was] given their original materials." *(Ibid n#39)* He goes on to say that "As far as I know, the Hampshire witches only befriended two Gardnerian High Priestesses — Sheila [Saperton] and Ray Bone. This is assuming, of course, that Eddie's story is true and that he didn't manufacture the evidence. [But] I did see alleged correspondence between Eddie and the Hampshire witches."[52] *(Ibid n#39)* Bennie Geraci also confirms that Eddie told him about *Jana's* vouch at the time.[53]

"We were just the Huntington Coven, but when Eddie got the letter from Jana in 12/75 naming him the 'first bearer of the red garter, and thereby messenger of the Gods in America' we used to laugh and call ourselves the Huntington Coven of the Order of the Red Garter. I think there was some barely half serious thought to have Eddie make/wear a red garter, but it never came to fruition." *(Ibid n#2)* Despite this alleged imprimatur, it is unclear what path of British Traditional Witchcraft the Huntington Coven actually practiced, as *Jana's* first letter is clear that she considered Gardnerian Wica to be an unauthorized offshoot of the New Forest path that she practiced. *(Ibid n#44)*

As Bargren's hesitancy admits, there are problems with this story. Raymond Buckland, who has extensive contacts within British Traditional Witchcraft, has never heard of either *Jana* or the phraseology "Elders of the Craft in Southern Britain."[54] When presented with the language in these letters, Michael Howard, editor of the British Craft journal *The Cauldron*, also indicated that he believed them to be suspect.[55] Likewise, Philip Heselton, a British historian of Gardnerian Wica who has studied the New Forest area extensively, has never heard of *Jana*. Heselton believes that a coven could have existed in the New Forest area during the 1975-1976 period. If so, however, he strongly suspects that it had no connection with whatever had been going on in Highcliffe in the 1930s (i.e., the "Clutterbuck coven").[56]

Heselton examined copies of the *Jana* vouches, and he believes that they are fraudulent and originate in the United States, for several reasons. "Some of the phraseology does not sound genuine," Heselton writes. "'High Priestesses and High Priests of Hampshire,' for example, gives the impression of a highly-developed network of covens in the county of Hampshire, which I am certain there never was, and certainly not in 1975. They would not have emphasized their Priesthood in that way, anyway. Then the phrase 'Southern Britain' is one which I have never heard in my 63 years of living in England, neither inside nor outside the Craft. [The letters] seem to have been written by someone who has read 'High Magic's Aid,' because they use the terms 'Pentacle grade' and 'Red Garter,' neither of which are actually used in the Craft in England, certainly not in my experience." *(Ibid n#56)* There was one contemporaneous reference to the practice of the Messenger of the Gods wearing red garters, and that was Buckland's *Witchcraft from the Inside* (1971) in reference to alleged antique practices.[57] This book was carried by the Warlock Shop — and, though it does not vindicate the "Southern Britain" terminology, one should note a September 27, 1952 article by Allen Andrews in the British magazine *Illustrated*, which mentions a meeting of the "Southern Coven of British Witches" in the New Forest area.[58, 59]

Heselton continues, "With regard to the letters originating in America, this is suggested by the following evidence, which I admit is inconclusive. The spelling [of] 'recognize,' where the English would certainly write 'recognise.' The use of the term 'vouched for' ... this was never used in England, but it suggests a familiarity with that expression. 'So be it ardane' is, of course, used in the Craft Laws, which were probably invented by Gerald Gardner in 1957. That phrase never really caught on in England, but seems to be used a lot in American writings. The paper used is probably the size and certainly the shape of Junior Legal, 5 inches by 8 inches, which was a paper used in America but not in England. The signature 'Jana' seems characteristic of much American handwriting which I have seen, though this is, of course, very inconclusive." *(Ibid n#56)*

Although this does not conclusively prove deception, the evidence is compelling enough to call into question the authenticity of the warrants conveyed by the Jana letters. Eddie already had a record of misrepresenting his own bona fides and Craft history (the prime example being the true origins of the Traditionalist Gwyddoniaid he founded in 1972) and the Jana letters raise similar concerns. Eddie might certainly have had the motivation to do so since a vouch from Britain would appear to solve many of his problems in the political landscape of the local Craft community. However, inconsistencies in the evidence suggest that if a deception was perpetrated, Eddie may not have been its author, or perhaps not the sole author.

For example, there is the aforementioned *Jana* signature, which Heselton hinted, but was too polite to say, was rather slovenly. Conversely, Buczynski's handwriting was quite elegant. The *Jana* sample, which was consistent throughout the correspondence, does not match any of the extensive handwriting samples left behind by Eddie. One possibility, but with no proof, is that Eddie's High Priestess, Sheila Saperton, signed both letters. Rejected by the Long Island Line herself, Saperton would certainly have had sufficient motive to participate in a deception. Sheila claimed to have been in contact with a member of *Jana's* New Forest Coven in England, and to have spoken with this person on the phone when visiting the country in the late 1970s in an unsuccessful attempt to set up a meeting. Yet Sheila also stated that it was Eddie who "acted as the go-between for the New Forest Coven and those of us who are the direct descendents." *(Ibid n#42)* However, the *Jana* correspondence appears to indicate that the warrants were the product of *Jana's* coven and three others, which denotes a level of organization that Heselton believes was lacking in the New Forest area at that time. If Heselton's analysis is correct and the *Jana* letters are fraudulent, Sheila's statements would appear to indicate that she was somehow in on the true story.

There are also issues with the Book of Shadows itself. The Huntington Coven Book of Shadows has a black list that is similar to the one provided at the front of Buczynski's book for The Wica. *(Ibid n#2, 48)* Indeed, there are some similarities between the Huntington Coven book and The Wica book. For example, some of the innovations on co-equality, election, and length of service which he imported into The Wica book from Buckland's Seax-Wica tradition can also be found in the Huntington Coven's book in a section called "Antimonies" [sic]. A note is also included in a separate training book called "Witchcraft – For the First Degree" stating that homosexuality is not a bar to the practice of the Craft so long as the person in question fulfills the polarity requirement of practicing with an opposite-sex partner in Circle.[60] *Jana's* August 4 letter to Buczynski refers to these innovations, but states that the book used by her coven does not contain them. Certain Laws in the Huntington Coven book have not been singled out for retention with underlining as was done in The Wica book. This could indicate that the Huntington Coven book is yet another variation of Buczynski's original Gardnerian Book of Shadows, perhaps one closer to its original form as received from Patricia Siero.

Also, the "Bales and Apies" section of the Huntington Coven book contains material that is not found in other traditions flowing from the Gardnerian rootstock. This is not a great hurdle in itself; one would expect some differences between a modern book that has passed through several initiated generations and one that is allegedly based on the "raw" foundations of the tradition. But the nature of the material itself raises questions. For example, the book speaks of "The Five Whistlers," whose advent is said to be a forewarning of dire peril and requires a convocation of Third Degree practitioners to dispel. Philip Heselton was unable to identify any stories relating to The Five Whistlers within the traditions of the New Forest area. *(Ibid n#56)* Will Kale of Paganism Studies.org, a group in Great Britain that documents the history of Neo-Paganism and Witchcraft in England, is likewise unfamiliar with The Five Whistlers.[61]

The Five Whistlers passage almost certainly derives from "The Seven Whistlers" of nineteenth century British folklore, referring to the calls made by a night-flying flock of birds that signal impending disaster for sailors or miners.[62] This legend was known in Leicestershire, Lancashire, Worcestershire and Shropshire counties in the Midlands and Northwest region of England. Hampshire, the stated county of origin for the Huntington Coven's materials, is located in the Southeast region of England.[63] While it is possible that the Huntington Coven's Book of Shadows is legitimate, it is also just as likely that anomalous folkloric elements were added to an existing Gardnerian Book of Shadows in order to make it appear to have come from the wilds of England. Buczynski had a Gardnerian book, obtained from his initiating high priestess, Patricia Siero, in 1973, and the Warlock Shop carried an extensive catalogue of folklore books covering the British Isles, including at least one book that specifically discusses the legend of The Seven Whistlers: A.R. Wright's *English Folklore* (London, 1928).[64,65]

Finally, there is the issue of the claim itself. Eddie could not legitimately claim a lineage based solely on a vouch from *Jana*. The claim might have passed muster if his dilemma was only that his original initiator, Patricia Siero, was just no longer willing to vouch for him. A vouch from a recognized Third Degree in England would have been sufficient to shore up his claim if his lineage were intact. However, aside from the consideration that no one seems to have heard of *Jana* (which would seem to undermine the point of this entire exercise), the simple fact is that Eddie's own initiation was voided when Judy Kneitel re-initiated Patricia Siero. This, in effect, broke the line according to Gardnerian philosophy, and all downline initiates who were not re-initiated by someone else were effectively "orphaned" and illegitimate, at least insofar as the recordkeeping was concerned. Because he had not actually been re-initiated by *Jana* (or by anyone else of standing in any flavor British Traditional Witchcraft), Buczynski simply had nothing for which to vouch.

Eddie had become involved in the Huntington Coven unbeknownst to Ria, with whom he was still in close contact. It is not clear why Eddie kept this involvement from Ria, or from Carol whom he met late in 1975. In August 1976, Eddie shared copies of the *Jana* letters with Ria while preparing a vouch acknowledging Ria's lineage from him.[66] Ria was never certain of how the *Jana* vouch came to be, but she accepted it at face value from Eddie, as was proper for a subordinate. Ria, in turn, shared the letters with Carol. Both women have since related the story, told to them by Eddie, that he brought their Book of Shadows (which is to say, the one used by the Huntington Coven and given to them along with the *Jana* vouches) over from the Old World and from Kentucky. *(Ibid n#20)* While none of this constitutes conclusive evidence of a deception, or by whom, it does raise serious questions as to the authenticity of the claimed lineage and the origins of the Book. Even considering these doubts, the Huntington Coven's Book of Shadows is still a useful means of practice for those who wish to follow it. If it works for the practitioner, who else is qualified to gainsay it?

Over the course of the year, several of the men in Buczynski's household had become intrigued with his spiritual activities, enough so that they began to explore Wica for themselves. Bennie joined the Huntington Coven mainly because he knew that it was so important to Eddie, and he wanted to become closer to his lover. He was brought into the Craft by Sheila Saperton on Long Island in June 1976, choosing the Craft name *Damien*, which he took from the main character of the movie *The Omen* (1976). Intrigued by Eddie and Bennie's trips out to Huntington, Joey Cupolo began to express an interest in Witchcraft shortly thereafter.

Joey already knew that Eddie was involved with Witchcraft. After all, it is somewhat difficult to hide anything among six roommates in a one-bedroom apartment. But Cupolo didn't really understand what that meant. "Eddie was living [at the apartment] for a while before he realized that I was interested," Joey recalled. "You see, I didn't *know* what Witchcraft was. I was like an everyday person thinking Witches are either fairy tales or Satanists. I was occult-minded, though. I was very into astrology and the tarot." Overcoming his initial surprise at Joey's interest, Eddie immediately started him on a crash course of education. "Before he [arranged to have me brought in], Eddie gave me basic books — [Frank Donovan's] *Never on a Broomstick*, Gerald Gardner's book *Witchcraft Today*, and another one. And the more that I read these things, the more interested I got."[67]

Cupolo dived right in, and Buczynski was impressed with his dedication. "Eddie, if he felt you were a Witch," Joey said, "would sometimes initiate you and then teach you later. If he didn't get that feeling, he might have you attend the Pagan Way first. But if he felt that you were a Witch at heart — and some people are — that was it. He would initiate you." *(Ibid n#67)* Cupolo was one who was on the fast track, and he wasn't destined for the Pagan Way until after he had become a Witch — and even then, he would be one of the teachers and guides in the group. Joey was initiated by Sheila in 1976, taking the Craft name *Osric*. "I found *Osric* in a baby book," Joey admitted. "I ended up changing later it to *Ozrik* because I liked the Wizard of Oz." *(Ibid n#67)*

Like clockwork, the three men would make the trek by train out to Huntington Station for rituals. Sheila had a pleasant home that she shared with her two teenage sons and a multitude of cats. "We had nice circles," Joey remembered. "[We'd take] a little ceremonial bath at night. And then we'd come downstairs and drink a little wine. We used to get high, sometimes, too. Oh yeah, honey, we were happy campers when we hit that circle. It was nice." *(Ibid n#67)* Rituals ran fairly late, and the guys would stay overnight at Sheila's home, waiting until the next day to take the train back to Queens.

While Bennie and Eddie got along well with Sheila, she and Joey tended to mix like oil and water. Joey remembers one conversation he had with Sheila regarding her lawn, which was always a mess, with weeds growing everywhere. When he asked her why she didn't maintain it, Sheila's reply was, "I'm a Pagan, and it's wrong to mess with nature." Joey retorted that she was just lazy and didn't want to mow, which did nothing to endear him to his high priestess. *(Ibid n#67)* "I don't think she ever cared for me," Joey admitted. Unfortunately, that tension would haunt their relationship to its end.

Getting along with the others didn't keep Eddie from pulling pranks on Sheila and the rest of the coven. Taking cleansing baths immediately prior to ritual was common in this time, and the practice is still followed by some traditions. In the article "Being a Witch Is," *Gwion* notes tongue-in-cheek that "Being a Witch is ... taking a ritual bath at the covenstead when seven other witches have just been in the tub."[68] The same was true of the Huntington Coven, Joey says, but with a twist inspired by the backroom bars the boys had visited. "I remember that Eddie would go, 'Did you remember to pee in the water?' And I'd go, 'Yeah.' That was the thing, we all peed in the water. My first golden showers, honey (laughing)." *(Ibid n#67)* Why did they do this? Perhaps because, deep down, all men are fourteen years old and occasionally enjoy pulling one over on the adults even if, as the high priest of the coven, he's supposed to be one of them.

In February 1976, Eddie accompanied Bennie for the first time on a visit to New Orleans for Mardi Gras. There he finally met Bennie's family. *(Ibid n#1)* Bennie had been going with Eddie to the Nascosto residence in Ozone Park for Sunday dinners for months, so it now was time for Eddie to meet his "in-laws." He was warmly accepted into Bennie's family, just as Bennie had been with his own, and the Geracis and Nascostos remain cordial to this day. The gist of this was that the relationship between the two men continued to deepen.

By the end of 1975, Buczynski and Geraci had begun searching for their own apartment. While they loved the other guys dearly, the old apartment was simply too crowded to afford enough privacy for two men in a fairly new relationship. More important, Eddie desperately needed elbow room — and a quiet space — for researching and writing. Eddie had a very focused attention but it was often challenged by their living conditions, as Joey Cupolo and Bennie Geraci admitted. "[Eddie] had to be a speed reader. He could read a book a day, and the best part about it is he knew what was in it. ... I swear to God, he could sit there and get himself wrapped up in one of his books..." Joey began. "And fix himself a Scotch about this tall," Bennie interrupted, using his hands to describe a highball glass. "He loved his Johnny Walker White." Joey continued, "And we could all be tap-dancing on his fucking head, and he's reading his book. He probably still knows what's going on around him, but he's concentrated on that book." *(Ibid n#67)*

Eddie was making the best money that he had ever earned in his life. The Christmas bonuses at J. Aron and Company were quite handsome, even for someone as low in the pecking order as Eddie. Between their two salaries, the couple had enough income to comfortably afford their own place. Upon their return to New York from New Orleans, they located a suitable apartment in a group of high-rise apartment buildings in Middle Village, New York. By March 1976, they had moved into Apt. T-40 at 84-35 62nd Drive. Eddie now had an actual office to which he could retreat in order to study and write. The apartment was ideal for other reasons. It was located close to Rego Park where Joey and Charlie remained, and was near Forest Park where Ria and Carol had set up house, and it was also large enough to host rituals and, equally important, parties.

While Eddie was involved with the Huntington Coven, Ria had continued to operate the Bronx Coven with her husband, David. Unfortunately, the Bronx Coven did not survive the year. Ria and Carol had become progressively friendlier with one another in the months since Bulzone was brought into the Craft, eventually resulting in an affair between the two women that ended the Farnhams' marriage. The Bronx Coven folded when Ria and Carol moved to an apartment on 108th Street in the Forest Hills neighborhood of Queens. *(Ibid n#20, 28)* Starting a new Forest Hills coven, Ria and Carol took turns acting as high priestess and used several men as high priest. She and Carol never suspected the existence of Eddie's Huntington Coven, even though they had regularly socialized with the boys at their apartment, and *vice versa*. And there were many parties.

One of the perks of Bennie's job at Chase Manhattan Bank was that corporate customers gave bank employees liquor vouchers every year at Christmastide. Bennie didn't really drink much, but that didn't keep him from redeeming the coupons for free booze. As a result, he usually accumulated quite a collection of liquor at the end of the year. Some of it, such as bottles of nice Scotch, he gave away to close friends like Eddie. To get rid of the rest of it, the guys would throw a party during the holidays. These were big affairs (there was an open bar, after all) and co-workers, people from the apartment building, and friends from the Neo-Pagan community would show up.

Bennie said that he and Eddie usually kept their bedroom locked during these parties, since a lot of strangers were usually roaming through the place. But this was no guarantee that things couldn't come up missing, and during one party someone raided one of the "special" ice trays for drinks. A co-worker with whom Eddie had had some trouble in the past was in attendance. Sitting in a chair drinking her cocktail, she suddenly stopped. A puzzled look came over her face as she pulled a piece of paper from her mouth. "There was a piece of paper with my name on it floating in my glass!" she exclaimed, showing the offending parchment to Eddie. Without batting an eye, Buczynski calmly collected the spoiled beverage and quipped "Party favor!" by way of explanation, before sauntering back to the kitchen to refresh the lady's drink and dispose of the remnant of the binding spell.[69]

At the end of 1975, Herman had asked Eddie if he would sign over his share of the Warlock Shop.[70] As he was no longer living there and was not likely to have the time or inclination to work there again full time, Buczynski acquiesced to Slater's request and gave it to him. "He just let Herman have the shop free and clear," Joey Cupolo asserts. "He didn't want no connection with it whatsoever. I told him he was an idiot." *(Ibid n#67)* It is likely that Herman was tying up loose ends in preparation for some big plans he had for the business.[71] Because Eddie Buczynski wasn't the only one who was getting ready to pull up stakes at the time. Herman Slater was scouting out a new location, too.

17. A gathering of Minoans and friends. Party at Eddie Buczynski and Bennie Geraci's Middle Village apartment, Queens. 1977. On the sofa are (left to right) Carol Bulzone, Joey Cupolo and Ria Farnham. On the floor are Bruce-Michael Gelbert (bearded) and Kim Schuller (above Gelbert).

18. The Magickal Childe, 35 West 19th Street, Chelsea, Manhattan. ca. 1997.

19. Magickal Childe "herb aisle" looking toward the Oils Office, with Priscilla the shop cat. ca. 1993.

20. Herman Slater in his perch at the Magickal Childe checkout counter. 1984.

21. (above, right) Magickal Childe "book aisle" looking toward the checkout counter with Steve Teischer in the background. ca. 1994.

22. Peter Conte mugging for the camera in the Magickal Childe Oils Office. ca. 1994.

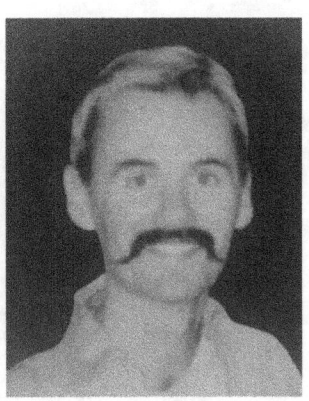

23. Clinton Stevens (aka "Chanel 13"), incense & potions master of the shop. ca. 1976

24. (left) Magickal Childe's famous "Hard Core New Age" banner hanging over the sidewalk. ca. 1994.

25. (right) Sala One Nine, a Spanish restaurant and bar now occupying 35 West 19th Street. 2012.

26. (left) The first catalog of the Warlock Shop (January 1973) and (right) an Abrahadabra catalog from the Magickal Childe (1979).

27. Eddie Buczynski (left) and Bennie Geraci, Middle Village, Queens. 1978.

28. Sheila Saperton (Lady Khrysis), sabbat at Buczynski and Geraci's Middle Village apartment. ca. 1976.

29. The first Minoan Sisterhood sabbat. Forest Hills, Queens. Late 1977.

30. First edition of the "Simon" Necronomicon. December 1977.

31. Herman Slater and friends, Magickal Childe Harvest Festival Samhain rite. October 1984.

32. Crowd scene on West 19th Street, Magickal Childe Harvest Festival. October 1984.

Chapter 23: The Dockside of the Force

A Magickal Childe is Born

One could argue that the Warlock Shop had outgrown its cramped Brooklyn Heights location almost from the moment it had opened in 1972. However, by the end of 1975 it had clearly outgrown its space on Henry Street. Herman's business sense told him that major changes were needed if he wanted his shop to flourish, because further growth simply wasn't possible given the limitations of the Brooklyn Heights storefront. While the current walk-in trade was reasonable, he knew it could be better in Manhattan, especially in a larger retail space. There, a whole customer base awaited; people who would never venture off the island into Brooklyn or the other boroughs, no matter how much he advertised in the *Village Voice*.[1] "I think the lease on 300 Henry was running out and Herman began to have dreams of expanding into what he called 'The A&P of the Occult,'" writes former employee Ken Dalton.[2] Slater began looking for another location for the expanding business, and advertising for the Warlock Shop in the *Voice* dropped precipitously beginning that summer. By November, Herman had ceased placing ads altogether.[3]

The only question was where to go. Greenwich Village, with its gradually gentrifying atmosphere, seemed an ideal location and offered a support network of overlapping subcultures and tourist trade; however, Village rents continued to rise despite the abysmal financial state of New York City.[4] Being thrifty, Slater ruled out that location for the store. One place that looked more promising was the West Side neighborhood of Chelsea located just south of the old "Devil's playground." The area was once home to the longshoremen who worked the piers to the west and butchers from the Meatpacking District, Chelsea was a working-class neighborhood fallen on hard times. By 1976, most shipping had left the lower West Side, and the area was now a new kind of playground: a decaying and sleazy amusement park for gay men seeking anonymous sexual encounters after the West Side leather bars closed for the night.[5] Herman occasionally frequented the nearby leather and hustler bars for rough trade and male prostitutes, so there was a certain convenience factor to be considered in moving the store there.[6] Furthermore, housing was still inexpensive in Chelsea, and the area was just beginning to experience an influx of gay men driven out of the Village by rising rents.

One drawback was that Chelsea in not yet a particularly safe area for gay men.[7] The residents of the neighborhood — Hispanics, blacks, and the descendants of working class Irish immigrants in the area — were generally not fond of the mostly gay, mostly white refugees moving in from the Village. Gay-bashings were common, particularly for men foolish enough to venture out alone at night on the wrong street while hitting the bar-tubs-trucks circuit. Gangs of young street toughs made life dangerous for people in the area, though some gay men organized for their own protection and gave as good as they got.[8]

Generally speaking, occult stores tend to thrive in the same places that gay bars, used bookstores, and subcultural establishments do. They are transitional places – fairly dark and gritty, and afflicted with shuttered storefronts, trash, drugs and crime – but are located on the fringes of the more "respectable" areas. In other words, they are just bad enough to keep the rents within reason, yet not scary enough to drive away the paying customers. Chelsea in late 1975 was just such a place. The prices were right, and Herman smelled a demographic change in the air that augured well for future business in the area. He found a suitable storefront on West 19th Street and signed a lease in November 1975. The Warlock Shop continued to process catalogue sales during this period, and this was the only source of income while the store moved locations. Unfortunately, mail order sales began to dry up earlier in 1975 because Herman could not afford to fund the printing and mailing of a new catalogue.

The property at 35 West 19th Street is a 1920s-era six-story structure. It was dirty and not much to look at back then, but it had a *lot* of floor space; roughly 2000 square feet, or four times the size of the old Warlock Shop. The floors overhead held five apartments served by a stairwell, elevator and foyer located on the west side of the first floor, but the rest of the first floor and part of the basement would be Herman's domain. The building's owner was indifferent to Slater's line of work, as long as he paid the rent on time and in full. The tenants upstairs weren't so fortunate, especially when they sought protection from their landlord under New York's tough "Loft Law" in 1983 as the area's changing demographics and rising rents finally threatened to push them out.[9] But the building had just changed hands in March 1975, only a few months before Herman started looking for space, and the new owner was willing to cut a deal in order to get the first floor occupied. A Tibetan temple (which the Dalai Lama actually visited) was located above the shop. The temple denizens developed good relations with Herman and came to buy all of their black candles from him.[10]

Ria, Carol and a number of others helped Herman prepare the new space through December and January, erecting shelves and moving new display cabinets into place. Slater was completely out of 300 Henry Street by the end of December, moving the contents of the store in a single weekend.[11] Eddie and Bennie went to the store a few times in January to help Herman unpack and arrange things.[12] Eddie introduced Joey Cupolo to Herman during one of these trips, explaining that Joey was his roommate and was beginning to study the Craft. Herman agreed to hire him to work at the store when it reopened.

Although Herman and Eddie ostensibly made their peace in 1975, Buczynski did not initially help out, or even hang out much, at the new location possibly because of Eddie's busy schedule or because of Herman's discomfort at seeing Eddie and Bennie together. Herman's eyes still lit up whenever Eddie visited the shop, like a high school girl with a crush.[13] However, Bennie remembers that although Herman was always civil to him when he visited, the shopkeeper always greeted him with a gimlet-eyed stare and a grunt when he walked through the door with Eddie. Bennie ended up calling Herman "Igor," but never within earshot of anyone but Eddie. When he first went with Eddie to the shop in Brooklyn Heights, Bennie couldn't figure out what was going on with Herman. "Eddie never told me that he and Herman used to be lovers," Bennie said. "He would tell me when I asked that Herman was his business partner, or used to be his partner."[14] Buczynski reluctantly admitted the truth, but only after Geraci had figured it out for himself.

There is some evidence that Eddie's continued popularity in the community grated on Slater's nerves even as he pined for the younger man's lost affection. "I remember that Herman seemed to be quite jealous sometimes of the attention and adoration that Eddie received," writes Karen Bartlett. "We were at the Magickal Childe one day and there was some kind of gathering going on, and Eddie was supposed to attend (this was quite some time after they split up). I remember asking Herman if Eddie was coming and when? Herman snapped at me saying 'He's not a saint yet! You have to die first!' ... Sometime after that Herman started selling pieces of Eddie's old Welsh Trad Robe to various people like it was a holy relic. He laughed about it."[15]

The size of the new location allowed for a much more flattering presentation of the merchandise. The store was entered via double doors on the right side of the shop front. A large display window filled the remainder of the façade. The cash register and checkout counter were to the left as one entered. This setup allowed Herman (or whoever was minding the front of the store) to keep an eye on everyone coming and going, and on the street out front. A pop machine was placed inside the double doors on the right, as was a community bulletin board and magazine racks. A large, wooden dragon, formerly a movie prop, hung suspended from the pressed-tin ceiling, its glassy glare almost as fierce as the basilisk-like one its owner often directed at the customers. Glass cases displaying jewelry, altar furniture (censers, patens, chalices, athames and candlesticks) and statues occupied the floor and the east and west walls just past the checkout area. Beyond this were bookcases filled with offerings from every spiritual path, including Neo-Paganism, Witchcraft, Ceremonial Magick, Christianity, Jewish mysticism and Satanism. Seven-foot-tall shelves were attached to the east wall, crammed with rows of half-gallon jars containing a huge selection of herbs, resins and exotic spell ingredients.[16,17]

Long-time employee Kathryn Frank, who started hanging out at the store in 1977, believes that the sheer volume and diversity of offerings made the store unique. "I don't know if there were similar stores at the time," she writes, "but certainly I think you could mark it as one of the earliest attempts to bring all religions under one roof. Some people criticized the fact that the [store] carried the *Satanic Bible* and other things; other people criticized other religious books and artifacts being made available. Herman's answer was generally, 'Screw them.' I really respected that."[18] However, some viewed Slater's cozy relationship with the Satanists with great mistrust, and this would eventually result in a rebellion against some in the Wiccan community. A decade later, Wiccan author Amber K would ask that her products "not be associated with some of the junk you sell."[19] Others in the New York community began a boycott of the store when Slater's defense of his marketing decisions led him to publicly insist on the similarities between Satanism and Witchcraft — a *verboten* topic of public discussion within the community since the earliest days of the Craft.[20, 21]

The dark things on offer extended beyond vending copies of the *Satanic Bible* to pimply-faced bridge and tunnel boys.[22] Like the Brooklyn location, the Chelsea store carried human skulls for sale. The skulls often came from overseas through middle men, and it isn't at all clear how they were obtained in their countries of origin or managed to clear customs into the United States. Slater admitted to writer Dan Greenburg in 1975 that grave robbers occasionally stopped by the Warlock Shop to sell him material, but that he refused to purchase anything that came from the consecrated ground of any religion because of the bad karma associated with it. The illegality of such transactions seemed to be of secondary concern.[23] Skulls sold for medical research in the United States are engraved with a registration number by respectable dealers in order to protect the owner in the event that the police are ever called in to investigate. The merchandise sold by Herman sometimes lacked this nicety. Kathryn Frank writes, "[T]here were many rumors as to where they came from — some said from Vietnamese people that United States soldiers had brought back, but who the hell knows? They definitely were real. I borrowed one once and ran it past some friends at the medical school I worked at in college, and they were like, 'Oh crap, Kathy, where the hell did you get this? That's a real human skull, and we totally can't handle this. We have medical grants to protect!'" *(Ibid n#18)*

But not all of the human bones were of questionable origin. Ken Dalton recalls receiving a shipment of skulls at the Warlock Shop from a legitimate supplier. But that in itself didn't guarantee the absence of controversy. "[Herman] got a shipment of skulls from a medical supply house, and put them in the display window," Dalton remembers. "He was upstairs that evening when 3 young Latinos came in and asked me 'How much for head in the window?' It was a new display and I didn't know the price. I couldn't resist, so I went to the back, yelled up the stairs to Herman, and said that there were 3 guys who '... wanted head in the window — how much?' Of course, Herman's initial response was 'Are they good looking?' (We eventually completed the sale without scandal.)" *(Ibid n#2)*

On February 13, 1976, the Warlock Shop was back in business in the new location and held a grand re-opening. Herman had been advertising the "new store" in both mundane and magickal publications such as the *Village Voice* and *Green Egg*, and had spent several months ordering and filling the shelves with goods. Mixed in with the skulls, bones, dried bats, and mummified cat's paws were "books, amulets & talismans, hooded robes & capes, crystal balls, tarot cards, chalices, swords, knives ... and all the paraphernalia needed by researcher or practitioner."[24, 25, 26] A wide variety of occult jewelry, some of it very high quality merchandise handmade by local artists and practitioners such as Bonnie Claremont, was also on display.[27] Unfortunately, everything didn't quite go as planned. "The opening day was a fiasco," Ken Dalton asserts. "Herman rented a Hammond organ with thoughts of Toccata and Fugue-y Phantom of the Opera mood music. He forgot to get someone to play the instrument, so I was pressed into service. (Uh, I'm not a keyboard player, anything with strings, sure. Keys? No.) Very few customers, no press, not much buzz at all." *(Ibid n#2)*

People who came through the new location either liked it or hated it. "The space on West 19th Street was enormous, far bigger than was needed," remembers Dalton, who worked there for the first two months after the move. "Still, whereas Henry Street had an old fashioned charm to it (Eddie swore it was haunted), the Manhattan store had no charm at all. It was too big, too cold and the overhead fluorescent lightning made it seem like K-Mart. West 19th Street was, at the time, full of warehouses for the garment industry. There were a lot of vacancies and the rent for so big a space wasn't too bad. Nevertheless, I hated that space." *(Ibid n#2)* But others had a different experience, and the store also appears to have mellowed with time. Many years later, *New York Times* reporter Dinitia Smith adeptly captured the enduring atmosphere of the location, writing:[28]

> *On a rainy afternoon, the [shop] has a mysterious look. A shaft of light falls across the sidewalk from the window. Inside is a trove of magic artifacts, crystals, herbs, talismans, books on necromancy and pagan rituals, stacked to the pressed tin ceiling. It is a slightly sinister place, but the air is filled with the sweet smell of cloves and cinnamon.*

"What I remember most about the shop ... was that it was fairly dark and gloomy, seeming to cater to the more gothic/grim aspects of occultism than those of celebration," writes Zanoni Silverknife. "I am sure that Herman was quite aware of what the public wanted or thought the Wiccan scene was about and stocked those things that would sell. But, I believe this was not the case when he first opened up shop. A business person tries to stay abreast of change or will go under, financially."[29] Employee Joe Klingon concurs that Slater liked to cultivate an ominous aura about the place. When he finally got the courage to enter the store for the first time, Klingon found Slater sitting behind the counter drinking coffee and reading the newspaper. "You don't have green skin, you don't have fangs, and you're not breathing fire and smoke," he exclaimed. "Depends on which day you catch me on," Herman replied.[30] While the gothic ambience was intentional, in an odd example of coincidence stamping its influence upon the gibbering reptilian portion of the brain, Slater had unintentionally moved the Warlock Shop to a location that was just blocks away from the setting of yet another H.P. Lovecraft story.[31]

With the move to the new storefront, Herman had expanded his already large display of tarot decks. One was issued by the Credo Company of Laguna, California. Painted by Marty Yeager, the "Yeager Tarot of Meditation" was highly unusual for this time in that it depicted the human figures on its card faces realistically and in the nude. Decidedly homoerotic in much of its imagery, the Yeager deck was well loved by many gay men of the day.[32] Eddie purchased a copy of the Yeager Tarot from Herman shortly after the store re-opened, and it quickly became one of his favorite decks, which he used as an alternative to his other favorite, the Aquarian Tarot.

Despite his protest over Z. Budapest charging money for tarot readings in 1975, less than a year later Herman had installed card readers in the Magickal Childe. Buczynski eventually read cards there for paying customers, as did artist Emma Davy, Ria Farnham, Carol Bulzone, Peter Conte and a host of others over the years. A sign in the front of the shop announced who was "on duty" doing readings, with their hours posted. A small, round table with a couple of chairs was located at the back of the store, at the end of the center aisle. Emma's daughter, Marianne, who as a teenager hung out in the shop while her mother did readings, recalls how exhausted her mother was after her shift. "Readings wore my mother out big time!" writes Marianne. "She was exhausted when she finished. She could have worked more hours and I got the feeling that Herman might have liked her to, but really it took so much out of her. ... I know she charged anywhere from 25 [dollars] and UP for readings. She used many types of readings also. Not just cards. She would ask to hold an object and often received images, words, [and] information that way, usually that brought a higher price. I have no idea what the Magickal Childe's cut was, but I know they were both happy with the deal."[30]

Aside from the marked increase in the size of the showroom, the biggest change brought about by the relocation was the shop now had a dedicated space for meetings, workshops, rituals and performances; activities that the Warlock Shop simply could not accommodate in Brooklyn Heights. *(Ibid n#27)* Inspired by the well-appointed spaces he had seen in places like Chicago's Pagan Way and El Sabarum, Herman set out to do them one better, New York style. At first the back room was not much to look at, but it was spacious and could hold a large number of people fairly comfortably. Sally Eaton recalled the early days of this space, writing:[34]

> *In early 1976 ... This is the point at which I first worked for Herman ... The move had taken place only months before. The rear of the store had not yet been partitioned into the Oil Office and Temple space, but was used as a storage area, and at times a sewing room where magical robes were made. Herman had a desk there, but the area was still fairly cluttered following the move.*

The back room was essentially a large, open space measuring about 25 feet by 17 feet, though it also contained a bathroom that was said to have had the best graffiti in New York City.[35] The door leading from the main part of the store to the back room was hidden by a big wardrobe containing racks of capes and robes, behind which was a short hallway that led to the meeting space. "Everybody always got a kick out of people freaking out when someone would come back into the store [from the back room]," laughs Kathryn Frank. "This big old wardrobe would swing open, and some people would practically be wetting themselves." *(Ibid n#18)*

Once the space had been cleared and cleansed to hold meetings, Herman aggressively marketed this resource to the community under the sound principle that anything that got people into the store would eventually increase sales, and it did. Starting in February, Slater began advertising the first of many years of free Sunday afternoon lectures at the new location. Herman led the show, with a Pagan Way lecture on the "Basics of Witchcraft" on Saturday, February 14. *(Ibid n#18)* Simon, the Ceremonial Magickian who had given lectures for Herman when the store was in Brooklyn Heights, followed him to Manhattan and continued sharing his knowledge with seekers. Billed as "Msgr. Simon – Slavonic Orthodox Church," his workshop on "The Pagan Roots of Christianity & Judaism" was the second lecture in the new space.[36] Until he left New York in 1984, Simon was one of the most prolific speakers at the shop.[37] Other lecturers included a wide gamut of local practitioners, such as Rolla Nordic, Malcolm Mills, Eugenia Macer-Story, Jerry Birnbaum, and Robert Hall, as well as authors traveling the lecture circuit to promote their latest book. The lectures offered that first year in Manhattan covered a full range of topics, including the Qabala, black magic (twice), sex magic (thrice!), exorcism, omens, talismanic magick, Chinese occultism, the tarot, clairvoyance and planetary astrology. "At the heyday of Magickal Childe's operation," writes Peter Levenda, "the Sunday afternoon lectures pulled in more than 150 people, packing the small room in the back of the store." *(Ibid n#1)*

Lectures became a very important part of the outreach and marketing of the store, much more than at the old Warlock Shop, since the clientele at the new location could meet right where the merchandise was (in contrast to Brooklyn Heights, where meetings had to be held blocks away from the merchandise). This advantageous association of lectures and sales does not speak ill of Slater's motives, which were on the whole as honorable as pragmatism allowed. During all the years he sold occult paraphernalia in New York City, Herman Slater was deeply committed to disseminating information to the public. But meeting spaces do not pay for themselves, particularly in Manhattan. As most of the workshops and concerts at the shop were either free or charged only a nominal fee (generally a dollar), the proceeds from the business were needed to pay for the meeting space and its lighting, heat, and water. The attendees also knew that when Herman did charge for a presentation, he expected the lecturer to give good value for that dollar.

The non-judgmental attitude of the store extended to the workshops presented there, which could, like the customers, stray into darker themes. Peter Levenda recalls teaching a workshop titled "The Occult & Fascism" that was attended by James Madole, head of the National Renaissance Party, a neo-fascist sect with occult-Theosophical leanings. Madole challenged Levenda to a debate on the topic, and then later claimed to have presented the workshop himself.[38, 39] Neo-fascists and Satanists were welcome customers just like anyone else, as long as they behaved themselves, and members of both groups did occasionally hang out at the store in Brooklyn Heights and Chelsea. This fact has somehow promulgated the erroneous belief that Anton LaVey was a regular visitor, and that he conducted meetings there with James Madole.[40] But while LaVey and Slater were frequent correspondents, the Church of Satan leader never visited either location of the shop. However, LaVey's New York lieutenant, Jay Solomon, did occasionally visit the store and is known to have spoken with such people as James Madole while there.[41] *(Ibid n#39)*

On Sunday July 25, Clinton "Chanel 13" Stevens presented a workshop on herbal magick and medicine.[42] The fey herbalist had hung out at the Warlock Shop in Brooklyn Heights for a couple of years, mixing oil blends and incense for Herman, and ended up following the store when Herman moved it to Chelsea. With Clinton's help, Herman expanded the selection of herbs and oils, greatly enhancing the alchemical nook he had set up to mix incense and oil blends. The new and improved "oils office" was installed against the back wall of the front room and provided with a mixing counter for what was essentially an occult pharmacy where oils, incense, spells could be prepared to order.

Around this time, while Clinton was coming in part-time to set up the new oils office, he recommended that Herman hire his good friend,

Broadway singer Sally Eaton, to help out at the new store. Clinton had always impressed Herman with his knowledge of herbs and oils, so he hired Eaton on the spot to help with the mixing and other jobs. Joey Cupolo also assisted Clinton at the back counter. "To be honest, that was the part that I loved," Cupolo recalled. "People would ask for something and we'd fix it ourselves right there in front of them. Clinton was the best. Me, I had to go into my files. He would go right out of his memory. Clinton was invaluable. But Eddie was a good herbalist, too."[43]

With the larger store, Herman could offer Stevens a larger role in running the oils office as the resident "Celtic — Afro — Carib Herbalist on Staff."[44] As *Chanel 13*, Stevens mixed special orders of incense, powders, oils, washes, and the odd spell for the shop's clients. A *New York Times* article in October 1976 noted that "Clinton, who is originally from New Orleans, is initiated in the rites of demonology." *(Ibid n#35)* While wildly inaccurate, this type of press coverage helped develop the mystique of the shop and its workers. More importantly, in the move to Chelsea, Clinton's famous Formulary card file was collated and re-typed for the new shop. It had been added to over the past couple of years, but nearly all of the original cards were in Clinton's own handwriting.[45] Although he was a popular fixture at the shop, Clinton's greatest claim to fame would eventually come from the information in that card file. Ria Farnham adored Clinton, whom she referred to as "my Louisiana swamp Witch."[46] Farnham had been exposed to Santeria growing up in the Bronx, and Stevens broadened her knowledge by introducing her to Vodoun and to the Véve, which are the magickal seals of the Vodoun Gods.[47]

This latter bit of knowledge came in handy when Ria mistakenly placed a large order for seven-day candles with candle inserts from Crusader, a candle wholesaler in Brooklyn. Knowing that Herman would go ballistic at the costly mistake, since he would not be able to sell this more expensive stock quickly, Ria worked quickly to make them more saleable. Using an athame, ritual oils and glitter, Ria removed several candles from their insert sleeves and applied some basic candle magick to her dilemma. Carving spells into the candles using Vévés, runes and other designs, Ria selected appropriate oils to anoint them, and then applied colored glitter to the now sticky surface for effect (both magickal and aesthetic). The resulting "enchanted candle" was a value-added product that no other store was offering. Slater was so impressed by the finished product that he forgave Ria. He also added enchanted candles to the Magickal Child's product line, and Ria was soon carving them next to Clinton in the oils office.[48, 49]

As the year progressed, business in the new location was adequate, but Herman felt that there was definitely room for improvement. More Manhattan customers visited Chelsea than were ever willing to venture into Brooklyn Heights; however, the neighborhood would be playing catch-up to Herman's expectations for years to come. The area was still rough, and the name "Warlock Shop" did little to help the store's public image. Herman had been thinking about changing the name of the business for some time. The name-calling and finger-pointing during the Witch Wars of the previous years, when the shop and its owners had been tarred with the Saxon "oath-breaker" epithet, left a residuum that Slater felt the need to jettison, or at least play down. The "warlock" label also conjured up visions of B-movie horror schlock, simultaneously instilling a less salubrious and, to some, less serious image that put off folks with more discriminating sensibilities.

"Chanel told me Herman was sick of hearing Wiccan newbies remind him that the term 'Warlock' is a pejorative often taken to mean 'traitor and oath-breaker,'" recalls Sally Eaton. "Of course 'warlock' is also a Gardnerian technical term — nothing Herman could have explained to the rubes who constantly bugged him about it." *(Ibid n#34)* At that time, Herman was also in talks with Malcolm Mills and Cindy Brodkin about taking over the catalogue sales as a separate enterprise. Neither Mills nor Brodkin cared for the Warlock Shop moniker; they wanted something less dark that would attract more customers.[50] And while Herman generally didn't give a damn about what other people thought, he was a firm believer in the adage that business is business. So he was open to the suggestion to change the name.

An event in late July provided him with the inspiration for a new name for the store. On July 27, the Superior Court in Calaveras County, California decided a court case in favor of one Grady McMurtry, a student of Aleister Crowley in the O.T.O. The Court turned over to McMurtry's O.T.O. Association the archives of the O.T.O. and the library and papers of Aleister Crowley, which had been in the possession of the widow of the last O.T.O. leader when she died. Jim Wasserman, who managed Slater's account for Samuel Weiser, was involved on the periphery of the current O.T.O. struggle, and Wasserman probably mentioned to Slater what was afoot in California.

Now Slater was a long-time admirer of Crowley's work, having a genuine affinity for the genius of a man who was, much like himself, equal parts Magus, P.T. Barnum, and punk. Remembering Jim's news as he was casting about for a new image, the mischievous and shrewd Slater was inspired to use the O.T.O. conflict to his advantage. Choosing a name from the very heart of Crowley's magickal theories that best described his own attempt to place his imprimatur on the occult world of New York, Slater proposed to Mills and Brodkin that the Warlock Shop be renamed the "Magickal Childe." Malcolm, a student of Crowleyian ceremonial magick, reacted favorably. In fact, he was quite insistent that the name needed to change if there was any hope of growing the business. *(Ibid n#50)* Thus was a Magickal Childe born.

The August 2, 1976 edition of the *Village Voice* marked the first appearance of the store as the "Warlock Shop (Magickal Childe)."[51] By the next edition of the *Voice*, however, the names were reversed to read "Magickal Childe (Warlock Shop)."[52] Over the next several months, the store was advertised as "formerly the Warlock Shop" in the Voice Bulletin Board, thus maintaining continuity for its existing customers. This qualifier was eliminated from Voice Bulletin Board ads by the beginning of November, though the Warlock Shop reference would remain in graphical ads, and even on the store's shopping bags, for the remainder of its existence. New customers referred to the shop as "the Childe," but to the old-timers, the store would always be the Warlock Shop. Once you build a brand name, it is hard to let it go.

"The re-naming of the store to something Thelemic was serendipitous, implying a break with the 'witch wars' which disrupted the Brooklyn store," writes Eaton. "The witchy Beardsley satyr remained its logo, however, no doubt for continuity." *(Ibid n#34)* Slater adopted a new slogan to describe the shop's philosophy — "Hard Core New Age" — in order to distinguish the Magickal Childe from the "fluffier" aspects of the genre (though he catered to one and all). The slogan was eventually emblazoned on a large golden-yellow banner that hung outside the shop, visible to the passing traffic on West 19th Street, until its final day of operation. This in-your-face philosophy was also reflected in a sign posted just inside the shop door. Next to a drawing of the Mother Goddess were the words:[53,54]

**IF YOU ARE
A BIGOT:**
RACIALLY
RELIGIOUSLY
ETHNICALLY
SEXUALLY OR OTHERWISE
FUCK OFF!

By late 1975, the catalogue sales of Earth Religions Supplies had withered away to almost nothing, primarily because of Slater's continued inability to scrape together the funds to produce new catalogues in a timely manner and mail them to prospective customers. Part of the problem was the financial hole the store fell into in mid-1974, but just as important, Slater had never been able to keep an accurate set of books. Alan Cabal, who worked at the Childe for several years, describes the state of the store's finances thusly: "The [account] books, such as they were, consisted mainly of scraps of paper stuffed into shopping bags. There was no earthly way anyone but Herman could make any sense of it." *(Ibid n#27)* Judith McNally agrees. "I'd never ask him to set up a budget for me," she wrote. "He'd be completely honest but, ye gods, he was disorganized!"[55] Malcolm Mills also concurs, noting that "Herman seemed to be oblivious to the IRS, perhaps because his father worked for them. He did file taxes so far as I know, but his returns were based on fantasy figures."[56] It didn't help matters that Herman was in the habit of paying himself directly from the till whenever he needed spending money, and that he was notorious for not leaving enough cash in the register to make change for the paying customers.

When the demands became too much, Slater sometimes fantasized about chucking it all and moving on with his life. Ken Dalton writes, "Toward the end [of my dealings with him in 1976], Herman became more openly interested in the financial aspect of the Craft. He was looking to either sell the shop or take on investors, publish the Gardnerian [book], or otherwise go commercial." *(Ibid n#2)* Herman ended up selling an interest in the Magickal Childe to a former worker named Jack about the time that Dalton was leaving his employ. "He often spoke of selling the store and moving to upstate New York, buying an old church and setting up a business there," remembers Kathryn Frank. "But when people were interested in buying he made it clear that he would not sell the mail order business, so people backed off. Herman often said to me, 'That's where the real money is. You've got to have the store so you can let people know you exist, but the mail order is the money maker.'" *(Ibid n#18)* Yet by late summer Slater had finally come to an agreement with Malcolm Mills and Cindy Brodkin on their takeover of the Magickal Childe's mail order business. Mills had some experience in the direct mail business, and Cindy Brodkin, daughter of television producer Herbert Brodkin, had the capital to float the business until it became profitable. They both thought that it would be an interesting business opportunity. Herman was not a partner in the venture; Mills' and Brodkin's attorneys felt it would be too risky to have him as a shareholder because his liabilities could transfer to the other partners. The role of the Magickal Childe was limited to providing Mills and Brodkin with the store mailing list and serving as their supplier. Malcolm and Cindy prepared the catalogues and collected the money, while Herman processed the orders and handled the shipping.

In September, Brodkin and Mills moved into separate lofts at 37 West 19th Street, next door to the Magickal Childe, the better to both manage the mail order business and keep an eye on Herman. Malcolm set aside two rooms in his place for the new firm, which they named Abrahadabra. Although Slater had originally advertised a "giant new 1976 mail order catalogue" to be released in mid-April, Abrahadabra did not begin operating until early 1977. The venture ended up being quite successful, turning a profit in its first year.[57,58] *(Ibid n#10, 50, 56)* Despite a fairly amicable start, by the time Abrahadabra's association with the Magickal Childe ended in 1980, Mills had become thoroughly fed up with Slater's way of doing business, and Mills and Brodkin weren't speaking to each other. *(Ibid n#50)* After the Abrahadabra partnership collapsed, the Magickal Childe reclaimed its mail order operations and continued to publish catalogues until 1993.[59]

With the new store came a growth in staff, and turnover became a bigger problem for Slater than it had been at the old location. A certain level of impersonality also developed both because of staff turnover and for other reasons. "The staff was made up of very different types of people, some who were very welcoming, others not so much," Kathryn Frank explains. "Sometimes there was a strong sense of, well, we're the coolest people in the room (and of course this was often true), and some condescension to newcomers at times. But that was short lived if you kept coming, didn't make yourself out to be superior (I'm talking clientele here), and proved to be actually open to new ideas." *(Ibid n#18)*

Customers from those times also spoke of occasional tension between the gay men on staff and the straight customers, and vice versa. Herman seemed to prefer lesbians and gay men as staffers, and though he did not draw his help exclusively from the gay community, the gay staff could be somewhat distant to some of the straight clientele. Larry Kirwan recalls, "Many of the gay men in particular seemed a bit insular or locked into their own community. There was a definite feeling amongst the gay men that they were different than those of us of who might have been merely straight or adventurous, while we didn't give a goddamn one way or the other. It wasn't something that was troubling. That schism was reflected all across West Village society then."[60] Joey Cupolo, one of those gay employees, recalled his time as a Magickal Childe employee fondly. "I've had a lot of jobs in my life, and that was the only job that I looked forward to going to work. I loved working that place. Herman gave me keys and at first we didn't open until noon, which is wonderful. And that's a nice time to open," he said, laughing, "because them Witches are like vampires. They ain't coming out in the daytime." *(Ibid n#43)*

But not everyone had such a fun time working for Herman. While he could be supportive and helpful to staff, especially to those he thought were really trying (or to whom he was attracted), he could also be cantankerous and arbitrary. Employees who were fired because they crossed wires or wits with Slater could generally get back into his good graces after tempers cooled. But those who were kicked out for stealing from him or messing with his business were persona non grata as far as Herman was concerned, and were tossed out on their ear if they dared to show their face around the store again. As employee Laura Austan noted, "Herman erased people" who ripped him off.[61] Curt Bargren recalls an argument between Bobbi Willis (Craft name *Heather*) and Herman Slater in the late 1970s. Herman bragged of putting "the curse of the Goddess" on Willis, who subsequently became a bag lady on the streets of New York.[62] Their vicious fight apparently started when Slater and Willis were both attracted to the same man. Surprisingly enough, several years later Willis ended up working for Herman at the Magickal Childe, where she stayed for the next eight years. If her employment also resulted from the curse, those on Slater's bad side might note that it proved marvelously efficacious.

Kathryn Frank says the Magickal Childe was a place where people were accepted regardless of their sexual orientation or race. Slater had fought in 1974 to ensure that the Craft community did not discriminate. But even though all races were welcome and did patronize the store, Frank says that "it was more white than anything else, although of course the store carried Vodoun books and paraphernalia, and Santeria. ... There was certainly no racial bias that I ever heard of, although some [customers] took offense that such stuff was carried in the store. And again, both Herman and Eddie's response was basically, 'Fine. Go start your own damn store and you can put whatever you want in it.'" *(Ibid n#18)* Herman defended Vodoun and its practitioners, writing, "Do not get scared and imagine that voodoo is what you have seen in the movies or on television. Media depictions of voodoo are slanted, uninformed and generally grotesque."[63] Despite its color-blindness, the store was once picketed by a small group of black men who objected to its promotion of the occult. Protesters stopped Tarot reader Emma Davy one night as she left the store and asked, "Don't you know what they're doing in there?" She earnestly replied, "No. What?" which stopped them cold and gave her a good chuckle on the way home. *(Ibid n#18)*

The Magickal Club House

Many folks who frequented the shop at its new location also socialized a few blocks away at the Bells of Hell, an Irish ex-pat bar that was run in the 1970s by legendary proto-shock-jock Malachy McCourt.[64] Located at 105 West 13th Street, the Bells was frequented by hard-drinking would-be novelists, journalists, lawyers, communists, folk-singers, Irish republican activists, occultists, gays and lesbians, and anarchists.[65] Many rock journalists drank in the outside bar, including Lester Bangs, Billy Altman, and Nick Tosches. Turner & Kirwan of Wexford played as the Bells' house band for several years. Larry Kirwan, who was a student of Simon's at the Magickal Childe in late 1976, went on to become the front man for the Irish rock group Black 47. The band memorialized the bar in the song "Bells of Hell" on their CD *Elvis Murphy's Green Suede Shoes* (2005). Larry notes, *(Ibid n#60)*

> The Bells of Hell was a total blast. It attracted more of the younger, drug influenced community and every other nut that happened to swing around the Village. Sometimes I would look down on the audience through a haze of smoke and think *"Jesus, how the hell did we attract such a crowd of oddballs?"* Then again, I was one of them.

In the autumn of 1976, at Kirwan's invitation, Simon and a number of other fellow-travelers began hitting the Bells on Friday and Saturday nights to listen to the band and hang out afterwards. Under Simon's influence, and with help from Judith McNally and many others, they eventually formed a social club of sorts that they nicknamed StarGroup One. Its goal, according to Simon, was to disseminate occult knowledge and help liberate New Yorkers from the corrupt power structure of the day; a sort of agit-prop for the occult movement. StarGroup One was truly a construct of its time. Alan Cabal wrote that it was "inspired by the *Illuminatus* books of Robert Anton Wilson and Robert Shea and Timothy Leary's exopsychology theory of the eight-circuit brain." *(Ibid n#27)*

StarGroup One eventually organized parties and arranged concerts and performances in the back rooms of the Bells and the Magickal Childe. One such party, held in July 1978, is described by Giani Siri:[66, 67]

> *In June of '78, at one of the concerts there was a discussion about a birthday party to be held in July for someone named Rose Kelly. They needed a cake. Amy Sefton knew that I was a decent baker and pretty good at cake decoration. I volunteered along with Amy to make the cake. Here's where it got weird for me. I had perceived from the other regulars at the Bells, that this was a surprise party for Rose. To this day I cannot tell you why or how I hit upon the cake decoration that Amy confirmed would be perfect: A sun shield flanked by horns of Isis with a rose in the center of the shield. Amy and I transported this huge cake on the day of the party – July 22, 1978 – to The Bells. Everyone said it was perfect. The cake was set in a place of honor. Simon and Judith McNally began the festivities. I waited for the guest of honor to arrive. A few minutes into the event I realized this woman for whom I'd baked this cake had been dead for over 40 years, and been married to someone named Aleister Crowley. As they talked about her biography and I learned Yeats had been part of the Golden Dawn, that soothed me a bit. But as the observance continued and the events of the Cairo working were memorialized I got very spooked because I could not give any rational explanation for how I'd developed the symbol I'd put on the cake. Cue the Twilight Zone music. Some very special and powerful things happened in and around that evening. I don't know what had happened before that night but that was when I joined StarGroup One.*

StarGroup One's membership was fluid and eclectic, running the gamut of the fringe-artistic-occult subculture of New York. Larry Kirwan notes, "We were able to turn out numbers and provided a focal point for many in the occult community." *(Ibid n#60)* The loose but effective union included Judith McNally, Larry Kirwan, Pierce Turner, Chris Claremont of X-Men fame, his then-wife Bonnie, journalist and writer Alan Cabal (Bonnie's future husband), Marvel Comics writer Allyn Brodsky, avant-garde poet and performer Copernicus, cloudwalker Philippe Petit, Amy Sefton and her husband, the science fiction artist known as "Freff" (Connor Freff Cochran), and many others.[68, 69] *(Ibid n#66)* A great deal of creative ferment was generated by this artistic-occult commingling. Giani Siri, for example, began a project called the StarGroup Tarot to memorialize many denizens of the New York occult community; this project eventually evolved into *The New York Tarot*. Freff contributed a painting to the *Fantasy Showcase Tarot Deck* published by Bruce Pelz in 1980. Simon went on to publish the most infamous, and arguably one of the most popular, occult books from the 1970s, the *Necronomicon*. The activities of StarGroup One allowed its members to fill the downtime between earning a living and practicing magick with some good, hard-drinking fun.

The Dan Greenberg book *Something's There* was published early in 1976. Greenberg had interviewed Herman Slater and members of the Children of Branwen for the book in 1975 while the Warlock Shop was still in Brooklyn Heights. To promote the book, Greenberg organized a day-long Tour of Occult New York, which was auctioned off as part of a Public Television fundraiser for Channel 13 in May. The occult tour, which took place on September 1, featured a Welsh full moon ritual that was conducted at the Magickal Childe by Sarna Svendsen's Passaic Coven. The event, complete with a photo of the Welsh rite, was written up in *The New York Times*, thereby satisfying Slater's hope for some free publicity for the new store.[70]

A public ritual was held at the Magickal Childe on October 31, 1976 to honor the Neo-Pagan Sabbat of Samhain.[71] The rite was performed by Margot Adler's Manhattan Pagan Way in the back room of the Childe, followed by a potluck dinner and party. Among the attendees was future Witchcraft high priestess and author Judy Harrow who, as a newcomer to the Craft, was attending her first public ritual.[72] This was the beginning of what would become an annual community event in Chelsea and the start of the tradition of throwing a Witches Ball in New York City at Hallowe'en. The Hallows Festival would gradually grow into a public ritual and street party in the 1980s, with West 19th Street being closed between 5th and 6th Avenues. Herman would use the opportunity to raise funds for various causes, such as bidding to rescue people from a mock Inquisition in order to send occult books to a library in Montana. He would often attend the event in drag, appearing one year as Laurie Cabot and another as Barbara Bush.[73, 74] Slater was also known to do tarot readings for Hallowe'en fundraisers at the Theater for the New City, where Eugenia Macer-Story is still featured each year.[75]

Kathryn Frank tells an amusing story of how Slater dealt with troublemakers at the event. "One year, when he was officiating at the casting of a Circle, some bridge and tunnel boys started jeering and making fun. People tried to hush them, but they kept it up. All of a sudden, Herman, wearing full regalia and a horned helmet, the whole nine yards, [and] wielding this massive sword he had just used to cast the Circle, broke the Circle and took off after them. They freaked out and started running away, with Herman chasing them all the way down the block, swinging this frigging scimitar! Cheers rose from the crowd, applause broke out, then Herman calmly returned to the Circle, repaired the breach and continued on with the ritual." *(Ibid n#18)*

In later years, the Hallows Festival became so large that Slater hired the New York City chapter of the Hell's Angels to act as security, undoubtedly preventing any more disruptive ballyhooing (given the mis-memories of what had happened at Altamont in 1969). The President of the chapter, Sandy Alexander, became a semi-regular face at the Childe.[76] The press attended these spectacles and took notes, pictures and film footage for their obligatory Hallowe'en stories. Film of the festival's 1985 Samhain ritual even appeared in a documentary on Witchcraft and Satanism.[77] "The Press was always around for better or worse," writes Peter Conte. "[And] movies were a pain in the ass as they took up too much time [to film]" and interfered with the workers' ability to make money.[78] But despite these drawbacks of fame (or infamy), the shop and its various events provided a cozy gathering place for practitioners of the various spiritual paths that made the Childe their home.

Slater also wasn't opposed to holding events at other nearby venues when the situation warranted it. Playwright Eugenia Macer-Story recalls that Slater produced one of her plays a few doors down from the Childe. "There is the production of my mini-musical by Herman at the Inferno Disco on Hallowe'en in about 1980," Eugenia writes. "The Inferno Disco was a wild venue. I had never been there before. Herman booked as one of the acts my mini-musical *Red Riding Hood's Revenge*, and we played to a capacity house. ... This play later was published and won recognition from a theatrical magazine. At the time, one of the O.T.O. people approached me portentously and declared – 'You KNOW, there is nowhere else they would let you STAGE this.' Maybe not." *(Ibid n#18)*

It wasn't long before the Magickal Childe became the *de rigueur* destination for many visitors to Manhattan. Not all of these people were serious practitioners; many, in fact, were dabblers or sightseers. Larry Kirwan notes that quite a few of the people hanging around the Childe "had little interest in the time and discipline it took to master various techniques. They liked to talk the talk, as they say, but were too interested in sex and drugs to do any of the serious walking. This is not a particular put down of the Childe and the hangers on that it attracted, but more a statement of the general philosophy of the times. Some of the rest of us were no less interested in the wildness but were seeking other forms of knowledge, not to mention, power." *(Ibid n#60)*

Despite this criticism — which, if one really wanted to press the point home, could be leveled at many occult shops, or Christian churches for that matter — many people who were seriously involved in the occult also made the pilgrimage to the Magickal Childe. They included occult authors, such as Raymond Buckland and Francis King. Larry Kirwan attended lectures on ceremonial magick there. Sally Eaton, the original "hippy Witch" in the Broadway production of *Hair*, worked and hung out at the shop. Margot Adler, who had not yet written her ground-breaking book *Drawing Down the Moon*, was a Childe regular, as were Hans Holzer and Rolla Nordic.

The hip and beautiful people also dropped by, such as Norman Mailer and his assistant Judith McNally who, as an initiate of Welsh Witchcraft and Gardnerian Wica, often dragged the author to the musical shows held in the rear of the store. Deborah Harry of the rock group Blondie came in a number of times for herbs and other items to help her bandmate and significant other, Chris Stein, when he was suffering from pemphigus in 1983. *(Ibid n#18)* John Lennon and Yoko Ono, who were said to be interested in the Tarot and the religion of ancient Kemet, were occasional customers (before John was gunned down by a lunatic fan in 1980), as was movie producer Roy Radin (before Roy was gunned down in a soured film deal in 1983).[79,80] George Harrison and Paul McCartney were also said to drop by from time to time until an "aspiring actress" who was working the counter said something rude to McCartney. *(Ibid n#43)* WNBC-TV news co-anchor Sue Simmons regularly had her fortune read in the back. *(Ibid n#33)* William S. Burroughs, Alan Ginsberg and Harry Smith would also pop in from time to time.[81] *(Ibid #76)* Writers and directors over the years also used the Magickal Childe as a setting or inspiration for their own work. These included Roberta Findlay and Robert Bierman, who filmed portions of their horror flicks *The Oracle* (1985) and *Vampire's Kiss* (1989), respectively, in the shop; and Steve Patterson, the writer and director of the film *Drawing Down the Moon* (1997), who used the shop as a research source.[82] "We had virtually everyone who was an A list celebrity show up at one time or another, from famous fashion designers to musicians to movie stars, always incognito," claims Peter Levenda. *(Ibid n#1)*

Typical of the types of encounters one could expect at the Magickal Childe is a story from Joey Cupolo. *(Ibid n#43)* Late in the day on Christmas Eve in 1976, Joey and Clinton were sitting behind the counter at the Childe just toking up and relaxing. Business was slow that day, since most of the store's customers had done their shopping before Winter Solstice, several days earlier. As Joey told it, "in the early dusk a black limousine pulled up in front of the store, and this skinny guy with beady eyes wearing wire rim glasses and a rabbit fur coat gets out of the car and comes into the store. He greets Clinton by name in this British accent and thanks him, saying 'Oh Clinton, by the way, that spell worked very well.'" The "skinny guy" was John Lennon doing a bit of late Christmas shopping for Yoko Ono. Lennon purchased a human skull and some pewter artifacts. "He wanted me to wrap the skull, and we had no wrapping paper," Joey said. "I'm shaking. We had some posters, so I used posters to wrap it. And [Lennon] says 'That's very ... unusual.' He seemed to like me. He said to Clinton 'I get a good vibe from him, even though he does shake a lot.' And Clinton said, 'I think he might be a little nervous being around you.'"

Sally Eaton, too, recalls being alone in the Childe one afternoon in 1976 when Lennon stepped out of a cab and came in. "In one of the glass cases Herman had three flint knives purported to have come from a Neolithic barrow in the north of England. 'Pycti' athames, I think he called them, and I think they were like $100 each. Lennon was fascinated and bought two of them." *(Ibid n#45)*

To explain its popularity, one needs to understand that the Magickal Childe wasn't just a place to shop. The store also functioned as a community center. According to Kathryn Frank, the Childe was run like a combination business, club house and hangout. *(Ibid n#18)* It was a place where you could go to hear the latest gossip, and sometimes to people-watch, and it was the scene of some really great parties, with lots of drugs and drink and carrying on, laughter, and a refined form of cattiness or bitchiness between different groups, leanings and genders. *(Ibid n#60)* On another level, it was something like an occult spa, a place where you could go to renew yourself.

Not everyone agreed with this opinion. Ken Dalton felt the Magickal Childe didn't have the same level of engagement with the community as the Warlock Shop did in Brooklyn Heights. "I never felt that there was any real connection to the community. No vibe there. Also ... things were becoming a bit more fragmented by then; the community was, in my opinion, beginning to splinter." *(Ibid n#2)* However, Larry Kirwan remarks that the shop offered people a chance to start over. "There was a feeling that when you entered the Magickal Childe you abandoned your past life," writes Kirwan. "I knew nothing of Herman's past, where he came from, nor did I give a continental hoot. Likewise with Al Cabal and all the others that I met in there. You could start a new life crossing that doorstep and we often did. There was definitely a sense of complete freedom in that store. I miss it." *(Ibid n#60)*

Woody Allen might have been thinking of the Magickal Childe when he wrote, "There is no question that there is an unseen world. The problem is, how far is it from midtown and how late is it open?"[83] In the case of the Childe, it served its Midtown neighbors 'till 8 PM, seven days a week.

Chapter 24: The End of the Line

In the Grip of the Devil

That the Magickal Childe would put limits on its hours of operation (and a ho-hum closing time of 8 PM at that) seems to go against the whole pop cultural construct of the nocturnal Witch, up until the wee hours stirring spells by candlelight. But Witches, while romantically pigeonholed by the outside observer as overwhelmingly "Otherworldly" by nature, are really far more focused on this world than on any other one. In marked contrast to the many shades of Christianity, whose adherents sometimes eschew earthly pleasures in lieu of the bright and shining future that their death and salvation holds (or claim that they do, at any rate), the Witch and Neo-Pagan generally live in this world and make what they can of this life. In other words, all (spell)work and no play makes Endora a very dull Witch, indeed. The sexual permissiveness that swept the country in the 1970s applied to the members of this community as much as it did anyone of the younger generation. After all, Herman and his staff liked to "get some" every now and again, too.

Slater, in particular, seemed willing to blur the lines between business and pleasure more often than was perhaps prudent. One of his former workers, Laura Austan, noted that Slater could be a demanding taskmaster, especially for those employees who were, quite literally, under him:[1]

> Working for Herman was tough. He got his every penny's worth of everything. That included people he employed for the shop or his bedroom. ... These [hustlers] would also have a job with the store in some capacity for as long as his interest held. Usually they'd be the general gopher, but they'd sometimes end up the Shipping Clerk or floor worker. The regular staff referred to them as 'The Dogwalker.' That was partially correct, as Herman had 2 or 3 Salukis all the time and couldn't walk them with the tubercular hip he had. So someone had to walk them. Herman's apartment on West 16th Street was a revolving door of hustlers, drug addicts, clingons and admirers.

Bennie Geraci concurs. "Herman would pick up these strays at the bars and take them in, and they would work for him at the shop," Geraci remembers. "Eddie would see a new boy working at the shop and ask Herman, 'So where did you pick up this number?' And Herman would hem and haw about what bar he had visited recently."[2] Alan Cabal's assessment of Slater's peccadilloes is more acerbic, characterizing the string of boyfriends that Herman dragged through the front door of the Magickal Childe as drug-addicted rough trade who he picked up at the

Haymarket Saloon (a hustler bar on 8th Avenue allegedly run by the Mob). "He'd keep them around until they ripped him off, then give them the boot and move on to the next one," Cabal wrote. "He liked them big and stupid, a total contrast with Eddie's graceful and intelligent demeanor."[3] Musician Kenny Klein also remembers this foible of Slater's. "Herman always had young men working for him, and often he would make one or another the store manager," Klein writes. "I never knew any of their names, other than Eric Pryor, who ended up turning on the Pagan community and becoming a TV evangelist who was anti-Pagan."[4]

Seventeen-year-old Eric Pryor was one of the young men Herman took under his hawk's wing in 1977. A native of Suffren, New York, Pryor had run away from home at the age of fourteen, according to his uncle, Pau Roefs, "to live a life of debauchery, prostitution, drugs, alcohol, violence and Satan worship."[5] Pryor claimed that his first exposure to the occult was Hans Holzer's book *The Witchcraft Report*. Upon reaching New York City, Pryor, like so many runaways before and since, turned to street prostitution in order to survive, and this, in all likelihood, is how he came to cross paths with Herman Slater.[6] As he had done with other hustlers, Herman made a project out of the street kid, giving him a part-time job at the Magickal Childe in return for sexual favors. While working at the Childe, Pryor was initiated into the Earth Star coven of the Welsh tradition that was being run out of the back room of the Magickal Childe by Herman and his high priestess Maria Parra.[7] This was not an unusual development according to many others, including Kenny Klein, who recalls, "Herman had a long line of men that he'd initiated, most known or thought to be his lovers. Many were teens. Some went on to become very prominent members of the Pagan community."[8]

Pryor would later move to California and claim to be a major leader in the Neo-Pagan community, with thousands of followers. When that shtick failed to conjure up any dividends from the West Coast Neo-Pagans, he made a very public conversion to Evangelical Christianity, which proved to be somewhat more lucrative.[9, 10] In an example of the chickens coming home to roost, Pryor named Slater as a pervert in a series of anti-occult presentations to police departments and churches in the United States and Canada. In a 1991 seminar on "Satanic Crime" he gave in Richmond, British Columbia, Pryor identified Herman as "the top gun" in the Neo-Pagan community, and described him as "a big time homosexual who is into S&M and bondage" who also sold "snuff" videos (pornography in which one of the participants is murdered) through his Magickal Childe catalogues.[11] After the high tide of the Satanic ritual abuse scam had passed, Pryor quietly settled down to preach in Carson City, Nevada. He was struck by a truck and killed while crossing the street one day in 2009 — a true case of karma running over one's dogma if ever there was one.[12]

Notwithstanding the rumors of what went on at the Childe, and despite its underlying mystique, manning a cash register in a Witchcraft store just wasn't as likely to get you laid as actually venturing out to the bars and discos after work. New York wasn't known as "the city that never sleeps" for nothing, and in the sexual Seventies "sleep" seemed more of a euphemism than ever before. Former ABC 20/20 producer/director Joseph Lovett characterized the decade as "the most libertine period that the Western world has ever seen since Rome."[13] Known as the "Golden Age of Promiscuity," it was the definitive decade of Aleister Crowley, especially with regard to the gay community.

Because of the anti-sodomy laws throughout much of the United States, the sexual revolution came much later for gays and lesbians than it had for everyone else.[14] Thus, if Stonewall represented the popping of a cork, the decade that followed was the foaming of the champagne as the pressure of generations was suddenly, and wildly, released. It was Crowley who had recorded the words of the spirit Aiwass in 1904, writing, "Be goodly therefore: dress ye all in fine apparel; eat rich foods and drink sweet wines and wines that foam! Also, take your fill and will of love as ye will, when, where and with whom ye will!"[15] And they did.

Lest anyone think that his admonition had somehow omitted the unspeakable vice of the Greeks, Crowley was quick to rid them of their ignorance. Crowley promoted the belief that all roads lead inevitably to the center, and encouraged every person to follow their own path through life and not bow to the pressure of society or religion. "The homosexual must not blaspheme his nature and commit spiritual suicide by suppressing love or attempting to pervert it, as ignorance and fear, shame and weakness, so often induce him to do," Crowley exhorted. "Whatever the act which expresses the soul, that act and no other is right."[16] That seems fairly clear.

Not everyone treated Aleister's egalitarian philosophy with equanimity. Crowley's own literary executor, John Symonds, bluntly disparaged the Great Beast's appetites and his attraction to the modern world. In his introduction to a reprint of Crowley's volume of erotic poetry, *White Stains*, Symonds exhibited a rigid, post-Wildean disdain of his erstwhile benefactor's morals, writing,[17]

> *[Aleister Crowley] was swamped by the Dionysian aspect of his nature, and lacked the other, the Apollonian side which supplied the balance and made the wholeness of classical man. Hence the abhorrence in which he was held by all except those fringe personalities who themselves approached his uninhibited forms of behavior, and his fascination for the youth of today when everything has broken loose and a large portion of mankind is in the grip of the Devil.*

Symonds certainly wasn't alone in this opinion. Fellow Englishman Alastair Cooke, in summarizing the age of free love in the United States, disgustedly observed in one *Letter from America* (1977) that perhaps the public's fascination with sex and pornography had finally run its course. "Maybe ... we shall try again to make a fair and practical definition of freedom of speech that will manage to rid us of the clutter of filth that floats along with the First Amendment and is marketed for lucre in the name of liberty."[18] Many were far too busy getting it on (or making lucre) to listen to such nattering; most of all the homosexuals, who were still generally treated like human garbage whether they abstained from the act or not. Dismissing the disgust of religious fundamentalists, author Jack Fritscher wrote, "Everything they say is true; but we weren't guilty, because it wasn't sin. It was liberation after years of oppression."[19]

But at a deeper level, below the queasiness exhibited by social critics of the day, beneath even the writhing bodies upon which their critical gazes were fixed in horror, one must ask whether there was some force at work which seemed bent on unhinging society in a very primeval way. Perhaps Dionysos, the original Vine, whose powers and place of pride had been press-ganged for the better part of two millennia in the service of the Christian God, sought to re-balance the human equation between the rational and the irrational. Freed after such a long absence by the madness of Nietzsche and the poetry of the Beats, the hips of Elvis and the lips of Jagger, His return might threaten to cause modern pillars of society, like those of the ancient Thebans, to lose their heads — and nothing causes people to lose (or even loose) their heads quite like good, old-fashioned boot-knocking sex. Author Emile Schurmacher in his book *Witchcraft in America Today* (1970) questioned whether the relaxation of sexual mores beginning in the 1960s actually led to the resurgence of interest in Witchcraft.[20] Like the Greek King Pentheus of old, the conservatives of this era railed against an ancient and untamable God of indestructible life, also to no avail.

It is ironic that although American right-wingers smeared everyone on the Left as perverts and/or communists, in fact the Socialists, New Left and, to a lesser extent, the Hippies had never been all that comfortable with homosexuals either. The Young Socialists Alliance was known to have expelled a gay member, and the Peaceniks had tried to prevent the GLF from displaying its banner at an anti-war protest.[21] Carl Wittman, who had authored *A Gay Manifesto* in 1970, had become disillusioned by the homophobia of the New Left by the mid-1960s. Recalling Tom Hayden's announcement that homosexuality and marijuana would not be tolerated in those working with the Students for a Democratic Society (SDS) in Newark, Wittman would eventually transform his anger over this betrayal of liberalism into a call for action.[22] Other movement leaders, such as Abbie Hoffman, were equally and unapologetically homophobic in their choice of language.[23, 24]

As the newspaper *Come Out!* lamented in 1971, "A few brothers and sisters have moved to the country or back into other closets in the movement (peace closets, [Socialist Worker's Party] closets, etc.).

Although all of these people still maintain a Gay identity, they are still not struggling around issues that are Gay issues. Going back into left straight organizations as an open Gay person is like naming your own oppression."[25] By some accounts, however, the inability of many Hippies to connect with or even acknowledge the needs of gays wasn't so much rooted in homophobia, although that certainly existed too, as it was a product of the heterosexual cluelessness of American society in general. This point was lampooned in the 1974 movie *The Groove Tube*.[26]

In pre-Stonewall days, establishments such as bars, restaurants and bathhouses that catered, albeit reluctantly, to gays were often owned and operated by the Mob. Beginning in the late 1960s, gay activists began lobbying for homosexuals to get involved and supplant organized crime in this niche market.[27] After the riots at the Stonewall Inn, which made that establishment a poster child for all Mob-controlled gay bars, gay men and lesbians slowly began to open their own places. The goal was for homosexuals to look out for their own interests, to control their own spaces and to cut out the criminal element, which was seen as yet another mechanism of oppression. But even in these new venues, problems still cropped up. Accusations of discrimination against customers based on class or race were noted in some gay-owned and operated businesses, particularly bars and bathhouses.[28] One early effort to sidestep corporate control of gay culture in New York was the advent of the GAA's weekly dances in 1971 held at a converted firehouse at 99 Wooster Street in Manhattan. The firehouse was destroyed by person or persons unknown (rumored at the time to be the Mob) in an arson attack in 1974, but by that point gay sex had already become industrialized in the Big Apple.

After Stonewall, the number of bars and bathhouses catering to gay and bi men increased dramatically. When capitalism was merged with a long-repressed sex drive, sleazier (and far more interesting) venues were bound to manifest. The old places for meeting people were still there — the piano bars and restaurants, the public restrooms, the adult theatres and peep shows, and the bathhouses that had catered to gay clientele in New York for almost a century. Indeed, there is some indication that public sex may have actually increased in the wake of Stonewall, due in part to raids on gay bars prompted by the Knapp Commission in 1970. For the back-to-nature types, there were the parks — Forest Park, Morningside Park, Riverside Park, and the Bridle Path and Ramble in Central Park, to name but a few — as well as numerous pocket parks where one could usually find denizens up for a quick game of pocket pool. The Ramble itself had been known as a gay cruising spot for at least fifty years by this time; however, according to Morty Manford, a former President of the GAA, arrests for public sex skyrocketed during the early 1970s, with forty-five men taken in on sodomy charges during one month in 1974 from the Bridle Path and Ramble alone.[29]

Subway "tea rooms" were also still as popular as ever, to the point where the Broadway Arms bathhouse eventually installed an IRTearoom that simulated the subway experience for its customers.[30] Then there were the ancient bath houses, such as the Everard and the Mt. Morris, and the up-and-comers like the New St. Mark's and Man's Country. Arthur Bell, in a *Village Voice* article on gay bathhouse culture in 1970s New York, noted how anonymous sexual encounters had changed over the decades. But by opening a window into a hitherto unknown world for most *Voice* readers, the article earned Bell the scorn of gay activists and sex club habitués alike (not that these were mutually exclusive callings) for exposing a seedy, yet venerable and very real, underside of gay life.[31]

A new sexual subculture involving BDSM had also emerged, stemming from an earlier biker subculture from the late 1950s – early 1960s (illustrated by Kenneth Anger's film *Scorpio Rising*, 1964) to become what the Village Voice in 1975 termed "the dark side of gay liberation."[32] A number of gay bars sprang up to cater to this crowd, many of them in the Meatpacking District and Chelsea where rent was cheap. Such bars as the International Stud, Anvil, Mineshaft (which gave new meaning to "snakes and ladders"), Toilet, Triangle, Sewer, Warehouse, Badlands and Crisco Disco offered spaces where back-room deals could be closed while on one's knees.[33, 34, 35] The International Stud (117 Perry Street), its own back room made famous in Harvey Fierstein's play and movie, *Torch Song Trilogy*, was one of Eddie and Bennie's favorite places to hang out, as was the Limelight (also in Manhattan) and Pep McGuire's, a disco bar in Queens not far from their apartment where they would dance the night away to songs like Donna Summers' "I Feel Love." Sunday was reserved for another bar, the Badlands.[36]

A hypermasculinized clone culture had begun to infiltrate the gay community nationwide. "On any given day," railed Arthur Evans, "Castro Street [in San Francisco] is filled with a conformist mob of male impersonators decked out in denim, leather, and even Nazi-like uniforms."[37] The same thing was happening in New York, where reporter Jonathon Mahler wrote that, "femme chic had given way to macho chic." The literary magazine *Christopher Street* observed that "It is getting exceedingly difficult to tell a homosexual from a longshoreman."[38] As objects of adoration, starlets and divas were out. Cops, the military and blue collar workers were in. "So what if it's only an accountant from Passaic dressed as a forest ranger?" Richard Goldstein rhetorically asked in the *Village Voice*. "The idea is to live on the edge beyond the pale of Bloomingdale's."[39] It is this movement that explains both the look and the popularity of the musical group *The Village People*. Gay men fetishized the oppressor, upped its amperage, overturned it, and took it from behind.

This sexual freedom came at a cost, because as the bars and baths multiplied, people seemed to lose their emotional connection with one another. In a space of approximately six years, the community had graduated from a time of furtive assignations, where people hesitated to give out their real names to sexual partners for fear of blackmail and arrest, to one where no one actually cared who you were because they were already moving on to the next person in the queue. It was an age of supermarket sex and commoditized touch — smell it, squeeze it, put it down, move on and pick up another. Looking back from that vantage point, what passed for homosexual culture in the previous decades seemed almost quaint by comparison. Not everyone dove headfirst into those dark waters, of course, as shown by ads in the *Village Voice* Bulletin Board that lamented the dehumanization of the bar scene. But many did. By 1975, the Mayor's office was trying to rein in the growth in the sex industry in New York to no avail. The problem, from the perspective of the powers that be, was that public sex had simply become *too* public by the mid-1970s. From the perspective of the participants, those in power were, at best, busybodies, and at worst fascist oppressors.

Given the repression that homosexuals had endured for centuries in the Western world, public sex — in parks, public restrooms, even in doorways and alleys — had, in many cases, been the only way in which men could actually meet and share moments of intimacy. This was particularly true for gay men who had been forced by social or family pressures to marry and raise children and who thus lacked a private space for trysts. The public venues, though dangerous, became enshrined in the homosexual subculture for the freedom from social mores. It is perhaps counterintuitive, then, that despite the newfound openness and the widening choice of businesses catering to gay men, public sex was more popular than ever. But patronizing a gay bar was no guarantee of avoiding arrest and ruin; police raids on New York bars began to seriously decline only in the latter half of the 1970s — and then mostly because of a lack of manpower (the city had laid off five thousand officers in 1975, for economic reasons) rather than from any dawning acceptance on the part of the police or the city fathers. However, harassment did sometimes flare up again at election time.

The decimated New York shipping industry, in combination with the close proximity of the leather clubs which occupied cheap spaces in the Meatpacking District, gave rise to the "Casbah" — an area on the Hudson River just west of the district from 14th Street south to Christopher Street. The abandoned and decaying docks and warehouses, dangerous remnants of the shipping industry from the first half of the twentieth century, were used as a sexual playground by gay men and hustlers. Armed robberies, beatings and the occasional accidental death were the risks men seemed willing to take in order to score. A series of high-profile attacks on gay men in Central Park's Ramble by gangs of young toughs armed with baseball bats occurred in the summer of 1978, emphasizing the risks inherent in public sex.[40] Joey Cupolo says that their roommate, Kevin McClung, used to go to the docks. "And those places were dangerous. There were holes in the floor, and you fall in a hole and you're in the water. ... These queens, if there was an empty spot in New York, they tricked," Joey said.[41] Empty meat and produce delivery trucks parked overnight underneath the structure of the abandoned-in-place Highline and along West Avenue were also used as gathering places for anonymous sex. Sex in the trucks was already an open secret by 1974, as demonstrated by its appearance in *Lovers*, an off-off Broadway musical review by Peter Del Valle and Steven Sterner.[42, 43]

Travel between the leather clubs, the trucks, and the docks was a regular sexual circuit for many gay and bi men in 1970s Manhattan. *(Ibid n#13)* If one were to draw a straight line between the northern and southern ends of the "Casbah," and then extend lines eastward from those points to the Magickal Childe on West 19th Street, an equilateral triangle would be formed (a Devil's Triangle, a conservative preacher might shout) that encompassed one of the sleaziest and most electrifying sections of New York City for the few short years that it was at its peak. Calling out the Devil in this is not an untoward deed for, at its heart, this area and others like it throughout the Western world represented a very real rebellion against those who had set themselves up as both the purveyors of society's mores and the mouthpieces of Heaven.

Herman Slater, who was a sometime denizen of this nighttime world, had relocated his shop to within a few blocks of this sexual playground. He may have done so deliberately, or perhaps it was just a welcome happenstance that the requisite retail space opened up so close to his favorite stomping grounds such as the Eagle, where he would pick up rough trade. It should come as no surprise that Eddie, along with Bennie and the others in his close circle, were also known to venture into the Meatpacking District, particularly after the shop reopened in the new space. Joey worked at the Childe, after all, and Eddie taught there and helped out on occasion. The bathhouses and back room bars were sometimes the focus of group outings by the roommates.

Joey Cupolo and Bennie Geraci reminisced about some of those excursions in a 2004 interview. "One day we got up to the door of the Toilet, and they told me and Charlie that the Toilet's closed, but the Sewer's open across the street," Joey recalled, laughing. "We used to go to these back room places. We'd have to go downstairs. That was scary enough going downstairs..." Bennie interjected, "That was the Underground." "No," Joey disagreed, "not the one that you had to knock on the door, and they lashed you up in slings ... You know, what they did in the warehouses on that street across from the docks. It was like caverns almost downstairs." Bennie said, "Yeah, remember, you used to have to climb up ladders and everything?" Joey replied, "Yeah, and one day I just got too paranoid and said 'If there's a fire, honey, we're dead meat. Dead fuckin' meat.'" Bennie exclaimed, "The Mineshaft!" finally remembering the name of the bar. "Oh, *that's* the one!" Joey agreed. "Honey, that was a

nasty fuckin' place ... New York was definitely an education (laughing)."
(Ibid n#41)

Hollywood attempted to provide just such an education to the American public (whether it was ready for it or not) when Warner Brothers released the William Friedkin movie *Cruising* (1980), starring Al Pacino. The movie, which was loosely based on a series of gay murders in New York City between 1962 and 1979, depicted sleazy scenes of backroom and public sex between gay men. The gay community protested the filming throughout the summer of 1979, attempting to disrupt the production with noise and lights. Protests continued unabated during the film's release. But for all the criticism that *Cruising* garnered, Bennie says that the New York scene that he and Eddie frequented in the 1970s was very much reflected in the film.[44] It should have, seeing as Friedkin used three bars in the Meatpacking District — the Mineshaft, Anvil, and Ramrod — for his pre-production research.

But even recognizing that the dark, dangerous world depicted in *Cruising* may have been exaggerated for effect, Cupolo was right to be concerned about their safety at these venues. Many baths and bars, particularly those that were operated "off the books," were often uninspected by code enforcement, the fire marshal or the health department, and were dangerously overcrowded, with poor lighting and unmarked and inadequate escape routes. On May 25, 1977, the gay community was rocked by a fire that broke out at the Everard Baths that killed nine men and injured twelve. The "Ever-Hard," located at 26-30 West 28th Street in Tin Pan Alley, was housed in a building that originally functioned as a church. By World War I, however, the Everard had begun to serve an entirely different sort of congregation.

Just four years before the Everard fire, on June 24, 1973, a fire in the Upstairs Lounge, a gay bar in New Orleans, took thirty-two lives and injured many more. Bennie Geraci who, with Charlie Dandelakis, had once lived only a block away from that bar in New Orleans and occasionally patronized it, recalls collections being taken up in New York gay bars for the victims of the Upstairs Lounge fire. Now fire had struck the Everard, which was an occasional stomping ground for Bennie, Eddie and rest of the gang. The tragedy shook them all, making the men much more conscious of their surroundings. After the Everard Baths fire, Bennie notes, "We always looked for where the exits were located, and requested rooms near the exits."[45]

Fires, muggings, and dangerous structures weren't the only hazards. Even before the spectre of the Human Immunodeficiency Virus (HIV), gay and bi men in 1970s-era New York had to deal with a number of sexually-transmitted diseases that rampaged through the community, spread by men who engaged in sex with multiple partners each evening. It wasn't uncommon for gay men to have all the anonymous sex they could squeeze into a weekend, and then head to their personal physician or the local health clinic for treatment after being exposed to whatever was circulating at the time. *(Ibid n#13)* Eddie and his friends weren't immune to the "love bugs" that were the scourge of the sex scene. "We all went there at one time or another, me and Joey and Charlie," Bennie said. "It wasn't every week, you know, but we had to go get fixed up. ... Eddie too. We were all real active."

Rising Expectations

Eddie had been sexually active for at least a decade by this time, so was certainly no playground Pollyanna. This no-strings-attached approach to sexuality had absolutely no effect on his relationship with Bennie; the two men were committed to one another and always went home together, even if they shared their bodies with others during their prowls. But as the gay scene changed with the times, so did Eddie's thinking about the mind, body, heart and spirit. It was hard not to experience a certain sense of exhilaration and empowerment when repeatedly confronted by bars full of sweating and half-naked men, bodies dancing and hearts pounding to a primal, Dionysian beat. Many gay men felt that they hadn't really started living until the Seventies came along and broke the molds for what constituted acceptable social behavior within their community.

To help gay men seize control of their own destinies in the evolving arena of sexuality and relationships, Lige Clarke and Jack Nichols published a book based on the questions that readers had submitted to them as editors of the newspaper Gay and via their "Homosexual Citizen" column in *Screw* magazine. Called *Roommates Can't Always Be Lovers: An Intimate Guide to Male-Male Relationships* (1974), it was one of the first gay self-help books published in the United States. Nichols followed this up with *Men's Liberation: A New Definition of Masculinity* (1975). Men's Liberation would question many of the assumptions of what makes a man in modern society by offering new paradigms for the concepts of gender, sex roles, emotions, playfulness, domination, cooperation and masculinity. Excited by the newfound freedoms for post-Stonewall gay men, yet frustrated by a lack of guidance specific to gay men in taking advantage of those freedoms, author David Loovis set out to create it for himself and others with *Gay Spirit* (1974). "This book," Loovis wrote, "is to help you who are already homosexual achieve fullest gratification from being homosexual."[46] To do this, Loovis insisted that it was most important to maintain a sensual aura about oneself. In those hedonistic times, a man almost had to go out of his way to not project a sensual aura.

This equation of sensuality with spirituality, a concept accepted at face value by many within the Hippie movement of the 1960s, was now coming into its own within the post-Stonewall gay community. Despite the wishes of the Marxists sprinkled throughout the gay rights movement, it was inevitable that homosexuals would begin translating these new experiences into spiritual codes for living. Gay men and lesbians were breaking new ground by moving from simply accepting or embracing their sexuality to celebrating it through life-affirming ritual and worship. In the subterranean world of S/M, with its rites, traditions, pass codes and symbolism, gay men were beginning to adopt the language of spirituality and worship to bring its adherents into a greater communion with each other and the Universe. The leather and S&M scene were nothing new; Life magazine had described the Tool Box, a San Francisco bar that catered to this subculture in 1964.[47, 48]

Lige Clark and Jack Nichols, who were no fans of this trend, observed, "It is no coincidence that many in the S/M crowd are religiously oriented and are known to attend churches. The dogma of atonement, involving as it does agony as a payment for 'sins,' is not foreign to them. Nor is it a coincidence that the element of punishment for the performance of sexual acts (and as a corollary to their enjoyment) is paramount in sadomasochistic ritual."[49] But Mark Thompson had a different take on the matter, noting that "S/M actually means 'sex magic'. It is their art and craft and means of taking a shamanic journey into the 'other world' of personal and collective myth. It is in that secret place where the healing occurs."[50]

On the other end of the sensual-sexual-spiritual spectrum was the California-based Order of the Golden Calf. An offshoot of the PsyVen, the Order was described as an "all-Gay, anti-Jesus Freak, pro-Life, pro-Joy Pagan cult."[51] According to Robert Anton Wilson, the members of the Order "had a magnificent gold (or imitation gold) statue of a calf and carried it around to places where other sects were proselytizing on the streets. There they would do an Adoration of the Calf, distribute leaflets describing their idol as 'the first victim of monotheistic bigotry,' and urge everybody else to 'lighten up your act a little.'"[52, 53] Perhaps because of the Order's activities, PsyVen was later characterized as a "gay church" that co-sponsored orgies in Berkeley.[54]

The Order's Bacchic rites put forth the confident, celebratory and open face of a new concept — that of "gay spirit." In *The Island Dialogues* (1973), Llee Heflin echoed the earlier writings of Aleister Crowley, making a case for a loving Universe that not only acknowledges homosexuality, but expects it. From the perspective of ceremonial magick, Heflin proposed a mystic, sensual, intimate spirituality in which gay men can celebrate their love for one another. "I do mean plainly and clearly that man loving man in perfect correlation of flesh emotions intellect and spirit is the ideal loving for man," Heflin wrote. "In the language of men this means plainly that men are to know each other sexually in the flesh at the same time that they know each other sexually in their emotions sexually in their intellects and sexually in their spirits. ... I tell you that two men so loving can create an Universe."[55]

Buczynski was certainly aware of these developments, since such books as *The Island Dialogues* were being sold by the Warlock Shop and marketed in the *Earth Religion News*. By August 1974, these concepts were beginning to filter into the pages of the newspaper itself. An article titled "Gay Magick? Dat Ol' Gay Magick Got You in its Spell?" discussed in positive terms Crowley's XI° working within the O.T.O. and its application to gay men. The author chided those who characterized the homosexual rite as "unnatural," saying that they simply do not understand the nature of the Universe. "To the true adept," he wrote, "all such arbitrary divisions are symptoms of incomplete enlightenment." In this, the author hewed closely to Crowley's own teachings on the mysteries inherent in the homosexual act. Nevertheless, the article warned that quantity was not the equal of quality. "In terms of magick, the heterosexual driven by blind lust and the homosexual motivated by a need to conquer an endless string of 'numbers' will never make it through to magickal enlightenment. Their literalness of the interpretation of the sexual experience precludes their ever mastering the higher mysteries of sexuality."[56] In other words, celebration was not a substitute for knowledge, understanding or, ultimately, wisdom, even though it could be a key to obtaining all of those things.

The scene in the Meatpacking District and, indeed, throughout New York and the larger cities of the United States was one means of breaking and sweeping away the chains of social taboo that had long bound many gay men for so long. But the more sensitive amongst these congregants, the Neo-Pagans and the mystics, the recovering Catholics, wandering Jews, budding Buddhists and their like, translated this fleshly experience into one of spiritual evolution where, in the words of Heflin, "the conflict between the Spirit and the Flesh, between God and Man is resolved in a genuinely satisfying way." Heflin and other like-minded explorers mapped out a new spiritual terrain for gay men, one in which the "Tantric sexual nature of God and the Universe is shown so that the Piscean lie against loving can at last be expelled."[57,58]

Those of a Neo-Pagan bent were not the only ones drawn to spiritual pursuits during this period. By the late 1970s and early 1980s, some ten years after the Stonewall riots, gay men had begun to join the Catholic Church in increasing numbers.[59] Nevertheless, throughout the Seventies gay men and lesbians were more apt to challenge the institutions and rules designed to keep them down, silent, and in their previous (preferably invisible) place in society. In one of the earliest protests involving Neo-Pagans and homosexuals, a Philadelphia group calling itself "Pagans & Atheists" picketed St. Patrick's Cathedral in New York City in 1974. A photograph of the event shows two participants holding signs decorated with images of the Cretan Snake Goddess and bearing the slogans "Return to Matriarchy" and "Burn Churches! Not Witches and Faggots." Citing John Robertson's book *Pagan Christs* (1903), the group argued that the only parts of Christianity worth keeping had originally been stolen from the Pagan religions of old, so it would be better to go back to the source rather than maintaining an oppressive charade.[60] In an article published in the January 10, 1976 issue of *Gay Community News*, the group called for a return to the Old Religion:[61]

> *There is no salvation in Christianity; only a continuation of our oppression as queers and as women. As free entities. As androgynes. As pagans and atheists. As goddess worshippers. As earth lovers, as matriarchy seekers. The goddess lives. Paganism now!*

Before leaving New York in early 1972, Arthur Evans, the former strategist of the GAA, had begun researching and writing about the political ramifications of Witchcraft and its historical connection to the social standing of homosexuals. Evans published several installments of his manuscript in *Out* magazine in 1973 and in the *Fag Rag* in 1974. These essays formed the basis of his groundbreaking book, *Witchcraft and the Gay Counterculture* (1978). Calling for nothing short of a revolution, the activist envisioned "a post-industrial communist nature-society where gay culture can flourish free from repression and exploitation."[62] Evans' impatience with the pace of change in modern society was rooted in the same rising feeling of freedom and a burgeoning desire which others also felt, to no longer compromise who and what they were. "Like butterflies, we are emerging from the shells of our past restricted existence," he wrote in the book's concluding lines. "We are re-discovering the ancient magic that was once the birth right of all human beings. We are re-learning how to talk to the worms and the stars. We are taking flight on the wings of self-determination."[63] *(Ibid n#62)*

In comparison to this heady stuff, the gay adherents of British Traditional Witchcraft could never achieve Loovis' "fullest gratification from being homosexual," for their sexuality was at best invisible in their spiritual lives, and at worst anathema to it. Since first becoming involved in Witchcraft in 1972, Eddie had willingly toed the party line when it came to operating with a female magickal partner, a rule that was observed by all existing Craft traditions, including his own Traditionalist Gwyddoniaid and The Wica. However, with the increasing openness and freedom of the gay subculture, he began to chafe at this limitation. A related issue that angered him was that the concept of an all-male coven was still rejected as illegitimate. "Eddie said that he was getting sick and tired that the Gardnerians could be all female [in a coven] if they wanted, but they weren't allowed to be all male," recalled Joey Cupolo. *(Ibid n#41)* While all-female covens were not universally accepted either, the point remained that some were. Polarity, some felt, was being used as an excuse to exclude some people, but not others. In the case of gay men, the result could be dehumanizing and anything but spiritually uplifting.

On the surface, the members of the Huntington Coven appeared to be relatively comfortable with the presence of Eddie, Bennie and Joey in skyclad Circles with them. But there is some indication that the male members of the coven were uneasy and that a tightly-knit group of three openly gay men in the coven, one of whom was their high priest, may have been too much for them. Their disquiet became more pronounced when Eddie began pushing to incorporate gay-friendly aspects to their rituals, and the coven resisted any suggestions to experiment with homoerotic elements. At no time was this clearer than when Eddie told Sheila Saperton in the spring of 1976 that he wished to elevate Bennie to the Third Degree himself within the Huntington Coven Circle.

At one level, this was a reasonable request. It was not uncommon for one half of a heterosexual couple who were lovers as well as working partners, either wife/husband or boyfriend/girlfriend, to initiate and elevate their lover/spouse if they were of sufficient level to do so. Such initiations often occurred whether or not the initiator was the high priestess or high priest of the coven in question, as allowances were often made to accommodate the feelings of those involved. However, this approach had never been taken for a gay or lesbian couple.

Within the traditional Craft, females were tasked with initiating and elevating males, and *vice versa*. Most heterosexuals considered homosexuality to be a surface phenomenon (a choice) rather than a fixed trait, which is why they were generally unsympathetic to the plight of the homosexual practitioner in the interpretation of Craft practices. They felt the homosexuals, after all, should always be able to modify their behavior in order to conform to the rules that the heterosexuals made up — a fantasy promulgated to this day by right-wing Christians who argue that gays and lesbians should remain chaste (and miserable and alone). This opinion was strengthened by the fact that homosexuals were already required to toe the boy-girl working arrangements of these groups. Yet that stance was and remains intellectually dishonest, because it refuses to recognize the basic structures that comprise a human personality. It also fails to acknowledge the fact that many of those same heterosexuals making that argument could not have changed their own behavior in favor of a homosexual orientation if they had been required to do so (at least not outside of a prison, boys school, or seminary). Ken Dalton and Eddie had many discussions about the problems of being accepted as a gay man in the Craft.

Ken Dalton:[64]

> *Eddie was genuinely torn up about this issue. As one of the most genuine people I've ever had the privilege to know, Eddie recognized and keenly felt the inherent disconnect in his orientation and life style to the normative values and practices of the Craft. He struggled with this and as time went on his*

frustration became increasingly apparent. He talked about his wish to be able to express the fullness of his being in the Circle, but recognized that the structure of the Craft simply did not encompass this. Certainly he was not closeted or reticent about expressing himself; there was no question that he was an extremely proud, openly gay man. Similarly, he never tried to impose his orientation on anyone else. The issue, as I saw it, was that Eddie was unique. He was so special, so knowledgeable, so loving to all that there was never a question or objection to what he did or who he was, either in or out of the Circle. The difficulty was that Eddie was not concerned just about himself, he knew that he was golden and would be welcomed by all; his concern was for others who were perhaps not so extraordinary. He recognized that the quotidian mass of the LBTG world (as we now refer to it) did not enjoy the same level of love and acceptance.

Yet Buczynski's concern about the place of gays in the Craft soon ran headlong into the realities inherent in his own practice, casting this issue in very personal terms. Elevation to the Third Degree in the Craft generally involves the performance of the *Hieros Gamos* (the Sacred Marriage, or Great Rite) between the one conducting the ceremony and the one going through the transformation. In traditional covens, this rite involves the actual sex act; however, since Buczynski was the high priest of the Huntington Coven, the Great Rite was only performed symbolically using the chalice and the athame to represent the female and male essence, respectively. *(Ibid n#41)* "As an example of his level of discomfort with the 'requirements' of the Craft," says Ken Dalton, "take a look at Lady Jana's letter to Eddie of 8/4/75 where she obliquely refers to his 'particular situation' as not being uncommon and permissible so long as his behavior in the Circle was according to the [Book of Shadows]." *(Ibid n#64)*

But for Bennie's elevation to Third Degree, Eddie insisted on performing the *Hieros Gamos* instead of Sheila. That was simply too much for the coven. Sheila in particular felt not only that Eddie was usurping her role as high priestess (and, truth be told, he was), but also that he was turning the tradition upside down. She refused to countenance it, and bolstered her position by citing the opinion of the unseen *Jana*, who is said to have written from England to say that this was simply not their way. Practically speaking, it was unrealistic for Eddie to think he could perform the ritual as he intended within a coven that was ostensibly British Traditional Witchcraft in nature. By the same token, if Buczynski had been calling the shots as the putative mouthpiece of *Jana*, he could have simply produced a supposed letter from Great Britain supporting his decision and then just gone ahead and conducted the rite as he saw fit. The fact that events unfolded otherwise tends support the conclusion that

Buczynski was not, in fact, *Jana* (or, at any rate, not playing that role completely on his own).

Reflecting on this event in 2005, Sheila Saperton wrote, "I hope you understand that Eddie kept his vows ... This IS a fertility religion and can only be male to female and not the same sex. That does not mean that any of the participants would not allow same sex relationships outside of the Circle. This is not discriminatory, but if one part is to be carried out so must it all. ... Eddie wanted to share the Craft in a way that was comfortable for him and I do respect him for that."[65] Saperton was correct, in that Eddie was beginning to realize just how personally important it was for him to be able to integrate his ecstatic vision of gay sexuality into his spirituality, and how untenable that vision was within traditional Wica.

The final straw came at the Summer Solstice ritual; or, more to the point, immediately following it. During the night, while everyone else was sleeping, one of Sheila's teenaged sons ended up fooling around with Joey in a manner similar to what many hormonally hopped-up teenaged boys do. Sheila found out after the teen confessed, and she exploded in anger telling Cupolo to leave her house and the coven. Eddie, who knew that the kid was something of a flirt and had probably instigated the event, stood by Joey. Cupolo believes that the fact that he was probably the least-liked of the three Queens residents probably sealed his fate: "I think that's why she over-reacted with the incident." *(Ibid n#41)* Most mothers would probably disagree with that characterization. Regardless, in the intersection of Sheila's capacity as both the high priestess of the coven and an aggrieved mother, the role of mother won out.

On returning home, Eddie sat down and marshaled his thoughts for his next move. He didn't waste much time pondering what his response to Saperton would be; he believed that his defense of Joey's indiscretion and his own failed attempt to elevate Bennie had irreparably damaged his position as high priest of the coven. Dalton recalls the point when Buczynski decided on his course of action.

Ken Dalton: *(Ibid n#64)*

> *I was with him one night and he simply said, "I'm leaving the Craft." I thought he was joking; he wasn't. He said that he was tired of feeling like a second class citizen and that he felt that his energies were needed elsewhere, to finalize the formation and attend the birth of a specific and declared gay version of pagan spirituality. He also said that to do so, he needed to make a clean break from the Craft, including his straight friends from the past in the Cult. It was like a funeral of sorts. He gave away many of his old tools and paraphernalia. He gifted me with the altar statue of the Goddess which he had used for years. It's still in my bedroom today. He gave me a hug, a kiss on the cheek and I never saw him again.*

Buczynski composed a letter of resignation and mailed off by the end of the month, with a copy to Joey Cupolo. Summing up all of his frustrations with Wica's stance on homosexuality, he could just have easily been addressing the Vatican and his own forestalled attempt to become a Jesuit priest:[66]

> *I entered the Craft against the wishes of practically everyone in the Craft. I proved to them, and to those that followed that, regardless of my private life, I was one of the most accomplished and skillful Priests of the Great Goddess. For many years I have struggled against their own hypocrisy and Dark-age, perverted morals. Nothing has changed, and I find even amongst those who say to the contrary, a most bigoted opinion of the Male Homosexual.*
>
> *I am tired of being looked-down-upon by upper middle class Suburbanites whose ideas of morals are mate-swapping romps in the nude. This is what the recognized Craft is today. I find only one exception, our coven — and even there I can feel the attitude that we, the Homosexuals, are 'different' (yuch!!!) Well, you're all right — we are different — so different that we have no right to worship as you do. I am sure that many of the 'Men' in the coven are constantly afraid of being 'approached' and just wouldn't know what to do. Your fears may now end!*
>
> *For countless Centuries in every Pagan society, the male homosexual constituted a special and separate Priesthood of the Great Mother. Therefore, there is nothing wrong with me serving Her. However, the Laws of the very Religion of which I am a Titular Head condemns my form of Love and Physical expression. Be that as it may, I cannot look down upon these Laws, for they are believed and followed by many serious people throughout the world. But I ask myself, What am I doing Here — it is a denial of my very Nature — it is me saying that my way is the wrong way for me even though I continue in that way. I cannot remain a traitor to myself and my own people. It is not necessary for me to abandon the Service of my Goddess; that will continue in the privacy of my own home — in my own way.*
>
> *I love all of you dearly, and if you truly love me, you will understand what I am saying. I cannot continue as the High Priest or active member of The Craft, therefore, I Gwydion, High Priest of the Huntington Coven, hereby do resign from said coven.*
>
> *I will always be a Witch, and I am proud of that. I will always wish to participate in Circles if I am invited ... that will never end. But as I have stated above, I cannot continue to be a Traitor to Myself, My Own People, or the Goddess that I worship.*

The letter was said to have devastated Sheila, who had relied upon Eddie for his leadership skills and knowledge within the coven.[67] Joey places the blame for the split squarely on Sheila, not on the mythical *Jana*, saying "We came to realize that as open minded as they tried to act, they still had reservations about the gay thing. It's too bad that she wasn't open-minded. She did depend on Eddie a lot." *(Ibid n#41)* Although their relationship was damaged, Sheila and Eddie did not completely sever all ties with one another. In late November 1977, for example, Buczynski granted a favor to Saperton and elevated one of her female initiates to the Third Degree.[68]

For several years now, Buczynski had been studying the "special and separate Priesthoods of the Great Mother" to which he had referred in his resignation letter. In so doing, he had accumulated a wealth of knowledge that had coalesced around the nucleus of an idea. This was confirmed by Ken Dalton, who wrote, "[Eddie] began to become more interested in starting his own tradition, specifically geared to gay and lesbian pagans."[69] Starting in late June, Eddie pulled together his notes and began a fierce writing campaign, which was foreshadowed by the note he had penned at the end of the copy of the resignation letter he sent to Cupolo: *(Ibid n#68)*

> *Joey, I'm sure Charlie would like to see this too! New cult is SUPER NEAT — you'll Love it! Love, Eddie*

Chapter 25: A Place of Our Own

Crafting the Minoan Tradition

Eddie Buczynski had examined a number of Bronze Age civilizations for inspiration over the years, beginning with the ancient Egyptians whose civilization he had idolized as a youth. Welsh initiate Judith McNally recalled Buczynski speaking to her about the needs of gay practitioners four years before he resigned from the Huntington Coven. "Certainly, Ed was wrestling with the practical problems of making the Craft hospitable to GLBT pagans," wrote McNally, "and I even recall his once saying that 'someday' he might dig into the single-sex mystery cults and see if enough could be found to revive or create a gay and lesbian trad. So even that early — 1972 — the idea occurred to him, though it would be a long while before he had the leisure to put it together."[1]

The problems he had been having within Gardnerian Wica in 1973 may have further spurred his interest in this subject. Rightly or wrongly, Eddie believed that his sexuality had exacerbated the problems he had encountered within the Craft, if not the unspoken impetus for much of the animosity. Certainly by 1973 he had fixed his interest solely upon ancient Greece, with an eye toward Minoan Crete and its theorized antecedents in Anatolia. Eddie confirmed this timing in 1977, when he wrote about his decision to leave British Traditional Witchcraft in order to pursue the creation of a spiritual path that would not require him to deny his nature:[2]

> *Finally, sick of all the shit flying back and forth from coven to coven (mainly concerning me), along with threats, death curses, slander, etc., I decided that, in order to find fulfillment in my religious beliefs, I must find a pagan cult which would welcome me as I am — a proud gay man. I began to research ancient religions involving the worship of the Mother Goddess. ... All I needed now was to find a place in which I could function openly and freely as myself. Most of the pagan Mother Goddess cults of antiquity were overtly tolerant of homosexuals; most had a homosexual priesthood. But none seemed quite right. I continued my search. In 1973 I discovered the answer on an island in the Mediterranean: Crete, the home of the Minoan civilization. In three years [by 1976] I had learned enough about Minoan worship of the Great Mother and Her Divine Son (the patron of homosexual men) to know for certain that here was the root of European witchcraft as we know it today.*

What had inspired Eddie to pick the Minoan civilization, as described by British archaeologist Arthur Evans, as his template? One possibility was that the Minoan society, with its mythologized peaceful, Goddess-worshipping pre-patriarchal civilization, was a phenomenon of current popular culture. Since the late 1960s, Crete had been calling to young, disenfranchised Americans who were intent on dropping out of the rat race in exchange for a simpler way of life. This was much to the chagrin of the Greeks, who looked askance at the hordes of penniless Hippies that took up residence in their seaside caves and beaches.[3] Since the mid-1960s, feminists had seized upon the archaeological evidence of Goddess-centered societies in places like ancient Crete and the Cyclades to bolster their political case for a rebirth of woman-centered spirituality, and the myth of a Universal Matriarchal Age was hypothesized in the work of nineteenth century scientist and writer Karl Pearson.[4] Other influences in this field included the writings of Frederick Nietzsche (*The Birth of Tragedy*, 1872) and Knossos excavator Arthur Evans (*The Mycenaean Pillar Cult and Its Mediterranean Relations with Illustrations from Recent Cretan Finds*, 1901).

But the person most responsible for first defining the intersection of Evans' work on Crete and the concept of the Great Mother Goddess was Classicist and feminist author Jane Harrison, whose *Prolegomena to a Study of Greek Religion* (1903) and *Themis: A Study of the Social Origins of Greek Religion* (1912) laid out the case for a peaceful Minoan culture guided by a priesthood devoted to the Goddess. This concept was continually developed and refined throughout the twentieth century with such books as Erich Neumann's *The Great Mother* (1955), which provided an in-depth assessment of the archetype of the Great Mother Goddess; Sibylle von Cles-Reden's *The Realm of the Great Goddess* (1960), which posited a "world-wide religion of the earth's dawn age"; and Helen Diner's *Mothers and Amazons* (1965), which presented a history of the sacred Feminine.[5,6,7] The anthropologist Marija Gimbutas followed a decade later, documenting evidence of Goddess worship throughout prehistoric Europe and inspiring feminists to seek alternative spiritual paths.[8]

Within the occult community, Crete figured prominently in the mythology of lost Atlantis, as demonstrated by a 1958 article in *Fate* magazine that touched on Plato's retelling of Solon's story of a great and powerful island located in the western sea that was wiped out by the Gods. Its author, Curtis Fuller, noted that the Minoans were a technologically advanced, yet highly artistic and naturalistic people who faded from history after the incursions of more warlike peoples. Unlike many other writers, however, Curtis acknowledged that the Cretans were not pacifists.[9] Eddie and others believed that both lost Atlantis and Priam's conquered Troy had ties to the Witchcraft that eventually developed in Great Britain.

Crete had also figured in the dreams and fantasies of many other people over the years, including Gerald Gardner, Ed Fitch, and Frederick Adams. Gardner is said to have believed that he had been a lowly worshipper of the Cretan Mother Goddess in a past life.[10] Considering his homophobia, this assertion is somewhat ironic, given the eventual use that Buczynski made of the Minoan Priesthood. Another such dreamer was W. Holman Keith, formerly of the Temple of Aphrodite on Long Island, who published *Divinity as the Eternal Feminine* (1960), which argued for the rekindling of Goddess worship within the context of a heterosexual social matrix that was tolerant of homosexuals.[11] Keith's writings would exert some influence on the shape of Fred Adams' Feraferia.

Late twentieth century feminism would also lay its claim to the Minoan dream. While this concept had first surfaced in Johann Jakob Bachofen's *Mother Right* (1861), historian Cathy Gere reports that the concept was repurposed to support various social movements in the twentieth century. "In the 1950s ancient Crete was reinvented as a beatnik Eden of creative spontaneity and existential joy," writes Gere. "At the end of the next decade, these neo-Dionysians were reborn as the exemplary peaceniks of the ancient world before emerging from their hippie haven to star in an outrageous feminist fable about the matriarchal beginnings of culture."[12] Gere contends that the impact of the modernist interpretation of ancient Crete was even more widespread. "My first exposure to Minoan Crete was thoroughly pagan – an activist from Greenham Common Women's Peace Camp gave me one of those tomes of pacifist matriarchal prehistory to read in the eighties," she writes, "and I was intrigued enough to go to Arthur Evans's work, from which I realized that the modernists invented everything that we associate with the counter-culture, including neo-paganism."[13] With the advent of the 1970s, feminists began pushing for a gynocentric spirituality to balance out what they perceived as several thousand years of patriarchal control and tyranny. In 1973, Mary Daly published *Beyond God the Father: Toward a Philosophy of Women's Liberation*, a manifesto calling for women to break free of what she termed the dis-ease of phallocracy and the oppression of Christolatry.[14]

Z. Budapest's Susan B. Anthony Coven No. 1 in Los Angeles, California was using the Minoan Snake Goddess as one of its symbols in newsletters by the early 1970s. Her publication of *The Feminist Book of Lights and Shadows* (1975) demonstrated that a same-sex coven based in part on the worship of the Cretan Mother Goddess was possible.[15] Merlin Stone provided Minoan examples (amongst others) of patriarchy's usurpation of the power of the Great Mother Goddess in her book *When God was a Woman* (1976).[16] Cretan iconography and feminist-lesbian spirituality had gone hand in hand since at least 1970, although the adoption of the labrys (double-headed axe) came several years earlier – though it was used as a symbol of Amazonian power, not of ancient Crete.[17] But Buczynski, while a feminist at heart, was no more willing to be pushed off the island of Crete by lesbian separatists than by prudish straight archaeologists. He may have emulated Dionysos, but no modern-day Lykurgos would cow him.

Already enamored of the history of Classical Greece, Eddie would have found Crete to be the ideal marriage between two civilizations that he had adored since youth, combining the familiar Hellenic God-forms with the magic and mystery of ancient Kemet. Historians and archaeologists have long known that Kemet influenced the Minoan civilization, called Keftiu by the Egyptians. Certainly the two lands had traded with one another, and there is evidence to support a Minoan presence in Egypt in the early Eighteenth Dynasty under Pharaoh Ahmose I (ca. 1550-1525 BCE).[18] Arthur Evans, the archaeologist who discovered the ruins of Knossos, believed that the similarities between the two civilizations may have resulted from the colonization of the island by Egyptians. "The proto-Egyptian in Early Minoan Crete is, in fact, so clearly defined and so intensive in its nature as almost to suggest something more than such a connection as might have been brought about by primitive commerce."[19] Evans' theory is not universally accepted, for commerce even in those dim recesses of time appears to have been anything but primitive; however, most scholars believe that there is evidence supporting a long-standing and mutually beneficial relationship between the two lands.

Eddie's association with the CES a few years earlier had whetted his appetite for a spiritual philosophy that was rooted in the ancient Near East. One of Buczynski's immediate influences for his choice of Crete as a template, and perhaps the most important one from within the Neo-Pagan community, was Frederick Adams. In 1967, Adams and others founded Feraferia, a Hellenistic-inspired Neo-Pagan spiritual tradition that Svetlana Butyrin, Adams' partner, described as "Paradisal, Minoan and Megalithic" in nature.[20, 21] The mythology of Minoan Crete, particularly pertaining to the Minoan Mother Goddess, provided an important basis for Adams' work in Feraferia. In December 1973, Adams wrote a multi-page article on Minoan Goddess worship, "The Mother God of Crete," that was published in the first edition of the *Earth Religion News*.

Adams set the tone in his first paragraph, writing, "On the Island of Crete, a truly erotic civilization flowered millennia before Christ."[22] Painting a picture of a peaceful, nature-loving people who were in touch with the cycles of life and death, he describes an almost idyllic society where bare-breasted priestesses worshipped Goddesses of hearth, mountain and subterranean realm. The Goddesses, aided by a young vegetation God, maintained a harmonious balance in the lives of their people. "Religion penetrated every phase of their daily life," Adams wrote. "But this religion was not grim, gloomy or at war with instinct. On the contrary, it expanded life gloriously and showered rainbow hues of fully discharging libido on everything with which the Minoans associated themselves." *(Ibid n#22)*

Written at the height of the sexual revolution, these words were like a siren call to young men and women that could lead, not to shipwreck and ruin, but to the primordial garden of delight. The article focused on the heterosexual aspect of Goddess worship, but not because Adams was anti-gay — rather, he simply loved and adored women. Adams concludes by asserting that this dream is yet within our grasp, and that the Minoan Mother Goddess "still patiently follows our sun in search of the next dawning of her erotic covenant, which weds man and all nature."[23]

Fred Adams would later write two further articles discussing the influence of the Minoan civilization on his beloved Feraferia.[24, 25] But it was Adams' first article that likely stimulated Buczynski's imagination on the subject of pre-Classical, pre-patriarchal religion in the Aegean, and set his feet on the path toward developing a cult that would allow him to, in Saperton's words, share the Craft in a way that was comfortable for him. But even before Adam's initial article appeared in late 1973, Buczynski already showed signs of homing in on the Minoans. Ria Rivera notes that Eddie had assigned her to construct and perform a ritual and feast preparatory to her initiation (ultimately aborted) into Gardnerian Wica in December 1973. Ria prepared and conducted what she described as a Minoan ritual on March 15 of that year. The date coincided with the Roman Festival of Ops, but the rite was dedicated to the Goddess Rhea. Held in the small ritual space in the back room on the second floor of the Warlock Shop, the rite included a feast of pork cooked with dates and figs, served with minted beer.[26]

From the time Adams' article was published, Eddie began researching Aegean archaeology, Greek mythology and historical novels to glean the details from which he could formulate the mythos of his new spiritual path.[27, 28] With the problems he encountered in the Huntington coven, Buczynski intensified his research throughout the summer of 1976.[29] He spent a great deal of time combing through the stacks at the New York Public Library, and writing down his ideas at his desk in the office of the Middle Village apartment. Using ancient Crete as his model, he called this new spiritual path the Minoan Brotherhood.[30]

Bennie Geraci believes that Eddie had been planning something along these lines for some time. "He was determined that he was going to get the Minoan Brotherhood started, I think, before he even met me [in 1974]," Geraci writes. "He was always into the Greeks. He had it in his mind. He always had Greek and Minoan archaeology books that he was reading. I know that because they were in my room and I could see what he was reading. He didn't discuss it, but every now and then he'd say 'Look at this!' or 'Look at that!' or he'd talk a lot about Knossos."[31] Ken Dalton recalls many conversations with Eddie in 1975 and 1976 about his idea of forming a gay men's tradition based on the mythology of Minoan Crete.

Ken Dalton:[32]

It was at about this time that he began to talk to me about forming an alternative to the Craft — of course, you now know this as the Minoan Brotherhood. I do think that I may have been one of the earliest persons with whom Eddie discussed the possibilities, it was a nascent thought at that time, and he spoke of this as a parallel to the Craft. I don't think that in the beginning he contemplated leaving the Craft or that the Brotherhood would, for him, supplant the Craft. ...

We spoke a fair bit about this concept. ... Since I was in college at the time he asked me on a few occasions to check references for him or to look up some details or historical details. ... I gave him a copy of the Homeric Hymns. He really loved those, and thought that he might incorporate some of those into the liturgy he was developing. Nevertheless, he never told me much about the inner workings of his plan. We discussed the concept of the Kouros figure [the physical embodiment of the young, male God] and its symbolism, the symbolism of the double axe, etc.

In choosing the Minoan civilization as the model for his new spiritual tradition, Buczynski essentially had three goals in mind. The first and foremost of these was to provide a setting in which gay men could worship the Gods free of Western expectations for what it means to be a man, including the gender and polarity strictures laid down by British Traditional Witchcraft and other advocates of heterosexual fertility rites under which he had chafed for the last several years. The second objective was to provide a meaningful way to facilitate this worship that was internally consistent with the culture he used as his model. The third goal was to ensure that the first two goals would be in harmony with the female creative and nurturing principle of the Universe. The success of the first two goals was not assured in the 1970s, for a variety of reasons. As for the third, until the conservative backlash of the early 1980s, American society and culture were already slowly moving in this direction.

The Intersection of Sex, Love, and Spirit

For homosexuals, two great struggles occurred simultaneously in the 1970s. The first was the political and public relations fight to convince straight society that being "gay was okay," in Frank Kameny's words. This was a campaign for equal rights in employment, for equal access to goods and services, and for the elimination of the sodomy statutes that critics used to justify denying homosexuals their right to function as contributing members of society. More fundamentally, it was a crusade for their right to be left alone so that everyone could live their lives as they saw fit without the interference of government busybodies.

The second struggle lay in convincing the gay community itself that being gay was okay. This problem occupied a good deal of Eddie's thinking. As noted earlier, the American Psychiatric Association had only removed homosexuality from its list of mental and emotional disorders in 1973, and it would be more than a decade before a simple majority of the American electorate caught up with this new paradigm. Oppression of gay men in particular was still rampant throughout most of the United States, including New York City. All mainstream cultural references pointed to heterosexuality as the normative state, and references to homosexuality, where they could be found at all, were overwhelmingly negative. One example was the October 8, 1974 episode of the popular ABC television show *Marcus Welby, MD*. The episode, named "The Outrage," was about a junior high school boy who was taken on school camping trip and raped by his science teacher. True to its name, this show provoked outrage in gay communities around the country, and it was pulled by ABC affiliates in Philadelphia and Boston. The issue was not that such things do not happen, but that the subject matter played into the public's fear of gay men associating with children. Furthermore, the episode included no contrast with heterosexual assaults on children, which are overwhelmingly more numerous by comparison.

Because of this barrage of negativity, many gay and bisexual men were prey to self-esteem issues that manifested in destructive behaviors, such as drug abuse and sexual addiction, or the feeling that they deserved what society dished out to them. These issues were a problem even in New York City, with its burgeoning social outlets for gay men; partly because of the macho environment in which so many men were raised, but also because of the continual influx of damaged young men from the provinces who also bore the programmed scars of their upbringing.

Eddie pointed a finger at the root cause of this problem in a paper he later wrote for those inquiring about membership in his new group. "Our Balance has been disrupted, and Society, with its Patriarchal Homosexual-Taboo is mainly responsible for this," Buczynski asserted. "These Taboos stem from the Patriarchal Religions (Christianity and Judaism as an example)."[33] Buczynski further pointed to those things that hold back gay men from experiencing the ecstatic and from being in harmony with nature, writing, "Now as Christians, Jews, or Moslems, etc., we cannot reach these states. The Masculine Principle, exalted almost exclusively in these Religions, creates a Repressive, fear-inducing atmosphere. Especially to a Gay man, functioning is almost impossible under the characteristic influences of Guilt, Pity, and Condemnation in these Religions."[34] *(Ibid n#33)*

But Buczynski firmly believed that the battle was not with the Christian God, against whom he admonished Minoan initiates not to speak, but rather against the abuses of His followers in their hatred, ignorance, and persecution of homosexuals. *(Ibid n#30)* As a bumper sticker that became popular in the 1980s after the rise of the Christian right would later put it, "Jesus, save me from your followers." British Traditional Witchcraft, in Eddie's opinion, was just as incapable of rectifying this problem, for he found "the Witch-Cult to contain Sexual Bigotry and Moral Hypocrisy, (very similar, in fact, to the very Judeo-Christian standards which they claim to despise)." *(Ibid n#30)* What Eddie was looking for was a "path for the individual who realizes the need for regaining a Balance in their lives, conducive to Happiness and Peace of Mind — to be in Harmony with the Eternal Scheme of the Universe in order to fully realize that we ourselves are 'God.'"[35] In this, Buczynski borrowed from the central tenet of the CAW, the pass phrase of which was "Thou art God/dess."

The goal, then, was to free gay men from the shackles of an Abrahamist mindset and to restore balance to their lives through the application of a new spiritual paradigm. Achieving this goal was partly a psychological struggle. In this Eddie took inspiration from the writings of John Lauritsen, a gay activist in the 1970s who had co-authored a history of the early gay rights movement, and from Leo Martello, who had worked with Lauritsen in the GLF.[36] Evidence of this influence can be found in Buczynski's writings after the founding of the Minoan Brotherhood. Lauritsen had self-published a pamphlet titled *Religious Roots of the Taboo on Homosexuality* that Eddie insisted all initiates and prospective members alike must read.[37] Another example is Mitch Walker's book *Men Loving Men*.

When *Men Loving Men* came out in 1977, it so impressed Buczynski that he exhorted those inquiring about membership in the Minoan Brotherhood to read it first before contacting him again.[38] *(Ibid n#35)* In 1976, Walker published a paper on Uranian psychology that exerted a major influence on the approach to sex and relationships he took in *Men Loving Men*.[39] Walker wrote of "the Double," the unconscious spirit-force that functions as "the secret gay love-source in the mind." The force he writes about is the mystical aspect of homosexuality, which "has to do with magic, with fantastic powers beyond our ordinary daily living."[40] This magic wasn't to be selfishly hoarded, but to be used in the service of others. "Because of the essential equality basic to gay love (inherent in the Double), and because gay people are outcast from the society and its constricting consciousness, they have a spiritual potential for realizing the Androgyne within," Walker asserted. "This is a great gift and a burden, because with it comes a responsibility to help ourselves and humanity become more whole and harmonious."[41, 42] This last concept resonated strongly with Eddie, who would exhort future initiates in the Brotherhood to act as Priests to the gay community.

That year also saw the publication of *The Joy of Gay Sex*.[43] These two books, with their forthright treatment of gay sex as natural, loving and free, marked a sea change in how sex between men was viewed within the gay community itself, translating the countercultural concept of free love into the language of gay men. More importantly, it was a declaration of guilt-free love. As ceremonial magickian Katon Shual writes, "The first and perhaps most significant step is to start viewing one's sexuality as Magical and allow all things to reinforce this intention. Thus any sexual act is also a Magical ritual."[44] This concept spontaneously played itself out in the West Side bars and bathhouses that Eddie frequented on the weekends.

For over a century, Classical Greek and Hellenic civilization had been held up as a model for discourse on homosexuality. Hilary Fraser notes that this dialogue, based on Plato's *Symposium*, began in the 1850s and was fully established by the 1880s.[45] It wasn't until the publication of K.J. Dover's *Greek Homosexuality* (1977) that the Victorian shawl was finally ripped away to allow for a serious study of the "unspeakable vice of the Greeks."[46] Unfortunately, Dover's book did not appear until some months after the Minoan Brotherhood was established, and so wasn't initially available for Eddie's use. Other writers on the comparatively new subject of gay Witchcraft did not manifest until the early 1980s, at which point the trend of promoting Witchcraft and Neo-Paganism as life-affirming spiritual alternatives for gay men was already fairly well established.[47] The earlier writings of Edward Carpenter, John Addington Symonds, and others were available to Eddie, as were the Greek myths as related by Graves and others.[48, 49] But while these fixed Eddie's attention on ancient *Hellas* as a source of homoerotic myths from which he could draw inspiration, they did not specifically advance the concept of a Cretan homeland wherein gay men *as* gay men could worship Pagan Gods. So whence came this central theme that formed the basis of the Minoan Brotherhood?

Buczynski certainly wasn't the first man to attempt to grow a spiritual path for gay men from the rootstock of Greek mythology. Eighty years earlier, the poet and writer George Cecil Ives founded The Order of Chaeronea in an effort to promote unity and forward-thinking social and political policies among like-minded homosexuals in Edwardian England.[50] Ives pursued a life-long struggle for homosexual rights, which he termed "the Cause." With the public humiliation of Oscar Wilde in 1895, his quest and the hope even for an open dialogue on the subject suffered a serious setback. In 1897, Ives came to the realization that a clandestine means was needed to continue the work for homosexual rights. Using a romanticized ideal of Greek homosexual spirituality, Ives and others strove to form a global chain of lovers, building on the ideal of an army of lovers first realized by the Theban Band; the ancient Greek fighting force of 144 pair-bounded lover-warriors who provided inspiration to early promoters of gay rights. Ives was himself the author of several books important to the modern gay rights movement and to the linkage of Pagan ideals with the struggle for sexual freedom. These include *The Graeco-Roman View of Youth* (1926), *Eros' Throne* (1900) and *Book of Chains* (1897), all of which were long out of print and quite rare by Eddie's time.

Unfortunately for The Order of Chaeronea, the time was not yet ripe for such a group to survive, let alone flourish; it needed another time and place, and a different set of social circumstances, to take root. Ives passed away in 1950, his Order having faded from the landscape many years before. His papers, including some of the Order's documents, were purchased by the University of Texas at Austin in 1977; however, Eddie would not have had access to or even knowledge of this material when he was writing his core materials in 1976. So if the paths first broken by his Victorian forebears lay blocked, what inspired Buczynski's adaptation of Bronze Age Crete?

Strange Bedfellows

Buczynski, like so many Craft teachers, was fond of making reading lists for his students, and this fondness extended to his newly-founded Minoan Brotherhood. The reading lists in the first documents compiled by him for students of the new tradition provide some insights into his thought process during the first years of the Minoan Brotherhood. For example, the first Minoan Book of Shadows, or what is known as the "proto-book" dating from late 1976, recommends the following books: *(Ibid n#30)*

> Evans, Sir Arthur. *The Palace of Minos.*
> Gardner, Gerald. *Witchcraft Today.*
> Graves, Robert. *The Greek Myths (Volume I).*
> Graves, Robert. *The White Goddess.*
> Mylonas, George. *Eleusis and the Eleusinian Mysteries.*
> Nilson, Martin P. *A History of Greek Religion.*
> Nilson, Martin P. *Minoan-Mycenaean Religion, and Its Survival in Greek Religion.*
> Pendlebury, John D. S. *The Archaeology of Crete.*
> Renault, Mary. *The Bull from the Sea.*
> Renault, Mary. *The King Must Die.*
> Vanggaard, Thorkil. *Phallos.*

Minoan reading lists published in early to mid-1977 included the following additional titles:[51] *(Ibid n#35)*

> Finley, Moses. *Early Greece: The Bronze and Archaic Ages.*
> Hawkes, Jacquetta. *The Dawn of the Gods.*
> Lauritsen, John. *Religious Roots of the Taboo on Homosexuality.*
> Moody, R.A., *Life After Life.*
> Swann, T.B. *How Are the Mighty Fallen.*
> Willetts, R.F. *Everyday Life in Ancient Crete.*

The cited works can be roughly divided into four categories: fictional works, mythology, history and archaeology, and the occult. Many of the books straddle more than one field. One thing that stands out in these lists is that although many of the books are grounded in historical evidence and scholarship, several are works of popular fiction. This is not necessarily a black mark, as mythology is itself, to some extent, a body of fictional portrayals and morality plays designed to teach spiritual and cultural lessons. Indeed, time has a tendency to render even the most disgraceful or inane stories respectable (one may look no further than the Old Testament, with its tales of rapine, slaughter, and post-justified land theft, for proof). A Neo-Pagan instance of creative inspiration from a work of fiction may be found in the CAW, initiated in 1962 by Tim Zell and Lance Christie based on an interpretation of Robert A. Heinlein's *Stranger in a Strange Land*.[52] In Eddie's case, inspiration came from a number of fictional sources.

Mary Renault was well known among gay readers for her frequent use of homosexual protagonists in her historical novels. As Eddie noted, her novel *The King Must Die* "contains a great deal of information on both the attitudes towards homosexuality in ancient Crete and Goddess worship — the State religion — in ancient Crete and amongst the early Greeks (Mycenaeans)." *The King Must Die* and *The Bull from the Sea* are still considered required reading by many in the Minoan Brotherhood.[53] Science fiction and fantasy author Thomas Burnett Swann's book *How Are the Mighty Fallen* depicts a gay relationship between the Biblical Jonathan and David, a story that Eddie likely intended as a means of overturning Christian moral interpretations of homosexual relationships in the minds of those seeking information on the Minoan Brotherhood.[54]

Although not referenced in the reading list, one of Eddie's favorite novels was Robert Graves' *Watch the North Wind Rise*.[55] Written in the year of Buczynski's birth while Graves was still mourning the loss of his son in World War II, the novel studies a utopian anthropological experiment based in part on the supposed matriarchal society of ancient Crete. Graves incorporated themes from his seminal work *The White Goddess* into the novel, including the concepts of a great Mother Goddess, the sacred year and the ritual sacrifice of the Year King. Not surprisingly, the book was considered to be "very basic to Feraferian ideology," according to W. Holman Keith.[56] As indicated by the inclusion of *The White Goddess* on the reading list, and in concord with the opinion of other Wiccans of the 1960s and 1970s, Graves' ideas resonated with Eddie and played a strong role in shaping the underlying structure of the cultus he was attempting to create for gay men. However, Buczynski cautioned his students to "beware, Graves is just a little bit anti-gay." *(Ibid n#30)*

"New Crete," as Graves called the mythical society in *Watch the North Wind Rise*, was not a paradise for all. The mores and idiosyncrasies of its citizens stood in marked contrast to the comparative rough-and-tumble of their spiritual forebears of the Bronze Age Aegean. Its multitudinous rules governing a citizen's every waking moment remind one more of Confucianism than a religion bound to both land and Gods with ties of blood and rustic pragmatism. These rules, as laid out in the story, were an unwritten body of law designed to ensure the smooth functioning of society within the Goddess-centered and technophobic blueprint its architects developed in response to decades of world war driven by schismatic Christianity. But capital punishment was present even in this otherwise loving and gentle utopia. When the protagonist of the novel inquires about the continued existence of capital punishment, the Witch who acted as his guide defended the practice by saying that only "bad people" were killed. Asked what she meant by bad, the woman explained, "Bad is when, for example, a calf is born with two heads, or a hen crows and doesn't lay eggs. Or when a man behaves like a woman." Shocked, the man replied, "What, you kill your poor homosexuals? That seems a bit hard."[37] That seems a bit of an understatement.

Notwithstanding the mild disapproval of Graves' character, it seems clear that openly homosexual men — or at least effeminate or receptive ones — were not welcome in this future Pagan vision any more than they generally were in the Neo-Paganism of Eddie's present. Graves' portrayal ran counter to Buczynski's understanding of a Minoan society where the homosexuality of Goddess-worshipping men was accepted and celebrated.

The scholarly texts cited in the Minoan reading lists were primarily meant to provide the prospective student and the initiate with background information on the art, culture and religious practices of the Minoans, as supported by research and archaeological discoveries. Nilson's *Minoan-Mycenaean Religion, and Its Survival in Greek Religion*, for example, was the standard text on the religious beliefs and ritual practices of ancient Crete until Nanno Marinatos' *Minoan Religion* was published in 1993.[58] The Warlock Shop was already carrying Nilson's book by late 1973 for the then princely sum of $22.[59] Its presence in the shop inventory probably resulted from Buczynski's interest in the work, as the book was both dry and expensive and would not have been a fast seller from Slater's point of view.

Apart from Nilson, Eddie's most important academic source appears to have been the Classicist R. F. Willetts, whose *Everyday Life in Ancient Crete* is cited in the reading list.[60] Willetts was one of the leading experts on ancient Crete in the 1950s and 1960s, and one of the first modern scholars to write on the subject of homosexuality in Cretan society in a matter-of-fact way.[61] His 1965 book *Ancient Crete* unquestioningly supports the contention of Ephoros, as reported by the Roman historian Strabo, that aristocratic youth in ancient Crete were subjected to a homoerotic initiation rite that had elements of the Zeus-Ganymede myth (e.g., ritual abduction, bestowing of gifts):[62, 63]

The love affairs of the Cretan youths, as they are described by Ephoros, were also imbued with characteristically archaic features.

They centered upon a kind of mock 'marriage' by abduction — but of a younger by an older boy.

Classical scholar Dr. Robert B. Koehl states that Willetts' ideas on the subject were at first not given the wide attention that they deserved, due to both the subject matter and the politics of the time.[64] Willetts, says Koehl, "wrote in the late 1950's-1960's and was highly regarded by some but shunned by most for his outspoken communism," writing extensively on the lessons that Classical studies could impart to the movement. This association would not have dissuaded Buczynski, because much of the underground sociopolitical landscape in New York City at that time, particularly in his beloved Greenwich Village, was still heavily influenced by the Marxist philosophy underlying much of the anti-war and social rights movements.

Koehl generally supports Willetts' position with his analyses of Minoan artifacts, such as the so-called Chieftain Cup, but believes the abduction myth may actually be linked to the earlier legend of King Minos, rather than to the Dorian invasion and the subsequent Zeus-Ganymede myth.[65, 66] This idea is not without its critics. Dr. William Percy, for example, believes that homosexual initiation practices were a post-Minoan, even post-Mycenaean, addition to Cretan society.[67] Dr. Koehl acknowledges this, but notes: *(Ibid n#64)*

Willetts, like all other scholars, up until today, regard [homosexual initiation] as a Dorian institution; brought to Crete by the Dorian/Spartan conquerors in the Dark Ages (anywhere from 1100 [BCE] onwards). But no one suspected the root was Minoan (or interpeted the famous description by Ephoros as having Minoan roots) until I connected it with the imagery on the Chieftain Cup.

By constructing the ritual and initiatory structure of the Minoan Brotherhood in 1976 on the basis of homoerotic practices of Minoan Crete, Eddie, in Dr. Koehl's words, "was remarkably intuitive, in any case. You know, 'it takes one to know one.'" *(Ibid n#64)* Buczynski also adapted the research into sex magick that he had conducted during his stint with the CES so that it could be applied to homosexual men. He did this with the understanding that one is more likely to succeed in using one's sexuality as a magickal practice if an actual ritual framework is used to reinforce this intent. Eddie would later explain the Minoan Brotherhood to interested seekers "as a Mystery/initiatory cult which erotically celebrates Life through male love." *(Ibid n#28)*

While Buczynski's goal was to craft a tradition to meet the needs of gay men, he wanted to do so in a way that restored a sense of balance to the worldview of the men who chose to follow this path. In his opinion, the mistake of both the Abrahamists and the feminists (and to a certain extent the Gardnerians) was in empowering one sex to the detriment of the other. In Eddie's view, it was important for men and women to acknowledge that both sexes were necessary (and equal) components of the whole. It was not necessarily easy for Eddie to raise these issues at the time, because gay men resented the prominent opinions of some feminists who unfairly lumped them in with the men who acted as oppressors to both groups. As with race, there were also entrenched gender bias issues within the gay community that made the argument a difficult one to carry. But Eddie made a passionate case for including the feminine element in the Minoan Brotherhood in his essay "Why Would a Gay Man Worship a Goddess?" *(Ibid n#33)*

> *Looking around us, everywhere, only a fool or a Blindman could disregard the Balance in Nature which emanates from the Total Harmony of the Universe. There is Male and Female, Dark and Light, Creative and Destructive, Dry and Wet etc. et al. It is the "NATURAL ORDER OF THINGS."*
>
> *We, as Gay Men, have, in many cases, disrupted the Harmonious balance of our minds by becoming too pre-occupied with "One side of the coin" so to speak.....very nearly forgetting the Other side. Now, I'm not trying to say that our Sexual Preferences are 'wrong'. On the contrary, they are very much 'Right' for us. But no Man is an island, and we cannot blank out the Feminine Principle which is fifty percent of all Nature merely because we physically enjoy the Male and do not Sexually desire the Female. ...*
>
> *In the Minoan Brotherhood, when we are in the Sacred Grove, all men, doing our "thing", we are worshipping the Gods which we have found to be within each other. ... However, if we didn't bring in the "other half" in some way, we would be defeating our own purposes of Harmony and the working of Magick (which requires total balance and harmony) by being "one-sided".*

Eddie concluded that the principle of polarity is necessary, even within a single-sex Circle, in order for gay men to be whole. He felt that by losing sight of the Divine Feminine, gay men would not only dishonor the Gods but risk failing in their works. The heterosexual practitioners who scoffed at gay men's ability to work magick were speaking and writing from a position of utter ignorance because, as many have pointed out, gay men (and lesbians) carry both polarities within them just as all people do. The difference between the homosexual and the heterosexual was that the homosexual practitioner was often more experienced at using this capability, and certainly far more accepting of its use by a working partner of the same sex.

Buczynski's goal was to create a tradition that translated the ancient concept of men's mysteries into a vibrant and modern practice. In the West, the concept of separate men's and women's mysteries has often been avoided, even reviled. Eddie's genius was to look back to the basis for human magick, the blood, the seed and the union of the two. The Gardnerians had figured out the latter as the basis for their fertility cult, but were essentially blind to the power inherent in the first two or their relevance to modern peoples. Many so-called "primitive" societies maintained this link to their spiritual root stock, which had been lost in the West once sex was considered dirty and situations of same-sex eroticism perverse. Neo-Pagans, even gay ones, were not immune to these feelings, given their upbringing in a society that devalued the feelings of men. Welsh initiate Gwilym Dafydd recalled a 1975 conversation in which Buczynski explained how he thought such a sex-segregated spiritual tradition could function:[68]

> *All forms of consenting-adult human sexuality, including both (i.) curiosity-based exploration, free from society's labels, and (ii.) the sublimizing of this exploration expressed through the ritual arts, hold a key for re-connecting with ancient Mysteries that unlock Magickal (Transformational) and Worshipful (Transcendental) potential. Put another way, people of legal age can choose to practice Deity-connected sex-play, or choose to symbolize this in ritual, for religious fulfillment, and this is in every way as valid as Judeo-Christian-Islamic prayer practices, or those of the polytheistic beliefs of Asia, Africa, or the Pacific islands, or those of the indigenous peoples of North and South America. Doing so cannot and does not characterize a seeker's sexuality as exclusively straight, bi, or gay, because the Myths that expound these Mysteries present the Gods as assuming all of these various roles at different stages of Their stories (e.g., the Stag-Boar-Wolf Welsh Degrees, or the Twelve Labours of Herakles). At the human level, for example, straight-identifying men would not expect to encounter any practices during a Minoan Brotherhood ritual that exceeded the bounds of male pubescent play, adolescent exploration, college fraternities, or post-sports celebration, but would probably be best advised not to attend a Minoan ritual if such things had offended them in the past or were likely to do so. At the same time, those who identify with alternate sexualities need not feel excluded from the witch-cult, as they had felt in the past from being rejected by bigoted churches and covens alike. This, at least, was how [Eddie's ideas] were described to me in the summer/fall of 1975.*

Yet Eddie had changed his mind on this point after the Huntington Coven imbroglio of 1976, deciding instead to make the Minoan Brotherhood more explicitly queer in its core mythos and practices. In choosing Minoan Crete, Buczynski had concluded "the Minoan Cult of Rhea to be, perhaps, the most Joyous and Beautiful, and also strikingly similar to the Witch Cult" of which he was a member.[69] He used British Traditional Witchcraft as the starting framework for Minoan rituals, and indeed a number of lingering traces of that tradition can be seen in the resulting ritual structure.

Aside from his familiarity with that ritual process, Eddie justified the adaptation by citing a theory that Minoan ritual magick was spread to the British Isles by Bronze Age traders and thereby affected the native spiritual practices that eventually became Gardnerian Wica.[70] This assertion was based on a claim by Gerald Gardner and others, who believed that there was a demonstrable link between British Traditional Witchcraft and the practices of the ancient Greeks. Buczynski noted that in *Witchcraft Today*, Gardner provided "an excellent chapter comparing the Witch-cult with the ancient Greek Mysteries, which they probably sprung [sic] from." *(Ibid n#30)* Aubrey Wyatt, a student of Buczynski's from 1979-1982, explains the connection that Eddie saw between these disparate places.

Aubrey Wyatt:[71, 72]

Around the time that Eddie and I met and became friends there was some worry in the Neo-pagan, Craft community. Word was out that some of the "scholarship" of people from the past was not sound, not true, or exaggerated. Robert Graves (Homophobe that he was) had addressed this in the "White Goddess." Others had not. Many in the community worried about the repercussions, and there were some. So, Eddie wanted to make sure that the basis of our "Mythos" was founded in scholarship and sound. The idea being that it would encompass intuitive, ecstatic, visions (Dionysos) and sound scholarship (Apollo). We started with myths from Delphi and from the Orphics because there was more info available in these areas. Plus, historically, up until the time of Hellenistic Greece the Priests at Delphi were still brought in from Crete. This is where we started, but we moved on as we learned more. ...

Eddie had me read numerous books. I read books by Gerald Gardner and Raymond Buckland, "The Golden Ass," Frazier's "Golden Bough" and "The White Goddess" by Robert Graves. This book by Mr. Graves was the "primary source" for the three of us. For you see, [Eddie's efforts were] born from a search for the beginnings of the European Spiritual Tradition and the part gay men held within that tradition. Tracing European origins is tricky business, but it seems to be integrally tied to the Danaan Tribes. And there is a major connection between the Minoans nd the Welsh, well all Celts in fact. Graves book documents these connections. And, in the myth of Europa she is taken to Crete by Zeus in the form of a white bull. White bulls, of course, are sacred to Poseidon. Most scholars now think Zeus, Poseidon, and Dionysus were all one in Crete. But it was Graves who wrote: "This mythological rigmarole adds up to an identification of the Israelite Jehovah of Tabor, or Atabyrius, with Dionysus the Danaan White Bull-God: an identification which rests on respectable Classical authority." ...

Along these lines, Dudley Young in his book "Origins of the Sacred: The Ecstasies of Love and War" writes, "I suspect that the Cretan bull was quite possibly a match for his cousin Osiris, and that his major mysteries were imported, distorted, dispersed, and shared among Zeus, Poseidon, and Dionysus, the three Mycenaean bull gods." The Brits have a myth that says they are descendants who sailed there from Troy, that's why even today, Britannia wears a Trojan helmet. There is evidence of that trade and communications between Troy and Crete was extensive, and that both their roots reach back to the culture of Catal Huyuk. A piece of ceramic from the Neolithic period "portrays a human figure with hands raised in the epiphany gesture as it appears in Minoan-Mycenaean art and also very much earlier in Catal Huyuk" (from Walter Burkert, "Greek Religion").

However, if there is such a link, it is more likely an artifact of recent origin through the influence and activities of the Masonic Lodge system in Great Britain and ceremonialists such as the Golden Dawn, the O.T.O., and other fellow travelers. But by emphasizing Gardner's supposed Cretan connection, Eddie probably hoped to establish the *bona fides* for a modern homosexual Witchcraft tradition.

Information gleaned from the research was pieced together and modified for modern usage in order to construct "a complete, structured Pagan Mystery Religion geared entirely towards the Homosexual." Eddie did the lion's share of the writing and research. Joey Cupolo helped adapt the ritual layout of British Traditional Witchcraft to meet the needs of the new tradition. The ritual year was modified to align the sabbats more closely with holy days of ancient Greece. Symbols, tools, Goddesses and Gods were based in part on interpretations from the ancient Aegean, with the pantheon structured around the worship of the Great Mother and Her Divine Son. Observances of the Men's (and later Women's) Mysteries, including rites of initiation and advancement, were strictly to be maintained as sex-segregated rites.

Eddie and Joey used Bennie as a sounding board, and had him review the resulting drafts of the Book before concurring with the final results.[73] Others also assisted the project in small ways. Herman was used as a foil for some of Eddie's ideas, and although Khem Caigan never saw the final product, he read the early material Eddie had worked on in the summer of 1976. Khem was an assistant to filmmaker, artist, and occultist Harry Smith throughout the 1970s and early 1980s, and together, the two men had compiled a concordance of the Enochian alphabet. With that ceremonial leaning in mind, Caigan had encouraged Eddie to make the Minoan materials more intellectual, which is to say ceremonial, in nature. Caigan recalls that Eddie decided to not take his advice, feeling that the entire system would become far too cerebral.[74] Simon confirms that, despite his bookishness, Eddie had no background in ceremonial magick and no desire to train others in it.[75]

Buczynski may have felt that by over-intellectualizing the system he would risk losing touch with the ecstatic current that he believed was vitally important in breaking the bonds of Judeo-Christian dogma with which most gay men grew up. He wanted, instead, to restore the balance between the Apollonian and the Dionysian. This sense of restoration fits with Eddie's readings of Minoan archaeology, which had characterized the Dionysian cult that swept across Greece in the sixth century BCE as a return to the ecstatic worship of the Cretan Mother Goddess.[76] In this vision of the past, the snake was not under the control of Delphian Apollo; rather, it was nurtured at the breast of the Great Mother, who reigned over the riotous struggle of unending life and death. J.R.R. Tolkien's Galadriel might well have been describing such a figure when referring to a vision of herself as an elemental Queen, "beautiful and terrible as the Morning and the Night!"[77]

Eddie represented this Cretan Mother Goddess as a single figure — the Goddess Rhea — Who is said to have formed mankind from the dirt She scraped from under Her nails as she lay on the ground during Her pained birthing of what came to be called the Olympian Gods. Yet Buczynski also incorporated various other Goddesses into his mythology as aspects of Rhea, each with Her own attributes and responsibility over different domains of Creation and human endeavor. In this, Eddie was following the example set by Minoan archaeologist Arthur Evans, who had insisted that the Cretan Mother Goddess be depicted as a single image comprising the different aspects he had encountered in engravings, statuary and paintings during his excavations.[78] Modern Wicca, which follows a similar template of a composite Mother Goddess, draws its inspiration from the works of Graves and Murray, which are themselves derivative of Evans on this point.

Cathy Gere, author of the groundbreaking book on the genesis of the Minoan myth, *Knossos and the Prophets of Modernism* (2009), credits Evans' own repressed homosexuality for many of the modern interpretations of Minoan culture. "[Evans] was an Edwardian perpetual boy-man," writes Gere, "whose frivolous, androgynous, goddess-worshipping Minoans seem more at home in the decadent cabaret of Weimar Berlin than at any Nuremberg rally."[79, 80] This didn't stop the Nazis from attempting to appropriate the early Greek civilizations as an example of superior Aryan culture, but the Minoan bull proved to be much longer lived than their fascist bullshit.

As a Priest of Isis in the CES, Eddie would also have noted several interesting parallels between Kemetic religious beliefs and those attributed to Minoan Crete. One such similarity is the Isis-Horus relationship, which found its corollary in Eddie's adoption of the Great Mother and Divine Son in his tradition. To Buczynski, a civilization centered on the worship of a strong Mother Goddess by androgynous, feminine men "unbearded and slim-waisted, with hair streaming down beneath their shoulders," would have seemed like heaven. In the Minoan Brotherhood, the Divine Son and Consort of Rhea is called Asterion, also known as the Starry One and the Earth-Shaker. Depicted as the Bull of Heaven and, alternatively, as a bull-headed man, Buczynski conceived Asterion as the patron of men who love men. It was through His auspices, in secret rites held under the watchful and approving eye of the Mother, that gay and bisexual men would begin to reclaim the magic and power they had held when the world was young and before a minor desert storm god had developed an attitude problem. In Greek mythology, Asterion was the King of Crete, the consort of the demi-Goddess Europa, and the stepfather of Europa's three sons by Zeus — Minos, Rhadamanthus and Sarpedon. So the story goes, Asterion was willing to divide his kingdom among the sons of Zeus upon his death, but the three young men quarreled over the affections of a beautiful youth (isn't that always the case?) and Asterion ended up awarding the island to Minos.

Had Minos proved himself worthy by winning the contest and the boy? And, if so, does this story of ancient boy-love track in some way with Robert Koehl's theory of the homoerotic abduction of youths and initiation into manhood supposedly practiced by the ancient Minoans? The answer is lost in time, but however Minos came by the throne, he lived to regret his victory. Minos, the stepson of a bull-headed man, eventually became the stepfather of a bull-headed man in the form of another Asterius, the Minotaur, through an unfortunate dalliance between his wife Pasiphäe and a sacred bull of Poseidon. As Robert Callasso so eloquently notes in *The Marriage of Cadmus and Harmony* (1993), bulls are intimately entwined with the Minoan story.[81]

While bulls were worshipped in other lands of the ancient Near East, including Eddie's beloved Egypt, the bull in prehistoric Crete appears to have occupied a central role as both an object of cultic interest and as a sacrificial victim. Bull imagery is found everywhere in Minoan art, from seal stones, to cups, and frescoes to stone carvings, bulls and their horns are a dominant theme in Minoan culture at its height of power. The bull is associated with both Zeus and Dionysos, who numbers amongst His epithets Βουγενες, or "Bull-born." In ancient Crete in particular, the relationship between these two Gods is both complex and overlapping, and perhaps even syncretic. Both Zeus and Dionysos were said to have been birthed on Crete and hidden in caves to protect them while growing up, and both were protected by a sacred band of spirit-youth attendees called the Kouretes, which was also the name given to the Priests of Rhea. In Mycenaean Linear B, Zeus is represented as *Di-wo*, while Dionysos is *Di-wo-ni-so-jo*.

Archaeologist Emily Vermeule notes that the Greek story of the Cretan Zeus may have been an attempt to reconcile their mythology with the older Cretan myth of the Minoan Divine Youth.[82] This Young God was almost always depicted in Minoan iconography as a beardless youth, which is also how Dionysos is often portrayed. Perhaps this beautiful Divine Youth was the same one whose favor allowed Minos to claim his kingdom. If one follows the trail back far enough, the Young God depicted in Cretan imagery is one whose powers are both vegetal and seasonal, and one who also demonstrates a mastery over animals; all characteristics held in common with Dionysos. Ephipany is yet another trait which the Cretan Divine Youth shares with the God of the Vine.[83] There is also some indication that the bull-headed rhytons found on Crete may have been used to pour ritual libations of wine, or perhaps even blood, and where wine and blood are spilled, their trails often lead back to the epiphanic, ecstatic Dionysos.

Buczynski saw in the clues left behind by the ancient Minoans traces of this ecstatic and homo-erotic spirituality. He hoped that his Minoan spiritual path, conceived as it was during the sexual revolution of New York's gay community, would be able to channel some of this Dionysian energy toward a similar restoration of ecstatic worship of the Great Mother in a manner that would benefit the gay community. Between the lesbian feminist spirituality on one side and gay male groups like the Minoan Brotherhood on the other, there began the barest movement towards the development of a "homosexu-laity" within the Neo-Pagan community. The need for community and service was a point Eddie consistently emphasized in his writings of the time, stressing the need for Minoan initiates not to remain aloof but rather to serve "our people" and become involved in the political struggle for gay rights. Eddie continued to write and revise the Minoan Brotherhood Book of Shadows, which he titled *The Book of the Mysteries*, through the end of 1976, and, with Bennie, he conducted trial runs of the rituals in their new apartment in order to check their feel and flow.[84]

Chapter 26: Gay Spirit

The Founding of the Minoan Tradition

On the chill New Year's Day of 1977, three men met in the candlelit living room of the Middle Village apartment to perform a magickal ritual. The furniture had been moved back out of the way, save for a low sturdy coffee table that would act as the altar. Amidst a thin grey haze of equal parts incense and pot smoke, Eddie Buczynski, Joseph Cupolo, and Bennie Geraci set up the altar to the specifications that Eddie had devised in the previous months. Shivering slightly in the cool air, for the men were skyclad, they purified the space, set the wards, and generated the energy necessary to call upon the Gods to witness their rite. By the end of the ritual, the men were running with sweat and brimming with energy. The Minoan Brotherhood, the first tradition of the modern era devoted solely to the spiritual well-being of gay men, was formed. Joey and Bennie were initiated, and Joey was elevated to the Sublime Degree within the Brotherhood.[1,2]

With the completion of this first ritual, the three men had also founded the first coven of the Brotherhood, Knossos Grove; named in honor of the ancient city-state of the same name in Minoan Crete. *(Ibid n#1)* As Buczynski would later recall,[3]

> *[In] January of 1977, the 'Minoan Brotherhood' emerged, a true form of pagan witchcraft for gay men, which boasts a beginning over four thousand years ago in a world of peace, love, and harmony. ... Whether gay pagan religions become an integral part of gay society or not, its nice to know that some of us, as gay people, can, in this ancient and happy way, through a religion that glorifies the life-style that we have chosen to live, try our hand at helping to recreate that time of bliss which once existed under the Great Mother, and aid in the rebalancing of our diseased world.*

Eddie's optimism notwithstanding, gay Pagan religions, which still exist within today's gay community, never became what anyone could call an integral part of gay society. In the first years of the Minoan Brotherhood, Knossos Grove never had more than five active members at any one time.[4] And most Minoan covens down through the years never functioned effectively with more than about that same number of men. But the rituals, when everyone was "on," were quite powerful and sexually ecstatic. Wine, pot and music were used to enhance the mood. "We used to play Jethro Tull's 'Songs from the Wood' sometimes when we had a circle," Joey remembered.[5] As an initiate from 1980 recalled, "I know it's frowned on by a lot of Pagans now, but we smoked before rituals. And Eddie put Belladonna and pot in the incense."[6]

Eddie envisioned that Knossos Grove would be the Mother Grove of the tradition. Far from abandoning the lineage-based system practiced by Gardnerians in the United States, Eddie chose to embrace it and set up the record-keeping criteria necessary to keep track of who was brought into the tradition. The thought was that these initiation records would be sent to the Mother Grove for safekeeping and could eventually be used by Minoans as a lineage database, similar to what the Long Island Gardnerians were setting up for their initiates.

Also similar to Gardnerian Wica, Eddie set up the Minoan Brotherhood so that each Grove functioned autonomously within the framework of the Laws of the tradition. A high priest would always be answerable to his initiator. However, the machinations and power trips he had both observed and experienced during the past five years, where people were cast from their spiritual traditions for political reasons — or just mere pissiness on the part of an upline matriarch — left a sour taste in Buczynski's mouth and influenced the shape of his creation. For this reason, he chose to exercise a light hand in the operation of downline covens, and instead attempted to promote a consensus process within each Grove through the use of a Council, and within the tradition via an annual meeting of the Third Degree High Priests. One example of his choices was Eddie's refusal to include a Rite of Reculade in the Minoan *Book of the Mysteries,* which was a clear break with other Witchcraft traditions of the day. Buczynski had, over the course of the last three years, left a considerable record of disparaging remarks and writings concerning the many failings and hypocrisies of Gardnerian Wica, and he wanted no repeat of the things that had consumed so much time and energy within that path. If any Minoan were to question Buczynski's sincerity in abandoning that path, Eddie removed all doubt by warning initiates in the bluntest of terms to respect but give wide berth to the followers of Gardnerian Wica.

Shortly after the founding of the Brotherhood, Eddie began writing informational material to pass out to men who might be interested in joining the tradition. The booklet he created provided a basic background of what the Brotherhood was about and why it had been founded. A suggested reading list was provided, as was a questionnaire that was closely modeled on the one used for the Pagan Way.[7] This introductory packet was ready for distribution by the beginning of February. Filling out the questionnaire was not a requirement for membership; answering the questions in a face-to-face meeting with the members of the Grove would also suffice. Such a meeting was always required anyway, and a man's acceptance for initiation into a Grove was predicated on the consensus of all the current initiates in that group.

The first new man was brought in at the Sabbat ritual on the first of February. Kim Schuller had been interested in the Craft and had visited the Magickal Childe several times in 1976, commuting from his apartment in Brooklyn. He eventually developed a friendship with Joey, who, in early 1977, invited Kim to meet with his coven in Queens. What Joey had failed to mention was that it was an all-male group. So when Kim showed up at the apartment, the first thing that struck him was, "Where are the girls?" Schuller was bisexual and was dating a man named Gilbert at the time, so he quickly adapted to the concept of an all-male coven. He hit it off with Eddie and Bennie right away, and asked to be brought into the Minoan Brotherhood. Kim was initiated on March 3 and took the Craft name *Sky*, which seemed a decent fit with both his bright blue eyes and his laid-back Seventies outlook on life.[8]

Later in the month, Eddie took time to attend Herman's open house for the Magickal Childe. The shop owner had scheduled the event, most likely with a twinkle in his eye, for Friday February 13. At this point, the Childe had been open for exactly one year, and the event was a re-birthday party of sorts to celebrate the shop's success at its new location. While Eddie and Herman were on good terms at this time, there was some friction between the former lovers, possibly because of Herman's disagreement with Eddie's decision to leave Gardnerian Wica and his own Welsh tradition in order to work within the Minoan Brotherhood.[9] Herman did have a legitimate point, from his perspective. He tended to believe that sexuality was a separate issue from spirituality. After all, wasn't that what he and Eddie had been fighting for over the past several years — the right to participate in British Traditional Witchcraft and its related branches without undue consideration of where gay men parked either of their heads outside of Circle?

It wasn't that Slater wasn't in favor of gay liberation, for he supported the changes that were taking place within the gay community and was a long-time friend of gay activist Leo Martello, and it is important to note that Leo backed Herman in his position.[10] Martello was a bit of a prude by the standards of the day. His own Witchcraft tradition neither practiced in the nude nor engaged in sex within their rituals, and he was skeptical of those that did, suspecting that they were merely trying to "use the Craft as a means of fornication."[11] Thus, in Martello's eyes, the sexuality of the practitioner was irrelevant unless one was more interested in mate-swapping and perversion than in worshipping the Gods.

Slater's friendship with other gay and bisexual Pagans extended across the nation, and a number of these contacts also appear to have backed this position, either tacitly or directly. One example was David White (Craft name *Merlin*) who, with his wife Lady Sintana, led the Ravenwood Coven in Atlanta, Georgia. Apart from attending a psychic convention that they hosted in the late 1970s, Herman's friendship with this couple was such that he actually acted as a witness for some of the coven's Third Degree elevations.[12,13] Ravenwood's elder high priest was a well-respected leader in the Craft, and he was also a gay man who eventually became involved in the long-running Atlanta-based Gay Spirit Visions conference. Nevertheless, White's public face in the Craft was both closeted and traditionalist.[14] Another gay Pagan correspondent of Slater's was Harold Moss, the co-founder of the CES. Moss, later writing about his thoughts on Buczynski's founding of a same-sex spiritual tradition, stated, "I thought of it as Ed's retirement from serious work."[15]

There were (and remain) two schools of thought. One, maintained by Harold Moss, Herman Slater, Leo Martello and others, was that homosexuality was natural, normal and irrelevant to the practice of spiritual work. The other, promoted by those such as Arthur Evans, Harry Hay, and Eddie Buczynski, essentially argued that homosexuality was a manifestation of spirituality and thus worthy of celebration within that context. Slater's dislike of the Minoan Brotherhood may also have been colored by his opinion of what he referred to as the West Coast approach to feminist Witchcraft. In Herman's eyes, what Eddie was doing was no different from what Z. Budapest, whom he detested, had been advocating.[16,17] However, his objections did not prevent Slater from stocking the Magickal Childe with the incenses and oils which Eddie had developed for use in Minoan rituals. Business, after all, was business.

Eddie, who was done trying to mold himself to the polarized boy-girl expectations of others, was passionate in defending sex-segregated rituals as being just as valid as mixed-sex ones. The low-level, though unexpected, resistance he encountered did nothing to dissuade him from working to attract other gay men to his new spiritual path. But while Herman and the others had a point, Eddie's vision was also valid, for he was providing a venue for sex-segregated rituals that also instilled a sense of awareness of the sacred power of the Goddess and the duty owed to Her by men. His vision was also more expansive than that of Z. Budapest and the Dianics, for Eddie's plans included the eventual creation of a female path for the celebration of Women's Mysteries and, ultimately, a place where both halves of the spiritual community could come together in worship. But before he could do this, Buczynski had to build up Knossos Grove into a stable coven and work out any remaining kinks in the system of rituals, and for that he needed a few more men.

Bruce-Michael Gelbert was working part-time at the Oscar Wilde Bookstore at 291 Mercer Street in Greenwich Village in 1977, and wrote freelance articles for a publication in Boston in his spare time. Having been raised as an Orthodox Jew, Bruce-Michael had lapsed in his practice and was of uncommitted spirituality at the time. Gelbert was a cultured and educated man, having worked in the Metropolitan Opera from 1968 until 1974. He was working at the Oscar Wilde counter in early February when Eddie walked in with a few copies of the Minoan Brotherhood handouts he had prepared for distribution. Eddie asked Gelbert if it was okay to post a Minoan Brotherhood notice on the shop's community bulletin board. Bruce-Michael had met Kim a week or so earlier and thus had already heard of the group, so he agreed to let Eddie leave some copies at the bookstore. Gelbert took a copy for himself out of curiosity. Having explored different spiritual philosophies in a search for something that could appeal to his inner fire, Bruce-Michael read the material and was impressed with the thought that had gone into it and the philosophy expressed there. He struck up a conversation with Eddie and the two hit it off at once. Gelbert told Busczynski that he was interested in the Brotherhood, and he was invited to visit with the other men later in the month. The dark-haired, dark-eyed man radiated an easy sexuality and serious mien that impressed the others, and by the end of February he had been initiated. He took the Craft name *Dov*.[18]

Another means that Eddie had envisioned for bringing gay and bi men to the Minoan Brotherhood was to host a feast after sabbat, much as many other covens did and, indeed, still do. Given Eddie's love of history, it should come as no surprise that the parties Eddie and Bennie hosted after Circle were patterned after the ancient Roman orgy. The term "orgy" brings to mind the image of a sexual free-for-all, and that is certainly how the Seventies defined the concept; one need look no further than the Psychedelic Venus Church to see the concept wrought into living flesh. However, what occurred at the Middle Village apartment was more closely aligned with the orgies of Classical Rome. The altar and other religious accoutrements were cleared away before the guests arrived. The parties — akin to Dionysian rites, with food, booze, buzz and plenty of easy sexual energy — were a reflection of the times, though mild in comparison to the offerings available in most back room bars and bathhouses of the day.

Initially, the "orgies" were cozy, laid-back affairs involving just the coven members and a few select guests, such as prospective initiates and gay and bisexual initiates of other Witchcraft traditions, such as Gardnerian Wica and Traditionalist Gwyddoniaid. But as time went on, they were opened to a wider circle of friends and acquaintances, such as lesbians, straight women, and even straight men, not all of whom were even Pagan. There was a definite sexual energy underlying these gatherings, and it was not uncommon, just as happened during the Roman orgies upon which these parties were modeled, for trysts and tricks to occur. In a 2004 interview, Joey jokingly referred to Knossos Grove as "Gwydion and Damien, the Minoan back room." Bennie's response was, "Don't believe that! [pause] After Circle, maybe." *(Ibid n#4)* Aubrey Wyatt noted that when the sexual energy swamped everything else in the room, Eddie referred to that time as when the "Lady" (meaning the Mother Goddess) took over. "It was, as I have said, another time," Wyatt noted. *(Ibid n#6)*

It was Eddie's "after Circle" methods that unfortunately proved to be too much for Joey, who felt that the Brotherhood could easily stray into a distracting licentiousness, given the cultural trends of the day. Joey was no prude by a long shot, but he felt that the emphasis should remain on homoerotic ritual and magick, and less on the celebratory aftermath, which could, after all, be had in the Village via a short train trip. Sometimes they did take that trip. Bruce-Michael Gelbert remembers one night after Circle when the Brothers went to the Mineshaft near the Magickal Childe in order to work off their sexual energy. A man came up to Gelbert and, smelling the lingering aroma of incense on his skin, asked if he'd just come there from church. "After a fashion," Gelbert answered with a grin. *(Ibid n#18)*

To his credit, Eddie didn't emphasize the wild aspect of the Minoan Brotherhood in order to gain converts, although it might have grown by leaps and bounds during this period if he had. To paraphrase a character in a popular television show, if a religion comes along that encourages you to get hammered, run naked through the woods, have sex with whoever and whatever, and it's all part of getting closer to God, what more could one ask for?[19] But if Buczynski had taken that route, the Minoans would likely have burnt themselves out within a short span of years, just as did Psychedelic Venus Church. Nevertheless, Joey was troubled by the direction that it was taking, and he agonized over what to do.

Even though he'd only been active in Knossos Grove for less than a half-dozen rituals, Cupolo decided that the best course was to leave so that he could run a Grove in his own way. *(Ibid n#5)* As in most Witchcraft traditions, a man who has achieved the "Sublime Degree" is permitted to hive from his home coven in order to start his own group. Cupolo wasn't even sure that he'd be in New York much longer anyway. Charlie was beginning to tire of New York City and was working on a job transfer to a Chase branch back in New Orleans. He hoped to persuade Joey to move back there with him later that year.

By the end of February, Joey informed Eddie of his intent to split off and form Phaistos Grove, named for another of the great Minoan city-states. Buczynski was saddened that Cupolo wished to leave, but was consoled by the thought that the existence of two Groves would help establish the Minoan Brotherhood that much sooner. Eddie gave his blessings, and went so far as to amend Joey's vouch document to both acknowledge the formation of the new Grove and to name Cupolo as the first initiate and co-founder of the Minoan Brotherhood in recognition of the work he had done with Eddie on *The Book of the Mysteries*, including his drafting the ritual framework designed to honor the *Kouros*, who is the physical embodiment of the young male God. *(Ibid n#2)*

Late in February, Eddie and Bennie went shopping for wedding bands. The couple had been contemplating tying the knot for some months and had decided that the time was right. Gay marriage was not a new topic, even in the 1970s. For example, historian George Chauncey documented gay marriages in New York dating back to the early twentieth century in his book *Gay New York* (1994). In 1962, *New York Daily News* reporter Jess

Stearn wrote about a gay marriage ceremony in his despicable best-selling book, *The Sixth Man*.[20] The following year, Randy Lloyd published an article titled "Let's Push Homophile Marriage" in *One* magazine, the organ of the Mattachine Society. Lige Clarke and Jack Nichols, as editors of the newspaper *Gay*, received a number of letters from gay men seeking advice on marrying or adopting their lovers.[21]

Although not debated at nearly the level of intensity and consequence as in the years after the turn of the next millennium, gay marriage in the late 1970s was still considered to be a particularly radical act — not merely because it went against social convention, but also because the gay community was almost entirely unsupportive of the concept. Many gay activists, particularly those who were heavily influenced by the Marxist ideology that was in vogue at the time, considered marriage to be an archaic institution that had no application to them. Gays and lesbians who wished to marry were accused of aping the heterosexuals and were considered to be decidedly unliberated in their worldview, if not even detrimental and distracting to the cause. This attitude still has not changed for some.

Straight society, in turn, was horrified at the thought of gay men marrying, and that attitude has only changed marginally over the years, as demonstrated by the success of the Republican Party at rallying evangelical votes in the first years of the twenty-first century by using the topic to disguise their own moral shortcomings and lack of vision. But even in the Seventies, some futurists, such as Alvin Toffler, were trying to prepare society for the eventuality of gay marriage. Toffler's seminal book *Future Shock* was made into a documentary of the same name in 1972, and this film depicted a homosexual marriage ceremony as a matter of fact that the public had better get used to thinking about.[22] Just a few years earlier, Federico Fellini's film *Satyricon* (1969) held up for ridicule the shipboard marriage of Encolpio to a man old enough to be his grandfather. It is likely that the director intended the audience to scorn the hypocrisy of the pederast, who solemnly told the young Encolpio that *he* must now give up boys, rather than targeting the act of homosexual marriage itself.

Eddie and Bennie chose a pair of white, yellow and red gold braided rings, which they exchanged with one another in a private marriage rite held in their apartment during the full moon of Saturday, March 5, where they vowed to stay together as long as they loved one another. The ritual they used was a Minoan Brotherhood marriage ceremony that Eddie had written into the Brotherhood's *Book of the Mysteries*. Though prepared specifically for Bennie and him, Eddie, by including it in the Book, made the rite available to others in the Brotherhood who might wish to use it.[23] They did not announce the ceremony to friends until afterwards. The next day when the two lovers went to Eddie's parents' home for the regular Sunday family dinner together, the eagle-eyed Marie noticed the rings and commented on their beauty. "Is everyone wearing those these days?" she asked. "No," Eddie replied, "just Bennie and me." Marie nodded sagely, and Bennie was pretty sure that she understood the rings' significance.[24]

On March 10, 1977, the New York City police department announced that a serial killer targeting young women and young couples was working in the New York suburbs. The killer, who would eventually come to be known as the "Son of Sam," was a slovenly postal employee named David Berkowitz.[25] Bennie notes that the members of their little groups were all worried about this development. Ria and Carol in particular, being lithe young women with long dark hair, fit the profile of the killer's victims to date. Their concern was certainly justified, not only on that basis, but also because the killer was believed to be hunting in their section of Queens, having shot three people in Forest Hills that January and March. Though the men were likely safe from the killer's deadly attentions, they were still uneasy about this development. Some, like Eddie, with his thin build and long hair, were perhaps more at risk of being mistaken for women from behind at night than the other men, although there was never an incident where Berkowitz made this mistake during his spree; the men he attacked were always in the company of a woman. Nevertheless, 1977 proved to be a year when a healthy dollop of paranoia was fashionable.

In April, Kim Schuller met Eddie and Bennie's next door neighbor, Lisa Marie, at a party at their place. Kim was, by nature, a somewhat passive man and an intellectual, and he found Lisa Marie's strength and intelligence quite attractive. The two soon began dating and as the spring progressed into summer, they spent more and more time together. At last, Kim was practically living in Lisa Marie's apartment. Eddie believed that their budding relationship was adversely affected the energy of their Minoan rituals, observing to Bruce-Michael that the Circles "just weren't working." *(Ibid n#18)* The rituals seemed lackluster and the erotic magick wasn't happening the way that it should. Buczynski attributed the dullness to Kim's drifting into a relationship with a woman. He addressed his concerns to Kim, complaining that there was no spark in the rituals anymore, and suggested that Kim might be better off going out on his own or joining a mixed-sex coven if he was going to pursue relations with women. Kim felt rejected and hurt by this criticism, and he responded by leaving the Grove by the beginning of summer. *(Ibid n#8, 18)*

Eddie wasn't the only person uncomfortable with Kim's budding relationship. *Village Voice* columnist Arthur Bell was "pretty heavily invested in *Sky*," according to Gelbert. *(Ibid n#18)* Bell had dated the younger man for several months, taking him to cultural events throughout the city that were open to Bell because of his wide-ranging social connections. Shortly after the relationship between Kim and Lisa Marie became serious, Bruce-Michael ran into Arthur at a book publishing party on the Upper West Side. Bell took Gelbert aside and the two went for walk in Riverside Park to discuss the "problem with *Sky*." He railed over the situation to Gelbert, telling him that he felt betrayed by the fact that Kim had "left us for a woman." *(Ibid n#18)*

This attitude concerning bisexuals was prevalent in the 1970s. Many gay activists regarded bisexuality as a copout and a repressive remnant of the closet, rather than the legitimate sexual orientation that it is. Leo Martello, when asked by Hans Holzer to explain the difference between a homosexual and a bisexual, summed up this attitude. "Well, the difference between a homosexual and a bisexual is that a homosexual has the guts to say so and the bisexual doesn't."[26] Kim, for his part, felt himself betrayed by those he looked upon as friends, spiritual mentors and, in some cases, sex partners. Eddie's stand on Kim's gravitation toward the heterosexual side of his bisexuality was therefore not particularly shocking in the context of the gay community of that era, but it was unsettling — given his previously-stated opinion on the need to attain balance between the male and female.

Buczynski's position was also not universally accepted within Knossos Grove. Bennie was very unhappy with Kim's departure, and not just how it occurred, and he let Eddie know it in no uncertain terms.[27] In an attempt to make amends, Eddie sat down and wrote a complete mixed-sex Minoan Book of Shadows just for Kim and Lisa Marie to use. However, Kim and Lisa Marie never actually used it.[28] After Kim left the Grove, he and Lisa Marie attended the Manhattan Pagan Way a few times at Margot Adler's Central Park West apartment. But over the next year or so, they drifted away from Paganism, settled down, married and moved out of the city.[29]

Sometime in May, Bruce-Michael leapt at an opportunity to join the writing staff of a new gay publication — *GaysWeek*, also known as the *New York Gay News*. Gelbert was excited for this opportunity to write for a local publisher, as was Eddie.[30] "See? Good things are happening to you," he gleefully told the writer. Eddie asked Bruce to consider writing an article on gay Witchcraft for the newspaper, and Bruce replied "Why don't you do one instead?" The publisher initially showed some resistance to Eddie's submission, saying that some of the information he presented needed to be taken on faith, but Bruce persuaded the publisher to overlook his qualms, and the article was eventually published. Eddie's goal was to discuss the discrimination faced by some gay men within the Craft, and it ended with a notice that the Minoan Brotherhood had been founded to help gay men address this issue. *(Ibid n#8)*

In response to Eddie's article, Leo Martello wrote a letter that was published in the next issue of the newspaper. In a typical Leo fashion, Martello noted that he had not been mentioned in the article despite his long-standing struggle against gay and lesbian discrimination in the Craft and elsewhere. Even though the article had been intended to advertise the existence of the Minoan Brotherhood, the practice of which Martello was already on record as having disapproved, Buczynski dutifully apologized for having omitted the Sicilian's contributions to the cause when he replied in the July 4 edition.[31, 32] This publicity caught the eye of a *New York Newsday* reporter, who asked Eddie to grant him an interview on the subject of gay Witchcraft. But Eddie, perhaps recalling the unpleasantness associated with the 1973 *National Star* article, declined the request on the basis that he had nothing more to say to the straight world on the subject, especially since he believed that his words would be twisted in the escalating tabloid environment of the era.[33]

On the same day as the Everard bathhouse fire in New York, the San Francisco school board voted 7-0 to begin normalizing the treatment of homosexuality by including objective information on it in the San Francisco Public Schools sex education programs — so the politics of homosexuality turned out to be a hot topic that summer. By 1977 many observers believed that the "Stonewall energy," the accumulated anger and sense of injustice that had empowered the gay community and fueled its demands for civil rights since 1969, was pretty much spent as a political force in New York City. The lessening of police and liquor control crackdowns on gay and lesbian social venues had somewhat eased the pressures driving the movement, but not necessarily because of social tolerance, although there was more of a live-and-let-live attitude in the years following the Stonewall riots. In reality, New York City had furloughed a significant number of its police in response to its budget crisis, and the remaining officers simply had better things to do than to bust gay bars.

Tolerance certainly wasn't the same as civil rights, as critics like Arthur Bell pointed out when lamenting the six times that a gay rights bill had been defeated before the New York City Council.[34] But with the increasing tolerance and decreasing pressure, most gay men had simply become more interested in indulging in their new-found freedoms than in storming the Bastille. However, the social pendulum began to swing back at about the same time: reporter Jonathon Mahler characterized 1977 as the last great year of nonreproductive unprotected sex.[35] While it would be several years before HIV, with its incredibly long incubation period, would begin to bring down the house like termites gnawing from within, by late that spring the reactionary evangelical politics that had been rumbling in the distance for nearly a decade suddenly broke like a storm. The place was Miami-Dade County in Florida, and the trigger was a starched, perky and self-righteous orange juice peddler named Anita Bryant.

With their limited world view, some conservatives certainly saw much to fear in the world in the late 1970s, whether it was the legal availability of contraception and abortion on demand, or the shameless visibility of Witches and homosexuals.[36] Inspired by a wave of gay rights ordinances enacted in major cities across the nation, gay activists in Dade County, Florida had begun to flex their political muscles in 1976. Following a successful campaign to elect sympathetic members to the County Commission in November, activists moved forward with their plan to codify gay rights into law. In January 1977, over the protests of evangelical preachers, the Dade County commissioners voted to extend civil rights in public accommodations to gays. Opponents said that the civil rights ordinance was the opening that gays were looking for to exploit children under cover of government-mandated legitimacy. One of the main opponents to the law was singer Anita Bryant, who formed a political action group called "Save Our Children." Believing that homosexuality was a force for evil in the United States, Bryant conducted a campaign to rally the public behind an effort to repeal the ordinance.

As a popular gospel singer, Bryant stood for wholesomeness and purity. That was why the Florida Citrus Growers Association used her to advertise orange juice; an odd juxtaposition, given that orange juice commercials in the sexual Seventies included one featuring a long, hard tanker truck called "The Big O." Nevertheless, she proved to be an effective campaigner. Among Bryant's assertions was, "If gays are granted rights, next we'll have to give rights to prostitutes and to people who sleep with St. Bernards and to nailbiters." It thus became easy for opponents to trivialize the beneficiaries of the ordinance while simultaneously casting them as monstrosities. By trading on the public's fears of homosexual "recruitment" and child molestation, Bryant's campaign resulted in a repeal of the Dade County ordinance by an overwhelming margin of 69% to 31% on June 7, 1977. For her efforts, *Hustler* magazine named Bryant the Asshole of the Month.[37]

That evening, on hearing of the Florida repeal drive's success, thousands of gay men and lesbians in New York City gathered in front of the Stonewall Inn before marching to former Congresswoman Bella Abzug's townhouse to voice their opposition.[38] They were angry not only because of the prejudicial and dirty campaign waged by the recall petition's supporters, but also because a conservative government in Florida had at least passed a gay rights measure while the supposedly liberal establishment in New York City had failed to do so over and over again. The following day, Bryant incongruously stated, "In victory, we shall not be vindictive. We shall continue to seek help and change for homosexuals, whose sick and sad values belie the word 'gay' which they pathetically use to cover their unhappy lives." Emboldened by her victory, the singer pushed for a ban against adoption by gays, which also passed by an overwhelming margin. But Bryant's early victories began to galvanize opposition to her efforts.

After her initial successes at the Dade County polls, Anita Bryant attempted to take her message to a national audience, and it was at this point her campaign began to falter. She was greeted with protests at her stops, becoming one of the first persons to be "pied" as a political act when a protestor nailed her in the face in Des Moines, Iowa. Gay activists also organized a juice boycott and a campaign of letter-writing to the Florida Citrus Growers Association. Some protesters enclosed two-dollar bills and requested a copy of a nonexistent pamphlet linking orange juice with homosexuality. Bryant's personal and professional life began to crumble.

Though the actual economic impact of the orange juice boycott was debatable, it drew unwelcome attention to that industry and made Bryant's employers uneasy about her highly visible position as their spokesperson. She began losing sponsors and then complained that she was a victim of discrimination, the irony and hypocrisy of which was not lost on her critics. *(Ibid n#34)* When her staple contract with the Florida Citrus Commission was allowed to lapse in 1979, it was obvious that Anita had become a "radioactive" property. Bryant's marriage finally crumbled in 1980, partly because of the excessive time she devoted to her Christian activism. Ironically, her divorce and subsequent remarriage weakened her support among conservative Christians, and Bryant was forced to declare bankruptcy and faded from the political scene.

Bryant and her "Save Our Children" campaign presented Eddie with the first opportunity to exercise his belief that the Minoan Brotherhood should be priests to their people. In the run-up to the 1977 Dade County vote, Eddie had organized the members of the Brotherhood to perform a magickal working against Anita Bryant. In a dark moon ritual on May 17, they asked the Gods to reflect the singer's hatred back upon her. *(Ibid n#4)* While it would be rash to link what subsequently happened to Bryant with this ritual act, there are certainly grounds for thinking that the magickal law of return, expressed by the folk saying that "what goes around comes around," might have something to do with her subsequent nosedive in popularity.[39]

The lasting legacy of Anita Bryant's ill-begotten foray into politics is twofold. Bryant's actions helped repoliticize gay communities across the country, providing a *cause célèbre* for activists that bridged the gap between the late 1970s and the horror that the election of Ronald Reagan engendered amongst progressives in 1980. The modern entry of Evangelical Christians into United States political discourse can also arguably be laid at the Bryant's feet like a bouquet of dead roses. California State Senator John Briggs came away from the Dade County vote with a burning desire to build on the success of Bryant's efforts with a plebiscite against homosexual school teachers in California. Although Briggs' opportunistic effort, known as Proposition 6, ultimately failed at the polls, it helped spread a message of fear and intolerance from coast to coast.[40]

Within two years of traveling to Miami to help Bryant in her opposition to the Dade County ordinance, the Reverend Jerry Falwell became the head of a new organization that called itself the "Moral Majority." Although Falwell went on to work against the civil and humanitarian rights of the nation's gay and lesbian citizens for the next two decades, it was Anita Bryant who, like Sister Aimee a generation prior, led conservative Christians into politics under the rubric of domestic social issues.[41] The apocalypse once predicted by Bryant should Dade County recognize its gay and lesbian citizens has yet to manifest — that is, if one doesn't hold the disastrous aftermath of Florida's botched role in the 2000 Presidential election to the same Biblical standard as plagues of blood and frogs.

Endings and Beginnings

Biblical plagues would probably have provided a respite for New Yorkers during the hot summer of 1977. At 9:27 PM on the steamy evening of Wednesday July 13, the power grid serving metropolitan New York City and Long Island collapsed through a combination of incompetence on the part of electric supplier Consolidated Edison and just plain bad luck. Power wasn't completely restored to the city until 10:39 PM the following evening. Manhattan, Queens and Staten Island came through the emergency relatively unscathed in comparison to the rest of the city, but no borough was without at least some damage. Riots, looting and arson wracked the Bronx and Brooklyn. In all, 3,776 people were arrested for looting and other assorted crimes. Whole blocks of shops were looted and torched in the twenty-four hours of madness and pandemonium that followed.[42]

Bennie will never forget the 1977 blackout. He had just gotten home from his evening walk, and it was a very hot night. "I was listening to Diana Ross' *Love Hangover* and had the stereo cranked up when everything went out," he remembered. "We had the only lit apartment with all the candles we had. As I can recall, [Lisa Marie] came over and we partied all night, drank wine and got high."[43] It was peaceful in Forest Hills, but eerie in the unaccustomed darkness. Queens suffered less than other areas, but even so, there was looting in some isolated places. The power stayed off through the next day, meaning that there was no work, or even any means to get to work with all of the trains and subways down. Eddie was upset by the blackout, not because of the inconvenience and the lost income, but because his ice spells had all melted and had to be redone immediately after the power was restored. Bennie notes that Eddie "was worried about some of the people that he had restraints on."[44]

Though Joey was gone from Knossos Grove, he remained busy in the Craft and, specifically, in the Brotherhood. He initiated his first man, Kenny, in June 1977. *(Ibid n#5)* As a favor to Eddie, Ria gave Joey his Second and Third Degrees in Wica. This was considered a necessity if Cupolo ever wanted to run a Wica coven, in addition to Phaistos Grove, because the men had left the Huntington Coven when Joey was still only a Wiccan First Degree. Ria took Eddie's word that Joey had been initiated, but she had no idea that the men had been involved with Sheila's coven.[45]

In honor of his Third Degree, Clinton Stevens made Joey a silver pendant.[46]

Clinton helped Joey secure a part-time position at Weiser Books to help supplement his income, but Joey didn't like working there. "All I did was sit in the basement and pack books and ship out," Cupolo groused. "They'd get so mad at me because I'd have my little incense and my candles burning down there. They'd say, 'Oh you people and your Witch stuff!' And we're in a fucking occult bookstore. Give me a break! And you think the weirdoes came into Magickal Childe..." *(Ibid n#46)*

Clinton and Joey had become good friends through their workplace interactions at the Magickal Childe. Joey had a great deal of respect for the New Orleans native. "He lived in a Manhattan loft, and in that loft were hundreds and hundreds of plants," Joey recalled. "He even had an orange tree. [He] and his roommate, Stephen Machon, both had green thumbs and were amazing. And [Clinton] was into everything. He was a ballet dancer, he had buns of fire. He was from New Orleans, but he had no accent whatsoever because he said he had fought so hard to get rid of his Southern accent. He did *not* want to be known as a Southerner, but he did love New Orleans.'" *(Ibid n#4)*

According to Sally Eaton, Stevens shared a SoHo loft in the Worth Street area with his roommate and good friend, Stephen Machon.[47] Joey also hit it off with Machon, who was a former Bostonian. With a doctorate in music and a master's in biochemistry, Machon was a genius in Cupolo's eyes. Machon, in turn, idolized Stevens. He told Joey a story about the time that his father was on his deathbed with cancer. Clinton and his Santeria friends came to the hospital dressed very flamboyantly, went into the sickroom and closed the curtain around the bed. From behind the curtain all that could be heard were the sounds of chanting and shaking rattles. "The next day," Joey said, "the doctors were a wreck because [Machon's] father had completely recovered. He had no trace of cancer left in his body. And Steven Machon said 'I was sold.'" *(Ibid n#4)*

Joey thought that Clinton was a genius, too, and not just in mixing oils and incenses. Like Eddie, "Clinton was a speed reader," Joey Cupolo remembers. Stevens knew little about astrology when the two first met. "He found out I was into astrology. He went home that night, [and] he'd gotten himself one of the biggest, fattest books he could find. And the next day he was an expert. And I said, 'You mean you learned this in one frigging night?' And he said, 'I want to be interested in what you're interested in.' And I said, 'Jesus, you know more than I do, already. Gods, give me a break.'" *(Ibid n#4)*

While Joey was fascinated with Clinton's talent and intellect, Stevens was himself infatuated with Cupolo. His budding romantic interest in Joey was beginning to make the latter uncomfortable. Joey liked Clinton as a friend, but he was already in a relationship with Charlie, and it was obvious that Clinton was looking for much more. Earlier in the year, Clinton broached the idea of the two men going into business together. The plan was to open a shop that was a combination occult store, consignment shop and art gallery. "Clinton and I were going to open the shop in the Soho district, back when you could afford a shop [there]."[48] *(Ibid n#5)* It seemed like a dream opportunity. Joey wasn't doing very well financially for himself in the city, going from one low-paying job to another in a city that demanded much of its residents. In a heart-to-heart conversation with Carol Bulzone, Cupolo confessed his frustrations with his lot. In her raspy smoker's voice, Carol asked "Did you ever hear the song 'If you can make it here, you can make it anywhere?'" Joey replied, "Well, I *haven't* made it here, honey. So let me give it a fucking try somewhere else." *(Ibid n#4)*

It is possible that with Clinton Stevens' backing and creativity, Cupolo might have eventually hit upon that elusive formula for success in New York. But the prospect of even closer ties with Clinton was ultimately what caused Joey to rabbit out of the city. "He was really, really, really upset when I left New York," Joey remembered. "He couldn't stand it. He went to a lot of trouble to raise the money for us to open that shop in SoHo. In a way, it was best that I left because it was getting to be kind of a sticky situation because I knew how he felt about me. And I didn't feel that way about him, and he knew that. ... I kind of messed everything up when I left New York." *(Ibid n#4, 5)*

Charlie's job transfer finally came through in May 1978, and he and Joey made plans to move to New Orleans the next month. Even though Clinton had no desire to live there again, he was upset when he found that the two were moving to New Orleans. 'You're going back to *my* birthplace," Clinton complained. *(Ibid n#4)* Hurt though he might be, Clinton still looked out for his friend. As their depature time drew near, Joey and Charlie had still been unable to sell three rooms of furniture that they needed to unload in order to help finance the move. They were beginning to feel dejected, as they had hoped to get at least get a couple hundred dollars for the lot despite having spent much more. As Cupolo remembers, "All of a sudden people started coming through the house saying, 'I want that. I want that. I want that.' And then I get a phone call, and it was Clinton. And he asks, 'So, how is your sale going? Pretty good, huh?' Now I was in Queens and he was in Manhattan, and [so he couldn't have just sent his friends over to buy stuff]. Clinton says, 'Oh I did a little something.' I tell you something, that Santeria magic is fucking powerful." *(Ibid n#4)*

Cupolo and Dandelakis left New York just weeks ahead of the big blackout. With Joey's departure, Buczynski lost his main sounding board. Joey continued corresponding with Eddie through 1978, but the letters grew less frequent as the men grew apart, then finally stopped altogether. Deciding early on that the original Minoan book was not quite to his liking, Buczynski spent much of the year tinkering with the rituals and rewriting it.

He also penned an explanatory preface to the Book that was to be used in the training of new initiates.[49]

One of the biggest changes he proposed was designed to remedy the situation that arose when Kim was belittled and forced to leave the Grove. The qualifications for membership in the tradition were modified to allow other than explicitly gay men to enter the Minoan Brotherhood. With this change, bisexuals, and even straight men who were self-assured and open-minded enough to practice homoerotic magick with gay men, would be allowed to join.[50] Another change removed the labrys as a ritual tool from the hands of men. Although it was originally used in Minoan Brotherhood rituals, Eddie decided that it was more appropriate, based on the available archaeological evidence, to reserve its use solely for the high priestesses of the cult. Many of these changes were confirmed in the first annual November Council of the Minoan Brotherhood, the Third Degree group that Buczynski had set up to maintain the tradition.[51, 52]

The Brotherhood's initial use of the labrys attracted the attention of Clinton Stevens. "Clinton was very interested in the brotherhood," Joey stated. "He felt there was a connection with Chango." *(Ibid n#46)* The connection that Clinton perceived was likely due to the fact that the double-bladed axe was also a symbol of the Santerian Orisha. Eddie also began incorporating slightly more ceremonial influences into his teachings, adding some of the materials that Khem Caigan had advocated.[53] Credit for the hints of planetary magick and references to Crowley's 777 can be laid at Khem's feet. Buczynski also developed an enthusiastic interest in the Kabbalah at this time, one that he was eager to share with others such as Joey. *(Ibid n#33)*

Joey and Kim may have left Knossos, but new men soon came into the Grove, including John D'Antoni and a fellow named Lance. It was around this time that Eddie expanded his Craft name in the Brotherhood to Gwydion-Hyakinthos. Later, it was not uncommon for Minoan in initiates to have three names, one for each Degree. "As it was explained to me," recalled Aubrey Wyatt, "your First Degree name captures your essence, your Second Degree name defines your mission, your calling, and your Third Degree is your dedication to the God/dess you have chosen to serve." *(Ibid n#6)*

In line with his desire to develop a complete magico-religious path, Eddie began drafting a Book of Shadows for the female branch — the Minoan Sisterhood — of what would eventually be called the Minoan tradition. Eddie stated that once the Minoan Brotherhood was established, "the Minoan Sisterhood followed soon after, after negotiations with lesbian High Priestesses of the British cult who were seeking the same ideals." *(Ibid n#3)* Ria and Carol, the high priestesses in question, were excited to work with Eddie in crafting the Minoan Sisterhood. Eddie took the Minoan Brotherhood book, changed it in a number of places to reflect his perception of what would constitute a celebration of the Women's

Mysteries, and then handed the skeleton of a Book of Shadows over to the ladies.[54] However, Ria and Carol were bemused by some of Eddie's ideas on what should comprise the Women's Mysteries. Conferring between themselves, the ladies decided that they weren't terribly comfortable with some of the material as it was written, and were nonplussed by other notions. To be fair, Eddie had given the book to them with the understanding that they should modify it to suit their needs, and they did so from about mid-1977 through mid-1978.[55]

Progress, however, was slow. Writing to Joey Cupolo in November of 1977, Buczynski lamented, "The Sisterhood seems to be going nowhere — I wish Kat [Carol] and Rhea would start doing something." *(Ibid n#33)* Eddie's frustration seemed to stem from his desire to quickly see the Minoan tradition to its logical completion. After the terrible incident with Kim, Buczynski had realized that he had violated his own injunction to seek a balance between the sexes in the Minoan current of worship. In an attempt to rectify that situation, he proposed that there be a middle ground where Minoan Brothers and Sisters could come together to worship in much the same way as a tribal society wherein the members of the men's houses and women's houses would gather for village festivals. Writing to Joey, Eddie said, "We are also trying to start 'The Cult of Rhea' — a Male-Female Minoan Cult. If you want a copy of the Rituals, let me know & I'll Xerox them." *(Ibid n#33)* Eddie had offered a set of those rituals to Joey again in December 1977, but Cupolo never received them. *(Ibid n#51)*

The Cult of Rhea rituals to which Eddie referred were almost certainly related to those which he had written for Kim and Lisa Marie after Kim left Knossos Grove. The absence of initiation and elevation rites in that Book of Shadows clearly indicates that it was not meant to stand alone, and that the men and the women who came together within those rituals were expected to be initiates of the Minoan Brotherhood and Minoan Sisterhood. *(Ibid n#50)* But as slowly as the development of the Sisterhood was progressing, the Cult of Rhea was getting nowhere at all. Joey stated that he left New York before the Sisterhood had gotten off the ground. Bennie could not recall any mixed-sex circles between the men of Knossos Grove and Ria and Carol's group after the Sisterhood formed, although the idea was being discussed in 1978. "These were long-term plans that never came to fruition," Bennie said. *(Ibid n#4)* Although they never really held joint Brotherhood-Sisterhood sabbats, there were still occasional mixed-sex Wiccan gatherings. One of these, held at Ria and Carol's Forest Hills apartment at Ostara of 1978, was memorable for Eddie popping in through the kitchen window with a basketful of red-dyed eggs.

The women eventually got their Book of Shadows into a passable form (although both Carol and Ria admit that it still isn't 100 percent "complete"), and they began initiating women into the cult in the spring of 1978. *(Ibid n#54)* A Third Degree Gardnerian named Chris, who had been in the Pagan Way with Ria a few years earlier, was the first woman initiated into the Sisterhood by Ria and Carol. They brought her in on the advisement of Eddie. *(Ibid n#55)* Emma Davy, who read tarot cards at the Magickal Childe, was another of their first initiates. Although Emma was a straight woman, she felt drawn to the energy implicit in a women's tradition.

Emma was also a bit of a character, as Ria remembers. "We had a little refrigerator in the oils office," Ria writes. "A lady who Emma didn't like brought in a very decadent chocolate cake for Herman and the staff from a French bakery in the Village. Emma looked at that cake and, knowing that Herman was supposed to be watching his weight and diet, said 'This cake wasn't bought with love.' She placed the cake on the floor and did a tarantella on it saying, 'Take that, you bitch!'[56] Emma wasn't the only character brought into the Sisterhood during this period. Lady Heather, another Minoan initiate, taught classes on "bitchcraft" at the Magickal Childe that were reportedly well attended. Other future initiates would include Wiccan authors Loretta Orion, Lexa Roséan, and Phyllis Curott.

Eddie and Bennie had settled into a very comfortable, if unconventional, married home life. On October 6, 1977, they took Eddie's parents to Radio City Music Hall to see "A Very Special Night with Linda Ronstadt" (Ronstadt being Eddie's favorite musician). Eddie had also begun teaching part-time once more at Magickal Childe, this time heading a class on Near Eastern religions, with about 30 students. Eddie had confided to Joey that he planned to move Bennie and himself out of "this redneck neighborhood" and into a Brooklyn Heights brownstone. However, by December, they had decided against moving and re-decorated instead. *(Ibid n#51)* Finances likely played a large role in this. While both Bennie and Eddie were making decent money, Eddie's credit was destroyed from his time with Herman and the Warlock Shop.

Herman, however, positively thrived in his new location, as did the Childe. Eugenia Macer-Story recalls how good Herman looked at the Magickal Childe Samhain festival that year. "I was struck by the *difference* between Samhain Herman and healer Herman," writes Eugenia. "He was wearing a scarlet silk cloak and a Robin-Hood like black outfit and looked very sensual, very handsome. I thought at the time this was his younger self emerging for the occasion."[57]

Sponsored by the Earth Star Temple Association, Inc., the Pan-Pagan Hallows Festival was held at the shop on the afternoon of October 30, 1977. The festival, which was advertised as being for Goddess Worshippers only, offered ritual, music, songs, dance, drama (a given), and a potluck. Macer-Story noted that people were in costume and that the event was held throughout the store, not just in the back room. This marked the first mention of Earth Star Temple in conjunction with the Magickal Childe.[58, 59] "Earth Star Temple was a Pagan Way group hosted by the Welsh tradition and led by Lady Maria Parra," notes Sally Eaton. "Margot Adler, Kenny [Klein] & Tzipporah, and many other Pagan luminaries lectured and performed there."[60] By placing the management and scheduling of the back room under a separate entity, Herman hoped to draw a distinction between the business aspects of the shop and the education and outreach activities in the newly-installed temple space. The need for this separation became apparent after the local O.T.O. chapter later began using the back room as their main meeting place. But, for all practical purposes, Herman Slater remained the person in charge of the space.

By late in the fall of 1977, Bruce-Michael Gelbert decided to drop out of Knossos Grove in favor of other pursuits. Gelbert ultimately didn't stick with the Brotherhood, mainly because he felt the path suffered from just too much of a reaction against Christianity. Eddie had tried to keep such reactions out of the tradition, telling the men that if blame was to be apportioned for the treatment of gays at the hands of the Christians, it should be aimed at the worshippers and not at their God. However, the Bryant debacle had pretty much set the tone for dealings between the Christian faith community and the gay community in 1977, and most gay men weren't feeling the love from or toward the former. For their part, Christians didn't even know of the miniscule Minoan Brotherhood's existence at this time, and it is hard to see how they would have cared about either the good will or animosity of its members if they did. Their ignorance of the Brotherhood changed in the early 1990s when Wiccan-*cum*-Christian evangelical Eric Pryor began gadding about the country lecturing on Satanic occult conspiracies.

In years to come, Pryor would claim that during his time as a Witch and hustler in New York City he had been "a kept man in the temple" and had practiced "Minoan magic."[61] As to the former assertion, Pryor was presumably referring to the Earth Star Temple located in the Magickal Childe. Given his hustling background and the fact that Slater had given him a job (no matter how short its duration), there is some minor support for Pryor's claim to have been a "kept man." And, although it is doubtful that he would have been allowed to use either location of the store as a crash pad, given his background, he would not have been the first homeless employee to do so. As to his claim of practicing "Minoan magic," Pryor would certainly have heard about the Minoan Brotherhood while working at the Magickal Childe in 1977, but he was not an initiate and had never attended a Minoan Brotherhood rite, even as a guest. Therefore, whatever Pryor had been practicing had nothing whatsoever to do with Buczynski's Cretan Witchcraft tradition. Pryor also specifically mentioned the Minoan Brotherhood in his talks, explaining that "a Minoan is a gay occultist" (which is true, as far as it goes) and that "all great Pagan leaders were at one time in the Minoan Brotherhood" (which is utterly false).

Pryor named as Minoan initiates the likes of Raymond Buckland, which surely came as a surprise to the happily-married heterosexual.[62]

While the evidence for Pryor's homo-Satanic fantasies may have fallen short, there were things of a darker nature manifesting in the shadowed, dusty corners of the shop on West 19th Street in 1977. On the longest night of that year, the Magickal Childe would act as a gothic birthing chair for one of the most controversial occult publishing projects of the 1970s.

Chapter 27: The Necronomicon Affair

The Lively Story of a Dead-Name Dropper

> *Those who are intuitively gifted must resort to reason more than those who aren't. Those who discard logic, who refuse to use their minds in a schizophrenic pursuit of the unknown are apt to end up more "psycho" than "psychic."*
>
> –Leo Martello

On December 22, 1977, the wan winter sun illuminated a book that had appeared in the West 19th Street window of the Magickal Childe. The book, glimpsed through glass streaked with the grimy exhalations of the city, had been both eagerly and skeptically anticipated for several years by a subset of the occult practitioners in New York City and beyond. What has since come to be known as the Simon *Necronomicon* or, or vulgarly, the "Simonomicon," was finally released to the public that Thursday.[1] The book, edited (some say written) by a long-time habitué of the shop, Simon, was the latest in a line of tomes to have carried a name originally invented by the horror writer H.P. Lovecraft as a literary device. It would prove to be the most memorable, persistent and financially successful of the highly questionable lot.

The occult horror in which Lovecraft indulged can best be described as the clashing forces of light and dark; of extra-dimensional travelers oozing across the vast, cold voids of space and time; of maddened, gibbering, tentacular shadows, the scratching of rats within dilapidated walls, of ululating rituals to obscene gods in crumbling temples; and of swarthy, shifty foreigners in league with vaguely amphibioid, bug-eyed men with a fondness for damp, rotting ports like Red Hook in Brooklyn. Within this Lovecraftian milieu was a grimoire of blasphemous, occult knowledge that was said to open the pathways between our world and the dark dimensions to which mad elder gods were banished in ages long past. In Lovecraft's stories, men who would unleash these evil forces upon mankind pursued this tome, seeking the rewards of power and glory that they imagined would await them. In other words, it was a book sought primarily by madmen and assholes. This fictional work is the original Necronomicon.

The trail of the Simon *Necronomicon* starts several years earlier when the Warlock Shop was still in Brooklyn Heights. An ad in the Yule 1973 edition of the *Earth Religion News* offered two books for sale:[2]

> The Necronomicon (original script) $30
> The Necronomicon (translation ... lmtd. edition) $15

(Translation not yet in print ... advanced orders being taken)

The most likely candidate for "The Necronomicon (original script)" named in the ad is L. Sprague de Camp's *Al Azif: The Necronomicon*, which was published in January 1973 and was reportedly sold in the store. The limited edition "translation" for which the Warlock Shop took advance orders was almost certainly the book that ended up being published a full four years later as the Simon *Necronomicon*.[3]

Almost a year before the ad appeared in *Earth Religion News*, Simon had approached Herman Slater with a business proposition: If Simon gave him the translation of a manuscript purported to be a rare treatise on magick, could Herman publish it? In return for participating in the deal, Simon offered to split any profits equally with the Warlock Shop.[4] It may be that Simon had no knowledge of Lovecraft or the Necronomicon, as he has claimed, and that it was Herman Slater's idea to emphasize the manuscript's similarities to H.P. Lovecraft's dread tome.[5,6] Whether Simon actually presented Herman with a rare eighth or ninth century manuscript written in Demotic Greek and phoneticized Babylonian and Sumerian that had been stolen by defrocked Orthodox priests, as he has maintained for the last thirty years, or whether he outlined a proposal to stage an elaborate hoax, as the book's critics have long insisted, may never be known. However, this much is clear: either business proposition would have appealed equally to the feisty and irreverent shopkeeper. Simon later wrote that Slater believed that associating the Warlock Shop with the *Necronomicon* would boost the store's profile, and time has certainly borne this out. For better or worse, Herman accepted the offer wholeheartedly, and he has reaped the notoriety of that decision to this day.

Simon began work on the *Necronomicon* manuscript in early 1973. The Warlock Shop and the Friends of the Craft had already begun to make an international name for themselves by participating in the widely-celebrated "Occult" exhibit at the Museum of American Folk Art in Manhattan that January. The first catalogue of the shop was published at roughly the same time as Simon's offer to Herman, thus beginning a mail order business that would put the Warlock Shop on the map from coast to coast. Herman, inveterate gossip that he was, began to spread word among select people in the community that he had a line on the "real thing." This clearly was jumping the gun, as the manuscript was nowhere near ready for publication. By mid-1973, Herman was already becoming frustrated at the pace of Simon's progress. He had hoped that it would be a quick and easy project, and one that would have already begun generating a little extra income for the store. Herman didn't have the ready cash to publish the book himself, even if the manuscript had been ready, but he was cultivating connections that might eventually be able to underwrite the project. In an attempt to pressure Simon to speed up his work, Slater asked him to put together a prospectus that he could show to a well-heeled customer who might be interested in fronting the money for the publication of the book. However, rather than publishing a derivative work, this customer was more interested in buying the original manuscript to add to his own collection. Since neither Slater nor (purportedly) Simon owned the original manuscript, Herman's effort ultimately fell through. This wasn't a great loss from Simon's perspective, as there was still so much work left to do.

A great deal of print and many pixels on internet discussion groups have been spent debating the authenticity of the manuscript that Simon allegedly presented to Slater. But whether the Simon *Necronomicon* was genuine or a hoax, or something in between, certain skills would be needed to help prepare a workable, and marketable, manuscript for eventual typesetting and publication. Translators and persons schooled in Near Eastern history were needed, either to research ancient texts and archaeological papers in order to translate and incorporate enough historical material into the book to make a forgery plausible, or else to translate an actual ancient manuscript in a way that rendered its contents accessible to a modern reader.

Translation, after all, is not as simple as consulting lexicons of words and making basic substitutions. There is an art to producing understandable text from any foreign language. If the reader doubts this, he or she should try converting a random sentence from a foreign language into Standard English using any of the machine utilities on the internet. Some concepts, including slang, wordplay and antique usage, may not be directly translatable between cultures without the interpretation of a knowledgeable individual. While many translators can produce serviceable texts, imbuing the resultant product with an artistry and subtlety to rival the original requires the expertise of a specialist who can also contextualize the ideas being communicated. Ask any two Classicists to debate the relative merits of a translation of the *Odyssey* by Richmond Lattimore and one by Robert Graves and you will soon understand the essence of the problem. Furthermore, most priests do not make particularly good translators. They simply don't exercise the skill often enough to become proficient, and their field of interest is generally too narrow to provide the depth of knowledge that is the mark of a good translator. At best, they may be able to gamely fumble their way through New Testament Greek, which is different from Homeric Greek, which is different from Attic Greek, and so forth. Thus, even if one were constructing a forgery using authentic material as "filler," one still would need the help of skilled translators to do so — assuming, that is, that one actually cared whether they did a good job. Simon, as the editor of the tome, recognized this limitation, and acknowledges the participation of several translators in this endeavor, including Ms. I. Celms and Ms. N. Papaspyrou, as well as a "Mr. X" and a "Mr. Y."[7]

Apart from language, questions of ritual and mythology needed to be resolved. Simon admits there were gaps in the manuscript that required the skills of experienced ritualists to fill.[8] But again, these skills would be necessary whether one was constructing a forgery or dealing with an actual manuscript of ancient magick. If a forgery is to be believable, the writer must marry a mythology, supported by enough accepted information to make it at least casually plausible, with a workable religious and ritual system. If it is an authentic manuscript of great age, there is yet another problem. Pre-Christian magickal grimoires and formularies are quite rare and generally fragmentary. The details of ancient magickal rituals are often poorly represented in surviving documentation, not only because of the secrecy that is "part of the traditional ritual procedure used in approaching the gods for help," but also because many such ancient documents failed to survive, particularly after the ascendancy of Christianity.[9] We are left to surmise many practices from religious texts, which may only provide clues as to the power structures being accessed in ritual, and from any remaining physical evidence of these rites, such as curse tablets and protective amulets, which generally provide no information on the circumstances of their preparation.

From what we do know of ancient magickal practices (and we actually do know a great deal, despite the fragmentary record), magick in the ancient Near East and Europe was quite similar to modern Western practices. Hellenistic magic, for example, was very eclectic, much like the Neo-Pagan practices of today, "borrowing freely from the religions and practices of other cultures."[10] There were differences as well. Historians Ankarloo and Clark note that magick in ancient Greece, despite its "rebellious, anti-social nature, was directly dependent on, and formed in accordance with, the norms and values of society itself."[11] This is certainly less true of modern practitioners. Regardless of the number of people who consult their daily horoscope in the morning newspaper (and it is in the millions), those who publicly admit to practicing magick in Western societies are almost universally treated on par with people who insist that the CIA is reading their brainwaves, rather than as persons with access to hidden sources of knowledge or power. Still, the similarities between ancient rites and modern practices would make it somewhat easier for an editor to bridge the identified gaps of a real manuscript, or else to plug the gaping holes of a hoax.

Jerry Birnbaum was one consultant who helped re-imagine ancient practices in modern terms. A frequent lecturer on the Kabbalah at the Warlock Shop, Jerry's role was acknowledged in the Necronomicon as someone "who aided in some of the preliminary practical research concerning the powers of the Book, and its dangers." *(Ibid n#7)* Another consultant was Norman Mailer's assistant, Judith McNally. Judith was a Welsh high priestess "whose thorough knowledge and understanding of Craft folklore aided the editor in assuming a proper perspective toward this work." *(Ibid n#7)* Peter Levenda also spent time at the University of Pennsylvania Library researching Sumerian material, such as seals and mythology.[12] Others included archaeology students at the University of Pennsylvania. Those who were eventually given portions of the completed manuscript to critique included Gardnerian high priestess Bonnie Claremont.[13]

A detailed analysis of the Simon *Necronomicon* by a university-trained Sumerologist would likely prove quite interesting in identifying exactly what was taken from the resources listed in the bibliography, or others not listed, and rooting out what is spurious, inconsistent, or even revelatory in nature.[14] The fact that no serious scholars of ancient magick, religion or literature have bothered to analyze and publish their findings on the Simon *Necronomicon* should not be construed on its face as a rejection of its authenticity, but it certainly does not bode well. Both the absence of an original manuscript and the contamination of any original material by obviously modern filler would hopelessly complicate any academic study of the work. The complaints of the book's critics regarding errors and inconsistencies in God-names and attributes are well taken; however, such errors, where they exist, could be the result of poor translation and transposition, both within the original manuscript and in modern usages, and of sloppy research rather than of outright fraud (although this does not make for a strong case against outright fraud, either). As Simon readily admits, there was little money and no fame, at least of the type sought by most academicians who value their tenure, in consulting on this project. *(Ibid n#12)* Still, absence of criticism from these ranks should not be taken as a tacit endorsement.

Work on the manuscript dragged on through 1973 and 1974. Herman tried to interest several publishing firms in the project during this time, but he kept encountering closed doors. The editors all expressed a similar skepticism of the book's *bona fides*. Questionable provenance wasn't necessarily a deal-breaker in the world of book publishing, but the recent experience of Clifford Irving's fraudulent autobiography of Howard Hughes perhaps remained a bit too fresh in everyone's mind. Regardless of these setbacks, Herman kept the pressure on Simon with advertisements drumming up advance orders for the book in *Earth Religion News* and the store's catalogue.[15]

As 1974 blurred into 1975 with no *Necronomicon* manuscript yet in hand. Slater began to despair of ever seeing any revenue from the project. He had made some modest advance sales for the book since the very first ad in 1973, but had had to stall impatient customers with excuses about production difficulties. Refunding the orders was certainly an option, but that would have been akin to admitting that the book announcement was nothing but a stunt. It also would have meant parting with a buck, which not only went against Herman's basic business sense but was also problematic because money was perennially tight. Simon acknowledges the understandable irritation that these delays provoked, thanking "all those patient Pagans and Friends of the Craft who waited, and waited for the eventual publication of this tome." *(Ibid n#7)* The "Friends of the Craft" reference was directed to the core habitués of the store, including Slater himself.

Most of the work on the book manuscript — the translations, in-fill, arranging and editing — had finally been completed by the summer of 1975. During the final push for the manuscript's completion, which had taken over an unhealthy chunk of his life, Simon had been hospitalized with a punctured lung.[16] As summer drifted toward autumn, he got to the point where he just wanted the book finished and off his plate. Simon completed the Introduction to the book on October 12, 1975, the 100th anniversary of Aleister Crowley's birth.[17] Crowley and Ceremonial Magick were a hot topic in occult circles, and Simon's notes in the Introduction to the book demonstrate Crowley's influence on his own magickal explorations and training.[18, 19] The mysterious Mr. X whom Simon mentioned in the acknowledgements was most likely William Siebert, a Thelemite and one-time O.T.O. initiate who tended to favor Kenneth Grant's philosophical interpretation of Crowley's work. Mr. X's ideas, as well as those of Jack Parsons and Kenneth Grant, influenced Simon's discussion of Crowley in the Introduction.[20, 21] It is not surprising then that homage was paid to the "Demon PERDURABO" (Crowley's name for himself) in the book. *(Ibid n#7)* Since Crowley considered himself the reincarnation of Eliphas Lévi, one of the occult writers whose work Lovecraft is known to have used in his horror stories, it is perhaps fitting that the Great Beast's shadow would fall upon the completed manuscript.[22] Relieved of his burden, Simon finally went on to other things.

So 1975 yielded to 1976, and Simon decided to let Herman keep a copy of the manuscript at the store to "flog to publishers." Unfortunately, legitimate publishers still showed no interest. The manuscript languished, locked in a dark cabinet under the Magickal Childe's checkout counter, to be pulled out from time to time as an idle curiosity to interested visitors. One day that summer, a couple of fellows walked in off the hot street looking for some mischief. Larry K. Barnes, and his childhood friend Bruce, looked amusedly at the wares on display — the skulls, the herbs, the grimoires, and athames, swords, statues, and chalices. Thinking to have a go at the man behind the counter, Larry asked with a lopsided grin and a bit of quiver in his voice if the store had a copy of the Necronomicon for sale. Without batting an eye, Herman reached down and unlocked the cabinet. Extracting Simon's manuscript and slapping it down on the counter before the two men, he said "Sure" and stifled his own smirk.

Barnes, eyes bulging, leafed through the manuscript, looking at the rituals, incantations, and what appeared to be twisted angelic seals. He muttered that it couldn't be a real manuscript, that the Necronomicon was just something that Lovecraft made up. Slater casually mentioned that he had been unsuccessfully looking for a publisher for the past couple of years. Larry got a wild look in his eye, which was not an uncommon occurrence where he was concerned. A strapping, athletic young man, he radiated bodily health while simultaneously vibrating with otherworldly energies that originated from within an overactive, intensely artistic imagination that was powered, at least in part, by illicit drugs. But the Barnes family had printer's ink in their blood. Larry's father owned a printing company, Barnes Graphics, at 233 Spring Street. As he clutched the manuscript, Larry's mind whirled at the possibilities.

Later that day, Simon and Herman were talking about an unrelated topic and Slater said that he had had an interesting visitor that Simon should meet. That night Simon traveled to Barnes' comfortable Manhattan apartment. There, amid the alien bric-a-brac that marked the great obsession of Barnes' life, and with the manuscript as a catalyst, the two men found common cause and friendship. Simon had finally found an enthusiastic backer and now had the necessary resources to publish the *Necronomicon*.

Once they had a tentative commitment from Barnes to underwrite the book's production, Simon and several others associated with the project formed a company, Schlangekraft, Inc., to act as the publisher. Barnes had originally tried to buy the manuscript outright, but Simon refused. The deal they eventually negotiated was that Barnes Graphics would receive a fifty-percent stake in all future royalties after Larry's initial investment was paid off via sales. Schlangekraft, Inc. would receive the remaining fifty percent. In a nod to his original agreement with Simon, and in consideration of his work in finding a publisher, Slater was guaranteed a sole distributorship with standard reseller discount on the first edition of the book. The Magickal Childe would leverage its promotional resources — its extensive mailing list, the Abrahadabra catalogue, and the store itself — to sell the book. They were finally in business.[23]

To design the book, Slater suggested that Barnes bring Jim Wasserman onto the project. Wasserman had moved to New York City in 1973, where he began working at Samuel Weiser's Bookstore handling accounts. These included that of the Warlock Shop, which is how Slater first came to meet him. After six months, Wasserman's writing talents and knowledge of occult literature gained him influence with Donald Weiser, the head of the firm. Jim moved to Weiser's publishing department, where he proved to have a talent for the job and began to edit manuscripts for upcoming release. Sally Eaton worked with him on one such project — the Weiser reprints of *Ophiel's Art & Practice* series. Increasingly, his efforts were directed toward projects involving Aleister Crowley, whose teachings Wasserman passionately embraced.[24] Among the Crowley books he had worked on for Donald Weiser was the 1975 edition of *The Commentaries of AL* (the so-called Equinox, Volume V, Number 1) that was edited by Marcello Ramos Motta of Brazil. Jim eventually rose to the position of General Manager and Editor-in-Chief before leaving Weiser's to establish his own book production and graphic design firm, Studio 31.[25] *(Ibid n#24)* His job on this project would be to arrange the entire look of the *Necronomicon*, from typeface to layout to illustrations to cover.[26]

The style of the book was also destined to be heavily influenced by Larry Barnes, who had studied art and had taste for the florid and horrid. Larry believed that an over-the-top presentation would ultimately be more successful than the subdued design favored by Simon and the others, and most independent observers believe in hindsight that he was correct in this.[27] Thus, for example, the first printing was styled as a grimoire of old, or at least one as imagined by a graphic artist with roots in the horror comic genre, with a silver-stamped black leather cover and black ribbon page marker. It was designed to be as much a statement as a book.

To tackle the illustrations of the seals and to design the cover illustration and other touches, Wasserman turned to Khem Caigan.[28] A friend and sometime student of ceremonial magickian Harry Smith, Khem had worked with Wasserman doing illustration at Weiser's and was currently staying on Jim's couch in his third floor walkup at 21 Howard Street. One day Wasserman asked Khem if he'd like to work on the *Necronomicon*. Caigan scoffed at the idea, saying that the book was an invention of Lovecraft's. Jim took the young artist to the Magickal Childe, and there in the basement they met with Slater and Simon. Khem looked over the sketches for the seals and decided that the project was just weird enough to be interesting. Agreeing to the assignment, he set about the task of turning the seals in Simon's manuscript into photo-ready images from which printing plates could be etched. As Khem recalled years later,[29]

> *I took the manuscript back to the loft, dug up some pencils, a quill pen, straight-edge, compass, and some india ink. I cobbled together a drafting table from some boards, and set to work on a rough draft of the cover. The New York Public Library provided a few touches that I introduced to what was a typewritten & hand-illustrated manuscript. I viewed many examples of Coptic & Demotic magical papyri, including the Gnostic 'Book of Jeu' with its Gates & Seals. The title lettering was inspired by the underground comics & posters of Rick Griffin – kinda rubbery looking, with claws. I adapted the border from an old Coptic text, with bars added to the vesicae giving a suggestion of eyes peering out of the page. The sigils needed some re-scaling and thickening, and I enclosed them in circles after the fashion of the Seals to be found in some mediaeval grimoires. The 'Humwawa' seal looked tatty, so I rendered it a bit more 'intestinal'. The 'Urillia'/R'lyeh text was shabby, so the calligraphy was touched up. I created the 'Elder Sign' by superimposing the three signs "carved upon the grey stone, that was the Gate to the Outside", and enclosing them*

in a circle. And I did the initial capital letters for the chapters, wrapping them up in Art Nouveau-esque bandages.

Wasserman subcontracted a new firm, Feint Type, to typeset the manuscript for printing. *(Ibid n#26)* Bonny Nielsen and Lia Colla, the owners of the company, lived on the second floor of the same building on Howard Street as Jim. A few weeks previous, Caigan had helped the women move a used linotype machine they had purchased from Weiser's up to their loft. Wasserman had taken the book manuscript and produced the layouts and technical instructions for the typesetters. Neilsen and Colla took the templates Jim had created and started setting the type for the book.[30]

As the first set of galleys was being printed, William S. Burroughs dropped by Feint Type. He had heard that a version of the Necronomicon was being printed and decided to venture forth from his apartment (called "the Bunker") at the YMCA building on Bowery to check it out. He sat down and read the book through, commenting that it was "good shit." Simon and Barnes were thrilled with the verdict, and Larry asked the Beat writer if he'd consider writing a recommendation for the book. Both men were surprised when Burroughs, who generally refused such requests, agreed. Thus, the book promotions were able to proclaim,[31]

> *Let the secrets of the ages be revealed. The publication of the Necronomicon may well be a landmark in the liberation of the human spirit.*
>
> –William S. Burroughs

Slater handled the initial publicity for the book, promoting it in the Abrahadabra catalogue, which was sent all over the United States and Canada, and many places overseas. Barnes eventually involved himself in promoting the first hardcover trade edition of the book, placing ads in national magazine such as *Omni, National Lampoon,* and *Psychology Today.*[32] This edition of the book retailed for $50, a far cry from the $15 price tag touted in the original 1973 advertisement in *Earth Religion News.*[33] The cost of producing the deluxe first edition was somewhat alarming, and both friends and nay-sayers expressed their doubt that the book would pay for itself. The partners forged ahead regardless, and were vindicated when heavy advance sales of the book through the Abrahadabra catalogue made the first edition a success before it even went to print.

Simon originally wanted the book to come out on October 12, 1977, which was the 92nd anniversary of Aleister Crowley's birthday and would have marked two years since the completion of the manuscript. Production delays made that date impossible to keep, however, so Simon felt that the next auspicious date to roll out the book would be December

1, which would mark the 30th anniversary of Crowley's passing. With that date in mind, the fledgling StarGroup One organized its first event as a celebration of the book's release. The publishing party was held just down the block from the Magickal Childe at the Disco Inferno at 5 West 19th Street.[34] The event, with its food, booze, and musical acts (Turner & Kirwan of Wexford and Mike Kramer's band The Workers) lasted well into the night and was a great success. Unfortunately, production delays had once again pushed back the book delivery date.[35] With no copy of the actual book available for the kick off, Barnes improvised a mock-up of the *Necronomicon* with the ornate first edition silver-stamped leather cover for the curious guests to gawk at.

The book was finally ready on Winter Solstice, and it went on sale in the Magickal Childe on December 22, 1977.[36] The run of the deluxe first edition comprised 666 signed and numbered copies with silver-stamped leather covers. It sold out almost immediately. A limited cloth-bound first trade edition of 1333 copies of the book was also issued in 1977, this one also with a silver-stamped black cover. Reaction to the book was instant, and ran the gamut from wild praise to sneering dismissal. Khem Caigan remembers asking his mentor, Harry Smith, for his impression of the book. Harry replied, with typical aplomb, "We-ell ... if you *like* that sort of thing, then that's *just* the sort of thing you'll like." *(Ibid n#29)* Others were less sanguine. J. Gordon Melton, the Christian academician and scholar of modern spiritual movements who was known as a relatively balanced writer on the modern occult movement, was uncomplimentary about the book's value to the spiritual seeker in his 1978 review of the *Necronomicon* for *Fate Magazine*. But, as they say, there is no such thing as bad publicity, and any review that suggested the potential danger of using the book was pure gold for sales.

On December 12, ahead of the book's publication, Simon gave the first of several lectures on the *Necronomicon* at the Magickal Childe.[37] He would continue to lecture on the book periodically over the years as reader demand dictated, usually in combination with some topic touching on Ceremonial Magick. "We held elaborate 'book parties' and other promotional events to which the [O.T.O.] was invited and at which the Order and Thelema in general were introduced to the public," Simon remembers. "Our 'public' at the time consisted of a diverse audience of science fiction enthusiasts, Tolkienoids, *Illuminatus!* true believers, and various artistic and musical types."[38] Some of these events were held in the Earth Star Temple, while others occurred at the Bells of Hell in the West Village.

A revised hardcover edition of 3333 copies in leather was published in late 1979. Each edition of the book sold out rapidly, and some copies were even sold in Great Britain via the Askin publishing operation of occult authors Francis King and Stephen Skinner.[39] Larry Barnes had tried to sell the trade paperback rights to the book in 1977, initially with no more success than Slater's earlier efforts. But once the book proved a success in its hardcover editions, Avon bought the rights to the book, and in 1980 the Simon *Necronomicon* was finally published in paperback for the masses. Revised hardcover editions in black leather and cloth were issued in 2008.

Ceremonial magickians, Lovecraft aficionados, and pimply-faced Satanist wannabes weren't the only ones buying and using the book. Neo-Pagans, who were normally reticent to experiment with grimoires and treatises derived from the Judeo-Christian spiritual tradition, were also "walking the gates" as Simon recalled in a 2002 interview. "The Necronomicon seemed to offer a system of magic that was outside this tradition, that was purely 'pagan' inside and out," Simon wrote. "It was thus embraced by many pagans as a suitable technique of ceremonial magic that would not compromise their own beliefs and that could be used with impunity by pagans."[40] This wasn't revisionist speculation on Simon's part. In response to a perceived demand for instruction on this very topic, he had written a two-part article on the subject of Neo-Pagan ceremonial magick that ran in *Earth Religion News* in 1974 and 1976 well before the *Necronomicon* was published.[41,42] And Jerry Birnbaum, one of the people in the acknowledgements section of the book, was a Neo-Pagan who helped in the writing and worked with the system in order to provide feedback to the editors.[43]

A companion volume to the *Necronomicon* was released by Magickal Childe Publishing in 1981. Titled the *Report on the Necronomicon*, the book was initially the brainchild of Larry Barnes and Herman Slater, who had hoped to capitalize on the paperback success of Avon's reprinting of the *Necronomicon*. Simon wrote the *Report*, which was a slim volume in comparison to the *Necronomicon* itself. However, it proved to be a good seller, if somewhat less so than its namesake. The pamphlet was eventually re-printed by Magickal Childe Publishing as the *Necronomicon Spellbook* in 1987, before being purchased and re-issued by Avon Books in October 1998.[44] Another volume in the series, *The Gates of the Necronomicon*, was to be published by Magickal Childe Publishing in 1992. The book had been written by Simon, typeset, and readied for galleys, and was advertised in the Abrahadabra catalogues for May and July of that year. Unfortunately, Slater's death in July 1992 forestalled the issuance of the book, and the manuscript vanished.[45] Simon was eventually able to recreate it, and the book was published by Avon in late 2006.

Shortly after the *Report on the Necronomicon* was published, Simon dropped out of sight for various personal reasons, including the persistent stalkers that the notoriety of his association with the *Necronomicon* had attracted.[46] The Simon *Necronomicon* has remained in print for the last 30 years, and in that time it has reportedly sold over eight hundred thousand copies worldwide. During this run it has inspired supporters to sing its praises and detractors to damn its lies. It has moved into the collective spiritual toolkit of Satanists and chaos magickians in particular, who are always on the lookout for a means to twist their thinking out of what they view as the quicksand mindset of blasé conformity. This association with chaos magick may ultimately explain why William S. Burroughs endorsed the book.

Burroughs was said to have been involved for the last decade of his life in the Magical Pact of the Illuminates of Thanateros (IOT), an umbrella group in the chaos magick movement. Peter Carroll coined the term "chaos magick" in his 1978 book *Liber Null* to describe a branch of ritual magick that promotes the idea that any belief system can provide the ritualist with the necessary focus for exerting his Will on the fabric of reality.[47] Even belief systems that are known to be fictional can be used to this end. The Simon *Necronomicon*, as a magickal grimoire, provides sufficient detail and plausibility in its ritual system to make it an attractive tool even for chaos magickians who otherwise have serious reservations about its patrimony. It didn't hurt that the Simon *Necronomicon* conveniently appeared at the dawn of the chaos movement. Burroughs often used drugs as a tool to wrench his own perceptions out of phase with those of his fellow man. A paperback grimoire would certainly present a less expensive route to this state of consciousness than a heroin habit, and may even be less dangerous, at least in theory. In any regard, one can just as easily perish in one's own bathroom; just ask the shade of Elvis. No one ever accused him of gate-crashing the sunken island of R'lyeh.

Being involved in the initial splash of the *Necronomicon* release provided some synergistic benefits to Slater and the Magickal Childe. The increased publicity and foot traffic through the store helped sales, especially when Herman diligently worked to capitalize on the concomitant notoriety spawned by the book by looking for ways to sell material related, however remotely, to the book. A customer recalls walking into the store one day and hearing Slater on the phone, presumably with a statuary supplier, yelling "I want Pazuzu! Give me Pazuzu!"[48] Magickal Childe Publishing later cashed in on the burgeoning Chaos Magick market by printing Adrian Savage's *An Introduction to Chaos Magick* (1988).[49]

An interesting side note to this discussion of the chaos magick movement highlights the contributions of one of its early unintended heroes, Danish physicist and mathematician Per Bak. While working at Brookhaven National Laboratory on Long Island during the period when the Simon *Necronomicon* was being edited, Per Bak began the inquiry that eventually led to his theory of "self-organizing criticality." This theory states that there appears to be a law of nature by which new forms come into being spontaneously from old forms.[50] Some chaos magickians point to this as proof of the efficacy of quantum magick, though most quantum physicists wouldn't be caught dead defending that position. However, the really interesting part of the story, at least to a conspiracy theorist, is that, in the language of Kemet, *per bak* is the ancient name of the city of Denderah, where the famous ceiling relief of the Egyptian zodiac was discovered. This is the same Denderah zodiac to which Simon refers in the Preface to the Second Edition of the *Necronomicon*.[51] At this titillating intersection of chaos magick and conspiracy theories, perhaps the moral of the story is that, rather than seeing a Shoggoth behind every extra-angled doorway, sometimes coincidences are simply to be borne with aplomb. *Tekeli-li!*

This leads us to the beauty of the Simon *Necronomicon* and, in that beauty, truth; or a facet of the truth, at any rate. For had the story of Simon's book not, with the willful help of its editor/contributor/author over the years, been so thoroughly twisted around so many disparate and unlikely co-themes — Lovecraft, Crowley, Sumer, assassination, UFOs, murder cults, suicides, drugs, perversion, theft and insanity — it might have sunk beneath the surface of oily, troubled waters like a failed depth charge shortly after its release, just as the other Necronomicons have, a curiosity of its times and nothing more. The simultaneous combination of all these bizarre threads, careening as they do like drug-maddened rats through dank and darkened mazes, provides a royal repast for the gibbering paranoid lurking within us all. This loopy, tangled skein, festooned on dead trees like the guts of a murder victim, makes the story too implausible *not* to be true at some level, doesn't it?

In *Dead Names: the Dark History of the Necronomicon* (2006), Simon disputes any charges that the *Necronomicon* is a work fraught with evil — and then, chapter by chapter, he throws up a fog of death and mayhem that follows in the wake of the book project, striking down both participants and innocent bystanders, obscuring the storyline and kicking sand in the faces of supporters and detractors alike. This combination of conspiracy and sleight-of-hand is pure *Illuminatus! Trilogy* in its styling. It is a pity that more critics haven't appreciated the lengths to which Simon has gone to pay homage to a body of work that he so clearly admires. Indeed, one might argue that Simon has endeavored throughout the *Necronomicon* and its attendant books to summon up from the collective unconscious a fourth volume of Wilson's hideous, illustrious trilogy. As the chaos magickians might say, "Fake it until you make it."

Concerning "The Necronomicon Files"

It is necessary to go an extra step in this chapter to address the particulars of a myth that has been circulated regarding how the Simon *Necronomicon* came to be. According to a story presented in the book *The Necronomicon Files*, the Simon *Necronomicon* was the unfortunate result of a drunken party at the Warlock Shop in Brooklyn Heights. As the story goes, a group of people sat around one evening during a post-lecture party and made up the tome in response to a *what-if* game gone wrong. The challenge was supposedly to produce a fraudulent *Necronomicon* designed to fool a credulous public and capitalize on the current popularity of H.P. Lovecraft, who had lived a few blocks from the shop during the mid-1920s.[52]

This creation myth has a "Necronomicon group" — comprised of Eddie Buczynski, Herman Slater, Leo Martello, and unnamed others — spontaneously forming at the Warlock Shop that night. Buczynski allegedly took notes while others dictated their thoughts on what information such a book would contain. Herman is said to have afterwards taken the notes, copyrighted them, and then quickly rushed the book into print before any of those who had had a hand in the project could object. Slater's goal was allegedly to make as much money as he could before the hoax was revealed by the outraged or concerned party-goers. Eddie was said to have claimed that he had no prior knowledge of Herman's planned actions. It is also alleged that Buczynski then subsequently used the *Necronomicon* to train newcomers to the Craft and, more troubling, that the book was purposefully designed by Buczynski and the other named individuals to trap and harm the unwary in some crude exercise of occult Darwinism. The problems with this story are manifest and are addressed to some extent in Simon's *Dead Names*.[53]

If this creative free-for-all happened as stated, the party at which the concept was both proposed and then acted upon would have had to occur before the first ad for the book, which is to say before Yule of 1973. Since the Simon *Necronomicon* was not released until Yule of 1977 (almost four years later) there is no support for the allegation that anyone "rushed" the book into print. Another considerable problem with this myth is that the book is far too complex to have sprung fully-formed, like Athena from the head of Zeus, in the course of a single evening, particularly through the actions of an inebriated *ad hoc* committee. It is doubtful that even a workable outline for such a book could have been achieved in that time and under those conditions, let alone the development of the sigils and other detailed information presented in the *Necronomicon*. Such a project would have taken even a knowledgeable person several months to write and edit.

However, it is possible that, in the course of a discussion at the Warlock Shop, the germ of an idea may have been created, and that this idea may have later been turned into a book proposal that eventually became the Simon *Necronomicon*. It should be noted that Simon has consistently denied this allegation, and there is no proof that such a meeting ever took place. *(Ibid n#53)* But even if the book had been conceptualized at any such gathering, that is a far cry from the tale as told by *The Necronomicon Files* of a ready manuscript being rushed into print ahead of a storm of recriminations. As has been pointed out, whoever translated the text, or spun it out of whole cloth, had the better part of four years in which to do so before the Simon *Necronomicon* finally hit the shelves in late 1977. Hardly a rush job!

It is also improbable that people such as Herman Slater, Leo Martello and Eddie Buczynski ever co-conspired to write the book, though they certainly would have had knowledge of the project's existence. Indeed, it is rather naïve to even suggest, as Gonce's source in *The Necronomicon Files* does, that Herman would be able to prepare a book project without Eddie's knowledge, given their personal relationship, their business partnership and the cramped confines of their home and office above the Warlock Shop. Martello, an insider at the store who had circled with Eddie and Herman in the Traditionalist Gwyddoniaid, would have heard of such a project, but except for the acknowledgement in the *Necronomicon* that Slater inspired the work to be completed by dint of his "encouragement and constant kvetching," there is no proof that any of these men were ever involved in writing the book. *(Ibid n#7)* Furthermore, neither Buczynski nor Martello is mentioned in the *Necronomicon*'s acknowledgements. Given that Simon, the book's editor, willingly acknowledged the efforts of so many other people, there really isn't any logical reason that he would have denied Eddie's or Leo's role in that project, if either man actually had one.

Herman Slater had a strong personality, and if he had written or edited the *Necronomicon*, he almost certainly would have named himself its editor or contributor just as he had done on a number of other projects, such as the controversial *Book of Pagan Rituals* (née *Pagan Rituals I* and *Pagan Rituals II*). Slater would also have ensured that credit was given to his former lover, if Buczynski had actually participated, because the two men remained on fairly good terms until the latter's death long after the book's publication.[54] In addition, Slater, and presumably Simon, would have known better than to fail to mention Leo Martello's role in the project, if there was one, given Leo's prickly temperament and tendency to publicly scourge anyone he believed to have slighted him. Such an eruption would surely have "queered the pitch" for the book, as it were. That none of these things occurred is yet another indication that the story related in *The Necronomicon Files* is faulty.

Another problem with the tale is that Herman Slater, in point of fact, neither published nor copyrighted the *Necronomicon*. The original book was published by Schlangekraft, Inc., which was never an imprint of either the Warlock Shop or the Magickal Childe, the publishing vehicles of which were Earth Religions Supplies, Inc. and Magickal Childe Publishing, Inc., respectively. Indeed, the Magickal Childe did not begin to print books until 1981, three years after the *Necronomicon* was released. The copyright holder of the *Necronomicon* is listed as "Simon." New books in the *Necronomicon* series continued to be published by Avon Books into the new millennium under the Simon *nom de plume* and copyright, even though those named by Harms and Gonce had passed away before these books were issued.⁵⁵ Simon also continues his correspondence with select persons and posts to discussion groups to this day, including those associated with the authors of *The Necronomicon Files*. Therefore, Slater clearly could not have used the name Simon as an alias, nor is there any indication that Slater exercised any editorial control whatsoever over the book's contents. As to whether Simon is, or is not, the alias of occult writer Peter Levenda as has been widely speculated, Peter has this to say on the subject: "Simon and I do occasionally share a drink together." And a mirror too, perhaps; but in this one instance it may be best to just let sleeping sorcerers lay undisturbed.⁵⁶

Reacting to the publication of *The Necronomicon Files* in 1998, Simon has consistently denied that Buczynski, Martello or Slater had anything to do with writing the *Necronomicon*.⁵⁷ The fact that everyone who was close to Eddie during this period — Bennie Geraci, Joseph Cupolo, Ria Farnham (the latter of whom worked at both locations of the occult store) — denies the claim that Eddie worked on the *Necronomicon* further bolsters Simon's assertion that he did not.⁵⁸,⁵⁹ Khem Caigan, who *was* involved, at least peripherally, in the project and who knew both Buczynski and Slater, states that neither man had anything to do with writing the Simon *Necronomicon*.⁶⁰ Khem and Simon do not appear to publicly agree with many things these days on the history of that book, but they are in concord on this one point.

As has been previously discussed, the Minoan Brotherhood materials of the 1976-1977 period are devoid of virtually all elements related to ceremonial magick other than those intrinsic to the rituals of Wica. This focus reflects Eddie's relative disinterest in the topic until late 1977 when, with Khem Caigan's encouragement, he began to cultivate an interest in the Kaballah. Indeed, Welsh tradition initiate Judith McNally, who knew Eddie quite well during the period when *The Necronomicon Files* alleges the *Necronomicon* to be written, categorically stated that "he gave ceremonial magicians a wide berth when I knew him."⁶¹ Both Simon and Caigan confirm that Buczynski had no interest in ceremonial magick.⁶² *(Ibid n#60)* There is also no indication in any of Buczynski's surviving papers that he used information from the Simon *Necronomicon* to train people or to set traps for the unwary, even as examples to demonstrate what not to do, or that he perpetrated any of the other malicious actions claimed in the Harms and Gonce book.⁶³ Such actions, if the happened, would indeed be ethically scandalous behavior. Fortunately, they did not.

The source of these claims rests with just one person, known in *The Necronomicon Files* as *Nestor*. It may be a coincidence that *Nestor* was the public name used by *Thain*, who was also known as Gerald Fisher, formerly of the Louisville Coven of Gardnerian Wica. Fisher was blacklisted in the Book of Shadows of Eddie's New York Coven of Witches in 1974, which is an indication of the rancor that existed at one time between the two men. If the *Nestor* in question is indeed *Thain* (and this is by no means confirmed), then it may well be that there are still some unsettled issues between the men in question.[64, 65] Given how *Nestor*'s claims are presented in *The Necronomicon Files*, there is certainly a suggestion of personal animus at work to besmirch the reputations of those individuals named in the book — persons who are now all conveniently deceased and thus unable to defend themselves.

H.P. Lovecraft and the Necronomicon

Speculators down through the years have explored the possibility that Lovecraft accessed rare, occult reference works from which he either drew the gist of the Necronomicon, or perhaps even encountered a grimoire by that name from sources associated with the Golden Dawn or other mystical organizations. This is highly unlikely. Lovecraft is known to have mentioned Elizabethan occultist John Dee and incorporated information from such contemporary books as Eliphas Lévi's *The History of Magic* in his writing, for example in *The Case of Charles Dexter Ward*.[66] However, despite his use of occult concepts and terminology to bolster his stories, Lovecraft had little empathy for occultists or their view of reality. In a letter to writer Clark Ashton Smith, he stated, "I am, indeed, an absolute materialist so far as actual belief goes; with not a shred of credence in any form of supernaturalism — religion, spiritualism, transcendentalism, metempsychosis, or immortality." He wrote sneeringly of "the junk sold at an occultist's book shop in 46th St.," of "the psychic lunatic fringe" and "these crack-brained cults" with their "free booklets & 'literature'." He placed his name on their "sucker lists" in order to obtain free literature to use in his writing.[67]

It is certainly possible that Lovecraft had encountered works on magic, demonology and diabolism during his forays through the bookshops of New York, Cleveland and Providence, and that such books inspired the author during the creative process. However, there is some doubt as to whether Lovecraft even had the skills in Hebrew, Latin and ancient Greek necessary to decipher any truly exotic magickal texts that he might have come across.[68, 69] But even if he had the requisite knowledge, he would have treated the information contained therein as mere grist for his pulp mill, and would otherwise given the documents no credence whatsoever. Regardless of what resources may have been available to him, Lovecraft's surviving letters clearly document the fictional nature of the Necronomicon he cited in his stories, and he freely admitted to more than one correspondent that the name came to him in a dream.[70] Since the 1970s, some have supposed that Lovecraft's active and rich dream states were utilized as a sort of trance-mediumship by these so-called elder gods to feed him the images that he used in his stories.[71] This belief not only denigrates the in-born creativity of the writer, reducing him to little more than a Dictaphone for agencies unknown and unknowable, but it also forms the basis of a self-referential chain of causality that cannot be tested objectively. If one is susceptible to such circular argument, it is far easier (and more socially acceptable within the dominant culture of our times) to follow a Christian path of Biblical inerrancy than one devoted to mad gods that up until recently existed only within the pages of pulp fiction.

Few people believe that any extant version of the Necronomicon is actually based upon a manuscript of eldritch knowledge, stolen or otherwise. However, the authenticity of the Simon version, let alone any connection (however tenuous) it may have to the nightmarish Lovecraftian vision of such a grimoire, isn't really germane to this tale; nor is it entirely the point when one is considering the book strictly on its own merits. As Simon and many others have pointed out, all books of spiritual exploration must by necessity start somewhere. It is enough to document here how Simon's manuscript and book passed through the lives of our subjects, thus leaving the determination of their ultimate patrimony to the partisans on either side of the debate, who are certainly not known for their reticence on the subject. As to the efficacy of the rituals and mythology of the Simon *Necronomicon* when used as directed (or otherwise, as the case may be), judgment is best left to the individual wielder of that dread paperback. A magickal working, after all, is only as good as the practitioner's commitment to seeing it through to its ultimate conclusion. That being the case, one might be forgiven for wishing certain of these individuals upon themselves, as Leo Martello might say, given their sometimes dubious motives for utilizing the book.

There is an intrinsic power to words and in the repetition, visualization, and transmutation of words and ideas, regardless of their source. This point is driven home when we consider the parable of a certain mythology of semi-Semitic origin and how it has evolved over time. An addition to its foundational book, writ large on golden leaves no less, was allegedly discovered under a rock in the Western hemisphere less than 200 years ago. Those who believed in the authenticity of that golden book were persecuted, sometimes killed, and driven into the wilderness by the authorities. And yet, despite the initial gnashing of teeth by the established cults of the day, the spiritual path that sprang from that golden book is now arguably considered a member of that family of faiths, with over ten million adherents worldwide. Contrast this with the continued popularity of the Simon *Necronomicon* over the past 30 years, and one might be tempted to conclude that the difference between elder gods and elders of another sort is sometimes as subtle as the addition or subtraction of a few tentacles. Thus endeth the lesson.

Some confusion admittedly remains regarding the provenance of the Simon *Necronomicon*. One thing, however, is certain: H.P. Lovecraft played no role in the production of any published version of that blasphemous tome, other than to lend the fictional underpinnings and a name upon which later authors would hang their own interpretations. It is tempting to warn readers to accept no substitutes; but if history is any indication, they won't listen. However, if any of Lovecraft's contemporaneous admirers had ever expressed to him a belief in the book's authenticity, they would have been unceremoniously lumped into "the psychic lunatic fringe" that Lovecraft so despised.

Man, once surrendering his reason, has no remaining guard against absurdities the most monstrous, and like a ship without rudder, is the sport of every wind.

−Thomas Jefferson

Chapter 28: Babalon Comes to Babylon

The Rebirth of the O.T.O.

Apart from gay Witches breaking their shackles and the emergence of dark books of debatable provenance, New York City in 1977 also played host to a vital and energetic fraternal and religious organization that had just eight years earlier been on the verge of extinction. The Ordo Templi Orientis (O.T.O.), a mystical initiatory tradition with some similarities to Masonic organizations, had been founded in Germany or Austria sometime around the turn of the twentieth century. Aleister Crowley, a ceremonial magickian from England, took over the O.T.O. in 1925 from the deceased OHO, Theodor Reuss. Crowley spent the rest of his life trying to build the Order into a strong international organization, including the establishment of lodges in the United States. Unfortunately, the intervention of World War II critically damaged the O.T.O. in Europe. Crowley passed away in 1947, his life's work largely in ruins at the hands of the Fascists and internal squabbling. His successor, Karl Germer, emigrated to the United States after the war. In his capacity as the OHO, Germer functioned as little more than a caretaker of the Order during his tenure, and the O.T.O. drifted toward senescence and obscurity. Germer passed away in 1962 without naming a successor.

Just before the invasion of Normandy, Aleister Crowley had met a young American soldier named Grady McMurtry. McMurtry, who had loaned Crowley a month's worth of pay during those bleak years in order to secure a supply of pre-war paper for the publication of the *Book of Thoth*, impressed the older man with his life experience and with his interest in the O.T.O. He was brought into the Order by Crowley himself and became a valued correspondent of the so-called "wickedest man in the world." Crowley eventually conferred the IX° of O.T.O. upon McMurtry and made him a Sovereign Grand Inspector General of the Order. In 1944, Crowley broached the idea of appointing McMurtry as the "Caliph" (deputy) of the Order, against the possibility that Germer might die before naming an heir. This was a shrewd move on the part of Crowley, who was 69 years old and in declining health. Given the instability of Europe in the post-war years and the competing European factions within the Order, he may have felt that transferring the functional control of the O.T.O. to a robust, awakened America was the best chance for the Order's long-term survival. Germer was informed of Crowley's intentions and had no serious objections so long as his own place as OHO after Crowley was secure. McMurtry, who had by this time rotated back to the States and was living in California, was presented with papers to that effect in March and April of 1946. In June 1947, shortly before his death, Crowley once more informed McMurtry that he should keep himself in readiness to succeed Germer as the OHO if it became necessary.[1]

Germer and McMurtry worked together within Agapé Lodge in Los Angeles, which at the time was the only operational lodge of the O.T.O. in existence. The men had a falling out in 1957, and they eventually lost contact with one another when the McMurtry left California for a new job on the East Coast. After Germer passed away in 1962, his wife Sascha and O.T.O. member Frederic Mellinger were named the executors of his estate with regard to the property that Germer had held in trust for the O.T.O. Sascha attempted to discharge her probate obligation by transferring the archives of the Order and a library of Crowley materials, including manuscripts of published and unpublished writings, to Hermann Metzger of Switzerland in 1963 based on his claim of being the current OHO. Mellinger blocked the transfer, ostensibly on the grounds that Metzger's claim was invalid. The materials remained with Mrs. Germer, who eventually severed all ties with the remaining members of the Order. Grady McMurtry was not informed of Karl Germer's death until 1969, whereupon in June of that year he exercised the charters that Aleister Crowley had bestowed upon him and assumed the title "Caliph Hymenaeus Alpha IX°, X°." He was supported in his actions by Dr. Israel Regardie and Gerald Yorke, the two most prominent surviving members of the Order. Regardie and Yorke were not only personal friends of Crowley, but also understood the man's thought processes and knew what he would likely have wanted done under the circumstances. *(Ibid n#1)*

Upon assuming leadership of the so-called Caliphate, McMurtry invited the surviving O.T.O. members to help him re-establish regular operations of the O.T.O. Germer's caretaker administration of the Order, and the leaderless period after his death, had driven the O.T.O. to the brink of extinction. Fewer than a dozen O.T.O. members remained in the United States, several of whom would pass away within the next few years. The situation in Europe and elsewhere was not much better. No active O.T.O. body with a demonstrable connection to Crowley's organization existed anywhere in the world, so the first order of business was to re-establish a functioning governing body and immediately begin growing the membership.

Attempts were made to advertise the Order's continued existence in the hopes of attracting new members. These efforts included the publication of Crowley's Thoth Tarot, illustrated by Lady Frieda Harris, which was a legacy that Crowley left to McMurtry in payment for the loan to Crowley during McMurtry's stint in England in World War II.[2] The membership-building activities centered on The College of Thelema in Dublin, California and the Kaaba Clerk House in San Francisco in 1969 and 1970. In 1971, McMurtry registered the Ordo Templi Orientis Association as a legal entity in the State of California. The recruiting efforts were met with mixed success, and recruitment activities were eventually transferred to Berkeley, California, where they limped along as McMurtry divided his time between his job on the East Coast and the O.T.O. on the West Coast. *(Ibid n#1)* Llee Heflin, who was initiated by Grady McMurtry and Mildred Burlingame in 1969, recalled that there wasn't an organization to speak of at that time.[3] The O.T.O. itself reported that as of early 1977, it was teetering on the brink of extinction, with the organization down to around six members and having no official functioning bodies.[4]

In the early 1970s, a number of pretenders to Crowley's throne emerged. Among them was the aforementioned Hermann Metzger, who headed an occult group in Switzerland. Metzger emerged from post-war Europe claiming to be a remnant of the O.T.O. membership from the time of the organization's co-founder, Theodore Reuss. Karl Germer had taken an interest in Metzger's work and had initiated correspondence with him and a program of training to inculcate him in the O.T.O. as reorganized under Crowley, but this was never completed to the satisfaction of his tutor, Frederic Mellinger, who blocked the transfer of the O.T.O. archives to Metzger in his capacity as co-executor of Karl Germer's estate.

Kenneth Grant was another contender for the post. A writer of some renown on Crowleyan magickal philosophy, Grant headed what he classified as an O.T.O. group in London. However, Aleister Crowley's friend and former secretary, Israel Regardie, challenged Grant's claim to the OHO O.T.O., and even his status as a member of the O.T.O., by printing the text of Karl Germer's expulsion of him. Dated July 20, 1955, Germer's letter to Grant reads, "You are notified that the very small and limited authority I gave you at one time to establish a Camp of O.T.O. in the valley of London is withdrawn, and I formally expel you from membership in the Ordo Templi Orientis."[5] Germer, who on Crowley's authority had assumed the office of OHO upon the master's death in 1947, had the authority to discipline wayward members. Grant, although not without his own supporters both in the United States and abroad, ultimately did not prevail in his claims.[6]

Yet another claimant to Crowley's mantle was Louis T. Culling, who stated that he and the Ordo Templi Astarte (O.T.A.), with whom he worked, were the only legitimate representatives of the O.T.O. in the United States. Culling wrote that he was the last legitimate holder of an O.T.O. charter and that Karl Germer's claim to being the legitimate OHO was fraudulent. He similarly dismissed Grady McMurtry's subsequent claim of being the head of the Order. Culling said that his passing on of his charter to the O.T.A. on March 21, 1972 "puts an end to the McMurtrey's [sic] claims of being head of the O.T.O. McMurtrey [sic] does not hold a dispensation."[7] Unfortunately for Culling and the O.T.A., their hand was weaker than nearly everyone else's at the table. A 1957 letter from Karl Germer stated that Culling was no more than a II° in the

Order, and was thus in no position to occupy the post of OHO, which could be held by no one under the rank of IX°.[8]

In an article published in the October 1974 edition of *Gnostica News*, McMurtry presented to the greater community his *bona fides* to function in the capacity of the "Caliph" for the purposes of restructuring and reviving the O.T.O. *(Ibid n#8)* While this presentation of his credentials did nothing to silence the critics, he was at least aboveboard in laying out his position. The next year saw the beginning of a turn in the Order's fortunes.

Since the aborted attempt to transfer them to Hermann Metzger in 1963, the O.T.O. materials had remained in the possession of Sascha Germer in Los Angeles. Upon Sascha's death in April of 1975, the material was held in probate and in danger of being scattered, lost or destroyed. There was evidence that Germer's home had already been broken into on at least one occasion and the materials rifled through by persons unknown.[9] Helen Parsons Smith, the ex-wife of Jack Parsons and one of the last remaining members of the O.T.O.'s Agapé Lodge, wrote of her concerns to McMurtry. It was the peril of the Germer materials that finally fixed Grady McMurtry's unwavering attention on the work that needed to be done in California. McMurtry promptly quit his job in Washington, DC and moved to the West Coast in order to devote his energy to preserving the O.T.O. archives and Crowley material. He and Smith were joined in this task by another former Agapé member, Phyllis Seckler.

Other individuals were also becoming interested in the papers and documents from the Germer estate, the most aggressive being a Brazilian named Marcello Ramos Motta. Motta was a former student and initiate of Crowley's mystical order, called Astrum Argentum (A∴A∴), under Karl Germer. Upon Germer's death, Motta believed himself to be the chosen leader of the O.T.O. on the basis of an alleged conversation Germer had had with his wife where Motta was referred to as "the one to follow." Whatever Germer may have meant by such a statement, Motta's interpretation – that he was the new OHO O.T.O. – was impossible, not only because Germer had not officially named a successor, but also for the simple reason that Motta had never even been initiated into the O.T.O. and therefore lacked any standing to assert his claim.

Nevertheless, Motta established his own version of the Order, known as Society Ordo Templi Orientis (S.O.T.O.), in Brazil and began recruiting students so he could expand S.O.T.O. into other countries. He had also published Crowley's *Blue Equinox* in Brazil, and *The Commentaries of AL, being The Equinox*, Volume V, Number 1. The latter was published by Samuel Weiser, Inc. in 1975, and Donald Weiser, as the largest publisher of Crowley material in the United States, most definitely felt that he had a horse in this race. Weiser's interests were manifest, as any decision regarding the ownership of the Crowley materials would have an immediate impact on their publication in the United States into the foreseeable future.

In 1976, McMurtry's O.T.O. Association was in the process of attempting to establish its claim to the O.T.O. portion of the Germer estate. Don Weiser sent Jim Wasserman to California during the last half of July for business, including a meeting with Grady McMurtry to discuss re-issuing the Thoth Tarot in conjunction with Stuart Kaplan of U.S. Games Systems.[10] While in the area, Wasserman was instructed to spend a few days investigating the claims of the various parties pertaining to the Crowley library and O.T.O. archives and report back to his employer on the legal terrain.

Wasserman also happened to be on very good terms with Motta, whom he had met and corresponded with, first in his role as General Manager and Managing Editor of Weiser's, and then as Motta's student in the A∴A∴. Motta gave Wasserman his power of attorney and asked him to assert Motta's claims to the material in the Germer estate as the legitimate OHO O.T.O. Jim met with Helen Smith and Phyllis Seckler on July 14, and later with Grady McMurtry, and he believed that all three people were sincere and legitimate initiates of the O.T.O. who wanted to protect the material in the best interests of the Order. If the three of them worked in together with Motta, and with the publishing resources of Weiser behind them, Wasserman believed that the world would be on the brink of a "Golden Age of Thelema."[11]

Motta, on the other hand, was convinced that McMurtry was a fraud. He warned Wasserman to trust none of the California people, and to do his best to cut a deal to secure Motta's access to the Crowley material. Wasserman, having met with the O.T.O. members, believed that Motta was both mistaken about their intentions and ignorant of who had the real authority with regard to both the Order and the materials. In a letter to Motta dated July 18, he stated that "McMurtry's credentials were absolutely real and so far superior to anything that Mr. Motta possessed that [Motta] had better recognize [McMurtry] for his own self-interest as well." *(Ibid n#11)* He followed this up on July 19 with another letter spelling out the reality of the situation in more personal terms and informing Motta that he was so convinced of McMurtry's legitimacy that he had "placed his own spiritual life on the line" to prove it to Motta by taking the O.T.O. Minerval degree at McMurtry's hand on the evening of Sunday July 18, 1976.

Motta's response to what he characterized as Wasserman's betrayal was to simultaneously rescind his power of attorney on July 27, 1976 and order Wasserman to present a demand that the O.T.O. Association photocopy the entire archives and turn the copies over to Motta. This the O.T.O. Association steadfastly refused to do for several reasons, not the least of which was that the Order would effectively lose control of the materials once they left the country. Motta had also failed to offer any compensation for what would have been a prohibitively expensive and time-consuming task. Regardless of the questioned legitimacy of Motta's claims, he was already too late, for on that same day the Superior Court in Calaveras County, California recognized Grady McMurtry as the authorized representative of the O.T.O. for the purposes of probating the estate. An order was issued for delivery of the remaining O.T.O. archives that had been in Sascha Germer's keeping into the hands of the O.T.O. Association.

This was by no means the end of the legal wrangling, which went on for many more years. Bill Heidrick, the former secretary of the O.T.O. Association, recalled the struggles that the organization, publishers, and others had with regard to the unsettled state of the various O.T.O. copyrights in the ensuing years. "Prior to [1985], O.T.O. claimed but usually could not effectively enforce copyright control. We mainly granted permission as a support and approval procedure, up until then. This included defense of publishers and authors who had been threatened with suit by [John] Symonds or by Motta. In the case of the Magickal Childe, I don't recall such matters for books, but there was such a matter involving essential oil preparations. O.T.O. did license use of the O.T.O. logo (lamen) and trademarks for Herman [Slater's] brand of Abramelin Oil. Our Trademarks were registered early on, from the O.T.O. Association days in California, before incorporation. Motta tried to suppress sales of the Magickal Childe's Abramelin Oil bearing the O.T.O. trademarks, and we interceded with the New York City government to protect Herman's usage of the trademarks in that way."[12]

Others also felt Motta's sting. Even before Motta lost his chance at the O.T.O. archives, relations had begun to sour between him and his erstwhile publisher, Samuel Weiser, Inc. Motta sued Weiser for copyright and trademark infringement concerning the many Crowley works that they had published, claiming that Weiser was cheating him, and demanding greater recognition and a greater share in the marketing of his own book. *(Ibid n#10)* While not a party to the suit, the O.T.O. presented testimony in support of the defendant. Weiser won the case when Motta's S.O.T.O. was unable to meet the test of legal existence after claiming in court that S.O.T.O. was continuation of Crowley's O.T.O.[13]

At this same time, the O.T.O. served Motta with papers for a copyright infringement and defamation suit to be heard in the 9th Federal District Court in San Francisco. That case was concluded in 1985, with McMurtry's O.T.O. being recognized by the Court to be the legal continuation of Aleister Crowley's O.T.O. It was awarded the exclusive ownership of the names, trademarks, copyrights and other assets of the Order, and Grady McMurtry was recognized by the Court as the legitimate OHO O.T.O. The victory was bittersweet, for Grady died of congestive heart failure on the day that the ruling was released to the public. In the late 1980s and early 1990s, the O.T.O. cleared the final impediments of ownership of the Crowley copyrights with the British Crown Receiver.[14] *(Ibid n#1)* In 2002, the British High Court, in *Ordo Templi Orientis v. John Symonds, Anthony Naylor and Mandrake Press*, found that the O.T.O. was the sole owner of the copyrights for all of the works of Aleister Crowley.[15]

There are those who believe that this fight was all about money. But in 1974, long before the battle over the copyrights had begun, McMurtry wrote of his concern over the adulteration of Crowley's works that was taking place at the time. *(Ibid n#8)* The only way to effectively protect the purity of this legacy was to exercise control over its publication. Bill Heidrick observes that "[The] O.T.O.'s never made back as much on royalties as it cost to clear title and defend copyright — especially when you include the cost of buying things like Crowley typescripts for editing new releases like *Book 4*. Still, that's to be expected. Doing the work is the intent, not living off it even as an organization."[16]

Once the initial fight to re-establish the O.T.O. and to secure the archives was won in 1976, the Order redoubled its efforts to build the membership. The O.T.O. Supreme Council aimed to establishing several regional initiation sites in the United States, focusing on areas where there was sufficient interest to establish and grow the Order. In principle, this meant trying to get a foothold in major urban areas, such as New York City, Chicago and Los Angeles. The expansion into the Big Apple resulted from a small set of initiations that took place at Grady McMurtry's home in Berkeley, California in May 1977. This group of newcomers included some people from New York. Two initiates of the O.T.O. were already present in the state, including Jim Wasserman, who had returned to New York City from that remarkable 1976 business trip with a personal commitment to revitalizing the O.T.O. The New York initiates agreed to work with the new members in order to establish two proto-lodges in 1977. One proto-lodge, the Allen Bennett Chapter, was established in Syracuse, New York. It eventually became the Ra Hoor Khuit Lodge at the end of 1978. The other, Mobius Chapter, was established in New York City, becoming Lashtal Lodge by early 1979. *(Ibid n#14)*

A Magickal Partnershop

There was already some interest in the O.T.O. within New York's occult community. A new generation of Thelemic devotees, weaned on Weiser reprints, Anger films, and the crypto-ceremonial lyrics of Led Zeppelin were a happening-in-waiting. Samuel Weiser had done a decent trade in Crowley works since 1971. Under the editorship of Martin Nixon, *Oriflamme — A Review of Magick* had begun publication in New York by The Society for the Propagation of Truth in September of 1974.[17] Herman Slater's and Eddie Buczynski's Earth Religions Supplies imprint published the first United States edition of Aleister Crowley's *White Stains* in 1974.[18]

Lectures on ceremonial magick and Crowley by Simon and others had been quite popular at the Warlock Shop, and trade in Crowleyana had been steadily picking up throughout the 1970s. Slater had gotten to know and respect Jim Wasserman beginning in 1973 from his business dealings with Samuel Weiser, Inc. Herman knew an expanding market when he saw one. Staking his store's future in part on a rising silver star, Slater renamed it the Magickal Childe in 1976 after a central tenet of Crowleyian magick, thus grounding the British occultist's legacy in the earthly realm of commerce. The O.T.O.'s time had come.

Slater took the extra step of inviting the O.T.O. to use the back room of the Magickal Childe, a step that was supposedly greeted with horror by the owner of Samuel Weiser Books. "Donald Weiser LOATHED the O.T.O., and I remember sitting with him and Herman when he warned us not to have anything to do with them," recalls Malcolm Mills.[19] Weiser's concern may have been heightened by the thought of the then-pretender to the Crowley copyrights bedding down with a potential publishing competitor. Unsurprisingly, Slater thought that it made good business sense, and the local chapter began meeting and teaching workshops at the store. The earliest publicized meeting of the O.T.O. at the Magickal Childe was held on October 8, 1977. This lecture, sponsored by the Mobius Chapter, was advertized as an O.T.O. Orientation Meeting and discussed such topics as initiation and the Gnostic Mass.[20] Grady McMurtry began to spend a great deal of time shuttling among the newly-founded O.T.O. groups around the country, including New York City, giving lectures and conducting initiations. His trips were usually whirlwind affairs, measured in a few days, not all of which were necessarily spent at the same location. *(Ibid n#16)* McMurtry gave a number of presentations at the Magickal Childe, almost literally bringing down the house on one occasion when he collapsed a projector screen on top of himself during a slide show.[21]

Simon held many classes to which members of the Order were invited and through which the O.T.O. was promoted. "We held events on days of Thelemic and Pagan importance such as Beltane, Crowleymas, Rose Kelly's birthday, etc. That was in 1977, 1978 when Mr. Dowling was running [Lashtal Lodge]. And so it goes. I continued to hold classes — gratis — for the Order until about 1982 or so," Simon recalled in a 2002 interview. "There were classes in ceremonial magic, Tantra, Eastern mysticism, even apostolic succession! They were heavily attended, and the atmosphere at the time was positive, cheerful, energetic and ... muscular. Discussions were wide-ranging, free form and very informative for everyone. You would find Kenneth Anger in attendance one day, Quentin Crisp another, and we all felt we were accomplishing something."[22]

Not everyone was happy with the way things were developing. Politics also began to intrude as the Order under McMurtry worked to secure its primacy as the unbroken line of Crowley's organization. Those attempting to revive the O.T.O. reasoned that if the Order was to survive in a form recognizable to its creator, something had to be done to wrench it back onto the tracks and away from the disorganized mess that had developed under Germer's care. One means of doing this was to revert to the "rulebook" of the Order, *The Equinox Volume 3, Number 1* (also known as the *Blue Equinox*). Published by Aleister Crowley in 1919, the *Blue Equinox* sets forth the principles of the Order. The action of McMurtry and his supporters in reinstating these principles was reasonable, for Crowley would never have sanctioned the current situation. But many Crowley aficionados, dabblers and hangers-on, and even some solid initiates, had grown accustomed to this free-wheeling chaos and resented any attempt by a central authority to re-assert control. Or, to be more accurate, some of them resented any central authority that was not themselves. Like a boulder thrown into a stream, the attempt to impose order caused even more whorls of chaos in its wake, at least for the short term.

"I objected strenuously to the 'Blue Equinox' mentality of the McMurtry faction, finding in it an unhealthy whiff of fascism," Simon said in a 2002 interview for *Behutet* magazine. "I could not imagine how such a gaggle of warmed-over hippies would have embraced the noxious philosophy of the *Blue Equinox* regulations, so I guess I still harbor an unseemly 60's mind-set, unattractive of one in my advanced years I'm sure!" *(Ibid n#22)* While Simon's observation seems valid from the vantage point of the 1960s and 1970s, where everyone expected to be able to do their own thing without undue interference from others, it must be remembered that this "noxious philosophy" was also of Crowley's devising. Thus, it could be argued that the *Blue Equinox* regulations were completely in concord with the goals of a group that was attempting to ensure the O.T.O.'s survival. Even Marcello Motta could not credibly fault the regulations, having edited and re-issued them in Brazil in the 1970s. Motta's biggest objection appeared to be that he, and not McMurtry, should be the one to implement them as OHO O.T.O.

Despite charges of fascism, it should come as no surprise that the O.T.O. had a strong countercultural element that was in concert with the times. For the most part this element was quite useful from a Crowleyian perspective, allowing practitioners to break patterns of behavior that prevented them from advancing in their work. Hard drugs were one means that Crowley used to accomplish this goal. However, in Crowley's time the use of these substances was much less prevalent than it had become in the 1970s, and certainly not as widely accepted by society — or at least by such a major subcultural element thereof — as was the case during the Order's revival. Heroin, methamphetamine and mescaline (later LSD) had been filtering into the occult community since the 1950s, and some members of the Order not only didn't resist this trend, but often seemed inordinately drawn into it during this period. According to Alan

Cabal, "At that time there was a pretty clear distinction between the OTO crowd and the Golden Dawn bunch: the former being drug-crazed libertines indulging in all forms of depravity and debauchery, and the latter being your basic sexually repressed white-light blissninnies."[23]

While Cabal takes a certain artistic license in his description, the underlying premise is essentially sound. The result was conflict as certain individuals and groups were destabilized under the influence of drugs. Their level of drug use was often in marked contrast to the Wiccans, who generally (though by no means always) tended to be stoners, 'shroomers, and wine-bibbers, and who didn't seem to need drugs as an excuse for conflict. There was a noticeable change when William Breeze (*Hymenaeus Beta*) was elected to head the O.T.O. after Grady McMurtry passed away in 1985. "Maybe he was elected Outer Head of the Order because he's Grady's antithesis — respectable and successful in the mundane world, with no history of flakiness or drugs," Sally Eaton speculated. "Bonnie [Cabal] agreed, and once quipped, 'O.T.O. used to be a sex-and-drugs cult, but now it's a cult of typesetters.'"[24] One detects a certain wistfulness in this observation.

Due to conflicts in personality and approach, the state of affairs between Mobius Chapter in New York City and the Grand Lodge in Berkeley was strained at best, and became more so after the Chapter evolved to become Lashtal Lodge. Before the year was out, the Grand Lodge had begun planning for the establishment of yet another lodge in the New York metropolitan area. One of those who was reportedly disaffected by the state of affairs between New York and California was Jim Wasserman. Jim had remained active in the O.T.O. and continued to develop his relationship with its major players and his expertise in Crowley's works. He supervised the Weiser edition of *The Book of the Law* in 1976 and midwifed the publication of an improved second edition of the Thoth Tarot deck in 1977, for which he contributed the instructional booklet.[25] *(Ibid n#14)*

The year 1979 proved to be significant for the O.T.O. The Order was incorporated under the laws of the State of California on March 26, thus helping to lay the legal groundwork for its final win in federal court against Grady McMurtry's nemesis, Marcello Motta. On September 21, the O.T.O. Supreme Council granted Jim Wasserman a charter authorizing him to operate and administer a new encampment (Camp) of the O.T.O. He was championed in this effort by Grady McMurtry and Bill Heidrick. The primary reason for establishing Tahuti Camp was to provide an alternative to Lashtal Lodge so that people had a choice between the different personalities and management styles of the two groups. *(Ibid n#14)* A Natal Working, involving a magical "Oath of Encampment," that consecrated Tahuti Camp was performed on Sunday, October 21, 1979.

Tahuti Camp was placed under the supervision of Lashtal Lodge for a probationary period, giving Tahuti some time as a subordinate group in the O.T.O. hierarchy for it to develop until it could stand on its own.[26] *(Ibid n#16)* Lashtal Lodge must certainly have considered this to be a galling state of affairs, since the Grand Lodge had established the camp within Lashtal's recruitment area so soon after Lashtal's elevation to Lodge status. This awkward arrangement caused some friction between the two groups, especially because they both occasionally used the Earth Star Temple space in the rear of the Magickal Childe. Nevertheless, Tahuti became a Chapter on November 29, 1980 with the proviso that it would only become completely independent of the supervision of Lashtal Lodge when the Tahuti Master received his IXth degree. This emancipation occurred in 1981.[27]

The first Tahuti Lodge Master was Jim Wasserman, who had lobbied for and shepherded the fledgling group from its inception. Members of the early Lodge included Richard Gernon, Alan and Bonnie Cabal, Jim Garvey, Maxine Janoff, Sherry Lane and Andrea Lacedonia. *(Ibid n#10)* Others who drifted in and out of the Tahuti in those days included Margot Adler, who received her Minerval in 1982, and Abrahadabra co-owner Cindy Brodkin, who was nicknamed "Eris" by the O.T.O. members; a punning allusion to the fact that she was an heiress.[28] *(Ibid n#10)* Musicologist, artist and writer Harry Smith lived in Chelsea near the Childe, and he was active in the Tahuti Lodge and its events at the shop. The impact of Tahuti Lodge in the revitalization of the O.T.O. on the East Coast cannot be overestimated. Bill Heidrick states with some certainty that "without Tahuti, O.T.O.'s presence in New York City would have faded." *(Ibid n#14)*

Herman Slater and the Magickal Childe likewise had a positive impact in nurturing and promoting the O.T.O. during this critical period of its history. Before the O.T.O. began meeting in New York City, the Warlock Shop and, later, the Magickal Childe had hosted lectures on Aleister Crowley and ceremonial magick. Once the O.T.O. had awakened from its period of dormancy, Slater offered a safe, neutral meeting ground for the Order's groups. Lashtal Lodge, for example, was invited to perform a Thelemic ritual at the Magickal Childe's fifth annual Pagan Samhain Festival on October 26, 1980.[29] Tahuti members were deeply involved in the activities of the StarGroup One social circle that hung out at the Childe and the Bells of Hell. Bill Heidrick states that Slater's influence on the growth of the O.T.O. under McMurtry was "positive on the whole in New York City and only a little less so nationally. Herman offered a local place to hold meetings and interest new people. His sales of O.T.O. publications and of general ritual supplies [also] helped."[30] *(Ibid n#14)* Jim Wasserman notes that Herman and Grady were also quite friendly, and their friendship helped to cement a relationship early on between the Childe and the Grand Lodge.[31]

The Childe became the main meeting place for Tahuti Lodge functions beginning in early 1981. The Lodge Master and the owner of the

Magickal Childe had been friends and sometime business associates for six years at this point. Wasserman needed a stable and inexpensive meeting place that met his minimum facility needs with regard to hosting lectures, rituals, and other events. Herman didn't mind the group's activities, which he found interesting, and he appreciated the business that the group brought his way. Slater's philosophy of freedom of religion included all religions. Thus, one could find an O.T.O. Lodge, a Pagan Way Grove, any of several different Witchcraft covens, or even a Satanist group meeting in the Earth Star Temple, depending on the day one happened to walk into the Childe.

This relationship between the Magickal Childe and Tahuti Lodge quickly evolved over the next several months. By early summer, Wasserman wanted to up the stakes in the partnership by rennovating Earth Star Temple to better support Tahuti's activities. The room had changed little since the oils office and the meeting space had been set up in mid-1976. While the room was adequate for holding regular classes and events, Tahuti Lodge required a special Masonic-style countercharge floor of black and white tiles, as well as an altar, to enable the group to present the Gnostic Mass in the store on a regular basis. As this was a central requirement for a Lodge of the O.T.O., Wasserman's request was not an idle one. However, meeting this requirement would dramatically change the look of the Earth Star Temple space. *(Ibid n#10)*

Slater initially balked at allowing Tahuti Lodge to radically modify the space, which, after all, was used mainly by Witchcraft groups such as the Welsh Pagan Way. He didn't mind hosting occasional O.T.O. lectures and rituals at the Childe, but he was worried that the perception that he was favoring the O.T.O. to this extent might negatively impact his relations with the Wiccans, especially given that those two parts of the occult community sometimes didn't mix well. Herman discussed his concerns with the Abrahadabra catalogue co-owner, Malcolm Mills, who was himself an aficionado of Crowley's works. Mills told Slater to go ahead and do it: "Herman and I had a long discussion about it and [he] wondered if it was too much of a diversion from the Wiccan emphasis of the shop. I mostly agreed to let them in because I liked Al Cabal."[32,33]

Jim Wasserman, Kent Finne, and others painted the walls and laid the tessellated floor tiles during the summer of 1981. A Gnostic Mass altar with a three-step dais was also constructed. The O.T.O. paid for the renovation out of a combination of Lodge funds and donations to the Ecclesia Gnostica Catholica (E.G.C.), which was the organ within the O.T.O. responsible for performing the Gnostic Mass.[34] *(Ibid n#10)* The overall effect was stunning, and the Magickal Childe was approached by photographers and filmmakers for the opportunity to capture the Earth Star Temple on film. These included Allan Tannenbaum, the chief photographer of the *SoHo Weekly News*, who displays a 1981 photograph of Herman Slater and Maria Parra next to the Gnostic altar in his book *New York in the 70s* (2003), and Director Damon Santostefano, who filmed Slater in the back room of the Magickal Childe for a documentary, *Satanism and Witchcraft* (1987).

Things didn't always go smoothly with the Tahuti Lodge meeting under Slater's roof. In 1982, a violent disagreement between some former members of the Lodge and its leadership threatened to make things very difficult for Herman and his store, yet he stood his ground and continued to provide Tahuti with a safe place to meet. "That's one thing for which I'm forever grateful," Wasserman writes. "He did it at a time when we were in trouble. He could have alienated a lot of people, and he supported us."[35]

Slater participated in Gnostic Masses in the back of the store with Grady McMurtry, Jim and Wileda Wasserman, Richard Gernon, Jim Garvey and others, and eventually he asked to be initiated. With Jim Wasserman as a witness, Slater took the O.T.O. Minerval Degree at Tahuti Lodge from Grady McMurtry on September 18, 1983.[36] He never took another degree, and William Breeze, who would succeed McMurtry as the OHO O.T.O. in 1985, characterizes Slater's initiation "as a fraternal wanting-to-belong thing."[37] *(Ibid n#12)* Slater friend Sally Eaton concurs. Herman's "self-image as godfather of the New York Occult scene would certainly allow him to accept initiations as tributary honoraria. Any O.T.O. initiations he took were almost certainly of this nature," states Eaton. "[It was] just enough to smugly assure folks that he was indeed a member of O.T.O. Herman was a widely-read eclectic occultist, who 'collected' initiations long before it became fashionable. He would always have maintained an interest in Crowley as a popular, sexually radical author. But all that overblown hierarchic stuff just wasn't Herman's style — his first love was Wicca, which is simple, spontaneous, and not subject to corporate oversight. I can't imagine Herman wasting much time or energy on any organization he couldn't control or make money on." *(Ibid n#10)*

Despite his disdain of "overblown hierarchic stuff," Herman's interest in the Order was sufficient for him to request, and be granted, an O.T.O. camp charter. "The more he knew about it, the more he wanted to get involved and wanted his own Camp," said Wasserman who, as Tahuti Lodge Master, signed Slater's application. *(Ibid n#36)* Earth Star Camp was officially recognized by the O.T.O. Supreme Council on February 25, 1984. Earth Star never performed any initiations, nor did it perform the Gnostic Mass. Herman left the O.T.O. activities that occurred in the store up to Tahuti Lodge; did not seek Earth Star's elevation to Lodge status, nor did he assume active leadership of an encampment as might otherwise be expected. *(Ibid n#10)* "He was pretty much a one man camp," remembers Jim Wasserman. "He had a charter because he was so strategically located and had a store." *(Ibid n#36)*

The rationale for Herman's desire to have an O.T.O. encampment associated with the store was complex. Certainly part of it was a matter of pure business acumen. But he was also genuinely interested in being a community resource. As Bill Heidrick explains, "At the time, O.T.O. 'Camp' was a catch-all minimum level type of O.T.O. group. Most of them functioned as study groups, proto-bodies expected to advance as membership and services developed to higher level O.T.O. groups, contact points for the general public (that would include Earth Star) and even some experimental pre-internet e-bodies (back in the days of BBS's [electronic bulletin board systems]). Herman did have some kinds of O.T.O. events at the shop under 'Earth Star', but mainly he was doing that for co-publicity, both for O.T.O. and for his shop. In other words, it was primarily a hosting venue for other O.T.O. bodies and a place where people could go to get further contacts with other O.T.O. bodies or Grand Lodge. There were announcements of seminars at Earth Star in the O.T.O. Grand Lodge members' periodical." *(Ibid n#12)*

Wasserman concurs, noting that Tahuti Lodge tried to provide as much information to Herman as possible in order to help him communicate with his customers who had questions about the Order. *(Ibid n#36)* It was this special status as a disseminator of information that allowed Earth Star Camp to survive when, in 1985, the Order closed other such official bodies that did not have more than one member.[38] Still, Slater had an impish streak when it came to his relationship with the O.T.O. Breeze remembers Herman keeping a not-for-sale copy of Francis King's book *The Secret Rituals of the O.T.O.* (1973) "in the window of the shop [just] to wind me up." But the OHO met the characteristic tail-tweak with aplomb and refused to be baited. *(Ibid n#37)* Despite Slater's irreverence, his connections with the O.T.O. proved useful by allowing Magickal Childe Publishing to put out several choice Crowley titles, including the *Goetia of Solomon the King* (1989) and *Magick in Theory and Practice* (1990).

Vanity was likely another factor in Slater's request for a Camp charter, for his was the only occult supply store to be accorded such an honor. Finally, the wily businessman may have been planning for some future day when the Magickal Childe and Tahuti Lodge would part ways. This finally occurred in 1984, when a disagreement between Slater and Wasserman, aggravated by Slater's decision to convert the back room of the Childe into book storage, marked the end of the Lodge's association with the shop. Being a separate encampment allowed the Magickal Childe to keep a toe in, as it were. But whatever Slater's ultimate intentions, Earth Star Camp never became more than a public relations and marketing tool for Magickal Childe, and its charter went inactive shortly before the Camp Master's death in 1992.[39] Tahuti Lodge eventually moved into its own space, and continues to this day. It celebrated its silver anniversary in 2004, in small part a testament to Herman Slater's desire to promote religious freedom and diversity.

Chapter 29: Letting Go of the Life That Was Planned

The Dionysian Meets the Apollonian

Nineteen seventy-seven drifted into 1978 with little change in the settled domesticity of Eddie and Bennie's home life. Eddie continued to work at J. Aron, while Bennie maintained his position at Chase Manhattan. Bennie was content with things the way they were, but there is some indication that Eddie was beginning to feel tied down. "Eddie hated his job, but he loved the freedom it gave him," Bennie remembered. "He was outside walking all over during the day because he was a messenger, and it gave him time to go visit the library and bookstores to do the stuff he was into."[1] Eddie remained active teaching and helping out at the Magickal Childe, and they both continued to circle in Knossos Grove.

To build up some muscle mass, Buczynski, who had always been slender rather than muscular, joined the Sheridan Square Gym in 1977. He had been doggedly stopping off there after leaving J. Aron to work out several times a week. During one workout session in August 1978, he met a handsome Italian man named Gene Muto. After earning his MA in Theatre from the University of Connecticut, Gene had moved to New York and was an off-off-Broadway director who tended bar on the side. Eddie was attracted to the bearish and charming man on a very primal level, and the feeling was mutual. The men struck up a conversation that quickly developed into an affair.[2]

Eddie normally got off work at 4 PM, worked out, and then headed home by 6 PM. But Eddie began coming home later and later until, when Bennie questioned him, he finally admitted that he had met someone who was interested in playing with him, and Bennie was okay with that because he trusted Eddie. In the very beginning, the men were a committed couple and didn't play around. After a couple of years, they began to play both together and separately in what today would be described as an "open relationship."[3] But there were rules in this dance: both men would resist falling for other men, and they would always return home to one another. This equation became unbalanced as Eddie continued to spend more and more time away from home. Finally, in September 1978, Eddie came home from work and told Bennie that, even though he still loved Bennie, he was also in love with Gene. According to Bennie, Eddie told him, "I love you and will always love you and never leave you," but Geraci was taken completely unaware by Buczynski's pronouncement and was emotionally shattered by it.

Buczynski's behavior up to that point had been as a solicitous and caring lover, the kind of man who would show up at his lover's workplace every year with a birthday cake. *(Ibid n#1)* Yet there had been indications that Eddie could be somewhat disingenuous in discussing the details of his relationships with others. "When Eddie and I first met, he didn't tell me that Herman [used to be] his lover," Geraci said. "He would tell me when I asked that Herman was his business partner, or used to be his partner. And later on I was like, 'Bitch, that was your lover.' [And Eddie replied], 'Well, yeah, but I really didn't love him like I love you.' And I said, 'Well don't fucking tell me he wasn't your lover.'" *(Ibid n#1)*

Buczynski seems to have genuinely hoped that Geraci would accept the news of his love for Muto with some equanimity. This optimism would certainly be in line with the opinion of several friends who said that Eddie was by nature polyamorous. If so, he overestimated Geraci's flexibility on the subject. No matter how open-minded they may be, if you are going to marry a southern boy (or girl, for that matter), you will inevitably fetch up against a wall built by many generations of in-born tradition if you attempt to independently expand the parameters of the marriage bed. When Bennie went to retire for the evening, Eddie tried to accompany him. The New Orleans native said, "Where do you think you're going?" Eddie replied "I'm coming to bed," to which Bennie replied "Not to this bed, you're not." *(Ibid n#1)* From that point onward, the marriage was essentially over. Eddie began spending more time, and nights, with Gene. "We had an open relationship," Bennie said in a 2010 interview. "But we had ground rules. Coming home and telling me that he was in love with someone he was messing with on the side went outside them. ... He wanted to have his cake and eat it too."[4]

From September 1978 onwards, the relationship between the two men had deteriorated. Bennie still loved Eddie, but he was not going to stand for another man enagaging the affections of his mate. It is also clear that Eddie still had feelings for Bennie, but that he wanted more than Bennie was able to give him. Shortly after Eddie's revelation, Bennie realized that this wasn't just a phase or a fling. As Eddie had done so many times before in his spiritual life, the reset button had been punched and he had moved on. Bennie resigned himself to the fact that it was now time to move on with his own life as well, and concluded that the best way to do so would be to make a clean break with New York and its, now painful, reminders. Charlie had already moved back to New Orleans, and although Bennie still had friends and a career in New York, the Big Easy was calling him home. To this end, he began making plans to move back to New Orleans. But complications soon arose.

Eddie and Bennie shared a checking account and an apartment, but everything was in Geraci's name because Buczynski's credit was in a shambles as a result of his involvement with Herman Slater and the Warlock Shop. Bennie knew that moving out before Buczynski could get his feet under him would have left Eddie in a real bind, particularly with regard to the apartment and utilities. While another man might not have given a second thought to making an ex-lover sleep in the bed of his own making, Bennie just couldn't find it in his heart to do that to Eddie. "I was going to leave sooner," Bennie said, "but Eddie suggested that I stay at least until December when he got his year-end bonus so that he could settle up what he owed to me. I agreed and stayed until February [1979]." *(Ibid n#1, 4)* This delay also allowed Eddie to get the lease and utilities transferred into his own name.

In preparation for a trip he needed to take to Arizona, Gene Muto sublet his apartment at 106 West 13th Street and moved in with Buczynski and Geraci for a few weeks. *(Ibid n#2)* With other men, this arrangement could have caused a great deal of friction, but they all managed to get along even though it must surely have been galling from Bennie's perspective. After Gene left for Arizona, home life returned to some semblance of normalcy. Right before Christmas, Eddie took Bennie to see *The Treasures of Tutankhamun* exhibit that ran at the Metropolitan Museum of Art from December 18, 1987 through April 14, 1979. Geraci recalled that Buczynski, with his long-held interest in ancient Egypt, was very eager to see the show. Eddie bought Bennie a set of Egyptian-themed towels from the museum store after touring the exhibit.[5]

Eddie went out west in late December to visit Gene, and the two of them traveled to Las Vegas and the Grand Canyon. They returned to New York City in late January 1979 and Gene took back his apartment and picked up a new job at an airline reservation desk. That job lasted almost a year before the airline folded, after which he took a job with a popular bar in Chelsea called Chelsea Place. Having settled up financially with Eddie, Bennie left New York in February, but not before suffering one more humiliation when Eddie asked to buy back Bennie's wedding ring so that he could give it to Gene. Bennie just gave it to him and left. Eddie's family was sad over the breakup, according to Frank Buczynski, because they had all grown very fond of Bennie.[6] Shortly after Bennie left New York, Eddie moved out of the Middle Village apartment and into the small West 13th Street walkup where Gene lived, just across from the Bells of Hell. The old apartment was sublet, completely furnished, to Eddie's brother, Frank, and two of Frank's friends.

Gene's apartment was very small, in a way that only a New Yorker or a resident of Tokyo truly understands, with a living area containing a loft bed over a built-in closet. It also held a sofa (custom-built by Gene because no regular sofa would fit in there) and a small writing desk. There was also a tiny eat-in kitchen just big enough to fit four people at the table, and a small bathroom. Eddie had a party in the apartment one night when Gene was working at the bar in Chelsea, and he had somehow managed to fit thirty guests in there. People were so packed into the place, said Gene, that "if someone wanted to smoke pot, they'd have to go outside because there was no way for them [to raise their arms] to light it." *(Ibid n#2)*

Now that he had Eddie all to himself, Gene proceeded to dun him on all of the changes he expected Eddie to make in his life. It nearly drove Eddie to despair. Writing to Ria and Carol on March 31, he begged for the couple's help in calming his relationship with Muto. "Think of a way, something, anything I can do to stop this," Buczynski wrote. "Gene has changed my life — radically. And he expects a great deal of me, and adjustment and acclimation. The main problem being I can't handle all of it at one time, and it's causing friction between us which frightens me." Buczynski agonized over the fact that Muto was being hypercritical of everything, and that nothing Eddie did was good enough. He hinted in the letter that this included pressure on him to give up Witchcraft, but Buczynski reassured the women that, "I'm blessed greatly and I'm hanging on strong."[7]

But while Eddie stayed as true to the Craft as he could, he ended up leaving his part-time position at the Magickal Childe shortly after moving in with Gene. *(Ibid n#2)* And his contacts with friends in the Craft also began to suffer. His friends were sad at Buczynski's withdrawal. "We didn't see Eddie as often when he was with Gene," said Carol Bulzone.[8] Gene Muto admitted this to be the case. "We sort of disassociated ourselves from his circle of friends because he knew that I don't like Witchcraft," Muto stated in a 2004 interview. "I don't mean this to be insulting in any way, but I always thought that was so much horseshit. And he had a lot of energy and natural intelligence, and was very bright, and [I thought] that he should focus his creativity and intelligence on something more fruitful. He had a lot of energy and he needed something to do, so he made up stuff. That wasn't going to get him anywhere in a serious life and career. He'd still be working in a commodities place running messages, and doing [Witchcraft] on the side, as opposed to a serious course of study." *(Ibid n#2)*

The situation reportedly infuriated Herman, who believed that Gene was trying to pressure Eddie to return to Catholicism.[9] Gene denies this, describing himself as being "to the left of Marx" at this point in his life, and asserting that Eddie was on the political left too. Muto and his brothers had grown up ostensibly Catholic, but his mother had yanked them all out of Catholic school after she got into a fight with one of the priests, a situation remarkably similar to what Bennie had gone through in New Orleans as a youth. By the time Gene was 15 or 16, he considered himself an atheist, and viewed spiritual pursuits with something of a jaundiced eye. *(Ibid n#2)* But basic human nature may have been yet another reason for Muto's animosity to the Craft, apart from his pragmatic or politico-philosophical objections to its practice. One friend of Eddie's asserted that Gene "was not pleased that Eddie was into Witchcraft, and he wasn't happy about the 'sexual magic' that happened in and after circles."[10]

In Gene's defense, he honestly did mean well for Eddie, and Buczynski was motivated enough to take and pass the New York graduate equivalency diploma (GED) exam later that year, thereby earning his high school diploma 15 years after dropping out of school. *(Ibid n#2)* Eddie's younger brother, Tommy, also received his GED at the same time, according to Frank Buczynski. *(Ibid n#6)* But the fact remains that Eddie was not ready just yet to move on from Witchcraft and the Minoan Brotherhood to other things. What Gene viewed as, quite literally, bullheadedness on Buczynski's part led to some friction within their relationship, as demonstrated by Eddie's letter to Ria and Carol, but it was never enough to place it in jeopardy. It was certainly not enough to drive the Brotherhood onto a reef, as had happened towards the end of Eddie's time with Bennie.

Eddie and Bennie's deteriorating relationship had had a deleterious effect on Knossos Grove, which met very little between mid-1978 and early 1979.[11] The men's lack of interest wasn't surprising given the state of things but, as a result, the number of active members continued to shrink during those troubled times. Eddie did bring in one new member later in 1979, a darkly handsome Italian named Tony Fiara (Craft name *Hyacinthus*). Tony would later prove to be an important choice for Eddie in terms of both the history and continuity of the tradition. But by the end of the year, Fiara and Buczynski were all that remained of the active membership of the Minoan Brotherhood in New York City.

During this same period, beginning with a Labor Day gathering in Benson, Arizona, two hundred gay and bisexual men from around the country were organizing a vibrant spiritual movement that would eventually become known as the Radical Faeries.[12] The Radical Faeries were influenced in large part by the liberationist philosophy of event organizers like Harry Hay, John Burnside, Don Kilhefner and Mitch Walker; espousers of what the mainstream might label a Marxist mindset who were also not above playing dress-up or playing in the mud (and sometimes both simultaneously). Gay activist and author Arthur Evans, who had formed a Neo-Pagan "Faery Circle" in the fall of 1975 after moving to the San Francisco Bay area, also affected this movement through the publication of his manuscript for *Witchcraft and the Gay Counterculture*.

The rise of the Radical Faeries offered a new type of spiritual movement to gay men, one whose members might (or might not) occasionally make use of the tools of Witchcraft, but who otherwise cared little for its trappings (e.g., the lineage, tradition, or control issues). The new-born Faeries, upon leaving Benson, Arizona in 1979, travelled back to their homes across the nation and began to form new groups and immediately eclipsed the Minoan Brotherhood, which remained confined to New York City, in both size and influence. It is unknown whether Eddie was aware of this development, but if he had been he would have applauded the effort, for the Faeries provided yet another safe harbor in which gay men could openly worship and celebrate. Regardless, Buczynski stuck with his beloved Minoans and soldiered on through his latest difficulties.

The Second Coming of Knossos Grove

Eddie never used the West 13th Street apartment for group rituals. One reason was that the new place was considerably smaller than the Middle Village apartment and simply wasn't large enough to accommodate rituals. Gene's dismissive opinion of Witchcraft was also a likely factor in Buczynski's decision to begin using the Earth Star Temple in the rear of the Magickal Childe to convene his Minoan Brotherhood Circles in 1979. The Childe was convenient from his perspective, being only six blocks north of the new apartment, and Herman could never say no to Eddie. But however convenient the Earth Star Temple was, it would never be an ideal location because it was a semi-public space that could be used only during business hours. It also had no real facilities for ritual bathing. This problem was solved later that year when Tony Fiara moved into the East Village, squatting in an abandoned apartment building on East 13th Street between Avenues A and B.[13] This proved to be a much better location, even though it was farther away than the Childe, and Fiara ended up hosting Minoan Brotherhood rituals there until 1982.

Toward the end of 1979, Eddie met a newcomer to the Magickal Childe who would eventually become interested in, and initiated into, the Minoan Brotherhood. Aubrey Wyatt had come to Witchcraft via a circuitous route, as did many gay men during that period. "I've had dreams, visions, and mystical experiences since childhood. So did my mother's mother. In fact, she was declared insane and institutionalized, so I learned early to keep my 'experiences' secret," Wyatt admitted. "It wasn't until my Junior year at College that I finally broke down and told my lover/professor about them. We were in rehearsals for *A Midsummer Night's Dream*. He was very understanding and introduced me to several alternative spiritual paths. I read the complete works of Jung and *The Birth of Tragedy* by Nietzsche. He also introduced me to Mary Renault and I read all her books, including *The King Must Die* and *The Bull from the Sea*, two historical novels (though from a Greek perspective) about Minoan/Mycenaean culture and myth. After graduation and summer theatre, I moved to New York City in August, 1979. There I met another man who became my lover/mentor. He followed the 'Old Religion' combined with studies of the Hermetic [Kabbalah]. I also became fascinated with discovering my roots, personal family, and collective culture. [My lover] directed me to The Magickal Childe, where I first met Eddie."[14]

Wyatt's naturally curious intellect, combined with his knowledge of Greek mythology, sparked Buczynski's interest in the young actor. With Eddie's help and direction, Aubrey learned that his grandparents had provided him with a solid mix of Scottish, Irish and Welsh ancestry. Eddie also informed Aubrey that all of the younger man's family surnames were connected in one way or another to the Old Religion, including the Wyatt surname, which Margaret Murray specifically mentioned in one of her books. Buczynski suggested that Wyatt read Murray's *God of the Witches* and *The Witch Cult of Western Europe*, in addition to a book on Druids that Aubrey purchased from the Childe and one on the Kabbalah he got from Weiser's. After several long visits to the Magickal Childe, Eddie began asking Aubrey to meet with him outside the shop.

"We talked a lot about classical myth," Wyatt recalled in 2003. "I was in the theatre and very into the mythology of Dionysus. [Although] Dionysus's origins are hard to track, there was evidence that he may have come from Thrace. Eddie thought otherwise [and], as usual his intuition and scholarship were right on the money, as most scholars now believe that he originated in Crete. I had recently read Nietzsche's *The Birth of Tragedy* that compares/contrasts the influences of Dionysus and Apollo in theatre. I knew they were worshiped together at Delphi and found this fact most intriguing. Most of the 'Gay relationships' in Classical myth are between the Divine and mortals. The possibility of two Gods being lovers was exciting." *(Ibid n#14)*

Buczynski was apparently impressed enough with Wyatt's progress by late November to inform him of the existence of his gay male Witchcraft tradition. Eddie had hoped that Aubrey would be interested in joining, and he was not disappointed in Wyatt's reaction. "At that time there were only two members (Eddie and Tony) and he really wanted to find a third," writes Wyatt. "I remember he enticed me by hinting that the rituals would be 'dramatic' and he'd like for me to perform the role of 'the God' and that it would basically be as Dionysus. I agreed. He called Tony, who met us, and we talked more." Aubrey was initiated on Friday, January 4, 1980 after the first full moon of the month, taking the Craft name *Ariel*. He was elevated quickly in two consecutive full-moon rituals performed in Tony Fiara's apartment. The Second Degree rite was held on the Friday, February 1, 1980 right after January's blue moon, and the Third Degree ritual took place on Saturday, 1 March 1980, the first full moon of March. Eddie and Tony made much ado about the fact that Aubrey's Third Degree ritual was held in a blue moon month. *(Ibid n#14)*

Wyatt recalled the night of his initiation, including Buczynski's decision to start anew by reforming Knossos Grove:[15]

> *The first coven of Minoan Brothers was named, dedicated, and we performed our first ritual on Friday, January 4th, 1980. After my initiation, there were now three of us. So, after my*

initiation, Eddie led a ritual where the coven was named Knossos Grove, and part of the ritual included the "creation of a Magickal Childe" from the essence of two Priests under the watchful eye of the third, who was the God/dess. Eddie performed the ritual, Tony and I provided the seed that was to nurture and grow into a "Brotherhood of Gay Minoan Brothers."

Eddie, for some reason, did not deem it necessary to inform Aubrey that the Minoan Brotherhood had already been in existence for several years at this point. Wyatt was surprised to learn, many years later, that Eddie had actually been working with Knossos Grove since the beginning of 1977. "If there were others initiated before Tony and me, I neither know them, nor ever heard of them," he asserted.[16] The explanation may be found in the simple fact that Eddie, as much as he loved history, was not one to linger in the past, or at least not his own. Those who had left for other things simply weren't the focus of his attention; those who were present, were. This was a pattern for Buczynski since the "big breakup" of the Welsh tradition in 1973. The rebirthing ritual of Knossos Grove was designed to make it stick around for the long haul this time.

Minoan ritual during this period focused on the worship of Apollo and Dionysus as sacred lovers. "Eddie and I talked a great deal about the fact they shared the Temple at Delphi — and the relationship between the Sun-God and the Earth/Underworld God," writes Wyatt. "I know Tony was really into Apollo, and that Hyacinthus was one of Apollo's mortal lovers. The balance between our passions for Apollo and Dionysus was one of the reasons Eddie really wanted me to join the Grove." *(Ibid n#10, 16)* Aubrey served as the masculine aspect of the Divine during his first year in the Brotherhood, and as the feminine aspect during the second. *(Ibid n#10)* Rituals often involved a lot of jokes and playing around. At first, Wyatt found this to be irreverent, and told the others so. But Eddie explained that Neo-Pagan ritual wasn't like church, and that it was okay to have some fun.[17]

Knossos Grove began to slowly grow once more during 1980. Wyatt noted that there was a never-ending cycle of people coming in, leaving, and returning once more. *(Ibid n#10)* It was during this period, shortly after Aubrey's initiation, that Tony Fiara brought in his lover, Larry Schneider. Eddie initiated Jeffrey Whitfield (Craft name *Hermes*) sometime that summer. "Jeffrey was a Tibetan monk," remembers Artie Jamison. "He was the one who taught us the chants to Lakshmi and a few of the other Deities. He was a wonderful spirit; absolutely marvelous spirit. He accepted everyone else. He had a great wisdom from Tibet, [and] I think that made him who he was to tell you the truth. ... Calm, soothing, and his magicks were unbelievable. Man, this kid could make a formula out of nuthin. And it worked."[18] Whitfield had previously received formal training in Tibetan Buddhism in California, and had met Eddie when

Jeffrey was attending the Tibetan temple located above the Magickal Childe. Whitfield moved in with Fiara and Schneider for a short while, which made things somewhat easier when it came to holding Sabbats.[19] Buczynski also brought in a Spanish fellow whose name is lost to time, but who is remembered for joining primarily because he wanted to learn magick in order to persuade his lover return to him.[20]

Buczynski had been giving some thought to revisiting the Cult of Rhea/Cult of the Double Axe mixed-sex branch of the Minoan tradition. He and the other men had held several joint sabbats with Ria and Carol at their place in Forest Hills during this time. But, aware that the time involved in taking on another group such as the Cult of Rhea would likely cause problems at home, Eddie ultimately abandoned the idea of a distinct Cult of Rhea, and the new rituals were never written. Any remaining thought of bringing forth a third, mixed-sex branch of the Minoan tradition permanently faded from Eddie's attention after this time.

Formulae for Success

The Magickal Childe continued to do well in Chelsea, despite a serious setback when the Abrahadabra mail order partnership collapsed in 1980 over differences between the partners, and between the partnership and Slater himself. Malcolm Mills characterized Slater as a man who could be very witty and charming at times but "was also unethical, unscrupulous and vicious."[21] According to Mills, "We handed the mail order business back to Herman."[22] Slater somehow managed to jump-start the catalogue once again, and the Magickal Childe continued to publish it on a regular basis until 1993.[23] He also decided that the demand for supplies was high enough in the hinterlands to justify branching out into more festivals and book shows, including to one of the few larger Neo-Pagan gatherings that was not held in a hotel.

Magickal Childe had a vendor's booth at the fourth annual Pan Pagan Festival, which was held August 21-24, 1980.[24] Originally scheduled to be held in Baraboo, Wisconsin, the festival was moved at the last minute to Lake Holiday, Indiana to accommodate the unexpectedly large number of registrants.[25] This Pan Pagan Festival was notable for the blowup surrounding Z. Budapest's women's-only ritual and for the report that a majority of the festival community held anti-gay opinions following a survey of attitudes that had been conducted at Pan Pagan 1979.[26] Even aside from these issues, it was a wonder that the metaphorical tent didn't come crashing down due merely to the simultaneous presence of Herman Slater and Z. Budapest at the event.

In addition to reaching out into the Neo-Pagan community through appearances at gatherings, Slater continued to experiment with publishing books and pamphlets. His experiences under the Earth Religions Supplies, Inc. imprint had whetted his appetite. Slater formed Magickal Childe

Publishing with the express purpose of bringing to market more high-quality books that were written by people in the community itself. In time, he would bring a number of books to print in the United States from well-known authors, including titles by Gerald Gardner, Aleister Crowley, and Janet and Stewart Farrar. For his pilot project, Herman decided to produce something in house, and he began pulling together material for it throughout 1980. By the beginning of 1981, Herman had accumulated enough recipes to begin laying out what came to be the first volume of *The Magickal Formulary.*[27]

One reason often given for his deciding to publish the Formulary is that the shop was in dire financial straits and that Herman needed to raise some quick cash to deal with taxes and other bills, and he did have tax troubles in 1981. But the Childe, like most occult shops, was always walking a financial tightrope, and as any publisher will tell you (and Herman knew this from personal experience) printing a book is the wrong way to go about raising funds if time is of the essence. Selling the publishing rights to another publisher might have made some quick cash, but Slater opted instead to keep the copyright for the book with his Magickal Childe Publishing imprint. In all likelihood, Herman was merely sticking to form by bringing a product to market that he thought customers would buy. This isn't to say that he wasn't out to make a buck on the deal. The success of the Simon *Necronomicon* taught him, if nothing else, that those who printed popular high quality books could make a tidy profit if they were willing to be patient. It was a lesson that would pay off handsomely in the long run.

The Formulary was heavily marketed as containing the secret formulae of the Magickal Childe, the inner workings and treasures with which a desperate Slater was loath to part. While it is true that much of the book was based on recipes in use at the Magickal Childe, some of it came from other published formularies. There were some curious discrepancies in the published material. One of the criticisms most often leveled at *The Magickal Formulary* by knowledgeable practitioners is that, while a large number of the formulae appear to be based on those traditionally used in Santeria, Brujeria and New Orleans Vodou, many are missing key ingredients. Others point out that some ingredients are hopelessly muddled together with no apparent rhyme or reason. Much of this confusion can be attributed to the source of many of those formulae: Clinton Stevens.

Clinton kept the large Formulary card file at his "occult pharmacy" in the shop to guide him in his crafting. However, most of that information was in the form of shortcuts; mnemonic devices that were designed to jog their owner's memory during the preparations. In many cases, the spirits to be invoked during preparation, the proportions of the ingredients, and even key ingredients themselves were missing from these file cards. As Eaton explains it, "More than one person (including Clinton himself) told me that many recipes in the Formulary were incomplete. There were ingredients and steps in the preparation which were deliberately withheld to keep Herman from passing them along to the next oil office employee."[28] That Herman would simply sell the contents of the card file had apparently never occurred to Clinton.

Some of the formulae appearing in the book were gibberish from their inception. Joe Cupolo recalls a number of occasions in 1976 and 1977 where Herman would pester Clinton for the formulae of various mixtures that could be applied to specific uses. Clinton would rattle off lists of ingredients, which Slater would dutifully jot down. After one of these sessions, when Cupolo asked if he could have those formulae too, the herbalist rolled his eyes and smiled, saying, "Those spells aren't for shit. I just did that for Herman, because he wouldn't leave me alone."[29] This may help to explain why some of the mixtures have left experienced practitioners scratching their heads in puzzlement. Gwilym Dafydd notes:[30]

> *Clinton's Anna Riva material got mixed indiscriminately with European Traditional Witchcraft recipes, just because they were jumbled in that one crumbly index-card Rolodex everybody referred to. Thus you have Galangal, Squill, Saturn Root, etc., in shared cocktail mixes with lemony Santero floor washes and bayberry-based controlling/ commanding/ compelling oils. Toss in some Big Easy shoelaces, Palm Sunday palm leaves, and 100% herbal graveyard dirt, and you've thoroughly confused Old World and New World traditions until no one can tell which is which. This is why you get Smudged nowadays for an allegedly Wiccan ritual, and also why the art of incense preparation has disappeared as thoroughly as Khat shipments from Yemen.*

In Slater's acknowledgements in the *Formulary*, Clinton Stevens is thanked first among others, which included Paul Huson, Anna Riva and Marie Laveau.[31] Clinton had, after all, been the heart and soul of the shop's oil office since 1973. "Herman exploited and capitalized on [Clinton's] knowledge — almost all of the stuff in the Formulary was Clinton's to begin with and he was furious that Herman published it," Sally Eaton recalls. "But Clinton was too generous with his expertise. Herman may have rationalized that the card file was (sort of) public domain after it had been in the store for so long."[32] Stevens had developed most of the formulae well before he worked for Slater, and he clearly considered them to be his personal property.[33,34] Therefore, on finding out in 1981 that Slater had been using the card file without his permission, Stevens saw no reason to correct any of Herman's errors. Clinton continued to remain close with Carol and Ria, but he would never forgive Herman Slater. *(Ibid n#32)*

As Slater edged closer to publishing *The Magickal Formulary*, he began casting about for someone to head up the project. Enter Kathryn Frank, who had been hanging out at the Magickal Childe since 1977. When she wasn't promoting punk rock bands through CBGB and Trouser Press, Frank worked as a photo-typesetter.[35] Slater recognized that her skills would be invaluable to the Formulary project. Kathryn's employer allowed her to use the company's machine to set up the book, as long as Slater paid for the paper (which was quite expensive).

"Herman enlisted me and one of the store's managers, Timmy Hough [also known as Tim Wallace or Hough-Wallace], to edit and get the book printed," Frank recalls. Tim was also a makeup/hair guy who worked a lot in New York City and Europe. He did Annie Lennox's makeup for her first few Eurythmics videos and toured with Boy George.[36] "[Herman] handed us four sets (Rolodex cards, notebooks and such) of recipes for incenses, oils and other things (how he got them, I don't know). It took a while, but we managed to put it all together alphabetically and create the book. ... Tim and I were listed as the Copy Editors, [and] I also got credit for the typesetting. Bonnie Claremont did the paste-up work."[37] *The Magickal Formulary* was issued in March 1981, thereby becoming the first imprint of Magickal Childe Publishing. In July 1987, Herman expanded and re-issued the book as *The Magickal Formulary Books I and II*. Changes included additional recipes, details on how to run spells and set up an altar, and other little extras.[38]

Hough and Frank exerted one other small influence on the Formulary that has gone uncredited. A lady named Valerie who worked at the Childe kept having affairs with the gay men who also worked there in an effort to change their sexual orientation. In her honor Hough, himself a gay man, created a formula for "Aunt Valerie's Healing Oil" that contained valerian, lavender, and asafoetida (which, because of its noxious smell, is used to control and banish demons in ceremonial magick). Frank writes, "The instructions read: *This old Polish formula* (Valerie being Polish) *is a special 'homophobic' blend which aids in the instant cure of homosexuality. Use copiously*. At my insistence, we told Herman before the book went to be published. He cracked up, Valerie's attempts being well known and commented upon, and decided to include it." *(Ibid n#37)* It is unclear to this day whether Timmy intended the asafoetida in the formula to banish the homosexuality (represented by the lavender) or Valerie (represented by the valerian root) from the gay men's lives. Regardless of its mistakes, omissions, inside jokes, and outright plagiarism, *The Magickal Formulary* was destined to become legend.

By this point "legendary," or at any rate "celebrated," aptly describes the annual Samhain Festival hosted by the Magickal Childe. The fifth annual festival, organized by the Magickal Childe in conjunction with the Earth Star Temple, was held on the afternoon of Sunday, October 26, 1980.[39] The event, which was held at the Disco Inferno, surpassed even

1979's massive gathering, which was itself reportedly attended by 700 people. The 1980 festival was notable for the diverse cast of characters involved in its production. Jim Alan and Selena Fox of Circle Sanctuary in Wisconsin performed selections of Neo-Pagan music with De-Anna Alba. Also performing were Margot Adler and Tziporah, as well as the Major Thinkers, which was the New Wave band that Larry Kirwan and Pierce Turner had formed out of their long-running band, Turner and Kirwan of Wexford, that often played the Bells of Hell. The master of ceremonies for the event was Simon, and the Convocation was conducted by Leo Martello. Lashtal Lodge O.T.O. conducted a Thelemic ritual, and Slater's Welsh Earth Star Temple performed the sabbatic rite. It is not an overstatement to say that the Childe's Samhain festivals had become the social event of the year for the Neo-Pagan community in New York City.

Despite the lively and growing occult scene in New York, Eddie had continued his gradual withdrawal from it in 1980, mainly because of continued pressure from Gene who, not unreasonably, wanted to spend more time with his lover. But while Eddie may have begun disengaging from the greater community, his withdrawal did not extend to the Minoan Brotherhood; at least for the moment. Knossos Grove had grown large enough that there were more than enough members to share all the roles and duties. Even so, everyone clearly understood that Knossos "really was Eddie's baby."[40]

But Gene apparently had other ideas. Given that it was Eddie's passion for the archaeology and art of ancient Greece that was feeding his current interest in Witchcraft and involvement in the Minoan Brotherhood, Muto decided to dig a new channel for that energy in the hope that it would lead to "something more fruitful." In May 1980, he took Eddie on a whirlwind trip to Greece, including the sites of Crete, thereby clothing the dry bones of Buczynski's history and archaeology books with living flesh. "It was a horrible trip for both of us in the sense that it was our first trip to Europe. We got a tour [package]. ... It was really pretty comprehensive, and it really wasn't that bad. The food was bad but the hotels were okay. Looking in retrospect, we didn't know what to expect. We did the Greek thing. We took bus trips, and I know we went to Delphi and some other places. But part of this trip was going to Crete, and he of course was in his glory. We went to Knossos. And I remember that one night, I think it was at Delphi but it might have been Crete, where he sat up all night on the balcony of the hotel room. I said 'I'm going to bed.' (laughing) Of course, he got cold." *(Ibid n#2)* Together, the two men learned how to swim through the culture of another country. It was as if a star had burst to life behind Buczynski's eyes, and he would never again look at the world the same way.

Buczynski returned with a purpose in life. Before Greece, his aspirations had been limited to essentially the same goal he had had in high school — to be a Priest. These were the dreams of a boy from a

Catholic family in Queens who had few real opportunities to advance in life. Even so, Eddie had dreamed of going to college, even as a child. "He always wanted to go to college," said Terry Gianniotis. "He was always thinking or trying to figure out how to get there."[41] After the trip to Greece, some inner limitation seems to have been broken, and the world that opened up before him was one where academic accomplishments were his for the taking, if he only the Will to reach for them.

"When Eddie went to Crete, it completely changed his life, and the direction of the Grove," writes Aubrey Wyatt. "Indeed, after Crete Eddie was inspired and decided to go back to school." *(Ibid n#16)* Eddie would later write that "Travelling around the country had been one of the deciding factors in my choosing Aegean archaeology as a major field of study in school. Although short, it was a pleasant and stimulating trip."[42] Despite these assertions, it is evident that Buczynski had been moving toward academia for some time. His intense study of Egyptian and Aegean archaeological textbooks over the past six years, the pressures placed on him by his lover, and even his enthralled examination of the King Tut artifacts at the Met (the nationwide tour of which had inspired a number of young people to take up the trowel and field book as a career) likely all played a role in convincing him to consider a formal career in archaeology.

Eddie filled out an application for the fall quarter at Hunter College, part of the City University of New York (CUNY). Hunter was close to home, being located on the Upper East Side. It had been making a name for itself in the world of classics for the past decade, thanks in no small part to the efforts of the socially adept head of its Department of Classical and Oriental Studies. Hunter had recently succeeded in adding a degree in archaeology to its offerings, which would have drawn Buczynski's eye to its curriculum. Eddie's choice of major was met with some consternation. "Much to my chagrin, he ended up doing archaeology," said Muto, laughing. "I said, 'Great. What the fuck are you going to do with that?'" *(Ibid n#2)*

Nevertheless, to his delight and amazement, the former high school dropout was accepted for the fall quarter. While Buczynski and his family were excited, Muto remarked it really wasn't all that surprising that he had gotten in. "I think at the time they had an open door policy, [that is] the CUNY system," said Gene. "Which means that if you had a high school degree, you could go." *(Ibid n#2)* This in no way disparages the school, which after all offered many students such as Eddie the opportunity for a higher education than they might not have had otherwise. Buczynski would remain at Hunter for next five years pursuing coursework in classics and ancient history.

Eddie realized that beginning school in the fall would require a serious rearrangement of his schedule, one that would force him to choose among his various interests and commitments, curtailing or eliminating anything that didn't support his academic pursuit. One of the things that had to go was his leadership of the Minoan Brotherhood. This wasn't a decision he took lightly, and unlike other situations in which he chose to abruptly change his course, in this he refused to just cut and run. The reason for this change in Buczynski's *modus operandi* is complex, but distilled down to its essence, his ties to the Minoan Brotherhood were intimately bound up in his emotional and intellectual commitment to a career in archaeology. He could not simply abandon the Brotherhood to the winds of fate without undermining in his own mind the very basis for his choice to go on to college. Mentally, however, Eddie had already retired from the public face of the Craft.[48] With Athena playing the part of both Siren and Muse, Buczynski headed off to school.

33. Eddie Buczynski, off the coast of Capri, Italy. 1980.

34. (left) Eddie Buczynski and Gene Muto, Rego Park, Queens. ca. late 1978.

35. (above) Tony Fiara in his apartment, Lower East Side, Manhattan. ca. 1981.

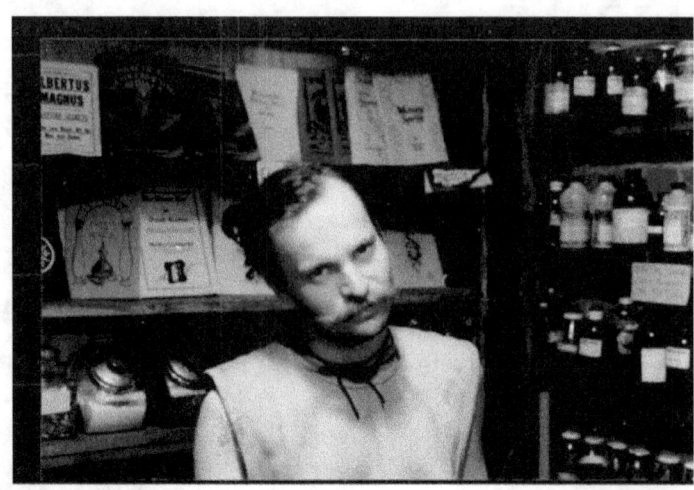

36. Jeffrey Whitfield in the Oils Office, Enchantments, East Village, Manhattan. ca. 1983.

37. Enchantments, 341 East 9th Street, Manhattan, October 2004.

38. Maria Parra and Herman Slater, Earth Star Temple, Magickal Childe. 1981.

39. ASCSA Summer Session. Eddie Buczynski (right) and classmates at Mrs. Panayiota's restaurant, Arachova, Greece. July 1982.

40. Ria Farnham (left) and Carol Bulzone, first Enchantments Witches Ball. October 1982.

41. Eddie Buczynski (right), Hunter College CUNY graduation, Madison Square Garden. May 1985.

42. Eddie Buczynski (left), graduation from Bryn Mawr College, May 1988.

43. Statue of Pallas Athena with votive offerings, Thomas Great Hall, Bryn Mawr College. November 2004.

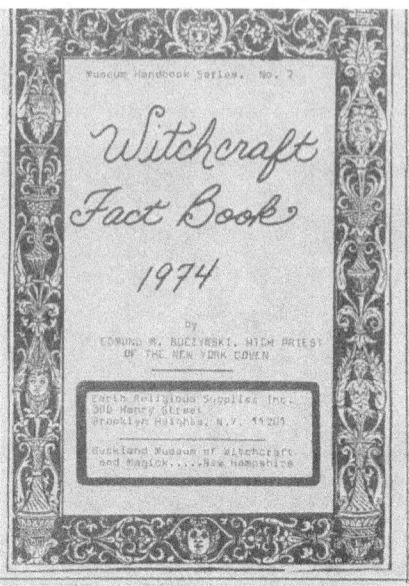 

44. The 1974 First edition of Eddie Buczynski's *Witchcraft Fact Book* and the 1984 edition.

45. Eddie Buczynski obituary written by Herman Slater. March 1989

46. Edmund Buczynski Memorial Bookplate, Bryn Mawr College, 1989.

Regius Senex

Chapter 30: The Hunter College Years

Learning from History

In September 1980, Eddie began classes at Hunter College in the Department of Classical and Oriental Studies or, as Department Head Clairève Grandjouan jokingly referred to it, "The Department of Funny Alphabets." Grandjouan was a world renowned scholar in the field of archaeology. After graduating from Bryn Mawr College with a BA in Archaeology in 1950, she became a member of the American School of Classical Studies at Athens (ASCSA). Earning her PhD from Bryn Mawr in 1955, she eventually moved on to the Archaeological Institute of America (AIA), where she served in the post of General Secretary from 1962-1968. The AIA was headquartered at New York University, so she took up residence in Greenwich Village, renting an apartment on Waverly Place that she would occupy from 1962 until her death.

Having been home-schooled by brilliant and highly-cultured parents who were also educational theorists, Grandjouan had vowed never to take up teaching as a career. Yet when offered a position in the Classics Department of Hunter College in 1968, she resigned her post at the AIA and never looked back. In 1969, Grandjouan became the Chair of the Department and embarked on a campaign of reorganization and expansion that turned it into a vital and respected institution. At the same time, she was a well-loved lecturer of history and archaeology in New York City, known for popularizing her subject matter and engaging audiences across all strata of the community with her own unique blend of humor and empathy. As Marjorie Venit, author of a biographical paper on Clairève, puts it, "playfulness to Grandjouan was a concrete and palpable component of daily life."[1] Professor Tamara Green, who had served under Grandjouan, called her one of the most creative scholars she had ever known.[2]

As a long-time Greenwich Village resident who lived just a short walk from the Stonewall Inn, Grandjouan had seen the gay rights revolution and the rise of that community in her neighborhood. As a world traveler and child of "gay Paree," she was very open-minded to the presence of an openly gay man in her department. It helped that Eddie was an intelligent student who was both personable and intimately engaged in the subject matter, and yet as one who was handicapped by starting college so late in life, he would have naturally attracted Clairève's interest. She became Buczynski's self-appointed mentor at the school. Buczynski was immediately drawn to the matronly and good-hearted professor, who he came to refer to as his "personal Athena" (the Greek Goddess of wisdom). "He talked about her a lot," Gene Muto remembers. "She was a real mentor. He really admired her."[3]

Muto helped his lover with school expenses. Phyllis Saretta, who lived down the street from the men and who would attend classes with and befriend Eddie beginning in 1982, wrote that, "Gene was completely supportive of him, and his academic future. He made sure Eddie had all the tools he needed in order to pursue his academic career."[4] Buczynski's income from his job at J. Aron was also used to help underwrite his college expenses.

Buczynski made the most of the opportunity, throwing himself into his studies. Tamara Green believed that Eddie's late blooming actually conferred more benefit than handicap. "Like most older students," she said, "he was more settled and knew what he wanted out of life." *(Ibid n#2)* It didn't take long at all for Buczynski to prove himself on that score. He ended up in the Thomas Hunter Honors Program, which required him to maintain a grade point average of at least 3.65. This was a remarkable achievement for someone who at one time didn't think that he'd even go to college. "[Eddie] told me that he didn't grow up thinking that he was academically capable, or gifted, or anything and that he kind of felt like he had squandered some of his youth," remembered James Wright, a professor of Minoan and Mycenaean archaeology. "He found his way into Hunter, and once he met Clairève Grandjouan it was all over. I think she saw that he was a smart, enthusiastic person. Hunter's a great place like that. There are all these incredibly bright people in New York who are growing up in that great city in a real rough and tumble sort of way. But the City University of New York system is right there for them. And the faculty is great at taking these raw diamonds and starting to burnish them and cut them ... So Hunter's a great sort of story, and Eddie is a part of that tradition."[5]

Not everything came easy for Buczynski. He struggled to make up for a lack of foreign language skills, which were an absolute necessity for one who, like Eddie, had his eye on a career in archaeology. He did well in French during his time at Hunter because he had taken it in high school and was able to pick it up again. But, according to Gene, he just got through German by the skin of his teeth because he'd had to start from scratch.[6] Nevertheless, Tamara Green said that Eddie was an enormously enthusiastic student who was passionate about archaeology, especially about the Minoans. "Every paper he ever wrote was about the Minoans," she recalls. But she never quite understood where he got his passion for ancient Crete. *(Ibid n#2)* Her puzzlement is in itself baffling, for Eddie later credited Tamara with providing him the inspiration to academically pursue a study of the Minoan religion that had so captured his imagination a few years before.[7]

Crete weighed heavily on Eddie's mind from the fall of 1980 through the spring of 1981 as he tried to figure out to whom to give over the leadership of his beloved Minoan Brotherhood. Either no one within Knossos Grove wanted the responsibility or none were ready for it in

Eddie's opinion, for he ended up approaching a Gardnerian Third Degree named Michael Thorn (Craft name *Eliphas*). Thorn had formed an experimental coven, Kathexis Anthropos, on Long Island in 1981. It was quite controversial within Gardnerian circles first and foremost because the coven was composed entirely of gay men. The only exception to this was when they made use of a visiting high priestess for the performance of initiations and elevations so that the members would not run afoul of Gardnerian lineage rules.[8]

Despite this concession, many Gardnerians still greeted the notion of a gay men's coven with disdain and skepticism. "I don't think 'renting a priestess' from another coven just for initiations and elevations, in the manner of the New York gay men's coven, would achieve very much apart from ensuring their position in the Gardnerian lineage," opined Frederic Lamond. "Balancing energies cannot be achieved in a simple initiation ceremony: it requires continuous example and training in subsequent coven meetings, which a 'rented priestess' would be unable to do in a gay men's coven."[9]

Kathexis Anthropos wasn't the only magickal group founded around this time to serve the gay community. Gay poet Ian Young helped to organize The Hermetic Order of the Silver Sword in Toronto on April 2, 1982. Based on the practices of the Hermetic Order of the Golden Dawn, the Order provided a safe space for homosexuals to practice ceremonial magick.[10] But magickal groups which catered to the needs of gays and lesbians were still quite rare, and the prevailing attitude in the occult community toward them continued to be one of caution, if not outright dismissal.

But it was just this sort of attitude, voiced by people who were not themselves gay and yet who styled themselves experts on what homosexuals were and were not capable of doing, that Thorn sought to disprove with Kathexis Anthropos. The coven operated under two basic principles. "These were kind of revolutionary back then, but they aren't now," Thorn recalled. "One was that 'gay is okay,' and that was a big leap for some people. And that also the Goddess and the God were in everyone, and so everyone had both energies and polarities. It's just a matter of manifesting them. So this was pretty shocking and pretty upsetting to lots of people, and they were horrified."[11]

It was this willingness to experiment that attracted Thorn to Buczynski's attention. "Eddie and I were in touch because he wanted to pass on the Minoan tradition," Thorn recalled in a 2006 interview. "And he thought that since I was doing this gay thing, that I might want to take it over. I thought about it for a while, and then I said 'Well, I really want to do the Gardnerian thing. I don't really want to do the Minoan thing. I want to still be a Gardnerian and still do the Gardnerian thing [Kathexis Anthropos] and see where it goes.'" *(Ibid n#11)* One thing that put him off was the sexual test that Buczynski wanted to impose to see if Thorn was up to the challenge and sufficiently laid back to work comfortably within the sexually-charged space of Minoan ritual. Between what he called the "casting couch" and the rumors of the after-Sabbat "magickal orgies" that he said were going on at the time, Thorn just didn't feel right for the position.

Michael graciously declined Eddie's offer, and the two men parted ways on amicable terms.[12] Unfortunately, Kathexis Anthropos was ultimately not very successful, and the coven ended up converting to a mixed-sex group in 1983. This conversion had nothing to do with the men's ability to adequately perform ritual, for they were successful at this by all accounts. Nor did it have anything to do with the coven's membership, which Thorn characterized as a good group of guys. He just wasn't able to attract a large enough group because, "in general, gay men just weren't interested in spirituality. Eddie did better [at that]." *(Ibid n#11)* However, Eddie was only marginally better at attracting and keeping members, and even he was not consistent in this respect.

The sexually-charged aspect of Minoan practice also troubled Aubrey Wyatt, who had begun to withdraw from Knossos Grove earlier that year. "I was in a relationship at the time, and the ritual became more and more sexual in a way that I wasn't comfortable with," Wyatt writes. "I started worshiping alone. Eddie, Tony and I remained friends. I didn't judge their actions, but just didn't want to participate. Later, I got very involved in the Theater and, as happens in New York, saw little and then none of Eddie and Tony."[13]

By the end of the spring of 1981, Eddie decided that he could wait no longer to make a decision about the future of the coven. In a letter addressed to the group, Buczynski stepped down as the Minos of Knossos Grove and unceremoniously handed the reins over to Tony Fiara.[14] Larry Schneider was named the cup-bearer, or Fiara's assistant. With his duty discharged, Eddie withdrew from the day-to-day decisions of the grove. The five remaining men worked to keep the tradition alive. Nonmembers, particularly men who had the potential to become members, including initiates of other Witchcraft traditions, were occasionally welcomed to participate as guests. Eddie would himself come back several times to participate in sabbats as time permitted.

One of these visits was recounted by H. Bruce Baldwin, a guest of Knossos Grove in late 1981. Baldwin had met Buczynski at the Warlock Shop around 1974, and he made a point to stop there and, later, at the Magickal Childe whenever he made the trip into the city. During one visit in late 1982, Bruce met Carol Bulzone in the East Village where she was advertising a Minoan Sisterhood meeting. Inquiring about it, Carol told him of the Sisterhood and its sibling tradition, the Minoan Brotherhood. The idea of a gay men's Witchcraft tradition appealed to Baldwin, and armed with Tony Fiara's contact information, he called the Minos of Knossos Grove and asked if he could learn more about the group. Fiara and Schneider agreed to meet with Baldwin, and after a long conversation, the men decided to stay in touch. The next time Baldwin was in the city, he was invited to attend a coven sabbat as a guest.[15]

"I was invited to come to a meeting of the Brotherhood, but told that I would have to wait for the end of the ritual to be admitted," Baldwin wrote in 2005. "When I arrived I was told that I would be waiting with someone that was no longer an active member, a young man named Ed. He looked vaguely familiar, and so as the Grove began its rituals we waited outside the temple and talked. It took a while but I finally recovered the memory that this was the same young man, now a few years older and a little more filled out, and even more attractive, that I remembered from the Warlock Shop. ... What I didn't know at the time was that he was the founder of the [Minoan Brotherhood]. So we knew that we would need to be skyclad for the ritual, and Ed suggested that we undress each other, to my amusement. So we did. What happened next was a memorable occasion of having a wonderfully magickal encounter with a man that was not only Gay but was a Witch as well — the first such encounter of my life. ... He said that we were in all likelihood influenced by the energies in the temple not 15 feet away from us. Unfortunately, that was the last time that I would see him." *(Ibid n#15)*

Knossos Grove began to shrink once more, with Kenton Neidel being the last man brought in by Tony shortly after Eddie's departure. By 1982, the only regular Minoan attendees at Sabbats were Tony and Larry. "I do remember at the time that Tony explained to me that many Minoan students had been drawn away to the attraction of a surviving Hawaiian Men's tradition. I can't remember who was teaching this [Hawaiian tradition]," recalled Welsh initiate Gwilym Dafydd. "Thus, by 1982 the Sabbats at Tony's apartment consisted of Tony, Larry, their extra-toed cats, and myself (as an invited guest from the Welsh tradition)."[16]

One possible source for this purported "Hawaiian men's tradition" is Regnier Winsel and Robert Talbert, who operated a voice studio together for many years on West 72nd Street in New York.[17] In his regular *Gnostica News* column in 1972, Leo Martello reported on a trip that the two men had taken together to Haiti "where they were initiated into a Voodoo ceremony and were permitted to take photographs."[18] Martello characterized Winsel as a "Kahuna High Priest" in the article. Unlike the Hawaiian men's tradition, no trace of which remains, interest in the Minoan Brotherhood would periodically flare up like air striking a banked coal, next in 1985 and then off and on again through the following decades. The spark that Eddie had struck would never quite burn out, and yet it would also never quite catch on within the gay community as he had hoped that it would.

During the spring of 1981, when time-share satyrs were looking forward to their annual hunt of doe-eyed office boys through the Meat Rack on Fire Island, a little-noticed article was published in the British medical journal The Lancet about a group of eight young men in New York City who had come down with a relatively rare form of cancer usually seen in elderly men in the Mediterranean.[19] In June and July, the Centers for Disease Control and Prevention (CDC) issued two articles in its Morbidity and Mortality Weekly Report on clusters of unusual infections in men located in Los Angeles, San Francisco and New York. Several commonalities were noted in these men, including infections with cytomegalovirus, Pneumocystis carinii (now called Pneumocystis jirovecii) pneumonia, Kaposi's sarcoma, and oral candidiasis, as well as severe defects in their immunological systems, particularly their T cell lymphocytes. What made the reports stand out was that all of the cases involved sexually active gay men.[20,21]

The New York Times, sensing that something unusual was afoot, published the first mainstream media article on the topic in its Health section on July 3.[22] Titled "Rare Cancer Seen in 41 Homosexuals," the article caused a ripple of unease in New York's gay establishment, and this concern gradually spread throughout the remainder of the community with whispers of a "gay cancer" and speculation on who might have it. By late 1981, with over a hundred similar cases turning up on both coasts, evidence was mounting that the problem was widespread. The CDC classified the new disease as an epidemic, and the media began referring to the syndrome as gay-related immune deficiency (GRID). This association of the disease with homosexuality persisted, even though by late 1981 cases began turning up in both men and women, in intravenous drug users, in those dependent on blood products such as hemophiliacs and surgical patients, and in Miami's Haitian community. It was not until 1982 that doctors finally settled on acquired immune deficiency syndrome, or AIDS, as the term to describe the phenomenon they were witnessing.

While these were the early days of the public's awareness of what would become a worldwide epidemic, it was not the beginning of the epidemic itself. What no one understood then was that by the time the first cases of AIDS in the United States were diagnosed in 1981, more than two hundred and fifty thousand Americans may have already been infected with the human immunodeficiency virus (or "HIV," as it came to be known) that causes the disease, primarily because of the extraordinarily long incubation period — up to a decade — between infection by HIV and manifestation of the range of opportunistic infections and symptoms that characterize the onset of AIDS.[23]

What is now known about the epidemiology of the disease is that it had successfully entered the human population at least twice, including once in the African country of Cameroon as early as the 1930s. This case probably resulted from a hunter being bitten by or exposed to the blood of an infected chimp, as hunters in the region often make use of primates for "bushmeat." One or more infected people eventually traveled from Cameroon to the Belgian Congo (now Zaire). In that country, in the city of

Kinshasa, the first human definitively known to have been infected with HIV was a man who had had his blood stored in 1959 as part of a medical study.[24, 25] By the mid-1960s, men and women were beginning to die of a mysterious wasting disease that was called "slim" in central Africa and was eventually linked to AIDS.

It is likely that HIV was eventually carried to Haiti sometime after 1960 as aid workers and advisors shuttled back and forth between the two countries after the Belgian Congo achieved its independence.[26] From Haiti, the virus entered the United States through Haitian immigrants, American men who traveled to Haiti to engage in sex, some other as yet unidentified vector or, more likely, all of the above. Haiti was a known travel destination for gay sex tourists in the 1960s, given the unsympathetic legal and political climate for homosexuals in the United States, so it is not inconceivable that this could have been a vector for the transmission of HIV.[27] However, immigration to the United States from Latin America and the Caribbean was also on the rise after the passage of the Immigration and Nationality Act of 1965. It is therefore likely that the virus had entered the United States from Haiti and elsewhere many times via several routes throughout the 1960s.[28] And New York City of the 1960s, with its incipient gay community and growing population of Caribbean immigrants, was ideally suited for the introduction of the virus.

Once here, HIV slowly built up a reservoir of infected individuals until the demographics of a key population changed in a way that conferred a significant advantage in the transmission of the virus. This change occurred in the late 1960s and early 1970s with the sexual liberation that swept the nation's youth, particularly in gay communities across the country in the years following the Stonewall riots. Many years later, Dr. Anthony Fauci of the National Institutes of Health summarized the situation: "[I]t just so happened that at the time of the evolving of the permissiveness of sexuality among the gay community back in that period of time, after they had just essentially been able to win their freedom to express themselves sexually as they wanted to do in society — unfortunately, it came at a time when a virus was introduced."[29]

Herman Slater went into the hospital in late 1981, dogged with a persistent infection that he just wasn't able to shake. After an extensive regimen of antibiotics had knocked it down and he was finally released to return to work, Slater told Ria that he thought that the doctors were nuts. They had informed him that the reason he was having such a tough time fighting off the infection was because he had some kind of "gay disease."[30] Media reports of the new disease troubled Eddie deeply, but there is no indication that the onset of HIV/AIDS had any influence whatsoever in his continued pullback from the Neo-Pagan community. Buczynski had already embarked down a new path that would monopolize much of his time for the next seven years, and his involvement in Witchcraft dwindled in direct proportion to the commitments he had already made to his heavy academic and work schedules.

This isn't to say that Eddie cut off all ties to the community. He still corresponded with and occasionally visited friends, especially when their shared interests lay outside the boundaries of Witchcraft and its interminable politics. One such person was Kathryn Frank, who had recently moved from New York to Great Britain to work as a punk rock promoter. Buczynski wrote to Frank in October urging her to take a side trip to Greece. "I do miss you and Timmy [Hough] & Francis [Dreux, Tim's lover]," Eddie wrote. "Melina went home to Greece so, it seems, all of my friends are in Europe now — I hope I'm next!!! I'm gettin' pretty damned lonely here. I'll be in school in Athens in the summer — maybe we can meet somewhere on the continent for Holidays."[31]

In this Eddie referred to his summer trip to attend a session of the ASCS, the premiere training academy for American archaeologists and classical historians. To attend a summer session at the ASCSA, one needed a recommendation from one of the founding institutions and had to pass an entrance exam. The exam was not a great hurdle for Eddie, and Clairève Grandjouan, a long-time member of the illustrious school, believed in him enough to submit his name for consideration without reservation. That Eddie had been tapped by Grandjouan to attend the June 1982 summer session of the ASCSA was a measure of how much he had impressed the Department Head after his first year, with both his grades and his devotion to the subject matter.

Other things were afoot in Eddie's life that fall. His next youngest brother, Frank, was married the second week of October. By all accounts, the reception was a happy affair for the family. "It was a smashing success," Buczynski noted. "I danced all night and was so high on blow and booze that I thought I'd never come down." *(Ibid n#31)* Muto had also begun his doctoral work at New York University and was up for a teaching position as an associate professor in the drama department at Central Connecticut State University in New Britain, Connecticut. The men were making tentative plans to move to New Haven in February, and talked about buying a Jeep so that Eddie could commute to school at Hunter. *(Ibid n#31)* Unfortunately, the position, and their plans, fell through and they continued making do with the cramped apartment on West 13th Street.

By this point in their relationship, the stress of Eddie's and Gene's first months together had long since passed, and the two had fallen into a steady routine of home, school, work and socializing. Eddie would work and go to school during the day and study at night. Gene would typically have classes at night, and work on the weekends. They even adopted two cats — a stretch given their cramped quarters — which Eddie named Maybelle and Grimalkin. The men regularly entertained small groups of people at the apartment, such as Eddie's family, and fellow classmates and friends, such as Dana Matera, Laura Calderone and Catherine Gorlin.

Phyllis Saretta, who met Eddie at school in late 1982, writes, "Bobby, my late fiancé/partner in life and I socialized with Gene and Eddie a couple of times. We went to dinner and to the theatre. Gene and Eddie were very close. I think Eddie really looked up to him." *(Ibid n#4)*

After their May 1980 trip to Greece, the two had later decided to follow it up with a two-week package tour of Italy, visiting Rome, Sorrento, Naples, Capri and other cities. While it was interesting, the trip was grueling, with the crowded bus usually pulling in to the hotels late at night. After that, Buczynski and Muto vowed to plan their own trips from then on. *(Ibid n#6)* After a few such trips to Europe, both men had come to appreciate the many New York restaurants that served fare from other cultures. One of their favorites was an Argentine restaurant called El Gaucho in the Village. Eddie and Gene had developed a taste for Spanish cuisine after taking a two-week driving trip in southern Spain and Portugal in January 1981. As they sipped drinks in a little Spanish bar while watching Ronald Reagan's inauguration, one of the locals asked Gene, *¿Señor Reagan es para los ricos, no?* Muto, with some disgust, replied, *Sí, para los ricos*. *(Ibid n#6)*

In the spring of 1982, Eddie happily busied himself getting ready for his anticipated June trip to Athens. His joy was shattered when, after several months of illness, Professor Clairève Grandjouan suddenly passed away on Memorial Day weekend. She was only 52. Dr. Susan Rotroff succeeded her as the archaeologist in the Classics Department of Hunter College."[32, 33] Tamara Green, who had been acting head of the department during Grandjouan's illness, assumed the position after her death, becoming Eddie's de facto advisor at the same time. *(Ibid n#2)* The department was grief-stricken, and Eddie was heartsick. Because it was Clairève who had recommended him for the summer session at the ASCSA, and who had also authorized the Archaeology Department at Hunter to finance it, the trip would be a bittersweet salute to her generosity. *(Ibid n#2)* Buczynski vowed that he would do everything in his power to justify her faith in him and to "do her proud."[34]

To Hellas and Back

Eddie approached his trip to Greece with both excitement and trepidation. On the one hand, he was thrilled with the chance to delve into the archaeological sites of ancient Greece from the working side of the barricades, speak with working archaeologists and researchers, and have a degree of access to the monuments not normally granted to the masses of tourists who overwhelm the sites at the height of summer. On the other hand, he worried that he might not make the grade, and that the realities on the ground might sweep away his naïve concept of what it meant to be a researcher out in the field.

"More than an ordinary adventure (if there truly is an adventure that is 'ordinary'), this would be a test for me," Buczynski wrote in 1982. "If I had already taken a big step to when I decided to start college in my early thirties, the decision to pursue a course of study in Classical Archaeology was an enormous one. It had all looked very good on paper in a New York City classroom, but just how it would work out for me in the actual field remained to be seen. By the very nature of their work it isn't difficult to figure out that archaeologists are made of 'sterner stuff,' but just how stern that stuff is, I had no idea." *(Ibid n#34)*

Even though the Director of Summer Session II, Dr. John Fischer (Wabash College), had tried to prepare the attendees for the brutality of navigating archaeological sites in Greece at the height of summer — the heat, the climbing, the tourists, the long days and tight schedule — Buczynski was still struck by the harshness of it all on June 27 when he stepped off the plane at Ellinikon International Airport into the heat wave that was roasting Athens that June. "It was 115 degrees on the day that I arrived — how does anyone prepare for that?" *(Ibid n#34)*

Eddie also expressed uncertainty about his mental readiness for the effort he was about to undertake. Various washout scenarios stormed through his mind in the taxi from the airport to Kolonaki, the upscale shopping and residential district clustered at the base of Lykavittos Hill where the school is located. All of his worries focused on a single question — would he be strong enough, smart enough to survive the session? Buczynski's trepidation was understandable. The ASCSA was then, and remains today, one of the world's most prestigious archaeological schools.

Founded in 1881 by a consortium of nine American universities in collaboration with leading businessmen, and built on land deeded by the Greek government, the ASCSA was designed to provide graduate students and scholars from affiliated North American colleges and universities with a base for the advanced study of all aspects of Greek culture, from antiquity to the present day. It is the largest of the fourteen foreign institutes located in Athens, and is charged with responsibility for oversight of excavations in Corinth and the Athenian Agora. The School's primary function is to introduce graduate students in an academic-year program, as well as undergraduates and secondary school teachers in summer sessions, to the sites and monuments of Greek civilization.[35, 36]

As the cab sped away after dropping him at the front gates on Souidias Street, Buczynski paused to calm his mind. Resolving to do the best that he could, Eddie squared his sweaty, exhausted shoulders and dragged himself and his luggage out of the sweltering heat and into the marginally cooler academic sanctuary. He and other arrivals were checked in and assigned their rooms in the dormitory, a process that had been repeated for the past century. Late that afternoon, there was an optional opportunity for the attendees to climb to the top of Lykavittos Hill, which legend explains as a large stone dropped by the Goddess Athena when She was constructing the Acropolis. The long and exhausting ascent to the top of the hill was an ominous taste of things to come over the next six weeks, but those who finished the climb were rewarded with a spectacular view of Athens laid out at their feet.

The orientation meeting was held early on Monday, June 28, followed by tours of the libraries.[37] Dr. John Fischer of Wabash College was an efficient session leader and, according to Dr. Susan Rotroff, an affable, good-humored man and "a true people person."[38] But Fischer was all business in briefing the attendees on the expectations and goals for the session, for the schedule set for both students and support staff for the next six weeks was nothing short of brutal, with only two and a half days of free time reserved for the students in the scorching heat of the Grecian summer. An ASCSA summer session is, in essence, a boot camp for archaeologists and classical scholars, and they must be dedicated and in decent physical shape to see it through to the end.[39]

John Fischer noted in his report to the ASCSA board that this session "group was very good, [with a] good sense of camaraderie." *(Ibid n#37)* It isn't surprising, then, that it didn't take long for Buczynski to make friends, and he was soon part of a small circle of students that included Sue Salay, Lena Hatzichronoglou, and Jytte Willumstad. A fellow student from Hunter College who was attending the session, Jytte was originally from Denmark. She was a slight, shy woman, described by others in the session as a rather delicate traveler. Eddie hadn't known her before the trip, but he immediately befriended the younger woman, who seemed to be having trouble adjusting.

Eddie's efforts on her behalf were remembered by several fellow students, one of whom was Alden Smith. While studying for his MA at the University of Vermont, Smith had won what is now called the Brent M. Froberg Scholarship, which allowed him to attend to the ASCSA summer session.[40] Smith wrote in 2004, "I remember Eddie distinctly. He was a vibrant individual, interesting to speak with and deeply interested in and committed to his archaeological studies. I know he had hopes for a career in classics."[41] He continued, "[Jytte] didn't make friends too easily and yet Eddie befriended her. This was a mark of [his] kind demeanor and gentle character."[42]

Another session attendee, Lena Hatzichronoglou, remembers Buczynski with considerable affection. A native of Athens who was studying for her doctorate at Johns Hopkins University in Baltimore, Lena used the trip that summer as both a learning experience and an opportunity to visit with her family while she was in country. "I remember [Eddie] very fondly as a very beautiful, handsome young man that all the Greek female maids were in love with," recalled Hatzichronoglou with a smile. "They admired his blue eyes and his beauty, and so did the rest of us. You see I was the only Greek person in the group, and the Greeks in school came and talked to me [about him]. I remember him most specifically during our meal times when we sat at the table and joked and laughed a lot together."[43] Even though Eddie was more interested in Koúroi, he was too much of a gentleman, social butterfly, and flirt to shun the attentions of the Koúrai at the school. However, he did shave his mustache halfway through the session, making him look less like a Greenwich Village clone and more like the grinning, mischievous youth he was at heart. *(Ibid n#43)*

The itinerary for the session was ambitious, and the group started out first thing Tuesday morning with a trip to the National Museum, where they were given a quick tour of the classical exhibits and were able to speak with staff. *(Ibid n#37)* The afternoon was spent at the Athenian Agora excavations overseen by the school. The next day, the group explored the Acropolis, the South Slope, the Pnyx, and Philopappos. It was here that Eddie would first meet Dr Susan Rotroff, who took time out of her busy schedule to lecture to the students on the Areopagos, Pnyx, and Philopappos. Dr Rotroff would later join the staff at Hunter College in 1983.

Eddie and Gene's tour of Greece in the spring of 1980 had been only a warm-up to the in-depth introduction that Eddie and the others were now given to some of the most recognizable archaeological treasures on the planet. If he had not already been ensnared years before, Buczynski would have fallen in love. As it was, he knew within these first few days in the session that he had made the right decision to travel to Greece that summer, and had definitely made the correct choice of career. He was finally in his element — but the elements were about to assert themselves in their lives. On Thursday, July 1, they would begin their first trek outside of the comforts of the city, for they were venturing to Crete.

The students were given leave to spend Thursday morning and afternoon as they chose. Most, if not all, of them chose to pack for the excursion. Eddie made use of the facilities at the school to prepare a handout for one of his scheduled site presentations. Each student was required to give two reports, generally about twenty minutes in length, on the monuments or sites that the session visited. These assignments were divided up among the students, and Eddie had been selected to give a report on one of the Cretan sites. This was not a random happenstance: the session Director did have the leeway to consider students' personal interests when making the assignments, and no one could fail to notice, after an hour with Eddie, that he had a passion for Minoan Crete.

The ferry departed from Piraeus shortly after 5 PM for an overnight sea voyage to Herakleion, Crete. The ferries between Athens and Crete are large vessels that carry many passengers and vehicles. The boarding process close to departure time resembles a crazed circus with masses of people, porters, baggage, and drivers jockeying for position. The trip took nine hours, during which the students were strongly encouraged to get some sleep, because they needed to hit the ground running once they reached port.

Very early on Friday, the group disembarked from the ferry at Herakleion, where they met their bus. They quickly loaded their baggage and themselves, and immediately took off for ancient Knossos, the splendorous dream that Buczynski had held fixed in his inner sight for the past six years. They spent the entire afternoon prowling through the Herakleion Museum, which held many of the objects that Eddie had made icons of veneration in the Minoan tradition. He was in Heaven; a Heaven on earth. Once they were through for the day, the group was bussed back to Herakleion and the comforts of their hotel.

The school staff had meticulously planned the summer sessions to make the greatest use of the students' time for the out-of-town excursions. Travel time between sites was of particular concern, and could easily eat up much of the day. Changing hotels every night added to the stress of the trips. One way that the staff chose to maximize time on site and minimize traveling was to base the group in one town located near a number of sites. From their hotel, the group could mount day expeditions to different sites over several days, rather than changing hotels every night. John Fischer noted that, "This proved especially pleasant in Nafplion, Herakleion, Olympia and Delphi. [The] students got a chance to get to know the towns better." *(Ibid n#37)*

To keep the students from dragging, the schedule was arranged so as to alternate long days with short ones. Rest stops and swimming (a social necessity as much as a welcome respite during the baking heat, where both people and fish could "go off" very quickly) were scheduled as time permitted. In past years, a group picnic was arranged for midday meals. This summer, however, most meals were taken in local restaurants, which had the added advantage of immersing the students in the local culture wherever they went. The food was inexpensive and good, according to Fischer, and the hotels they stayed in were very good. One unexpected delight was the firm contracted to transport the group from place to place, Kostas Zomopoulos and his son. "They were friendly, safe, reliable, prompt and breakdown and argument free (a definite change from previous suppliers)," wrote Fischer. *(Ibid n#37)*

One thing the staff couldn't plan for was sites that didn't always abide by their posted operating times. This was, and remains, a common problem in Greece, and it posed an obvious problem for the school when trying to keep to a schedule. Nevertheless, the group managed to visit every site, even if they weren't able to devote as much time as they had hoped. The school also arranged ahead of time with archaeologists at various digs, museums, and conservatories to meet with the students to give them the benefit of their own experience in the field. A large number of these scholars took time from their busy schedules to speak to the group at the different sites.

Saturday, July 3 had the group exploring Phaistos, Ayia Triadha, Kommos and Gortyn (famous for its wall of ancient post-Minoan laws). On Sunday and Monday, the group did a whirlwind tour of Káto Zákros, Palaiókastro, Kritsá and Nirou Khani. As Fischer later recalled, "Kato Zakro was a very long day. The students thought it was worthwhile, but long days tend to be rushed and [do] not afford the students the time to see things at leisure. This is compounded by the site hours, which ran from 9 AM to 3 PM, which didn't leave much viewing time or time to reflect on what they were seeing." *(Ibid n#37)* Eddie, however, was fully prepared for the site, which constituted one of his two required reports. Káto Zákros was the last major Minoan palace structure to be excavated and studied in modern times, and it had the most artifacts found intact in situ following its collapse, including trade goods from ancient Kemet. One of the artifacts uncovered, a magnificent bull's head rhyton, was a particular favorite of Eddie's. The site is approached through a river gorge named Pharángi ton Nekrón (Gorge of the Dead) by the locals because of the Minoan cave burials in its walls.[44]

Even with the limited time they had to examine the site, the students managed to touch on the major points of the ruined palace and its associated city precinct, which covered an area of about two acres. With Zákros bay and the remnants of the Minoan harbor as a backdrop, Eddie celebrated July 4th by giving a report on the archaeological significance of the site and the materials discovered there. Fischer recalled that Eddie's report on Káto Zákros was excellent.[45] Alden Smith agrees, writing "I certainly recall that he gave a first rate oral report at Kato Zakro in Crete. His handout was the best produced of any student on the program. He was deeply interested in Minoan civilization and I think he planned to specialize in it." *(Ibid n#41)*

Tuesday had them at the central Cretan site of Arkhanes in the morning. Today it's a grape and olive processing region, but in ancient times it was a trading hub and the location of a Minoan palace. That afternoon, the students and their baggage went aboard the Herakleion ferry for the 5 PM overnight return voyage to Piraeus. After the relative coolness of the island, the summer heat of Athens reasserted itself with a vengeance. They were given another free morning to recover from the trip, after which they assembled at the National Museum for more lectures. A day trip to Brauron, Thorikos and Sounion followed on Thursday, while all of Friday was spent at the school's excavations at the Athenian Agora attending lectures on site oversight, conservation and study. The attendees were barely settled back in their dorm rooms before they had to pack up and head out on the road once more.

Saturday was spent on a bus trip north to visit the sites of Dáfni, Eleutherai, Plateía, Leuktra, and Kabeiron. Staying overnight in Thebes, they then traveled to the excavations in Thebes before continuing on to Orchomenos, Gla and Thermopylae, where Leonidas and his Spartan troops and allies perished defending the Greek alliance against the Persians. Gla is a barren limestone outcropping that holds a fifty-six acre complex with nearly two miles of fortifications. The citadel was apparently an important food production and storage center in Mycenaean times.[46] The area surrounding the ridge was once a lake, drained by the Mycenaeans in a remarkable feat of prehistoric engineering in order to provide the fertile fields that produced the grain that was stored and safeguarded in the guarded silos of ancient Gla.

In July and August, Athenians normally abandon the oven-like heat of the city for holidays in the country or on the islands, where cooler temperatures are said to prevail. The session attendees therefore looked forward to this next excursion out into the countryside and away from the bread oven that was Athens. However, the hoped-for respite appears to have been lacking. Sunday, July 11 must have been a brutally hot, dry, and long day, based on what Eddie later wrote of their visit to the site: "All of us left Greece happier and better individuals — after all, being now made of 'sterner stuff,' after all, we survived Gla!" *(Ibid n#34)*

The troop dragged themselves into their hotel in Volos that evening, and the next day set forth for the Volos Museum, Dhimini, Sesklo and Pelion. After staying in Volos one more night, they traveled to Demetrias, Phthiotic Thebes, and Lamía on Tuesday, July 13. After staying overnight in Lamía, they headed for Kalapodi, Levadheia, and Chaeronea. The field of Chaeronea is the place where, in 338 BCE, forces under King Phillip II of Macedon and his son, Prince Alexander (Alexander the Great), defeated an alliance of Greek city-states under Athens and Thebes. Fighting for Thebes was the Sacred Band, a hoplite infantry formation made up of 300 pair-bonded lovers. They were defeated almost to a man, and a lion monument was erected over their gravesite. Seeing that ancient lion, restored in the early twentieth century by Hellenists, would have affected Eddie deeply. It isn't out of character to believe that he may have gathered a small bunch of wildflowers to leave at their grave, or perhaps placed a small stone, Kadesh for sacred comrades.

They stayed three nights in Delphi, hopping from site to site to site and covering the Delphi Museum, the Sanctuary of Apollo, Arachova and Athena Pronaia. Eddie gave his second oral report here, this time on the Siphnian Treasury. John Fischer recalled that this report was also excellent. *(Ibid n#45)* Buczynski would have been particularly drawn to Delphi because of its mythic ties to Crete. Apollo is associated with Delphi through his epithet Delphinios, the dolphin, which relates the tale of his arrival at the sanctuary in the form of a dolphin bearing Cretan priests upon his back to found his sanctuary. The students were given a free afternoon on their final day in the area, which they used to explore the local culture.

"While at Delphi, we visited Arachova as a group," remembered Lena Hatzichronoglou, "and someone mentioned this restaurant which was way up the hill. Our gang climbed all the way up to visit Mrs. Panayiota and taste her food. We were not disappointed." *(Ibid n#43)* It had to be very good food, indeed, for the students not to begrudge the climb up the slopes of Mount Parnassos after all of the climbing and hiking that they had already put in on this leg of the journey. Fortunately, the views of the surrounding countryside were fantastic and perfectly complemented the food, wine, and camaraderie of the evening.

Saturday, July 17 saw the group back in Athens, with visits to Hosios Loukas, Chalkis, Eretria and Amphiareion. Sunday was a rare day of rest, but they were back at it on Monday with follow-up trips to the Acropolis and the Athenian Agora, and a lecture on Athens under the Romans. Day trips were scheduled on Tuesday, July 20 for Aigosthena and Eleusis. The sanctuary of Eleusis operated for almost two thousand years to initiate men and women into the mysteries of the cult of Demeter and Persephone. Eddie picked up several common stones from the ground and brought them back home, providing him with a connection to one of the oldest continuously-operated ceremonial sites of ancient Europe. It is unlikely that he would have risked doing so had he not still had an active connection to Neo-Pagan spirituality. Picking up stones is frowned upon at all of the archaeological sites; or, as ASCSA Director Henry Immerwahr warned students, "You can step on the antiquities, but you cannot pick them up and say, 'Look what I found.'"[47] The remainder of the week was spent with short trips to Kerameikos, the National Museum, Olympieion, the Ilissos area, Peiraeus and the Peiraeus Museum, and the Naval Museum. A film was presented on Thursday evening, with Michael and Susan Katsev of the Institute of Nautical Archaeology in the school's Loring Hall.

The final road trip of the summer session began on Friday, July 23, with a bus ride to the Peloponnesos. They visited Kenchreai, Isthmia, Perachora and Corinth, staying two nights in New Corinth. The next three nights saw them using Nauplion as their base while exploring Nemea, Nauplion, Epidauros, the Franchthi Cave, Halieis, Asine, Argive Heraion, Argos, Lerna, and Mycenae. Next to Crete, Mycenae was probably the next most important site in all of Greece from Eddie's perspective, given its connection to late Minoan culture. Walking through the cyclopean lion gate would have sent a shiver through his body, knowing that he was treading on the same ground as King Agamemnon of old.

On Wednesday, they toured the Argos Museum, Tegea and Mistra, before overnighting in Sparta. With the sunrise, came Sparta, the Sparta Museum, Kalamata and Methone. From Methone, the group traveled Pylos and the Palace of Nestor on Friday, followed by the Chora Museum, Messene and Megalopolis. They slept in Andritsaina and then swung south for Bassai and Olympia, home of the Gods and of the temple and athletic complex dedicated to them. After two nights in Olympia, they returned to Athens on Monday, August 2 for stops at Patras and Sikyon.

Tuesday was one of the rare free days for the attendees, who rushed about getting in some last-minute shopping and exploring ahead of the session end. These last five days were a whirlwind of activity, with stops at the Acropolis (for a third and final time), the Epigraphical Museum, and the Numismatic Museum. Day trips were taken to Aegina, Ikaria, Marathon, Vrana and Rhamnous. On Saturday, they ended with a lecture on Byzantine Athens by Beata Panagopoulou. On Saturday, August 8, students took an optional exam before vacating their rooms and heading to the airport for home.

Session Director John Fischer, in his report to the ASCSA board, characterized the students as an "agile and lively group that bore up well to the heat generally without complaints" and with "cheerful and consistent good humor." *(Ibid n#37)* As for Buczynski, Fischer noted in 2004, "I recall him with great fondness. He was lively, committed, interested and a real spark plug. He gave the session a real boost and vitality, as well as a remarkable intellectual commitment to things Greek, which is an absolute requisite for such an intense program. When you wed that to his liveliness, he made a wonderful student." *(Ibid n#45)*

Eddie must have impressed the school staff as well, for he was asked to write the traditional Session II report from the students' perspective for the school newsletter. While the ASCSA had asked him for a personal view, Eddie chose to provide an article that reflected his understanding of what the group as a whole gleaned from the session. Buczynski's thoughtful words indicate that Clairève Grandjouan had chosen well: *(Ibid n#34)*

> *Being able to see and experience the actual material culture of a people who, up until now, existed for us only in the written word or photographs in a book, and to have integrated ourselves into both the continuity and the changes in that culture (as modern Greek life surely demonstrates), renewed in all of us the covenant we made with Academia – the promise that these extraordinary intellectual achievements of Man are not only very much alive but are really worth the effort to understand. The realization that we are part of that ongoing adventure of accomplishment is both exciting and comforting. ... For our class, the Summer Session was the final approach to an important crossroads in our lives: whether or not to continue in Classical Studies. All of us successfully reached that crossroads by school's end. Some, including myself, were inspired to continue; some, to turn in new directions.*

Laurels to the Victor

Newly energized, Eddie returned to New York in early August and re-dedicated himself to his studies. Every summer thereafter at Hunter, Buczynski took classes emphasizing an introduction into field archaeology. These classes were lecture and classroom oriented; Eddie himself never had the opportunity to conduct field work in excavations despite his desire to do so. *(Ibid n#2)* During the ASCSA summer session, he had taken fifteen rolls of slides documenting the various sites he had visited. Like Grandjouan, Eddie had come to appreciate the usefulness of photographs to illustrate points. Also like her, many of his slides included shots of the local wildflowers.[48]

Eddie and Gene took a trip to Baltimore in late summer to have dinner with Lena Hatzichronoglou, where his summer session classmate was now finishing her doctoral studies at Johns Hopkins. Eddie and Lena exchanged letters and cards for the next several months before they both got too busy and drifted apart. During the fall 1982 semester, Eddie wrote to say that school was going well so far. Addressing Lena as γλυκά μον (sweet one), he informed her, "I'm reading Plato and loving it (and doing surprisingly well)." *(Ibid n#48)* He wrote to her once again late that year to say that school was keeping him extremely busy.[49]

That fall Eddie met Phyllis Saretta. Phyllis was a new archaeology major in Eddie's department and, it turns out, lived on the same block of West 13th Street, though closer to 7th Avenue. Over the next three years, Phyllis and Eddie would often travel to classes at Hunter together. "Eddie was a caring and good-natured person," Saretta remembers. "He was very lively, and likeable. In fact, before I actually met him, I used to see him in the cafeteria at Hunter sitting with a group of the archaeology/classics students. He stood out to me as a person with leadership abilities." (*Ibid n#4*) Tamara Green confirms this, writing, "In college, Eddie was popular and had a wide circle of friends. He served as a mentor to the younger students." *(Ibid n#2)* Buczynski could be a very good friend indeed, as Saretta illustrates with two recollections.

Phyllis Saretta: *(Ibid n#4)*

> *We saw each other practically every day, or at least spoke on the phone. ... Personally, he did a lot for me. When I was ill with bronchitis, I had to miss 5 weeks of classes. He would get the assignments for me and pick up my answers and bring it in to the professor (we lived on the same street). When I recovered, though still very weak, he took me to school many times in a taxi. He also came over one day to bring me chicken soup which he had made himself. I could go on and on about the many loving things he did for me. ... One summer, he and I did a summer tutorial together in Koine Greek with Professor Tamara Green. It*

was really wonderful. I had mentioned to him that the textbook that I had to use for Classical Greek was different from the one he had learned from, and that I wished I had that textbook. The next thing I knew, he purchased it for me, and wrote an inscription inside to me. He also bought me a very good German dictionary for graduation, because I was required to learn German for graduate school.

After the fall semester ended, Eddie and Gene took a month-long winter tour of Greece and Italy. "As soon as he came back [from the summer session] I said 'Let's go back to Greece,'" Muto recalled. The men spent New Year's Eve there, and crisscrossed the countryside retracing Eddie's steps from his July stay. "We went to Corinth, Thebes, and ... Mycenae. And then we went to Crete. We drove all through Crete. Then we went to Italy for a couple of weeks." *(Ibid n#6)* This time it was Eddie who served as the tour guide of the archaeological sites, fortified by the knowledge of his earlier trip that year. Eddie wrote Lena once more, this time from Europe in January 1983, to say that school had progressed from merely keeping him busy to outright "murder." He submitted his application to participate in the ASCSA excavations of the Athenian Agora, hoping to go back to Greece once again during the summer of 1983.[50]

As it turns out, Eddie was not chosen to assist with the work at the Athenian Agora that summer, which is just as well in one respect, for that permitted him to be in New York when Bennie Geraci returned from New Orleans for a visit. Bennie travelled with David Roberts, who had moved back to New Orleans earlier that year. Eddie and Gene treated the two travelers to dinner at a very nice restaurant in Midtown. As Bennie saw how Eddie and Gene interacted, he finally realized that it really was over for him, and he was okay with that. Eddie extracted a promise from Bennie to see him before he returned to New Orleans, but Bennie never fulfilled that promise, which upset Eddie. He didn't know it yet but, as the dinner party broke up, it was the last time Bennie would ever lay eyes on his former lover.

Buczynski remained in contact with a select number of his Craft friends, including Herman Slater. By all accounts, Slater was continuing to do well for himself, despite a fight that had begun the previous year between the residential tenants and the landlord of the building occupied by the Magickal Childe. The tenants had banded together in 1983 to defend themselves from what they claimed was the owner's neglect and depredation. Organizing as the Harmonious Tenants Association, the residents applied for protection under New York City's Loft Law. The fight went on for the next decade, and although it included the mysterious cessation of utilities and services for the rest of the building, it didn't seem to affect the commercial space occupied by the Childe.[51]

Buczynski wasn't the only busy bee during the summer of 1982. Ria and Carol had been making big plans since the previous year. To no one's great surprise, 1981 had seen Slater going through yet another cycle of tax troubles. As Alan Cabal recalls, "Every now and then the issue of unpaid sales taxes would pop up and he'd threaten to sell the shop, but he never did."[52] This time was different, however, in that he had a serious buyer at hand when he made the announcement. Carol and Ria asked Herman if he would sell out to them, and the Magickal Childe's master noncommittally replied that if they could raise the cash he'd consider the offer.

This left the two women, who like so many New Yorkers lived from paycheck to paycheck, with the task of trying to figure out how to raise several thousand dollars to make a down payment on the store. The women had tried to get something like this off the ground for a couple of years. They had originally batted around the idea with Eddie and Bennie of opening their own shop called Incantations, Inc.[53] When informed of their latest plans, Richard Gernon, who had recently inherited the Mastership of Tahuti Lodge from Jim Wasserman, offered to help them work magick to make it happen. Closing up shop early one night while Herman was away, Ria and Carol were led through an invocation of Mercury by Richard, who censed the space with a mixture of red wine and storax that he cooked off in a metal spoon over a lit candle. The women conducted a Venus ritual several nights later. It wasn't until some time later that they learned that Gernon was so adept at cooking material in a spoon because of his heroin addiction.[54]

Throughout 1982, the women were very successful at raising capital. With several thousand dollars in hand, they went back to Herman and made him an offer on the shop. By that time, however, Slater was out of trouble and no longer interested in selling. Ria and Carol were devastated and doubted that he'd ever follow through on any offer to sell out, and they were probably correct. The truth was that while Herman sometimes dreamed aloud of buying a farm and moving to the country, the reality was that the store had become his raison d'être, and without it he'd have been left rudderless.

Frustrated by Herman's on-again, off-again attitude toward selling the store, they gave up on the idea of running the Magickal Childe and instead focused on starting up their own business. They found a suitable location in the East Village and used the money they had raised to rent it. Calling on friends to help, including several of the Minoan Brothers, they made it ready in secret. One of the Minoans who helped was Jeffery Whitfield, who ended up becoming their oils and incense master. In late 1982, Carol and Ria quit the Magickal Childe and opened Enchantments, Inc. at 341 East 9th Street. "My partner Carol and I wanted to bring more of the Craft to the public," Ria explained in a 1987 documentary interview. "But we actually opened it up to the dedication of the Gods so that we could bring forth Their name and Their laws [and] love ... So it was actually opened up more as a dedication to the spiritual work that we have ahead of us."[55]

Whatever their motivation for striking out on their own, the women, fearing Slater's wrath, left a resignation letter at the Magickal Childe while he was out rather than offering their resignations in person.[56] When Herman found out what they had done, he was furious; whether this was for setting themselves up in competition with him or for the gutless way in which they had done it, it's difficult to say. In all honesty, however, this outcome was his own fault. As the one who had raised their expectations, he had no one to blame but himself when, after he failed to follow through, they seized the initiative for themselves — and he would have just as likely done the same thing had he been in their shoes.

The women opened Enchantments on September 7, 1982. At 2 o'clock that very morning, Ria was awakened from a restless sleep by a phone call. On the other end of the line was a New York City police officer who was responding to a burglar alarm at the Magickal Childe. Stumbling around in the dark, the officer had managed to find the phone and an employee list that still showed Ria as a store manager. "Don't hang up on me, lady! Please don't hang up!" the cop begged the groggy Witch. "I'm in here in the dark and I can't find the lights. And this place is creeping me out!" Ria took pity on the man and guided him to the light switch, which was located in the robe cabinet in the back of the store that doubled as a hidden door to the back room. After flipping on the lights, Ria heard the policeman moan, "Oh God! It was better with the lights off!"[57]

Ria noted that it was fortunate that the police had called her and established an alibi for the two women. "I know how Herman thought," Ria said, "and he would have immediately suspected that Carol and I were responsible for the break-in given that we were opening our own store that day." *(Ibid n#57)* Slater cooled down after several months, assisted in no small part by the diplomacy of Jim Wasserman, who persuaded the old grouch to come to the East Village location in 1983 and make up with them. *(Ibid n#54)* According Carol Bulzone, Herman concluded, "You'll be the girls' store, and we'll be the boys' store. It'll be fine."[58]

In late 1983, Herman asked Eddie to let him republish the *Witchcraft Fact* Book through Magickal Childe Publishing. Whereas the old version had been printed in pamphlet form for the past 10 years, this time Herman planned to release it as a high-quality paperback and enlisted Wasserman's Studio 31 as the book's designer.[59] The book was released in June 1984. In the biographical blurb on the back cover, Herman noted that "Ed is currently involved in anthropology. He has gone underground as far as his involvement in Earth religions."[60]

As far as most of his classmates and professors were concerned, Eddie was underground, for there seemed to be nothing out of the ordinary about his spiritual life. "I knew that Eddie had at one time been heavily involved with the occult," wrote Phyllis Saretta, "but by the time I met him [in 1982], I believe he was not involved with it anymore. In fact, he didn't speak about it at all, and was completely engrossed in his new 'life,' so to speak." *(Ibid n#4)* Buczynski may not have spoken of it, but he was not quite as underground as Slater had claimed. In 1983 he wrote a substantial paper, *Liber Ubrarum* [sic]: *the Book of Shadows with commentary*, for a class with Tamara Green.[61] The Latin name *Liber Umbrarum* means, literally, "Book of Shadows," and is taken from the final section of Doreen Valiente's 1978 book *Witchcraft for Tomorrow*. Eddie's paper analyzed selected rituals from the *Gardnerian Book of Shadows*. An appendix of the paper contained the *Gardnerian Book of Shadows*, which a Gardnerian initiate would have known to be a violation of his oath. This incident appears to confirm that Eddie no longer considered himself a member of Gardnerian Wica, or necessarily bound by its Laws.

In August, Eddie was laid off from his job at J. Aron, joining almost twenty percent of his fellow employees in the futures unit of Goldman Sachs.[62] *(Ibid n#6)* The investment banking house had purchased J. Aron in November 1981 for a price reported at the time to be slightly more than $100 million, which was a princely sum at that time. Goldman Sachs had purchased J. Aron at the frenzied height of gold and silver futures trading, which was probably not their smartest move.[63] Buczynski didn't remain unemployed for long, picking up a student assistant position in the Classics office at Hunter. *(Ibid n#38)* While he would miss the great year-end bonuses at J. Aron, the Classics office position suited him far better from an academic standpoint.

In a concession to Eddie's new job status, the two men rented a cottage in Newport, Rhode Island and relaxed on the beach after summer semester classes ended in 1983. This proved marginally less expensive than traveling abroad. *(Ibid n#6)* Realistically speaking, however, Eddie's employment change didn't slow the adventures of the two all that much. In late summer 1984, they once more rented a cottage in Newport, Rhode Island. That winter they traveled to Mexico, flying into Mexico City, and then on to Merida to see Chichen Itza, and to Cancun to see Tolun. *(Ibid n#6)* Phyllis Saretta had by this point become a trusted friend who was able to look after Maybelle and Grimalkin when they were gone. *(Ibid n#4)*

Buczynski made another new friend at the start of fall semester 1983 when Susan Rotroff, whom he had met in Greece the previous summer, joined the Classics department as an assistant professor. Rotroff quickly came to like the good-humored native of Queens. "I remember Eddie very, very fondly," Rotroff wrote in 2004. "He was a fixture of the department of Classics at Hunter when I arrived in 1983 and was a very welcoming presence to me as a new faculty member at that time. ... [He] was always fun to talk to, and always had a good and funny comment on the craziness of Hunter and the department. I remember one day when the secretary, Shirley Aronoff, was in a particularly desperate mood (probably [due to] beginning-of-semester chaos) and I think there may have been some crisis about her many cats (the departmental office at Hunter was chiefly decorated with pictures of cats). I remember Eddie rolling his eyes and saying to me, 'This I need like a hole in the head!' thereby summarizing exactly what I was thinking myself — but in such a nice way." *(Ibid n#38)*

Some in the Neo-Pagan community believed that a hole in his head was exactly what Herman Slater had developed in late 1984, when he shut down the Earth Star Temple space in the back of the Magickal Childe. This move ran counter to his previous philosophy that bringing in customers through workshops, rituals, and meetings would help sustain the business. In both of its incarnations, the shop had been sponsoring workshops and rituals for twelve years, and had both educated several generations of Neo-Pagans and brought them into the shop to buy things. However, this came to an abrupt end when Slater claimed that he needed the space for storage for the burgeoning wholesale operations of Magickal Childe Publishing.

But Herman hadn't gone off the deep end. Sales were often brisk at the store and via catalogue, but one of Magickal Childe's fastest-growing sources of profit were the deals that Herman would forge at book shows across the country to supply other book stores with the products of his publishing business. At its height, Laura Austan claimed that the wholesale book portion of the enterprise would end up raking in upwards of a million dollars a year. By contrast, even though the store was doing well (a thousand dollars a day on a slow day to as much as ten times that around the holidays) it was only a cash cow to Magickal Childe Publishing's alleged gold mine.[64] However, former Childe employee Randy Jones does not believe that the publishing business was ever that profitable and, even if it was this did not translate into money in the bank. "You have to realize that the MC was not run like your typical business — we were constantly robbing Peter to pay Paul," writes Jones. "There was never any money — it went out as fast as it came in. Although Herman had a BA in Business Management, he was good at business and lousy at management. We were all paid off the books (what books?). When I was the manager/bookkeeper, if we had $5000 in the bank that was unusual."[65] Herman appears to confirm this in a 1987 documentary interview. "It's not making a profit, I can guarantee you that!" Slater said, laughing. "We basically break even, and that's about it." *(Ibid n#55)*

The downside of this business was that the publisher was generally expected to pay royalties, especially to living authors, and there were suspicions that Magickal Childe Publishing did not always live up to its side of the bargain.[66] But whether this failing was due to Herman's notoriously bad bookkeeping skills, or to other motives, remains unclear. "Lots of people felt Herman cheated them," noted Kathryn Frank, who was in charge of the publishing side of the business. "However, one must keep in mind that many/most of the people Herman was dealing with were, well, let's say not worldly. Herman was a business man, aside from many other aspects of his being, but he was most definitely a business man and I think a lot of people just didn't understand what that means. Basically, you get to be the dickhead who tells people they're not going to get the money they think their things are worth."[67] That may be true. But the fact remains that more than one person who went into business with Slater characterized him in unflattering terms afterward. Yet in a community that had a bad habit of tearing down anyone who stuck their head up too far, Slater was also conscious of the strains under which new authors could be operating. "What Herman used to tell new authors," writes Laura Austan, "was to do a self-defense & protection ritual (Denning & Phillips) as soon as a contract was signed when you've written a Craft book."[68]

Although it was hard to argue with his reasoning concerning the back room, his action ended an outreach program that stretched back to shortly after the Warlock Shop opened in Brooklyn Heights in 1972. Laura Austan credits the eviction of spiritual activities and workshops from the premises in favor of pure commerce as the beginning of a long, slow decline in the fortunes of the Magickal Childe.[69] Fortunately for the community, other entities continued to fill this need, including InnerVision, which was in its nineteenth year in 1984, and the School of Mystical Sciences, which celebrated its 10th anniversary in 1985.[70, 71] The back room was stripped of its altars and other accoutrements and filled with slapdash shelving to store the current titles, such as *A Witches Bible Compleat*, and popular backlist titles, such as Gerald Gardner's *Meaning of Witchcraft*. This shelving can be seen in the movie *The Oracle* (1987). A large painting of Lady Rowen by Emma Davy, which had hung in the temple for several years, was given to Kathryn Frank.[72]

It was at this time that friends of Herman Slater began noticing some subtle personality changes in the cranky shopkeeper. It was nothing that they could really put their finger on, but Slater was becoming even more prickly and paranoid. Some attributed it to the amount of money allegedly flowing through the shop, which was liable to make any thinking person look over his shoulder. By the late 1980s, the Magickal Childe was being burgled at least once a month. The frequency increased after a number of the employees had become junkies (some of whom Slater suspected of engineering the break-ins). He had taken to keeping a gun and a blanket under his desk at the Childe, and he occasionally came to the shop in the middle of the night to sleep behind the counter.[73]

Herman's problems were the furthest thing from Eddie's mind as he steadfastly plodded through his classes from 1984 into 1985. Buczynski continued to do very well in his studies, remaining on the honors list as he raced to the graduation finish line, but other things were troubling his thoughts during this period. What came to be known as the AIDS crisis seemed at times to monopolize the news throughout 1985. In January, the

U.S Food and Drug Administration approved and licensed the first blood test for HIV. Later that year, sexually-active gay men were barred from donating blood. Ryan White, a thirteen-year-old junior high student was barred from school due to concerns about his infection with HIV, which as a hemophiliac he had contracted from a tainted blood transfusion. In July, film star Rock Hudson became the first public figure to acknowledge that he had AIDS. He died in October, two weeks after his long-time friend President Reagan publicly mentioned *AIDS* for the first time. By the end of the year, AIDS cases had been reported in every populated continent in the world. In the United States alone, 20,470 cases of AIDS had been reported, and 8,161 people had died.

The results of a national poll undertaken in 1985 showed that seventy-two percent of Americans were in favor of mandatory testing of everyone for HIV. Fifty-one percent of respondents favored quarantining HIV positive individuals, with fifteen percent in favor of tattooing those infected with HIV (the question about tattooing was an attempt to gauge support for the vile suggestion made by conservative commentator William F. Buckley, Jr. that was reminiscent of a similar practice undertaken by the Nazis).[74] Politician Lyndon LaRouche advocated interning HIV-positive individuals in so-called treatment centers that critics referred to as concentration camps. Given the proposals of people such as Buckley, LaRouche, and their ilk the reticence of those at risk to be tested and to have their HIV status known by any government agency was understandable.

Susan Rotroff recalled a conversation she had had with Eddie while he was still at Hunter College: "[He] told me he was worried about his health, because he had been promiscuous as a younger man. But everything seemed OK at that time." *(Ibid n#38)* However, Phyllis Saretta had observed that Eddie got sick frequently during the last years of his undergraduate studies. *(Ibid n#4)* By the end of the year, the Mineshaft, one of the backroom bars where Eddie and Bennie used to hang out, became the first sacrifice to the new post-AIDS reality when it was padlocked by order of Mayor Koch on November 7, 1985. Bathhouses and bars on both coasts began closing as politicians cast about for something, anything, to slow or stop the progression of the disease.[75]

In the spring of 1985, the graduating students' hearts turned to college applications and job interviews. In Eddie's case, efforts were geared toward graduate school rather than to the job market. He applied to several schools, but his first choice was Bryn Mawr College, the alma mater of his beloved advisor, Clairève Grandjouan. Eddie's motivation to seek out Bryn Mawr was simple, according to Gene Muto: "[Clairève] had gone to Bryn Mawr, and that was one of the key reasons that he wanted to go there." *(Ibid n#6)* It was Eddie's firm belief that his mentor would have wanted him to attend Bryn Mawr, and he was bound and determined to get in there. His acceptance there seemed even more likely when he was elected to Phi Beta Kappa at Hunter in the spring of 1985. The criteria for being elected to this honor are that one must take several semesters of a foreign language and maintain an overall minimum grade point average of 3.75.[76] Eddie easily met these requirements, and he felt confident that he would also successfully pass the hurdles for graduate school.

According to Brunilde Sismondo Ridgway, a retired professor in the Department of Classical and Near Eastern Archaeology at Bryn Mawr College, the prospective student to Bryn Mawr's graduate program had to possess sufficient academic credentials, be recommended for the slot, successfully navigate a series of interviews by the faculty and the current graduate students, and pass the requisite admissions exams, including tests in ancient languages. "You simply could not be a successful student without a grasp of the languages of the ancient near east, including Greek and Latin," asserts Ridgway. "You also need a working knowledge of French and German..." given that much of the literature is in those languages.[77] While Eddie had made good progress in his language skills, he still struggled with German.

After Eddie had sent in his applications, he was informed that that he had become the first winner of the new Mellon Fellowship sponsored by the Andrew Mellon Foundation. *(Ibid n#2)* This award guaranteed that he would be financially able to attend graduate school, because it provided full payment of tuition and fees, plus a small stipend on which to live. The excitement surrounding his impending graduation was dampened when he was informed by Bryn Mawr College that his application had been rejected. Since Grandjouan's death, Eddie had focused on her desire to see him study at her alma mater. To be informed that he would not was a severe blow.

Tamara Green, however, wasn't willing to let the matter rest. She made a telephone call to her colleagues at Bryn Mawr's Department of Classical and Near Eastern Archaeology to ask why Eddie hadn't made the cut. Brunilde Ridgway was very apologetic, knowing that Eddie's former mentor Clairève, herself a distinguished "Mawrter," had wanted him to attend the college. The late professor's opinion certainly carried a great deal of weight. But Ridgway informed Green that, while Buczynski's application was flawless in every other respect, his language skills were just not up to par for the school. Tamara asked if it would make a difference in their considerations if they knew that Eddie had just been awarded the Mellon Fellowship. There was a pause on the other end of the phone before Brunilda asked Tamara to give her ten minutes. After quickly conferring with the other Department members, Ridgway called back to inform Green that they would indeed give him a chance. Eddie was accepted at Bryn Mawr College, becoming the second graduate of Hunter's new Department of Archaeology to go on to graduate school. *(Ibid n#2)* Despite his success, the celebratory atmosphere was somewhat muted, after he had come so close to not succeeding. *(Ibid n#6)*

It was a bright, sunny day in May when Eddie finally crossed the stage at Madison Square Garden to receive his BA with a triple major in Special Honors, Classical Studies and History.[78] The keynote speaker was Congresswoman and former Vice Presidential candidate Geraldine Ferraro. When Ferraro read off the names of the Phi Beta Kappas during the ceremony, Eddie Buczynski, the only male member of that class of honorees, was omitted from the list. Eddie's parents were terribly hurt by this, and Marie wanted to give Ferraro a piece of her mind after the ceremony for not reading his name, but Eddie told them to let it go.[79] He had better things to do than worry about petty slights. This was a day for celebrating, and the family certainly had good reason to do so, for he was the first of their family to graduate from college. Eddie went off to Bryn Mawr that summer, taking the cats with him. Gene continued to occupy the West 13th Street apartment, which was now much quieter and just a little less crowded.

Chapter 31: The Bryn Mawr College Years

The Lure of Bryn Mawr College

The small village of Bryn Mawr, whose name means "high hill" in Welsh, is appropriately nestled in the forested hills of Pennsylvania eleven miles west of Philadelphia in an area of the state settled predominantly by Welsh Quakers in the mid 1600s. Founded in 1683, Bryn Mawr is a bustling upscale town of old Tudor, frame and stone homes, ancient trees, and small shops sitting athwart the main thoroughfare of Lancaster Avenue; a place where the local Jaguar dealer is plopped down next to the convenience store, and where the quaint train station still actively serves to connect the community to distant Philadelphia. It is wedged cheek by jowl amongst the towns of Rosemont, Haverford and Villanova, all of which, like Bryn Mawr, have small private universities named for them. If one ventures off of Lancaster Avenue and wanders up North Merion Avenue, the street gradually narrows and large trees crowd in close as if to guard a secret. Over a bridge and around a bend, the trees suddenly part like the curtain of a proscenium to reveal a shining gothic cathedral of flying buttresses, stained glass and waving flags. The Goodhart Theatre, a basilica of the performing arts, is a foretaste of what awaits the visitor within the magickal inner world of Bryn Mawr College.

The 135 acres of Bryn Mawr College clearly comprise one of the most beautiful college campuses in the United States. Crossing its boundary is like stepping through the looking glass into a world of Welsh castles, soaring oaks, rustling ancient pines, and green, green hills. Its crenelated battlements, looking as if Caernarfon Castle had been transplanted from Wales to Pennsylvania, were designed by the Philadelphia architecture firm Cope & Stewardson and represent the first examples of the "collegiate gothic" style of architecture that later influenced the design of many college campuses in the United States. The rolling hills of the campus function as an academic pasture, where young minds are plumped on the rich forage of Yeats and Plutarch, enzyme chemistry and Anatolian archaeology, child psychology and classical Greek sculpture. The school is blessed, as Richmond Lattimore explains, with "fresh lawns and towers not of ivory."[1]

Bryn Mawr College was founded in 1885 at the bequest of Joseph W. Taylor, a Quaker physician, who saw a pressing need to facilitate "the advanced education of females." Other women's colleges existed in the United States at the time, but until the advent of Bryn Mawr College the graduate education of women through the PhD level was exceedingly rare. The college was originally established with a secondary mission, that being to inculcate conservative young women in the beliefs of the Society of Friends. But early in its history, the school's second President, M. Cary Thomas, and a majority of the Trustees steered the institution toward a non-denominational path, allowing the school to compete academically with certain European institutions and the great universities. However, this change was not accomplished without resistance, and President Thomas was forced to defend her decision from the pressure of some trustees who wished to return the school to a more conservative path. On one occasion she refused the demand, made on religious grounds, to omit Shakespeare's and other Elizabethan plays from the school's lectures and library and from the students' private rooms. Despite this change and the subsequent challenges, the school continues to honor key Quaker principles, such as freedom of conscience and freedom of inquiry, and strongly emphasizes consensus-building, peace studies and conflict resolution.

Living up to this moral framework, while easy in theory, has proved quite costly to the college during periods of social unrest. On two occasions in the college's history, the Bryn Mawr trustees were forced to make the difficult decision of sticking to the school's founding principles and risking the loss of educational grants and student loan monies, rather than capitulating to the government's attempts to coerce institutions of higher learning into complying with dictates that challenged the freedom of its students. In the 1950s, during the communist witch hunts driven by the likes of Senator Joseph McCarthy and the House Un-American Activities Committee, Congress required students applying for college loans to sign a loyalty oath to the United States and an affidavit denying membership in the Communist Party. In the 1960s, at the height of student protests against the Vietnam War, colleges were required to report student protesters or face the loss of government scholarship support. In both cases, Bryn Mawr College led the nation by refusing to comply and instead made up the lost funding through donations. In the latter case, the government eventually lost a court challenge that had claimed the requirement to be unconstitutional.[2]

Bryn Mawr's history includes many such instances, from the support of the women's suffrage movement at the turn of the twentieth century, to the promotion of labor rights and establishment in the 1920s of the first PhD program in social work in the country, and the sponsorship of academic refugees from the fascist dictatorships of Spain, Italy and Germany in the 1930s and 1940s. Such dedication to a higher moral principle, while rare even in the lofty province of academia, is the birthmark of an institution that prides itself on an Old World style of education, and it is something that has virtually disappeared from today's halls of higher learning.

This social conscience would have appealed to Eddie Buczynski at a very basic level. As Gene Muto noted many years later, Eddie possessed a left-leaning worldview that found little resonance with the predatory practices of the Republican right that had swept the country in the 1980s with the election of Ronald Reagan.[3] Bryn Mawr's commitment to social equality and community service fit in both with the post-Vatican II social activist Catholicism of the United States, which informed his early adult life in the 1960s, and with the basic principles of the magick that he practiced in occult settings from the 1970s onward. To manifest change in this world required not only commitment and discipline in the mental and spiritual realms, but also action on the physical plane. From that standpoint, Bryn Mawr was an ideal setting in which to study and prosper.

Beginning in the mid-to-late 1960s, college campuses across the United States became laboratories for social experimentation and activism. In particular, young adults were more open to exploring alternative ways of expressing themselves sexually. Bryn Mawr, like most venerable old schools, had a mixed record in this regard. While not possessing a *laissez faire* approach to personal conduct (as demonstrated by the high regard in which its jointly-administered student-faculty honors code was held), the school historically strove to balance personal conscience and choice with societal expectations of conduct in line with its Quaker roots. Thus, while the early days of the college saw efforts to crack down on women smoking in their rooms and shimmying in and out of dormitory windows at night to avoid being caught out after curfew, they also witnessed the then unique experiment of student self-government, begun in 1892 and continuing to the present. However, most of the moral strictures placed upon students had essentially vanished from Bryn Mawr well before the 1980s, as they had in most other schools in the United States.

Although Bryn Mawr's graduate school of Arts and Sciences had been co-educational since 1931, the undergraduate college remains the domain of women to this day. This dedication to women also extends to non-traditional students, who are served by the McBride Scholars Program for those who have come to higher education later in life. As a women's undergraduate school, it shares its place of honor with the other so-called Seven Sisters Colleges — Mt. Holyoke, Wellesley, Barnard, Vassar, Radcliffe and Smith.[4] Sex-segregated institutions have long been recognized as places that provide opportunities for men or women to explore same sex relationships, and Bryn Mawr has been no exception. Indeed, the college can arguably be said to have had a lesbian presence on campus for 100 years by the time Eddie arrived, spanning from the appointment of M. Carey Thomas as dean of the as yet unborn school in 1883 to the activities of the Lesbian Support Group that existed in 1985 when he enrolled.[5] The feminist movement of the 1970s, in conjunction with the long-standing tradition of personal empowerment promoted by the school, had fostered a very liberal setting in which students could experiment in their social development, and this attitude naturally permeated to the graduate schools. Eddie's professors, graduate classmates and undergraduate contemporaries confirm that Bryn Mawr in the mid-to-late 1980s was known as a safe haven for gays and lesbians. As one "Mawrter" put it, the undergraduate folk wisdom was that if you hadn't slept with someone of your own gender before you went there, you would by the time you graduated.[6] Or, as an inside joke states:[7]

> Q: *What do you call it when a Bryn Mawr woman comes out?*
> A: *Her sophomore year.*

While obviously said in jest, the attitude underlying these statements demonstrates a generally non-judgmental and accepting atmosphere that would have been essential to one who had come to sexual maturity in the hothouse environment of New York City in the 1960s and 1970s as Eddie had.

Climbing the Acropolis

As ground-breaking as Bryn Mawr has been over the years, it remains a campus steeped in tradition. One saying has it that anything that happens twice on the campus becomes a tradition. It is certainly true that the college possesses some unique, beautiful and quite esoteric customs and rituals that work to simultaneously charm and bind the community together. As with the school's unique student-led government, its traditions also arise as a manifestation of the will of the student body. College President Nancy J. Vickers notes that Bryn Mawr "is an intensely built community ... in part because traditions are student run and so much a part of the life of the College."[8] Most of these activities are solely within the domain of the undergraduate school, where Traditions Mistresses ensure that the lore of the college is passed from one generation of students to the next. By holding true to its traditions, Bryn Mawr has reinforced the place of women as the glue that holds society together. Francine du Plessix Gray states that "By our fidelity to the historic female need to safeguard the past, we will wrap the tomorrow of tomorrow, we will preserve the quality of quality."[9]

Bryn Mawr has historically attracted an independent sort of student; one with an appreciation for the antique, unconventional and even quirky. Thus, for example, we see the excitement and affection with which the students, faculty and surrounding community generally greet the annual May Day celebrations, a tradition dating back to 1904. Where else in these days in the United States, other than in the rituals of Neo-Pagan gatherings or the festivities of certain Germanic societies, does one see a community come together to dance around the Maypole in order to bring the summer in? Yet at Bryn Mawr, after the traditional breakfast of strawberries and cream and a parade led by bagpipers and the college President, each class dances at its own Maypole bedecked in its class color on the Merion

Green. Afterwards, Morris dancers trot their ancient steps, the freshwomen gather flowers for the upper classes, the seniors race their hoops, the actors present their plays, and the musicians play and sing their songs. The closest collegiate approximation to this celebration would be a homecoming weekend, and yet that comparison would do a grave injustice, for Bryn Mawr's May Day is an observation of a gentler, courtlier ideal by far.

In the 1970s and 1980s, the school attracted a large number of students who prided themselves on a deep knowledge of things medieval and Celtic, including ancient folkloric practices and rituals.[10] Among these students was Eddie who, having once danced the Maypole with his fellow Witches in Central Park, would have cherished the Pagan fertility ritual at the root of Bryn Mawr's May Day tradition. The mystical current of another Bryn Mawr tradition would also have resonated with him. In mid-November at Lantern Night, the sophomores present each freshwoman with a lantern in a complex and beautiful night ritual of colored lights and song. Each lantern has glass panes tinted in one color signifying the owner's school class. The colors (light blue, red, dark blue, and green) together with the purple that all McBride Scholars receive, are designed to represent the elements of Greek hermetic magick — air, fire, water, earth, and spirit, respectively. While not a direct participant of this ceremony himself, being a graduate student and a male, Eddie would have appreciated the ritual and its magickal symbolism.

That Pagan symbolism abounds at Bryn Mawr is not surprising; the school has continued to foster the concept of a classical education long after it has gone out of vogue with the increasingly compartmentalized and industrial mindset of American higher learning. Such "casual Paganism," starting with Renaissance Europe's rediscovery of its past and influenced by the splintering of the Enlightenment into the romantic, aesthetic and decadent movements, was a mark of a late Victorian university education that was steeped in the arts and of the classics read in their native tongues. In remembrance of this transition, Bryn Mawr continues to sing its traditional songs in ancient Greek and is (alas!) one of the last schools in the United States to do so. Two of these songs honor and call upon the Goddesses of Victory and of Wisdom. Of Victory, they sing:[11]

> *Anassa Kata, kalo kale,*
> *Ia ia ia Nike,*
> *Bryn Mawr, Bryn Mawr, Bryn Mawr!*
>
> *(Queen, descend, I invoke You, Fair One,*
> *Hail, hail, hail, Victory,*
> *Bryn Mawr, Bryn Mawr, Bryn Mawr!)*

The Anassa Kata is used by the students to invoke the Greek Goddess Nike to see them to victory, and is traditionally started by the seniors and taken up by the other students at sporting events and at other times throughout the year. It is a rousing call. But the most beloved school song is arguably the hymn to Pallas Athena, the Goddess of wisdom and Matron of the college:[12]

Pallas Athena thea,
Mathe matos kais thenous,
Se par hemeies imen
Hiru-sousai soi deine.

(Pallas Athena, Goddess of learning and strength
We come to You to worship You, dread Goddess.)

Makarize, ai-toumen
Hemin sophian didou
Hemin syngignou aei
Makar thea akoue.

(Bless us we pray; give us wisdom.
Be with us always, Blessed Goddess, hear!)

Hierize nyn tous lykhnous
Aei phanos phaoien
Lampry nontes ten hodon
Melan phanon poi-ountes.

(Sanctify our lanterns now, to shine forever clearly,
Lighting the way, making bright the dark.)

The hymn to Athena is sung at all formal school occasions, including the Step-sings that are held during the major traditions, such as Parade Night and Lantern Night, alumnae reunions and graduation ceremonies. It dates to the turn of the twentieth century and was a source of controversy when it was sung at a Chapel lecture in 1904. A Trustee of the school and his daughter made an enraged complaint to President Thomas at that time, saying that "it was irreverent and pagan and a hymn to a heathen goddess, sung like a benediction standing."[13]

President Thomas shrugged off the complaint. When in her twenty-second year, Thomas had become heavily influenced by the writings of such authors as Algernon Charles Swinburne.[14] Swinburne, a Victorian poet of the aesthetic movement, celebrated and explored the concepts of Paganism and unconventional eroticism. It is not difficult, therefore, to understand the tolerance with which a college administration headed by

Thomas greeted the birth of such "irreverent" traditions, and may even have had an unconscious hand in encouraging them.[15] Pallas Athena continues to be "sung like a benediction standing" at Bryn Mawr by strong women in honor of a strong role model, Pagan Goddess or no.

A ten-foot-tall statue of Pallas Athena resides on campus in a sunlit corner of Thomas Great Hall. In that cavernous neo-Gothic temple of dark wainscoting, rich carpets, bright flags and diamond-paned windows, the students make votive offerings to Her throughout the year for guidance, wisdom, sporting triumphs and the inevitable help on tests and term papers. On the night before May Day, the Traditions Mistresses are said to conduct rituals designed to propitiate Athena in the hope of a dry May Day. "It's a site of ritual," explains archaeology professor James Wright. "There are always offerings to Athena. It's extraordinary. It's really extraordinary."[16]

Athena's familiar owl, whose name may well be σοφός ("sophos," or wisdom), roosts in the keystone of the arch of Rockefeller Hall, much as its living model continues to make its home in the nooks and crannies of the Acropolis.[17] She is found in carvings here and there throughout the campus, and is present in triplicate upon the school crest.[18] The owl, said by some to be a primeval form of the Goddess Athena, is the protector of the school.[19] In the past, one of the duties of the Traditions Mistresses was to provide for the "care and feeding" of the owl. At the beginning of the school year, the Mistresses would process clockwise around the campus to "wake" the owl, and at the end of the year they would process counterclockwise to put the owl back to sleep. Witchcraft practitioners will, of course, recognize in these rituals a reflection of their own magickal practices — the clockwise or "sunwise" (i.e., deosil, in Wiccan parlance) invocation of a Power and the counterclockwise (i.e., widdershins) dismissal of the invoked Power when it is no longer needed. In truth, by "waking" the owl one is really invoking the spirit of wisdom, or Sophia, that lies at the heart of Bryn Mawr's traditions in order to guide the faculty and students on their path to knowledge in the service of humankind:[20]

> *Sophias philai paromen,*
> *Philokaloumen met euteleias,*
> *Philosophoumen aneu malakias*
> *Plouto ergou kairo crometha.*
> *Athlon ariston kai kindunon tonde kalliston nomizomen.*
> *Enthoumometha orthos hosa praxomen orthos.*
> *Kalon to athlon kai elpis megale, elpis megale.*
> *Elpis megale, nai megale.*
>
> *(Friends of wisdom, let us gather.*
> *We love beauty with simplicity.*
> *We love wisdom without softness.*

*We use our talent to accomplish deeds.
This is the finest achievement,
And this is the venture we consider noble.
We have proper pride
In what we have achieved.
The achievement is worthy,
And our hope is great, hope is great.
Hope is great, yea, great.)*

A Pagan current does indeed run just below the school's Judeo-Christian veneer; however, it does so mainly as an outgrowth of the quest for knowledge as expressed within a Socratic framework of inquiry. Students at Bryn Mawr are generally expected to take an active role in their own education and in the development of their campus community. They are also expected to have the maturity and drive to undergo a regimen of self-directed inquiry, particularly at the graduate level, that is augmented by the challenges and guidance of their professors. This approach to education is one of the most valuable legacies of the ancient Greeks, and it can be intimidating for those accustomed to being led by the hand and spoon-fed their studies. Eddie Buczynski would have found this concept quite appealing in his pursuit of knowledge, for it is the same spirit of intellectual exploration that he practiced throughout his adult life and encouraged in his Craft students in the 1970s and early 1980s.

Towers Not of Ivory

The dog days of summer lay heavy on both New York and Philadelphia in July 1985 when Eddie packed up his belongings and moved to Pennsylvania's "high hill." This move marked a sea change in Eddie's relationship with Gene. From this point on, each man would be living on his own. Gene fully supported Eddie's decision to move to Bryn Mawr, even though they would be apart. Gene himself was trying to decide where his own career would lead, as he finished his doctoral work in theatre at NYU. Being apart for an extended period of time is rarely easy on a relationship, but Gene noted many years later that both men were mature adults and trusted one another implicitly. *(Ibid n#3)*

Graduate students were not obligated to make use of the school housing at Bryn Mawr College. As an older student who had been on his own for quite a while, Eddie preferred to have his own place. Eileen Markson, the head of the Rhys Carpenter Library at Bryn Mawr, received a note from Tamara Green in the summer of 1985 asking her to help Eddie find a place to live. Eileen gave him a number of leads, and he settled on a small but cozy one-bedroom apartment at Thornbrook Manor.[21] The Thornbrook, located at 819 Montgomery Avenue just down the street from Eileen's home, was an older apartment complex of neatly kept three-story brick buildings that were partially camouflaged from the street by brooding, ancient pine trees that grew up close to its walls.

Montgomery Avenue is a heavily traveled, tree-lined thoroughfare of large homes, apartments and administrative buildings located just south of campus. The ground-floor apartment that Eddie chose was ideally located, being a mere two blocks from campus, and one block north of the Bryn Mawr train station and the downtown shopping district. Muto hauled Eddie's possessions and helped him to get established, and also brought the cats to keep him company. In short order, Buczynski had managed to fix up the place in, as Eileen noted, "charming good taste." *(Ibid n#21)* He covered the hardwood floors with area rugs and filled the apartment with bookcases overflowing with his books on history, archaeology, art, religion and the occult.

The small living room just inside the door was converted for use as an office. There he placed his faithful writing desk and trusty old typewriter, which was soon supplanted by an Apple Macintosh with an ImageWriter printer. He also had a video player, still a rarity in those days. The combined kitchen/dining area had no dining table, serving instead as the living room in lieu of the area which Eddie had converted into office space. Eddie established a shrine to the Minoan Mother Goddess at shoulder height on one of the bookcase shelves in the makeshift living room, something he had not had room for (or felt the freedom to do) in the tiny New York apartment. Before long, the kitchen window that overlooked the courtyard was filled with plants, just as Eddie had filled the windows of every other apartment in which he had lived. Overall, it was luxuriously spacious in comparison to the apartment he had shared with Gene, and Maybelle and Grimalkin finally had some room to roam.

Aside from his summer stint at the ASCSA in 1982, this was the first time that Eddie had ever been away from New York City and his friends for any significant length of time. He was both nervous and excited at his prospects in graduate school. These feelings were compounded somewhat by a slight, and quite unfounded, sense of inferiority that Eddie felt because of his late academic start in life. *(Ibid n#16)* At 38, he was one of the oldest students on campus. Nevertheless, Eddie was delighted at the opportunity to study there. He took the challenge in stride — and challenging it was.

According to Brunilde Ridgway, Rhys Carpenter Professor Emerita of Archaeology at Bryn Mawr College, the school's course of study in archaeology was "more rigorous than prestigious."[22] This is perhaps a bit of modesty on the award-winning professor's part. In 1983, Bryn Mawr's Department of Classical and Near Eastern Archaeology was ranked among the ten best in the country by the Conference Board of Associated Research Councils, along with the graduate departments of art history, Greek and Latin.[23] Together, these separate departments formed an incredibly strong interdisciplinary matrix of great academic depth. The importance of having a working knowledge in the academic fields touching upon one's chosen area has long been recognized at Bryn Mawr. Archaeology students have historically been encouraged to broaden their studies with coursework in all of these adjoining areas that together make up what we refer to as "the classics." As Mawrter Emily Vermeule put it:[24]

> *The student of tragedy must know history; the student of archaeology must know Lucretius and Homer. Bryn Mawr was a place that expected good ancient languages of its art historians in the ancient field and a knowledge of vase painting by students of myth.*

This interdisciplinary approach, in combination with the school's concomitant drive toward academic excellence and original thought, formed an unshakable foundation for the archaeology curriculum at Bryn Mawr. At its founding in 1885, the school had established an archaeology curriculum; by 1896, it had become the art and archaeology department. Classical archaeology as a discipline assumed its place as an independent department at Bryn Mawr in 1914, becoming one of the first such established in the country. The school began participating in the mission of the ASCSA and at the Classical School of the American Academy in Rome very early on, and its faculty members have taught at and directed them both at various times throughout their respective histories.[25, 26] Since its earliest days, Bryn Mawr has maintained archaeological digs throughout the Near East, from Cilicia to Anatolia, from Greece to Crete. For a college of its size, its influence in the field of Classical and Near Eastern archaeology in research, publications and graduate progeny has far exceeded all expectations save, perhaps, those of Bryn Mawr herself. It was into this storied environment that the boy from Queens stepped.

When Eddie enrolled in 1985, the department was headed by the distinguished Dr. Machteld J. Mellink. Machteld was a world-renowned expert on Anatolian archaeology and recent past chair of the AIA, which was the post that Eddie's previous mentor, Clairève Grandjouan, had previously held.[27] Machteld had spent many years excavating sites in Turkey, studying the Bronze Age civilizations of the coast, including that of Troy, and investigating the influence of that part of the world on the cultural cross-fertilization of the Eurasian land mass. In 1934, Bryn Mawr became the first United States college to organize a dig in Turkey at Tarsus.[28] From 1949, when she came to teach at Bryn Mawr, Mellink gladly continued that effort by participating in digs at Tarsus and Gordion and leading the excavation of Elmali, and she used the opportunity to train new generations of students in the nuts and bolts of field work. *(Ibid n#27)*

Mellink was tough, exemplifying the Bryn Mawr tradition of fielding intelligent and self-sufficient women, whether it be a Hetty Goldman (BA, 1903) excavating Mediterranean sites at the start of the Graeco-Turkish

War or a Katherine Hepburn (BA, 1928) shooting on location in the Belgian Congo for the film *The African Queen*. After spending long hours at the dig site by day, Machteld would spend the evening writing her widely-read Turkish archaeological newsletter by flashlight. *(Ibid n#28)* In her rare free time, she might be found dancing in Tarsus or racing horses across the Anatolian plateau. She was not without a sense of humor, having once convinced 500 cruise passengers that she was having an affair with a fellow passenger, whom she mischievously named Heinrich Schliemann.[29] Eddie adored her.

In accordance with the expectations of its Chair and its own long history of excellence, the Department of Classical and Near Eastern Archaeology laid out a tough curriculum that demanded the best of its students. Eddie was forced to spend time early in his studies playing catch-up in the basics of archaeology because his time at Hunter College gave him a stronger background in the Classics. *(Ibid n#22)* His weak grasp of the German language was also a handicap in his primary studies. Much of the research in Classical and Near Eastern archaeology is published in French and German, as those two countries fielded many of the premiere archaeologists during the nineteenth century and much of the twentieth. He spent much valuable time gaining the proficiency he needed to carry on his studies.

Besides providing new students with any necessary remedial help, the archaeology professors had yet another burden thrust upon them by the mass media of the 1980s, that being to administer a dose of reality on the subject of their chosen career. The film *Raiders of the Lost Ark* was released in theatres in June 1981, and later *Indiana Jones and the Temple of Doom* in May 1984. The Indiana Jones movies came on the heels of the massively popular touring exhibit of priceless artifacts from the tomb of Pharaoh Tutankhamen that stormed the United States from 1976 to 1979.[30] In the wake of those events, archaeology programs across the country were forced by necessity to throw cold water in the faces of a few starry-eyed incoming students who dreamed of a romantic life as a bullwhip-toting treasure seeker in a battered fedora.[31,32]

In the introductory briefing for prospective graduate students, the Bryn Mawr professors made it quite clear that archaeology comprised three-quarters research in the dusty library stacks and one-quarter backbreaking, dirty field work. Furthermore, even after all the hard work of graduate school, it was tough to get a job, because there were few openings in any given year, and even when a graduate did manage to land a position, there was not a lot of money in it. *(Ibid n#22)* To paraphrase Harrison Ford's character, the closest that an archaeologist ever gets to an actual "X marks the spot" is when he or she obtains an official's signature on the necessary excavation permits required by the host government.[33] Fortunately Eddie's interest in the field was not motivated by the mass media or the prospect of great riches. He had developed his love affair with both books and Near Eastern history early in life.

As in other new environments to which he was exposed, the Queens native rapidly made new friends among his fellow students and professors. "He had a charm about him," said his lover, Gene Muto, an assessment with which many who had met Buczynski agreed. *(Ibid n#3)* "I remember Eddie with great fondness," wrote Pamela Webb, a faculty member of Bryn Mawr who was, in 1985, a fellow graduate student at the college. "I was a student at Hunter before Eddie entered the program there. I was the first student to convince Professor Clairève Grandjouan to write a letter of recommendation to her alma mater, Bryn Mawr College. A few years later, I believe Eddie became only the second person to be accepted from Hunter into the graduate program at Bryn Mawr. So he and I felt we were part of a very small, very special group. Clairève had received her Ph.D. at Bryn Mawr with Bruni Ridgway, one of the most illustrious scholars in the field of Greek sculpture in the twentieth century. Clairève, too, was world renowned, and both Eddie and I considered it a privilege to be able study with these remarkable scholars."[34]

Ridgway downplays such lofty praise, but she, too, believed that Buczynski had found inspiration from Clairève Grandjouan, who Brunilde described as a tremendously inspiring teacher. *(Ibid n#22)* But Ridgway was an inspiring teacher in her own right. A student of the formidable classical art historian Rhys Carpenter at Bryn Mawr, she continued to advance her mentor's work throughout her own career, becoming, by the time Eddie entered the college, one of the world's foremost experts of ancient Greek statuary. It was Carpenter who, at the behest of Bryn Mawr President Martha Carey Thomas, established the Department of Classical Archaeology at the college in 1914. Thus, it could be argued that Buczynski and Webb were both the beneficiaries of a long line of academic giants.

"Bryn Mawr's program had the reputation of being one of the best," writes Michael Hornum. "So it would have been a challenge to get into, and this does speak well for Eddie's intelligence and commitment. His greatest academic interest appeared to be in Minoan civilization. He was a good student and diligent researcher in my collaborations with him. ... Professionally, Eddie and I collaborated on a couple of seminar papers."[35] Asli Özyar, a former graduate classmate who is now a professor of history at Boğaziçi University in Turkey, concurs, citing a high-quality paper on the Early Bronze Age West Anatolian Coast as an example of Buczynski's capabilities.[36] Asli, the last of Machteld Mellink's graduate advisees, is in a good position to judge, for after graduation she was charged with defining for the Turkish government the ten key areas of Anatolian archaeology that require future investigation. Janice Kamrin, then a University of Pennsylvania student taking classes at Bryn Mawr, notes that Eddie "was very serious about [his studies], dedicated to it, and seemed to be very good. We were all Bryn Mawrters together, and you don't make it there unless you know your stuff. ... His class presentations were excellent. ... As a colleague, Eddie was also very generous with time and expertise."[37]

Kamrin, who was a highly-regarded assistant to Dr. Zahi Hawass in Egypt's Supreme Council of Antiquities until the Arab Spring of 2011, remembers Eddie, whom she first met in a seminar with Machteld Mellink about Aegean archaeology, with great fondness. "Although I did not know him for a long time, we got fairly close rapidly, because he was such an open, unpretentious, warm person," recalls Kamrin. "We had great fun in class, which was very intellectually stimulating and from which we all learned a lot, and also hung out together — Eddie, myself, and two of the other students from the class especially. We were also drawn together more intensely by the attempted suicide of one of our small gang — she didn't show up to class one day, and had left a variety of 'clues' with us, especially with Eddie. So at break time we went down to her apartment, and basically got there just in time. That sort of thing does tend to break down barriers, not that Eddie really had many to start with." *(Ibid n#37)*

Ridgway describes Eddie as a very kind and sensitive man. To illustrate this point, she also cites the attempted suicide by the student, whom she described as a lesbian from Sweden. Eddie attempted to help the woman, drawing on his experience in counseling coven members, bolstered as it was with his own experience as a gay man who had attempted suicide in the past. In the end, however, the student was sent back to her home country. Eddie's thoughtfulness also manifested itself in his studies. "Eddie was very talented and artistically sensitive," Ridgway notes. "He was concerned with the human side of his studies." *(Ibid n#22)* In this, Buczynski might be said to be carrying on the tradition set by the Department's founder, Rhys Carpenter, who had argued for the humanistic value of archaeology.

Another of Eddie's friends and fellow students, Nathan Meyer, concurs with this assessment of a very human side to Eddie's approach to the material. "[Eddie was] engaging, full of laughter and ease about himself and life. ... I remember him as having primarily an emotional or intuitive relationship to the art and iconography, but being smart enough and disciplined enough to know there was more than that in terms of empirical data," wrote Meyer. "He was on a full scholarship, I believe, and you could tell he was very keen in his mind. It was just that being smart was not the biggest part of Eddie; it was very much subordinate to his intuitive feel for things. I knew also that he had come from an a-traditional background in terms of academics but had succeeded marvelously in a traditional world. I liked that. You have to realize that in our same classes there were some folks who had been born with a silver spoon in their mouth (or perhaps elsewhere) and Eddie just sort of glided over/around that."[38]

Kamrin characterized Buczynski as "Warm, giving, funny, [with] little tolerance for bullshit. Just a lovely man." *(Ibid n#37)* Asli Özyar remembers Eddie as someone who went well out of his way to help his fellows, a man who was about as far away from an entitlement mentality as one could get. "He was always cheerful and a good friend. ... I was the newcomer, coming from Turkey, overseas that is, and was trying to find out about the college and graduate school and everything. He was extremely helpful and friendly, a bit like an older brother. Once, I wanted to take an anthropology course at University of Pennsylvania and he was interested in using the [University] library. So we took the local train and went there together, he helped me to register there, as well." *(Ibid n#36)*

The additional pressures inherent in graduate school certainly hadn't dampened Buczynski's sense of humor. Alice Donohue relates an ongoing scheme she and Eddie concocted on how to become rich and toss their worries to the winds. "From time to time we discussed, with appropriate mimed juicing motions, a project to become tycoons through making and marketing Uncle Eddie's Homemade Clam Juice with Juicy Bits of Clam; it seemed funny after a day of reading excavation reports."[39] The real joke was that peddling clam juice was probably more likely to make one rich than writing those excavation reports, and yet somehow this reality has failed to discourage generations of highly dedicated archaeologists, including Eddie and Alice.

Even more than his time at Hunter, Eddie's class comprised a very close group of students who were very supportive of him and each other. *(Ibid n#22)* James Wright, current Chair of the Department, remembers this as being a highly energetic period in the Department's history. "[Eddie] was very much beloved by students here and socialized with them," Wright says. "I don't think that he was the life of the party, but he added much to the social mix. And that was a time when we had a really — well I shouldn't say that it was a time when we had a really great social group of students as if we don't have that today — but there was something *tremendous* about the students then, partly perhaps [because] I had a big program in Greece that attracted a lot of students to the program. They were very committed, they were very well trained, [and] they made seminars work at a very high level. ... And so it was a dynamic period, and he added to that with his interest and enthusiasm." *(Ibid n#16)*

"[Eddie was] full of laughter and ease about himself and life. ... I remember him as being just wonderfully engaging and interesting to be next to," writes Nathan Meyer. "I remember him secondarily as being GAY! in a very traditional setting and being utterly comfortable with that. ... He made absolutely no attempt to disguise it, which of course at that time was a political statement itself. I remember discussing only in the context of a bigger story his connection to the gay community. I had lived in [San Francisco] in the Castro and had a gay brother so perhaps it was just not so relevant to the way we interacted. I can say that I never perceived any difference in the way Eddie was treated by the Bryn Mawr faculty." *(Ibid n#38)*

Classmate Michael Hornum concurs, noting, "I remember Eddie as bright, personable, and funny. ... He made no attempt to hide [his sexual orientation], and I don't remember it causing him any problems. In fact, sometimes his orientation made for humorous and insightful comments on his part — I remember one in which several graduate students (myself included) were debating whether a particular ancient image was circumcised or not, and Eddie commented something like, 'I have seen many a phallus and this one definitely was circumcised.' I think Bryn Mawr was quite liberal about sexual orientation." *(Ibid n#35)*

Like the undergraduate school, Bryn Mawr's graduate schools were fairly open to the presence of gay and lesbian students at the time. A case in point was recent graduate Paul Rehak, who earned his MA at Bryn Mawr in 1980 and his PhD there in 1985, just ahead of Eddie's arrival. Rehak was a popular student with an inquisitive mind in the Department of Classical and Near Eastern Archaeology, whose own research interests included ancient sexuality and gender roles. Machteld Mellink and Brunilde Ridgway were quite fond of him. As an openly gay man who was very active in Philadelphia, where he lived while in school, Rehak may have broken ground for Buczynski in the Department.[40,41] But, as noted, it isn't as if Bryn Mawr College was particularly closed-minded on this subject.

"He was completely accepted," says Professor James Wright. "It wasn't an issue, partly because it's a women's college, but partly because the whole issue of sexuality had already been dealt with here by and large. There are lesbians at this school; there always have been. And I think by that time people were open about it." For his part, Wright had absolutely no problem with Buczynski's sexual orientation, since the teacher who had brought Wright into the field of archaeology was himself a gay man who Jim greatly respected. "So, personally, to me it just was in no way an issue. But not in the sense that I would have ignored it. But rather it was something that could be talked about if one wanted to talk about it. Eddie was quite open about it. He didn't hide it; he didn't advertise it. He just was who he was. And that was fine." *(Ibid n#16)*

Eddie and his fellow students started their long school days with coffee in the commons. "I first met Eddie in the large communal gathering hall at Bryn Mawr College," recalls Nathan Meyer. "It was the place where every morning (at least in 1986) there was a bad coffee and cake donut breakfast served. Food was not the point; gathering was the point." *(Ibid n#38)* Classmate Pamela Webb writes, "My fondest memory of Eddie was sitting at one of the small round tables in Thomas Great Hall every morning between 10 and 11 during campus coffee hour. We railed at the imbecilities of the Reagan administration, shared our stories, and laughed a lot." *(Ibid n#34)*

The remainder of a typical day was spent in lectures and seminars, interspersed with long hours of research in the Art and Archaeology

Library (later replaced by the Rhys Carpenter Library). "Many students were there late into the night," remembers Michael Hornum. *(Ibid n#35)* Eddie became a familiar face at the library, not only because of his own studies there, but from his Bibliographical Assistant position in the department. *(Ibid n#21)* In the process, he also became good friends with the head librarian, Eileen Markson, who lived only a block away from his apartment. Eileen had been Clairève Grandjouan's best friend at Bryn Mawr, and this would also have provided a link between Eddie and her. *(Ibid n#16)*

Still, the students didn't spend all of their time at the grindstone. They had one another over to their apartments for dinner and relaxed at department get-togethers. *(Ibid n#35)* And there were the undergraduate activities, especially the May Day celebrations that would have intrigued Eddie. But they were far too busy to simply "hang out." Despite being fully engaged in graduate school, Buczynski managed to keep up a long-running correspondence with distant friends, fellow students and former professors. Tamara Green recalls receiving many enthusiastic postcards from Greece.[42] Hunter classmate Phyllis Saretta says that when Eddie went off to Bryn Mawr, "We spoke on the phone quite often. He wanted me to visit him in Pennsylvania and stay with him, but I never had the opportunity to do so. He also sent me some postcards. But when he came to New York we spent some time together."[43] Buczynski also managed to keep up a workout regimen to stay in shape — a hard thing to do in graduate school, which is a world renowned for pasty-skinned mole people. "He loved to talk about working out," remembers Asli Özyar. "He liked to hear that he looked very young for his age. I was 16 years younger, and he looked almost my equal, or so I thought." *(Ibid n#36)*

Hornum, Meyer and Markson took turns looking after Eddie's apartment and the cats when he was travelling, which was several times a year. During the winter break of 1985, Eddie and Gene spent time in Egypt and Israel. "We both hated Israel but loved Egypt," said Gene Muto. "We took a cruise on the Nile. When we got to Jerusalem it was like a fucking prisoner camp. We got lost on the sabbat in a car in the Hassidic section and they wanted to stone us. And we couldn't get out. It was like a maze. We went to Tel Aviv that afternoon and Tel Aviv was absolutely terrific. It was exactly what we were looking for. In Jerusalem the food was great. The first Middle Eastern meal you get is like thirty things to eat. But the second time it gets to be old. In Tel Aviv, we ate Russian and Slavic, German, and everything.

"In Egypt we went to the major attractions, but we also went to Abu Simbel, which not everybody does. We took a flight there. We had some real adventures. It was not a new plane, that's for sure. And the airport was literally a Quonset hut. We took a bus [from the airport] to Abu Simbel, and on the bus on the way back they said 'Oh, your plane is gone.'" *(Ibid n#3)* Gene and Eddie weren't quite on the verge of panic, but they were seriously debating what they were going to do, since there was no hotel nearby and no other way back to Cairo. But they needn't have worried. As their bus rounded the Quonset hut, they saw the plane tucked away inside. Eddie ended up loaning the slides he took on this trip to Michael Hornum, who used them in his own studies. *(Ibid n#35)*

From the beginning of fall semester 1985, Eddie began to formulate the idea for his master's thesis. His original intention was to find and isolate a marine aspect in Minoan cult, an idea which grew out of a long-standing interest in Minoan religion that predated even his development of the Minoan Brotherhood in 1976. Buczynski had also experimented with the use of sea shells, especially tritons, in Neo-Pagan ritual, and this informed his choice of topic. Cretan archaeological discoveries also pointed to the important role of marine mollusks, such as the *Murex*, in the economy of Middle Minoan Crete. His thesis advisor, Machteld Mellink, cautioned him that such a comprehensive effort would be beyond the scope of a master's thesis. The process for the master's program is less formal than that for the doctorate, according to Brunilde Ridgway. However, the candidate was still required to write a thesis under supervision and then defend it before a committee.

Buczynski was still puzzling over how to limit his topic when he and Dr. Mellink attended a lecture on October 18 by Judith Shackleton of the University of Cambridge. Her subject, the archaeological interpretation of non-utilitarian uses of marine shells, inspired Eddie to look at the practical, artistic and cultic uses of marine shells in ancient Crete from the Neolithic through the Late Minoan periods. This subject had heretofore received very little attention. With the help of the aforementioned Mrs. Shackleton and Mr. David S. Reese, also a resident at the University of Cambridge and one of the world's foremost experts on the economic and biological aspects of mollusks in ancient Crete, Buczynski was off to a good start on his research.[44] Though passionate in general about archaeology, Eddie's true interest was in Minoan Crete, said Brunilde Ridgway, and Eddie's passion for the Minoan civilization was encouraged by Machteld, who loved the topic of his master's thesis. *(Ibid n#22, 36)*

During the spring semester of 1986, Eddie started to get the itch to teach Witchcraft again and wanted to try to start a Minoan Brotherhood Grove in the greater Philadelphia area. It was unlikely that he would find any takers for a gay men's coven in Bryn Mawr, so in March Eddie travelled the short distance by train to Philadelphia, where there was a large and diverse gay community. He left an advertisement for the Minoan Brotherhood in the postings section of a three-ring binder maintained by Giovanni's Room, a well-established gay bookstore. Within a week, a young student at the University of Pennsylvania, Kevin Moscrip, replied:[45]

> *I wrote him a letter, to which he responded. I was the first and from what I understand only to respond to the ad. We met a*

week or so later at the restaurant next door to Giovanni's Room, and had lunch or a snack or something, at which time we discussed who I was, what I had done magickally and spiritually and why I was interested in the Brotherhood. After the discussion, Eddie wanted to bring me in right away. I asked him to slow down and help me understand the commitment I was making. So over the spring and summer, I worked with him, reading books he recommended and asking him questions. He showed me the Laws, to help me understand what I was committing to uphold.

By the end of the summer, Buczynski and Moscrip both felt that Kevin was ready to be initiated into the Minoan Brotherhood. This took place on October 8, 1986. There is an open question as to why Buczynski wanted to pick up where he had left off in the Craft. By this time, he had arguably been away from active practice of Witchcraft for five years. The passing of his first teacher and high priestess, Gwen Thompson, from cancer in May undoubtedly had him reminiscing about the old days. His master's thesis, in which he was investigating the Minoan use of seashells in religious practices, also had him thinking of his beloved creation, the Minoan Brotherhood. But openly-practicing Neo-Pagans were a rarity then, as now, in the field of archaeology, and would have been viewed with considerable skepticism and concern about their objectivity, something to which Christian or Jewish archaeologists would rarely be subjected.

"He told me he missed it," writes Moscrip, explaining Buczynski's own rationale for deciding to teach once more. "She [the Goddess] was calling him back; [and] he missed being in circle. He missed working Magick, so he was responding to his heart's yearning, and starting up a grove again. ... I think he was doing it on the sly from Gene." *(Ibid n#4.5)* Gene Muto had finished graduate school in the spring of 1986, shortly after Eddie decided to get involved again in the Minoan Brotherhood. As his time in school was drawing to a close, Muto began searching for a job but could find nothing nearby. Although he would have liked to take a position in Philadelphia so that he and Eddie could take an apartment together, Gene knew that just wasn't going to happen in the current job market.

When an opportunity opened up in Augusta, Georgia for a tenure track position, Muto ended up taking it in August 1986. To celebrate Muto's graduation, Eddie and Gene took a trip to Cancun to explore Copal and Tolun, which was one of Gene's favorite sites. *(Ibid n#3)* By the end of the summer, Gene, who had despised Eddie's practice of Witchcraft, had settled in Augusta. Eddie came down for a visit, and Gene continued travelling to Bryn Mawr and New York every Christmas and when he had breaks from teaching. According to Muto, the distance didn't affect their relationship: "He was busy in graduate school, and I was busy teaching. We were adult enough and old enough — I was thirty-six when I left New York, he would have been thirty-seven." *(Ibid n#3)* But that understanding, as in the past, didn't quite extend to Eddie's interactions with his Minoan students, and didn't prevent him and Kevin from getting to know each other better over the summer. *(Ibid n#45)*

With Gene now settled far away in Georgia and unlikely to pop in on him on the weekend, Eddie may have taken this as a sign that his decision to reconvene his practice was acceptable to the Gods. Eddie's apartment was a decent size to host a small coven, so the two men weren't crowded when conducting the rites. He resisted the urge to tart up his apartment in nouveau Pagan décor, maintaining only a small Minoan Snake Goddess statue and labrys shrine with some seashells in the living room. Upon seeing it, most fellow students and professors would merely have assumed these items to be related to his graduate studies and deep interest in the Minoan civilization. "There were some candles about, and I recall some incense burners, but it was really very modest and normal from what I recall," writes Nathan Meyer. *(Ibid n#38)* A wooden, metal-banded footlocker was used for the altar. After rituals, Eddie used it to store his ritual tools and *Book of the Mysteries*, which he had begun to revise yet again to reflect information from his college studies."[46] *(Ibid n#45)*

Still, the few people at Bryn Mawr with whom he had discussed his Neo-Pagan past would see more to the room than might otherwise meet the eye. "[His occult interests] came up in small ways," Meyer remembers. "I stayed at his apartment so I was sort of in tune with various interests. The whole occult thing came up but in a very muted way ... it was just part of the whole fabric of Eddie. It was not like he walked around tooting it. It just was. Again, perhaps because I just took it in stride it was just there and not a big deal." Meyer continues, "I was aware that Eddie had that side to him but it was not something we discussed in much detail. I certainly had no idea how extensive it was. Both Eddie and I were into Minoan art and iconography and we discussed some of the 'pagan' ritual symbology. ... I always knew there was a lot more there than I had access to. Not because he hid things but just because he had lived a lot that I had not been around to witness and you can only yak so much a day." *(Ibid n#38)*

Michael Hornum was also aware of Eddie's past involvement with Wicca. "We had some overlapping academic interests, and also some overlapping religious interests — I was a student of Neo-Platonism, and through it had come to have respect for ancient 'paganism.' Since Eddie was into 'Wicca,' we had some rapport there as well. ... He did give me a paperback book he had done on Wicca [the *Witchcraft Fact Book*]. ... We did discuss his Wicca activities." *(Ibid n#35)* While there was certainly some nostalgia behind his move to once more pick up the athame and chalice, Eddie may also have had a concern that his failure to keep his faith with the Gods may have cost him dearly. Buczynski was dogged by a series of short illnesses during this time. It could be that, at a subconscious level, he was trying to make amends for abandoning his spiritual practices so that he could find some comfort in the face of terrifying possibilities.

Back in New York City, one portion of Buczynski's past was already starting to come unraveled as AIDS swept through the gay community. The first Knossos Grove member to fall ill was Tony Fiara. Tony gave up the leadership of Knossos Grove to Jeffrey Whitfield, who moved the coven's rituals and meetings a few blocks away to Enchantments, where he still worked. But Whitfield had his own problems, the primary one being a coke addiction. For a while he was able to hold his life together, making incense, oils, and enchanted candles in the back of the shop. He regularly made "protection from arrest" candles for his coke dealer — that is, until she began providing him with adulterated product that made him sick, after which it is rumored that he carved her a candle while chanting over it, "May she be protected BEHIND BARS!" Soon thereafter, it is said that the dealer was arrested and Jeffrey was forced to find a new source for his blow.

Eventually, however, Whitfield's life began to completely fall apart. He couldn't possibly make enough money carving candles to support his coke habit, even if his work hadn't begun to suffer from his erratic behavior. Jeffrey had been homeless on and off over the preceding two years as he battled his drug addiction. His condition was aggravated by untreated diseases associated with AIDS and a sometimes violent dementia that was gradually worsening over time as the disease advanced. When he was evicted a final time for non-payment of rent, Carol and Ria allowed him to stay in a small shed located in the enclosed garden behind Enchantments that they used for classes and rituals. But the women began to lose patience with his deteriorating job performance and grew concerned about his increasingly violent temper. Feeling both persecuted and paranoid, Jeffrey abandoned his job and shelter at Enchantments during the summer of 1987, living on a bench in Tompkins Square Park and regularly being jumped for whatever he had on him as he struggled against both disease and madness. It was there that Jeffrey was found by Maria Parra, who convinced him to go to the hospital.[47]

To those who had known him, Whitfield's condition was an incredibly disheartening change in what had once been a very warm and caring personality. Jeffrey refused to speak to Ria and Carol, nor would he communicate with anyone from the Minoan Brotherhood, believing that his brothers had abandoned and deceived him. In his final months, he attempted to refocus his personal practice on the Tibetan Buddhism of his past. In October, Whitfield died of complications from AIDS, becoming the first Minoan brother known to have succumbed to the disease. Sadly, he would not be the last. Whitfield was cremated on Samhain, and his passing was honored with an ancestor ritual attended by Ria, Carol, and others who had known and worked with him.[48] *(Ibid n#47)* By the end of 1986, a total of 11,932 deaths nationwide had been attributed to AIDS.

Shortly after Jeffrey Whitfield's death, Ria received a phone call from Larry Schneider, Tony Fiara's former lover. After Fiara developed AIDS, Schneider had fled New York City for what he had hoped would be the relative safety of Seattle, Washington. But for Larry there was no escape. Screaming at Ria Farnham that he was sick, he claimed that the Minoan brothers had all infected each other and that everyone was going to die. He urged Farnham to leave the evils of Witchcraft behind and seek the forgiveness of Christ. Ria hung up on him in disgust, but she was troubled by his words. *(Ibid n#48)*

Chapter 32: A Bull at the End

Time Sends a Warning Call

During Christmas break at the end of 1986, Eddie and Gene took a trip to Cartagena de Indias, Colombia. "We stayed in this nice hotel and Cartagena was just terrific," remembered Muto, noting that they met up with another group of Americans while they were down there and hung out at the various bars and restaurants together. Eddie had a blast, and was able to relax away from the pressure of school. The two men ate as the natives did, from street vendors and in cantinas frequented by the locals. The food was great, and neither of them suffered any ill effects. "This was before all of the Medellin [drug cartel] shit," Gene recalls. "Cartagena was a lot of fun."[1] Neither Buczynski nor Muto, as a gay couple, but especially not Buczynski as a gay Witch, would have had a very relaxing stay in Cartagena in earlier days. The Spanish crown had established the city as the center for the Holy Inquisition in the Americas in 1610, a place it occupied until the Spanish were driven from the region by Simón Bolívar. When Eddie came back to Bryn Mawr, he dove back into his classes and thesis work with a vengeance. As time permitted, he also continued to teach Kevin Moscrip Minoan Witchcraft.

In March 1987, Buczynski came down with a severe case of shingles and then developed oral candidiasis, a yeast infection of the mouth also known as "thrush." Both of these conditions are known to manifest in persons who are under a great deal of stress, as one might expect of a graduate student. But both conditions are also telltale signs of a compromised immune system, such as one might encounter in a person being treated for cancer, or one infected with HIV. While the bout left Eddie debilitated and in great pain, it also pushed home the point that he could no longer afford to continue ignoring the gathering warning signs that he was ill.[2] Kevin Moscrip, recalling the 1986-1987 time period, writes, "He didn't mention anything to me about being sick. He didn't look actively sick when I knew him that I could tell."[3] But Eddie's college friends at Bryn Mawr and, as previously noted, Hunter had already begun to suspect that Eddie was not a well man.

Nathan Meyer recalls, "I knew he was ill even that first year at Bryn Mawr. ... Eddie told me he had shingles and he always had a certain look of pain or stress around his eyes and mouth. I knew he was struggling at some level. ... He was also just not well overall, one could tell."[4] Pamela Webb likewise believed that Eddie was in trouble from early in their friendship. "Within a few months of meeting Eddie, I suspected that he might be ill," she writes. "My ex-husband is an oncologist/hematologist who owned the only HIV testing equipment in the Philadelphia area at the time (other than the University of Pennsylvania). Consequently, I was very aware of the HIV-AIDS situation in the early 1980s. I spoke with Eddie several times about taking a blood test, although I never mentioned my suspicions that he might have HIV. He wouldn't consider it. I think he had his own suspicions, and may have been fearful of receiving bad news."[5]

Eddie, as the founder and a follower of a Witchcraft tradition modeled on pre-Hellenic Minoan cult practices, felt a special connection with Athena and had been making offerings to Her statue in Thomas Great Hall since his arrival at the school.[6] "I was aware of the Athena statue and also aware that students made offerings there," writes Nathan Meyer. "I was quite naïve about that sort of thing so did not think much of it. Eddie may have been the one who told me about it — or it could have been one of the undergrads I worked with. I do not recall him specifically talking about his own practices ... but there was always a bit of a smile and twinkle in his eye that let you know there was more 'there' there." *(Ibid n#4)*

Eddie may well have increased his supplications to the Goddess as his pain increased. If he did so, he was no different from others in his situation across the country. Wiccans at this time were mobilizing to help where they could. A Seattle Witch named John Yohalem described the efforts in 1987 of local Wiccans to help people living with AIDS, speaking to author James McCourt. "Everyone designed rituals around AIDS: Rituals for a Cure, for understanding, rituals to send energy to distant Positives — Witches love to send magical healing energy, it is our favorite thing — rituals to zap coven members in travail, rituals to build T-helper cells (these might not have been a good idea, anti-virally speaking)," writes Yohalem. "They really thought they could beat AIDS by sending energy; it was a major theological crisis when they couldn't. Not that allopathic medicine was helping much either, at that point. Scientists were as frantic as we were."[7]

Lest anyone think poorly of Eddie or, indeed, of any Wiccan or Neo-Pagan for resorting to prayers of supplication to their Gods in response to the AIDS crisis, it should be noted that this is really no different from Christians seeking the intercession of their God under similar circumstances. Openly gay San Francisco Supervisor and former Methodist minister Harry Britt told *The New York Times* in 1985, "You do what you have to do to save your life. ... Our spirituality has developed more as these young men have begun to think about dying. It is a trying thing when you get a pimple on your face or feel a bit weak and you realize that may be the beginning of something that will take your life."[8] The position taken by the Neo-Pagan community and by most Christians such as Britt was certainly more empathetic than, and indeed morally superior to, that taken by people like evangelical preacher Jerry Falwell, who smugly and self-righteously proclaimed that "AIDS is not just God's punishment for homosexuals; it is God's punishment for the society that tolerates homosexuals."[9]

Eddie had previously arranged by phone to provide further Minoan Brotherhood instruction to Kevin Moscrip during spring break, but by the time the Spring Equinox rolled around, Eddie was depressed and in so much pain that he was simply unable to continue. Moscrip made the long bicycle trip from Philadelphia up to Bryn Mawr for the meeting, only to be turned away by a note taped to Eddie's kitchen window next to the building entry door. In the note, Eddie apologized but said that he could no longer meet with Kevin. Puzzled, Moscrip rapped on the kitchen window and on the outer door trying to get Buczynski to speak with him, but there was no acknowledgement. Kevin left Bryn Mawr confused, disappointed and hurt, and without a clue as to why he had been turned out. He was never able to re-establish contact with Eddie again after that.[10] While one may ascribe pain and depression as Eddie's reasons for refusing to continue teaching Kevin, Eddie may also have decided, perhaps even subconsciously, to drive Kevin away in order to save his life.

Illness continued to dog Buczynski's steps throughout the year. "I remember he had several medicines he was taking at the time," writes Nathan Meyer. "But he had a strong spirit and that was what I remember the most." *(Ibid n#4)* Despite his spirit and sense of humor, the opportunistic infections were beginning to take their toll. Eddie had last seen Ria Farnham and Carol Bulzone in 1986 during a trip to New York when he stopped by Enchantments. At that time he had given Carol a big hug, but didn't say much to anyone, and Bulzone now recalls that it was almost as if Buczynski was saying goodbye. If his classmates are correct, Eddie was probably distracted by pain even then.

Eddie had continued to write to Carol and Ria sporadically afterward, but these communiqués ended early in the summer of 1987 with one final letter. In it, Eddie told the women that he was sick and that no one else yet knew of his condition. He told them that he would probably never see them again, but he wanted them both to know that he loved them. Ria reportedly moaned aloud and ran from the room when she saw the letter, reading between the lines at what Eddie wasn't openly telling them.[11] But Carol refused to believe it. "I didn't know what he meant by it," Bulzone said. "I was praying that it wasn't — the deadly thing — you know? I thought, 'The Goddess would never do that to Eddie. Not Eddie.'"[12] It was in this letter that Eddie also informed the stunned women that he was returning to the Catholicism of his youth. Eddie had begun attending services at Our Mother of Good Counsel Parish on just a short distance from his apartment. In choosing this church, Eddie may have subconsciously recalled the words of his biological father, to seek out the Mother and pray to Her when troubled.

Ria and Carol were undergoing their own struggles that year, with Ria wishing to fulfill a deathbed promise she had made to her mother to have a child. Carol objected to these plans, and the resulting turmoil culminated in their decision on September 17 to formally end their relationship. Shortly afterward, Ria sold her half of Enchantments, Inc. to Carol and set out in pursuit of motherhood. In 1986, she had self-published her first book, *The Enchanted Candle*, based upon the candle-dressing techniques she had developed while working at the Magickal Childe. To make ends meet during her quest, she relied heavily on sales of her book and a part-time job doing tarot readings at Original Products, a large botanica in the Bronx.

Soon after writing to Ria and Carol, Eddie screwed up the courage to call Bennie. He had likely been putting this off because he didn't want to hear that Bennie might also have been infected. As Bennie listened to Eddie explain what he had been going through, his heart fell. "Oh Bennie! Don't ever get this, whatever you do," Geraci recalled his former lover as saying. "Needless to say, it hit me like a ton of bricks because he was pretty sick at the time. And I didn't have the heart to tell him that I was [HIV] positive also."[13, 14]

Bennie had known that he was HIV positive for almost two years, having been diagnosed in August 1985. He had gotten himself tested right after finding out that David Roberts had tested positive for HIV. Roberts passed away from complications associated with AIDS early in 1987. By the time Eddie called, Bennie had been experiencing a low grade fever for over a year and had begun taking AZT, the first HIV medication approved by the Food and Drug Administration.[15] After he hung up the phone, Bennie sat and cried for a long time. *(Ibid n#14)*

During summer break, Gene and Eddie rented a cottage for two weeks on Cape Cod once more. *(Ibid n#1)* Aside from reading, travel was what Eddie loved most of all. Because of those experiences, "Eddie enjoyed every minute of the rest of his life," said his mother.[16] Upon his return to Bryn Mawr, Eddie made one final push to complete his master's thesis. Buczynski's artistic sensitivity, combined with his passion for the subject matter, seems to have struck a chord with his thesis committee. "Machteld worked with Eddie throughout and was quite proud of what he was doing — especially the beautiful drawing of the conch-shell that Eddie used as the cover of his thesis," Brunilde Ridgway writes. "[James Wright] contributed advice, while Machteld was still the supervisor ... the primary professor."[17] The triton drawing that Eddie rendered seems to have captivated many people. "He was fascinated with triton shells; he was obsessed with the triton, or conch," James Wright remembers. "And he had made a magnificent drawing of one for his master's thesis. ... He was quite taken with them, and that's obviously something that had happened when he was travelling on the American School summer session."[18]

The stress of finishing up the thesis was no doubt sizeable, because Buczynski was a perfectionist. "He was a good student, a hard working student, who prepared his reports with great thoroughness. He was confident in his presentation. He was organized in what he was going to say," said James Wright, adding, with a laugh, "and he tended to talk about what he was most interested in, too." *(Ibid n#18)* Eddie turned out several versions of the thesis on his trusty dot matrix printer before he was satisfied with the final version. It was with a huge sense of relief that he submitted the final report in September 1987. Once it was safely in the review committee's hands, Buczynski was able to devote all of his attention to his final two semesters of classwork.

By November, however, the cumulative effects of his various illnesses, aggravated by the stress of completing his thesis, overwhelmed him. He collapsed and was admitted to Bryn Mawr Hospital with *Pneumocystis jirovecii* pneumonia (then called *Pneumocystis carinii*, or PCP), a type of pneumonia often associated with immunocompromised individuals. *(Ibid n#2)* While in the hospital, Buczynski was finally tested for HIV, and he was confirmed to be infected. Eddie had invested so much time in hiding from the truth that, once it was out, there was a certain sense of relief on his part. The first phone call that he made to convey the news was to Gene, who immediately made arrangements to visit.

The second call Eddie made was to his mother, who was understandably upset but who perhaps didn't fully understand the ramifications of his diagnosis at the time. *(Ibid n#1)* Her attitude may be partially due to how Eddie approached his illness. "He was very determined to stay really strong," said Terry Gianniotis, who also found out about Eddie's infection around this time. "He was determined to stay strong for his mother. He was determined to beat it."[19] Eddie had a good support system to assist him in the effort, both at school and at home. In the coming year, his mother and stepfather would periodically visit from New York City to help care for him during particularly bad bouts. Marie recalled that during one visit, the apartment was filled with yellow roses (Eddie's favorite) that had been sent or brought by friends. There were so many flowers, she confided, that the apartment unsettlingly resembled a funeral parlor.[20]

Unlike some gay couples whose relationships are shattered when one or both partners are diagnosed with HIV, Gene's support of Eddie never wavered. "Gene and Eddie were devoted to one another," writes Brunilde Ridgway, who recalled that Gene did what he could to ensure that Eddie was getting the proper care, despite the geographical distance between them.[21] Gene recalls that Eddie "was extremely gregarious and a hypochondriac, so he loved the attention in the beginning." *(Ibid n#1)* But his illness was finally taking its toll on his ability to carry out his class assignments. "His pneumonia did affect his studies and activity," said Michael Hornum. "My friendship with him was affected to the extent that I am not particularly good with sick people, so I didn't spend that much time with him." *(Ibid n#2)* Others did, however, including Kevin Glowacki, Nathan Meyer, Eileen Markson, and various professors.

Eddie was released from the hospital just before Thanksgiving. He was supposed to visit with his brother, Frank, and his family over the holiday, but he ultimately decided against it. He was weak, and still sick enough that he didn't want to chance infecting Frank's newborn baby with a lingering respiratory illness.[22] Instead, he spent the time at home with his parents, where he asked for a holiday goose instead of the traditional turkey. Marie stated that she knew nothing about geese, so Terry Gianniotis' mother went to the chicken market for her and picked out a plump bird, which Eddie insisted on preparing for family and favored neighbors. *(Ibid n#19, 20)* Over Christmas break, Eddie and Gene took a trip to Santorini, the ancient volcanic island of Minoan Thera. They stayed at the home of the parents of the housekeeper of some friends of theirs. The whitewashed home was perched high up the cliff face, and partially carved out of the exposed rock of the blasted volcanic crater. It was utterly beautiful and peaceful. *(Ibid n#1)* Machteld Mellink's last scheduled teaching year at Bryn Mawr before retirement was academic year 1987-1988, coinciding with Eddie's last year in the master's degree program. In preparation for retirement, Machteld began stepping back from her duties, with Brunilde Ridgway taking over as the Department chair. In December, Ridgway attended the annual meeting of the AIA in New York to interview possible candidates for Machteld's position. Whoever would be chosen for that slot had some rather large shoes to fill. Just that year Machteld had begun providing advice to attorney Larry Kaye in his suit against the Metropolitan Museum of Art in New York on behalf of the Turkish government to recover the Lydian Hoard, a collection of valuable artifacts that were alleged to have been illegally removed from the Anatolian plain in the 1960s.[23,24] This was a crowning achievement in her life-long devotion to Anatolian archaeology. Despite her decreasing duties, Machteld remained on board as the primary supervisor of Eddie's thesis, assisted to a large extent by James Wright as the Minoan expert on the teaching staff.[25]

Buczynski finished up his final class assignments in April and May. In April, he stood before the thesis committee to defend his work. "The process for the MA is less formal than for the PhD," writes Brunilde Ridgway. "After submitting the thesis, the candidate took both a written and an oral examination, usually by April (Commencement is in May). The latter consisted primarily of a discussion of the thesis, so that the writer could receive comments from people other than the supervisor. The committee consisted of three members: the supervisor, another member of the department that has knowledge of the candidate's field, and a third member (also from the Department) who is closest in subject matter to the main field. I seem to remember reading Eddie's thesis, and therefore I am likely to have been a member of that committee. The degree is officially conferred at the Commencement ceremony." *(Ibid n#25)*

Michael Hornum adds that, in defense of the thesis, "Questions from faculty are fielded. Since most Bryn Mawr graduate students go on to take PhD exams, write [a] dissertation, and defend that, I think that the MA defense was more of a chance for faculty to see if the student had 'what it takes' to go on and for the student to get a 'taste' of what would come later in a more intensive way. So, I don't think MA defense was as rigorous as it would be in a terminal MA program [where the student is not going on to a PhD program]." *(Ibid n#2)*

Buczynski successfully defended his thesis that April and passed the written examination, thus earning his degree and making him eligible to go on to the doctoral program if he so chose. On Sunday, May 15, 1988, Eddie walked across the stage and was awarded with a Master of Arts in Classical and Near Eastern Archaeology. The weather that day was comfortable for the graduates, who were running around in suits and robes. The grass lawns and tree leaves of the beautiful campus were that living electric green of late spring, providing a perfect backdrop for the joyous occasion. Eddie's parents and Gene were in town to attend the ceremony, and his family was extremely proud of their eldest son as he took the diploma and shook the hand of the College President. Buczynski had purchased a new suit for the occasion and "he looked smashing that day" according to Eileen Markson, who went out to dinner afterward with Eddie, Gene and the Nascostos to celebrate. After graduation, Eddie and Gene flew to Cancun to once more explore Copal and Tolun. *(Ibid n#1)*

Eddie planned to continue his studies at Bryn Mawr, and immediately after returning from Mexico he began his pre-doctoral studies in Classical and Near Eastern Archaeology. James Wright was the expert in the Minoan and Mycenaean areas at the college. Since Eddie was intent on furthering his research into the Minoan civilization, Wright was scheduled to work with Eddie as his doctoral thesis advisor.

James Wright: *(Ibid n#18)*

> *He was a student of Clairève Grandjouan at Hunter, and she was a very dynamic and charismatic woman who just instilled in him this tremendous love and interest in the past. And also, she was very unique in her own way. Not someone who would follow any normal path but, rather, follow her passions. And that's something that Eddie clearly inherited from her — that if he was really interested in something, he should go that direction — which is a way of saying that sometimes it may have seemed to some of us who were teaching him, advising him that he was a little hard to advise because he had a fixed idea about where he was going. And so I was eager to work with him, because I thought that as he prepared for the preliminary examinations — and there would have been at least one of them, if not two under me (in other words he would have done something Bronze Age in general, and*

specifically on the Minoans) — he would have had to read much more broadly in the field, and to cover it so that he could pass his special exam. And then out of that would have come, presumably, a dissertation topic.

As to what Eddie eventually hoped to do once he had completed the program, the unanimous answer from classmates, professors and family members alike was that he had expressed an intense desire to teach archaeology. *(Ibid n#1, 22)* Unfortunately, events quickly began to conspire against him. In late May, Buczynski developed flu-like symptoms that he could not shake. This was later assumed to have been the beginnings of a *Toxoplasma gondii* infection. Brunilde Ridgway was preparing for a trip to Greece in August when she stopped by Eddie's apartment for a visit. "Eddie had had several bouts of respiratory infections and fever before I went to Greece, and once I visited him at his apartment and he was quite worried," Ridgway recalls. *(Ibid n#21)* She asked him "Why do you worry?" and he replied that he was afraid because his promiscuity in the New York City baths in the 1970s was finally catching up with him. *(Ibid n#17)* Ridgway reassured Eddie and said that she would see him on her return in December. She left in late August for Greece as an Elizabeth A. Whitehead Visiting Professor at the ASCSA. While there, Ridgway also planned to interview new candidates to fill Professor Mellink's position at Bryn Mawr.

James Wright had gone to Greece that summer and returned in August right before Brunilde Ridgway headed out. Wright recalls that "by October, [Eddie] was finding it increasingly difficult to function. He was sick in the apartment he was living in ... and I went over to talk about what we could do and to see how we could manage this, and he wanted to undertake [his pre-doctoral studies]." *(Ibid n#18)* But by the end of October, just as Eddie was getting into the broad research that would form the basis of his special exam in the doctoral program, he was hospitalized with a severe case of toxoplasmosis. Marie recalled that she and Edward were in town looking after their son right before Hallowe'en when Eddie took a nasty fall in the apartment. Realizing that something was wrong, Edward took Eddie to the Bryn Mawr hospital, where it was discovered that the younger man had become partially paralyzed on his right side.[26]

Caused by an infection with a protozoan — *Toxoplasma gondii* — toxoplasmosis causes brain lesions in some humans. The etiology within the human body wasn't completely understood at the time, but greater numbers of immunocompromised individuals were contracting it as the AIDS crisis evolved. "I did not visit him at the hospital," Nathan Meyer remembers. "Eddie was really ill, and I seem to recall that visiting was sort of touch and go as to whether we could. AIDS was pretty new then still and people were pretty freaked. I seem to recall that he was in some sort of isolation ward." *(Ibid n#4)* Despite the precautions that were in place then, Eileen Markson did visit with Eddie several times.

Eddie had become quite close to Eileen Markson and her mother, both of whom had gone well out of their way to take care of him, the apartment, and the cats during his illnesses. He called from his hospital room and asked Eileen to stop by because he had something "really hot" for the two women. When Markson arrived, Eddie gave her and her mother two tickets to see Linda Ronstadt in concert.[27] Asli Özyar also visited a few times and was heartbroken when she saw his condition. Eddie had always been so proud of his body-building, and for her it was like watching a dashing older brother slowly wither away.[28] Asli, who had moved into the apartment next to Eddie's earlier that fall, ended up sharing responsibilities with Eileen in caring for Maybelle and Grimalkin while Eddie was hospitalized. It was Maybelle and Grimalkin who may have, unfortunately, contributed to their master's condition, for cat litter boxes were a suspected disease vector for *Toxoplasma gondii*.

Once released from the hospital, Eddie was confined to his apartment with an intravenous drip to combat the infection. A priest visited once a week to administer communion via the church's shut-ins program. If Marie was present, the priest offered her communion as well, but she always politely refused. *(Ibid n#20)* Buczynski was still very weak after his hospital stay, and the paralysis was an additional burden because he could no longer use his right hand for eating, writing, drawing, or dressing himself. "He said to me 'Why did it have to be my right hand?'" Marie remembers. "He had a lot of difficulty trying to eat, but when I offered to help cut up his food to make it easier for him to pick up with his left hand, he refused and became frustrated. He wanted to do it himself." *(Ibid n#20)*

It was at this time that Eddie began to experience changes in his personality. "I went and visited him once," says James Wright, "and it was very painful, because the cyst in his brain (I found this out later) ... was in a position where it affected his ability to socialize. So he really didn't want people around him, and I thought 'Why would he be pushing away from us when people are trying to comfort and help him?' And I found it distressing and frustrating because I didn't know what was going on. Of course, he didn't either. And I think that everybody who had to deal with him as he got more ill had to face this. As he increasingly withdrew, I guess his mother most of all was devastated by it." *(Ibid n#18)*

According to Gene, the hospital had assigned an absolutely terrific caretaker named Robert to check up on him. *(Ibid n#1)* Between Robert, Eileen and a few other friends, Eddie was able to get by. The toxoplasmosis had begun to affect his right side. He needed help dressing, and walking was becoming difficult. It was at this time that Eddie realized that he simply couldn't continue with his pre-doctoral work. James Wright notes that, while Eddie never officially withdrew from the doctoral program, everyone realized that he wasn't coming back. *(Ibid n#18)*

Queen, Descend

Just before Christmas 1988, Eddie's parents made another trip up to Bryn Mawr by train to spend the holidays with him. The Nascostos were shocked at how thin Eddie, who had always been lithe, had become. The bout of toxoplasmosis had increasingly weakened the right side of his body, and he had great difficulty in getting around. Marie was ever the optimist, as mothers usually are, and hoped against hope that her son would be able to ride out this latest challenge. She reminisced with him, sharing family and neighborhood gossip, and attempted to stimulate his waning appetite. Eddie was still undergoing some fairly dramatic personality changes. With successive bouts of illness he was becoming withdrawn and irritable. This and the weakness on his right side were both symptoms of the brain lesions caused by a serious toxoplasmosis infection.[29] *(Ibid n#18)*

Gene Muto traveled up from Augusta to spend his break week between Christmas and New Year's with Eddie, arriving before Christmas Eve as the Nascostos were preparing to leave. Marie and Edward filled Gene in on Eddie's status, then said goodbye to their son and went to the train station. After the Nascostos left for their return trip to Queens, Eddie's health began to deteriorate once more, and he became dazed and unsteady. Gene realized that his lover was in serious trouble. On Christmas Eve, he bundled Eddie up and took him back to Bryn Mawr Hospital. There the doctors had to struggle just to stabilize him, and the prognosis was not good. They explained to Gene that, given Eddie's underlying immune-compromised system, there just wasn't much hope for reversing the effects of the brain damage caused by the ongoing parasitic infection.[30] In short, Eddie was beginning to lose the fight. It was the time of the ancient *Angeronalia*, when the world holds its breath on the knife edge of rebirth; and like its namesake whom Eddie had secretly worshipped — the Goddess who suffered in silence — he, too, was falling still.

After Eddie was settled into the hospital, Gene returned to the apartment. Over the next several days, as he shuttled back and forth between apartment and hospital room, it became obvious that Eddie would no longer be capable of living by himself. The doctors were not optimistic that he would even recover from this latest bout, and as each day passed it began to look more and more to them, and to Gene, that Eddie might not last until the end of the year. Although Bryn Mawr Hospital was small, and more cutting-edge care could have been provided in Philadelphia, the local hospital did a wonderful job of looking after Eddie. A patient advocate was assigned to his case. A young graduate of Bryn Mawr's Social Work program, she was, according to Gene, very sensitive to Eddie's condition and a great help to them both.

James Wright sent a pot of cyclamen for Eddie's room. Originating from the hillsides of Greece, where it grows wild and blooms through the winter, the flower would have brightened the otherwise sterile room and reminded Eddie of the wonderful times he had had in Europe. *(Ibid n#18)* A few days before New Year's, Gene called Eileen Markson to say that Eddie was asking for her. Eddie had resisted prior suggestions that he allow others to pay visits while he was in the hospital and had turned down requests by professors, such as Brunilde Ridgway and classmates like Kevin Glowacki, both of whom had come back from Greece on December 15. Even requests from Eddie's own family were turned down. *(Ibid n#17)* As Gene later said, it wasn't so much that Eddie looked haggard and just didn't want anyone to see him; the disease was really affecting his mind, causing him to change from being very gregarious to being very introverted. *(Ibid n#1)* Nevertheless, he had finally decided to see Eileen, as she had been his closest and dearest friend during his time at Bryn Mawr.

Eileen was grateful for the opportunity to see him once more, and bundled up for the journey through the cold to Bryn Mawr Hospital. She was incredibly saddened by the sight of Eddie's decline, but she refused to let it show. Mentally and emotionally, Eddie was at a high point and was upbeat and optimistic throughout her visit, despite his debilitated state. The unspoken knowledge, however, was that these were the last opportunities for them to see one another. Eddie was saying his goodbyes. *(Ibid n#27)* Eddie also called Tamara Green from the hospital, and although she noted that he still seemed upbeat and optimistic, it was obvious that he was fading.[31] Muto confirms this, noting, "[Eddie had] a sense of joy about life, almost until the very end." *(Ibid n#1)*

Gene pulled Eileen aside and asked if she would come to the apartment later to help dispose of some of Eddie's possessions. She came over and went through the extensive collection of archaeology and history books that Eddie had so lovingly collected over the last 20 years. She set aside those that could be added to the archaeology stacks at Bryn Mawr College and saw to their transfer to the library. Not surprisingly, most of these covered Minoan and ancient Aegean topics. Gene packed up what personal belongings and clothes of Eddie's he could carry in the car, deciding to leave the furniture as it was just too impractical and bulky to haul. He offered to Eileen anything that remained of Eddie's things, and she took a small English teapot as a memento. *(Ibid n#27)* Eileen made arrangements to liquidate what was left in a yard sale.

As the year dwindled down, Gene divided his time between watching over Eddie, tidying up Eddie's remaining affairs, and readying himself both for spring quarter classes at Augusta State University and what he assumed would be his lover's passing. However, Eddie ended up surprising everyone by rallying, his health improving to a point where it was deemed safe to move him. The decision was made to transport him to Augusta, where it would be easier for Gene to take care of him. With the New Year came the time for Gene to head back to Augusta State to begin teaching. He and the hospital patient advocate made arrangements to move Eddie in early January. Then, satisfied that things were under control on that end, Gene loaded the car and headed back to Georgia with Maybelle and Grimalkin. Eddie made the 700-mile journey two weeks later in a private ambulance arranged by Bryn Mawr Hospital. *(Ibid n#1)* His stepfather, Ed, had planned to accompany him on the trip, but a work commitment came up that couldn't be avoided, and so Eddie rode down in the company of two emergency medical technicians. Marie was furious, but there was nothing to be done about it.

Gene lived in a one-bedroom flat in the Hickman Arms Apartments in Augusta. Installing Eddie in the apartment would make things a little tight, but still manageable. Fortunately, the size of the apartment also guaranteed that Eddie could walk to any location within it, even with his mobility issues. He arrived exhausted from the twelve-hour ambulance trip, which was made nonstop, except for refueling and rest breaks for the two emergency techs who alternated as drivers.

A few days after Eddie arrived, Gene took him to the Medical College of Georgia for an evaluation to determine the best course for care. Eddie was impatient and upset during the visit. Like many who are in the end stage of a terminal illness, he was feeling very ill and irritable, and he absolutely hated sitting around waiting rooms wasting his precious remaining time. The level of care in Augusta also wasn't what Eddie had become accustomed to at Bryn Mawr Hospital. While Bryn Mawr was small and may have had limited access to cutting-edge treatments in fighting AIDS, it more than made up for that with a very personalized touch. In Augusta, Eddie's treatment was more impersonal and institutional in nature, which didn't sit well with him.

After the evaluation, the hospital referred them to a local palliative care physician, Dr. Michael Willoughby, who was, in Gene's words, "full of shit" regarding the realities of Eddie's condition. *(Ibid n#1)* This characterization is perhaps unfair, as one of the jobs of any doctor is to try to keep up his patient's flagging spirits and energy, and the gritty realities inherent in caring for an end-stage AIDS patient were still new ground for many physicians at that time even in larger cities, let alone in Augusta, Georgia. Still, Gene's main complaint stems from the sense that it is better to be respectfully honest when dealing with patients who are in the terminal stages of a disease like AIDS than to promote unrealistic optimism.

A rotating team of home health aides from St. Joseph Hospice was organized to care for Eddie at the apartment, thereby freeing up some of Gene's time so that he could focus both on teaching, which was making considerable demands on his time, and on clearing any obstacles to meeting Eddie's needs. However, the most important thing was that someone would be able to watch over Eddie on and off throughout the day. With his paralysis and declining health, Eddie increasingly needed help to do the most basic things, such as dressing, eating, going to the bathroom and moving about.

It was in these last few months of Eddie's life that the tragedy of his situation truly hit home. A once promising life and all of his plans for the future were now shrunk to a day-to-day struggle for survival as he fought a rearguard action against an implacable enemy. Confined to the apartment, Eddie's life mostly revolved around pharmaceutical regimens, fitful naps, exhortations to eat and a dulling of his once bright star. Paralysis stole the use of his right hand, preventing him from writing or drawing, two activities he loved most in the world, and made holding and manipulating the pages of a book difficult, if not impossible. The cumulative effects of the toxoplasmosis infection also proved a steady drain on the considerable reservoir of intellectual curiosity that had driven Eddie's voracious reading habit, thereby robbing him of yet another pursuit that he had so loved in life.

Eddie still managed to keep in touch with the outside world, though he could no longer pen or type the many letters and note cards that he once enjoyed sending to friends and family. He spoke by telephone with friends several times while in Augusta, including his childhood friend, Terry; and he spoke often with his mother and stepfather. "I did speak to him from there a couple of times, but he soon became too ill to communicate," recalls Phyllis Saretta.[32] Gene worked constantly to keep Eddie engaged in life. The health care aides from St. Joseph Hospice also provided some company for Eddie, though clearly some were better at their job than others.[33]

The St. Joseph Hospice was located on the grounds of the St. Joseph Hospital, a non-profit hospital in Augusta that was affiliated with the Catholic Church. Apart from the health care aides, members of the Roman Catholic clergy were available on staff to provide pastoral care for those being served by the facility. The priests and nuns acted as grief counselors or just someone with whom patients or family members could speak. One of the priests on call for the hospice was Father John O'Brien. The 43-year-old Irish Catholic served at the Church of the Most Holy Trinity, a parish serving a multiracial but mostly black congregation in downtown Augusta. Together with Sister Josephine Slevin, Father O'Brien provided grief counseling at area hospitals, including St. Joseph's.[34]

In February 1989, Eddie expressed a desire to continue his rapprochement with the religion of his childhood. Gene contacted St. Joseph's with the request, and Father John and Sister Josephine were sent out to the apartment to speak with Eddie. Despite his failing health, Eddie retained the spiritual inquisitiveness that marked so much of his adult life. One of the concepts that he held dear was the parallel he saw between Mary and the Great Mother Goddess. This is not an unusual belief in the Neo-Pagan community, particularly for those who had grown up Catholic. Eddie had remarked to more than one friend over the years on the similarities between the two religious figures. Certainly many scholars have noted this, pointing to paintings and sculpture of Madonna and child as the continuation of a theme stretching back to ancient times, when statues of the Goddess Isis suckling the young God Horus were venerated. In truth, the idea of the female as the font of life is as old as humankind, and Eddie was able to take some comfort in this.

He met with both priest and nun in weekly sessions where he discussed the path he had taken after leaving the church in the 1960s. Presumably these talks included a dialogue on his occult studies, as well as his homosexuality. Eddie really liked the brogue-voiced Father John, who was his contemporary in age. On the other hand, Sister Josephine "drove Eddie nuts" for some reason, though he eventually came to like the 50-year-old nun as well. After several meetings, the priest and Eddie were in accord as to Eddie's desire to rejoin the church, and in late February Eddie made his confession of reconciliation. *(Ibid n#34)*

Also in February, Gene broached the subject of Eddie's wishes regarding his burial arrangements. Eddie said that he very much wanted to be interred with his biological father. Gene contacted the Long Island National Cemetery in Farmingdale, New York, where Eddie's father was buried, to see if this was possible. *(Ibid n#1)* As the weeks passed, the need for an answer to this question became more urgent. Eddie's health continued its steady decline throughout the month. The paralysis worsened on the right side of body, further limiting his mobility. He complained constantly to the physician about various pains, and he was plagued with nausea and a series of minor skin rashes and itching, caused in part by the drugs intended to control the toxoplasmosis. In the struggle to maintain Eddie's weight against the wasting syndrome emblematic of AIDS, Gene and the aides alternated between bribing and bullying him to consume canned dietary supplements.

By the second week of March, Eddie's breathing had become quite labored, and Dr. Willoughby noted that Eddie was beginning to suffer from congestive heart failure.[35] Further, it appeared that the toxoplasmosis was no longer responding to the drug therapy. He informed Gene that Eddie was approaching the end stage of his fight. When Eddie's breathing rate fell below a certain point, Dr. Willoughby told Gene, he was to immediately bring Eddie to the hospice. It was at this time that the Long Island National Cemetery finally replied to Eddie's request to be interred with his father. His request was denied, and the rejection seemed to pull the last wind from Eddie's sails.[36] His dyspnea became more pronounced, and within a few days it reached the point that Dr. Willoughby had said to watch for. On March 13, Muto made the decision to drive the dazed and weak Buczynski to St. Joseph's, where he was admitted to the hospice. Over the next three days he became delirious as the lesions caused by the toxoplasmosis began to cause severe swelling in his brain.

Gene spent his free time keeping watch over Eddie, who was drifting in and out of consciousness and laboring for each breath. By the night of March 15, Eddie had slipped into a coma and was unaware of Gene's presence. At a little after 8 o'clock on the morning of Thursday, March 16, Gene stopped by the hospice to check on Eddie before heading to the university. As he slipped his hand around one of Eddie's, the warm but slowly cooling flesh told him that Eddie had left it a short time earlier. His first reaction was dazed surprise. "I remember thinking to myself 'Oh! He's gone.' Just that." There was an immediate sense of relief that the struggle was finally over, but it would be days before Gene would come to grips with the fact that Eddie had passed. *(Ibid n#1)* He informed the duty nurse, who then located Dr. Willoughby to make the pronouncement. The cause of death was listed as Acquired Immunodeficiency Syndrome with the contributing factor of central nervous system toxoplasmosis.[37] Edmund Buczynski, Jr. had returned to the Mother.

Δεν ελπίζω τίποτε. Δεν φοβάμαι τίποτε. Είμαι λεύτερος.[38]

"I hope for nothing. I fear nothing. I am free."

Senex Et Puer

Chapter 33: Epilogue

Empty Jugs and Empty Cups

On discovering that Eddie had passed, Gene Muto informed the university that he would not be in to work that day. In the first of a long string of telephone calls, he broke the news to Eddie's mother. Despite the considerable forewarning of this outcome, Marie was devastated. "Marie, God bless her, was in denial right up to the very end," says Gene.[1] "I know that she was locked in her bedroom for weeks, I think. Probably months [after Eddie passed]," recalls Terry Gianniotis.[2,3] But one can understand her grief. She had not only lost her first husband at an early age, but now had lost his namesake, her firstborn son, well ahead of his time. Eileen Markson believes that Marie may also have felt somewhat shut out at the end, partly because of Eddie's personality changes and perhaps also because of the vast distance between New York and Augusta, and this deepened her sense of despair at Eddie's loss.[4]

The Nascostos were in no condition to discuss funeral and burial arrangements, and they were too far away to be of much immediate help regardless. It is possible that Marie's long-standing aversion to funerals played some part in this reluctance to address the issue, but there may have been a more tragic reason. "I think that she was also embarrassed that he had died from AIDS," speculates Eddie's childhood friend, Terry Gianniotis, continuing, "And she didn't want that said out loud. ... She was petrified of the neighbors on [the] street, what they were going to think." *(Ibid n#2)* As difficult as it may be to believe that community prejudice could be responsible for stifling a family's need to memorialize its dead, such was the case throughout the United States in the early years of the AIDS crisis, and sadly, it remains true in some communities to this day. Gene, as the executor of the estate, took charge of the arrangements and ordered Eddie's cremation. The body was picked up from St. John's by the Thomas L. King Funeral Home, which transported it directly to Southern Funeral & Cremation.[5] The ashes were returned to Muto within a few days.[6]

Gene also called Eileen Markson at Bryn Mawr College, who then went through the Department of Classical and Near Eastern Archaeology to inform the professors of Eddie's passing. There was great sadness at the news, and at the loss of someone who they all believed would have eventually made a talented and sensitive professor in that field.[7] The waste was heart-breaking in its measure. "I remember hearing [about] it from a friend at Bryn Mawr, perhaps a professor," recalls Nathan Meyer. "I remember being sad, but also somewhat feeling that it was inevitable given what I had witnessed in [San Francisco]."[8]

Eddie's "little sister," Asli Özyar, who was pursuing her own doctoral studies at Bryn Mawr at the time of Eddie's death, summarized the feelings of their fellow students and professors, writing, "I am sorry to have lost a warm friend and a potentially good scholar." *(Ibid n#7)*

Michael Hornum says, "I think I heard from other students, and I believe that Gene later contacted me to let me know that I could keep some slides of travels in Israel and Egypt that Eddie had lent me."[9] Various other friends were also contacted in the coming days. Gene notified Dana Matera of Eddie's death and asked her to tell a list of others in New York City, including Phyllis Saretta, Rita Rose, and Laura Calderone.[10] He also called Tamara Green at Hunter College, who then spread the word among Eddie's other undergraduate professors and those of his former fellow classmates who remained in the area. It was Green who told a student who had past ties to the Magickal Childe of Eddie's death within days of the event.[11]

When he learned of Buczynski's passing, the student rushed to give Slater the bad news. By his own admission, he and Slater were not on speaking terms at the time of his phone call. Therefore Herman's first reaction was anger at hearing what he had to say. Slater, likely suspecting that the message was motivated by revenge, ended up screaming that the caller was lying. *(Ibid n#11)* Slater eventually calmed down and accepted the truth that the man he had never stopped loving was really gone. He later posted a notice on the community bulletin board just inside the front door of the Magickal Childe. It was the only obituary that Eddie would receive.[12]

The word filtered out into the occult community after that. Ria Farnham and Carol Bulzone were each told by Herman, who called them with the news. Many of Eddie's friends and students in the occult community felt that he had left them in the lurch when he went off to college. Most had heard little or nothing from him over the past several years, though a number of them had secretly hoped that he would eventually find his way back to them. Up to this point, most of the occult community of New York City — the center of Eddie's life for a decade — had not even been aware that he was sick. They were now confronted with the fact that he was gone, and that he would never be coming back — and to find out that he had passed from the disease that was currently ravaging so many of their friends in New York was like a body blow to many.

Gene spent the days and weeks following Eddie's death clearing up the last details and disposing of Eddie's things. He gave Eddie's clothes, leftover medicines, and remaining supplements to Sister Josephine to do with as she saw fit. The books that he had given to Bryn Mawr were catalogued and added to the stacks of what eventually became the new Rhys Carpenter Library. Eileen Markson took the painting of the triton shell that Eddie had created for the title page of his master's thesis and had the Bryn Mawr graphics department produce a sepia-tone bookplate to commemorate the donation.[13] "I think of him whenever I find a book with the memorial bookplate," writes former classmate Alice Donohue, now a professor in Bryn Mawr's Department of Classical and Near Eastern Archaeology.[14]

The boxes of slides that Eddie had taken during his ASCSA summer session and on subsequent trips to Greece were donated to Hunter College to supplement the vast collection begun by his beloved undergraduate mentor, Clairève Grandjouan. Other items, such as Eddie's address book, were sent to his mother. After Buczynski's death, Gene is rumored to have destroyed the measures and coven records that Eddie had collected over the years.[15] The destruction of the records was a particularly sad loss for the Minoan Brotherhood. Gene does not recall taking this action, and in all likelihood it may have been Eileen Markson who disposed of any remaining papers and whatever else remained after the apartment sale she had arranged when Eddie was moved. Regardless of who accomplished the task, the Brotherhood owes him or her a debt of gratitude despite the irreplaceable loss of information. After all, they had no one with whom to entrust this material, and the Brotherhood's arcana — measures, vouches, and the like — should not go wandering into the wrong hands.

A few weeks after Eddie's passing, Gene called Marie and delicately asked what she would like done with the remains since the cemetery had rejected Eddie's request to be interred with his father. He had at first thought of scattering Eddie's ashes in the Mediterranean ocean off the coast of his beloved Crete. Marie was uneasy about that idea, however, so Gene ultimately decided that he would hold onto Eddie's ashes until he himself passed, and that they would eventually be interred together. There is something poetic and proper in this that Eddie would have appreciated. As the ghost of Patroclus implored Achilles, "[L]et one single vessel, the golden, two-handled urn the lady your mother gave you, hold both our ashes" (*Iliad*, XXIII, 91-92).[16] Marie did not object to this plan.

No memorial service was held anywhere at that time for the 42-year-old. The Nascostos were too grief-stricken to think of holding a service, but the failure to do so had consequences that reached far beyond the members of Eddie's immediate family. "I remember going to someone else's funeral sometime after Eddie had passed away, and I felt like the funeral was more for Eddie," remembered Gianniotis. "I mean, there was no way to grieve." *(Ibid n#2)* Eddie's professors at Bryn Mawr had discussed holding a ceremony at the college in the fall when more of the staff and students would be on campus, but once classes began people became too distracted to follow through on the idea. A year or two after Eddie's death, Bryn Mawr held an AIDS remembrance, and several of Eddie's professors and friends wrote testimonials to him in the service book.[17] In 1991, Dr. Wright presented a paper at "The Origins and Ancient History of Wine" conference held at the Robert Mondavi Winery. Entitled "Empty Jugs and Empty Cups: The Social Role of Wine in Minoan and Mycenaean Societies," the paper was dedicated to Eddie's memory.[18]

Most surprising of all, no public memorial was held within the occult community of New York immediately after his death, though many of Eddie's friends grieved in private. The Minoan Brotherhood no longer maintained a consistently active presence in New York City at this point in its history, with several of its members facing or having already lost their own battles against AIDS, and others having moved on to other things. The Minoan Sisterhood carried on as always, though weakened by the competition between its co-founders following the breakup of their relationship. Both Ria and Carol bitterly mourned Eddie's loss. Herman mostly kept his feelings to himself; however, he refused to allow any criticism of Eddie to take place within earshot. Though Buczynski had been absent from the New York occult scene for some years, his death allowed many of the old accusations to resurface, with some people smugly observing that the grinding wheels of Karma were unavoidable. This sort of talk infuriated Slater, who threw himself into protecting the memory of the friend who could no longer defend himself.

Marie sought some sense of closure over the next two months as she began going through Eddie's address book. In an extraordinary act of kindness and courage, she sat down and began calling each of the people listed in the book to tell them of her son's death. One of those she contacted, Phyllis Saretta, vividly remembers the phone call to this day, describing Marie as being utterly heartbroken. *(Ibid n#10)* This was a venture into the unknown for her, as Marie had met very few of Eddie's friends; he had only introduced people to his tightly-knit family that were very, very close to him, partly to protect his mother from a lot of the controversy, and the crazy, that was part and parcel of the Neo-Pagan community. But it also fit with his general tendency to compartmentalize his life.

Bennie Geraci was one of the first people Marie contacted. He and his family had stayed on good terms with the Nascostos since Bennie and Eddie's breakup, exchanging cards and phone calls several times a year. Bennie had heard nothing of Eddie since they spoke in 1987 – not because Bennie didn't care, but because he felt sidelined as Eddie became busy in graduate school. Regardless, Bennie had no clue that Eddie had become gravely ill, so the news that Eddie had died stunned him. "Actually, I was kind of in shock, and it was hard for me to accept. Even though I had long gotten over him, I still had a deep love for him. I didn't call Marie back for a good while afterwards."[19]

Eileen Markson, James Wright, Tamara Green and other professors at Bryn Mawr College and Hunter College also received phone calls from Marie, and many still receive follow-up calls or cards once or twice a year. In a letter to Jim Wright after Eddie's death, Marie expressed great bitterness over Eddie's loss. She wrote of her anger at the Catholic Church, blaming its stance on homosexuality for driving him away. *(Ibid n#17)* She felt that if Eddie had remained with the church, he might not have become infected and been stolen from her. This rather remarkable admission reflects the depth of her loss.

Herman Slater's talk with Marie was a catharsis. She knew of him when he and Eddie were together, but she had never really had gotten to know him well. Her phone call meant a great deal to the otherwise hard-bitten businessman, and his face always softened when he spoke of her afterwards. They spoke several more times over the remaining years of his life. Immediately after learning of Eddie's death, Herman retreated to his West 16th Street apartment to brood and write. "I'll never forget when he got the news of Eddie's death; he stayed home for days, and didn't abuse anyone for weeks," Slater friend and former Childe employee Laura Austan remembers. "He was so quiet. He felt he owed Eddie more than he let on. ... Herman never got over Eddie. And his guilt was palpable when he spoke of him."[20]

Slater published some of Eddie's writings in a book titled *Pagan Rituals III* in December 1989, dedicating it to the defense of Eddie's memory in the occult community. Comprising *The Witchcraft Fact Book* in its entirety, as well as some Outer Court materials that Eddie had written for the Pagan Way that was taught at the Magickal Childe and Warlock Shop, the book is probably most memorable for its introduction. Penned in March immediately following word of Eddie's death, Slater's text blasted the Craft community and its treatment of Buczynski and, implicitly, himself.[21]

But Herman did not escape the disease that had claimed his former lover and friend, and his health rapidly declined over the next year. Laura Austan explains that no one really understood what was going on with him, including Slater himself. "Herman's illness began with untreated syphilis," says Austan. "It was the syphilis that warped his personality. Both it and [the] AIDS weren't diagnosed until the fall of 1990. He'd been going to a doc who just wrote scrip after scrip [for barbiturates to deal with symptoms instead of assessing the underlying cause], and when he began going down I got him to go to my doc, who found the syphilis and HIV."[22] Roger Pratt recalls a 1990 memorial circle held on the first anniversary of Buczynski's death to which Herman was invited. Slater was, unfortunately, too ill to attend; however, Leo Martello and several others did pay their respects.[23]

Long-time friend Peter Levenda notes that Herman appeared to undergo some personality changes towards the end. "He developed some strange friendships in his last year or so, people who did not seem to be involved in the occult or paganism," Levenda remembers. "I often wonder if his illness caused him to question his spirituality, to harden his heart against it or to become more intolerant of New Age thinking. He may have begun to see it as more closely linked to his fantasy and science fiction reading of years before than he would have liked: and the occult (and religion in general perhaps) as more wishful thinking than anything he could rely upon in the days and weeks to come of his illness. This is pure speculation on my part, but I sensed him drawing away from the spiritual aspect of the Craft while still retaining many of his social contacts within the various groups. This type of ambivalence is not unusual, though, in a person undergoing such tremendous stress."[24]

"I was stunned when he was diagnosed with HIV," writes Judith McNally. "Granted, he was part of that first generation of AIDS patients who 'came by it honestly' — that is, had NO idea their lifestyle was unsafe. Before I met Herman, he'd had a nasty bout with TB that settled in the bone; was laid up for months with hip replacement surgery and other treatment, and for the rest of his life walked with a limp (about which he was needlessly self-conscious.) It seemed to me he had already *done* the illness thing and learned those lessons — it seemed manifestly unfair he was hit with another brutal, chronic illness that would eventually kill him."[25]

By early 1992, Slater's illness had progressed to where he was simply unable to supervise the business any longer. At that point, the day-to-day operation of the Magickal Childe was left in the care of one of the employees, who oversaw it during the last months of Herman's life. It was the beginning of the end for the shop, according to Laura Austan. "[He] didn't order anything, but kept taking mail orders which couldn't be filled," she asserts. "He pocketed the money and nobody saw it again. The daily receipts went to him, then were never seen again."[26]

Herman was eventually confined to the AIDS ward at St. Vincent's Hospital, where he spent his remaining weeks. The summer solstice of 1992 marked his twentieth anniversary as the master of the shop, but by this time he was beyond caring. Ria came to see him one final time shortly before his death and was shocked by his appearance. "I went in his room," Ria said in a 2001 interview. "He [had] lost a tremendous amount of weight; he was very thin and bird-like and shaking. He was chubby before — robust, energetic, loud and very Jewish. ... He said, 'Is that little Lady Rhea?' I broke down and cried. He bridged our years with a few words. He was my High Priest, my teacher, my mentor. We talked. I told him I loved him and to hang in there. He said, 'Oh dear, just leave things as they are. This is the way it's going to be.'"[27]

Slater succumbed a few days later, on July 9, 1992. A memorial service in the Welsh tradition was held at the Gay and Lesbian Community Center on West 13th Street. A Jewish service, with many friends and family, was also held, and on July 12 the Tahuti Lodge of the O.T.O. conducted a Greater Feast for Slater in honor of his service to the O.T.O. and the New York City occult community.[28] One final absurdity was visited upon Herman at the memorial when Hal Geller, "God of Beer" (so nicknamed because that's what is tattooed on his arm), popped open a can of malt at the end of the service and took a swig. Hal, who once upon a time had been a member of the Children of Branwen, declared to the room, "That was for Herman. The rest is for me."[29]

According to Laura Austan, Slater didn't die a pauper, noting that "Herman had 50 grand in his apartment when he died."[30] Kathryn Frank remembers that Herman's apartment was full of collectibles. "[It] was crammed with the *most* amazing stuff," Frank writes. "After all, he had first pick of anything that came through the store."[31] Regardless of Slater's personal circumstances, upon his passing, conditions at the shop, which had been struggling in his absence, went from bad to worse. "Things went downhill when Herman passed away," writes former Childe employee Peter Conte. "He was good at making money, not handling money. ... He left the Childe in a state of financial chaos."[32] Laura Austan concurs with this opinion.

Laura Austan: *(Ibid n#20)*

When Herman died he left the shop to 5 employees — Anthony Passaro, who'd been there for 8+ years, doing the office things; Anthony's mother Barbara; Steve Teischer, his old friend who'd been running the register; a guy named Jesus (Tony), who disappeared; and Emily Brinkerhoff, a young girl and daughter of Linda — all of whom were working there when Herman died. ... [L]ittle by little, the place fell apart. ... The shop had been broken into on a regular basis; the till was always short. Everything came COD. The phone was shut off. I came back at the end of '93, and even the herb shelves were sparse. We began inventing new incense blends because we didn't have the ingredients for the Formulary's demands. Then the books became few. It was slowly dying. ...

There was bitterness all over at the whole thing, including from Herman's family, who felt cheated. Especially his nephew. They even fought over his cane. Herman's ritual tools and other belongings were sold at the Childe. I made the sale signs. Still makes me sick. ...

I left for good in February of '95 when Anthony & I had a fight, he fired me, and I said, "Enough." When I last visited in '98, ... the Childe was a shell. Steve died a couple of years ago; I don't know where Anthony or the rest of the gang are now.

The Magickal Childe closed as a brick-and-mortar shop in February 1999.[33] The space was vacant until 2004, when the 35 West 19th Street storefront was taken over by the Spanish restaurant Sala One-Nine. According to Matthew Sawicki, who visited the location during its reconstruction, the workers refurbishing the space were a bit spooked by the atmosphere and wondering what had previously gone on in the back room as they scraped Egyptian designs off of the windows where the kitchen was being installed. One of the restaurant employees recently noted that "there is something that hangs around the place that most of us have encountered in one way or another. ... It isn't bad at all. ... We (the staff) have always felt a very benevolent soul protecting the place [and] we try to honor that in little ways." Steve Teischer's brother, Joel, is said to have inherited the Childe's remaining publishing rights upon Steve's death. A phantom of the Magickal Childe still exists, selling copies of the Formularies on the internet.

To the very end, Herman still had a bit of a public image problem, with the Magickal Childe being called New York's "dark" occult shop and Slater himself referred to as "Manhattan's ace warlock" by *New York* magazine shortly before his death.[34] The murmured recriminations that had surfaced at Eddie's death were nothing compared to the outpouring of venom that arose upon Slater's passing. Some in the New York City occult community trumpeted their satisfaction at his death, while others bragged openly that they or their coven had actively worked magick to bring it about.[35] In the case of the former, it is a wonder that anyone would admit to being so mean-spirited. With the latter, it is hard to fathom why anyone would profess to be such an incompetent magickal practitioner that it would take upwards of a decade for their spellworkings to manifest. Truly this is a case where those in question never quite made it to the apex of the Witches Pyramid (which advises the practitioner to "Keep Silent"), or bothered to conform to the Wiccan Rede to which many of them putatively subscribed.[36]

Judith McNally was blunt in her assessment of such people, writing, "I have been frankly amazed how, after his death, people came out of the woodwork to criticize him. And some of those screeching the loudest seemed happy enough to do business with him when he was alive. Much of the trash-talk strikes me as just that — trash — which says far more about his detractors than about Herman."[37] Peter Conte writes that "They all ([or] most) hated his guts, but there would have been NO Occult in NYC [without Herman], or at least not as strong." *(Ibid 32)* But not everyone hated Herman's guts. A member of the Ravenwood Coven in Atlanta, Georgia recalled Herman with great fondness, writing that the shopkeeper used to tell him, "If you want the real stuff, buy the cheap stuff. It's real. I would even give it away to ones that I feel are true seekers. The rest of it pays the rent."[38]

In casting about for a lesson to be drawn from this situation, one might refer to Woody Allen's film *Oedipus Wrecks* (1989), in which he lightly skewers the occult subculture of his native New York. A failed actress and ex-waitress plays a psychic named Treva who cons the protagonist, Sheldon, into performing a series of bizarre rituals with masks, magic powders and dancing to avert a personal crisis that has the entire city talking about him. Finally, fed up with the paces she puts him through, Sheldon confronts Treva, who confesses to being a fraud with no powers who was just in it for the money. Sheldon consoles her with the thought that if she had moved to California, she'd probably "have a swimming pool and your own church!"[39] Those are certainly better odds than could be had in New York, where the best she'd probably end up with is her own occult supplies store, a pile of past due notices, and the enmity of half the city's occult community. Herman, who once averred that he was just a simple Jewish businessman, understood, as everyone who's ever owned or operated an occult shop does, that it takes a lot of work and often some very special circumstances to turn a real profit in that line of business.

"As well as being one of the real characters of all time, [Herman] was a hardnosed business man amongst many people who had little (or no) awareness of how things get done in the real world," writes Kathryn Frank. "I always thought that was one of the reasons he and I had a good relationship — I had real-life jobs in publishing and other fields and understood more about how a store stays in business, and I respected his ability to 'herd cats' as they say. Gosh, sometimes I miss him and Eddie and Emma and that store so damned much! It was like the most fun clubhouse a wild girl could ask for. Always a scandal going on, cool stuff to buy, and a certain cachet to telling people, 'Oh sure, I know Magickal Childe. I run their publishing business.' Actually, that still impresses some people today."[40]

The Minoan Brotherhood skated to the edge of extinction several times after its founder left for college, mainly because its men moved on to other things. Despite its founder's hopes, it has never been a particularly large or influential spiritual tradition (the total number of initiates only surpassed a hundred in 2006). By the late 1990s, only two Minoan Third Degree high priests were still teaching; however, with the turn of the twenty-first century, interest in the Brotherhood began to wax once more. Today there are active Groves in California, Indiana, Michigan, Massachusetts, New York, Ohio, and Toronto, Canada. The Minoan Sisterhood continues to teach women in the greater New York City area, where it has been centered since its founding. The Wica tradition of Witchcraft also operates several covens in New York and elsewhere, as does the Traditionalist Gwyddoniaid.

After working for several years at Original Products in the Bronx, Ria Farnham opened her own occult supply store, Magickal Realms, on

Perry Street in Greenwich Village in 1992. In 1994 she moved the store to the Bronx and once again took up the teaching of Gardnerian Witchcraft, Wica, and the Minoan Sisterhood from that location, as well as Pagan Way classes. Magickal Realms' most notable products are the enchanted candles prepared in much the same way as when she first began the practice at the Magickal Childe. In 2011 Ms. Farnham became Ms. Rivera after marrying her long-time spouse, Sandra Rivera, shortly after gay marriage was legalized in New York State. Like Ria, Carol Bulzone taught Gardnerian Witchcraft, Wica, and the Minoan Sisterhood from Enchantments, as well as Pagan Way classes. Carol ran Enchantments until 2004, when she sold it to her store managers and went into semi-retirement. She operated a small shop called The Broomstick in Liberty, New York for a few years after.

Also passing over around the same time as Eddie Buczynski was Clinton Stevens, the potions and incense wizard of the Warlock Shop and Magickal Childe. Dying in New York City in April 1989 after his own long struggle with AIDS, Stevens, like Buczynski, had returned to the Catholicism of his youth shortly beforehand. To be honest, though, having practiced Santeria for so many years, he hadn't actually strayed all that far from his roots. Clinton had held his own against the plague for several years by using his herbal knowledge, according to long-time friend Sally Eaton. In his final years, Stevens and his roommate, Stephen Machon, had become very active in the New York chapter of the AIDS protest group ACT-UP.[41] "I was out of touch with Clinton after 1976, although he remained close with Cat & Rhea," writes Eaton. "I did manage to renew acquaintance with Clinton's close friend and roommate, Stephen Machon, a month or so after Clinton's death. Stephen made me promise never to tell Herman that Clinton had died, so clearly there was residual bitterness over the Formulary [almost] a decade later."[42]

Leo Martello passed away in June 2000 from cancer. Isaac Bonewits followed him into the Summerlands in 2010, while Owen Rachleff and Hans Holzer both passed over in 2009. Tommy and Judy Kneitel retired from the Craft in the 1990s and moved to Florida in 2004. Tommy succumbed to cancer in late 2008 and is missed by many Gardnerian initiates throughout the United States. After his publication of *The Tree*, Raymond Buckland went on to write many more books on various aspects of Neo-Pagan spirituality, and he remains one of the most successful Neo-Pagan authors of all time. He lives with his wife in northeastern Ohio and still presents workshops around the country.

Kay Smith remains largely retired from the Craft, and she performs occasional cabaret acts at the reconstituted Stonewall Inn and at other venues around Manhattan. Many in the New York City area consider her to be the Witch Queen of the local Craft community, a title at which she irascibly scoffs. Many people who spit at Eddie's name will go out of their way to acknowledge Kay's contribution. This is not only ungallant (and quite disrespectful from a Celtic perspective, where the Glorious Dead are to be honored), but it is also an act of willful ignorance to refuse recognition of the role played by Eddie as a wellspring of the Welsh tradition. Kay notes that this attitude puzzles her greatly.

Renate Springer eventually retired from the Craft and moved back to Germany, where she lives with her husband. She enjoys going out dancing with her friends. Sheila Saperton passed away from cancer in 2006. Peter Levenda has become something of an expert on the occult entanglements of the Third Reich, publishing books on the subject and appearing in documentaries on the subject that appear in various venues, including the History Channel. His drinking buddy, Simon, continues to publish books related to the Necronomicon phenomenon and other occult topics.

Margot Adler embarked on a successful career in broadcasting, first for Pacifica Radio and later for National Public Radio, where she currently works as a correspondent based in the New York Bureau. *Drawing Down the Moon*, which arguably launched her onto the national media stage, remains one of the most influential books documenting the rise of Neo-Paganism in the United States. Its latest revision was published in 2006.

Tamara Green continues to head Clairève Grandjouan's "Department of Funny Alphabets" at Hunter College, CUNY. After retiring from Bryn Mawr College in 1988, Machteld Mellink became an emeritus professor and for several years continued her research in the archaeology of Turkey, where she is still considered a something of a national hero for aiding in the return of the Lydian Hoard from the New York Metropolitan Museum of Art.[43,44] She was awarded the AIA Gold Medal for Distinguished Archaeological Achievement in 1991, and the AIA subsequently established a lectureship in her name. Brunilde Ridgway retired from Bryn Mawr College in 1997 and is currently an emeritus professor at the school. She received an AIA Gold Medal in 1988. James Wright now heads the Department of Classical and Near Eastern Archaeology at Bryn Mawr College. Eileen Markson retired as Director of the Rhys Carpenter Library at Bryn Mawr College in 2004.

Bennie Geraci continues to live in reasonably good health in Louisiana, and is now dealing with some of the very same issues faced by everyone else who is fortunate enough to grow older. Joey Cupolo and Charlie Dandelakis still live together as roommates, now residing in Florida after escaping New Orleans ahead of Hurricane Katrina. Sky eventually married Lisa Marie before moving to Connecticut, where they raised a child and live happily together. Bruce-Michael Gelbert is an opera reviewer who divides his time between Manhattan and Fire Island.

Gene Muto left Augusta State University in 1998 and now maintains a busy teaching and directing schedule as the head of the theatre department at Longwood University. Muto still enjoys international travel, and he has escorted groups of students to Europe to study theatre history.

Frank became the second Buczynski child to graduate from college, earning a degree in chemistry and settling down to raise a family. Tommy Nascosto continued to hone the guitar skills Eddie taught him until he was good enough to play backing for such bands as Joan Jett and the Blackhearts. He currently plays in a goth rock band fronted by his wife. Marie and Ed Nascosto still reside in their little house in Ozone Park, Queens. They miss their eldest son very much.

The Legacy and Lessons of Eddie Buczynski

Arthur Schlesinger once said that we must regard man as neither brute nor angel. Eddie Buczynski — as his family, close friends, lovers and acquaintances assured this author time and again — was no saint. He was a man and, as a man, he must by definition hang suspended somewhere between the ideals of heavenly perfection and the failures of hellish defect. Being human, we all have the capacity to have one foot in the clouds while the other is firmly planted in the dung heap. Thus, to portray Buczynski as something other than a fallible being is to disrespect his memory and to lose sight of the lessons his life offers us. Therefore, this author has chosen to view his subject from a place of humanity; not salaciously, and yet with his warts intact. It is with that understanding firmly in mind that this book was conceived: neither a hagiography/panegyric of Eddie's life and times, nor an attempt at a repudiation or exposé. Steering the middle way in an endeavor of this nature is much harder than one might imagine, as forming a bond with one's subject is a risk that every writer of a biographical work inevitably faces. And Eddie Buczynski is, admittedly, a charmer even in death.

Eddie's life touched many different people and areas of interest, and did so in a way that prevented almost anyone who met him from ever seeing more than an incomplete picture of the man. It was astounding, as the research into his life unfolded, to discover that most of his occult and mundane acquaintances knew very little about Eddie, was outside of their immediate interactions with him. His political beliefs; who his friends and family were; his childhood stories; how he came to Witchcraft and to archaeology; or even how he met his various loves — these are all details that we usually take for granted when interacting with our friends. And yet Eddie was a cipher to many of those with whom he shared some of his most profound spiritual and academic experiences; indeed, it seems clear that very few ever came close to actually *knowing* him as a person. How much harder, then, is it for the complete stranger, when faced by a daunting jumble of jigsaw puzzle pieces, to assemble a full picture of just what this man was all about?

What does one say, after all, when confronted with someone who, sixteen years after dropping out of high school, becomes an honors student in college within mere months of earning his GED, and who eventually goes on to win a full scholarship to a prestigious graduate school? Or someone who, though at one time aspiring to be a Jesuit priest, instead created three distinct living traditions of Witchcraft and who, further worked within four other Neo-Pagan spiritual traditions? Eddie Buczynski's life represents an intersection between worlds both modern and ancient, Christian and Pagan, homosexual and heterosexual. Reconciling these disparate aspects of his life and personality is necessary for anyone wishing to understand the man and his motivations, and yet the man standing at the confluence of these forces has been an enigma to most for the better part of forty years.

Mawrter Emily Vermeule, in her keynote address before the American Philological Association — "Archaeology and Philology: The Dirt and the Word" — said that "a number of scholars in the field of archaeology would never have entered that world of Dirt, with its stones and heat and hard living and hard prickly social life only cooled by beer and swimming, unless we had been fired, when younger, by the pleasures of the Word and its gripping images of the past. No one would willingly, or knowingly spend the summers of a life away from home … unless we had a deep abiding love for the Classics and cared with some kind of passion to see still hidden classical remains at first hand."[45]

In Vermeule's words we find a key to understanding what made Buczynski tick, for this passion for the past was at the very heart of who Eddie Buczynski was. This is not to be confused with some romantic ideal of living *in* the past. Eddie, after all, was a modern man raised in and perfectly content to live within a modern maelstrom of a city. Rather, Eddie's passion was geared toward excavating the past, first from the dry pages of his beloved books, and later (or so he had planned) from the dry soils of foreign lands. In both cases, he aspired to discover aspects of the past that were relevant, first and foremost to himself, and only later to others. By doing so, he hoped to distract himself from the depressing reality of his biological father's early death and to discover some hope for his own future.

Eddie's love of history, and especially for the pre-Classical civilizations of the Mediterranean, was rooted in his childhood memories of times spent with his biological father roaming the galleries of New York's museums. According to his later writings, the museum explorations he undertook with his father were some of his earliest happy memories. It is understandable, then, that he would use these recollections as the foundation upon which to build the structure of his intellectual world after his father's death. The artifacts, ruins, stories and Gods of ancient civilizations were the touchstones he used to connect his own past with that of the peoples and places he chose to study. Long before Buczynski entered academia, his keen mind that allowed him to grasp the subtle nuances of what he was reading in archaeology and history books that were written well above his supposed grade. But he also had the tender heart of a poet and an innate artistic sensitivity. Together, this intellect and sensitivity formed the basis of his single greatest gift — an ability to look behind the facts in order to open up vistas of what living in the ancient world might have been like and how we could use this knowledge to render our own lives richer and more complete.

It was this natural curiosity that first led Eddie to explore spirituality early in his life, when he had decided to pursue the priesthood in the Roman Catholic Church. Buczynski stated that he chose Catholicism mainly because he thought that the religions of the Pagan peoples he admired — the Greeks, the Romans, the Egyptians — were no more. As a Catholic, he had been immersed from birth in rituals that had been handed down for millennia, rituals that use trappings not so different from what our Pagan ancestors used (mainly because they were modeled on the earlier ones) in order to establish sacred space and worshipful attitudes. Three years after his father's death, he chose to transfer to a Catholic High School as a first step in his preparation for the priesthood, and this decision was the fulcrum upon which the rest of Buczynski's life would turn.

Our lives are, in the main, constructed from the choices we make throughout our time on the material plane. Do we turn right or left? Do we study for a test or goof off? Do we ask her out? Or him? Or do we sit home alone instead and eat a pint of ice cream? Join the Army or go to college? Wear a condom or take a chance? Each choice carves a new temporal path, leading to a causal chain of further choices that can diverge dramatically from one's original course, parallel it, or eventually rejoin it at some point downstream. Given this reality, it is fair to say that if the Catholic Church had been more accepting of young homosexual men (especially the bright and inquisitive ones, and not just those who could be counted on to keep their mouths shut after vespers), and if he had been beaten up somewhat less by his Catholic classmates for being a bit too light in his patent leather shoes, Eddie might have quietly lived his life as a Jesuit priest, and all that subsequently came to pass might never have been.

But such was not to be because, to paraphrase E.M. Forster, the Roman Catholic Church has always been disinclined to accept human nature.[46] Within the body of Holy Mother Church, homosexuals are treated as "disordered individuals" by men who for the most part have no personal understanding of what a healthy "ordered" sexual relationship can or even should be. Catholicism, like most of the various sects of the Abrahamic faiths, struggles with the very idea of homosexuality. Stripped of its smothering cloak of Old Testament tribal ignorance and the centuries of dogma arising from New Testament hair-splitters, both of which so often treat the existence of the *other* as repugnant and a *casus belli* for spiritual warfare, Christianity is at its heart a religion of love. But given the unfortunate wording (or unfortunate interpretations) that reviles people whose only crime is to exist as Nature intended them, there will always be a struggle between the Christians' calling to minister to homosexuals and the compunction to condemn them.

Homosexuals instinctively know that their sexual orientation isn't a choice in the same way that they know that the sun will rise in the morning. It is not just their opinion in an argument, as if two people were quibbling over whether today's sky is turquoise or robin's egg blue. It is a profound statement of fact by a person who can see the sky to a blind man whose only understanding of the sky and of color are the words written several thousand years before by someone who was himself blue-yellow colorblind. Neo-Pagan religions rarely possess such a religious driver for the condemnation of homosexuals, and when discrimination does occur (as in the case of Ceremonial Magick and Gardnerian Wica in their early days, and among a few small-minded people even today) it is generally due to the predilection of the individual rather than to any dogmatic mandate rooted in ancient myth or history. It should be noted that the Neo-Pagan paths mostly managed to work through this period of immaturity at a remarkably fast pace in the latter half of the twentieth century, unlike the "big three" Abrahamic faiths, which are, on the whole, still floundering over issues of sexuality and gender after several thousand years.

Religious scholar J. Gordon Melton raised an interesting question in 1975 when he asked, "Why do most Witches seem to come from Roman Catholic and Jewish backgrounds?"[47] Margot Adler disputed the basis for this characterization, writing that the Neo-Pagan community was a diverse mix of former Catholics, Protestants, Jews, and the unchurched.[48] Adler's point notwithstanding, the underlying rationale for gay and lesbian former Catholics who have taken up the chalice and the blade seems pretty straightforward: they are spiritual people imbued with a deep love and appreciation for ritual who are in search of a spiritual home that speaks to them and gives the meaning, hope, comfort and support to their lives that Christianity was unable to provide.

As has been shown, gay men and lesbians were not the only ones seeking this answer in the 1960s. But in the special case of homosexuals, the question that the obstinate gainsayers of human nature should really be asking themselves is why anyone of that orientation would want to rub elbows or break bread with those who spend their time and energy trying to convince them that they are vile creatures doomed to an eternity of damnation and punishment. It should come as no surprise, then, that so many GLBT people have rejected the church — any church — as a source of solace when it seems to hold them in such low esteem. Indeed, the true miracle (or insanity, in the opinions of Lige Clark and

Jack Nichols) was that so many homosexuals still clung to the skirts of such an abusive and hateful parent in the 1960s and beyond when so many alternative choices were becoming available.

While Eddie's venture into Witchcraft was at least partially motivated by his own inability to become a Jesuit Priest, it was more fundamentally a reaction to what he saw happening in the Roman Catholic Church, especially in its failure to live up to the promise of change that was implied in the original goals of Vatican II. His choice was also informed by what he saw and experienced in the microcosm of Greenwich Village during his sojourn there. Author Annie Gottlieb wrote, "For those who experienced the Sixties as a war, or a party, or a trip, they ended. For those who experienced them as a spiritual awakening, they were only the beginning."[49] In Eddie's case, his spiritual quest for the priesthood was sidetracked onto a divergent spiritual path that was even more intimately entangled with his love of ancient history. In *The Witchcraft Fact Book*, Eddie explained why Witchcraft was a valid choice for modern people.

Edmund M. Buczynski:[50]

WHY THE NEED FOR WITCHES TODAY?
The answer is simple. The Earth needs it!
Look at the state of religion today. Rituals being changed and misunderstood. Saints being dropped from the books (because they were merely Old Gods in disguise). People being treated like Cattle instead of intelligent individuals. There's small wonder why the churches and synagogues have been abandoned by the young. Turned off by hypocrisy, blatant religious bigotry, anti-scientific thinking, and repressive moral codes which are imposed without reasons for the imposition being given, today's young people are looking for something relevant to the real world. And this is why many turn to Wica — the religion of Nature; the religion of the Real World.

The hypocrisy about which Eddie wrote was clear to many in New York City during the 1960s, where a church whose fundamental tenets proclaimed love and peace for all mankind was supporting a war in Southeast Asia. Repressive moral codes were also being enforced by the power structure of a New York Diocese that was itself controlled by a right-wing Cardinal whose own homosexuality was an open secret and a source of derisive fodder for local wags. Eddie's contempt for the actions of his childhood church was stronger than many gay Catholics, possibly because he was forced to abandon his dream of becoming a Jesuit priest. It was almost as if, after surviving the last handful of pills in his multiple suicide attempts, a light bulb finally switched on in his mind, leading him to conclude that the Church's and society's rejection of him were measures of their failure to live up to their own ideals, and not due to any fault on his part. Despite this contempt, he was always careful to lay any blame for wrongful actions on the worshippers who make up a church, coven, or temple, and not on the God(s) whom the worshippers purportedly honored.

The fact that Eddie drifted back to the Catholicism of his youth in his final days does not invalidate the spiritual pursuits of his adult life. There is certainly some indication that he despaired during the summer of 1987 after he first became seriously ill, and he may even have believed that the Gods had abandoned him then — and yet Eddie never took down his Minoan altar to the Goddess during his stay in Bryn Mawr. Once in Augusta, Georgia, under exceedingly trying circumstances and with very few options available to him, it should come as no surprise that he would turn to his childhood religion in order to find some modicum of spiritual comfort in his last months. After all, it was his biological father who had told him in his youth to seek out the Mother of God in times of need.[51]

There is no doubt that Eddie was sincere in his desire to rejoin the Catholic Church, a body that he had never wished to leave in the first place. But one should be cautious and not read too much into this rapprochement, for it would take more than a final sprinkle of water to wash away Buczynski's fundamental beliefs. If Eddie was able to find comfort in those aspects of Catholicism that resonated with the Neo-Pagan practices of his adult life, it was not an act of disingenuousness on his part. As Diana Paxson writes at the end of Marion Zimmer Bradley's *Mists of Avalon*, "a student of the Mysteries [can] find truth and inspiration in both Christianity and Paganism. The vision at the end of *Mists* in which the Goddess takes the form of the Virgin Mary expresses a truth beyond dogma."[52]

> *Eddie's legacy can be felt throughout the Craft community. Because of him the spread of the Craft in the City accelerated. Upon the shoulders of Eddie, Gwen, the Bucklands, and others, the Craft of the early 70's was built and grew. The lesson is that Eddie was never satisfied. I think even in his death, he was not spiritually settled. The lesson was also to stop searching without for spiritual wholeness, because in the end, it is between you and the Gods, not you and your many traditions.*[53]

–Andrew Theitic, NECTW Archivist and elder; Minoan Brotherhood elder; Editor, The Witches' Almanac

It took seven years of wandering through the pleasurable iniquities of 1960s-era Greenwich Village, punctuated by an unsuccessful attempt at reconciliation with the Church, before Eddie found his way to Witchcraft. It took Witchcraft roughly the same amount of time from the point when it putatively and publicly reached these shores to develop to where it would become accessible to the likes of him. But once Buczynski started down that path it was not at a leisurely stroll but, rather, at the full run of a stampeding bull. The search for spiritual knowledge or "truth" can itself be almost akin to an addiction — a ready excuse for aimlessness, dissolution or noncommittal frippery — that does little but fill a person's soul with spiritual junk food as a means of killing time between the darkness of womb and tomb. In some ways, some of the so-called "degree collectors" in the Neo-Pagan movement have much in common with hoarders, only they are less likely to be crushed under piles of newspaper than they are stacks of Pagan *tchotchkes*, books, and certificates of accomplishment. Both groups ultimately risk being eaten by their cats in the end.

But one can also look at this process as a learning experience (assuming that one is actually learning something and not just being promoted from grade to grade like a dull child in a failing school system). Though Eddie's search also exhibited elements of aimlessness, it was through this rapid-fire process of discovery as he moved from one group to the next that he was able to build upon the key principles that would underlie his work in the Traditionalist Gwyddoniaid, the Wica, the Church of the Eternal Source, and, finally, the Minoan Brotherhood and Sisterhood. Some observers believed Buczynski's progress through the various groups he formed, led or participated in to be an aimless game of hopscotch. But with each step Eddie was gathering and applying useful knowledge and experience. Taking a line from Seneca, "If a man knows not what harbor he seeks, then any wind is the right wind."

> *All I know is that Eddie made us learn our rituals. They were beautiful celebrations of life and love.*[54]
>
> **–Kay Flagg (Lady Vivienne), Witch Queen and elder, Traditionalist Gwyddoniaid**

> *Eddie was Eddie. He did as he wished to do and felt was right. He was inventive and colorful and definitely his own person. He encouraged me to think for myself and not bow down under some rule of another person. He was truly an Aquarian who, I wish, could have helped us to usher in the Aquarian Age. Indeed, I think perhaps that he did! Witness the Minoan Brotherhood that he organized and formed! ... He is, of course, always on my Sav'n Altar with other pictures of the Ancestors for, indeed, he is an ancestor of mine in the Craft.*[55]
>
> **–Zanoni Silverknife, Co-founder, Georgian Tradition of Witchcraft**

That Buczynski took what Gwen Thompson gave him and modified it for his own use, there is no question. Hermes is, after all, the God of thieves as well as the guardian of esoteric knowledge. But Eddie didn't keep what he was given; rather, like Prometheus, he passed this gift on to others in the Welsh tradition. By co-opting Thompson's materials in so thoughtless a manner, he unnecessarily made enemies; but his hubris also gave birth to the poetic rituals of the Traditionalist Gwyddoniaid, which gave joy to so many others. It was only through this ongoing process of learning and adaptation that he was able to go where others had not. Eddie was not the only offender of this nature during this period, and to single him out for censure on this point when so many other perps have walked, including some who were remanded to the custody of their grandmothers, seems injudicious at best. Welsh initiate Judith McNally acknowledged this point in Buczynski's favor. "In creating the Minoan Sisterhood/Brotherhood, he obviously started something that any number of people found valuable and could build on," McNally wrote in 2005. "If he reached that point via a twisted road — well, it's only fair to ask how many people's lives, subjected to the scrutiny of a good biographer, would prove flawless?"[56]

> *As far as Eddie's legacy, I would use one word — Eternal. There will always be generations of children who will be searching for the things that he left behind — the Welsh tradition, the Wica, the Minoan Brotherhood and Minoan Sisterhood. He left us a great legacy in the Craft and in the love of the Gods. I loved Eddie with all my heart, and I still miss him.*[57]
>
> **–Ria Rivera (Lady Rhea), author; Co-founder and elder, Minoan Sisterhood**

> *I totally support the Wiccan revival and [Eddie and Herman] were both pioneers and providers who made it possible. Earth Religion News and the Warlock Shop and Magickal Childe catalogs gave this entire country access to ideas and books and tools they had never dreamed of, just like Sears did for isolated farmers in earlier times. They helped create the infrastructure of the Craft they loved, and the Welsh tradition lives on!*[58]
>
> **–Robert Carey, Children of Branwen; Co-editor, Mandragora**

> *Ed seemed to feel that the Gardnerian community was unfairly hostile to gay men, and I guess he came up with a solution. I think the success of the Minoan tradition in NY helped allay those feelings, though I think he died not knowing*

how important he had been to the NY Pagan community. He was a legend from the moment I became aware of him, and was held in awe by many in the NY scene.[59]

–Kenny Klein, musician; author; elder, Blue Star Wicca

Neither Eddie Buczynski nor Herman Slater created anything unique with the Warlock Shop or the Magickal Childe. There were other occult shops in New York City and, indeed, around the country at the time. Their first mail order catalogue, while impressive for 1972, was also not a new idea, for stores like Gnostica in Minneapolis had similar offerings, though admittedly nowhere near as comprehensive as that of the Warlock Shop. Nor was the outreach program exclusive to them, for other shops were also functioning as ad hoc speaker's bureaus, issuing newsletters, printing books, and providing workshops and rituals for the education of the public.

The distinction to be made with regard to Buczynski and Slater is that these two men provided all of these things together under one roof, and did so within the largest media market in the United States during a period when Witchcraft had captured the imagination of the public. To this day, New York, with its alignment of politics, culture, media, human capital, and business, arguably ranks as the world's most influential city.[60] As with real estate, it is all about location, although in this case it was as much a function of the temporal as the geographical. Thus were they able to associate their (anti-)establishment with the public face of Witchcraft and draw to it the diverse crowd of celebrities, practitioners, fringe walkers, whack jobs, everyday people, touristas and media representatives as one can conjure up only in a city like New York. This is not to belittle their accomplishments, for they really did the hard work to make it all come together, and it was done successfully for twenty years, after all. While one may occasionally fault them for their methods, one cannot argue with their success.

He was a seeker. He was always in search of — everything. He was never satisfied with one path, with only one way of doing things. He always went the extra mile, digging deep. Many a night he'd be reading thick, thick, thick college textbooks. He loved it. He was a scholar.[61]

–Bennie Geraci, former lover; Minoan Brotherhood elder

Many of Eddie's Neo-Pagan friends have lamented his leaving their community behind in exchange for college, and some of them continue to blame Gene Muto for Buczynski's decision to do so. This judgment is unfair to Gene, despite his own personal misgivings on the subject of Witchcraft and Neo-Paganism, and it also disrespects Eddie's own capacity to make the informed decisions that affected his life. It is clear that Eddie had never really adhered to Gene's insistence that he "put aside childish things" and abandon Witchcraft entirely. He opted instead to take the middle path by refocusing the energies he had formerly devoted to the Neo-Pagan community at large on the narrower scholarly track that satisfied the same basic intellectual drives that had first led him to Witchcraft.

The Neo-Pagan community of Eddie's day was not by and large an intellectual one, and although change has come in that respect over the intervening years, it could not then have hoped to captivate his attention indefinitely.[62] He was simply too insatiably curious. In all likelihood, the intense research he had conducted before founding the Minoan Brotherhood had already begun to swing him around like a compass needle toward an academic career. It is almost certain that if Muto had not come along, Buczynski would still have found his way to the registrar's office before long. Once in college, he thrived as never before in his entire life. It is not presumptuous to state that Eddie had finally come into his destiny. As the poet e.e. cummings noted, it takes courage to grow up and become what you really are.

> *God knows where he might have ended up. Because he did have such a strong interest [in the Minoan civilization] he might have, for example, ended up getting involved in some of the scientific analyses that had to do with food and marine remains, and so forth. He would certainly have gone much more deeply into Minoan religion. Just a few years after he died a monograph on Minoan religion came out. And I think there were lots of areas in which we would have seen intellectual growth, because he was interested in a topic that needed a lot of work, [and] still needs a lot of work.*[63]
>
> **–Dr. James Wright, Chair, Department of Classical and Near Eastern Archaeology, Bryn Mawr College**

Eddie would likely have made an excellent archaeology professor, for he did love to teach, and teaching was the track upon which he had set his feet some seventeen years before his death with his first coven in Brooklyn Heights. But any prognostication of his success in teaching is based not only on his innate ability to charm others, nor solely on the application of his keen intellect. Rather, Eddie had a way of breathing life into the past, of bringing to it a sense of continuity and new-found appreciation for its beauty. He did this because the Gods Who formed the basis of his studies were to him not dry citations in the pages of academic monographs, nor were They to be found solely in the carvings of shattered temples and tombs. His strength was based in his worship of those Gods as manifest and undying principles in the World. Eddie would have brought his love of the spiritual aspects of the Minoan civilization to his teaching and made the subject both alluring and relevant to his students.

This is a discomforting thought for many archaeologists and historians, who are suspicious of anyone who grows *too* close to their subject and "goes native," as it were. But Buczynski was not blind to the need for objectivity. As classmate Nathan Meyer confirms, Eddie recognized the importance of remaining within the boundaries established by the empirical data. Still, his experiences in the occult allowed him an additional degree of freedom to search "outside the box" for answers, giving him an intuitive feel for Pagan ritual that few others in his field may have had. His intuitive grasp of the spiritual was not out of line with Bryn Mawr's interdisciplinary approach to archaeology, and it would probably have made him a better field archaeologist as well as a first-rate professor. The true tragedy is that we'll just never know what his full range of capabilities might have been to inspire future generations of scholars.

> *The first thing that I had heard before [Eddie's death] was that he had gone back to school, that he had done the whole archaeology thing. And I was really impressed and happy about that. I thought "Wow, that's great!" ... It just seemed to me that was just about the best thing that he ever could have decided to do. ... I have to admit my first reaction was "He broke away. He got out." He figured out a way to translate this into the real world in a really powerful way, and I was extremely excited by that. It was like it was a symbol for me or something very powerful. And then, I don't remember when I heard that he got sick, but I remember [thinking] "Oh my God. Here he was, he was branching out, he was going to really make it. Here he was going to be a Pagan in the scholarly world and all that kind of stuff, and that was going to be really far out." And I was just sad about it.[64]*

–Margot Adler, Craft elder; author; broadcaster

> *I missed Eddie as the Minoan Brotherhood was formed, but always returned and checked in with Eddie and, after he passed, with Herman until he too passed. I'd say two-thirds (plus) of all my covenmates and extended Craft, etc. pals died of AIDS in a short time. It was devastating — utterly.[65]*

–Denny Sargent, Children of Branwen; Co-editor, Mandragora

Eddie's sexuality was the source of much of his creativity and the impetus for his founding the Minoan Brotherhood. It was, in combination with his intellectual curiosity and fascination with history, one of the main reasons that he had chosen to explore the spirituality of modern Witchcraft in lieu of Christianity. Despite his mother's belief that the Catholic Church's dislike of homosexuality was the root cause of Eddie's death, there is no reason to think that he would have survived the plague had he remained in the church from the 1960s onwards. Tragically, many gay and bisexual Catholics have died of AIDS, including a number of Catholic priests. While there is no clear-cut proof that Buczynski would have violated a vow of celibacy had he been admitted into the Jesuits, it seems unlikely that he could have maintained such a vow indefinitely, for at heart, Eddie was a joyously sexual creature.

"I remember a gentle, loving being, filled with vitality; a gay man who had a quiet, but intense presence," writes H. Bruce Baldwin, one of the very last men Eddie touched in Minoan sacred space. "That he was willing to share himself with me was a gift that I hold in my memory, for that evening not only did I share a special physical moment but a spiritual moment as well. It is something that I have been able to share with few."[66] It is a cruel irony that the very openness and sexual freedom that had inspired Eddie to create the Minoan Brotherhood would also set up the circumstances of the disaster that was to afflict the gay community in the following decade and beyond. It is akin to celebrating the Mass only to later discover that someone had poisoned the Host and wine.

Writing in 1999, Minoan Brotherhood initiate Kenton Neidel reflected on the impact of AIDS on the gay community. "The epidemic took so many of my brothers, and I was very happy to find out that the Minoans still exist in one form or another," Neidel wrote. "I'm sure we passed around the bug as freely as we passed around our love ... Living with AIDS for the past 12 years, some of my non-Pagan friends attribute my longevity to my spirituality, which is pure bullshit. I don't even know what spirituality is anymore. I lived because I did."[67]

The spectre of AIDS has colored our understanding of what has taken place within the gay community for the past thirty years. From our current vantage point, we are tempted to view with dismay or horror the path that Eddie Buczynski chose for the Minoan Brotherhood from the time it was founded until society in general, and the gay community in particular, got a handle on the causative agent of the disease and how it was spread. But hindsight all too often strays into judgment, which is an obtuse and decidedly unfair response, particularly when considering a previously unknown disease that arose without warning to devastate an entire community.

Nevertheless, Kenton's remembrances are a chilling echo of Larry Schneider's words to Ria Farnham in 1987. Schneider claimed that the Minoan brothers had all infected one another and that everyone associated with the group was going to die. But not everyone did die, although some did. A number of others continue to live with HIV/AIDS, but others were not infected, and many of the original initiates are still alive, as are members from subsequent incarnations of Knossos and other Minoan groves. Did the practices of the Minoan Brotherhood significantly increase the likelihood that its members would become infected with HIV? Given the sexual mysticism implicit in the premise of the tradition and the period in which it arose, it would be difficult to argue that participating in certain Minoan practices had no effect on the potential for exposing individual members to HIV. However, it is doubtful that these practices were any more likely to have spread the disease among the individuals comprising the tradition's membership than any of the other vectors that were already present within their lives as members of the gay community of New York City during that era.

The simple fact is that those in question were all sexually-active gay men who engaged in the same sexual behaviors as thousands of their peers throughout the community, and the activities that took place outside the confines of the Minoan groves and their rites occurred much more often and with many more sexual partners than within them. Minoan initiates were, for the most part, not choirboys (which is not to say that choirboys were immune to the same temptations or not afforded the same opportunities to experiment as other men their age). What this means is that although certain practices of that time period are now considered to be "unsafe," the overall contribution of those practices to the risk profile of the individual members was dwarfed by the sheer scale of the men's outside sexual activities. The men who were attracted to and actively sought out the Minoan Brotherhood and who went on to develop AIDS were in all likelihood either already infected with the disease before participating in the tradition or would have become so anyway due to the rampant promiscuity inherent in the mainstream gay liberation movement. This is neither a criticism of those practices or individuals, nor of those times, but merely an acknowledgement of what was actually occurring in the community.

It should also be noted that the Minoan Brotherhood was not the only magickal group during this period to participate in practices "which erotically celebrate Life"[68]. Of particular interest are the traditional Witchcraft covens, many of which engaged in very similar activities.[69] However, there are two major differences between the established practices of the Wiccan covens and those of the Minoan groves. First is that traditional covens generally relied upon established heterosexual mixed-sex working partners, and that these participants were often as not also committed monogamous couples. Minoan groves, by contrast, tended to be much more fluid with respect to working partners. Although the Minoans made provisions to accommodate committed working partners, this was more prevalent after the advent of AIDS rather than before.

The other divergence between the practices of the two groups was that mixed-sex couples often used condoms, largely because the feminist movement's drive to allow women to control their own fertility and child-bearing.[70] Conversely, gay and bisexual couples of the period, being unconcerned about pregnancy, did not use condoms. Even though condoms might have helped curb the rampant transmission of other STDs such as syphilis and gonorrhea, which were at epidemic proportions within the community by the late 1970s, gay men rebelled against using them in their drive for sexual freedom. Indeed, the first mention of what came to be known as "safe(r) sex" in response to the AIDS crisis didn't appear in the gay press until about 1983.[71]

Thus, before the advent of AIDS, gay men were actively discouraged from using prophylactics by a peer pressure born of the exigencies of a liberation sexuality, and backed by thousands of years of male custom and practice. This remained unaffected by the changes demanded of straight men by the women's liberation movement. Indeed, this position was so deeply engrained that large numbers of gay and bisexual men still resisted using condoms even after the need for protection became obvious by the mid-1980s. It is within this context that certain practices of the Minoan Brotherhood, as conceived by Buczynski, should be examined, rather than in the harsh light of our present understanding of the costs of those practices. The ramifications, after all, are based upon factors that the men at that time could not reasonably have been expected to anticipate, let alone accommodate.

He was and is in my mind a great Gay Genius. He taught us the Craft, the will to gather up and lead people. He was a gay activist for sure in his political views, but a spiritual leader in his heart. That's what I remember.[72]

–Joe Caldiero (Max), Traditionalist Gwyddoniaid, Gardnerian Tradition

What he left behind was a bunch of wonderful traditions that suited many different people in different ways, and I think it just goes to prove to the world that you don't have to be straight to love the Goddess. The most important thing was the love of the Goddess, and the idea of perfect love and perfect trust. He never really — with all this bullshit going on, people attacking other people — he never, never, never relinquished his perfect love and perfect trust. And to tell you the truth, I think he did the Minoan tradition, not only because it had its validity through history, but because there was a need for it at the time. ... I think what he decided was that it was important that the gay community have something.[72]

–Artie Jamison, Traditionalist Gwyddoniaid elder

I think [the Minoans] are too secretive. I understand the reasons for the Brotherhood's secrecy. But frankly, I think [their] desire for secrecy has become a sickness. In the beginning, this tradition was playful and open. Eddie would talk to anyone who would listen. And, for a tradition that was intended to reach out to gay men and has been riddled with losses from AIDS, I'm a bit perturbed by the brothers' unwillingness to open to people. ... Suicide among gay teens is still the highest in the country. Gay men suffer in isolation, risk infection, and participate in 'life-threatening' behaviors. Why not take a proactive stance? ... Work to nurture your gay brothers, teach them, help them change, grow spiritually. That would be truer to your roots. This secrecy thing is tied to the 'Burning Times' in Europe. So, keep people's identities secret, but not the tradition. It's historically incorrect [to do so].[74]

–Aubrey Wyatt, Minoan Brotherhood elder

Eddie's final gift to modern Witchcraft — the Minoan tradition — was, like him, a product of the times. Conceived during a period when the freedom of expression for gay sexuality was just coming into its own, and when gay men (and to a certain extent lesbians) were still being denied entry into many Witchcraft traditions, the Minoan tradition was Eddie's vision of gay activism translated into religion. Buczynski never meant for the Minoans to be an exclusive club of initiates that looked down with snobbish indifference on non-members, something that they are occasionally accused of today. When he enjoined them to be priests not just to each other, but also to "our people," he was telling initiates of his path to get out into the streets and minister to a gay community that was still in desperate need of guidance and help.

Helping others is by definition, and of necessity, a much larger act than merely pushing them towards any particular spiritual pursuit, a complaint that has often been leveled against Christian proselytizers, among others. It is the act of leading by setting a good example, of providing aid and comfort while expecting nothing in return, and of fighting for the rights of others to live and love and worship as they choose, even if their ways are not our own. As Aubrey Wyatt notes, this need has not diminished in the intervening years, despite the political and social progress the gay community has made. The most holy persons on the planet are not necessarily the ones with titles and followers, but those who are unafraid to roll up their sleeves and do the necessary and often dirty work to make life better for others, and not merely for themselves or their coterie of friends and supporters. Eddie Buczynski's true impact on the world lies with those who walk the talk; who have taken his teachings to heart and who have striven to make a difference in the world. Some notable examples of Buczynski's legacy in this regard include:

- **Kenton Neidel,** former Executive Director of the Hand in Hand community AIDS support program in Santa Fe, NM; volunteer at the Southwest CARE Center in Santa Fe, NM (treatment of HIV and AIDS); homeless advocate and volunteer in various communities; Minoan Brotherhood initiate. Passed away on March 12, 2003.[75,76]
- **Ria Rivera,** author of *The Enchanted Candle* and *The Enchanted Formulary*; founder of The Pagan Center of New York and The Bronx Buddhist Center; high priestess and elder in Traditionalist Gwyddoniaid; high priestess and elder in The Wica; co-founder (with Carol Bulzone and Eddie Buczynski) of the Minoan Sisterhood.
- **Adam Donaldson Powell,** artist, poet, author of *Gaytude: a poetic journey around the world*, *Le Paradis*, and *Three-legged Waltz;* national public advocate for people with AIDS for the country of Norway; Norwegian representative at the 2004 UN special session on HIV/AIDS (UNGASS); Minoan Brotherhood high priest.
- **Phyllis Curott,** author of *Book of Shadows*, *Witch Crafting*, and *The Love Spell*; attorney for the Lady Liberty League; keynote speaker at the 1993 and 2004 Parliament of World Religions; member of the United Nations' Non-Governmental Organization Committee on the Status of Women; President Emerita of Covenant of the Goddess; Minoan Sisterhood high priestess.
- **Paul Larson,** author Psychological healing: Historical and philosophical foundations of professional psychology (in press); Professor, The Chicago School of Professional Psychology; attorney; Pagan Prison Minister in the States of Wisconsin and Illinois; coordinator for the Between the Worlds Men's Community; Circle Sanctuary Ordained Minister; Minoan Brotherhood initiate.
- **Lexa Rosean,** author of *The Supermarket Sorceress*, *Easy Enchantments*, *Tarot Power*, and others; playwright, *I Married a Lesbian Witch*; poet; professional tango dancer and instructor in New York City and Europe, and leader and role model for the queer tango movement; professional cartomancer and astrologer; high priestess in The Wica; Minoan Sisterhood high priestess.

ଓ **Gary Suto,** fashion designer; founder of the New York Gay Men's Open Pagan Circle; volunteer in The Pagan Center of New York and The Bronx Buddhist Center; coordinator for the Between the Worlds Men's Community; former coordinator of San Francisco Pagan Pride Day; high priest in The Wica; Minoan Brotherhood high priest.

Lawrence D. Bell said, "Show me a man who cannot bother to do little things and I'll show you a man who cannot be trusted to do big things." Human nature dictates that there will always be certain practitioners of every spiritual tradition who "cannot be trusted to do big things," and those spiritually descended from Edmund Buczynski – or Gerald Gardner, Gwen Thompson, Alex Sanders, Buddha, Abraham, Mohammed, Christ or a host of others – are certainly no different. As human beings, we are no more than that which we leave behind, for good or for ill. Once we are gone, it is up to those who come after to either build on our works or tear them down. We each are both blessed and cursed with the gift of free will, and thus have the means to fight the ephemeral destructive forces of vanity, greed, hate and ignorance. We have within us the power to create a world in which hatred, discrimination, Witch Wars, lies, banishments, curses, ego trips and hypocrisy do not exist.

> *He was one of the most outgoing, friendliest people I had ever met and I liked him immediately. ... The lesson [of his life]? To love openly and to be genuinely present not only to and with others, but also with himself. His engagement to the world was complete and without reservation. Would that we were all so engaged.*[77]

–Ken Dalton, Craft elder; attorney

"Within this gorgeous spacious structure are many mansions," wrote Mawrter Emily Vermeule, "[and] in the mansions a particular private room for each one of us; and we might as well be neighborly about it, even friends." *(Ibid n#44)* Can those who remain behind, regardless of their religion or spiritual practice, their politics or native land, their social status or age, race or sexual orientation, come together in peace in order to transform this world into such a neighborly place, one which is full of the happiness and joy that Buczynski wrote of as the natural state of mankind?[78] From generation to generation, hope springs eternal that such will be the case.

Robert Calasso, in his marvelous book *The Marriage of Cadmus and Harmony*, writes that "In any Cretan story, there's a bull at the beginning and a bull at the end."[79] But it is important to remember that these stories always close with the bull dying at the height of his power in sacrifice to the Gods and in sacrifice to itself. When Edmund Buczynski, Jr. passed away at age 42, he left a legacy: the living embodiment of the love, honor and respect that he believed was due not only to the Gods of our ancestors, but to each one of us from the other. The sun has now set on his mortal frame, and Eddie has become one with those Glorious Dead, as the Witch-kin call them. But though his flesh may have fallen into darkness and corruption, the sun continues to shine on his essence through the words and deeds, family and loves, friends and even foes that he has left behind. For the Bull of Heaven stamps his foot, and the resulting ripples spread out across the galaxy of human thought, never to dampen or die — or so the ancient Egyptians believed — for as long as the name lives on.

Y Gwir yn Erbyn Y Byd
"The Truth against the World"[80]

Chapter Notes

Acknowledgements

[1] Buczynski, Edmund M. "Summer Session 1982: Going Forward, Looking Back — A Personal View." *American School of Classical Studies at Athens Newsletter* (ASCSA NL) (Fall 1982) 1. Web.

[2] Author's Note: The names of several living individuals mentioned in this book have been pseudonymized to protect their privacy.

Proemium

[1] R.F. Willetts, "Hermes," entry in Richard Cavendish (ed.), *Man, Myth and Magic: An Illustrated Encyclopedia of the Supernatural.* New York: Marshall Cavendish Corp. 1970. 1289.

Notes for Chapter 1

[1] Nascosto, Marie. Telephone interview. 8 December 2010.

[2] Nascosto, Marie. Letter to the author. 29 January 2007. MS.

[3] Muto, Gene. Personal interview. 28 October 2004.

[4] Natal horoscope run by Malcolm Mills. Mills, Malcom. Message to the author. 19 March 2011. Email.

[5] Natal horoscope interpretation by Julie Scott-Schudin. Scott-Schudin, Julie. Personal interview. 19 March 2011.

[6] Plutarch. "Of Natural Affection towards One's Offspring." Moralia.

[7] "Fifteenth Census of the United States: 1930, Population Schedule (Brooklyn Borough)." United States Department of Commerce — Bureau of the Census. 8 April 1930.

[8] Carpenter, Natalie. "Buczynski, Edmund." Letter to the author. United States National Personnel Records Center (St. Louis). 25 January 2006.

[9] "US Naval Armed Guard Center, Brooklyn, N.Y." [booklet]. New York: New York Telephone Company. 1945.

[10] Nascosto, Marie. Telephone interview. 9 December 2010.

[11] Cooper, Sherod. Liberty Ship. Annapolis: Naval Institute Press 1997. 2

[12] Cooper. Liberty Ship. 28-29.

[13] Nascosto, Marie. Letter to the author. 9 May 2008. MS.

[14] "Curb of Smallpox 'A Miracle' says Health Commissioner." New York Times (NYT) (26 April 1947). Web.

[15] "Ozone Park: They Were 'Yearning to Breathe Free'." New York Newsday. Web (www.newsday.com/extras/lihistory/spectown/hist0010w.htm).

[16] Shaman, Diana. "If You're Thinking of Living In Ozone Park; Changing Faces, Enduring Values." NYT (5 October 2003).

[17] Seyfried, Vincent. *The Story of Woodhaven and Ozone Park (Queens Community Series).* New York: Woodhaven Cultural and Historical Society. 1985. 61.

[18] Gianniotis, Terry. Telephone interview. 16 October 2011.

[19] Buczynski, Frank. Telephone interview. 8 May 2008.

[20] Buczynski, Edmund. "Edmund Michael Buczynski" autobiographical paper. 28 September 1974. MS. Ed Buczynski File. Church of the Eternal Source Archives (Arch. CES).

[21] North, Erika [Judith McNally]. Message to the author. 30 November 2005. Email.

[22] Siri, Giani. Message to the author. 9 April 2007. Email.
[23] "National Gravesite Locator." National Cemetery Administration. Web (gravelocator.cem.va.gov).
[24] Geraci, Bennie. Message to the author. 26 April 2006. Email.
[25] Nascosto, Marie. Letter to the author. 27 December 2006. MS.
[26] North, Erika [Judith McNally]. Message to the author. 30 November 2005. Email.

Notes for Chapter 2

[1] Leek, Sybil. *The Complete Art of Witchcraft*. New York: The World Publishing Company. 1971. 15.
[2] Bourne, Lois. *Dancing with Witches*. London: Robert Hale. 2006. 91.
[3] Valiente, Doreen. *Where Witchcraft Lives*. London: The Aquarian Press. 1962. p. 81. It is certainly possible that Valiente excluded any mention of Gardner for both reasons; however, human nature being what it is, which is the more likely motivator?
[4] Davis, Morgan. "Monique Wilson & The Gardner Estate." geraldgardner.com (http://www.geraldgardner.com/Monique_Wilson.pdf, accessed 7 May 2008).
[5] Buckland, Raymond. Message to the author. 11 October 2008. Email.
[6] Starchild, Zera. "Raymond Buckland, the Father of American Wicca." Doorway Publication and Gifts. 2007. Web (http://doorwaypublications.com/interview.html, accessed 24 September 2008).
[7] Olwen [Monique Wilson]. Gardnerian Wica vouch of Rowen [Rosemary Buckland]. Perth, Scotland. 30 November 1963. MS.
[8] This occurred shortly after the passing of Dr. Margaret Murray (age 100) on November 14, 1963. Dr. Murray's treatise on the survival of Witchcraft, *The Witch Cult in Western Europe*, helped spur the growth of Witchcraft and was a major influence on Raymond Buckland's early studies.
[9] Heselton, Philip. *Witchfather: A Life Of Gerald Gardner*. (Volume 2: From Witch-Cult to Wicca.) Loughborough: Thoth Productions. 2012. 632. Print.
[10] Buckland, Raymond. From his up-coming autobiography, as yet untitled. Copyright Raymond Buckland 2010, with permission.
[11] Kobler, John. "Out for a Night at the Local Caldron." Saturday Evening Post 239.23 (5 November 1966) 78. Print.
[12] Morton was eventually arrested and deported back to England. His exploits formed the basis for Nathaniel Hawthorne's story "The Maypole of Merrymount." Tweed, Thomas (Editor). *Retelling U.S. Religious History*. Berkeley: University of California Press. 1997. 3, 182. Most historians believe that Morton's actions were designed to mock the Puritans rather than to revive pre-Christian rites. But rebellion against the status quo has often ushered in periods of spiritual awakening, even within Christianity itself. And the maypole, as a Pagan phallic symbol, was sure to inflame Puritan ire.
[13] "Watson's Annals" records four mystic hermits living in the Philadelphia area by 1700. "Mystics in the Early History of Philadelphia." *Behutet* 11 (Autumn 2001).
[14] Horowitz, Mitch. *Occult America: White House Séances, Ouija Circles, Masons, and the Secret, Mystic History of Our Nation*. New York: Bantam Books. 2009. 1-2.
[15] See: Hark, Ann. Hex Marks the Spot. New York: J. B. Lippincott Company. 1938.

Lewis, Arthur. *Hex: a Spell-Binding Account of Witchcraft and Murder in Pennsylvania.* New York: Trident Press. 1969.

[16] Haining, Peter. *The Anatomy of Witchcraft.* New York: Taplinger Publishing Company. 1972. 100-101.

[17] "Root workers" are, literally, those who work magic with plant parts, among other items. Horowitz. Occult America. 2009. 119-120.

[18] Jefferson, Thomas. (Adrienne Koch and William Peden, eds). *The Life and Selected Writings of Thomas Jefferson.* New York: Modern Library Classics. 1998.

[19] Horowitz. Occult America. 2009. 53-54.

[20] Jenkins, Phillip. *Mystics and Messiahs: Cults and New Religions in American History.* Oxford: Oxford University Press. 2001. 71.

[21] Owen, Alex. *The Place of Enchantment: British Occultism and the Culture of the Modern.* Chicago: University of Chicago Press. 2004. 4.

[22] Gordon, Mel. *Voluptuous Panic: The Erotic World of Weimar Berlin.* Los Angeles: Feral House. 2006. 221.

[23] "Alpha et Omega." Wikipedia. Web (http://en.wikipedia.org/wiki/Alpha_et_Omega, accessed 13 October 2008).

[24] Gilbert, R.A. *The Golden Dawn Scrapbook: The Rise and Fall of a Magical Order.* New York: Samuel Weiser, Inc. 1997. 195-196.

[25] A box of occult items washed ashore and was discovered in early October 1966 in Bracklesham Bay, Sussex, England. It was later identified as the remnants of Golden Dawn regalia which had been buried on a seaside clifftop at the closure of the Order. "'Witches Box' from the Sea." Fate 20.3 (March 1967) 62. The Weschcke Library. Llewellyn Worldwide. Woodbridge. (Wesc. Lib. Llew.).

[26] Horowitz. Occult America. 2009. 211-215.

[27] Horowitz. Occult America. 2009. 211.

[28] King, Francis. *Megatherion: The Magickal World of Aleister Crowley.* England: Creation Books. 2004. 117.

[29] Carter, John. Sex and Rockets: *The Occult World of Jack Parsons.* Los Angeles: Feral House. 2004. 33-34.

[30] "Bonus Item" (Minutes of the Agapé Lodge, September 21, 1935). Magical Link V:2 (1985) 2. Earth Religion Archives. Circle Sanctuary. Mt. Horeb. (Arch. Circ. Sanc).

[31] Ad Veritatum. "An Interview with Caliph Hymenaeus Beta X°." Magical Link VI.1 (January 1986) 2. (Arch. Circ. Sanc).

[32] Trask, Nigel. "Hounding the King of the Devil Cults around the Globe." Ogden Standard Examiner. 22 April 1928.

[33] Stephensen, P.R. and Israel Regardie. *The Legend of Aleister Crowley.* St. Paul: Llewellyn Publications. 1970. 116-125.

[34] Wilson, Colin. *Aleister Crowley: The Nature of the Beast.* London: Aeon Books. 2005. 115.

[35] Grant, Kenneth. *Aleister Crowley: The Hidden God.* New York: Samuel Weiser. 1974. 93.

[36] Jenkins. Mystics and Messiahs. 2001. 8.

[37] The American Society for Psychical Research (ASPR) was founded in Boston in 1885, later reorganizing and moving to New York City in 1905. The ASPR is the oldest psychical research organization in the United States. Its

[38] Haining. The Anatomy of Witchcraft. 99.

benefactors over the years have included the inventor of the Xerox machine, Chester Carlson. Source: ASPR website (http://www.aspr.com).

[39] Lovecraft used information from such contemporary books as Eliphas Levi's "The History of Magic" in his writing (e.g., The Case of Charles Dexter Ward). Joshi, S. and David Schultz, eds. H.P. Lovecraft, Letters from New York. San Francisco: Night Shade Books. 2005, 292. Despite this, Lovecraft had little empathy for occultists or their ideas of reality, stating "I am, indeed, an absolute materialist so far as actual belief goes; with not a shred of credence in any form of supernaturalism — religion, spiritualism, transcendentalism, metempsychosis, or immortality." Lovecraft, H. P. Letter to Clark Ashton Smith. Brooklyn, New York. 9 October 1925. Web.

[40] Ware, Caroline. Greenwich Village 1920-1930. New York: Harper Colophon Books. 1965. 173, 189-190. [Reprinted from the original 1935 report.]

[41] Schurmacher, Emile. *Witchcraft in America Today.* New York: Paperback Library. 1970. 46-52.

[42] "Witchcraft in Brooklyn: Queer Contracts Exposed by Record Book of Fortune Teller." NYT (25 March 1900) Np. Web.

[43] "Capt. O'Reilly Worsted in Occult Science Case: Arrested Mrs. Georgia Donovan, a Brooklyn Seeress." NYT (13 May 1903) Np. Web.

[44] "One Thousand Fortune Tellers Plying Their Trade in New York City." NYT (12 December 1909) Np. Web.

[45] Adams' two astrology books, *Astrology: Your Place in the Sun* (1927) and *Astrology: Your Place Among the Stars* (1930), were based upon the manuscript that Aleister Crowley wrote which eventually became *Liber 536, The General Principles of Astrology.* Crowley, Aleister and Evangeline Adams. *The General Principles of Astrology.* Newburyport: Red Wheel/Weiser. 2002. pp. xvii, xx.

[46] Greenwich Village. Dir. Walter Lang. Twentieth Century Fox, 1944. The $5 fee Carmen Miranda's character charges per reading is equivalent to over $60 in 2008 dollars, yet another example to audiences of the day of the extravagance and exotic nature of the fortune teller. Minimum wage, after all, was only 30 cents an hour in 1944.

[47] "Declared to be a Witch: A Singular Case in the Recorder's Court at Paterson, N.J." NYT (25 July 1895) Np. Web.

[48] "Nugent Luckstone in Tombs with Him: Post Office Inspectors Get Supreme Ruler of Iridescent Order of Iris." NYT (15 March 1914) Np. Web.

[49] Wallace, C.H. *Witchcraft in the World Today.* New York: Award Books. 1967. 82.

[50] Harney, Scott. *Esoteric Guide to New York.* New York: Esoteric Guides. 2003. 167.

[51] "Seize Price Lists of Voodoo Doctor — Police Get Circulars Offering 'Wishing Dust' and Lucky Charms to Negroes at $1 to $1,000." NYT (13 August 1923) Np. Web.

[52] Brandon, George. *Santeria from Africa to the New World.* Bloomington: Indiana University Press. 1993. 104.

[53] For examples, see: Bach, Marcus. *Strange Altars.* New York: The Bobbs-Merrill Company. 1952.

Wright, Harry. *Witness to Witchcraft.* New York: Funk & Wagnalls. 1957.

54. Robertson, Nan. "City Bars Sale of 'Voodoo Objects' in Its Markets; Venders of Religions Articles Found Selling Talismans, Hexes and Love Potions." NYT (17 August 1962) 24. Web.
55. Maple, Eric. *The Dark World of Witches*. A.S. New York: Barnes & Company. 1962. 194.
56. It seems that few things have changed in 40 years. Wallace. *Witchcraft in the World Today*. 1967. 89.
57. Schurmacher, Emile. *Witchcraft in America Today*. New York: Paperback Library. 1970. 156-157.
58. Schurmacher. *Witchcraft in America Today*. 1970. 46-47.
59. LeBlanc, Rena. "Voodoo in Suburbia." Probe the Unknown 2.4 (Fall 1974) 20-22. Print. (Wesc. Lib. Llew.).
60. Clifton, Chas. *Her Hidden Children: The Rise of Wicca and Paganism in America*. Lanham: AltaMira Press. 2006. 129.
61. Adler, Margot. *Drawing Down the Moon: Witches, Druids, Goddess Worshippers, and Other Pagans in America Today*. Penguin Books. 1986. 233-236.
62. "Church of Aphrodite, Goddess of Love, is Chartered in New York." LIFE (4 December 1939) 101.
63. Clifton. *Her Hidden Children*. 2006. 139-142.
64. Pendderwen, Gwydion [Tom DeLong]. "Introduction." Thorns of the Blood Rose (Victor Anderson). San Leandro: Privately Published. 1980.
65. Adler. *Drawing Down the Moon*. 1986. 288-293.
66. Moss, Harold. Message to the author. 18 August 2008. Email.
67. Kelly, Aidan. *Crafting the Art of Magic (Book I): A History of Modern Witchcraft, 1939-1964*. St. Paul: Llewellyn Publications. 1991. 21-26; and others.
68. "Personal." *Pentagram* (5). London: BM/Eleusis. December 1965. 19.
69. Wilson, Joseph B. "Warts And All: The Spiritual Autobiography of Joseph B Wilson," Part Five (Draft). 2003. (http://www.toteg.org/ Joseph/5Warts.html, accessed 23 February 2008).
70. Wilson, Joseph B. "The Foundations of 1734: The Words of Joseph B. Wilson." *1734 Witchcraft*. 1999. (http://www.1734-witchcraft.org/, accessed 14 October 2008).
71. Leek, Sybil. *Diary of a Witch*. Englewood Cliffs: Prentice-Hall. 1968. 124-125.
72. Leek, Sybil. *A Shop in the High Street*. New York: David Mckay Co. 1964.
73. Not everyone was receptive to her message. Leek writes of numerous offers for interviews which were subsequently withdrawn when station executives began to fret about what their sponsors would say of being associated with a Witch. Leek. Diary of a Witch. 176-177.
74. Buckland, Raymond. *Witchcraft...The Religion* (Museum Handbook Series. No. 1). Bay Shore: The Buckland Museum of Witchcraft & Magick. 1966.
75. "Scotland's Underground Witches." Fate 15.4 (April 1962) 83. Print. (Wesc. Lib. Llew.).
76. "Real Witches at Work: English pagans keep an old cult alive." LIFE 57.20 (13 November 1964) 55. Print. Even more surprising was that not a single letter to the editor concerning these articles, either pro or con, was printed in the month following their publication.
77. Bone, Ray. "We Witches are Simple People." LIFE 57.20 (13 November 1964) 60. Print.

[78] Hughes, Pennethorne. *Witchcraft.* Maryland: Penguin Books. 1965. p. 217.
[79] "Bewitching Tale about Witches." LIFE 45.21 (24 November 1958) 66-69.Print.
[80] Jones, Leslie Ellen. *From Witch to Wicca.* Cold Spring Harbor: Cold Spring Press. 2004. 172.
[81] Ehrenstein, David. *Open Secret.* New York: William Morrow and Company. 1998. 84.
[82] Haining. *The Anatomy of Witchcraft.* 101-102.
[83] Roberts, Susan. *Witches USA.* New York: Dell Publishing. 1971. 107.
[84] Leek. *Diary of a Witch.* 114, 115, 127.
[85] Leek. *Diary of a Witch.* 128-136.
[86] Wallace. *Witchcraft in the World Today.* 96.
[87] Paul Lynde allowed himself to be "touched" by Witchcraft again many years later in his television show The Paul Lynde Halloween Special (1976), starring Margaret Hamilton (as the Wicked Witch of the West from the movie The Wizard of Oz) and Billie Hayes (as Witchiepoo from the children's television show H.R.Pufnstuf). Florence Henderson sang a disco rendition of "That Old Black Magic." The special was an underground classic due to it being the national television appearance of the rock band KISS.

Notes for Chapter 3

[1] Margolis, Jon. *The Last Innocent Year: America in 1964.* New York: William Morrow and Company. 1999. viii.
[2] Wetzsteon, Ross. *Republic of Dreams: Greenwich Village: The American Bohemia, 1910-1960.* New York: Simon & Schuster. 2003. ix, xvi
[3] Chauncey, George. *Gay New York: Gender, Urban Culture, and the Making of the Gay Male World, 1890-1940.* New York: Basic Books. 1995. 234.
[4] "History of SROs and Homelessness in New York." Supportive Housing Network of New York. Web. (http://www.shnny.org/what_is_history.html, accessed 16 August 2009).
[5] Newfield, Jack. "MacDougal at Midnight: A Street Under Pressure." Village Voice 10.25 (8 April 1965) 1, 25. Microfilm (MCF). Columbus Metropolitan Library Tech Center (Cols. Met. Lib).
[6] Sanders, Ed. *Fug You.* Da Capo: New York. 2011. 74-75. Print.
[7] Polsky, Ned. *Hustlers, Beats, and Others.* New York: Anchor Books. 1969. 148.
[8] Waldron, Eli. "The new American capital of Bohemia." Saturday Evening Post 237.20 (23 May 1964) 98. Print.
[9] But nothing lasts forever. In 1992, Village Voice writer C. Carr noted the latest diaspora, this time from "the faux bohemia once known as the East Village Scene". A victim of its own success just like Greenwich Village before it, gentrification displaced those who had come before, bringing with it higher rents and degrading the social matrix upon which artistic exiles depend for inspiration and support. "For the first time in 150 years," Carr wrote, "bohemia can't be pinpointed on a map." Thus, by 1993 and the first public reading of Jonathon Larson's musical Rent, which portrayed the dying days of this Boehme, his work was arguably already a period piece (based on a much earlier period piece).

Carr, C. "The Bohemian Diaspora." Village Voice 38.5 (4 February 1992) 26-31. MCF. (Cols. Met. Lib).

[10] Sanders. *Fug You.* 258-259.

[11] Ellwood, Robert. *The Fifties Spiritual Marketplace: American Religion in a Decade of Conflict.* New Brunswick: Rutgers University Press. 1997. 163-164, 173.

[12] Love, Robert. *The Great Oom: The Improbable Birth of Yoga in America.* New York: Viking Press. 2010. 69.

[13] Hedgepeth, William. "Inside the Hippie Movement." Look 31.17 (22 August 1967) 64. Print. While Look was speaking to the spiritual side of the movement, The Saturday Evening Post was playing up the drug aspect of the subculture, and darkly labeling it "The Hippie Cult." Didion, Joan. "The Hippie Generation." Saturday Evening Post 240.19 (23 September 1967). Np.

[14] Partridge, William. *The Hippie Ghetto: The Natural History of a Subculture (Case Studies in Cultural Anthropology).* New York: Holt, Rinehart and Winston, Inc. 1973. 81.

[15] Kerouac, Jack. "After Me, the Deluge." Los Angeles Times. October 26, 1969. V1, 44, 45, 61.

[16] "The Hippies." Firing Line with William F. Buckley Jr. WOR-TV. 3 September 1968.

[17] Polsky. *Hustlers, Beats, and Others.* 1969. 148-151.

[18] White, Edmund. *City Boy.* New York: Bloomsbury. 2009. 5.

[19] Star, Jack. "The Sad 'Gay' Life." Look. January 10, 1967. 30-33.

[20] Stearn, Jess. *The Sixth Man.* New York: MacFadden Book. 1965. 205-206.

[21] Gianniotis, Terry. Message to the author. 2 November 2011. Email.

[22] Jamison, Artie. Personal interview. 28 April 2006.

[23] Van Ronk, Dave. *The Mayor of MacDougal Street: A Memoir.* Cambridge: Da Capo Press. 2006. 148-149.

[24] Polsky. *Hustlers, Beats, and Others.* 1969. 78-79.

[25] Kisseloff, Jeff. "Jim Fouratt." *Generation on Fire — Voices of Protest from the 1960's: An Oral History.* Web. (http://www.generationonfire.com/fouratt.html, accessed 28 May 2010).

[26] This wasn't even the first time that this had happened. A similar situation had occurred in the Village during the 1920s-1930s, with the influx of Bohemians and tour buses, and retaliation by the resident population. Ware. Greenwich Village 1920-1930. 1965. 96.

[27] Herbert, Brian. *Dreamer of Dune: The Biography of Frank Herbert.* New York: Tor Books. 2004. 85, 181, 184.

[28] Stevens, Jay. *Storming Heaven: LSD and the American Dream.* Grove Press. 1998. 208.

[29] Rundquist, Thomas. *Sex, Drugs in Religions: An Uncensored Bibliography.* Danvers: Nova Media, Inc. 2004. 103.

[30] Buczynski. "Edmund Michael Buczynski" autobiographical paper. 1974. CES.

[31] Evans, Arthur. BIOGRAPHICAL SKETCH. Web (http://www.webcastro.com/evans1.htm#biography, accessed 2 July 2009).

[32] Stearn. *The Sixth Man.* 1965. 121, 156.

[33] Buczynski, Frank. Telephone interview. 8 May 2008.

[34] North, Erika [Judith McNally]. Message to the author. 30 November 2005. Email.

[35] Buczynski, Eddie. Letter to Joseph Cupolo. 1 December 1977. MS.

36 Jessup, John K. "New Currents Swirling Around Peter's Rock." *Life* 59.25 (17 December 1965) 76. Print.
37 Spencer, Steven M. "The Birth Control Revolution." *Saturday Evening Post* 239.2 (15 January 1966) 22. Print.
38 Zoll, Rachel. "Study: Homosexuality, celibacy didn't cause abuse." 18 May 2011. Web (http://www.msnbc.msn.com/id/43076289/ns/politics/t/study-homosexuality-celibacy-didnt-cause-abuse/, accessed 25 May 2011).
39 Fritscher, Jack. *Mapplethorpe: Assault with a Deadly Camera*. Mamaroneck: Hastings House. 1994. 158.
40 Allen, Peter Lewis. *The Wages of Sin: Sex and Disease, Past and Present*. Chicago: University of Chicago Press. 2000. 139-140. The stance of Pope Paul VI on birth control, promulgated as it was by a man who did not even participate in the reproductive process, led President Nixon's Agriculture Secretary, Earl Butz, to sarcastically quip in 1974, "He no play-a the game, he no make-a the rules."
41 An interest in the occult was not necessarily a disqualification to service, particularly in a scholarly Order such as the Jesuits. The Rev. Lawrence L. Cassidy, SJ, taught courses on the occult at St. Peter's College in New Jersey. Fr. Cassidy (d. 2006) was a well-known adherent of astrology, and wrote several papers on the compatibility of the practice with Christian belief.
42 The process continues to this day, with Roe v. Wade, 410 United States 113 (1973) establishing the right to abortion, and Lawrence v. Texas, 539 US 558 (2003) which overturned sodomy laws across the country.
43 Alterman, Eric. "Altercation: The Punditocracy vs. History." www.msnbc.com. August 10, 2006. Web. A lingering, and unfortunate, side effect of this phenomenon was a muted and ineffective anti-war movement in the face of George W. Bush's Iraq adventure, even when two-thirds of the country was finally opposed to the war by 2006.
44 Peter Levenda notes "This is perhaps only comprehensible to those of us who grew up in New York City which had been for years under the thrall of Cardinal Spellman, one of the most powerful men in the country in those days, who was an unabashed supporter of the war." Levenda, Peter. Message to the author. 29 August 2005.
45 The writer Michelangelo Signorile refers to Spellman as being "one of the most notorious, powerful and sexually voracious homosexuals in the American Catholic Church's history." Signorile, Michelangelo. "Cardinal Spellman's Dark Legacy." New York Press (19:9). March 1-7, 2006.
46 Radio personality and barman Malachy McCourt often mocked the hypocrisies of the late Cardinal Spellman, including his closeted homosexuality and his trip to Vietnam to bless the guns of United States forces used in the conflict. McCourt remarked that Spellman was the target of a Viet Cong assassination attempt in Saigon: "They sent him a poisoned altar boy" (a joke that Herman Slater would often repeat years after Spellman's death). Spellman was also referred to as the "Cardinal of Vaseline." See: McCourt, Malachy. *A Monk Swimming: A Memoir*. New York: Hyperion. 1999.
47 Cooney, John. *The American Pope: The Life and Times of Francis Cardinal Spellman*. New York: Crown Publishers. 1984.
48 To be fair, support for the Vietnam War within the Catholic Church was hardly a required article of faith, and even Rome eventually grew wary of

Spellman's cheerleading of the slaughter. Many within the church became active in the anti-war movement. In one example, 50 nuns lay down in protest outside St. Patrick's Cathedral before mass on Sunday, April 30, 1972. Village Voice 17.18 (May 4, 1972). MCF. (Cols. Met. Lib). Another example is Emmaus House, an experimental community formed in Harlem in 1965 by Father David Kirk (d. 2007), who was a Melkite Catholic.

[49] Jessup, John K. "New Currents Swirling Around Peter's Rock." Life 59.25 (17 December 1965) 76. Print.

[50] Buchanan, Henry A. and Bob. W. Brown. "The Ecumenical Movement Threatens Protestantism." Saturday Evening Post 237.37 (24 October 1964) 10, 15. Print.

[51] Melton, J. Gordon. "Beyond Millennialism: The New Age Transformed." Presented at the conference on New Age in the Old World held at the Institut Oecumenique de Bossey, Celigny, Switzerland. July 17-21, 2000.

[52] Melton, J. Gordon. "Toward a History of Magical Religion in the United States." *Green Egg* 8.73 (September 1975) 33. Print. From the collection of Alaric Terrason (Coll. A.Terr.).

[53] Elwood, Robert S. *The Sixties Spiritual Awakening.* New Brunswick: Rutgers University Press. 1994. 202-203.

[54] Holzer, Hans. *The Directory of the Occult.* Chicago: Henry Regnery Company. 1974. 3, 4.

[55] Ehrenhalt, Alan. "The Faustian Generation." Newsweek (24 July 2006) Np. Web-Exclusive Commentary. (http://www.newsweek.com/2006/07/23/the-faustian-generation.html, 25 accessed July 2006).

[56] Ironically, the modern evangelical movement in the United States began at roughly this time, in part due to the horrified reaction of religious conservatives at this social unrest and loss of Christian gravitas, and in part to reassert Christianity's relevance to a modern world and to re-energize the faithful.

[57] Bayly, Joseph. *What About Horoscopes?* Colorado Springs: David C. Cook Publishing Company. 1970.

[58] "The Occult: A Substitute Faith." Time (Monday 19 June 1972) Np. Web (http://www.time.com/time/magazine/article/0,9171,877779,00.html, accessed 22 December 2007)

[59] *Hippies, Hypocrisy and Happiness.* Pasadena: Ambassador College Press. 1968. 20-21.

[60] Roszak, Theodore. "Politics of the Nervous System." The Nation. 1 April 1968. Reprinted in Goodman, Mitchell (ed.). The Movement Toward a New America. New York: Alfred A. Knopf. 1972. pp. 648-651.

[61] Partridge. *The Hippie Ghetto.* 1973. 10.

[62] It was the movement of blacks into his neighborhood, for example, that prompted Carmine Fatico, a capo of the Gambino crime syndicate, to move the base for his operations from Brooklyn to Ozone Park in Queens in the early 1970s. Capeci, Jerry. *Gotti: Rise and Fall.* Chicago: Onyx Books. 1996. 156.

[63] Lewis, James R. and Jesper Aagaard Petersen, eds. *Controversial New Religions.* New York: Oxford University Press, USA. 2004. 102.

[64] Heine, Bill. "Summoning of the Leopard Demon: a Magical Memoir of the Sixties." Bill Heine website. 2006. Web (http://www.billheine.com/selectedmemoirso.html, accessed 21 January 2010).

[65] Power, Lisa. *No Bath but Plenty of Bubbles: An Oral History of the Gay Liberation Front 1970-1973.* New York: Cassell. 1995. 17.
[66] Kisselloff, Jeff. "Jim Fouratt" in Generation on Fire — Voices of Protest from the 1960's: An Oral History (http://www.generationonfire.com/ fouratt.html, accessed 28 May 2010).
[67] Chappell, Vere. *Sexual Outlaw, Erotic Mystic: The Essential Ida Craddock.* San Francisco: Weiser. 2010.
[68] Chappell, Vere (ed.). *Lunar and Sex Worship.* York Beach: Teitan Press. 2011.
[69] Banes, Sally. *Greenwich Village 1963: Avant-Garde Performance and the Effervescent Body.* Durham: Duke University Press. 1993. 249-250.
[70] Koestenbaum, Wayne. *Andy Warhol: A Penguin Life.* New York: Viking Books. 2001. 147-148.
[71] Baumgarten, Marjorie and Louis Black. "Ondine on Edie, On Warhol, on Ondine" (A 'Chronicle' Reprint). Austin Chronicle. 17 October 2003. Web.
[72] "Light in the Heart of Darkness." Esquire LXXIII.3 (March 1970) 122. Print.
[73] Fritscher, John. *Popular Witchcraft.* Secaucus: Citadel Press. 1973. 44.
[74] Bockris, Victor. *Warhol: The Biography.* New York: De Capo Press. 2003.
[75] Warhol, Andy and Pat Hackett. *POPism: The Warhol '60s.* New York: Harper Colophon. 1983.
[76] Eaton, Sally. Message to the author. 23 January 2008. Email.
[77] While it's likely a coincidence, before settling on the name The Velvet Underground, Reed and Cale cycled through several other iterations of the band, including The Warlocks (1965). Bockris, Victor and Gerard Malanga. *Up-Tight: The Velvet Underground Story.* New York: Omnibus Press. 1983. 20.
[78] Warhol and Hackett. *POPism.* 1983. 289-290.
[79] Name, Billy. Message to the author. 14 April 2006. Email.
[80] Robinson, Esther B. "Billy Name — After Andy was Shot." A Walk into the Sea. Arthouse Films. 2007.
[81] Macer-Story, Eugenia. Message to the author. 13 January 2009. Email.
[82] "Witchcraft — Spirits." NYT (6 December 1855) Np. Web.
[83] Buckland, Raymond. *Witchcraft from the Inside.* St. Paul: Llewellyn Publications. 1971. 55.
[84] Institute for Research. Advertisement. Village Voice 11.30 (19 May 1966) 2. MCF. (Cols. Met. Lib).
[85] Institute for Research. Advertisement. Village Voice 10.13 (14 January 1965) 12. MCF. (Cols. Met. Lib).
[86] Wallace. *Witchcraft in the World Today.* 1967. 83.
[87] Sherwood, Debbie. *The Story of a Happy Witch.* New York: Magnum Books. 1973. 71-85. Sherwood describes the class in detail in the chapter "I Studied to be a Witch at NYU."
[88] Sanders. *Fug You.* 129.
[89] Farrell, Barry. "The Other Culture." LIFE 62.7 (17 February 1967) 94. Print.
[90] Sanders. *Fug You.* 150.
[91] Allyn, David. *Make Love, Not War.* New York: Little, Brown and Company. 2000. 44.
[92] Peace Eye Bookstore Advertisement. Village Voice 14.41 (24 July 1969) 6. MCF. (Cols. Met. Lib).
[93] Smith, Patti. *Just Kids.* New York: HarperCollins. 2010. 115. Print.

[94] Lachman, Gary. *Turn Off Your Mind: The Mystic Sixties and the Dark Side of the Age of Aquarius.* New York: The Disinformation Company. 2003. 378.

[95] Weschcke, Carl. Message to the author. 6 August 2009. Email.

[96] Wallace. *Witchcraft in the World Today.* 93.

[97] By 1996, Llewellyn alone had sales of around $12 million. Rybak, Deborah Caulfield. "The Alchemist's Revenge." City Pages (13 November 1996) Np. Web.

[98] Pauwel, Louis and Jacques Bergier. *The Morning of the Magicians.* New York: Stein and Day. 1960.

[99] Gault, R. T. "The Quixotic Dialectical Metaphysical Manifesto: Morning of the Magicians." The Absolute Elsewhere: Fantastic, Visionary, and Esoteric Literature in the 1960s and 1970s. Web (http://www.cafes.net/ditch/motm1.htm, accessed 1 December 2008).

[100] Phoenix, Jack. "Gary Lachman: Music, Magick and Mind." Fortean Times 220 (February 2002) Np. Web. (www.forteantimes.com/features/interviews/40/gary_lachman.html, accessed 1 December 2008.)

[101] Wilson, Doric. Message to the author. 5 June 2010. Email.

[102] Crespy, David and Edward Albee. *Off-Off-Broadway Explosion: How Provocative Playwrights of the 1960's Ignited a New American Theatre.* New York: Back Stage Books. 2003. 37.

[103] Horn, Barbara. *The Age of Hair: Evolution and Impact of Broadway's First Rock Musical.* Santa Barbara: Greenwood Press. 1991.

[104] *Dionysus in 69 – The Performance Group.* New York: Farrar, Straus and Giroux. 1970.

[105] De Palma, Brian and Richard Schechner (Directors). *Dionysus.* Sigma III Corporation (Distributors). 1970. The film received an "X" rating from the MCAA for frontal nudity and adult situations.

[106] Bottom, Stephen J. *Playing Underground: A Critical History of the 1960s Off-Off-Broadway Movement.* Ann Arbor: University of Michigan Press. 2004. 249

[107] Anger, Kenneth. *The Films of Kenneth Anger: Volume Two* (book). Fantoma Films. 2007. 22.

[108] Schreck, Nikolas. *The Satanic Screen: An Illustrated Guide to the Devil in Cinema.* England: Creation Books. 2000. 130.

[109] Case, George. *Jimmy Page: Magus, Musician, Man.* New York: Hal Leonard Books. 2007. 121.

[110] Led Zeppelin. "Led Zeppelin IV" (informally known as ZOSO). Atlantic Records. 1971. Writer Erik Davis called it "the greatest spell of the 1970s." David, Erik. "Led Zeppelin IV." *33 1/3 Greatest Hits, Volume 1.* New York: Continuum. 2006. 201.

[111] Harvey, Doug. "Dismembering Harry Smith." LA Weekly (May 4, 2001) Np. Web.

[112] Igliori, Paola. *American Magus: Harry Smith.* New York: Inanout Press. 1966.

[113] On December 6, 1969, a free concert at the Altamont Speedway in northern California resulted in four deaths, including one homicide. Altamont, with its commingled violence and heavy drug use, is often cited as the symbolic end of the Hippie era and the death of the Woodstock Nation.

[114] Watson, Stephen. *The Birth of the Beat Generation.* New York: Pantheon Books. 1995. 298.

[115] Didion, Joan. "The Hippie Generation." Saturday Evening Post 240.19 (23 September 1967) Np. Web. "Hashbury" was a play on words referring to the rampant drug use in Haight-Ashbury, the district that served as ground zero for the Hippie subculture in San Francisco, California.
[116] "Speed Kills." Time (20 October 1967) Np. Web.
[117] Lukas, J. Anthony. "The Two Worlds of Linda Fitzpatrick." NYT (16 October 1967) Np. Web.
[118] One of those accused of the murders was 25 year old Donald Ramsey, an adherent of the Yoruban religion who lived in the building. Sanders. *Fug You.* 272-273.
[119] Buckland. *Witchcraft from the Inside.* 74.
[120] Smith, Susy. *Today's Witches.* Englewood: Prentice-Hall. 1970. 139.
[121] Nemeton advertisement. *Gnostica News* 5.4 (1976) 18. Print. (Wesc. Lib. Llew.).
[122] Pendderwen, Gwydion. "Dry Mouth Musings..." *Green Egg* 8.76 (February 1976) 23. Print. (Coll. A.Terr.).
[123] Wasson, R. Gordon, et al. *The Road to Eleusis: Unveiling the Secret of the Mysteries.*
Hoffman, Albert, et al. *Psychoactive Sacramentals: Essays on Entheogens and Religion.*
Schultes, Richard Evans, et al. *Plants of the Gods: Their Sacred, Healing, and Hallucinogenic Powers.*
McKenna, Terence. *Food of the Gods: The Search for the Original Tree of Knowledge A Radical History of Plants, Drugs, and Human Evolution.*
Ott, Jonathan. *Pharmacotheon.*
Pendell, Dale. *Pharmako/Poeia, Pharmako/Gnosis, and Pharmako/Dynamis.*
[124] This isn't to say that there aren't also native hucksters afoot on the lecture circuit; there undoubtedly are. Human nature is, after all, very human.
[125] Austan, Laura. Message to the author. 19 February 2011. Email. Austan's observation of the involvement of gay men in the Spiritualist movement is interesting in light of Cliff Bias' rooms in the Ansonia Hotel. A grand old residential hotel, the original basement of the Ansonia was a Turkish bath that was converted in the 1960s into a famous gay bathhouse – the Continental Baths – thus allowing spirits to be raised in other ways.
[126] Warhol and Hackett. *POPism.* 1983. 255.
[127] Montgomery, Ruth. *A Gift of Prophecy: the Phenomenal Jeane Dixon.* New York: William Morrow. 1965.
[128] Smyth, Frank. *Modern Witchcraft.* New York:Harrow Books.1973.p. 15.
[129] Horowitz. Occult America. 2009. 253-254.
[130] Eliade, Mircea. *Occultism, Witchcraft and Cultural Fashions.* Chicago: University of Chicago Press. 1978. 59.
[131] Eighth Street Bookshop. Advertisement. Village Voice 14.12 (2 January 1969) 6. MCF. (Cols. Met. Lib).
[132] Macer-Story, Eugenia. Message to the author. 14 January 2009. Email.
[133] O'Neil, Paul. "The Wreck of a Monstrous 'Family.'" LIFE 67.25 (19 December 1969) 22, 26. Print.
[134] "Honi soit qui mal y pense." Esquire LXXIII.3 (March 1970) 99-123. Print.
[135] Like all such rumors, this one is apocryphal at best, and more likely pure poppycock. The House of Windsor, current head of the Order, certainly makes no claims of any such ties to the occult.

[136] Roberts. *Witches, USA.* 41-47.
[137] International Association of Machinists and Aerospace Workers. "IAM Organizers Accused of 'Witchcraft'." The Machinist XXIII.31 (10 October 1968) 2. Web.
[138] International Association of Machinists and Aerospace Workers. "Nixon Firm Linked to Witchcraft Case." The Machinist XXIII.33 (24 October 1968) 5. Web.
[139] Buckland, Raymond. From his up-coming autobiography, as yet untitled. Copyright Raymond Buckland 2010, with permission.
[140] Roberts. *Witches, USA.* 137.
[141] Schreck, Nikolas. *The Satanic Screen: An Illustrated Guide to the Devil in Cinema.* England: Creation Books. 2000. 133-139, 145-146.
[142] Cochrane, Robert. "The Craft Today." Pentagram 2 (November 1964) 8. Electronic.
[143] Herlihy, James Leo. *Season of the Witch.* New York: Simon and Schuster. 1971.
[144] Rolling Stone 84 (10 June 1971) 52.
[145] "Witchcraft." Google Labs Books Ngram Viewer. Web (http://ngrams.googlelabs.com/graph?content=Witchcraft&year_start=1800&year_end=2000&corpus=0&smoothing=3, accessed 2 January 2011).
[146] Huebner, Louise. *Power Through Witchcraft.* New York: Nash Publishing Corp. 1969.
[147] Buckland, Raymond. *Ancient & Modern Witchcraft.* Secaucus: Castle Books. 1970.
Johns, June. *King of the Witches: The World of Alex Sanders.* New York: Coward-McCann. 1970.
[148] Leek, Sybil. *The Complete Art of Witchcraft.* Cleveland: The World Publishing Company. 1971. Buckland, Raymond. Witchcraft from the Inside. St. Paul: Llewellyn Publications. 1971.
Bonewits, P. E. I. *Real Magic.* New York: Berkley. 1971.
Farrar, Stewart. *What Witches Do.* New York: Coward, McCann and Geoghegan. 1971.
[149] Crowley, Aleister (Kenneth Grant and John Symonds, eds). *Confessions of Aleister Crowley.* New York: Bantam. 1971.
Crowley, Aleister. *Moonchild.* New York: Avon. 1971.
Regardie, Israel, ed. *The Golden Dawn* (4th edition). St. Paul: Llewellyn Publications. 1971.
Wilson, Colin. *The Occult.* New York: Random House. 1971.
[150] Dass, Ram (Richard Alpert). *Be Here Now.* New York: Lama Foundation/Harper and Row. 1971.
[151] Many kids and young adults in the 1960s, including this author, had their first real exposure to the occult (apart from fairy tales, Walt Disney, and Dark Shadows) through the Ouija talking board. Friends and I played with it up until its appearance in Peter Blatty's The Exorcist (1973), after which their enthusiasm waned considerably. Parker Brothers estimates that they have sold over ten million Ouija boards since 1967.
[152] Sloane, Leonard. "Witches, Zodiac, Occult Newest Trend for Toys." NYT (8 March 1970) 1, 19. Web.
[153] Johns, June. *King of the Witches: The World of Alex Sanders.* New York: Coward-McCann. 1969. 140. This linkage of UFOs with the occult continued

to be made throughout the 1970s and early 1980s by authors such as psychic playwright Eugenia Macer-Story (Congratulations the UFO Reality, 1978) and UFO-logist Timothy Green Beckley (MIB Aliens Among Us, 1971 and Psychic & UFO Revelations in the Last Days, 1980).

[154] Flying Saucer News Bookstore. Advertisement. Village Voice 14.43 (7 August 1969) 6. MCF. (Cols. Met. Lib).

[155] Flying Saucer News Bookstore. Advertisement. Village Voice 14.49 (18 September 1969) 27. MCF. (Cols. Met. Lib).

[156] "Psychic Seminar." Calendar item. Village Voice 14.45 (4 September 1969) 6. MCF. (Cols. Met. Lib).

[157] The Universe Book Club. Advertisement. Flying Saucers: The Magazine of Space Conquest 28 (February 1960). Back cover. Print.

[158] The Universe Book Club. Advertisement. Flying Saucers and UFOs 1969 (3). 1969. Back cover. Print.

[159] Hynek, J. Allen. "Are Flying Saucers Real?" Saturday Evening Post 239.26 (17 December 1966) 17-21. Print.

[160] Däniken, Erich von. *Chariots of the Gods.* New York: Bantam. 1968. According to the von Däniken website (www.daniken.com), Erich's books have been translated into 32 languages, and have sold 63 million copies worldwide.

[161] Leslie, Desmond and George Adamski. Flying Saucers Have Landed. New York: The British Book Centre. 1953.

[162] Jung, C.G. Flying Saucers. New York: MJF Books. 1978.

[163] Jenkins. Mystics and Messiahs. 2001. 73.

[164] Parker, Ian. "Letter from Cairo: The Pharaoh." New Yorker 85.37 (16 November 2009) 58. Print.

[165] Examples include "The Cult of Dionysus" (Spring 1948), "Isis, Goddess of Sex" (November 1949), "The Ancient Rites of Pan" (September 1950), "Pagan Rites of May Day" (June 1953), "Ancient Crete — Wonderful Land of the Sea Kings" (July 1957), "The Mysteries of Attis" (November 1957), "Pagan Rites of Pan" (December 1958), and "Witches Out of Hiding" (June 1964). (Wesc. Lib. Llew.).

[166] Steiger, Brad. "How Strange Were the Paperbacks." *Gnostica News* 4.8 (June 1975) 44. Print. (Wesc. Lib. Llew.).

[167] Strausbaugh, John. "MUSIC; Sidewalk Hero, On the Horns of a Revival." NYT (28 October 2007) Np. Web.

[168] Scotto, Robert. Message to the author. 11 April 2008. Email.

[169] Scotto, Robert. *Moondog: The Viking of 6th Avenue.* Los Angeles: Process Media. 2007. 152, 165.

[170] Scotto. *Moondog.* 145.

[171] Inominandum [Miller, Jason]. "Simon Speaks: Part II." *Behutet* 17 (2003) p. 13. Print.

[172] Clifton. *Her Hidden Children.* 2006. 139-142.

[173] Keith, W. Holman. *Divinity as the Eternal Feminine.* New York: Pageant Press. 1960.

[174] References to Heinlein's terminology from the story, including "grok-ing" and "sharing water," had begun showing up in the Village Voice by early 1966, indicating that others were already taking a spiritual interest in the novel prior to the advent of CAW. Advertisement. Village Voice 11.32 (26 May 1966) 2. MCF. (Cols. Met. Lib).

[175] Adler. *Drawing Down the Moon.* 1986. 288-293.
[176] Zell-Ravenheart, Oberon. "CAW — Report to Waterkin: The Third Phoenix Resurrection." CAWeb. 21 February 2006. Web (http://original.caw.org/articles/ReportToWaterKin.html, accessed 26 October 2008).
[177] Fritscher, Jack. *Popular Witchcraft: Straight from the Witch's Mouth.* Bowling Green: Popular Press. 2004. 130.
[178] Pendderwen, Gwydion. [Tom DeLong]. "Introduction." Thorns of the Blood Rose (Anderson, Victor). Privately Published. 1980.
[179] Kampel, Stewart. "Ah, Halloween! A Time to Take Off Clothes." NYT (31 October 1971) 1. Web.
[180] Martello, Leo. *Black Magic, Satanism & Voodoo.* Secaucus: Castle Books, Inc. 1973. 115.
[181] Wallace. *Witchcraft in the World Today.* 86.
[182] Burke, Tom. "Princess Leda's Castle in the Air." Esquire LXXIII.3 (March 1970) 107. Print.
[183] "Real Witches at Work: English Pagans Keep an Old Cult Alive. A High Priestess Talks About Her Witchcraft." LIFE (13 November 1964) 55. Print.
[184] Examples include: "The Good Witch of the West — Los Angeles' Official Sorceress Casts Only Kindly Spell." LIFE (10 April 1970). This article covered Louise Huebner.
"Witchcraft is Rising." Look (24 August 1971). An appropriately Satanic-looking Anton LeVey stared out at the reader, skull in hand. Other occult figures of the day were also covered in this article, including Long Island resident Raymond Buckland.
[185] Smyth. *Modern Witchcraft.* p. 99.
[186] Nascosto, Tom. Message to the author. 18 February 2008. Email.
[187] Buczynski, Edmund M. Volume One: Liber Ubrarum [sic] — The Book of Shadows with Commentary (Unpublished Paper). December 1983. P. ii. MS.
[188] Buckland Witchcraft lecture Advertisement. Village Voice 14.49 (18 September 1969) 27. MCF. (Cols. Met. Lib).
[189] Klemesrud, Judy. "Witchcraft: Some People Find It a Serious Matter." NYT (31 October 1969) Np. Web.

Notes for Chapter 4
Biographical information concerning Leo Martello's childhood and early adulthood was adapted from: Martello, Leo. *What it Means to Be a Witch.* New York: Privately Published. ca. 1973. 1-7.
[1] Bruno, Lori. "The Biography of Leo Martello." Trinacrian Rose Church and Grove. 2006. NP. Web (www.trinacrianrose.org).
[2] Martello, Leo. *Witchcraft: The Old Religion.* New York: University Books. 1973. 33.
[3] Martello. *It's Written in the Stars.* 1966. 5.
[4] Martello, Leo. *Your Pen Personality.* New York: Hero Press. 1961.
[5] Martello, Leo "Introduction." *The Secrets of Ancient Witchcraft with the Witches Tarot* (Arnold Crowther, Patricia Crowther). Secaucus: Citadel Press. 1974. 14.
[6] Martello, Leo. *It's Written in the Cards.* New York: Key Publishing Company. 1964.

[7] Martello, Leo. *How to Prevent Psychic Blackmail: The Philosophy of Psychselfism*. New York: Hero Press. 1966.
[8] Austan, Laura. Message to the author. 19 February 2011. Email.
[9] Hammel, Lisa. "Need an Occultist? Name Your Choice." NYT (28 November 1970) 34. Web.
[10] Carey was interviewed by Joy Miller, AP Women's editor, October 29, 1967 for a Hallowe'en piece on the rise of the occult in the United States See: Martello, Leo. *Weird Ways of Witchcraft*. Secaucus: Castle Books. 1972. 50. Martin Carey went on to draw the occult Mandala that appeared in the August 1968 issue of The Digger Papers.
[11] Fritscher, John. *Popular Witchcraft*. Secaucus: Citadel Press. 1973. 41
[12] Michael Bowen (artist). Web (en.wikipedia.org/wiki/Michael_ Bowen_(artist), accessed 19 October 2009).
[13] Sanders. *Fug You*. 278-280.
[14] The rite included the purification of the participants, consecration of the four directions, casting a circle, invocation of Powers and Spirits, prayers for the soldiers, offerings, raising of energy, and performance of the magickal working. This ritual format would be recognized by anyone versed in a Western esoteric tradition. Ed Sanders, who believed that the Pentagon did, in fact, levitate, is rumored to have said that the war was not halted because the building should also have been rotated.
Campbell, Marc. "44th Anniversary of the the [sic] Exorcism of the Pentagon." Dangerous Minds (16 October 2011). Web (http://www.dangerousminds.net/comments/44th_anniversary_of_the_the_exorcism_of_the_pentagon/, accessed 18 October 2011).
[15] This direct action is covered in a documentary film. The Sixth Side of the Pentagon. Chris Marker and François Reichenbach. Les Films du Jeudi. 1967.
[16] Sanders. *Fug You*. 311-312.
[17] Huebner, Louise. "The LA Witches Story, Part I." Louise Huebner: The Official Witch of Los Angeles. 2003. Web (http://www.mentorhuebnerart.com/ witchstuff/officialwitch.shtml).
[18] Schurmacher, Emile. *Witchcraft in America Today*. New York: Paperback Library. 1970. 9.
[19] Eaton, Sally. Message to the author. 23 January 2008. Email.
[20] Martello, Leo. *Hidden World of Hypnotism*. New York: HC Publishers, Inc. 1969.
[21] Martello. *Weird Ways of Witchcraft*. New York: HC Publishers. 1969.
[22] Sears, James. *Rebels, Rubyfruit, and Rhinestones: Queering Space in the Stonewall South*. New Brunswick: Rutgers University Press. 2001. 20-33.
[23] Sears, James. *Behind the Mask of the Mattachine: The Hal Call Chronicles and the Early Movement for Homosexual Emancipation*. New York: Harrington Park Press. 2006. xiv and xii.
[24] Sears. *Rebels, Rubyfruit, and Rhinestones*. 25-26.
[25] Martello, Leo. *Weird Ways of Witchcraft*. 1972. 116-124.
[26] Campbell, J. Louis. *Jack Nichols Gay Pioneer: "Have You Heard My Message?"* New York: Harrington Park Press. 2007. 103.
[27] Campbell. Jack Nichols *Gay Pioneer*. 102.
[28] Clarke, Lige and Jack Nichols. *I Have More Fun With You Than Anybody*. New York: St. Martin's Press. 1972. 29.

[29] Hershman, Florence. *Witchcraft USA.* Peacock Press. 1971. 22-26.
[30] Campbell. Jack Nichols, *Gay Pioneer.* 103.
[31] Campbell. Jack Nichols, *Gay Pioneer.* 104.
[32] Thompson, Mark. *Long Road to Freedom: The Advocate History of the Gay and Lesbian Movement.* New York: St. Martin's Press. 1994. 66.
[33] Star, Jack. "The Sad 'Gay' Life." Look (10 January 1967) 30-33. Print.
[34] Loughery, John. *The Other Side of Silence — Men's Lives and Gay Identities: A Twentieth-Century History.* New York: Owl Books. 1998. 303-320.
[35] Sismondo, Christine. *America Walks into a Bar: A Spirited History of Taverns and Saloons, Speakeasies and Grog Shops.* New York: Oxford University Press. 2011. 250-264.
[36] "Get the Mafia and the Cops Out of Gay Bars." Homophile Youth Movement (HYMN). July 1969? From: Marotta, Toby. Revisiting Stonewall. Web (www.tobymarotta.com/flyer/index.htm, accessed 6 July 2009).
[37] "Scenes." Village Voice 11.34 (9 June 1966) 6, 7. MCF. (Cols. Met. Lib).
[38] Sismondo. *America Walks into a Bar.* 2011. 261-262.
[39] Caldiero, Joe. Message to the author. 8 February 2010. Email.
[40] Liscoe, Kevan. "Scared No More." Village Voice 14.39 (10 July 1969) 4. MCF. (Cols. Met. Lib).
[41] Carter, David. *Stonewall: The Riots That Sparked the Gay Revolution.* New York: St. Martin's Press. 2001. 125.
[42] Jamison, Artie. Personal interview. 26 April 2006. The assertion by one correspondent that Eddie Buczynski may have also witnessed the upheaval is reasonable, given his frequenting the area, but this has not been independently confirmed. Truthfully, with the passage of time it becomes harder to determine which is more numerous — Stonewall riot participants or reincarnated Atlantean high priestesses.
[43] Carter. *Stonewall.* 182-194.
[44] Truscott IV, Lucian. "Gay Power Comes to Sheridan Square." Village Voice 14.38 (3 July 1969) 18. MCF. (Cols. Met. Lib).
[45] One of the initial organizers of the Mattachine Foundation, Harry Hay, became involved in a form of spirituality in the 1970s that emphasized a version of Neo-Paganism based on the Native American two-spirit individual. He eventually founded the Radical Faerie movement with his companion John Burnside and a small circle of friends at the site of Sri Ram Ashram in Arizona on Labor Day weekend in 1979.
[46] Lauritsen, John and David Thorstad. *The Early Homosexual Rights Movement (1864-1935).* New York: Times Change Press. 1974. 5.
[47] Frank Kameny, a leader of the Washington, DC chapter of Mattachine, admits that the organization had badly miscalculated the dramatic shift in attitudes amongst younger homosexuals. "By the time of Stonewall, we had fifty to sixty gay groups in the country," he said. "A year later there was at least fifteen hundred. By two years later, to the extent that a count could be made, it was twenty-five hundred." Carter. *Stonewall.* 251.
[48] Eisenbach, David. *Gay Power: An American Revolution.* New York: Carroll & Graf Publishers. 2006. 118-119.
[49] Martello, Leo. "A Positive Image for the Homosexual." Come Out! A Newspaper By and For the Gay Community (14 November 1969) 16. Web.
[50] Hodges, Andrew and David Hutter. *With Downcast Gays: Aspects of Homosexual Self-Oppression.* London: Pomegranate Press. 1974.

[51] Evans and Bell were lovers, and lived in Greenwich Village not far from where the Stonewall riots took place. In 1971, Arthur Bell would become a writer on topics of interest to the gay community for The Village Voice, and would later publish two books on his experiences in the gay community. Arthur Evans left New York in 1972, eventually moving to San Francisco in 1975, where he would become involved in Neo-Pagan queer spirituality. Evans published two books of interest to queer Pagans — Witchcraft and the Gay Counterculture (Fag Rag Books, 1978) and The God of Ecstasy: Sex-roles and the Madness of Dionysos (St. Martin's Press, 1988).
[52] Martello, Leo. Letter. Gaysweek (20 June 1977). From the collection of Bruce-Michael Gelbert (Coll. BMG).
[53] Tanit. "Leo Martello: Il Mago." Earth Religion News (ERN) 1.2 (February 1974) 22. Print. (Arch. Circ. Sanc).
[54] Peck, Abe. *Uncovering the Sixties: The Life and Times of the Underground.* New York: Citadel Press. 1991. 219.
[55] Carter. *Stonewall.* 226.
[56] Brown, Mike and Michael Tallman, Leo Louis Martello (Staff writers). "The Summer of Gay Power and the Village Voice Exposed!" COME OUT! A Newspaper By and For the Gay Community 1.1 (14 November 1969).
[57] Lauritsen, John. "The First Gay Liberation Front Demonstration." GayToday VIII.167. Web (http://www.gaytoday.com/viewpoint/011904vp.asp).
[58] Loughery. *The Other Side of Silence.* 321-329.
[59] Carter. *Stonewall.* 215-232.
[60] Nichols, Ross. "How Martin Duberman Twisted New York History." Greenwich Village Gazette VI.XXVI. Web.
[61] Sears, James. *Rebels, Rubyfruit, and Rhinestones.* 29-30.
[62] Teal, Donn. *The Gay Militants: How Gay Liberation Began in America, 1969-1971.* New York: Stein and Day. 1971. 105.
[63] Star, Jack. "The Faces of the Boys in the Band." Look 33.24 (2 December 1969) 62-67. Print.
[64] Star, Jack. "A Changing View of Homosexuality?" Look 33.24 (2 December 1969) 68. Print.
[65] The second President of the GAA, Rich Wandel, eventually went on to become a Third Degree high priest in Gardnerian Wica, and the founder of the New York LGBT Community Center National History Archive. Wandel, Rich. Message to the author. 22 February 2009. Email.
[66] Evans eventually left New York City first for Washington State in April 1972, before moving to San Francisco in 1975. In 1978, he published the first in-depth look at the historical relationship between Witchcraft and homosexuals — Witchcraft and the Gay Counterculture. In his acknowledgements, "Leo Martello, friend and witch" heads the list. Arthur writes that it was Martello "who first suggested to me in 1970 that there was a link between witchcraft and the history of feminism." Evans, Arthur. Witchcraft and the Gay Counterculture. San Francisco: Fag Rag Books. 1978. P. 170.
[67] Miller, Merle. *On Being Different: What it means to be a homosexual.* New York: Random House. 1971. 37-38.
[68] Carter. *Stonewall.* 234-237.
[69] Martello, Leo. "The Gay Witch." GAY (1 December 1969) Np. From the collection of John Lauritsen.

70 In 1972, Martello began writing another Witchcraft-oriented column, this time in *Gnostica News*, an organ of Llewellyn Publishing. Called "Wicca-Basket," Leo's column was patterned after Randy Wicker's news and analysis column, "Wicker Basket," that was published in Gay. Campbell. Jack Nichols *Gay Pioneer*. 137.

71 Sears, James. *Rebels, Rubyfruit, and Rhinestones*. 30-31.

72 Gay Power (founded in September 1969) and GAY each had approximately 25,000 readers. Carter. *Stonewall*. 242.

73 Campbell. Jack Nichols *Gay Pioneer*. 139.

74 Barteldes, Ernest. "Jack Nichols, Gay Pioneer: An Interview." Greenwich Village Gazette VI.XXVI (27 July 2001) Np. Web (http://www.gvny.com/columns/barteldes/barteldes07-27-01.html).

75 Martello, Leo Louis. "Raid Victim Impaled on Fence." Advocate. April 29-May 9, 1970. pp. 1, 6.

76 Teal. *The Gay Militants*. 1971. 226

77 Teal. *The Gay Militants*. 1971. 229.

78 *Weird Ways of Witchcraft*, which had originally been issued by HC Publishers in 1969, was updated and re-released in 1972 by Castle Books, and covered some of the additional occurrences of 1970-71, including the 1970 "Witch-In" in Central Park.

79 Martello, Leo. "Book Review: Witches USA. ... So They Say." ERN 1.4 (June 1974) 62. Print. (Arch. Circ. Sanc).

80 Clarke and Nichols. *I Have More Fun with You Than Anybody*. 151.

81 Clifton. *Her Hidden Children*. 2006. 42-43.

82 Clarke and Nichols. I Have More Fun with You Than Anybody." p. 40.

83 Weinraub, Bernard. "10,000 Chant 'L-O-V-E'; L-O-V-E IS THEME OF PARK 'BE-IN'." NYT (27 March 1967) 1. Web.

84 Martello. Witchcraft: *The Old Religion*. 1973. 23-25.

85 Martello. Witchcraft: *The Old Religion*. 1973. 24.

86 Hershman. *Witchcraft USA*. 1971. 61.

87 Holzer, Hans. *Witches: True Encounters with Wicca, Wizards, Covens, Cults, and Magick*. New York: Black Dog & Leventhal Publishers. 2005. 68.

88 Pratt, Roger. Message to the author. 17 June 2010. Email.

89 For many years after, Martello complained that no Pagan or Craft group came to his aid during this event. *Green Egg* editor Tim Zell noted that his newspaper was, as far as he knew, the only one to congratulate Martello on his success. Zell, Tim. Editorial Note. *Green Egg* 5.47 (11 May 1972) 13. Print. Archives of *Green Egg* Magazine. Church of All Worlds. Cotati. (Arch. GE CAW).

90 Martello. *Weird Ways of Witchcraft*. 1972. 20-22.

91 Adam, Barry. *The Rise of a Gay and Lesbian Movement*. Boston: Twayne Publishers. 1987. 78.

92 Highleyman, Liz. "PAST Out: Who was Carl Wittman?" *LETTERS From CAMP Rehoboth* 16.4 (5 May 2006). Web (http://www.camprehoboth.com/issue05_05_06/past_out.htm). Wittman later acquired land in Wolf Creek, Oregon and moved there in 1971. In 1973, with his lover Allan Troxler, he helped establish RFD magazine, a country journal for gay men, which debuted in 1974. The Wolf Creek location eventually became the site of the first Radical Faerie sanctuary, just as RFD became the voice of the Radical Faerie happening.

[93] Wittman, Carl. *Refugees from Amerika: A Gay Manifesto.* San Francisco: Red Butterfly Collective. 1970.
[94] Lauritsen, John. Message to the author. 2 August 2007. Email.
[95] The London chapter of the Gay Liberation Front, inspired perhaps by Wittman's essay, printed their own GLF Manifesto in 1971. See: Gardiner, James. *Who's the Pretty Boy Then?: One Hundred & Fifty Years of Gay Life in Pictures.* London: Serpent's Tail. 1998. 142.
[96] Solanas, Valerie. *SCUM Manifesto.* New York: Self-Published. 1967.
[97] See: Rhodes, Jacqueline. *Radical Feminism, Writing, and Critical Agency: From Manifesto to Modern* (SUNY Series in Feminist Criticism and Theory). New York: State University of New York Press. 2005. 28, 36. In 1969, the Redstockings issued their own (Bitch) Manifesto.
[98] "W.I.T.C.H." *Green Egg* 7.65 (September 1974) 18. Print. (Coll. A.Terr.).
[99] Freeman, Jo. W.I.T.C.H. — The Women's International Terrorist Conspiracy from Hell. Web (http://www.jofreeman.com/photos/witch.html, accessed 25 May 2010).
[100] Smith, Susy. *Today's Witches.* Englewood Cliffs:Prentice-Hall.1970. 2.
[101] Durbin, Karen. "Alphabet Soup." WIN (January 1970). Reprinted in Goodman, Mitchell, ed. *The Movement Toward a New America.* New York: Alfred A. Knopf. 1972. 67.
[102] Teal. *The Gay Militants.* 1971. 261-262
[103] "Vast Outpouring of Political Support." GAY (9 November 1970) Np.
[104] Homophile Discussion Group. Advertisement. Village Voice 14.38 (3 July 1969) 2. MCF. (Cols. Met. Lib).
[105] Clarke and Nichols. *I Have More Fun with You Than Anybody.* 138-139.
[106] Clarke and Nichols. *I Have More Fun with You Than Anybody.* 134-135.
[107] Teal. *The Gay Militants.* 1971. 260-261.
[108] Martello. *Weird Ways of Witchcraft.* 1972. 120.

Notes for Chapter 5
[1] Soror Charis. "Herman Slater: 'Thee Magickal Childe'" (Part I). *Behutet* 10 (Summer 2001) 2. Print.
[2] Jones, Randy. Message to the author. 29 July 2009. Email.
[3] Warlock Shop. Advertisement. *Green Egg* 9.77 (March 1976) 48. Print. (Coll. A.Terr.). In the ad, Slater noted that the Warlock Shop was established in 1965.
[4] Greenberg, Dan. *Something's There: My Adventures in the Occult.* New York: DoubleDay. 1976. 86.
[5] Rivera, Ria. Personal interview. 30 October 2004.
[6] "The Unlikely Story of the Monk and the Warlock." Uncommon Sense Ministries, Inc. NP. Web (http://usminc.org/necronomicon.html, accessed 10 February 2012).
[7] Austan, Laura. Message to the author. 19 February 2011. Email.
[8] Eaton, Sally. Message to the author. 12 April 2006. Email. Martello and Slater generally remained friends until Herman's death in 1992.
[9] Rachleff, Owen S. The Occult Conceit. New York: Bell Publishing Company. 1971. p. 119. While the author may have been referring to another shop in Manhattan, it is also possible that Slater's shop had gone out of business between the time when Rachleff wrote about it and when the book was

published. Certainly the anonymous shopkeeper's attitude aligned with Herman's at that time, as did the macabre taste in stock.

10. Goro, Herb and Ellen Stock. "Atlantic Avenue: Boulevard of Brooklyn Dreamers." *New York* 6.29 (16 July 1973) 46. Web (http://books.google.com/books?id=7uYCAAAAMBAJ&lpg=PA46&ots=Xqf wA3Z0Jj&dq, accessed 23 May 2011).
11. Slater, Herman. Letter (dated 1/28/76). *Green Egg* 9.77 (March 1976) 41. Print. (Coll. A.Terr.).
12. Frank, Ann. Letter. *Green Egg* 9.77 (March 1976) 41. Print. (Coll. A.Terr.). Frank notes "that Herman's 'conversion' to Paganism took place while he was seriously ill in a hospital bed several years ago", and "the rapid metamorphosis that took place (with the help of a certain E.B. [Eddie Buczynski], who is in fact a homosexual) since he first opened the Warlock Shop."
13. Jamison, Artie. Telephone interview. 26 April 2006.
14. Silverknife, Zanoni. Message to the author. 13 July 2004. Email.
15. Pratt, Roger. Message to the author. 15 June 2010. Email.
16. Mills, Malcolm. Message to the author. 3 August 2007. Email.
17. Dalton, Ken. Message to the author. 30 January 2012. Email.
18. Weschcke, Carl. Message to the author. 10 August 2007. Email.
19. Moss, Harold. Message to the author. 29 August 2008. Email.
20. Kneitel, Tommy. Message to the author. 10 September 2004. Email.
21. Kirwan, Larry. Message to the author. 28 February 2007. Email.
22. North, Erika [Judith McNally]. Message to the author. 30 November 2005. Email.
23. Bulzone, Carol. Telephone interview. 2 November 2004.
24. Flagg (Smith), Kay. Personal interview. 31 October 2004.
25. Soror Charis. "Herman Slater: 'Thee Magickal Childe'" (Part I). *Behutet* 10 (Summer 2001) 3. Print.
26. North, Erika [Judith McNally]. Message to the author. 16 April 2006. Email.
27. North, Erika [Judith McNally]. Message to the author. 29 November 2005. Email.
28. Levenda, Peter. Message to the author. 29 August 2005. Email.
29. Fitch, Ed. Message to the author. 21 April 2004. Email.
30. "Coven Contacts." *Gnostica News* 3.8 (21 March 1974) 10. Print. (Wesc. Lib. Llew.). Contains a notice from the Louisville, Kentucky Gardnerian coven, preferring couples.
31. Mary Nesnick was a First Degree initiate of the Buckland's Brentwood, New York coven in 1967 before she allegedly left the group under less than salutary conditions.
32. Helios. Message to the author. 21 April 2004. Email.
33. Buczynski, Edmund Michael. "Witchcraft Today and the Homosexual." *Gaysweek* (13 June 1977) 10. (Coll. BMG).
34. Caldiero, Joe. Message to the author. 8 February 2010. Email.
35. Thompson, Gwen. Letter. *Green Egg* 7.62 (May 1974) 40. Print. (Coll. A.Terr.).
36. Mathiesen, Robert and Thetic. The Rede of the Wiccae: Adriana Porter, Gwen Thompson, and the Birth of a Tradition of Witchcraft. Providence: Olympian Press. 2005. 4. Note: From this point forward, Phyllis Ruth

Thompson (née Healy) will be referred to as Gwen Thompson in order to avoid confusion.

Notes for Chapter 6
[1] Adler. *Drawing Down the Moon.* 1986. 87.
[2] Mathiesen and Thetic. The Rede of the Wiccae. 2005. pp. 5-7.
[3] Theitic, [Andrew]. "The New England Covens of Traditionalist Witches (N.E.C.T.W.)." The Witches' Voice, Pagan Traditions. 28 January 2001. Web (http://www.witchvox.com/va/dt_va.html?a=usri&c=trads&id=9085).
[4] Lady Gwynne [Gwen Thompson]. "Let it Be Known." Letter to listed distribution. 16 May 1985. MS.
[5] Helios. Message to the author. 21 April 2004. Email.
[6] Martello, Leo. "Wicca-Basket." *Gnostica News* 3.3 (21 October 1973) 17. Print. (Wesc. Lib. Llew.).
[7] "Lineage Outskirts — DC's Lineage." Web (http://www.nightwing.awebspider.com/lineagemandrake.htm, accessed 2 September 2009).
[8] Fitch, Ed. "Of Traditions, Anti-Quality, and Ego Trips." ERN 1.2 (February 1974) 23. Print.
[9] Martello, Leo. "Wicca-Basket." *Gnostica News* 3.1 (21 August 1973) 27. Print. (Wesc. Lib. Llew.).
[10] Slater, Herman. Letter. Magickal Childe Spring 87 Supplement. Spring 1987.
[11] William Wheeler recalls Leo Martello telling him that Leo helped Gwen write her Third Degree rite. Wheeler, William. Message to the author. 11 July 2007. Email.
[12] Theitic, Andrew. Message to the author. 4 February 2007. Email.
[13] HERMES DIONYSUS [Edmund Buczynski]. The Cauldron (New England Covens of Traditionalist Witches Book of Shadows). North Haven/Brooklyn Heights: Unpublished MS. 1972? P. 1. MS.
[14] North, Erika [Judith McNally]. Message to the author. 30 November 2005. Email.
[15] Eddie's copy of The Cauldron lists the owner's name as HERMES in Theban runes and DIONYSUS in Enochian. The use of the Craft name "Hermes" identifies it as Buczynski's copy of Gwen's Traditionalist book. It can be dated to circa 1972 based upon the printing dates of the books referenced in the main body of the required book list located in the back.
[16] "Cowan" is a pejorative word referring to a non-Witch. Its use derives from Freemasonry, where it refers to a pretender or interloper. The term has generally fallen from favor, being replaced with "Mundane" or, more recently (and less seriously), "Muggle" in reference to the Harry Potter series of books by author J.K. Rowling.
[17] HERMES DIONYSUS [Edmund Buczynski]. *The Cauldron.* 1972? 39-40. MS.
[18] The mythology of modern Witchcraft often presents the Roman Catholic Inquisition and the heresy trials that occurred during the Protestant Reformation as the "Burning Times" when anywhere from tens of thousands to millions of Witches, mid-wives and self-sufficient women were murdered by Christians to terrify and retain their hold upon the common people.
[19] Pratchett, Terry. *Witches Abroad.* New York: HarperTorch. 2002. 16.
[20] Tuan. Message to the author. 13 March 2005. Email.
[21] Silverknife, Zanoni. Message to the author. 13 July 2004. Email.

[22] Holzer, Hans. *The Witchcraft Report.* New York: Ace Books. 1973. 133.
[23] HERMES DIONYSUS [Edmund Buczynski]. *The Cauldron.* 201-206.
[24] Slater, Herman. Letter. *Green Egg* 5.50 (5 October 1972) 10. Print. (Arch. GE CAW).
[25] Bartlett, Karen. Message to the author. 26 March 2007. Email.
[26] The Kinsey Scale, developed by researcher Alfred Kinsey, et al. in his landmark study Sexual Behavior in the Human Male (1948), attempts to define a man's sexual orientation based upon a history of his sexual contacts. The scale runs from 0, or exclusively heterosexual, to 6, or exclusively homosexual.
[27] Buczynski, Edmund Michael. "Witchcraft Today and the Homosexual." Gaysweek (13 June 1977) 10-11. (Coll. BMG).
[28] Jamison, Artie. Telephone interview. 24 January 2004.
[29] HERMES DIONYSUS [Edmund Buczynski]. "To Approach the Priesthood." The Cauldron. Pp. 41-42. MS.
[30] Pratt, Roger. Message to the author. 15 June 2010. Email.

Notes for Chapter 7

[1] "The Great City." The Saturday Evening Post 237.20 (23 May 1964) 25. Print.
[2] Astor, Gerald. "New York: Dream or Nightmare?" Look 33.7 (1 April 1969) 61. Print.
[3] "Business Records: Bankruptcy Proceedings." NYT (4 January 1972) 50. Print.
[4] Levenda, Peter. Message to the author. 28 March 2006. Email.
[5] Buckland, Raymond. *Witchcraft from the Inside.* St. Paul: Llewellyn. 1971. 83.
[6] Kampel, Stewart. "Ah, Halloween! A Time to Take Off Clothes." NYT (31 October 1971) 12. Web.
[7] Fritscher. *Popular Witchcraft.* 1973. 85.
[8] North, Erika [Judith McNally]. Message to the author. 16 April 2006. Email.
[9] Wallace. *Witchcraft in the World Today.* 1967. 85-86.
[10] Cover Story "The Occult: A Substitute Faith." Time (Monday 19 June 1972) Np. Web (http://www.time.com/time/magazine/article/0,9171,877779,00.html, accessed 22 December 2007).
[11] The Brentano's on 5th Avenue was probably the first mainstream bookstore chain to have a separate occult section. The séance for the press was held on June 15, 1970. See: Hershman, Florence. Witchcraft USA. New York: Tower Books. p. 143. This Brentano's is famous for another reason, for it was the same bookstore where Patti Smith and Robert Mapplethorpe had worked in 1968.
[12] However, by 1974 the "Mystique Boutique" would disappear, with its occult offerings melding in with all of the other mundane selections as the novelty dissipated. Source: Smith, Marcella. Message to the author. 5 September 2006. Email.
[13] Weschcke, Carl. Message to the author. 10 August 2007. Email.
[14] Moss, Harold. Message to the author. 18 August 2008. Email.
[15] Gwilym Dafydd HHH. Message to the author. 30 July 2006. Email.
[16] Wallace. *Witchcraft in the World Today.* 1967. 83.
[17] Klemesrud, Judy. "Witchcraft: Some People Find It a Serious Matter." NYT (31 October 1969) Np. Web.
[18] Guberman, Ira D. "Mysteries of the Occult Examined in L.I.U. Course." NYT (31 October 1971) Np. Web.

[19] "Occult Interests and Jersey City Priest." NYT (12 March 1972) Np. Web.
[20] Aquino, Michael. The Church of Satan (5th Edition). San Francisco: Self-published. 2002. pp. 225, 299.
[21] There have been several founding dates cited for the Warlock Shop, and nearly all of them have been wrong. Peter Levenda has stated that the store could not have opened any earlier than 1972, as that was the year that he had moved to Brooklyn Heights and the store was not yet open at that time. No advertisements for the Warlock Shop had appeared in The Village Voice, Herman Slater's preferred advertising venue, prior to August 1972. Corroboration also comes from Slater himself, who stated that the Warlock Shop first opened in 1972. Sources: An Introduction to Witchcraft. Herman Slater. The Magickal Childe. 1987. Videocassette; Slater, Herman. Letter. *Green Egg* 5.50 (5 October 1972) 10. Print. (Arch. GE CAW).
[22] Carey, Robert. Message to the author. 24 April 2007. Email.
[23] Lovecraft made these remarks in reference to his story "*The Horror at Red Hook*" (1925) that was modeled on the dock and warehouse district of that name to the southwest of Brooklyn Heights. See: Lovecraft, H. P. Letter to Clark Ashton Smith. 9 October 1925. Web.
[24] Simon. *Dead Names: The Dark History of the Necronomicon*. New York: Avon Books. 2006. 88.
[25] Simon. *Dead Names*. 2006. 87.
[26] Cabal, Alan. "The Doom that Came to Chelsea." NEWS & COLUMNS section. New York Press 16.23 (3 June 2003) Np. Web.
[27] Soror Charis. "Herman Slater: 'Thee Magickal Childe'" (Part I). *Behutet* 10 (Summer 2001) 2. Print.
[28] Levenda, Peter. Message to the author. 29 August 2005. Email.
[29] Levenda, Peter. Message to the author. 26 May 2011. Email. Two of these were Book of Runes and Magickal Alphabets, which were part of the Magus Manuscript Series edited by Simon and self-published in 1973.
[30] "Ed Buczynski – His Warlock Shop is a Satanist Supermarket." National Star (2 March 1974) Np. Slater is quoted in the article as saying "A year and a half ago [June 1972] we had $2000 invested in the store."
[31] Goro, Herb and Ellen Stock. "Atlantic Avenue: Boulevard of Brooklyn Dreamers." New York 6.29 (16 July 1973) 46. Web(http://books.google.com/books?id=7uYCAAAAMBAJ&lpg=PA46&ots=XqfwA3Z0Jj&dq, accessed 23 May 2011).
[32] Eaton, Sally. Message to the author. 21 January 2008. Email.
[33] Pratt, Roger. Message to the author. 15 June 2010. Email.
[34] Caldiero, Joe. Message to the author. 8 February 2010. Email.
[35] Dalton, Ken. Message to the author. 30 January 2012. Email.
[36] Frank, Kathryn. Message to the author. 6 January 2010. Email.
[37] [Slater, Herman and Ed Buczynski]. "The Warlock Shop" (flier). Brooklyn: Self-published. Late 1972? MS.
[38] The meaning of the word "Warlock" continues to be debated in the Neo-Pagan community. For an example, see: Sinir. "What is a Warlock?" *Green Egg* 142 (December 2007) 32. Web (http://www.greeneggzine.com/ISSUES/2007_06_YULE/142_GE_YULE2007.pdf).
[39] Hephaestos and Hermes [Herman Slater and Ed Buczynski]. *The Warlock Shop/Earth Religions Supply Catalogue*. Brooklyn: Self-published. January 1973. 2.

[40] Philip Heseltine (Peter Warlock) was involved in the popular occult practices of his day — spiritualism, automatic writing, and the Ouija. He was contemporary and friend of D.H. Lawrence and William Butler Yeats, both of whom were also involved in the occult. And like Yeats, Heseltine was interested in Celtic mythology. Smith, Barry. "Frederick Delius and Peter Warlock: A Friendship Revealed." Oxford University Press. 2000. 248; and Talbot, John. Review of "The Collected Letters of Peter Warlock." Tempo 60.235 (2006) 61. Web.

[41] The Peter Warlock Society. Web (http://www.peterwarlock.org/WARLOCK.HTM).

[42] British novelist Mary Butts, a student of Aleister Crowley and a credited co-author with him of the 1912 work Magick (Book 4), asserted that it was Heseltine who originally introduced her to the occult.

[43] The City of New York, Housing and Development Administration, Certificate of Occupancy No. 216383, 300 Henry Street, Brooklyn. 17 February 1976. Web.

[44] "Residential Sales." NYT (4 November 2001) Np. Web.

[45] Soror Charis. "Herman Slater 'Thee Magickal Childe'" (Part I). *Behutet* 10 (Summer 2001) 3-4. Print.

[46] Eaton, Sally. Message to the author. 12 April 2006. Email.

[47] An advertisement in August 1973 confirms that Eddie and Herman were co-proprietors of the store. Source: Earth Religions Supply, Inc. (Warlock Shop Division). Advertisement. New Broom: A Journal of Witchcraft 1.3 (Lammas 1973) Np. Print. (Arch. Circ. Sanc).

[48] Leo Martello refers to Herman and Eddie as partners and co-owners of the Warlock Shop. Source: Martello, Leo. Witchcraft: The Old Religion. 1973. p. 171.

[49] This was the beginning of a trend throughout Herman's life, where he would date younger men to whom he would occasionally offer part-ownership in the store. With the exception of Eddie, these arrangements were almost always disastrous according to his friends.

[50] Peter Levenda stated that he had access to all of the business invoices from the 1972-1973 timeframe after offering to help Herman set up an accounting system for The Warlock Shop, and that Eddie's name was on none of the paperwork he saw. Source: Levenda, Peter. Message to the author. 29 August 2005. Email.

[51] Lowenstein, Kenny. Telephone interview. 25 January 2004.

[52] Jamison, Artie. Telephone interview. 24 January 2004.

[53] Slater, Herman. Letter. *Green Egg* 5.50 (5 October 1972) 10. Print. (Arch. GE CAW).

[54] John (Sonny) Wojtowicz (d. 2006), along with Sal Naturile (d. 1972) and an unnamed individual, robbed the Chase Manhattan bank at East Third Street and Avenue P in Brooklyn in order to pay for sex reassignment surgery for Wojtowicz' transsexual girlfriend, Elizabeth (Liz) Debbie Eden (d. 1987).

[55] While several people familiar with the Warlock Shop from the period say that the criminals either planned the heist at the shop while browsing the stacks (unlikely given the small size of the shop and Herman's watchful eye) or met there before proceeding to the bank (also unlikely, given the distance between the two locations), the only evidence that comes close to substantiating these claims is a recollection by Magickal Childe employee

Randy Jones. Jones writes, "Actually the day Sonny robbed the bank he had been at Herman's apartment. [And] Liz (the transvestite) lived in my X's, Steven [Teischer]'s, boarding house in Brooklyn. Steven always said Liz was a nice girl." Source: Jones, Randy. Message to the author. 29 July 2009. Email.

[56] Tanit. "Leo Martello: Il Mago." ERN 1.2 (February 1974) 18. Print. (Arch. Circ. Sanc).

[57] Kneitel, Tommy. Message to the author. 10 September 2004. Email.

[58] Dalton, Ken. Message to the author. 30 January 2012. Email.

[59] Soror Charis. "Herman Slater 'Thee Magickal Childe'" (Part II). *Behutet* 11 (Autumn 2001) 12. Print.

[60] Greenberg, Dan. *Something's There.* 1976. 85.

[61] Soror Charis. "Herman Slater 'Thee Magickal Childe'" (Part I). *Behutet* 10 (Summer 2001) 7. Print.

[62] Bulzone, Carol. Telephone interview. 2 November 2004.

[63] Flagg (Smith), Kay. Personal interview. 31 October 2004.

[64] Slater, Herman. Letter. *Green Egg* 5.50 (5 October 1972) 10. Print. (Arch. GE CAW).

[65] Warlock Shop Advertisement. Village Voice 17.33 (17 August 1972) 9. MCF. (Cols. Met. Lib).

[66] Soror Charis. "Herman Slater: 'Thee Magickal Childe'" (Part I). *Behutet* 10 (Summer 2001) 4. Print.

[67] Warlock Shop. Advertisement. Village Voice 17.44 (2 November 1972) 14. MCF. (Cols. Met. Lib).

[68] Taurus-Risen Co. Advertisement. Village Voice 17.42 (19 October 1972) 8. MCF. (Cols. Met. Lib).

[69] Taurus-Risen Co. Advertisement. Village Voice 17.43 (26 October 1972) 10. MCF. (Cols. Met. Lib).

[70] The Blessed Be Shop. Advertisement. Village Voice 17.40 (5 October 1972) 14. MCF. (Cols. Met. Lib).

[71] "Walli" was Walli Elmlark, a Witch who taught classes at the New York School of Occult Arts and Sciences. He was also an avant-garde recording artist who appeared on two King Crimson compilations, and who co-authored Rock raps of the 70's (1972) with UFOlogist and author Timothy Green Beckley. There is an amusing anecdote of Walli's attempt to help David Bowie exorcise a demonic swimming pool in Los Angeles in the 1970s. See: Bowie, Angela. *Backstage Passes: Life on the Wild Side with David Bowie.* New York: Cooper Square Press. 2000.

[72] Warlock Shop/Friends of the Craft Advertisement. Village Voice 17.42 (19 October 1972) 15. MCF. (Cols. Met. Lib).

[73] Simon. *Dead Names.* 118.

[74] Chauncey. *Gay New York.* 1995. 151.

[75] The "Vaseline Flats" apartment building sits on the SW corner of Joralemon Street and Columbia Place just across the Brooklyn Queens Expressway viaduct from the former printing plant and warehouse bought by the Watchtower Bible & Tract Society in 1983. In the early 1970s, the building was rather shabby and under rent control. It has since been completely refurbished, and appears to be co-ops. Source: Ward, Jim. Message to the author. 15 August 2005. Email.

[76] Soror Charis. "Herman Slater 'Thee Magickal Childe'" (Part I). *Behutet* 10 (Summer 2001) 4-5. Print.

[77] Flagg (Smith), Kay. Message to the author. 17 August 2009. Email.
[78] Cheiron. Message to the author. 23 August 23, 2004. Email.
[79] Martello. *Witchcraft: The Old Religion*. 1973. 173-174.
[80] This invocation was given by Doreen Valiente at the Pentagram dinner held in London on October 3, 1963. "Fifty at Pentagram Dinner." Pentagram 2 (November 1964). p. 1. Web.
[81] Simon. *Dead Names*. 2006. 94.

Notes for Chapter 8

[1] Book advertisement. ERN 15 (August 1974) 17. Print. (Arch. Circ. Sanc).
[2] Gwilym Dafydd HHH. Message to the author. 27 July 2007. Email.
[3] Carey, Robert. Message to the author. 24 March 2007. Email.
[4] Ria Rivera [née Farnham], a Welsh initiate from early 1973, confirmed Thompson's influence on the tradition, writing, "The Welsh Tradition is derived from the teachings of the *Mabinogian*, the four lost books of Welsh, Celtic and Druidic magic. It was brought here by Gwen Thompson." See: Lady Rhea [Ria Rivera]. "The Crystal Ball" in Wildman, Laura (ed.). *Celebrating the Pagan Soul*. New York: Citadel Press. 2005. P. 97.
[5] Simon noted that he saw some pages from Eddie's draft Welsh rituals in the early days of the Warlock Shop. See: Simon. "ECCE!" ERN 1.1 (December 1973) 2. Print. (Arch. Circ. Sanc).
[6] Helios. Message to the author. 21 April 2004. Email.
[7] Flagg (Smith), Kay. Message to the author. 28 July 2004. Email.
[8] Carey, Robert. Message to the author. 24 March 2007. Email.
[9] North, Erika [Judith McNally]. Message to the author. 30 November 2005. Email.
[10] Theitic, Andrew. Message to the author. 4 February 2007. Email.
[11] Martello. *Witchcraft: The Old Religion*. 1973. 175.
[12] Owen Rowley states that he was initiated by Gwen Thompson in October of 1972, and that Eddie had been gone for about a month at that point. Source: Rowley, Owen. Message to the author. 6 August 2009. Email.
[13] Flagg (Smith), Kay. Personal interview. 31 October 2004.
[14] "[Hela was] the one other person Eddie told that story to in my presence. I remember because when we swore to 'fall upon our blades rather than reveal the secrets' Eddie smiled. Later after the Circle he told her the story." Presumably, the athame story was one of the secrets the initiates were being asked to keep. Source: (Cf. n#7).
[15] Cheiron. Message to the author. 23 August 2004. Email.
[16] Lady Gwynne [Gwen Thompson]. "Let it Be Known." Letter. 16 May 1985. MS.
[17] The Welsh Book of Shadows used in this comparison was an original copy given to Joseph Cupolo by Eddie Buczynski in 1975 or 1976. Source: Gwydion [Eddie Buczynski]. Traditionalist Gwyddoniaid Book of Shadows. Brooklyn Heights: Unpublished MS. 1972. MS.
[18] Mathiesen and Thetic. *The Rede of the Wiccae*. 2005. 51.
[19] HERMES DIONYSUS [Edmund Buczynski]. *The Cauldron*. 1972? 208. MS.
[20] Thompson, Gwen. Letter. *Green Egg* 8.72 (August 1975) 44. Print. (Coll. A.Terr.). It should also be noted that every student of Second Degree and higher was "a former First Degree student."

21 The next leaf of the book, what would have been pages 209-210, has been roughly torn from the volume. However, an examination of the blank leaf that follows (pages 211-212) shows light indentations indicative of the text that was written on the leaf that had been removed from the book. The book passed through the hands of several persons related to both Buczynski's and Thompson's traditions after having left his keeping, any one of whom may have taken the liberty to remove the leaf. Source: HERMES DIONYSUS [Edmund Buczynski]. The Cauldron. 1972?

22 According to one source, Martello's claim that he wrote the Welsh Third Degree ritual is circumstantially supported based on the presence of Leo's handwriting in the first copy of Eddie's Welsh book. Source: (Cf. n#6). This recollection is close to one held by William Wheeler, who states that Martello spoke of helping Gwen Thompson write her Third Degree [i.e., Elder] ritual. Source: Wheeler, William. Message to the author. 11 July 2007. Email.

23 Wheeler, William. Message to the author. 11 July 2007. Email. William Wheeler states that Leo Martello spoke of lending money to Gwen Thompson, and that the funds were either not repaid or were a long time coming.

24 Martello, Leo. "Wicca-Basket." *Gnostica News* 3.2 (21 October 1973) 17. Print. (Wesc. Lib. Llew.).

25 Martello, Leo. Letter. *Green Egg* 6.58 (October 1973) 45. Print. (Coll. A.Terr.).

26 Others also report on Thompson's negativity during this period. See: Lineage Outskirts — DC's Lineage. Web (http://www.nightwing.awebspider.com/lineagemandrake.htm, accessed 2 September 2009).

27 Gwen had also begun moving in with friends in various cities during this same time frame, first in Gatlinburg, TN in late 1973, and then in Saugus, MA. Sources: Thompson, Gwen. Letter. *Green Egg* 6.59 (December 1973) 42. Print. (Coll. A.Terr.).
Thompson, Gwen. Letter. *Green Egg* 8.71 (June 1975) 39. Print. (Coll. A.Terr.).

28 In an alternative telling of the story, William Wheeler writes that Leo Martello stated that he had assisted Gwen Thompson in drafting the N.E.C.T.W. Third Degree ritual. Source: (Cf. n#23).

29 Hermes [Edmund Buczynski]. Traditionalist Gwyddoniaid vouch of Vivianne [Kay Flagg (Smith)]. Brooklyn Heights, New York. 8 October 1972.

30 Kay Smith would eventually choose Goewyn as the name by which she would be known within the Tradition when she split from Eddie to lead a new Welsh coven at midsummer in 1973.

31 [Buczynski, Edmund]. *Traditionalist Gwyddoniaid Book of Shadows*. Brooklyn Heights: Unpublished MS. 1972. 2. MS.

32 Carey, Robert. Message to the author. 3 April 2007. Email.

33 Warlock Shop/Friends of the Craft Advertisement. Village Voice 17.42 (19 October 1972) 15. MCF. (Cols. Met. Lib).

34 Martello, Leo. "Wicca-Basket." *Gnostica News* 2.3 (21 November 1972) 21. Print. (Wesc. Lib. Llew.). Martello also mentioned having put in an appearance at Gwen Thompson's Samhain rite that same day.

35 Martello, Leo. "Wicca-Basket." *Gnostica News* 24 (21 December 1972) 21. Print. (Wesc. Lib. Llew.).

[36] Poiel. "Wiccan Sects." *Gnostica News* 2.7 (21 May 1973) 20. Print. (Wesc. Lib. Llew.).
[37] Source: (Cf. n#31). The cross-quarter sabbat of Oimelc, or Imbolc, is held on or about February 1st, while Midsummer is held on or about June 21st.
[38] Holzer. *The Witchcraft Report*. 1973. 37.
[39] Raymond Buckland asserts that Eddie did not train with his coven. Source: Buckland, Raymond. Message to the author. 5 February 2004. Email.
[40] North, Erika [Judith McNally]. Message to the author. 11 December 2005. Email. The age of majority in New York State in 1965 was 21.
[41] Spock. Letter. *Green Egg* 7.61 (March 1974) 52. Print. (Coll. A.Terr.).
[42] Theitic, Andrew. Message to the author. 26 February 2007. Email.
[43] Buczynski, Edmund. *Volume One: Liber Ubrarum [sic] — The Book of Shadows with Commentary*. i-iii.
[44] Buczynski. "Edmund Michael Buczynski" autobiographical paper. 1974. (Arch. CES).
[45] Guerra, Elizabeth with Janet Farrar. *Stewart Farrar: Writer on a Broomstick*. Arcata: R.J. Stewart Books. 2008. 99.
[46] Horowitz. *Occult America*. 2009. 52-53.
[47] Cuhulain, Kerr. *Witch Hunts: Out of the Broom Closet*. Casper: Spiral Publishing. 2005. 68.
[48] Adler, Margot. *Drawing Down the Moon*. 1986. 88.
[49] This is a practice similar to that of Gardnerian Wica, where the measure is combined with the hair and blood of the initiate after the oath is taken.
[50] For example, Tommy and Judy Kneitel, and Raymond Buckland, though not Welsh initiates, all have in their possession copies of the Traditionalist Gwyddoniaid Book of Shadows — gifts to them from Eddie Buczynski himself. This author has several different versions of the Welsh book, gifted to him from various sources who received them from Buczynski, and was even offered by Kay Flagg, the Welsh Witch Queen, a chance to copy her own book (the offer was respectfully declined due to the book's fragility). Sources: (Cf. n#39); Kneitel, Tommy. Message to the author. 10 September 2004. Email.
[51] Many Witchcraft traditions allow for the addition, but not the removal, of material from the Book of Shadows. This is one way in which traditions evolve over time, and why the lines between traditions tend to become blurred.
[52] Kelly, Aidan. *Inventing Witchcraft: A Case Study in the Creation of a New Religion*. Loughborough: Thoth Publications. 2007. 266.
[53] Hutton, Ronald. *Triumph of the Moon: A History of Modern Pagan Witchcraft*. Oxford: Oxford University Press. 1999. 238-239.
[54] Real problems arise when a holder of these materials passes away, or when they pass on the materials to their own students, who may not have a personal tie to the originators of the works or even know from whence the materials came.
[55] Silverknife, Zanoni. Message to the author. 13 July 2004. Email.
[56] Silverknife, Zanoni. Message to the author. 2 July 2004. Email.
[57] Moondancer. Message to the author. 1 July 2004. Email.
[58] Silverknife, Zanoni. Message to the author. 14 July 2004. Email.
[60] Clifton, Chas. Message to the author. 21 May 2012. Email.
[61] Bowman, Marion. "Reinventing the Celts." *Religion* 23 (1993) 147-156.

[62] Colton, Charles Caleb. *Lacon, or Many Things In Few Words, addressed to those who think.* Volume 1 (No. 183) 1820.

Notes for Chapter 9

[1] Martello. *Witchcraft: The Old Religion.* 1973. 192.
[2] Buckland, Raymond. *Witchcraft from the Inside.* 1995. 151.
[3] Fitch, Ed. A Grimoire of Shadows: Witchcraft, Paganism & Magick. St. Paul: Llewellyn Publications. 1996. p. xi.
[4] Buckland, Raymond. From his up-coming autobiography, as yet untitled. Copyright Raymond Buckland 2010, with permission.
[5] SilverWitch, Sylvana. "Ed Fitch: Revealing the Craft." Widdershins 1.2 (Litha 1995) Np. Web (http://www.widdershins.org/vol1iss2/2.htm, accessed 20 December 2007).
[6] Fitch. *A Grimoire of Shadows.* 1996. xi-xii.
[7] Editorial. Zetetic 1.1 (Fall/Winter 1976) 4.
[8] Lady Sheba [Jessica Wicker Bell]. The Book of Shadows. St. Paul: Llewellyn Publications. 1971.
[9] Buckland. *Witchcraft from the Inside.* 1995. 150.
[10] Sevarg, Luba. The Do-It-Yourself Witchcraft Guide. New York: Award Books. 1971.
[11] Wallace. Witchcraft in the World Today. 1967. 83.
[12] Wilson, Joseph. "Re: A word for poor departed Herman Slater." Lucky Mojo Curio Company (Catherine Yronwode). 27 March 2003. Web (http://www.luckymojo.com/esoteric/religion/neo-paganism/var200303hermanslater.txt, accessed 21 December 2007).
[13] Yeardo. "The Pagan Way and its Goals." *Green Egg* 6.59 (December 1973) 34, 36. Print. (Coll. A.Terr.).
[14] Clifton. *Her Hidden Children.* 2006. 23-24.
[15] "Wiccan Covens: TWPT Talks to Judy Harrow." Wiccan/Pagan Times. 2001. Web (http://www.twpt.com/harrow.htm, accessed 12 January 2008).
[16] Nightshade, Jonathon. Message to the author. 21 February 2012. Email.
[17] Helios. Message to the author. 21 April 2004. Email.
[18] Dalton, Ken. Message to the author. 30 January 2012. Email.
[19] Martello. *Witchcraft: The Old Religion.* 1973. 177.
[20] Holzer. *The Witchcraft Report.* 1973. 39.
[21] Flagg (Smith), Kay. Personal interview. 31 October 2004.
[22] Poiel. "Wiccan Sects." *Gnostica News* (2:7). 21 May 1973. 20.
[23] Martello. *Witchcraft: The Old Religion.* 1973. 185.
[24] Carey, Robert. Message to the author. 24 March 2007. Email.
[25] Lady Sheba [Jessica Wicker Bell]. *The Book of Shadows.* 2006 (1971). 3-35.
[26] This did not prevent the owners of the Warlock Shop from openly questioning, as they did in 1974, whether Lady Sheba lied about her Craft lineage and the source of her materials. Source: "Sheba a Fraud?" ERN 1.3 (February 1974) 1. Print. (Arch. Circ. Sanc).
[27] "Wiccan Sects." *Gnostica News* (2:7). 21 May 1973. 20. (Wesc. Lib. Llew.).
[28] Holzer. *The Witchcraft Report.* 1973. 38.
[29] Adler, Margot. Presentation at Pagan Spirit Gathering. 25 June 2005.
[30] North, Erika [Judith McNally]. Message to the author. 30 November 2005. Email.

[31] "Under One Cover Entire Pagan Way Rituals." Advertisement. ERN (1:3). March 1974. 26. Print. (Arch. Circ. Sanc).
[32] Earth Religious Supplies, Inc. (Warlock Shop Division). Advertisement. *Green Egg* 7.63 (June 1974) 53. Print. (Coll. A.Terr.). The ad mentions "Now Available in Hard & Soft Cover ENTIRE PAGAN WAY RITUALS $5 & $3 plus ship".
[33] [Slater, Herman (ed.)]. *A Book of Pagan Rituals.* New York: Samuel Weiser, Inc. 1978. Copyright notice.
[34] Nightshade, Jonathon. Message to the author (Part I & II). 18 February 2012. Email.
[35] Gwydion [Edmund Buczynski]. "A Visit to a Temple or a House is Not Only a Home." ERN 1.4 (June 1974) 29-30. Print. (Arch. Circ. Sanc).
[36] Unattributed [Ed Fitch, Tony Kelly, William Gray, et al.]. Book of Pagan Rituals (Friends of the Craft-Version Vol. I). Brooklyn: Earth Religious Supplies. 1974. P. 1. Print. From the Collection of Jonathon Nightshade (Coll. J. Night.). The overleaf of Nightshade's copy of Volume I, which he inherited from Donna Cole Schultz, is autographed by Herman Slater and Ed Buczynski. The notice on the title page states "Printed at cost by: Earth Religious Supplies." No copyright is claimed, and the title page clearly states "From Pagan Way Materiel."
[37] Slater, Herman. *A Book of Rituals (Advanced).* Brooklyn: Earth Religious Supplies. 1975. Print. P. 1. (Coll. J. Night.). This volume also notes that it is "From Pagan Way Materiel."
[38] Slater, Herman. Letter (dated April 23, 1975). *Green Egg* 8.71 (June 1975) 42. Print. (Coll. A.Terr.).
[39] Slater, Herman (ed.). *Pagan Rituals III: Outer Court Training Coven.* New York: Magickal Childe Publishing, Inc. 1989. 11.
[40] Hansen, John M. "Re: A word for poor departed Herman Slater." Lucky Mojo Curio Company (Catherine Yronwode). 29 March 2003. Web (http://www.luckymojo.com/esoteric/religion/neo-paganism/var200303hermanslater.txt, accessed 21 December 2007).
[41] Slater. *Pagan Rituals III.* 10.
[42] Wilson, Joseph B. "Warts And All: The Spiritual Autobiography of Joseph B Wilson," Part Fifteen (Draft). 2003. Web (http://www.toteg.org/Joseph/15Warts.html, accessed 23 February 2008).
[43] Weinraub, Bernard. "Secret Agent Testifies at Captain's Trial." NYT (11 July 1971) Np. Web.
[44] Wilson, Joseph B. "Warts And All: The Spiritual Autobiography of Joseph B Wilson," Part Seventeen (Draft). 2003. Web (http://www.toteg.org/Joseph/17Warts.html, accessed 23 February 2008).
[45] Holzer. *The Directory of the OCCULT.* 1974. 171.
[46] Martello. *Black Magick, Satanism & Voodoo.* 1973. 84-90, 181.

Notes for Chapter 10
[1] Carey, Robert. Message to the author. 24 March 2007. Email.
[2] Carey, Robert. Message to the author. 3 April 2007. Email.
[3] Holzer. *The Witchcraft Report.* 1973. 9.
[4] Bartlett (Chieco), Karen. Message to the author. 26 March 2007. Email.
[5] Bartlett (Chieco), Karen. Message to the author. 13 January 2008. Email.
[6] Martello. *Witchcraft: The Old Religion.* 1973. 177.

[7] Vivienne/Goewyn [Kay Flagg (Smith)] and Arawn [Terry Parker]. Traditionalist Gwyddoniaid vouch of Katrin [Melda Tamarack]. Brooklyn Heights, New York. 28 October 1973.
[8] Silverknife, Zanoni. Message to the author. 13 July 2004. Email.
[9] Silverknife, Zanoni. Message to the author. 14 July 2004. Email.
[10] Greenberg. *Something's There.* 1976. 99-114.

Notes for Chapter 11
[1] Leek, Sybil. *The Complete Art of Witchcraft.* New York: The World Publishing Company. 1971. 15.
[2] Roberts, Susan. *Witches USA.* 129, 135, 136.
[3] Buckland, Raymond. *Witchcraft from the Inside.* St. Paul: Llewellyn Publications. 1995. 150.
[4] Holzer, Hans. *The Truth About Witchcraft.* Garden City: Doubleday. 1971. 86-90.
[5] Andro. Letter. *Green Egg* 6.60 (February 1974) 47. Print. (Coll. A.Terr.). Andro alleged that Rosemary Buckland had done no initiations for 2 or 3 years after her mistake at bringing in "Noodnick" (Mary Nesnick).
[6] Eaton, Sally. Message to the author. 12 April 2006. Email.
[7] Adler, Margot. Personal interview. 30 October 2004.
[8] Kneitel, Tommy. Message to the author. 30 January 2005. Email.
[9] Buckland. *Witchcraft from the Inside.* 1971. 76.
[10] Kneitel, Tommy. Message to the author. 10 September 2004. Email.
[11] Kneitel, Tommy. Message to the author. 11 September 2004. Email.
[12] Martello. *Witchcraft: The Old Religion.* 1973. 190-191.
[13] (Cf. n#6) Candy Darling, born James Lawrence Slattery (d. 1974), was a transvestite film star and pop celebrity of the late 1960s through early 1970s.
[14] Eaton, Sally. Message to the author. 23 January 2008. Email.
[15] Lady Rhea [Ria Rivera]. "The Crystal Ball." Wildman. *Celebrating the Pagan Soul.* 2005. 98.
[16] Holzer. *The Witchcraft Report.* 1973. 37.
[17] Buczynski had expressed contempt for Holzer's previous book, *The New Pagans* (1972), referring to the author's description of Paganism as "sewage" and of "literally perfuming our philosophies and values with the smell of bullshit." Buczynski, Ed. Letter. *Green Egg* 5.48 (30 June 1972) 2. Print. (Arch. GE CAW).
[18] Levenda, Peter. Message to the author. 29 August 2005. Email.
[19] Martello. *Witchcraft: The Old Religion.* 1973. 201.

Notes for Chapter 12
[1] Martello. *Witchcraft: The Old Religion.* 1973. 177.
[2] Flagg (Smith), Kay. Message to the author. 18 October 2004. Email.
[3] Adler, Margot. Personal interview. 30 October 2004.
[4] First published in 1931, Margaret Murray's book was reprinted in 1952 shortly before Gerald Gardner published *Witchcraft Today* (1954). Murray, Margaret. *The God of the Witches.* Herefordshire: Castle Hill Books. 1952.1
[5] Martello. *Witchcraft: The Old Religion.* 1973. 181.
[6] Poiel. "Wiccan Sects." *Gnostica News* 2.7 (21 May 1973) 20. Print. (Wesc. Lib. Llew.).

[7] Holzer. *The Witchcraft Report.* 1973. 37.
[8] Helios. Message to the author. 21 April 2004. Email.
[9] Adler. *Drawing Down the Moon.* 1986. 89.
[10] For a discussion of this phenomenon, see: Hutton. *Triumph of the Moon.* 1999. 291-298.
[11] Lamond, Frederic. "Memories of Gerald Gardner" in Wildman, Laura (ed.). *Celebrating the Pagan Soul.* New York: Citadel Press. 2005. 94.
[12] Hutton. *Triumph of the Moon.* 1999. 288.
[13] Rose, Elliot. *A Razor for a Goat.* Toronto: University of Toronto Press. 1989. 150.
[14] Pendderwen, Gwydion [Tom DeLong]. Letter. *Green Egg* 6.60 (February 1974) 40. Print. (Coll. A.Terr.).
[15] North, Erika [Judith McNally]. Message to the author. 3 December 2005. Email.
[16] Bourne. *Dancing with Witches.* 2006. 93.
[17] Rose. *A Razor for a Goat.* 1989. 151.
[18] Martello. *Witchcraft: The Old Religion.* 1973. 20. Martello took a six month sabbatical from the Welsh coven beginning in April 1973, leaving the country to study with Arnold and Patricia Crowther in England. He returned to the United States later that year with a Third Degree in British Traditional Witchcraft from the Crowthers.
[19] Martello, Leo. "Wicca-Basket." *Gnostica News* 2.4 (21 December 1972) 21. Print. (Wesc. Lib. Llew.).
[20] Martello. *Witchcraft: The Old Religion.* 1973. 172-173.
[21] Buczynski. *Volume One: Liber Ubrarum [sic] – The Book of Shadows with Commentary.* iv.
[22] McCullough, Colleen. *The Grass Crown.* New York: William Morrow & Co. 1991. 956.
[23] Spock. Letter. *Green Egg* 7.61 (March 1974) 52. Print. (Coll. A.Terr.).
[24] Theitic, Andrew. Message to the author. 4 February 2007. Email.
[25] Kneitel, Tommy. Message to the author. 10 September 2004. Email.
[26] Lowenstein, Kenny. Telephone interview. 25 January 2004.
[27] Tommy Kneitel publicly claimed Branwen as a high priestess of his line. Phoenix [Tommy Kneitel]. "Gardnerian Aspects" 1.3. *Green Egg* 6.59 (December 1973) 35. Print. (Coll. A.Terr.).
[28] Helios. Message to the author. 14 April 2004. Email.
[29] Slater. *Pagan Rituals III.* 13.
[30] Pratt, Roger. Message to the author. 15 June 2010. Email.
[31] Pratt, Roger. Message to the author. 17 June 2010. Email.
[32] Martello, Leo. "Wicca-Basket." *Gnostica News* 2.7 (21 May 1973) 16. Print. (Wesc. Lib. Llew.).
[33] Exemplified by Lady Seana [Siobhan] being elevated to Third Degree and becoming the high priestess of the Order of the Silver Wheel coven on May 2, 1973. Lady Seana. Notice. Order of the Silver Wheel, Brooklyn Heights, New York. 2 May 1973.
[34] Vivienne/Goewyn [Kay Flagg (Smith)]. Traditionalist Gwyddoniaid vouch of Dylan/Arawn [Terry Parker]. Brooklyn Heights, New York. 20 June 1973.
[35] Tasha Catt [Athena] was elevated by Kay to Third Degree on August 15, 1973. Vivienne/Goewyn [Kay Flagg (Smith)]. Traditionalist Gwyddoniaid vouch of Athena [Tasha Catt]. Brooklyn Heights, New York. 15 August 1973. MS.

Melda Tannen [Katrin] was elevated to Third Degree on October 28, 1973. Vivienne/Goewyn [Kay Flagg (Smith)]. Traditionalist Gwyddoniaid vouch of Katrin [Melda Tannen]. Brooklyn Heights, NY. October 28, 1973. MS.

[36] Lady Vivienne and Hermes [Kay Flagg (Smith) and Eddie Buczynski]. "Welsh Traditionalist Witchcraft." New Broom I.3 (August 1973) 9. Print. (Arch. Circ. Sanc).

[37] Holzer. *The New Pagans.* New York: Doubleday & Company. 1972. 1-10. Holzer had expressed doubts as to whether the 26-year-old Parker would be able to hold it together by himself.

[38] Flagg (Smith), Kay. Message to the author. 28 July 2004. Email.

[39] Gillette, Devyn Christopher. *Home Again: An Introduction To Blue Star Wicca.* 1 March 1998. Web (http://www.thesgc.talktalk.net/bluestarwicca/homeagain.html, accessed 8 March 2008).

[40] Eddie and Herman leveled this accusation at Simon. Referring to Eddie as "Grand Magus Lord-of-the-Woods Chief Taxus Exemptus Pontifex Minimus Drwg Gwraig Buczynski," Simon sniffed that he had only seen a few pages of the work in progress in the early days of the Warlock Shop and had then promptly forgotten them. Drwg Gwraig means "evil woman" in Welsh. Source: Simon. "ECCE!" ERN 1.1 (December 1973) 2. Print. (Arch. Circ. Sanc).

[41] Gwilym Dafydd HHH. Message to the author. 23 July 2007. Email.

[42] Inominandum [Miller, Jason]. "Simon Speaks: Part II." *Behutet* 17 (Spring 2003) 8. Print.

[43] Caigan, Khem. Telephone interview. 3 April 2006.

[44] Adler, Margot. Letter. *Green Egg* 7.61 (March 1974) 39. Print. (Coll. A.Terr.).

[45] Adler. *Drawing Down the Moon.* 2006. 131.

[46] (Cf. n#25). As has been demonstrated, only Branwen and Bryce's Outer Court coven left. So Kneitel was incorrect in his assertion that "most of Eddie's Welsh people also walked out and sought Gardnerian initiation."

Notes for Chapter 13

[1] Martello, Leo. Letter. *Green Egg* 6.60 (February 1974) 41. Print. (Coll. A.Terr.).

[2] Crowther, Patricia and Arnold Crowther. *The Secrets of Ancient Witchcraft with the Witches Tarot.* University Books, Inc. 1974. 7-17.

[3] Critchley, Steven. Message to the author. 16 June 2010. Email.

[4] Slater. *Pagan Rituals III.* 13.

[5] Kneitel, Tommy. Message to the author. 10 September 2004. Email.

[6] Theo [Fran Fisher]. Gardnerian Wica vouch of Sira [Patricia Siero]. Louisville, Kentucky. June 30, 1973. MS.

[7] Rowen [Rosemary Buckland]. Gardnerian Wica vouch of Theo [Fran Fisher]. Brentwood, New York. 5 August 1965. MS. Theo (Fran Fisher) is not to be confused with Theos (Judy Kneitel), who appeared on the scene many years later.

[8] Starchild, Zera. "Raymond Buckland, the Father of American Wicca." Doorway Publication and Gifts. Web (http://doorwaypublications.com/interview.html).

[9] Buckland, Raymond. From his up-coming autobiography, as yet untitled. Copyright Raymond Buckland 2010, with permission.

[10] Fitch, Ed. Message to the author. 21 April 2004. Email.

[11] Slater. *Pagan Rituals III.* 1989. 13.
[12] The likely date for this ritual would have been Saturday 7 July 1973, as that evening would have seen a first quarter moon.
[13] Hela [Renate Springer]. Gardnerian Wica vouch of Gwydion [Ed Buczynski]. Brooklyn Heights, New York. 11 July 1973. MS. The document states that Gwydion has attained the "Sublime Degree" (i.e., Third Degree).
[14] Rivera, Ria. Telephone interview. 30 January 2004.
[15] Slater, Herman. Letter. *Green Egg* 7.61 (March 1974) 53. Print. (Coll. A.Terr.).
[16] Springer, Renate. Telephone interview. 26 November 2005.
[17] Levenda, Peter. Message to the author. 29 August 2005. Email.
[18] Sira [Patrician Siero]. Gardnerian Wica vouch of Hela [Renate Springer]. Paterson, New Jersey. 30 June 1973. MS.
[19] Springer, Renate. Telephone interview. 27 November 2005.
[20] Hela [Renate Springer]. Gardnerian Wica vouch of Gwydion [Ed Buczynski]. Brooklyn Heights, New York. 11 July 1973. MS. This document names Gwydion elder and high priest of the Brooklyn Heights Coven of the New York Covendom.
[21] Frank, Kathryn. Message to the author. 19 May 2010. Email.
[22] Pratt, Roger. Message to the author. 15 June 2010. Email.
[23] Pratt, Roger. Message to the author. 17 June 2010. Email.
[24] Hela [Renate Springer]. Gardnerian Wica vouch of Goewyn [Kay Flagg (Smith)]. Cherry Grove, New York. 12 September 1973. MS.
[25] (Cf. n#8). Buckland states categorically that "The very first coven to branch off from ours was in 1965 ... with Fran and Gerry Fisher [*Theo* and *Thain*] from Kentucky."
[26] Buckland, Raymond. Message to Curt Bargren. 17 December 2010. Email.
[27] Buckland, Raymond. Message to the author. 11 October 2008. Email.
[28] Hutton, Ronald. Message to the author. 19 October 2005. Email.
[29] Heselton, Philip. Message to the author. 21 August 2009.
[30] Lamond, Frederic. Message to the author. 11 January 2007. Email.
[31] Heselton, Philip. Message to the author. 25 August 2009. Email.
[32] Slater. Pagan Rituals III. 12-13.
[33] Buckland. Ancient & Modern Witchcraft. 1970. p. 176. This same complaint continues to be voiced four decades later.
[34] Kneitel, Tommy. Message to the author. 30 January 2005. Email.
[35] Buckland, Raymond. Message to the author. 3 April 2008. Email.
[36] Buckland, Raymond. Message to the author. 26 October 2004. Email.
[37] (Cf. n#.7). An examination of the signature shows a distinct difference between it and the calligraphy of the text and examples of Raymond Buckland's handwriting in the author's possession.
[38] Buckland, Raymond. *Witchcraft... The Religion.* New York: The Buckland Museum of Witchcraft & Magick. 1966. 13. Print.
[39] Thain [Gerald Fisher]. "Gardnerian Wicca Inc." *ERN* 1.1 (December 1973) 2. Print. (Arch. Circ. Sanc).
[40] Fitch. A Grimoire of Shadows. 1998. p. xv.
[41] (Cf. n#9). This coven was, according to Buckland, the coven of Theo and Thain.
[42] Regardless of what practitioners of Gardnerian Wica may otherwise claim, the act of using an initiate's measure against him or her is by their own definition

a form of "black magick," as its indisputable purpose is malefic — that is, to cause irreparable harm to the person in question.

43 Of course, the problem with an initiator denying an initiate who has such a paper vouch is that the irrefutable proof presented by the latter constitutes a lie on the part of the former — at least in the eyes of the disinterested observer. This messy paper trail, so destructive to the concept of plausible deniability, may explain why many high priestesses and high priests have stopped issuing paper vouches altogether.

44 Crowther, Patricia and Arnold Crowther. *The Witches Speak*. New York: Samuel Weiser, Inc.. 1976. 97.

45 It is worth noting that Eddie Buczynski never published the Gardnerian Book of Shadows, even though he was certainly given ample reason in the coming to renounce any loyalty he might have held for the tradition in the coming years.

46 Eaton, Sally. Message to the author. 12 April 2006. Email.

47 Buczynski, Ed. "America's Own Stonehenge: Mystery Hill New Hampshire." *ERN* 1.1 (December 1973) 16. Print. (Arch. Circ. Sanc).

48 Advertisement for the "Buckland Museum of Witchcraft and Magick." ERN 1.1 (December 1973) 12. Print. (Arch. Circ. Sanc). The museum later failed due to a lack of visitors in this remote area and the inability of Ray to make a living at running it.

49 Buckland, Raymond. "Birth of a Tradition or the Coming of the Seax-Wicca." ERN 1.1 (December 1973) 1. Print. (Arch. Circ. Sanc).

50 Buckland, Raymond. *The Tree: the Complete Book of Saxon Witchcraft*. New York: Samuel Weiser, Inc. 1974.

51 Buckland, Raymond. "Seax-Wica: Official Information Sheet No. 1." *Green Egg* 7.62 (February 1974) 11. Print. (Coll. A.Terr.).

52 Buckland, Raymond. "Birth of a Tradition or the Coming of the Seax-Wicca." ERN 1.1 (December 1973) 16. Print. (Arch. Circ. Sanc).This welcome is in stark contrast to the misinterpretation of Buckland's original intentions and the abuse heaped upon gays in Seax-Wica by a later Stieward of that tradition. Source: Daven's Journal. Web (http://davensjournal.com/index.htm?dissassociation.xhtml&2, accessed 7 May 2008).

53 Phoenix. "Gardnerian Aspects: Newsletter of the Gardnerian Tradition." *Green Egg* 7.63 (June 1974) 18. Print. (Coll. A.Terr.).

54 (Cf. n#34). It should be noted that, despite Tommy Kneitel's assertion, Eddie's claim to Gardnerian lineage and the Commack coven's rejection of same actually predated Buckland's debut of Seax-Wica by many months.

55 In 1975, Buckland made note of this break by sardonically posting a poem of friendship sent to him by the Kneitels in November of 1972 shortly before they took over the Long Island coven from Rosemary and him. Raymond appended an editorial note stating "...ah! how easily they forget!" Phoenix and Theos [Tommy and Judy Kneitel]. "To Robat." Seax-Wica Voys 2 (Yule-Imbolc 1975) 10. Print. (Arch. Circ. Sanc).

56 Buckland, Raymond. "First Edition Comments." ERN 1.2 (February 1974) 5. Print. (Arch. Circ. Sanc).

57 Buckland, Raymond. Message to the author. 21 June 2003. Email.

58 Lady Arianne. Letter. *Green Egg* 8.76 (February 1976) 31. Print. (Coll. A.Terr.). Interestingly enough, the Occult Shop owned by Abraxas, which had existed in Smithtown, New York since 1970, was burned out shortly after

Notes for Chapter 14

[1] Hodges, Andrew. *Alan Turing: The Enigma.* New York: Walker & Company. 2000.
[2] For an in-depth examination of this topic, see: Owen, Alex. *The Place of Enchantment: British Occultism and the Culture of the Modern* (Chapter Three: Sexual Politics). Chicago: University of Chicago Press. 2004. 85-113.
[3] Fortune, Dion. *Sane Occultism.* New York: Weiser Books. 1973.
[4] Fortune, Dion. *The Cosmic Doctrine.* Chetenham: Helios Book Service. 1966.
[5] King. Megatherion. 33.
[6] The so-called "Paris Workings." See: Owen. *The Place of Enchantment.* 2004. 186-220.
[7] Urban, Hugh. "Unleashing the Beast: Aleister Crowley, Tantra and Sex Magic in Late Victorian England." Esoterica V (2003) Np. Web.
[8] Grant, Kenneth. *Aleister Crowley: The Hidden God.* New York: Weiser. 1974. p. 68. (Wesc. Lib. Llew.).
[9] Conner, Randy, et al. *Cassell's Encyclopedia of Queer Myth, Symbol and Spirit: Gay, Lesbian, Bisexual and Transgender Lore.* London: Cassell & Company. 1997. 257.
[10] Owen. *The Place of Enchantment,* 106-109.
[11] King, Francis. *Sexuality, Magic and Perversion.* Secaucus: Citadel Press. 1972. 190-193.
[12] D'Arch Smith, Timothy. *The Books of the Beast: Essays on Aleister Crowley, Montague Summers, Francis Barrett and Others.* Lancaster: Crucible. 1987. 75-88.
[13] Grant, Kenneth. *Nightside of Eden.* London: Skoob Books. 1995. 146.
[14] Sherry, Robert Brett. "Crowley, Bisexual? — Investigating the Love Life of The Great Beast 666, Part I." *Behutet* 40 (Winter 2008) 9. Print.
[15] "A Brief Biography of Frater Thabion" [Carroll "Poke" Runyon]. Welcome to the OTA. Web (http://www.templeofastarte.com, accessed 23 January 2010).
[16] Frater Aleyin [Carroll "Poke" Runyon]. "What is the O∴T∴A∴?" *Gnostica News* 4.2 (October 1974) 10. Print. (Wesc. Lib. Llew.).
[17] "What is the O∴T∴A∴?" *Gnostica News* 2.5 (21 March 1973) 2. Print. (Wesc. Lib. Llew.).
[18] Holzer. The New Pagans. 1972. 143.
[19] Clifton. Her Hidden Children. 2006. 151-152.
[20] Sitch, Ed [Ed Fitch]. "California Pagans Meet." ERN 1.4 (June 1974) 2. Print. (Arch. Circ. Sanc).
[21] "Point-Counterpoint: Spurious O.T.O. Dispensation." *Gnostica News* 5.4 (1976) 86. Print. (Wesc. Lib. Llew.).
[22] Bennu Phoenix Temple Advertisement in "Occult Sources." *Gnostica News* 3.10 (21 May 1974) 29. Print. (Wesc. Lib. Llew.).
[23] Lewis, James. *Satanism Today: An Encyclopedia of Religion, Folklore, and Popular Culture.* Santa Barbara: ABC-CLIO. 2001. 113.
[24] Palmer, John. "Aleister Crowley and the Golden Dawn." *Gnostica News* 4.3 (November 1974) 28-30. Print. (Wesc. Lib. Llew.).

[25] Regardie, Israel. Letter. *Gnostica News* 4.5 (January 1975) 12. Print. (Wesc. Lib. Llew.).
[26] Hansford, Phillip. Letter. *Gnostica News* 4.5 (January 1975) 12. Print. (Wesc. Lib. Llew.).
[27] Heflin, Llee (777). *The Island Dialogues: Liber Alal – Live Loving, Living Love, Light, A Book from Darkness.* San Francisco: Level Press. 1973.
[28] Koenig, P.R. "XI° -- Per Aftera Ad Astra, Anal Intercourse and the O.T.O." Web (http://user.cyberlink.ch/~koenig/sunrise/xi.htm, accessed 2 September 2009).
[29] Metacalus. "Counterpoint: The Fallacies of Sexism in Magick." *Gnostica News* 4.6 (February 1975) 21. Print. (Wesc. Lib. Llew.).
[30] Clarke, Lige and Jack Nichols. *Roommates Can't Always Be Lovers: An Intimate Guide to Male-Male Relationships.* New York: St. Martin's Press. 1974. 58.
[31] Unattributed ["!"]. "Gay Magick?" *ERN* 1.5 (August 1974) 16. Print. (Arch. Circ. Sanc).
[32] Zell-Ravenheart, Oberon. Message to the author. 20 August 2009. Email.
[33] Moss, Harold. Message to the author. 18 August 2008. Email.
[34] Kelly, Aidan. *Hippie Commie Beatnik Witches: A Social History of the New Reformed Orthodox Order of the Golden Dawn.* Tacoma: Hierophant Wordsmith Press. 2011. 83.
[35] Fritscher, Jack. *Popular Witchcraft: Straight from the Witch's Mouth.* Madison: University of Wisconsin Press. 2004. xiii.
[36] Graves, Robert. *The White Goddess: A Historical Grammar of Poetic Myth.* New York: Creative Age. 1948. 10-12.
[37] Forster, E.M. *Maurice.* New York: W.W. Norton & Co. 2005. 51.
[38] Graves, Robert. *Goodbye to All That.* New York: Anchor. 1958. 19. It is curious that, despite his stated distaste of the practice, Graves still managed to carry on close friendships with known homosexual men throughout his adult life, such as with British poet Siegfried Sassoon.
[39] Ankarloo. *Witchcraft and Magic in Europe: The Twentieth Century.* 1999. 52.
[40] Bourne herself did not think much of homosexual practitioners, either, believing that they did not possess Witchy auras. Source: Bourne, Lois. *Dancing with Witches.* London: Robert Hale. 2006. 38.
[41] Gardner, Gerald. *Witchcraft Today.* Newport Pagnell: Mercury (Restivo Enterprises). 1999. 13.
[42] See: Kelly, Aidan. *Crafting the Art of Magic, Book I: A History of Modern Witchcraft, 1939-1964* (Llewellyn's Modern Witchcraft Series). St. Paul: Llewellyn Publications. 1991.
Hutton, Ronald. *The Triumph of the Moon.* Oxford: Oxford University Press. 1999.
[43] This refers to the Book of Shadows (a compendium of ritual, laws, and mythos) compiled by Gerald Gardner with additions in the mid-1950s by his one-time high priestess Doreen Valiente.
[44] Harvey, Graham. *Contemporary Paganism: Listening People, Speaking Earth.* New York: New York University Press. 1997.
[45] Hutton. *The Triumph of the Moon* (Chapter 18: Uncle Sam and the Goddess).1999.
[46] In 1989, Doreen Valiente recanted her earlier beliefs regarding homosexuality in the Craft community. "Homosexuality, we were told, was abhorrent to the

Goddess, and Her curse would fall upon the people of the same sex who tried to work together. For a long time I believed this; but today I question it. Why should a people be 'abhorrent to the Goddess' for being born the way they are?" Source: Valiente, Doreen. *The Rebirth of Witchcraft*. Blaine: Phoenix Publishing. 1989. 183-184.

[47] Poiel. "Wiccan Sects." *Gnostica News* 2.7 (21 May 1973) 20. Print. (Wesc. Lib. Llew.).

[48] Hutton. *Triumph of the Moon*. 1999. 371.

[49] Score, John (ed.). *The Wiccan* 11 (8 June 1970) 5-6.

[50] Martello. *Black Magick, Satanism & Voodoo*. 1973. 108.

[51] Martello. *Weird Ways of Witchcraft*. 1972. 20-22.

[52] On the September 14, 1994 edition of the 700 Club, Pat Robertson asserted that "Many of those people involved with Adolf Hitler were satanists. Many of them were homosexuals. The two seem to go together." Bull, Chris and John Gallagher. *Perfect Enemies*. New York: Crown Publishers. 1996. 276.

[53] Shual, Katon. *Sexual Magick*. Oxford: Mandrake. 1989. 10.

[54] Cholla. "Who Cannot Hex Cannot Heal." *Feri Tradition: Witcheye — A Journal of Feri Uprising*. 2000. Web (http://www.feritradition.org/witcheye/hex.html, accessed 4 February 2012).

[55] Aaronovitch, Ben. *Moon Over Soho*. New York: DelRey. 2011. 88.

[56] Bonewits, Isaac. "Editorial: An Occultist of Another Color." *Gnostica News* 4.6 (February 1975) 2. Print. (Wesc. Lib. Llew.). See also: Vairanatha, Acharya. "Madam Blavatsky, the Theosophists, and Racism." *Gnostica News* 4.9 (July 1975) 15, 39. Print. (Wesc. Lib. Llew.).

[57] Patterson, George. Letter. *Green Egg* 7.62 (May 1974) 41. Print. (Coll. A.Terr.).

[58] Slater. *Pagan Rituals III*. 1989. 13-14.

[59] Zotique, Jonathon. "A Manifesto of Ideals for the New Age." *Green Egg* 6.55 (June 1973) 11-14. Print. (Arch. GE CAW).

[60] According to Tim Zell, Jonathan Zotique abandoned Wicca completely by August of 1973. He was subsequently ordained as a Bishop in 1976. In 1989, Zotique founded the Ancient British Church in North America (The Autocephalous Glastonbury Rite in Diaspora), which served the spiritual needs of homosexuals, transsexuals, prostitutes and drug addicts. He passed away in 1998 at the age of 54. Source: North American Old Roman Catholic Church. Web (http://netministries.org/see/churches/ch11962?frame=N, accessed 18 October 2009).

[61] Wyllie, Nan. Letter. *Green Egg* 6.57 (September 1973) 36. Print. (Arch. GE CAW).

[62] Dymond, Roy. Letter. *Green Egg* 6.57 (September 1973) 36-37. Print. (Arch. GE CAW).

[63] Martello, Leo. "The Gay Pagan." *Green Egg* 6.56 (August 1973) 21-22. Print. (Arch. GE CAW).

[64] Frost, Gavin and Yvonne Frost. "The Craft and Homosexuality: A New Look at an Old Topic." *Green Egg* 6.57 (September 1973) 25. Print. (Arch. GE CAW).

[65] Ironically, this theory entered into modern thought in the 1860s with the early philosophy of homosexual activist and sex researcher Karl-Heinrich Ulrichs. His term "Urning" was employed to denote 'a female psyche in a male body.'

See: Kaylor, Michael M. *Secreted Desires: The Major Uranians: Hopkins, Pater and Wilde.* Brno: Masaryk University. 2006. xiii, footnote.
66 Mann, Horace. *Thoughts: Selected from the Writings of Horace Mann.* Boston: H.B. Fuller and Company. 1867. 143.
67 Kight, Morris. Letter. *Green Egg* 6.58 (October 1973) 43-44. Print. (Arch. GE CAW).
68 Martello, Leo. Letter. *Green Egg* 6.58 (October 1973) 44-45. Print. (Arch. GE CAW).
69 Martello, Leo. "Wicca-Basket." *Gnostica News* 3.5 (21 December 1973) 16. Print. (Wesc. Lib. Llew.).
70 Spock. Letter. *Green Egg* 7.61 (March 1974) 52. Print. (Coll. A.Terr.).
71 Zell-Ravenheart, Oberon. Message to the author. 19 August 2009. Email.
72 Slater, et al. Letter. *Green Egg* 7.62 (May 1974) 34. Print. (Coll. A.Terr.).
73 Zell-Ravenheart, Oberon. Message to the author. 20 August 2009. Email.
74 Laws 155 and 156 from: Lady Sheba [Jessica Wicker Bell]. The Book of Shadows. 2006 (1971).
75 "The Brotherhood Messenger." *Gnostica News* 2.8 (21 June 1973) 21. Print. (Wesc. Lib. Llew.).
76 Kelly, Aidan. *Crafting the Art of Magic, Book I: A History of Modern Witchcraft, 1939-1964* (Llewellyn's Modern Witchcraft Series). St. Paul: Llewellyn Publications. 1991. 103-107.
77 Luhrmann, T. M. *Persuasions of the Witch's Craft: Ritual Magic in Contemporary England.* Cambridge: Harvard University Press. 1989. 64.
78 Nelson, Ray. "A Personal Report of the Pan Pagan Festival Held in Lake Holiday, IN August 21-25, 1980." RFD (25). Fall/Winter 1980. p. 21. Print.
79 Robert [Frederic Lamond]. "Living in Harmony with Nature." *Green Egg* 26.103 (Winter 1993-1994). 31. Print. Some Gardnerians, such as Frederic Lamond, continued to argue against the place of gays in the natural order well into the 1990s.
80 Martello. *Black Magick, Satanism & Voodoo.* 1973. 109. See also: Freedland, Nat. The Occult Explosion. New York: G.P. Putnam's Sons. 1972.
81 Holzer. *The Directory of the OCCULT.* 1974. 180.
82 Johns, June. *King of the Witches.* New York: Coward-McCann. 1969. 50-52.
83 Ankarloo, Bengt (ed.) *Witchcraft and Magic in Europe: The Twentieth Century.* Philadelphia: University of Pennsylvania Press. 1999. 60.
84 Hutton. *Triumph of the Moon.* 1999. 339.
85 Keith, W. Holman. *Divinity as the Eternal Feminine.* New York: Pageant Press, Inc.. 1960. 151.
86 Bagemihl, Bruce. *Biological Exuberance: Animal Homosexuality and Natural Diversity.* New York: St. Martin's Press. 1999. 2.
87 This thinking, promulgated by Theosophists such as C.W. Leadbeater and Annie Besant in the late 1800s, had some affect on the writings of contemporary sexologists, including Havelock Ellis and Edward Carpenter. See: Dixon, Joy. "Sexology and the Occult: Sexuality and Subjectivity in Theosophy's New Age." *Journal of the History of Sexuality* 7.3 (1997) 409-433. Print.
88 Martello. *Black Magick, Satanism & Voodoo.* 1973. 110-111. The dating of this letter by John Score to Leo Martello was probably not mere happenstance. Given the high profile of Martello's activism in pursuit of gay

rights, it was more likely to have been a deliberate attempt at twitching the tail of the good doctor.

[89] Martello. *Black Magick, Satanism & Voodoo.* 1973. 111.

[90] Martello. *Black Magick, Satanism & Voodoo.* 1973. 104.

[91] Buckland. *Ancient & Modern Witchcraft.* 1970. 176 Buckland reversed his opinion on this subject late in 1973, and was roundly criticized for it within the Craft community at the time.

[92] Adler. *Drawing Down the Moon.* 1981. 146.

[93] Pendderwen, Gwydion. "Dry Mouth Musings..." *Green Egg* 8.76 (February 1976) 23. Print. (Coll. A.Terr.).

[94] McFarland, Morgan. Letter. *Green Egg* 9.78 (May 1976) 36, 38-39. Print. (Coll. A.Terr.). McFarland wrote that less than half of Dianic covens and groves were women-only, with the remainder being mixed sex.

[95] White, Edmund. *City Boy.* New York: Bloomsbury. 2009. 231.

[96] "Skyclad" is a term used in Traditional Witchcraft to refer literally to being clothed only with the sky (i.e., naked). Not all traditions chose to practice in this manner, and even in those that did there could be some disparity. Photographs of rituals led by Alex Sanders, for example, almost always show him clothed while his coveners are naked.

[97] Louise Huebner in an interview with the National Insider on June 29, 1970. See: Martello. *Black Magick, Satanism & Voodoo.* 1973. 64. Huebner's opinion might be summarized by *Scratch a Witch, find a faggot.*

[98] Martello covered this in several of his books, including *Weird Ways of Witchcraft* (1972, 216-221), *Black Magick, Satanism & Voodoo.* (1973, 111-113), and *Witchcraft: The Old Religion* (1973, 99-102). For a fairly comprehensive overview on this topic, see: Conner, Randy. *Blossom of Bone: Reclaiming the Connections Between Homoeroticism and the Sacred.* New York: Harper Collins. 1993.

[99] Kaiser, Charles. "The APA decision December 1973: declassification of homosexuality as an illness, Charles Kaiser argues, was the gay movement's most revolutionary moment — Bold beginnings." *Advocate.* 12 November 2002.

[100] Kameny, Frank. "The Campaign Against the 'Sickness Question' 1964 — 1973." *The Rainbow History Project.* 8 July 2006. Web (http://www.rainbowhistory.org/APA.htm).

[101] One of the first published efforts by a so-called "ex-gay" was William Aaron's *Straight: A Heterosexual Talks About His Homosexual Past* (Double Day, 1972).

[102] Herman, Ellen and Martin Duberman (ed.). *Psychiatry, Psychology, and Homosexuality.* New York: Chelsea House Publishers. 1995. 102-113.

[103] Homosexuality was removed from the 10th revision of the World Health Organization's International Statistical Classification of Diseases and Related Health Problems (ICD-10), as endorsed by the Forty-third World Health Assembly on May 17, 1990.

[104] *The Celluloid Closet.* Epstein, Rob and Jeffrey Friedman. Home Box Office/Arte. 1995.

[105] Lawrence et al. v. Texas, No. 02-102, June 26, 2003. This ruling, decided on the eve of the 34th anniversary of the Stonewall riots, invalidated the remaining sodomy laws in all states, the District of Columbia, and United States territories and possessions.

[106] Interestingly enough, despite being the birthplace of the modern gay rights movement, New York's sodomy statute would not be declared unconstitutional in state court until 1980, and the law would not be repealed by the legislature until 2000. See: Summersgill, Bob. Sodomy Laws. Web (www.sodomylaws.org)

[107] Robinson, Lucy. "Carnival of the Oppressed: The Angry Brigade and the Gay Liberation Front." *Journal of Contemporary History* 6 (August 2003) Np. Web.

[108] Robinson. Tom. "Interview." Glad to be Gay – Tom Robinson. 8 October 2009. Web (http://gladtobegay.net/interview-tom-robinson/, accessed 20 May 2010).

[109] Buckland. *Witchcraft from the Inside.* 1971. 80.

[110] Power. *No Bath But Plenty of Bubbles.* 9.

[111] Robinson, Tom. "Glad to be Gay" (1976). *Rising Free.* 1978. Album.

[112] Power. *No Bath But Plenty of Bubbles.* 18-19, 294.

[113] Moss, Harold. "Guest Editorial." ERN 1.4 (June 1974) 3. Print. (Arch. Circ. Sanc).

[114] Slater, Herman. "Occult Consumer Information." ERN 1.3 (March 1974) 2. Print. (Arch. Circ. Sanc).

[115] Moss, Harold. Message to the author. 19 September 2008. Email.

[116] Critchley, Steven. Message to the author. 16 June 2010. Email.

[117] Moss, Harold. "Guest Editorial." ERN 1.4 (June 1974) 3. Print. (Arch. Circ. Sanc).

[118] This was still occurring even 20 years later, as demonstrated by the following two examples. In 1991, alleged former-Wiccan-turned-evangelical-preacher Eric Pryor claimed that "homosexuality and occultism go hand in hand" and that the Pagan community had strong ties to radical gay groups. Pryor suggested that the violence which evangelicals at that time were alleging as being perpetrated by occultists across the country was due to the influence of homosexuals in the Craft. According to Pryor, "most [Pagan] leaders are homosexual or bisexual." Pryor fingered the Magickal Childe occult store in New York City as a major player in this homosexual conspiracy. Cuhulain, Kerr. "Eric Pryor: Part 3." The Witches' Voice. 29 July 2002. Web (http://www.witchvox.com/va/dt_va.html?a=cabc&c=whs&id=4359, accessed 31 May 2010).

In the second example, the religion editor of the National Review, Fr. Richard Neuhaus, labeled the Magickal Childe and its owners as satanic in a 1992 article. Upset with the Irish Lesbian and Gay Organization protest over its discrimination by the Ancient Order of Hibernians in their annual St. Patrick's Day parade, Neuhaus used a rickety train of logic to link the shop's posted disapproval of bigotry as evidence that Satan promoted political correctness (PC), writing, "PC has the stated aim of reducing the prejudices that can turn nasty and truly evil. On the other hand, recent experience [of gay Irish groups protesting their exclusion from the parade] tells us that PC in fact exacerbates prejudice and unleashes hatreds on a grand scale." In effect, Neuhaus was saying that it was the gay men and lesbians who were the violent ones for attacking with their heads the brickbats of their opponents. Neuhaus, Richard. "Magickal city." *National Review.* 27 April 1992. Web.

[119] Moore, Martin. *Sex and Modern Witchcraft.* Los Angeles: Echelon Book Publishers. 1969. 100, 146-151.

[120] Fritscher, Jack. *Popular Witchcraft: Straight from the Witch's Mouth.* Secaucus: Lyle Stuart. 1973. 107-115.
[121] Newton, Jeremiah. Message to the author. 22 January 2010. Web.
[122] Martello. *Black Magick, Satanism & Voodoo.* 1973. 95-98.
[123] Burke, Tom. "Princess Leda's Castle in the Air." Esquire LXXIII.3 (March 1970) 107. Print.
[124] Gavin Arthur Memorial Page. Web (www.solsticepoint.com/astrologersmemorial/arthus.html, accessed 22 October 2009). Gavin Arthur (aka Chester Alan Arthur III, d. 1972) was the author of The Circle of Sex (1966), which examines the range of human sexuality. He cast the horoscope that determined the date for the first Human Be-In held in San Francisco on January 14, 1967.
[125] *Satanis: The Devil's Mass.* Dir. Ray Laurent. 1969.
[126] Footage of Bonewits' role as a Satanic acolyte also appears in two other documentaries. See: *The Occult Experience.* Dir. Frank Heimans. Cinetel Productions, Ltd. 1985; *Fangoria Magazine Scream Greats, Volume 2: Satanism and Witchcraft.* Dir. Damon Santostefano. Paramount Home Video. 1987.
[127] LaVey, Anton Szandor. *The Satanic Bible.* New York: Avon Books. 1976. 67.
[128] *Fangoria Magazine Scream Greats, Volume 2: Satanism and Witchcraft.* Dir. Damon Santostefano. Paramount Home Video. 1987.
[129] Aquino, Michael. *The Church of Satan* (5th Edition). San Francisco: Self-published. 2002. 225, 299. Barrett (d. 1998) eventually resigned from the Church of Satan to become the high priest of the Temple of Set, a splinter group founded in 1975 by Michael Aquino and others who left the CoS.
[130] Martello. *Black Magick, Satanism & Voodoo.* 1973. 107.
[131] The Church of Satan and its fellow travelers still offer sanctuary to like-minded gay men, a late example being British writer and musician Marc Almond.
[132] *Sex Ritual of the Occult.* Dir. Robert Caramico. 1970.
[133] Lamond, Frederic. *Fifty Years of Wicca.* Stathe: Green Magic. 2004. 86.
[134] Martello. *Black Magick, Satanism & Voodoo.* 1973. 109.
[135] Lamond. *Fifty Years of Wicca.* 79.
[136] Buckland, Raymond. Message to the author. 3 April 2008. Email.
[137] Nightshade, Jonathon. Message to the author. 17 February 2012. Email.
[138] Brita. Interview with Eliphas, High Priest of Kathexis Anthropos. The Hidden Path V.4 (October 1982) 27. Print. (Arch. Circ. Sanc).
[139] Leek, Sybil. *The Complete Art of Witchcraft.* Cleveland: World Publishing Company. 1971. 174.
[140] The Charge of the Goddess reads: "Let My worship be within the heart that rejoiceth for behold, all acts of love and pleasure are My rituals."
[141] Fritscher. *Popular Witchcraft.* Madison: University of Wisconsin Press. 2004. 138.
[142] "An Instant Cure." Time (Monday, 1 April 1974) Np. Web. The Board's ruling was placed before the association's 21,000 members for a vote in April of 1974, where it passed and became medical policy, effectively eliminating homosexuality, per se, as a mental illness from the medical lexicon.
[143] Buczynski, Edmund Michael. "Witchcraft Today and the Homosexual." *Gaysweek* (13 June 1977) 10. (Coll. BMG). To be fair, it must be iterated that the homophobia within Gardnerian Wica originated with Gerald

Gardner and others, not with Monique Wilson, although she is said to have continued the persecution.
[144] Eaton, Sally. Message to the author. 12 April 2006. Email.
[145] Eaton, Sally. Message to the author. 18 December 2010. Email. Eaton adds, "Olwen's purported homophobia has been widely discussed in the American Craft. Back in the 1960's English witches couldn't understand what Uncle Gerald saw in her. ... My personal theory (highly speculative, though) is that some of the homophobia may have been Olwen's over-reaction to Alex Sanders' ad hoc proclamation of himself as 'King of the Witches.'"
[146] Kneitel, Tommy. Message to the author. 10 September 2004. Email.
[147] Levenda, Peter. Message to the author. 29 August 2005. Email.
[148] Buckland, Raymond. "Ray Buckland Reverses Stand on Homosexuality." ERN 1.1 (December 1973) 1. Print. (Arch. Circ. Sanc).
[149] Martello. *Witchcraft: The Old Religion.* 1973. 200-202.
[150] Thorn, Michael [Michael Harismedes]. Message to the author. 19 January 2006. Email.
[151] Adler, Margot. Personal interview. 30 October 2004.
[152] Pratt, Roger. Message to the author. 16 June 2010. Email.
[153] Martello, Leo. "My Cauldron of Contempt." ERN 1.4 (June 1974) 32-33. Print. (Arch. Circ. Sanc).
[154] Springer, Renate. Message to the author. 26 November 2005. Email. While Renate herself may not have had these feelings, not everyone within her own coven was as open-minded.

Notes for Chapter 15

[1] Kneitel, Tommy. Message to the author. 10 September 2004. Email.
[2] This did not settle matters by any means. Fallout from Patricia's decision continued well into 1974, when Lady Sarna announced that she is hiving from Lady Sira of Patterson, New Jersey to form her own coven in Passaic, New Jersey, and acknowledging Lady Goewyn [Kay Flagg (Smith)] as her Witch-Queen. See: Announcement. ERN 1.4 (June 1974) 53. Print. (Arch. Circ. Sanc).
[3] Thain [Gerald Fisher]. "Gardnerian Wicca Inc." *ERN* 1.1 (December 1973) 2. Print. (Arch. Circ. Sanc).
[4] Starchild, Zera. "Raymond Buckland, the Father of American Wicca." Doorway Publication and Gifts. Web (http://doorwaypublications.com/interview.html, accessed 24 September 2008).
[5] Thain [Gerald Fisher]. "Gardnerian Wicca Inc." *ERN* 1.1 (December 1973) 2. Print. (Arch. Circ. Sanc).
[6] Front Cover. *ERN* 1.1 (December 1973) 1. Print. (Arch. Circ. Sanc).Unfortunately, the placement of this statement was done without the prior knowledge or consent of the Fishers. Slater and Buczynski were thus forced to print a retraction in the next issue of the newspaper. "In Apologia..." *ERN* 1.2 (February 1974) 5. Print. (Arch. Circ. Sanc).
[7] Fitch, Ed. Message to the author. 21 April 2004. Email.
[8] Helios. Message to the author. 21 April 2004. Email.
[9] Conte, Peter. Message to the author. 31 May 2011. Email.
[10] Slater. *Pagan Rituals III.* 1989. 13.
[11] Illustration. *ERN* 1.1 (December 1973) 15. Print. (Arch. Circ. Sanc).

[12] Buckland, Raymond. "Birth of a Tradition or the Coming of the Seax-Wicca." ERN 1.1 (December 1973) 1. Print. (Arch. Circ. Sanc).

[13] Buckland, Raymond. From his up-coming autobiography, as yet untitled. Copyright Raymond Buckland 2010, with permission.

[14] Inominandum [Miller, Jason]. "Simon Speaks: Part II." *Behutet* 17 (Spring 2003) 7. Print.

[15] Soror Charis. "Herman Slater: 'Thee Magickal Childe'" (Part I). *Behutet* 10 (Summer 2001) 2, 3. Print.

[16] Theos [Judy Kneitel]. "Notes from a Gardnerian High Priestess." The New Broom I.3 (Lammas 1973) 5. Print. (Arch. Circ. Sanc).

[17] Lowenstein, Kenny. Telephone interview. 25 January 2004.

[18] Piñero, Miguel. *Short Eyes: A Play.* New York: Hill and Wang. 1975. "Short Eyes" won the New York Drama Critics Circle award as the best play of the 1973-74 season. The Tombs was closed by a judge's order in 1974 for its inhumane conditions.

[19] Caigan, Khem. Telephone interview. 3 April 2005.

[20] North, Erika [Judith McNally]. Message to the author. 30 November 2005. Email.

[21] Cheiron. Message to the author. 23 August 2004. Email.

[22] Martello, Leo. "Wicca-Basket." *Gnostica News* 3.10 (21 May 1974) 22. Print. (Wesc. Lib. Llew.).

[23] Fate 29.1 (January 1976) 127; Fate 29.6 (June 1976) 127; Fate 28.9 (September 1975) 128; *Gnostica News* 4.9 (July 1975) 45. (Wesc. Lib. Llew.).

[24] Crowther, Patricia. *Witchblood! The Diary of a High Priestess!* New York: House of Collectibles. 1974. 5. That this statement was quoted by legendary scrapper Leo Martello in his introduction to Patricia's biography might be considered ironic to some.

[25] Rivera, Ria. Telephone interview. 30 January 2004.

[26] "One thing that was interesting was that three of us were on television. It was Herman, Eddie and I. I forgot the channel, though. It was really interesting, we were talking about the Wica. ... It was [listed] in TV Guide." Source: Springer, Renate. Telephone interview. 26 November 2005.

[27] Simon. *Dead Names.* 2006. 93.

[28] Flagg (Smith), Kay. Personal interview. 31 October 2004.

[29] Rivera, Ria. Message to the author. 24 January 2004. Email.

[30] Springer, Renate. Telephone interview. 26 November 2005.

[31] Frank, Kathryn. Message to the author. 19 May 2010. Email.

[32] Indeed, the increasing divergence of practices within Gardnerian Wica, including the discontinuation of scourging and the Great Rite within some covens, eventually prompted one group of elders, including Rosemary Buckland and the Kneitels, to issue what came to be known as the "October Letter" which defined what they considered to constitute valid practices and practitioners within the Gardnerian tradition. It was not well received by all Gardnerians. Sources: Rhiannon, et al. Letter. *The Hidden Path VIII.* 4 (Samhain 1985) 16. Print; Jana and Eldwyn. "A Response." The Hidden Path IX.1 (Imbolc 1986) 25-26. Print.

[33] Adler, Margot. Personal interview. 30 October 2004. Adler notes that "there was this sort of you know ... heterosexual trip about the way it believed [the Gardnerian tradition] should be practiced." Margot's own Gardnerian high

priest was a gay man named Bruce Kenyon (Craft name *Lear*). "What was weird was that Bruce ended up being the most conservative Gardnerian. It later turned out that unbeknownst to even me the [October letter] was written by Bruce Kenyon. I found out a year later that he was, in his spare time, basically being sort of the whipping person to get the Gardnerians back in line."

[34] Rivera, Ria. Personal interview. 30 October 2004.
[35] Rivera, Ria. Telephone interview. 30 January 2004.
[36] Rivera, Ria. Message to the author. 27 February 2010. Email.
[37] Lady Rhea [Ria Rivera]. "The Crystal Ball." Wildman. *Celebrating the Pagan Soul.* 2005. 96-97.
[38] Rivera, Ria. Message to the author. 30 September 2004. Email.
[39] (Cf. n#30). Though she no longer practices, Renate evinces the philosophy of Popeye, declaring, "I am what I am. I'm always gonna be what I am — a high priestess." Once a Witch, always a Witch.
[40] Front Cover. *ERN* 1.3 (March 1974) Print. (Arch. Circ. Sanc).
[41] Sanders, Ed. "Priestess." Beer Cans on the Moon. Reprise Records. 1972. CD.
[42] Nemorensis, Rex [Charles Cardell]. Witch. Surrey: Dumblecott Magick Productions. 1964.
[43] Nemorensis, Rex [Charles Cardell]. "Rex Nemorensis." *ERN* 1.6-8 (October 1976?) 154-174. Print. (Arch. Circ. Sanc).
[44] Martello. *Black Magic, Satanism & Voodoo.* 1973. 80.
[45] Fitch, Ed. "Of Traditions, Anti-Quality, and Ego Trips." *ERN* 1.2 (February 1974) 23, 26. Print. (Arch. Circ. Sanc).
[46] Kneitel, Tommy. Message to the author. 30 January 2005. Email.

Notes for Chapter 16
[1] Paulsen, Kathryn. *The Complete Book of Magic and Witchcraft.* New York: New American Library. 1970.
[2] Polanski, Roman (Director, Screenplay). *Rosemary's Baby.* Paramount. 1968.
[3] *The Modern Witch's Spellbook* by Sarah Lyddon Morrison (D. McKay, 1971) had an entire section on "Hate Magic" that included instruction on how "To Maim and Kill" and methods for successful grave robbing to obtain spell ingredients. Paul Huson's *Mastering Witchcraft* (HarperCollins, 1970) also had guidance on vengeance and attack, in addition to information on spells, rituals, and forming covens.
[4] "Rosemary's Baby — From best seller to movie chiller." Look 32.13 (25 June 1968) 91. Print.
[5] Melton, J. Gordon. "Towards a History of Magical Religion in the United States." *Green Egg* 8.73 (September 1975) 32-33. Print. (Coll. A.Terr.). For a religious scholar, Melton has been unusually fair-minded on the subject of minority religions for the last 30 years, a stance which has earned him a reputation, rightly or wrongly, as a "cult apologist" from some quarters of Christian academia.
[6] *Sex Ritual of the Occult.* Dir. Robert Caramico. 1970.
[7] Leek. *The Complete Art of Witchcraft.* 1971. 13.
[8] "Burn Occult Books." *Green Egg* 7.61 (March 1974) 7. Print. (Coll. A.Terr.).
[9] Gnosticus. "Book Burnings: An Insult to Humanity." *Gnostica News* 4.8 (June 1975) 2. Print. (Wesc. Lib. Llew.).

[10] One example is a city normally associated with leftist thought — Berkeley, California — which passed a ban in April of 1975. Source: St. Clair, David. "Los Angeles Witch-Hunt 1975." Fate 28.9 (September 1975) 81. Print. (Wesc. Lib. Llew.).

[11] Hunter, Frederic. "Rising Cults: Will They Influence America?" *Christian Science Monitor* (22 November 1974) Np. Web.

[12] Bonewits, Isaac. "Witchburning Now & Then." *Gnostica News* 3.6 (21 January 1974) 10, 16. Print. (Wesc. Lib. Llew.).

[13] It is also ironic that those fundamentalist Christians who believe in the power of imprecatory prayer to bring down their enemies are participating in the same practice they accuse practitioners of Witchcraft of performing.

[14] Holzer. *The Witchcraft Report.* 1973. 155-156.

[15] Bonewits, Isaac. "Witchburning Now & Then." *Gnostica News* 3.6 (21 January 1974) 10. Print. (Wesc. Lib. Llew.).

[16] Morris Cerullo eventually got into hot water regarding his faith-healing claims, fundraising efforts, and targeting of Jewish people for conversion. Warnke's claims of being a Satanic high priest were debunked in an exposé by the Christian magazine Cornerstone in 1992. Trott, Jon and Mike Hertenstein. "Selling Satan: The Tragic History of Mike Warnke." Cornerstone 98 (July 1992) np. Web (http://www.cornerstonemag.com/features/iss098/sellingsatan.htm, accessed 7 April 2011).

[17] Rice, Andrew. "Up Close, Michele Bachmann's Secret-Agent Political Organizer Looked More like Elmer Gantry than James Bond." *Capital New York.* 17 August 2011. Np. Web (www.capitalnewyork.com/article/culture/2011/08/3015443/close-michele-bachmanns-secret-agent-organizer-looked-more, accessed 18 August 2001).

[18] Bonewits, Isaac. "Witchburning Now & Then." *Gnostica News* 3.6 (21 January 1974) 10. Print. (Wesc. Lib. Llew.).

[19] Martello, Leo. "Wicca-Basket." *Gnostica News* 2.5 (21 February 1973) 16. Print. (Wesc. Lib. Llew.).

[20] Such evangelical sideshows still occur. Witness Kimberly Daniels of Jacksonville, Florida, who has traveled the countryside preaching against Witches and homosexuals from a 30-foot Winnebago dubbed "The Demon Buster Mobile." Despite its high baloney content, Daniels' vehicle should not be confused with the Oscar Meyer Weinermobile.

[21] Almost 30 years later, this trivialization by the media was still a problem. Margot Adler addressed the issue in 2000, writing, "Earth-based spirituality will finally have won the respect it deserves when interviewers ask us to address the hard questions of our age — during every season of the year." Adler, Margot. "Witches, Pagans, and the Media: Media interest doesn't equal media respect." Belief.net. 2000. Web (http://www.beliefnet.com/Faiths/Pagan-and-Earth-Based/2000/12/Witches-Pagans-And-The-Media.aspx, accessed 23 November 2009).

[22] "Ed Buczynski — His Warlock Shop is a Satanist Supermarket." *National Star* (2 March 1974). From the Collection of Renate Springer.

[23] Abraxas. Letter. *Green Egg* 7.63 (June 1974) 52. Print. (Coll. A.Terr.).

[24] Slater, Herman. Letter. *Green Egg* 7.63 (June 1974) 55. Print. (Coll. A.Terr.).

[25] "Playboy Potpourri: That Old Black Magic." *Playboy* 20.10 (October 1973) 215. Print.

[26] Martello, Leo. "Wicca-Basket." *Gnostica News* 3.5 (21 December 1973) 16. Print. (Wesc. Lib. Llew.).
[27] "Witchcraft is Rising" (cover story). Look (24 August 1971). Print.
[28] Carey, Robert. Message to the author. 24 March 2007. Email.
[29] Martello, Leo. "Wicca-Basket." *Gnostica News* 3.5 (21 December 1973) 21. Print. (Wesc. Lib. Llew.).
[30] Frost, Gavin. Letter. *Green Egg* 7.61 (March 1974) 39. Print. (Coll. A.Terr.).
[31] Holzer. *The Witchcraft Report*. 1973.p. 179. Fancy attire is actually quite common these days across the country at Neo-Pagan festivals, where one can see attendees costumed as Greeks, Romans, Egyptians, people from the Renaissance, wizards, pirates, faeries, dragons, warriors, vampires, sarongs, or nothing at all. As Pagan festivals in part owe their start to the science fiction and fantasy convention circuit, one could reasonably argue that Tim and Morning Glory were simply ahead of their time.
[32] Martello. *Black Magic, Satanism & Voodoo*. 1973. 65.
[33] Flagg (Smith), Kay. Personal interview. 31 October 2004.
[34] Rabinovitch, Shelly (editor). *The Encyclopedia of Modern Witchcraft and Neo-Paganism*. New York: Kensington Books. 2003. 24.
[35] Rachleff, Owen S. *The Occult Conceit*. New York: Bell Publishing Company. 1971. xvii.
[36] Martello, Leo. "Wicca-Basket." *Gnostica News* 2.4 (21 December 1972) 21. Print. (Wesc. Lib. Llew.).
[37] "The Occult: A Substitute Faith" (Cover Story). *Time* (19 June 1972) Np. Web (http://www.time.com/time/magazine/article/0,9171,877779,00.html, accessed 22 December 2007).
[38] The lectures were held at 7:30 PM every Wednesday during November 1972 at the First Unitarian Church (also known as The Church of the Savior), located at 121 Pierrepont Street in Brooklyn Heights at the corner of Monroe Place. Source: Warlock Shop/Friends of the Craft Advertisement. *Village Voice* 17.42 (19 October 1972) 15. MCF. (Cols. Met. Lib).
[39] In 1981, Raymond Buckland publicly complained that a tape of a lecture given by him on Gardnerian Wica was being sold in the Warlock Shop without his permission. Whether permission had been granted earlier and was withdrawn at a later date because of a title change (from "The Precepts and Practice of Gardnerian Witchcraft" to "Secrets of Gardnerian Witchcraft," thereby implying that he had violated his Gardnerian oaths after switching to Seax Wica) is unknown. However, the former tape appears in the 1973 catalogue of the store almost 8 years prior to Buckland's complaint. Source: Buckland, Raymond. Letter. Seax Wica Voys (Samhain 1981) 11. Print. (Arch. Circ. Sanc).
[40] Martello. *Witchcraft: The Old Religion*. 1973. 172.
[41] Introduction to Witchcraft & Satanism. Herman Slater (producer). New York: Magickal Childe. 1987. VHS.
[42] Aquino, Michael. *The Church of Satan (5th Edition)*. San Francisco: Self-published. 2002. 228.
Martello, Leo. WICA Newsletter 20 (1972).
[43] Carey, Robert. "The Great Draculeff Tapes." ERN 1.2 (February 1974) 3. Print. (Arch. Circ. Sanc).
[44] Martello, Leo. Letter. *Green Egg* 6.60 (February 1974) 38-39. Print. (Coll. A.Terr.).

[45] Unattributed [Slater, Herman]. "Witch Zaps TV Network." ERN 1.1 (December 1973) 1. Print. (Arch. Circ. Sanc). It's doubtless unsettling for the Fox Network, which now owns the Metromedia stations, to be reminded of WTTG's fling with the likes of Gore Vidal.

[46] Case in point is the homosexual rape of a teenage boy that appeared in the October 1974 episode of the popular television show Marcus Welby, MD. Titled "The Outrage," the show caused considerable outrage within the gay community when it aired, fomenting a boycott of the show, a letter-writing campaign against the network and its sponsors, and spurring the eventual creation of the Gay and Lesbian Alliance Against Defamation (GLAAD).

[47] Haining. *Anatomy of Witchcraft*. 1972. 111.

[48] Phoenix [Tommy Kneitel]. "Gardnerian Aspects" 1.7. *Green Egg* 7.62 (May 1974) 23. Print. (Coll. A.Terr.).

[49] Bonewits, Isaac. "A.A.D.L. News." *Gnostica News* (4:1). September 1974. 21. Print. (Wesc. Lib. Llew.).

[50] Bonewits, Isaac. "Aquarian Anti-Defamation League (of California) November 7, 1973 CE Activity Report to the Aquarian Media." *Green Egg* 6.60 (February 1974) 9. Print. (Coll. A.Terr.).

[51] Bonewits, Isaac. "A.A.D.L. News." *Gnostica News* 4.8 (June 1975) 41. Print. (Wesc. Lib. Llew.).

[52] Bonewits, Isaac. "A.A.D.L. News." *Gnostica News* 4.9 (July 1975) 22, 44. Print. (Wesc. Lib. Llew.).

[53] Now considered a cult classic, Simon is a black comedy that was long rumored to have been loosely based on the life of southern California occultist Carroll "Poke" Runyon (Order of the Temple of Astarte, OTA). However, lead actor Andrew Prine stated in the documentary Simon Says (Maljack Productions, 2008) that the film was actually based on the life of the film's writer, Robert Phippeny, who was purportedly a "warlock." The film's title was a play on June Johns' 1969 biography of Alex Sanders. Warhol Factory anti-ingénue Ultra Violet played a Wiccan high priestess whose ceremony was interrupted and ridiculed by Prine's character.

[54] Simon's sidekick, Turk, was a hustler he met in jail. When Turk asked his cellmate if he knew "Hercules," Simon thought a moment, and then said "Herakles ... Hylas" referring to Herakles' male companion and lover. In a later scene, Simon flogged another man in order to "charge his wand."

[55] Hardy, Robin (Director). *The Wicker Man*. British Lion. 1973.

[56] Aquino, Michael. *The Church of Satan (5th Edition)*. San Francisco: Self-published. 2002. 224-225.

[57] Frank, Kathryn. Message to the author. 6 January 2010. Email.

[58] OCCULT (exhibit handout). New York: Museum of American Folk Art. 16 January 1973.

[59] Simon. *Dead Names*. 2006. 135.

[60] Reif, Rita. "Blessed by Witches, an Occult Show is Unveiled." NYT (17 January 1973) 34. MS.

[61] "What's New in Art" (Lectures "WITCHCRAFT"). NYT (25 February 1973) Np. Web.

[62] The Clarion 3. *Museum of American Folk Art*. Summer 1973.

[63] Wertkin Gerard C. (ed.). *Encyclopedia of American Folk Art*. London: Routledge. 2003.

⁶⁴ Hephaestos and Hermes [Herman Slater and Ed Buczynski]. "The Warlock Shop/Earth Religions Supply Catalogue." Brooklyn: Earth Religions Supplies. January 1973. MS.
Slater, Herman and Ed Buczynski. "The Warlock Shop" (flier). Brooklyn: Earth Religions Supplies. Ca. late 1972. MS.
Slater, Herman. "PRESS RELEASE." Brooklyn: Earth Religions Supplies. January 1973? MS.
⁶⁵ The American Folk Art Museum (née Museum of American Folk Art) is to be commended for preserving this material in its file on the OCCULT exhibit. This ephemera would likely have vanished without the Museum's stewardship.
⁶⁶ Schurmacher. *Witchcraft in America* Today. 159.
⁶⁷ Holzer. *The Directory of the OCCULT.* 1974. 181.
⁶⁸ Soror Charis. "Herman Slater: 'Thee Magickal Childe'" (Part II). *Behutet* 11 (Autumn 2001) 9. Print.
⁶⁹ Honigman, Andrew. Message to the author. 1 May 2008. Email.
⁷⁰ Adler's project was eventually published as *Drawing Down the Moon* (1979). Adler, Margot. Letter. *Green Egg* 8.76 (February 1976) 32-36. Print. (Coll. A.Terr.).
⁷¹ Adler, Margot. Personal interview. 30 October 2004.
⁷² Margot Adler notes that her own covens during that period were not sustaining her intellectually, and this was her driving motivation to search out others of like mind in the Pagan community. "The *Green Egg* and Nemeton gave us the intellectual underpinnings of a broad Pagan movement with theology, philosophy, debates on very esoteric issues. ... I think the carping was there, but the real purpose of that forum was to give a wide view to those of us who were searching desperately in the ashes for a real deep Pagan world. And there it was. My covens were not sustaining me intellectually. And to know there were people out there like [Isaac] Bonewits and Harold [Moss] and Aiden [Kelly] and Fred [Adams], Penny [Novack], and on and on, it was so intoxicating!" Adler, Margot. Message to the author. 11 May 2011. Email.
⁷³ ERN 1:6-8 (1976) Inside Front Cover. Print. (Arch. Circ. Sanc).
⁷⁴ Adler. *Drawing Down the Moon.* 1981. 340.
⁷⁵ Slater. *Pagan Rituals III.* 1989. 11.
⁷⁶ Slater, Herman. Letter. *Green Egg* 8.71 (June 1975) 42. Print. (Coll. A.Terr.).
⁷⁷ Phoenix [Tommy Kneitel]. "Legend of the 'Witches Farthing.'" ERN 1.1 (December 1973) 7. Print. (Arch. Circ. Sanc).
⁷⁸ Kneitel, Tommy. Message to the author. 11 September 2004. Email.
⁷⁹ Kneitel's article appeared in the final issue of the newspaper. Tom Kneitel (Phoenix). "Tibetan Magic & Demon Possession." ERN 1.6-8 (October 1976?) 35-37. It should be noted in the interest of accuracy that a native form of shamanism does exist in Tibet, even if Tommy was not a practitioner of it.
⁸⁰ Soror Charis. "Herman Slater 'Thee Magickal Childe'" (Part II). *Behutet* 10 (Autumn 2001) 13. Print.
⁸¹ North, Erika [Judith McNally]. Message to the author. 30 November 2005. Email.
⁸² Adler, Margot. Letter. *Green Egg* 7.62 (May 1974) 37-38. Print. (Coll. A.Terr.).
⁸³ Margot Adler notes that "[Weinstein] doesn't really get enough credit in general because, like Sybil Leek, she was really very self made. But she was

one of the wisest Witches I know, and her book [*Positive Magic*, 1978] is really important, particularly Chapter 8." Adler, Margot. Message to the author. 11 May 2011. Email.

[84] Martello, Leo. Letter. *Green Egg* 8.72 (August 1975) 34. Print. (Coll. A.Terr.).

[85] Called The Magickal Mystery Tour, Slater's weekly cable television program would appear on the public access Manhattan Neighborhood Network in 1987 and featured interviews, rituals, music, and other aspects of the occult.

[86] Slater, Herman. Letter. *Green Egg* 7.63 (June 1974) 53. Print. (Coll. A.Terr.).

[87] Jamison, Artie. Telephone interview. 24 January 2004.

[88] "HELP...!" *Green Egg* 8.71 (June 1975) 4. Print. (Coll. A.Terr.).

[89] "Editorial Giggles." *Green Egg* 9.77 (March 1976) 24. Print. (Coll. A.Terr.).

[90] "Editorial Giggles." *Green Egg* 9.79 (June 1976) 29. Print. (Coll. A.Terr.).

[91] Weschcke, Carl. Message to the author. 10 August 2007. Email.

[92] Simon. *Dead Names*. 2006. 25.

[93] Fitch, Ed. "Of Traditions, Anti-Quality, and Ego Trips." *ERN* 1.2 (February 1974) 23, 26. Print. (Arch. Circ. Sanc).

[94] Phoenix [Tommy Kneitel]. "Gardnerian Aspects" 1.4. *Green Egg* 6.60 (February 1974) 25. Print. (Coll. A.Terr.).

[95] Phoenix [Tommy Kneitel]. "Gardnerian Aspects" 1.3. *Green Egg* 6.59 (December 1973) 35. Print. (Coll. A.Terr.).

[96] Kneitel, however, wasn't above participating in the very actions he criticized, as shown by his own letters to *Green Egg* which called into question the validity of Raymond Buckland's doctorate in anthropology. See: Kneitel, Thomas S. [Phoenix]. Letter. *Green Egg* 8.74 (October 1975) 54. Print. (Coll. A.Terr.).

[97] Phoenix [Tommy Kneitel]. "Gardnerian Aspects" 1.7. *Green Egg* 7.62 (May 1974) 24. Print. (Coll. A.Terr.).

[98] Leek. *The Complete Art of Witchcraft*. 1971. 15.

[99] Holzer. *The Witchcraft Report*. 1973. 180-182.

[100] Even Holzer's supporters had to admit that his fact-checking hadn't been consistently adequate.

[101] Holzer. *The Witchcraft Report*. 1973. 178.

[102] Adler. *Drawing Down the Moon*. 1981. 294-295.

[103] Moss, Harold. Message to the author. 18 August 2008. Email.

[104] Theos [Judy Kneitel]. "Notes from a Gardnerian High Priestess." The New Broom I.3 (Lammas 1973) 5. Print. (Arch. Circ. Sanc).

[105] Zell, Morning Glory. Editorial. *Green Egg* 8.72 (August 1975) 37. Print. (Coll. A.Terr.).

[106] Moss, Harold. Message to the author. 29 August 2008. Email.

[107] Melton, J. Gordon. "Toward a History of Magical Religion in the United States: Part II." *Green Egg* 8.71 (June 1975) 18. Print. (Coll. A.Terr.).

[108] Holzer. *The Witchcraft Report*. 1973. 188-189.

[109] Holzer. *The Directory of the OCCULT*. 1974. 188.

[110] Carey, Robert. Letter. *Green Egg* 7.62 (May 1974) 50. Print. (Coll. A.Terr.). The precocious 16-year-old elsewhere noted that "In the modern Craft the 'Raising of the Ire' is performed more frequently than the 'Drawing Down of the Moon.'" Carey, Robert. "The Great Draculeff Tapes." ERN 1.2 (February 1974) 3. Print. (Arch. Circ. Sanc).

[111] Sargent, Denny. Letter. *Green Egg* 7.68 (February 1975) 52. Print. (Coll. A.Terr.).

[112] Moss, Harold. Letter. *Green Egg* 7.61 (March 1974) 41. Print. (Coll. A.Terr.).
[113] Editorial Staff. "OPEN LETTER TO WHOM IT MAY CONCERN." *Green Egg* 7.61 (March 1974) 33. Print. (Coll. A.Terr.).
[114] Martello, Leo. Letter. *Green Egg* 7.61 (March 1974) 43. Print. (Coll. A.Terr.).
[115] Martello was himself certainly not without detractors. In a scathing 1974 review of *Weird Ways of Witchcraft* and *Black Magic, Satanism & Voodoo* in *Gnostica News*, Isaac Bonewits labeled Martello's work as misleading, disorganized, gossipy and overly ego-centric (whereas *Witchcraft: The Old Religion*, was merely criticized as the product of Leo's "neurotic insecurity"). Martello was himself a regular columnist of *Gnostica News* at the time. Bonewits, P.E.I. "Third Time's the Charm!" *Gnostica News* 3.11 (21 June 1974) 24. Print. (Wesc. Lib. Llew.).
[116] Eaton, Sally. Message to the author. 12 April 2006. Email. Sally's opinion carries a certain weight in the discussion. A good friend of the late Herman Slater, she is also an ex-wife of Ar nDraiocht Fein (ADF) co-founder Isaac Bonewits. She originated the role of the Hippie Witch, also known as the "Carbon Monoxide Girl," for her rendition of the song "Air" in the original Broadway production of Hair.
[117] Gardner, Gerald Brosseau. *Witchcraft Today*. Rider And Company, London. 1954. *Witchcraft Today* was heavily influenced by Margaret Murray's book *The God of the Witches*, which had been reprinted in 1952 shortly before Gerald Gardner's work. It is now accepted that the vast majority of the victims of these persecutions were not Witches at all in any classical or modern definition of the word.
[118] Simon. *Dead Names*. 2006. 94-95.
[119] WADL was eventually prodded by the Jewish Anti-Defamation League to rename itself twice since its founding, becoming the "Witches Anti-Discrimination Lobby" in the mid 1990s, and finally the "Alternative Religions Educational Network" (AREN) in 2000.
[120] "Aquarian Anti-Defamation League News." *Green Egg* 8.74 (October 1975) 19. Print. (Coll. A.Terr.).
[121] Advertisement for the Aquarian Anti-Defamation League. *Green Egg* 8.69 (March 1975) 49. Print. (Coll. A.Terr.).
[122] Holzer. *The Directory of the OCCULT*. 1974. 171.
[123] Pendderwen, Gwydion. "Dry Mouth Musings..." *Green Egg* 8.76 (February 1976) 23. Print. (Coll. A.Terr.).
[124] Gottlieb, Annie. *Do You Believe in Magic?* New York: Times Books. 1987. 195. Wilkus believes that the Nixon and Reagan Presidencies both resulted from this phenomenon.
[125] Inominandum [Miller, Jason]. "Simon Speaks: Part I." *Behutet* 16 (Winter 2002-2003) 11-12. Print.
[126] Konrath, Jacob. "The World's Strangest Convention." *Real* 17.3 (August 1966) 24-25, 66, 70. Print.
[127] Ad for the Space Age Club of Chicago, Inc. Flying Saucers FS-16 (August 1960) 57. Print.
[128] Mayer, Ken. "The History of the Kingdom of The West Pre-History." The Origins of the SCA. Web (http://history.westkingdom.org/Year0/index.htm, accessed 10 January 2010).

129. Holzer. *The Truth About Witchcraft.* 1971. 78.
130. Pratt, Roger. Message to the author. 17 June 2010. Email.
131. Pratt, Roger. Message to the author. 18 June 2010. Email.
132. Martello. Black Magic, Satanism & Voodoo. 1973. P. 185.
133. Zell, Tim. Editorial Note. *Green Egg* 5.47 (11 May 1972) 13. Print. (Coll. A.Terr.).
134. Advertisement. *Village Voice* 17.43 (26 October 1972) 44. Print. MCF. (Cols. Met. Lib).
135. "Satan's Celebration — A Rock and Occult Festival" (Flier: dated 31 October 1973). This Ain't the Summer of Love blog. Web (http://www.magictramps.com/images/_full/_flyers/17.jpg, accessed 15 June 2010).
136. Advertisement for "Edgar Allen Poe's 5th Annual Bizarre Bazaar." Village Voice 21.38 (20 September 1976) 2. Print. MCF. (Cols. Met. Lib).
137. Advertisement for "Friends of the Craft." *Village Voice* 17.43 (26 October 1972) 12. Print. MCF. (Cols. Met. Lib).
138. Martello, Leo. "Book Review: Witches USA. ... So They Say." ERN 1.4 (August 1974) 62. Print. (Arch. Circ. Sanc).
139. "Eugenia Macer-Story." Eullee.com: The Playwrights Database. Web (http://www.doollee.com/PlaywrightsM/macer-story-eugenia.html, accessed 17 July 2010).
140. Weschcke, Carl. Message to the author. 5 July 2007. Email.
141. "Occult Festival." *Gnostica News* 1 (1 September 1971) 1-2. Print. (Wesc. Lib. Llew.).
142. Weschcke, Carl. Message to the author. 7 January 2008. Email.
143. "Fourth Annual Pan-Pagan Festival." Seax Wicca Voys 1(out of sequence) (Beltane 1980) 4. Print. (Arch. Circ. Sanc).
144. Adler. Drawing Down the Moon. 1981. 384-385
145. "Second Annual Rites of Spring Pagan Festival." Seax Wicca Voys 1 (out of sequence) (Beltane 1980) 4. Print. (Arch. Circ. Sanc).
146. "Wisconsin Midsummer Celebration." Seax Wicca Voys 1 (out of sequence). Beltane 1980. p. 4. Print. (Arch. Circ. Sanc).
147. Seax Wicca Voys 1 (out of sequence) (Beltane 1980) 2. Print. (Arch. Circ. Sanc).
148. "FAQs." Starwood Festival. Web (http://www.rosencomet.com/starwood/faq.html, accessed 3 January 2010.
149. Adler. *Drawing Down the Moon.* 1981. 278.
150. Poland, Jefferson F. & Valerie Alison. *The Records of the San Francisco Sexual Freedom League.* New York: The Olympia Press, Inc. 1971. Poland was known variously in the community as Rev. Jefferson "Fuck" Poland and Rev. Jefferson Clitlick.
151. Marinacci, Michael. "Sex, Drugs and Hindu Gods: The Story of the Psychedelic Venus Church." 1998. Web (http://pw1.netcom.com/~mikalm/psyven.htm, accessed 16 January 2010 via the Internet archive).
152. Poland & Alison. *The Records of the San Francisco Sexual Freedom League.* Olympia Press. 1971.
153. Marinacci, Michael. "Sex, Drugs and Hindu Gods: The Story of the Psychedelic Venus Church." 1998. Web (http://pw1.netcom.com/~mikalm/psyven.htm, accessed 16 January 2010 via the Internet archive).

[154] Review of the BooHoo Bible. *Rolling Stone* 103 (2 March 1972) 68. See also: Kleps, Art. *The BooHoo Bible.* Toad Books. 1972.

[155] "Remember [CAW] was a mix of Heinlein (a right wing SF writer), [Ayn] Rand (a very right wing writer), and Maslow. Yes, libertarian, totally, free sex and drugs but, until later when Zell got the environmental bug, Zell would have been as anti-communist as any right winger." Adler, Margot. Message to the author. 11 May 2011. Email.

[156] Clifton. *Her Hidden Children.* 2006. 151-152.

[157] Holzer. *The Witchcraft Report.* 1973. 183-184.

[158] That same year, Wicker helped Fugs founder Ed Sanders and Beat poet Allen Ginsberg organize the Committee to Legalize Marijuana (LeMar). Sanders. *Fug You.* 115. Print.

[159] Sanders. *Fug You.* 82. Print.

[160] Allyn, David. *Make Love, Not War.* New York: Little, Brown and Company. 2000. 44.

[161] Adler. *Drawing Down the Moon.* 1981. 366.

[162] Martello, Leo. "Wicca-Basket." *Gnostica News* 2.3 (21 November 1972) 25. Print. (Wesc. Lib. Llew.).

[163] (Cf. n#103). Adams' support of the expulsion was particularly confusing, given Feraferia's record as a very sex positive group. Yet, its rites were generally kept out of the mainstream sight, and were exclusively heterosexual in orientation.

[164] Holzer. *The New Pagans.* 1972. 66-68. Holzer explicitly mentioned that homosexual men were allowed to participate in PsyVen activities, as if this fact helped to underpin his argument that the group was degenerate. His lack of objectivity can further be discerned by an examination of his coverage of PsyVen and the OTA in the book, with the former being lumped in with "Warlocks and Devils" and the latter with "The Masters of Magic."

[165] Martello. *Witchcraft, the Old Religion.* 1973. 253.

[166] Adler. *Drawing Down the Moon.* 1981. 366 (cf n#17).

[167] Martello. *Black Magic, Satanism, & Voodoo.* 1973. 55.

[168] Martello. *Witchcraft the Old Religion.* 1973. 29.

[169] Frank, Kathryn. Message to the author. 7 January 2010. Email.

[170] Holzer. *The New Pagans.* 1972. 103.

[171] Clifton. *Her Hidden Children.* 2006. 150.

[172] Moss, Harold. "Guest Editorial." ERN 1.4 (June 1974) 4. Print. (Arch. Circ. Sanc).

[173] Moss, Harold. Letter, to listed distribution. "The Council of Earth Religions." 4 January 1973. MS. (Arch. CES).

[174] Moss, Harold. Letter. *Green Egg* 8.70 (May 1975) 40. Print. (Coll. A.Terr.).

[175] "The Gnostic Aquarian Society." *Gnostica News* 2.3 (21 November 1972) 17. Print. (Wesc. Lib. Llew.).

[176] Gnosticus [Carl Weschcke]. "Witchmeet." *Gnostica News* 3.3 (21 October 1973) 14. Print. (Wesc. Lib. Llew.).

[177] Frost, Gavin and Yvonne Frost. *The Witch's Bible.* Los Angeles: Nash Publishing. 1972. Nash Publishing was also responsible for Louise Huebner's *Power Through Witchcraft* (1969), which advocated grave robbing in order to procure ingredients to work curses. *The Witch's Bible* has since been renamed the *Good Witch's Bible.*

[178] Frost and Frost. *The Witch's Bible.* 1972. 70, 189.

[179] Janet and Stewart Farrar avoided much of the controversy faced by the Frosts by naming their own 1980s-era book *A Witches' Bible* — and by having it published and marketed by Herman Slater. Once "Bible" had been used in the name of a Witchcraft for the first time, much of the disgust and outrage had worn off. By the time *A Wiccan Bible* (2003) appeared, the term had lost all of its edgy cachet, and the effort was seen more as an attempt to copycat prior efforts.

[180] "Editorial from '*Green Egg*'." ERN 1.3 (March 1974) 5. Print. (Arch. Circ. Sanc).

[181] Frost and Frost. *The Witch's Bible*. 1972. 83-86, 129-130.

[182] Frost and Frost. *The Witch's Bible*. 1972. 84.

[183] Frost and Frost. *The Witch's Bible*. 1972. 181.

[184] Frost and Frost. *The Witch's Bible*. 1972. 190-191.

[185] Frost, Gavin and Yvonne Frost. "The Craft and Homosexuality: A New Look at an Old Topic." *Green Egg* 6.57 (September 1973) 25. Print. (Arch. GE CAW).

[186] Holzer. *The Witchcraft Report*. 1973. 88.

[187] Frost and Frost. *The Witch's Bible*. 1972. 22.

[188] Frost and Frost. *The Witch's Bible*. 1972. 75, 305.

[189] Adler. *Drawing Down the Moon*. 1981. 123.

[190] Levenda, Peter. Message to the author. 29 August 2005. Email.

[191] This letter was later reprinted in *Green Egg*. Slater, Herman. Letter. *Green Egg* 6.53 (21 March 1973) 9. Print. (Arch. GE CAW).

[192] Moss, Harold. Letter, to listed distribution. "The Council of Earth Religions." 4 January 1973. MS. (Arch. CES).

[193] Gnosticus [Carl Weschcke]. "Editorial Comment." *Gnostica News* 2.5 (21 February 1973) 2. Print. (Wesc. Lib. Llew.).

[194] Adler. *Drawing Down the Moon*. 1981. 97.

[195] Holzer. *The Witchcraft Report*. 1973. 190.

[196] Frost, Gavin and Yvonne Frost. Letter. *Green Egg* 6.53 (21 March 1973) 10. Print. (Arch. GE CAW).

[197] Slater, Herman. Letter. *Green Egg* 6.53 (21 March 1973) 10. Print.

[198] Holzer. *The Witchcraft Report*. 1973. 191.

[199] Frost and Frost. *The Witch's Bible*. 1972. 13.

[200] Holzer. *The Witchcraft Report*. 1973. 192-193.

[201] It also should be noted that, although Wheatley had at one time resided in Lymington near the New Forest (and some of his stories were set there), he hadn't even lived in the area since 1968.

[202] Jenkins. *Mystics and Messiahs*. 2001. 174.

[203] Aquino, Michael. "Horns Across the Water: Satanism in Britain and America." Web (http://www.necronomi.com/magic/satanism/horns.set.txt, accessed 19 May 2010).

[204] Holzer. *The Witchcraft Report*. 1973. 193-194.

[205] Martello. *Witchcraft: The Old Religion*. 1973. 88.

[206] Warlock Shop advertisement. *Gnostica News* 2.8 (21 June 1973) 19. Print. (Wesc. Lib. Llew.).

[207] Gnosticus [Carl Weschcke]. "Witchmeet." *Gnostica News* 3.3 (21 October 1973) 14. Print. (Wesc. Lib. Llew.).

[208] El Draco. Letter. *Green Egg* 7.61 (March 1974) 49. Print. (Coll. A.Terr.).

209 Slater, Herman. "From the Inner Plain" [sic]. ERN 1.3 (March 1974) 2. Print. (Arch. Circ. Sanc).
210 Slater, Herman. "Directions That This is Going." ERN 1.1 (December 1973) 2. Print. (Arch. Circ. Sanc).
211 Zell, Tim. Editor's Note. *Green Egg* 6.59 (December 1973) 39. Print. (Coll. A.Terr.).
212 The Frosts, in an interview with Margot Adler in the late 1970s, confirmed that they did not consider themselves Pagan, primarily because they did not involve themselves with "stone gods" (i.e., idols). Adler. *Drawing Down the Moon*. 1981. 124.
213 Pendderwen, Gwydion [Tom DeLong]. Letter. *Green Egg* 6.60 (February 1974) 40. Print. (Coll. A.Terr.).
214 Slater, Herman. Letter. *Green Egg* 7.61 (March 1974) 53. Print. (Coll. A.Terr.).
215 Zell, Tim. Editorial. *Green Egg* 7.61 (March 1974) 53. Print. (Coll. A.Terr.).
216 Spock. Letter. *Green Egg* 7.61 (March 1974) 52. Print. (Coll. A.Terr.).
217 Zell-Ravenheart, Oberon. Message to the author. 19 August 2009. Email.
218 Warlock Shop advertisement. *Gnostica News* 3.9 (21 April 1974) 28. Print. (Wesc. Lib. Llew.).
219 Buczynski, Edmund. "A Visit to a Temple or A House is not Only a Home." ERN 1.4 (June 1974) 29-30. Print. (Arch. Circ. Sanc).
220 Scheiber, Lewis. "Impressions of a Witchmeet." ERN 1.4 (June 1974) 44. Print. (Arch. Circ. Sanc).
221 Wildgrube, Donald. Message to the author. 5 April 2007. Letter.
222 Zell, Tim. "Paganism, Witchcraft and Neo-Paganism: The Old Religion and the New Religion." ERN 1.3 (March 1974) 8-10. Print. (Arch. Circ. Sanc).
223 Scheiber, Lewis. "Impressions of a Witchmeet." ERN 1.4 (June 1974) 45. Print. (Arch. Circ. Sanc).
224 Slater, Herman. "Publisher's Editorial." ERN 1.4 (June 1974) 3. Print. (Arch. Circ. Sanc).
225 Weschcke, Carl. Message to the author. 4 July 2007. Email.
226 Weschcke, Carl. Message to the author. 11 May 2010. Email.
227 "Principles of Wiccan Belief." *Green Egg* 7.64 (August 1974) 32. Print. (Coll. A.Terr.).
228 Sitch, Ed. "California Pagans Meet." ERN 1.4 (June 1974) 2. Print. (Arch. Circ. Sanc).
229 Ravenwolf, Silver. *To Ride a Silver Broomstick*. St. Paul: Llewellyn Publications. 2000. 284.
230 "Spring Witchmeet 1974 – Witches Unite in Unique Policy Decisions." *Gnostica News* 3.10 (21 May 1974) 19. Print. (Wesc. Lib. Llew.).
231 Harlow, Alison. Letter. *Green Egg* 9.78 (May 1976) 48-49. Print. (Coll. A.Terr.).
232 Frost, Gavin. "Witchcraft The Oldest New Religion." ERN 1.4 (June 1974) 12-15. Print. (Arch. Circ. Sanc).
233 Bonewits, Isaac. "My Satanic Adventure." ERN 1.4 (June 1974) 7-9. Print. (Arch. Circ. Sanc).
234 Unfortunately, this proposal attracted little interest apart from those elders already situated in their camp. See: Smith, Kay. "Announcement to All of the Third Degree." ERN 1.2 (February 1974) 4. Print. (Arch. Circ. Sanc).

[235] Inominandum [Miller, Jason]. "Simon Speaks, Part II." *Behutet* 17 (Spring 2003) 8. Print.
[236] Caigan, Khem. Telephone interview. 3 April 2006.
[237] Gwilym Dafydd HHH. Message to the author. 30 July 2007. Email.
[238] "Applying Traditional Therapies, Rituals and Systems." PaganNews.com. Web (http://www.pagannews.com/gyf.shtml, accessed 28 April 2010).
[239] "What Might Gavin and Yvonne Frost Say at Your Event? A Current Lecture Menu: The Myth-History of Modern Wicca." The Church and School of Wicca. Web (http://www.wicca.org/gavinandyvonne/menu.html, accessed 28 April 2010). First, as has been demonstrated, there was no trial. Second, Lady Sheba was sick and was not even present at the event. Third, and most ironic, Carl Weschcke had supported the Frost's right to call themselves whatever they wanted, and had not been in favor of a trial, and yet they continue to blame him for the situation. Finally, Gavin had entered Circle with Herman during the Witchmeet and agreed that the mutual recriminations would cease. They obviously haven't.
[240] Pitzl-Waters, Jason. "Sacrificing the Frosts." The Wild Hunt blog. 25 June 2007. Web (http://wildhunt.org/blog/2007/06/sacrificing-frosts.html, accessed 17 May 2010.).
[241] Crisp, Quentin. *The Naked Civil Servant*. New York: Holt, Rinehart, & Winston. 1977.

Notes for Chapter 17

[1] Jane Cicciotto's Craft name has been variously spelled as both Coreatha and Koreatha.
[2] Buczynski, Ed. "America's Own Stonehenge: Mystery Hill New Hampshire." ERN 1.1 (December 1973) 16. Print. (Arch. Circ. Sanc).
[3] Rivera, Ria. Message to the author. 24 January 2004.
[4] A note should be made here regarding the seeming discrepancy of Ria Rivera's [Rhea's] elevation to Third Degree, which she has in the past claimed as dating to 1973. Eddie had not provided Ria with a vouch when he had elevated her to Third Degree in 1974. In 1976, she asked for and received a vouch from Eddie which seemed to imply that she had only attained the Third Degree on August 9th of that year, the date he wrote the paper for her. This caused some confusion, as Ria had been a practicing high priestess for several years by that point. Eddie attempted to clarify the matter by issuing yet another vouch, dated August 22nd; however, that paper indicated that Ria was made a Third Degree in 1973. This is a mis-remembrance on Eddie's part. Ria states that she was made a Third Degree at Imbolc (early February). As Eddie had not yet begun practicing Gardnerian Wica with Renate Springer in February 1973, and the Yule breakup which delayed the initiation of David and Ria occurred in December of that same year, the year cited by Eddie for granting Ria a Third Degree (1973) was simply not possible. It is clear that Eddie had misremembered the 1973 date as the year he had elevated Ria to Third rather than the date when he had actually initiated her. In any case, given that the dates are within roughly a month of one another and given that she had not initiated anyone in the period between her initiation and elevations, the discrepancy does not truly matter. Sources: Gwydion [Edmund Buczynski]. The Wica vouch of Rhea [Ria Farnham]. Middle Village, Queens, New York. 9 August 1976. MS. Gwydion [Edmund

Buczynski]. "To whom it may concern." The Wica vouch of Rhea [Ria Farnham]. Middle Village, Queens, New York. 22 August 1976. MS.

[5] Lady Diana. Notice of fealty to Goewyn [Kay Flagg (Smith)]. Brooklyn Heights, New York. 19 January 1974.

[6] Goewyn [Kay Flagg (Smith)]. The Wica vouch of Sarna. Riverside, New York. 21 March 1974. MS.

[7] Rivera, Ria. Personal interview. 30 October 2004.

[8] Unattributed [Buczynski, Edmund]. *The New York Coven of Witches Book of Shadows (The Wica)*. Brooklyn, New York. ca. 1974. 19. MS.

[9] Unattributed [Buczynski, Edmund]. *The New York Coven of Witches Book of Shadows (The Wica)*. ca. 1974. 16. MS.

[10] Sawicki, Matthew. Message to the author. 26 March 2009. Email.

[11] Buckland, Raymond. *The Tree: The Complete Book of Saxon Witchcraft*. New York: Weiser Books. 1974. 28.

[12] Buckland, Raymond. *The Tree: The Complete Book of (Saxon) Witchcraft*. Unpublished Manuscript. Undated [1974]. From the Collection of Ken Dalton (Coll. K. Dal.).

[13] Buckland, Raymond. "Birth of a Tradition or the Coming of the Seax-Wicca." ERN 1.1 (December 1973) 1+. Print. (Arch. Circ. Sanc).

[14] Buczynski, Ed. "America's Own Stonehenge: Mystery Hill New Hampshire." ERN 1.1 (December 1973) 16. Print. (Arch. Circ. Sanc).

[15] Buckland, Raymond. "Birth of a Tradition or the Coming of the Seax-Wicca." ERN 1.1 (December 1973) 16. Print. (Arch. Circ. Sanc).

[16] Unattributed [Buczynski, Edmund]. "The New York Coven of Witches." ERN 1.3 (March 1974) 12. Print. (Arch. Circ. Sanc).

[17] Gwydion [Buczynski, Edmund]. *The New York Coven of Witches Book of Shadows (The Wica)*. ca. 1974. 1-2. MS. The wording in the Book of Shadows is identical to that in the article published in the Spring Equinox 1974 edition of ERN.

[18] Horowitz. *Occult America*. 2009. 212.

[19] Slater. *Pagan Rituals III*. 1989. 13.

[20] Cassals, Ferran. "Bring Back the Horned God." ERN 1.5 (August 1974) 3. Print. (Arch. Circ. Sanc).

[21] Buczynski. *The New York Coven of Witches Book of Shadows (The Wica)*. 20. MS.

[22] Unattributed [Slater, Herman?]. "The Power Trip." ERN 1.1 (December 1973) 4. Print. (Arch. Circ. Sanc).

[23] Caigan, Khem. Telephone interview. 3 April 2006.

[24] Slater, Herman. "House Editorial." ERN 1.3 (March 1974) 3. Print. (Arch. Circ. Sanc).

[25] Eaton, Sally. Message to the author. 27 February 2008. Email.

[26] Rivera, Ria. Message to the author. 20 February 2004. Email.

[27] Spock. Letter. *Green Egg* 7.61 (March 1974) 52. Print. (Coll. A.Terr.).

[28] Slater, et al. Letter. *Green Egg* 7.62 (May 1974) 34. Print. (Coll. A.Terr.).

[29] Coreatha [Jane Cicciotto]. "Poppet Magick." ERN 1.3 (March 1974) 23. Print. (Arch. Circ. Sanc).

[30] Coreatha [Jane Cicciotto]. "Poppet Magick for Healing." ERN 1.4 (June 1974) 15. Print. (Arch. Circ. Sanc).

[31] Buckland, Raymond. (ed.) "Seax Wica." ERN 1.4 (June 1974) 49-52. Print. (Arch. Circ. Sanc).

[32] Buckland, Raymond. (ed.) Seax-Wica Voys 2 (Yule-Imbolc 1975). Print. (Arch. Circ. Sanc).

[33] Buckland, Raymond. Message to the author. 5 February 2004. Email.

[34] Advertisement "Sword Designed by the Late Dr. Brousseau Gardner!" ERN 1.3 (March 1974) 19. Print. (Arch. Circ. Sanc).

[35] Unattributed [Slater, Herman?]. "Watch Out England: Con Man On The Loose." ERN 1.4 (June 1974) 28. Print. (Arch. Circ. Sanc).

[36] Johns, June. *King of the Witches: The World of Alex Sanders*. New York: Coward-McCann, Inc. 1969. 143.

[37] Ankarloo and Clark (eds.). *Witchcraft and Magic in Europe: The Twentieth Century*. 1999. 59-60.

[38] Unattributed [Slater, Herman?]. "In Apologia." ERN 1.4 (June 1974) 27. Print. (Arch. Circ. Sanc).

[39] Front Cover. ERN 1.4 (June 1974) Print. (Arch. Circ. Sanc).

[40] Laffont, Jean-Pierre. "Le Grande Retour a la Nature." *ERN* 1.5 (August 1974) 18-21. Print. (Arch. Circ. Sanc).

[41] Lady Gwen [Gwen Thompson]. "Wiccan-Pagan Potporri." *Green Egg* 8.69 (March 1975) 9. Print. (Coll. A.Terr.).

[42] "Witches in Britain: Britain's Witches Make a Comeback." *Weekend Telegraph* 35 (21 May 1965) Np. Web.

[43] "Real Witches at Work: English pagans keep an old cult alive." LIFE 5.20 (13 November 1964) 55. Print.

[44] Woodward, Wilcock. "England's Nude Witch Cult." *Swank* (March 1966) Np. Web. Swank was and remains a United States "men's magazine." As such, it was arguably a far more deleterious forum for the Craft than *Green Egg* or *Earth Religion News* ever were.

[45] Thompson would eventually criticize *Green Egg* for this as well. *Green Egg* was not shipped in a plain brown wrapper, and the staff did not appear to be particularly sympathetic to the plight of subscribers in rural areas of the country who complained that nude cover art was causing them problems. See: Thompson, Gwen. Letter. *Green Egg* 9.79 (June 1976) 37. Print. (Coll. A.Terr.).

[46] Crowley, Aleister. *White Stains*. Brooklyn Heights: Earth Religions Supply, Inc. 1974.

[47] Advertisement for a limited edition "Under One Cover Entire Pagan Way Rituals." ERN 1.3 (March 1974) 26. Print. (Arch. Circ. Sanc).

[48] *Witchcraft Fact Book*. Advertisement. ERN 1.3 (March 1974) 26. Print. (Arch. Circ. Sanc).This is not to be confused with an earlier *Witchcraft Fact Book*, also in pamphlet form, that had been published by Mary Nesnick and Mary Smith.

Notes for Chapter 18

[1] Unattributed. "The Wiccan Rede." ERN 1.3 (March 1974) 11. Print. (Arch. Circ. Sanc).

[2] Lady Gwen [Thompson, Gwen]. "Wiccan-Pagan Potporri." *Green Egg* 8.69 (March 1975) 9-11. Print. (Coll. A.Terr.).

[3] The N.E.C.T.W. archivist confirmed that Gwen was referring to Eddie Buczynski when writing about the Rede appearing in 1974. Source: Theitic, Andrew. Message to the author. 4 February 2007. Email.

[4] Lady Gwen [Thompson, Gwen]. "Wiccan-Pagan Potporri." *Green Egg* 8.69 (March 1975) 10. Print. (Coll. A.Terr.).
[5] Gwydion [Buczynski, Edmund]. *Traditionalist Gwyddoniaid Book of Shadows*. Brooklyn Heights: Unpublished MS. 1972. 5-7. MS.
[6] HERMES DIONYSUS [Buczynski, Edmund]. *The Cauldron* (New England Covens of Traditionalist Witches Book of Shadows). North Haven/Brooklyn Heights: Unpublished MS. 1972? pp. 97-99. MS.
[7] Mathiesen and Theitic. *The Rede of the Wiccae*. 2005. 68-70.
[8] Hutton. *Triumph of the Moon*. 1999. 249.
[9] Valiente. *The Rebirth of Witchcraft*. 1989. 65-74.
[10] Kelly. *Crafting the Art of Magic, Book I*. 1991. 103-107.
[11] Kelly. *Crafting the Art of Magic, Book I*. 1991. 54.
[12] Scire [Gardner, Gerald Brousseau]. *High Magic's Aid*. London: Michael Houghton. 1949. 182.
[13] Scire [Gardner, Gerald Brousseau]. *High Magic's Aid*. 1949. 188.
[14] "Rule of Three (Wiccan)." Wikipedia. Web (http://en.wikipedia.org/wiki/Rule_of_Three_(Wiccan), accessed 11 July 2008).
[15] "Fifty at Pentagram Dinner." *Pentagram* 2 (November 1964) 7. Electronic.
[16] Coughlin, John. "Part 3: Eight Words..." The Wiccan Rede: A Historical Journey. 2002. Web (http://www.waningmoon.com/ethics/rede3.shtml, accessed 9 July 2008).
[17] Glass, it should be noted, had a letter published in the same issue of the *Pentagram* in which Valiente's couplet appeared (indeed, it was printed on the very same page as the couplet). Glass was seeking input on a Witchcraft book (likely *Witchcraft: The Sixth Sense*) that she had been contracted to write. Source: "Author's Query." *Pentagram* 2 (November 1964) 7. Electronic.
[18] Glass, Justine. *Witchcraft: The Sixth Sense*. London: Neville Spearman. 1965. 58.
[19] Caigan, Khem. Telephone interview. 3 April 2006.
[20] Thompson, Gwen. Letter. *Green Egg* 8.71 (June 1975) 39. Print. (Coll. A.Terr.).
[21] Thompson, Gwen. Letter. *Green Egg* 8.72 (August 1975) 44-45. Print. (Coll. A.Terr.).
[22] Zell, Tim. Editorial. *Green Egg* 8.72 (August 1975) 45. Print. (Coll. A.Terr.).
[23] Unfortunately for Thompson (d. 1986), the association of her tradition with the Welsh tradition would continue to be repeated in future years, first in a 1997 issue of *Green Egg*, and then in a 2009 reprint of her original article in the book *Green Egg* Omelette.
"Rede of the Wiccae." *Green Egg* 29.121 (November-December 1997) 9. Print.
Dalley, Kirsten and Oberon Zell-Ravenheart (eds.). *Green Egg Omelette*. Franklin Lakes: New Page Books. 2009. 49.
[24] Theitic, Andrew. Message to the author. 4 February 2007. Email.
[25] Slater. *Pagan Rituals III*. 1989. 11.
[26] Gawr, Rhuddlwm [William Wheeler]. Message to the author. 10 July 2007. Email. Margot Adler noted in *Drawing Down the Moon* (1981) that this guide was rife with errors, listing groups that were extinct and people who were no longer Pagan, as well as many who hadn't given their permission to be listed. See: Adler. *Drawing Down the Moon*. 1981. 409.

[27] Gawr, Rhuddlwm [William Wheeler]. Message to the author. 11 July 2007. Email.
[28] (Ibid n#26). Interestingly enough, Betws-y-coed is the same area in Wales where Gavin and Yvonne Frost claim to have received the material for their tradition of Celtic Wicca.
[29] Wheeler published both *The Way* and its companion volume, *The Quest*, in 1985. See:
Gawr, Rhuddlwm. *The Way: A Discovery of the Grail of Immortality*. Athens: Camelot Press. 1985.
Gawr, Rhuddlwm. *The Quest: The Search for the Grail of Immortality*. Athens: Camelot Press. 1985.
[30] Theitic, Andrew. Message to the author. 17 July 2008. Email.
[31] Theitic, Andrew. Message to the author. 12 August 2008. Email.
[32] Theitic, Andrew. Message to the author. 18 July 2008. Email.
[33] Theitic, Andrew. Message to the author. 19 July 2008. Email.
[34] Helios. Message to the author. 21 April 2004. Email.
[35] Gawr, Rhuddlwm. *The Cauldron: Celtic Mythology and Witchcraft*. Athens: Camelot Press, Ltd. 1989.

Notes for Chapter 19

[1] Adler. *Drawing Down the Moon*. 1986. 270.
[2] "Rev. Harold Moss — Priest of Horus." *Church of the Eternal Source*. Web (http://home.earthlink.net/~ceswebhq/Bios/moss.htm, accessed 12 August 2008).
[3] Wildgrube, Don. Letter to the author. 5 April 2007. MS.
[4] Holzer. *The Witchcraft Report*. 1973. 114.
[5] Moss, Harold. Message to the author. 18 August 2008. Email.
[6] Moss, Harold. Letter to Edmund Buczynski. 5 August 1974. MS. (Arch. CES).
[7] Moss, Harold. Message to the author. 29 August 2008. Email.
[8] "We dealt quite a bit with [Burt and Jane Cicciotto], unbeknownst to us [allegedly] struggling heroin addicts who predictably fell off the wagon and everything they had built collapsed. I blew up at Herman over the phone for recommending them to us and he shrugged it all off." Source: (Ibid n#5).
[9] Moss, Harold. Letter to Edmund Buczynski. 31 July 1974. MS. (Arch. CES).
[10] In an article in the June 1974 edition of ERN, he signed himself as "Edmund Buczynski, C.E.S." See: Buczynski, Edmund. "A Visit to a Temple or A House is not Only a Home." ERN 1.4 (June 1974) 29-30. Print. (Arch. Circ. Sanc).
[11] Buczynski, Edmund. Letter to Harold Moss. 28 September 1974. MS. (Arch. CES). Moss, Harold. Message to the author. 29 August 2008. Email.
[12] Buczynski, Edmund. "Edmund Michael Buczynski" Autobiographical paper. 28 September 1974. MS. (Arch. CES).
[13] Buczynski, Edmund Michael. "Witchcraft Today and the Homosexual." Gaysweek (13 June 1977) 11. (Coll. BMG).
[14] Moss, Harold. Letter. ERN 1.4 (June 1974) 4. Print. (Arch. Circ. Sanc).
[15] Holzer. *The Witchcraft Report*. 1973. 112.
[16] Bartlett, Karen. Message to the author. 22 December 2008. Email.
[17] Buczynski, Ed. Letter. KHEPERA [*Green Egg* 7.63 (June 1974) 31]. Print. (Coll. A.Terr.).

[18] Budge, E.A. Wallis. *From Fetish to God in Ancient Egypt.* Oxford: Oxford University Press. 1934. 66.
[19] Buczynski, Edmund. Message to Harold Moss. 7 August 1974. Letter.
[20] Ankh em Ma'at [Moss, Harold]. Letter. ERN 1.4 (June 1974) 18. Print. (Arch. Circ. Sanc).
[21] [Buczynski, Edmund (ed.)]. "Esbat." ERN 1.4 (June 1974) 19, 22. Print. (Arch. Circ. Sanc).
[22] [Buczynski, Edmund (ed.)]. "Esbat." ERN 1.5 (August 1974) 24. Print. (Arch. Circ. Sanc).
[23] Carey, Robert. Message to the author. 24 March 2007. Email.
[24] Buczynski, Edmund. Letter to Harold Moss. 6 September 1974. MS. (Arch. CES).
[25] Unattributed [Buczynski, Edmund]. *Volume Number One: The Temple Ritual.* Brooklyn Heights: Unpublished MS. ca. early September 1974. (Arch. CES).
[26] Unattributed [Buczynski, Edmund]. *Volume Number Two: The Rituals of Khem.* Brooklyn Heights: Unpublished MS. ca. early September 1974. (Arch. CES).
[27] Moss, Harold. Letter to Edmund Buczynski. 18 March 1975. MS. (Arch. CES).
[28] Cheiron. Message to the author. 23 August 2004. Email.
[29] Moss, Harold. Letter to Edmund Buczynski. 5 August 1974. MS. (Arch. CES).
[30] Buczynski, Edmund. Letter to Harold Moss. 7 August 1974. MS. (Arch. CES).
[31] Myron, Ron. "Incense, Herbs & Stones." ERN 1.5 (August 1974) 26-27. Print. (Arch. Circ. Sanc).
[32] Buczynski, Edmund. Letter to Ron Myron. 12 August 1974. MS. (Arch. CES).
[33] Moss, Harold. Letter. ERN 1.4 (June 1974) 4. Print. (Arch. Circ. Sanc).
[34] Myron, Ron. Letter. *Green Egg* 9.77 (March 1976) 34. Print. (Coll. A.Terr.).
[35] Bartlett, Karen. Message to the author. 26 March 2007. Email.
[36] Caldiero, Joe. Message to the author. 8 February 2010. Email. The bath was Man's Country, 53 Pierrepont Street.
[37] North, Erika [Judith McNally]. Message to the author. 30 November 2005. Email.
[38] [Buczynski, Edmund (ed.)]. "Esbat." ERN 1.4 (June 1974) 18. Print. (Arch. Circ. Sanc).
[39] Fitch, Ed. Message to the author. 21 April 2004. Email.
[40] ERN 1.5 (August 1974) 2. Print. (Arch. Circ. Sanc).
[41] Bartlett, Karen. Message to the author. 26 March 2007. Email.
[42] Dalton, Ken. Message to the author. 30 January 2012. Email
[43] Nascosto, Tom. Message to the author. 18 February 2008. Email.
[44] Buczynski, Edmund. Letter to Jim Kimble. October 1974? MS. (Arch. CES).

Notes for Chapter 20

[1] The American cottage industry of Armageddon speculators has long held that New York City represents the "Babylon" mentioned in the New Testament (Revelation 14:8); "Babylon is fallen, is fallen, that great city." Even the Satanists have gotten in on the act. When the Church of Satan relocated its headquarters to New York City's Hell's Kitchen in 2001, CoS Magister Peter Gilmore justified the move by saying "New York is the perfect city for a Satanist to live in ... It is secular, it is Babylon." Knipfel, Jim. "ALAS,

BABYLON: Is NYC still evil enough for the Church of Satan? Whither Hades-on-the-Hudson?" NY Press. Web (http://www.nypress.com/18/23/news&columns/knipfel.cfm, accessed 21 February 2008).

[2] The dunes were an "all man's land" so well known for its heavy cruising and anonymous sex that it was dubbed the "Meat Rack." While it was certainly a more expensive and less convenient destination than cruising the Rambles in Central Park, it was also considerably less dangerous and far more exotic.

[3] Stearn, Jess. *The Sixth Man.* New York: Macfadden-Bartell Corporation. 1962.

[4] Shapiro, Peter. *Turn the Beat Around: The Secret History of Disco.* London: Faber & Faber. 2005. 66.

[5] Dalton, Ken. Message to the author. 13 December 2011. Email.

[6] Welty, Eudora. "The Petrified Man" in *A Curtain of Green* and other stories. Harvest Books. 1979. 44.

Notes for Chapter 21

[1] Geraci, Bennie. Message to the author. 12 July 2009. Email.

[2] Buczynski, Edmund. Letter to Ron Myron. Early February 1975? MS. (Arch. CES).

[3] Moss, Harold. Letter. *Green Egg* 8.74 (October 1975) p. 37. Print. (Coll. A.Terr.).

[4] Geraci, Bennie. Message to the author. 28 September 2008. Email.

[5] Buczynski, Edmund. Letter to Ron Myron. Mid February 1975? MS. (Arch. CES).

[6] Moss, Harold. Letter to Edmund Buczynski. 18 March 1975. MS. (Arch. CES).

[7] Adler. *Drawing Down the Moon.* 1986. 267, 271-273.

[8] Moss, Harold. Message to the author. 18 August 2008. Email.

[9] Buczynski, Eddie. Letter to Harold Moss. 25 April 1975. MS. (Arch. CES).

[10] Moss, Harold. Letter to Edmund Buczynski. 30 April 1975. MS. (Arch. CES).

[11] Martha Adler was on record as having an antipathy towards homosexuals practicing Witchcraft. While there is no evidence that she allowed this predisposition to interfere with her signing off on Eddie's certificate, the fact remains that the certificate was never completed. Martello. *Black Magick, Satanism & Voodoo.* 1973. 109.

[12] Myron, Ron. Letter to Eddie Buczynski. 5 June 1975. MS. (Arch. CES).

[13] Buczynski, Eddie. Letter to Ron Myron. 23 June 1975. MS. (Arch. CES).

[14] Buczynski, Eddie. Letter to Harold Moss. 1 August 1975. MS. (Arch. CES).

[15] (Ibid n#4). Bennie notes that the first time that Eddie set foot in New Orleans was during a visit to meet Geraci's family in early 1976.

[16] [Buczynski, Edmund (ed.)]. "Esbat." ERN 1.6-8 (October 1976?) 69-79. Print. (Arch. Circ. Sanc).

[17] Myron, Ron. Letter. *Green Egg* 9.77 (March 1976) 34. Print. (Coll. A.Terr.).

[18] Moss, Harold. Letter. *Green Egg* 9.80 (December 1976) 56. Print. (Coll. A.Terr.).

Notes for Chapter 22

[1] Frank, Kathryn. Message to the author. 25 September 2009. Email.

[2] Dalton, Ken. Message to the author. 30 January 2012. Email

[3] Carey, Robert. Message to the author. 24 April 2007. Email.

[4] Soror Charis. "Herman Slater: 'Thee Magickal Childe'" (Part I). *Behutet* 10 (Summer 2001) 3. Print.
[5] Cheiron. Message to the author. 23 August 2004. Email.
[6] Rivera, Ria. Telephone interview. 5 February 2004.
[7] Slater, Herman. *An Introduction to Witchcraft & Satanism*. New York: Magickal Childe Publishing, Inc. 1987. Videocassette.
[8] Soror Charis. "Herman Slater: 'Thee Magickal Childe'" (Part I). *Behutet* 10 (Summer 2001) 7. Print.
[9] Soror Charis. "Herman Slater: 'Thee Magickal Childe'" (Part II). *Behutet* 11 (Autumn 2001) 12. Print.
[10] Cordova, Jeanne. "Police arrest feminist witch, vow to close Feminist Wicca." *Green Egg* 8.70 (May 1975) 7-8 [reprinted from: Los Angeles Free Press (28 February 1975)]. Print. (Coll. A.Terr.).
[11] Alison of Nemeton. "The Trial of Zee Budapest." *Gnostica News* 4.8 (June 1975) 40. Print. (Wesc. Lib. Llew.).
[12] For a partial listing of state laws on the books at the time, see: Bonewits, Isaac. "Witchburning Now & Then." *Gnostica News* 3.6 (21 January 1974) 6, 8. Print. (Wesc. Lib. Llew.).
[13] St. Clair, David. "Los Angeles Witch-Hunt 1975." Fate 28.9 (September 1975) 78. Print. (Wesc. Lib. Llew.).
[14] Walker, Lee. "Heresy Trial of Z Budapest." *Green Egg* 8.72 (August 1975) 5-8. Print. (Coll. A.Terr.).
[15] Slater, Herman. Letter. *Green Egg* 8.72 (August 1975) 43. Print. (Coll. A.Terr.).
[16] Slater, Herman. Letter. *Green Egg* 8.74 (October 1975) 44. Print. (Coll. A.Terr.).
[17] "Ed Buczynski. His Warlock Shop is a Satanist Supermarket." *National Star* (2 March 1974) Np. From the Collection of Renate Springer.
[18] Holzer. *The Directory of the OCCULT*. 1974. 181. Little did Holzer suspect that the finances of the Warlock Shop were, at this point, a literal house of cards, albeit tarot cards.
[19] Slater, Herman. Letter. *Green Egg* 8.73 (September 1975) 37. Print. (Coll. A.Terr.).
[20] Bulzone, Carol. Telephone interview. 2 November 2004.
[21] Lauritsen, John. "Dangerous Trends in Feminism: Disruptions, Censorship, Bigotry." Paper delivered to the Gay Academic Union Conference IV in New York City. 27 November 1976. It should be noted that this same accusation was often made during this era and later, and with no small justification, by lesbians concerning their treatment at the hands of gay men. And some feminists were also just as quick to put down lesbians. See (http://en.wikipedia.org/wiki/Lavender_Menace).
[22] This saying would become not only a popular feminist bumper sticker but also the title of Ulrich's book on women's history. Ulrich, Laurel. *Well-Behaved Women Seldom Make History*. New York: Alfred Knopf. 2007.
[23] Budapest, Z. Letter. *Green Egg* 8.73 (September 1975) 37-38. Print. (Coll. A.Terr.).
[24] Zell, Tim. Editorial. *Green Egg* 8.73 (September 1975) 38. Print. (Coll. A.Terr.).
[25] Frost, Gavin. Letter. *Green Egg* 8.73 (September 1975) 45. Print. (Coll. A.Terr.).

[26] Bonewits, Isaac. Letter. *Green Egg* 8.74 (October 1975) 41-42. Print. (Coll. A.Terr.).
[27] Slater *Pagan Rituals III*. 1989. 14.
[28] Rivera, Ria. Telephone Interview. 30 January 2004.
[29] Rivera, Ria. Message to the author. 24 January 2004. Email.
[30] Unattributed [Saperton, Sheila]. "NAJ" MS. Huntington Station: Unpublished MS. 1976. pp. 4, 11. MS.
[31] Bargren, Curt. Message to the author. 17 December 2010. Email.
[32] Buckland, Raymond. "Seax-Wica: Official Information Sheet No. 1." *Green Egg* 7.62 (May 1974) 11. Print. (Coll. A.Terr.).
[33] Khrysis [Saperton, Sheila]. "Seax Wicca: First Initiate." ERN 1.4 (June 1974) 49. Print. (Arch. Circ. Sanc).
[34] Buckland, Raymond. "Seax Wicca." ERN 1.5 (August 1974) 44. Print. (Arch. Circ. Sanc).
[35] Saperton, Sheila. "Seax-Wica, Long Island Coven." Letter. Undated [August 1974]. Print. (Coll. K. Dal.).
[36] Buckland, Raymond. *THE TREE: The Complete Book of (Saxon) Witchcraft*. Unpublished MS. Undated [1974]. MS. (Coll. K. Dal.).
[37] Bargren, Curt. Message to the author. 19 March 2005. Email.
[38] Phoenix [Kneitel, Tommy]. "Gardnerian Aspects." *Green Egg* 7.63 (June 1974) 18. Print. (Coll. A.Terr.).
[39] Bargren, Curt. Message to the author. 18 March 2005. Email.
[40] Dalton, Ken. Message to the author. 13 December 2011. Email.
[41] Bargren, Curt. Message to the author. 18 December 2010. Email.
[42] Saperton, Sheila. Message to the author. 30 March 2005. Email.
[43] Jana. Witchcraft Vouch [British Traditional Witchcraft] to Gwydion [Edmund Buczynski]. Hampshire, England. 22 August 1975. MS. (Coll. R. Riv.).
[44] Jana. Letter to Gwydion [Buczynski, Eddie]. 4 August 1975. MS. (Coll. K. Dal.).
[45] Jana. Letter to Gwydion [Buczynski, Eddie]. 22 August 1975. MS. (Coll. K. Dal.).
[46] As with the prior claims of the Traditionalist Gwyddoniaid, the twelfth-century British Isles are again presented as the crèche from which arise the Book of Shadows of a system headed by Buczynski. Unattributed [Saperton, Sheila]. "NAJ" MS. Huntington Station: Unpublished MS. 1976. 10. MS.
[47] Gwydion [Buczynski, Edmund]. Letter to the Huntington Coven. June 1976. MS.
[48] Book of Shadows [Huntington Coven of the Hampshire Tradition]. Huntington Station/Rego Park: Unpublished MS. Undated [1975]. MS. (Coll. K. Dal.).
[49] Gwydion [Buczynski, Eddie]. Gardnerian Wica vouch of Godwyn. Rego Park, New York. 26 December 1975.
[50] Godwyn. Gardnerian Wica vouch of Cerdic [Dalton, Ken]. Rego Park, New York. 27 December 1975.
[51] Jana. Announcement. Hampshire, England. December 1975.
[52] Bargren, Curt. Message to the author. 19 March 2005. Email.
[53] Geraci, Bennie. Message to the author. 3 December 2009. Email.
[54] Buckland, Raymond. Message to the author. 15 October 2004. Email.
[55] Howard, Michael. Message to the author. 2 February 2004. Email.
[56] Heselton, Philip. Message to the author. 21 August 2009. Email.

[57] Buckland. *Witchcraft from the Inside*. 1971. 87-88.
[58] Dearnaley, Roger. "An Annotated Chronology and Bibliography of the Early Gardnerian Craft" (a work in progress). 2000. Web (http://www.thewica.co.uk/an_annotated_chronology_and_bibl.htm#RebirthOfWitchcraft, accessed 1 June 2010).
[59] It should be noted for clarity's sake that Heselton has also documented the existence of a "Southern Coven" operating in the Highcliffe area, but he does not believe this to be tied to the purported group in question. Source: Heselton, Philip. *Gerald Gardner and the Cauldron of Inspiration: An Investigation into the Sources of Gardnerian Witchcraft*. Milverton: Capall Bann Publishing. 2003. 261-266.
[60] Unattributed [Buczynski, Eddie]. *Witchcraft — For the First Degree* (The Huntington Coven of the Hampshire Tradition). Rego Park/Huntington Station: Unpublished MS. Undated (1975). MS. (Coll. K. Dal.).
[61] Kale, Will. Message to the author. 20 July 2009. Email.
[62] Buckland, Raymond. *The Weiser Field Guide to Ghosts*. San Francisco: Red Wheel/Weiser. 2009.117-118.
[63] Eddie's copy of the Bales and Apies book which was used along with the Huntington Coven Book of Shadows contains a map of the counties of England. Pasted on the inside front cover of the book, this map has the counties of Southern England picked out in black ink, with the county of Hampshire outlined in red ink. An arrow on the following page points to this map, with the accompanying words: "The Witches of Hampshire were influenced by the Belgae, Regnenses, Atrebates, Durotriges, and Cantiaci." See: Unattributed [Buczynski, Edmund]. Bales and Apies (The Huntington Coven). Rego Park/Huntington Station: Unpublished MS. Undated (1975). MS.; and (Ibid n#48).
[64] Warlock Shop. Advertisement. ERN 1.3 (March 1974) 25. Print. (Arch. Circ. Sanc).
[65] Wright, A.R. *English Folklore*. London: Benn. 1928.
[66] Gwydion [Edmund Buczynski]. Wica vouch of Lady Rhea [Ria Farnham]. 9 August 1976. MS.
[67] Geraci, Bennie and Joseph Cupolo. Personal interview. 14 November 2004.
[68] Gwion. "Being a Witch Is." ERN 1.2 (February 1974) 12.
[69] Geraci, Bennie. Message to the author. 12 July 2009. Email.
[70] Rivera, Ria. Message to the author. 18 January 2004. Email.
[71] Mills, Malcolm. Message to the author. 4 August 2007. Email.

Notes for Chapter 23
[1] Levenda, Peter. Message to the author. 29 August 2005. Email.
[2] Dalton, Ken. Message to the author. 30 January 2012. Email.
[3] The last ad for the Brooklyn Heights location was placed November 3, 1975. Warlock Shop Advertisement. Village Voice 20.44 (3 November 1975) 18. MCF. (Cols. Met. Lib).
[4] While the finances of New York City were undergoing a melt-down after President Ford told the city to "drop dead" in May, rents on the island were, somewhat incongruously, continuing to rise. The rent for merchant spaces in the West Village has only gotten worse with time. In 2004, the Manhattan rent for a space comparable to that of the Warlock Shop (~450 sq. ft.) was

[5] *Gay Sex in the 70s.* Dir. Joseph F. Lovett. Wolfe Video. 2005.

[6] Cabal, Alan. "The Doom that Came to Chelsea." *New York Press*, NEWS & COLUMNS. 16.23 (4-10 June 2003) Np. Web.

[7] Few places are what could reasonably be thought of as "safe" in a metropolis such as New York City. The author visited the former location of the Magickal Childe in 2005 with Ria and her partner, Sandra, and had to avoid a pool of blood on the sidewalk just down the block where it looked as if someone had been knifed not long before.

[8] Shernoff, Michael. "Early Gay Activism in Chelsea: Building a Queer Neighborhood." LGNY 57 (6 July 1997) Np. Web (http://www.gaypsychotherapy.com/history.htm).

[9] Rhine, Arthur. "Loft to Luxury." Letter. *NYT* (21 March 1993).

[10] Mills, Malcolm. Message to the author. 8 August 2007. Email.

[11] The wooden façade of the 300 Henry Street building was replaced with brick in 1976. The building eventually went condo and was sold in 2001 for $399,000, a price that would probably have astounded Slater and Buczynski. Source: "Residential Sales." NYT (4 November 2001) Np. Web.

[12] Geraci, Bennie. Message to the author. 27 January 2007. Email.

[13] Cheiron. Message to the author. 23 August 2004. Email.

[14] Geraci, Bennie. Message to the author 20 May 2010. Email.

[15] Bartlett, Karen. Message to the author 26 March 2007. Email.

[16] Rivera, Ria. Personal interview. 30 October 2004.

[17] "Inside Occult New York." NYT (31 October 1976) Np. Web.

[18] Frank, Kathryn. Message to the author. 6 January 2010. Email.

[19] Amber K. Letter. Magickal Childe Spring 87 Supplement. Spring 1987. 1.

[20] Slater, Herman. Letter. Magickal Childe Spring 87 Supplement. Spring 1987.1.

[21] Harismides, M. Letter. Magickal Childe Fall 87 Supplement. Fall 1987. 1.

[22] Rivera, Ria. Telephone interview. 26 May 2011. Rivera states, "I remember when Alan Cabal worked at the shop, and he used to tell me that we'd go through a case — that's 144 books — of the Satanic Bible in a week." How many of those books were shoplifted by adolescents who were too afraid to be seen purchasing a copy is a figure lost to the dustbins of time.

[23] Greenburg, Dan. *Something's There*. Garden City: Doubleday & Company. 1976. 84.

[24] Warlock Shop Advertisement. Village Voice 21.7 (16 February 1976) 44. MCF. (Cols. Met. Lib).

[25] Warlock Shop Advertisement. *Green Egg* 9.77 (March 1976) 48. Print. (Coll. A.Terr.).

[26] Greenberg, Dan. *Something's There: My Adventures in the Occult.* New York: DoubleDay. 1976. 84. Slater complained to Penthouse writer Dan Greenberg about the increasing difficulties associated with importing quality human bones because of concerns that they were being looted from foreign gravesites.

[27] Cabal, Alan. "The Doom that Came to Chelsea." NEWS & COLUMNS section. New York Press 16.23 (3 June 2003) Np. Web.

[28] Smith, Dinitia. "Finding Personal Spaces in Public Places." NYT (17May 1996) Np. Web.

[29] Silverknife, Zanoni. Message to the author. 13 July 2004. Email.
[30] Soror Charis. "Herman Slater: 'Thee Magickal Childe'" (Part I). *Behutet* 10 (Summer 2001) 6. Print.
[31] The H.P. Lovecraft horror story "Cool Air" was set in the building located at 317 West 14th Street, which was the one-time residence of H.P. Lovecraft's friend George Kirk.
[32] Yeager, Marty and Kenneth Hickenbottom. *The Yeager Tarot of Meditation*. Laguna: Credo Company. 1975. When the rights to the Yeager Tarot were sold to United States Games Systems, Inc., the management ordered much of the full frontal nudity to be covered up by crudely painting short pants on the male figures before the deck was republished in 1983.
[33] Davy, Marianne. Message to the author. 20 May 2010. Email.
[34] Eaton, Sally. Message to the author. 21 January 2008. Email.
[35] "Inside Occult New York." NYT (31 October 1976) Np. Web.
[36] Warlock Shop Advertisement. Village Voice 21.9 (1 March 1976). p. 2. MCF. (Cols. Met. Lib).
[37] Simon. *Dead Names*. 2006. 305.
[38] "NRP Leader Gives Lecture on 'The Occult & Fascism' at New York's Warlock Shop." The National Renaissance Bulletin (June-July-August 1977). Reports that Madole met with Anton LaVey at the Warlock Shop are also highly suspect, as LaVey never visited either location of the store.
[39] Levenda, Peter. Message to the author. 26 May 2011. Email. Despite his commitment to diversity, it is unlikely that the Jewish shopkeeper would have invited the anti-Semitic NRP leader to speak at his establishment (or buddied around with him as has been implied by various persons on the web). Madole's organization was involved in a number of anti-Semitic protests in New York City in the 1970s. Levenda writes, "Herman Slater was a devout anti-Nazi. ... Slater thought Madole was evil and ridiculous. While Slater would have had the chutzpah to offer a workshop to Madole, just to see what would happen, to my knowledge he never did."
[40] Goodrich-Clarke, Nicholas. *Black Sun: Aryan Cults, Esoteric Nazism, and the Politics of Identity*. New York: NYU Press. 2003. 83.
[41] Rivera, Ria. Telephone interview. 26 May 2011. Ria likewise confirms that, while Slater and LaVey were correspondents, the latter never visited either location of the store. Ria recalled that, "When I asked him about the thick file of correspondence he had [with LaVey], Herman said 'He's not a Satanist! He's a psychologist!'"
[42] Warlock Shop Advertisement. Village Voice 21.29 (19 July 1976) 2. MCF. (Cols. Met. Lib).
[43] Geraci, Bennie and Joseph Cupolo. Personal interview. 14 November 2004.
[44] Warlock Shop Advertisement. Village Voice 21.30 (19 July 1976) 37. MCF. (Cols. Met. Lib).
[45] Eaton, Sally. Message to the author. 23 January 2008. Email.
[46] Rivera, Ria. Telephone interview. 5 February 2004.
[47] Lady Rhea [Ria Rivera]. "The Crystal Ball" in Wildman, Laura (ed.). *Celebrating the Pagan Soul*. New York: Citadel Press. 2005. 98-99.
[48] Soror Charis. "Herman Slater: 'Thee Magickal Childe'" (Part I). *Behutet* 10 (Summer 2001) 7. Print.
[49] Lady Rhea. *The Enchanted Candle*. New York: Citadel Press. 2004.
[50] Mills, Malcolm. Message to the author. 3 August 2007. Email.

51 Magickal Childe (Warlock Shop) Advertisement. Village Voice 21.31 (2 August 1976) 2. MCF. (Cols. Met. Lib).
52 Magickal Childe (Warlock Shop) Advertisement. Village Voice 21.32 (9 August 1976) 2, 29. MCF. (Cols. Met. Lib).
53 *The Oracle.* Dir. Robert Bierman. Shriek Show. 1985.
54 For a twisted interpretation of this declaration, see: Neuhaus, Richard. "Magickal city." National Review (27 April 1992) Np. Web.
55 North, Erika [Judith McNally]. Message to the author. 30 November 2005. Email.
56 Mills, Malcolm. Message to the author. 5 Aug 2007. Email.
57 Mills, Malcolm. Message to the author. 4 August 2007. Email.
58 Warlock Shop. Advertisement. *Green Egg* 9.77 (March 1976) 48. Print. (Coll. A.Terr.).
59 Austan, Laura. Message to the author. 9 December 2010. Email.
60 Kirwan, Larry. Message to the author. 28 February 2007. Email.
61 Austan, Laura. Message to the author. 29 November 2010. Email.
62 Bargren, Curt. Message to the author. 2 December 2010. Email.
63 Slater, Herman (ed.). *Magickal Formulary Spellbook — Book II.* New York: Magickal Childe (www.magickalchilde.com). 2004. 1.
64 Malachy McCourt, brother of Pulitzer Prize winner Frank McCourt (author of "Angela's Ashes"), was an infamous talk radio personality on New York's WMCA. Amongst his more notable targets were the Catholic Church (especially Joseph Cardinal Spellman), the Vietnam War, and Richard Nixon. In a commentary on the Saturday Night Massacre in 1973 where Nixon fired special prosecutor Archibald Cox and several other administration officials, McCourt drew howls of protest for calling the President a "Cox Sacker" on the air.
65 Kirwan, Larry. *Green Suede Shoes: An Irish-American Odyssey.* New York: Thunder's Mouth Press. 2005.
66 Siri, Giani. Message to the author. 9 April 2007. Email.
67 The "Cairo working" is the event where the entity whom Aleister Crowley referred to as "Aiwass" dictated through him to Rose Kelly the material that became Liber AL vel Legis, or "The Book of the Law" — the foundation of Thelemic practice. This occurred on three consecutive days beginning on April 8, 1904.
68 Simon. *Dead Names.* 2006. 134, 156-157.
69 Siri, Giani. *The New York Tarot.* Smyrna: Sirius Endeavors. 1987.
70 Klemesrud, Judy. "6 Witches and Channel 13 Auction Fan Turn Out for a 'Full-Moon Ceremony'." NYT (2 September 1976) Np. Web.
71 Magickal Childe Advertisement. *Village Voice* 21.44 (1 November 1976) 2. MCF. (Cols. Met. Lib). Note: the ad appeared the day after the event occurred.
72 "Wiccan Covens: TWPT Talks to Judy Harrow." Wiccan/Pagan Times. 2001. Web (http://www.twpt.com/harrow.htm, accessed 12 January 2008).
73 Soror Charis. "Herman Slater: 'Thee Magickal Childe'" (Part II). *Behutet* 11 (Autumn 2001) 13. Print.
74 The Witches Ball migrated from place to place as venues closed and rental fees fluctuated. In 1987, it was held at The Limelight, a deconsecrated Episcopal Church cum disco located at 656 Avenue of the Americas. The

Limelight's claim to fame was as the setting for the true-life story behind the film *Party Monster* (2003).
[75] Macer-Story, Eugenia. Message to the author. 13 January 2009. Email.
[76] Caigan, Khem. Telephone interview. 3 April 2006.
[77] *Fangoria Magazine Scream Greats, Volume 2: Satanism and Witchcraft.* Dir. Damon Santostefano. Paramount Home Video. 1987. Herman Slater and Ria Farnham both appeared in this film, though this would not be Herman's only film credit. Apart from appearing in a video produced by the Magickal Childe, he is said to have designed the large cauldron in which a cannibal witch cooks actress Dana Michele in the film The Nutzoids at Cannibal Cove (1989).
[78] Conte, Peter. Message to the author. 31 May 2011. Email.
[79] Simon. *Dead Names.* 2006. 124.
[80] Levenda, Peter. *Sinister Forces: A Grimoire of American Political Witchcraft (Book Two).* Oregon: TrineDay. 2007. 253.
[81] Eaton, Sally. Message to the author. 12 April 2006. Email.
[82] One popular, yet highly unlikely and completely unsubstantiated rumor had the Disney megaconglomerate offering to buy the contents of the Magickal Childe lock, stock and cauldron for a proposed Witchcraft installation at Walt Disney World.
[83] Allen, Woody. *Without Feathers.* New York: Ballantine Books. 1986. 11.

Notes for Chapter 24
[1] Austan, Laura. "Herman Slater." Austanspace. 23 February 2009. Web (http://austanspace.blogspot.com/2009/02/herman-slater.html, accessed 2 November 2010).
[2] Bennie, Geraci. Message to the author. 20 May 2010. Email.
[3] Cabal, Alan. "The Doom that Came to Chelsea." NEWS & COLUMNS section. New York Press 16.23 (3 June 2003) Np. Web.
[4] Klein, Kenny. Message to the author. 10 April 2006. Email. Klein was once married to Tzipora Katz, who did a lot of business with the Magickal Childe selling incense and other goods through her business, Tzipora and the Wizard. The two began a musical career, and eventually sold tapes of their music to the Childe as well.
[5] Cuhulain, Kerr. "Eric Pryor: Part 1." The Witches' Voice. 29 July 2002. Web (http://www.witchvox.com/va/dt_va.html?a=cabc&c=whs&id=4357, accessed 31 May 2010).
[6] Cuhulain, Kerr. "Eric Pryor: Part 2." The Witches' Voice. 29 July 2002. Web (http://www.witchvox.com/va/dt_va.html?a=cabc&c=whs&id=4358, accessed 31 May 2010).
[7] Unattributed. New York Welsh Tradition Lineage. Undated [1993?].
[8] (Ibid n#4). Klein was once married to Tzipora Katz, who did a lot of business with the Magickal Childe selling incense and other goods through her business, Tzipora and the Wizard at East 33rd Street and 3rd Avenue in the East Village. The two began a musical career, and eventually sold tapes of their music to the Childe as well.
[9] O'Brien, Dave. "Reborn Again?" San Jose Mercury News (14 December 1991) Np. Web.
[10] Marsh, Eric. "Eric Pryor, the 'Witch that Switched'." Eric's World (13 December 2009). Web

(http://www.ericmarsh.info/Erics_World/My_Blog/Entries/2009/12/13_Eric_Pryor,_The_Witch_That_Switched.html, accessed 31 May 2010).

11. Kerr Cuhulain, who has written extensively about Pryor and his claims, examined a number of Magickal Childe catalogues and found this to be untrue. Source: Cuhulain, Kerr. "Eric Pryor: Part 3." The Witches' Voice (29 July 2002). Web (http://www.witchvox.com/va/dt_va.html?a=cabc&c=whs&id=4359, accessed 31 May 2010).

12. Gaines, Adrienne. "Wiccan-Turned-Bible Teacher Eric Pryor Dies." Charisma (16 June 2009). Web (http://www.charismamag.com/index.php/news/22317-wiccan-turned-bible-teacher-eric-pryor-dies, accessed 6 June 2010).

13. *Gay Sex in the 70s*. Dir. Joseph Lovett. Lovett Productions. 2005.

14. This included the State of New York, which did not rescind its sodomy law until 2000, even though it had been held unenforceable by the courts since 1998.

15. Crowley, Aleister. *The Book of the Law: sub figura Liber AL vel Legis*. New York: Samuel Weiser, Inc. 1987. Chapter One, Stanza 51.

16. Crowley, Aleister; Louis Wilkinson and Hymenaeus Beta (eds.). *The Law is for All: The Authorized Popular Commentary to The Book of the Law*. Tempe: New Falcon Publications. 1998. 52, 68.

17. Crowley, Aleister. *White Stains*. London: Duckworth. 1993. x. This also proves that the philosophy of *Friedrich Nietzsche* can be used just as easily to lobby against Pagan influences as it can to favor them.

18. Corliss, Richard. "That Old Feeling: Cooke's Tour." Time (30 March 2004). Web.

19. Fritscher, Jack. *Mapplethorpe: Assault with a Deadly Camera*. Mamaroneck: Hastings House. 1994. 121.

20. Schurmacher, Emile. *Witchcraft in America Today*. New York: Paperback Library. 1970. 53.

21. Peck. *Uncovering the Sixties*. 1991. 219.

22. Highleyman, Liz. "PAST Out: Who was Carl Wittman?" *LETTERS From CAMP Rehoboth* 16.4. Web (http://www.camprehoboth.com/issue05_05_06/past_out.htm, accessed 5 May 2006).

23. Power. *No Bath but Plenty of Bubbles*. 17.

24. Kisseloff, Jeff. "Jim Fouratt." Generation on Fire — Voices of Protest from the 1960's: An Oral History. Web (http://www.generationonfire.com/fouratt.html, accessed 28 May 2010).

25. "What's Happening?" *Come Out!* 2.76 (late January 1971?) 3. Web.

26. *The Groove Tube*. Dir. Ken Shapiro. Levitt-Pickman. 1974. Refer to "The Dealers" scene with Ken Shapiro and Richard Belzer.

27. "Get the Mafia and the Cops Out of Gay Bars" (flyer). Homophile Youth Movement (HYMN). (July 1969?). Marotta, Toby. Revisiting Stonewall. Web (www.tobymarotta.com/flyer/index.htm, accessed 6 July 2009).

28. Evans. *Witchcraft and the Gay Counterculture*. 1978. 138, 140.

29. Ireland, Doug. "Rendezvous in the ramble." New York Magazine (July 24, 1978). Np. Web (http://nymag.com/print/?/features/47179/, accessed 20 September 2011).

30. Mahler, Jonathon. *Ladies and Gentlemen, the Bronx is Burning*. New York: Picador. 2005. 128.

[31] Bell, Arthur. "The Bath Life Gets Respectability." *Village Voice* 21.39 (27 September 1976) 19-20. MCF. (Cols. Met. Lib).
[32] Goldstein, Richard. "S&M: The Dark Side of Gay Liberation." *Village Voice* 20.27 (7 July 1975) 10-13. MCF. (Cols. Met. Lib).
[33] Mahler. *Ladies and Gentlemen, the Bronx is Burning.* 2005. 126-128.
[34] Schwartzberg, Stephen. *The Crisis of Meaning: How Gay Men Are Making Sense of AIDS* Oxford: Oxford University Press. 1996.
[35] Moore, Patrick. *Beyond Shame: Reclaiming the Abandoned History of Radical Gay Sexuality.* Boston: Beacon Press. 2004.
[36] Geraci, Bennie. Message to the author. 12 June 2010. Email.
[37] Evans. *Witchcraft and the Gay Counterculture.* 124-125.
[38] Mahler. *Ladies and Gentlemen, the Bronx is Burning.* 2005. 127.
[39] Goldstein. "S&M: The Dark Side of Gay Liberation." *Village Voice* 20.27 (7 July 1975) p. 11.
[40] Ireland. "Rendezvous in the ramble." *New York Magazine* (July 24, 1978). NP.
[41] Geraci, Bennie and Joseph Cupolo. Personal interview. 14 November 2004.
[42] Del Valle, Peter and Steven Sterner. *Lovers: The Musical That Proves It's No Longer Sad To Be Gay.* New York: TOSOS Theatre Company. 1974.
[43] Wilson, Doric. Message to the author. 5 June 2010. Email.
[44] Geraci, Bennie. Message to the author. 5 June 2004. Email.
[45] Geraci, Bennie. Message to the author. 21 March 2007. Email.
[46] Loovis, David. *Gay Spirit: A Guide to Becoming a Sensuous Homosexual.* New York: Strawberry Hill Publishing. 1974. 25.
[47] Sismondo. *America Walks into a Bar.* 2011. 257.
[48] Welch, Paul. "Homosexuality in America." Life (June 26, 1964).
[49] Clarke and Nichols. *Roommates Can't Always Be Lovers.* 1974. 79.
[50] Thompson, Mark. *Leatherfolk: Radical Sex, People, Politics and Practice.* New York: Alyson Books. 2001. xxi. As quoted in Moore, Patrick. *Beyond Shame: Reclaiming the History of Radical Gay Sexuality.* Boston: Beacon Press. 2004. 27.
[51] Sitch, Ed and Herman Slater. "California Pagans Meet." ERN 1.4 (June 1974) 2. Print. (Arch. Circ. Sanc).
[52] Wilson, Robert Anton. *Coincidance: A Head Test.* Las Vegas: New Falcon Publications. 1991. 200.
[53] A photograph of the golden calf can be found in the Summer 2008 issue of RFD magazine.
[54] *Before Stonewall: The Making of a Gay and Lesbian Community.* Dir. Greta Schiller. First Run Features. 1985. DVD.
[55] Heflin. *The Island Dialogues* (Liber ALAL). 1973. 50.
[56] Unattributed. "Gay Magick? Dat Ol' Gay Magick Got You in its Spell?" ERN 1.5 (August 1974) 16. Print. (Arch. Circ. Sanc).
[57] Heflin. *The Island Dialogues* (Liber ALAL). 1973. Back matter.
[58] This evolution continued into the new millennium, propagating through music, art, literature and film. For an example of older myths being made new, refer to the song "The Origin of Love" from John Cameron Mitchell's film *Hedwig and the Angry Inch* (2001), which retells Plato's story of the origin of the sexes from The Symposium.

[59] Zoll, Rachel. "Study: Homosexuality, celibacy didn't cause abuse." 18 May 2011. Web (http://www.msnbc.msn.com/id/43076289/ns/politics/t/study-homosexuality-celibacy-didnt-cause-abuse/, accessed 25 May 2011).
[60] Robertson John. *Pagan Christs*. University Books. 1967 reprint.
[61] Mecca, Tommi Avicolli (ed.). *Smash the Church, Smash the State: The Early Years of Gay Liberation*. San Francisco: City Lights Books. 242-245.
[62] Evans. *Witchcraft and the Gay Counterculture*. 1978. 155.
[63] Evans, Arthur. "San Francisco Art Commission Helps Publish Gay-Positive Philosophy Book." WEBCASTRO. Web (http://www.webcastro.com/evans1.htm, accessed 11 June 2010.) In late 1975, Evans formed the San Francisco Faery Circle, which combined neo-pagan consciousness, gay sensibility, and ritual play. He presented a series of public lectures in 1976 entitled "Faeries," based on his earlier research. These efforts fed into the creation of the Radical Faeries in 1977.
[64] Dalton, Ken. Message to the author. 30 January 2012. Email
[65] Saperton, Sheila. Message to the author. 30 March 2005. Email.
[66] Gwydion [Buczynski, Edmund]. Letter to the Huntington Coven. June 1976. MS.
[67] Cupolo, Joseph. Message to the author. 14 January 2004. Email.
[68] Buczynski, Eddie. Letter to Joseph Cupolo. 1 December 1977. MS.
[69] Dalton, Ken. Message to the author. 13 December 2011. Email.

Notes for Chapter 25
[1] North, Erika [Judith McNally]. Message to the author. 30 November 2005. Email.
[2] Buczynski, Edmund Michael. "Witchcraft Today and the Homosexual." *Gaysweek* (13 June 1977) 11. (Coll. BMG).
[3] Thompson, Thomas. "Crete: A Stop in the New Odyssey." Life 65.3 (19 July 1968) 20-29. Print.
[4] Pearson, Karl. "Woman as Witch." Gnostica News 4.6 (February 1975) 1, 36, 37, 38, 39. Print. (Wesc. Lib. Llew.). Karl Pearson is considered to be the author most responsible for the theory of the "Universal Matriarchal Age." He was also a proponent of human eugenics, and an advocate of committing open warfare on so-called "inferior races."
[5] Neumann, Erich. *The Great Mother: An Analysis of the Archetype*. New York: Pantheon Books. 1955.
[6] von Cles-Reden, Sibylle. *The Realm of the Great Goddess*. Schauberg: Verlag M. Dumont. 1960.
[7] Diner, Helen (Bertha Eckstein-Diener). *Mothers and Amazons*. New York: Julian Press. 1965.
[8] Gimbutas, Marija. *The Gods and Goddesses of Old Europe 7000 to 3500 BC: Myths, Legends and Cult Images*. London: Thames and Hudson. 1974.
[9] Fuller, Curtis. "Ancient Crete — Land of the Sea Kings." Fate 10.7 (July 1957) 18-26. Print. (Wesc. Lib. Llew.).
[10] Bourne. *Dancing with Witches*. 45.
[11] Keith, W. Holman. *Divinity as the Eternal Feminine*. New York: Pageant Press. 1960.
[12] Gere, Cathy. *Knossos and the Prophets of Modernism*. Chicago: University of Chicago Press. 2009. 209.
[13] Gere, Cathreina. Message to the author. 16 October 2009. Email.

[14] Daly, Mary. *Beyond God the Father: Toward a Philosophy of Women's Liberation.* Boston: Beacon Press. 1973.
[15] Budapest, Zsuzsanna. *The Feminist Book of Lights and Shadows.* Los Angeles: Feminist Wicca. 1975.
[16] Stone, Merlin. *When God Was a Woman.* New York: Dorset Press. 1976.
[17] Budapest, Zsuzsanna. Message to the author. 25 September 2006. Email.
[18] "Minoan Paintings in Avaris, Egypt." The Thera Foundation. 2006. Web (http://www.therafoundation.org/articles/art/minoanpaintingsinavarisegypt, 4 accessed July 2010).
[19] Leadbeater, Charles. W. *Glimpses of Masonic History.* New York: Gramercy. 1998. 54.
[20] Butyrin. Svetlana. Letter. *Green Egg* 6.59 (December 1973) 36. Print. (Coll. A.Terr.).
[21] A photograph of a Feraferian priestess holding a labrys — a ritual double-bladed axe associated with Minoan Crete — and a statue of the Minoan Snake Goddess appears in Holzer, Hans. *Witches: True Encounters with Wicca, Wizards, Covens, Cults, and Magick.* New York: Black Dog & Levanthal Publishers. 2005. 12.
[22] Adams, Frederick. "The Mother God of Crete." ERN 1.1 (December 1973) 4, 14-15. Print. (Arch. Circ. Sanc).
[23] Adams, Frederick. "Crete." ERN 1.2 (February 1974) 26. Print. (Arch. Circ. Sanc).
[24] Adams, Frederick. "Feraferia." ERN 1.5 (August 1974) 49. Print. (Arch. Circ. Sanc).
[25] Adams, Frederick. "Feraferia for Beginners." ERN 1.5 (August 1974) 51. Print. (Arch. Circ. Sanc).
[26] Rivera, Ria. Telephone interview. 30 January 2004.
[27] Buczynski, Edmund Michael. "Witchcraft Today and the Homosexual." *GaysWeek* 17 (13 June 1977) 10. (Coll. BMG).
[28] Unattributed [Buczynski, Edmund]. "The Minoan Brotherhood" (Booklet and Questionnaire). Middle Village: Self-published. January 1977? MS.
[29] Buczynski, Edmund Michael. "Witchcraft Today and the Homosexual." GaysWeek 17 (13 June 1977) 11. (Coll. BMG).
[30] Unattributed [Buczynski, Edmund]. "The Children of Rhea (The Minoan Brotherhood)." Middle Village: Self-published. 1976. MS.
[31] Geraci, Bennie and Joseph Cupolo. Personal interview. 14 November 2004.
[32] Dalton, Ken. Message to the author. 30 January 2012. Email
[33] Unattributed [Buczynski, Edmund]. "Why Would a Gay Man Worship a Goddess?" Middle Village: Self-published. 1977. MS.
[34] Matthew Todd notes that this remains a problem in the gay community decades later, writing, "I believe that this is the final phase of gay liberation, a process that started 50 years ago on the streets of New York and London, but continues with its most important part — really, truly learning to love ourselves." Todd, Matthew. "How to Be Gay & Happy." Attitudes 196 (September 2010) 61. Print.
[35] [Buczynski]. "The Minoan Brotherhood" (Booklet and Questionnaire). 1977.
[36] Lauritsen, John and David Thorstad. *The Early Homosexual Rights Movement (1864-1935).* New York: Times Change Press. 1974. From 1985-1996, Lauritsen covered the AIDS crisis as a free-lance investigative journalist for the New York Native.

[37] Lauritsen, John. "Religious Roots of the Taboo on Homosexuality: A materialist view." New York: Self-published. 1974. MS. Lauritsen later expanded this pamphlet into a book-length "defense of male love from a secular humanist perspective." Lauritsen, John. *A Freethinker's Primer of Male Love.* East Haven: Inland Book Company. 1994.
[38] Walker, Mitch. *Men Loving Men.* San Francisco: The Gay Sunshine Press. 1977.
[39] Walker, Mitch. "The Double: An Archetypal Configuration." *An Annual of Archetypal Psychology and Jungian Thought* (Spring 1976).
[40] Walker. *Men Loving Men.* 1977. 146-147.
[41] Walker. *Men Loving Men.* 1977. 148.
[42] In 1979, Mitch Walker would put this to the test by helping to found the Radical Faeries with Harry Hay, John Burnside, and Don Kilhefner. Walker's theories of the spiritual essence of gayness would find its way into his 1980 book *Visionary Love.* Walker, Mitch. *Visionary Love: A Spirit Book of Gay Mythology.* San Francisco: TreeRoots Press. 1980.
[43] Silverstein, Charles and Felice Picano. *The Joy of Gay Sex: an Intimate Guide for Gay Men to the Pleasures of a Gay Lifestyle.* Avenel: Outlet. 1977.
[44] Shual. *Sexual Magick.* 1989. 36.
[45] Fraser, Hilary. "Victorian poetry and historicism" in *The Cambridge Companion to Victorian Poetry* (J. Bristow, ed.). Cambridge: Cambridge University Press. 2006. 122.
[46] Dover, Kenneth J. *Greek Homosexuality.* Cambridge: Harvard University Press. 1977.
[47] Two forefathers of this topic include: Mitch Walker (*Visionary Love: A Spirit Book of Gay Mythology and Transmutational Faerie*, 1980) and Arthur Evans (*Witchcraft and the Gay Counterculture*, 1981).
[48] Example: Carpenter, Edward. *Iolaus: An Anthology Of Friendship.* (1902).
[49] Example: Symonds, John Addington. *A Problem in Greek Ethics: Studies in Sexual Inversion.* (1883).
[50] Conner, Randy, et. al. *Cassell's Encyclopedia of Queer Myth, Symbol and Spirit.* London: Cassell & Co. 1998. 257.
[51] Unattributed [Buczynski, Edmund]. *Minoan Brotherhood Book of the Mysteries.* Middle Village: Unpublished MS. 1977. MS.
[52] Adler. *Drawing Down the Moon.* 1979. 270-275.
[53] Evangeline Walton, whose work had so inspired Eddie in his crafting of the Welsh tradition, had developed a trilogy of books centered on the Theseus myth in the late 1940s. Unfortunately, she kept her books off the market when Mary Renault published her own Theseus novels in 1958 and 1962. The first of Walton's Theseus trilogy — *The Sword is Forged* — was not published until 1982, some five years after the birth of the Minoan Brotherhood. But for Renault's successful publication of the Theseus story, Walton's work might also have played a part in Buczynski's development of the Minoan tradition.
[54] From 1964 to 1977, Swann also published a series of Cretan-inspired fantasy novels — *Cry Silver Bells* (1977), *The Forest of Forever* (1971), and *Day of the Minotaur* (1966) — collectively known as "The Minotaur Trilogy."
[55] Caigan, Khem. Telephone interview. 3 April 2006. Khem has a copy of this book that Eddie gifted him around this time. The book was published in

England under the title *Seven Days in New Crete* (London: Cassell & Co., 1949).
[56] Martello. *Black Magic, Satanism & Voodoo.* 1973. 138.
[57] Graves, Robert. *The Golden Fleece* and *Watch the North Wind Rise.* Manchester: Carcanet Press. 2004. 425.
[58] Marinatos, Nanno. *Minoan Religion: Ritual, Image, and Symbol.* Columbia: University of South Carolina Press. 1993.
[59] Warlock Shop Advertisement. ERN 1.1 (December 1973) 6. Print. (Arch. Circ. Sanc).
[60] Willetts, R.F. *Everyday Life in Ancient Crete.* New York: Putnam. 1969.
[61] Willetts wasn't the only such writer. Another was Classical Greek scholar Robert Flacelière, whose 1960 book *L'Amour en Grèce* devoted a chapter to the history of paederasty and homosexual love in Greece, including ancient Crete. Flacelière, Robert. *Love in Ancient Greece.* New York: Crown Publishers, Inc.. 1962. 62-100.
[62] Percy, William A. *Pederasty and Pedagogy in Archaic Greece.* Chicago: University of Illinois Press. 1996.
[63] Willetts, R. F. *Ancient Crete: A Social History from Early Times Until the Roman Occupation.* London: Routledge and Kegan Paul. 1965. 116.
[64] Koehl, Robert. Message to the author. 2 December 2006. Email. For an example, see Willetts, R. F. "The World of Homer." *Our History.* London: History Group of the Communist Party. 1964. Np. Web.
[65] Koehl, Robert. "The Chieftain Cup and a Minoan 'Rite of Passage'." *Journal of Hellenic Studies* 106 (1986) 99-110. Print.
[66] Koehl, Robert. "Ephoros and Ritualized Homosexuality in Bronze Age Crete. Queer Representations." *Reading Lives, Reading Cultures* (ed. M. Duberman) (New York, 1997) 7-13. Print.
[67] Percy. *Pederasty and Pedagogy in Archaic Greece.* 1996. 22-26.
[68] Gwilym Dafydd HHH. Message to the author. 23 July 2007. Email.
[69] (Ibid n#30). The Witch Cult he refers to is Gardnerian Wica.
[70] (Ibid n#35). There is some anectdotal support for this diffusion theory of Greek thought to the British Isles. See also: Cunliffe, Barry. The Extraordinary Voyage of Pytheas the Greek. New York: Penguin Books. 2002.
[71] Wyatt, Aubrey. Message to the author. 5 January 2004. Email.
[72] Wyatt, Aubrey. "Minoan History Part 2." Message to the author. 11 December 2003. Email.
[73] Geraci, Bennie and Joseph Cupolo. Personal interview. 14 November 2004.
[74] Caigan, Khem. Telephone interview. 3 April 2006.
[75] Simon. *Dead Names.* 2006. 299.
[76] Gere. *Knossos and the Prophets of Modernism.* 2009. 46.
[77] Tolkien, J.R.R. *The Lord of the Rings.* New York: Houghton Mifflin. 2004. 366.
[78] Gere. *Knossos and the Prophets of Modernism.* 2009. 81.
[79] Gere. *Knossos and the Prophets of Modernism.* 2009. 12, 49, 80.
[80] For further details, see: MacGillivray, J. Alexander. *Minotaur: Sir Arthur Evans and the Archaeology of the Minoan Myth.* London: Jonathon Cape. 2000.
[81] Calasso, Robert. *The Marriage of Cadmus and Harmony.* New York: Knopf. 1993. 21.

[82] Vermeule, Emily. "A Gold Minoan Double Axe." Bulletin of the Museum of Fine Arts 57.307 (1959: 4-16) 6.
[83] Marinatos. *Minoan Religion*. 1993. 175-179.
[84] Geraci, Bennie. Message to the author. 27 January 2007. Email.

Notes for Chapter 26

[1] Minos Gwydion [Buczynski, Edmund]. Foundation Document of the Minoan Brotherhood. Middle Village: Unpublished MS. 1 January 1977. MS.
[2] Minos Gwydion [Buczynski, Edmund]. Minoan Brotherhood vouch of Ozric [Cupolo, Joseph]. 1 January 1977. MS.
[3] Buczynski, Edmund Michael. "Witchcraft Today and the Homosexual." Gaysweek (13 June 1977) 11. (Coll. BMG).
[4] Geraci, Bennie and Joseph Cupolo. Personal interview. 14 November 2004.
[5] Cupolo, Joseph. Message to the author. 15 January 2004. Email.
[6] Wyatt, Aubrey. "Minoan History Part 2." Message to the author. 11 December 2003. Email.
[7] [Buczynski]. "The Minoan Brotherhood" (Booklet and Questionnaire). January 1977? MS.
[8] Schuller, Kim. Personal interview. 28 April 2006.
[9] Helios. Message to the author. 15 May 2004.
[10] Rivera, Ria. Message to the author. 21 February 2007. Email.
[11] Martello. *Witchcraft: The Old Religion*. 1973. 101.
[12] Davis, Michael. Message to the author. 5 October 2011. Email.
[13] Lord Starhawk. Posting on "Herman Slater." Magickal Childe. ND. Web (http://www.magickalchilde.com/herman.html, accessed 10/10/2011).
[14] Foster, Star. "The Passing of Lord Merlin." *Pantheon*, the Pagan blog at Patheos. 2 October 2011. Web (http://www.patheos.com/community/paganportal/2011/10/02/the-passing-of-lord-merlin/, accessed 10/10/2011).
[15] Moss, Harold. Message to the author. 18 August 2008. Email.
[16] Slater, Herman. Letter. *Green Egg* 8.72 (August 1975) 43. Print. (Coll. A.Terr.).
[17] Slater, Herman. Letter. *Green Egg* 8.74 (October 1975) 44. Print. (Coll. A.Terr.).
[18] Gelbert, Bruce-Michael. Personal interview. 29 April 2006.
[19] *True Blood* "Frenzy." Dir. Daniel Minahan. Home Box Office. 2009.
[20] Stearn, Jess. *The Sixth Man*. New York: MacFadden Books. 1962. 167-169.
[21] Clarke and Nichols. *Roommates Can't Always Be Lovers*. 1974. 142, 163.
[22] *Future Shock*. Dir. Alexander Grasshoff and Ken Rosen (Writer). Metromedia Producers Corporation (MPC). 1972. As a closeted high school student, the author recalls seeing this film in class and being both shocked and excited by the possibilities.
[23] Many Minoan Brothers had long wondered why a marriage ritual was included in the Minoan Brotherhood Book of Shadows. This 1977 rite may mark one of the earliest documented gay Pagan handfastings and gay Pagan handfasting ritual layouts in modern times. They are quite common today.
[24] Geraci, Bennie. Message to the author. 20 January 2004. Email.
[25] Mahler, Jonathon. *Ladies and Gentlemen, the Bronx is Burning*. New York: Picador. 2006. 248.
[26] Holzer. *The Witchcraft Report*. 1973. 46.
[27] Geraci, Bennie. Message to the author. 28 April 2006. Email.

[28] Geraci, Bennie. Message to the author. 29 April 2006. Email.
[29] (Ibid n#8). Kim and Lisa Marie packed the Book of Shadows away and forgot about it until they were asked to be interviewed for this biography almost 29 years later.
[30] *GaysWeek* didn't last very long, running only from 1977 until its demise in 1979.
[31] Martello, Louis Leo. Letter. *GaysWeek* 18 (20 June 1977) Np. (Coll. BMG).
[32] Buczynski, Edmund Michael. Letter. GaysWeek 20 (4 July 1977) 6. (Coll. BMG). When Bruce-Michael Gelbert pointed out that Martello's name was misspelled in Eddie's letter, Eddie's response was a smile and a chuckle.
[33] Eddie Buczynski. Letter to Joe Cupolo. 11 November 1977. MS.
[34] Bell, Arthur. "Anita Bryant's Ire and Brimstone Village Voice 22.14 (4 April 1977) p. 11. MCF. (Cols. Met. Lib).
[35] Mahler. *Ladies and Gentlemen, the Bronx is Burning*. 126.
[36] A segment of the Christian conservative population would become more frustrated and radicalized. By the early 1980s, the worst of these groups (e.g., the Covenant, the Sword and the Arm of the Lord Church) advocated the killing of unrepentant homosexuals and Witches. See: "Cult Forms Army to Kill God's Enemies." Seax Wica Voys 8 (Imbolc 1982) 1. Print. (Arch. Circ. Sanc).
[37] "Bits & Pieces: Asshole of the Month." *Hustler* 4.1 (1977) 17. In this same issue, Hustler publisher Larry Flynt came out strongly in support of gay rights (7). It is interesting to note that straight pornographers such as Flynt and *Screw* publisher Al Goldstein were often better examples of Christ's exhortation to treat others as they would wish to be treated than were grandstanding moralizers like Bryant.
[38] Mahler. *Ladies and Gentlemen, the Bronx is Burning*. 2006. 131.
[39] In 1998, Dade County partially reversed the damage done by Bryant, passing an anti-bias ordinance that included sexual orientation. That ordinance withstood a recall challenge by fifty-six percent of the vote in 2002, showing that the times had indeed changed. The statute forbidding adoptions by gay persons in Florida, however, remains in effect.
[40] Dochuk, Darren. *From Bible Belt to Sun Belt: Plain-Folk Religion, Grassroots Politics, and the Rise of Evangelical Conservatism*. New York: W.W. Norton & Co. 2011. 380-383.
[41] Sutton, Matthew. *Aimee Semple McPherson and the Resurrection of Christian America*. Boston: Harvard University Press. 2007.
[42] Mahler. *Ladies and Gentlemen, the Bronx is Burning*. 2006. 187-205, 214-223.
[43] Geraci, Bennie. Message to the author. 25 July 2006. Email.
[44] (Ibid n#43) Geraci, Bennie. Message to the author. 25 July 2006. Email. "Restraints" or "restraining orders" is a tongue-in-cheek way of referring to magickal bindings of those who wish you harm.
[45] Lady Rhea [Farnham, Ria]. The Wica vouch of Osric [Joey Cupolo]. Forest Hills, New York. 20 June 1977. MS.
[46] Cupolo, Joseph. Message to the author. 14 January 2004. Email.
[47] Eaton, Sally. Message to the author. 14 December 2010. Email.
[48] Cupolo, Joseph. Message to the author. 12 June 2010. Email.
[49] Unattributed [Buczynski, Edmund]. "Initiate's Booklet." Middle Village: Unpublished MS. 1977? MS.

[50] [Buczynski]. *The Minoan Brotherhood Book of the Mysteries.* Middle Village: Unpublished MS. 1977. MS

[51] Buczynski, Edmund. Letter to Joseph Cupolo. 1 December 1, 1977. MS.

[52] Buczynski, Edmund (unattributed). "The First Annual November Council: Decisions." Middle Village: Unpublished MS. 1 November 1977. MS. This turned out to be the one and only meeting of the tradition's representatives during Eddie's lifetime.

[53] Caigan, Khem. Telephone interview. 3 April 2006.

[54] Bulzone, Carol. Telephone interview. 2 November 2004.

[55] Rivera, Ria. Telephone interview. 30 January 2004.

[56] Rivera, Ria. Telephone interview. 13 June 2010.

[57] Macer-Story, Eugenia. Message to the author. 13 January 2009. Email.

[58] Magickal Childe Advertisement. Village Voice 22.44 (31 October 1977) 2. MCF. (Cols. Met. Lib).

[59] Macer-Story, Eugenia. Message to the author. 14 January 2009. Email.

[60] Eaton, Sally. Message to the author. 21 January 2008. Email.

[61] Cuhulain, Kerr. "Eric Pryor: Part 2." The Witches' Voice. 29 July 2002. Web (http://www.witchvox.com/va/dt_va.html?a=cabc&c=whs&id=4358, accessed 31 May 2010).

[62] Cuhulain, Kerr. "Eric Pryor: Part 3." The Witches' Voice. 29 July 2002. Web (http://www.witchvox.com/va/dt_va.html?a=cabc&c=whs&id=4359, accessed 31 May 2010).

Notes for Chapter 27

[1] The book discussed in this chapter will be referred to as the "Simon Necronomicon" to differentiate it from both the Lovecraftian literary vehicle and the other Necronomicons that have been published over the years.

[2] Advertisement. ERN 1.1 (December 1973) p. 6. Print. (Arch. Circ. Sanc).

[3] It should be noted that this was not the earliest mention of the Necronomicon in connection with the Warlock Shop. The January 1973 store catalogue lists the following:

The Necronomicon   Abdul Albazrad $12.50
(Ltd. Printing, Advanced orders taken)

The listing of Abdul Albazrad (sic) as its author and the failure to mention that it was a "translation" undoubtedly marks this book as the L. Sprague de Camp Necronomicon, which was in the process of being published at the same time that the *Earth Religions Supply* catalogue was being prepared in late 1972. The December 1973 Advertisement in the *Earth Religion News* for the "Translation not yet in print" could not refer to the L. Sprague de Camp book because by that time Al Azif: The Necronomicon had already been in print for nearly a year. The $12.50 price in the January 1973 catalogue also tracks well with the $15 price in the December 1973 *Earth Religion News* ad. Source: Hephaestos and Hermes [Slater, Herman and Edmund Buczynski]. "The Warlock Shop/Earth Religions Supply Catalogue." Brooklyn: Self-published. January 1973. 7.

[4] Simon. *Dead Names.* 2006. 98.

[5] Simon. *Dead Names.* 2006. 98-101.

[6] It is known that while Herman Slater was laid up recovering from his tuberculosis surgery in 1971, he read occult fiction and fantasy voraciously.

One of his favorite authors at that time was H.P. Lovecraft, whose works were being re-issued that year.

[7] Simon. *Necronomicon.* 1977. v.
[8] Simon. *Dead Names.* 2006. 102.
[9] Faraone, Christopher and Dirk Obbink (eds.). *Magika Hiera: Ancient Greek Magic & Religion.* New York: Oxford University Press. 17.
[10] Luck, Georg. *Arcana Mundi: Magic and the Occult in the Greek and Roman Worlds.* Baltimore: The Johns Hopkins University Press. 1985. 24.
[11] Ankarloo, Bengt and Stuart Clark. *Witchcraft and Magic in Europe: Ancient Greece and Rome.* Philadelphia: University of Pennsylvania Press. 1999. xii.
[12] Simon. *Dead Names.* 2006. 104-105.
[13] Cabal, Alan. "The Doom that Came to Chelsea." NEWS & COLUMNS section. *New York Press* 16.23 (3 June 2003) Np. Web.
[14] Simon. *Necronomicon.* 1977. lv-lvi.
[15] Advertisement. ERN 1.5 (August 1974) 5. Print. (Arch. Circ. Sanc).
[16] Simon. *Necronomicon.* 1977. xxxi
[17] Simon. *Dead Names.* 2006. 30
[18] Simon. *Necronomicon.* 1977. xi-xxx
[19] Simon. *Dead Names.* 2006. 150
[20] Simon. *Dead Names.* 2006. pp. 210-211
[21] Alobar [Siebert, William]. Message to the author. 24 February 2007. Email. Alobar states "I went to a workshop on alchemy by Simon at the Warlock Shop & Herman introduced us. Simon asked if I would pull together a set of correspondences for his not-yet-published Necronomicon along the lines of Crowley's Liber 777, but it never got beyond the initial discussion phase."
[22] Crowley, Aleister. *White Stains.* London: Duckworth. 1993. vii.
[23] Simon. *Dead Names.* 2006. 144, 146
[24] Eaton, Sally. Message to the author. 21 January 2008. Email.
[25] Source: "Wasserman Biography." Studio 31. Web (http://www.studio31.com/jimw.htm). Wasserman's book production company (Studio 31/Royal Type) continued to generate titles (e.g., reprints of Gerald Gardner's books) for Magickal Childe into the 1990s.
[26] Simon. *Necronomicon.* 1977. ii.
[27] Simon. *Dead Names.* 2006. 142-143. Simon and Slater had preferred an understated film noir look.
[28] (Ibid n#26). Khem Caigan is credited as "Khem Set Rising."
[29] Caigan, Khem. "The Simonomicon (& Me)." 1999. Web (http://web.archive.org/web/20021003213342/http://home.flash.net/~khem/Simonomicon.html, accessed 30 September 2007).
[30] Caigan, Khem. Telephone interview. 3 April 2006.
[31] Simon. *Necronomicon.* New York: Avon. 1980. Back Cover.
[32] Simon. *Dead Names.* 2006. 159
[33] Fifty dollars was a king's ransom to a poor college student in 1977, else this author (who vividly remembers seeing the ads in Omni and National Lampoon) would in all likelihood have purchased a copy back then. A first edition today cannot be had for under about $750, and even second editions in cloth have been known to fetch close to $1000.
[34] Simon. *Dead Names.* 2006. 148.
[35] Kirwan, Larry. Message to the author. 28 February 2007. Email.
[36] Simon. *Dead Names.* 2006. 158.

[37] Magickal Childe Advertisement. *Village Voice* 22.49 (5 December 1977) 2. MCF. (Cols. Met. Lib).
[38] Inominandum [Miller, Jason]. "Simon Speaks: Part I." *Behutet* 16 (Winter 2002-2003) 9-10. Print.
[39] Skinner, Steven. Message to the author. 26 September 2007. Email.
[40] *Inominandum* [Miller, Jason]. "Simon Speaks: Part I." 12.
[41] Simon. "A Short Primer on Pagan Ceremonial Magick." ERN 1.5 (August 1974) 42. Print. (Arch. Circ. Sanc).
[42] Simon. "A Short Primer on Pagan Ceremonial Magick." ERN 1.6-8 (October 1976) 30-31. Print. (Arch. Circ. Sanc).
[43] Levenda, Peter. Message to the author. 28 March 2006. Email.
[44] Simon. *Dead Names*. 2006. 268
[45] Simon. *Dead Names*. 2006. 266-267.
[46] *Inominandum* [Miller, Jason]. "Simon Speaks: Part I." 8-9.
[47] Khem Caigan notes that chaos magick has its roots in the magickal surrealists such as Kenneth Grant and his Typhonian O.T.O. Source: Caigan. "The Simonomicon (& Me)."
[48] Aside from being the daimon represented by the statue unearthed at the beginning of The Exorcist (1973), Pazuzu is an entity of Assyrian/Babylonian origin listed in the Simon Necronomicon. Farber, Phil. Reader Comments. February 3, 2012. Llewellyn Blogs: Magick: Kraig, Donald Michael. "Guard the Mysteries Reveal Them Constantly." February 3, 2012. Web (http://www.llewellyn.com/blog/2012/02/guard-the-mysteries-reveal-them-constantly/, accessed 3 February 2012).
[49] Savage, Adrian. *An Introduction to Chaos Magick*. New York: Magickal Childe Publishing, Inc. 1988.
[50] Bak, Per, Kurt Weisenfeld and Chao Tang "Self-organized criticality: An explanation of 1/f noise." Physical Review Letters 59.4 (1987) 381-384. Web.
[51] Simon. *Necronomicon*. 1977. viii.
[52] Harms, Daniel and John Gonce III. *The Necronomicon Files*. Boston: Weiser Books. 2003. 173-196.
[53] Simon. *Dead Names*. 2006. 297-304.
[54] Slater's impassioned defense of Buczynski's memory in the preface to Pagan Rituals III alone should rebuff any suggestion that he would deny Eddie any recognition honestly due him. See: Slater. *Pagan Rituals III*. 1989.
[55] For example: Simon. *Dead Names: The Dark History of the Necronomicon* (Avon Books, 2006); and Simon. *The Gates of the Necronomicon* (Avon Books, 2006).
[56] Alan Cabal, in his marvelously entertaining memoir of those times in the New York Post — *The Doom That Came to Chelsea* — writes that Simon was not just the editor but the author of the Necronomicon published under his imprimatur. Cabal's ex wife, Bonnie Claremont, worked on the Necronomicon manuscript. See: Cabal, Alan. "The Doom that Came to Chelsea." NEWS & COLUMNS section. New York Press 16.23 (3 June 2003) Np. Web.
[57] Simon. *Dead Names*. 2006. 297-300.
[58] Geraci, Bennie and Joseph Cupolo. Personal interview. 14 November 2004.
[59] Rivera, Ria. Message to the author. 18 January 2004. Email.
[60] Caigan, Khem. Telephone interview. June 2005.

61. North, Erika [Judith McNally]. Message to the author. 30 November 2005. Email.
62. Simon. *Dead Names.* P. 299.
63. Harms and Gonce. *The Necronomicon Files.* 2004. 175-176.
64. Gwydion [Buczynski, Edmund]. The Wica Book of Shadows." Forest Hills: Unpublished MS. 1974? MS.
65. Helios. Message to the author. 14 April 2004. Email. Gerald Fisher is said to have become a "Hard Gard" and turned against Buczynski and Slater in the ongoing tit-for-tat between them and the Long Island Line of Gardnerian Wica. Thus, if the Nestor referred to by Harms and Gonce is the same person who was blacklisted by Buczynski, then there are ample personal reasons to suspect the source of information beyond the fact that, as a resident of Kentucky, it is unlikely that Fisher could have been present at or privy to the goings-on in the back room of the Warlock Shop in Brooklyn Heights, New York in 1972. Even Hard Gards cannot claim to have mastered the art of bilocation.
66. Joshi, S. and David Schultz (eds). *H.P. Lovecraft, Letters from New York.* San Francisco: Night Shade Books. 2005. 292.
67. Lovecraft, H. P. Letter to Clark Ashton Smith. 9 October 1925. Web. It was not long after this letter was written that Samuel Weiser was first founded as a used bookstore in 1926 on 4th Avenue in Manhattan. It soon became an antiquarian specialist in Esoteric books and "Orientalia."
68. Joshi, S.T. *H.P. Lovecraft: The Decline of the West.* Starmont House, Mercer Island, WA. 1990.
69. Rottensteiner, Franz. "Lovecraft as Philosopher." *Science Fiction Studies#56* 19.1 (March 1992).
70. Example: Lovecraft, H. P. Letter to Harry O. Fischer. February 1937. For many examples of Lovecraft's correspondence regarding the Necronomicon, this author recommends the interested reader to visit: Loucks, Donovan. "The H.P. Lovecraft Archive: Quotes Regarding the Necronomicon from Lovecraft's Letters." Web (http://www.hplovecraft.com/creation/necron/letters.asp).
71. Lovecraft, H. P., Anthony Raven, and Stephen Fabian. *The Occult Lovecraft.* Saddle River: Gerry de la Ree. 1975.

Notes for Chapter 28
1. Sabazius X° and AMT IX°. "History of Ordo Templi Orientis." United States Grand Lodge, Ordo Templi Orientis. Web (http://oto-usa.org/history.html, accessed 23 January 2006).
2. As Grady had survived D-Day, and Aleister was unable to immediately pay back the loan, Crowley assigned the rights to the Book of Thoth and its accompanying Tarot deck to the young soldier. This was upheld by Gerald Yorke, Crowley's British literary executor, allowing Grady to arrange for the first full-color edition of the deck, published by Llewellyn in 1970. Eaton, Sally. Message to the author. 21 January 2008.
3. Koenig, P.R. "XI° -- Per Aftera Ad Astra, Anal Intercourse and the O.T.O." Web (http://user.cyberlink.ch/~koenig/sunrise/xi.htm, accessed 2 September 2009).
4. "Features & Editorial." *Magickal Link* IV.4 (April 1984) 1. Print. (Arch. Circ. Sanc).

[5] Regardie, Israel. Letter. *Gnostica News* 5.2 (February 1976) 4. Print. (Wesc. Lib. Llew.).
[6] Carter, Randolph. Letter. *Gnostica News* 4.12 (November-December 1975) 2. Print. (Wesc. Lib. Llew.).
[7] Culling, Louis T. Letter. *Gnostica News* 2.4 (21 December 1972) 2. Print. (Wesc. Lib. Llew.).
[8] Hymenaeus Alpha (Grady McMurtry). "Aleister Crowley's Ordo Templi Orientis." *Gnostica News* 4.2 (October 1974) 15. Print. (Wesc. Lib. Llew.).
[9] It was not known how much material had been lost during this period. Some was eventually recovered, including Crowley's original manuscript for *Liber AL vel Legis (The Book of the Law)* in 1985.
[10] Eaton, Sally. Message to the author. 21 January 2008. Email.
[11] Palmer, Nancy J. (Reporter). REPORTER'S TRANSCRIPT OF PROCEEDINGS OF COURT TRIAL IN THE United States DISTRICT COURT FOR THE NORTHERN DISTRICT OF CALIFORNIA BEFORE THE HONORABLE CHARLES A. LEGGE, JUDGE. Grady McMurtry, et al. vs. Society Ordo Templi Orientis, et al. CIVIL NO. C-83-5434 (VOLUME I, PAGES 375 – 496). Wednesday, May 15, 1985. MORNING SESSION.
[12] Heidrick, Bill. Message to the author. 24 January 2008. Email. John Symonds was Aleister Crowley's literary executor.
[13] "Grand Lodge Report." *Magical Link* 5.2 (1985) 7. Print. (Arch. Circ. Sanc).
[14] Heidrick, Bill. Message to the author. 14 February 2008. Email.
[15] Wikipedia Entry: Ordo Templi Orientis (http://en.wikipedia.org/wiki/Ordo_Templi_Orientis). Accessed February 19, 2008.
[16] Heidrick, Bill. Message to the author. 15 February 2008. Email.
[17] *Oriflamme*. Advertisement. *Green Egg* 7.64 (August 1974) 55. Print. (Coll. A.Terr.). Nixon and the Society had no connection to the O.T.O., and Oriflamme eventually ceased publication after the O.T.O.'s newsletter Magickal Link began in 1981.
[18] Crowley, Aleister. *White Stains*. Brooklyn: Earth Religions Supply, Inc. 1974.
[19] Mills, Malcolm. Message to the author. 4 August 2007. Email.
[20] Magickal Childe Advertisement. Village Voice 22.41 (10 October 1977) 2. MCF. (Cols. Met. Lib). Note: the ad appeared several days after the event, a not-uncommon occurrence according to several people.
[21] Carey, Robert. Message to the author. 24 April 2007. Email.
[22] *Inominandum* [Miller, Jason]. "Simon Speaks: Part I." *Behutet* 16 (Winter 2002-2003) 9-10. Print.
[23] Cabal, Alan. "A Gay Old Time: Out and About in Chelsea." *New York Press* (8 June 2001) Np. Web.
[24] Eaton, Sally. Message to the author. 23 January 2008. Email.
[25] "Biographical Page." James Wasserman Books. Web (http://jameswassermanbooks.com/bio.htm, accessed 18 February 2008).
[26] "Tahuti Lodge Ordo Templi Orientis in the Valley of New York City." Web (http://tahutilodge.org/history.php, accessed 15 February 2008).
[27] (Ibid n#16). In the parlance of today's O.T.O., the Tahuti Chapter of 1980 would now be called an "Oasis", as the term "Chapter" is currently reserved for a type of non-public access O.T.O. body.
[28] Mills, Malcolm. Message to the author. 8 August 2007. Email.

²⁹ "Fifth Annual Pagan Samhain Festival." Announcement. Seax-Wica Voys 1 (Beltane 1980) 4. Print. (Arch. Circ. Sanc).
³⁰ Sales of O.T.O. materials at the Magickal Childe did not appear constitute a very large cash flow for the Order. Financial records cited by Heidrick show slightly less than $1200 in receipts from these transactions between 1980 and 1986, comprising sales of cassette tapes, newsletters, and copies of Liber 777. Source: Heidrick, Bill. Message to the author. 24 January 2008. Email.
³¹ Wasserman, Jim. Message to Dennis Stevens. 13 February 2007. Email.
³² Mills, Malcolm. Message to the author. 5 August 2007. Email.
³³ "At the time we took over the mail order (our company was called Abrahadabra and we mailed catalogs under that name), the O.T.O. wasn't particularly prominent in the shop. ... I do recall that at one point some of the O.T.O. members decided to throw a hissy-fit because we were using Abrahadabra as the name of our company. Cindy and I thought they were being ridiculous and actually considered trademarking the name. I remember telling Herman (who thought the trademark idea was very funny) that if the O.T.O. wished to use the word, they could come to me for permission. Ultimately we decided it wasn't worth the $500 to trademark it, although we did a search and found it was available." Source: Mills, Malcolm. Message to the author. 3 August 2007. Email.
³⁴ Soror Charis. "Herman Slater: 'Thee Magickal Childe'" (Part II). *Behutet* 11 (Autumn 2001) 9. Print.
³⁵ Soror Charis. "Herman Slater: 'Thee Magickal Childe'" (Part I). *Behutet* 10 (Summer 2001) 7. Print.
³⁶ Soror Charis. "Herman Slater: 'Thee Magickal Childe'" (Part II). *Behutet* 11 (Autumn 2001) 10. Print.
³⁷ Hymenaeus Beta, Frater Superior, Caliph, O.T.O. Message to Dennis Stevens. 12 February 2007. Email.
³⁸ Grand Treasurer General. "Grand Lodge Report, December 30, 1985." Magical Link VI.1 (January 1986) 4. Print. (Arch. Circ. Sanc).
³⁹ (Ibid n#12). Bill Heidrick notes, "The last listing for Earth Star Camp was given in the O.T.O. Magical Link of Winter '91 (end of that year), and so the Camp actually ended a little before Herman passed away around the middle of the next year. Herman had essentially handed-off management of the store to others, and there was no O.T.O. camp at that address in the last months of his life."

Notes for Chapter 29
¹ Geraci, Bennie. Message to the author. 20 May 2010. Email.
² Muto, Gene. Personal interview. 28 October 2004.
³ Geraci, Bennie. Personal interview. 17 January 2004. Email.
⁴ Geraci, Bennie. Message to the author. 13 June 2010. Email.
⁵ Geraci, Bennie. Telephone interview. 21 July 2011.
⁶ Buczynski, Frank. Telephone interview. 8 May 2008.
⁷ Bulzone, Carol. Telephone interview. 2 November 2004.
⁸ Bulzone, Carol. Telephone interview. 2 November 2004.
⁹ Cheiron. Message to the author. 23 August 2004. Email.
¹⁰ Wyatt, Aubrey. Message to the author. November 30, 2003.
¹¹ Geraci, Bennie. Message to the author. 10 May 2008. Email.

12. Kilhefner, Don. "The Radical Faeries at Thirty (+ one)." Gay and Lesbian Review XVII.5 (September-October 2010) 17-21. Print.
13. Helios. Message to the author. 11 April 2004. While the apartment is remembered as being on East 13th Street near Avenue C, it was more likely between Avenues A and B where several long-standing squats were located.
14. Wyatt, Aubrey. "Minoan Brotherhood History, 1st Installment." Message to the author. 11 December 2003. Email.
15. Wyatt, Aubrey. Message to the author. January 4, 2004. Email.
16. Wyatt, Aubrey. "Minoan History Part 3." Message to the author. 11 December 2003. Email.
17. Wyatt, Aubrey. "Minoan History Part 2." Message to the author. 11 December 2003. Email.
18. Jamison, Artie. Telephone interview. 24 January 2004.
19. Rivera, Ria. Message to the author. 18 January 2004. Email.
20. Helios. Message to the author. 21 April 2004. Email.
21. Mills, Malcolm. Message to the author. 3 August 2007. Email.
22. Mills, Malcolm. Message to the author. 4 August 2007. Email.
23. Austans, Laura. Message to the author. 9 December 2010. Email.
24. Terrason, Alaric. Message to the author. 11 March 2007. Email.
25. "Fourth Annual Pan Pagan Festival." *Seax Wicca Voys* 1 (Beltane 1980) 4. Print. (Arch. Circ. Sanc).
26. Nelson, Ray. "A Personal Report of the Pan Pagan Festival Held in Lake Holiday, IN August 21-25, 1980." *RFD* 25 (Fall/Winter 1980) 21. Print.
27. Slater, Herman (ed.). *The Magickal Formulary*. New York: Magickal Childe Publishing. 1981.
28. Eaton, Sally. Message to the author. 27 February 2008. Email.
29. Geraci, Bennie and Joseph Cupolo. Personal interview. 14 November 2004. Email.
30. Gwilym Dafydd HHH. Message to the author. 28 July 2007. Email.
31. Slater. The Magickal Formulary. 1981. P. ii.
32. Eaton, Sally. Message to the author. 23 January 2008. Email.
33. Eaton, Sally. Message to the author. 12 April 2006. Email.
34. Rivera, Ria. Message to the author. 20 January 2004. Email.
35. Frank, Kathryn. Message to the author. 16 February 2011. Email. Frank, at British rocker Tom Robinson's suggestion, brought the Rock Against Racism movement to the States from Great Britain in 1979.
36. Frank, Kathryn. Message to the author. 6 November 2010. Email. Tim Hough briefly dated Tom Robinson.
37. Frank, Kathryn. Message to the author. 6 January 2010. Email.
38. Frank, Kathryn. Message to the author. 27 August 2009. Email.
39. "Fifth Annual Pagan Samhain Festival." *Seax Wicca Voys* 1 (Beltane 1980) 4. Print. (Arch. Circ. Sanc).
40. Wyatt, Aubrey. Message to the author. 30 November 2003. Email.
41. Gianniotis, Terry. Telephone interview. 16 October 2011.
42. Buczynski, Edmund M. "Summer Session 1982: Going Forward, Looking Back — A Personal View." ASCSA NL (Fall 1982) 1. Web.
43. Buczynski. *Volume One: Liber Ubrarum [sic] — The Book of Shadows with Commentary*. New York: Unpublished MS. P. ii, iii. MS. This paper, written by Eddie in 1983, asserted that he had left the Craft in 1980, and yet this was clearly not the case. Buczynski would continue to lead Knossos Grove

through at least the first half of 1981, and participate in sabbats for a short period thereafter.

Notes for Chapter 30
1. Venit, Marjorie Susan. "Biography of Clairève Grandjouan." *Breaking Ground: Women in Old World Archaeology*. Web (http://www.brown.edu/breakingground, accessed 21 October 2010).
2. Green, Tamara. Telephone interview. 28 April 2004.
3. Muto, Gene. Personal interview. 29 October 2004.
4. Saretta, Phyllis. Message to the author. 1 September 2004. Email.
5. Wright, James. Personal interview. 6 November 2004.
6. Muto, Gene. Personal interview. 29 October 2004.
7. Buczynski, Edmund. "The Practical, Artistic and Cultic Use of Marine Shells in Minoan Crete." Diss. Bryn Mawr College. September 1987. P. iii. MS.
8. Brita. *Interview with Eliphas [Michael Thorn]*. *The Hidden Path* V.4 (Samhain 1982) 25-27. Print. (Arch. Circ. Sanc).
9. Lamond, Frederic. *Fifty Years of Wicca*. Sutton Mallet: Green Magic. 2004. 121.
10. "The Hermetic Order of the Silver Sword." Circle of the Free Spirit. Web (http://circleofthefreespirit.org/AvatarTemple.htm, accessed 29 March 2012).
11. Thorn, Michael. Telephone interview. 19 January 2006.
12. By 1984, Michael Thorn would end up guesting on a regular basis with another Minoan Brotherhood grove in New York City. However, he never took a degree in the tradition. Source: (Ibid n#10).
13. Wyatt, Aubrey. Message to the author. 30 November 2003. Email.
14. Helios. Message to the author. 21 April 2004. Email.
15. Baldwin, H. Bruce. Message to the author. 5 September 2005. Email.
16. Gwilym Dafydd HHH. Message to the author. 12 January 2004. Email.
17. Talbert, Robert. "Master Voice Builder Takes on Major Repair Job." Education Update VIII.2 (October 2002) 7. Web (http://www.educationupdate.com/archives/2002/oct02/issue/assets/EdUpdate_Oct02.pdf, accessed 2 November 2010). See also: Winsel, Regnier. The Anatomy of Voice: An Illustrated Manual of Vocal Training. Hicksville: Exposition Press. 1966. Winsel passed away at age 72 in the Bronx on April 1, 1988.
18. Martello. Leo. "Wicca-Basket." *Gnostica News* 2.4 (21 December 1972) 21. Print. (Wesc. Lib. Llew.). Winsel passed away at age 73 in the Bronx on April 1, 1988.
19. Hymes, K.B., Greene, J. B., Marcus, A., et al. 'Kaposi's sarcoma in homosexual men: A report of eight cases." *Lancet* 2 (March 1981) 598-600.
20. "Pneumocystis Pneumonia — Los Angeles." *Morbidity and Mortality Weekly Report* 30 (5 June 1981) 250-252. Web.
21. "Kaposi's Sarcoma and Pneumocystis Pneumonia Among Homosexual Men — New York City and California." *Morbidity and Mortality Weekly Report* 30 (4 July 1981) 305-308.
22. Altman, Lawrence K. "Rare Cancer Seen in 41 Homosexuals." NYT (3 July 1981) Np. Web.
23. Curran, Jim. Interview. *Frontline: The Age of AIDS*. Dir. Greg Barker, William Cran. PBS/WGCH Boston. 2006. Video.

[24] "Scientists trace AIDS origin to wild chimps: Gene tests match virus in primates in Cameroon to first known human case." MSNBC (Associated Press). 25 May 2006. Web.

[25] Neergaard, Lauran. "Scientists Confirm Origins of HIV." Associated Press. 25 May 2006. Web.

[26] M. Thomas P. Gilbert, Andrew Rambaut, Gabriela Wlasiuk, Thomas J. Spira, Arthur E. Pitchenik, and Michael Worobey. "The emergence of HIV/AIDS in the Americas and beyond." *Proceedings of the National Academy of Sciences* (31 October 2007) Np. Web.

[27] Bazell, Robert. "Research rewrites first chapter of AIDS in United States: Don't blame 'Patient Zero' or Haitians for the epidemic." NBC News. 6 November 2007. Np. Web.

[28] One recent study points to 1969 as being the earliest point at which the virus had successfully established itself in the United States population from Haiti. Source: Worobey, et al. "The emergence of HIV/AIDS in the Americas and beyond." The irony of Worobey's 1969 dating has been smirkingly noted by more than one conservative wag/homophobe, given its significance to the Stonewall riots and the modern gay rights movement. However, at least one confirmed case of the disease is known from Saint Louis as early as 1968, thereby rendering the sound bite not merely callous, but moot. Source: Kolata, Gina. "Boy's 1969 Death Suggests AIDS Invaded United States Several Times." NYT (29 October 1987) Np. Web.

[29] Fauci, Anthony. Interview. "Frontline: The Age of AIDS." Dir. Greg Barker, William Cran. PBS/WGCH Boston. 2006. Video.

[30] Rivera, Ria. Telephone interview. 30 January 2004. It should be noted that there was no test for the anti-bodies associated with HIV in 1981, so the doctors could only speculate on the underlying cause of Slater's illness.

[31] Buczynski, Edmund. Letter to Kathryn Frank. 18 October 1981. MS. From the Collection of Kathryn Frank (Coll. K. Fra.).

[32] Grandjouan, Clairève (Eileen Markson and Susan Rotroff). *Hellenistic Relief Molds from the Athenian Agora (Hesperia: Supplement XXIII)*. Princeton: American School of Classical Studies at Athens. 1989. xv-xvii.

[33] "Clairève Grandjouan, 52, Dies; Taught Archaeology at Hunter." NYT (8 June 1982) Np. Web.

[34] Buczynski, Edmund M. "Summer Session 1982: Going Forward, Looking Back — A Personal View." ASCSA NL (Fall 1982) 1, 4. Web.

[35] "About the ASCSA." American School of Classical Studies at Athens. Web (http://www.ascsa.edu.gr/index.php/about/, accessed 7 November 2010).

[36] "Mission and History." American School of Classical Studies at Athens. Web (http://www.ascsa.edu.gr/index.php/About/history, retrieved 7 November 2010).

[37] Fischer, Dr. John. "Report of the Director of Summer Session II, 1982 — Summer Session Schedule." Letter to the Director, American School of Classical Studies at Athens. 1982. MS. From the Collection of Dr. John Fischer (Coll. J. Fisc.).

[38] Rotroff, Susan. Message to the author. 30 August 2004. Email.

[39] "Programs, Summer Sessions, A Typical Day." American School of Classical Studies at Athens. Web (http://www.ascsa.edu.gr/index.php/programs/Summer, accessed 7 November 2010).

[40] "About the Lecturer." Monmouth College Department of Classics. Web (department.monm.edu/classics/Department/FoxLecture/biography_of_alden_smith.htm, retrieved November 4, 2010).
[41] Smith, Alden. Message to the author. 8 August 2004. Email.
[42] Smith, Alden. Message to the author. 9 August 2004. Email.
[43] Hatzichronoglou, Lena. Message to the author. 5 August 2004. Email.
[44] Cameron, Pat. *Blue Guide: Crete (7th Ed.)*. London: A & C Black Publishers. 2003. 282-283.
[45] Fischer, John. Message to the author. 3 August 2004. Email.
[46] Mee, Christopher and Antony Spawforth. *Oxford Archaeological Guides: Greece*. Oxford: Oxford University Press. 2001. 324-326.
[47] "Summer Session: Another View." ASCSA NL (Fall 1982) 4. Web.
[48] Buczynski, Eddie. Letter to Lena Hatzichronoglou. 19 September 1982. MS. From the Collection of Lena Hatzichchronoglou (Coll. L. Chro.).
[49] Buczynski, Eddie. Letter to Lena Hatzichronoglou. December 1982. MS. (Coll. L. Chro.).
[50] Buczynski, Eddie. Letter to Lena Hatzichronoglou. January 1983. MS. (Coll. L. Chro.).
[51] Rhine, Arthur. "Loft to Luxury." Letter. NYT (21 March 1993) Np. Web.
[52] Cabal, Alan. "The Doom that Came to Chelsea." NEWS & COLUMNS section. New York Press 16.23 (3 June 2003) Np. Web.
[53] Rivera, Ria. Telephone interview. 30 January 2004.
[54] Soror Charis. "Herman Slater: 'Thee Magickal Childe'" (Part II). *Behutet* 11 (Autumn 2001) 14. Print.
[55] *Fangoria Magazine Scream Greats, Volume 2: Satanism and Witchcraft*. Dir. Damon Santostefano. Paramount Home Video. 1987.
[56] Rivera, Ria. Telephone interview. 5 February 2004.
[57] Rivera, Ria. Telephone interview. 1 April 2011.
[58] Bulzone, Carol. Telephone interview. 2 November 2004.
[59] Soror Charis. "Herman Slater: 'Thee Magickal Childe'" (Part II). *Behutet* 11 (Autumn 2001) 9. Print.
[60] Buczynski, Ed. *Witchcraft Fact Book*. New York: Magickal Childe Publishing. 1984.
[61] Buczynski, Edmund. *Liber Ubrarum [sic]: the Book of Shadows with commentary*. New York: Unpublished MS. 1983. MS.
[62] Endlich, Lisa. *Goldman Sachs: The Culture of Success*. New York: Simon & Schuster. 2000. 99.
[63] It's a small consolation, perhaps, but this miscalculation would eventually be dwarfed by the company's catastrophic errors in judgment during the subprime housing bubble in the early years of the twenty-first century.
[64] Austan, Laura. Message to the author. 9 December 2010. Email.
[65] Jones, Randy. Message to the author. 29 July 2009. Email.
[66] Farrar, Janet. Message to the author. 9 November 2010. Email.
[67] Frank, Kathryn. Message to the author. 11 November 2010. Email.
[68] Austan, Laura. Message to the author. 19 February 2011. Austan was referring to Denning, Melita, and Osborne Phillips. *The Llewellyn Practical Guide to Psychic Self-Defense & Well-Being*. St. Paul: Llewellyn Publications. 1983.
[69] Austan, Laura. Message to the author. 30 November 2010. Email.
[70] Innervision Advertisement. Village Voice 29.1 (3 January 1984) 31. MCF. (Cols. Met. Lib).

[71] School of Mystical Sciences Advertisement. Village Voice 30.1 (1 January 1985) 36. MCF. (Cols. Met. Lib).
[72] Frank, Kathryn. Message to the author. 10 December 2010. Email.
[73] Austan, Laura. Message to the author. 9 December 2010. Email.
[74] "HIV/AIDS Facts & Statistics – Timeline of the Epidemic (1985)." *AIDS Project of Los Angeles*. Web (http://www.apla.org/facts/timeline.html#1985, accessed 6 November 2010).
[75] Henican, Ellis. "City Padlocks Gay Club, Warns Others in AIDS Drive." Newsday, Combined edition. (8 November 1985) 5. Web.
[76] Hillery, Mark. Telephone interview. 16 January 2006.
[77] Ridgway, Brunilde. Telephone interview. 4 August 2004.
[78] Green, Tamara. Message to the author. 17 March 2011. Email.
[79] Nascosto, Marie. Letter to the author. 27 December 2006. MS.

Notes for Chapter 31
[1] Lattimore, Richmond. "Impressions of Bryn Mawr." 1978. This was a poem read at the inauguration of Mary Patterson McPhearson as President of Bryn Mawr College.
[2] Labalme, Patricia (Ed.). *A Century Recalled: Essays in Honor of Bryn Mawr College*. Bryn Mawr: Bryn Mawr College Library. 1987. 49-50.
[3] Muto, Gene. Personal interview. 29 October 2004.
[4] Since Buczynski's day, the seven sisters have dwindled down to just four discrete and fully functional hold-outs: Smith, Wellesley, Mt. Holyoke and Bryn Mawr.
[5] Horowitz, Helen. *The Power and Passion of M. Carey Thomas*. Champaign: University of Illinois Press. 1999. 170-172.
[6] Moore, Julia. Message to the author. 2005. Email.
[7] Wieglosz, Ruth, "Competitive College" in Howard, Kim and Annie Stevens *Out & About Campus: Personal Accounts by Lesbian, Gay, Bisexual & Transgender College Students*. New York: Alyson Publications. 2000. 56.
[8] From *"A Spirit of Consensus," Bryn Mawr Alumnae Bulletin* (Winter 1998). Bryn Mawr College. Bryn Mawr, PA.
[9] Labalme. *A Century Recalled*. 1987. 117.
[10] Moore, Julia. Message to the author. 11 December 2004. Email.
[11] The Anassa Kata, also known as the Bryn Mawr College Cheer, from the Bryn Mawr College website.
[12] Pallas Athena, from the Bryn Mawr College website.
[13] Bessette, Alicia. *"Come and See: Religious diversity invites new ways of knowing to Bryn Mawr." Bryn Mawr Alumnae Bulletin* (Winter 2000) Np. Web.
[14] Horowitz. *The Power and Passion of M. Carey Thomas*. 1999. 84-85.
[15] President M. Cary Thomas made a point of emphasizing the Pagan origins of the May Day tradition in her 1915 May Day chapel address. From: (Ibid n#13).
[16] Wright, James. Personal interview. 6 November 2004.
[17] Sophos or *wise*.
[18] Athena's owl is a popular mascot for those of a historical bent. It's also present on the seal of the Archaeological Institute of America.
[19] One of Athena's epithets is "Glaukôpis" meaning with eyes like a glaux or owl. It is usually taken to mean owl-eyed, gray-eyed or blue-eyed.

[20] The Bryn Mawr College song *Sophias*. From the Bryn Mawr College website.
[21] Markson, Eileen. Message to the author. 12 January 2005. Email.
[22] Ridgway, Brunilde. Telephone interview. 4 August 2004.
[23] Labalme. *A Century Recalled.* 1987. 142.
[24] Labalme. *A Century Recalled.* 1987. 164.
[25] Labalme. *A Century Recalled.* 1987. 167.
[26] "Graduate Program in Archaeology." Bryn Mawr College Department of Classical and Near Eastern Archaeology. Web (www.brynmawr.edu/gradgroup/archaeology/).
[27] Archaeological Institute of America. Web (www.archaeological.org). Ms. Mellink held the post of president of the AIA from 1980-1984.
[28] "The Mellink Eras: Machteld J. Mellink and the timeline of Anatolian archaeology." *Bryn Mawr Alumnae Newsletter* (Winter 1998) Np. Web (http://www.brynmawr.edu/alumnae/bulletin/mellink.htm).
[29] Labalme. *A Century Recalled.* 1987. 172. Heinrich Schliemann, the famed excavator of the sites of ancient Troy and Mycenae, had passed away in 1890. Surprisingly, one of the more credulous passengers asked "Dr. Schliemann" when he would be returning to his interesting work at Troy.
[30] The "King Tut" exhibition drew an estimated 8 million viewers during its seven-city American run, and inspired a minor pop craze, from songs by Steve Martin and the Bangles to a renewed interest in Egyptian mythology in the Neo-Pagan community and a brisk business in imported decorative faux Pharaonic tchotchkes, that continues to this day.
[31] Tribble, Scott. "Raiders of the Lost Ark. St. James Encyclopedia of Popular Culture. Farmington Hills: Gale Group. 2000. Ironically enough, the Archaeological Institute of America (AIA) elected Harrison Ford, who portrayed the adventure-seeking Indiana Jones, to its board of directors in 2008. Source: "'Indy' gets elected to archaeological board." MSNBC: Associated Press (15 May 2008) Np. Web (http://www.msnbc.msn.com/id/24656327/, accessed 15 May 2008.)
[32] This phenomenon did not originate in the imaginations of Steven Spielberg or George Lucas. Michael Balter, in his book on the archaeology of Çatalhöyük, *The Goddess and the Bull* (15), points to a real, as opposed to fictional, archaeologist who inspired a comparative level of enthusiasm with a similar methodology — the aforementioned Heinrich Schliemann. Balter, Michael. *The Goddess and the Bull: Catalhoyuk: An Archaeological Journey to the Dawn of Civilization.* New York: Free Press. 2004. 15)
[33] Boam, Jeff (screenplay), George Lucas and Menno Meyjes (story). *Indiana Jones and the Last Crusade.* Los Angeles: Paramount Pictures. 1989.
[34] Webb, Pamela. Message to the author. 10 May 2004. Email.
[35] Hornum, Michael. Message to the author. 8 February 2005. Email.
[36] Özyar, Asli. Message to the author. 29 November 2004. Email.
[37] Kamrin, Janice. Message to the author. 6 November 2005. Email.
[38] Meyer, Nathan. Message to the author. 7 January 2007. Email.
[39] Donohue, Alice. Message to the author. 31 August 2004. Email.
[40] Younger, John. Message to the author. 22 October 2010. Email.
[41] An ardent supporter of the Lambda Classical Caucus (LCC), Paul Rehak died in 2004 due to complications from a heart attack and AIDS. He served as co-chair of the LCC with his partner John Younger from 1994-1998. The Rehak Award, named in Paul's memory, honors the excellence of a publication

relating to the LCC's mission, including, but not limited to, homosocial and homoerotic relationships and environments, ancient sexuality and gender roles, and representation of the gendered body. From: "Paul Rehak, 8 March 1954 – 5 June 2004." University of Kansas – John G. Younger. Web (http://www.people.ku.edu/~jyounger/prehak/, accessed 19 November 2010).

[42] Green, Tamara. Telephone interview. 28 April 2004. Email.
[43] Saretta, Phyllis. Message to the author. 1 September 2004. Email.
[44] Buczynski, Edmund. "The Practical, Artistic and Cultic Use of Marine Shells in Minoan Crete." Diss. Bryn Mawr College. September 1987.
[45] Moscrip, Kevin. Message to the author. 3 February 2004. Email.
[46] Agapemitera, Minos Xeiron. *The Book of Minos* (Boston MS). Boston: Unpublished MS. February 1996. 3. MS.
[47] Rivera, Ria. Telephone interview. 5 February 2004.
[48] Rivera, Ria. Telephone interview. 30 January 2004.

Notes for Chapter 32

[1] Muto, Gene. Personal interview. 29 October 2004.
[2] Hornum, Michael. Message to the author. 8 February 2005. Email.
[3] Moscrip, Kevin. Message to the author. 3 February 2004. Email.
[4] Meyer, Nathan. Message to the author. 7 January 2007. Email.
[5] Webb, Pamela. Message to the author. 10 May 2004. Email.
[6] The statue currently standing in Thomas Great Hall is a replacement of the one Eddie faced; the one from his day now quietly rests in a high stairwell niche in the Rhys Carpenter Library.
[7] McCourt, James. *Queer Street*. W.W. New York: Norton and Company. 2004. 436-438.
[8] Turner, Wallace. "AIDS Impact Wide in San Francisco." NYT (28 May 1985) Np. Web.
[9] Press, Bill. "Press: The sad legacy of Jerry Falwell." Milford Daily News (18 May 2007) Np. Web.
[10] (Ibid n#3). It wasn't until 1992 that Moscrip was able to locate another Minoan Brotherhood teacher, this time on the west coast, in order to continue his training.
[11] Helios. Message to the author. 4 April 2004. Email.
[12] Bulzone, Carol. Telephone interview. 2 November 2004.
[13] Geraci, Bennie. Message to the author. 22 January 2004. Email.
[14] Geraci, Bennie. Message to the author. 2 February 2007. Email.
[15] Bennie had started on AZT during the clinical trial prior to its FDA approval. "I had a fever (low grade) for over a year and that didn't start right off the get go when I was diagnosed," he recalled. The regimen for the Glaxo Wellcome drug (also known as zidovudine and Retrovir®) was demanding, with doses being required every four hours around the clock and without exception. The drug also caused nausea and had a pronounced toxicity that not every patient was able to tolerate, and it was very expensive (and even fewer patients were able to tolerate that side-effect than the toxicity). Nevertheless, AZT represented hope to people desperate for a treatment.
[16] Nascosto, Marie. Letter to the author. 27 December 2006. MS.
[17] Ridgway, Brunilde. Message to the author. 27 January 2005. Email.
[18] Wright, James. Personal interview. 6 November 2004.
[19] Gianniotis, Terry. Telephone interview. 16 October 2011.

²⁰ Nascosto, Marie. Telephone interview. 25 October 2011.
²¹ Ridgway, Brunilde. Telephone interview. 4 August 2004.
²² Buczynski, Frank. Telephone interview. 8 May 2008.
²³ Post, Leonard. "Law's True Art" in The National Law Journal. January 13, 2003.
²⁴ "The Mellink Eras: Machteld J. Mellink and the timeline of Anatolian archaeology." Bryn Mawr Alumnae Bulletin (Winter 1998) Np. Web (http://www.brynmawr.edu/Alumnae/bulletin/mellink.htm, accessed 8 November 2004).
²⁵ Ridgway, Brunilde. Message to the author. 28 January 2005. Email.
²⁶ Nascosto, Marie. Telephone interview. 27 October 2011.
²⁷ Markson, Eileen. Telephone interview. 23 April 2004.
²⁸ Özyar, Asli. Message to the author. 29 November 2004. Email.
²⁹ According to the toxo factsheet by the Gay Men's Health Crisis (www.gmhc.org), some of the symptoms of toxo can include one-sided weakness or numbness, difficulty walking and talking, and mood and personality changes. These symptoms will get worse and progress to paralysis, coma and death unless the infection is properly treated.
³⁰ The drugs used to combat the toxoplasma gondii organism, pyrimethamine and sulfadiazine, only act as suppressers. As they do not eliminate the infection, relapses after the treatment period are likely to occur in someone in Eddie's state. Eddie's December relapse is a case in point. The drugs themselves have serious side effects, such as bone marrow toxicity. Sulfadiazine can also cause rashes and fever. Cook, Nathaniel. "Toxoplasma gondii: Takes a licking and keeps on ticking." *Davidson College* (21 April 2000) Np. Web.
³¹ Green, Tamara. Personal interview. 28 April 2004.
³² Saretta Phyllis. Message to the author. 1 September 2004. Email.
³³ One was clearly a dud from Gene's perspective, and was removed within a week for performance issues. Source: Muto, Gene. Personal interview. 29 October 2004.
³⁴ O'Brien, Father John. Telephone interview. 21 January 2005.
³⁵ Of the type known as "congestive heart failure, symptomatic at rest."
³⁶ (Ibid n#1). It is unclear what the basis for denial would have been, given that the Long Island National Cemetery has a stated policy allowing for family members to be interred with their loved ones.
³⁷ "Certificate of Death, State File No. 009608." State of Georgia. 16 March 1989. By the end of 1989, a total of 27,408 deaths nationwide would be attributed to AIDS.
³⁸ The epitaph of renowned Cretan author Nikos Kazantzakis.

Notes for Chapter 33
¹ Muto, Gene. Personal interview. 29 October 2004.
² Gianniotis, Terry. Telephone interview. 16 October 2011.
³ Marie confirmed that she suffered from bouts of crying and refused to leave the house for weeks after learning of Eddie's death. Nascosto, Marie. Telephone interview. 30 January 2012.
⁴ Markson, Eileen. Telephone interview. 23 April 2004.
⁵ "Certificate of Death, State File No. 009608." State of Georgia. 16 March 1989.
⁶ Muto, Gene. Personal interview. 29 October 2004.

[7] Özyar, Asli. Message to the author. 29 November 2004. Email.
[8] Meyer, Nathan. Message to the author. 7 January 2007.
[9] Hornum, Michael. Message to the author. 8 February 2005. Email.
[10] Saretta, Phyllis. Message to the author. 1 September 2004. Email.
[11] Cheiron. Message to the author. 23 August 2004. Email.
[12] Slater, Herman. Obituary notice for Ed Buczynski. *Magickal New York*: Unpublished MS. March 1989? The Collections of Andrew Theitic and Alisha Engeleit.
[13] Markson, Eileen. Letter to Marie Nascosto. 17 July 1989. MS.
[14] Donohue, Alice. Message to the author. 31 August 2004. Email.
[15] Wyatt, Aubrey. "Minoan History Part 3." Message to the author. 11 December 2003. Email.
[16] Percy. *Pederasty and Pedagogy in Archaic Greece*. 39.
[17] Wright, James. Personal interview. 6 November 2004.
[18] Wright, James. "Empty Jugs and Empty Cups: The Social Role of Wine in Minoan and Mycenaean Societies." McGovern, Patrick (ed.), et al. *Origins and Ancient History of Wine (Food and Nutrition in History and Anthropology)*. Abington: Routledge. 2000. 307.
[19] Geraci, Bennie. Telephone interview. 20 January 2004.
[20] Austan, Laura. Message to the author. 7 November 2010. Email.
[21] Slater. *Pagan Rituals III*. 1989. 9-14.
[22] Austan, Laura. Message to the author. 5 November 2010. Email.
[23] Pratt, Roger. Message to the author. 17 June 2010. Email.
[24] Levenda, Peter. Message to the author. 29 August 2005. Email.
[25] North, Erika [Judith McNally]. Message to the author. 29 November 2005. Email.
[26] Austan, Laura. Message to the author. 8 November 2010. Email.
[27] Soror Charis. "Herman Slater 'Thee Magickal Childe'" (Part II). *Behutet* 11 (Autumn 2001) 4-15. Print.
[28] "News & Notes: Herman Slater Dies." *Magical Link* 6.1 (Spring 1992) 1. Print. (Arch. Circ. Sanc).
[29] Rivera, Ria. Telephone interview. 13 June 2010.
[30] Austan, Laura. Message to the author. 9 December 2010. Email.
[31] Frank, Kathryn. Message to the author. 11 December 2010. Email.
[32] Conte, Peter. Message to the author. 31 May 2011. Email.
[33] Soror Charis. "Herman Slater: 'Thee Magickal Childe'" (Part II). *Behutet* 11 (Autumn 2001) 15. Print.
[34] Ickes, Bob. "Books & Paper: Occult Books." New York 25.19 (11 May 1992) 67. Web (http://books.google.com/books?id=4eQCAAAAMBAJ&lpg =PA67&dq, accessed 23 May 2011).
[35] Caigan, Khem. Telephone interview. 3 April 2006.
[36] The Witches Pyramid illustrates the philosophy behind working magick, beginning with 'To Know," progressing through 'To Will' and 'To Dare,' and ending with 'To Keep Silent.' As with so many things in life, magickal aptitude is generally equated to be inversely proportional to the claimant's gum-flapping prowess.
[37] North, Erika [Judith McNally]. Message to the author. 30 November 2005. Email.
[38] Lord Starhawk. Posting on "Herman Slater." Magickal Childe. Web (http://www.magickalchilde.com/herman.html, accessed 10/10/2011).

[39] Lee, Sander H. *Eighteen Woody Allen Films Analyzed: Anguish, God, and Existentialism.* Jefferson: McFarland & Company, Inc. 2002. 137.
[40] Frank, Kathryn. Message to the author. 12 November 2010. Email.
[41] Eaton, Sally. Message to the author. 14 December 2010. Email.
[42] Eaton, Sally. Message to the author. 23 January 2008. Email.
[43] Post, Leonard. "Law's True Art." *National Law Journal* (13 January 2003) Np. Web
[44] "The Mellink Eras: Machteld J. Mellink and the timeline of Anatolian archaeology." *Bryn Mawr Alumnae Bulletin* (Winter 1998) Np. Web (http://www.brynmawr.edu/Alumnae/bulletin/mellink.htm, accessed 8 November 2004).
[45] Vermeule, Emily. "Archaeology and Philology: The Dirt and the Word." American Philological Association Presidential Address. 1995. Web (http://www.apaclassics.org/Publications/PresTalks/VERMEULE.html)
[46] Forster, E.M. *Maurice.* W.W. Norton & Co. 2005. P. 211.
[47] Melton, J. Gordon. "Toward a History of Magical Religion in the United States." *Green Egg* 8.73 (September 1975) 33. Print. (Coll. A.Terr.).
[48] Adler. *Drawing Down the Moon.* 1986. 311.
[49] Gottlieb, Annie. *Do You Believe in Magic?* New York: Times Books. 1987. 194.
[50] Buczynski. *The Witchcraft Fact Book.* 1984. 21.
[51] Buczynski, Edmund. "Edmund Michael Buczynski" (autobiographical paper). New York: Unpublished MS. 28 September 1974. MS. Edmund Buczynski File. Church of the Eternal Source Archives.MS.
[52] Paxson, Diana. "A Letter from Diana L. Paxson." Bradley, Marion Zimmer. *The Mists of Avalon.* New York: Knopf. 1982. 883.
[53] Theitic, Andrew. Message to the author. 4 February 2007. Email.
[54] Flagg (Smith), Kay. Message to the author. 18 October 2004. Email.
[55] Silverknife, Zanoni. Message to the author. 13 July 2004. Email.
[56] North, Erika [Judith McNally]. Message to the author. 3 December 2005. Email.
[57] Rivera, Ria. Telephone interview. 28 November 2010. Email.
[58] Carey, Robert. Message to the author. 23 April 2007. Email.
[59] Klein, Kenny. Message to author. 10 April 2006. Email.
[60] "The Most Influential Cities." *National Geographic.* December 2011. 24-26. Print.
[61] Geraci, Bennie. Message to the author. 15 June 2010. Email.
[62] Margot Adler notes that her own covens during that period were not sustaining her intellectually, and this was her driving motivation to search out others of like mind in the Pagan community via such organs as *Green Egg* and Nemeton Newsletter. Adler, Margot. Message to the author. 11 May 2011. Email.
[63] (Ibid n#17). The monograph in question (Marinatos, Nanno. *Minoan Religion: Ritual, Image, and Symbol [Studies in Comparative Religion].* Columbia: University of South Carolina Press. 1993.) is on the Minoan Brotherhood recommended reading list.
[64] Adler, Margot. Personal interview. 30 October 2004.
[65] Sargent, Denny. Message to the author. 25 February 2007. Email.
[66] Baldwin, H. Bruce. Message to the author. 5 September 2005. Email.

67. Kenton Neidel, as reported on June 19, 1999. Neidel would himself pass from the disease less than four years after writing these words.
68. Unattributed [Buczynski, Edmund]. "The Minoan Brotherhood" (Booklet and Questionnaire) Middle Village: Self-published January 1977? MS.
69. Certain rites within Crowleyian ceremonial magick would also be considered unsafe, including unprotected heterosexual sex magick, the homosexual initiation into the XI° O.T.O. (i.e., per aftera ad astra), and the ritual consumption of bodily fluids (i.e., menstrual blood and semen) between working partners. Like the Wiccans, the majority of ceremonial magickians were heterosexual. However, a not insignificant number of members within this magickal community in New York City were also heroin users. IV drug use was later identified as a transmission vector for HIV due to the sharing of needles.
70. It should be noted that this was not universally true. In Introduction to Witchcraft (1987), Herman Slater criticized the Neo-Pagan festival circuit, and Wiccans in particular, for promoting an atmosphere of unsafe promiscuity that had the very real potential to spread AIDS within the heterosexual population of the Neo-Pagan community. *An Introduction to Witchcraft & Satanism.* Herman Slater (Producer). New York: Magickal Childe. 2007. VHS.
71. "Gay Doctors Recommend Steps for Blood Donation, 'Healthful' Sex." The Advocate (Issue 366). April 28, 1983. Print.
72. Caldiero, Joe. Message to the author. 8 February 2010. Email.
73. Jamison, Artie. Telephone interview. 24 January 2004.
74. Wyatt, Aubrey. "Minoan History, Part 1." Message to the author. 11 December 2003. Email.
75. "Obituaries – KENTON H. NEIDEL." Albuquerque Journal North (20 April 2003) Np. Web.
76. Enright, Nancy (SW CARE Center). Telephone interview. 11 November 2010.
77. Dalton, Ken. Message to the author. 30 January 2012. Email.
78. Buczynski. *The Witchcraft Fact Book.* 1974. 23.
79. Calasso, Robert. The Marriage of Cadmus and Harmony. New York: Knopf. 1993. 21.
80. The motto of Eddie Buczynski's Traditionalist Gwyddoniaid.

Bibliography

Aaronovitch, Ben. *Moon Over Soho*. New York: DelRey. 2011.

Adam, Barry. *The Rise of a Gay and Lesbian Movement*. Boston: Twayne Publishers. 1987.

Adler, Margot. Drawing Down the Moon: Witches, Druids, Goddess-Worshippers, and Other Pagans in America Today. Boston: Beacon Press. 1979, 1986.

---. New York: Penguin. 2006.

Allyn, David. *Make Love, Not War*. Little, Brown and Company. 2000.

Anderson, Victor. *Thorns of the Blood Rose*. San Leandro: Privately Published. 1980.

Ankarloo, Bengt (ed.) *Witchcraft and Magic in Europe: The Twentieth Century*. Philadelphia: University of Pennsylvania Press. 1999.

Ankarloo, Bengt and Stuart Clark. *Witchcraft and Magic in Europe: Ancient Greece and Rome*. Philadelphia: University of Pennsylvania Press. 1999.

Asbury, Herbert. The French Quarter: An Informal History of the New Orleans Underworld. New York: Thunder's Mouth Press. 2003.

Aquino, Michael. *The Church of Satan* (5th Edition). San Francisco, CA. 2002.

Bagemihl, Bruce. Biological Exuberance: Animal Homosexuality and Natural Diversity. New York: St. Martin's Press. 1999.

Balter, Michael. *The Goddess and the Bull*. New York: Free Press. 2005.

Banes, Sally. Greenwich Village 1963: *Avant-Garde Performance and the Effervescent Body*. Durham: Duke University Press. 1993.

Lady Sheba [Bell, Jessica Wicker]. *The Book of Shadows*. Minneapolis: Llewelyn Publications. 2006 (1971).

---. *The Grimoire of Lady Sheba*. Minneapolis: Llewellyn Publications. 1972.

Bessette, Alicia. *"Come and See: Religious diversity invites new ways of knowing to Bryn Mawr" Bryn Mawr Alumnae Bulletin* (Winter 2000). Bryn Mawr College.

Blanchard, Mary. *Oscar Wilde's America: Counterculture in the Gilded Age*. New Haven: Yale University Press. 1998.

Blincoe, Deborah and John Forrest (Editors). *Prejudice and Pride: Lesbian and Gay Traditions in America*. New York: New York Folklore Society. 1993.

Bockris, Victor and Gerard Malanga. *Up-Tight: The Velvet Underground Story*. New York: Omnibus Press. 1983.

Bockris, Victor. *Warhol: The Biography*. New York: De Capo Press. 2003.

Bottom, Stephen J. Playing Underground: A Critical History of the 1960s Off-Off-Broadway Movement. Ann Arbor: University of Michigan Press. 2004.

Bowman, Marion. "Reinventing the Celts", *Religion* 23, 1993.

"A Spirit of Consensus." Bryn Mawr Alumnae Bulletin (Winter 1998). Bryn Mawr College.

"The Mellink Eras." *Bryn Mawr Alumnae Bulletin* (Winter 1998). Bryn Mawr College.

"Commencement: The One Hundred and Third Academic Year." Bryn Mawr College. May 15, 1988.

Buckland, Raymond. *Ancient & Modern Witchcraft*. Secaucus: Castle Books. 1970.

---. Autobiography Manuscript (untitled). 2010.

---. *Witchcraft from the Inside*. Minneapolis: Llewellyn Publications. 1971.

—, 1995.

---. *Witchcraft...The Religion*. New York: The Buckland Museum of Witchcraft & Magick. 1966.

---. *The Weiser Field Guide to Ghosts*. San Francisco: Red Wheel/Weiser. 2009.

---. The Witch Book: The Encyclopedia of Witchcraft, Wicca, and Neo-Paganism. Visible Ink Press. 2002.

Buczynski, Edmund [Unattributed]. *Bales and Apies*. The Huntington Coven, Huntington, NY. ca. 1976.

---. [as *Gwydion*, et al]. *Book of Shadows* (unpublished manuscript). New York Coven of Witches (the Wica). Forest Hills, NY. Ca. 1973-74.

---. [as *Hermes Dionysus*]. *The Cauldron* (Celtic Traditionalist Witchcraft Book of Shadows). North Haven, CT/Brooklyn Heights, NY. Ca. 1972.

---. [Unattributed]. *The Children of Rhea (The Minoan Brotherhood)* (unpublished manuscript). Knossos Grove, Middle Village, NY. 1976.

---. [as "Un-nefer, Priest of Isis"]. "Esbat" 1.1. *Earth Religion News* 1.5. (August Eve 1974).

---. [as *Gwydion*]. *Friends of the Craft: The Welsh Tradition Lecture* (Cassette Tape). New York: Magickal Childe Publishing, Inc. (originally Earth Religions Supplies). 1972.

---. *Volume One: Liber Ubrarum* [sic] *— The Book of Shadows with Commentary* (Unpublished Paper). New York: Hunter College. December 1983.

---. [Unattributed]. *The Minoan Brotherhood* (Booklet and Questionnaire). Middle Village: Knossos Grove. 1977.

---. [as *Gwydion*]. *The Minoan Brotherhood Book of Shadows* (unpublished manuscript). Middle Village: Knossos Grove. 1977.

---. [as *Gwydion*]. *The New York Coven of Witches* (explanation for interested seekers). Brooklyn Heights. ca. 1974.

---. *The Practical, Artistic and Cultic Use of Marine Shells in Minoan Crete*. Masters Thesis in Archaeology (Thesis Committee Copy). Bryn Mawr: Bryn Mawr College. September 1987.

---. "Summer Session 1982: Going Forward, Looking Back — A Personal View." *American School of Classical Studies at Athens Newsletter* (Fall 1982). Athens: ASCSA. 1982.

---. *The Witchcraft Fact Book* (No. 2 in the 'Museum Handbook Series'). Brooklyn: Earth Religious Supplies, Inc. 1974.

---. *The Witchcraft Fact Book*. New York: Magickal Childe. 1984.

---. "Witchcraft Today and the Homosexual." *GaysWeek* 17 (13 June 1977) 10-11.

---. [Unattributed]. *Why Would a Gay Man Worship a Goddess?* Middle Village: Knossos Grove. 1977.

Budge, E.A. Wallis. *From Fetish to God in Ancient Egypt*. Oxford: Oxford University Press. 1934.

Bull, Chris and John Gallagher. *Perfect Enemies*. New York: Crown Publishers. 1996.

Cabal, Alan. "The Doom that came to Chelsea." *New York Press* 16.23 (6/4/2003 – 6/10/2003).

Calasso, Robert. *The Marriage of Cadmus and Harmony*. New York: New York: Vintage. 1994.

Cameron, Pat. *Blue Guide: Crete* (7th Ed.). London: A & C Black Publishers. 2003.

Campbell, J. Louis. *Jack Nichols, Gay Pioneer*. New York: Routledge. 2006.

Capeci, Jerry. *Gotti: Rise and Fall*. New York: Onyx Books. 1996.

Carter, David. *Stonewall: The Riots That Sparked the Gay Revolution*. New York: St. Martin's Press. 2004.

Carter, John. Sex and Rockets: The Occult World of Jack Parsons. Los Angeles: Feral House. 2004.

Case, George. *Jimmy Page: Magus, Musician, Man*. New York: Hal Leonard Books. 2007.

Chappell, Vere. Sexual Outlaw, Erotic Mystic: The Essential Ida Craddock. San Francisco: Weiser. 2010.

Chappell, Vere (ed.). *Lunar and Sex Worship*. York Beach: Teitan Press. 2011.

Charters, Ann (Ed.). *The Portable Sixties Reader*. New York: Penguin Books. 2003.

Chauncey, George. Gay New York: Gender, Urban Culture, and the Making of the Gay Male World, 1890-1940. New York: Basic Books. 1995.

Clarke, Lige and Jack Nichols. *I Have More Fun with You Than Anybody*. New York: St. Martin's Press. 1972.

---. Roommates Can't Always Be Lovers: An Intimate Guide to Male-Male Relationships. New York: St. Martin's Press. 1974.

Clifton, Charles. Her Hidden Children: The Rise of Wicca and Paganism in America. Lanham: AltaMira Press. 2006.

Colton, Charles Caleb. Lacon, Or Many Things In Few Words, addressed to those who think. Volume I (No. 183) 1820.

Conner, Randy. Blossom of Bone: Reclaiming the Connections Between Homoeroticism and the Sacred. New York: Harper Collins. 1993.

---; David Sparks; Mariya Sparks. Cassell's Encyclopedia of Queer Myth, Symbol and Spirit: Gay, Lesbian, Bisexual and Transgender Lore. London: Cassell & Co. 1998.

Cook, Nathaniel. "*Toxoplasma gondii*: Takes a licking and keeps on ticking." Charlotte: Davidson College. April 21, 2000.

Cooney, John. The American Pope: The Life and Times of Francis Cardinal Spellman. New York: Times Books. 1984.

Cooper, Sherod. *Liberty Ship*. Annapolis: Naval Institute Press. 1997.

Crespy, David and Edward Albee. Off-Off-Broadway Explosion: How Provocative Playwrights of the 1960's Ignited a New American Theatre. New York: Back Stage Books. 2003.

Crowley, Aleister. *The Book of the Law: sub figura Liber AL vel Legis*. New York: Samuel Weiser, Inc. 1987.

---. *White Stains*. London: Duckworth. 1993.

---; Evangeline Adams. *The General Principles of Astrology*. York Beach: Red Wheel/Weiser. 2002

---; Louis Wilkinson and Hymenaeus Beta (eds.). *The Law is for All: The Authorized Popular Commentary to The Book of the Law*. Tempe: New Falcon Publications. 1998.

Crowther, Patricia and Arnold Crowther. *The Secrets of Ancient Witchcraft with the Witches Tarot*. Secaucus: University Books, Inc. 1974.

---. *The Witches Speak*. New York: Samuel Weiser, Inc. 1976.

Cuhulain, Kerr. *Witch Hunts: Out of the Broom Closet*. Casper: Spiral Publishing. 2005.

Cunliffe, Barry. *The Extraordinary Voyage of Pytheas the Greek*. New York: Penguin Books. 2002.

Daly, Mary. Beyond God the Father: Toward a Philosophy of Women's Liberation. Boston: Beacon Press. 1973.

D'Arch Smith, Timothy. The Books of the Beast: Essays on Aleister Crowley, Mantague Summers, Francis Barrett and Others. Lancaster: Crucible. 1987.

de Camp, L. Sprague and Abdul Alhazed. *Al Azif: The Necronomicon*. Philadelphia: Owlswick Press. 1973.

Diner, Helen (Bertha Eckstein-Diener). *Mothers and Amazons*. New York: Julian Press. 1965.

Dochuk, Darren. From Bible Belt to Sun Belt: Plain-Folk Religion, Grassroots Politics, and the Rise of Evangelical Conservatism. New York: W.W. Norton & Co. 2011.

Dover, Kenneth J. *Greek Homosexuality*. New Haven: Harvard University Press. 1977.

Ehrenstein, David. *Open Secret*. New York: William Morrow and Company. 1998.

Eisenbach, David. *Gay Power: An American Revolution*. New York: Carroll & Graf Publishers. 2006.

Eliade, Mircea. *Occultism, Witchcraft and Cultural Fashions.* Chicago: University of Chicago Press. 1978.

Eller, Cynthia. *Living in the Lap of the Goddess.* Boston: Beacon Press. 2005.

Ellwood, Robert. The Fifties Spiritual Marketplace: American Religion in a Decade of Conflict. New Brunswick: Rutgers University Press. 1997.

---. The Sixties Spiritual Awakening: American Religion Moving from Modern to Postmodern. New Brunswick: Rutgers University Press. 1994.

Endlich, Lisa. *Goldman Sachs: The Culture of Success.* New York: Simon & Schuster. 2000.

Evans, Arthur. *Witchcraft and the Gay Counterculture.* Boston: Fag Rag Books. 1978.

Ficino, Marsilio. *Meditations on the Soul, Selected Letters of Marsilio Ficino.* Rochester: Inner Traditions International. 1997.

Fitch, Ed. *A Grimoire of Shadows: Witchcraft, Paganism & Magick.* St. Paul: Llewellyn Publications. 1998.

Flacelière, Robert. *L'Amour en Grèce.* Paris: Librairie Hachette. 1960.

Forster, E.M. *Maurice.* New York: W.W. Norton & Co. 2005.

Fortune, Dion. *The Cosmic Doctrine.* Chetenham: Helios Book Service, United Kingdom. 1966.

---. *Sane Occultism.* New York: Weiser Books. 1973.

Foldy, Michael. The Trials of Oscar Wilde: Deviance, Morality, and Late-Victorian Society. New Haven: Yale University Press. 1997.

Fraser, Hilary. "Victorian poetry and historicism." *The Cambridge Companion to Victorian Poetry,* ed. J. Bristow. Cambridge: Cambridge University Press. 2006.

Fritscher, Jack. *Popular Witchcraft: Straight from the Witch's Mouth.* Secaucus: Lyle Stuart. 1973 (Madison: University of Wisconsin Press. 2004).

Frost, Gavin. *The Witch's Bible* (since renamed *Good Witch's Bible*). Los Angeles: Nash Publishing. 1972.

Fuller, Jean. *The Magical Dilemma of Victor Neuburg.* South Cockerington: Mandrake. 1990.

Gardiner, James. Who's the Pretty Boy Then?: One Hundred & Fifty Years of Gay Life in Pictures. London: Serpent's Tail. 1998.

Gardner, Gerald. *Witchcraft Today.* Newport Pagnell: Mercury (Restivo Enterprises). 1999.

Gawr, Rhuddlwm. *The Cauldron: Celtic Mythology and Witchcraft.* Smyrna: Camelot Press, Ltd. 1989.

---. The Way: The Discovery of the Grail of Immortality. Smyrna: Camelot Press, Ltd. 1985.

Gere, Cathy. *Knossos & the Prophets of Modernism.* Chicago: University of Chicago Press. 2009.

Gimbutas, Marija. The Gods and Goddesses of Old Europe 7000 to 3500 BC: Myths, Legends and Cult Images. London: Thames and Hudson. 1974.

GMHC Fact Sheet: Toxoplasmosis (Toxo). Gay Men's Health Crisis (www.gmhc.org), New York, NY. 2003.

Glass, Justine. *Witchcraft: The Sixth Sense*. London: Neville Spearman. 1965.

Gleichauf, Justin F. *Unsung Sailors: The Naval Armed Guard in World War II*. Annapolis: Naval Institute Press. 1990.

Goodman, Mitchell (ed.). *The Movement Toward a New America*. New York: Alfred A. Knopf. 1972.

Goodrich-Clarke, Nicholas. Black Sun: Aryan Cults, Esoteric Nazism, and the Politics of Identity. New York: NYU Press. 2003.

Gordon, Mel. Voluptuous Panic: The Erotic World of Weimar Berlin. Los Angeles: Feral House. 2006.

Gottlieb, Annie. *Do You Believe in Magic?* New York: Times Books. 1987.

Grandjouan, Clairève (completed by Eileen Markson and Susan Rotroff). *Hellenistic Relief Molds from the Athenian Agora* (*Hesperia*: Supplement XXIII). Princeton: American School of Classical Studies at Athens. 1989.

Grant, Kenneth. *Aleister Crowley: The Hidden God*. New York: Samuel Weiser. 1974.

---. *Nightside of Eden*. London: Skoob Books. 1995.

Graves, Robert. *The Golden Fleece and Watch the North Wind Rise*. Manchester: Carcanet Press. 2004.

Greenberg, Dan. Something's There: My Adventures in the Occult. New York: DoubleDay. 1976.

Haining, Peter. *The Anatomy of Witchcraft*. New York: Taplinger Publishing Company. 1972.

Hark, Ann. *Hex Marks the Spot*. New York: J. B. Lippincott Company. 1938.

Harms, Daniel; John Gonce III. *The Necronomincon Files*. Boston: Weiser Books. 2003.

Harney, Scott. *Esoteric Guide to New York*. New York: Esoteric Guides. 2003.

Harvey, Graham. *Contemporary Paganism: Listening People, Speaking Earth*. New York: New York University Press. 1997.

Heflin, Llee (777). The Island Dialogues: Liber Alal – Live Loving, Living Love, Light, A Book from Darkness. San Francisco: Level Press. 1973.

Henican, Ellis. "City Padlocks Gay Club, Warns Others in AIDS Drive" in *New York Newsday* (Combined editions). Long Island, NY, Nov 8, 1985.

Herman, Ellen and Martin Duberman (ed.). *Psychiatry, Psychology, and Homosexuality*. New York: Chelsea House Publishers. 1995.

Hershman, Florence. *Witchcraft USA*. Peacock Press. 1971.

Heselton, Philip. Gerald Gardner and the Cauldron of Inspiration: An Investigation into the Sources of Gardnerian Witchcraft. Milverton: Capall Bann Publishing. 2003.

Heselton, Philip. Wiccan Roots: Gerald Gardner and the Modern Witchcraft Revival. Milverton: Capall Bann Publishing. 2001.

Heselton, Philip. Witchfather: A Life of Gerald Gardner. (Volume 2: From Witch-Cult to Wicca). Loughborough: Thoth Publications, 2012.

Hodges, Andrew. *Alan Turing: The Enigma.* New York: Walker & Company. 2000.

Holzer, Hans. *The Directory of the OCCULT.* Chicago: Henry Regnery. 1974.

---. *The New Pagans.* Garden City: Doubleday. 1972.

---. *The Truth About Witchcraft.* Garden City: Doubleday. 1971.

---. Witches: True Encounters with Wicca, Wizards, Covens, Cults, and Magick. New York: Black Dog & Leventhal Publishers. 2002.

---. *The Witchcraft Report.* New York: Ace Books. 1973.

Horowitz, Helen. *The Power and Passion of M. Carey Thomas.* Champaign: University of Illinois Press. 1999.

Horowitz, Mitch. Occult America: White House Séances, Ouija Circles, Masons, and the Secret, Mystic History of Our Nation. New York: Bantam Books. 2009.

Howard, Kim; Annie Stevens. Out & About Campus: Personal Accounts by Lesbian, Gay, Bisexual & Transgender College Students. New York: Alyson Publications. 2000.

Huebner, Louise. *Power Through Witchcraft.* New York: Nash Publishing Corp. 1969.

Huson, Paul. Mastering Witchcraft: A Practical Guide for Witches, Warlocks and Covens. New York: G.P. Putnam's Sons. NY. 1970.

Hutton, Ronald. The Triumph of the Moon: A History of Modern Pagan Witchcraft. Oxford: Oxford University Press. 1999.

Inominandum [Miller, Jason]. "Simon Speaks: Part I." *Behutet* 16 (Winter 2002-2003) Philadelphia: O.T.O Thelesis Camp.

---. "Simon Speaks: Part II." *Behutet* 17 (Spring 2003) Philadelphia: O.T.O Thelesis Camp.

Jefferson, Thomas and Adrienne Koch and William Peden (eds). *The Life and Selected Writings of Thomas Jefferson.* New York: Modern Library Classics. 1998.

Jenkins, Phillip. Mystics and Messiahs: Cults and New Religions in American History. Oxford: Oxford University Press. 2001.

Johns, June. King of the Witches: The World of Alex Sanders. London: Peter Davies. 1969.

Jones, Leslie Ellen. *From Witch to Wicca.* Cold Spring Harbor: Cold Spring Press. 2004.

Joshi, S.; David Schultz (eds). *H.P. Lovecraft, Letters from New York.* San Francisco: Night Shade Books. 2005.

Joshi, S.T. *H.P. Lovecraft: The Decline of the West.* Mercer Island: Starmont House. 1990.

Jung, C.G. *Flying Saucers.* New York: MJF Books. 1978.

Kaiser, Charles. *The Gay Metropolis: 1940-1996.* New York: Houghton Mifflin Company. 1997.

Keith, W. Holman. *Divinity as the Eternal Feminine.* New York: Pageant Press. 1960.

Kelly, Aidan. *Crafting the Art of Magic, Book I: A History of Modern Witchcraft, 1939-1964* (Llewellyn's Modern Witchcraft Series). St. Paul: Llewellyn Publications. 1991.

---. Hippie Commie Beatnik Witches: A Social History of the New Reformed Orthodox Order of the Golden Dawn. Tacoma: Hierophant Wordsmith Press. 2011.

---. Inventing Witchcraft: A Case Study in the Creation of a New Religion. Loughborough: Thoth Publications. 2007.

King, Francis. Megatherion: The Magickal World of Aleister Crowley. England: Creation Books. 2004.

Kirwan, Larry. *Green Suede Shoes: An Irish-American Odyssey.* New York: Thunder's Mouth Press. 2005.

Kirwan, Larry (Black 47). *Elvis Murphy's Green Suede Shoes* (CD). Gadfly. 2005.

Koehl, Robert. "The Chieftain Cup and a Minoan 'Rite of Passage'." *Journal of Hellenic Studies* 106 (1986) 99-110.

---. "Ephoros and Ritualized Homosexuality in Bronze Age Crete." *Queer Representations: Reading Lives, Reading Cultures,* ed. M. Duberman (New York, 1997).

Koestenbaum, Wayne. *Andy Warhol: A Penguin Life.* New York: Viking Books. 2001.

Labalme, Patricia (Ed.). *A Century Recalled: Essays in Honor of Bryn Mawr College.* Bryn Mawr: Bryn Mawr College Library. 1987.

Lachman, Gary. Turn Off Your Mind: The Mystic Sixties and the Dark Side of the Age of Aquarius. New York: The Disinformation Company. 2003.

Lamond, Frederic. *Fifty Years Of Wicca.* Sutton Mallet: Green Magic. 2005.

Lauritsen, John; David Thorstad. *The Early Homosexual Rights Movement (1864-1935).* New York: Times Change Press. 1974.

---. Religious Roots of the Taboo on Homosexuality: A materialist view. New York: Self-published. 1974.

---. *A Freethinker's Primer of Male Love.* East Haven: Inland Book Company. 1994.

LaVey, Anton Szandor. *The Satanic Bible.* New York: Avon Books. 1976.

Leadbeater, Charles. W. *Glimpses of Masonic History.* New York: Gramercy. 1998.

Leek, Sybil. *The Complete Art of Witchcraft.* New York: World Publishing Company. 1971.

---. *Diary of a Witch.* Englewood Cliffs: Prentice-Hall. 1968.

Levenda, Peter. Sinister Forces: A Grimoire of American Political Witchcraft (Book Two). Oregon: TrineDay. 2007.

Loovis, David. *Gay Spirit: A Guide to Becoming a Sensuous Homosexual.* New York: Strawberry Hill Publishing. 1974.

Loughery, John. The Other Side of Silence — Men's Lives and Gay Identities: A Twentieth-Century History. New York: Owl Books. 1998.

Love, Robert. The Great Oom: The Improbable Birth of Yoga in America. New York: Viking Press. 2010.

Lovecraft, H. P., Anthony Raven, and Stephen Fabian. *The Occult Lovecraft.* Saddle River: Gerry de la Ree. 1975.

Luck, Georg. *Arcana Mundi: Magic and the Occult in the Greek and Roman Worlds.* Baltimore: The Johns Hopkins University Press. 1985.

Luhrmann, T. M. Persuasions of the Witch's Craft: Ritual Magic in Contemporary England. Cambridge: Harvard University Press. 1989.

MacGillivray, J. Alexander. Minotaur: Sir Arthur Evans and the Archaeology of the Minoan Myth. London: Jonathon Cape. 2000.

Mahler, Jonathon. *Ladies and Gentlemen, the Bronx Is Burning.* New York: Picador. 2006.

Mann, Horace. *Thoughts: Selected from the Writings of Horace Mann.* Boston: H.B. Fuller and Company. 1867.

Margolis, Jon. *The Last Innocent Year: America in 1964.* New York: William Morrow and Company. 1999.

Marinatos, Nanno. *Minoan Religion: Ritual, Image, and Symbol.* Columbia: University of South Carolina Press. 1993.

Martello, Leo. *Black Magick, Satanism & Voodoo.* Secaucus: Castle Books, Inc. 1973.

---. How to Prevent Psychic Blackmail: The Philosophy of Psychoselfism. New York: Hero Press. 1966.

---. *It's Written in the Stars.* New York: Key Publishing Company. 1966.

---. *It's Written in the Cards.* New York: Key Publishing Company 1964.

---. *Hidden World of Hypnotism.* New York: HC Publishers, Inc. (Allograph). 1969.

---. *Weird Ways of Witchcraft.* Secaucus: Castle Books. 1969.

---. *What it Means to Be a Witch.* New York: Privately Published. ca. 1973.

---. *Witchcraft: The Old Religion.* New York: University Books. 1973.

---. *Your Pen Personality.* New York: Hero Press. 1961.

Mathiesen, Robert and Theitic. The Rede of the Wiccae: Adriana Porter, Gwen Thompson and the Birth of a Tradition of Witchcraft. Providence: Olympian Press. 2005.

McCourt, James. *Queer Street: The Rise and Fall of an American Culture, 1947-1985.* New York: W.W. Norton & Company. 2003.

McCourt, Malachy. *A Monk Swimming: A Memoir*. New York: Hyperion. 1999.

Mee, Christopher and Antony Spawforth. *Oxford Archaeological Guides: Greece*. Oxford: Oxford University Press. 2001.

Miller, Merle. On Being Different: What it means to be a homosexual. New York: Random House. 1971.

Minos Xeiron Agapemitera. *The Book of Minos* (Boston Manuscript). Temenos Asterfaede, Boston, MA. February 1, 1996.

Moore, Patrick. Beyond Shame: Reclaiming the History of Radical Gay Sexuality. Boston: Beacon Press. 2004.

Morrison, Sarah. *The Modern Witch's Spellbook*. New York: David McKay Company. 1971.

Newton, Esther. Cherry Grove, Fire Island: Sixty Years in America's First Gay and Lesbian Town. Boston: Beacon Press. 1993.

Owen, Alex. The Place of Enchantment: British Occultism and the Culture of the Modern. Chicago: The University of Chicago Press. 2004.

Ozone-Howard Chamber of Commerce: http://www.queenschamber.org/QueensInfo/NeighborhoodPages/ozonepark.html)

"Ozone Park: They Were `Yearning to Breathe Free'" in *New York Newsday* (http://www.newsday.com/extras/lihistory/spectown/hist0010w.htm)

Partridge, William. *The Hippie Ghetto: The Natural History of a Subculture* (Case Studies in Cultural Anthropology). New York: Holt, Rinehart and Winston, Inc. 1973.

Pauwel, Louis and Jacques Bergier. *The Morning of the Magicians*. New York: Stein and Day. 1960.

Peck, Abe. Uncovering the Sixties: The Life and Times of the Underground. New York: Citadel Press. 1991.

Percy, William A. *Pederasty and Pedagogy in Archaic Greece*. Chicago: University of Illinois Press. 1996.

Polsky, Ned. *Hustlers, Beats and Others*. New York: Anchor Books. 1969.

Power, Lisa. No Bath but Plenty of Bubbles: An Oral History of the Gay Liberation Front 1970-1973. New York: Cassell. 1995.

Rabinovitch, Shelly (editor). *The Encyclopedia of Modern Witchcraft and Neo-Paganism*. New York: Kensington Books. 2003.

Rachleff, Owen S. *The Occult Conceit*. New York: Bell Publishing Company. 1971.

Ravenwolf, Silver. *To Ride a Silver Broomstick*. St. Paul: Llewellyn Publications. 2000.

Rhea, Lady. *The Enchanted Candle*. New York: Citadel Press. 2004.

Rhodes, Jacqueline. *Radical Feminism, Writing, and Critical Agency: From Manifesto to Modern* (SUNY Series in Feminist Criticism and Theory). New York: State University of New York Press. 2005.

Roberts, Susan. *Witches USA*. New York: Dell Publishing. 1971.

---. *Witches USA*. Hollywood: Phoenix House. 1974.

Rose, Elliot. *A Razor for a Goat*. Toronto: University of Toronto Press. 1989.

Rottensteiner, Franz. "Lovecraft as Philosopher." *Science Fiction Studies #56* 19.1 (March 1992) Greencastle: SF-TH Inc. at DePauw University.

Sanders, Ed. Fug You: An Informal History of the Peace Eye Bookstore, the Fuck You Press, the Fugs, and Counterculture in the Lower East Side. New York: Da Capo Press. 2011.

Schurmacher, Emile. *Witchcraft in America Today*. New York: Paperback Library. 1970.

Sears, James. Behind the Mask of the Mattachine: The Hal Call Chronicles and the Early Movement for Homosexual Emancipation. New York: Harrington Park Press. 2006.

Sears, James. Rebels, Rubyfruit, and Rhinestones: Queering Space in the Stonewall South. New Brunswick: Rutgers University Press. 2001.

Seyfried, Vincent. *The Story of Woodhaven and Ozone Park* (Queens Community Series). Flushing: Queens Historical Society. 1991.

Shaman, Diana. "If You're Thinking of Living In Ozone Park; Changing Faces, Enduring Values." *New York Times* (October 5, 2003).

Shapiro, Peter. Turn the Beat Around: The Secret History of Disco. London: Faber & Faber. 2005.

Shilts, Randy. And the Band Played On: Politics, People and the AIDS Epidemic. New York: St. Martins Press. 1987.

---. Conduct Unbecoming: Gays and Lesbians in the United States Military. New York: St. Martin's Press. 1997.

Shual, Katon. *Sexual Magick*. Oxford: Mandrake. 1989.

Signorile, Michelangelo. "Cardinal Spellman's Dark Legacy." *New York Press* 19.9 (March 1-7, 2006).

Simon. Dead Names: The Dark History of the Necronomicon. New York: Avon Books. 2006.

---. *The Gates of the Necronomicon*. New York: Avon Books. 2006.

---. *Necronomicon*. New York: Avon Books. 1980.

---. *The Necronomicon Report*. New York: Magickal Childe Publishing. 1981, 1987.

---. *The Necronomicon Spellbook*. New York: Avon Books. 1998.

Silverstein, Charles and Felice Picano. The Joy of Gay Sex: an Intimate Guide for Gay Men to the Pleasures of a Gay Lifestyle. Avenel: Outlet. 1977.

Sismondo, Christine. America Walks into a Bar: A Spirited History of Taverns and Saloons, Speakeasies and Grog Shops. New York: Oxford University Press. 2011.

Slater, Herman. *An Introduction to Witchcraft* (VHS Tape). New York: Magickal Childe Publishing, Inc. 1987.

Unattributed [Herman Slater (Ed.)]. *Book of Pagan Rituals* (Friends of the Craft-Version Vol. I). Brooklyn: Earth Religious Supplies. 1974. [The authorship of this work is in dispute.]

--- (Ed.). *A Book of Rituals (Advanced)*. Brooklyn: Earth Religious Supplies. 1975. [The authorship of this work is in dispute.]

--- (Ed.). *A Book of Pagan Rituals*. York Beach: Samuel Weiser, Inc. 1978.

--- (Ed.). *The Magickal Formulary*. New York: Magickal Childe Publishing, Inc. 1981.

--- (Ed.). *The Magickal Formulary Spellbook — Book II*. www.magickalchilde.com. 2004.

--- (Ed.) and Edmund M. Buczynski (unattributed author). *Pagan Rituals III: Outer Court Training Coven*. New York: Magickal Childe Publishing, Inc. 1989.

---[as *Hephaestos*]; Edmund Buczynski [as *Hermes*]. *The Warlock Shop/Earth Religions Supplies Catalogue*. Brooklyn Heights: Earth Religious Supplies. January 1973.

Smith, Patti. *Just Kids*. New York: Harper Collins. 2010.

Smith, Susy. *Today's Witches*. Englewood Cliffs: Prentice-Hall. 1970.

Smyth, Frank. *Modern Witchcraft*. New York: Harrow Books. 1973.

Solanas, Valerie. *SCUM Manifesto*. New York: Self-Published. 1967. [Latest edition: AK Press, San Francisco, CA. 1996.]

Soror Charis. "Herman Slater 'Thee Magickal Childe' (Part 1)" *Behutet* 10 (Summer Solstice 2001) Philadelphia: O.T.O Thelesis Camp.

---. "Herman Slater 'Thee Magickal Childe' (Part 2)." *Behutet* 11 (Autumn Equinox 2001). Philadelphia: O.T.O Thelesis Camp.

Stephensen, P.R. and Israel Regardie. *The Legend of Aleister Crowley*. St. Paul: Llewellyn Publications. 1970.

Stone, Merlin. *When God Was a Woman*. New York: Dorset Press. 1976.

Teal, Donn. The Gay Militants: How Gay Liberation Began in America, 1969-1971. New York: St. Martin's Press. 1995.

Thompson, Mark. Leatherfolk: Radical Sex, People, Politics and Practice. New York: Alyson Books. 2001.

Thompson, Mark. Long Road to Freedom: The Advocate History of the Gay and Lesbian Movement. New York: St. Martin's Press. 1994.

Tolkien, J.R.R. *The Lord of the Rings*. New York: Houghton Mifflin. 2004.

Tribble, Scott. "Raiders of the Lost Ark" entry in *St. James Encyclopedia of Popular Culture*. Farmington Hills: Gale Group. 2000.

Tweed, Thomas (Editor). *Retelling United States Religious History*. Berkeley: University of California Press. 1997.

Urban, Hugh. "Unleashing the Beast: Aleister Crowley, Tantra and Sex Magic in Late Victorian England." *Esoterica* V (2003) East Lansing: Michigan State University Press.

Valiente, Doreen. *The Rebirth of Witchcraft.* Blaine: Phoenix Publishing, WA. 1989.

Vermeule, Emily. "Archaeology and Philology: The Dirt and the Word." American Philological Association Presidential Address 1995. APA Website (www.apaclassics.org/Publications/PresTalks/VERMEULE.html)

von Cles-Reden, Sibylle. *The Realm of the Great Goddess.* Schauberg: Verlag M. Dumont. 1960.

Walker, Mitch. *Men Loving Men.* San Francisco: The Gay Sunshine Press. 1977.

Wallace, C.H. *Witchcraft in the World Today.* New York: Award Books. 1967.

Ware, Caroline. *Greenwich Village 1920-1930.* New York: Harper Colophon Books. 1965.

Warhol, Andy and Pat Hackett. *POPism: The Warhol '60s.* New York: Harper Colophon Books. 1983.

Watson, Stephen. *The Birth of the Beat Generation.* New York: Pantheon Books. 1995.

Welty, Eudora. "The Petrified Man" in *A Curtain of Green and other stories.* Harvest Books. 1979.

White, Edmund. *City Boy.* New York: Bloomsbury. 2009.

Wildman, Laura (Ed.). *Celebrating the Pagan Soul.* New York: Citadel Press. 2005

Willetts, R.F. *Everyday Life in Ancient Crete.* New York: Putnam. 1969.

Willetts, R. F. Ancient Crete: A Social History from Early Times Until the Roman Occupation. London: Routledge and Kegan Paul. 1965.

---. "The World of Homer." *Our History.* London: History Group of the Communist Party. 1964.

Wilson, Colin. *Aleister Crowley: The Nature of the Beast.* London: Aeon Books. 2005

Wilson, Robert Anton. *Coincidance: A Head Test.* Tempe: New Falcon Publications. 1991.

Wittman, Carl. *Refugees from Amerika: A Gay Manifesto.* San Francisco: Red Butterfly Collective. 1970.

Woods, William and Diane Binson. *Gay Bathhouses and Public Health Policy.* New York: Harrington Park Press. 2003.

Wright, James. "Empty Jugs and Empty Cups: The Social Role of Wine in Minoan and Mycenaean Societies." *Origins and Ancient History of Wine* (Food and Nutrition in History and Anthropology). McGovern, Patrick (Editor). London: Routledge. 2000.

Photo Credits

Figure 0. Title Page. Photographer: Margot Adler. Courtesy of the photographer.

Figure 1. Page 102. Photographer: unknown. Courtesy of the Buczynski/Nascosto family.

Figure 2. Page 102. Photograph attributed to Herman Slater. From the collection of Kay Flagg.

Figure 3. Page 102. Photographer: Sardi Klein. Art: George Arthur. Courtesy of Pat Garrard (*Capitalist Reporter*). From the collection of Alisha Engeleit.

Figure 4. Page 102. Photographer: Jean-Pierre Laffont. Courtesy of the photographer.

Figure 5. Page 103. Photographer: Jean-Pierre Laffont. Courtesy of the photographer.

Figure 6. Page 103. Photographer: Jean-Pierre Laffont. Courtesy of the photographer.

Figure 7. Page 104. Photographer: Jean-Pierre Laffont. Courtesy of the photographer.

Figure 8. Page 104. Photograph attributed to Herman Slater. From the collection of Kay Flagg.

Figure 9. Page 105. Photograph attributed to Herman Slater. From the collection of Karen Bartlett.

Figure 10. Page 105. Photograph attributed to Herman Slater. From the collection of Kay Flagg.

Figure 11. Page 105. Still from the film *Fangoria Scream Greats Volume 2: Satanism and Witchcraft*. 1986. Courtesy of *Fangoria* magazine.

Figure 12. Page 105. Still from the film *The Occult Experience* (1985). Courtesy of Cinetel Productions.

Figure 13. Page 106. From the author's collection.

Figure 14. Page 106. Photographer: Llewellyn Worldwide. Courtesy of Llewellyn Worldwide. From the collection of Harold Moss.

Figure 15. Page 107. From the author's collection.

Figure 16. Page 107. Photographer: Jean-Pierre Laffont. Courtesy of the photographer.

Figure 17. Page 341. Photographer: Bennie Geraci. Courtesy of the photographer.

Figure 18. Page 341. Photographer: Flaming Pablum (http://vassifer.blogs.com). Courtesy of the photographer.

Figure 19 Page 342. Photographer: Laura Austan. Courtesy of the photographer.

Figure 20. Page 342. Still from the film *Fangoria Scream Greats Volume 2: Satanism and Witchcraft* (1986). Courtesy of *Fangoria* magazine.

Figure 21. Page 342. Photographer: Laura Austan. Courtesy of the photographer and Derek & Lisa Harrison.

Figure 22. Page 343. Laura Austan. Courtesy of the photographer.

Figure 23. Page 343. Photographer: Sally Eaton. Courtesy of the photographer.

Figure 24. Page 343. Photographer: Laura Austan. Courtesy of the photographer.

Figure 25. Page 343. Photographer: Colleen Quinn. Courtesy of the photographer and Sala One Nine.

Figure 26. Page 344. From the author's collection.

Figure 27. Page 344. Photographer: unknown. From the collection of Bennie Geraci.

Figure 28. Page 344. Photographer: Bennie Geraci. Courtesy of the photographer.

Figure 29. Page 345. From the author's collection.

Figure 30. Page 345. Photo attributed to Ria Farnham. From the collection of Carol Bulzone.

Figure 31. Page 345. Still from the film *The Occult Experience* (1985). Courtesy of Cinetel Productions.

Figure 32. Page 345. Still from the film *The Occult Experience* (1985). Courtesy of Cinetel Productions.

Figure 33. Page 471. Photographer: Gene Muto. From the collection of the Buczynski/Nascosto family.

Figure 34. Page 471. Photographer: Bennie Geraci. Courtesy of the photographer.

Figure 35. Page 471. Photographer: H. Bruce Baldwin. Courtesy of the photographer.

Figure 36. Page 472. Photographer: unknown. From the collection of Carol Bulzone.

Figure 37. Page 472. Photographer: Michael Lloyd. Courtesy of the author.

Figure 38. Page 473. Photographer: Allan Tannenbaum (www.sohoblues.com). Courtesy of the photographer.

Figure 39. Page 473. Photographer: unknown. From the collection of Lena Hatzichronoglou.

Figure 40. Page 474. Photographer: unknown. From the collection of Carol Bulzone.

Figure 41. Page 474. Marie Nascosto. Courtesy of the photographer.

Figure 42. Page 475. Marie Nascosto. Courtesy of the photographer.

Figure 43. Page 475. Photographer: Michael Lloyd. Courtesy of the author.

Figure 44. Page 476. From the author's collection.

Figure 45. Page 476. Attributed to Herman Slater. From the collection of Andrew Theitic.

Figure 46. Page 476. Courtesy of Eileen Markson and Bryn Mawr College.

Publications of Earth Religions Supplies and Magickal Childe Publishing

Bertiaux, Michael. *The Voudon Gnostic Workbook.* New York: Magickal Childe Publishing, Inc. 1988.

Buczynski, Edmund M. *Witchcraft Fact Book* (No. 2 in the 'Museum Handbook Series'). Brooklyn: Earth Religions Supplies. 1974. Pamphlet.

---. *Witchcraft Fact Book.* New York: Magickal Childe Publishing, Inc. 1976-1984. Pamphlet.

---. *Witchcraft Fact Book.* New York: Magickal Childe Publishing, Inc. 1984.

Casaubon, Meric. A True & Faithful Relation of What passed for many Yeers Between Dr. John Dee (A Mathematician of Great Fame in Q. Elizabeth and King James their Reignes) and Some Spirits. New York: Magickal Childe Publishing, Inc. 1992.

Conte, Peter and Herman Slater (Eds.). *The Hoodoo Bible: The Complete Compendium of Southern Folk Magic.* New York: Magickal Childe Publishing, Inc. 1997. [This title was released five years after Slater's death and no more than a few copies were ever printed.]

Crowley, Aleister. *The Book of the Goetia of Solomon the King.* New York: Magickal Childe Publishing, Inc. 1989.

---. *The Book of the Law: sub figura Liber AL vel Legis.* New York: Ordo Templi Orientis and Magickal Childe Publishing, Inc. 1990.

---. *Magick in Theory and Practice.* New York: Magickal Childe Publishing, Inc. 1990, 1991.

---. *Rites of Eleusis: As Performed at Caxton Hall.* New York: Magickal Childe Publishing, Inc. 1990.

---. *White Stains.* Earth Religions Supplies, Brooklyn Heights, NY. 1974.

Earth Religion News (Vol. 1, No. 1). Brooklyn: Earth Religions Supplies. December 1973.

Earth Religion News (Vol. 1, No. 2). Brooklyn: Earth Religions Supplies. February 1974.

Earth Religion News (Vol. 1, No. 3). Brooklyn: Earth Religions Supplies. March 1974.

Earth Religion News (Vol. 1, No. 4). Brooklyn: Earth Religions Supplies. June 1974.

Earth Religion News (Vol. 1, No. 5). Brooklyn: Earth Religions Supplies. August 1974.

Earth Religion News (Vol. 1, No. 6-8 combined). Brooklyn: Earth Religions Supplies. (October 1976?).

Farrar, Janet and Stewart A. *A Witches Bible Compleat.* New York: Magickal Childe Publishing, Inc. 1987, 1991, 1995.

---. Witches Bible, Volume I: The Sabbats and Rites for Birth, Marriage and Death. New York: Magickal Childe Publishing, Inc. 1984.

---. *Witches Bible, Volume II: The Rituals.* New York: Magickal Childe Publishing, Inc. 1984.

---. *Witches Bible, Volumes I and II* (Boxed Set). New York: Magickal Childe Publishing, Inc. 1984.

Gardner, Gerald B. *The Meaning of Witchcraft.* New York: Magickal Childe Publishing, Inc. 1982, 1988, 1991.

---. *Witchcraft Today.* New York: Magickal Childe Publishing, Inc. 1980, 1982, 1988, 1989.

Gawr, Rhuddlwm. *1980 Pagan, Occult, New Age Directory.* New York: Magickal Childe Publishing, Inc. 1980.

Lady Sara. *The Book of Light.* Brooklyn: Earth Religions Supplies. 1974.

Levender [Levenda, Peter], [Herman] Slater, Goulavitch. *Books of Runes & Magickal Alphabets & Cypher.* Brooklyn: Earth Religions Supplies. 1975.

White Witch Doctor [Mills, Malcolm]. *The Use of Voodoo Potions & Herbs.* New York: Magickal Childe Publishing, Inc.

---. *Voodoo Love Secrets.* New York: Magickal Childe Publishing, Inc. 1980.

Nordic, Rolla. *The Tarot Shows the Path.* New York: Magickal Childe Publishing, Inc. 1990.

Randolph, Pascal Beverly. *Sexual Magic.* New York: Magickal Childe Publishing, Inc. 1988.

Sanders, Alex. *The Alex Sanders Lectures.* New York: Magickal Childe Publishing, Inc.. 1984.

Savage, Adrian. *An Introduction to Chaos Magick.* New York: Magickal Childe Publishing, Inc. 1988, 1989.

Simon. *Necronomicon Report.* New York: Magickal Childe Publishing, Inc. 1981.

---. *Necronomicon Spellbook* (formerly *Necronomicon Report*). New York: Magickal Childe Publishing, Inc. 1987, 1988.

---. *Red Dragon: Le Dragon Rouge* (Magickal Manuscript Series). New York: Magickal Childe Publishing, Inc. 1992.

Slater, Herman. *Introduction to Witchcraft: A Political and Spiritual Discourse* (VHS Tape). New York: Magickal Childe Publishing, Inc. 1988.

--- (Ed.). *The Magickal Formulary.* New York: Magickal Childe Publishing, Inc. 1981.

--- (Ed.). *Magickal Formulary Spellbook, Book I.* New York: Magickal Childe Publishing, Inc. 1981, 1987.

--- (Ed.). *Magickal Formulary Spellbook, Book II.* New York: Magickal Childe Publishing, Inc. 1987.

Unattributed [Herman Slater (Ed.)]. *Book of Pagan Rituals* (Friends of the Craft-Version Vol. I). Brooklyn: Earth Religious Supplies. 1974. [The authorship of this work is in dispute.]

--- (Ed.). *A Book of Rituals (Advanced)* [Vol. II]. Brooklyn: Earth Religious Supplies. 1975. [The authorship of this work is in dispute.]

--- (Ed.) *Pagan Rituals I and II* (combined). Brooklyn: Earth Religious Supplies. 1974.

--- (Ed.) *Pagan Rituals III: Outer Court Training Coven.* New York: Magickal Childe Publishing, Inc. 1989.

Index

Abington Township School District v. Schempp, 36
Abrahadabra (catalog), 344, 357, 429, 431, 433, 452, 453, 464, 657
Achilles, 547
Acropolis, 489, 490, 494, 495, 509, 512
Adams, Frederick, 20, 59, 295, 384, 386
Adler, Margot, x, 105, 141, 155, 156, 158, 159, 162, 163, 164, 167, 200, 211, 235, 238, 242, 243, 244, 248, 256, 261, 361, 363, 411, 421, 452, 468, 555, 559, 566, 603, 605, 607, 617, 618, 620, 623, 629, 633, 667
Adler, Martha, 139, 197, 301, 302, 315, 318, 636
Aesthetic Movement, 16, 181
Alexander the Great, 493
Allen, Woody, 364, 553, 667
Alpha et Omega, 16, 182, 576
Altman, Billy, 359
American Academy in Rome, 515
American Hypnotism Academy, 65
American Psychiatric Association (APA), 185, 201, 388
American Psychological Association, 201
An Introduction to Chaos Magick (book), 434, 654
Ancient and Modern Witchcraft (book), 209
Anderson, Victor, 20, 60, 191, 578, 588
Angeli Blanca, Angeli Negro (film), 221
Anger, Kenneth, 48, 67, 221, 370, 449, 584
Angerona (Goddess), 153
Ansonia Hotel, 51, 66, 88, 585
Apollo (God), 398, 400, 462, 463, 493
Aquarian Anti-Defamation League (AADL), 231, 232, 246, 247, 326, 622, 625
Aquarian Arrow (newsletter), 196
Aquino, Michael, 206, 230, 232, 597, 616, 621, 622, 628
Araujo, Gwen, 183
Archaeological Institute of America (AIA), 479, 662, 663
Archaeology, v, vi, viii, 3, 387, 392, 400, 427, 468, 469, 470, 479, 480, 496, 506, 512, 514, 515, 516, 522, 514-23, 532, 534, 537, 555, 556, 557, 558, 565, 566, 663, 665, 667
Art and Archaeology Library, 521
Arthur, Gavin, 205, 616

Association of Cymmry Wicca, 252
Assumption College, 64
Astrology, 52, 110, 577
Astrum Argentum (A\A\), 445
Athanor Fellowship, 252
Athena, Pallas (Goddess), 325, 436, 470, 475, 479, 488, 493, 511, 512, 528, 662
Athenian Agora, 488, 490, 492, 494, 497, 660
Athens, Greece, 188, 479, 486, 487, 488, 489, 490, 492, 493, 494, 495, 660
Augusta State University, 537, 555
Austan, Laura, 51, 52, 66, 88, 358, 365, 501, 502, 549, 550, 551, 585, 589, 593, 642, 643, 661, 662, 666
Baal Sathanas, 269
Babalon, 17
Bachofen, Johann J., 385
Bailey, Alice, 43
Baldwin, H. Bruce, 482, 483, 567, 659, 667
Balsiger, Dave, 225
Banes, Sally, 42, 583
Bangs, Lester, 359
Barnes Graphics, 429
Barnes, Larry, 428, 429, 430, 431, 432, 433, 578
Barnum, P.T., 355
Barrett, Ronald, 110, 206, 610, 616
Bartlett, Karen, 99, 146, 300, 304, 305, 348, 596, 604, 634, 635, 640
Bath houses. *See* Gay bars and bath houses
Bayly, Joseph, 40, 582
Beatles, The, 12
Beatnik, 26, 28
Beats, 27, 28, 29, 30, 32, 41, 42, 368
Beckley, Timothy Green, 56, 250, 587, 599
Behutet (magazine), 184, 450, 575, 587, 593, 594, 597, 598, 599, 607, 610, 618, 623, 625, 630, 637, 641, 642, 654, 656, 657, 661, 666
Bell, Arthur, 75, 76, 77, 370, 410, 412, 591, 645, 651
Bell, Book and Candle (play, movie), 24, 26
Bell, Jessica Wicker. *See* Lady Sheba
Bell, Lawrence D., 572
Bells of Hell (club), 251, 359, 432, 452, 458, 468
Bennu Phoenix Temple, 185, 610

Bergier, Jacques, 47, 584
Berkowitz, David (Son of Sam), 410
Bewitched (television), 26, 39
Beyond (magazine), 58, 291, 348
Beyond God the Father (book), 385, 647
Bierman, Robert, 363, 642
Birnbaum, Jerry, 352, 426, 433
Birth control, iv, 34, 581
Birth of Tragedy, The (book), 384, 461, 462
Black Arts, The (book), 57
Black list, 282, 336
Black magic, 135, 191, 192, 199, 207, 223, 266, 352, 609
Black Magic, Satanism and Voodoo (book), 250
Black Panthers, 37, 76
Blavatsky, Madame, 16, 41, 316, 612
Blondie (band), 363
Blue Equinox (book), 445, 450
Blue Star Wica, 165
Bone, Eleanor, 14, 22, 173, 228, 331
Bonewits, Isaac, 56, 192, 205, 224, 232, 246, 274, 275, 326, 554, 586, 612, 616, 620, 622, 623, 625, 629, 637, 638
Book of Chains (book), 391
Book of Shadows, ix, 15, 94, 96, 122, 125, 126, 129, 130, 132, 133, 134, 136, 137, 138, 140, 157, 159, 160, 162, 164, 166, 177, 189, 190, 197, 214, 219, 278, 279, 280, 281, 282, 289, 292, 293, 294, 298, 332, 333, 336, 337, 379, 392, 402, 411, 418, 419, 438, 500, 595, 600, 602, 609, 611, 633, 638, 639, 650, 655
Book of Shadows, The (book), 137, 290, 571, 603, 613
Book of the Law (book), 120, 451, 642, 644, 656
Botanica, 19, 109, 530
Bourne, Lois, 161, 173, 190, 207, 575, 606, 611, 646
Bowers, Roy (Robert Cochran), 21
Boy-love, 184, 189
Boys in the Band, The (play/film), 70, 76, 202, 591
Bracelin, Jack, 190
Bradley, Marion Zimmer, 561, 667
Breeze, William *(Hymenaeus Beta)*, 451, 454, 455
Briggs, John, 414
British Heroin Program, 284
Britt, Harry, 528
Broadway, 24, 48, 52, 70, 76, 224, 354, 363
Brodkin, Cindy, 355, 357, 452
Brodsky, Allyn, 361
Bronx Coven, 340
Bronx, New York, 4, 19, 62, 100, 101, 109, 116, 139, 284, 316, 326, 327, 340, 354, 415, 530, 553, 571, 572, 659
Bronze Age Aegean, 393
Brooklyn Heights Coven, 155, 165, 170, 216, 217, 277, 608
Brooklyn Heights, Brooklyn, 6, 89, 91, 102, 104, 105, 110, 111, 119, 123, 128, 129, 135, 139, 141, 155, 158, 167, 170, 179, 212, 216, 217, 229, 265, 275, 277, 284, 300, 306, 315, 316, 326, 328, 346, 348, 351, 352, 353, 354, 361, 364, 420, 423, 435, 502, 565, 595, 597, 600, 601, 605, 606, 608, 621, 631, 632, 633, 635, 639, 655
Brooklyn Pagan Way, ix, 139, 156, 167
Brooklyn, New York, 1, 3, 18, 19, 52, 62, 87, 107, 119, 133, 139, 148, 153, 156, 165, 170, 219, 235, 285, 296, 330, 333, 349, 354, 356, 405, 415, 423, 574, 577, 582, 594, 597, 598, 599, 604, 623, 631, 652, 656
Brothers of the Sacred Heart, 8
Brubaker, Ginny, 270
Bruce, Lenny, 254
Brujo, 154
Bryant, Anita, 412, 413, 414, 421, 651
Bryn Mawr College, 475, 479, 503–24, 506, 520, 537, 545, 549, 555, 565, 659, 662, 663, 664
Bryn Mawr Hospital, 531, 536, 537, 538
Bryn Mawr, Pennsylvania, 475, 479, 506, 514, 662
Buckland, Raymond *(Robat)*, v, 12–15, 21, 22, 26, 50, 54, 56, 60, 61, 63, 66, 108, 116, 120, 130, 135, 136, 137, 145, 151, 152, 159, 169, 171, 172, 173, 174, 177, 179, 199, 202, 207, 209, 212, 213, 221, 227, 229, 232, 233, 234, 237, 279, 281, 283, 291, 328, 330, 334, 363, 398, 422, 554, 575, 586, 588, 602, 603, 607, 608, 617, 618, 621, 624
  break with Commack Coven, 172, 177, 178, 213
  Brentwood Coven, 150, 151, 152, 171, 173, 175, 207, 330
  Buckland Museum of Witchcraft and Magick, 22, 54, 60, 178, 287, 609
Buckland, Rosemary *(Rowen)*, v, 12, 120, 150, 156, 168, 171, 172, 173, 175, 177, 179, 211, 212, 575, 605, 607, 618
Buckley, William F., 30, 503, 580
Buczynski, Edmund Sr.

marriage to Marie Mauro, 2
Buczynski, Edmund, Jr.
  AIDS and, 502, 528, 534, 538, 540, 545, 664
  as Gwydion, 128, 129, 280, 332, 333, 381, 407, 418, 600, 604, 608, 630, 631, 633, 638, 639, 646, 650, 655
  as Gwydion-Hyakinthos, 418
  as Hermes, vii, 95, 98, 128, 165, 563, 595, 597, 601, 607, 623, 652
  as Un-Nefer, 300
  ASCSA summer session, 489, 496, 547
  Bryn Mawr College admission, 475, 503, 504, 517
  Catholicism and, vi, 6, 8, 508, 529, 558, 561
  founding of the Minoan Brotherhood, 393, 404, 383-408, 411, 650
  founding of the Traditionalist Gwyddoniaid, 128, 130, 140, 159, 160, 163
  founding of The Wica, 279, 280, 282, 283, 336, 377, 553, 571, 630, 631, 651
  graduation from Bryn Mawr College, 475
  graduation from Hunter College, 474, 516
  Hunter College admission, 469, 474
  Huntington Coven and, 329, 331, 333, 334, 336, 337, 339, 340, 378, 379, 381, 383, 398, 415, 638, 639, 646
  John Adams H. S., 9, 11
  Monsignor McClancy Mem. H. S., 8
  natal horoscope, 1
  suicide attempts, 10, 560
  Witchcraft Fact Book, 287, 476, 499, 524, 549, 560, 632, 661, 667, 668
Buczynski, Frank, 8, 10, 458, 460
Budapest, Zsuzsanna, 181, 190, 196, 199, 200, 249, 323, 324, 325, 326, 351, 385, 406, 464, 637, 647
Budge, E.A. Wallis, 300, 635
Bull from the Sea, The (book), 392, 393, 461
Bulzone, Carol *(Miw-Sekhmet)*, 92, 326, 340, 341, 351, 417, 459, 474, 482, 499, 529, 546, 554, 594, 599, 637, 652, 657, 661, 664
Burning Times, 97, 193, 235, 246, 570, 595
Burroughs, William S., 25, 363, 431, 434
Butyrin, Svetlana, 386, 647
Butz, Earl, 581

Cabal, Alan, 356, 360, 361, 364, 365, 451, 452, 453, 498, 597, 640, 643, 653, 654, 656, 661
Cabalists, 239
Cabot, Laurie, 326, 327, 361
Caffe Cino, 48
Cage, John, 43
Caigan, Khem, 166, 275, 292, 400, 418, 430, 431, 432, 438, 607, 618, 630, 631, 633, 643, 648, 649, 652, 653, 654, 666
Caldiero, Joe, x, 71, 72, 73, 75, 93, 113, 304, 569, 590, 594, 597, 635, 668
Callasso, Robert, 401
Cameroon, Africa, 484, 660
Campbell, Joseph, vi, 30, 589, 590
Cardell, Charles (Rex Nemorensis), 219, 619
Carey, Martin, 67, 589
Carey, Robert, 110, 114, 120, 129, 145, 146, 147, 148, 227, 233, 234, 244, 301, 563
Carpenter, Edward (gay activist), 183, 391, 613
Carpenter, Rhys (archaeologist), 513, 514, 517, 518, 521, 546, 555, 664
Carson, Rachel, 37, 366
Carter, Henry, 293, 294, 576
Casbah (Hudson River docks), 371, 372
Case, Paul Foster, 17, 281, 577
Cassals, Ferran, 281, 631
Castaneda, Carlos, 51
Castro, The, 370, 519
Cauldron, The (book), 94, 96, 99, 100, 122, 124, 125, 126, 127, 134, 159, 290, 291, 292, 293, 294, 334, 595, 596, 600, 601, 633, 634
Celtic Traditionalist Witchcraft, 94, 132, 291
Central Park, New York, 31, 45, 63, 79, 80, 81, 82, 87, 147, 154, 167, 309, 310, 369, 371, 411, 510, 592, 636
Ceremonial Magick, 67, 166, 183, 185, 186, 191, 348, 352, 428, 432, 559, 654
Cerullo, Morris, 225, 620
Chaos Magick, 434
Chase Bank, 315
Cheetah (club), 250
Chelsea, Manhattan, 251, 312, 341, 346, 347, 349, 353, 354, 361, 370, 452, 458, 464, 597, 614, 640, 643, 653, 654, 656, 661
Cherry Grove, Fire Island, 171, 310, 311, 312, 608
Chicago Temple of the Pagan Way, 142, 270, 275

Chicago, Illinois, 16, 20, 37, 60, 84, 100, 109, 139, 142, 249, 270, 275, 352, 448, 571, 576, 581, 582, 585, 610, 625, 646, 649
Chieco, Eddie *(Fenris)*, 146, 148, 149
Children of Branwen, 105, 145, 146, 147, 148, 165, 305, 361, 551, 563, 566
Christian Science Monitor (newspaper), 224, 620
Christopher Street (magazine), 370
Christopher Street Gay Liberation Day, 79
Chubb, Ralph, 183
Church of All Worlds (CAW), 20, 60, 79, 187, 196, 228, 234, 236, 243, 245, 249, 252, 254, 255, 256, 257, 272, 274, 293, 390, 393, 587, 588, 592, 596, 597, 598, 599, 605, 612, 613, 627, 628
Church of Aphrodite, 20, 578
Church of Satan (CoS), 48, 60, 110, 116, 205, 206, 221, 230, 232, 266, 353, 597, 616, 621, 622, 635
Church of the Eternal Source (C.E.S.), ix, 20, 187, 188, 252, 295-304, 317, 562, 574, 634, 667
Church of Wicca, 259, 262, 265, 268, 269
Cicciotto, Burt, 270, 296, 297, 317, 322, 634
Cicciotto, Jane *(Coreatha)*, 270, 277, 283, 284, 285, 296, 299, 317, 630, 631, 634
Circle Network News (magazine), 236
Circle Sanctuary, 197, 236, 252, 468, 571, 576
Claremont, Chris, 361, 467
Clark, Tom, 36
Clarke, Elijah, 68, 69, 70, 75, 76, 77, 78, 79, 80, 85, 86, 161, 181, 374, 409, 589, 592, 593, 611, 641, 645, 650
Classical and Near Eastern Archaeology, 504, 514, 516, 520, 533, 545, 547, 555, 565, 663
Cloven Hoof (newsletter), 206, 232
Cochran, Connor, 361
Cohn, Roy, 38
Cold War, 4, 57, 158, 246, 248
Colla, Lia, 431
Come Out! (newspaper), 75, 368, 590, 644
Commack Coven, 155, 166, 167, 172, 177, 178, 180, 213, 215
Communism, 29, 38
Complete Art of Witchcraft (book), 208, 575, 586, 605, 616, 619, 624
Complete Witch, The (book), 221
Coney Island Hospital, 1
Conte, Peter, 213, 343, 351, 362, 551, 552, 617, 643, 666

Continental Witchcraft, 87
Copernicus (performer), 361
Cosmic Doctrine, The (book), 182, 610
Council of American Witches (COAW), 258, 273, 274
  Principles of Wiccan Belief, 273, 274, 276, 629
Council of Earth Religions (COER), 256, 257, 258, 259, 262, 272, 296, 627, 628
Council of Themis, 245, 252, 253, 255, 256, 257, 258, 263
Counterculture
  anti-war movement, iv, 30, 37, 38, 59, 67, 71, 248, 581, 582
Coven of Kyarliad, 165
Craddock, Ida, 42, 583
Crete, Greece, viii, 383, 384, 385, 386, 387, 392, 393, 394, 395, 398, 399, 401, 402, 462, 468, 469, 480, 490, 492, 493, 494, 497, 515, 522, 547, 587, 646, 647, 649, 661
Crisp, Quentin, 276, 449
Critchley, Steven, 168, 204, 607, 615
Crowley, Aleister, 3, 16, 17, 27, 32, 41, 42, 43, 44, 47, 48, 49, 50, 56, 90, 120, 132, 148, 179, 183, 184, 185, 186, 187, 190, 200, 286, 316, 355, 360, 367, 375, 376, 418, 428, 429, 431, 435, 442-54, 455, 465, 576, 577, 586, 598, 610, 632, 642, 644, 653, 655, 656
  Abbey of Thelema, 17
Crowley, Vivienne, 164, 234
Crowther, Arnold, 168, 588, 606, 607, 609, 618
Crowther, Patricia, 14, 168, 172, 176, 204, 215, 588, 606, 607, 609, 618
Crystal Well (newsletter), 138, 236
Culling, Louis T., 444, 656
Cult of Rhea/Cult of the Double Axe, 464
Cunningham, Sara, 264, 295, 299
Cupolo, Joey *(Osric/Ozrik)*, 312, 337, 338, 339, 340, 341, 347, 354, 358, 363, 371, 372, 373, 377, 380, 381, 382, 399, 403, 408, 415, 416, 417, 419, 438, 466, 555, 580, 600, 639, 641, 645, 646, 647, 649, 650, 651, 652, 654, 658
Curott, Phyllis, 420, 571
Cybele (Goddess), 188, 189, 194
Dafydd, Gwilym, 166, 276, 397, 466, 483, 596, 600, 607, 630, 649, 658, 659
Dalton, Ken, 91, 113, 117, 139, 305, 306, 313, 321, 328, 329, 330, 333, 346, 349, 350, 357, 364, 378, 379, 380, 382, 387, 572, 594, 597, 599, 603, 631, 635, 636, 638, 639, 646, 647, 668

Daly, Mary, 385, 647
Dancing with Witches (book), 161, 190, 575, 606, 611, 646
Dandelakis, Charlie, 309, 373, 417, 555
Dark of the Moon (play), 24
Dark Shadows (television), 26, 39, 586
Darling, Candy, 43, 154, 181, 205, 605
Daughters of Bilitis, 74, 201
Davy, Emma, 351, 359, 420, 502
Dee, John, Dr., 41, 439
DeLong, Tom (Gwydion Pendderwen), 50, 132, 139, 160, 200, 247, 269, 578, 588, 606, 629
Delphi, Greece, 398, 462, 463, 468, 491, 493
Devil and Mr. Smith, The (book), 225
Dianic Tradition, 200
Dionysus (God), 399, 462, 463, 587
Dionysus in 69 (play, film), 48, 584
Directory of the OCCULT, The (book), 242, 245, 604, 613, 623, 624, 625, 637
Divinity as the Eternal Feminine (book), 60, 385, 587, 613, 646
Dixon, Jeanne, 52, 323, 585, 613
Do-It-Yourself Witchcraft Guide (book), 137, 603
Donohue, Alice, 519, 547, 663, 666
Donovan, Frank, 338, 577
Dover, K. J., 391, 648
Drawing Down the Moon (book), 167, 235, 363, 555, 578, 588, 595, 602, 606, 607, 614, 623, 624, 626, 627, 628, 629, 633, 634, 636, 648, 667
Drawing Down the Moon (film), 363
Dylan, Bob, 29, 58
Dymond, Roy, 193, 612
Eaglen, Arthur, 207
Earth Day (1970), 37, 79
Earth Religion News (newspaper), 50, 107, 143, 178, 187, 210, 211, 212, 213, 216, 217, 219, 236, 237, 238, 240, 268, 269, 272, 275, 279, 281, 283, 284, 285, 286, 288, 289, 290, 292, 299, 300, 303, 304, 305, 319, 323, 324, 328, 330, 376, 386, 423, 424, 427, 431, 433, 563, 591, 632, 652
Earth Religions Supplies, Inc., 108, 142, 143, 234, 235, 236, 286, 297, 323, 356, 437, 448, 464, 623
Earth Star Temple, 420, 421, 432, 452, 453, 461, 467, 501
East Village/Lower East Side, Manhattan, 28, 29, 32, 33, 41, 45, 46, 49, 67, 69, 87, 250, 461, 472, 482, 498, 499, 579, 643

Eaton, Sally, 43, 46, 48, 68, 90, 113, 115, 154, 155, 209, 245, 352, 354, 355, 356, 363, 364, 416, 421, 429, 451, 454, 465, 466, 554, 583, 589, 593, 597, 598, 605, 609, 617, 625, 631, 641, 643, 651, 652, 653, 655, 656, 658, 667
Ecclesia Gnostica Catholica, 453
Ehrenhalt, Alan, 40, 582
Eliade, Mircea, 30, 585
Elle (magazine), 285
Ellwood, Robert, 29, 580
Elmlark, Walli, 599
Enchantments, Inc., 472, 474, 498, 499, 525, 529, 530, 554
Enderle, Herman, 139, 142, 143, 207, 270
Engeleit, Joe, 146, 666
English Folklore (book), 337, 639
Epperson v. Arkansas, 36
Erasmus of Rotterdam, 41
Esbat (newsletter), 300, 302, 304, 305, 319, 635, 636
Evangelical Christianity, 40, 223, 224, 366, 414
Evans, Arthur (archaeologist, author), 383, 384, 385, 386, 392, 400, 649
Evans, Arthur (author, gay activist), 33, 75, 76, 77, 370, 377, 406, 460, 580, 591, 644, 645, 646, 648
Everyday Life in Ancient Crete (book), 392, 394, 649
Evil eye, 18
Ex-gays, 195, 201
Eye of Horus, 46
Fag Rag (newspaper), 377, 591
Falwell, Jerry, 414, 528, 664
Fantasy Showcase Tarot Deck, 361
Farnham, David *(Ammon)*, 103, 104, 146, 216, 217, 218, 277, 284, 326
Farnham, Ria *(Rhea)*, 117, 149, 154, 216, 218, 284, 300, 321, 341, 351, 354, 438, 474, 526, 529, 546, 553, 567, 630, 631, 639, 643
Fate (magazine), 22, 25, 50, 57, 58, 215, 224, 323, 384, 432, 576, 578, 618, 620, 637, 646
Fauci, Anthony MD, 485, 660
FBI, Counter Intelligence Program, 46, 247, 254
Feint Type, 431
Fellini, Federico, 53, 409
Fellowship of Hesperides, 20, 59
Feminine Mystique, The (book), 42
Feminism, 385, 591
Feraferia, 59, 79, 198, 236, 252, 255, 256, 257, 295, 301, 385, 386, 387, 627, 647

Feri Tradition, 191, 612
Ferraro, Geraldine, 505
Festival of Occult Arts, 79, 251
Fiara, Tony, 460, 461, 462, 463, 471, 482, 525, 526
Findlay, Robert, 363
Finne, Kent, 453
Fire Island, New York, 171, 310, 311, 312, 483, 555
Firing Line (television), 30, 580
First Amendment, U.S. Constitution, 36, 81, 82, 83, 224, 368
Firth, Violet (Dion Fortune), 47, 136, 182, 204
Fischer, John, 488, 489, 491, 492, 493, 495, 655, 660, 661
Fisher, Fran *(Theo)*, 14, 93, 106, 138, 168, 171, 173, 174, 177, 178, 209, 212, 607
Fisher, Gerry *(Thain)*, 14, 93, 138, 169, 608, 655
  as Nestor, 438
Fitch, Ed, ix, 95, 132, 136, 138, 139, 140, 142, 143, 175, 213, 214, 220, 240, 305, 384, 594, 595, 603, 604, 607, 608, 610, 617, 619, 624, 635
Flaming Creatures (film), 28
Florida Citrus Growers Association, 413
Forest Hills, Queens, 340, 345, 410, 415, 419, 464, 651, 655
Forster, E.M., 188, 558, 611, 667
Fouratt, Jim, 32, 42, 75, 580, 583, 644
Frank, Kathryn, 114, 115, 170, 217, 232, 256, 348, 349, 352, 357, 358, 359, 362, 364, 467, 486, 501, 502, 551, 553, 660
Freemasonry, v, 595
Freud, Sigmund, 199
Friedan, Betty, 42
Fritscher, Jack, 35, 43, 108, 208, 368, 581, 583, 588, 589, 596, 611, 616, 644
Frost, Gavin and Yvonne, 185, 194, 267, 259-67, 268, 269, 273, 275, 276, 295, 305, 325, 612, 621, 627, 628, 629, 630, 634, 637
  Church and School of Wicca, 185, 259, 265, 266, 267, 275, 276, 630
  Witchmeet, 269, 270, 271, 272, 273, 274, 275, 276, 629, 630
Fugs, The (band), 46, 67, 254, 627
Fuller, Curtis, 384, 613, 646
Future Shock (film), 409, 650
Ganymede (Demigod), 394, 395
Gardner, Gerald Brosseau, vi, 12, 14, 15, 20, 21, 22, 23, 61, 62, 131, 137, 150, 159, 160, 161, 164, 168, 172, 173, 179, 187, 190, 196, 197, 207, 219, 237, 241, 246, 247, 261, 282, 283, 290, 291, 331, 335, 338, 384, 392, 398, 399, 465, 502, 572, 575, 605, 606, 611, 617, 625, 632, 633, 639, 653
  homophobia of, 189
  Witchcraft Museum, 14, 22
Gardnerian Wica, iv, v, 12, 15, 22, 23, 55, 56, 60, 65, 93, 106, 114, 116, 126, 132, 136, 137, 140, 150, 151, 156, 162, 164, 167, 168, 169, 170, 172, 173, 174, 175, 177, 178, 179, 181, 190, 191, 199, 200, 212, 213, 216, 217, 219, 221, 229, 260, 277, 278, 279, 281, 284, 289, 290, 296, 298, 325, 330, 331, 333, 334, 363, 383, 387, 398, 404, 405, 407, 438, 500, 559, 575, 591, 602, 607, 608, 616, 621, 630, 638, 649, 655
  Kentucky Line, 168, 169, 212
  Long Island Line, 168, 171, 212, 217, 219, 277, 282, 289, 298, 330, 332, 335, 655
  October Letter, 618
  Whitecroft Line, 173
Gates of the Necronomicon (book), 433, 654
Gay (newspaper), 592
Gay Activists Alliance (GAA), 77, 78, 79, 87, 116, 325, 369, 377, 591
Gay bars and bath houses, 31, 70, 78, 90, 123, 129, 309, 311, 347, 369, 370, 371, 373, 412
  Anvil, 370, 373
  Badlands, 311, 370
  Continental Baths, 311, 585
  Crisco Disco, 370
  Everard, 370, 373, 412
  Ice Palace, 311, 312
  International Stud, 311, 370
  Julius, 311
  Knapp Commission, and, 369
  Limelight, 311, 370, 642
  Mineshaft, 370, 372, 373, 408, 503
  Mt. Morris, 370
  Ninth Circle, 311
  Pierrepont Baths, 304
  Sewer, 370, 372
  Stonewall Inn, 71, 74, 311, 369, 413, 479, 554
  Toilet, 370, 372
  Tool Box, 375
  Uncle Paul's, 91
  Warehouse, 370
Gay Community News (newspaper), 377

Gay Liberation Front (GLF), 37, 74, 75, 76, 77, 79, 85, 87, 195, 202, 203, 325, 368, 390, 583, 591, 593, 615
Gay Manifesto (book), 368, 593
Gay New York (book), 408, 579, 599
Gay Spirit (book), 374, 406, 645
Gaysweek (newspaper), 591, 594, 596, 616, 634, 646, 650
Gelbert, Bruce-Michael *(Dov)*, 341, 406, 408, 410, 411, 421, 555, 591, 650, 651
Geller, Hal, 146, 551
Genet, Jean, 28
Georgian Tradition, 293, 562
Geraci, Bennie (Damian), 308, 314, 319, 334, 339, 341, 344, 348, 365, 372, 373, 387, 403, 438, 456, 457, 458, 497, 530, 548, 555, 564, 575, 636, 638, 639, 640, 641, 643, 645, 647, 649, 650, 651, 654, 657, 658, 664, 666, 667
Gere, Cathy, 385, 400, 646, 649
Germer, Karl, 48, 184, 442, 443, 444, 445, 446, 447, 450
Germer, Sascha, 443, 445, 447
Gernon, Richard, 452, 454, 498
Ghost Hunter (magazine), 25
Gianniotis, Terry, 5, 6, 7, 9, 10, 63, 469, 531, 532, 545, 547, 574, 580, 658, 664, 665
Gibran, Kahlil, 30
Giles, Thomas, 138, 139
Gimbutas, Marija, 384, 646
Ginsberg, Alan, 24, 32, 67, 68, 74, 255, 363, 627
Gittings, Barbara, 201
Gla, Greece, 492, 493
Global Village, 82, 238
Glowacki, Kevin, 531, 537
Gnostic Aquarian Festival (Gnosticon), 251
Gnostic Mass, 449, 453, 454
Gnostica News (newspaper), 50, 129, 159, 185, 195, 196, 205, 215, 224, 236, 246, 263, 266, 268, 269, 270, 274, 445, 483, 585, 587, 592, 594, 595, 601, 602, 603, 605, 606, 610, 611, 612, 613, 618, 619, 620, 621, 622, 625, 626, 627, 628, 629, 637, 646, 656, 659
Golden Bough, The (book), 47, 398
Golden Dawn, v, 16, 44, 47, 56, 132, 183, 185, 187, 281, 360, 399, 439, 451, 576, 586, 610, 611
Goldstein, Richard, 69, 77, 370, 645, 651
Gotham Book Mart, 46
Graeco-Roman View of Youth, The (book), 391

Graham, Billy, 224
Grandjouan, Clairève, 479, 480, 486, 487, 495, 496, 503, 504, 515, 517, 521, 533, 547, 555, 659, 660
Grandmother tales, 95, 131
Grant, Kenneth, 56, 148, 184, 428, 444, 576, 586, 610, 654
Graves, Robert, 49, 188, 393, 398, 425
Gray, William Gordon, 142, 604
Great Britain, United Kingdom, 15, 16, 22, 41, 122, 181, 190, 202, 247, 279, 284, 285, 286, 331, 333, 384, 486
Great Mother Goddess, 384, 385
Great Mother, The (book), 646
Great Rite (Hieros Gamos), 99, 123, 140, 194, 204, 216, 217, 259, 379, 618
Greek Homosexuality (book), 391, 648
Green Egg (magazine), 50, 60, 99, 118, 160, 162, 180, 192, 194, 195, 196, 200, 224, 228, 234, 235, 236, 238, 240, 242, 243, 244, 245, 250, 255, 257, 261, 268, 269, 275, 283, 285, 289, 290, 292, 295, 300, 303, 315, 323, 325, 328, 330, 350, 582, 585, 592, 593, 594, 596, 597, 598, 599, 600, 601, 602, 603, 604, 605, 606, 607, 608, 609, 612, 613, 614, 619, 620, 621, 622, 623, 624, 625, 626, 627, 628, 629, 631, 632, 633, 634, 635, 636, 637, 638, 640, 642, 647, 650, 656, 667
Green, Tamara, 479, 480, 487, 496, 500, 504, 513, 521, 537, 546, 549, 555, 659, 662, 664, 665
Greenberg, Dan, 90, 148, 361, 593, 599, 605, 640
Greenwich Village, Manhattan, vi, 11, 17, 18, 19, 24, 25, 26, 27, 28, 29, 30, 31, 33, 41, 42, 55, 61, 66, 67, 71, 74, 88, 89, 130, 311, 346, 395, 406, 479, 490, 554, 560, 561, 577, 579, 580, 583, 591, 592
Gretna, Louisiana, 308
Grimoire of Shadows (book), 138, 175, 603, 608
Griswold v. Connecticut, 36
Groove Tube, The (film), 369, 644
Hair (musical), 48, 52, 363, 584, 625
Hall, Dwight, 163
Hall, Robert, 352
Hardin, Louis Thomas (Moondog), 58
Hare Krishna movement, 41
Harris, Frieda, 443
Harris, William, 233, 443
Harrison, Donald, 295
Harrison, George, 41, 363
Harrow, Judy, 138, 361, 585, 603, 642
Hatzichronoglou, Lena, 489, 493, 496, 661

Hawass, Zahi Dr., 57, 518
Hay, Harry, 406, 460, 590, 648
Hazel, Witch, 81, 82, 250
Hebrew Qaballah, 320
Hedgepeth, William, 30, 580
Heflin, Llee, 186, 375, 376, 444, 611, 645
Heidrick, William, 447, 448, 451, 452, 455, 656, 657
Heine, Bill, 41, 582
Heinlein, Robert, 36, 60, 249, 393, 587, 627
Hellenic Order, 255
Helluva Town (television), 79, 80
Hemphill, Herbert Jr., 233
Hepburn, Katherine, 516
Herakleion, Crete, 490, 491, 492
Herakles (Demigod), 397, 622
Herbert, Frank, 32, 67, 580
Herlihy, James, 55, 586
Hermes (God), vii, 95, 563, 574, 597
Hermetic Order of the Golden Dawn, 16, 131, 183, 481
Hermetic Order of the Silver Sword, 481, 659
Heseltine, Philip, 114, 598
Heselton, Philip, 172, 173, 334, 335, 336, 608, 638, 639
Hexerei, 80
Hickman Arms Apartments, 538
Hidden Path, The (newsletter), 208, 236, 240, 616, 618, 659
Hirsig, Leah (the Scarlet Woman), 17
History of Magic, The (book), 439, 577, 667
Hofmann, Albert, 32
Holzer, Hans, 25, 39, 61, 105, 129, 130, 141, 145, 151, 155, 159, 165, 223, 228, 234, 242, 243, 244, 245, 250, 255, 256, 262, 263, 264, 266, 269, 299, 324, 363, 366, 411, 554, 582, 592, 596, 602, 603, 604, 605, 606, 607, 610, 613, 620, 621, 623, 624, 625, 626, 627, 628, 634, 637, 647, 650
Homosexuality
  BDSM and leather, 187, 346, 370, 371, 372, 375
  Marxist ideology and, 76, 84, 395, 409, 460
Hornum, Michael, 517, 520, 521, 522, 524, 531, 533, 546, 663, 664, 666
Horus (God), 295, 303, 401, 540, 634
Hotfoot Jackson (book), 25
House Un-American Activities Committee, 4, 507

How Are the Mighty Fallen (book), 392, 393
Huebner, Louise, 56, 68, 200, 228, 586, 588, 589, 614, 627
Hughes, Pennethorne, 23, 427, 579
Human Immunodeficiency Virus (HIV), 149, 189, 373, 412, 483–85, 503, 527, 530, 531, 549, 550, 568, 571, 660, 662, 668
  Acquired Immune Deficiency Syndrome (AIDS), ix, x, 149, 182, 189, 483–86, 502, 503, 525, 526, 528, 530, 534, 538, 540, 545, 547, 548, 549, 550, 554, 566, 567, 568, 569, 570, 571, 645, 647, 659, 660, 662, 663, 664, 665, 668
  AZT, 530, 664
  Pneumocystis jirovecii/Pneumocystis carinii/PCP, 484, 531
Hunter College (City University of New York), 65, 88, 469, 474, 479, 487, 489, 490, 503, 516, 546, 547, 549, 555
Huntington Coven, 329, 331, 333, 334, 336, 337, 339, 340, 378, 379, 381, 383, 398, 415, 638, 639, 646
Huson, Paul, 466, 619
Hustler (magazine), 413, 651
Hutchinson, James LeRoy, 29, 50
Hutton, Ronald, 160, 172, 197, 602, 606, 608, 611, 612, 613, 633
I Ching (book), 44, 47
I Married a Witch (film), 24, 26
Immigration and Nationality Act of 1965, 41, 485
Inauguration of the Pleasure Dome, The (film), 48
Inferno Disco, 251, 362
InnerVision, 109, 233, 502
International Society for Krishna Consciousness, 41
Introduction to Witchcraft (film), 621, 668
Invocation of My Demon Brother (film), 48
Iridescent Order of the Iris, 18
Isis (Goddess), 189, 298, 300, 302, 303, 315, 316, 317, 318, 319, 320, 360, 401, 540, 587
Island Dialogues, The (book), 186, 375, 611, 645
Isle of Man, 14, 22
Itkin, Michael, 33
Ives, George Cecil, 183, 184, 391
J. Aron and Company, 315, 339

Jamison, Artie *(Tammuz)*, 73, 116, 146, 147, 239, 463, 570, 580, 590, 594, 596, 598, 624, 658, 668
Jana (British Witch), 331, 332, 333, 334, 335, 336, 337, 379, 382, 618, 638
Jersey City, 31, 110, 597
Jethro Tull (band), 49, 403
John, June, 56, 290, 622
Jones, Leslie Ellen, 24
Jones, Randy, 91, 501, 599
Joy of Gay Sex (book), 390, 648
Julian (book), 95, 241, 646
Jung, C.G., 30, 47, 57, 461, 587
Kale, Will, 336, 639
Kameny, Franklin, 69, 77, 201, 388, 590, 614
Kamrin, Janice, 517, 518, 663
Karma, 548
Kaster, Joseph, 46, 110
Katz, Tzipora, 643
Kaye, Larry, 532
Keith, W. Holman, 20, 59, 198, 257, 385, 393
Kelly, Tony, 139, 142, 604
Kemble, Jim, 272, 295, 298, 306
Kemet, 295, 300, 320, 363, 386, 435, 492
Kerouac, Jack, 5, 24, 30, 49, 580
Kessler, Bruce, 232
Keystone Communal (play), 48
King Must Die, The (book), 392, 393, 461
King of the Witches (book), 56, 232, 290, 586, 613, 632
King Pentheus, 368
King, Francis, 363, 432, 455, 493, 576, 599, 610
Kirwan, Larry, 92, 358, 359, 360, 362, 363, 364, 432, 468, 594, 642, 653
Klein, Kenny, 366, 421, 564, 643, 667
Kleps, Art, 253, 627
Klingon, Joe, 351
Knapp Commission, 369
Kneitel, Judy *(Theos)*, 135, 156, 164, 171, 174, 210, 211, 212, 214, 215, 217, 298, 337, 554, 602, 607, 609, 618, 624
Kneitel, Tommy *(Phoenix)*, 91, 116, 117, 152, 153, 154, 156, 162, 164, 167, 168, 171, 174, 178, 179, 209, 210, 213, 214, 216, 220, 231, 237, 241, 242, 244, 248, 275, 298, 328, 554, 594, 599, 602, 605, 606, 607, 608, 609, 617, 619, 622, 623, 624, 638
Knight, Morris, 85
Knossos and the Prophets of Modernism (book), 400, 646, 649

Knossos, Crete, 384, 386, 387, 403, 404, 406, 407, 408, 411, 415, 418, 419, 421, 456, 460, 462, 463, 468, 480, 482, 483, 491, 525, 568, 646, 658
Koehl, Robert B., 395, 401, 649
Korythalia (newsletter), 236
Krishna Consciousness, 41, 316
Kupferberg, Tuli, 254
Kyle, Charlie (Poule d'Eaux), 310
La Vecchia, 65, 162
Lady Sheba, 137, 140, 196, 274, 276, 290, 603, 613, 630
Laffont, Jean-Pierre, 285, 632
Lamond, Frederic, 160, 172, 206, 207, 481, 606, 608, 613, 616, 659
Lancet, The (journal), 484, 659
LaRouche, Lyndon, 503
Larson, Paul, 571, 579
Lattimore, Richmond, 425, 506, 662
Lauritsen, John, 74, 75, 84, 325, 390, 392, 590, 591, 593, 637, 647, 648
Laveau, Marie, 466
LaVey, Anton, 48, 49, 60, 205, 206, 221, 227, 266, 353, 616, 641
Law of Return, 276
Leary, Timothy, 32, 36, 248, 360
Lee, Christopher, 232, 667
Leek, Sybil, 21, 25, 26, 50, 52, 56, 57, 61, 63, 67, 150, 208, 223, 224, 227, 228, 242, 250, 264, 323, 575, 578, 579, 586, 605, 616, 619, 623, 624
Lennon, John, 363, 364
Leo, Alan, 43
Lesser Key of Solomon, The (book), 42
Lessing, Kitty, 93
Levenda, Peter, 92, 112, 155, 169, 209, 229, 261, 272, 352, 353, 363, 427, 438, 549, 555, 581, 594, 596, 597, 598, 605, 608, 617, 628, 639, 641, 643, 654, 666
Lévi, Eliphas, 428, 439
Lewis, H Spencer, 17, 576, 610, 629
Liber Ubrarum (paper), 500, 588, 602, 606, 658, 661
Liberation Theology, 33
Life (magazine), 20, 22, 24, 33, 46, 53, 375, 581, 582, 645, 646
Linear B, 402
Liscoe, Kevan, 74, 590
Little Grove of Ganymede, 193
Llewellyn (publisher), 47, 109, 159, 224, 234, 235, 236, 251, 252, 258, 266, 269, 271, 576, 578, 583, 584, 586, 592, 596, 603, 605, 611, 613, 629, 654, 655
LLOYD, RANDY, viii, 409
Long Island Church of Aphrodite, 20, 59

Long Island National Cemetery, 540, 665
Look (magazine), 25, 30, 61, 70, 76, 227, 580, 588, 590, 591, 596, 619, 621
Loovis, David, 374, 377, 645
Los Angeles Free Press, 637
Los Angeles Free Press (newspaper), 266
Los Angeles, California, 17, 56, 61, 68, 70, 74, 85, 109, 195, 200, 234, 323, 385, 443, 445, 448, 484, 576, 580, 587, 588, 589, 599, 615, 620, 627, 637, 647, 659, 663
Louisville Coven, 171, 212, 257, 438
Louisville, Kentucky, 14, 93, 138, 139, 168, 169, 171, 172, 175, 179, 212, 257, 438, 594, 607
Lovecraft, H.P., 18, 47, 58, 90, 111, 351, 423, 424, 428, 430, 433, 435, 436, 439, 440, 577, 597, 641, 653, 655
Lovers (musical), 372, 645
Lowenstein, Kenny *(Loic)*, 116, 120, 163, 165, 214, 598, 606, 618
Lucifer Rising (film), 48, 49
Mabinogian, The (book), 600
Macer-Story, Eugenia, 45, 52, 251, 352, 361, 362, 420, 583, 585, 587, 626, 643, 652
Machen, Arthur, 47, 122
Machon, Stephen, 416, 554
Madden, Terry, 100, 116
Madison Square Garden, 7, 474, 505
Madole, James, 353, 641
Magic Lantern Cycle (films), 48
Magickal Childe, 341, 342, 343, 344, 345, 346–64, 365, 366, 372, 405, 406, 408, 416, 420, 421, 422, 423, 428, 429, 430, 432, 433, 434, 437, 447, 453, 448–55, 459, 461, 462, 464, 465, 467, 473, 482, 497, 498, 499, 501, 502, 530, 546, 549, 550, 552, 553, 554, 563, 564, 593, 594, 597, 598, 599, 604, 615, 618, 621, 623, 637, 640, 641, 642, 643, 644, 650, 652, 653, 654, 656, 657, 658, 661, 666, 668
   Earth Star Temple and, 420, 421, 432, 452, 453, 461, 467, 501
   Harvest Festival and, 345
   Magickal Childe Publishing, 433, 434, 437, 455, 465, 467, 499, 501, 604, 637, 654, 658, 661
Magickal Formulary (book), 465, 467, 642, 658
Magickal Realms, 553
Maiden (coven position), 14, 128, 147, 158
Mailer, Norman, 26, 67, 123, 363, 426
Mandragora (newsletter), 563, 566
Manford, Morty, 369

Manhattan, 11, 22, 27, 31, 33, 34, 35, 36, 38, 43, 56, 58, 63, 67, 69, 87, 89, 90, 109, 110, 111, 116, 119, 139, 165, 166, 167, 214, 250, 310, 316, 340, 341, 346, 350, 352, 353, 354, 361, 362, 369, 370, 372, 411, 415, 416, 417, 424, 429, 456, 472, 552, 554, 555, 593, 598, 624, 639, 655
Manhattan House of Detention, 214
Manpower, 89
Mapplethorpe, Robert, 47, 205, 310, 581, 596, 644
Margolis, Jon, 27, 579
Marie, Lisa, 410, 411, 415, 419, 555, 651
Marijuana (pot), 27, 32, 33, 50, 253, 254, 368, 403, 458
Marinatos, Nanno, 394, 649, 650, 667
Markson, Eileen, 513, 521, 531, 533, 535, 537, 545, 546, 547, 549, 555, 660, 663, 665, 666
Martello, Leo, ix, 47, 56, 63, 64–70, 74, 75, 76, 77, 78, 79, 80, 81, 82, 83, 84, 85, 86, 87, 88, 89, 90, 94, 95, 105, 108, 116, 120, 127, 128, 129, 131, 132, 156, 159, 161, 162, 165, 168, 181, 191, 192, 193, 194, 195, 198, 199, 203, 204, 205, 207, 208, 210, 211, 215, 217, 219, 227, 228, 229, 230, 231, 234, 238, 241, 243, 245, 246, 250, 251, 256, 260, 266, 269, 275, 282, 283, 390, 405, 406, 411, 423, 436, 437, 438, 440, 468, 483, 549, 554, 588, 589, 590, 591, 592, 593, 595, 598, 599, 600, 601, 603, 604, 605, 606, 607, 612, 613, 614, 616, 617, 618, 619, 620, 621, 624, 625, 626, 627, 628, 636, 649, 650, 651, 659
Marvel Comics, 361
Matera, Dana, 486, 546
Mathers, Moina, 280
Mathers, Samuel Liddell MacGregor, 16, 183, 280
Mathiesen, Robert, 290, 594, 595, 600, 633
Mattachine Society, 69, 74, 409
McBride Scholars Program, 508
McCarthy, Joseph, 38, 68, 246, 247, 507
McCartney, Paul, 363
McClung, Kevin, 311, 371
McFarland, Morgan, 200, 614
McMartin Preschool scandal, 225
McMillan and Wife (television), 230, 231
McMurtry, Grady (Hymenaeus Alpha), 186, 355, 442, 443, 444, 445, 446, 447, 448, 449, 450, 451, 452, 454, 656
   Thoth Tarot, 443, 446, 451

McNally, Judith, 92, 96, 100, 104, 108, 123, 124, 125, 130, 141, 155, 160, 215, 238, 304, 356, 360, 361, 363, 383, 426, 438, 550, 552, 563, 574, 575, 580, 594, 595, 596, 600, 602, 603, 606, 618, 623, 635, 642, 646, 655, 666, 667
Meaning of Witchcraft (book), 502
Meatpacking District, 346, 370, 371, 372, 373, 376
Medical College of Georgia, 538
Mellinger, Frederic, 443, 444
Mellink, Machteld, 515, 517, 518, 520, 522, 532, 534, 555, 663, 665, 667
Melton, J. Gordon, 39, 222, 244, 432, 559, 582, 619, 624, 667
Men Loving Men (book), 390, 648
Metacalus, 186, 208, 611
Metzger, Hermann, 443, 444, 445
Meyer, Nathan, 518, 519, 520, 521, 524, 527, 528, 529, 531, 534, 545, 566, 663, 664, 666
Miami-Dade, Florida, 412
Middle Village, Queens, 339, 341, 344, 387, 403, 407, 458, 461, 630, 631, 647, 648, 650
Midwest Pagan Council, 252
Mills, Malcolm, 91, 352, 355, 356, 357, 449, 453, 464, 574, 594, 639, 640, 641, 642, 656, 657, 658
Minneapolis Coven of Lothlorian, 252
Minoan Brotherhood, ix, 383–422, 438, 460, 461, 463, 468, 470, 480, 482, 483, 522, 523, 525, 529, 547, 548, 553, 561, 562, 563, 564, 565, 566, 567, 568, 569, 570, 571, 572, 647, 648, 650, 652, 658, 659, 664, 667
   Asterion (God), 401
   Book of the Mysteries, 402, 408, 409, 524, 648, 652
   Knossos Grove, 403, 404, 406, 407, 408, 411, 415, 419, 421, 456, 460, 461, 462, 463, 468, 480, 482, 483, 525, 658
   Kouros, 388, 408
   Phaistos Grove, 408, 415
   Rhadamanthus, 401
   Rhea (Goddess), 387, 398, 400, 401, 402, 419, 464, 631, 647
Minoan Crete, vi, 189, 383, 385, 386, 387, 395, 398, 401, 403, 490, 522, 647, 659, 664
Minoan Religion (book), 394, 649, 650, 667
Minoan Sisterhood, 345, 418, 419, 482, 548, 553, 554, 563, 571

Minoan Thera, 532
Minoan Tradition, 383, 403
Minoan-Mycenaean Religion, and Its Survival in Greek Religion (book), 392, 394
Minos, 395, 401, 402, 482, 650, 664
Miranda, Carmen, 18, 577
Mists of Avalon (book), 561, 667
Morganwg, Iolo, 122
Morning of the Magicians, The (book), 47, 584
Morningside Park, 369
Moscrip, Kevin, 522, 523, 527, 529, 664
Moss, Harold, 20, 91, 106, 187, 204, 243, 244, 254, 256, 257, 258, 262, 272, 295–303, 306, 315, 317, 318, 319, 330, 406, 578, 594, 596, 611, 615, 623, 624, 625, 627, 628, 634, 635, 636, 650
Mother Right (book), 385
Mothers and Amazons (book), 384, 646
Motta, Marcello, 429, 445, 446, 447, 450, 451
Murex, 522
Murray, Margaret, 14, 132, 137, 159, 222, 247, 400, 462, 575, 605, 625
Museum of American Folk Art, 233, 424, 622, 623
Muto, Gene, 456, 457, 458, 459, 468, 469, 471, 479, 480, 486, 487, 497, 503, 507, 514, 517, 521, 523, 527, 536, 537, 540, 545, 555, 564, 565, 574, 657, 659, 662, 664, 665
Myron, Ron, 302, 303, 314, 315, 317, 318, 320, 635, 636
Mystic (magazine), 58
Naked Witch, The (film), 26
Name, Billy, 42, 43, 44, 46, 181, 583
Nascosto, Edward, 7, 8
Nascosto, Marie (see also Buczynski, Marie), 574, 575, 662, 664, 665, 666
Nascosto, Tommy, 10, 556, 588, 635
National Lampoon (magazine), 431, 653
National Organization for Women, 37
National Renaissance Party, 353
National Star, 285, 597
National Star (tabloid), 226, 227, 324, 412, 620, 637
Naval Armed Guard, 2, 574
Necronomicon (Simon), 345, 361, 423–41, 465, 555, 597, 652, 653, 654, 655
   chaos magick and, 434, 435, 654
Necronomicon Files, The (book), 435, 436, 437, 438, 654, 655
Necronomicon Spellbook (book), 433
Neidel, Kenton, 483, 567, 571, 668

Nema, Soror, 148
Nemeton (newsletter), 236, 240, 623, 667
Neo-Paganism (contemporary Paganism), iv, v, viii, ix, x, 6, 60, 78, 79, 155, 165, 187, 194, 221, 223, 225, 227, 228, 229, 231, 235, 239, 241, 243, 248, 249, 254, 257, 263, 272, 274, 333, 348, 391, 394, 411, 555
Nero, Claudia *(Branwen)*, 158, 168
Nero, Gerard *(Bryce)*, 158, 168
Nesnick, Mary *(Dionysia)*, 93, 99, 136, 151, 157, 165, 213, 594, 605, 632
Neuhaus, Fr. Richard, 615, 642
Neumann, Erich, 30, 384, 646
New Age, iv, 16, 39, 47, 56, 57, 60, 67, 108, 186, 188, 192, 239, 244, 249, 343, 356, 550, 582, 612, 613
New Broom, The (newsletter), 240, 598, 607, 618, 624
New Forest Coven, 333, 335
New Orleans, Louisiana, 15, 154, 251, 308, 309, 312, 313, 319, 339, 354, 373, 408, 416, 417, 457, 459, 465, 497, 555, 636
New Pagans, The (book), 165, 242, 243, 245, 256, 605, 607, 610, 627
New York Coffeehouse Law, 28
New York Coven of Witches, 107, 280, 281, 438, 631
New York in the 70s (book), 454
New York Metropolitan Museum of Art, 316, 555
New York Tarot, 361, 642
New York Temple/School (CES), 187, 239, 243, 252, 254, 256, 257, 258, 263, 272, 275, 295–303, 303, 314, 315, 316, 317, 318, 319, 320, 326, 327, 331, 386, 395, 401, 406, 574, 580, 602, 627, 628, 634, 635, 636
New York Times (newspaper), 18, 19, 50, 63, 233, 311, 350, 354, 361, 484, 528, 574
New York University, 45, 78, 88, 89, 90, 110, 228, 479, 486, 611
Newton, Jeremiah, 616
Nichols, John, 69, 70, 75, 76, 77, 78, 80, 85, 86, 201, 374, 375, 409, 560, 589, 590, 591, 592, 593, 611, 645, 650
Nielson, Jacquie, 238
Nielson, John, 238
Nietzsche, 368, 384, 461, 462, 644
Nightshade, Jonathon, 142, 603, 604, 616
Nike (Goddess), 510, 511
Nixon, Martin, 448, 581
Nixon, Richard, 38, 52, 53, 282, 642
Nordic, Rolla, 61, 229, 352, 363

North Haven, Connecticut, 94, 95, 96, 124, 129, 131, 134, 595, 633
Occult Bookstores
  4th Avenue (New York), 18, 25, 655
  Church of Light, 109
  Controversial, 109
  Gnostica, 109, 251, 252, 564, 646
  Gotham Book Mart, 46
  Orientalia, 25, 43, 46, 655
  Peace Eye, 46, 67, 583
  Samuel Weiser Books, 46, 236, 449
OCCULT exhibit (1973), 233, 234, 623
Occult Experience, The (film), 616
Odyssey (book), 425, 642, 646
Oedipus Wrecks (film), 553
Oesopus Island, 17
Olcott, Henry, 16
Olympian Gods, 400
Omen, The (film), 337
Omni (magazine), 431, 653
Ondine, 43, 583
One (magazine), 409
Ono, Yoko, 363, 364
Ops (Roman Festival), 387
Oracle, The (film), 363, 502, 642
Order of Chaeronea, 183, 184, 391
Order of the Golden Calf, 185, 253, 375
Order of the Magi, 20
Order of the Red Garter, 334
Ordo Templi Astarte (O.T.A.), 444
Ordo Templi Orientis (O.T.O.), v, ix, 3, 16, 17, 44, 47, 148, 177, 179, 183, 184, 186, 187, 355, 362, 376, 399, 421, 428, 432, 442–55, 468, 551, 610, 611, 654, 655, 656, 657, 668
  Earth Star Temple and, 420, 421, 432, 452, 453, 461, 467, 501
  Lashtal Lodge, 448, 449, 451, 452, 468
  Mobius Chapter, 448, 449, 451
  Tahuti Lodge, 452, 453, 454, 455, 498, 551, 656
Oriflamme (newsletter), 236, 448, 656
Original Products, 109, 530, 553
Orion, Loretta, 420
Orwell, George, 40
Oscar Wilde Bookstore, 406
Osiris (God), 300, 303, 399
Owen, Ruth Wynn, 21, 207, 554
Owles, Jim, 76, 77
Ozone Park, Queens, 4, 5, 7, 9, 10, 11, 31, 34, 62, 91, 102, 111, 305, 306, 307, 321, 339, 556, 574, 582
Özyar, Asli, 517, 518, 521, 535, 546, 663, 665, 666
Pagan Christs (book), 376, 646

Pagan Rituals (books), 141, 142, 294, 326, 437, 549, 604, 606, 607, 608, 612, 617, 623, 631, 633, 638, 654, 666
Pagan Spirit Gathering, 252, 603
Pagan Way, ix, 100, 101, 116, 120, 132, 135–44, 145, 146, 147, 158, 167, 171, 175, 177, 216, 218, 229, 238, 239, 257, 270, 271, 286, 301, 316, 328, 338, 352, 361, 404, 411, 420, 453, 549, 554, 603, 604, 632
Pagan, Occult, New Age Directory (book), 293
Page, Jimmy, 49, 584
Palmer, John Phillips, 185, 186, 610, 656
Pan Pagan Festival, 464, 613, 658
Parker, Terry *(Dylan/Arawn)*, 165, 170, 301, 605, 606, 607
Parra, Maria, 149, 366, 421, 453, 473, 525
Parsons, Jack, 428, 576
Partridge, William, 30, 40, 58, 580, 582
Passaic Coven, 281, 361
Patroclus, 547
Patterson, George, 98, 132, 133, 192, 363, 612, 617, 662
Paxson, Diana, 249, 561, 667
Peaceniks, 368
Pelz, Bruce, 361
Pentagram, The (newsletter), 21, 291, 578, 586, 600, 633
Percy, Willam, 395, 649, 666
Perry, Rev. Troy, 86
Petit, Philippe, 361
Pharaoh Ahmose I, 386
Pharaoh Akhenaten, 295
Pharaoh Tutankhamen, 516
Phi Beta Kappa, 504, 505
Philadelphia, 17, 42, 138, 139, 142, 165, 257, 318, 376, 389, 506, 513, 520, 522, 523, 527, 529, 536, 575, 613, 653
Philbin, Regis, 264
Pink Floyd (band), 49
Plant, Robert, 49
Plato, 384, 391, 496, 645
Podber, Dorothy, 43
Poland, Rev. Jefferson, 253, 254, 255, 258, 626
Polsky, Ned, 32, 579, 580
Porter, Adriana, 94, 290, 291, 594
Powell, Adam Donaldson, 571
Pratchett, Terry, 97, 595
Pratt, Roger, 82, 91, 100, 101, 113, 164, 170, 173, 211, 250, 260, 549, 592, 594, 596, 597, 606, 608, 617, 626, 666
Prima, Diane de, 43, 255
Prophet, The (book), 30

Proposition 6, 414
Pryor, Eric, 366, 421, 422, 615, 643, 644, 652
Psychedelic Peace Fellowship, 33
Psychedelic Venus Church, 185, 187, 252, 258, 407, 408, 626
  Order of the Golden Calf, 185, 253, 375
Psychic Awareness Weekend, 251
Psychology Today (magazine), 431
Queens, New York, 3, 4, 8, 31, 33, 73, 87, 102, 110, 119, 213, 310, 311, 313, 321, 326, 330, 338, 340, 341, 344, 345, 370, 380, 405, 410, 415, 417, 469, 471, 500, 515, 517, 536, 556, 574, 582, 599, 630, 631
Quest, The (book), 294, 634
Rachleff, Owen, 228, 230, 262, 554, 593, 621
Racism, 192, 612, 658
Radical Faeries, 460, 646, 648, 658
Radin, Roy, 363
Rainbow Coven, 257
Ravenspirit, Michael, 101
Reagan, Ronald, 51, 52, 414, 487, 503, 508, 520, 625
Realm of the Great Goddess (book), 384, 646
Reed, Lou, 43, 583
Reese, David M., 522
Regardie, Israel, 17, 47, 56, 61, 185, 443, 444, 576, 586, 611, 656
Rego Park, Queens, 110, 310, 333, 339, 471, 638, 639
Renault, Mary, 392, 393, 461, 648
Reuss, Theodore, 442, 444
Rhys Carpenter Library (Bryn Mawr College), 546, 555, 664
Rider-Waite-Smith tarot, 17
Ridgway, Brunilde, 504, 514, 517, 518, 520, 522, 530, 531, 532, 534, 537, 555, 662, 663, 664, 665
Right Hand Path, 182
Rimbaud, Arthur, 48, 50
Rite of Reculade, 404
Rites of Spring, 252, 626
Riva, Anna, 466
Riverside Coven, 171
Riverside Park, 369, 410
Roberts, David, 309, 311, 312, 497, 530
Roberts, Susan, 136, 139, 151, 251
Robertson, John, 376, 578, 612, 646
Robinson, Tom, 203, 583, 615, 658
Rockefeller Hall, 512

Roman Catholic Church, 181, 229, 558, 560, 612
  Brothers of the Sacred Heart, 8
  Jesuits (Societas Iesu), 8, 62, 567, 581
  Vatican II, 34, 35, 38, 130, 508, 560
  Virgin Mary, 6, 561
Ronno, Frances, 146
Ronstadt, Linda, 420
Rose, Elliot, 160, 161
Roséan, Lexa, 420
Rosicrucian, 15, 17, 164
Roszak, Theodore, 40, 582
Rotroff, Susan, 487, 489, 490, 500, 503, 660
Rowley, Owen, 600
Runyon, Carroll, 184, 245, 253, 254, 255, 256, 258, 610, 622
Sala One Nine, 343
Salay, Sue, 489
Salem, Massachusetts, 83, 85, 284, 326
Salucca, Mike and Patty, 326
San Francisco, California, 17, 41, 49, 60, 74, 83, 85, 109, 205, 254, 309, 370, 375, 412, 443, 447, 460, 484, 519, 528, 545, 572, 577, 583, 585, 591, 593, 597, 616, 621, 622, 639, 646, 648, 655, 664
Sanders, Alex, 56, 60, 131, 197, 199, 209, 265, 284, 285, 572, 579, 580, 586, 614, 617, 619, 622, 632
Sanders, Ed, 29, 45, 46, 67, 219, 255, 589, 627
Sanders, Maxine, 284
Santeria, 19, 354, 359, 416, 417, 465, 554, 577
Santerian Orisha, 418
Santorini, Greece, 532
Santostefano, Damon, 454, 616, 643, 661
Saperton, Sheila *(Khrysis)*, 328, 329, 330, 331, 332, 333, 334, 335, 337, 344, 378, 380, 382, 387, 555, 638, 646
Saretta, Phyllis, 480, 487, 496, 500, 503, 521, 539, 546, 548, 659, 664, 665, 666
Sargent, Denny, 146, 148, 244, 301, 566, 624, 667
Satan Seller, The (book), 225
Satanic Bible, The (book), 205, 206, 221, 349, 616, 640
Satanic panic, 225
Satanic Rituals, The (book), 221
Satanism, v, 16, 19, 39, 53, 55, 60, 135, 150, 205, 206, 221, 223, 224, 226, 227, 231, 232, 250, 348, 362, 454, 621, 626, 628, 668
Satanism and Witchcraft (film), 454, 616, 643, 661
Satyricon (film), 409
Savage, Adrian, 434, 654
Save Our Children, 413, 414
Sawicki, Matthew, 552, 631
Sayville, New York, 312
Schechner, Richard, 48, 584
Scheiber, Lewis, 272, 629
Schlangekraft, Inc., 429, 437
Schliemann, Heinrich, 516, 663
Schneider, Larry, 463, 482, 483, 526, 567
Schuller, Kim *(Sky)*, 341, 405, 410
Schultz, Donna Cole, 100, 139, 142, 143, 173, 207, 211, 577, 604, 655
Score, John (M), 139, 191, 198, 199, 203, 204, 211, 274, 279, 282, 612, 613
Scorpio Rising (film), 370
Screw (magazine), 69, 77, 85, 374, 651
Season of the Witch (book), 55, 586
Seax-Wica, 178, 275, 279, 283, 328, 329, 330, 336, 609, 632, 638, 657
Second Ecumenical Council of the Vatican (Vatican II), 34, 35, 38, 130, 508, 560
Sedgwick, Edie, 43
Sefton, Amy, 360, 361
Seventh Ray (newslatter), 236
Sex magick, 183, 184, 185, 187, 260, 320, 395, 668
Sex Ritual of the Occult (film), 206, 223, 616, 619
Shackleton, Judith, 522
Shamanism, 51
Shanks, Robert, 186
Shea, Robert, 360
Sheep Meadow, Central Park, 79, 80, 81, 82
Sheridan Square, Manhattan, 72, 79, 456, 590
Sherlock, Bonnie, 132
Short Eyes (play), 214, 618
Siero, Patricia *(Sira)*, 168, 169, 170, 177, 212, 277, 278, 281, 331, 336, 337, 607
Silent Spring (book), 37
Silverknife, Zanoni, 98, 132, 133, 147, 350, 562, 594, 595, 602, 605, 641, 667
Simon (author), 59, 119, 165, 166, 214, 216, 233, 240, 248, 249, 275, 303, 345, 352, 359, 360, 361, 400, 431, 433, 437, 423-41, 449, 450, 465, 468, 555, 597, 599, 600, 607, 618, 622, 624, 625, 641, 642, 643, 649, 652, 653, 654, 655, 656, 661
Siri, Giani, 6, 360, 361, 575, 642
Sister Josephine, 539, 540, 546
Sixth Man, The (book), 188, 311, 409, 580, 636, 650

Skinner, Stephen, 432, 654
Skyclad, 22, 140, 145, 200, 219, 284, 285, 329, 378, 403, 483
Slater, Herman, ix, 87-93, 97, 99, 102, 122, 128, 133, 139, 142, 143, 144, 145, 147, 148, 152, 154, 160, 165, 168, 169, 170, 171, 172, 173, 174, 179, 192, 195, 204, 208, 209, 210, 212, 213, 214, 216, 217, 218, 219, 226, 229, 230, 231, 233, 234, 235, 236, 237, 238, 239, 241, 242, 244, 251, 269, 277, 279, 283, 285, 286, 289, 292, 293, 294, 295, 296, 298, 300, 304, 305, 306, 314, 319, 321, 322, 323, 324, 325, 326, 340, 342, 345, 346, 357, 365, 366, 372, 394, 405, 406, 421, 424, 425, 427, 428, 429, 430, 431, 433, 434, 436, 437, 438, 447, 448, 449, 452, 453, 454, 455, 457, 464, 465, 466, 467, 468, 473, 476, 485, 497, 498, 499, 500, 501, 502, 546, 548, 549, 564, 581, 593, 594, 596, 597, 598, 599, 603, 604, 606, 607, 608, 612, 613, 615, 617, 618, 620, 621, 622, 623, 624, 625, 628, 629, 631, 632, 633, 637, 638, 640, 641, 642, 643, 645, 650, 652, 653, 654, 655, 657, 658, 660, 661, 666, 668
and Magickal Childe store, 346-64
and Warlock Shop, 108-19
Book of Pagan Rituals controversy, 143, 437, 604
campaign against the Frosts, 259-76
death of, 549-53
Smith, Alden, 148, 158, 446, 489, 492, 577, 661
Smith, Dinitia, 350, 640
Smith, Harry, 41, 47, 49, 67, 363, 400, 430, 432, 452, 584
Smith, Hershel, 225, 226
Smith, Jack, 28
Smith, Kay (Flagg) *(Vivienne)*, 92, 104, 118, 119, 123, 125, 128, 139, 140, 147, 165, 170, 218, 228, 275, 277, 301, 554, 562, 601, 602, 605, 606, 607, 608, 617, 631
Smith, Patti, 46, 596
Society for Creative Anachronism (SCA), 80, 249, 625
Socrates, 188, 189
Solomon, Jay, 353
Songs from the Wood (album), 49, 403
Southern Coven of British Witches, 335
Spare, Austin Osman, 148
Spellman, Francis Cardinal, 35, 38, 581, 582, 642
Spiritual Independents Movement, 66
Spiritualism, 16, 188

Springer, Renate *(Hela)*, 169, 171, 211, 215, 216, 217, 219, 277, 298, 555, 608, 617, 618, 620, 630, 637
St. Joseph Hospital, 539
St. Mary Gate of Heaven Parish, 7
StarGroup One, 360, 432
Starhawk, 68, 235
Starry One, 401
Starwood Festival, 626
Stearn, Jess, 188, 311, 409, 580, 636, 650
Stein, Chris, 363
Stein, Gertrude, vii
Stevens, Clinton (Chanel 13), 43, 154, 343, 353, 354, 416, 417, 418, 465, 466, 554, 657
Stone, Merlin, 385, 647
Stonewall Inn/Riots, iv, 37, 71-74, 76, 77, 78, 79, 85, 89, 184, 195, 198, 199, 201, 202, 203, 208, 231, 246, 311, 367, 369, 374, 376, 412, 413, 485, 590, 591, 614, 644, 645, 660
Stranger in a Strange Land (book), 60, 249, 393
Strega, 18, 65
Stuart, Sylvester, 132
Students for a Democratic Society, 83, 368
Studio 31, 234, 430, 499, 653
Sufi, 30, 320
Summerisle, Lord, 232
Susan B. Anthony Coven, 190, 385
Suto, Gary, 572
Svendsen, Sarna, 361
Swann, Thomas Burnett, 392, 393, 648
Sygma Photo News Agency, 285
Symonds, John (Crowley literary executor), 56, 367, 447, 448, 586, 656
Symonds, John Addington (gay activist), 391, 648
Symposium (Plato's), 391, 645
Talbert, Robert, 483, 659
Tamarack, Melda, 147, 301, 605
Tantra, 50, 252, 449, 610
Tao, 44, 320
Tarot, The (book), 17, 58
Taylor, Joseph W., 506
Temple of Aphrodite, Long Island, 197, 385
Temple of Spiritual Guidance, 66
The Amazing Randi, 45
Their Satanic Majesties Request (album), 48
Theitic, Andrew, 123, 125, 166, 293, 294, 561, 595, 600, 602, 606, 632, 633, 634, 666, 667
Thelema, 17, 184, 236, 432, 443, 446

Themis: A Study of the Social Origins of Greek Religion (book), 384
Theosophy, v, 16, 184, 613
Third Reich, 555
Thomas Great Hall, 475, 512, 520, 528, 664
Thomas Hunter Honors Program, 480
Thomas, Martha Carey, 517
Thompson, Gwen (Phyllis Ruth) Wiccan Rede, and, 289, 292
Thoreau, Henry David, 16, 30
Thorn, Michael, 211, 481, 482, 617, 659
Thornbrook Manor, 513
Threefold Law, 291
Tibetan Book of the Dead (book), 43, 47
Tibetan Buddhism, 463, 525
Toffler, Alvin, 409
Tolun, Mexico, 500, 523, 533
Tombs, The, 214, 618
Torch Song Trilogy (play), 370
Tosches, Nick, 359
Traditionalist Gwyddoniaid, 104, 105, 128, 130, 140, 141, 157, 158–67, 168, 171, 177, 190, 192, 213, 257, 265, 272, 283, 289, 292, 293, 294, 295, 335, 377, 407, 437, 553, 562, 563, 569, 570, 571, 600, 601, 602, 605, 606, 633, 638, 668
    Children of Branwen, 105, 145, 146, 147, 148, 165, 305, 361, 551, 566
Transcendental Meditation, 29
Trask, Nigel, 17, 576
Tree, The (book), 178, 279, 328, 329, 554, 609, 631
Triumph of the Moon (book), 160, 172, 602, 606, 611, 612, 613, 633
Troy, 384, 399, 515, 663
Truth About Witchcraft, The (book), 151, 223, 242, 605, 626
Turner, Pierce, 359, 361, 432, 468
Tyet, 300
UFOs, and the occult, 57, 435, 586, 587
UFOs, and the Occult, 56
Ulrich, Laurel Tatcher, 325, 637
University of Pennsylvania, 427, 517, 519, 522, 527, 613, 653
Valiente, Doreen, 13, 14, 172, 190, 219, 241, 290, 291, 500, 575, 600, 611, 633
Van Druten, John, 24, 25, 26
Vaseline Flats, 119, 123, 147, 218, 599
Velikovsky, Immanuel, 57
Vice Versa (newsletter), 4
Victorian England, 183, 610
Vidal, Gore, 95, 231, 241, 622
Vietnam War, 38, 46, 68, 158, 507, 581, 642

Village Voice (newspaper), 63, 75, 108, 118, 129, 137, 218, 327, 346, 350, 355, 370, 371, 410, 579, 580, 582, 583, 585, 587, 588, 590, 591, 593, 597, 599, 601, 621, 626, 639, 640, 641, 642, 645, 651, 652, 654, 656, 661, 662
Vodoun, 15, 223, 354, 359
W.I.T.C.H. Manifesto, 84
Waite, Arthur Edward, 17
Waldron, Eli, 29, 579
Wallace, C. H., 26, 60, 467, 577, 578, 579, 583, 596
Wandel, Rich, 591
Warhol Factory, 154, 622
Warhol, Andy, 42, 43, 48, 49, 52, 59, 310, 583, 585, 622
Warlock (coven position), 114
Warlock (definition), 69, 113, 114, 355, 597, 641
Warlock Shop, 102, 103, 104, 111, 119, 120, 108–21, 123, 129, 135, 139, 141, 142, 145, 146, 147, 152, 153, 154, 155, 163, 166, 167, 168, 169, 170, 172, 179, 195, 210, 211, 212, 214, 216, 217, 218, 219, 226, 229, 230, 233, 234, 235, 236, 237, 242, 251, 260, 261, 265, 266, 269, 270, 271, 275, 277, 283, 284, 285, 286, 292, 297, 300, 304, 305, 306, 315, 321, 322, 324, 325, 326, 327, 328, 335, 337, 340, 344, 346, 347, 349, 350, 351, 353, 355, 361, 364, 375, 387, 394, 420, 423, 424, 426, 429, 435, 436, 437, 449, 452, 457, 482, 483, 502, 549, 554, 563, 564, 593, 594, 597, 598, 599, 600, 601, 603, 604, 607, 620, 621, 623, 628, 629, 637, 639, 640, 641, 642, 649, 652, 653, 655
    Earth Religions Supplies catalog, 234, 297, 323
Warnke, Mike, 225, 227, 620
Washington Square, 17
Wasserman, Jim, 234, 322, 355, 429, 430, 431, 446, 448, 449, 451, 452, 453, 454, 455, 498, 499, 653, 656, 657
Watch the North Wind Rise (book), 393, 649
Waxing Moon, The (newsletter), 21, 136, 291
Way, The (book), 146, 293, 294, 634
Webb, Pamela, 517, 520, 527, 663, 664
Wein, Chuck, 43
Weinstein, Marion, 238, 623
Weirs Beach, New Hampshire, 178, 328
Weiser, Donald, 47, 143, 322, 429, 445, 446, 449

Weiser, Samuel, 25, 47, 56, 108, 143, 235, 286, 322, 355, 416, 429, 430, 431, 445, 446, 447, 448, 449, 451, 462, 655
Welsh Outer Court, 158, 163, 289
Welsh Traditionalist Witchcraft, 125, 128, 139, 147, 165, 229, 607
Weschcke, Carl *(Gnosticus)*, 47, 91, 109, 224, 240, 251, 258, 259, 263, 267, 271, 272, 273, 274, 276, 576, 584, 594, 596, 624, 626, 627, 628, 629, 630
West Indies Botanical Garden, 19
Wetzsteon, Ross, 27, 579
Wheeler, William *(Rhuddlwm Gawr)*, 127, 293, 294, 595, 601, 633, 634
When God was a Woman (book), 385
Whistlers, 336
White Goddess, The (book), 49, 188, 189, 392, 393, 398, 611
White Stains (book), 286, 367, 448, 632, 644, 653, 656
White, David *(Merlin)*, 405
White, Edmund, 31
White, Ryan, 503
Whitfield, Jeffrey, 463, 472, 498, 525, 526
Whitman, Walt, 16, 30
Wiccan Rede, 207, 288, 289, 290, 291, 292, 552, 632, 633
Wicker Man, The (film), 232, 622
Wicker, Randy, 254, 592
Wilde, Constance, 183
Wilde, Oscar, iv, 16, 181, 183, 264, 391
Willetts, R.F., 392, 394, 395, 574, 649
Willis, Bobbi, 358
Willoughby, Michael M.D., 538, 540, 541
Wilson, Campbell *(Loic)*, 14, 15, 22
Wilson, Doric, 48
Wilson, Monique *(Olwen)*, 13, 14, 15, 22, 172, 173, 174, 179, 209, 282, 291, 331, 575, 617
Wilson, Robert Anton, 148, 360, 375
Winsel, Regnier, 483, 659
Winter, Orion de, 43
Witchcraft and the Gay Counterculture (book), 377, 460, 591, 644, 645, 646, 648
Witchcraft for Tomorrow (book), 500
Witchcraft in America Today (book), 368, 577, 578, 589, 623, 644
Witchcraft Report, The (book), 129, 155, 242, 243, 244, 245, 256, 264, 266, 366, 596, 602, 603, 604, 605, 606, 620, 621, 624, 627, 628, 634, 650
Witchcraft Today (book), 13, 20, 23, 62, 190, 207, 246, 338, 392, 398, 594, 596, 605, 611, 616, 625, 634, 646, 650

Witchcraft: The Old Religion (book), 266, 588, 592, 598, 600, 603, 604, 605, 606, 614, 617, 621, 625, 650
Witchcraft: The Sixth Sense (book), 291, 633
Witches Anti-Defamation League (WADL), 83, 231, 246
Witches Ball, 251, 326, 361, 474, 642
Witches Bible Compleat, A (book), 502
Witches Pyramid, 552, 666
Witches, USA (book), 136, 251, 474, 592, 605
Witchmeet, 106, 142, 259, 266-76, 283, 295, 296, 298, 627, 628, 629, 630
Witchmobile, 225, 226
Wittman, Carl, 83, 84, 368, 592, 593, 644
Wojtowicz, John, 116, 598
Wolfenden Report, 202
Woodroofe, John (Arthur Avalon), 43
Woodstock, 326, 329, 584
World War I, 2, 4, 16, 17, 19, 27, 59, 373
World War II, 17, 38, 45, 57, 95, 182, 309, 393, 442, 443
Worlds in Collision (book), 57
Worthington, Madge, 207
Wright, A. R., 337, 519, 520, 577, 639
Wright, Elbee, 142
Wright, James, 480, 512, 519, 520, 530, 531, 532, 533, 534, 535, 536, 549, 555, 565
Wyatt, Aubrey, 398, 407, 418, 461, 462, 463, 469, 482, 570, 649, 650, 657, 658, 659, 666, 668
Yeager Tarot of Meditation, 351, 641
Yeager, Marty, 351, 641
Yemaya House, 110
Yippies, 85, 256
YMCA, 31, 431
Yogi, Maharishi Mahesh, 29, 50
Yohalem, John, 528
Yorke, Gerald, 443, 655
Young Socialists Alliance, 368
Zell, Julie (Morning Glory), 195, 228, 244, 249, 269, 271, 272, 274, 621, 624
Zell, Tim (Otter/Oberon), 20, 187, 196, 225, 228, 243, 244, 245, 249, 250, 255, 256, 267, 268, 269, 270, 271, 272, 273, 274, 292, 325, 393, 588, 592, 611, 612, 613, 624, 626, 627, 629, 633, 637
Zen Buddhism, 19, 29, 41
Zeus (God), viii, 394, 395, 399, 401, 402, 436
Zielinsky, Tommy *(Pygmalion)*, 133
Ziprin, Lionel, 41
Zotique, Jonathon, 192, 193, 194, 612

 Michael Lloyd is an engineer and writer with long-standing ties to GLBT and contemporary Pagan communities. He is the co-founder and former co-facilitator (2002–2011) of the Between The Worlds Men's Gathering, a spiritual retreat for men who love men. A long-time resident of Columbus, Ohio, Michael was named in the 2011 *Who's Who of GLBT Columbus*.

www.ingramcontent.com/pod-product-compliance
Lightning Source LLC
Chambersburg PA
CBHW052038290426
44111CB00011B/1544